HANDBOOK

OF

Family Therapy

VOLUME II

Edited by

Alan S. Gurman, Ph.D.

Professor,
Department of Psychiatry,
University of Wisconsin Medical School

and

David P. Kniskern, Psy.D.

Private Practice
Cincinnati, Ohio

Published in 1991 by
Routledge
Taylor & Francis Group
270 Madison Avenue
New York, NY 10016

Published in Great Britain by
Routledge
Taylor & Francis Group
2 Park Square
Milton Park, Abingdon
Oxon OX14 4RN

Printed in the United States of America on acid-free paper
15 14 13 12 11 10 9 8

International Standard Book Number-10: 0-87630-642-3-8 (Hardcover)
International Standard Book Number-13: 978-07630-642-0 (Hardcover)
Library of Congress Card Number 80-20357

Library of Congress Cataloging-in-Publication Data

Handbook of family therapy
  Includes bibliographical references and index.
   ISBN 0-87630-242-8 (v. 1)
   ISBN 0-87630-642-3 (v. 2)
   1. Family psychology. I. Gurman, Alan S. II. Kniskern, David. P.
RC488.5.H33   1991
616.89'156   80-20357

Taylor & Francis Group
is the Academic Division of T&F Informa plc.

Visit the Taylor & Francis Web site at
http://www.taylorandfrancis.com

and the Routledge Web site at
http://www.routledge-ny.com

To Our Families:

Gerri, Jesse and Ted

and

Rebecca, Jonathan and Ethan

Contents

About the Editors ix
Contributors xi
Preface xv

PART I: *Historical and Conceptual Foundations*

1. The History of Professional Marriage and Family Therapy 3
   Carlfred B. Broderick, Ph.D., and *Sandra S. Schrader, Ph.D.*

2. Systems Theory, Cybernetics, and Epistemology 41
   Herta A. Guttman, M.D.

PART II: *Models of Family Therapy*

3. Behavioral Family Therapy 65
   Ian R. H. Falloon, M.D.

4. Behavioral Marital Therapy 96
   Amy Holtzworth-Munroe, Ph.D., and *Neil S. Jacobson, Ph.D.*

5. Bowen Theory and Therapy 134
   Edwin H. Friedman, D.D.

6. Brief Therapy: The MRI Approach 171
   Lynn Segal, L.C.S.W.

7. Contextual Therapy 200
   Ivan Boszormenyi-Nagy, M.D., Judith Grunebaum,
   L.I.C.S.W., B.C.D., and *David Ulrich, Ph.D.*

8. Ericksonian Family Therapy 239
   Stephen R. Lankton, M.S.W., Carol H. Lankton, M.A.,
   and *William J. Matthews, Ph.D.*

9. Focal Family Therapy: Joining Systems Theory with
   Psychodynamic Understanding   284
   *Arnon Bentovim, F.R.C. Psych., and Warren Kinston,
   M.R.C. Psych.*

10. The Milan Systemic Approach to Family Therapy   325
    *David Campbell, Ph.D., Rosalind Draper, A.A.P.S.W., and
    Elaine Crutchley, M.R.C. Psych.*

11. Family Psychoeducational Treatment   363
    William R. McFarlane, M.D.

12. Strategic Family Therapy   396
    Cloé Madanes

13. Structural Family Therapy   417
    Jorge Colapinto

14. Symbolic-Experiential Family Therapy   444
    Laura Giat Roberto, Psy.D.

PART III: *Special Issues and Applications*

15. Family Therapy as the Emerging Context for Sex Therapy   479
    Marilyn J. Mason, Ph.D.

16. Treating Divorce in Family-Therapy Practice   508
    Craig A. Everett, Ph.D., and Sandra S. Volgy, Ph.D.

17. Promoting Healthy Functioning in Divorced and
    Remarried Families   525
    Froma Walsh, Ph.D.

18. Ethnicity and Family Therapy   546
    *Monica McGoldrick, M.S.W., Nydia Garcia Preto, M.S.W.,
    Paulette Moore Hines, Ph.D., and Evelyn Lee, Ed.D.*

19. A Family–Larger-System Perspective   583
    Evan Imber-Black, Ph.D.

20. Values and Ethics in Family Therapy   606
    William J. Doherty, Ph.D., and Pauline G. Boss, Ph.D.

21. Training and Supervision in Family Therapy:
    A Comprehensive and Critical Analysis   638
    Howard A. Liddle, Ed.D.

Name Index   698
Subject Index   705

About the Editors

ALAN S. GURMAN, PH.D., Professor of Psychiatry at the University of Wisconsin Medical School, is the Director of the Psychiatric Outpatient Clinic and Co-Director of the Couples/Family Clinic. He is a graduate of the Boston Latin School (1963), Boston University (B.A., 1967), and Columbia University (Ph.D., 1971). The recipient of distinguished career awards in family therapy research from both the American Association for Marriage and Family Therapy (AAMFT) and the American Family Therapy Association (AFTA), he is a Fellow of the American Psychological Association and the AAMFT. He has served as President of the Society for Psychotherapy Research, a member of the AFTA Board of Directors, and a member of the Advisory Board of the Society for the Exploration of Psychotherapy Integration. Dr. Gurman is also the author of over 100 publications, has edited or written nine books, including *Effective Psychotherapy: A Handbook of Research* (with A. Razin), *Clinical Handbook of Marital Therapy* (with N. Jacobson), and *Theory and Practice of Brief Therapy* (with S. Budman), and was the Editor of the *Journal of Marital and Family Therapy* from 1982 to 1990. In 1983, he was identified as the fifth most frequently cited author in family therapy. A Diplomate of the American Board of Family Psychology, he maintains an active practice of marital, family, and individual psychotherapy.

DAVID P. KNISKERN received his Psy.D. degree from the University of Illinois. After a Predoctoral and Postdoctoral Fellowship in the Department of Psychiatry at the University of Wisconsin Medical School, he joined the faculty of the Department of Psychiatry at the University of Cincinnati College of Medicine. While at the University of Cincinnati, he coordinated marital/family therapy training and was the Director of the Psychology Division. He is the author of numerous articles and chapters about clinical and research aspects of family therapy and has also edited *From Psyche to System: The Evolving Therapy of Carl Whitaker* (with J. Neill), and *Handbook of Family Therapy* (with A. Gurman). Dr. Kniskern is a member of several journal editorial boards and has served as a member of the American Association for Marriage and Family Therapy's (AAMFT) National Advisory Committee on Standards for Education and Training. In 1978, Dr. Kniskern was corecipient (with Dr. Gurman) of the award for "Outstanding Research Contribution in Marital and Family Therapy" of the AAMFT. Since 1987, Dr. Kniskern has been engaged in full-time private practice in Cincinnati. He also consults to several agencies and teaches at the Southern Ohio Family Institute.

Contributors

ARNON BENTOVIM, F.R.C. Psych.
Consultant Psychiatrist
The Hospital for Sick Children
  and
The Tavistock Clinic
  and
Senior Lecturer (Hon.)
Institute of Child Health
London, England

PAULINE G. BOSS, Ph.D.
Professor
Department of Family Social Science
University of Minnesota
St. Paul, Minn.

IVAN BOSZORMENYI-NAGY, M.D.
Director, Institute for Contextual Growth
Ambler, Penn.
  and
Professor and Chief, Family Therapy Section
Hahnemann University
Philadelphia, Penn.

CARLFRED B. BRODERICK, Ph.D.
Professor and Director, Marriage and Family
  Therapy Program
Department of Sociology
  and
Co-Director
The Human Relations Center
University of Southern California
Los Angeles, Calif.

DAVID CAMPBELL, Ph.D.
Principal Clinical Psychologist
Tavistock Clinic
  and
Consultant, King's Consulting Partners
King's College
London, England

JORGE COLAPINTO
Faculty
Family Studies
New York, N.Y.

ELAINE CRUTCHLEY, M.R.C. Psych.
Consultant Child and Adolescent Psychiatrist
Child and Family Consultation Service
Frimley Park Hospital
Frimley, England

WILLIAM J. DOHERTY, Ph.D.
Professor
Department of Family Social Science
University of Minnesota
St. Paul, Minn.

ROSALIND DRAPER, A.A.P.S.W.
Senior Clinical Lecturer
Tavistock Clinic
  and
Consultant, King's Consulting Partners
King's College
London, England

CRAIG A. EVERETT, Ph.D.
Marital and Family Therapist
Private Practice
    and
Director
Arizona Institute of Family Therapy
Tucson, Ariz.

IAN R.H. FALLOON, M.D.
Director
Buckingham Project
22 High Street
Buckingham, England

EDWIN H. FRIEDMAN, D.D.
Private Practice
Bethesda, Md.

JUDITH GRUNEBAUM, L.I.C.S.W., B.C.D.
Executive Committee and Faculty
Couples and Family Center of the Cambridge
    Hospital and Lecturer on Psychiatry
Harvard Medical School
Cambridge, Mass.
    and
Supervisor and Therapist
Boston University Student Mental Health Clinic
Boston, Mass.

ALAN S. GURMAN, Ph.D.
Professor and Director, Outpatient Clinic
Department of Psychiatry
University of Wisconsin Medical School
Madison, Wisc.

HERTA A. GUTTMAN, M.D.
Professor of Psychiatry
McGill University
    and
Psychiatrist-in-Chief
Royal Victoria Hospital
Director
Allan Memorial Institute
Montreal, Quebec, Canada

PAULETTE MOORE HINES, Ph.D.
Project Director, Office of Prevention Services
University of Medicine & Dentistry of New
    Jersey
Community Mental Health Center at
    Piscataway
Piscataway, N.J.

AMY HOLTZWORTH-MUNROE, Ph.D.
Assistant Professor
Department of Psychology
Indiana University
Bloomington, Ind.

EVAN IMBER-BLACK, Ph.D.
Associate Professor and Director of Family and
    Group Therapy
Department of Psychiatry
Albert Einstein College of Medicine
Bronx, N.Y.

NEIL S. JACOBSON, Ph.D.
Professor
Department of Psychology
University of Washington
Seattle, Wash.

WARREN KINSTON, M.R.C. Psych.
Director
Sigma Centre
Brunel University
Uxbridge, Middlesex
    and
Honorary Consultant Psychotherapist
Hospital for Sick Children
London, England

DAVID P. KNISKERN, Psy.D.
Private Practice
    and
Consultant, Southern Ohio Family Institute
Cincinnati, Ohio

CAROL H. LANKTON, M.A.
Private Practice
Gulf Breeze, Fla.

STEPHEN R. LANKTON, M.S.W.
Private Practice
Gulf Breeze, Fla.

EVELYN LEE, Ed.D.
Assistant Clinical Professor
Department of Psychiatry
University of California
San Francisco, Calif.

HOWARD A. LIDDLE, Ed.D.
Professor, Counseling Psychology
and
Director, Adolescents and Families Project
Temple University
Philadelphia, Penn.

CLOÉ MADANES
Co-Director
Family Therapy Institute of Washington, D.C.
Washington, D.C.

MARILYN J. MASON, Ph.D.
Clinical Faculty
Department of Family Social Sciences
School of Human Ecology
University of Minnesota
St. Paul, Minn.

WILLIAM J. MATTHEWS, Ph.D.
Associate Professor of Counseling Psychology
University of Massachusetts
Amherst, Mass.

WILLIAM R. McFARLANE, M.D.
Director
Biosocial Treatment Research Division
New York State Psychiatric Institute
and
Associate Clinical Professor of Psychiatry
College of Physicians and Surgeons
Columbia University
New York, N.Y.

MONICA McGOLDRICK, M.S.W.
Associate Professor and Director of Family Training
Department of Psychiatry
University of Medicine & Dentistry of New Jersey
Robert Wood Johnson Medical School and Community Mental Health Center at Piscataway
and
Staff, Family Institute of Westchester
Piscataway, N.J.

NYDIA GARCIA PRETO, M.S.W.
Director, Adolescent Day Hospital
Faculty, Family Training Program
University of Medicine & Dentistry of New Jersey
Community Mental Health Center at Piscataway
Piscataway, N.J.

LAURA GIAT ROBERTO, Psy.D.
Adjunct Associate Professor
Department of Psychiatry and Behavioral Sciences
Eastern Virginia Medical School
Norfolk, Va.

SANDRA S. SCHRADER, Ph.D.
Private Practice
Coventry, Conn.

LYNN SEGAL, L.C.S.W.
Private Practice
Senior Research Associate
Mental Research Institute
Palo Alto, Calif.

DAVID ULRICH, Ph.D.
Private Practice
Stamford and Lyme, Conn.

SANDRA S. VOLGY, Ph.D.
Clinical Psychologist and Family Therapist
Private Practice
Tucson, Ariz.

FROMA WALSH, Ph.D.
Professor
School of Social Service Administration and Department of Psychiatry
and
Co-Director
Center for Family Health
University of Chicago
Chicago, Ill.

Preface

In 1978, we began to lay plans for bringing together the first comprehensive textbook presentation of the dominant conceptual and clinical influences on the field of family therapy. The reception of our 1981 *Handbook of Family Therapy* has been extremely gratifying to us, and the *Handbook* has become a standard primary reference source in the field, widely adopted in both university and freestanding institute training centers. Just as individuals and families must evolve and change with the needs of succeeding generations and decades, so, too, must such a volume: hence, the birth of the *Handbook of Family Therapy, Volume II*.

Let us look briefly at some of the concrete indices of change in the family therapy field in the past decade, for these changes parallel the richness of the conceptual and clinical advances in the field in that period. In 1981, there existed almost two dozen family therapy journals, while at this writing there exist about two times that number; in 1979, the membership of the American Association for Marriage and Family Therapy (AAMFT) was about 7,500; by 1990, it had increased to over 17,000. In the last decade, family therapy training has gained a more solid foothold in traditional psychiatry, clinical psychology, social work, and nursing graduate training programs, has greatly expanded its national training accreditation program at both masters and doctoral levels, and has proliferated a seemingly endless panoply of short-term training programs, lectures, and workshops. In addition, family therapy (in the United States, at least) has received increased legal recognition as an autonomous mental health profession via a series of legislative victories involving licensure.

Amid all these rapidly accumulating professional/political changes, the conceptual and clinical practice frontiers of the field have been pushed forward as well. The present *Handbook, Volume II*, attempts to reflect these advances.

At this point, a few words about the title of this volume are in order. We originally conceived of our editorial task as revising the original *Handbook*. Yet, as we settled upon what topics we wanted to be included in the present volume and which potential authors we hoped would write these chapters, and as we read what our ultimate roster of authors had written, we realized that this volume was, in truth, *both* a revised *Handbook and* a new book unto itself. Thus, over 85 percent of the authors in the new *Handbook* were not contributors to the original volume, and slightly over half of the topics addressed in the present *Handbook* were either not included in the original book, or were included with such vastly different emphases that their present counterparts constitute genuinely different treatments of the domains in question. In summary, our aim with *Volume II* has been to augment and extend the contents of the first *Handbook*, not to supplant it.

In general, those clinical points of view that were articulated in chapters in the first *Handbook* but do not appear here are those which, while continuing to be of significant interest to numbers of family therapists, have not greatly expanded their spheres of influence in the last decade.

The new chapters of *Volume II* that appear anew reflect increasing concern in the field with basic theoretical underpinnings (Guttman, "Systems Theory, Cybernetics, and Epistemology"); special issues that have assumed much greater importance in clinical practice in recent years (Walsh, "Remarried Families"; McGoldrick et al., "Ethnicity"; Mason, "Sexuality"; Imber-Black, "Larger Systems"); the contemporary "wings" of well-established "schools" (Madanes, "Strategic Therapy"; Lankton et al., "Ericksonian Therapy"); the ascendancy to prominence of new schools of therapy (McFarlane, "Psychoeducational"; Campbell et al., "Milan Systemic"); the extensions and refinements of established family treatment approaches by a generation of new clinical scholars (Roberto, "Symbolic-Experiential Therapy"; Falloon, "Behavioral Therapy"; Friedman, "Bowen Theory"; Segal, "Brief Therapy"; Bentovim & Kinston, "Psychodynamics and Systems Theory"; Colapinto, "Structural Therapy"); and the increasing sophistication of the field in specialized areas of professional and clinical concern (Doherty & Boss, "Values and Ethics"; Liddle, "Training and Supervision").

Readers who are familiar with the first *Handbook* will recognize that our organization of the chapters on the major models of family therapy has changed dramatically. Whereas we originally divided the schools of treatment into four subcategories, in the present volume, we simply present these approaches in alphabetical order. While there are certainly enormous differences among many major approaches to family therapy on questions of vital clinical importance, it is our view that most schools of family therapy are now much less "pure" than they were 10 years ago and that most of these chapters reflect the increasing synthesis in clinical theory in the field, especially at the technical level.

As in the first *Handbook*, we have written a number of "Editors' Notes" in each chapter, the purposes of which are: (1) to point out the similarities and differences between an author's thinking and the views of other contributors to this volume; (2) to challenge a contributor's idea or conclusion on the basis of our own thinking or clinical experience, or to refer the interested reader to ideas published elsewhere for further study of an issue; and (3) to offer our own views on some very basic clinical matters. We hope that these notes will stimulate relevant empirical study and useful critical thought.

One of the structural aspects of the original *Handbook* that was particularly appealing to many readers was our inclusion in the Preface of a set of quite detailed "Guidelines for Contributors" that the authors of the chapters on the "major models" were asked to follow. These Guidelines provide a framework for the comparative study of these theories of family therapy. As before, we did not expect each author to address each listed item in the Guidelines, but to use them as primary anchoring themes for the presentation of his or her point of view. In addition to some smaller changes from the original Guidelines, three more readily apparent changes will be noted. First, the "major models" chapters no longer contain brief sections on training; rather, we decided that since training is undergoing so many changes within many schools of family therapy, our readership would be better served by our new comprehensive chapter on supervision and training. This chapter touches on some specifics of training within various schools and also examines a broad array of philosophic and technical considerations, which need to be considered by all approaches.

Likewise, the chapters in *Volume II* do not contain a section on research. As with training considerations, it was our judgment that changes on the empirical front of the field are happening so rapidly that this section would be too quickly outdated. Moreover, a parallel decision not to include our own updated chapter on family therapy research was based on our belief that the field is better served by more frequent journal updates, which describe advances in specific areas of family therapy. Also, despite the greater specificity of family therapy knowledge of late, we find that the broad conclusions contained in the research chapter in the original *Handbook*, and in our 1986 chapter with Pinsof in Garfield and Bergin's *Handbook of Psychotherapy and Behavior Change* (New York: Wiley), are still valid. Finally, most of the contributors to this volume responded to our preference that they include a brief case illustration of their treatment approach in order to enhance and clarify the relevance of their theoretical discussions for clinical practice.

Our revised Guidelines for Authors, then, were as follows:

I. BACKGROUND OF THE APPROACH

Purpose: To place the approach in historical perspective both within the field of psychotherapy in general and within the area of marital-family therapy in particular.

Points to include:

(1) Cite the major influences that contributed to the development of the approach, e.g., people, books, research, theories, conferences.

(2) The therapeutic forms, if any, that were forerunners of the approach, e.g., play therapy, psychoanalysis, desensitization, etc.

(3) Type of patients with whom the approach was initially developed, and speculations as to why.

(4) Early theoretical speculations and/or therapy techniques.

II. THE HEALTHY OR WELL-FUNCTIONING MARRIAGE OR FAMILY

Purpose: To describe within your theoretical framework how a healthy family/marriage operates, or what is indicative of smooth operation.

Points to include:

(1) How are functional roles defined within a healthy family/marriage? Gender roles?

(2) How are problems solved?

(3) What markers are characteristic of the family life-cycle?

(4) Describe how a healthy family changes over time.

(5) How is affection/sexuality handled?

(6) What levels of intimacy and separateness are found?

(7) How dependent or autonomous are family members? Describe the "organization" of the healthy family/marriage in terms of boundaries, alliances and the like.

(8) Relationships with extended family.

(9) Relationships with non-family members.

(10) In your theoretical framework, how much emphasis is given to ethnic and/or socioeconomic differences? If emphasized strongly, discuss the role of such factors.

(11) Are there other dimensions that need to be considered in describing the healthy family/marriage?

III. THE PATHOLOGICAL OR DYSFUNCTIONAL MARRIAGE OR FAMILY

Purpose: To describe the way in which pathological functioning is conceptualized within the approach.

Points to include:

(1) Describe any formal or informal system for diagnosing or typing families.

(2) What leads to family or marital dysfunction? Individual dysfunction?

(3) How do symptoms develop? How are they maintained?

(4) What determines the type of symptom to appear?

(5) Why are some people symptomatic and not others? Alternatively, what is the systemic role of the "identified patient"?

(6) Can there be "well" members in pathological marriages/families?

(7) Are there other dimensions that need to be considered in describing dysfunctional families/marriages?

IV. THE ASSESSMENT OF SYSTEM FUNCTIONING AND DYSFUNCTION

Purpose: To describe the methods, whether formal or informal, used to gain an understanding of a particular marriage's or family's style or pattern of interaction, symptomatology and adaptive resources.

Points to include:

(1) At what *unit* levels is assessment made (e.g., individual, dyadic, triadic, family system, family/extended system interface [e.g., schools, other helping professionals])?

(2) At what *psychological* levels is assessment made (e.g., intrapsychic, behavioral)?

(3) What tests, devices, questionnaires,

or observations are typically used?

(4) Is assessment separate from treatment or integrated with it? E.g., what is the temporal relation between assessment and treatment?

(5) What is the role of the verbal interview as contrasted, e.g., with home visits, structured interaction tasks, etc.?

(6) To what extent do issues of ethnicity and life-cycle changes influence your assessment?

(7) Are family strengths/resources a focus of your assessment? If so, in what way?

(8) What other dimensions or factors are typically involved in assessing family/marital dysfunction?

V. GOAL-SETTING

Purpose: To describe the nature of therapeutic goals established and the process by which they are established.

Points to include:

(1) Are there treatment goals that apply to all or most cases for which the treatment is appropriate (see XI, Treatment Applicability) regardless of between-family differences, or regardless of presenting problem or symptom?

(2) Of the number of possible goals for a given family/couple, how are the central goals selected for this couple/family? How are they prioritized?

(3) Do you distinguish between intermediate or mediating goals and ultimate goals?

(4) Who determines the goals of treatment? Therapist, family, other? Both? How are differences in goals resolved? To what extent and in what ways are therapist values involved in goal setting?

(5) Is it important that treatment goals be discussed with the family/couple explicitly? If yes, why? If no, why not?

(6) At what level of psychological experience are goals established, e.g., are

they described in overt, motoric terms, in affective-cognitive terms, etc.?

VI. THE STRUCTURE OF THE THERAPY PROCESS

Purpose: To describe the treatment setting, frequency, and duration of treatment characteristic of your approach.

Points to include:

(1) Is treatment conjoint, concurrent, three generational, individual, etc.? Why? Are combined therapies used, e.g., individual psychotherapy plus family therapy?

(2) Are psychotropic medications ever used within your method of family/marital therapy? What are the incations/contraindications for such use?

(3) How many therapists are usually involved? From your perspective, what are the advantages (or disadvantages) of using co-therapists? Are treatment teams often or sometimes used? If "yes," what are the specific advantages of team treatment in the theoretical framework of your treatment approach?

(4) What is the spatial arrangement within the therapy room? Is it a significant structural aspect of therapy?

(5) Is therapy time-limited or unlimited? Why? Ideal models aside, how long does therapy typically last?

(6) How often are sessions typically held?

(7) How are decisions about therapy structure made? Who makes these decisions?

VII. THE ROLE OF THE THERAPIST

Purpose: To describe the stance the therapist takes with the family/couple.

Points to include:

(1) To what degree does the therapist overtly control sessions? How active/directive is the therapist?

(2) Does the therapist assume reponsi-

bility for bringing about the changes desired? Is responsibility left to the family/couple? Is responsibility shared?

(3) Do patients talk predominantly to the therapist or to each other?

(4) Does the therapist use self-disclosure? What limits are imposed on therapist self-disclosure?

(5) Does the therapist "join" the family or remain outside?

(6) Does the therapist's role change as therapy progresses? Does it change as termination approaches?

(4) What are the clinical skills or other therapist attributes most essential to successful therapy in your approach?

VIII. TECHNIQUES OF MARITAL-FAMILY THERAPY

Purpose: To describe techniques and strategies always or frequently used in a particular approach to marital-family therapy and their tactical purposes.

Points to include:

(1) How structured are therapy sessions?

(2) What techniques or strategies are used to join the family or to create a treatment alliance?

(3) What techniques or strategies lead to changes in structure or transactional pattern? Identify, describe and illustrate major commonly used techniques.

(4) Are "homework" or other out of session tasks used?

(5) How is the decision made to use a particular technique or strategy at a particular time? Are different techniques used for different family/marital problems?

(6) What are the most commonly encountered forms of resistance to change? How are these dealt with?

(7) What are both the most common *and* the most serious technical errors a therapist can make operating within your therapeutic approach?

(8) On what basis is termination decided and how is termination effected?

IX. CURATIVE FACTORS IN MARITAL-FAMILY THERAPY/MECHANISMS OF CHANGE

Purpose: To describe the factors, i.e., mechanisms of change, that lead to change in families/couples and to assess their relative importance.

Points to include:

(1) Do patients need insight or understanding in order to change? (Differentiate between historical-genetic insight and interactional insight.)

(2) Are interpretations of any sort important and, if so, do they take history (genetics) into account? If interpretations of any kind are used, are they seen as reflecting a psychological "reality," or are they viewed rather as a pragmatic tool for effecting change?

(3) Is the learning of new interpersonal skills seen as important? If so, are these skills taught in didactic fashion, or are they shaped as approximations occur naturalistically in treatment?

(4) Does the therapist's personality or psychological health play an important part?

(5) What other therapist factors influence the course and outcome of the treatment? Are there certain kinds of therapists who are ideally suited to work according to this approach; are there others for whom the approach is probably a poor "fit"?

(6) How important are techniques?

(7) Is transference utilized?

(8) Is countertransference utilized? Is it seen as a major risk in marital/family therapy?

(9) Must each family member change? Is change in an "identified patient" (where relevant) possible without interactional or systemic change? Does systemic change necessarily lead to change in symptoms?

(10) What factors or variables enhance or

limit the probability of successful treatment in your approach?

(11) What characterizes "good/successful" vs. "bad/unsuccessful" termination of therapy?

(12) What aspects of your therapy are *not* unique to your approach, i.e., characterize all effective family therapy?

X. SPECIAL ISSUES IN MARITAL THERAPY

Purpose: To identify any major issues (theoretical, technical, etc.) which need to be considered in the treatment of marital problems, yet which do not follow from mere extensions of preceding material.

Points to include:

(1) Are there areas of assessment which need to be considered in this approach's treatment of marital problems that differ from the treatment of family problems?

(2) Does your approach to treatment include goals that are specific to the nature of marriage (as compared to other intimate relationships)?

(3) Are there particular aspects of the structure of the therapy process with couples that differ from the treatment of families?

(4) In your approach, are there commonly used techniques in the treatment of marital conflict that are different from those used in the treatment of families?

XI. TREATMENT APPLICABILITY

Purpose: To describe those families/couples for whom your approach is particularly relevant.

Points to include:

(1) For what families/couples is your approach particularly relevant?

(2) For what families/couples is your approach either not appropriate or of uncertain relevance? E.g., is it less relevant for severely disturbed families or families with a seriously dis-

turbed member, for marital and/or sexual problems, families with non-traditional structures? Why?

(3) When, if ever, would a referral be made for either another (i.e., different) type of marital/family therapy, or for an entirely different treatment, e.g., hypnotherapy, chemotherapy?

(4) When would *no* treatment (of any sort) be recommended?

(5) Are there aspects of your approach that raise particular ethical issues that are different from those raised by family therapy in general?

(6) How is the outcome, or effectiveness, of therapy in this model evaluated in clinical practice?

For (1) and (2), discussion in terms of syndromes, family "types," identified patient types, symptom severity, etc., would be appropriate.

XII. CASE ILLUSTRATION

Purpose: To illustrate the clinical application of this model of family therapy by detailing the major assessment, structural, technical and relational elements of the process of treating a family viewed as typical, or representative, of the kinds of families for whom this approach is appropriate.

Points to include:

(1) Relevant case background (e.g., presenting problem, referral source, previous treatment history).

(2) Description of relevant aspects of your clinical assessment: family functioning, family structure, dysfunctional interaction, resources, individual dynamics/characteristics (including how this description was arrived at).

(3) Description of the process and content of goal setting.

(4) Highlight the major themes, patterns, etc., of the therapy of this family over the whole course of treatment. Describe the structure of ther-

apy, the techniques used, the role and activity of the therapist, etc.

Note: Do *not* describe the treatment of a "star case," in which therapy progresses perfectly. Select a case which, while successful, also illustrates the typical course of events in your therapy.

Editing this second volume of the *Handbook* has been a consuming yet invigorating experience for us. Like a family living through a series of inevitable major stressors and transitions, we and our authors collectively have dealt with, at our rough count, about two dozen major life events in the past four years, including significant geographical moves, divorces and marriages, births, deaths, and illnesses. We want to thank all of our contributors for both their hardy persistence and their dignified forbearance in bringing this *Handbook of Family Therapy, Volume II* to fruition.

ALAN S. GURMAN
Madison, Wisconsin
DAVID P. KNISKERN
Cincinnati, Ohio
August, 1991

PART I

Historical and Conceptual Foundations

CHAPTER 1

The History of Professional Marriage and Family Therapy*

Carlfred B. Broderick, Ph.D., and Sandra S. Schrader, Ph.D.

It seems likely that people have been listening to each other's family problems and responding with commiseration and advice as long as there have been families. It seems equally likely that as soon as humankind became prosperous enough to develop specialized professions (the chief, the priest, the physician, the prostitute), many of these worthies included giving advice on family matters among their duties and prerogatives. Only in our own century and our own culture, however, has a profession developed whose sole purpose is to deal with problems between family members. Doubtless it was an inevitable development. The temper of the times had become such as to encourage attempts to intervene in every social problem. From Pro-

hibition to Social Security, from the community mental health movement to the women's rights movement, we have been a nation boldly (if not always wisely) committed to finding cures for new and old social ills. The family received particular attention as the divorce and juvenile delinquency rates rose dramatically decade after decade. Indeed, as we shall see, marital therapy and family therapy are only two of the many related movements that grew up in response to evident social needs. The social-hygiene movement, the family-life-education movement, the child-guidance and parent-education movements, and an array of new psychotherapeutic modalities such as group, brief, and behavioral approaches all emerged within a narrow span of decades in response to the same compelling historic currents.

The present cluster of cross-borrowing, overlapping professions that deal with the relation-

* Beverly Farb, A.B. did the library research for this chapter.

3

ships among family members began as at least four largely independent movements.[1] The oldest of these is the *marriage-counseling* movement. It grew out of the attempts of many in the various helping professions (medicine, psychology, education, social work, the ministry, law) to address the widely acknowledged increase in marital and sexual problems of the post–World War I era. The new movement was pragmatic and eclectic. In nearly every case, marriage counseling was the auxiliary activity of a professional whose primary commitment was elsewhere.

The *sex-therapy* movement is the youngest of the four in that the document that may be thought of as the movement's founding chapter (*Human Sexual Inadequacy* by William Masters and Virginia Johnson) was published only in 1970. Yet its roots reach back as early as any of the others, and many of the key figures in the development of marriage counseling were also forerunners of the sex-therapy movement.

The other two movements, *marital therapy* and *family therapy*, both trace their origins to the development of social psychiatry in America after World War II. The pioneers were mostly psychiatrists who dared to break the rules requiring a therapist to see no more than one member of a family at a time.

In this chapter, we shall attempt to trace the evolution of each of these four movements and their progressive amalgamation into contemporary training and practice. Before doing so, however, it may be helpful to sketch some of the closely related historical developments.

THE SOCIAL-WORK MOVEMENT

The history of social work has been inextricably interwoven from the beginning with the history of interventions into marriages and families. Social workers have by turns been the most daring

pioneers and the most passive "Johnny come lately's" in the whole parade of professionals.

Social historians date the beginning of social work in this country to the founding of the first citywide charity organization in Buffalo, N.Y., in 1877 (Rich, 1956). Modeling themselves after similar organizations in Great Britain, early American societies concerned themselves primarily with aiding the poor at a time when there was little government investment in what has since come to be called "welfare." From the beginning, it was observed, however, that the proper unit of concern for these societies was not the single client but the family. "Work with families" was the phrase used in the earliest descriptions of the casework activities of these organizations (Rich, 1956, p. 13). As Robert Treat Paine (1899), president of the Boston Associated Charities, put it in his first annual report, "Each one of the 7,716 cases reported is a human family with human lives, cares, and woes" (p. 355).

One of the early pioneers in the conversion of a volunteer service into a profession requiring advanced training was Zilpha D. Smith. In 1890 she wrote of her colleagues, "Most of you deal with poor persons or defective *individuals*, removed from family relationships. We deal with the *family* as a whole, usually working to keep it together, but sometimes helping to break it up into units and to place them in your care."

But perhaps the greatest champion of looking at the whole family and its need was Mary Richmond, originally the general secretary of the Baltimore Charity Organization Society, and eventually one of the main organizers of the profession at the national level. Her 1908 publication of a case record of a widow and four children followed over nine years (she entitled it *A Real Story of a Real Family*) set a new standard of family-oriented case record keeping among social workers (Rich, 1956). In her influential book *Social Diagnosis* (Richmond, 1917), she quoted the Swiss neuropathologist Paul Dubois as referring "to this necessity of not confining one's therapeutic efforts to the patient alone, but extending it to those who live with them. This is often the one way to obtain complete and lasting results" (Dubois, 1907). Then she elaborated, "In some forms of social work, notably family rebuilding, a client's social relations are so likely to be all important that family case workers welcome the opportunity to see at the

---

[1] *Editors' Note.* Broderick has indicated to us elsewhere (Broderick, 1979) three criteria that define a profession: (1) self-awareness and the identity of a body of experts; (2) a set of skills requiring advanced training and established standards of performance; and (3) a recognition of this body of experts and the utility of their expert service by the larger society.

very beginning of intercourse several of the members of the family assembled in their own home environment, acting and reacting upon one another, each taking a share in the development of the client's story, each revealing in ways other than words social facts of real significance" (Richmond, 1917, p. 137). In 1928 she wrote a paper, "Concern of the Community with Marriage" (Richmond, 1928), that further stressed the importance of dealing with relationships as well as individual problems.

As early as 1911, enough social-work agencies had begun to specialize in the treatment of marriages and families that a group of them formed the alliance that has come to be known as the Family Service Associations of America (Barker, 1984, p. 11). This was the agency that in 1943 produced the first volume entirely devoted to marriage counseling. Titled *Report of the FSAA Committee on Marriage Counseling*, it was a substantial handbook for training social workers in counseling with couples. The report considered both psychoanalytic and sociological constructs and insights in addition to many practical guidelines on how to proceed clinically. As an in-house publication, it was not widely read outside of the agency that produced it, but it is a testimony to the fact that the field of social work never abandoned its involvement with families.

Indeed, the case could be made that both marriage counseling and family therapy had their origins as subspecialties within the broader field of social casework. That this is not the prevailing view is probably the result of at least two historical realities. First, traditionally the field of social work has not packaged its intellectual and clinical wares for export into the broader community. Its practitioners have been less likely to write books for general consumption (e.g., the 1943 *Report* cited earlier), to give widely advertised workshops, or to seek leadership positions in multiprofessional organizations.

The second factor was the establishment in the 1920s of the orthopsychiatry movement, which gave shape and legitimacy to the status structure of the clinical professions. Psychiatrists with their M.D. degrees were in charge, clinical psychologists with their Ph.D.s were in the middle, and social workers with their B.S.W.s and M.S.W.s were on the bottom, with little or no influence. Moreover, the orthopsychiatric thrust was focused on the psychodynamics of the

individual, not on the relationships among family members. Without doubt, this movement set back the development of whole-family therapy within the social-work profession several decades. The proceedings of the first roundtable discussions of the American Orthopsychiatric Association in 1930 were a harbinger of the decades to follow. In their discussion of that occasion, John Spiegel and Norman Bell (1959, p. 116) have written:

A psychiatrist, a social worker and a clinical psychologist spoke in this panel discussion, about treatment of behavior and personality problems in children. Alone among the three discussants, the social worker, Charlotte Towle, dealt with the problems and the family in dynamic fashion. She was articulate and direct concerning the family, saying in part "Treatment cannot be given to any member of the family without affecting the entire group. In some cases the entire family must be drawn into treatment. Approach to this or that member or centering treatment on a certain individual cannot be a random thing" (Towle, 1948).

The prolonged discussion that followed dealt largely in whether notes should be made in front of the patient. No reference to Towle's ideas was made at all. The whole issue of the dynamic formulation and handling of family relationships simply dropped out of sight.

The point may be further documented by Florence T. Waite's summary of 50 years of casework practice published in 1941. As she pointed out:

Family casework had moved beyond the older emphasis on trying to know and be in touch with several family members. It had developed a clinical orientation and tended to concentrate on the individual because: (1) competitiveness and jealousy existed among family members; (2) seeing the whole family blurred the autonomy of the individual and the worker was apt to take over the family too completely and overpoweringly; (3) society has increased its emphasis on the individual even at the expense of his membership in the family and society at large. (As summarized in Sherman, 1961, pp. 19–20)

While that view doubtless overstates the retreat of social workers from relationship counseling for this period, it does appear to be true that from the decades of the '30s forward, they have never, as a profession, taken the lead in the marriage- and family-therapy movement. They have, however, at every point, provided a substantial part of the professional cadre actually seeing couples and families in the various pioneering programs that we shall describe later. It seems likely that their actual contribution is much greater than present accounts give them credit for (cf. Guerin, 1976; Kaslow, 1979).

Although, as we have seen, the potential existed for the field to grow out of social-casework experience, the evidence is that two quite separate social movements provided the actual historical roots of both the early marriage-counseling movement and the more recent sex-therapy movement. One was the sexual-reform movement that flourished in Europe in the post–World War I era. The other was the family-life-education movement that developed in the '30s and '40s in the United States.

THE SEXUAL-REFORM MOVEMENT OF THE POST–WORLD WAR I ERA

A number of Europeans and Americans participated in the movement to establish human sexuality as a scientific field and to free men and women from disabling sexual ignorance, fear, and inhibition. Preeminent among these were Havelock Ellis of Great Britain and Magnus Hirschfeld of Germany. More than any others, they paved the way for working with couples in a practical way on the sexual problems of everyday life.

Havelock Ellis was a remarkable man. He was a physician who also produced some of the most widely acclaimed translations of the Greek dramatic poets. Raised in Victorian prudery, largely without a father's influence, he vowed to do all within his power to spare others the ignorance of and discomfort in sexual matters he had experienced as a young man. In all, he produced seven volumes covering almost every imaginable aspect of sexual behavior. His writing was literate, well reasoned, and well documented, but beyond that he was remarkably free from the moralizing that previous sexual scholars had indulged in, and he livened up his text with literally hundreds of excerpts from sexual histories he had collected over the years. Decades

in advance of his time, he worked personally with individuals (mostly women) in helping them overcome their sexual fears.

Ellis saw himself as something of a secular high priest of sex and refused to charge for consultations. Yet he saw scores of sexually unhappy people and was in correspondence with hundreds more. His approach varied from patient to patient, but two elements were common to most of his encounters: (1) he listened with acceptance and personal supportiveness, reassuring the individual that his or her personal experiences and fears were not unique; and (2) he recommended reading (usually of his own published work) to help further allay anxiety and to be exposed to a scientific and informed perspective on the matter.

Because he wrote the first major work on homosexuality (or sexual inversion as he preferred to call it), many of his clients were homosexuals of both sexes. Among his heterosexual clientele, most were women who were attracted, apparently, not only by his scientific scholarship and liberated views, but also by his striking leonine appearance coupled with a gentle personal style. When he felt it would be accepted, he sometimes personally introduced these women into his own version of nondemand sexual pleasuring. He considered himself impotent through most of his adult life and this awareness contributed to his confidence that these approaches would not be misconstrued as mere seduction. It is curious by contemporary standards that he never saw couples as clients, nor did he, so far as is recorded, instruct husbands and wives in how to enlarge their mutual repertoire of sexual approaches. (See his biography, *The Sage of Sex*, by Calder-Marshall [1959], especially pp. 173–174 and 238–243, for a fuller description of his approach.)

His German counterpart, Magnus Hirschfeld, founded the Institute of Sexual Science in Berlin in 1918 and together with Ellis and August Forel founded the World League for Sexual Reform. Between 1921 and 1932, this group convened five meetings of the International Congress for Sexual Reform on a Scientific Basis. Literally thousands of physicians from all over the world visited his center in the 15 years of its existence. He culminated his career with a five-volume work, *Geschlechtskunde* (*Sex Education*) (1930), which reported his conclusions based on analyzing 10,000 questionnaires filled out by men and women who came to him for advice.

As part of his wide-ranging interest in sexual reform, he instituted the first German Marriage Consultation Bureau (Hirschfeld, 1940) and was instrumental in influencing his Austrian colleague, Dr. Karl Kautsky, to set up the first publicly funded Center for Sexual Advice in Vienna (Stone, 1949). The movement grew and by 1932 there were hundreds of centers throughout Germany, Austria, Switzerland, The Netherlands, and the Scandinavian countries. Although it appears that the emphasis in these centers was on contraceptive and eugenic counseling, it is clear that psychological and relational matters were routinely discussed (Hoenig, 1978). These early sex and marital counselors listened to problems empathically, gave reassurances as to normality, and information on contraceptive and sexual practices, and assigned readings (including Ellis').

When Hitler took over Germany, then Austria, and then most of Europe, one of his earliest actions was to destroy Hirschfeld's original center (Hirschfeld was a Jew) and to convert the publicly owned centers to "Health and Racial Hygiene Bureaus." Their revised function was to interview all applicants for marriage licenses as to their emotional, intellectual, physical, and genealogical fitness for marriage and reproduction. It must be counted one of the bitter ironies of that era that the movement that began as an idealistic effort to assist couples and families with information and counseling ended as the instrumentality through which the Nazis prevented intermarriage between "Aryans" and "non-Aryans" and implemented the sterilization of "mental and physical defectives" and, as the world was eventually to learn, of Jews.

Some insight into the murky thinking of those times may be gained by a few excerpts from an article by the American eugenicist Marie Kopp, writing in the *Journal of Heredity* in 1938, six years into the new program.

The European approach to the counseling of individuals, couples, and families differs fundamentally from the American attitude toward these functions. In the United States of America, marriage counseling to date has in the main been concerned with the solution of the problems related to the psychology and physiology of sex, reproduction, family, and racial

relationships. In Europe, on the other hand, the main objectives are the betterment of the biological stock. To accomplish this purpose, those most unfit for marriage are dissuaded or prevented from marriage and procreation and those most fit are encouraged to shoulder the responsibilities of parenthood. . . . (p. 154)

The contemporary marital counseling in Germany typifies the new European service in its concern with the biological improvement of its people. The counseling of individuals presenting psychological or sociomedical problems of adjustment, on the other hand, is no longer a major concern of services operating under municipal and state auspices. . . . (p. 158)

The counseling bureaus formerly sponsored by the various German municipalities and by political, social, and commercial groups have ceased to exist. . . . (p. 159)

As we shall see below, the concept developed by Hirschfeld and others did survive, but in America and England rather than in the lands of its first flowering.

Meanwhile, another development was taking place in America, which, while having no direct clinical aspect, nevertheless played an important role in paving the way for the eventual establishment of modern sex therapy; sex was becoming a legitimate arena for scientific research. Kinsey, Pomeroy, and Martin (1948) list 16 studies of human sexuality published in America before 1940. These, together with the published works of Ellis, Hirschfeld, and others, constituted a pool of scientific knowledge upon which physicians, social hygienists, and others could draw in counseling couples with sexual problems.

THE FAMILY-LIFE-EDUCATION MOVEMENT

As a nation, Americans tend to have great faith in education as a vehicle for addressing social problems. As early as 1883, mothers' groups had begun to come together to discuss how to incorporate the best pedagogic principles into their own parenting (Groves & Groves, 1947). In 1908 in Washington, D.C., the constitutional convention, so to speak, of the American Home Economics Association took place and courses began increasingly to be instituted in high schools and colleges that were calculated to improve American homemaking. It is true that at first emphasis was heavily upon cooking, sewing, and money management, but relational aspects of the married woman's role were always there as an explicit (though often neglected) category within the discipline. With the passage of the Smith-Lever Act of 1914 and the Smith-Hughes Act of 1917, the home-economics perspective was given further visibility. These acts provided federal grants to establish and maintain county home-demonstration agents as part of the state agricultural extension programs and vocational home-economics instruction in high schools throughout the country.

In 1923, Vassar College introduced the first preparation for parenthood course at the college level (Groves & Groves, 1947). But with the changing mores governing sex, courtship, and marriage, college students were more interested in the relationships between the sexes than in the parental role. Inevitably, educators sensitive to their students' felt needs attempted to respond. Preeminent among these was Ernest R. Groves. In 1920, he founded the Sociology Department at Boston University, having previously served as professor of sociology and dean of the College of Liberal Arts at the University of New Hampshire (and before that as a minister and pastoral counselor). After two years at the new job, his dean asked him to head a team of academics and medical practitioners to develop a course on preparation for marriage for which the students had pressed. Groves agreed. It is a measure of the temper of the times that, one by one, the other members of the team dropped out "lest it be misunderstood and hurt their reputations." In the end, Groves gave the course himself under the title "The Family and Its Social Functions" (Green, 1986). It was basically a sociology-of-the-family course with an applied emphasis. In 1927, however, he moved to the University of North Carolina and there designed and taught for the first time a fully "functional" course in marriage and family relations for college credit. Institutionally oriented courses on the family had been offered at U.S. universities at least since 1893 when Charles R. Henderson taught a course on the family at the University of Chicago (Mudd, 1951, p. 6). By 1908, a survey by Bernard had determined that about 20 such courses were being offered across the nation

(Bernard, 1908). Groves' new "functional" approach differed from traditional approaches in several important ways: (1) it was eclectic, drawing upon law, biology, medicine, home economics, and psychology as well as sociology; (2) it was practical, being shaped to the needs of the students rather than to the theoretical or empirical investments of the academic profession; and (3) it was unabashedly intended to be remedial and cautionary—that is, its intent was not only to analyze and describe, but to *improve* the courtship and marriage of the students involved.

Groves pioneered in a number of additional related areas. He was the first to introduce psychoanalytic concepts into the sociological literature, publishing articles on the relationship between the two fields in both sociological and psychoanalytical journals in 1916 and 1917. He coauthored (with Phyllis Blanchard) the first text on mental hygiene in 1930 and the first college text on marriage in 1931. He founded the Groves Conference on the Conservation of Marriage and the Family in 1934 and in 1937 taught the first university-level course in marriage counseling at Duke University (Green, 1986). It is not surprising that he became perhaps the key figure in the founding of the American Association of Marriage Counselors in 1942.

Meanwhile, on the West Coast, family-life education was being promoted by another pioneer. Beginning in 1930, Paul Popenoe set up a series of all-day workshops that toured university campuses and churches in Southern California and elsewhere with a wide list of lecture-discussion topics available in serial or concurrent sessions. For example, the following typical program was offered on the University of Southern California campus on March 3, 1934 (American Institute of Family Relations [AIFR], 1934).

Morning Addresses:
Women's Jobs or Women's Homes, The Family in a Changing Social Situation

Afternoon Roundtables:
Guiding Youth in the Ethics of Sex, Getting Acquainted, Premarital Examinations, What Makes Personality, Sex Education of Children in the Home, Voluntary Sterilization, Extracurricular Activities, Current Family Literature, Shall Parenthood Be Penalized?, The Problem of Movies, The Technique of Counseling, The Choice of a Mate, Improving Di-

vorce Courts, Teaching Family Relations, Censorship, Social Hygiene

Evening Sessions:
Love before Marriage, Love in Early Married Life, and Love after 40.

Popenoe and his colleagues conducted 100 such workshops between 1930 and 1940 in what must have been one of the most active family-life-education efforts in the country (AIFR, 1940).

It is clear that from the beginning the philosophy and goals of family-life educators were very similar to those of the early marriage counselors and it is no surprise to learn that the two functions were often performed by the same people. Students in college courses and workshops with a functional focus would frequently make appointments with their instructors to pursue these matters further in private. As a consequence, those teaching such courses found themselves doing a substantial amount of premarital and marital counseling with their students. This was done almost always without fee and usually without any professional training in the techniques of counseling. A survey of those who taught such courses in 1948 (by then functional courses were taught in 632 colleges and universities) showed that they were mainly either home economists who had expanded their definition of their discipline or sociologists who had risked being identified with a nontraditional (and, some said, nonacademic) approach to the family. A few psychologists, notably Cliff Adams at Pennsylvania State University, also joined in (Bowman, 1949).

By the time of Ernest Groves' death in 1946, the field of family-life education was well established with a dozen textbooks available to choose from, a professional association to belong to (the National Council of Family Relations [NCFR], founded in 1938 by Paul Sayre) and a professional journal, *Marriage and Family Living*[2] (founded in 1939, as an organ of NCFR).

Even today, the relationship between family-life education and marriage and family therapy is reflected in the number of universities that

offer degree programs in each area within a single department.

HISTORY OF THE MARRIAGE-COUNSELING PROFESSION

It has been noted that, in the early years, marriage and premarriage counseling was often the auxiliary activity of a college professor. It was equally likely to be the auxiliary occupation of a range of other professionals, including lawyers, social workers, and physicians. One group of physicians that played a particularly central role in the early shaping of the field of marriage counseling were members of the growing specialty of obstetrics and gynecology. Like the family-life educators, these professionals were viewed as "experts" who ought to have answers for people with sexual and other marital problems. As a result, many gynecologists saw sexual and marital counseling as one important aspect of their profession. As late as 1950, over one quarter of the members of the American Association of Marriage Counselors were gynecologists and an almost equal proportion were in other medical specialties.

Phase I: 1929–1932, The Pioneers

Two different marriage-counseling centers, one on each coast, claim to have been the first in America. Both were influenced by Hirschfeld and his pioneering work in Germany. One claimant was Paul Popenoe, who uncontestedly opened the doors of the American Institute of Family Relations in Los Angeles in February 1930. He was initially the sole member of the staff, supported by a committee of 40 local backers and by the $3-per-hour fee that he charged for consultation (not a trivial amount in that year of the Great Depression) and $100-per-workshop program.

Popenoe, a biologist specializing in human heredity, came to this new enterprise from the social-hygiene movement, having been the executive secretary of the American Social Hygiene Association in New York City. A eugenics activist, he was a member of the American Genetic Association and became the editor of the

---

[2] In 1964 this became the *Journal of Marriage and the Family*.

Journal of Heredity (Peacock, 1977; Popenoe, 1975). (In fact, he was editor when Kopp published her piece on the new approaches to counseling in Nazi Germany.) He claims the distinction of being the first to introduce the phrase "marriage counseling" into the English language, that being his translation from the German *Eheberatungsstellen*, the term used for marital consultation centers in Vienna and elsewhere in Europe (Popenoe, 1975). Probably more than any other person, he promoted public recognition of the marriage-counseling profession through such means as the monthly article in the *Ladies' Home Journal*, "Can This Marriage Be Saved?" (begun in 1945 and still continuing) and on early television, providing case materials for "Divorce Court," a popular semi-documentary of the 1940s and 1950s.

The other claimants, Abraham and Hannah Stone, date their beginning differently in different places. In 1949, Abraham Stone published a short history of the field, listing his New York City clinic as commencing operations in 1929 just a few months prior to Popenoe. About the same time, his clinic filled out a survey form for Emily Mudd's book on marriage counseling that lists a 1930 opening date (several months after Popenoe) (Mudd, 1951, p. 293). Doubtless, a case could be made for either date since the Stones had been doing marriage counseling in their roles as physicians for some years prior to this. In any case, whether in 1929 or 1930, and whether first or second by a few months, it is agreed that they began operations in the New York Labor Temple and in 1932 moved to the Community Church of New York where they ran an ecumenical marriage center for many years.

A third pioneer, Emily Hartshorne Mudd, established the Marriage Council of Philadelphia in 1932. Dr. Mudd was committed to research on the marriage-counseling process and in 1939 was the first, so far as we know, to develop a continuing program of evaluative studies (Mudd, 1951). She was among the first to publish a book in the field (1951) and she collaborated in the first case book (Mudd, Stone, Karpf, & Nelson, 1958). She was also one of the three or four people most responsible for the founding of the American Association of Marriage Counselors.

Phase II: 1934–1945, The Establishment of the American Association of Marriage Counselors

In 1934, Lester Dearborn, a social hygienist and sex counselor with the Boston YMCA, invited Dr. Mudd to Boston to discuss the formation of a professional organization whose goals would be "to establish standards, exchange information and special knowledge about marital and family relations" (Humphrey, 1978). Nothing came of the meeting at that time and Dearborn later approached Abraham Stone on the matter, but again without results. Finally, he got in touch with Ernest Groves, who responded to the idea and, in April 1942 at the annual invitational Conference on Conservation of Marriage and the Family, which he had instigated at Chapel Hill, N.C., Groves proposed the establishment of a professional association for marriage counselors (Humphrey, 1978). Later that year, Dearborn and a colleague, psychiatrist Dr. Robert Laidlaw, invited six others to join them in an organizational meeting on June 20. Besides the conveners, attending were Drs. Ernest and Gladys Groves, Emily (Stuart) Mudd, Dr. Abraham Stone, Dr. Robert L. Dickenson, and Dr. Valerie Parker (Mudd & Fowler, 1976).

For the next three years, they met annually but informally under the chairmanship of Lester Dearborn. Then, in April 1945, they formally elected Ernest Groves the first president, Lester Dearborn first vice-president, Emily Mudd second vice-president, and Robert W. Laidlaw secretary-treasurer (Mudd & Fowler, 1976). The purpose of the organization was stated as follows:

The American Association of Marriage Counselors [AAMC] is a professional organization which concentrates its work specifically on marriage counseling. It has this stated purpose in the bylaws: to establish and maintain professional standards in marriage counseling. This purpose shall be furthered by meetings, clinical sessions, publications and research. Membership in it is open to those who meet its detailed requirements for clinicians in the field or for affiliates whose work in this or related fields is outstanding and for associates whose background, training, and beginning practice are sufficiently advanced to enable them to gain professionally by meeting with the more experienced counselors. (Mudd & Fowler, 1976, p. 433)

Meanwhile, across the Atlantic in London, England, David and Vera Mace, together with a few like-minded friends, were searching for a solution, or at least a constructive response, to the growing domestic conflicts they observed as a result of, first, the Depression, and then of World War II. In 1938, they formed the first Marriage Guidance Council. By 1943, it had become the National Guidance Council of Great Britain. It provided marital intervention from an organizational format that differed markedly from the German and American models. Their idea was for a few professionals to train and supervise a much larger number of lay people. These paraprofessionals (as we would call them today) would be able to provide counseling at a much reduced cost, which would bring the service into the earning range of the English working-class couple. By 1944 they had developed a syllabus for training marriage counselors and had established a system that still operates today, not only in Great Britain, but in many of the British Commonwealth countries (Mace, 1945, 1948).

Phase III: 1946–1965,
The Construction of a Profession

In 1932, there were three functioning centers for marriage counseling. Fifteen years later, in 1947, Ernest Groves listed 15 that he felt were "representative and nationally recognized." In addition to the original three in Los Angeles, Philadelphia, and New York, there were four additional New York centers plus others in Boston, Chicago, Detroit, Cincinnati, Cleveland, Washington, D.C., Chapel Hill, N.C., and San Francisco (Groves & Groves, 1947).

This group of pioneers also produced the first marriage-counseling textbooks aimed at a general professional audience. These included *Marriage and Family Counseling* (1945) by Rabbi Sydney Goldstein, who, in addition to being an early associate of the Stones and chairman of the Jewish Institute on Marriage and the Family (New York), served a term as president of the National Council on Family Relations; *Marriage Counseling Practice* (1948) by John Cuber, one of the academics of the group; *Marriage Counseling* (1948) by David Mace, who, in addition

to his work in Great Britain, was a "foreign corresponding member" of AAMC almost from its founding; and, as has been previously noted, *The Practice of Marriage Counseling* (1951) by Emily Mudd of the Marriage Council of Philadelphia.

In 1948 a joint committee of the AAMC and the National Council on Family Relations, under the chairmanship of Abraham Stone, proposed a set of standards for marriage counselors (see Figure 1-1).

As Nichols (1979) has noted, the course of development from a more or less naively service-oriented group to a fledgling profession can be traced in the sequence of standards for training issued by the organization over the years. Their first target of concern was standards for marriage counselors (1949) (see Figure 1-1); next their concern shifted to standards for marriage-counseling centers (1953), then for training centers for postgraduate professional marriage counselors (1959) and related doctoral programs with a major in marriage counseling (1962). It is perhaps also a sign of maturity that in 1962 a code of ethics was formally adopted (Mudd & Fowler, 1976).

In 1956 the association accredited three training centers: Marriage Council of Philadelphia, the Merrill-Palmer School in Detroit, and the Menninger Clinic in Topeka, Kansas.

With all of these achievements, it might be supposed that by the early 1960s the new profession had established a reasonably clear identity and philosophy of treatment. Unhappily, the evidence is that these clarities were slow in coming. For example, a study of case records from three of the pioneering clinics (one on the East Coast, one in the Midwest, and one on the West Coast) found that conjoint couple interviews constituted only 5 percent of their practice in 1940, 9 percent in 1950, and 15 percent in 1960 (Michaelson, 1963). While these increases were statistically significant because of the large numbers of cases, they are not very impressive. Even more disappointing is the datum that conjoint whole-family interviews dropped over this same period from 5 percent to 3 percent to 1 percent. Clearly, the modal approach was still the one-on-one interview with an individual about his or her family problems.

Other research from the very end of this pe-

Marriage Counseling Report of the Joint Subcommittee on Standards for Marriage Counselors of the National Council on Family Relations and The American Association of Marriage Counselors

Abraham Stone, M.D., Chairman
Janet Fowler Nelson, Secretary

Gladys H. Groves	Emily Hartshorne Mudd
Sophia J. Kleegman, M.D.	Reverend Otis R. Rice
Robert W. Laidlaw, M.D.	Anna Budd Ware
Herbert D. Lamson	

Marriage counseling is here regarded as a specialized field of family counseling which centers largely on the interpersonal relationship between husband and wife. It involves many disciplines and is interprofessional in character. Those who wish to enter this field, however, whether physician, clergyman, psychiatrist or social worker, require a common body of scientific knowledge, techniques and qualifications.

Standards for acceptable and recognized marriage counselors, are herewith presented in terms of academic training, professional experience and qualifications, and personal qualifications.

1. Academic Training
   a. Every marriage counselor shall have a graduate or professional degree from an aproved institution as minimum qualification. This degree shall be in one of the following fields: education, home economics, law, medicine, nursing, psychology, religion, social anthropology, social work, and sociology.
   b. Whatever the field of major emphasis, there shall be included accredited training in: psychology of personality development; elements of psychiatry; human biology, including the fundamentals of sex anatomy, physiology and genetics; sociology of marriage and the family; legal aspects of marriage and the family; and counseling techniques.

2. Professional Experience and Qualifications
   a. The candidate shall have had at least three years of recognized professional experience subsequent to obtaining his degree. In addition, he shall have had actual experience as a clinical assistant in marriage counseling under approved supervision.
   b. A candidate's qualifications shall include:
   • Diagnostic skill in differentiating between the superficial and the deeper level types of maladjustment, and the ability to recognize when the latter type requires referral to other specialists.
   • A scientific attitude toward individual variation and deviation, especially in the field of human sex behavior, and the ability to discuss sexual problems objectively.

3. Personal Qualifications
   a. The candidate shall possess personal and professional integrity in accordance with accepted ethical standards.
   b. The candidate shall have an attitude of interest, warmth, and kindness toward people, combined with a high degree of integration and emotional maturity.
   c. The personal experience of marriage and parenthood is a decided asset.

Figure 1-1. AAMC/National Council on Family Relations standards for marriage counselors (From *Marriage and Family Living, 11,* 5, 1949)

riod suggested part of the reason for the slowness of change. A 1965 survey of AAMC members (Alexander, 1968) showed that only 25 percent of them identified themselves primarily as marriage counselors. For the remainder, it was an auxiliary activity. Table 1-1 shows that those whose primary professional identity was as "marriage counselor" saw the most couples and/or families and the fewest individuals. Those who identified themselves as clinicians from another profession (medicine, psychology, social work) saw the largest number of individuals. The third

group (mostly academics who taught marriage and family courses) fell in between.[3]

Perhaps this lack of a clear commitment to any particular clinical philosophy, together with the scattered loyalties of its members, contributed to the difficulties of the professional asso-

---

[3] *Editors' Note.* Since Alexander's data are now more than three decades old, it would be informative to see an update on these trends, both within the membership of the AAMFT and among non-AAMFT members who regularly do marital and/or family therapy.

TABLE 1-1

Percent of AAMC Members in 1965 by Primary
Professional Identification and Treatment Modality

| Treatment Modality | Primary Professional Identification | | |
	Marriage Counselor (N = 75)	Other Therapist (N = 114)	Nonclinical Professional (N = 93)
Individual	11	46	19
Marriage	63	30	56
Family	23	23	17
Other*	3	1	8
Total	100	100	100

* Modified to absorb rounding percents. (From Alexander, 1968, Table 15, p. 157.)

TABLE 1-2

Frequency of Publications on Marital Therapy
in Selected Periods

| Period | Number of Publications* | | Cumulative Frequency |
	N	%	
Pre-1940	5	(1.2)	5
1940–1948	11	(2.7)	16
1949–1951	16	(3.8)	32
1952–1954	16	(3.8)	48
1955–1957	21	(5.0)	69
1958–1960	29	(7.0)	98
1961–1963	45	(10.9)	143
1964–1966	68	(16.4)	211
1967–1969	119	(28.7)	330
1970–1972†	85	(20.5)	415
Total	415	(100.0)	

* Numbers in parentheses indicate the percent of the total number of publications occurring in each period.
† This period extends through August 1972 only; hence, the number of publications in this period will need to be adjusted upward later. (From Gurman, 1973, Table 1, p. 49.)

ciation set up by the early practitioners. In any case, despite the significant achievements of its early years of existence, the AAMC fell on hard times in the late 1950s. It was forced to close the doors of its headquarters office in New York because it could no longer pay its bills. Providentially, in 1960, David and Vera Mace (who had immigrated to America in 1949) were persuaded to adopt the ailing organization and to operate it out of their New Jersey home for several years until it once more became self-sufficient.

While this drama was being played out on the East Coast, a scenario of perhaps equal significance to the future of the profession was being enacted on the West Coast. There, a determined band of Southern California marriage counselors successfully lobbied their state legislature to set up licensing for the profession. Among the members of this group were James A. Peterson, the founder of the first Ph.D. training center for marriage counselors in the western United States (at the University of California in 1953); Clinton Phillips, at that time director of the American Institute of Family Relations, which Popenoe had founded in 1930 (and later himself the founder of the California Family Studies Center); and James Rue, who became a leader of the free-standing California Association of Marriage and Family Counselors. To this day, the California Association has not chosen to affiliate with the national organization, but nevertheless has prospered and in 1990 claimed a membership of almost 18,000 members.

With the passage in 1963 of the California law licensing marriage, family, and child counselors, for the first time it became unlawful for an untrained person to set up practice as a marriage or family counselor in that state. The legislature also established for the first time a legally recognized, family-oriented clinical profession that was separate from social work, psychology, and psychiatry. It may be said that with the enactment of that law, the marriage-counseling movement took a major step toward becoming a full-fledged profession.

Phase IV: 1966–1975, Consolidation and Maturation as a Profession

At the beginning of this decade of consolidation and maturation, the fledgling profession of marriage counseling still lacked a coherent theoretical foundation or body of scholarship. This was well documented by Gurman's (1973) comprehensive survey of all professional articles on marriage counseling and therapy done from the beginning through 1972 (see Table 1-2).

It can be seen that the growth of a body of clinical literature was very slow prior to 1960 and that all of the literature prior to 1963 constituted fewer items than were published in the following six years (1964–1969). Two other observations about literature in the field are appropriate. First, when Gurman examined the journals in which these articles (through 1972) appeared, he noted that "the heterogeneity of the professional discipline represented . . . is striking: psychiatric, psychological, social work, and sociological journals are all included" (Gurman, 1973, p. 49). He found over 50 journals represented among these professions.

Even more disconcerting is Goodman's (1973) analysis of that subset of 170 marriage-counseling articles published between 1931 and 1968 that present research findings. She noted that 28 percent contained no references, while this occurred in only 9.5 percent of the articles she drew from the scientific literature in more academic fields.[4] The average number of references per marriage-counseling article was six (compared with 15 among the scientific articles). Cross-referencing was minimal.

Only 54 of the 170 papers were cited by other papers within the population. In other words 68% of the papers constituting the field received no citations in the relevant research literature. . . . There were only 116 instances of cross-referencing and a fifth of them were self-citations. . . . Only fifteen of the papers were cited three or more times, seven being the highest number of citations received by any paper in the population. (Goodman, 1973, p. 112)

What these data make apparent is that there was no cohesive body of marriage-counseling professionals who followed each other's work, built upon each other's experiences, or critiqued each other's theories. Until 1975, the year that marks the end of this period, there was no central journal for the field.[5] In that year, the organization established the *Journal of Marital and Family Counseling* (renamed the *Journal of Marriage and Family Therapy* in 1979), with William Nichols as its first editor. But prior to that event (and for some time afterward), each practitioner played to his or her own home discipline, for the most part untouched by the work of marriage counselors from different disciplines who published in journals he or she never read.

The chief focusing mechanisms in the field were the annual meetings of the AAMC itself and also of the Counseling Section (founded in 1962) of the National Council on Family Relations, which boasted almost as many members as the AAMC in these years (Jewson, 1970).

One of the benefits of the multidisciplinary nature of the field was the proliferation of approaches to marital problems. A number of behavioral approaches were developed by therapists such as Richard Stuart (1969, 1975, 1976), David Knox (1971), and the Oregon group (Weiss, Hops, & Patterson, 1973; Jacobson & Martin, 1976). (For a later and fuller development of these approaches see Jacobson and Margolin [1979] and Holtzworth-Munroe and Jacobson, Chapter 4).

Couples communications workshops proliferated as a sort of short-term group approach to marital problems. Among the most carefully developed of these were the Minnesota Couples Communications Program (Miller, Nunnally, & Wackman, 1975, 1976) and the conjugal-therapy groups developed by Guerney and his colleagues at Pennsylvania State University (Guerney, 1977).

Still another variant that focused on prevention rather than cure was the marital enrichment movement in its many manifestations (Mace & Mace, 1976; Otto, 1975).

But perhaps the most influential force in the marriage-counseling movement during the 1960s and early 1970s was the confluence of the other three movements, as marriage counselors became aware of them.[6] In the early '60s, many of the pioneers of the family-therapy movement (whom we shall discuss below) were invited to address the annual meetings of the AAMC. Nathan Ackerman, John Bell, Virginia Satir, Sanford N. Sherman, John Warkentin, and others made clinical presentations on the new, whole-family approaches. The impact was sufficient that in 1964 the AAMC approached the editorial board of the journal *Family Process*, which had only recently been founded by Jackson and his Palo Alto group together with Ackerman and his

---

[4] Goodman's "more academic fields" are identified as "fields based on the classical scientific model: emphasizing elemental analysis, using extensive controls, and directed toward producing prediction based on universal laws deduced from empirical findings" (Goodman, 1973, p. 111). They are not specified beyond this definition.

[5] *Editors' Note.* When the first edition of this *Handbook* was published in 1981, there existed almost a dozen English-language family-therapy journals and about a half-dozen foreign-language journals. As of 1990, we are aware of the existence of at least 15 of the former and a dozen of the latter types of family-therapy journals.

---

[6] *Editors' Note.* It is interesting to note that while the *Journal of Marriage and Family Counseling* grew out of the marriage-counseling movement, almost half the articles in its first two volumes were on *family* therapy.

New York group as the basic organ of the family-therapy movement. The marriage-counseling organization wanted to join as the third sponsor of the journal. The offer was refused (Humphrey, 1978), but the interest of AAMC members in the exciting new field of family therapy did not end, and in 1970 they changed the name of their organization to reflect their broadened perspective, becoming the American Association of Marriage *and Family* Counselors (AAMFC).

William Masters and Virginia Johnson were also invited speakers at annual meetings during the late 1960s, although the cause of general amalgamation with the sex-therapy field was set back at least a decade by AAMC's shortsighted rejection of the application of these two giants for membership. It seems that neither of them had received any training as relationship counselors and the committee on membership could not see any reason to make an exception in their case. (This was prior to the publication of their 1970 book and resulted in their refusing to make any further presentations to the group or to respond to later invitations to resubmit their applications.)

The confluence of all of these forces resulted in a paradoxical situation. By 1975, the field of marriage counseling had finally achieved enough sense of professional identity to support its own professional organization and to found its own journal. On the other hand, the strong currents of amalgamation among the four movements threatened to swallow it whole. As it turned out, the AAMFC itself survived and thrives today (having again changed its name, in 1978, to the American Association for Marriage and Family *Therapy*, or AAMFT), but the marriage-counseling movement has become so merged with the more dynamic family-therapy movement that it has all but lost its separate sense of identity. As one evidence of that, the speakers (Sluzki & Bloch, 1984) invited to keynote the 40th anniversary of the founding of AAMC were luminaries from the family-therapy movement, and, in their review of the significant events in the history of the marriage- and family-therapy field, failed to note the founding of the AAMC among them.

THE HISTORY OF SEX THERAPY

In a later section of the chapter, we shall review the development of social psychiatry as a major source for the ideas developed in the marriage- and family-therapy movements. It played little or no part in the development of modern sex therapy. To Freud and his successors, sexual problems were symptoms of underlying neuroses that needed to be exorcised through intensive, long-term analytic reshaping of the psyche. As we have already indicated, however, an alternative approach to the treatment of sexual disorders developed in Europe during the 1920s and 1930s that was more direct and pragmatic. Among the founders of this movement were Havelock Ellis in England and Magnus Hirschfeld in Germany.

In general, sexual counseling in America closely followed the patterns set in Europe. Most practitioners came to the field from the social-hygiene movement (for example, Paul Popenoe in Los Angeles and Lester Dearborn in Boston) or from medicine (for example, Abraham Stone in New York and Robert L. Dickinson). Without a doubt, special note should be given to the work of Dickinson. He was an extraordinary scientist and counselor in the area of human sexuality. A gynecologist, he systematically sketched the pelvic anatomy of each of his thousands of patients and of many males as well. His 1933 publication, *Human Sexual Anatomy*, and its 1949 expansion and revision illustrate and document the anatomy of the human pelvis in its most diverse manifestations. He even anticipated Masters by using a penis-sized test tube to simulate intercourse from various angles and depths of penetration, thus permitting a clear correlation between what could be observed internally and the sensation reported by the patient. Beyond his observational data, he interviewed thousands of his patients on their sex histories and current practices (Dickinson & Beam, 1931, 1934). It is doubtful that anyone before him was in a position to counsel couples on their sexual problems with more authority.

Thus, when he became one of the founding members of the AAMC, he brought a wealth of sophisticated knowledge on the sexual aspects of marriage to that small group of professionals. It is not surprising that the third meeting of the

AAMC in the mid-1940s had as its topic, "Clinical Techniques in the Treatment of Frigidity" (Humphrey, 1978).

The American with sexual problems in the 1930s and 1940s thus had some chance of finding a counselor who was at least informed as to the scientific knowledge available at that time. By modern standards, these were, perhaps, not very effective sex therapists. Still, it seems probable that individuals or couples consulting one of these specialists would have received a great deal better help than if they had consulted their pastor or family doctor, or even their psychotherapist, if the professional in question lacked specialized training in this field.

The monumental work of Alfred Kinsey and his associates (1948, 1953) added immeasurably to the knowledge base upon which sex therapists had to draw. That research team took comprehensive lifetime sex histories from literally thousands of American men and women across a broad spectrum of social backgrounds. Their findings and the publicity that attended the publication of those findings raised the consciousness of Americans concerning their own sexual biases and behavior as nothing before or since has done.

As important as Kinsey's work was in the development of the field, it was, however, overshadowed by the contributions of Masters and Johnson (1966, 1970). William H. Masters was a research-oriented gynecologist who had been interested in the physiology of sexual functioning since his medical school days. He had apprenticed, in effect, in the laboratory of one of the outstanding authorities on pelvic anatomy in the world at that time, George Washington Carver of the University of Rochester School of Medicine. Carver advised him that if he was serious about this interest, he owed it to himself, first, to wait until he was at least 40 before becoming involved in sex research; second, to preface it by earning a reputation as a scientist in some other, less controversial field; and, third, not to consider pursuing such research until he had the support of a major medical school or university (Brecher, 1971).

Masters came close to keeping this counsel. By 1954, when he entered into the project that was to make him famous, he had, indeed, achieved prominence in his profession through his research on hormone replacement in older women and the development of a nonsurgical procedure for creating a vagina in women who had been born without one; also, he was a research professor at the Washington University School of Medicine. He did lack two years of being 40, but he was encouraged to hasten his project by the positive reception of Kinsey's *Sexual Behavior in the Human Female* the year before (1953).

In 1955, he decided it would be important to add a female coinvestigator to the project. He applied to the University Placement Bureau and they sent over a Virginia Johnson, recently divorced and looking for a way to support her young family. She seemed serious and mature and had a manner that he felt would put female subjects at ease. He hired her and they have remained partners in research and therapy and eventually in marriage.

The results of their work began to be published in the late '50s and early '60s and reprints were quickly circulated among those doing couple counseling. The articles were purposely written in the most obtuse medical jargon so as to certify the intent to write for a medical audience and not for popular consumption. Their book *Human Sexual Response* (1966) followed the same format. Both the authors and the publishers were astonished at the sales volume. It is difficult to believe that many of the 300,000 who bought the book were able to understand what they read. If they found it difficult, however, they got a great deal of help from the media. Popularizations appeared in a number of widely read magazines and the authors were interviewed on popular talk shows. More important for this history, Masters and Johnson did literally dozens of presentations at various professional meetings, explaining their findings to physicians, therapists, and educators of all kinds.

It is difficult to overestimate the impact of this work on those working with couples and their sex problems. One concrete consequence was the founding in 1967 of the American Association of Sex Educators and Counselors (AASEC) with Patricia Schiller as its head. It became the first organization to set up standards of certification for sex therapists, in 1972 (AASEC, 1973), and granted the first certificates the following year.

But it was Masters and Johnson's second book, *Human Sexual Inadequacy* (1970), that set forth their clinical applications of their earlier findings and revolutionized the field. Not only did Masters and Johnson begin to train others in their methods at their center in St. Louis, but within months many others had begun to offer training in their own derivative versions of the new approach.

Actually, the approaches utilized by Masters and Johnson were not entirely new. A technique very similar to the one they recommended for dealing with premature ejaculation had been put forth by J. H. Semans in 1956. In 1958, a systematic behavioral approach (of individual, not conjoint, treatment) based on many of the same principles they used had been spelled out in a book by Wolpe, *Psychotherapy by Reciprocal Inhibition*. Neither of these innovative works had the impact on the field that *Human Sexual Inadequacy* had. In recent years, however, sex therapists have turned to those earlier contributions and found them helpful. One whole wing of the sex-therapy movement that is represented by behavior therapists finds more to model in Wolpe than in the St. Louis approach (LoPiccolo & LoPiccolo, 1978).

Feminists have repudiated the view that the best unit of diagnosis and treatment is the couple. Rather, they encourage women to meet together in groups and, through discussion and the assignment of masturbatory exercises, take responsibility for their own sexuality. Hite (1976) and others have also objected to the view that women who cannot have an orgasm in intercourse (that is, without direct clitorial stimulation) are other than typical and normal. They insist that it is sexist to suppose that women should find intercourse as enjoyable as more direct forms of stimulation. In these emphases, they follow behavioral approaches to sexual therapy rather than Masters and Johnson's approach.

Since 1970, a veritable deluge of workshops, short courses, and the like have been offered, scores of sex clinics have been opened, books have proliferated, two journals have been founded (*Journal of Sex and Marital Therapy; Journal of Sex Education and Therapy*), and the AASEC has set up standards for certifying qualified sex therapists. Although the youngest of the four therapeutic movements we have discussed, it is clear that the impact of sex therapy on the broader profession has been no less than the others.

THE DEVELOPMENT OF SOCIAL PSYCHIATRY[7]

Psychoanalysis, as it was initially propounded by Freud, placed instinctual libidinal drive at the center of its explanation of human behavior. Although Freud recognized the importance of early familial relationships in shaping the personality (the prime example being the oedipal rivalry), still, several of his students felt that he underemphasized social elements. Among the most outspoken were Alfred Adler and Carl Jung.

About 1910, Adler became the first of Freud's pupils to challenge him openly on these matters, offering an alternative and more socially rooted theory of psychodynamics (Adler, 1917). He held that the driving dynamic of life was the deeply internalized sense of inferiority to which we all fell heir by virtue of being born small and helpless. Rather than sexual drive, we were motivated by a compulsion to achieve feelings of adequacy and power. In this struggle, we might follow one of two paths. We might flee into illness from which we dominate and manipulate those around us through weakness (a strategy later theorists called metacomplementarity (Watzlawick, Beavin, & Jackson, 1967). Alternatively, we might engage those around us in a more open struggle for power. In this second case, Adler foreshadowed the theories of most contemporary family therapists, who also attempt to explain individual pathology as a by-product of family conflict. Indeed, Adler may have been the first of Freud's disciples to break the rules about seeing members of the same family. He did not publish his experiences with this daring new format, but he did encourage his own disciple, Rudolph Dreikurs, to pursue this approach in a more systematic fashion (Dreikurs, 1948, 1949a, 1951).

Jung also took the position that a child's personality was a product not only of the direct experience with each parent, but also of the relationship between them.

In 1910, he spelled out this concept in more contemporary sounding terms:

---

[7] This discussion is heavily indebted to the treatment of this subject by Thompson (1951).

The concealed discord between the parents, the secret worry, the regressed hidden wishes, all of these produce in the individual a certain affective state which slowly but severely, though unconsciously, works its way into the child's mind, producing therein the same conditions and hence the same reactions to external stimuli . . . The more sensitive and moldable the child, the deeper the impression. (Jung, 1910, pp. 246–247)

Another Jungian concept that places the role of social expectations in sharp focus is the *persona* (or *mask*) each person assumes in social situations in order to meet the expectations of others. This concept is closely allied with those being developed independently by the influential social psychologists Mead (1934) and Cooley (1909) in this same general period.

In the 1920s, Rank introduced innovations in style that were more appropriate to family therapy than traditional techniques had been. He focused more on what was happening in the session itself and less on what had happened years before; he introduced his own personality and feelings into sessions rather than remaining detached and fostering idealization; and he set a definite time limit to treatment (Thompson, 1951).

In the 1930s, as Hitler gradually forced analysts to leave continental Europe, a strong community of analysts developed in America. These men and women were more in touch with the work of anthropologists and sociologists than their predecessors had been and these influences were manifest in varying degrees in their theories and therapeutic approaches. Among the most influential to emerge from this cross-fertilization were Erich Fromm (1941, 1947) and Harry Stack Sullivan (1947, 1953).

Fromm's emphasis was on the interaction between a person and society. He echoed Jung's insights into social *customs*: "The most beautiful as well as the most ugly inclinations of man are not a part of a fixed and biologically given human nature but result from the social process which creates man" (Fromm, 1941, p. 12). His emphasis in the development of individuality foreshadowed the work of Bowen and others on the importance of differentiation from the family.

Sullivan was the most interpersonally oriented of all of the American analysts. He was definitely influenced by early social psychol-
ogists such as Mead and Cooley. For example, one of his central concepts is the notion that, before learning to communicate in symbols, a child experiences the mother's emotions through "empathy." Maternal anger or disapproval of any kind is transmitted to the child as anxiety and insecurity. The concept of self is shaped by the parts of one's behavior that others respond to, positively or negatively. Sullivan uses the term "reflected appraisals" to indicate much the same process as "looking-glass self" (Cooley, 1909) or "generalized other" (Mead, 1934) referred to in social psychology. His theory of child development, far more than Freud's or any other analyst's at that time, reflected the child as growing in response to shifting social situations as he or she matures.

Two other aspects of Sullivan's work provided important precedents and foundations for the innovators who were to follow. First, he was among the first to assert and to demonstrate that schizophrenia could be treated by psychotherapy. Several of the founders of family therapy were initially engaged in a Sullivanian approach to the treatment of schizophrenia (e.g., Bowen and Jackson). Second, he was first and foremost a clinician rather than a theorist; that is, he refused to be impressed by any theory that could not be demonstrated in practical work with patients (Thompson, 1951). Without doubt, this disposition to trust one's experience instead of the reigning dogma characterizes the founders of all of the movements discussed in this chapter.

Other analysts made important contributions toward the establishment of a social emphasis in psychiatry, and by midcentury, when the family-therapy pioneers were beginning to experiment, there was a well-established bias in that direction among American analysts. The work of Fromm-Reichmann (1950), Horney (1937, 1939), and Thompson (1951), in particular, led to greater understanding of the relationship between a patient's behavior and his or her familial experiences and interactions. For a more detailed account of the conceptual roots of the movement, see Miller and Sobelman (1985).

FROM CLASSICAL ANALYSIS TO CONJOINT MARITAL THERAPY

Psychoanalysis by its very nature is concerned with the internal dynamics of the human psyche, and with an analysis of the patient–therapist relationship. Freud left a legacy of conviction that it was counterproductive and dangerous for a therapist to become involved with more than one member of the same family. It is not clear from his writing what exactly prompted him to feel so strongly on the matter. It is known that on at least one occasion he did undertake the analysis of a husband and wife simultaneously. They were James and Alex Strachey, who later became his English translators (Stone, 1971). Perhaps the experience was a difficult one for him. In any case, he wrote:

When it comes to the treatment of relationships I must confess myself utterly at a loss and I have altogether little faith in any individual therapy of them. (Freud, 1912)

and later he commented further:

When the husband's resistance is added to that of the wife, efforts are made fruitless and therapy is prematurely broken off, . . . We had undertaken something which under existing conditions was impossible to carry out. (Freud, 1915)

This negative assessment became virtually a doctrine among analysts. In 1938, a survey of British analysts found that almost without exception they accepted the prohibition against analyzing members of the same family (Glover, 1955).

On the other hand, it should be noted that a minority felt that there were extenuating circumstances under which this might be permissible (for the most part, when families insisted) and we must assume that some had attempted it without reaping the dire consequences others feared would attend such a practice. As late as 1956, even such a forward-looking analyst as Kubie wrote:

The concurrent analysis of husband and wife . . . may be of great value when conducted independently by two psychoanalysts; but experienced psychoanalysts generally regard as unwise the simultaneous treatment of both husband and wife by one analyst . . . it makes the task of both patients harder. In the end one or the other is likely to lose his confidence in the impartiality of the analyst and the analysis of the patient will suffer accordingly. Therefore, since it is usually wise not to postpone the analysis of one until after the other is finished, it is well to send the second patient to another psychoanalyst as soon as possible. (Kubie, 1956, pp. 36–37)

In addition to concern about impartiality, analysts were centrally concerned with the complications of multiple transference and countertransference problems. Mittlemann (1956) further cautioned that the concurrent analysis of both members of a marriage by the same analyst required a good memory to keep straight what had been learned from each. In the even more radical modality of conjoint therapy, the concern was that neither would be willing to deal candidly with sensitive material in the presence of the other spouse. It is probable that none of these objections could have been successfully met on theoretical grounds. However, as increasing numbers of analysts found occasions to break the rules for special cases, it became clear that, in practice, these problems could be overcome and that therapy sometimes actually went faster.

It appears that the first report on the psychoanalysis of married couples was made by Clarence Oberndorf, a New York analyst, at a meeting of the American Psychiatric Association in 1931 (Sager, 1966). The paper was published in expanded form in 1938 and described the sequential analysis of five married couples (Oberndorf, 1938). In 1933 he read a paper titled "Folie à Deux" before the New York Neurological Society (published the following year as Oberndorf, 1934), which attempted to spell out a theory of interactive or emergent neuroses in a marriage.

In 1936, the Ninth International Congress of Psychoanalysis met in Nyon, Switzerland, with the theme, "Family Neuroses and the Neurotic Family." Sager's summary of the conference and its impact is succinct:

Laforgue, the main speaker, reported on his experience in analyzing simultaneously several members of one family. He showed how two partners in a marriage unconsciously communicate how they support their complementary neurosis. . . . Leuba, at the same Congress, discussed his analytic experience with 14 families and made the first attempt at a systematic "family diagnosis." These early reports unfortunately got sidetracked in the subsequent development of psychoanalysis . . . . (Sager, 1966, p. 459)

Perhaps the intervention of World War II deflected the attention of the psychoanalytic community from the issue. In any case, soon after the end of that conflict, in 1948, Bela Mittlemann of the New York Psychoanalytic Institute published the first accounts of concurrent marital therapies in America. Earlier (1944) he had contributed a theoretical paper elaborating on Oberndorf's concept of *folie à deux*. He wrote, "Because of the continuous and intimate nature of marriage every neurosis in a married person is strongly anchored in the married relationship." Mittlemann continued, "It is a useful and at times indispensable therapeutic measure to concentrate the analytic discussions on these complementary patterns and, if necessary, to have both mates treated" (Mittlemann, 1944, p. 491).

At about this time, Henry Dicks and his colleagues at the Tavistock Clinic in England had set up a Family Psychiatric Unit, staffed by psychiatric social workers who worked toward the reconciliation of couples referred by the divorce courts. They soon after brought under the Tavistock umbrella the Family Discussion Bureau, a marital casework agency directed by Dr. Michael Balint and Enid Balint. Although these clinics were modeled after the American marriage-counseling centers discussed in the previous section, their inclusion in the services of a respected psychiatric facility such as the Tavistock Clinic added impetus to the movement among psychiatrists (Dicks, 1964). Another milestone was passed in 1956 with the publication by Victor Eisenstein, director of the New Jersey Neuropsychiatric Institute, of an edited book titled *Neurotic Interaction in Marriage*. In 1959, Don Jackson coined the term "conjoint therapy" to describe a therapist meeting conjointly with a husband and wife (Jackson, 1959).

The movement continued as a force among psychoanalysts into the 1960s with major articles appearing in psychiatric texts (e.g., Green, 1965; Green, Broadhurst, & Lustig, 1965; Laidlaw,

1956) and journals (e.g., Rodgers, 1965; Watson, 1963), and even in the new journal *Family Process* (Carroll, Cambor, Leopold, Miller, & Reis, 1963). In 1965 the Society of Medical Psychoanalysis held a symposium on psychoanalysis and marriage (Sager, 1966). Nevertheless, increasingly in the 1960s and 1970s, the movement was absorbed into the more broadly based family-therapy movement. Probably Sager's excellent 1966 history of the movement (upon which we have drawn shamelessly) was written at the very zenith of its independent development.

THE FAMILY-THERAPY MOVEMENT

Precursors

The family-therapy movement, like the marital-therapy movement, grew out of the general field of psychiatry. Within that broad discipline, we have already outlined some of the major elements that prepared the way for what was to follow. Certain published works seem to have been particularly seminal if we are to credit the footnotes in the writings of the earliest pioneers. A series of papers over the years emphasized the importance of the family in the etiology and management of serious emotional difficulties. In addition to some of Freud's early work on the Oedipus complex and related ideas, some of the most frequently cited were: (1) Flugel's (1921) *The Psychoanalytic Study of the Family*, which discussed the individual analysis of various family members; (2) Moreno's work over the decades of the 1930s and 1940s with group psychodrama methods, including work with married couples and other family members (Moreno, 1934, 1940, 1952); (3) Ackerman's (1938) article "The Unity of the Family"; and (4) Richardson's (1945) influential book *Patients Have Families*.

In 1949, John Bowlby published an article, "The Study and Reduction of Group Tension in the Family," in which he described conjoint family interviews used as auxiliary to individual interviews at the Tavistock Child Guidance Clinic. Apparently this technique developed out of frustration with a young teenager he had in treatment who was making very little progress.

After two years of weekly treatment sessions, very many of which were missed, I decided to confront the main actors with the problem as I saw it. Thus I planned a session in which I could see father, mother and boy together. This proved a very interesting and valuable session . . . and a turning point in the case. (1949, pp. 19–20)

Noting that this approach was really only an adaptation of group-therapy techniques already developed by others, he went on to reassure his readers that he and his colleagues at Tavistock considered the family application of these techniques still experimental. "Though we rarely employ it more than once or twice in a particular case, we are coming to use it almost as a routine after the initial examination and before treatment is inaugurated" (p. 20).

There is no contemporary evidence that this paper, published in a new, and at that time not very widely read, journal, was seen by any of the Americans who were active in founding the family-therapy movement. As we shall see, however, by an odd quirk, the work at Tavistock served as a major stimulus to the development of this new approach in the United States.

There is some evidence that other therapists in Hungary and elsewhere were also beginning to see whole families at this time, but none of this information made its way across the Atlantic until years later (Silverman & Silverman, 1962). In the United States, Rudolf Dreikurs of the Community Child Guidance Center of Chicago, a disciple of Adler, seems to have developed a program very similar to the one at Tavistock in this same period. We have found very few references to his work, however, aside from a footnote in Bell (1967), and it appears that his innovative approaches also contributed less than they might have to the movement as it actually emerged (see Dreikurs, 1948, 1949a, 1949b, 1950, and 1951). More recently, there has been some renewed interest in Adlerian thought in family therapy (Sherman & Dinkmeyer, 1987).

The Founding Decade: 1952–1961

As every historian of the family-therapy movement has noted (e.g., Guerin, 1976; Kaslow, 1979), it began in a dozen places at once among independent-minded therapists and researchers in many parts of the country. By the end of the 1950s, however, it had emerged as a connected movement whose members exchanged correspondence and visits and began to cite one another in footnotes. We have arbitrarily chosen the decade 1952–1961 as the founding decade because 1952 seems to be the year in which a number of the pioneers made major steps toward establishing conjoint family therapy as a treatment approach and because 1961 is the year that nearly all of them finally met together in a body to prepare the way for the first "state of the art" joint handbook (Ackerman, Beatman, & Sherman, 1967) and to found a common journal, *Family Process*, which first appeared in 1962.

John Bell

Among the many claimants for the title "father of family therapy," perhaps none has better credentials than John Bell. By all odds the best statement on how he got into the business was reported in a *Saturday Evening Post* interview with him.

In August of 1951, Dr. John Bell—then a professor of psychology at Clark University in Worcester, Massachusetts—had been staying as a house guest at the home of Dr. John Sutherland, medical director of the famed Tavistock Clinic in London. One afternoon, while Mrs. Sutherland and Mrs. Bell were preparing tea and the Sutherland and Bell children were playing in a nearby room, the British doctor started describing some recent studies in his institution.

"I've been meaning to tell you about the work of one of our psychiatrists" [Bowlby], he said. "He's been having the whole family of the patient come in."

At that moment the two wives entered with the tea tray, and the conversation changed. But a few days later, sailing home to the United States, Dr. Bell recalled the idea of "having the whole family of the patient come in."

"Long afterward," he said a few months ago, "I learned I'd misunderstood Jack Sutherland. He was actually talking about seeing all the family members individually, with an occasional conference with the whole family. But it was my impression that his colleague was seeing the entire family together at each session. It was a startling thought to me—after all, nobody was doing a thing like that—but it sounded appealing. I decided to try it myself."

Back at Clark University Dr. Bell was asked to consult on the case of a 13-year-old boy who had been expelled from a Western Massachusetts school because of "violent behavioral problems." He decided to work not only with the patient, but also with his parents and his two sisters. The father, a bank official, took a dim view of the proposal, but finally agreed to participate.

"It's a lot of nonsense," he said. "It's Billy who has the trouble. The rest of the family is fine."

By the second session it became clear that the rest of the family was far from fine. The mother was revealed as a rigid perfectionist with strong feelings of hostility towards her son, an adopted child. The father, unable to cope with his wife, had taken to drinking. As the parents drifted apart, the son developed problems.

"The basic problem involved the entire family unit," Dr. Bell reported, "and it was with this entire unit that I decided to work."

Early in 1953 he made his first report to a group of fellow psychologists, describing the successful use of the new family approach on this and nine other families. Unfortunately his preliminary account wasn't published in a national scientific journal. Dr. Bell—now an official of the National Institute of Mental Health in San Francisco—continued his pioneering work, but most psychotherapists were unaware of it. (Silverman and Silverman, 1962)

Something of Bell's character and of his relation to the rest of the field is reflected in his preface to the 1972 paperback version of Ackerman's early landmark publication, *The Psychodynamics of Family Life*. He wrote, in part,

When Arthur Rosenthal asked me to write a foreword to this new paperback edition of the late Nat Ackerman's classic book, I accepted immediately and without reservation.

Why had I reacted so fast? Out of the past came painful memories. I recalled how this book, when I first confronted it in 1958, had provoked in me sharply hostile reactions. My own ideas of the family and family therapy seemed to me to have gone beyond those of Ackerman, and to have been more revolutionary. As our differences emerged in public and were followed by years of competitive sparring, they raised barriers to professional and personal openness. Was I now really welcoming a public chance to expose old wounds?

But the later years brought about a change in our relations. The publication of *Family Process* threw us together as colleagues. A friendship of growing closeness and trust began and deepened, terminated too soon by his sudden death. This mutual respect and affection led us to reconsider our differences and contentions. (Bell, 1972)

Among Bell's most respected contributions is his book *Family Group Therapy* (1961). It constituted, in effect, a handbook of family therapy, and, together with the 1958 Ackerman volume he chose to ignore, constituted one of the founding documents of the profession.

Nathan W. Ackerman

Ackerman came to family therapy from the field of child psychiatry. Some appreciation for the distance he came in his career can be gained from his description of his own training.

During the nineteen thirties, while I was undergoing medical and specialty training, the worst chore for the resident physician in neurology and psychiatry was a weekly duty to visit with the patient's relatives and to report progress. In those days, this was felt to be an unmitigated bore, an inescapable nuisance, having no bearing whatever on the medical care and treatment of the patient. It was tacitly understood among young physicians that the main incentive for contact with the family was gently to prepare the way for obtaining ultimately from the family, on the decease of the patient, a signed authorization for autopsy. This is a backward glance on the then dominant emphasis on brain pathology as connected with mental illness, also on the extraordinary transformation of the medical attitude toward relatives. (Ackerman, 1967, p. 126)

His own view was sharply revised when, soon after finishing his residency, he became involved in an extensive study of mental health problems among the unemployed in a depression-struck mining town in western Pennsylvania.

I went to see, first hand, the mental health effects on the families of unemployed miners. This experience was a shocker; I was startlingly awakened to the limitless, unexplored territory in the relations of family life and health. I studied 25 families in which the father, the sole breadwinner in the mining community, had been without work for between two and five years. The miners, long habituated to unemployment, idled away their empty hours on the street corner, or in the neighborhood saloon. They felt defeated and degraded. They clung to one another to give and take comfort and to pass away the endless days of inactivity. Humiliated by their failure as providers, they stayed away from home; they felt shamed before their wives. The wives and mothers, harassed by insecurity and want from day to day, irritably rejected their husbands; they punished them by refusing sexual relations. The man who could no longer bring home his pay envelope was no longer the head of the family. He lost his position of respect and authority in the family; the woman drove him into the streets. Often, she turned for comfort to her first son. Mother and son then usurped the leadership position within the family. Among these unemployed miners, there were guilty depressions, hypochondriacal fears, psychosomatic crises, sexual disorders, and crippled self-esteem. Not infrequently, these men were publicly condemned as deserters. The configuration for family life was radically altered by the miner's inability to fulfill his habitual role as provider. (Ackerman, 1967, p. 126)

This experience plus others convinced him that emotional problems could be generated by the immediate environment as well as by the dynamics of the psyche. He carried this perception with him when he joined the psychiatric staff at Southard School, which was a facility for disturbed children associated with the Menninger Clinic in Topeka, Kansas. By 1937, he was the chief psychiatrist of the Child Guidance Clinic. While he adopted the prevailing orthopsychiatric principle that the psychiatrist saw the patient and the social worker saw the mother, by the mid-1940s he noted a growing flexibility in the field and a single therapist would sometimes see both. In his own private practice, he began to experiment with this procedure, and in a few cases he independently discovered, as Bowlby had, that an interview with the entire family could be exceptionally helpful in breaking through an impasse with a difficult child. His special contribution, however, was that he did not leave it at the level of a daring pragmatic innovation. For four years he conducted seminars around the issue of the relationship between the illness of a child and the mothering and fathering the child received. He began to see the family as the proper unit of diagnosis and treatment and began sending his staff on home visits to study the family (Guerin, 1976). His 1950 article with Sobel, "Family Diagnosis: An Approach to the Pre-School Child," is held by some to be the founding document of the family-therapy movement (Kaslow, 1980).

In 1955, he organized and chaired the first session on family diagnosis held at the meetings of the American Orthopsychiatric Association.

In 1957, he opened the Family Mental Health Clinic at Jewish Family Services in New York City. This led, in 1960, to the founding of the Family Institute (after his death renamed the Ackerman Institute). Meanwhile, in 1958, he had published the first book-length treatment of diagnosis and treatment of family relationships, *The Psychodynamics of Family Life*.

Ackerman's influence was by no means limited to those whom he trained in his institute, however. As a consultant to Israel Zwerling and his staff at Albert Einstein Medical School, he played a major role in shaping the work of that distinguished group (Nichols, 1984), and when Salvador Minuchin came to work at Wiltwick School in New York City, Ackerman was one of his early consultants and models (Hoffman, 1981).

In 1961, he joined with Don Jackson of Palo Alto to found the most influential and unifying journal in the field, *Family Process*.

Christian F. Midelfort

Christian Midelfort is an interesting example of what happens to a pioneer who remains largely isolated from a developing movement. Few have stronger claims as founding fathers. In the preface to his 1957 book *The Family in Psychotherapy*, arguably the first book fully dedicated to the topic, he writes:

As a participant in today's development of psychiatry, I have reported in this book my own results with family therapy in various types of mental illness. My development of this approach was first based on techniques I observed in my father's practice. . . .

To my knowledge the first place in this country to make use of this type of family therapy was the Lutheran Hospital in LaCrosse, Wisconsin. At this hospital relatives of psychiatric patients stayed as nurses aides and companions in consistent attendance to supervise occupational, recreational, and insulin therapies, to minimize suicidal risk, fear, aggression, and insecurity and to take part in therapeutic interviews with patient and psychiatrist. . . . Family treatment is also extended to the out-patient department for all types of mental illness. (Midelfort, 1957, pp. v–vi)

He delivered a paper on the use of family-therapy techniques at the American Psychiatric Association meeting in 1952, possibly the first such paper ever presented to a professional psychiatric meeting in the United States. Part of his unique contribution to the field was his emphasis on religious and ethnic factors in the healing process. He believed that the chief strengths of every family lay in its roots and traditions, a sort of mirror image of the view that these are the chief source of a family's pathology (Yost, 1986). Nevertheless, his situation as a staff psychiatrist in a small Wisconsin community, and later as a lecturer at the Lutheran Theological Seminary in St. Paul, Minn., did not lend itself to his taking part in the network of innovators that began to exchange visits, tapes, and materials in the 1957–1962 period. He was never on the board of *Family Process*, never participated in the seminal meetings throughout the '60s, and did not operate a training center that might have produced disciples. As a result, his influence has been minimal and few contemporary family therapists are aware of his contributions.

Theodore Lidz

Lidz was another of the founders who was analytically trained. In the early '40s, while on the staff of Johns Hopkins University, he became interested in the families of schizophrenics. He found that they tended to come from homes that were, almost without exception, beleaguered by instability and strife (Lidz & Lidz, 1949). When he moved to Yale in 1951, he sharpened his focus and together with a colleague began studying a small group of young hospitalized schizophrenics and their families intently. Following analytic concepts more closely than some of the others, he became especially concerned with the failure of these families to develop appropriate internal structure and role differentiation.

Lidz was the first to explore systematically the role of *fathers* in the process of schizmogenesis (Lidz, Perker, & Cornelison, 1956; Lidz, Cornelison, Fleck, & Terry, 1957a). And he was among the first to identify destructive relationships *between* the parents (as contrasted to between parent and child) as a major issue. In some cases, he found the parents to be distant and hostile toward each other (the condition he labeled "schism"). In others there was a tendency for the mother to become domineering in a destructive way (the condition he labeled "skew"). He felt that the first condition was hardest on male children and the second on females (Lidz et al., 1957b).

Lidz reported his work in 1955 in Washington and at national meetings in 1956 and 1957. He became acquainted with the similar research and treatment interests of Jackson, Bowen, Wynne, and Ackerman. In 1961 he was one of those who agreed to be a consulting editor of *Family Process*.

For a more extended account of his professional life and contributions to the family-therapy movement, see Nichols (1984).

Lyman C. Wynne[8]

Of all the pioneers, perhaps none was so fully prepared by formal training to become a family researcher and therapist as Lyman Wynne. In 1948, after having received his medical training at Harvard, he entered the graduate Department of Social Relations for a Ph.D. Those four years brought him into interaction with many of the leaders in the field of sociology, social psychology, and social anthropology. Among them he found himself most intrigued with the ideas of Talcott Parsons, including his view of personality as a subsystem within a larger family system. Concurrently, he was working with Erich Lindemann at the Massachusetts General Hospital and the Human Relations Service at Wellesley, one of the earliest full-service mental health clinics in America. He saw several patients with severe psychoses and with the further complication of ulcerative colitis. It became evident to Lindemann's team that family events were almost always at the root of colitis attacks in this population. Wynne saw his first whole families in 1947 as ancillary to the treatment of these seriously afflicted patients. Lindemann's work on grief in families and his theories of family structure, complete with social orbits, family splits, and many other concepts, seemed to fit right in with what Wynne was learning academically.

---

[8] Much of this material is based on an interview with Wynne, January 26, 1979, in Los Angeles.

In 1952, he took a position as a psychiatrist with John Clauson's Laboratory of Socioenvironmental Studies at the National Institute of Mental Health (NIMH) in Bethesda, Md. It was there, and at the Prince George County (Md.) Mental Health Clinic, that he began working intensively with the families of mental patients. Initially, he saw whole families only when individual treatment or joint interviews with the mother and patient were not effective. Gradually, however, he began to apply Parsons' notion of family systems to the situations he faced and eventually worked out his own theory of family structure of schizophrenic patients (Wynne, 1961; Wynne, Ryckoff, Day, & Hirsch, 1958).

At about this time (1954), Murray Bowen came to NIMH as head of an in-house research project on hospitalized schizophrenic patients and their families. Although they worked in separate sections and did not always see eye to eye on their approaches to families, Wynne found in Bowen the first colleague who shared his interest in the family as a unit of treatment. When Bowen left NIMH two years later, Wynne assumed leadership of the in-house family-research section as well as his own project.

But Wynne's first real indication that this approach was more widely practiced came at the 1956 and 1957 meetings of the American Psychiatric Association in Chicago. There he and Bowen met with Don Jackson, Theodore Lidz, and Ackerman. One of the immediate results of this encounter was the exchange, in 1959, of videotapes of family-counseling sessions between Jackson and Wynne (see Jackson, Riskin, and Satir [1961] for the Palo Alto reviews of the Wynne tapes). It took several close viewings of the tape Jackson sent before the Bethesda group finally concluded that it was a swindle. The tape from Palo Alto was a simulated session (starring Virginia Satir as mother). When confronted with this deception, Jackson confessed, but pleaded that this was just like the families they actually saw and illustrated the double bind especially well. Wynne continued interchange with Palo Alto and several of the other centers in the following years and was on the first board of editors of *Family Process*. Eventually (1971), he moved from NIMH to the University of Rochester Medical School, where he has continued his work with the families of schizophrenics.

An excellent summary of Wynne's research approaches and contributions to the developing field can be found in Nichols (1984).

Murray Bowen

Like the majority of the pioneers, Bowen was a psychiatrist who specialized in treating psychotic children. Like Ackerman, he got started toward family therapy while working at Menninger. Like Midelfort, he felt the parents, and especially mothers, should be required to live in the hospital with their disturbed child, and in 1951 he requested the use of a cottage on the grounds at Menninger for this purpose (Guerin, 1976). It soon became evident that it would be still more helpful if fathers could be added, but after a few attempts, he abandoned that approach as too complicated at that time. Instead, he concentrated on the "symbiosis," as he termed it, between the ill child and the mother.

In 1954, he joined Lyman Wynne at NIMH and began a research project that involved having the families of schizophrenic youngsters live in the hospital. A pair of journalists with the *Saturday Evening Post* interviewed Bowen about his project and reported:

Seven complete families participated in the project, which ran from 1954 to 1959. Usually there were two or three families in the hospital's special unit at the same time. Husband and wife occupied one room, and the children were in other rooms nearby. All families ate in a common dining room and shared the same lounge and recreation room. In some instances the father went to work each morning and returned to the hospital at night. In others, the father took a leave of absence from his job. The subjects were under the observation of a 20-member team of psychiatrists, social workers, nurses and attendants, some of them working seven days a week in eight-hour shifts. Family privacy was respected but nurses were nearby and on call. (Silverman & Silverman, 1962)

Initially, the project provided separate therapists for the various family members. However, quoting from his own account of events:

After a year, all families were started in family psychotherapy, the only form of therapy for newly admitted families. The old families continued their already-established individual therapy and began going to family psychotherapy sessions, too. Family therapy for the new families was alive and fast moving, and progress was more rapid than with any other therapy. The other families were not making progress in either individual or family psychotherapy. In family sessions their attitude was, "I'll take up my problems with *my* therapist." But their individual therapy was also slow, both patients and parents expecting the other to deal with significant issues. After a few months, all individual psychotherapy was discontinued. (Bowen, 1976, p. 228)

The new procedure was soon adopted in his private practice. His first patient to be switched over:

. . . was a bright young husband with a phobic reaction in a compulsive personality who was making steady progress after six months of psychoanalysis for four hours a week. The dilemma was discussed with the project consultant, who was a senior psychoanalyst. The therapist said:

"This man has a good chance for one of the better psychoanalytic results in three to four years with a total of 600 to 700 hours. There is also a good chance his wife will develop enough problems in two years to refer her to another analyst for three to four years. About six years from now, after 1,000 or more combined psychoanalytic hours, they should have their lives in reasonable order. How can I in good conscience continue this long and expensive course when I know within me that I can accomplish far more in less time with different approach? On the other hand, how can I in good conscience take a chance and suggest something new and untried when I know the chances are good with the proved psychoanalytic method?"

The consultant mused about analysts who hold onto patients too long and wondered how the husband and wife would react to the questions. The issue was discussed with the patient, and one week later his wife accompanied him to her first session. The clinical method used was analysis of the intrapsychic process in one and then the analysis of the corresponding emotional reaction in the other. They continued the family therapy sessions three times a week for 18 months for a total of 203 hours. The result was far better than would ordinarily be expected with 600 hours of psychoanalysis for each. (Bowen, 1976, p. 230)

Already in 1956, however, Bowen began to feel that the administration of NIMH was not supportive of his new approach. He attributed this to the institute's being wary of his flouting the conventions of traditional psychiatric practice (Guerin, 1976). In any case, he finally moved to Georgetown University, only a few miles away, with the hope of continuing his project there. As it turned out, his sponsor there died in the midst of the transfer and he was never able to get his staff moved over.

Once settled in his new surroundings, he instituted one of the first training programs for family therapists. Although focusing on the relationships among all family members, his practice gradually narrowed to work with couples, helping them to differentiate from each other and from their families of origin, as well as sponsoring their children's independence and growth (Nichols, 1984). Bowen also distinguished himself from other family therapists in his modeling of his model. In 1971, he made what has become a famous trip home to his own extended family in Pennsylvania to deal with his own unfinished business with them. (For a detailed description and analysis of this experience, see his 1972 "Anonymous" paper.) This trip became the prototype of those he has recommended to clients who have similar problems of unresolved issues with their families of orientation. He continued at Georgetown until his death in 1990 and remained, since the spring of 1957 (when he presented reports of his research at both the family session of orthopsychiatric meetings in March and the American Psychiatric Association meetings in May), a major influence in the field.

Carl A. Whitaker

From the beginning, Carl Whitaker has been noted as the most irreverent and whimsical of the founding fathers. In recent years, he has developed this approach into a finely honed therapy of the absurd—a therapy in which he often seems to drive a family sane by appearing more mad than they. It was in keeping with this character, then, to be one of those who early risked violating the conventions of traditional psychotherapy. He himself attributes his creative efforts to "a deficit of psychiatric training related to personnel shortages in World War II" (Whitaker & Keith, 1982, p. 43). In 1943 he and John Warkentin, then practicing psychiatry in Oak Ridge, Tenn., began bringing spouses and eventually children into sessions with their patients. In 1946, he moved to Atlanta (as chief of psychiatry at Emory) and partly shifted his emphasis to work with schizophrenics (Guerin, 1976). Here, too, he found that involving the families was useful. At the same time he embarked on a project of what he called "dual therapy" (i.e., conjoint marital therapy) and in 1958 published a report on 30 couples he had seen between 1955 and 1957 (Whitaker, 1958).

Whitaker might well be credited with having called the first meeting of the family-therapy movement. According to his own account (published in the first edition of this *Handbook*, p. 189):

Our staff work [at Emory] with schizophrenic patients eventuated in a series of ten four-day conferences on the treatment of schizophrenia. . . . The conferences centered on intensive treatment of one schizophrenic and a schizophrenic and his family for the four days. Two interviews were carried out each day by a subgroup, while the rest watched through a one-way mirror. We spent the rest of the day and night discussing the interviews. The tenth conference was held at Sea Island, Georgia (1955), and included Gregory Bateson and Don Jackson [together with John Rosen and Albert Scheflen from Pennsylvania]. This meeting led to the publication of *Psychotherapy of Chronic Schizophrenic Patients*. (Whitaker, 1958)

As the family-therapy movement developed, Whitaker was part of the central network from the beginning, having been on the first board of editors of *Family Process*. He was one of the first to extend the clinical definition of family to include grandparents, as well as collateral kin, all of whom he would invite for weekend workshops around a particular individual's or nuclear family's problem. In 1965, he moved from Atlanta to become a professor in the Department of Psychiatry at the University of Wisconsin Medical School, and became professor emeritus in 1982.

The Palo Alto Group:
Gregory Bateson, Jay Haley,
John Weakland, Don D. Jackson,
Virginia Satir

It would be hard to imagine five more richly individual persons than those in this group, yet their early contributions are so intertwined that it is impossible to outline the history of one without introducing the others.

In the beginning was Gregory Bateson. It is ironic that although he is considered by many to be one of the founders of the field of family therapy, he had very little interest in the subject. He was not a therapist, but an anthropologist and philosopher. He was the son of one of the foremost biologists of the time (William Bateson, the man who introduced the word "genetics" into the English language) and was himself a protean intellect. Long before he turned his attention to the issues of family dynamics, he had accumulated backgrounds in an incredible variety of intellectual endeavors, all of which he brought to bear on each new problem he addressed. He had studied the kinship structure of tribes in Bali and in New Guinea (with his wife, Margaret Mead), and he had investigated the social and communication behavior of otters and other animals. He was one of the intellectual coterie who developed modern systems theory and cybernetics and he had studied and debated the philosophy of such men as Bertrand Russell and Alfred North Whitehead. Of even more obvious relevance to his later contributions, he was a colleague of and frequent correspondent with several of the germinal thinkers in the field of psychology and psychiatry, particularly psychologist Kurt Lewin (the developer of psychological field theory) and psychiatrist Harry Stack Sullivan (as already noted, one of the most creative integrators of sociological and psychodynamic concepts) (Lippset, 1980). In fact, before launching the project that resulted in his identification as one of the founding fathers of family therapy, he had already coauthored a volume with Jurgen Ruesch titled *Communication: The Matrix of Psychiatry* (Ruesch & Bateson, 1951).

It is a happy circumstance that the process by which Bateson moved from these concerns into an interest in family dynamics is well documented. It began with his fascination with some of the paradoxical aspects of communication. Whitehead and Russell (1910) had developed the concept of hierarchies of logical types as a means of resolving the paradoxical qualities of statements such as the classic "I am lying." Like all paradoxes, the harder one thinks about it, the more disoriented one feels. It is true only if it is false and false only if it is true. Using the theory of logical types, however, it becomes clear that the paradox consists of two contradictory statements that elude comparison because they are at different logical levels. There is the evident content of the statement, "I am lying," and there is also the framing statement (or meta-statement as it came to be called), which is not spelled out explicitly but is inherent in all human discourse, namely, "I expect you to believe what I say to you." When the metamessage is made explicit, the original statement loses some of its mind-boggling paradoxical qualities and assumes the qualities of a mere pair of contradictory statements (A is true/A is not true).

Bateson was impressed with the number of situations in which similar paradoxes were present. Among his otters, the metamessage "this is only play" made it possible for the animals to participate in realistic mock fights without fear or error. The apparently absurd verbalizations of schizophrenics had some of this same quality. Humor, especially certain types of humor such as repartée between a ventriloquist and a dummy or between puppets, seemed rich with paradoxical material, as also did hypnosis. In 1952, Bateson succeeded in getting a Rockefeller Foundation grant to pursue his studies in this area, and with this money he assembled a staff with variegated backgrounds and talents.

Among his earliest appointments were Jay Haley and John Weakland. Haley's background was in communication. He had most recently been engaged in analyzing fantasy sequences in popular movies using a logical model somewhat similar to that which intrigued Bateson. Weakland had begun his career as a chemical engineer but had turned to anthropology, with special interest in China and in Chinese films.

One of Haley's early assignments was to attend a workshop offered by Milton Erickson, the remarkable hypnotherapist (Haley, 1976). That fateful meeting resulted in a relationship that led finally to Haley's becoming Erickson's chief expositor and intellectual biographer. Erickson's methods, in turn, provided the foundation for the paradoxical approach to family therapy that became the trademark of the Palo Alto branch of the movement.

In 1954, the Rockefeller grant ran out and it became clear that it would not be renewed. The pragmatics of finding alternative funding pushed the team members to narrow their focus to a more glamorous subissue and they chose schizophrenia. The application proposed the investigation of the premise that schizophrenia was the product of children's being caught in paradoxical binds by a mother who "is driven not only to punish the children's demand for love, but also to punish any indication which the child may give that he knows that he is not loved" (Haley, 1976, p. 67).

The reformulated research project was funded by a Macy Foundation grant and one of the first expenditures was to bring Don Jackson, a psychiatrist, into the project as clinical consultant on the problem of doing therapy with schizophrenics. Jackson had spent the previous three years as a psychiatric resident at Chestnut Lodge in Rockville, Md. (Guerin, 1976), where he was supervised by Sullivan, who emphasized the interpersonal aspects of psychiatric problems. His own work had emphasized the importance of the family homeostatic mechanisms.

In 1956, the team of Bateson, Jackson, Haley, and Weakland generated one of the most discussed papers in the history of psychiatry, "Toward a Theory of Schizophrenia." In it, they introduced the concept of the double bind as the crucial familial determinant of schizophrenia in children. As unlikely as it may seem, to this point they had never actually observed the families of their schizophrenic subjects. Haley notes that it had not yet occurred to them that mental disorders could be caused by current interaction in families (rather than in childhood [Haley, 1987]). However, Haley, who had been interviewing the Veterans Administration patients utilized as subjects in the project, serendipitously noted that one of them had severe anxiety attacks following each of his mother's visits. This led to the systematic observation of mothers' visits to their sons at the facility and provided a dramatic new insight into their understanding of how the double bind operates in current, and not merely historical, life (Haley, 1976). As a result, in 1956, the team started having conjoint sessions with the families of schizophrenics, videotaping them for further analysis as part of the research project.

In 1957, Jackson met John Bell and also Charles Fulweiler, who introduced him to the one-way mirror as a mechanism for interactive supervision (Haley, 1987).

The year 1959 was pivotal for Jackson and for the movement. Jackson published his paper on conjoint family therapy, arguing that it was more effective than seeing family members individually (Jackson, 1959). While remaining a consultant to the Bateson project, he set up the independent Mental Research Institute (MRI), which was much more sharply focused on family therapy per se. That year also, Virginia Satir came from Chicago to join him in the new institute.

Satir was the only one of the pioneers who was a woman and the only one whose background was in social work. Independently of each of the others, she had begun to see families in her private practice in Chicago as early as 1951. According to Bunny Duhl, the first conjoint session was an accident:

A mother of a disturbed young woman Satir had been seeing, who had been improving, called her and threatened to sue Satir for alienating her daughter's affection. Satir asked her to come in with her daughter; she then saw the same behavior between the girl and her mother that Satir had originally experienced between her daughter and herself. She soon asked for the husband and son to join the mother and daughter, and from then on began seeing families of people with many types of problems, from learning disorders and somatic illness to schizophrenics. (Duhl, 1983, p. 10)

Subsequently (1955), she instituted a training program for residents at the Illinois State Psychiatric Institute. As she later wrote, "I worked on a systems approach long before I understood anything about it and before I even heard a name for it. Then in 1957 I read Don Jackson's article 'Toward a Theory of Schizophrenics' and I began to know what was going on" (Satir, Stachowiak, & Taschman, 1977, p. 165).

In 1960, Jackson attended the seminal meeting of family therapists in New York and agreed with Nathan Ackerman to have MRI and the Family Institute jointly sponsor a new journal, *Family Process*. Jay Haley was appointed the first editor and the first issue came out in 1962. As we have noted before, this publication has been the chief unifying influence in the movement ever since. Satir, as her later writing shows, was greatly influenced by the Palo Alto group, although she was not at all intimidated by it. For example, she could borrow a useful concept such as "metamessage" and give it a freer interpretation that fit more easily into her own view of family interaction. (Compare, for example, her use of the concept in *Conjoint Family Therapy* [1964] with other publications of the group such as Watzlawick, Beavin, and Jackson [1967].) During the mid-'60s she gradually disengaged from the MRI as she became more and more involved with the human-growth movement and eventually became fully involved with the Esalen Institute at Big Sur, Calif. Probably more than any other early founder, she was responsible for popularizing the movement. She had a flair for clear, nontechnical exposition and charismatic presentation that led her to address tens of thousands in person, hundreds of thousands through her books, and millions through the media.

In 1962, at the close of the Bateson project, Haley and Weakland joined MRI. Then, in 1967, Haley left to join Minuchin in Philadelphia at the Philadelphia Child Guidance Clinic.

In January 1968, Don Jackson died, thereby depriving the field of one of its most articulate and creative forces. Gregory Bateson spent his later years studying animal behavior at the Marine Institute in Hawaii, and died in 1980 at the age of 76. Virginia Satir died in 1988.

The Philadelphia Group: Ivan Boszormenyi-Nagy and Associates

The department of Family Psychiatry at the Eastern Pennsylvania Psychiatric Institute (EPPI) was one of the chief centers of research and training in the family-therapy movement. Nagy, like several of the other founding fathers, was a psychiatrist devoted to the therapy of psychotics, and to the integration of family therapy with psychotherapy as a whole. As administrator of an interprofessional, interacademic center, he was able to assemble an impressive group of associates who helped to make Philadelphia a major early center of family therapy. James Framo, Gerald Zuk, Geraldine Spark, David Rubinstein, Barbara Krasner, Margaret Cotroneo, Leon Robinson, Geraldine Lincoln-Grossman, and Oscar Weiner were among them.

This group was instrumental in the founding of the Family Institute of Philadelphia, with Nagy as its first full-term president. Members of the department were also responsible for the first organized training program held in a European country (Holland, 1967), and for a number of early national conferences in family therapy in the United States. Literally thousands of professionals were trained at this center before the Commonwealth of Pennsylvania abruptly closed this leading psychiatric research and training institution in 1980. Among this group's earlier contributions was the volume entitled *Intensive Family Therapy* (Boszormenyi-Nagy & Framo, 1965). Nagy's major position statement on the premises of what has later become contextual therapy (see Chapter 7, this volume), an integrative approach, is *Invisible Loyalties* (Boszormenyi-Nagy & Spark, 1973). Nagy and some of his associates continue to be affiliated with both Hahnemann University and their private training institutes, locally and nationally.

The "Second Wave": 1962–1977

With the publication of *Family Process* in 1962, the family-therapy field may be said to have entered a new era. The pioneers continued to be active and to wield enormous influence on the movement, but they were joined by new talents, many of whom were their own proteges. By the end of 1977, a national association, the American Family Therapy Association (AFTA), had been founded; a number of training centers were well established, books advocating one or another strategy of intervention were proliferating; competing "schools" of therapy were becoming differentiated out of the range of possibilities; and textbooks had begun to appear, summarizing the available options.

It is impossible to do justice to the proliferation of programs and personalities that emerged during this period, but it may be useful to highlight a few of the more influential centers and some of the most often-cited figures associated with them.

New York City

It would be fair to say that New York and Philadelphia served as the two eastern capitals of the family-therapy movement during the crucial 15-year period considered here. At the heart of the New York establishment was Nathan Ack-

erman. Charismatic, innovative, and assertive, he was the dominant personality in the field on the East Coast until his death in 1971. In 1965, he had founded the Family Institute of New York, and this became his chief base of training operations. However, he was also active as a consultant and mentor in the other two centers.

When *Family Process* was first jointly published by the Ackerman and Jackson groups, as already noted, the first editor was Jay Haley from the Palo Alto group. When Haley stepped down from the post in 1969, Ackerman saw to it that the second editor was one of his own colleagues, the able Donald Block. Two years later, when Ackerman died, Block succeeded him as director of the Family Institute, changing its name to the Ackerman Institute of Family Therapy. Throughout this period and to the present day, this institute has been one of the major training facilities in the field.

A second New York City center was at the Albert Einstein College of Medicine and the affiliated Bronx State Hospital. Israel Zwerling, who had been greatly influenced by Ackerman, together with Marilyn Mendelson, who had been analyzed by Jackson, founded the Family Studies Section in the Department of Psychiatry in the early 1960s (Kaslow, 1980). Ackerman continued as a consultant to the group until his death. Andrew Ferber became director of the program in 1964 and Philip Guerin, a protege of Bowen, became director of training in 1970. An impressive roster of contemporary family therapists of note received their training at the facility.

The third center in New York that had particular impact in the field during this period was the Wiltwyck School for Boys. During the early 1960s, Edgar Auerswald and Salvador Minuchin came together as staff psychiatrists in the facility for delinquent boys, and with encouragement and direction from Ackerman, undertook a major research project on the dynamics of poor families (Minuchin, Auerswald, King, & Rabinowitz, 1964; Auerswald, 1968, 1975). They became increasingly impressed with the observation that the mental health problems of many of the Puerto Rican families in the study were more a product of their displaced immigrant status than of psychodynamic problems. When the families were given more information about their new surroundings and assisted in establishing a new network of supportive friends, their symptoms tended to disappear. Minuchin was a native of Argentina and received his medical training there but came to New York for his analytic training. There followed a stint working with children in Israel who had been displaced by the turmoil in that troubled land. It was there that he first became impressed with the importance of working with families when possible, and when he returned to New York to take the position at Wiltwyck, he was determined to expand his involvement with the families of the disadvantaged boys in this new setting (Nichols, 1984). He was aware of the family work of Ackerman and others with articulate middle-class families, but saw his challenge as finding a way to intervene helpfully in families with little or no education and multiple problems and disadvantages. The project resulted in a book, *Families of the Slums*, jointly written by Minuchin and his colleagues in the project, Braulio Montalvo, Bernard Guerney, Bernice Rosman, and Florence Schumer (1967). As a result of this work, Minuchin had the opportunity to become director of the Philadelphia Child Guidance Clinic where his concepts matured and his contributions expanded.

Philadelphia

When Minuchin went to Philadelphia to head the Philadelphia Child Guidance Clinic, he brought Montalvo and Rosman with him and was joined by Jay Haley of the Palo Alto group. Together they developed a unique program for training members of the local Black community as paraprofessional family therapists. Part of their success in this endeavor was due to the innovative training and "on line" supervision programs they developed. It was their modus operandi to have a supervisor (or more often a supervisory team composed of other trainees plus senior staff) interrupt a therapy session with suggestions for redirection. Initially, they simply came to the door, but eventually they used phones and even "bugs" in the ear, modeling their approach after the techniques used by football coaches in calling plays to their quarterbacks.

The contributions of the Minuchin–Haley team were substantive as well as methodologi-

cal. The therapeutic approach that came to be known as "structural therapy" emerged out of their interaction. In addition to carrying over the communications and systems elements developed earlier at MRI, they gave added emphasis to the realignment of the counterproductive family coalitions and tied their theory also to a family developmental framework (Haley, 1971; Minuchin, 1974). Minuchin also pursued his special interest in family-induced psychosomatic disorders including, especially, anorexia nervosa (Minuchin, Rosman, & Baker, 1978).

Meanwhile, the family therapists at EPPI had discovered a group of colleagues at the Philadelphia Psychiatric Center (Friedman, John Sonne, Lincoln, Oscar Weiner) who were also beginning to do conjoint family work, and in 1964 they were amalgamated into the Family Institute of Philadelphia (intended to be the Philadelphia counterpart of Ackerman's Family Institute of New York) (Kaslow, 1980). Many contemporary therapists of note began their career as family therapists at the institute—among them Gerald Zuk, one of the few psychologists who has become an important theorist of the movement (see, for example, Zuk, 1971). Another innovator was Ross Speck, who, together with his associates, developed a short-term intervention called network therapy (Speck, 1967; Speck & Oblan, 1967; Speck & Attneave, 1972). In this approach, the extended family, friends, neighbors, school counselors, probation officers, and anyone else who impinged on the family are all brought together on a single occasion. Again, they may meet partly together and partly in subgroups. It is undeniably impossible to ignore the impact of such a gathering on the family being helped.

Boston

The founding of the Boston Family Institute in 1969 is illustrative and typical of the way the field was developing in this "second wave" period. The two leading figures, Fred Duhl and David Kantor, like the original pioneers, had had experience with families but no training in family therapy. Fred Duhl, a psychiatrist, had, however, like Lyman Wynne before him, worked with Erich Lindemann at the Massachusetts General Hospital and had first seen whole families in that context as an auxiliary intervention to treating psychotic outpatients. Also, he knew Edgar Auerswald, and as often as possible throughout the early '60s, Duhl would get together with Auerswald to compare notes and discuss the exciting new developments in family and community psychiatry (Duhl, 1983). Kantor, a psychologist, had a background not in medicine but in group work and psychodrama. In 1965, he had begun his in-depth study of a small group of normal and schizophrenic families, which resulted in the landmark volume *Inside the Family* (Kantor & Lehr, 1975).

In 1967, Kantor and Duhl decided jointly to offer training in family therapy to the psychiatric residents at Boston State Hospital. The experiment faded for lack of interest on the trainees' part. However, Kantor and Duhl learned a great deal from the experience, and two years later, together with a small group of similarly minded associates, they established the Boston Family Institute and began teaching from their own experience and from what they could learn about what others had been doing (Duhl, 1983). In the course of time, this group created dramatic new expressive techniques, such as family sculpting.

Palo Alto

The Mental Research Institute that Jackson had founded in 1959 thrived during the early 1960s, producing a great number and variety of provocative papers (see Jackson's two volumes of collected essays from the group [1968] and Haley's [1976] account of the intellectual ferment that produced them). The years 1967 and 1968 were pivotal for this group. Watzlawick, Beavin, and Jackson brought out the influential book *Pragmatics of Human Communication* in 1967, to some degree summarizing the theoretical work of the group to that point. However, with Haley's move to Philadelphia in 1967 and Jackson's untimely death in 1968, the group went through a period of crisis and reorganization. The new leadership that emerged has proved productive in its own right, however. Among the best known are Paul Watzlawick, Arthur Bodin, John Weakland, and Richard Fisch, who, under the directorship of Fisch, established the Brief Therapy Center at MRI in

1967. This effort to establish strategies for the briefest possible effective interventions with seriously disturbed clients produced two additional volumes that have had a major impact on the field, *Change—Principles of Problem Formation* by Watzlawick, Weakland, and Fisch (1974) and, more recently, *The Tactics of Change: Doing Therapy Briefly* by Fisch, Weakland, and Segal (1982).

Among the other innovators at MRI during this period were Carlos Sluzki, who did more than anyone else outside of the original group to critique and refine the concept of the double bind (and, who became the third editor of *Family Process*, succeeding Donald Bloch in 1983). Also, Jules Riskin pioneered during this period in the development of instruments to measure family interaction (Riskin & Faunce, 1970) and in the dynamics of normal (or, as he called them, "nonlabeled") families (Riskin, 1976).

Galveston, Texas

Far removed from the family-therapy centers on the East and West coasts, a team of clinicians in isolated Galveston, Texas, developed one of the most innovative family-therapy approaches to come out of this early period. Robert McGregor, a clinical psychologist—together with Agnes Ritchie, M.S.W., and others—was working as part of an orthopsychiatric team dealing with a geographically scattered clientele of juvenile offenders and their multiproblem families. They hit upon the strategy of virtually storming the family with a team of professionals (prototypically, a social worker, a psychologist, and a psychiatric intern, each accompanied by a trainee from his or her own discipline). In a fast-paced, two-day intervention with both conjoint and divided sessions, this team attempted to make a lasting impact on a delinquent child and the family. They called their approach "multiple-impact therapy" (Ritchie, 1960; MacGregor et al., 1964; MacGregor, 1967).

Milan, Italy

Meanwhile, in Milan, Italy, Mara Selvini Palazzoli, a psychiatrist trained in child analysis, was working with anorectic girls and their mothers. She became aware of the work of Bateson's group and also of Ackerman's institute, and in 1967, together with three associates (Luigi Boscolo, Guiliana Prata, and Gianfranco Cecchin) founded the Institute for Family Studies in Milan. As in Galveston, the Milan clients came from long distances and, like the Texans, the Milan associates (as they preferred to be called) developed a short-term intensive set of interventions that demanded the attendance of the whole family at 10 all-day sessions, spaced a month apart. In 1977, the final year of the period under consideration, they toured the family-therapy centers of the United States. That tour, plus the English-language book outlining their methods that appeared the following year (Selvini Palazzoli, Boscolo, Cecchin, & Prata, 1978), had a major impact on the mainstream family-therapy movement in the United States (Nichols, 1984). The subsequent history of this dynamic group, its splitting up into two separate teams (Selvini and Prata in one group and Boscolo and Cecchin in the other), the participants' shift away from their initial focus on eating disorders and so forth are detailed in Chapter 10 in this volume by Campbell, Draper, and Crutchley.

Chicago, Illinois

Two centers for training family therapists developed in Chicago during this period. In 1968, Charles Kramer founded the Family Institute of Chicago. Kramer was an analyst who, like Duhl in Boston, was never trained in family therapy but was in communication with the innovators at professional meetings. His program eventually affiliated with the Department of Psychiatry at Northwestern Medical School (Nichols, 1984). The second Chicago training center during this period was Irving Borstein's program at the Institute for Juvenile Research. Borstein was heavily influenced by Carl Whitaker, who served as a consultant to the program in its early years.

The Founding of AFTA

In the midst of all of this proliferation, in 1977 a subgroup of the *Family Process* editors and friends organized into the American Family Therapy Association (AFTA). Its first officers were Murray Bowen, president; John Spiegel, vice-president; Gerald Berenson, executive vice-president; James Framo, secretary; and Geraldine Spark, treasurer. It has grown and prospered in the years since its founding. In some ways, it has served as a counterpoint to AAMFT and its all-embracing universalism, providing a more exclusive forum for those who identify themselves with the original family-therapy movement.[9]

THE CURRENT SCENE: MID-1970S TO THE PRESENT

History is best viewed from a distance. Doubtlessly, the most recent developments in our field will be seen most clearly and evaluated most meaningfully by those to come. Yet even with our foreshortened perspective, some unfolding issues seem too important to overlook.

Out of the long list that might be considered here, we feel that half a dozen issues have been particularly focal for the profession in its most recent period: (1) the issue of *homogenization* versus *specialization*, (2) the related question of *ecumenicism* versus *denominationalism*, (3) the increasing *internationalization* of the field, (4) *gender issues*, (5) the question of *empirical validation* for the claims of practitioners, and, finally, (6) *ethical and legal issues*.

Homogenization versus Specialization

There is no unanimous opinion on the issue of whether *all* relational therapists need to be trained in *each* of the major configurations (families, couples, individuals), *each* of the major approaches (such as structural, object relations, behavioral), and *each* of the areas of specialization (sex therapy, divorce mediation, substance abuse, child abuse, etc.). It seems to us that, for the most part, the field is moving away from

---

[9] *Editors' Note.* Framo (1989) provides a rich and fascinating summary of the early history (and prehistory) of AFTA, based on the detailed minutes he kept as the association's secretary.

the proliferation of narrowly trained specialists. Rather, most family therapists are being exposed to an overview of the whole field and required to develop basic skills as relational therapist. Then, after becoming licensed or certified as a general practitioner (to draw on the terminology of the "medical model"), perhaps one might proceed to specialize in a field of special interest through further training or internship opportunities.

In 1978, the AAMFT was commissioned by the U.S. Department of Health, Education and Welfare to set up standards for certification of training programs in marriage and family therapy. It established a 10-member Commission on Accreditation for Marriage and Family Therapy Education together with a 21-member National Advisory Committee on Standards for Education and Training. Appointments to these bodies have ranged across the four professions and it is not overly surprising that the result has been a set of training standards that requires a comprehensive curriculum. This same philosophy of breadth in training requirements is increasingly being reflected in the licensure requirements of states. (These are, of course, related phenomena, as the AAMFT is virtually always consulted by legislative staff members when questions of contemporary standards for professional training are under review.)

In view of this development, it seems likely that specialties will increasingly be constructed on a foundation of general training rather than as an alternative to it.

Secularization versus Denominationalism

Recent years have witnessed the increase in two opposite tendencies within the field. On the one hand, there is the rise of what might be called "denominationalism," that is, the calcification of the divisions in the field among the various schools (or "denominations") of therapists. As Carlos Sluzki put it (1983):

During the last ten years, we have witnessed a Balkanization of the field into sectors based on political rather than scientific boundaries. We have also seen the rise of a "star" system, based on maintaining those artificial boundaries for political-economic reasons. The consequence of all this has been the development of more and more "brand-name" models and increased bickering about whose technique washes whiter.

Virtually every textbook and handbook (including this one) has come to identify a set of schools of therapy, each with its major historical figures and current advocates. Students must learn to distinguish each from the other and to identify major therapists according to the school to which they belong. Undeniably, these types of distinctions facilitate the organization of courses and curricula and lend themselves to examination questions (e.g., "Compare experiential, strategic, and object relations approaches as they deal with transference and countertransference. 1 hour"). They also provide a shorthand for identifying strangers at professional conferences ("I'm a Bowenian with functionalist overtones. What are you?").

It is our view, however, that the future belongs to the opposite tendency, which might be called secularization (or perhaps ecumenicism). This trend toward integration in the field of family therapy is increasingly pronounced each year. There has been, as yet, no generally successful effort to accomplish conceptual and clinical integration on a grand scale, but it is our observation that integration occurs regularly in the actual practice of therapists. For many contemporary family therapists, the process of integration begins during their training years.

Although there are still strong networks of therapists loyal to one or another pioneer, particularly in the areas of family therapy and sex therapy, the enormous majority of marriage, family, and sex therapists today are trained in secular settings, that is, in programs that impartially have them read a wide range of current textbooks rather than those representing only one view. Perhaps the university or agency will invite Haley or Bowen or Satir or Stuart or Masters for a special workshop, and for a period of weeks everyone is a convert to that philosophy. These men and women are charismatic and articulate. But after a series of such appearances, learning from such specialized workshops tends to become integrated into the therapists' own views.

There is food for thought in the closing comments of Salvador Minuchin as he addressed the

1985 Conference on the Evolution of Psycho-therapy in Phoenix, Ariz.:

A therapist therefore joins the family in a thera-peutic system and tries to help the family actualize alternative ways of being. The therapeutic goal is to expand the family members' repertory of responses to the complexities of life. Within this framework the possibilities are many and varied, as are the voices that speak to me. Today, they are the way I do ther-apy. Clearly the voices I hear do not mean that every-thing is the same or that eclecticism is beautiful. The demands of a situation, and one's own possibilities and limitations, still operate selectively. Perhaps this is like the harmonic context of a melody. Within that context, a theme appears, is taken up by other voices, and can reappear in counterpoint or in inversion. *Within the possibilities open to us, the best in us always learns from the best of others.* (Minuchin, 1987, p. 14)

It is our observation, also, that real therapists working with real families in the real world use every bit of repertoire they have that is consis-tent with the conditions of different clinical sit-uations and their own character and style. It is true that there is little integration in the liter-ature, but it is also true that nearly every prac-titioner is his or her own showcase of tailored integration.

Internationalization

We have already noted the Milan therapists and the impact they have had and are having on the field. Today, however, it must be acknowl-edged that there are major talents and training programs in many countries. In an editorial marking the 25th anniversary of *Family Process*, Carlos Sluzki notes that the quarter century has produced not only another dozen U.S. journals and a half-dozen major U.S. newsletters, but also family-therapy journals and newsletters in Argentina, Australia, Belgium, Canada, Fin-land, France, Germany, Great Britain, Israel, Italy, Japan, New Zealand, Norway, Portugal, and Switzerland. It may be assumed that there are relevant publications in other nations that did not come to his attention. Moreover, the number of practitioners in several of these coun-tries currently exceeds the entire membership of the profession 25 years ago. For example, the

British Association for Family Therapy has over 1,000 members.

Some of these national family-therapy move-ments, such as in Italy and Great Britain, have strong indigenous roots. Others may be almost entirely rooted in the works of one or more of the pioneers we have surveyed. None are un-influenced by the major currents in the field, but they, in turn, have been having an effect on the mainstream American scene. What sells in Philadelphia or Palo Alto may not sell in Tokyo or Buenos Aires or Tel Aviv—at least not without modification and challenge.

At the same time, the special values and cir-cumstances of the various ethnic groups in America have, in these past few years, raised the consciousness of many to the need for flex-ibility and innovative adaptation. This move-ment is reflected in the spate of books and articles on interethnic issues in relational ther-apy (for example, the volume edited by Monica McGoldrick, John Pearce, and Joseph Giordano in 1982) and in the inclusion of a course in this in the AAMFT's recommended curriculum for training centers. It has been unsettling for many to discover that much of what passed for ther-apeutic truth in their own training is actually a set of very particular ethnocentric values about what is good and true for families. The easy an-swer that we simply work within the value sys-tem of the family has proved to be challenging and unsettling when the value system of the family may include a patriarchal structure or voodoo beliefs or "child abuse."

The impact of these issues on the field has only begun to be felt.

Gender Issues

By the mid-1970s, it had become evident that many of the basic assumptions and practices of family therapy were at odds with the tenets of the feminist movement. The first paper chal-lenging the family-therapy establishment from a feminist perspective to appear in *Family Pro-cess* was by Rachel Hare-Mustin in 1978. Since then, there has been an ongoing dialogue in the pages of the various family-therapy journals and at sessions of professional meetings on this issue. Perhaps no set of authors identified the major points of conflict so concisely as Judith Libow,

Pamela Raskin, and Barbara Caust writing in the *American Journal of Family Therapy* in 1982. They cite the propensity of most family therapists to focus on ongoing, reciprocal circular causation, while the feminist therapist focuses on the linear causation of historic sexism and structural inequities. Similarly, they note that while family therapists intervene with the goal of improving relationships and patterns of interaction, the feminist therapist's goal is, rather, "to facilitate the growth of a strong, competent woman who has enhanced control over resources" and "to increase the ability of women to work together politically to change society and its institutions" (p. 8). The family therapist is seen as utilizing *expert* power to achieve the changes he or she seeks while feminists are committed to utilizing *referent* power (which highlights the commonality of all women's experiences). Finally, the family therapist is committed to work within the framework of the ethnic, social, and religious values of the client family whereas the feminist therapist is committed to challenge those values that directly or indirectly support sexism.

These issues are far from resolved and sessions devoted to these questions are currently among the best attended and most spirited at professional meetings.

Empirical Verification

We have already noted that many of the pioneers in the various movements that evolved into the present field of marriage and family therapy began as researchers. Havelock Ellis, Magnus Hirshfeld, and William Masters were scientists before they attempted therapeutic intervention. Gregory Bateson, Theodore Lidz and Lyman Wynne began as researchers into the familial roots of schizophrenia. Nevertheless, the early years of clinical development in the various fields were not distinguished by a major investment in evaluative research. (The exception is the ongoing-research component of the Masters and Johnson clinical program.) The great body of research on treatment outcomes has been produced since the mid-1970s. In this volume, Gurman, Kniskern, and Pinsof survey this literature, and conclude that while the main point, that family therapy is an effective style of

intervention, has been well established, we are far from having established the reciprocal feedback between researcher and therapist that would most effectively move the discipline forward.

Ethical and Legal Issues

The ethics of clinical practice were first outlined in the Oath of Hippocrates (ca. 460–370 B.C.), which even today is administered to medical graduates in an abbreviated version. Marriage and family therapists, like all other practitioners, are required (paraphrasing) to "lead your lives and practice your art in uprightness and honor; that whatsoever life you shall enter it shall be for the good of that individual to the utmost of your power, you holding yourself aloof from wrong, from corruption, from the tempting of others to vice . . . that what you shall see and hear of the lives of men which is private you will keep inviolably secret."

In recent decades, these basic principles have been elaborated upon and refined. Since interventions *intended* for the good of the patient can have unintended hurtful consequences or side effects, the principle of *informed consent* has developed. Under this principle, the practitioner is required to inform the patient in advance of the type and degree of risk the patient assumes in accepting a given intervention.[10]

The responsibility of the clinician was also extended by the famous Tarasoff decision and its successors, which held that the obligation to protect the confidentiality of the therapy session is secondary to the obligation to protect others (or the patient himself or herself) from planned violence. More recently still, the obligation of confidentiality has been modified by laws requiring the reporting of any knowledge or suspicion of child abuse or elder abuse.

Beyond these general issues that affect every helping profession equally, relational therapists must deal with issues unique to the conditions of their practice. When seeing couples or families in conjoint sessions, it is not always clear that any given intervention will have the same

---

[10] *Editors' Note.* These matters are greatly elaborated in this volume by Doherty and Boss, Chapter 20.

effect on all family members. Whose good is paramount when not all are benefitted? When information comes separately from one family member, when is it ethical to share it with other family members? These are not easy questions, but guidelines are emerging. In many cases, the issues are raised and resolved by legislators or judges. In other cases, the profession itself is the agent of resolution. At this printing, the most recent summary of the current guidelines for ethical practice is the 1985 edition of the *AAMFT Code of Ethical Principles for Marriage and Family Therapists*.[11]

These guidelines have not gone unchallenged, however. Susan Green and James Hansen (1986) surveyed a sample of family therapists and determined that there are a number of salient ethical issues of concern to practitioners that are not covered in the AAMFT document. Among these are questions involving the ethics of pressuring reluctant family members to participate in therapy, seeing one member of a family when others are not present, and sharing one's values and biases with the family. The official guidelines (as well as standard references in the field) have also been criticized by Donald and Robert Wendorf (1985) as being insufficiently sensitive to systemic as contrasted with traditional linear approaches to therapy. For example, they explore the issue of family secrets as a question of family rules and metaphors, rather than as a matter, primarily, of confidentiality. Without doubt, these issues, and others that will yet arise, will continue to generate discussion among practitioners in the field.

SUMMING UP

In this brief survey of the history of the field of marriage and family therapy, we have traced its roots to a variety of earlier movements and personalities. Even between the first and the present editions of this *Handbook*, a wealth of new historical information has become available as various participants in some of the pioneering programs have published their own accounts of significant events and as scholars have sifted through early documents. Thus, our history evolves even as the field itself evolves. It is good that it is so.

We are a profession in search of wisdom, and wisdom is seldom rootless.

REFERENCES

Ackerman, N.W. (1938). The unity of the family. *Archives of Pediatrics, 55,* 51–62.

Ackerman, N.W. (1958). *The psychodynamics of family life.* New York: Basic Books.

Ackerman, N.W. (1967). The emergence of family diagnosis and treatment: a personal view. *Psychotherapy, 4,* 125–129.

Ackerman, N.W., Beatman, F.L., & Sherman, S.N. (Eds.) (1967). *Expanding theory and practice in family therapy.* New York: Family Service Association of America.

Ackerman, N.W., & Sobel, R. (1950). Family diagnosis: An Approach to the pre-school child. *American Journal of Orthopsychiatry, 20*(4), 744–753.

Adler, A. (1917). *The neurotic constitution* (authorized translation by Bernard Blueck and John E. Lind). New York: Mofatt, Yard & Co.

Alexander, F. (1968). *An empirical study on the differential influence of self-concept on the professional behavior of marriage counselors.* Unpublished doctoral dissertation, University of Southern California.

American Association of Sex Educators and Counselors (1973). *Professional training and preparation of sex counselors and sex therapists.* Washington, DC: American Association of Sex Educators and Counselors.

American Institute of Family Relations (1934, March 3). *Program for Southern California Conference on Education for Family Life,* University of Southern California. (From the archives of the institute).

American Institute of Family Relations (1940, Oct. 4, 5). *Final program: The 100th Conference of the American Institute of Family Relations on the Successful Family.* Occidental College, Los Angeles. (From the archives of the institute).

American Institute of Family Relations (1970). *Fact sheet.* (From the archives of the institute.)

Auerswald, E.H. (1968). Interdisciplinary vs. ecological approach. *Family Process, 7,* 202–215.

Barker, R.L. (1984). *Treating couples in crisis: Fundamentals and practice in marital therapy.* New York: Free Press. London: Collier Macmillan.

Bateson, G., Jackson, D.D., Haley, J., & Weakland, J.H. (1956). Toward a theory of schizophrenia. *Behavioral Science,* 251–264.

Bell, J.E. (1961). *Family group therapy.* (Public Health Monograph #64, U.S. Department of Health, Education and Welfare). Washington, DC: U.S. Government Printing Office.

Bell, J.E. (1967). Family group therapy—A new treatment method for children. *Family Process, 6,* 254–263.

Bell, J.E. Preface. (1972). In N.W. Ackerman, *The psychodynamics of family life.* New York: Basic Books. (Originally published in 1958.)

Bernard, L.L. (1908). The teaching of sociology in the United States. *American Journal of Sociology, 15,* 164–213.

Boszormenyi-Nagy, I., & Framo, J. (Eds.) (1965). *Intensive family therapy.* New York: Harper & Row.

Boszormenyi-Nagy, I., & Spark, G. (1975). *Invisible loyalties.* New York: Harper & Row.

Bowen, M. (1976). Family therapy and family group therapy. In

---

[11] Available from AAMFT, 1100 17th St., NW, 10th Floor, Washington, DC 20036.

D.H.L. Olson (Ed.), *Treating relationships*. Lake Mills, IA: Graphic.

Bowlby, J. (1949). The study and reduction of group tension in the family. *Human Relations, 2,* 123–128.

Bowman, H. (1942). *Marriage for moderns*. New York: McGraw-Hill, 1942.

Bowman, H. (1949). *Marriage education in college*. New York: Social Hygiene Association.

Brecher, E.M. (1971). *The sex researchers*. New York: New American Library.

Calder-Marshall, A. (1959). *The sage of sex*. New York: Putnam.

Carroll, E.J., Cambor, C.G., Leopold, J.V., Miller, M.D., & Reis, W.J. (1963). Psychotherapy of marital couples. *Family Process, 2,* 25–33.

Clark, R. (1973). *Ellen Swallow: The woman who founded ecology*. Chicago: Follett.

Cooley, C.H. (1909). *Social organization*. New York: Scribner's.

Cooley, C.H. (1956). *Human nature and the social order*. Glencoe, IL: Free Press. (Originally published, 1909.)

Cuber, J. (1948). *Marriage counseling practice*. New York: Appleton-Century-Crofts.

Dickinson, R.L. (1949). *Human sex anatomy*. Baltimore: Williams & Wilkins, 1933. (Revised and expanded, 1949.)

Dickinson, R.L. & Beam, L. (1931). *A thousand marriages*. Baltimore: Williams & Wilkins.

Dickinson, R.L. & Beam, L. (1934). *The single women*. Baltimore: Williams & Wilkins.

Dicks, H.V. (1964). Concepts of marital diagnosis and therapy as developed at the Tavistock Family Psychiatric Clinic, London, England. In E.M. Nash, L. Jessner, & D.W. Abse (Eds.), *Marriage counseling in medical practice*. Chapel Hill: University of North Carolina Press.

Dreikurs, R. (1948). *The challenge of parenthood*. New York: Duell, Sloan, & Pearce.

Dreikurs, R. (1949a). Counseling for family adjustment. *Individual Psychology Bulletin, 7,* 119–137.

Dreikurs, R. (1949b). Psychotherapy through child guidance. *Nervous Child, 8,* 311–328.

Dreikurs, R. (1950). Technique and dynamics of multiple psychotherapy. *Psychiatric Quarterly, 24,* 788–799.

Dreikurs, R. (1951). Family group therapy in the Chicago Community Child Guidance Center. *Mental Hygiene, 35,* 291–301.

Dubois, P. (1907). *The psychoneuroses and their moral treatment* (S.E. Jelliffe & W.A. White, Eds. and trans.). New York: Funk & Wagnalls.

Eisenstein, V.W. (Ed.), (1956). *Neurotic interaction in marriage*. New York: Basic Books.

Ellis, H. (1936). *Studies in the psychology of sex*. New York: Random House.

Flugel, J.C. (1921). *The psycho-analytic study of the family*. London: Hogarth Press.

Folsom, J.K. (1943). *The family and democratic society*. New York: Wiley.

Freud, S. (1912). [*Recommendations for physicians on the psychoanalytic method of treatment*] (J. Riviere, trans.) Zentralblatt, Bd. II. Reprinted in Sammlung, Vierte Folge.

Freud, S. (1915). *General introduction to psychoanalysis*. New York: Liveright.

Freud, S. (1938). [The transformation of puberty] In A.A. Brill (Ed. and trans.). *The basic writings*. New York: Modern Library.

Fromm, E. (1941). *Escape from freedom*. New York: Farrar & Rinehart.

Fromm, E. (1947). *Man for himself*. New York: Rinehart.

Fromm-Reichmann, F. (1950). *Principles of intensive psychotherapy*. Chicago: University of Chicago Press.

Glover, E. (1955). *The technique of psycho-analysis*. New York: International Universities Press.

Goldenberg, I., & Goldenberg, H. (1985). *Family therapy: An overview* (2nd ed.). Monterey, CA: Brooks/Cole.

Goldstein, S.E. (1945). *Marriage and family counseling*. New York: McGraw-Hill.

Goodman, E.S. (1973). Marriage counseling a science: Some research considerations. *Family Coordinator, 22,* 111–116.

Green, B.L. (1965). Introduction: A multi-operational approach to marital problems. In B.L. Green (Ed.), *The psychotherapies of marital disharmony*. New York: Free Press.

Green, B.L., Broadhurst, B.P., & Lustig, N. (1965). Treatment of marital disharmony: The use of individual, concurrent, and co-joint sessions as a "combined approach." In B.L. Green (Ed.), *The psychotherapies of marital disharmony*. New York: Free Press.

Green, J.T. (1985). Ernest R. Groves: Explorer and pioneer in marriage and family life education and marriage counseling. In P. Dial & R. Jewson (Eds.), *In praise of fifty years: The Groves conference on the conservation of marriage and the family*. Lake Mills, IA: Graphic.

Green, S.L., & Hansen, J.C. (1986). Ethical dilemmas in family therapy. *Journal of Marriage and Family Therapy, 12,* 225–230.

Groves, E.R., & Groves, G.H. (1947). *The contemporary American family*. Chicago: Lippincott.

Guerin, P.J., Jr. (1976). Family therapy: The first twenty-five years. In P.J. Guerin, Jr. (Ed.), *Family therapy: Theory and practice*. New York: Gardner Press.

Guerney, B.G., Jr. (1964). Filial therapy: Description and rational. *Journal of Consulting Psychology, 28,* 303–310.

Guerney, B.G., Jr. (1977). *Relationship enhancement*. San Francisco: Josey-Bass.

Gurman, A.S. (1973). Marital therapy: Emerging trends in research and practice. *Family Process, 12,* 45–54.

Haley, J. (1971). Toward a theory of pathological systems. In G.H. Zuk & I. Boszormenyi-Nagy (Eds.), *Family theory and disturbed families*. Palo Alto, CA: Science & Behavior Books.

Haley, J. (1976). Development of theory: a history of a research project (Original, 1961). In C.E. Sluzki, & D.C. Ransom (Eds.), *Double bind: The foundation of a communicational approach to the family*. New York: Grune & Stratton.

Haley, J. (1987). Personal communication.

Hare-Mustin, R.T. (1978). A feminist approach to family therapy. *Family Process, 17,* 181–194.

Hirschfeld, M. (1930). *Geschlechtskunde*. (5 vols.). Stuttgart: J. Püttman Verlag.

Hirschfeld, M. (1940). *Sexual pathology: A study of derangements of the sexual instinct* (Original in 1932). (Authorized translation by Jerome Gibbs.) New York: Emerson Books.

Hite, S. (1976). *The Hite report*. New York: Macmillan.

Hoenig, J. (1978). Dramatic personae: Selected biographical sketches of 19th century pioneers in sexology. In J. Money & H. Musaph (Eds.), *Handbook of sexology, Vol. I*. New York: Elsevier.

Hoffman, L. (1981). *Foundations of family therapy: A conceptual framework for systems change*. New York: Basic Books.

Horney, K. (1937). *The neurotic personality of our time*. New York: Norton.

Horney, K. (1939). *New ways in psychoanalysis*. New York: Norton.

Humphrey, F.G. (1978). Presidential address for American Association for Marriage and Family Therapy. Houston, Texas.

Jackson, D.D. (1959). Family interaction, family homeostasis, and some implications for cojoint family therapy. In J. Masserman (Ed.), *Individual and family dynamics*. New York: Grune & Stratton.

Jackson, D.D. (Ed.) (1968). *Human communication, Vol. 1. Communication, family and marriage, Vol. 2 Theory, communication and change*. Palo Alto, CA: Science & Behavior Books.

Jackson, D.D., Riskin, J., & Satir, V.M. (1961). A method of analysis of a family interview. *Archives of General Psychiatry, 5,* 321–339.

Jacobson, N.S., & Margolin, G. (1979). *Marital therapy: Strategies based on social learning and behavioral exchange principles*. New York: Brunner/Mazel.

Jacobson, N.S., & Martin, B. (1976). Behavioral marriage therapy: current status. *Psychological Bulletin, 83,* 540–556.

Jewson, R. (1970). The National Council on Family Relations: Decade of the sixties. *Journal of Marriage and the Family, 32*, 610–615.

Jung, C. (1910). The association method. *The American Journal of Psychology, 21*, 219–269.

Kantor, D., & Lehr, W. (1975). *Inside the family*. San Francisco, CA: Jossey-Bass.

Kaslow, F.W. (1980). History of family therapy in the United States: A kaleidoscopic overview. *Marriage and Family Review, 3* (1/2), 77–111.

Kinsey, A.C., Pomeroy, W.E., & Martin, C.E. (1948). *Sexual behavior in the human male*. Philadelphia: W.B. Saunders.

Kinsey, A.C., Pomeroy, W.B., Martin, C.F., & Gebhard, P. (1953). *Sexual behavior in the human female*. Philadelphia: W.B. Saunders.

Knox, D. (1971). *Marriage happiness: A behavioral approach to counseling*. Champaign, IL: Research Press.

Kolevzon, M.S., & Green, R.G. (1985). *Family therapy models: Convergence and divergence*. New York: Springer.

Kopp, M.E. (1938). Marriage counseling in European countries: Present status and trends. *Journal of Heredity, 29*, 153–160.

Kubie, L.S. (1956). Psychoanalysis and marriage: Practical and theoretical issues. In V.W. Eisenstein (Ed.), *Neurotic interaction in marriage*. New York: Basic Books.

Laidlaw, R.W. (1956). The psychotherapy of marital problems. In V.W. Eisenstein (Ed.), *Neurotic interaction in marriage*. New York: Basic Books.

Landis, J.T., & Landis, M.G. (1948). *The marriage handbook*. New York: Prentice-Hall.

Landis, P.H. (1946). *Your marriage and family living*. New York: McGraw-Hill.

Lederer, W.J., & Jackson, D.D. (1968). *The mirages of marriage*. New York: Norton.

Libow, J.A., Raskin, P.A., and Caust, B.L. (1982). Feminist and family systems therapy: Are they irreconcilable? *American Journal of Family Therapy, 10*, 3–12.

Lidz, R.W., & Lidz, T. (1949). The family environment of schizophrenic patients. *American Journal of Psychiatry, 106*, 332–345.

Lidz, T., Cornelison, A.R., Fleck, S., & Terry, D. (1957a). The intrafamilial environment of the schizophrenic patient: 1. The father. *Psychiatry, 20*, 329–342.

Lidz, T., Cornelison, A., Fleck, S., & Terry, D. (1957b). The intrafamilial environment of schizophrenic patients: II marital schism and marital skew. *American Journal of Psychiatry, 114*, 241–248.

Lidz, T., Perker, B., & Cornelison, A. (1956). The rule of the father in the family environment of the schizophrenic patient. *American Journal of Psychiatry, 113*, 126–132.

LoPiccolo, J., & LoPiccolo, L. (1978). *Handbook of sex therapy*. New York: Plenum Press.

Mace, D.R. (1945). Marriage guidance in England. *Marriage and Family Living, 7*, 1–2, 5.

Mace, D.R. (1948). *Marriage counseling*. London: Churchill.

Mace, D.R., & Mace, V. (1976). Marriage enrichment—a preventative group approach for couples. In D.H.L. Olson (Ed.), *Treating relationships*. Lake Mills, IA: Graphic.

Mace, D.R., & Mace, V. (1986). Marriage enrichment—developing interpersonal potential. In P. Dial & R. Jewson (Eds.), *In praise of fifty years: The Groves conference on the conservation of marriage and the family*. Lake Mills, IA: Graphic.

MacGregor, R. (1967). Progress in multiple impact theory. In N.W. Ackerman, F.L. Beatman, & S.N. Sherman (Eds.), *Expanding theory and practice in family therapy*. New York: Family Service Association of America.

MacGregor, R., Ritchie, A.M., Serrano, A.C., Schuster, F.P., McDanald, E.C., & Goolishian, H.A. (1964). *Multiple impact therapy with families*. New York: McGraw-Hill.

Masters, W.H., & Johnson, V.E. (1966). *Human sexual response*. Boston: Little, Brown.

Masters, W.H., & Johnson, V.E. (1970). *Human sexual inadequacy*. Boston: Little, Brown.

McGoldrick, M., Pearce, J.K., & Giordano, J. (Eds.) (1982). *Ethnicity and family therapy*. New York: Guilford.

Mead, G.H. (1934). *Mind, self and society* (C.W. Morris, Ed.). Chicago: University of Chicago Press.

Michaelson, R. (1963). *An analysis of the changing focus of marriage counseling*. Unpublished doctoral dissertation, University of Southern California.

Midelfort, C.F. (1957). *The family in psychotherapy*. New York: McGraw-Hill.

Miller, D.R., & Sobelman, G. (1985). Models of the family: A critical review of alternatives. In L. L'Abate (Ed.), *The handbook of family psychology and therapy, Vol. 1* (pp. 3–35). Homewood, IL: Dorsey Press.

Miller, S., Nunnally, E.W., & Wackman, D.B. (1975). *Alive and aware: Improving communication in relationships*. Minneapolis: Interpersonal Communication Programs.

Miller, S., Nunnally, E.W., & Wackman, D.B. (1976). Minnesota Couples Communication Program (MCCP): Premarital and marital groups. In D.H.L. Olson (Ed.), *Treating relationships*. Lake Mills, IA: Graphic.

Minuchin, S. (1974). *Families and family therapy*. Cambridge, MA: Harvard University Press.

Minuchin, S. (1987). My many voices. In J.D. Zeig (Ed.), *The evolution of psychotherapy*. New York: Brunner/Mazel.

Minuchin, S., Auerswald, E., King, C., & Rabinowitz, C. (1964). The study of treatment of families that produce multiple acting-out boys. *American Journal of Orthopsychiatry, 34*, 125–133.

Minuchin, S., Montalvo, B., Guerney, B., Rosman, B., & Schumer, F. (1967). *Families of the slums*. New York: Basic Books.

Minuchin, S., Rosman, B.L., & Baker, L. (1978). *Psychosomatic families: Anorexia nervosa in context*. Cambridge, MA: Harvard University Press.

Mittlemann, B. (1944). Complementary neurotic reactions in intimate relationships. *Psychoanalytic Quarterly, 13*, 479–491.

Mittlemann, B. (1948). The concurrent analysis of married couples. *Psychoanalytic Quarterly, 17*, 182–197.

Mittlemann, B. (1956). Analysis of neurotic patterns in family relationships. In V.W. Eisenstein (Ed.), *Neurotic interaction in marriage*. New York: Basic Books.

Moreno, J.L. (1934). *Who shall survive?* Washington, DC: Nervous and Mental Diseases Publishing Co.

Moreno, J.L. (1940). Psychodramatic treatment of marriage problems. *Sociometry, 3*, 1.

Moreno, J.L. (1952). Psychodrama of a family conflict. *Group Psychotherapy, 5*, 20–37.

Mudd, E.H. (1955). *The practice of marriage counseling*. New York: Association Press.

Mudd, E.H., & Fowler, C.R. (1976). The AAMC and AAMFC: Nearly forty years of form and function. In B.N. Ard, Jr. (Ed.), *Handbook of marriage counseling* (2nd ed.). Palo Alto, CA: Science & Behavior Books.

Mudd, E.H., Stone, A., Karpf, M.J., & Nelson, J.F. (Eds.). (1958). *Marriage counseling: A casebook*. New York: Association Press.

Nichols, M. (1984). *Family therapy: Concepts and methods*. New York/London: Gardner Press.

Nichols, W. (1979). Doctoral programs in marital and family therapy. *Journal of Marital and Family Therapy, 5*, 23–28.

Oberndorf, C.P. (1934). Folie à deux. *International Journal of Psychoanalysis, 15*, 14.

Oberndorf, C.P. (1938). Psychoanalysis of married couples. *Psychoanalytic Review, 25*, 453–475.

Olson, D.H. (1970). Marital and family therapy: Integrative review and critique. *Journal of Marriage and the Family, 32*, 501–538.

Olson, D.H. (Ed.) (1976). *Treating relationships*. Lake Mills, IA: Graphic.

Otto, H. (1975). Marriage and family enrichment programs in North America—report and analysis. *Family Coordinator, 24*, 137–142.

Paine, R.T. (1899). *Proceedings of the National Conference on Charities and Corrections*, 1899, p. 355 (as cited in Rich, 1956, p. 18).

Peacock, E.C. (1977). The giant rests. *Family Life*, 1977, 37, 1:1.

Popenoe, P. (1975). The foreword. In American Institute of Family Relations (Ed.), *Techniques of marriage and family counseling, Vol. IV*. Los Angeles: American Institute of Family Relations.

Report of the FSAA Committee on Marriage Counseling. (1943). New York: Family Service Association of America.

Rich, M.E. (1956). *A belief in people: A history of family social work*. New York: Family Service Association of America.

Richardson, H.B. (1945). *Patients have families*. New York: Commonwealth Fund.

Richmond, M.E. (1917). *Social diagnosis*. New York: Russell Sage.

Richmond, M.E. (1928). Concern of the community with marriage. In M.E. Rich (Ed.), *Family life today: Papers presented at the Fiftieth Anniversary of Family Social Casework in America*. Boston: Houghton Mifflin.

Rithie, A. (1960). Multiple impact therapy: An experiment. *Social Work*, 5, 16–21.

Rodgers, T.C. (1965). A specific parameter: Concurrent psychotherapy of the spouse of analysand by the same analyst. *International Journal of Psychoanalysis*, 46, 237–243.

Sager, C.J. (1966). The treatment of married couples. In S. Arieti (Ed.) *American handbook of psychiatry*, Vol. III. New York: Basic Books.

Sager, C.J. (1976). *Marriage contracts and couple therapy*. New York: Brunner/Mazel.

Satir, V. (1964). *Conjoint family therapy*. Palo Alto, CA: Science & Behavior Books.

Satir, V., Stachowiak, J., & Taschman, H. (1977). *Helping families to change*. New York: Aronson.

Selvini Palazzoli, M., Boscolo, L., Cecchin, G., & Prata, G. (1978). *Paradox and counterparadox*. New York: Jason Aronson.

Semans, J.H. (1956). Premature ejaculation: A new approach. *Southern Medical Journal*, 49, 353–358.

Sherman, R., & Dinkmeyer, D. (1987). *Systems of family therapy: An Adlerian integration*. New York: Brunner/Mazel.

Sherman, S.N. (1961). The concept of the family in casework theory. In N.W. Ackerman, F.L. Beatman, & S.N. Sherman (Eds.), *Exploring the base for family therapy*. New York: Family Service Association of America.

Silverman, M., & Silverman, M. (1962, Nov.). Psychiatry inside the family circle. *Saturday Evening Post*, 46–51.

Sluzki, C.E. (1983). Interview on the state of the art. *Family Therapy Networker*, 7, (1), 24.

Sluzki, C.E. (1987). Family process: Mapping the journey over twenty-five years. *Family Process*, 26, 149–152.

Sluzki, C.E., & Bloch, D.A. (1984). *The roots of family therapy*. Presentation at the 42nd Annual Conference of the American Association for Marriage and Family Therapy, San Francisco.

Smith, Z.D. (1890). *Proceedings of the National Conference in Charities and Corrections*, 1890, p. 377 (as cited in Rich, 1956, p. 95).

Speck, R.V. (1967). Psychotherapy of the social network of a schizophrenic family. *Family Process*, 6, 208–214.

Speck, R.V., & Ohlan, J.L. (1967). The social networks of the family of schizophrenics. *American Journal of Orthopsychiatry*, 37, 206.

Spiegel, J.P., & Bell, N.W. (1959). The family of the psychiatric patient. In S. Arieti (Ed.), *American handbook of psychiatry Vol. 1*. New York: Basic Books.

Stone, A. (1949). Marriage education and marriage counseling in the United States. *Marriage and Family Living*, 11, 38–39, 50.

Stone, I. (1971). *The passions of the mind*. New York: Doubleday.

Stuart, R.B. (1969). Operant interpersonal treatment for marital discord. *Journal of Consulting and Clinical Psychology*, 33, 675–682.

Stuart, R.B. (1975). Behavioral remedies for marital ills. In A.S.

Gurman & D.G. Rice (Eds.), *Couples in conflict*. New York: Jason Aronson.

Stuart, R.B. (1976). An operant interpersonal program for couples. In D.H.L. Olson (Ed.), *Treating relationships*. Lake Mills, IA: Graphic.

Sullivan, H.S. (1947). *Conceptions of modern psychiatry*. Washington, DC: William Alanson White Psychiatric Foundation.

Sullivan, H.S. (1953). *Interpersonal theory of psychiatry*. New York: Norton.

Thompson, C. (1951). *Psychoanalysis: Evolution and development*. New York: Hermitage House.

Towle, C. (1948). Treatment of behavior and personality problems in children. The 1930 symposium: The social worker. *Orthopsychiatry 1927–1948*. New York: American Orthopsychiatric Association.

Waite, F.T. (1941). Casework: Today and fifty years ago. *The Family*, 21, 315–322.

Waller, W.W. (1938). *The family: A dynamic interpretation*. New York: Dial Press.

Watson, A.S. (1963). The conjoint psychotherapy of marriage partners. *American Journal of Orthopsychiatry*, 33, 912–922.

Watzlawick, P., Beavin, J.H., & Jackson, D.D. (1967). *Pragmatics of human communication*. New York: Norton.

Weiss, R.L., Hops, H., & Patterson, G.R. (1973). A framework for conceptualizing marital conflict: A' technology for altering it, some data for evaluating it. In L.A. Hamerlynck, L.C. Handy, & E.J. Mash (Eds.), *Behavior change: Methodology, concepts and practice*. Champaign, IL: Research Press.

Weiss, R.L., & Margolin, G. (1977). Assessment of marital conflict and accord. In A.R. Ciminero, K.S. Calhoun, & H.E. Adams (Eds.), *Handbook of behavioral assessment*. New York: Wiley.

Wendorf, D.J., & Wendorf, R.J. (1985). A systemic view of family therapy ethics. *Family Process*, 24, 443–453.

Whitaker, C.A. (1958a). Psychotherapy with couples. *American Journal of Psychotherapy*, 12, 18–23.

Whitaker, C.A. (Ed.). (1958b). *Psychotherapy of chronic schizophrenic patients*. Boston: Little, Brown.

Whitaker, C.A., & Keith, D.V. (1982). Experiential/symbolic family therapy. In A.M. Horne & M.M. Ohlsen (Eds.), *Family counseling and therapy*. Itasca, IL: Peacock.

Whitehead, A.N., & Russell, B. (1910). *Principia mathematica*. Cambridge, England: Cambridge University Press.

Wolpe, J. (1958). *Psychotherapy by reciprocal inhibition*. Stanford, CA: Stanford University Press.

Wynne, L. (1961). The study of intrafamilial alignments and splits in exploratory family therapy. In N.W. Ackerman, F.L. Beatman, & S.N. Sherman (Eds.), *Exploring the base for family therapy*. New York: Family Service Association of America.

Wynne, L., Ryckoff, I., Day, J., & Hirsch, S. (1958). Pseudo mutuality in the family relations of schizophrenics. *Psychiatry*, 21, 205–220.

Yost, J.L. (1986). For God, country and family: A personal tribute to Christian Fredrik Midelfort, M.D. *Family Process*, 25, 149–151.

Zuk, G.H. (1971). *Family therapy: A triadic-based approach*. New York: Behavioral Publications.

EDITORS' REFERENCES

Broderick, C.B. (1979). Personal communication.

Framo, J. (Winter, 1989). How AFTA got started. *American Family Therapy Association Newsletter*, 37, 10–15.

CHAPTER 2

Systems Theory, Cybernetics, and Epistemology

Herta A. Guttman, M.D.

General systems theory had its origins in the thinking of mathematicians, physicists, and engineers in the late 1940s and early 1950s, when technological developments made it possible to conceive of and build mechanical models approximating certain properties of the human brain. At that time, it was recognized that many different phenomena (both biological and non-biological) share the attributes of a system—that is, a unified whole that consists of interrelated parts, such that the whole can be identified as being different from the sum of its parts and any change in one part affects the rest of the system. General systems theory concerns itself with elucidating the functional and structural rules that can be considered valid for describing all systems, whatever their composition. These attributes include information processing, adaptation to changed circumstances, self-organization, and self-maintenance (Simon, Stierlin, & Wynne, 1985).

Norbert Wiener (1954) recognized that communication and self-regulation through communication are essential for the operation of systems. Information concerning the results of its past performance is reinserted into the system, thereby influencing its future behavior. This process is called *self-corrective feedback*. Wiener named the scientific investigation of these self-corrective phenomena *cybernetics*. It includes the study of self-regulation, self-reproduction, adaptation, information processing and storage, and goal-directed behavior (Simon et al., 1985).

EARLY BEGINNINGS: THE ROLE OF GREGORY BATESON

Gregory Bateson came into contact with cybernetic thinking at the Josiah Macy conferences, which were held during the 1950s and were attended by Wiener and other cyberneticians. Bateson immediately perceived the relevance of this way of thinking to the description of human interaction. An anthropologist, Bateson was particularly attracted to the idea that one could account for both the uniformity and the variability of human behavior in various cultures by assuming that they were rule-governed systems. He was interested in applying this perspective to the *Naven* ceremony, which he had witnessed among the Iatmul headhunters of New Guinea (Bateson, 1936). He felt he had insufficiently understood the significance of this ritual, in which boasting by one person about a culturally validated achievement would be met by "Naven" behavior—submissive, abnegatory behavior on the part of a man (men) who represent(s) the maternal lineage of the ceremony's protagonist. Bateson recognized that this ritual seemed to cement those kinship ties that were most fragile. Whereas the patrilineal tie was strong in this society, the link to the mother's clan, although extremely important, could be more easily broken if the mother's kinsmen were to challenge the boasting of the father's side of the family. This could have serious implications for the stability of the society. The "Naven" behavior of the mother's kinsmen "righted" a balance that was being put out of kilter by "masculine" boasting.

In his original study, Bateson recognized two types of behavior: *symmetrical behavior*, in which the protagonists are equal and which can escalate, thereby resulting in a disruption of the relationship; and *complementary behavior*, in which one person assumes a position opposite to the other's submissive or assertive stance, thereby stabilizing the relationship. Much later, after having become aware of cybernetic notions, Bateson rephrased these observations and stated that Iatmul society contained two kinds of forces: those that could propel the participants into a pattern of escalating antagonisms and the possible secession of a splinter group and those that supported accommodation and social cohesion (Bateson, 1936).

Bateson first named the process that includes both of these types of behavior *schismogenesis*, "a process of differentiation in the norms of individual behavior resulting from cumulative interaction between individuals" (Bateson, 1936, p. 175). In this process, "each party reacts to the reaction of the other" (Bateson, 1936, p. 189). He saw these forces as existing in a "dynamic equilibrium" with one another. Later, he found that cybernetic systems theory could explain this equilibrium with the notion of

self-governance, through *feedback*, whereby information that results from a given action is recursively fed back into the system and allows it to regulate its further activity in a modified manner. The first behavior pattern is an example of *positive feedback*, or information that increases the system's deviation from its original state; the second kind of behavior pattern is an example of *negative feedback*, or information that brings the system back to its original state and decreases deviation.

The son of a noted biologist, Bateson had a lifelong interest in the reciprocal accommodation between the organism and its ecological niche. He saw this as a fundamental process in all evolutionary development throughout the natural world, and believed that changes in organisms could be as important in determining the course of evolution as are those changes in the environment that produce evolutionary change in organisms (Bateson, 1979). His special strength was an acute awareness of the fundamental assumptions underlying general systems theory as it was then being articulated by Buckley (1968) and Bertalanffy (1968), that by observing systems one could formulate *rules* that could account for the functioning of interconnected parts. *This thinking represents a fundamental change from focusing on content, material substance, and the distribution of physical energy to considering pattern, process, and communication as being the essential elements of description and explanation.*

In order to test some of these ideas, Bateson sought and received funds for the study of communication processes in general, and those in families in particular, and formed the Palo Alto group (Haley, 1976). Bateson's involvement with family therapy was essentially limited to his participation in this project. He then moved on to the study of porpoises and their methods of communicating, both among themselves and with their human trainers. He was never interested in families or family therapy per se, but rather in overarching concepts that would describe and connect many varied types of behavior in many different types of natural systems. His ultimate goal was to develop a unitary view of nature, which could include mind and not just material substance (Bateson, 1972). The family and its communication patterns were one stop along the road of a more general intellectual and epistemological quest. However, as they developed, his ideas continued to influence family therapy. He made a unique and lasting contribution to the field.

THE ROLE OF THE PALO ALTO GROUP

The Palo Alto group was formed to study communication, in families in general and in families of schizophrenics in particular (Haley, 1976). It marked the beginning of a concern in psychiatric thinking with process and pattern rather than content. Heretofore, psychiatry had been influenced by neuropsychiatric reductionism on the one hand and by psychoanalytic concerns on the other. Both focused on underlying content, much as the physical and biological sciences had been concerned with laws governing matter rather than with laws governing process. The Palo Alto group's focus on the family system as a whole, rather than on a conglomerate of individuals, permitted the group to begin developing a new language that described supraindividual phenomena rather than processes within the individual, such as affects and motivation. *Family therapy thus became not just another therapeutic modality, but an important port of entry of new cybernetic ideas into psychiatric thinking.*[1] It heralded a paradigm shift: the individual and each successively more complex social group are viewed in relation to all the others, as a subsystem within many different contextual systems.

The Family as a Cybernetic System

Through their study of families, the members of the Palo Alto group perceived the advantage of describing the family not only as a system of interconnected parts, but also a *cybernetic system* that governs itself through feedback. Perhaps because they were studying families of young adult schizophrenics, they particularly emphasized *error-activated feedback*, that is, negative feedback that enables the system to "right" itself and to return to its original state whenever new, unbalancing information impinges on it. For instance, in the families of many schizophrenics, members behave the same no matter what their family's life stage. Many other observers have confirmed that certain schizophrenics' families are particularly rigid and have a particular propensity for utilizing negative feedback to return the system to its previous status (Ferreira & Winter, 1965; Mishler & Waxler, 1968; Reiss, 1981). The focus on schizophrenia probably explains why the Palo Alto group seems to have paid less attention to the implications of positive, deviation-amplifying feedback. Nevertheless, through the group's work, the fundamental cybernetic concept of self-governance in families became embedded in family-systems thinking (Haley, 1959b; Jackson, 1957).

The Family as a Homeostatic System

These observations led to the adoption of another cybernetic concept, that of *homeostasis*. In the 19th century, Claude Bernard (1859) postulated that warm-blooded animals, including human beings, tend to maintain a constant interior milieu (*milieu intérieur*) through the regulation of the pH of the blood and plasma, the hormonal balance, the distribution of various salts, and the balance of salts and water within the organism. The body preserves a narrowly defined equilibrium between its constituent elements, a condition of homeostasis that is maintained by many specific, automatic, self-regulating mechanisms. A broader cybernetic statement of this principle is that negative feedback maintains homeostasis in a system by reducing any deviation that results from the introduction of new information.

---

[1] *Editors' Note.* While this focusing on the family system "rather than" on the individuals was undoubtedly the major aspect of conceptual divergence that allowed the emergence of this new field, until only quite recently the individual had virtually become lost in the theoretical shuffle (cf. Nichols, 1987). In the last few years, we have often felt dismayed that neophyte family therapy students are not infrequently introduced to the idea that individuals are as much a part of family life as is family interaction, as though this were, somehow, a new idea.

The Family as a Rule-Governed System

The concept of homeostasis conveniently explains the tendency of families and other social systems to maintain a given configurational relationship among their constituent elements. Jackson (1957) elaborated on this as it applies to families and recognized that the mechanisms maintaining homeostasis operate according to certain rules that condition or "set" the range within which a given behavior can vary. One important rule he described was the *marital quid pro quo* ("something for something"), which ensures that each member of a couple stands to gain something from the relationship (Jackson, 1965). Sager and his co-workers (Sager et al., 1971) further elaborated on this concept, considering the quid pro quo to be fundamental to a marriage contract that is based not only on the partners' conscious expectations of, but also on their unconsciously dictated wishes for, recognition or compensation. They emphasized that the rules governing the marital relationship must be analyzed at several levels if they are to be fully understood.[2] This is an early example of the compatibility between psychodynamic concepts and systems principles, and illustrates the fact that the homeostatic *process* can exist within many contexts, linking many levels of functioning. In clinical contexts, it can include unconscious processes, cognitive mechanisms, behavior of various types, and electrical or physiochemical phenomena within the cells of the body.

Family rules may apply to different areas of family life. Some of these rules may function as *family myths*, designed to maintain family homeostatis (Ferreira, 1963). For instance, the myth of family harmony ("Our family does not quarrel") can maintain stability (Stierlin, 1973). When such a rule is transgressed, the homeostatic mechanisms of the family swing into action to bring the family system back to its former equilibrium.

The Symptomatic Family Member

The Palo Alto group began to believe that families that come to psychiatric attention may be "delegating" one family member to be the homeostatic component that brings the whole system "back on track" if one of its established rules is threatened. Whenever a deviation-amplifying piece of information is introduced (such as an argument between two people or a new need or life stage of one of the family members), the symptomatic person's behavior escalates. This can range from psychosomatic symptoms (Jackson & Yalom, 1966) to psychotic problems (Haley, 1959b). It often exacts a high price from the identified person. However, it allows the other family members to maintain their respective roles in the system because all other family problems or conflicts are laid aside in the face of this exigency. This thinking permitted the Palo Alto group to link various kinds of mental and physical symptoms to the systemic rules governing family systems.

Family Communication and Metacommunication

Because of the influence of cybernetic thinking, the Palo Alto group became interested in possible parallels between communication in families and information exchange in inanimate systems (Watzlawick, Beavin, & Jackson, 1967). This led to a focus on the digital and analogic languages described by computer scientists. In *digital communication*, each sign is discrete and is arbitrarily related to a particular meaning. For instance, if we consider words to be signs, there is no necessary relationship between their form and meaning other than that which has been attributed to them by semiotic convention. On the other hand, in *analogic communication*, the signs are continuous and not discrete, representing more or less of a given quality or quantity. Moreover, the signs are related to their meaning. For instance, a certain gesture directly conveys a specific emotion in a given culture.

The Palo Alto group recognized that, at the least, human communication can be divided into the verbal and the nonverbal. Seeing the parallel with the digital–analogic distinction, they characterized human verbal communication

---

[2] *Editors' Note.* In line with the previous "Editors' Note," it is indeed ironic that this central theme of one of family therapy's seminal early thinkers until recently had been all but overlooked or forgotten among marital and family therapists (Gurman, 1985). It is inevitable, yet most unfortunate, that conceptual politicization can so readily obscure fundamental truths.

as "digital" and nonverbal communication as "analogic." They observed that, in human development, there is a progression from the more diffuse, or analogic, to the more precise, or digital. Nevertheless, these are only *analogies*: verbal communication is not identical to "digital" computer language nor is nonverbal communication identical to "analogic" computer language.

In humans, the two channels of verbal and nonverbal communication usually are used simultaneously and constantly influence and condition each other. A verbal message can be "canceled out" by nonverbal communication. For instance, one family member may say to another, "I'm listening to you," and yet simultaneously turn to watch the television set. This type of phenomenon leads one to wonder how the two communication channels interact. What are the circumstances under which one or the other predominates? Perhaps one can resolve this question by postulating a further construct, that of metacommunication; that is, one channel conditions the other by being "above" it in some way. There are, therefore, different levels of communication.

One way of characterizing the different levels of a communication is to speak of the *report* (*digital*) and the *command* (*analogic*) aspects of a message. Each statement conveys not only informative content, but also a directive to the receiver as to how it is to be "read." This "reading" occurs with respect to a multiplicity of variables and contexts. For instance, the "command" aspect of a message may make a statement about the status relationship between the two communicants, about the sense or meaning (e.g., playful or serious, general or specific) that should be attributed to the statement, or whether the tone, the words, or the paraverbal behavior should be given primary importance. Often, both levels of the message are congruent so that the "command" reinforces the "report." However, as we have already seen, there are cases in which one level contradicts or contravenes the other.

As they continued to observe and recognize inconsistencies in the communication patterns of the individuals and families they were studying, Bateson and his group began to seek a theoretical construct that could account for these interactions in a more systemic way without resorting to concepts involving intrapsychic motivation (e.g., the conscious and the unconscious). They found such a construct in Whitehead and Russell's (1910/1913) theory of logical types.

This theory had been developed to account for the paradox posed by such statements as that of Epimenides, the Cretan, who said, "All Cretans are liars." If Epimenides is telling the truth, his statement is invalid, because he is a member of a class—the Cretans—who have been defined as liars. If Epimenides is telling a falsehood and all Cretans are *not* liars, his statement is invalid because he is including himself, a liar, in a description of all members of a class he says is truthful. To solve this problem, Whitehead and Russell proposed that statements about a class of things must be at a higher logical level than the class itself. They are *meta* to the class and do not include any member of that class.

From a systems perspective, such a conceptualization implies that there is a hierarchical organization of systems. Each system belongs to a class of systems, which, in turn, is a subsystem of a *metasystem*. The observer constructs a particular hierarchy by identifying the shared characteristics that are most relevant in demarcating classes.

When transposed to human communication, the theory of logical types gave the Palo Alto group the possibility of defining and ordering various classes of communication according to levels. By more clearly defining the parameters of clear and confused communication in families, they could begin to understand the speaker's irrelevancies and the receiver's *mystification* as being due to confusion in the categorizing and ordering of communication.

Can one really classify communication patterns in this way? Which is "meta"—nonverbal or verbal communication? Probably, the only sensible answer is a "constructivist" conclusion: the observer defines communication levels and their interrelationships (Segal, 1986; Foerster, 1984; Watzlawick, 1984). If one wants to know whether or not a verbal statement is being disqualified by a nonverbal message, one considers the nonverbal parameters to be "meta" to the verbal one. If one wonders whether a nonverbal message transmitted via a particular "channel" (e.g., tone of voice) is or is not being confirmed by another "channel" (e.g., movement), one observes the latter. In this case, movement is "meta" to tone.

In the language of communication, this process is called *punctuation*. Where does a sequence of actions begin? Where does it end? Who "causes" a certain event? Who is the actor and who is the recipient of the action? We "shift" reality according to the importance or level we accord some aspects rather than others. Reality is as we "punctuate" it.

The Theory of the Double Bind

The theory of the *double bind* is considered to be the definitive contribution of the Palo Alto group to the application of communication theory to the family and to schizophrenia. It includes many of the concepts that have already been mentioned: a rule-governed system, communication channels, metacommunication, logical types, and punctuation.

The most quoted example of the double bind stems from an observation of the interaction between a schizophrenic son and his mother when she visited him in the hospital (Bateson, Jackson, Haley, & Weakland, 1956). "He was glad to see her and impulsively put his arm around her shoulders, whereupon she stiffened. He withdrew his arm and she asked, 'Don't you love me any more?' He then blushed, and she said, 'Dear, you must not be so easily embarrassed and afraid of your feelings.' The patient was able to stay with her only a few minutes more, and following her departure, he assaulted an aide and was put in the tubs."

The riddle of this interaction lies not only in the incongruence of the mother's message, but in the fact that the son could not clearly and directly comment on it. The Palo Alto group concluded that the son's "violent craziness" was his comment on his mother's incongruence! By using a different "channel," at a different logical level, he was avoiding, not one, but two binds.

The first bind concerned the son's inability to comment on his mother's mixed message. The second bind, "meta" to the first, conditions or explains it: the son was in some way so dependent on his mother that he could not distance himself from her, either verbally or physically. In some way, the mother "bound" him and he was her "victim."

The Palo Alto group described many examples of such interactions. The group ultimately proposed the theory of the double bind, which defines the conditions that are necessary for such a situation to occur:

1. There must be two or more persons, one of whom is a "victim" and the other a "binder."
2. It must be a repeated experience.
3. There is a primary negative injunction.
4. There is a secondary injunction conflicting with the first one at a more abstract level, and, like the first, enforced by punishments or signals that threaten survival.
5. There is a tertiary negative injunction prohibiting the "victim" from escaping the field.
6. The complete set of ingredients is no longer necessary to set off the communication pattern once the "victim" has learned to perceive his or her universe in double-bind patterns.

In the example, the son is clearly dependent on his mother—he is the "victim." The primary negative injunction is conveyed by her body movement: "Do not express love for me." The secondary injunction, conflicting with the first, is: "You *should* express love for me." The tertiary injunction is: "Do not comment on my inconsistency. Do not notice that I have difficulty in deciding whether or not to have a loving relationship with you." The final criterion of the double bind (item 6) is not contained in this example.

The double-bind theory has been subjected to much theoretical scrutiny. There have been many attempts to operationalize it so as to conduct experiments to test its veracity (Olson, 1972). There have also been numerous objections to it, to which its authors have responded by clarifying certain aspects.

1. It is not systemically accurate to qualify one participant in an interaction as the "binder" and the other as the "victim." These roles arise out of a particular punctuation. The language of the original double bind belies a linear perspective, according to which the mother is the cause (is to blame for) her son's schizophrenic behavior. A truly systemic perspective assumes a reciprocal circularity in the relationship between two people.

The authors did retract and modify this aspect

of their original paper, noting that neither of the protagonists in this interaction was "responsible" for his or her role (Weakland, 1976; Bateson, Jackson, Haley, and Weakland, 1976). Nevertheless, on reading the original formulations of the Palo Alto group, it is striking to note how much they were influenced by the psychiatric thinking of their time. They allude to the "schizophrenogenic" mother (Fromm-Reichmann, 1948) and they do not include the father in a triadic perspective until some time later. Moreover, although espousing a systemic point of view, they are far more comfortable in imputing intrapsychic motivation and affects to the parent and the child than are many of today's systems therapists.

2. The tertiary injunction, prohibiting the "victim" from "escaping the field," should not be understood only in a literal sense, but also as a metaphor. Because of the intense survival value of a particular relationship, the receiver of the message cannot use any means of escape— either by actually distancing oneself in space or by verbally commenting on the relationship and thereby distancing oneself.

3. Whereas inconsistent messages (single binds) are quite common and easily identified, true double binds seem to be quite rare.

4. It is not true that double-bind situations per se are the only interactional correlates of the occurrence of increased psychotic behavior in schizophrenic patients when they are in close contact with their families. Many clinicians have observed that some schizophrenic patients can become more psychotic when intense affects are discussed in the family (Anderson, 1977; Guttman, 1973), when intense criticism is directly or indirectly expressed by family members (Brown, Birley, & Wing, 1972; Leff and Vaughn, 1985), or when a close family member is extremely ill or some other event threatens to separate the patient from that family member.

5. It has proved difficult to develop an experimental design that sufficiently approximates the double bind in order to (a) prove its existence or (b) prove that it is more common in certain types of families than in others. In any event, the results of these experiments have been inconclusive (Abeles, 1976).

Dell (1980) points out that the double-bind theory, properly understood, epitomizes systems theory's epistemological shift to observing pattern (the relationship between components) rather than content (the components themselves). Because this involves self-recursiveness, it may be impossible to follow the classical experimental model and to hold constant all variables except for one. It is impossible to determine causality with such a model, because each component is constantly shifting and influencing the other. Therefore, it might be impossible to hold double-bind interaction constant long enough to prove its existence.

At the end of their 10-year collaboration, the members of the Palo Alto group concluded that their work was basically a study of communication and the social learning of communication. Schizophrenia was one example, pursued both because of the patients' rich metaphorical and literal communications and because it attracted continued funding. However, the significance of this body of work extends much beyond schizophrenia. As Haley (1976) put it: "Instead of achieving a documentation of the theoretical approach of the research as was hoped, the experimental program resulted in introducing a small wedge into a new field, thereby following a pattern typical of this research project and perhaps inevitable in an exploratory field" (p. 94). The type of thinking that emerged from the work of this group has put a lasting imprint on the field. As a consequence, the systems approach and its advantages for the study of the family have become completely embedded in all aspects of family therapy.

THE LEGACY OF THE PALO ALTO GROUP: EARLY PROBLEMS

Issues of Control and Power

Early on, the members of the Palo Alto group were already struggling with and disagreeing about many of the issues that are still being debated in systems theory and family therapy. For instance, Haley (1976) points out that the term "control" implied different things to different people. He became increasingly convinced of a hierarchical paradigm, in which some family members controlled others and were more powerful in setting the rules for the system (Haley, 1976). Bateson, who abhorred the thought of power, saw control as a completely reciprocal and systemic phenomenon that does not have an originator or a recipient. He ultimately became disenchanted with working with psychiatrists, partly because he perceived them as being too complaisant with the notion of power —for instance, their role in the social control of patients (Bateson, 1976).

Issues of Levels and Language

Systems theory is basically a method of conceptualizing a configuration or a relationship. Each new method of conceptualizing requires a new language. Maturana (1978, 1984) has said, "We live in language," meaning that it is impossible to conceive of thought or of transmitting thoughts without adequately expressive language. The Palo Alto group was still tied to the language of the intrapsychic and had not yet really evolved a systemic metalanguage. There was a melange of different types of discourse. Sometimes they used language designed for inanimate cybernetic systems to describe animate human groups; sometimes they continued to use traditional psychodynamic language to describe their observations. For instance, Weakland emphasizes that the group's conclusions concur with the descriptions of Lidz (Lidz, Cornelison, Fleck, & Terry, 1957), who also often used the intrapsychic language of affect or motivation (Weakland, 1976).

In the same paper, Weakland also alludes to a new phenomenon: the direct observation of intrafamilial communication, as described by Wynne and his coworkers, who for the first time introduced family concepts such as "pseudomutuality" and the "rubber fence," which were derived from the direct observation of intrafamilial communication. The term "rubber fence" describes a family's characteristic tendency to include those persons, experiences, and values that are congruent with the family's myth about the harmony of its members' relationships and to extrude persons who threaten this myth (Simon et al., 1985). "Pseudomutuality" denotes a type of family relationship in which family unity is the primary value and individual members' thoughts, ideas, and feelings are subordinated to the family's shared needs and mythology. These terms mark the beginning of a vocabulary

that is specifically designed to describe the intimate human system of the family.

Issues of Causality

When describing the family, it is difficult to remain exclusively at the level of a whole system. At some point, it is necessary to focus on subsystems, in order to do justice to the interactional complexities clinicians must consider. For a long time, the language of intrapsychic motivation and feeling was taboo to some family-systems thinkers. They insisted that it was not "systemic" because the idea of circular, recursive feedback loops precludes punctuating any point in a feedback loop as being the cause of any specific subsequent event. Accordingly, it is theoretically incorrect to identify the motivation, thought, or action of any particular person as the cause of the behavior of another family member (Dell, 1982). This has come to be known as *linear thinking*. However, all along, other family therapists have continued using this language, insisting that the individual is a subsystem of the family and that one can legitimately include intrapsychic processes as well as behavior in a systemic description of the relationships between family members. At the very least, an individual's thoughts, fantasies, and feelings influence the context within which the thoughts, feelings, and behavior of other family members occur. One may not be entirely true to the complexity involved by describing this as a unidimensional, linear, cause–effect event, but one cannot completely exclude some notion of causality. This issue continues to be debated on a theoretical level (Guttman, 1986; Hoffman, 1985). Certainly, in the pragmatics of dealing with human situations, it is often virtually impossible not to attribute causality (or responsibility) more to one family member than to another (Dell, 1986; Imber-Black, 1986).

FROM MORPHOSTASIS TO MORPHOGENESIS

Positive, Deviation-Amplifying Feedback

In its early years, cybernetic theory dealt mainly with the mechanisms promoting homeostasis in systems. Indeed, a "control" view of systemic functioning tends inevitably to focus more on that which maintains sameness than that which promotes change. Although the implications of positive, deviation-amplifying feedback were recognized, less theoretical attention was devoted to them (Hoffman, 1971).

It is readily evident that, like other living systems, families undergo many transformations during their life span. *Morphogenesis* is just as much a fact of family life as is *morphostasis*, because change and adaptation are necessary for the family's survival (Speer, 1970; Wertheim, 1973, 1975). A theory of family systems must take into account the family's chronological development—its life cycle—and the impact of normative events such as birth or marriage and less normative events such as illness or unemployment.

In systems terms, these are deviation-amplifying events that activate positive feedback mechanisms. In response, there is an effect on some aspect of the family, for instance, its structure, the balance of power, or the rules governing some aspect of family life. One of two possible reactions then occurs: either there is a definitive change in the system or there is a return to the previous state because a deviation-reducing mechanism is brought into play. Systems thinkers speak of first-order and second-order change. *First-order change* refers to the system's tendency to return to a state that "balances out deviations and keeps the system at a constant level" (Simon et al., 1985, p. 34). That is, there is some change in the interrelationship of different elements of the system, but the basic rules and the original equilibrium are maintained. The second possibility is the occurrence of *second-order change*. This is a more radical response, the outcome being a definitive overall change in the rules about the rules governing the system, as well as in the interrelationships among elements constituting the system.

Sometimes both tendencies are clearly represented in the same family member. For instance, on the one hand, the rebellious adolescent is deviant to the family's *status quo ante* and as such is the carrier of positive feedback in the system. On the other hand, he or she also represents the negative feedback that maintains the family's static pattern of organization. Such a child both "pulls" the family into the future—into a different life-style, a changed pattern of rules, obligations, and satisfactions—and keeps the family "frozen" in its earlier *modus vivendi* because the family can label his or her behavior as "immature" and continue to behave as if it were a system with much younger children. For example, in therapy the parents may protest that they cannot allow the child a later curfew because he or she does not act responsibly enough to stay out so late in the evening. First-order change would occur if they were persuaded to relax the curfew and the child were to act less rebelliously and to resume confiding everything to the parent who depends on him or her for affective input. An example of second-order change would be if the adolescent were to come home on time for the new curfew, but were to continue to be more private about his or her life and the parents would begin to move closer to each other. Here, the family rules concerning proximity and distance between various dyads have significantly changed.

A family member who is chronically ill can also simultaneously represent forces pushing for change and for the status quo. On one level, the family must respond to the illness by reorganizing itself to care for this person; on another level, the presence of an ill member can reinforce the deviation-reducing, static tendency of the system by making it impossible to go beyond a certain point in changing family relationships as long as the primary rule is to care for the member who is ill.

The Origin of New Information

It is not easy to explain where new information originates and how it enters the system. If we assume that there is a range of closed and open systems, in a completely closed system, it is impossible for any new information to enter, whereas it is theoretically possible for all information to enter a completely open system.

Clearly, the "error-activated" information that constitutes deviation-reducing feedback can originate in the internal rules that govern the system's functioning. However, positive feedback is information that is new to the system and must be sufficiently powerful to amplify deviation from the system's previous rules. One source of such information can be the maturational changes in family members—particularly, but not exclusively, the children—as they experience life-cycle transitions. However, not all new information originates within the family. Rather, new ideas, attitudes, standards, and rules are brought into the family both via individual members and via various social institutions. This new information creates deviation-amplifying positive feedback that changes the system. All families are selective in their availability to new information and in their willingness to incorporate it. No family is either a completely open system or a completely closed system.

If it is difficult to explain how second-order change actually occurs in families, it is even more difficult to explain how new information originates in systems that influence the family. Many thinkers favor the idea of discontinuous "leaps," such that the rules governing the system's organization change radically and "all of a piece." This type of thinking seems to appeal particularly to those therapists and family theoreticians who focus on the more observable relationship or communicational properties of systems rather than on trying to know what is going on within a system or within the members of a system (e.g., Watzlawick, Weakland, & Fisch, 1974; Haley, 1980). From their vantage point, change seems to be discontinuous. Hoffman (1981) cites the observations of Ashby (1954) as an example of discontinuous change. Ashby describes "step-functions"—that is, phenomena in which change from one state to another seems to occur instantaneously, such as in the snapping of an elastic band. He contrasts such changes with those that seem to occur smoothly and continually, such as changes in the height of the column in a barometer. However, Ashby makes the point that "if the step-functions are not accessible to observation the change of the main variables from one form of behavior to another will seem to be spontaneous, for no change of state in the main variables can be assigned as its

cause" (Ashby, 1954, p. 89). This indicates that step-functions may simply seem to be discontinuous but are not really so. The same may be said of family members' behavior: the private, inner processes that may be governing their changed behavior, such as their thoughts, memories, and attitudes, are not easily available to the observer unless he or she considers subjective data to be relevant (Sigal, 1971).[3]

Explaining Change

Change, therefore, can be explained in various ways. Schools of family therapy that emphasize the relevance of the experiential dimension of people's lives identify inner experiences as the source of new ideas and ways of behaving that produce far-reaching changes in family functioning. Many family-therapy thinkers explain the occurrence of change by the idea of randomness. According to this model, new ideas or ways of behaving originate in chance variations in the environment (Dell, 1982). Family theorists who espouse this explanation refer to the observations of Prigogine (1976), who concluded that change in physiochemical systems can occur through the cumulative effect of chance variations in the milieu. The further the components are from the set point that controls the equilibrium of a given solution, the greater will be the possibility of variation and novelty. However, in much the same way as with Ashby's step-functions, a sudden change in a physiochemical solution can appear to the observer to be far more abrupt than it really is. Better knowledge of the minute processes occurring in such solutions might lead us to conclude that such change is strictly determined, rather than being random and spontaneous.

In any case, *the behavior of inanimate systems is not an adequate model for human systems.*[4]

---

[3] *Editors' Note.* Interestingly, a very similar controversy has colored the recent history of the clinical practice of behavior therapy. Subjective data assumed an increasingly important place in that field in the past decade, as the rising prominence of cognitive therapy illustrates.

[4] *Editors' Note.* While we quite agree, and suspect that most clinicians would also agree, the professional literature of family therapy too often seems to fail to grasp this essential distinction.

Human beings live in social relationships and are capable of imagination, abstract reasoning, and creativity. Hoffman (1985) says that a possible reason why family therapists focused exclusively on changing behaviors was that they were reacting against the prevailing intrapsychic focus on the psychodynamics of the individual. She reflects, "The pendulum seems to be swinging the other way. Mental phenomena have been brought back from a long exile, and ideas, beliefs, attitudes, feelings, premises, values and myths have been declared central again" (p. 190). It is neither convincing nor necessary to transfer explanations based on physiochemical chance to account for the occurrence of such social ideas as freedom, justice, and equality—as well as their opposites (Guttman, 1986; Maturana, 1984). Whereas it is difficult to identify the origins of new social forces that are the ultimate source of deviation-amplifying feedback, for any particular family the immediate origin of a new input is usually fairly clear.

Limitations of Family Morphogenesis

There are limitations to the possibilities for morphogenesis in families. Whereas a system's structure may change considerably, it must maintain its fundamental organization in order to continue belonging to a particular class of systems (Maturana & Varela, 1980; Varela, 1979). For instance, although the family can and must change its structure to accommodate effectively to different stages of the life cycle (Combrinck-Graham, 1985), morphogenesis and morphostasis must remain in some type of balance for a system to be recognizable as a family. Positive feedback theoretically can lead to runaways, which can completely alter the family's form. For instance, one can conceive that if one parent falls in love with someone else and leaves the family, the group which he or she leaves will still be so-named, but his or her single state will no longer be designated as "a family."

For the practicing therapist, the phenomenon of positive feedback has pragmatic as well as theoretical importance. It allows us to understand the family's history and presentation of problems in a supraindividual manner. We can define the precipitants of family distress as deviation-amplifying information that is in some way un-

comfortably morphogenic, perhaps because it threatens the members' trust in the family's continuing integrity and viability. Individual and group symptoms may be explained as attempts to reduce, slow down, or abolish change.

Whereas the family, or some family members, may fear and oppose second-order change, it may be possible first to obtain their cooperation in achieving first-order change: that is, some rearrangement of family relationships sufficient to remove the presenting symptom and to create enough comfort for the family to be able to continue developing at its own rate. Ultimately, this might lead to second-order reorganization of family relationships.

FAMILY MODELS AND SYSTEMS THEORY

All models of family therapy are systemic in nature in that they recognize the interconnectedness of individual, family, and social phenomena. They can differ in a number of respects (Madanes & Haley, 1977)—in their emphasis on intrapsychic constructs or on external behavior, in their emphasis on certain dimensions of family functioning, and in their definition of therapeutic goals. They also differ as to the preferred type of intervention and in underlying beliefs as to the curative factors in therapy. The choice of interventions is probably dictated by the particular goals of therapy that are most emphasized by a given model and also by its particular view of the nature of the family system.

In this section, we will briefly review several leading models of family therapy. Each model will be considered according to the particular systems concepts it emphasizes and the particular type of intervention it employs.[5]

The Psychoanalytic Model

The earliest family therapists were psychoanalysts who consciously tried to adapt their con-

---

[5] *Editors' Note.* Guttman's intent here was not to be either all-inclusive or exclusive, but to illustrate the use of systems concepts in a *range* of therapeutic methods.

cepts and methods to working with families.[6] They first attempted to transfer concepts from social psychology and sociological group theory, in the belief that the family could be understood as a special type of group, "the family group" (Ackerman, 1962). Early family therapists stressed the concept of roles, viewing them as being analogous to defenses—the compromise between the individual's intrapsychic needs and the requirements of the family. For instance, the reciprocity of unconscious needs, and so of roles, between various family members explained how they could be comfortable in maladaptive relationships as long as these were reciprocal and complementary.

Psychoanalytic therapists emphasized the unconscious and affectively determined nature of transactions between family members. These transactions are based on unconscious collusions, which permit each member to gratify some of his or her needs, drives, and fantasies (Ackerman, 1962). Reciprocal processes of blaming or scapegoating one family member were understood as originating in collusive projective identification between several family members, that is, one or more family members are projecting their own unwanted and disowned characteristics onto one or more other members (Ackerman, 1962; Dicks, 1967). This thinking has been articulated with ever-increasing sophistication by writers such as Dicks (1967), Paul (1967), and Sager (Sager et al., 1971).

Jackson (1957, 1965) was the first theorist to meld psychoanalytic concepts and systems theory. For him and the other members of the Palo Alto group, the family system consisted of the interplay in the interpersonal field of the unconscious needs of the family members. Family interaction operated mainly according to a homeostatic model and symptoms were perceived as being homeostatic mechanisms. Although the emphasis on systems theory encouraged focusing on the "here and now," early family theorists still attached importance to a historical perspective and to explaining how the system "got that way." For instance, Lidz (1973) explains that in certain children, schizophrenia results from both present marital conflict and the personal histories of each of the parents.

At first, the goals of psychoanalytically inspired family therapy were not articulated in a particularly systemic manner. There was some emphasis on increasing the quality and/or quantity of affective communication, but change was implicitly defined as increased insight, mutual empathy, and tolerance for other family members. One hotly debated point was whether "characterological growth" (i.e., second-order transformation) could occur through family therapy.

Psychoanalytic family therapists primarily employ the techniques of explanation and interpretation, linking family members' overt behavior to their underlying motives, drives, and affects, via the mechanisms of unconscious collusion, projection, and projective identification (Paul, 1967; Scharff & Scharff, 1987). Psychoanalytically oriented therapists were among the first to adapt the methods of Gestalt therapy, such as reenactment and family sculpting, to family therapy (Satir, 1964; Satir & Baldwin, 1983).

Today, the basic assumption of this model continues to be that unconscious and conscious aspects of family members' inner life form part of the systemic feedback loop that expresses itself in interaction, communication, and behavior.[7] This is predicated on the belief that the inner life is knowable, by both clients and therapists. Perhaps the most important change is that psychodynamically oriented family therapy, rather than being considered nonsystemic, is now recognized as a legitimate systems approach (Scharff & Scharff, 1987).[8]

---

[6] *Editors' Note.* This depends, perhaps, on one's criteria as to what constitutes a family therapist. As Broderick and Schrader (Chapter 1) delineate, social workers, marriage counselors, sexologists, and family-life educators had been significantly involved in clinical aspects of family life before psychoanalysts opened their offices to others than the analysand.

[7] *Editors' Note.* That is to say, that defenses are *both* interactional and intrapsychic.

[8] *Editors' Note.* We think psychodynamic/psychoanalytic family therapy *should* be thus recognized, yet we do not believe that these approaches are given much credence in large sectors of the field, especially in graduate-school family-therapy-training programs. Mainstream family therapy has spent so much time and energy differentiating itself from psychiatry, and national professional organizations (e.g., the American Association for Marriage and Family Therapy, in the United States) have spent so much time and energy earning legitimization of their members as mental health professionals that we doubt that psychodynamic models will gain much ascendance in training programs for some time to come.

The Structural Model

By the time structural family therapy was articulated in the late 1960s, systems theory was firmly in place as the basic underpinning of family therapy. Transactions between family members had been intensively studied, in terms of the instrumental and affective needs of the family members. Minuchin (1974) turned to the study of family structure, which he defines as "the invisible set of functional demands that organizes the ways in which family members interact" (p. 51). Structure denotes the family configuration that is produced when family members adopt specific amounts of proximity and distance to and from one another with respect to a given task or family event. Family structure changes according to the situation at hand. However, dysfunctional families seem to be more rigid in their structural range than are functional families.

Structural family therapists explicitly recognize life-cycle transitions as markers of family stress that necessitate accommodation to changed circumstances and that often precipitate the family's entry into therapy (Minuchin, 1974). Moreover, structural family theorists explicitly recognize the therapist's entry into the system as signifying a change, from the family system alone to a system consisting of family-plus-therapist (Minuchin & Fishman, 1981).

Structural family therapy focuses on the distribution of power in the system. It is a hierarchical model in which greater age usually confers higher status. However, grandparents usually do not have a more powerful position than do their adult children, if they are not making a significant economic contribution. The structural model also emphasizes flexibility in families. The members should be able to group and regroup into various subsystems according to the requirements of different situations. Whatever the configuration at a particular moment, there should be clear and well-defined boundaries between family members. Alliances and coalitions are recognized as being a fact of family life. However, they should be flexible.

The goal of structural family therapy is to restructure the system so as to permit the family to deal competently and in a competent and cooperative manner with those life tasks that are most salient at the particular time. It is behav-

iorally oriented and makes no explicit statement about the feelings and thoughts of family members. It articulates its goals in terms of action sequences and role behavior, constructing tasks and other interventions as a function of these goals.

The structural model is most explicit as concerns the deviation–minimizing feedback function of the presenting symptom and the need to "shake" the family out of its maladaptive stability. It is not as explicit as concerns positive feedback, although it implicitly recognizes the therapist as an agent of change and focuses heavily on the therapist's competence in designing interventions. There is no explicit demand for second-order change. Rather, there seems to be a strong implicit belief that small changes, enacted in sessions and promoted between sessions by task assignments, will bring the family to a better equilibrium in most cases and will lead to further-reaching changes in some cases. Structural family therapy has a basically pragmatic orientation, toward the most parsimonious solution for a given problem.

The Bowen Model

Family therapy based on the Bowen model has the distinctive characteristic of focusing on therapy with one adult individual, within his or her family context, rather than on conjoint therapy with the whole family. The basic premise of Bowen therapy is that the goal of individual development is autonomy and full differentiation from one's family of origin. Many individual problems are defined as originating in an arrest in this process. This is most obvious in families in which there is so little differentiation between members that Bowen (1966) spoke of an *undifferentiated ego mass*. He found this to be especially characteristic of families of schizophrenics. He believes that schizophrenic functioning arises out of successive marriages, across several generations, between poorly differentiated partners.

One of the main barriers to successful differentiation lies in an inability directly to confront disagreements with other family members for fear of their retaliation through *cutoffs*—cessation of direct contact. In order to express these feelings without this risk, two family members will triangulate another person—often of another generation—into their relationship whenever it is threatened (Guerin & Pendagast, 1976). Triangulation can also occur vis-à-vis an activity or a significant event, which in some way gives family members the possibility of expressing forbidden feelings. Implicit in Bowen theory is the belief that true individuation and differentiation can take place only through the "test" of confrontation. Bowen therapy specifically addresses methods (often indirect) of achieving this.

One method is to "coach" an individual to reenter the family with a specific agenda of changing some family rules, especially rules concerning appropriate behavior for preserving family loyalty. The ultimate goal of this unbalancing of homeostasis is to realign family relationships and facilitate greater differentiation.

The genogram has been most highly developed by Bowen therapists (Guerin, 1976), probably because the theory emphasizes the transgenerational repetition of a particular type of relationship in a particular family. By studying the genogram, therapist and client identify repetitious, adaptive, and maladaptive interactional patterns across the generations.

Although Bowen therapy focuses on one individual, it is highly systemic. The most important systems concepts it implements are homeostasis and reverberating circuits—patterns that become intensified as they are repeated and can have the characteristics of either positive or negative feedback. By making relatively small, nonthreatening moves, the identified person can produce positive feedback and effect relatively large changes in the family. The Bowen method has the advantage of encouraging the client to implement changes, since they first seem to be fairly innocuous.

Strategic Models

Although the differences and similarities between "strategic" and "systemic" family-therapy models are currently being debated, there seems to be sufficient clarity for a provisional differentiation between the two types of approach (MacKinnon, 1983). For the purposes of this chapter, the approaches of the Mental Research Institute (MRI) and of Jay Haley (1980) and Cloe Madanes (1980) will be considered to be examples of the strategic approach. The models of the Milan group (Selvini Palazzoli, Boscolo, Cecchin, & Prata, 1978, 1980a) and of the Ackerman Institute will be discussed under "Systemic Models."

Strategic therapy focuses on the resolution of the presenting problem. To that end, the symptom or the symptomatic situation is closely investigated. The MRI approach concentrates on delineating the homeostatic, "no change" forces operating in the family system (Watzlawick et al., 1974) on the assumption that "the solution is the problem" and that the family has already tried various methods of solving the problem. These have all failed, probably because they were simply "first-order" solutions that did not threaten family homeostasis, but simply rearranged it.

Haley (1980) emphasizes the implications of the family's stage in the life cycle. Much of his thinking is concerned with the presence or absence of age-appropriate and age-inappropriate hierarchical arrangements in families. He has been much influenced by methods of indirect hypnosis as practiced by Milton Erickson (Haley, 1973), particularly by the effectiveness of paradox. One of his best-known applications of paradox is to have the parents take control of a young adult whose rebellious behavior is pseudoautonomous. By truly controlling the behavior, the parents paradoxically "liberate" their child to become more truly differentiated from them (Haley, 1980).

The commonality among the strategic methods is their focus on the systemic ramifications of the presenting problem in order to offer a solution (which may be a task, a ritual, or some other prescription) that abolishes the symptom and, therefore, frees the system to realign itself more adaptively. These methods also share an ahistorical perspective with regard to the origins of family problems. They do not address intrapsychic or subjective experiences[9] and concentrate heavily on behavior. The systems concepts they emphasize are family rules and feedback.

---

[9] *Editors' Note.* Except as presenting problems.

Systemic Models

The Milan group has been most systematic in articulating and operationalizing the application of systems theory to family therapy, particularly as proposed by Bateson in his later writings (Selvini Palazzoli et al., 1978, 1980a; Tomm, 1984a). Rather than giving post-hoc systems explanations and descriptions of family phenomena, the members of this group started with these concepts and asked themselves how they applied to families. This is a particularly intriguing development in systemic thinking.

In their most influential paper (Selvini Palazzoli et al., 1980b), they consider Bateson's definition of information as *news of a difference*. This they translate into an interest in the "before" and "after" of family members' experience: How is a behavior, a family task, a family incident, a relationship between family members different now than it was in the past? How will it be different in the future? The divider between past, present, and future is assumed to be some critical family-life-cycle change, so the family members' answers lead to conclusions that relate present family functioning to the effect of this family life crisis.

To develop a systemic explanation, there must be information about all relationships in the family. From this information, a hypothesis is formulated about the possible origin of the presenting problem and the way in which it reveals dysfunctional relationships and attitudes among family members.

The circular questioning practiced by these groups represents the operationalization of the concept of circular feedback (Penn, 1982; Tomm, 1984b). Systems theory defines circular feedback as a response that is conditioned by everything that has gone before and that, in turn, evokes a response. The therapist's main activity is to pose questions, each of which is determined by the family members' answers to earlier questions. These circular questions have a major function in delineating the presenting problem and also may introduce possible new solutions for the problem.

Systemic therapists have also been influenced by the role of *paradox* in motivation and interaction, that is, by the contradiction between a person's or a family's avowed wish for change

and the tendency to resist change by maintaining the status quo, especially when confronted by a therapist. They do not consider the family system to be in any way deliberately compliant or defiant, any more than is the patient under hypnosis. Rather, the family system, by its nature, tends to resist change. The interventions of systemic family therapists are often guided by their perception of a given family's capacity for change through cooperation. Their criteria for resistant and nonresistant families have been especially well articulated by members of the training staff of the Ackerman Family Therapy Institute in New York City. For nonresistant, compliant families, the group uses direct interventions—advice, explanations, suggestions, interpretations, and tasks that are meant to be taken at face value and followed accordingly. For resistant, defiance-based families, the Ackerman group has developed a number of paradoxical interventions that are designed to circumvent the family's defiant attitude. Among these interventions are redefining (reframing) the problem, often through positive connotation; prescribing the symptom-producing interaction cycle; and restraining the family whenever change seems to be occurring (Papp, 1980).

Both the Milan and Ackerman groups assume that the family is making a desperate attempt to stabilize itself in the face of a crisis that threatens its previous equilibrium. They implicitly acknowledge the importance of power relations in the family, and they evaluate the potential cooperativeness of each family member, but particularly the attitude of the most powerful family member(s) (Selvini Palazzoli et al., 1980b, 1985). They try to take these factors into account when planning an intervention. When they have concluded that a family, or a certain family member, is resistant, the intervention is calculated to confront the resistance by making it impossible for the family member or members to state that they wish to change and yet continue the same course of action.

The two groups seem to differ, to some degree, in their emphasis on family history. The Milan group has retained a link with its psychoanalytic past and the members ask themselves whether or not the family's problems represent some transgression of certain family loyalties and traditions. The Ackerman group is more focused on the "here and now," but will acknowledge the role of duty and obligation among family members, if being dutiful may run counter to a family member's need for differentiation and autonomy.

Perhaps the most interesting and novel aspect of the Milan approach is that it acknowledges the unpredictability of family change. This point of view is influenced by the ideas of randomness and limited predictability, enunciated by Bateson and reinforced by the theories of Foerster (1984) and Prigogine (1976). Therefore, therapists can see themselves as introducing positive, deviation-amplifying feedback that increases randomness, the specific effect of which is, therefore, not predictable because the family can react in many different ways. It is only post hoc that the therapist seeks to explain a given family's reaction to an intervention, particularly if the family has not changed at all, or when it has become more, instead of less, symptomatic. In such cases, the hypothesis must be revised through more circular questioning (Penn, 1982). One of the primary goals of this questioning is to articulate the rules (particularly those concerning family loyalty across generations) that are maintaining problems for some or all of the family members.

To date, systemic therapists have provided the most innovative approach to operationalizing the abstruse ideas of systems theorists. They have also been most comprehensive in attempting to integrate many different concepts at different logical levels. Whether or not this endeavor produces better therapy outcomes remains the subject of a debate that ranges beyond systems theory to epistemological concerns (Cecchin, 1987).

THE EPISTEMOLOGY OF FAMILY THEORY AND THERAPY

With the development of a systems theory of family therapy, a number of different and potentially competing models of the family and of relevant therapeutic interventions has begun to emerge. In response to such a situation, one question that can arise is, which model best corresponds to the "truth"? In the history of psychotherapy, it has frequently been the tradition to

retreat into adhering to one particular school and to ignore or undermine the contributions of other views. To their credit, family therapists have not responded in this way to the challenge of different models. Rather, they have focused on epistemology, the discipline that attempts to define criteria for the truth of a given theory and that develops methods of determining whether these criteria are satisfied. Epistemology has also been defined as the study of the nature of knowledge and the limitations of any given theory of knowledge (Simon et al., 1985; Held & Pols, 1985).

Perhaps family therapists cannot so easily divide into schools because the family itself constantly presents them with epistemological dilemmas: Which member is telling the "truth"? Which paradigm or hypothesis will be most effective in guiding the interview or in sorting out the many pieces of information that deluge the family therapist? In families, the truth is multifaceted. For instance, it may be "true" that a child's intractable school phobia has the function of focusing the parents on this problem rather than on their unsatisfactory relationship. Furthermore, the child's symptom may also have the function of providing the mother with a companion, thereby compensating her for her husband's continuing primary allegiance to his own mother, who can continue to be contemptuous of her son's wife because she is an incompetent mother. At another level, the symptom may allow the father to project some of his own lack of courage onto his son and to be exasperated with him. Each of these statements about the family may be "true" in that the statement corresponds to a portion of the family's reality and can produce an intervention that may help the family. Yet it is impossible to assert that one statement is "truer" than another.[10]

Family therapy's interest in epistemology has also been motivated by a continued allegiance to Bateson's (1972, 1979) wish to develop a theory that can articulate principles unifying mind and nature. He hoped to do for biological phenomena what other sciences have succeeded in

---

[10] *Editors' Note.* But it is not impossible to assert that one theory of therapy makes propositions about the process of change that are more verifiable and empirically testable than those offered by another school.

achieving, that is, to articulate fundamental laws that explain and give coherence to varied physical phenomena. However, Bateson was often disheartened by the contrast between the internal coherence and interconnectedness of physical constructs and the fuzzy singularity of biopsychosocial constructs (Bateson, 1979).

Bateson stated that a fundamental operation of any theory of knowledge is to draw a distinction between what we can and cannot know; that is, what we can and cannot accept as proof of a thing's existence or veracity. Although he much admired the relative rigor of the natural sciences, Bateson nonetheless recognized that epistemological truth is ultimately subjective: "Epistemology is always and inevitably personal. The point of the probe is always in the heart of the explorer: What is my answer to the question of knowing?" (Bateson, 1979, p. 98). Bateson seems to have espoused a consensual, subjectively validated epistemology rather than to have believed in the possibility of a purely objective theory of knowledge.

Since Bateson, several other thinkers have become prominent in family therapy and have offered their answers to the question of knowing. Among the most influential are the constructivists, represented by Watzlawick (1984) and Foerster (Segal, 1986). They argue that the observer fashions reality according to his or her own perceptions and that these are conditioned by a variety of physiological and psychological factors. For family therapists, the advantage of this perspective is that it emphasizes that the observer's perceptions and activities are informed by his or her inner states and past experiences as much as by the process he or she is perceiving. The therapist must be considered as much an active participant *in* as an observer *of* the system. The problem with a strictly constructivist approach is how several observers can arrive at a consensus if reality is almost completely a function of each one's idiosyncratic constructions.

Another prominent contributor to the current epistemology of family therapy is Maturana (1978), whose biological experiments have led him to conclude that all organisms are *structure determined*; that is, they function in a manner that is defined by their particular organization or structure. All their behavior, including their relations with other organisms or with the inanimate environment, is limited by their structure-determined repertoire. Moreover, an organism can only maintain its organization by adapting to a surrounding "domain of existence" that limits its options for variability. This "domain" includes both animate and inanimate components of the environment. Therefore, what we perceive as change is simply structure-determined adaptation to the environment. Learning is, at most, accommodation to a new situation and can only occur within strictly defined limits.

This theory has definite implications for therapy. First, it raises the question as to whether one can truly change or effect change or whether what we call change is merely a type of adaptation. Such a view flies in the face of the possibility of second-order change. Second, such a theory defines and limits the therapist's potential activity. He or she must adapt interventions to be strictly congruent with the inherent possibilities of the family and its environment, helping the family to arrive at a realistic accommodation. Such a theory is most congruent with such family-therapy approaches as that of de Shazer (1982, 1985) and his colleagues. They focus on solutions to the complaints that are presented by clients, believing that minimal changes that can solve a given problem can also have a ripple effect on other areas of clients' lives. Nevertheless, their major focus remains on helping the client with a current, specified problem. They consider therapy terminated and successful when this problem has been satisfactorily resolved (de Shazer, 1982, 1985).

Although family therapy has not developed true schools of epistemology, there are certain discernible differences in primary focus that permit us to group family therapists to some extent. Keeney and Sprenkle (1982) broadly identify the aesthetic and the pragmatic schools of family therapy as subdivisions of an ecosystemic epistemology that is consonant with Bateson's (1979) comprehensive vision of nature as consisting of interconnected systems. However, they also accept the principle that some systems may be hierarchically ordered. They warn against reducing family-therapy theories to differences in techniques and stress that each approach makes a specific philosophical statement about the nature of families and the nature of reality.

Although they do not attach particular descriptive indicators or therapists' names to the two approaches, they clearly identify the "pragmatic" approaches as those that define the goal of family therapy as being the solution of a given problem through using various techniques of information gathering and intervention. The aesthetic forms of therapy have as their goal a more harmonious, growth-producing way of being for the family. They see the pragmatic effort as a legitimate activity, which should, however, be subsumed under the aesthetic approach because the latter has more global existential goals. The awareness of an overriding existential dimension to family life is also espoused by Allman (1982). Keeney and Sprenkle emphasize that, unless we maintain this awareness, even so aesthetic a therapy as that of Whitaker can be reduced to the pragmatics of "how to do it like Whitaker."

A preoccupation with preserving the ecosystemic purity of family therapy can seem either somewhat idealistic or needlessly pedantic. However, it has far-reaching and important implications. Family therapy represents not only a set of techniques or methods of treating families, but also a more inclusive approach to the entire healing process. The awareness of the systemic nature of human existence and of the ecological interconnectedness of human systems with one another and with physical systems constitutes a fundamental shift that has already had repercussions in medical practice and many other forms of biopsychosocial intervention (Marmor, 1983). It is important to preserve this basic perspective in order to be increasingly effective teachers and healers.

Moreover, there are certain epistemological questions that have direct relevance to the theory and practice of family therapy. Although therapists are not necessarily consistent with one another in each of their answers, these questions will probably remain central to contemporary family theory for some time, because they represent the dilemmas and unanswered conundrums of family-systems theory, and indeed, in some cases, of systems theory in general (Guttman, 1986).

One question is whether we can ever "know" what occurs within the components of a system or can only "know," through their manifest behavior and relationships, what occurs between them. In family-therapy terms, the question is whether the inner life and memories of family members do or do not constitute important information for the therapeutic process.

A related question is whether we can predict the effect of an intervention on a system if we do not know anything about the workings of its inner components and depend only on its external behavior as an indicator of the effect of input. This question relates to evaluating the family's response to therapeutic moves and has particular relevance to our belief in the possibility of evaluating family-therapy outcome. Those who espouse a strict circular approach do not believe that it is epistemologically feasible or relevant to specify the relevant intervening variables in family-therapy-outcome research (Gurman, 1983).

The concept of *circularity* is basic to systems theory. This means that systems are constantly modified by recursive circular feedback from multiple sources from within and from outside the system. When one describes the causal components of systemic change, it is not acceptable to espouse a linear view of causality that identifies only one factor as determining the subsequent behavior of a system. However, this paradigm of circularity may have disturbing implications when it is applied to family situations in which any form of abuse or oppression is occurring (Goldner, 1985; Taggart, 1985; Hare-Mustin, 1987; MacKinnon & Miller, 1987). Whereas one can acknowledge that extrasystemic factors may contribute to the behavior of the aggressor or the oppressor, this cannot be sufficient reason for absolving him or her of direct responsibility for a particular action. Moreover, from a practical perspective, it is necessary to address the problem in a linear manner, as if the abusive family member were the sole originator of the situation, and to deal with the family accordingly. Nevertheless, it can be argued that one may still maintain a multicausal, ecosystemic perspective that recognizes that hurtful behavior has roots both in the personal history of the perpetrator and in the values of the larger social system. This perspective is clearly necessary for preventive intervention.

There is a continuing debate as to whether ecosystems are or are not hierarchically organized. Whereas Keeney and Sprenkle (1982) recognize this possibility, others, starting with Bateson, reject the notion of hierarchy if it leads to the notion of power differentials within a system. Bateson accepted the theory of logical types, which is based on the premise of the hierarchical organization of classes, but he seems to have rejected the notion of social power on moral rather than on scientific grounds. On the basis of his research on the central nervous system, Maturana (1984) questions the belief that social power is hierarchically organized. However, he maintains that although there is no compelling rational basis for the assumption that social systems are organized according to the same model as biological or physical systems, hierarchy may still be a key factor in social organization.

This debate has important implications for the family because our everyday experience confirms that some members have more power than others, usually by virtue of their age or gender (Hare-Mustin, 1987). If we completely eschew the notion of power, we cannot account for situations such as the relation between parents or other adults and children or the relationship between abuser and abused. On the other hand, if our paradigm is constructed with the notion of power as a given, we will find ourselves contorting clinical presentations to fit this view; for example, the psychotic family member becomes either the most powerful family member (Haley, 1980) or the victim of another powerful family member (Bateson et al., 1976). This debate addresses a fundamental epistemological problem as to the legitimacy of fitting theories that arise out of physical or biological observations to psychosocial systems such as the family. Bateson's vision of a unified theory for all earthly phenomena may be simultaneously too simplistic and too grandiose.[11]

CONCLUSIONS

In and of themselves, epistemological theories can seem abstruse and very distant from the concerns of most family therapists. Moreover, the very notion of trying to define "truth" goes against the tradition of cultural relativism that

has been most consistently espoused by modern social science. It is, nevertheless, helpful periodically to question our preconceptions and assumptions in terms of their correspondence to reality, their theoretical coherence, and their usefulness (Guttman, 1986; Runions, 1984).

Because families are biopsychosocial systems par excellence, they can serve as a fertile testing ground for synthesizing theories of the kind Bateson hoped to develop. From that point of view, we can minimally conclude the following:

1. General systems theory has provided a fruitful paradigm shift that has enabled us to integrate a great deal of complex information and to develop a higher level of abstraction about the family as a group rather than as a mere aggregate of individuals.
2. Specific concepts of systems theory—particularly feedback, recursiveness, homeostasis, and morphogenesis—have proved to be pragmatically helpful. However, it is not yet completely clear whether they can be literally applied to families without some caveats as to their limitations.
3. Bateson's specific concepts—symmetry and complementarity, differences that create information, the unity of mind and nature—have provided fruitful opportunities to create new ways of conceptualizing family processes and to invent methods of interviewing and intervening.
4. The continuing sensitivity of family-therapy theorists to developments in the natural sciences promises continuing stimulation and, possibly, further practical developments in their application to family therapy.

In some ways, there is an analogy between Bateson's role in the 20th century and that of Descartes in the 17th century. Both were original thinkers who were concerned with issues of epistemology, with how we know and the assertions we can make about the nature of reality. Each left thoughts that were taken up and expanded upon by successive generations of thinkers, each of whom followed one aspect of the theory to its particular conclusion. In the case of Descartes, one group of followers consisted of empiricists and rationalists, such as Locke and Hume, and another group consisted of idealists, such as Kant and Hegel. In an analogous way,

---

[11] *Editors' Note.* Wow! Except in private, not-to-be quoted conversations, it is, indeed, rare to hear leaders in the field sing any tunes but those of unquestioning collegial praise.

Bateson's followers can be divided into the more empirically based, logical problem-solving family-systems theorists, such as Watzlawick, Haley, and de Shazer, and the aesthetic thinkers, who emphasize growth, coherence, and the realization of self within a larger ecosystemic context, such as Satir, Allman, Keeney, Bowen, and Paul. The contributions of these family-therapy theorists, it is hoped, will prove to be as long-lasting and as fruitful as have the philosophical systems left to us by Descartes and his successors.

Family therapy has been a long time coming. This makes it doubly amazing that it has moved forward so quickly within such a short period. It continues to have a dual mission: to develop better techniques and methods of helping people solve their problems and to test stimulating new ideas, coming from many different disciplines, about the nature of biopsychosocial systems and their relevance to human functioning. The second aspect makes it an especially exciting and creative enterprise (Guttman, 1989). As we move into the last decade of this century and toward the next millennium, family-systems theory and the epistemological inquiry that is associated with it will continue to develop in comprehensiveness and explanatory power.

REFERENCES

Abeles, G. (1976). Researching the unresearchable: Experimentation on the double bind. In C.E. Sluzki & D.C. Ransom (Eds.), *Double bind: The foundation of the communicational approach to the family.* New York: Grune & Stratton.

Ackerman, N.W. (1962). Family psychotherapy and psychoanalysis: The implications of difference. *Family Process, 1,* 30–43.

Allman, L.R. (1982). The aesthetic preference: Overcoming the pragmatic error. *Family Process, 21,* 43–56.

Anderson, C.M. (1977). Family intervention with severely disturbed in-patients. *Archives of General Psychiatry, 34,* 697–702.

Ashby, W.R. (1954). *Design for a brain.* New York: Wiley.

Bateson, G. (1936). *Naven: A survey of the problems suggested by a composite picture of the culture of a New Guinea tribe drawn from three points of view.* Cambridge, England: Cambridge University Press. (Second edition, Stanford, CA: Stanford University Press, 1958.)

Bateson, G. (1972). *Steps to an ecology of mind.* New York: Ballantine.

Bateson, G. (1976). Comments on Haley's "History." In C.E. Sluzki & D.C. Ransom (Eds.), *Double bind: The foundation of the communicational approach to the family.* New York: Grune & Stratton.

Bateson, G. (1979). *Mind and nature: A necessary unity.* New York: Dutton.

Bateson, G., Jackson, D.D., Haley, J., & Weakland, J.H. (1956).
Toward a theory of schizophrenia. *Behavioral Science, 1,* 251–264.

Bateson, G., Jackson, D.D., Haley, J., & Weakland, J.H. (1976). A note on the double bind. In C.E. Sluzki & D.C. Ransom (Eds.), *Double bind: The foundation of the communicational approach to the family.* New York: Grune & Stratton.

Bernard, C. (1859). *Leçons sur les propriétés physiologiques et les altérations pathologiques des liquides de l'organisme.* Paris: Ballière.

Bertalanffy, L. von (1968). *General systems theory.* New York: Braziller.

Bowen, M. (1966). The use of family theory in clinical practise. *Comprehensive Psychiatry, 7,* 345–374.

Brown, G.W., Birley, J.L.T., & Wing, J.K. (1972). Influence of family life on the course of schizophrenic disorders: A replication. *British Journal of Psychiatry, 121,* 241–258.

Buckley, W. (Ed.) (1968). *Modern systems research for the behavioral scientist: A sourcebook.* Chicago: Aldine.

Cecchin, G. (1987). Hypothesizing, circularity and neutrality revisited: An invitation to curiosity. *Family Process, 26,* 405–414.

Combrinck-Graham, L. (1985). A developmental model for family systems. *Family Process, 24,* 139–150.

Dell, P.F. (1980). Researching the family theories of schizophrenia: An exercise in epistemological confusion. *Family Process, 19,* 321–326.

Dell, P.F. (1982). Beyond homeostasis: Toward a concept of coherence. *Family Process, 21,* 21–41.

Dell, P.F. (1986a). In defense of "lineal causality." *Family Process, 25,* 513–522.

Dell, P.F. (1986b). Toward a foundation for addressing violence. *Family Process, 25,* 527–530.

de Shazer, S. (1982). *Patterns of brief family therapy.* New York: Guilford.

de Shazer, S. (1985). *Keys to solution in brief therapy.* New York: Norton.

Dicks, H.V. (1967). *Marital tensions: Clinical studies toward a psychological theory of interaction.* New York: Basic Books.

Ferreira, A.J. (1963). Family myth and homeostasis. *Archives of General Psychiatry, 9,* 457–463.

Ferreira, A.J., & Winter, W.D. (1965). Family interaction and decision-making. *Archives of General Psychiatry, 13,* 214–233.

Foerster, H. von (1984, April). How we perceive reality. Presented at the Conference on the Construction of Therapeutic Realities, Calgary, Alta., Canada.

Fromm-Reichmann, F. (1948). Notes on the development of treatment of schizophrenics by psychoanalytic psychotherapy. *Psychiatry, 11,* 263–273.

Goldner, V. (1985). Feminism and family therapy. *Family Process, 24,* 31–47.

Guerin, P.J., & Pendagast, E.G. (1976). Evaluation of family system and genogram. In P.J. Guerin (Ed.), *Family therapy: Theory and practice.* New York: Gardner Press.

Gurman, A.S. (1983). Family therapy and the "new epistemology." *Journal of Marital and Family Therapy, 9,* 227–234.

Guttman, H.A. (1973). A contraindication for family therapy: The prepsychotic or postpsychotic young adult and his parents. *Archives of General Psychiatry, 29,* 352–355.

Guttman, H.A. (1986). Epistemology, systems theories and the theory of family therapy. *American Journal of Family Therapy, 14,* 13–22.

Guttman, H.A. (1989). The augmentation of creativity: Epistemological concerns and the excitement of innovation in family therapy. *Journal of Family Psychology, 2,* 473–476.

Haley, J. (1959a). The family of the schizophrenic: A model system. *Journal of Nervous and Mental Disease, 129,* 357–374.

Haley, J. (1959b). The interactional description of schizophrenia. *Psychiatry, 22,* 321–332.

Haley, J. (1973). *Uncommon therapy: The psychiatric techniques of Milton H. Erickson, M.D.* New York: Norton.

Haley, J. (1976). Development of a theory: A history of a research project. In C.E. Sluzki & D.C. Ransom (Eds.), *Double bind: The foundation of the communicational approach to the family.* New York: Grune & Stratton.

Haley, J. (1980). *Leaving home: The therapy of disturbed young people.* New York: McGraw-Hill.

Hare-Mustin, R.T. (1987). The problem of gender in family therapy theory. *Family Process, 26,* 15–28.

Held, B., & Pols, B. (1985). The confusion about epistemology and "epistemology" and what to do about it. *Family Process, 241,* 509–516.

Hoffman, L. (1971). Deviation-amplifying processes in natural groups. In J. Haley (Ed.), *Changing families: A family therapy reader.* New York: Grune & Stratton.

Hoffman, L. (1981). *Foundations of family therapy: A conceptual framework for systems change.* New York: Basic Books.

Hoffman, L. (1985). Beyond power and control: Toward a "second order" family systems therapy. *Family Systems Medicine, 3,* 381–396.

Imber-Black, E. (1986). Maybe "lineal causality" needs another defense lawyer: A feminist response to Dell. *Family Process, 25,* 527–530.

Jackson, D.D. (1957). The question of family homeostasis. *Psychiatric Quarterly, Supplement 31,* 79–90.

Jackson, D.D. (1965). Family rules: The marital quid pro quo. *Archives of General Psychiatry, 12,* 589–594.

Jackson, D.D., & Yalom, I. (1966). Family research on the problem of ulcerative colitis. *Archives of General Psychiatry, 15,* 410–418.

Keeney, B.P., & Sprenkle, D.M. (1982). Ecosystemic epistemology: Critical implications for the aesthetics and pragmatics of family therapy. *Family Process, 21,* 1–20.

Leff, J., & Vaughn, C. (1985). *Expressed emotion in families: Its significance for mental illness.* New York: Guilford.

Lidz, T. (1973). *The origin and treatment of schizophrenic disorders.* New York: Basic Books.

Lidz, T., Cornelison, A.R., Fleck, S., & Terry, D. (1957). The intrafamilial environment of schizophrenic patients. II. Marital schism and marital skew. *American Journal of Psychiatry, 114,* 241–248.

MacKinnon, L. (1983). Contrasting strategic and Milan therapies. *Family Process, 22,* 425–444.

MacKinnon, L.K., & Miller, D. (1987). The new epistemology and the Milan approach: Feminist and sociopolitical considerations. *Journal of Marital and Family Therapy, 13,* 139–156.

Madanes, C. (1980). The prevention of rehospitalization of adolescents and young adults. *Family Process, 19,* 179–192.

Madanes, C., & Haley, J. (1977). Dimensions of family therapy. *Journal of Nervous and Mental Disease, 165,* 88–98.

Marmor, J. (1983). Systems thinking in psychiatry: Some theoretical and clinical implications. *American Journal of Psychiatry, 140,* 833–838.

Mashal, M., Feldman, R.B., & Segal, J.J. (1989). The unraveling of a treatment paradigm: A followup study of the Milan approach to family therapy. *Family Process, 28,* 457–470.

Maturana, H.R. (1978). Biology of language: The epistemology of reality. In G.A. Miller & E. Lennenberg (Eds.), *Psychology and biology of language and thought.* New York: Academic.

Maturana, H.R. (1984, April). The bringing forth of reality. Presented at the Conference on the Construction of Therapeutic Realities, Calgary, Alba., Canada.

Maturana, H.R., & Varela, F.J. (1980). *Autopoiesis and cognition: The realization of living.* Boston: Reidel.

Minuchin, S. (1974). *Families and family therapy.* Cambridge, MA: Harvard University Press.

Minuchin, S., & Fishman, H.C. (1981). *Family therapy techniques.* Cambridge, MA: Harvard University Press.

Mishler, E.G., & Waxler, N.E. (1968). *Interaction in families: An experimental study of family processes and schizophrenia.* New York: Wiley.

Olson, D.H. (1972). Empirically unbinding the double bind: A review of research and conceptual formulations. *Family Process, 11,* 69–94.

Papp, P. (1980). The Greek chorus and other techniques of paradoxical therapy. *Family Process, 19,* 45–57.

Paul, N.L. (1967). The role of mourning and empathy in conjoint marital therapy. In G.H. Zuk & I. Boszormeny-Nagy (Eds.), *Family therapy and disturbed families.* Palo Alto, CA: Science & Behavior Books.

Penn, P. (1982). Circular questioning. *Family Process, 21,* 267–280.

Prigogine, I. (1976). Order through fluctuation: Self-organization and social systems. In E. Jantsch & C.H. Waddington (Eds.), *Evolution and consciousness: Human systems in transition.* Reading, MA: Addison-Wesley.

Reiss, D. (1981). *The family's construction of reality.* Cambridge, MA: Harvard University Press.

Runions, J.E. (1984). Whatsoever things are true: Ways, means and values in modern psychiatry. *Canadian Journal of Psychiatry, 29,* 223–227.

Sager, C.J., Kaplan, H.S., Gundlach, R.H., Kremer, M., Lenz, R., & Royce, J.R. (1971). The marriage contract. *Family Process, 10,* 311–326.

Satir, V. (1964). *Conjoint family therapy: A guide to theory and technique.* Palo Alto, CA: Science & Behavior Books.

Satir, V., & Baldwin, M. (1983). *Satir step by step: A guide to creating change in families.* Palo Alto, CA: Science & Behavior Books.

Scharff, D.E., & Scharff, J.S. (1987). *Object relations family therapy.* Northvale, NJ: Aronson.

Segal, L. (1986). *The dream of reality: Heinz von Foerster's constructivism.* New York: Norton.

Selvini Palazzoli, M. (1985). The problem of the sibling as the referring person. *Journal of Marital and Family Therapy, 11,* 21–34.

Selvini Palazzoli, M., Boscolo, L., Cecchin, G., & Prata, G. (1978). *Paradox and counterparadox: A new model in the therapy of the family in schizophrenic transaction* (E.V. Burt, Trans.). New York: Aronson.

Selvini Palazzoli, M., Boscolo, L., Cecchin, G., & Prata, G. (1980a). Hypothesizing—circularity—neutrality: Three guidelines for the conductor of the session. *Family Process, 19,* 3–10.

Selvini Palazzoli, M., Boscolo, L., Cecchin, G., & Prata, G. (1980b). The problem of the referring person. *Journal of Marital and Family Therapy, 6,* 3–9.

Sigal, J. (1971). A simple dynamic model for family diagnostic interviewing. *Canadian Psychiatric Association Journal, 16,* 87–91.

Simon, F.B., Stierlin, H., & Wynne, L.C. (1985). *The language of family therapy: A systemic vocabulary and sourcebook.* New York: Family Process Press.

Sluzki, C.E., & Ransom, D.C. (Eds.) (1976a). *Double bind: The foundation of the communicational approach to the family.* New York: Grune & Stratton.

Sluzki, C.E., & Ransom, D.C. (1976b). Comment on Gina Abeles' review. In C.E. Sluzki & D.C. Ransom (Eds.), *Double bind: The foundation of the communicational approach to the family.* New York: Grune & Stratton.

Speer, D.C. (1970). Family systems: Morphostasis and morphogenesis: Or "is homeostasis enough?" *Family Process, 9,* 259–278.

Stierlin, H. (1973). Group fantasies and family myths—some theoretical and practical aspects. *Family Process, 12,* 111–125.

Stierlin, H. (1977). *Psychoanalysis and family therapy.* New York: Aronson.

Taggart, M. (1985). The feminist critique in epistemological perspective: Questions of context in family therapy. *Journal of Marital and Family Therapy, 11,* 113–126.

Tomm, K. (1984a). One perspective on the Milan systemic approach: Part I. Overview of development, theory and practice. *Journal of Marital and Family Therapy, 10*, 113–125.

Tomm, K. (1984b). One perspective on the Milan systemic approach: Part II. Description of session format, interviewing style and interventions. *Journal of Marital and Family Therapy, 10*, 253–277.

Varela, F.J. (1979). *Principles of biological autonomy.* New York: Elsevier, North Holland.

Watzlawick, P. (Ed.) (1984). *The invented reality: How do we know what we believe we know?* New York: Norton.

Watzlawick, P., Beavin, J.H., & Jackson, D.D. (1967). *Pragmatics of human communication: A study of interactional patterns, pathologies and paradoxes.* New York: Norton.

Watzlawick, P., Weakland, J.M., & Fisch, R. (1974). *Change: Principles of problem formation and problem resolution.* New York: Norton.

Weakland, J.M. (1976). The "double bind" hypothesis of schizophrenia and three-party interaction (1960). In C.E. Sluzki & D.C. Ransom (Eds.), *Double bind: The foundation of the communicational approach to the family.* New York: Grune & Stratton.

Wertheim, E.S. (1973). Family unit therapy and the science and typology of family systems. I. *Family Process, 12*, 361–376.

Wertheim, E.S. (1975). Family unit therapy and the science and typology of family systems. II. Further theoretical and practical considerations. *Family Process, 14*, 285–309.

Whitehead, A.N., & Russell, B. (1910/1913). *Principia mathematica.* Cambridge, England: Cambridge University Press.

Wiener, N. (1954). *Cybernetics, or control and communication in the animal and the machine* (2nd ed.). Cambridge, MA: Massachusetts Institute of Technology Press. (First edition, 1948, New York: Wiley.)

Wynne, L.C. (1970). Communication disorders and the quest for relatedness in families of schizophrenics. *American Journal of Psychoanalysis, 30*, 100–114.

Wynne, L.C., Rycoff, I.M., Day, J., & Hirsch, S.I. (1958). Pseudomutuality in the family relations of schizophrenics. *Psychiatry, 21*, 205–220.

EDITORS' REFERENCES

Gurman, A.S. (1985). Transition and tradition: A rural marriage in crisis. In A.S. Gurman (Ed.), *Casebook of marital therapy.* New York: Guilford.

Nichols, M.P. (1987). *The self in the system: Expanding the limits of family therapy.* New York: Brunner/Mazel.

PART II

Models of Family Therapy

CHAPTER 3

Behavioral Family Therapy

Ian R. H. Falloon, M.D.

Behavioral family therapy is a generic term for a number of therapeutic interventions that focus on the family unit and are derived from empirical studies. Although social learning theory was the major theoretical base for the earliest proponents of this approach, recent developments have incorporated a much broader set of paradigms derived from social psychology, sociology, cognitive psychology, and pathophysiology. *The key thread that binds these diverse perspectives is a demand for continual empirical challenge.* Every strategy, and every case, is subjected to empirical scrutiny that aims to define the specific therapeutic ingredients that facilitate the achievement of the specific benefits desired by the family. In other words, every family presents a new experiment with the potential to advance therapeutic frontiers.

For this reason, the development of behavioral family therapy has remained less dependent on charismatic promotion by a few innovative clinicians. Instead, progress has occurred on a much broader front with clinicians and researchers collaborating to consolidate an ever-expanding field of replicable knowledge.

HISTORICAL DEVELOPMENT

The earliest reports of behavioral family interventions were very simple case studies involving discrete problems with young children. Bedtime tantrums (Williams, 1959), nocturnal enuresis (Lovibond, 1963), aggressive behavior (Boardman, 1962), and language training in an autistic child (Risley & Wolf, 1967) were among the earliest attempts to involve the family unit in clinical intervention strategies. An exception to the focus on child-rearing issues was Wolpe's (1958) training spouses to assist in the desensitization of anxiety disorders.

All these early strategies were clearly individually focused. Family members were recognized as highly influential factors in the natural environment. From a learning-theory perspective, they were considered relevant sources of stimuli and responses. The manner in which they presented these eliciting stimuli and responded with reinforcement was considered to shape the behavior of other family members. Where deviant behavioral patterns were observed, it was assumed that their origins, and more especially their sustained performance, were a direct result of key family members' operant reinforcement. Thus, it was concluded that any strategy for modifying deviant behavior must involve changing the key family members' behavior. Parents and spouses were trained to eliminate the contingencies that maintained the deviant behavior and to employ different contingencies to prompt and support more desirable behavior patterns that were incompatible with the deviant behavior.

Such an analysis was derived directly from laboratory experiments involving animal learning. Family members were provided with clear instructions to respond to undesired behavior in a highly specific way. The therapist often demonstrated the specified response and the family member was encouraged to practice it during the session. Success was measured by the results observed during the treatment session, usually a count of the number of occasions the deviant behavior occurred during the session. Patterson and Brodsky (1966) described modifying the responses of the parents of a boy with multiple problems, including verbal aggression, kicking, and screaming, biting, and enuresis. They were taught to ignore inappropriate, undesirable behavior and to reward appropriate, desirable behavior. Within two weeks, the frequency of undesirable behavior had been reduced to tolerable levels while socially appropriate behavior was increased.

This approach to behavior disturbance in children was developed further by Gerald Patterson. Patterson recognized that the results of these laboratory-style experiments in behavior modification were somewhat limited in clinical practice and that the complexity of family life made the application of these operant strategies a much more difficult proposition in the home environment (Patterson, McNeal, Hawkins & Phelps, 1967). Furthermore, behavior patterns displayed in the clinic setting were analogous, but often far from identical, to those displayed in the home. He took the major step of transferring the assessment and intervention for families from the clinic to the home.

Methods of reliably recording family interaction patterns in the home were developed (Patterson, Reid, Jones, & Conger, 1975). The antecedents and consequences of episodes of undesired behavior were pinpointed and intervention strategies were based on these observations.

It was noted that the antecedents and responses were not entirely consistent. Where a consistent pattern was associated with repetitive performance of the specific undesired behavior, a clear formulation could be developed. Successful modification of the contingencies would then be expected to eliminate the undesired behavior, thereby offering proof for the formulation.

However, such straightforward associations between stimuli and responses were much rarer in the natural habitat of human families than they were in carefully controlled laboratory or clinical settings. Moreover, family members' perceptions of their behavior toward one another were often colored by cognitive and affective distortions, so that mere correction of undesired responses did not necessarily lead to increased family satisfaction. A child who behaved in the manner sought by the parents continued to be viewed as a bad child who was behaving appropriately to please the therapist and would inevitably lapse into his or her former bad ways as soon as the therapy ended. All too often, these pessimistic predictions were valid, although it could be argued that the pessimism of the parents was a major factor contributing to such short-lived changes. The early reports of dramatic success with operant conditioning methods seldom provided evidence of long-term benefits.

Patterson (1971) attempted to reduce the dependence on the therapist as the key mediator of family change by developing methods that sought to train family members to employ social-learning-theory strategies themselves. As early as 1967, he had described the need to intervene at several levels simultaneously before lasting changes in the family system were likely to take place (Patterson et al., 1967). It was not merely a matter of training parents to operate on a deviant child's behavior; the child required training to facilitate and respond to the parents' needs. Thus, the concept of *reciprocity* or quid pro quo was a key element in the earliest behavioral-family-therapy approaches.

The limited value of *coercion* in facilitating desired changes in families was observed by Patterson. Laboratory studies had demonstrated that coercive strategies produced, at best, only short-term suppression of behavior. A similar phenomenon was noted in families (Patterson & Hops, 1972). An escalation of negative responses (in lay terms, a heated quarrel!) was more likely to occur when one family member attempted to employ a coercive strategy to induce behavior change in another. Early strategies to counter the high frequency of coercive interactions in distressed families attempted to increase positive interaction between the warring factions, without any direct focus on the resolution of family conflicts. Exponents tended to promote the expression of positive feelings and mutually pleasing behaviors and to suppress arguments. Such an approach was of limited benefit to families where merely adopting more positive attitudes did not lead to improved problem resolution. Families with a long history of conflict and stress, who most needed professional assistance, were more likely to fall into this category, whereas those with acute, often transient, distress were more likely to benefit from reaffirmation of their basic positive feelings and attitudes toward each other. Such a phenomenon was likely to occur spontaneously or with minimal therapeutic guidance.

Richard Stuart (1969), a social worker, developed a strategy that aimed to promote a positive family milieu in distressed families. The *contingency contracting* approach focused on enhancing the reciprocal exchange of pleasing behaviors. This approach was well suited to redirecting the focus of marital dyads towards acknowledgement of positive interaction patterns, where a destructive spiral of coercion had developed. Stuart cited Thibaut and Kelley (1959) to support his view that:

The exact pattern of interaction which takes place between spouses is never accidental; it represents the most rewarding of all the available alternatives . . . it represents the best balance which each can achieve between individual and mutual rewards and costs. (p. 12)

The concept that families develop patterns of behavior that, while appearing counterproductive to the observer, nevertheless represent their best efforts to respond to their current circumstances is the cornerstone of behavioral family therapy. It is perhaps the key link between behavioral concepts of family systems and other systemic approaches to family intervention. Indeed, the ideas of reciprocity and balance echo the concepts of "quid pro quo" and "homeosta-

sis" described by Jackson (1965), which underpinned the early developments of most family-therapy models.

Stuart (1969) suggested that the most efficient strategy to change the homeostatic balance is for each family member to provide noncontingent (or unconditional) positive rewarding behavior to other family members, particularly those family members with whom he or she is experiencing conflict. In other words, a family member is more likely to change his or her behavior in order to please somebody who pleases him or her. Contrariwise, the motivation is less to please a person who is a source of coercive responses or one who appears to be providing contingent rewards only, that is, rewards conditional on the behavior change.

The interpersonal context into which Stuart applied operant conditioning paradigms was a crucial step. This "give to get" strategy assisted a family member to build up his or her potency as a mediator of change by focusing attention on the preexisting pleasing aspects of another person's behavior, as well as on that person's unmet needs, in the hope that such positive giving would be reciprocated by that person. In this way, the initial focus was removed from the presenting problems of the family to constructing an ambience in which mutual positive regard was maximal. Each family member was expected to take responsibility for change in others by initiating change in his or her own behavior first.

Contingency contracting was a strategy derived from these principles. Each family member drew up a list of behaviors that he or she was prepared to perform for each other family member. After some negotiation concerning the mutual desirability of specific behavior, a contract was drawn up among family members. At first Stuart (1969) suggested that tokens be exchanged as rewards for targeted desired behaviors. This allowed the person to earn a "credit" balance by frequent performance of desirable behavior for others. This credit could be exchanged later when that person was the recipient of desired behavior from others. Refinements of this approach dispensed with tokens and employed written, signed contract forms. Although Stuart's work has been devoted mainly to marital dyads, contingency contracting and the principles of enhancement of mutual positive regard as a precondition for effective problem resolution have been used widely throughout behavioral family therapy (e.g., Foster, Prinz, & O'Leary, 1983; Jacobson & Margolin, 1979; L'Abate, 1977; Patterson, 1971).

While Patterson, a psychologist, worked mainly with children, and Stuart, a social worker, with marital discord, the third major pioneer of behavioral family therapy, Robert Liberman, was a psychiatrist working mainly with the adult mentally ill. In a landmark paper entitled "Behavioral Approaches to Family and Couple Therapy" (Liberman, 1970), he described the application of an operant learning framework within the family system. His management of four cases with differing presenting symptoms—depression, intractable headache, social inadequacy, and marital distress—was outlined. Liberman added strategies derived from the imitative learning concepts of Bandura and Walters (1963) to contingency management and operant reinforcement. This included *role rehearsal* and *modeling* of alternative interpersonal communication patterns. Furthermore, he went to considerable lengths to emphasize that these techniques were employed within the context of a collaborative therapeutic alliance with detailed assessment of the functional relationships between presenting symptoms and family interaction patterns. In contrast to the stress Patterson had placed on observations of these patterns in parent–child transactions, Liberman conducted this assessment largely through a series of semistructured interviews with adult family members. Although charting of specific events was employed, this was conducted by the family members themselves. Efforts were made to target therapy to the enhancement of the quality of life of family members, not merely to the removal of symptoms.

The application of the methods of behavioral analysis that had been employed in adult psychiatry (Kanfer & Saslow, 1965) to a family unit broadened the scope of these interventions. Every member of the household became a legitimate focus for intervention, not merely to assist them in the resolution of problems, but also to help them to achieve short- and long-term goals in their lives. Furthermore, the behavioral analysis continued throughout therapy, enabling targeted goals, problems, and strategies to be modified as change or lack of change

became evident. Such feedback was highly specific and clearly structured and embodied the concept of the family as a system in which change in any one element was likely to cause change in every other element. However, it was assumed that a comprehensive behavioral analysis would enable the therapist to predict these changes before applying any intervention strategies, thereby embodying the scientific method.

As a psychiatrist practicing in a community mental health setting, Liberman saw the need to deal with extrafamilial issues that impinged on the family system. These included working with the educational, social-service, and medical agencies in the community so that the behavioral changes induced by family-therapy interventions were reinforced and maintained in settings outside the family.

In addition, he pioneered the approach now known as the psychoeducational approach (see Chapter 11). In a series of educational seminars, to which index patients and their families were invited, the nature and management of major mental disorders were explained. Families and patients were trained in specific strategies to cope with symptoms of the mental disorder. This included an understanding of the pathophysiology of the disorders and of the benefits and costs of drug therapy in their overall management (Falloon & Liberman, 1984).

Thus, it can be seen that the pioneering efforts of behavioral family therapists covered much of the field of mental health. The early approaches, although based on relatively simple psychological principles, were fairly complex in their application. The strategies were chosen after careful and often lengthy assessment of family functioning that aimed to predict the beneficial and detrimental changes that would occur as a consequence of the effective application of the strategy. These consequences were assessed, and the knowledge of their results provided further assessment upon which to choose subsequent interventions. The early exponents were concerned less about the theoretical concepts about family relationships than about the effectiveness of intervention strategies, and remarkably little attention was paid to the limiting factors that reduced the long-term benefits of these methods.

Recent developments in this field will be discussed later in this chapter. However, it is important to emphasize that the constraints of the scientific method, to which behavioral family therapy owes its advancement, ensure that development progresses in an evolutionary fashion. For this reason, it is not possible to define precise parameters of standard practice; rather, the major principles underlying current application will be outlined, with illustrations that provide a sample of the range of the approach.

WELL-FUNCTIONING FAMILY

Behavioral family therapy has tried to avoid explicit assumptions regarding the definition of a well-functioning family. From a learning-theory perspective, the most valid manner in which a family can be judged is from the results of its efforts in achieving the expected goals of each family member. The process by which those results are achieved is considered of secondary importance.[1]

Furthermore, the precise definition of a "family" is an issue that cannot be settled readily in objective terms. Is the issue determined by blood relationships, by cohabitation in a household, or by levels of intimacy in social relationships? The last concept is of greater significance to behavioral family therapists than the other two. In other words, "the family" in therapeutic terms is considered to be those individuals, whether biological relatives, members of the same household, or otherwise related, who are involved in interdependent close relationships.

In clinical practice, the precise boundaries that are drawn within a social network to constitute a family group tend to vary according to the specific presenting problem. For example, a sexual problem may involve merely two partners, either married, cohabiting, or engaged in regular dating, whereas the problem of an autistic child may involve the natural parents and siblings, house parents in a training home, other children living in the home, and teachers. In a study of the various combinations considered as functioning family units in a Chicago neighborhood more than 200 different combinations were found (Kellam, Ensminger, & Turner, 1977). Clearly, for research purposes, the traditional concept of mother, father, brother, and sister has been considered the norm. Modern concepts of families suggest that such a family is not the norm, possibly not even the most common family constellation. What is considered to be functioning for a single-parent family may vary considerably from that for a dual-parent unit.

Yet another basic problem in providing normative data on family functioning relates to ethnic and cultural expectations (see Chapter 19). Behavior considered desirable in one ethnic group may be considered highly deviant and destructive in another culture.

Leaving problems of definition aside, it is evident that behavioral family therapists have made some implicit assumptions about the adaptive value of specific family characteristics, at least within a North American Caucasian cultural framework. These assumptions have nearly all been construed from observations of distressed families and cannot be considered as definitive evidence of the real-life optimal functioning of families. A small body of research comparing parent–child and marital dyads presenting for help with marital distress with "non-distressed" controls has shown only limited validation for many of these constructs (Griest & Wells, 1983; Jacobson, Follette, & Elwood, 1984).

A review of the behavioral-family-therapy literature reveals that the focus of family intervention is on teaching specific interaction strategies or skills. The clinical context in which these strategies are applied appears to be a growing concern as the approach is employed in increasingly disturbed family units and its limitations are more readily recognized.

Expectations of Well-Functioning Families

It is assumed that optimal family functioning is facilitated by mutually shared goals and expectations. These include expectations for adequate resources for communal living, such as food, housing, clothing, and health care; sexual

[1] *Editors' Note.* This sounds like a value-free position about what constitutes a healthy family for a social-learning therapist, yet Falloon's confirmation of the importance of each family member's achieving his or her goals implies a model of the healthy/optimal family. Note that another school of therapy could endorse parental (or child) needs as primary, implying quite a different set of values.

interaction, procreation, and child-rearing functions; social, leisure, and recreational pursuits; moral expectations of religion, honesty, and loyalty; levels of dependence; and individual vocational, creative, intellectual, and personality development. A major consideration is the expectation that the family unit will provide support for the stresses associated with the expected transitional stages of life, as well as with stressful life events such as illness, incurrence of handicaps, or bereavement.

The level of agreement among all family members concerning the family's short-term and long-term goals is likely to predict the cohesiveness and organizational structure of the unit. Modern Western family living is somewhat devoid of clear societal expectations, leaving families in the position of having to construct their own goals, usually unaided. Legal constraints on marriage, child-rearing, interpersonal, behavior, and financial matters may be the only guidelines provided in many families, whereas families influenced by clear cultural or religious expectations may be expected to adhere rigidly to specific rules. Difficulties may arise both from a lack of specified, shared family expectations or from the excessive constraints of inflexible goals. It is not clear how much or how little sharing of family members' expectations is found in well-functioning families.

Structure and Style of Well-Functioning Families

Behavioral family therapists have shown particular concern for the concept of reciprocity in family relationships (Stuart, 1969). In a well-functioning family, it is assumed that each family member will influence every other family member in a mutually rewarding manner. This balance of interdependent relationships is considered to exist not merely in the marital dyad, but also between parents and children and among the children themselves (Foster & Hoier, 1982). The ability of a family member to dispense positive rewards to another person will determine his or her power to influence that person (Stuart, 1969). This includes the potency of that person to provide a model behavior that may be imitated by other family members (Liberman, 1970).

Coercive interaction patterns conform to similar reciprocal concepts (Patterson & Reid, 1970), but are assumed to be infrequent in the well-functioning family. This is not well substantiated. It is more likely that coercive interaction occurs in most families, but that it tends to escalate into destructive arguments in distressed families, whereas the nondistressed family manages to contain and control negative exchanges (Hahlweg, Baucom, & Markman, 1988; Wahler, Hughey, & Gordon, 1981).

The concept of boundaries (Minuchin, 1973) is implicit in behavioral family therapy. Very often, the major boundaries are made highly explicit by defining therapies in terms of sexual therapy, marital therapy, or parent training. However, the precise boundaries families choose for themselves are not of major concern to most behavioral family therapists. Provided that the arrangement is mutually rewarding for all individuals, no attempt is made to intervene directly. It is assumed that overinvolved interaction patterns where family members appear enmeshed in a highly intimate manner are satisfactory, provided that the mutual needs of each partner in the relationship are being met without coercion. However, where one partner experiences the other as domineering and intrusive, and as supressing his or her efforts to achieve expected life goals, the relationship is considered dysfunctional. Satisfactory "overinvolvement" is found in many situations—for example, in response to acute physical illness, with chronic major handicaps, after major life stress, during infancy, and during courtship and the early stages of cohabitation. With the exception of caring for a person with a chronic handicap, enmeshment is usually transient. Furthermore, it is crucial that the care of chronic handicapping conditions allows the handicapped person to maximize the achievement of functional goals within the constraints imposed by the disorder.

Concerns about the lack of intimacy and the excessive social distance between family members have tended to be an even greater problem for behavioral family therapists. Western societal values stress the achievement of autonomy and independence in mature adult development, without providing guidelines for how links with parents, siblings, in-laws, and friends are handled once emancipation has been attained. Many of the problems presented by newly married couples or new parents are associated with a lack of definition of the levels of intimacy involved in these relationships. A mother with a baby may feel a sense of failure if her mother or sister provides her with extensive assistance in the child's care. A husband may resent his wife's continued involvement in close friendships that antedated their marriage.

Without normative data concerning the boundaries in well-functioning family systems, it seems dangerous to speculate on this issue in a general manner. It is assumed that a wide range of interrelationships may be found to be satisfactory in different families at different times. Perhaps the ability to adjust mutually to the changing needs of family members in a flexible manner theoretically is most desirable (McAuley, 1988). However, the precise definitions of interdependence and appropriate levels of intimacy are elusive and can probably only be related to the precise context of the events in which they are observed (Arrington, Sullaway, & Christensen, 1988). Nevertheless, it is postulated that a well-functioning family shows concern about these issues and participates actively in the definition and redefinition of family style to meet the changing needs of all of its members.

Tolerance of Deviance

There is limited support for the hypothesis that nondistressed families tend to have a greater tolerance for behavior that deviates from their expected norms than do distressed families (Azrin, Naster, & Jones, 1973; Griest & Wells, 1983). It has been noted that parents who seek help for difficulties with their children include a subgroup whose members label normal behavior patterns as deviant (Griest & Wells, 1983). To some extent, this misperception of deviance is based on inadequate understanding. For example, a parent may have unrealistic expectations for a 2-year-old child to display total obedience (McAuley, 1987). On the other hand, an anxious or depressed parent may tend to focus attention on minor deviance (Griest et al., 1982), while a parent under stress as a result of marital discord or some other major environmental problem may scapegoat a child who displays minor deviations in behavior (Oltmanns, Broderick, & O'Leary, 1977). Behavioral family ther-

apists are beginning to accept that not all deviance is a direct result of parental mismanagement. A significant proportion of children are "difficult" to manage from birth (Thomas & Chess, 1977).[2] While a constitutional predisposition to deviance may be minimized by effective parenting, it is accepted that the behavior of some children may require specialized skills to handle effectively (Griest & Wells, 1983; McAuley, 1988).

It is evident that the manner in which families address deviant behavior is a highly complex phenomenon. Tolerance for clearly deviant behavior has been studied closely in research on coping with major mental disorders in adults. A clear, consistent association between family members' abilities to tolerate deviant behavior in schizophrenic and depressive disorders and the course of these disorders has been found (Vaughn & Leff, 1976). Families that respond to deviant behavior in a calm, tolerant manner help to minimize the disruption this behavior causes, whereas those that react in a distressed critical or highly overinvolved manner tend to amplify the behavioral deviance and potentially contribute to the severity of the disorder.

It may be assumed that a well-functioning family is able clearly to identify specific deviant behavior in its members, and having recognized the deviance, will be able to respond in a manner that will diminish the continuation or repetition of this behavior in an efficient manner. For minor deviance, this will take the form of minimizing the attention (or other forms of reinforcement) on the behavior or prompting alternative positive behavior. Major deviance will entail more extensive family-problem resolution.

When deviant behavior is associated with a chronic physical or mental handicap, the ability of the family to cope with this behavior is crucial. Relatively little is known about the way nondistressed patients and their families cope with such handicaps as severe development disorders, progressive physical illness, and dementias (Harris & Thorwarth, 1988; Zarit & Zarit, 1982).

---

[2] *Editors' Note.* As in Segal's (Chapter 6) discussion of the Mental Research Institute approach, Falloon is acknowledging that even in basically interactional approaches, not *all* problems need to be, or are appropriately, seen as interactionally based.

Crucial factors that appear to promote tolerance include a clear, shared understanding of the nature of the disorder, adequate family communication and problem-solving skills, and support from the extended social network and community as a whole.

Coping with Stress

The family is the primary resource for managing the stress of its members. This stress may be the result of factors within the family, including the illnesses and handicaps discussed above. In addition, stress arising outside the family is potentially detrimental to family members. Stress from events in the community and social network, such as loss of a job, breakup of a close friendship, or failure on an exam at school, may contribute to increased stress in the family unit. Optimal family functioning facilitates the resolution of these stresses and reduces the impact on the family unit. This is accomplished by effective family communication and problem solving relating to the specific stress.

The potential for the effective management of a major stress will depend on the preexisting levels of stress impinging on the family unit, as well as on the vulnerability of each family member at that time. Where preexisting stress levels are high and family members are highly vulnerable to stress, a relatively small additional stress may overwhelm the coping capacity of the family and place vulnerable family members at a high risk of stress-related disorders.

The well-functioning family provides its members with a highly efficient buffer against the trials and tribulations of life in the community and at the same time reduces the everyday stress of family living. It can be argued that such factors as nutrition and hygiene may be important considerations in family functioning, particularly where they reduce the constitutional vulnerability to physical illnesses. Basic family functions such as these frequently have been overlooked in family therapy, but in many cases they may provide invaluable links between family functioning and behavioral disturbance.

Finally, the well-functioning family provides support for members when they suffer illness. This caring role is complicated where both parents in a nuclear household are employed out-side the home. Nevertheless, it is assumed that primary care for sick members will reside within the family unit.

The behavioral approach seeks to clarify the manner in which the family unit provides support for and limitations on the goal-directed functioning of each of its members. In order to do this, the goals of family members must be clarified and specific examples of family functioning carefully analyzed to determine the precise dysfunctional responses. This microanalysis of family behavior may uncover a myriad of dysfunctional transactions. As a consequence, general statements about family dysfunction are hazardous. However, research studies have found a high prevalence for certain general patterns. These patterns will be summarized.

BEHAVIORAL ANALYSIS OF FAMILY DYSFUNCTION

The behavioral family therapist considers that every member of a system is doing his or her very best to cope with the precise contingencies that they perceive at any time, given the practical and emotional restraints they experience at that time (Falloon, Boyd, & McGill, 1984a). As a result of the positive connotation of the behavior of individual family members, it is very difficult to define dysfunction in a specific manner.[3] Rather, it is evident that at times the "best" responses of one family member may interfere with the progress of another family member toward achievement of his or her goals. Such a situation is seen clearly where one family member is suffering from a serious illness or handicap and other family members are expected to assist in the caregiving. However, where the context is less clearly defined, the responses of family members may be less readily understood.

Studies of families with children showing con-

---

[3] *Editors' Note.* Falloon's "positive connotation" is quite different from that of, e.g., the Milan systemic school of family therapy (cf. Campbell, Draper, & Crutchley, Chapter 10). Falloon's emphasis is on the therapist's acceptance and non-blaming of family members, whatever their behavior. While the Milanese "positive connotation" is also nonblaming, it is used to shift patients' attributions about themselves and others, not simply to be supportive.

duct difficulties have identified several common deficits. First, some family members have difficulties in their *recognition of deviant behavior* (Atkeson & Forehand, 1978; Cahill, 1978). At times, the behavior of young children that is within age-related norms is labeled as deviant and deviant behavior is not recognized as such. A similar phenomenon has been noted with respect to adult behavioral disturbance (Vaughn, 1977). These perceptual difficulties are enhanced by factors that interfere with cognition, such as depressive or anxiety disorders or high stress, as well as by a lack of understanding of normative functioning (Vaughn & Leff, 1981). The latter situation may arise when the family member has unclear expectations as a result of distorted personal development or merely a lack of adequate information. For example, a mother may believe that a child should be beaten whenever he or she whines because that was the way she and her siblings were treated; alternatively, a parent with a son who develops schizophrenia while away at college may believe his disorder was brought about by smoking marijuana and that his withdrawn behavior is merely the laziness of a college dropout. Thus, family dysfunction may result from entrenched attitudes derived from childhood experiences, as well as from a relatively straightforward lack of adequate information.

A second source of family deficits involves a *lack of clearly defined family rules.* A lack of rules is most prominent when the family is dealing with adolescent children (Barton & Alexander, 1981), but may be readily seen where drug or alcohol abuse occurs (Fichter & Postpischil, 1987), or with dementing elderly persons (Zarit & Zarit, 1980). The lack of a clear frame of reference for a family member who experiences problems of social judgment is highlighted in these situations. However, family rules may include more mundane considerations that surround the resolution of everyday family issues, such as the manner in which the family meets to discuss matters of concern and organizes basic household living. A lack of clear structure with regard to household management is a frequent source of family tension.

A third area where deficits are a common source of family dysfunction is in *emotional communication* among family members. The major deficiencies tend to be found in the low rate of expression of positive feelings coupled with an excess in the expression of negative feelings (Patterson, 1982; Vaughn & Leff, 1976). Very few family members have not acquired the skills involved in expressing positive feelings. The problem lies more in the recognition of pleasing, prosocial behavior performed by other family members and the expression of those feelings in a direct manner. Displeasing behavior is readily recognized and expressed in a hostile or coercive manner in these families, creating increased tension and reducing cooperative alliances among family members. High levels of coercive criticism and low levels of praise are found in most distressed families, regardless of whether the index problem is that of child rearing or of adult behavior (Alexander, 1973; Christensen, Phillips, Glasgow, & Johnson, 1983; Hooley, 1985; Patterson, 1982; Prinz & Kent, 1978; Vaughn & Leff, 1976).

It is assumed that well-functioning families do not suppress criticism of destructive behavior patterns, but rather express that criticism in a constructive manner that does not threaten the positive bonds between family members. In a similar manner, requests are made in a positive frame of reference rather than as a coercive demand. Thus, it is the *style* of negative communication that is usually deficient.[4] This includes family members who avoid direct expression of negative feelings, but instead express their displeasure toward others with indirect nonverbal gestures (Gottman, 1979). Another pattern of hostile criticism occurs where one or more family members become the victims of family-wide criticism, despite behavioral disturbance that differs insignificantly from that of other family members. In other words, they become the recipients of expressions of negative feelings that might be directed more appropriately toward the behavior of others. This scapegoating phenomenon places extreme pressure on the targeted person.

---

[4] *Editors' Note.* Of course, expressing criticism in a nonconstructive manner does not necessarily threaten positive bonds, and in some cases may strengthen them, as when the family's cultural or ethnic context defines affective intensity as showing caring involvement. Still, such supernormal sounding skills may be necessary for families to cope effectively and efficiently with problems of mental handicap, chronic psychiatric disorders, dementia, and the like—families of the sort the author deals with regularly.

A relatively rare communication problem is that of *excessive expression of noncontingent positive feelings*, accompanied by an intrusive expression of thoughts and feelings on behalf of the other person (Vaughn & Leff, 1976). This overinvolved pattern of emotional communication has been described in enmeshed or symbiotic relationships, and tends to smother attempts at individuation by the recipient of such responses. To assist an individual to maximize his or her creative potential, positive communication is considered most effective when it prompts and reinforces goal-directed behavior. In a similar manner, empathic expression is most effective when it assists a person to express his or her own thoughts and feelings in a clear, direct manner.

BEHAVIORAL ASSESSMENT OF FAMILY FUNCTIONING

Detailed, continuous assessment of family functioning is the framework upon which behavioral family therapy is constructed. Behavioral family interventions rely on assessment data to guide the therapy, to provide accurate feedback about the relative success of the program, and to allow modifications to be made that maximize the efficiency of treatment strategies. Assessment is a vital and integral component of the entire family-therapy process. Extensive reviews of behavioral family assessment have been completed in recent years (Arrington et al., 1988; Falloon et al., 1984b; Foster & Robin, 1987; McMahon & Forehand, 1987). A brief overview of this complex process will be provided in this chapter.

Behavioral assessment of family functioning is conducted on two main levels. The first level is an analysis of the presenting problems that seeks to pinpoint the specific behavioral deficits that underly these problem areas, and if modified, would lead to resolution of the problems. This is termed a *problem analysis*.

The second level of assessment is termed a *functional analysis*. This aims to uncover the interrelationships between those behavioral deficits and the interpersonal environment in which they are functionally relevant. The problem analysis defines the specific deficits of family functioning, while the functional analysis defines the context in which these deficits contribute to handicapping dysfunction.

The initial behavioral assessment may be straightforward and be accomplished in an hour or two. However, with complex family problems, it may extend to many hours of individual and conjoint interviews, naturalistic observations, and record keeping, spread over several weeks. This lengthy assessment phase is considered to have significant therapeutic potential and is regarded as the initial phase of behavioral family therapy. Even when the baseline assessment does not achieve any evident improvement in the presenting problems, the therapist seeks to develop a therapeutic alliance with all family members by demonstrating his or her genuine concern about understanding their personal difficulties and aspirations and unconditional respect for their current efforts at coping with the presenting problems.

Problem Analysis

The behavioral family therapist initiates assessment of the family functioning with the presenting problem. Few family members are able to specify the presenting issue in clear behavioral terms. Most tend to describe issues in broad terms, such as "Sam is disobedient," "John is lazy," "Sarah has gone off sex," or "Jane is very aggressive." The first task of behavioral assessment is to guide the family to describe the exact behaviors that are causing concern. This precise specification of the presenting problem is known as *pinpointing* (Patterson et al., 1975). The aim is to provide an unequivocal definition of the problem behavior that enables all family members and independent observers readily to agree on the occurrence of that target behavior.

In order to provide such specificity, presenting problems usually are defined in terms of overt behavioral acts rather than of emotional states or cognitions. However, wherever the specific feelings and thoughts that may accompany the behavioral act can be precisely specified, they are included in the definition. The ability to define such covert experience is limited in young children, but is usually a major part of the assessment of adolescent and adult problems.

In the course of pinpointing the presenting

problem, the therapist may uncover deficits that he or she may hypothesize as key factors that determine the presentation of the overt behavioral disturbance. An aggressive child may be unable to verbalize feelings of fear, a depressed housewife may be unable to discuss her lack of rewards for her everyday behavior with her husband, or a withdrawn young man may experience deficits in his thought processes that make it extremely difficult for him to initiate any constructive activity. The pinpointing process aims to uncover the crucial deficits that may contribute to the presenting problem. Ideally, one or two key deficits can be pinpointed and straightforward therapeutic interventions can quickly remedy the problem. In practice, many problems are more complex and require extensive detective work before they can be pinpointed in this manner.[5]

Most families present for treatment with one problem associated with one family member (the identified or index patient). However, very often the problem analysis reveals a plethora of deficits in other family members that may be contributing to the presenting problem, or to other distressing problems for the family. Furthermore, at times the index patient may not consider his or her behavior a problem, but instead may perceive it to be the best possible response to the issues. In order to assess the problem definition fully, it is necessary to interview each member of the household—first, to gain his or her perspective on the initial presenting problem, and then to facilitate the assessment of other significant family problems. It may be important to prioritize problems so that the most crucial are targeted for early intervention. For example, it has been noted that many children with conduct disorders as their presenting problems have depressed mothers (Griest, Forehand, Wells, & McMahon, 1980). In such cases, it may be important to pinpoint the nature of this maternal depression before addressing the child's conduct problems. Establishing the heirarchy of problems to be addressed in the intervention program is the responsibility of the

therapist, although he or she may present his or her formulation to the family for comment before deciding on the sequence of therapeutic strategies.

In addition to pinpointing the specific nature of the problem, the behavioral family therapist seeks to define how frequently it occurs. Once again, initial reports may prove highly unreliable. Families may be requested to keep records of the occurrence of a pinpointed problem behavior in order to specify its baseline frequency and to monitor the changes associated with subsequent therapy.

Although the focus of behavioral assessment is on the current nature of the presenting problem, the history of the development of that problem is often relevant. The importance of temperamental traits and personality in the development of child-rearing problems as well as in adult difficulties is clear (Rutter, 1987). Intellectual and biological deficits may also have a major bearing on the nature of the presenting problem and the choice of therapeutic intervention. Thus, in most cases where the presenting problem is severe behavioral disturbance of one family member, a traditional individual assessment of the identified patient is necessary prior to family assessment.

At the completion of the problem analysis, the therapist will have pinpointed one or more family problems, defined the frequency of their occurrence, and developed some preliminary hypotheses concerning the factors that may be contributing to the problems' occurrence and the distress associated with them.

Functional Analysis of Family Problems

The functional analysis of problem behavior extends the problem analysis to a systemic level. It aims to provide a formulation of the precise contexts in which the problem is likely to be most and least prominent.

In its most basic form, the functional analysis provides an understanding of the immediate antecedents and consequences of the problem behavior. At its most sophisticated, it seeks to reveal vulnerability factors and triggering stimuli that contribute in a covert way to the presentation of the problem behavior and its effect on the social environment.

---

[5] *Editors' Note.* Constructivists (e.g., Campbell et al., Chapter 10; Lankton et al., Chapter 8; and Segal, Chapter 6) would say that a therapist cocreates clinical problems, and does not discover or uncover them, as more positivistic behavior therapists see the matter.

Through interviews with family members and observations of the problem behavior, the behavioral family therapist may be able to pinpoint specific patterns of environmental and biological contingencies that precede and follow the targeted behavior with some consistency. It is assumed that these antecedents and consequences are functionally related to the problem behavior. The antecedents are discriminative stimuli that provide immediate triggers for the behavior, while the consequences are reinforcing stimuli that serve either to increase or to decrease the probability of a future occurrence of that specific behavior.

While clear-cut examples of classic antecedent → behavior → consequence are rare outside animal behavioral experiments, this basic assessment often provides clues to assist the therapist in formulating a basic intervention plan. For example, a child may repeatedly demand his or her mother's immediate attention when she is absorbed in another activity, and when she tells him or her to wait may respond with a temper tantrum, to which the mother will respond by giving the child the attention demanded, is a seemingly straightforward behavioral chain. However, it is unlikely that the precise stimuli and responses will be replicated repeatedly in the course of family interaction. Subtle variations in the way in which the child presents the initial request for the mother's attention, the levels of preoccupation she displays in her activity at the time of the request, and the nature of the attention that she provides all add to the complexity of this analysis.

Faced with the limitations of a simple operant conditioning model of environmental influence on problem behavior, behavioral family therapists have developed a more extensive approach to the assessment of family functioning. After the therapist has specified the immediate antecedents and consequences of the problem behavior, he or she attempts to answer the following questions:

1. How does this specific problem handicap this person (and/or the family) in everyday life?
2. What would happen if the problem were reduced in frequency?
3. What would this person (and his or her family) gain if the problem were resolved?
4. Who (or what) reinforces the problem with attention, sympathy, and support?
5. Under what circumstances is the specific problem reduced in intensity?
6. Under what circumstances is the specific problem increased in intensity?
7. What do family members currently do to cope with the problem?
8. What are the assets and deficits of the family as a problem-solving unit?

The first three questions concern the role that the problem plays in everyday family functioning. It is noted that the manner in which the family members perceive a problem will determine the extent to which it handicaps the index patient and the family. Problem behaviors regarded as threatening the emotional and physical security of the family tend to be associated with the greatest handicapping potential. These include threats of violence and suicide (Greenley, 1979).

It may be similarly perceived threats relating to childhood behavior that lead many parents to seek assistance when no abnormality can be observed in their children's functioning (Griest & Wells, 1983). Such negative perceptions are intensified when families are experiencing excessive stress, such as that associated with marital discord (Prinz, Foster, Kent, & O'Leary, 1979) or mental illness (Vaughn & Leff, 1976). Thus, the role that the individual and shared perceptions of family members play in defining and prioritizing problem behaviors must be considered in the behavioral assessment of the family. Further, stress factors that operate within the family unit, but do not impinge on the index patient directly, may increase the frequency of deviant behavior, at least as defined by the family at that time. For these reasons, it is crucial to identify the thoughts and feelings of all family members toward the index patient and his or her presenting problems and to identify all major problem issues within the family unit.

The manner in which problem behaviors are reinforced within family units is a complex process. In addition to the reinforcing responses that immediately follow a specific problem behavior, more remote reinforcers may play a part in creating a setting for problem behavior. These may include the tacit approval of aggressive behavior, particularly by males in the family, often accompanied by modeling of this behavior by other family members. Alternatively, behavior that is approved of in peer and cultural groups outside the family may be more difficult to modify at home.

The complexity of this functional analysis can be reduced by attempting to define two contrasting specific sets of contingencies: first, where the probability that the problem behavior will occur is minimal; and second, where the probability that the behavior will occur is maximal. Construction of a detailed profile of these cognitive–emotional, physiological–interpersonal contingencies tends to highlight the most relevant factors that surround the problem behavior. At times, it is possible to reconstruct these contingencies and to observe the emergence or recrudescence of the problem behavior.

A final component of the functional analysis is the assessment of the strengths and weaknesses of the family in coping with the problem behavior. It is rare that family members have not attempted, either individually or collectively, to employ strategies to minimize the handicaps associated with the behavior. These coping efforts can be examined in terms both of effective elements and of deficits. Frequently, the family already has excellent skills for coping with a problem behavior, but may not be using these skills in a manner that reduces distress. This misuse of skills may be caused by an inconsistency of application, a lack of persistence, expectations of immediate problem resolution, or a lack of coordination of family efforts. Shaping the family's existing coping skills is much easier than teaching new skills from scratch. For this reason, it is important to identify effective coping behavior or its components within the family unit.

It usually emerges that the problem behavior is present only a small part of the time and arises on a relatively small number of occasions when it might be expected. Therefore, most family interaction tends not to be related to the problem. The behavioral family therapist is concerned that the quality of life in the family is maximized during periods when the problem is not evident, as well as at times when the problem behavior is seen. It is assumed that distress and handicap will prove greatest in families where interaction unrelated to the problem is

unpleasant and unrewarding. In contrast, where everyday family interaction is pleasant or neutral the potential for constructive growth of personal talents is maximized. For this reason, the personal short-range goals of every family member are considered an important part of family assessment, particularly where the impairments in the index patient are long-term.

Many family members have no explicitly defined goals. Efforts to delineate specific goals for each family member help to establish the intervention as one that aims to enhance the quality of life of *every* family member, not merely that of the index patient. Furthermore, it is possible to assess how the family as a unit collaborates with each family member to facilitate that member's achievement of his or her life goals, or, alternatively, how the family unit deters members from their objectives.

Family members may propose unrealistic goals that are unlikely to be achieved within the constraints of their own abilities, their psychosocial context, or the time frame of the therapy program. The therapist encourages family members to shape achievable goals that will significantly enhance everyday functioning. A common thread runs through the behavioral assessment of family functioning—that is, the way in which the family unit resolves problems (and achieves goals) in a collaborative, constructive way. The manner in which a family structures its problem-solving, goal-achievement efforts can be assessed in three ways: (1) through interviews with individual family members; (2) through conjoint interviews about the way in which family problem-solving discussions are conducted; and (3) by observation of the family conducting a problem-solving discussion. The information gleaned from interviews is useful, but limited. For this reason, several efforts have been directed toward the development of standardized methods of observing the family unit engaged in problem solving. These have included training raters to sample family behavior in the family home (Patterson et al., 1975), setting up automated devices to record family behavior at home (Christensen, 1979), and observing discussions of problem issues in the clinic (Doane & Falloon, 1985; Robin, Kent, O'Leary, Foster, & Prinz, 1977). Home-based observations are extremely time-consuming, but provide samples of nonproblem interaction, as well as that which surrounds problem occurrence. Discussions of problem issues are less constrained than in the laboratory-test situation.

Where observations are recorded verbatim, they may be subjected to a wide range of coding systems that sample many aspects of problem-solving and communication-interaction patterns. In recent years, behavioral family therapists have tended to show more interest in problem-solving skills and to consider communication skills within the context of facilitating the problem-solving process. Methods of assessing patterns of interaction sequences have been developed that help delineate destructive and facilitatory communication in a more sophisticated manner than the earlier counts of the frequency of specific statements allowed (Hahlweg et al., 1988). Many of these methods can be adapted for use in everyday clinical practice as well as in research studies. For example, Falloon et al. (1984b) have employed a checklist to identify more specific components of communication and problem solving that are observed during the course of behavioral-family-therapy sessions, as well as in reports of interaction between sessions.

Continual Assessment

The initial phase of behavioral assessment of family functioning is complete once one or more functionally relevant problems or goals have been targeted, the contingencies that influence them have been postulated, the coping strategies that the family currently employs have been clarified, and the assets and deficits of family problem-solving functions have been observed. This assessment guides the therapist to formulate a treatment plan designed to find the most efficient way to facilitate problem resolution and/or goal achievement. Preference is given to shaping preexisting skills and strategies rather than training the family in new methods.

This initial assessment is only the first phase in behavioral assessment, which continues throughout therapy. Part of every treatment session is devoted to assessing the progress toward the targeted goals. An abbreviated form of the initial assessment may be repeated at each session, with more extensive reviews at predetermined intervals. This provides constant monitoring of the therapy process and allows early warning of lack of progress and assessment of the reasons for this, and permits a reformulation of the treatment approach to be achieved with maximum efficiency.

This continual specific assessment process is perhaps the most characteristic feature of behavioral family therapy. Within this framework, a broad range of intervention strategies can be deployed, including those developed by creative family therapists of all theoretical persuasions. All must be shown to assist a specific family with its specific targeted problems and goals in a clearly specified manner. In other words, each family represents a unique experiment for the therapist, who will have achieved a successful conclusion only when the targeted goals have been reached.[6]

STRUCTURE OF BEHAVIORAL FAMILY THERAPY

Behavioral family therapy is not constrained by any formal structures that define the therapeutic content—a statement that may confuse the reader who has learned of this approach from the scientific literature, where reports of carefully controlled experimental studies indicate highly structured applications of these methods. It is crucial not to confuse efforts to provide a highly consistent experimental replication of clinical methods with standard clinical practice. The structure of the behavioral approach in clinical practice is determined on a case-by-case basis, solely on the assumption that the structure chosen will prove the most efficient framework for the treatment of that family and the resolution of the family's unique problems. For this reason, a wide variety of structuring methods is employed.

Behavioral family therapy focuses on the precise manner in which family members communicate to resolve the wide range of stressors they encounter. For this reason, it is usual for all

---

[6] *Editors' Note.* It is interesting to note that therapists given to constructivism rather than to positivism would not even conceive of the *therapist* as having succeeded, but would emphasize the shared responsibility, or even attribute the success to the family.

family members living in the household to attend therapy sessions. However, this arrangement may be varied. Where stressors involve
the wider family or social network, persons living outside the immediate household may be
invited to participate, including grandparents,
siblings living away from home, aunts, uncles,
close friends, neighbors, colleagues from work,
teachers, social workers, family doctors, community nurses, and any other significant contacts. The nature of the therapy makes it difficult
to include large numbers in a therapy session
on a regular basis, however. More often, one or
two additional key persons may attend one or
more sessions to address a specific issue, and
homework to be done between sessions frequently involves one or more family members
carrying out specific problem-solving tasks with
persons in the extrafamilial network.

The individual goals of every family member
are targets for the treatment.[7] At times, these
goals may be highly personal and inappropriate for intergenerational problem solving, for
example, the resolution of sexual difficulties
between parents, obsessive-compulsive rumi-
nation, or prophylactic drug therapy for schizophrenia. Such problems may be addressed in an
individual or a marital context, where this seems
most appropriate. However, the indications for
the exclusive use of an individual or marital approach are extremely rare when a person is living in a family setting. In an excellent review of
the indications and contraindications for individual, marital, and family therapies, Crowe
(1988) concluded that there were no definite
rules to follow and that the choice was essentially
a matter of commonsense contracting between
therapist and family. Guidelines from research
studies are few. Bennum (1985) found that individual therapy was as effective as a conjoint
setting in resolving marital distress. Individual
therapy proved to be less effective than conjoint
family therapy for anorexia nervosa patients
whose illness had begun before 18 years of age,
but the two were equally effective in later-onset
cases (Russel et al., 1987).

A more recent trend in behavioral therapy is

to combine individually oriented strategies
within a conjoint family problem-solving framework. This is particularly useful where the
presenting problem is a specific psychopathol-
ogical syndrome, such as a specific phobic disorder (Cobb, McDonald, Marks, & Stern, 1980;
Hafner, 1987; Mathews, Gelder, & Johnston,
1981), severe depression (Falloon, 1975), or
schizophrenia (Falloon et al., 1984a, 1984b). In
most instances, the individual and family sessions are conducted by the same therapist. However, where day treatment is included in the
management plan, this may not be feasible.
Wherever possible, all aspects of treatment are
coordinated by one case manager who collaborates with the index patient and family. Efficient
communication and problem solving within the
professional network, as well as within the family
system, are considered vital in these cases. The
term "family management" has been coined
(Falloon et al., 1982) to emphasize the key part
that household members play in the overall care
of any member who suffers a mental disorder or
mental handicap.

Behavioral family therapy is concerned with
facilitating change in actual behavior in the
home environment. For this reason, at least
some assessment and treatment sessions are conducted in the home setting. Despite the added
cost of having the therapist journey to the family
home, there are several benefits, including
(1) increased efficiency in applying skills learned
in treatment sessions, (2) improved attendance
of "resistant" family members, (3) enhanced assessment of household stressors, and (4) more
relaxed participation by anxious family members. Whereas behavioral family therapists who
work with child-related disorders have long advocated home-based treatment (Patterson et al.,
1967; Harris & Thorwarth, 1988), those working
with adult presenting problems have been
slower to transfer sessions from hospitals and
clinics (Falloon, 1985). Once again, the indications and contraindications are supported by
scant empirical evidence and can be determined
solely according to clinical needs and constraints.

Multiple family group sessions form the basis for behavioral interventions that employ an
educative model. This includes many parent-
training approaches. Multiple family groups enable families with common presenting prob-

---

[7] *Editors' Note.* While behavioral therapy is highly goal-
focused, it is not necessarily brief; while adherence to clear
treatment foci encourages brevity, it does not require it.

lems—such as child-rearing difficulties, children with developmental disabilities, adolescent misbehavior, schizophrenia, or Alzheimer's disease—to share their methods of coping with these problems (Baker & McCurry, 1984; Dangel & Polster, 1984; Falloon & Liberman, 1982; Harris, 1983; Patterson, Cobb, & Ray, 1972; Zarit, 1988).

The limitations of the multifamily group setting in facilitating stable change in family behavior patterns are well recognized, particularly when the needs of severely disordered people are addressed. Thus, for the most part, behavioral family therapy is conducted in individual family groups with the multifamily setting being used as an adjunct for educative and supportive purposes or as a vehicle for dealing with minor family deficits. Despite the extensive use of these methods, surprisingly little research has been conducted to examine these issues in a systematic manner (Griest & Wells, 1983; Lutzker, McGimsey, McRae, & Campbell, 1983; McMahon & Forehand, 1987; Moreland, Schwebel, Beck, & Wells, 1982; Patterson, 1985).

Another issue where empirical evaluation is lacking concerns the number of therapists involved in behavioral-family-therapy sessions. Patterson (1985) has described the need for therapists to work in pairs with the families of children with severe, persistent conduct disorders. Falloon, Liberman, Lillie, and Vaughn (1980) employed three therapists in a group of three families with severely disabled schizophrenic members. However, for the most part, behavioral family therapy is conducted by solitary therapists. The clinical constraints of cost-effectiveness tend to govern this decision, particularly the untested assumption that doubling therapist time is likely to double therapeutic effectiveness. But testing this assumption would necessitate estimation of the indirect therapist time employed with each case (i.e., supervision, support groups, etc.), which may be reduced by cotherapy team work.

Behavioral family therapy is always contracted for a specific number of sessions at specific intervals. Educative courses aside, these decisions are determined by the behavioral assessment of the deficits and goals of each family and may vary enormously. Some families with persisting handicapping disorders may continue treatment for years. At all times, each family will be working toward a specific objective, which, when achieved, will necessitate renegotiation of the treatment contract. The session-by-session evaluation of progress toward specified goals permits a great deal of flexibility in these contracts. An initial contract for five sessions to resolve a school phobia may be reduced to three sessions when the problem is resolved quickly or may be extended by an additional 10 sessions when serious difficulties in the parents' marriage come to light. Sessions usually are an hour long and take place weekly. This allows the family time to complete between-sessions homework assignments. However, with families in crisis, daily sessions may be employed, and with families with chronic handicaps, weekly sessions may be too frequent. The varying capacity of key family members to learn new methods of resolving their problems is best served by a flexible scheduling of sessions to maximize therapeutic efficiency.

It may be concluded that, to date, behavioral family therapists have tended to focus on the technical skills of the therapeutic process, with limited consideration given to the structure in which these skills have been deployed. It seems doubtful that even after extensive research into these issues rigid guidelines will emerge. Nevertheless, knowledge of the comparative effectiveness of multiple family groups and conjoint sessions, home-based and clinic-based treatment, marital and family sessions, and paired or solitary therapists in resolving a selection of target problems would undoubtedly provide significant advancement in this field.

THE TECHNIQUES OF BEHAVIORAL FAMILY THERAPY

The behavioral approach is usually equated with specific behavior-change strategies such as contingency contracting, operant conditioning, and communication-skills training. It is undoubtedly true that while these strategies are employed frequently, and that research publications deal almost exclusively with the effectiveness of such strategies, the clinical practice of behavioral family therapy is characterized by a willingness to experiment with an unlimited range of interventions.[8] The only constraint placed on the application of any therapeutic strategy is that it be shown to produce the specific change that is targeted as the therapeutic goal for that family, preferably in the most efficient manner. In other words, each strategy is subjected to an experimental evaluation within the context of therapy. Studies that provide empirical validation of the efficacy of many intervention strategies in dealing with groups of families with broadly similar problems furnish some general guidelines to assist in the choice of major intervention strategies. However, the problems of families are so variable that the experienced behavioral family therapist will often have to draw upon his or her knowledge of psychological principles to create a strategy that addresses the specific constellation of family assets and deficits, problems and goals. The precise way in which a strategy is applied will be based on the initial and continuing assessment of the family's functioning. Specific feedback on the effectiveness of the technique is elicited both during the therapy session and when applied by the family in everyday activities. On the basis of this detailed feedback concerning progress toward the clearly defined family goals, the therapist makes the decision to continue the strategy, to modify the strategy, or to choose a new approach.

Despite the need to stress the manner in which strategies are tailored to specific family needs, a review of behavioral-family-therapy practice reveals that a relatively small number of interventions tend to form the basis for most therapeutic plans across a broad range of settings. They include education, communication and problem-solving training, operant conditioning approaches, and contingency management.

Education

Where family members show a significant lack of understanding of issues associated with their presenting problems, one or more sessions may be devoted to specific education. These educa-

tion modules may include general topics such as developmental milestones of children, the aging process, the principles of social learning theory, stress management, or specific topics related to a specific disorder, such as childhood autism, enuresis, schizophrenia, agoraphobia, or Alzheimer's disease.

The way in which the education is provided may range from a lecture to a group of families to an intimate discussion during which the index patient discloses his or her experiences of a disabling disorder. Visual aids, films, and videotapes, as well as books and handouts, may be utilized.

The goal of the education is to provide the family members with a clear rationale for the management of the targeted problem that may facilitate subsequent behavioral and cognitive change. In most cases, the education module is an introduction to a more extensive program of family intervention, but with highly competent problem-solving family units or with relatively straightforward presenting problems, the education itself may be a sufficient intervention to guide families to resolve their problems.

Communication Training

The behavioral approach emphasizes the need for clear, direct transfer of information about each family member's thoughts and feelings in the efficient resolution of problems and the achievement of personal goals. The expression of positive feelings is considered as important as the expression of negative feelings, and in distressed families, a deficit in the former may be more striking than in the latter. A family milieu in which negative feelings predominate is seldom conducive to collaborative problem resolution. As a result, most behavioral-family-therapy intervention programs seek to facilitate increases in the frequency of expressions of mutual positive feelings to provide an atmosphere in which problem issues can be discussed more readily.

Once the therapist is satisfied that the family has achieved sufficient mutual enhancement of positive interaction, the focus shifts to enhancing the quality of expression of negative feelings so that these can be employed as the basis for constructive problem resolution. In addition, fam-

---

[8] *Editors' Note.* And, indeed, this is *the* defining characteristic of all behavior therapy, not an inclination to call on clinical formulations based on learning theory.

ilies may receive training in making specific requests for behavior change rather than coercive demands, and in empathic listening skills, where deficits in these skills appear to detract from the efficient resolution of problems. With mentally handicapped or seriously mentally ill persons, family members may require training in communicating basic information (Falloon, 1975; Harris, 1986; Howlin, 1981; Hudson, 1978; Zarit, 1988).

The facilitation of communication skills involves a skill-training model. Family members are invited to describe and reenact their attempts to communicate their feelings and they receive supportive coaching from therapists and from other, more competent family members. Stress is placed on feedback that builds upon the person's strengths while providing constructive suggestions for overcoming weaknesses. Instructions, modeling, and positive reinforcement (e.g., praise) are used to enhance communication skills until a level of competence has been achieved that satisfies the family and therapist. These criteria will vary according to family background and current needs.

Congruent verbal and nonverbal expression is emphasized when expressing feelings. Family members with severe disabilities in interpersonal expression may benefit from individually tailored social-skills training. This may take place within the context of family therapy or in individual or group settings. The need to target the expression of negative feelings toward clearly defined problem areas where constructive problem resolution is feasible is stressed.

The therapist does not seek merely to facilitate competent performance of communication skills in the course of therapy sessions, but is satisfied only when clear evidence is provided that these skills have been performed as a part of everyday interactions. A variety of strategies have been developed to enhance the transfer of skills to everyday use, including providing written manuals and guidelines to use at home (Falloon et al., 1984; O'Dell, Krug, Patterson, & Faustman, 1980; Patterson, 1971), conducting sessions at home (Falloon et al., 1984; Herbert & Iwaniec, 1981; Howlin, 1981; Patterson, 1985), playing board games and computer games (Blechman, Rabin & McEnroe, 1986), and training in social-learning-theory principles (McMahon, Forehand, & Griest, 1981). However, the most common strategy used is that of assigning specific homework tasks to be completed between sessions (Falloon et al., 1984; Liberman, 1970; Foster et al., 1983). This homework involves the continued practice of skills rehearsed in the therapy sessions, accompanied by monitoring of performance on worksheets for discussion and feedback at the subsequent session. There is no clear consensus as to the relative merits of these generalization procedures, but the principle is clear—effective therapy produces sustained change in family behavior in the natural environment.

Problem-Solving Training

The early behavioral family therapists tended to focus on the manner in which family members communicated their needs and feelings to each other, including the way in which parents employed these communication skills to shape the behavior patterns they desired in their children (O'Dell, 1974). Recent developments have focused on the resolution of conflicts among family members. The content of the conflict issues found in families is highly variable, so that behavioral family therapists have moved toward assisting families to increase the efficiency of their own problem-resolution skills by adopting a consistent, structured approach. Rather than having the family depend on the therapist for novel plans to resolve problems, the therapist attempts to maximize the creative problem-solving potential of the family unit.

The problem-solving techniques employed in family and marital interventions are modifications of the approach outlined by D'Zurilla and Goldfried (1971). Detailed descriptions of these approaches are provided by Jacobson and Margolin (1979), Falloon and colleagues (1984), and Robin and Foster (1986). The method involves training the family to employ a multistep structured approach that includes defining a problem or goal in a clear manner, brainstorming a wide range of potential solutions, examining the benefits and "costs" of each proposed solution, choosing the solution that best fits the current needs and resources of the family, planning how to implement the chosen solution, and reviewing the implementation efforts.

Almost any problem or goal can be addressed

with this approach. The method facilitates a democratic discussion, with the equal participation of all family members, and ensures that the burden of coping with a difficult problem or achieving an arduous goal is shared by the entire family unit. It is difficult to involve very young children in the approach, but the principles can be employed by parents in handling conflicts with their children. For example, a parent of a child who has responded to a request with tantrum behavior may calmly invite the child to suggest some alternative responses he or she might employ in future, and rehearse how he or she might respond in a more desirable fashion.

The imposition of a high degree of structure often cuts across many inefficient patterns of family interaction, such as domineering or disruptive behavior. It may help to invite the family to nominate a person to chair the discussion and another to record notes on the discussion and plans for future review.

An essential prerequisite of structured problem-solving discussions is the ability of family members to communicate in a constructive manner. If a family is unable to discuss a "hot" issue in a reasonably calm way, has major deficits in expressive and receptive communication skills, or displays an excessive use of threats, accusations, or commands, such training may need to be preceded by several sessions of communication training. However, where these communication deficits are less pronounced and are unlikely to provoke serious disruptions in discussions, they may be addressed during the problem-solving sessions (Robin & Foster, 1986).

Once the structured approach has been introduced by the therapist, he or she tends to participate less actively during discussions and hands over to the family the responsibility for structuring the discussions, including the choice of the issues discussed in the sessions. Relatively low-key topics that involve most family members are chosen during the initial training sessions so that the family members can concentrate on the method before moving on to more stressful areas of emotional conflict, where high levels of tension may disrupt the learning process. At times of major family crisis, the therapist may be required to chair the family discussion and become an active participant in assisting the family to make plans to resolve the crisis. Once the crisis has been resolved, the therapist withdraws from active participation in order to facilitate the assimilation of the methods by the family unit.

Once more, the goal of therapy is to facilitate family-problem resolution in everyday life. The family is requested to build a weekly session for problem-solving discussions into the household program. This meeting should be free from disruptions and be held at a set time when all household members are able to attend on a regular basis. The agenda may include problems facing any household member—family conflicts, difficulties in the social network, or personal goals. Such a meeting does not preclude the use of a structured approach to problem resolution on a daily basis by family members.

This structured problem-solving approach appears to be very straightforward. In practice, few families are able to apply this structure to their problem-solving discussions without considerable coaching from a skilled therapist.

Operant Conditioning Strategies

Operant reinforcement strategies are used widely in behavioral family therapy, particularly in parent training with children and seriously disabled family members (Baker & McCurry, 1984; Falloon et al., 1984; Forehand & McMahon, 1981; Harris, 1987; Howlin, 1981; Herbert & Iwaniec, 1981; Patterson et al., 1975).

The most common approach involves teaching parents to use *shaping* and *time-out* procedures to increase desirable behavior patterns in their children. A typical program consists of several stages. First, parents are taught to attend to their children's behavior in a more precise manner so that they can discriminate between desirable and undesirable responses. They may be trained to keep records of specific behaviors. In the second step, parents are trained to provide specific verbal (praise) and nonverbal (smiles, hugs) rewards for specific desired responses, while ignoring undesirable responses. The third step consists of training parents to make specific requests for the child to perform specific desirable behaviors and to employ time-out procedures to minimize attention to undesired behaviors. Time-out may mean taking the child to his or her room or placing the child in a specific place, such as a chair, for a brief period. This enables the parent to minimize attention to undesirable behavior.

These skills are taught through instructions, behavior rehearsal, and therapist modeling. Constructive feedback and praise are provided. Videotaped feedback and bug-in-the-ear prompting may be used to facilitate skill acquisition. In some programs, training in the basic principles of social learning theory is provided to afford parents a rationale for the reinforcement strategies. Parents are instructed to employ the operant procedures in the home environment and to keep records of these efforts.

Contingency Contracting

A variation of operant reinforcement is the contingency contract. This strategy is widely used to replace hostile, coercive, blaming patterns of family behavior by cooperative, mutually pleasing behavior. A contract is drawn up by two or more family members that specifies the behaviors each desires the other to perform more frequently. The rewards that the recipient is willing to provide for the performance of the specific behaviors that are included in the contract are clearly specified. In this way, each person agrees both to give and to receive pleasing behaviors. A written agreement is signed by all persons involved. Implementation of the contract is reviewed at each treatment session and amendments added where necessary.

Contracts are usually based on increasing mutually rewarding behaviors, but on occasion, a contract may be made that concerns setting specific limits on undesirable behavior. Specific punishments are negotiated for specific undesirable behavior. For example, a teenager who angered her parents by frequently returning home late accepted that she would be grounded for five days for every half-hour she stayed out beyond the time she and her parents specified.

The *token economy system* is another strategy that is sometimes employed. A list of desired behaviors is drawn up for one or more family members. The performance of each specified behavior earns the family member a specific number of points or tokens. The points are exchanged for a range of rewards, with the value of each specified as an agreed-upon number of points. Undesired behavior can be punished by the deduction of points in a similarly specific way.

The operant methods are usually well understood by families, which tend to employ many of these principles in their everyday household management. However, they are seldom applied with the rigorous consistency that is used in behavioral family therapy. When structured in these highly specific ways, the power of these straightforward methods to effect mutually agreed-upon behavior change is considerable. The need for mutual contracts among all participants is stressed. One-sided attempts to modify another person's behavior seldom induce lasting change, and have usually been tried without success prior to referral for professional guidance.

THE ROLE OF THE THERAPIST

The interventions used in behavioral family therapy are highly specific, powerful mechanisms for change that can be readily learned by therapists. The efficient application of these strategies to family problems depends on two factors: (1) comprehensive assessment that enables an accurate selection of the appropriate interventions to fulfill the needs of each family, and (2) a sustained supportive therapeutic alliance. The first factor has been discussed repeatedly in this chapter. The second tends to be taken for granted in most dissertations on behavioral family therapies.

The therapeutic alliance in a family context depends not merely on the relationship between the therapist and the family members, but also on the interrelationships among the family members themselves. For this reason, the therapist must be highly competent in developing and maintaining a functional therapeutic milieu.

From the initial contact with the family to termination, the therapist displays respect for the family. In general terms, this involves an explicit contract to meet at a given place at a given time for a given length of time, with a specified agenda on a certain number of occasions. Any deviations from this structure are allowed only by agreement with the family. For example, if the initial contract was to assist with parenting skills and the therapist notes serious marital discord after several sessions, he or she does not change the content of therapy until this plan has been agreed to with the couple and the rationale for the change in terms of resolving the presenting problem is clearly understood.

The behavioral family therapist is taught to regard the responses that people make to any stimulus as the best ones they have available to fit the contingencies that surround that stimulus at that precise time. In other words, all family members are always doing their very best to cope with the contingencies of their life situation as they perceive them any point. The role of the therapist is not to confront the inadequacies of these best efforts, but to facilitate efforts to over-come manifest deficits and to improve the efficiency of the family members' responses. This commitment is made clear during the assessment phase, when the therapist expresses prime interest in the specific needs, goals, problems, strengths, and weaknesses of every family member and commits his or her efforts to assist each person to achieve that person's full creative potential. This commitment is maintained by constant reappraisal throughout therapy with the flexibility to modify therapist behavior as a direct consequence of the level of progress toward the family members' stated goals.

The therapist encourages family members to maximize their strengths by focusing his or her own feedback, as well as that of other family members, on all the efforts made to resolve problems and achieve goals. Failure is viewed as partial success and a behavioral analysis is conducted to define the strengths and weaknesses of such a plan in a constructive, nonjudgmental way.

Confrontation, coercion, and criticism of family behavior by the therapist are minimized. However, that does not prevent the therapist from expressing negative feelings toward the behavior of family members that displeases him or her. Consistent with the model of communication he or she is promoting for family use, the therapist expresses both positive and negative feelings in a direct, specific manner aimed at encouraging desirable behavior. The therapist accepts responsibility for any negative feelings toward family members and moves to resolve these feelings in the most efficient manner. Where serious problems are experienced, such

as poor compliance with homework assignments or hostility among family members, the therapist may chair a problem-solving discussion in an attempt to resolve this issue. Again, the format of such a discussion must conform with the one the family is expected to employ. This consistent use of the communication and problem-solving approaches by the therapist constitutes covert modeling. The therapist may draw attention to his or her modeled use of these skills in an effort to increase the potency of this modeling.

Studies of therapists' behaviors that are associated with family noncompliance or resistance to the therapeutic interventions have revealed that less experienced therapists, who tend to confront and to employ teaching methods that do not validate the current efforts that families are making, experience greater resistance in their sessions than do those whose supportive behavior is high (Patterson & Forgatch, 1985). Further validation of the key ingredients of the optimal therapeutic milieu in which to apply behavioral technology is required. Patterson (1985) has stressed the need for training in behavioral family therapy to include the specific clinical skill of developing and maintaining a therapeutic alliance, as well as training in behavioral strategies. These skills can be specified in more precise terms than the positive regard, warmth, and empathy that Truax and Carkhuff (1967) defined in the client-centered tradition two decades ago.

Another major source of resistance in behavioral family therapy appears to result from incomplete behavioral assessment and/or inflexibility in the treatment plans. Recognition that parent–child conflicts may result from a myriad of family problems, not merely from deficits in parenting skills, has led advocates of parent-training methods to broaden their training curricula. Marital counseling for marital discord, treatment for a depressed patient, and cognitive restructuring where a parent perceives a child's age-appropriate behavior as deviant have all been advocated as adjuncts to educative approaches (Griest et al., 1982; Griest & Wells, 1983; Morris, Alexander, & Waldron, 1987; Robin & Foster, 1986).

The need to match the therapeutic interventions to the key deficits of families, rather than fitting families into standardized intervention programs, is emphasized again. At times, it may be necessary to restructure the family members' definitions of the presenting problem. Where the behavioral analysis reveals key deficits that are not readily accepted as targets for intervention (e.g., a mother's overinvolved, or enmeshed, behavior toward her school-phobic child; a father's irritability and violent behavior after heavy drinking), the therapist may need to spend several sessions of cognitive restructuring until an effective therapeutic contract can be formulated (Morris et al., 1987; Robin & Foster, 1986).

Detailed behavioral assessment that continues throughout therapy assists in the prevention and early detection of resistant behavior. As a result, an experienced behavioral therapist does not believe resistance is an inevitable component of the therapy process, but rather is usually a reflection of suboptimal therapeutic skill.[9] Nevertheless, even experienced, skillful behavioral therapists encounter at least mild forms of resistance quite frequently. The strategies for handling this resistance have been reviewed extensively by Birchler (1988) and Morris and colleagues (Morris et al., 1988). Among the strategies advocated are monitoring the resistant behavior and ignoring it where it is infrequent or a minor disruption; providing reassurance, redirection, and repetition of rationale; conducting an analysis of the function of the resistance; solving the resistance problem with the family; using contingency contracting and limit setting; and relabeling resistant behavior as an effective strategy for coping with threatened change.

The termination of therapy is a process that is planned from the time of the initial assessment. Family members are told precisely how many sessions of what duration and frequency will be provided. They are reminded at each session that the therapy contract involves planning for independence from the therapist. Each homework assignment provides a rehearsal for this, particularly when family problem-solving meetings are scheduled between sessions. During sessions, the therapist hands over control to the family whenever possible. Several sessions before the final regular session, the therapist initiates a problem-solving discussion on the topic of planning for termination. The family may choose one or more follow-up sessions, continued telephone contact, or some other arrangement to assist in the maintenance of therapeutic gains. Once again, the needs of the family determine the nature of the plan. On occasion, the therapist may challenge unrealistic goals and assist family members to restructure them toward readily achievable objectives.

Therapist training in behavioral family therapy embodies the same social-learning-theory principles used in the therapy itself. Trainees receive workshop training in which they practice the therapeutic skills in role-played family sessions with instructions, modeling, constructive feedback, and positive reinforcement from an experienced therapist. Reading assignments include treatment manuals and descriptions of social-learning-theory principles. Several families are treated with close supervision from the trainer, either through a one-way screen, via video- or audiotaped recordings of sessions, or with a cotherapist. Basic competence is usually achieved within six months, although a high degree of skill may require two to three years of supervised practice. Systematic evaluation of therapist training in this approach is lacking at present. However, several attempts are currently under way to remedy this serious deficit (Falloon, 1987).

THERAPEUTIC FACTORS IN BEHAVIORAL FAMILY THERAPY

Behavioral family therapy aims to change specific targeted family problems or goals through the application of specific strategies. Each case is considered a unique experiment for the therapist, who seeks to devise the most efficient plan to achieve the targeted changes sought by the family. The highly specific matching of goals and strategies prevents a straightforward analysis of general therapeutic factors. Indeed, studies of groups of families tend to oversimplify the approach and to reduce clinical effectiveness. Despite these limitations, a number of controlled

---

[9] *Editors' Note.* Thus, to behavior therapists, resistance exists, but is largely a function of therapist factors. Contrast this view with that of psychoanalytic methods, in which patient variables are seen as central to resistance, and with some brief family-therapy methods, in which resistance is said not to exist (e.g., deShazer, 1985).

studies have been conducted that provide at least tentative evidence for the efficacy of several techniques as agents of change.

The combined structured-problem-solving and communication-training modules have been successfully incorporated into family interaction in families with deviant adolescents (Alexander, Barton, Schiavo, & Parsons, 1976; Robin et al., 1977) and cases of adult schizophrenia (Falloon, 1985). These changes in family-behavior patterns have been specifically associated with significant reductions in the severity of the presenting problems. Although in the two studies of adolescents the possibility exists that other elements of the therapy may have played a major part in the therapeutic benefits, process studies provided evidence that the specific enhancement of problem-solving and communication skills contributed to the therapeutic goals of behavioral family therapy in schizophrenia (Doane, Falloon, Goldstein, & Mintz, 1985; Doane, Goldstein, Miklowitz, & Falloon, 1986). The relative impact of communication skills and structured-problem-solving components has not been assessed.

The parent-training approach to child management consists of a series of strategies, which vary from center to center. There is evidence that various packages are effective in changing family behavior in the manner specified, and that this is associated with reductions in the presenting problems (Bernal, Klinnert, & Schultz, 1980; Fleischman, 1981; Forehand & King, 1977; Karoly & Rosenthal, 1977; Klein et al., 1977; Patterson, Chamberlain, & Reid, 1982). However, the precise therapeutic factors are not clear.

Evidence that the specific changes in parenting behavior that are induced in therapy fade soon after the end of parent training has led to studies of adjunct strategies that might contribute to stable changes in family behavior. Successful additives have included training in social learning principles (McMahon et al., 1981), written handouts (O'Dell et al., 1980), parental monitoring and self-reinforcement (Sanders & Glynn, 1981; Wells, Griest, & Forehand, 1980) and a number of sessions devoted to resolving parental problems (Griest et al., 1982).

This broadening of the educative parent-training approach, which is employed predominantly with presenting problems of childhood conduct,

has suggested that attempts to define interventions only in terms of achieving change in the behavior of the index patient tend to limit the effectiveness of the approach. Nevertheless, such an approach appears to help large numbers of families in a highly efficient manner. For this reason, it is important not to lose sight of the strengths of such an approach in improving the quality of living in many uncomplicated family systems, while advocating more complex methods for more complex family systems.

The skill-training methods employed in behavioral family therapy have been addressed in a series of studies on training families to employ time-out procedures (Flanagan, Adams, & Forehand, 1979; Nay, 1975; O'Dell et al., 1980). It may be concluded that modeling and rehearsal of the strategy with the use of written guidelines constitute the most effective training approach.

Insight in the classical sense is not considered a requirement for family change in this approach. Nevertheless, there is considerable support for the view that a clear understanding of the major factors contributing to the presenting problem, as well as a straightforward rationale for the therapeutic strategies, facilitates therapy (Falloon et al., 1984; Patterson, 1985; Robin & Foster, 1986).

There is no evidence that therapist variables such as personality, psychological health, or professional background play a major part in the success of behavioral family therapy. The most important therapist characteristic would seem to be the quality of the therapist's training and his or her maintenance of competence through continuing review (Patterson, 1985). Research into the training process is in its infancy, and in time a profile of the kind of person who is best suited to this approach may emerge.

INDICATIONS AND CONTRAINDICATIONS FOR BEHAVIORAL FAMILY THERAPY

Behavioral family therapy has been applied successfully in a wide range of disorders, in a wide range of styles. As well as providing the sole therapeutic approach, it has furnished the basis for comprehensive management of complex disorders and has been used as an adjunct therapy for other problems. The behavior therapist will wish to distinguish between enthusiastic case reports and well-controlled clinical trails in defining the benefits and limits of this approach. Although an empirical basis is employed in every case, there is a paucity of well-controlled trials of these methods, and very few that compare behavioral with other family-therapy approaches. Fortunately, several excellent studies have been initiated in recent years that should assist in establishing those areas where behavioral family therapy carries specific enduring benefits at low cost.

Behavioral family therapy has been demonstrated to have specific benefits in the treatment of conduct disorders of childhood and adolescence (Alexander et al., 1976; Forehand & King, 1977; Foster et al., 1983; Klein, Alexander, & Parsons, 1977; O'Dell et al., 1980; Patterson et al., 1982; Robin et al., 1977). Claims that the behavioral approach is more effective than other family therapies in the management of conduct disorders is more difficult to substantiate (Alexander et al., 1976; Robin, 1981). Behavioral family interventions have been considered valuable strategies in the long-term rehabilitation of children with developmental disorders (Baker & McCurry, 1984; Glahn & Chock, 1984; Harris & Thorwarth, 1988).

The clinical management of most adult mental disorders generally is most effective when psychosocial treatment is employed in combination with drug therapies (Falloon, Wilkinson, Burgess, & McLees, 1987). Behavioral family therapy has been reported as enhancing the management of schizophrenia (Curran, Faraone, & Graves, 1988; Falloon et al., 1985; Hudson, 1978; Tarrier, Barrowclough, Vaughn, Bamrah, & Freeman, 1986), depression (Falloon, 1975; Follette & Jacobson, 1988), anorexia nervosa (Fichter, 1977; Monti, Abrams, Kadden, & Cooney, 1988), senile dementia (Zarit, 1988), and alcoholism (Fichter & Postpischil, 1988). In all these reports, behavioral family therapy was employed within a comprehensive problem-oriented framework that included social casework, individual behavioral strategies, and education about mental disorders, in addition to pharmacotherapy. There is limited evidence that behavioral family therapy may make a specific contribution to the benefits associated with

these multimodal treatment regimens (Falloon, 1985; Tarrier et al., 1986).

The use of family behavioral intervention strategies as adjuncts to primary individual-based management has been advocated in the treatment of severe anxiety disorders. These have included agoraphobia (Hafner, 1988; Mathews et al., 1981) and obsessive-compulsive disorders (Hand, 1988). The family intervention tends to focus on the daily assistance household members can provide in implementing anxiety-management strategies with the index patient. However, an additional benefit of this family collaboration appears to be an improvement in family relationships and a reduction in household stress levels (Hafner, 1988).

Recent reports have questioned the long-term efficacy of parent-training procedures in the management of severe conduct disorders in children (Foster et al., 1983; Patterson & Forgatch, 1985). It has been suggested that the benefits may be enhanced by conducting a more thorough behavioral analysis that establishes the links between disturbed behavior in the children and discord between the parents, parental psychopathology (especially depression), and the manner in which parents perceive deviant behavior in their children (Griest & Wells, 1983; Robin & Foster, 1986). To date, no study has been reported that compares the standard parent-training approach with comprehensive behavioral family therapy.

There do not appear to be any absolute contraindications to behavioral family therapy. In the absence of published reports of the harmful effects of such therapy, it is worth noting the conditions under which this approach is likely to show the least benefits. Crowe (1988) has suggested that poor results are achieved when behavioral family therapy is applied where one family member is severely psychotic, where key family members are unable to attend therapy sessions, or where family members have a substance-abuse problem that they are unwilling to modify. In addition, Patterson and Forgatch (1985) have reported a lack of effectiveness of educative parent-training procedures in the treatment of severe conduct disorders in children. They have suggested that the reason for this lack of benefit is the fact that the conduct disorder is merely one expression of widespread family distress, including marital discord, serious parental psychopathology, and behavioral problems in siblings.

It is concluded that behavioral family therapy is most effective when it is employed in combination with other problem-oriented strategies and tailored in a highly specific manner to the strengths and weaknesses of each family unit. Further controlled research studies are needed to determine the relative indications for behavioral (and other) family therapies and the factors that predict a successful outcome. This research will enable therapists to apply these methods in the most efficient way. Without these data, family interventions are vulnerable to the vagaries of the marketplace, with their application depending more on successful promotion and swings of fashion than on the long-term benefits for and costs to the consumers and providers.

CASE ILLUSTRATION

Presenting Problem

James B., 9 years of age, was referred for treatment to a community-based mental health service by the educational psychologist. He had not attended school for three weeks after a period of intermittent absences. He lived at home with his mother, Susan; his father, Jack; and his older sister, Kate.

Assessment of Family Members Individually

Over the course of 10 days each household member was interviewed alone.

James was a healthy-looking, verbally expressive 8-year-old, who said he enjoyed school, but had experienced the onset of severe frontal headaches and dizziness during the spring term. He woke with these symptoms, which lessened as the day progressed. They became worse upon going to school and when his father and teacher shouted at him. He had difficulty concentrating at school. The headaches were made better by his resting quietly on the sofa and by his mother massaging his forehead. He could not identify any stress in his life prior to the onset of these symptoms.

He had previously enjoyed a full range of social activities with his friends and family, and was particularly interested in such sports as swimming and soccer. He had enjoyed visiting his friends' homes and having them play at his place. He was eager to return to an active life.

James' goals were to return to school and be able to concentrate on his lessons and to participate in sporting activities for two hours twice a week.

Susan B. was a 35-year-old homemaker. She appeared nervous and on edge during the interview. She said she had been surprised at James' illness and had taken him to the family physician on three occasions. All the tests had been normal. She noted that the headaches and dizziness were worse first thing in the morning. She said she had been very worried that he might be developing a brain tumor and had not been reassured when the doctor said there was nothing wrong. She became tearful and distressed when talking about this and said that her younger brother had died of meningitis at the age of 6. Further questioning revealed significant depressive symptoms, including feelings of guilt and worthlessness, poor appetite and sleep, and panic attacks. She attributed her depression to worry about her son's condition, although it was evident that her symptoms had preceded his disorder by several weeks. She said that she found her husband uncooperative and that it was difficult to discuss her problems with him, but she blamed herself for his behavior, stating that it was probably caused by her recent disinterest in sex.

She reported that she spent most of her days at home with her son and had limited contact with family or friends. She said that she had always preferred to keep to herself and felt most anxious in the company of others, especially outside her home. She tended to have more panic attacks in these situations and fewer when at home alone.

She had great difficulty in targeting goals for herself, finally agreeing to meet one friend or family member a week for one hour.

Jack B. was a 38-year-old store manager. He came late to the interview without apology. He said that he did not believe there was anything wrong with his son and that his wife should get him back to school immediately. He said that his wife had always been a worrier and that her current state did not seem any worse than usual. He agreed on a goal to converse with his wife for 10 minutes every evening.

Kate B. was a vivacious 14-year-old who reported no problems of her own. She expressed concern that James was taking after their mother. She spent much of her time visiting her two close girlfriends and said she could talk to their mothers much more easily than her own. She said that her father became fed up with her mother and at times he slapped her. On several occasions, she had tried to discuss these issues with her mother and father, without success. Her goals were to go on a school skiing trip and to complete a typing course.

Assessment of Family Functioning

Reports from family members suggested that the family had very limited problem-solving capacity. Indeed, it was very rare that both parents and children sat down together to discuss any issue. Family decisions were usually made by the father, without consultation, and the other family members did not usually carry out his orders unless threatened by him.

The therapist invited the family to attempt to resolve the issue of planning a family outing for the weekend (an activity in which Kate had expressed interest during her interview). During the discussion, mother and son said very little, while Kate made two suggestions before submitting to her father's domineering request to attend a soccer match. Effective communication and problem-solving skills were notably absent, with a high proportion of critical and coercive statements, particularly from Mr. B.

It was concluded that marital discord was probably a major factor in Mrs. B.'s depressive disorder and that she had developed an inappropriately dependent relationship with her son, James, to help her cope with this. The daughter, Kate, tended to avoid interaction with the family after finding that her efforts to mediate had proved unrewarding.

A provisional treatment plan was devised that involved (1) James' returning to school without delay, (2) communication and problem-solving training to enhance marital and family functioning, and (3) family-based management of Mrs. B.'s depressive disorder. The therapist agreed

to conduct 10 weekly family sessions of one hour each at the family's home.

Treatment

The initial phase of treatment involved solving the issue of James' return to school. The therapist led a problem-solving discussion at the family home to plan strategies for ensuring a successful reintegration into the school. It became evident that the mother's depression had made it difficult for her to get dressed in time to take James to school as she usually did. Kate agreed that she could take James on her way to her high school. The issue of how the mother could cope with being left all day on her own was then discussed. It was planned that she contact a close friend, who was a neighbor, discuss her current condition with her, and ask her if she would drop in for a cup of coffee and a chat each morning. The therapist noted that this plan far exceeded the goal Mrs. B. had targeted during her initial interview. He wondered whether she felt compelled to agree to this by the context of the family discussion. He did not detect any overt coercion or signs that Mrs. B. thought this new goal unrealistic, and he elected not to comment at this stage.

A week later, James had attended school once, but had felt so ill that he could not do any work, and he refused to return the next day. Mrs. B. had not contacted her neighbor. The therapist instructed James in a brief relaxation procedure. James found that this relieved his headache a little when he practiced it during the session. He was invited to employ this repeatedly when he felt a headache coming on. Further problem solving achieved a plan whereby James would go to school every day regardless of how he felt before, during, or after school. He would inform his teachers if he was unable to function in the classroom and would be able to receive medication in the school sick bay. Prior discussion between the therapist and the school authorities had established the feasibility of this plan.

The mother reported wanting to talk to her neighbor but could not find the courage to do this. She role-played having the planned conversation with her neighbor twice, with Kate taking the neighbor's part. She agreed to go to her neighbor immediately after the treatment session.

The following week, James had returned to school for three days. It was evident that neither he nor his sister received any praise for their efforts. Rather, Mr. B. had criticized both of his children for their failure to attend school on the previous Wednesday and Friday. The therapist explained that positive reinforcement in the form of praise is a very potent motivator and demonstrated how he might have responded on those occasions when James had succeeded in returning to school. He prompted Mr. B. to express his pleasure that James had gone to school for three days.

Mrs. B. had contacted her neighbor, Sandra, and was surprised to learn that Sandra had experienced a similar depression after the birth of her youngest child three years earlier. Sandra readily agreed to visit on a daily basis and took Susan on a shopping trip one day. However, Susan's sleep had deteriorated and, on further inquiry, she admitted thinking of taking a bottle of aspirin one evening with the clear intention of killing herself. An appointment was made with a psychiatrist and a course of antidepressants prescribed. She was asked to keep a record of her sleep on a daily basis, and this was used to monitor the effectiveness of the drugs. All other drugs were removed from the home. Her husband agreed to discuss her feelings with her for a few minutes every evening. He was instructed in the methods of inquiring about symptoms of depressed mood and hopelessness used in mental-state examinations.

The next week (fourth session), the therapist devoted the session to educating the family about the nature and treatment of depression. With the aid of a handout, he described the characteristic features of depression, theories of its etiology, and the rationale for combined drug and psychosocial treatment. Both parents expressed considerable interest, asking many clarifying questions. Mr. B. indicated surprise that his wife's difficulties were considered an illness, albeit one that could be largely brought on by life stress. He expressed remorse for his bullying behavior toward her, saying that he had probably made her worse. The therapist pointed out that Mr. B. had been doing his best to cope with his wife's behavior and that he could not be blamed for a lack of knowledge about a complex

and confusing disorder. Mr. B. then began to adopt a much more supportive attitude toward his wife, although at times he became frustrated with her and shouted at her in a hostile manner.

The next four sessions (sessions 5–8) were devoted to enhancing the communication skills of the family members. They were encouraged to reinforce all Mrs. B.'s efforts to engage in constructive activities, all James' efforts to rehabilitate himself at school, Kate's assistance with her brother and mother, and Mr. B.'s supportive behavior. Each family member completed a daily record of his or her expressions of positive feelings to one another and reenacted several of these interactions at the beginning of each session. They were coached in the use of positive requests for behavior change rather than demands (i.e., "I would like you to help me clear the table," versus, "Come on, James, help me clear the table!"). The children had little difficulty in adopting these skills. Mr. and Mrs. B. found it very hard to focus on everyday examples of constructive behavior. Both failed to record their efforts at expressing positive feelings. Part of two sessions was devoted to solving their difficulties, with some improvement in their compliance.

During this time, James had reestablished daily attendance at school and his headaches were less frequent and less severe. He had begun to participate in some sporting activities with his friends, but continued to avoid more rigorous games. Mrs. B. expressed her appreciation for her husband's attentiveness and found that she was able to open up to him about her feelings a little more. He said he felt uncomfortable playing "the psychiatrist" with her, and when it was evident that she no longer contemplated suicide, he was instructed to change his evening discussions to a conversation about his wife's daily activities. Mrs. B.'s sleep and appetite improved gradually.

The therapist decided to deal with the deficits Mr. and Mrs. B. had in expressing negative feelings within the context of teaching them to employ structured problem-solving procedures themselves. Sessions 9 and 10 were devoted to coaching the family in the problem-solving approach that the therapist had already used to deal with the initial family crisis. Mr. B. was selected to chair the family discussions and Kate agreed to record notes on the problem-solving worksheets provided by the therapist. The chairperson's role was explained as one of ensuring that all family members attended a weekly family meeting outside the therapy sessions, and that they stuck to the task of discussing one issue of concern in a systematic manner. The structure of this task tends to promote collaborative family interaction.

A review of progress after 10 sessions revealed that the goals of Mr. and Mrs. B. and James had been achieved, but that Kate had made little progress with her goals to go on a school trip and complete a typing course. She had postponed both events because she felt they would detract from her efforts to help at home. Her parents expressed their dismay that she had sacrificed her own goals to help them, but stated how much they had appreciated her help. The father offered to pay for a skiing trip the next year. She was encouraged to apply for a typing course during the next semester.

Mrs. B.'s depression was substantially improved, although she remained anxious in social situations and had occasional panic attacks. James continued to suffer headaches at times of stress, but was fully reintegrated into school and with his friends.

Although Mr. B. had made substantial progress in improving the marital relationship, some problems remained. Five further biweekly sessions were contracted to address these issues and to help Mrs. B.'s continued anxiety symptoms. Further assessment revealed that sexual contact between the couple had not been resumed, and that both partners were afraid to express any anger toward each other.

The therapist invited the couple to conduct its own problem-solving about the issue of re-establishing physical intimacy. This discussion led to an argument without any resolution plans. The main difficulty appeared to be Mr. B.'s demands that his wife engage in sexual intercourse at his request and her apprehension that this would often lead to her rejecting him. The therapist assisted them in solving this issue. This led to a plan whereby on one evening a week they would ensure that the children were in bed early. Mrs. B. would choose a mutually enjoyable activity, such as watching a videotaped movie, having a take-out meal, or playing cards. During this time, both partners would exchange expressions of positive feelings toward each other and avoid discussions of problems. They agreed to go to bed before 10:30 after showering. They would massage and caress each other without genital contact (the sensate focusing strategy of Masters and Johnson), and would proceed to intercourse only if Mrs. B. requested this. On other evenings, no discussion about sexual matters was permitted. Mr. B. expressed his skepticism about this plan, which was enthusiastically endorsed by his wife.

During the first two weeks, the plan was partially successful. A lengthy phone call from Mrs. B.'s sister interrupted the videotape they were watching and Mr. B. initiated intercourse before his wife requested it. However, both agreed that it had worked quite well. In subsequent weeks, various hitches in the plan occurred, but both partners expressed satisfaction that their sexual functioning was improving. Mr. B. requested that the frequency of sex be increased to two to three times a week. He agreed with his wife that it was more enjoyable when conducted in the relaxed manner they had now adopted and she consented to more frequent sexual intercourse, provided it was preceded by a "love-in"—the term they used to describe their presexual intimacy.

Two sessions were devoted to training Mr. and Mrs. B. in anxiety-management strategies to help Mrs. B. cope with her social anxiety and panic attacks. They were instructed to organize outings that provided exposure to the situation Mrs. B. feared most—eating in restaurants, attending sports functions, shopping in crowded shopping malls. Several strategies, including brief relaxation, respiratory control, and cognitive self-monitoring, were taught to Mrs. B. and Mr. B. was shown how to provide coaching and encouragement for his wife's efforts. Over the next four weeks, they engaged in seven exposure sessions during which Mrs. B. experienced four panic attacks. On each occasion, with the support of her husband, she managed to remain in the situation, cope with her severe anxiety, and experience its reduction from peak levels. Although she remained apprehensive in these situations, she gained confidence that she could cope with them and persuaded her husband to take her and the children to a restaurant on Mother's Day.

Two further sessions were conducted at monthly intervals at which progress was reviewed and behavioral strategies revised. Parents and children agreed that they had made substantial progress in overcoming their presenting problems and achieving their short-term goals. They said they appreciated the way in which the therapist had helped them to structure their problem-solving efforts and to tackle one problem after another. They continued to meet for family discussions after dinner each Monday. While these discussions did not always follow the six-step problem-solving guidelines, they did address specific issues in a systematic manner, keeping notes on their plans and reviewing progress. A follow-up phone call a year later revealed sustained improvement. Mrs. B. had suffered a recurrence of her depressive disorder with increased anxiety. However, with the assistance of her husband and children, she had been able to cope with this without undue distress and the disorder lasted little more than two weeks.

REFERENCES

Alexander, J.F. (1973). Defensive and supportive communications in normal and deviant families. *Journal of Consulting and Clinical Psychology, 40,* 223–231.

Alexander, J.F., Barton, C., Schiavo, R.S., & Parsons, B.V. (1976). Systems-behavior intervention with families of delinquents: Therapist characteristics, family behavior and outcome. *Journal of Consulting and Clinical Psychology, 44,* 656–664.

Arrington, A., Sullaway, M., & Christensen, A. (1988). Behavioral family assessment. In I.R.H. Falloon (Ed.), *Handbook of behavioral family therapy.* New York: Guilford Press.

Atkeson, B.M., & Forehand, R. (1978). Parent behavior training for problem children: An examination of studies using multiple outcome measures. *Journal of Abnormal Child Psychology, 6,* 449–460.

Azrin, N.H., Naster, B.J., & Jones, R. (1973). Reciprocity counselling: A rapid learning-based procedure for marital counselling. *Behavior Research and Therapy, 11,* 365–382.

Baker, B.L., & McCurry, M.C. (1984). School-based parent training: An alternative for parents predicted to demonstrate low teaching proficiency following group training. *Education and Training of the Mentally Retarded,* 261–267.

Bandura, A., & Walters, R. (1963). *Social learning and personality development.* New York: Holt, Rinehart & Winston.

Barton, C., & Alexander, J.F. (1981). Functional family therapy. In A.S. Gurman & D.P. Kniskern (Eds.), *Handbook of family therapy.* New York: Brunner/Mazel.

Bennum, I. (1985). Prediction and responsiveness in behavioral marital therapy. *Behavioural Psychotherapy, 13,* 186–201.

Bernal, M.E., Klinnert, M.D., & Schultz, L.A. (1980). Outcome evaluation of behavioral parent training and client-centered parent counselling for children with conduct problems. *Journal of Applied Behavioral Analysis, 13,* 677–691.

Birchler, G.R. (1988). Handling resistance to change in behavioral

marital therapy. In I.R.H. Falloon (Ed.), *Handbook of behavioral family therapy.* New York: Guilford Press.

Blechman, E.A., Rabin, C., & McEnroe, M.J. (1986). Family communication and problem solving with boardgames and computer games. In C.E. Schaeter & S.E. Reid (Eds.), *Game play.* New York: Wiley.

Boardman, W.K. (1962). Rusty: A brief behaviour disorder. *Journal of Consulting Psychology, 26,* 293–297.

Cahill, M.F. (1978). A search for the meaning of the "difficult" child. *Dissertation Abstracts International, 39,* 154.

Christensen, A. (1979). Naturalistic observation of families: A system for random audio recordings in the home. *Behavior Therapy, 10,* 418–422.

Christensen, A., Phillips, S., Glasgow, R.E., & Johnson, S.M. (1983). Parental characteristics and interactional dysfunction in families with child behavior problems: A preliminary investigation. *Journal of Abnormal Child Psychology, 11,* 153–166.

Cobb, J.P., McDonald, R., Marks, I.M., & Stern, R. (1980). Marital versus exposure therapy: Psychological treatments of co-existing marital and phobic-obsessive problems. *European Journal of Behavioural Analysis and Modification, 4,* 3–17.

Crowe, M. (1988). The indications for family, marital and sexual therapy. In I.R.H. Falloon (Ed.), *Handbook of behavioral family therapy.* New York: Guilford Press.

Curran, J.P., Faraone, S.V., & Graves, D.J. (1988). Behavioral family therapy in an acute inpatient setting. In I.R.H. Falloon (Ed.), *Handbook of behavioral family therapy.* New York: Guilford Press.

Dangel, R.F., & Polster, R.A. (Eds.) (1984). *Parent training: Foundations of research and practice.* New York: Guilford Press.

Doane, J.A., & Falloon, I.R.H. (1985). Assessing change in family interaction: Methodology and findings. In I.R.H. Falloon (Ed.), *Family management of schizophrenia.* Baltimore: Johns Hopkins University Press.

Doane, J.A., Falloon, I.R.H., Goldstein, M.J., & Mintz, J. (1985). Parental affective style and the treatment of schizophrenia. *Archives of General Psychiatry, 42,* 34–42.

Doane, J.A., Goldstein, M.J., Miklowitz, D.J., & Falloon, I.R.H. (1986). The impact of individual and family treatment on the affective climate of families of schizophrenics. *British Journal of Psychiatry, 148,* 279–287.

D'Zurilla, T.J., & Goldfried, M.R. (1971). Problem solving and behavior modification. *Journal of Abnormal Psychology, 78,* 107–126.

Falloon, I.R.H. (1975). The treatment of depression: A behavioural approach. *Psychotherapy and Psychosomatics, 25,* 69–75.

Falloon, I.R.H. (Ed.), (1985). *Family management of schizophrenia: A controlled study of clinical, social, family and economic benefits.* Baltimore: Johns Hopkins University Press.

Falloon, I.R.H. (1987). *Family care of schizophrenia: A training programme.* Proposal submitted to the Gatsby Trust, London.

Falloon, I.R.H., Boyd, J.L., & McGill, C.W. (Eds.) (1984a). *Family care of schizophrenia.* New York: Guilford Press.

Falloon, I.R.H., Boyd, J.L., & McGill, C.W. (Eds.) (1984b). Behavioral analysis and therapy: A framework for solving problems (Chap. 7). *Family care of schizophrenia.* New York: Guilford Press.

Falloon, I.R.H., Boyd, J.L., McGill, C.W., Razani, J., Moss, H.B., & Gilderman, A. (1982). Family management in the prevention of exacerbations of schizophrenia: A controlled study. *New England Journal of Medicine, 306,* 1437–1440.

Falloon, I.R.H., & Liberman, R.P. (1982). Behavioral family interventions in the management of chronic schizophrenia. In W.R. McFarlane & C.C. Beels (Eds.), *Family therapy in schizophrenia.* New York: Guilford Press.

Falloon, I.R.H., & Liberman, R.P. (1984). Interactions between drug and psychosocial therapy in schizophrenia. *Schizophrenia Bulletin, 9,* 543–554.

Falloon, I.R.H., Liberman, R.P., Lillie, F.J., & Vaughn, C.E.

(1981). Family therapy for relapsing schizophrenics and their families: A pilot study. *Family Process, 20,* 211–221.

Falloon, I.R.H., Wilkinson, G., Burgess, J.M., & McLees, S. (1987). Planning, development and evaluation of a community-based mental health service for adults. In D. Milne (Ed.), *Evaluative research in the adult mental health services.* London: Croom-Helm.

Fichter, M.M. (1977). An integrated hospital-community program for severe psychosomatic disease. Presented at the Fourth World Congress of Psychiatry, Honolulu, Hawaii.

Fichter, M.M., & Postpischil, F. (1988). Behavioral family therapy in alcoholism. In I.R.H. Falloon (Ed.), *Handbook of behavioral family therapy.* New York: Guilford Press.

Flanagan, S., Adams, H.E., & Forehand, R. (1979). A comparison of four instructional techniques for teaching parents to use time-out. *Behavior Therapy, 8,* 575–593.

Fleischman, M.J. (1981). A replication of Patterson's "Intervention for boys with conduct problems." *Journal of Consulting and Clinical Psychology, 49,* 342–351.

Follette, W.C., & Jacobson, N.S. (1988). Behavioral marital therapy in the treatment of depressive disorders. In I.R.H. Falloon (Ed.), *Handbook of behavioral family therapy.* New York: Guilford Press.

Forehand, R., & King, H.E. (1977). Non-compliant children: Effects of parent training on behavior and attitude change. *Behavior Modification, 1,* 93–108.

Foster, S.L., & Hoier, T.S. (1982). Behavioral and systems family therapies: A comparison of theoretical assumptions. *American Journal of Family Therapy, 10,* 13–23.

Foster, S.L., Prinz, R.J., & O'Leary, K.D. (1983). Impact of problem-solving communication training and generalization procedures on family conflict. *Child and Family Behavior Therapy, 5,* 1–23.

Foster, S.L., & Robin, A.L. (1987). Family conflict and communication in adolescence. In E.J. Marsh & L.G. Terdal (Eds.), *Behavioral assessment of childhood disorders* (2nd ed.). New York: Guilford Press.

Glahn, T.J., & Chock, P.N. (1984). Transitional teaching homes for developmentally disabled clients. In W.P. Christian, G.T. Hannah, & T.J. Glahn (Eds.), *Programming effective human services: Strategies for institutional change and client transition.* New York: Plenum Press.

Gottman, J.M. (1979). *Marital interaction: Experimental investigations.* New York: Academic Press.

Greenley, J.R. (1979). Family symptom tolerance and rehospitalization experiences of psychiatric patients. *Research in Community Mental Health, 1,* 357–386.

Griest, D.L., Forehand, R., Rogers, T., Briener, J., Furey, W., & Williams, C.A. (1982). Effects of parent enhancement therapy on the treatment outcome and generalization of a parent training program. *Behaviour, Research and Therapy, 20,* 429–436.

Griest, D.L., Forehand, R., Wells, K.C., & McMahon, R.J. (1980). An examination of differences between non-clinic and behavior-problem clinic-referred children and their mothers. *Journal of Abnormal Psychology, 89,* 497–500.

Griest, D.L., & Wells, K.C. (1983). Behavioral family therapy with conduct disorders in children. *Behavior Therapy, 14,* 37–53.

Hafner, R.J. (1988). Behavioral family interventions with anxiety disorder. In I.R.H. Falloon (Ed.), *Handbook of behavioral family therapy.* New York: Guilford Press.

Hahlweg, K., Baucom, D.H., & Markman, H. (1988). Recent advances in behavioral marital therapy and in preventing marital distress. In I.R.H. Falloon (Ed.), *Handbook of behavioral family therapy.* New York: Guilford Press.

Hand, I. (1988). Systemic-strategic behavior therapy for obsessive-compulsive patients and their families. In I.R.H. Falloon (Ed.), *Handbook of behavioral family therapy.* New York: Guilford Press.

Harris, S.L. (1983). *Families of the developmentally disabled: A guide to behavioral intervention.* New York: Pergamon Press.

Harris, S.L. (1986). Brief report: A 4- to 7-year questionnaire follow-up of participants in a training program for parents of autistic children. *Journal of Autism and Developmental Disorders, 16,* 377–383.

Harris, S.L., & Thorwarth-Bruey, C. (1988). Behavioral intervention for families of the developmentally disabled. In I.R.H. Falloon (Ed.), *Handbook of behavioral family therapy.* New York: Guilford Press.

Herbert, M., & Iwaniec, D. (1981). Behavioural psychotherapy in natural homesettings: An empirical study applied to conduct disordered and incontinent children. *Behavioural Psychotherapy, 9,* 55–76.

Hooley, J.M. (1985). *Criticism and depression.* Unpublished Ph.D. thesis, Oxford University.

Howlin, P.A. (1981). The results of a home-based language training programme with autistic children. *British Journal of Disorders of Communication, 16,* 73–88.

Hudson, B.L. (1978). Behavioral social work with schizophrenic patients in the community. *British Journal of Social Work, 8,* 159–170.

Jackson, D.D. (1965). Family rules. *Archives of General Psychiatry, 12,* 589–594.

Jacobson, N.S., Follette, W.C., & Elwood, R.W. (1984). Outcome research on behavioral marital therapy: A methodological and conceptual reappraisal. In K. Hahlweg & N.S. Jacobson (Eds.), *Marital interaction: Analysis and modification.* New York: Guilford Press.

Jacobson, N.S., & Margolin, G. (1979). *Marital therapy: Strategies based on social learning and behavior exchange principles.* New York: Brunner/Mazel.

Kanfer, F.H., & Saslow, G. (1965). Behavioral analysis: An alternative to diagnostic classification. *Archives of General Psychiatry, 12,* 529–538.

Karoly, P., & Rosenthal, M. (1977). Training parents in behavior modification: Effects on perceptions of family interaction and deviant child behavior. *Behavior Therapy, 8,* 406–410.

Kellam, S.G., Ensminger, M.E., & Turner, R.J. (1977). Family structure and the mental health of children. *Archives of General Psychiatry, 34,* 1012–1022.

Klein, N.C., Alexander, J.F., & Parsons, B.V. (1977). Impact of family systems intervention on recidivism and sibling delinquency: A model of primary prevention and program evaluation. *Journal of Consulting and Clinical Psychology, 45,* 469–474.

L'Abate, L. (1977). *Enrichment: Structured interventions with couples, families and groups.* Washington, DC: University Press of America.

Liberman, R.P. (1970). Behavioral approaches to family and couple therapy. *American Journal of Orthopsychiatry, 40,* 106–118.

Lovibond, S.H. (1963). The mechanism of conditioning treatment of enuresis. *Behavior, Research and Therapy, 1,* 17–21.

Lutzker, J.R., McGimsey, J.F., McRae, S., & Campbell, R.V. (1983). Behavioral parent training: There's so much to do. *Behavior Therapist, 6,* 110–112.

Mathews, A.M., Gelder, M.G., & Johnson, D.W. (1981). *Agoraphobia: Nature and treatment.* New York: Guilford Press.

McAuley, R.R. (1988). Behavioral parent training: Some thoughts about clinical application. In I.R.H. Falloon (Ed.), *Handbook of behavioral family therapy.* New York: Guilford Press.

McMahon, R.J., & Forehand, R. (1987). Conduct disorders. In E.J. Marsh & L.G. Terdal (Eds.), *Behavioral assessment of childhood disorders* (2nd ed.). New York: Guilford Press.

McMahon, R.J., Forehand, R., & Griest, D.L. (1981). Effects of knowledge of social learning principles on enhancing treatment outcome and generalization in a parent training program. *Journal of Consulting and Clinical Psychology, 49,* 526–532.

Minuchin, S. (1973). *Families and family therapy.* Cambridge, MA: Harvard University Press.

Monti, P.M., Abrams, D.B., Kadden, R., & Cooney, N. (1988). *Coping skills training in the treatment of alcohol abuse.* New York: Guilford Press.

Moreland, J.R., Schwebel, A.I., Beck, S., & Wells, R. (1982). Parents as therapists: A review of the behavior therapy parent training literature—1975 to 1981. *Behavior Modification, 6,* 250–275.

Morris, S.B., Alexander, J.F., & Waldron, H. (1988). Functional family therapy: Issues in clinical practice. In I.R.H. Falloon (Ed.), *Handbook of behavioral family therapy.* New York: Guilford Press.

Nay, W.R. (1975). A systematic comparison of instructional techniques for parents. *Behavior Therapy, 6,* 14–21.

O'Dell, S. (1974). Training parents in behavior modification: A review. *Psychological Bulletin, 81,* 418–433.7.

O'Dell, S.L., Krug, W.W., Patterson, J.N., & Faustman, W. (1980). An assessment of methods for training parents in the use of time-out. *Journal of Behavior Therapy and Experimental Psychiatry, 11,* 21–25.

Oltmanns, T.F., Broderick, J.E., & O'Leary, K.D. (1977). Marital adjustment and the efficacy of behavior therapy with children. *Journal of Consulting and Clinical Psychology, 45,* 724–729.

Patterson, G.R. (1971). *Families: Applications of social learning to family life.* Champaign, IL: Research Press.

Patterson, G.R. (1982). *Coercive family process: A social learning approach,* Vol. 3. Eugene, OR: Castalia.

Patterson, G.R. (1985). Beyond technology: The next stage in developing an empirical base for parent training. In L. L'Abate (Ed.), *Handbook of family psychology and therapy,* Vol. 2. Homewood, IL: Dorsey Press.

Patterson, G.R., & Brodsky, M. (1966). Behavior modification for a child with multiple problem behaviors. *Journal of Child Psychology and Psychiatry, 7,* 277–295.

Patterson, G.R., Chamberlain, P., & Reid, J.B. (1982). A comparative evaluation of a parent-training program. *Behavior Therapy, 13,* 638–650.

Patterson, G.R., Cobb, J.A., & Ray, R.S. (1972). A social engineering technology for retraining the families of aggressive boys. In H.E. Adams & I.P. Unikel (Eds.), *Issues and trends in behavior therapy.* Springfield, IL: C.C. Thomas.

Patterson, G.R., & Forgatch, M.S. (1985). Therapist behavior as a determinant for client non-compliance: A paradox for the behavior modifier. *Journal of Consulting and Clinical Psychology, 53,* 846–851.

Patterson, G.R., & Hops, H. (1972). Coercion, a game for two: Intervention techniques for marital conflict. In R.E. Ulrich & P. Mountjoy (Eds.), *The experimental analysis of social behavior.* New York: Appleton-Century-Crofts.

Patterson, G.R., McNeal, S., Hawkins, N., & Phelps, R. (1967). Reprogramming the social environment. *Journal of Child Psychology and Psychiatry, 8,* 181–195.

Patterson, G.R., & Reid, J.B. (1970). Reciprocity and coercion: Two facets of social systems. In C. Neuringer & J. Michael (Eds.), *Behavior modification in clinical psychology.* New York: Appleton-Century-Crofts.

Patterson, G.R., Reid, J.B., Jones, R.R., & Conger, R.E. (1975). *A social learning approach to family intervention. Volume 1: Families with aggressive children.* Eugene, OR: Castalia.

Prinz, R.J., Foster, S.L., Kent, R.M., & O'Leary, K.D. (1979). Multivariate assessment of conflict in distressed and non-distressed mother-adolescent dyads. *Journal of Applied Behavior Analysis, 12,* 691–700.

Prinz, R.J., & Kent, R.N. (1978). Recording parent-adolescent interactions without the use of frequency or interval-by-interval coding. *Behavior Therapy, 9,* 602–604.

Risley, T.R., & Wolf, M.M. (1967). Experimental manipulation of autistic behaviors and generalization into the home. In S.W. Bijou & D.M. Baer (Eds.), *Child development: Readings in experimental analysis.* New York: Appleton.

Robin, A.L. (1981). A controlled evaluation of problem-solving communication training with parent-adolescent conflict. *Behavior Therapy, 12,* 593–609.

Robin, A.L., & Foster, S.L. (1986). Problem-solving communication training: A behavioral family systems approach to parent-adolescent conflict. In P. Karoly & J.J. Stefferi (Eds.), *Adolescent behavior disorders.* Lexington, MA: Heath.

Robin, A.L., Kent, R., O'Leary, K.D., Foster, S.L., & Prinz, R.J. (1977). An approach to teaching parents and adolescents problem-solving communication skills: A preliminary report. *Behavior Therapy, 8,* 639–643.

Russell, C.F.M., Szmukker, C.I., Dare, C., Eisler, I. (1987). An evaluation of family therapy in anorexia nervosa and bulimia nervosa. *Archives of General Psychiatry, 44:* 1047–1056.

Rutter, M. (1987). Temperament, personality and personality disorder. *British Journal of Psychiatry, 150,* 443–458.

Sanders, M.R., & Glynn, T. (1981). Training parents in behavioral self-management: An analysis of generalization and maintenance. *Journal of Applied Behavior Analysis, 14,* 223–237.

Stuart, R.B. (1969). Operant-interpersonal treatment for marital discord. *Journal of Consulting and Clinical Psychology, 33,* 675–682.

Tarrier, N., Barrowclough, C., Vaughn, C.E., Bamrah, J., & Freeman, H.L. (1986). A controlled behavioural intervention to reduce schizophrenic relapse. Poster presentation at the Biennial Winter Workshop on Schizophrenia, Schladming, Austria.

Thibaut, J.W., & Kelley, H.H. (1959). *The social psychology of groups.* New York: Wiley.

Thomas, A., & Chess, S. (1977). *Temperament and development.* New York: Brunner/Mazel.

Truax, C.B., & Carkhuff, R.R. (1967). *Toward effective counseling and psychotherapy.* Chicago: Aldine.

Vaughn, C. (1977). Interaction characteristics in families of schizophrenic patients. In H. Katschnig (Ed.), *Die andere seite der schizophrenie.* Vienna: Urban & Schwarzenberg.

Vaughn, C.E., & Leff, J.P. (1976). The influence of family and social factors on the course of psychiatric illness: A comparison of schizophrenic and depressed neurotic patients. *British Journal of Psychiatry, 129,* 125–137.

Vaughn, C.E., & Leff, J.P. (1981). Patterns of emotional response in relatives of schizophrenic patients. *Schizophrenia Bulletin, 7,* 43–44.

Wahler, R.G., Hughes, J.B., & Gordon, J.S. (1981). Chronic patterns of mother-child coercion: Some differences between insular and non-insular families. *Analysis and Intervention in Developmental Disabilities, 1,* 145–156.

Wells, K.C., Griest, D.L., & Forehand, R. (1980). The use of a self-control package to enhance temporal generality of a parent training program. *Behaviour Research and Therapy, 18,* 345–358.

Williams, C.D. (1959). The elimination of tantrum behaviour by extinction procedures. *Journal of Abnormal and Social Psychology, 59,* 269.

Wolpe, J. (1958). *Psychotherapy by reciprocal inhibition.* Palo Alto, CA: Stanford University Press.

Zarit, S.H. (1988). Family interventions in senile dementia. In I.R.H. Falloon (Ed.), *Handbook of behavioral family therapy.* New York: Guilford Press.

Zarit, S.H., & Zarit, J.M. (1982). Families under stress: Interventions for caregivers of senile dementia patients. *Psychotherapy: Theory, Research and Practice, 19,* 461–471.

EDITORS' REFERENCE

de Shazer, S. (1985). *Keys to solution in brief therapy.* New York: W.W. Norton.

CHAPTER 4

Behavioral Marital Therapy

Amy Holtzworth-Munroe, Ph.D., and Neil S. Jacobson, Ph.D.

Behavioral marital therapy represents an amalgamation of many forces that have influenced the development of psychotherapy and behavior change procedures over the past 20 years. Its birth in the late 1960s represented a leap of faith, reflecting unbounded optimism that one could apply reinforcement principles to almost any clinical problem. In 1969, when Richard Stuart presented the first published data applying behavior therapy to marital problems, behavior therapy had survived its first full decade with a devoted band of enthusiastic adherents. A clearly detectable movement was under way to extend the applications to new domains of human misery and suffering.

The most obvious influence in the early development of behavioral marital therapy (BMT) was the operant conditioning approach used to modify the behavior of children (Patterson, 1974). As behavior modifiers began to train parents to modify the behavior of their children, they also collected data on the exchange of reinforcement and punishment among family members. Interest began to shift from the behavior of the individual deviant family member

(usually a child) to the interaction patterns of family members, including the marital dyad itself (Patterson & Hops, 1972; Patterson & Reid, 1970). Initial attempts to modify the behavior of distressed couples essentially transferred the operant principles used to modify children's behavior to the problems manifested by couples in distress.

This extrapolation from children to adults had certain limitations. In the treatment of children, parents had a great deal of control over the reinforcement contingencies. The therapist possessed no such control when treating married couples. Instead, the therapist had to induce couples to collaborate in producing an environment that was supportive of desirable relationship behavior. This required that the partners learn to negotiate with each other. Hence, the token-economy approach first suggested by Stuart (1969) was augmented by programs designed to teach couples communication and problem-solving skills (Patterson & Hops, 1972; Jacobson & Margolin, 1979). In a marital dyad, behavior exchanges are continuous, and the behavior of each member serves as both *antecedent* to and *consequence* of the behavior of the partner. As a result, any attempt to establish functional relationships between behavior and the environment by applying a unidirectional cause–effect model was unsatisfactory.[1] Thus, early investigators read and borrowed from theorists who had attempted to grapple with the complexities of understanding ongoing systems of two or more individuals (Thibaut & Kelley, 1959).

In this chapter, an attempt will be made to introduce the basic principles of BMT. In the initial section, a theoretical model of relationships and relationship distress will be presented. Then assessment techniques will be discussed. Later, we will detail the major elements of a behavioral approach to treating couples. Finally, a case will be presented that illustrates the approach.

Although this overview will not concentrate on research, documentation will be cited whenever it is available, and in some cases, important studies will be described. What distinguishes BMT from other approaches to treating couples is its commitment to empirical investigation as the optimal road to development. Despite its brief history, a substantial body of research has already been completed, helping to establish effective clinical procedures, firmer theoretical foundations, and assessment techniques of demonstrated utility.

SUCCESSFUL AND UNSUCCESSFUL MARITAL RELATIONSHIPS FROM A BEHAVIORAL PERSPECTIVE

A Behavioral Approach to Marital Therapy

What does it mean to say that an approach to treating couples is behavioral? First and foremost, behavioral approaches are contextual, much like the approaches to therapy that are derived from systems theory. The basic premise is that the behavior of both partners in a marital relationship is shaped, strengthened, weakened, and modified by environmental events, especially those events involving the other spouse. When we speak of events that cause one spouse to behave in a particular manner, we are typically referring to events that are external to that spouse. These causes include historical factors, the so-called learning history of that spouse, and events in the current environment that continuously influence the ongoing flow of transactions between the spouses. Since therapists cannot modify learning histories but can influence factors in the current environment of each spouse, the focus in therapy is on changing contingencies in the current environment. Thus, the focus is on the present, but the rationale for this focus is pragmatic rather than based on a devaluing of the importance of historical events in shaping adult behavior. We believe that all approaches to marital therapy, to the extent that they are successful, operate on current environmental contingencies regardless of the theory that dictates their course of intervention. The key to understanding these interventions is an analysis of how therapists are operating on the environment of the couples with whom they work. Even insight-oriented approaches actually effect change by altering contingencies of reinforcement.

Since each member of a marital relationship is subjected on a day-to-day basis to a variety of behaviors directed to him or her by the other partner, and since partner behaviors are often an extremely important part of what determines whether or not that person's life is satisfying, marital satisfaction and overall life satisfaction are highly related and often hard to separate. This dependence of each spouse on the partner's reinforcing and punishing properties dictates the terms of a *functional analysis* conducted by the behavioral marital therapist. The functional analysis of a marital relationship involves pinpointing the ways in which spouses simultaneously, mutually, and reciprocally act toward each other to affect their behavior toward each other and their degree of marital satisfaction.

The functional analysis constitutes the essence of a behavioral approach. As BMT moved away from an idiographic approach based on a func-

---

[1] *Editors' Note.* This point is so important that it deserves more than one reading. Behavioral marital therapy has frequently been described (and criticized) as being "too linear" in its views of marital interaction, almost always, in our view, because its critics have not grasped the inherently multidirectional, circular model of behavior maintenance and change that characterizes all social-learning theory. At a broader level, we believe that most marital and family therapists receive far too little exposure to learning theory applications to psychotherapy.

tional analysis and toward standardized techniques that were assumed to effect change across the entire population of distressed couples, the field lost touch with what is most essential to and valuable about a behavioral approach.

A truly behavioral approach to marital therapy does not become overly captivated by treatment technology. Techniques are never "behavioral" or "not behavioral." The important thing is whether or not the chosen intervention strategies attain goals dictated by the functional analysis. A paradoxical directive could be, in some instances, an ideal way to alter the contingencies of reinforcement and thereby create a context that supports new transactions between the spouses. Similarly, a session with each spouses's family of origin can at times be the best way to maximize the therapist's influence over a part of the environment that impinges powerfully on the couple's potential for a satisfying relationship. If other techniques are used more routinely, it is because they are viewed as more powerful ways to create an environment that will be supportive of desirable changes in the relationship.[2]

Cognition and BMT

Recent research on the role of cognition in marriage (Bradbury & Fincham, 1990; Baucom et al., 1989) has identified "cognition" and "affect" as important domains to which behavior therapists should pay attention. The idea has been promulgated that traditional behavioral approaches did not adequately take into account thoughts and feelings, and that the approach should be expanded to include methods for directly modifying dysfunctional cognitions and affective states. In fact, it is true that the early emphasis in BMT writings was on modifying observable behavior, with the belief (hope?) that behavior change would lead to desirable cognitive and affective changes. This belief was not based on any behavioral theory that we know of, and as clinicians discovered, there was no easily

predictable relationship between behavioral change and cognitive–affective change. However, those who use a behavioral approach to working with couples have no trouble including thoughts and feelings in its functional analysis. Viewed within a functional analytic framework, cognitive and affective phenomena can be primary or secondary targets of change, and to the extent that these phenomena are part of the problem, it would be foolish not to target them for change simply because they are not observable. Behaviorism (except for, perhaps, Watsonian behaviorism) has never excluded unobservables from its analyses. The idea that behaviorism means an exclusive focus on overt behavior is perhaps the single greatest misconception about behaviorism (Skinner, 1974). *There is no need to expand BMT to include a focus on cognition and affect. Behaviorism never excluded them in the first place.*

Thus, cognitive BMT (Baucom & Epstein, 1990) would be a redundant term were it not for the fact that much of the cognitive theory that has been proposed is, in fact, nonbehavioral. A behaviorist views thoughts and feelings as behaviors that are subject to the same types of influence as are observable behaviors. Thoughts and feelings are strengthened, weakened, modified, and shaped by events external to the organism in the same way that observable behaviors are. There are not three types of events that are of interest to clinicians— thoughts, feelings, and overt behaviors—but rather there are only behaviors, of which thoughts and feelings are two examples. The main distinguishing characteristic of thoughts and feelings is that they cannot be observed by anyone but the person experiencing them. Although thoughts and feelings can influence behavior in the same way that any two behaviors can influence each other, in the end they are a function of the same environmental contingencies that determine overt behaviors. Thus, whereas thoughts and feelings are viewed by behaviorists as behaviors that obey the same laws as other behaviors, cognitive behavioral marital therapists are dualistic in their view that cognitions are different types of phenomena and operate independently of the environment. Perhaps more important, the cognitive BMT view is that dysfunctional cognitions can, and often do, cause faulty marital interaction, whereas the

----

[2] *Editors' Note.* There are many ways to direct behavior. Thus, a therapist intervention that directs family behavior could be *directive* without being *behavioral*, two terms we think are often confused. An intervention is "behavioral" if it follows from a *functional analysis* of behavior.

behaviorist views all behaviors—cognitive, affective, and motoric—as ultimately dependent on the environment for their sustenance.

BMT and the Successful Marriage

Although early applications of learning theory to marriage paid little direct attention to describing the successful marriage, there have been a great many contributions to delineating the characteristics of distressed relationships (e.g., Gottman, 1979; Jacobson & Margolin, 1979; Patterson & Reid, 1970; Weiss, 1978). Most of the behavioral descriptions of healthy marriages are by extrapolation and inference from knowledge of distressed relationships. However, in recent years, investigators have begun to delineate the characteristics and determinants of successful marriages directly (Jacobson, Waldron, & Moore, 1980; Markman, 1981; Wills, Weiss, & Patterson, 1974).

In some respects, it is inconsistent with the principles of learning theory to define a successful marriage. This is so because it is believed that each partner brings into a relationship his or her own unique reinforcement history and his or her own goals for a long-term relationship. The model adopts a largely idiographic stance toward each couple's attempt to form and maintain a mutually satisfying relationship. Just as there are many routes to marital distress, similarly, there are many paths to marital satisfaction, and any general attempt to describe the successful marriage must take into account the wide divergence of standards and goals on which couples may base their union.

Every relationship is satisfying to the degree that the partners provide each other with benefits, and it is also true that the benefits must be great relative to the costs inherent in the relationship (Thibaut & Kelley, 1959). Costs are incurred whenever a couple attempts to sustain a long-term relationship, because there are certain reinforcers that are more easily attained by being alone. The costs of being in a particular relationship will vary directly with the benefits denied to a particular person as a result of entering into a state of relatedness. People whose reinforcers hinge primarily on the benefits that one can receive only from a relationship will experience the commitment to such a relationship as less costly than those who receive a substantial proportion of their daily reinforcement from activities that are incompatible with an intimate relationship.

Thus, any coupled individual has a minimum reward–cost ratio that determines the degree of satisfaction in a relationship. Thibaut and Kelley (1959) referred to this minimum standard as the *comparison level. A learning model posits that the rate of reinforcers received from the partner determines not only the degree of subjective satisfaction, but also the rate of rewards directed in return toward the partner.* This principle, that over time rewards given and received within a marital relationship are highly correlated, is termed *reciprocity,* and by now numerous investigations have supported the lawfulness of this phenomenon in couples (Gottman et al., 1976; Gottman, Markman, & Notarius, 1977; Gottman, 1979; Jacobson et al., 1980; Margolin & Wampold, 1981; Patterson & Reid, 1970; Wills et al., 1974). Thus, if we somehow had access to knowledge regarding the important reinforcers for a particular couple, we could predict with a substantial degree of accuracy how often one spouse would receive them on the basis of how often that partner provided them.

The analysis becomes further complicated by a need to evaluate the characteristics of the environment external to the partners' exchanges. This need follows from the observation that the persistence of a relationship depends to a large degree on the attractiveness of this environment, that is, the availability of comparable or superior reward–cost ratios if the person in question were not engaged in the current relationship.

Since both satisfaction with and persistence in a relationship depend on maintaining a high level of rewards relative to costs, success will depend on a couple's coping successfully with numerous obstacles to the maximization of this ratio. During the course of a relationship, couples are faced with factors that threaten either to deplete the current rate of rewarding exchange or to add to the incurred costs. Maintaining a high ratio is not much of a problem for couples during the early stages of a relationship, particularly given a large degree of initial attraction. Reinforcing value is at its peak, fueled by the novelty inherent in the exchanges and shared activities. Couples ensure during these periods that the contacts are as positive as possible. None of the costs inherent in a long-term commitment have been realized as yet. However, as the spouses spend more and more time together, interacting in a greater variety of situations, the costs begin to manifest themselves. For one thing, spouses experience each other in new roles, not all of which are inherently rewarding, as are the carefree activities characteristic of courtship. Moreover, as interdependence grows, the costs of being committed to someone become more prominent. Commitment entails that each spouse accommodate to the other. Inevitably, some of the indulgences of independence must be foregone.

It is only a matter of time before a couple is in conflict over some issue. A critical skill in maintaining a successful marriage is skill in conflict resolution (Jacobson & Margolin, 1979). Spouses who are not excessively alarmed or surprised by the occurrence of conflict will speak openly and directly to each other about conflict issues when the conflict occurs, and will establish this precedent early in their married life. When they do talk to each other about conflict, they will keep the issue in perspective and focus specifically on the behaviors that are of concern to them. They will attempt to understand the partner's point of view and listen carefully to what is being said. Spouses who respond less adaptively to the initial areas of conflict are bound to experience significant difficulties in maintaining a viable union.

One of the tragedies of the socialization process is that, while people are trained in numerous survival skills as a concomitant to becoming a mature adult, they receive little training in the skills necessary to sustain a viable relationship. One of the myths of our culture, so eloquently described by Lederer and Jackson (1968), is that relationship skills are unnecessary because love will conquer all. Couples in our society have been unprepared to handle conflict. Many experience it as a contradiction to the basis for their union. To acknowledge imperfections in the partner is viewed as being tantamount to a denial of love. Thus, many partners avoid discussing problems in their relationship, hoping that time will magically attenuate them. Other couples rightly choose to discuss their conflict areas, but do so in a way that simply adds to the discord. Such spouses attempt to coerce, threaten, intimidate, or humiliate their partners into behaving differently. Given their lack of preparedness and their stereotyped, idealized expectations, spouses feel cheated by a partner's undesirable behavior, and any precedent for constructive resolution of problems is drowned in a cacophony of accusation, blame, and fury.

But problem-solving or conflict-resolution skills account for only a part of the skills that couples need in order to be successful. Communication-skill level, however it is defined, differentiates between satisfied and dissatisfied couples more powerfully than any other class of relationship behavior (Jacobson et al., 1980). Communication skills also predict later marital satisfaction levels (Markman, 1981). Communication serves so many functions in a marriage that any attempt at delineation is bound to be too exclusive; writers of numerous theoretical persuasions have speculated on a number of these functions (Guerney, 1977; Haley, 1963; Jacobson & Margolin, 1979; Weiss, 1978). Similarly, the increased interest in sex therapy that followed the publication of Masters and Johnson's (1970) classic book has contributed to a recognition that sexual gratification and the continued growth and development of sexual interaction can be extremely important to long-term success in a marriage. Finally, there exists a variety of skills that couples must master in order to survive, although these skills seldom provide the basis for marital satisfaction; nor do couples marry in order to engage in these *instrumental behaviors* (cf. Weiss & Birchler, 1978). Nevertheless, many couples have failed to endure the consequences of inadequate financial management, household and domestic deficiencies, or conflicts over personal living habits.

Thus, the learning model places heavy emphasis on the skills necessary for enactment of relationship roles and functions. However, it is important to issue a caveat at this juncture. For many of these skill areas, it is likely that the more appropriate label would be "performance deficit" rather than "skill deficit." That is, the desirable transactions are not taking place, and it may be that, in many instances, the innate abilities are present despite the dysfunctional performance. We know, for example, that married partners can perform well as conflict resolvers when instructed to "act good" even if their uninstructed performance is in the dysfunctional range (e.g., Vincent, Freidman, Nugent, & Messerly, 1979); moreover, spouses in distressed marriages solve problems quite well when role-playing with strangers, thus suggesting that the abilities are present but the enactments are not occurring under the stimulus control of the partner's presence. The term "skill" may be a metaphor rather than a term to be taken literally. Moreover, it should be kept in mind that many skills are situation-specific. An overeater may have the self-control to resist fattening foods at home but not while traveling. Similarly, a spouse may know how to solve problems effectively but may not have been reinforced for enacting those "effective" behaviors in the presence of the spouse.

Whether these deficiencies are best conceptualized as skill or as performance deficits, it is obvious that one can combine exemplary skills to no avail if they do not have reinforcement value for one another.[3] People marry because of both the actual and perceived potential for the provision of benefits and rewards. During courtship, partners experience each other in a limited but often substantial number of situations, and each experiences the gratification obtained from the involvement. The commitment to cohabitation and/or marriage always involves both an appraisal of the adequacy of current outcomes and a forecast, albeit often implicit, regarding the continuance and expansion of such outcomes into new domains. Since it is considerably more difficult to maintain a high rate of rewards during the marriage than during courtship, successful marriages require more than an initially high rate of reciprocal reinforcement. *Successful couples adapt effectively to the requirements of day-to-day intimacy. In particular, they expand their reinforcement power by frequently acquiring new domains for positive exchange.* Spouses who depend on a limited quality and variety of reinforcers are bound to suffer the ill effects of satiation. As a result, over time their interaction becomes depleted of its prior reinforcement value. Successful couples cope with this inevitable reinforcement erosion by varying their shared activities, developing new common interests, expanding their sexual repertoires, and developing their communication to the point where the partners continue to interest each other.

To summarize, a number of factors have been identified that determine the long-term success of a marital relationship. All of them emphasize the capacity for adaptability, flexibility, and change. Spouses must be capable of evolving together and coping with the multitude of challenges and external forces that life imposes on them. These competencies can be learned. The model pays little attention to the learning history of either spouse prior to the initial meeting. However, the learning history plays a fundamental role in determining each partner's preferences for certain reinforcers and the standards each person presents as criteria for a satisfying relationship. It is also quite obvious that the success of a relationship requires a certain basic compatibility in reinforcement preferences and expectancies regarding marriage. *But, notwithstanding the partners' learning history, the development, maintenance, and enduring success of the relationship depend also on the characteristics of the partners' exchanges and the environmental forces to which they are subjected, and not just on preordained historically shaped personality characteristics.* Individual differences are important, to be sure, but what happens as a relationship evolves can be predicted to a large extent by the events that occur in the social environment produced by the partners' state of relatedness, and by the exogenous factors that sometimes facilitate and at other times impede their growth as a couple.

Reference has already been made to the role of the environment in shaping marital partners toward greater distance or increased intimacy. In addition to providing alternatives to the current relationship, the sociocultural milieu surrounding the couple can produce changes in the important reinforcers for one or both partners. These changes can be concordant or discordant,

---

[3] *Editors' Note.* Certainly, environmental contingencies (e.g., spousal nonreinforcement of desired behavior) may contribute to its low frequency. In our experience, such nonreinforcement does not usually follow from a lack of awareness of the need to reinforce desired behavior, but from anger about past (narcissistic) injuries. Moreover, spouses at times seem to "withold" their ability to problem solve, an ability that is often quite solid in *other* relationships (work colleagues, children, etc.). In these cases, the *internal* contingencies governing the "performance deficit" must be examined, whether in a functional analytic ("behavioral") way or in a psychodynamic manner.

so that either couples might continue to develop and evolve together or their experiences outside the home can create distance and conflict. One common contemporary example of the latter is the impact of the women's movement on marriage. The movement has changed the standards against which many women measure the adequacy of their marriage. Women have begun to demand egalitarian relationships, which involve changes in the division of labor with regard to both instrumental and noninstrumental tasks. Some marriages have not survived this escalation in demands. It is hardly surprising that partners change at different rates and in discordant directions. Given the omnipresent impact of the environment on behavior and the constant accommodation to social and cultural developments, it is testimony to couples' coping capacities that so many do remain together.

A Behavioral Analysis of Marital Distress

A behavioral model predicts that, despite heterogeneity in the antecedents of relationship distress, there are certain rather predictable, general distinctions between the exchanges of distressed and of nondistressed couples. Research in many laboratories has begun to test and confirm hypotheses regarding these differences. A brief summary of the distinctions follows.

First, whether the terms "reward" and "punishment" are defined by observers or by the spouses themselves, distressed couples engage in fewer rewarding exchanges and more punishing exchanges than do nondistressed couples. These differences are apparent both in their direct verbal communication (Birchler, Weiss, & Vincent, 1975; Gottman et al., 1976, 1977; Vincent, Weiss, & Birchler, 1975; Wills et al., 1974) and in the exchange of reinforcers other than verbal communication (Jacobson et al., 1980; Robinson & Price, 1980; Wills et al., 1974). Second, there is some evidence that the juxtaposition or patterning of exchanges may differ in distressed and nondistressed couples. Distressed spouses are more likely than nondistressed spouses to reciprocate the partner's use of punishment (cf. Gottman, 1979; Margolin & Wampold, 1981). It appears that many of these spouses are extremely sensitive to the partner's

use of punishment (Jacobson et al., 1980). Some authors have suggested that distressed couples are generally more reactive to immediate stimuli delivered by the partner, whether the impact of those stimuli is positive or negative (Jacobson & Margolin, 1979; Jacobson & Martin, 1976; Jacobson, Follette, & McDonald, 1982; Weiss, 1978). It has been suggested by Gottman and associates (Gottman et al., 1976) that nondistressed couples operate according to a "bank account" model of exchange, where rewards and punishments are deposited in a relationship account, and positive behavior is sustained without a need for quid pro quo exchanges. That is, the primary distinction between distressed and nondistressed marriages is the relatively high ratio of positive "deposits" to negative "withdrawals" found in nondistressed marriages. There is no immediate contingency linking these positive exchanges, and, in fact, it is the very absence of a contingent linkage in the context of frequent positive exchanges that characterizes nondistressed couples, according to this model.

Another way of describing this distinction between distressed and nondistressed couples is in terms of short-term versus long-term contingencies; that is, unhappy couples respond to immediate stimuli while satisfied couples are less likely to react to such stimuli alone and to respond instead to the reservoir of accumulated rewards. Currently, the evidence favors a qualification of this hypothesis. Although the tendency to respond to immediately preceding negative behavior is stronger in distressed couples, the distinction may not hold for positive behavior. Distressed couples are no more likely to reciprocate positive behavior than are nondistressed couples, and, in fact, may be even less likely to do so (Gottman et al., 1977; Jacobson et al., 1980, 1982). Perhaps, with regard to positive behavior, other factors counteract the tendency for distressed couples to be sensitive to immediate stimuli. For example, there is some evidence that distressed couples "selectively" notice and attend to negative behavior (Jacobson & Moore, 1981). To the extent that this is true, this selective attention may negate whatever tendency distressed couples might have to respond to positive behavior.

There is also some evidence that marital distress is associated with different topographical classes of rewards and punishments (Jacobson et al., 1980). Whereas direct communication seems to be salient for both types of couples, nondistressed couples provide reinforcement through positive communication. Positive communication, even when it does occur, does not appear to be as reinforcing to distressed couples. The reverse is true for negative communication. In distressed couples, the partners control each other's behavior through the presentation of negative communication and the withholding of positive communication. Such stimuli do not appear to be as compelling for nondistressed couples, when they do occur. Participation in shared activities provides an important reinforcing function for nondistressed couples, whereas such activities, even when they do take place, are not generally reinforcing for distressed couples. Overall, the results of preliminary research support the contention of behavior-exchange theory that unhappy couples tend to produce behavior change and compliance through aversive control tactics, that is, by strategically presenting punishment and withholding rewards.

Special mention should be made of the recent seminal contributions of John Gottman and his associates in their use of social psychophysiology to study affective processes in couples. Although, strictly speaking, the research is neither driven by a behavioral theory nor interpreted in the light of such a perspective, the work has implications for the theory and for behavioral interventions. Gottman and Levenson (Levenson & Gottman, 1983; Gottman & Levenson, 1985) have demonstrated that the linkage of spouses' physiological responding during marital interaction is correlated with concurrent levels of marital satisfaction. In addition, high autonomic arousal during conflict discussions was highly predictive of declines in marital satisfaction three years later. These and other findings have led Gottman (Gottman & Levenson, 1988) to produce an escape conditioning model to explain why distressed couples often tend to avoid conflict. Since husbands manifest strong sympathetic-nervous-system arousal during marital conflict, and the duration of this arousal is greater for men than for women, distressed husbands may wish to avoid the conflict that leads to this negative affect.

Finally, studies using longitudinal designs (e.g., Markman, 1981) have added to our understanding of marital distress. For example, Gottman and Krokoff (1989) provided evidence that conflict-resolution strategies that are good for couples in the short run might be bad for them in the long run, and vice versa. Specifically, "conflict engagement" is associated with marital distress in the short run but predicts improvements in marital satisfaction over time; in contrast, "withdrawal" from conflict is highly predictive of declines in marital satisfaction over time, although not related to it in the short run.

Marital Distress as an Outcome of Conflict Over Amount of Intimacy

Functional analyses can be molar as well as molecular. Response classes can unite topographically diverse behaviors around a theme of functional equivalence. As BMT began to shift its level of analysis from the molecular to the molar, certain themes began to emerge more prominently than others. In particular, conflicts over the optimal level of intimacy have emerged in our work as the most prominent interactional theme in distressed relationships (Christensen, 1988a, 1988b; Jacobson, 1989b). These conflicts take various forms, since there are multiple ways to seek closeness (e.g., asking for more feeling expression, canceling an independent activity, initiating affection) and various forms of distancing behavior (e.g., pursuing independent activities, refusing initiatives toward closeness). However, the dynamic that most impresses us is the one in which partners polarize one another via their efforts to pursue a given level of intimacy: this phenomenon has been well described from a variety of theoretical perspectives as the demand-withdrawal pattern, rejection–intrusion, or conflict over affiliation and independence (Jacobson & Margolin, 1979). Our analysis includes mention of this theme because it appears to unite what would otherwise be a diverse set of presenting complaints. It is, in our view, an important interactional dynamic in marriages that are not satisfying.

Gender Issues

Recent findings regarding gender differences in conflict engagement versus avoidance, satisfaction with traditional sex-linked roles, optimal level of intimacy, and expression of negative affect have compelled behavioral researchers to incorporate a gender-based perspective into behavioral theories (e.g., Markman & Kraft, 1989). As we have summarized elsewhere (Jacobson, 1983, 1989a, in press; Jacobson & Holtzworth-Munroe, 1986), a variety of gender differences have emerged from marital-interaction research: women tend to have many more complaints than do men regarding the quality of their current relationships; their complaints tend to take the form of requesting greater involvement and closeness from their husbands, whereas their husbands' complaints focus either on preserving the status quo, consolidating gender roles along traditional sex-linked lines, or creating greater separateness and autonomy for themselves; and women exhibit more negative affect and willingness to engage in conflict discussions than do their husbands. Altogether, these findings suggest a portrait of women as more inclined to seek therapy, less satisfied with the status quo of their relationships, inclined to show their dissatisfaction overtly, and pushing in particular for a closer, less traditional, more egalitarian relationship than currently exists. In contrast, husbands are generally disinclined to seek therapy, more satisfied with the status quo in their relationships, disinclined to engage in conflict with their wives, and oriented toward more traditional marriages, which, as we have argued elsewhere, perpetuate men's dominance and power (Jacobson, 1989b). Thus, any comprehensive behavioral account of marital distress must take these gender issues into account. Marital distress is thus related to the phenomenon of women seeking to move marriages in a less traditional, more egalitarian direction, while husbands either resist such movements or react against them by attempting to force movement in a direction that either consolidates or enhances traditional role structures.

Conclusion

The behavioral model of relationship success emphasizes the factors that are currently maintaining desirable and undesirable behavior, whether these factors involve the partner's behavior, the impact of the social environment, or person variables. Yet it is also a developmental model that attempts to link current conflict to antecedents in a couple's relationship history. In designing a marital therapy plan, this elucidation of antecedents is thought to greatly expand the ability of the therapist to aid his or her clients. The process of assessment attempts to uncover variables of both current and historical relevance.

BEHAVIORAL ASSESSMENT OF MARITAL DISCORD

In keeping with the emphasis in behavior therapy on the multidimensional assessment of verbal, physiological, and behavioral variables, the assessment of marital dysfunction includes a variety of procedures designed to evaluate both the strengths and the weaknesses of a relationship in terms of the partners' interactional behavior, the numerous and variegated ways that rewards and punishments are exchanged in the natural environment, and the spouses' subjective appraisals and feelings about the relationship. In addition, the social-learning model offers a set of hypotheses regarding the possible antecedent events and performance deficiencies that may be responsible for the current dysfunctional interaction. Thus, a number of performance areas are evaluated for their possible contributions to current distress: the ability of the spouses to discuss relationship problems; their current reinforcement value for one another; their skill in pinpointing the relevant reinforcers in their relationship; their general competencies in the areas of communication, sex, child rearing, and financial management; their strategies for utilizing their leisure time in an effective and personally satisfying manner; the distribution of roles and decision-making responsibilities; and prominent interactional themes. Behavioral assessment is characterized by a number of features that distinguish it from other approaches to assessment.

First, behavioral assessment is primarily concerned with identifying the current behavioral excesses and deficits that have produced the current dissatisfaction in the relationship and the variables that are responsible for their occurrence. These goals are based on the conviction that the common denominator in all distressed relationships is the relative absence of rewarding behaviors and/or the plethora of punishing behaviors. Whatever the basis for the current level of behavior exchange, the ultimate goal of therapy is to provide for behavior changes that will subsequently increase the satisfaction level in both partners. This requires a careful delineation of all problem areas and their controlling influences. Of course, often the target areas include cognitive and affective variables as well as observable interactional behavior.

Second, and following logically from the previous point, a behavioral assessment aspires toward the direct measurement of behavior in lieu of a focus on personality dynamics and the labeling of clients according to hypothesized underlying constructs. A behavioral analysis emphasizes description and the elucidation of functional relationships between behavior and its environmental covariates.

Third, the treatment plan that is ultimately adopted is directly related to the results of the initial assessment.

Fourth, behavioral assessment is continuous, taking place throughout treatment rather than simply terminating at the conclusion of the pretreatment phase. After a treatment plan has been formulated, the continued assessment provides both therapist and client with feedback regarding the progress toward early detection and modification of ineffective treatment plans.

With this background providing a unifying perspective, let us now examine the various strategies for collecting treatment-relevant information.

Interview

Jacobson and Margolin (1979) pointed out that much of the information required in order to understand the problems of a particular couple is more efficiently obtained through either written questionnaires or the direct observation of the couple's interaction than through a clinical interview per se. However, there are certain types of information that are not easily obtainable from other sources and are accessible through the interview format. For example, a developmental history of the relationship, which is important in determining the historical antecedents of the current distress, is best obtained through the interview. In addition, the interview is often a useful device for ascertaining details regarding behavioral sequences characterizing the relationship, along with the antecedents and consequences of those sequences. Finally, the initial interview serves important therapeutic as well as assessment functions (Jacobson & Margolin, 1979).

Self-Report Measures

We often employ three different types of assessment questionnaires: inventories yielding a global rating of marital satisfaction (Spanier, 1976); the Areas-of-Changes Questionnaire (A-C) (Weiss, Hops, & Patterson, 1973), which asks couples to indicate which of 34 partner behaviors they would like to see changed, as well as how much change is desired and the direction of the change (more–less); and the Marital Satisfaction Inventory (MSI; Snyder, 1979), a sort of MMPI for couples, which produces ratings of marital functioning on a variety of dimensions.

The Dyadic Adjustment Scale (DAS) (Spanier, 1976) provides a well-validated index of marital satisfaction, but is of limited value in a behavioral analysis because it does not yield specific information regarding the problem areas in the relationship. However, it does provide a reliable measure of global subjective satisfaction.

The A-C correlates highly with the DAS and is significantly more useful in pinpointing the behaviors that trouble each spouse. The MSI provides much more detailed information on perceived marital functioning and helps pinpoint strong and weak areas in the marriage.

Spouse Observation

Weiss and Patterson and their associates developed an instrument to aid couples in their collection of observational data in the home. The Spouse Observation Checklist (SOC; Weiss et al., 1973) consists of about 400 spouse behaviors grouped into 12 topographical categories: companionship, affection, consideration, communication, sex, coupling, child care, household responsibilities, financial management, work (school) activities, personal habits, self- and spouse independence. The task is for couples to check each behavior that occurs during a given 24-hour period. The instructions can be varied so that spouses are instructed either to record all behaviors that arise or to limit their recordings to those behaviors that have "pleasing" or "displeasing" effects on them. In addition, each spouse is instructed to give the relationship a daily rating on a scale of 1 to 9, based on overall satisfaction.

The SOC can serve a variety of assessment functions. First, it provides the therapist with daily frequencies of relevant behavior. Second, by correlating behavioral frequencies with daily satisfaction, it is possible to uncover the behaviors that seem to be most important to the satisfaction of each spouse. The SOC also provides a way to monitor the ongoing progress of therapy, since, by continuing the daily recordings during the treatment period, the therapist can observe relevant changes in areas targeted for intervention.

Direct Observation of Problem Solving and Communication

Since BMT places such a great emphasis on skills in conflict resolution and communication, direct observation of spouses' interactions is an important part of the assessment process. For the clinician, this observation is relatively informal, but nevertheless essential to the overall evaluation. For the clinical researcher, it means training observers to code spouses' interactional behavior reliably into relevant categories. The codes are then tallied to produce a profile of the couple's problem-solving ability, based on either the rate at which certain behaviors take place (reflections, verbal reinforcement, putdowns, etc.) or the sequence in which behaviors occur (e.g., the probability of the wife's complaining given that the husband has just complained). Whatever the resources of the assessor might be, the important point is that she or he aspires toward an unbiased, representative sample of the clients' interactional behavior.

Through the combined contributions of interviewing, self-report questionnaires, spouse observation, and observations of couple interaction, the relevant questions can be answered and a treatment plan formulated. By the time a pretreatment assessment has been completed, the therapist/assessor should have answered at least the following questions:

1. *Strengths and skills of the relationship*

What are the major strengths of this relationship? Specifically, what resources do these spouses have that explain their current level of commitment to the relationship?

What is each spouse's current capacity to reinforce the other?

What behaviors on the part of each spouse are highly valued by the other?

In what shared activities does the couple currently engage?

What common interests do they share?

What are the couple's competencies and skills in meeting the essential tasks of a relationship: problem solving, providing support and understanding, providing social reinforcement effectively, affording sexual satisfaction, child rearing and parenting, managing finances, taking care of household responsibilities, interacting with people outside the relationship?

2. *Presenting problems*

What are the major complaints, and how do these complaints translate into explicitly behavioral terms?

What behaviors occur too frequently or at inappropriate times from the standpoint of each spouse?

Under what conditions do these behaviors occur?

What are the reinforcers that are maintaining these behaviors?

What behaviors take place at less than the desired frequency or fail to take place at appropriate times from the standpoint of each spouse?

Under what conditions would each spouse like to see these behaviors take place?

What are the consequences of these behaviors currently, when they occur?

How did the current problems develop over time?

Is there a consensus on who makes important

decisions with regard to various areas of the relationship and what kinds of decisions are made collectively as opposed to unilaterally?

3. Sex and affection

Are the spouses physically attracted to each other?

Is either currently dissatisfied with the rate, quality, or diversity of their sex life together?

If sex is currently a problem, was there a time when it was mutually satisfying?

What are the sexual behaviors that seem to be associated with current dissatisfaction?

Are either or both partners dissatisfied with the amount or quality of nonsexual physical affection?

Are either or both partners currently engaged in an extramarital sexual relationship?

If so, is the uninvolved partner aware of the affair?

What is the couple's history regarding extramarital affairs?

4. Future prospects

Are the partners seeking therapy to improve their relationship, to separate, or to decide whether the relationship is worth working on?

What are each spouse's reasons for continuing the relationship despite current problems?

What steps has each spouse taken in the direction of divorce?

5. Assessment of social environment

What are each person's alternatives to the present relationship?

How attractive are these alternatives to each person?

Is the environment (parents, relatives, friends, work associates, children) supportive of either continuance or dissolution of the present relationship?

Are any of the children suffering from psychological problems of their own?

What would be the probable consequences of relationship dissolution for the children?

6. Individual functioning of each spouse

Does either spouse exhibit any severe emotional or behavioral problems?

Does either spouse present a psychiatric history of his or her own? Specify.

Have they been in therapy before, either alone or together? What kind of therapy? Outcome?

What is each spouse's past experience with intimate relationships?

How is the present relationship different?[4]

A vast amount of information is required in a thorough pretreatment assessment, considering that each of the above questions is, in reality, a summary question requiring a great deal of specific information. In our clinic, we typically devote three weeks to the pretreatment assessment. During this time, there are three therapist contacts: (1) initial conjoint interview focusing on a developmental history, (2) sessions at which one interviewer meets separately with each spouse, and (3) a session devoted solely to the assessment of communication and problem solving. Concurrently with this series of interviews, the clients are completing the SOC nightly at home. In addition, clients complete a variety of questionnaires regarding the relationship as well as questionnaires designed to assess their individual competencies and vulnerabilities.

At the conclusion of this pretreatment assessment period, the couple meets with the therapist(s) to receive treatment recommendations. During this meeting, the findings from the evaluation are summarized, and the therapist(s) either offer marital therapy along with a description of the treatment program or explain why marital therapy is contraindicated and suggest alternatives to the couple. It is left for the couple to decide, on the basis of the information received, whether or not to adhere to the therapist's recommendations. In most cases, adherence means committing oneself to a time-limited (about 20 weekly 60–90-minute sessions),[5] structured treatment program with specific goals designed to improve the relationship in accordance with the couple's verbally stated desires. To reiterate, assessment is not over once that commitment is made, but its scope changes as the subsequent assessment data serve primarily to

---

[4] *Editors' Note.* We think that this is an excellent assessment checklist for therapists of all persuasions, not just "behavioral."

[5] *Editors' Note.* To the list of several other myths about behavioral marital therapy that have been deflated in this chapter, the myth that BMT is either inherently or ideally "brief" may be added (see Budman & Gurman, 1988, for a detailed consideration of what constitutes "brief therapy").

provide feedback regarding progress and help the therapist to decide on modification of the treatment plan when such changes seem desirable. The treatment options provided by a social-learning perspective are described below.

GOAL SETTING:
THE ROUNDTABLE SESSION

Successful marital therapy is predicated on the spouses' willingness to work collaboratively to improve their relationship. Unfortunately, couples seldom enter therapy in a collaborative spirit. On the contrary, it is more typical for each spouse to expect the therapist to demand that the partner change without anticipating any mutuality in this change process. Thus, collaboration cannot be assumed, but must be fostered and shaped by the early contacts with the therapist. In addition the early sessions of therapy, beginning with the roundtable session, are dedicated to the creation of positive-outcome expectancies in both partners. It must be remembered that discord is usually at its peak when couples finally seek professional assistance; there is often a great deal of confusion, anxiety, and hopelessness connected with the request for help. To the extent that the therapist can produce an expectation on the part of each spouse that the treatment program can help the relationship, there will be some immediate therapeutic benefits in the amelioration of anxiety and hopelessness per se. Moreover, positive expectancies can help to lead to a positive outcome by enhancing the degree of behavioral commitment, that is, the willingness to respond appropriately to the therapist's directives and to persevere in the face of hard times during the course of therapy.

Even the just-described assessment phase of BMT is designed to create positive expectancies and build a collaborative set. In part, positive expectancies may be a serendipitous consequence of the thorough assessment procedures characterizing BMT. The therapist contributes by initially outlining the entire assessment process for the partners, explaining to them the rationale for each procedure. Clients benefit both from an informed understanding of why they are being asked to engage in various activities and from the imposition of an initial trial period between their initial contact with the therapist and the time when they must commit themselves to therapy. The former information alleviates much of the confusion and uncertainty regarding the content of therapy. The period of information gathering, devoid of any commitment to therapy, allows the couple time to become comfortable with the therapist; couples are seldom firmly committed to marital therapy when they first make contact, and when their tentativeness is supported, at least for the duration of the pretreatment assessment period, clients are less likely to experience the first few contacts as aversive.

The entire assessment period encourages spouses to identify and acknowledge the strengths of the relationship as well as the current problems. Since distressed couples tend to focus exclusively on their problems and often ignore positive elements in their relationship, the inducement to become reacquainted with both past and present benefits can serve to enhance spouses' commitment to the relationship and to foster collaboration during therapy.

The therapist's first direct attempt to build a collaborative set occurs at the roundtable session. By presenting an analysis of the relationship in learning terms, the therapist introduces a focus that implies reciprocal causality and mutual responsibility for the current problems. The description of their problems in a language that resists the attributing of blame to either partner, delivered as an objective and expert opinion, can enlarge each spouse's perspective and lead to a consideration of other views, facilitating the acceptance of mutual responsibility for maintaining the current distressed state. Although each spouse may enter therapy with an investment in viewing himself or herself as an innocent victim of the other's oppression, and is therefore unlikely to yield to a verbal exhortation, no matter how convincing, from the therapist, the broader perspective offered by the therapist usually fosters an awareness of alternatives and constitutes the first step toward acceptance of mutual responsibility. To the extent that an improved relationship is highly valued by the couple, collaborative behavior in therapy will be proportional to each spouse's acceptance of responsibility for creating and maintaining the current level of discord.

The second major strategy for enhancing spouses' collaborative behavior involves obtaining their commitment to following the therapist's instructions and then instructing them to collaborate. Although this strategy may seem excessively glib, it is extremely effective. Once couples have signed a written therapy contract committing themselves to following the therapist's instructions, most will act accordingly. There are a wide variety of behaviors that follow from a collaborative set, all of which add to the probability of a positive outcome. Instead of awaiting the emergence of such a set, the therapist can request the appropriate behaviors regardless of cognitive set. If couples do engage in these behaviors, the relationship is likely to improve, and collaboration will follow from these initial positive changes.

Finally, and most important, treatment sessions are graded so that, in the early stages, the requirements are less demanding and require minimal collaboration. These strategies, described later, are of low risk and have a high probability of success. Initial improvements resulting from such strategies will usually enhance collaboration and thereby prepare spouses for the more demanding phases of therapy where success requires collaboration.

STRUCTURE OF THERAPY AND GENERAL STRATEGIES

Structure

Therapy sessions are generally highly structured. At the beginning of each session, the therapist and couple work together to set a session agenda. Next, the homework from the previous session is reviewed. Then most of the remaining session time is spent on "new business," for example, focusing on the acquisition or practice of a particular skill or working on one specific problem area. Usually, this new business follows from the work completed in the previous session and the previous homework assignment. Sessions usually end with a summary of the session events and the presentation of a new homework assignment. The structure helps to keep both the therapist and the clients focused on the goals

initially set, ensuring that progress is made during the brief course of therapy.

Most therapy sessions are conjoint; however, it is not uncommon for spouses to be seen individually at times, either because an individual problem that is not completely related to the marriage is being treated simultaneously (e.g., depression) or because a particular directive or set of directives might be viewed as more effective if delivered to one spouse without the other being present. Cotherapy is occasionally utilized, especially for training purposes. However, we note the lack of evidence supporting the efficacy of cotherapy relative to one therapist, and at least one study demonstrates no differences between the two formats (Baucom & Mehlman, 1984). In light of the greater cost-effectiveness of having only one therapist, we would recommend cotherapy only under unusual circumstances, which are beyond the scope of this chapter.

In our clinical research setting, where standardized treatment packages are required, marital therapy consists of approximately 20 weekly sessions, each 60–90 minutes long. Near the end of therapy, sessions are faded, occurring less frequently, to foster the generalization and maintenance of gains acquired during therapy.

Recognizing that this structured version of BMT may be less than optimal for someone working in a clinical setting, we recently conducted a study comparing a structured, standardized version of our treatment package with a flexible condition in which the therapist could determine which components and interventions from our model would be utilized and how long couples would attend therapy. Therapists tended to keep couples in therapy longer in the flexible treatment. Interestingly, the results indicated that there were no differences in outcome for couples receiving the standard- versus the flexible-treatment package. However, at a six-month follow-up, it appeared that couples treated flexibly were less inclined to relapse and more inclined to show maintenance of treatment gains than were couples given the research-based treatment (Jacobson et al., 1989a). These results support our clinical intuitions. On the one hand, idiographic analyses consistent with a functional analytic framework are likely to maximize long-term outcome, and effective marital therapists must maintain technical flexibility.

On the other hand, there are certain types of problems that emerge so routinely that a standard technology will be broadly applicable. Here are some of its elements.

Instigating Positive Behavior Change

Given the empirically demonstrated differences between distressed and nondistressed couples in behavioral exchanges of reinforcers and punishers, therapists often begin therapy with an emphasis on the generation of positive changes in the couple's natural environment. The focus is initially on increasing positive behaviors, for several reasons. First, such assignments may be easier for couples to carry out as opposed to immediately working on major relationship problems. Second, this examination of, and increase in, positive actions helps to reverse the tendency of distressed spouses to track relationship events negatively. In addition, evidence suggests that as positive relationship behaviors increase in frequency, negative behaviors may decrease, without an explicit focus on these punishments. Third, behavior-exchange strategies provide couples with ways of overcoming the pernicious effects of reinforcement erosion.

Thus, the initial behavioral-exchange interventions are designed to have a short-term, but immediate, positive effect on the relationship. The resulting improvements in the relationship help to provide couples with encouragement and to foster the belief that change is possible. Such results increase the therapist's and the model's credibility, leading to increases in the spouses' willingness to collaborate with each other.

The behavioral-exchange interventions involve directives from the therapist for assignments to be implemented at home. During subsequent sessions, the homework assignments are debriefed. If the assignment went well, therapy may progress to the next assignment. However, if problems were encountered, troubleshooting may be necessary to examine the difficulties that prevented the couple from completing the assignment.

Communication and Problem-Solving Training

In the typical case, a great deal of therapy time is devoted to the acquisition of communication and problem-solving skills. In addition, we routinely include a focus on improving the quality of sexual and affectional interaction. Other skills (e.g., parenting or budgeting skills) may be taught, based on the needs of the individual couple. During these sessions, a didactic and psychoeducational orientation is frequently utilized. The therapist will present a skill and model its use, help the couple to acquire the skill by coaching and providing feedback, and ask the couple to practice the skill both during the session and at home.

Generalization and Maintenance

Throughout therapy, the therapist is aware of helping couples to generalize newly acquired skills to the home environment and explicitly fosters generalization through homework assignments. In addition, near the end of therapy, it is important to focus explicitly on generalization and maintenance, to ensure that the changes made in the relationship persist independently of the therapist. For example, the therapist decreases his or her involvement in therapy, fostering the couple's increasing responsibility for managing its affairs. Sessions are tapered, or faded, near the end of therapy, with the therapist meeting the couple less frequently, to observe how the spouses are managing problems on their own. Couples are encouraged to design and implement regular "home therapy sessions" during which they review their progress and solve any recent conflicts. During the final sessions, couples may be aided in anticipating future difficulties or stressors (e.g., the birth of the child, a spouse's returning to work) and may generate some ideas of how to handle such situations when they arise.

Attempts to help them generalize and maintain treatment gains have not been successful for all couples. A recent two-year follow-up of successfully treated couples found that about 30 percent of them had relapsed by that time. Perhaps such results should not have been surprising. After all, why should a short-term treatment program result in permanent changes in a relationship subjected to numerous influences other than therapy? Indeed, during interviews comparing couples that relapsed after therapy with those that maintained their treatment gains, it was discovered that the relapsers had experienced significantly more stressful life events during the period following therapy (Jacobson, Schmaling, & Holtzworth-Munroe, 1987). Since then, we have been experimenting with methods to enhance long-term-therapy outcomes. For example, maintenance sessions following formal termination, either at regular intervals or as needed by a couple when stressful life events occur, may help to pinpoint new problems and to reinforce previously learned skills, thus prolonging the positive effect of therapy (Jacobson, 1988).

THE ROLE OF THE THERAPIST

The successful therapist not only must deliver a technology, but, perhaps more important, must create a context in which this technology is likely to be successful. At each stage of therapy, the therapist must make a variety of clinical judgments and decisions, many of which cannot be anticipated in a textbook or at a seminar. Thus, while descriptions of this treatment approach may read like a "how-to" manual, a therapist's best technical efforts are likely to fail if not accompanied by various clinical skills.

Structuring Skills

BMT is time-limited and thus requires that a highly structured focus be maintained in order to utilize therapy time effectively. Therefore, the successful therapist must be active and directive. Agendas must be set, homework reviewed, and rules requiring collaboration enforced. Agenda setting is an important part of each therapy session. Therapists are reluctant to plan an agenda, believing that clients have the wisdom to begin the session by discussing issues of importance. However, in our experience, this often is not the case. Instead, clients may bring up material impulsively or refer to a recent event that is easily recalled but is of only peripheral importance. On the other hand, agendas are not imposed on clients but should be negotiated between the couple and the therapist. As such, they represent the therapist's attempt to implement a mutually agreed-upon treatment plan, by safeguarding discussion of the major issues in a couple's relationship.

In addition, the successful therapist realizes that when couples take control of the session and spouses' behavior deviates from the planned agenda, work on goals is not accomplished. Instead, destructive interactional patterns are usually perpetuated as the couple stops collaborating and begins fighting. The skillful therapist will interrupt couples who deviate from the agenda and rules. In addition, he or she will do so in a way that helps spouses to understand why they are being stopped and to regulate their own behavior in the future. Thus, when interrupting a client's destructive behavior, the therapist might ask, "Why am I stopping you?" This helps couples to develop an awareness of their rule violations.

The therapist must also structure the flow of therapy across sessions. Given the time-limited nature of therapy, the therapist must make sure that presenting problems are being addressed and initial goals and expectations are being met within the agreed-upon time frame of therapy. New problems may emerge over the course of therapy, requiring the renegotiation of treatment plans. However, given enough structure, these new goals may be incorporated into the existing therapy contract. In order to facilitate across-session structuring, the therapist must frequently "take inventory." This process, which should be conducted at the beginning of every third or fourth session, involves a formal review of progress made toward each treatment goal initially set for therapy. Thus, the couple is helped to examine the initial problem list and to identify what has improved and what changes still need to be made.

Instigative Skills

Structuring skills are a means to an end. They provide an environment that allows work on relationship issues to take place. However, once this environment is established, it becomes necessary for the therapist to help couples instigate changes within their relationship and in the natural environment. Three subcategories of instigative skills are most central.

Inducing a Collaborative Set

This topic has already been discussed.

Instigating Compliance with Homework Assignments

Homework is a crucial part of BMT. Changes in the home environment are induced by between-session work, and new skills, acquired during sessions, are generalized beyond the therapy hour. While couples do not always comply with homework assignments, we do not assume that noncompliance represents resistance to treatment goals. More often, assignments are not completed because the clients misunderstood them, forgot about them, or underestimated the importance of completing a particular assignment.[6] At other times, the immediate consequences of changing one's behavior may be aversive, perhaps involving time, effort, and a willingness to take risks, while the benefits are less tangible and more oriented toward the long term. Therefore, our model assumes that noncompliance is usually preventable through skillful clinical interventions.

At the heart of successful compliance induction are *stimulus-control strategies*. These are attempts on the part of the therapist to prevent noncompliance rather than to deal with it after the fact. Most of these strategies are designed to enhance the salience of the homework for spouses. Therapists often communicate in subtle ways that the task is not important by presenting the assignment tentatively or apologetically. Salience is maximized by verbally explicating the rationale for the assignment; eliciting explicit commitments for compliance from both spouses;

anticipating and repudiating potential excuses for noncompliance; anticipating, and even exaggerating, the aversiveness of the task; providing clients with verbatim, written descriptions of the assignment to take home with them; and calling clients during the week to check on adherence.

When noncompliance does occur, response-control strategies should be utilized to decrease the probability of future noncompliance. These strategies are designed to convey the message that noncompliance is a serious problem that is not to be ignored or taken lightly. Therefore, when noncompliance has taken place, it is a mistake to go on with business as usual, since such a strategy implies to the couple that homework is peripheral to marital therapy. In fact, the opposite is true, and often therapy cannot progress, since the agenda of a session depends on information from the homework assigned during the previous session. Therefore, couples must be informed that the agenda for the session will be postponed until the homework is completed. The rest of the session is then focused on a discussion of the compliance problem and how it can be solved, or it is utilized to have the couple complete the assignment. No other work is undertaken while noncompliance is still an issue. Couples quickly learn that therapy cannot progress on schedule unless they complete their assignments.

Promoting Generalization and Maintenance

In BMT, the therapist is initially very active and directive, particularly in the early and middle stages of therapy, when new skills are being taught. However, over the course of therapy, couples must learn to function as their own therapists, in order to generalize and maintain their changes in the natural environment. Once skills have been acquired, the therapist's influence must gradually fade. The therapist must be able to watch couples grapple with problems on their own, rather than jumping in to give feedback or input. In addition, the therapist must convey to the partners that they have the ability to keep their marital satisfaction high, to solve problems, and to deal with discouragement as it arises.

---

[6] *Editors' Note.* Of course, misunderstanding, forgetting, and so on, can each be a form of resistance. We underscore the obvious in order to emphasize that "resistance" is not a nasty word or idea, even though many (not just behavioral) family therapists seem almost phobic about the concept. Indeed, "resistance," or, more accurately, resistant behavior, is usually readily subject to a functional analysis.

Teaching Skills

Given the focus BMT places on the acquisition of new behavioral repertoires, it is essential that the therapist be a skillful teacher. New ideas and skills must be clearly explained to clients and psychological jargon should be avoided. In addition, the therapist must often repeat himself or herself, since the ideas being presented to clients are new to them and may be difficult to grasp. Therapists who are shy when it comes to repetition forget that most clients are not mental health professionals and do not process information about psychological issues as quickly as do therapists.

While such skills may help clients to change their behaviors, additional work is needed to ensure that couples understand the principles of and rationales for what they are learning. Therapists who simply prompt interactional changes in the therapy sessions can generate impressive short-term changes, but when therapy is over, the couple will be bereft of the skills that the program is attempting to impart. When therapy is having the intended effect, couples should leave with principles applicable to any new problems that might arise.[7] Being a good marital-therapy teacher means frequently shifting from specific examples to general principles, and then back to specifics. It also means actively involving clients in the learning process. Instead of preaching or lecturing, the effective therapist has couples do most of the work. Ultimately, the goal is to foster a stance toward therapy that is active and engaged rather than passive and quiescent.

Providing Emotional Nurturance

BMT is so structured that inexperienced therapists are often inclined to cling to the structure excessively, hoping that it will provide the answers when therapy does not appear to be going well. However, while structure is necessary, so is flexibility. The treatment approach loses cred-

ibility if applied too rigidly, and it is most effective when adapted to an individual couple's unique problems and needs. Clients often view rigid therapists as "cold" or "insensitive" to their situation.

The emotionally nurturant therapist provides clients with ample opportunity to express the range of affective experiences that underlie their seeking of therapeutic assistance and their reactions to therapy. In fact, the therapist should actively probe for these reactions by occasionally taking each spouse's "affective temperature." During the course of therapy, the therapist should directly assess the level of clients' involvement and their reactions to therapy. Concerns, reservations, and equivocal reactions must be specifically elicited and addressed. The therapist must be aware of nonverbal cues: when verbal and nonverbal affective responses do not match, probing is in order.

BMT TECHNIQUES

Behavior-Exchange Procedures

In the most generic sense of the term, behavior exchange in marital therapy refers to any procedure that directly helps spouses gain an increased frequency of desired behaviors from each other. Although there are many procedural variations among strategies of behavior exchange, two basic steps are common to all of them. First, behaviors described as desirable by one or both spouses are pinpointed. Second, there is some attempt to increase the frequency of these behaviors. In short, behavior exchange is a structured way for spouses to increase the benefits that they provide for each other.

Behavior-exchange procedures capitalize on whatever potential for reinforcement exists in the relationship. In directly instructing couples systematically to increase the rate of beneficial exchange, the therapist can immediately enhance each spouse's satisfaction without a great many costs accruing to either. The apparently simple and straightforward act of increasing positive behaviors can be a powerful therapeutic intervention because distressed couples, by the time they enter therapy, are often greatly underutilizing their current repertoire of rein-

---

[7] *Editors' Note.* We believe that this is one of BMT's major metavalues, above and beyond its empiricism, its clinical technology, etc.—i.e., that BMT is empowering and, thereby, preventative.

forcers. In some instances, each spouse is withholding positive behaviors as a strategy for minimizing the costs of a relationship that has been overrun with conflict. A characteristic stalemate often presents itself, in which couples lack an equitable, systematic face-saving way of reversing the destructive cycle of diminishing rewards. The numerous strategies for inducing an increase in positive behaviors provide a face-saving way of utilizing the resources already existing in their repertoires. Since spouses often retain a great deal of reinforcement potential for each other despite the small number of positive exchanges, behavior-exchange procedures provide a less intensive, relatively nondemanding basis for immediate improvement in the relationship, and they set the stage for whatever intensive work is later necessary to overcome deficits in various relationship skills. The induction of positive exchanges is frequently accompanied by training in techniques for recognizing and effectively providing reinforcement at critical times. Just as parents involved in a behavior-therapy program are often taught to conduct a functional analysis of the factors that control their children's behavior, distressed spouses can become sensitized to the contingencies that govern both their partner's and their own emission of positive behavior. Many strategies designed to increase the frequency of positive behavior also help partners relearn how to maximize their mutual reinforcing impact.

Behavior exchanges are ideally suited for the early stages of therapy, since they are both non-demanding and likely to generate positive changes that can serve as a foundation upon which other changes can be erected. However, several factors need to be considered when formulating intervention strategies in the early stages. First, since couples are unlikely to have adopted a collaborative posture this early, the intervention strategies must not pressure either partner into concessions on fundamental areas of disagreement. The behavior changes should be discrete, easily delivered, and exchangeable without the need for either extensive negotiation or new skill development on the part of either spouse. Second, since one of the purposes of behavior-exchange procedures is to foster subsequent collaboration, the procedures during these early stages of therapy should not assume or depend on collaboration. The inducement of

positive exchanges despite the virtual absence of collaboration challenges the ingenuity of even the seasoned marital therapist. Third, ideally the emphasis is on increasing positive rather than decreasing negative behavior (Weiss, 1978; Weiss et al., 1974). Usually, high-frequency or high-intensity negative behaviors are major reasons for seeking therapy, and their elimination can only coincide with the intensive collaborative effort in the later stages of therapy. A reduction in negative behaviors at this stage would require aversive control tactics (punishment or negative reinforcement), tactics that should not be encouraged even temporarily for couples already replete with high rates of negative exchanges.

Taking the above point into consideration, an important distinction can be made between two sets of behavior-exchange strategies. One is characterized by one spouse's asking the other to increase the frequency, intensity, or duration of particular reinforcing behaviors. The other occurs when each partner decides how to please the other more effectively. The distinction is that, in this latter case, the decision as to which behaviors are increased resides with the giver rather than the receiver.

This strategy is exemplified by an early intervention described by Jacobson and Margolin (1979). During a three-to-four-week baseline period, each spouse has been tracking the daily frequency of numerous spouse behaviors, based on the SOC. Currently, each has been rating each day on a 1–7 scale for overall relationship satisfaction. By correlating behavioral frequencies with daily satisfaction ratings, it is possible to pinpoint those behaviors that seem to be the most important determinants of daily satisfaction, that is, the "reinforcers" in the relationship (Jacobson et al., 1980; Wills et al., 1974). In therapy, spouses are instructed to form hypotheses regarding which behaviors on their part are most reinforcing to the partner. Then each is given the assignment of testing the hypotheses by systematically increasing some of the behaviors identified and observing the effects on the partner's daily satisfaction rating. The goal is to increase that rating. Each spouse is to conduct the experiment privately, without consultation with the partner, except to scan the partner's checklist each evening to observe the effects of the experiment.

This intervention, if implemented skillfully, almost always leads to a "spike" in the frequency of positive behavior for both spouses. The assignment is presented to the couple as a challenge; each spouse wants to demonstrate his or her capability to "please" the other.

There are many ways to vary the basic task of focusing spouses on pinpointing and increasing their delivery of positive behavior. Weiss and his associates (Weiss & Birchler, 1978; Weiss et al., 1973) ask couples to set up special "love days," on which one spouse attempts to double his or her output of "pleasing" behaviors. Similarly, Stuart (1980) has couples alternate "caring days," during which one spouse devotes the day to demonstrating his or her caring for the other in as many ways as possible. These methods differ from the strategies described above only in their focus on specific days as those targeted for change.

In addition to positive changes initiated by the giver, many persons derive benefit from learning to ask for changes in behavior from the partner. Because spouses may be unaccustomed to asking for such changes, they may assume that they should not have to do so, and that the other should somehow intuit what is wanted and provide it forthwith. Yet the direct communication of each person's desires is an important skill in maintaining a satisfying relationship. Other spouses do ask for changes in their partners, but the requests are so global or nebulous that it is unclear as to what is being requested. Behavior exchange requires that spouses learn to request change *directly by pinpointing* the precise behaviors that they wish to see occurring more often; thus, "I want to feel closer to you" might become, "I want you to tell me what you're feeling." "I want you to be more aware of my needs," may translate into, "Ask me what is wrong when you see that I'm upset." At times, requests as sublime as, "Be more tuned into the relationship" refer to such mundane desires as, "Help me with the dishes after dinner." Not always, certainly, but often, negative feelings can be directly tied to rewards that are being withheld.

In therapy, spouses practice asking for those behaviors that they want more often from each other. If possible, the requests are simple and straightforward; it is up to the receiver to decide whether to grant them. If the request requires extensive negotiation, it probably touches on some central relationship issues and is better reserved for later stages of therapy.

Various exercises are available to structure these exchanges. Weiss and Birchler (1978) have suggested that couples conduct a "cost–benefit analysis," in which each spouse rates the amount of benefit that would be obtained by the delivery of particular behaviors and the giver rates the "costs" to himself or herself inherent in providing the particular behavior. Here, it is hoped that exchanges can be arranged that reflect a balance between benefits and costs. At other times, couples might prefer to focus on a particular area, such as parenting, and each spouse requests specific behaviors from the other to improve their interaction regarding child-rearing decisions. These procedures tend to work best when each has the opportunity to refuse requests that are too costly. The exercise involves a high level of demand for compromise and few spouses refuse all requests. By minimizing the costs, yet inducing some concessions and change agreements, collaboration is more easily maintained.

We have come to believe that behavior-exchange exercises work better, especially in the early stages of therapy, when tasks are structured in such a way that givers rather than receivers decide which behaviors to change, when directives are general rather than specific, and when givers have a wide variety of choices regarding which behaviors to change. First, givers are asked to select behaviors they think would enhance the partner's daily satisfaction; there is a much greater likelihood that these behaviors, once delivered, will be reinforcing to the recipient. Second, change directives that are general rather than specific maximize the likelihood that spouses will comply with them. With initial directives that focus on the givers' initiating change and maximize the givers' options for how to change, subsequent sessions can incorporate input from the recipients in a way that maximizes the change-inducing potential of behavior-exchange exercises.

In addition to producing increases in positive behavior, these instigative interventions teach couples valuable skills that can be readily incorporated into their lives after therapy ends. First, they learn to monitor the quality of the relationship on a regular basis. Second, they learn how and when to intervene in a way that enhances relationship quality. Third, they learn the importance of engaging in these activities on a regular basis. Couples often assume that the maintenance of marital satisfaction can be accomplished without regular attention paid to it. Behavior-exchange exercises teach them that attention and hard work are required to maintain a high-quality relationship. Fourth, behavior-exchange strategies are effective antidotes to the problem of reinforcement erosion.

Thus far, the discussion has focused exclusively on behavior changes by one spouse as desired by the other. But behavior exchanges may also reflect couple deficits rather than behavior deficits in one or both spouses (Jacobson & Margolin, 1979). Mutual agreements to increase the rate of shared activities, the planning of leisure-time activities, and the acquisition of new hobbies or common interests can be beneficial to many couples who are deficient in any of these areas.

In closing this section on behavior-exchange procedures, the issue of compliance with therapist directives must be addressed (see Jacobson & Margolin, 1979, for a detailed discussion of this issue). Couples tend to be much more compliant with homework assignments when the task is explicitly made synonymous with therapy than when the link between these tasks and their in-session use is unclear or unspecified. When the treatment sessions center around the tasks engaged in at home, and when an incomplete assignment robs the therapy session of its agenda, noncompliance is rare. Once the therapist has invested the homework with this much importance, a spouse who does not comply is tacitly admitting that she or he is not interested in therapy.[8] Few spouses are willing to be implicated or blamed for interfering with the progress of therapy. Thus, the skill and ingenuity of the therapist should be directed at consistently and persistently defining the therapy session itself as attaining its *raison d'être* from the completion of assignments. Successful BMT is instigative and its fundamental business is the instigation of change in the natural environment. The sessions themselves, especially when the emphasis is on behavior exchange, are largely brainstorming sessions that plan strategies for enhancing the relationship in the natural environment. The therapist who can produce an ambiance of this nature will produce compliance.

Communication and Problem-Solving Training

From its inception, BMT has emphasized direct training in communication skills. Behavior therapy is far from unique in this regard since an emphasis on communication training has characterized psychoanalytic (Ables & Brandsma, 1977), systems theory (Satir, 1967), and Rogerian approaches (Guerney, 1977) to marital and family therapy. However, behavioral communication training is unique in a number of respects. First, it utilizes a systematic method of training adapted from other skill-training paradigms in behavior therapy. Second, the communication training tends to be change oriented rather than expression oriented. That is, whereas most approaches to communication training focus on communication per se (i.e., the expression and reception of feelings), behavior therapy teaches couples how to communicate *in order to facilitate the resolution of conflicts*. This is not to say that training in feeling expression is not important to behavioral therapists; on the contrary, many prominent writers in the field regularly include modules to help partners communicate support and understanding to each other (e.g., Weiss, 1978; Weiss & Birchler, 1978). The point is that problem solving receives great emphasis in behavior therapy; couples are taught strategies for resolving conflicts with the hope that these skills will help them cope with future conflict. Third, the specific skills that are taught include behavior-change principles de-emphasized by other approaches to communication training, such as pinpointing, shaping, and providing for the effective use of social reinforcement.

Regardless of the content of the treatment program, behaviorists have relied on a systematic method of communication training based on the concept of reinforced practice. The training method can be divided into three basic com-

---

[8] *Editors' Note.* Again, we wish to note that surface behavior does not routinely imply a particular depth meaning; e.g., "disinterest" may not be the issue, whereas fear, anger, and the like may be at issue.

ponents: instructions, feedback, and behavioral rehearsal.

Instructions

Any skill-training program has a content, and the training involves an attempt to impart that content to the clients. Behavioral communication training is no exception. This content can be presented to the couple verbally or by modeling the desired behavior. By modeling, we refer to the role-playing demonstration of the desired behavior by the therapist. Modeling is widely used for a number of reasons: it is an efficient way to demonstrate complex interactional skills; it provides the spouses with a face-saving way to change their behavior; and by imitating an esteemed role model, it allows the therapist to demonstrate in a compelling manner the facilitative effects of the new skills. With the therapist assuming the role of one spouse and role-playing with that spouse's partner, the interaction sequence usually proceeds more desirably, and it becomes clear that there are benefits to be derived from the adoption of these new behaviors.

If modeling is used to impart communication skills, the therapist must guard against mere imitation by the spouses. For the new behaviors to be useful in new situations, couples must learn the general principle behind the new behavior. Various strategies can be utilized to ensure that spouses are not just mindlessly imitating, but also are actively processing information and learning the "rules." For example, discussion can be encouraged after the modeling demonstration, with the spouses asked to pinpoint those aspects of the modeled behavior responsible for the enhanced interaction sequence.

Behavior Rehearsal

The dictum "practice makes perfect" is directly applicable to behavioral communication training. The rehearsal of those new behaviors modeled by the therapist is thought to be an essential component of the treatment program. As couples rehearse the new behaviors, they gradually achieve mastery of the new skills. Al-

though the therapist may prompt these new behaviors and reinforce their occurrence, ultimately the spouses must actively demonstrate their ability to enact them. Behavior rehearsal provides feedback to the therapist regarding the spouses' competencies, indicating the extent to which they are assimilating the didactic material.

Feedback

This is the final step in the training sequence. Spouses' practice attempts are followed by feedback from the therapist. Both desirable and undesirable aspects of their performance are underscored. The feedback can be either molecular, focusing on specific "behavioral units," or molar, focusing on a sequence of behavioral units and the relationships among them. In contrast to the type of feedback that might occur in a nonbehavioral treatment context, behavioral feedback tends to be descriptive rather than interpretive and tends to focus on the functional, as opposed to the content, characteristics of behavior. Thus, the therapist will point out the behavior ("You just interrupted her") and emphasize its impact. Feedback can be provided either verbally or through the use of tapes. Videotaped or audiotaped feedback often appears to be more powerful than simple verbal feedback; this is both an asset and a liability. Spouses can benefit greatly from viewing themselves from the perspective of an observer, but the feedback can be devastating. Couples should be prepared for the impact of videotaped feedback, and the therapist must provide support so that the feedback can be used constructively.

Problem-Solving Training

The entire training sequence can be thought of as a shaping process. Usually, the therapist's instructions are imperfectly adopted at first. With continued feedback, which includes reinforcement for all increments in desired communication, performance should gradually be refined and perfected. It appears that this shaping process, which includes both practice and performance-based feedback, in addition to the instructional content of the program, is necessary in order for couples to acquire new complex communication skills (Jacobson & Anderson, 1980). Although communication training depends on the instigation of new behaviors in the natural environment through the use of homework assignments, instigation is only part of the story.

Herein lies the essential distinction between skill-training and behavior-exchange procedures. Whereas the latter are content oriented, focusing on behavior change and, hence, instigative almost by definition, skill training is fundamentally concerned with the process of interaction and only secondarily concerned with the content of the behaviors serving as the focal point of discussion. However, problem-solving training has the virtue of effectively producing behavior change despite the process orientation. The relationship problems that serve as the raw material for problem-solving training tend to be those that are not easily amenable to behavior-exchange procedures. Some of these problems require negotiation because the recipient of the complaint will not agree to the request for change; others are refractory to simple behavior exchange because a statement of the problem does not immediately suggest a behavioral solution.

Problem-solving training is a very promising approach to teaching couples how to negotiate the solutions to problems in their relationship. It is often necessary because distressed couples tend to exacerbate rather than resolve their conflicts by discussing them. Conflict resolution can be circumvented by a number of communicative tactics prevalent in the repertoires of distressed couples. A common obstacle is the absence of a clear definition. The problem can be stated in abstract terms (e.g., "You seem to always want to humiliate me")[9] or the definition may be so global and all-encompassing that it communicates no specific information to the partner ("Our relationship is the pits"). The problem

may be "heard" in a way discrepant with the intent of the presenter; this can result from the receiver's deficiencies either in receiving or in accurately interpreting communication from the partner. Since negotiations between dissatisfied partners are often viewed as battles to be won rather than mutual problems to be solved, there is a tendency for the receiver to be inattentive and to listen to only portions of the speaker's remarks. Complaints that actually refer to very specific issues become accentuated and interpreted as total attacks. Actions are interpreted as reflecting malevolent intentions. Before much time has transpired, the spouses have alluded to every problem in their relationship, and they have created an overwhelming task that terminates with an exacerbation of discord.

Another common pattern, not mutually exclusive of the above, consists of emphasizing insight rather than behavior change. Couples often assume that if they can successfully trace a conflict to its historical roots, the problem will magically disappear. If insight is to be pursued as a goal in and of itself, then it should not be treated as a substitute for behavior change, although discussions of the past may be interesting, enlightening, and even enjoyable.

The most appropriate label for what is lacking in a distressed couple's problem-solving efforts is collaboration. Typically, each partner defends a position, and an implicit scoring system seems to be tabulating points. In such competitive struggles, there is a winner and a loser, but no relationship change.

The key to counteracting these behaviors is the establishment of a collaborative set. Behaviorists have been criticized (Gurman & Knudson, 1978) for the practice of discouraging angry interchanges during problem-solving negotiations, implying that our goal is to remove passion from marital interaction. *On the contrary, the behavior therapist's goal is not to eliminate anger and its concomitants from marriage, but simply to help couples discriminate between arguing and problem solving.* As previous sections of this chapter have indicated, therapy is usually structured in such a way as to postpone problem-solving training until a collaborative set has been firmly established, usually by positive changes that have already occurred. Problem-solving training is sufficiently charged that the maintenance of a collaborative set is a struggle. The

---

[9] *Editors' Note.* But note that abstractions do not automatically preclude good, clear problem definition, e.g., there are some married people who do, in fact, want to humiliate (or punish, or worry, or embarrass, etc.) their spouses! What seems essential to us in pinpointing behavior is that the problem definition capture the phenomenological essence of the situation, which may or may not require "behavioral" (vs. "abstract") description.

therapist attempts to increase spouses' awareness of their own behavior in this regard. When they stray from collaborating during a therapy session, the response is often to send them to a different part of the room designated as the "fight corner." Thus, spatial manipulations are used to sharpen the distinction between collaboration and noncollaboration. Similar procedures are practiced by couples at home; they are encouraged to use different parts of the home for fighting and for problem solving.

Problem-solving training is highly structured and controlled by a series of guidelines, which are specified elsewhere (Jacobson & Margolin, 1979) and will be described below. The structure and the guidelines provide cues for the acquisition of new behavior. By initially constraining spouses' behavior within this structure, the therapist minimizes the likelihood that destructive pretherapy interaction will intrude upon the problem-solving process.

The Problem-Solving Session

The program teaches that a problem-solving session has two distinct phases: one for problem definition and one for problem solution. During the definition phase, the goal is to arrive at a clear, specific statement of the problem. Suggested solutions are not allowed during this phase. Then, once the couple agrees that the problem has been defined, the discussion enters a solution phase, during which the effort is directed toward resolution of the problem. The use of two distinct phases facilitates the separation of tasks, which, when intertwined, disrupt and confuse the problem-solving process. By devoting a brief period solely to the careful description of the problem, without a premature attempt at resolution, communication tends to be sharpened. When effort can be concentrated on arriving at a mutual understanding of what the problem is, a major impediment to effective problem resolution has been circumvented. Because descriptive information is vague and ambiguous, spouses often operate with discrepant assumptions about the nature of the problem.

In order to foster a solution-focused discussion of behavior-change options, the solution phase is guided by the directive not to return to definitional issues. The goal of the problem-solving

session is to arrive at a decision that will eliminate the problem and improve the relationship.

In our training programs we recommend a set of guidelines, which can be parceled into three sets: general guidelines for problem-solving etiquette, guidelines for defining problems, and guidelines for solving problems.

General Guidelines

First, *discuss only one problem at a time.* Couples are instructed to limit a given problem-solving discussion to a focus on one problem. Although all relationship problems may seem to be connected, the task is to discuss one issue. It is much easier to resolve one problem than to attempt to solve two simultaneously. Attempts to interrelate multiple concerns in a single session limit the possibility of reaching any agreements, so complex and incoherent has the task become.

Second, *paraphrase.* Each spouse is encouraged to begin his or her response to the other's remark by summarizing what the other has said. Then the speaker indicates whether or not the summary was accurate. If not, the statement is repeated. Although such a directive might appear somewhat mechanical, the summary statement serves a number of important functions in a problem-solving discussion. The directive ensures that each person carefully listens to the other's remarks and immediately protects the couple from protracted miscommunication. In addition, interruptions are far less likely to occur. Finally, the summary statement increases the chances of each partner's adopting the other person's perspective.

Third, *avoid making inferences about the other person's motivation, attitudes, or feelings.* Problem solving is often hindered by mind reading. A particularly pernicious form of mind reading involves the inference of malevolent intentions from undesirable behavior. The proper focus of problem solving is on upsetting or undesirable behavior, not on speculative, unverifiable excursions into the other's head. The latter interferes with a collaborative set, since the partner often feels obliged to defend his or her intentions rather than accommodate to the other's complaint.

Fourth, *avoid verbal abuse and other aversive*

exchanges. When collaboration is constrained by cathartic attempts at revenge, humiliation, and other forms of punishment, effective problem solving is precluded.

Guidelines for Defining Problems

First, *when stating a problem, always begin with something positive.* Usually, the positive beginning includes an expression of appreciation for some other positive behavior or, better yet, some mention of certain aspects of the problem under discussion that are already "pleasing" to the spouse who is stating the problem. For example, instead of restricting the opening remark to, "You don't help me clean up after dinner," one might say, "I appreciate the way you've been helping me around the house lately. Don't think I haven't noticed. My only remaining gripe is that you don't help me clean up after dinner." To reinforce the notion that problems describe unwanted behavior rather than bad people, the person whose behavior is being criticized should be reminded that he or she is being criticized for one aspect of his or her behavior, not for being a failure as a spouse. Distressed spouses are particularly guilty of selectively tracking those behaviors that displease them and ignoring or not reinforcing the pleasing behaviors that already occur. The opening positive remark increases the likelihood that the problem will be received in the spirit of collaboration.

Second, when defining problems, *be specific.* Problems should be defined in precise, behavioral terms. "You don't want to sleep with me anymore," is more aptly defined by a specific behavioral deficit, for example, "Most of the time I initiate sex." Problem definitions that are vague and not anchored in the person's overt behavior leave room for doubt as to the specific actions that are upsetting. *Pinpointing,* a skill that is also emphasized as part of the behavior-exchange intervention continues to be emphasized in problem-solving training. Vague problem formulations are frowned upon, not only because they hinder communication efficiency, but also because they tend to inhibit collaboration. Defining a problem by describing the partner in terms of derogatory adjectives (e.g., "lazy"), personality-trait labels (e.g., "neurotic"), and overgeneralizations (e.g., "You

never treat me with respect") tend to produce defensive behavior in the partner, whereas a circumscribed comment on one's behavior is usually easier to accept.

Third, in stating a problem, *feeling expressions* are encouraged. The spouse who is pinpointing a problem is taught to include in his or her description an indication of the experiential impact of the problem. Partners tend to be more sympathetic to complaints when the negative impact is made explicit.

Fourth, *both partners are to acknowledge their role in perpetuating the problem.* This guideline is designed to intercept the tendency to try to justify one's behavior instead of simply accepting the other's formulation as a reflection of "the way she or he sees it." Admitting to one's role implies that the receiver simply admits to the occurrence or lack thereof of the behavior in question. It does not imply an acceptance of responsibility for changing. Furthermore, most relationship problems include contributions by both members; by admitting to being "part of the problem," the complainer increases the likelihood that the transgressor will become "part of the solution." The receiver's reaction to the initial problem formulation has important implications for the remaining discussion. When partners are truly collaborating and adhering to the present guidelines, the problem-definition phase will remain uncontaminated by attempts to deny the validity of a complaint. The issue is irrelevant to a problem definition, since, when a behavior is upsetting to one spouse, it is, a priori, valid. This does not necessarily imply that by "accepting" the complainer's formulation the receiver is committed to behavior change. The solution phase determines the actions to be taken. What is important is the purity of the definitional exchange and the necessity of not challenging the legitimacy of any problem, as long as one person is upset by a deficit or excess in the other's behavior.

Fifth, *problem definitions should be brief.* Ideally, the formulation stage will be limited to two exchanges. The first involves a statement of the problem by one partner, followed by a paraphrase, and culminating in a mutual understanding of the nature of the problem. Then the definition is broadened by each person's acknowledgment that the problem is an interactional one. Spouses are then ready to move into the solution phase of problem solving. The brevity of the definition phase constitutes an attempt to avoid the "verbal masturbation" that often occurs in partners' fixation on unnecessary explorations of the past. Extensive elaborations of the problem, including attributions of blame and tracing the problem's implications or its historical origins, are not avoided in principle, but they are eschewed as problem-solving strategy. This practice is part of the general attempt to isolate change-oriented discussions and separate them from other types of discussions that tend not to produce change agreements.

"What Is To Be Done?": Guidelines for Reaching Agreement

First, *once couples have defined a problem, the remaining discussion should be solution focused.* To ensure a solution focus, spouses are taught to generate solutions through the *brainstorming* technique. Couples brainstorm by generating as many proposed solutions as possible, without regard to their quality. The idea is to be imaginative and not censor solutions because, when considered privately, they seem silly or unworkable. To emphasize the lack of concern with quality, the therapist models and prompts the inclusion of a quota of patently absurd, humorous proposals on the overall list. In addition to inducing a structure that facilitates the maintenance of a solution focus, brainstorming disinhibits couples from a tendency to withhold proposals. Brainstorming is particularly useful when the couple is "stuck" in the solution phase. It often liberates spouses and enhances their production of creative suggestions. By its inclusion of "funny" and "absurd" solutions, it also adds levity to the problem-solving endeavor. It is important that the partners not evaluate the solutions as they are being generated. Once the list is complete, the absurd suggestions are eliminated, and the advantages and disadvantages of each remaining proposal can be evaluated.

Second, *behavior change should be based on mutuality and compromise.* This guideline summarizes a number of behaviors that couples are taught, all designed to produce an equitable change agreement following from a collaborative set. For example, a systematic set of procedures is specified for helping couples to go through the list of brainstormed solutions, evaluate their pros and cons and benefits and costs, and then come to a decision in each case regarding whether or not a particular proposal is to be included as part of the final change agreement.

Third, *final agreements should be in writing, and they should be very specific.* Any agreed-upon behavior change needs to be described in terms of frequency, duration, and the conditions under which the new behaviors are to occur. The agreement should also provide for cues that remind spouses of the terms to which they have agreed.

Summary and Conclusions Regarding Problem-Solving Training

Problem-solving training has been, in our experience, a very powerful treatment strategy for a wide variety of distressed couples. Systematic research into the efficacy of BMT seems to support our intuition (Jacobson, 1979, 1984; Jacobson & Follette, 1985; Jacobson et al., 1987). Its power seems to stem from two primary sources. First, it focuses simultaneously on *process* and *content*. Couples solve presenting problems as they acquire problem-solving skills, and, at the same time, they acquire skills that lead to more reinforcing interaction and allow them to solve their own problems more effectively in the future.

Second, problem-solving training epitomizes the reinforcing power of collaboration. In the process of mastering the art of solving relationship problems, spouses learn that they will be much happier working together on their relationship than in dealing with their conflicts as adversaries. The key to successful training lies in inducing spouses to behave as a team so that the advantages of collaboration have an opportunity to present themselves. Every guideline is designed to circumvent the typical strategies that couples use when they approach conflict resolution as adversaries. Reluctance to adopt specific guidelines defines the refusal to collaborate; any spouse who knowingly adopts the former stance must accept responsibility for the latter.

The therapist should notice that the rules and

guidelines are interdependent, so that the adoption of one facilitates performance of another. For example, when spouses obey the directive to refrain from problem solving at the time some undesirable behavior occurs, the conflict often disappears. Couples report that if they postpone the discussion to the next scheduled problem-solving session, by the time the session takes place, the problem seems trivial. The conflicts created by unproductive verbal exchanges can be considerably more destructive than the persistence of the problem that served as the impetus for the discussion. Thus, deferring the discussion to a prearranged problem-solving session diffuses it and often eliminates the need for the discussion; at the very least, it transfers the discussion from a situation likely to produce a negative outcome to one where the potential for a favorable settlement is much greater.

Perhaps the most difficult response class to modify in a problem-solving session is the tendency of spouses to defend themselves and their transgressions. The most common instance is the accused spouse's attempt to deny the legitimacy of the other's complaint, deny responsibility for the action or inaction for which he or she is being called to task, or enumerate circumstances that rendered the behavior beyond his or her control. The guidelines for problem definitions attempt to circumvent this tactic by designating the function of this phase as one of simply pinpointing the target behavior. The legitimacy is assumed, since one partner is upset, and there is no need for evaluation. The spirit of collaboration obviates an evaluative focus. This does not mean that the receiver of a complaint agrees with the problem, nor does acceptance of a problem definition obligate one to change. The solution phase will determine what is to be done about the problem. The point is that the destructive debate centering around the justifiability of the proposed problem is deflected. This is likely to frustrate spouses, but they will have the opportunity to evaluate the problem during the solution phase, when they consider the pros and cons of various strategies for solving the problem. The advantage of deferring this type of discussion until the solution phase is that, by this time, if all the guidelines have been followed, the response of the receiver of the complaint is likely to be mellowed. She or he has not been attacked, the complaint has been con-

fined to a specific pinpointed set of behaviors, and the mutuality of problem solving has remained intact.

Another fringe benefit of problem-solving training is that it forces spouses to confront their real goal in discussing relationship problems. If they cannot, will not, or do not observe the guidelines, they are tacitly endorsing the combative, adversary type of interaction. Angry exchanges occur in all relationships, and perhaps they are functional, but they do not lead to behavior change.[10]

The important discrimination couples must master is the difference between fighting and problem solving. It is not incumbent upon them to stop fighting, but simply to separate fighting from problem solving. If spouses are fighting rather than problem solving, they should be taught to acknowledge what they are doing, relabel the session as an argument, and reschedule the problem-solving session.

Finally, problem-solving training follows smoothly from the less intensive focus on increasing positive behavior that occurs earlier in therapy. Often, our treatment program begins with general instructions to identify and increase pleasing behavior, followed by a more specific focus on exchanging specific behaviors, and concluding with problem solving to deal with major problems. Spouses' success in prior, less demanding stages fosters greater collaboration in subsequent phases. Occasionally, the major presenting problems can be resolved without problem-solving training. In these instances, therapy can terminate, or, given an ambitious couple, problem-solving skills can be taught for preventative purposes.

At its best, problem-solving training is preventative as well as ameliorative. But in order for it to serve a preventative function, the therapist must ensure that couples are actually learning skills that can be applied in the natural environment, independently of the therapist.

---

[10] *Editors' Note.* But also note that combative interaction (surface level) does not *ipso facto* define a relationship as negative; e.g., at a depth level, combativeness may convey much-valued passion. Moreover, angry exchanges sometimes do lead to behavior change, e.g., when an over-controlled, inhibited couple begins to break a shared unconscious rule that anger, criticism, etc., must be avoided at all costs.

Generalization must be sufficiently programmed so that spouses continue to enact their newly acquired behaviors outside the therapist's office. A number of tactics can facilitate the process of generalization. First, termination should be gradual rather than abrupt. Rather than suddenly moving from weekly sessions to a cessation of therapist contact, sessions should be *faded*. As partners move from weekly to biweekly and then to monthly sessions, they are presented with the opportunity gradually to reassume control over their own marriage. Second, the therapist should become less active and directive as therapy progresses. If the clients are actually acquiring new skills rather than simply responding to cues provided by the therapist, they should exhibit an increased ability to deal effectively with relationship problems, even in the absence of direct guidance from the therapist. Third, the content of the change agreements or solutions should come from the couple. Fourth, the training must be structured so as to ensure the spouses' active involvement in the learning process. For example, spouses can be asked to critique the therapist's simulated problem-solving behavior, with the therapist role-playing either positive or negative problem-solving behaviors. In a performance-based treatment program, the therapist must ensure that the spouses are capable of functioning on their own so that the maintenance of treatment-derived gains will be possible even after termination.

Modification of Molar Interaction Patterns and Themes

One of the newest and most exciting aspects of our clinical research program involves the use of relationship themes as a therapeutic vehicle. Although these relationship themes were always part of our case conceptualization, their identification and direct use as an intervention tool were attempted only recently. Across the multitude of content areas that serve as the stimuli for marital conflict, it is usually possible to identify one recurring theme that unites these diverse content areas. In fact, our guess is that there are only a few major themes that characterize all marital disputes. These themes are explored with a series of strategies described below.

Troubleshooting: Cognitive and Affective Exploration

At times, even though couples learn to communicate more effectively during the course of therapy, communication skills remain under tight stimulus control. This means that as long as partners are under the control of "rules" for good communication, as in prescheduled problem-solving sessions, they do an excellent job of communicating; however, they may have intense, destructive arguments at other times. These rapidly escalating, reciprocal exchanges of negative affect begin so suddenly that they often seem to come out of nowhere. Indeed, it has been well documented that distressed couples are subject to these rapidly escalating negative interaction patterns even after they have responded favorably to marital therapy (Gottman, 1979; Hahlweg, Revenstorf, & Schindler, 1984). In addition to the cumulatively destructive impact these continuing arguments have on the relationship, they tend to undermine progress that has occurred during therapy in other areas. Moreover, when couples arrive for a therapy session still reeling from one of these arguments, it becomes difficult, if not impossible, to go on with the normal business of marital therapy.

In most cases, efforts aimed at teaching couples to apply their new communication skills during these spontaneous arguments will be unsuccessful. In the heat of battle, couples rarely opt to engage the skills, no matter how well rehearsed and perfected they might be. Similarly unsuccessful are attempts to teach these couples anger-management techniques using the self-instructional paradigm adapted by Novaco (1976). Whether attempting to transfer communication or anger-management skills, couples repeatedly demonstrate their inability to apply them in the more naturalistic situations. It is as if different contingencies are operating in the heat of battle than in those situations where resolving a conflict is the goal. During these arguments, the reinforcers are winning, saving face, or being right, rather than enjoying the more distal benefits of an improved relationship.

It seems that attempting to dissipate the conflict is the wrong therapeutic task in such situations. A goal that is both more feasible—and, in the long run, more beneficial—involves helping partners engage in a functional analysis of the high-conflict situation, which means identifying the variables that control their affective intensity and specifying all aspects of the interaction (i.e., behavioral, cognitive, and affective) that describe or define the contingency. Once contingencies are labeled, both therapist and clients gain more control over them. At the experiential level, the inability to specify and label controlling variables leads to bewilderment and confusion: spouses know that they are very upset but do not understand why the stakes are so high. Once contingencies are specified, the experience is one of enhanced understanding and subsequent relief. Ultimately, such a strategy allows for deintensification of the conflict and the possibility of productive problem solving.

The technique called troubleshooting (TS) resembles both the ego-analytic approach described by Wile (1981) and the emotion-focused therapy developed by Greenberg and Johnson (1988). In many ways, TS constitutes a strategy opposite to the classical BMT approach. Whereas most BMT techniques attempt to interrupt and diffuse coercive interaction, in TS there is no explicit effort to alter the escalation process. Instead, the primary goal is to label the cognitive and affective components of these arguments, as well as the variables controlling these components. The first step is to induce the couple to "get into" the dispute during a session. If the spouses have had an unresolved argument during the week, this can usually be accomplished simply by asking them to continue the discussion. Alternatively, the therapist might simply capitalize on a recurring dispute that arises during a session, so that induction is unnecessary. The process is most productive when the exploration occurs around issues that are both common and prototypical for a particular couple. Moreover, TS depends on the partners' being "upset." Without the experience of emotional upset, they are talking "about" a troublesome issue and the process becomes an academic exercise. When they are currently upset, they are experiencing the conflict, and there is no need to worry about generalization: the couple is already in the naturalistic situation! Without the emotional reaction that is characteristic of the conflict in the natural environ-

ment, it is difficult, if not impossible, to specify the relevant contingencies.

Once the couple has become embroiled in the conflict, the therapist interrupts the process by engaging in sequential dialogues with each spouse. These dialogues are aimed at an elaboration of the thoughts and feelings that transpire as the issue at hand is being discussed. The therapist attempts to elicit from each spouse the meaning that the issue has for him or her and the unexpressed affect associated with it. While the therapist elicits this information from one spouse, the other is asked simply to sit quietly and listen. Once both spouses have had the opportunity to elaborate thoroughly on their cognitive and affective states, the therapist usually attempts to identify factors that account for their existence.

The TS process seems to be a very productive way to use the material generated by escalation and it often leads to a reduction in destructive escalation. We think that all three steps play an important role in the efficacy of the technique. The first step ensures that any learning that occurs will be in a situation that is maximally relevant to those that present problems for the couple in the natural environment. The second step affords each spouse the opportunity to develop his or her position (Wile, 1981) without interruption, something spouses rarely have the opportunity to do when the therapist is not around. The experience reinforces each spouse for alternating the roles of elaborator and listener. When one spouse is elaborating on his or her thoughts and feelings, he or she has the experience of being listened to and understood by both therapist and partner. The labeling of cognitive and affective states, and the concomitant elucidation of controlling variables, clarifies the spouse's behavior for all parties. This clarification demystifies the interaction and creates a context in which each person's behavior "makes more sense." The listener typically experiences either a reduction in negative affect or a transfer from anger, contempt, and sadness to greater compassion, and sometimes even tenderness. Not only is the process reinforcing for both parties, but the information gained is valuable and helps to change the context in which future disputes occur.

Identification of Themes and Modification of Prototypical Interaction Patterns

In the process of piloting TS procedures, we found that couples who exhibited a tendency toward destructive arguments tended to repeat similar themes from argument to argument. If one looked over time at the continuity across arguments, it was usually possible to extract themes that cut across each conflict, regardless of the content. We then had the option of describing these interaction patterns to the couples as the first step in a series of therapeutic interventions. Intervention at the thematic level involved describing in great detail the characteristics of the recurring pattern and the role that each spouse played in it, followed by an attempt to get couples to self-monitor the occurrence of these patterns and then debrief them after the fact. Finally, attempts were made to rechoreograph these patterns through practice in the session and instigative tasks to be completed at home. At times, mere identification of the pattern helped to change it. More often, self-monitoring and debriefing helped couples rebound from, and ultimately become less likely to enact, the destructive arguments. When all else failed, the restructuring of interaction patterns through standard behavioral techniques has been successful with many couples.

The Politics of Working with Couples at the Thematic Level

It seems to us that the predominant theme around which couples struggle has to do with how much closeness or distance there will be in the relationship. These conflicts over intimacy in the relationship have already been described.

As research by Christensen (1988a, 1988b) has shown, this conflict is not independent of gender. It is much more common for women to be in the role of seeking more closeness and involvement, to appear to be making more demands for change in the relationship, and to be described by the partner as nagging and intrusive (see also Floyd & Markman, 1983; Margolin, Talovic, & Weinstein, 1983). Men are much more likely to be satisfied with the status quo

or to be seeking changes that would provide them with greater distance and autonomy; one of the corollaries of this pattern is the tendency for men to be conflict-avoidant (Gottman & Krokoff, 1989; Gottman & Levenson, 1988), to fend off the discussion of change, to be conservative forces in relationships bent on preserving things as they are.

These closeness–distance conflicts are also related to power. The distancing behavior typically characterizing men is both a manifestation of and a factor that perpetuates their dominance. Women ask for more from a position of weakness; men fend off these requests/demands from a position of strength derived in part from their control of economic resources, their inclination to avoid intimacy (which is inherently empowering, especially when pitted against a partner who wants more intimacy), and the structure of traditional marriages (Jacobson, 1983, 1989b).

Despite the success we have had with intervening at the thematic level, considerable clinical innovation remains necessary. We have already discovered that couples who are highly polarized on the closeness–distance issue are the most difficult to treat (Jacobson, Follette, & Pagel, 1986). In other words, when BMT is not successful, this may often be due to the perniciousness of these struggles over how much closeness there will be in the relationship. The modification of interaction patterns may not be sufficient unless change also occurs in the functions that these patterns serve: changing the function means maintaining or altering current levels of intimacy.

To the extent that this conflict over level of intimacy characterizes distressed couples, and to the extent that the conflict is based on gender, marital therapy becomes inherently political. Marital therapists must regularly confront the products of a patriarchal marital structure that manifests itself in a power differential favoring men. However spouses may present their complaints, a therapist who observes a structure that is oppressive to women either contributes to its perpetuation or works toward its removal. The latter means tampering with these gender-based intimacy structures and in other ways promoting egalitarian relationships. The alternative leads to the therapist's being complicit in the maintenance of an oppressive structure. It is difficult, if not impossible, to be apolitical when working with couples. Luckily, men also suffer from being cast in roles that teach them to be unexpressive, withdrawn, rejecting, and emotionally distant. Thus, everyone benefits from a therapist's proegalitarian stance. Perhaps our greatest technical challenge is to produce strategies capable of achieving these goals and to convince therapists to use them.

MECHANISMS OF CHANGE AND SPECIAL ISSUES: WHAT WE KNOW ABOUT WHETHER, HOW WELL, AND WHY BMT WORKS

BMT has been by far the most thoroughly researched approach to marital therapy (Baucom & Hoffman, 1986; Gurman, Kniskern, & Pinsof, 1986; Jacobson, 1978a). In fact, more high-quality research has been done on BMT than on all other approaches to marital therapy combined. It is also fair to say that BMT is the only approach to marital therapy whose efficacy has been clearly established. At last count, there were at least two dozen controlled-outcome studies conducted in at least five countries that consistently support the effectiveness of this approach relative to control groups (Hahlweg & Markman, 1988). No other approach to marital therapy has had its efficacy so clearly documented, although a few isolated studies have suggested the effectiveness of relationship-enhancement approaches (Guerney, 1977), emotion-focused marital therapy (Johnson & Greenberg, 1985), and insight-oriented marital therapy (Snyder & Wills, 1989). Virtually no empirical support exists for the efficacy of either structural or strategic versions of marital therapy.

From research conducted in our own clinical research centers, we also know that the efficacy of BMT cannot be attributed entirely to those nonspecific clinical factors that are common to all marital-therapy approaches (Jacobson, 1978b). That is, there is something about the unique content of BMT that accounts for the observed treatment effects.

We also have a rather good idea of how often BMT works. Based on the convergence of results across clinical trials, it appears that about two thirds of the couples improve substantially during the course of therapy, while about half of

them recover to the point where they are truly in the happily married range on measures of marital satisfaction (Jacobson, 1984; Jacobson & Follette, 1985; Jacobson et al., 1989a).

We have no idea how these results compare with those of other approaches, since comparable data are not available for other approaches. In the one comparative-outcome study involving insight-oriented marital therapy, improvement and recovery rates were roughly comparable in the behavioral and insight-oriented treatment groups (Snyder & Wills, 1989). However, in general, not much is known about the relative efficacy of BMT versus other approaches. Few comparative-outcome studies have been undertaken, and those that have been undertaken have not achieved consistent results. And many, if not most, have enough methodological problems associated with them to preclude definitive interpretation.

What accounts for the efficacy of BMT? What are the predictors of positive outcome? How durable are the effects? These are some of the questions we have been asking in our ongoing program of research. Based on results already available, it appears that either behavior exchange or communication and problem-solving training is sufficient by itself to elicit short-term outcomes that are equivalent to the effects of the entire treatment that combines both components. However, behavior exchange without communication and problem-solving training produces fairly rapid relapse and little continued progress beyond the acute treatment phase. In contrast, communication and problem-solving training, either alone or in combination with behavior exchange, results in minimal relapse over the first six months following therapy, and some couples (about one third) even continue to progress during the follow-up period. Over the long haul (one- to two-year follow-ups) the combined treatment holds up better than either component presented alone.

However, even in the combined treatment program, by the two-year follow-up, about 30 percent of the treatment responders have suffered a recurrence of marital problems. Even though couples as a group are still better off than they would have been without treatment, and even though about half of the couples are still doing well at the two-year follow-up, these recurrence rates are substantial. As a result of these and other types of converging data, many of our recent efforts have gone into the prevention of recurrence (Jacobson, 1989b). We have been working on the development of a maintenance treatment to be delivered periodically following formal termination. This maintenance treatment is designed to prevent recurrence by extending the stimulus control of the therapist beyond the period of formal termination and making the therapist available during stressful life events that take place after the end of therapy. Such stressful life events are good predictors of recurrence (Jacobson et al., 1987).

We still know very little about the types of couples who are most inclined to respond favorably to BMT. Unlike other investigators, we have not found that the ages of the partners or the length of marriage predicts outcome (Jacobson et al., 1984). The only individual difference variable that has consistently predicted outcome has already been mentioned: couples who are polarized in traditional gender-based ways on the question of how much closeness versus distance there will be in the relationship tend not to do as well as other couples. We do have clinical impressions about which couples are toughest, and these are summarized in the next section.

Finally, we have taken an interest in therapist, client, and other process variables in the therapy setting as predictors of outcome. Like other process researchers, we have found that client characteristics account for considerably more variance in outcome than do therapist characteristics (Fruzzetti & Jacobson, 1990; Holtzworth-Munroe, Jacobson, DeKlyen, & Whisman, 1989). Specifically, three dimensions of clients' behavior in the therapy session seem critical to successful therapy: their involvement and engagement during the session, the ability to form a collaborative set, and the extent to which they comply with homework.

APPLICABILITY

Marital therapy is not always indicated. Although it appears that a substantial majority of couples seeking therapy can benefit from a conjoint treatment program, not all couples are suited for marital therapy, nor will all couples

opt for such a treatment program, even when, from the therapist's perspective, they could benefit substantially from such a regimen.

First, marital therapy is not indicated, as the primary treatment, when the marital problems are primarily a consequence of a severe psychological or medical disturbance on the part of one spouse. Marital therapy can play an ancillary role in such instances, but an individually based treatment focusing on the dysfunctional individual will be the primary treatment. This phenomenon is exemplified by, but not exclusive to, many distressed couples in which one member is schizophrenic. At times, the assessment issues here are very complex and subtle. For example, clinical depression can be a response on the part of one spouse to a distressed marriage, or it can be functionally related to factors extraneous to the relationship. Marital distress may be observed in both instances, but in one case, marital therapy will serve as the primary treatment modality, whereas in the other case, it will play a subordinate role (Jacobson, Dobson, Fruzzetti, Schmaling, & Salusky, 1990; Jacobson, Holtzworth-Munroe, & Schmaling, 1989).

Second, when the primary precipitant of marital distress is one spouse's involvement in an extramarital sexual relationship, conjoint marital therapy may be futile as long as the affair continues. This does not mean that an extramarital affair is a "red flag" that should necessarily contradict a treatment plan based on conjoint marital therapy. It is obvious that many extramarital affairs are themselves precipitated by marital discord, and if the spouse having the affair is willing to stop all contact with the third party, marital therapy can be quite helpful. But a very attractive alternative to the marriage, such as a desirable new partner, creates insuperable difficulties for marital therapy if the spouse insists on continuing the affair while therapy is going on. Marital therapy is hard-pressed to compete with the novel reinforcers of a new relationship. BMT demands a great deal of commitment on the part of both spouses, and relationship enhancement is an unlikely outcome when one spouse is diverted from that task by the allure of a new partner.

Third, marital therapy is not indicated when one or both spouses do not want it, preferring instead to end the relationship. Although this may appear obvious, it is important to mention because therapists can easily shape their clients into accepting a treatment regimen designed to improve their relationship, despite extreme ambivalence on the part of the clients regarding the optimal path. The mandate of a marital therapist is to serve the interests of the clients, not to protect or foster the institution of marriage. If, at the conclusion of a pretreatment assessment, the clients decide that separation rather than marital therapy is the optimal path, some assistance from the therapist may still be indicated, but such assistance will take a very different form than that prescribed here. Divorce counseling is beyond the scope of this chapter, but it bears little resemblance to marital therapy in either its goals or tactics.[11]

Fourth, in addition to the above examples where marital therapy may be contraindicated, there are also times when, even though marital therapy is indicated, it assumes a form very different from the general procedures outlined in this chapter. In fact, BMT is a highly idiographic approach to marital therapy and the general procedures are little more than guidelines. One example of a clinical situation where the general format presented in this chapter requires extensive modification is the crisis situation. Occasionally, a couple enters therapy in acute crisis and the thorough pretreatment assessment must be discarded in favor of an immediate, directive intervention. When there are immediate risks of physical harm to one or both spouses, or when the day-to-day functioning is so severely impaired that immediate action must be taken, a crisis-intervention approach is preferred. The therapist might tell each spouse what to do for the next week, and these instructions might be formalized into a written contract. They may involve hospitalization of one spouse, a trial separation, a commitment to abstain from alcohol, or any set of instructions that seems necessary to modify the high level of stress. Later, when the crisis has been eased, other, more typical intervention strategies can be utilized. These crisis situations are the exception rather than the rule. Most couples are severely distressed when they first contact a mental health professional, but the situation is seldom so desperate that

immediate intervention is essential. Most couples stand to benefit much more from a carefully planned intervention based on a careful evaluation and assessment.

Finally, in those cases where marital therapy is indicated, are there instances when BMT is contraindicated? The model presented in this chapter attempts to encompass the gamut of marital problems and thus does not delimit itself. Theoretically, there is no marital problem that simultaneously indicates the need for marital therapy and contraindicates the use of a behavioral approach. However, in practice, some couples will find a behavioral framework for viewing their problems unacceptable. The tactics outlined in this chapter may appear mechanical, excessively contrived, and the like. Such couples may simply find this approach incompatible with their view of the world and will prefer an approach that makes more intuitive sense. Happily, although most spouses do not subscribe to a behavioristic view of the world, the efficiency and effectiveness of the procedures are usually sufficient to overcome initial reticence based on philosophical differences. However, now and then, we find a couple that believes that the cure is worse than the disease.

CASE ILLUSTRATION

Carl and Laura were in their mid-50's and had been married for eight years by the time they sought marital therapy. They were both in their second marriage. Carl's first wife had divorced him after 12 years of marriage and he now had two grown daughters. Laura's husband had died about one year prior to her meeting Carl, and she now had two grown sons.

After a brief honeymoon period characterized by a great deal of passion and romance, the relationship between Carl and Laura gradually deteriorated to the point to which their arguments were frequent and intensely destructive, with considerable verbal abuse on both sides and a few episodes of physical violence. This period of high conflict had been replaced over the past couple of years by mutual avoidance and withdrawal, with very little interaction or conversation and virtually no sex. On those occasions when Carl and Laura were forced to spend time

---

[11]*Editors' Note.* See Everett and Volgy (Chapter 16) for more detailed discussion of the differences between the two.

alone together, or when conversation was attempted, the arguments would recur.

As is the case with many distressed couples, their versions of how the relationship had gone awry were incompatible, as were their theories about what was needed to change in order for the relationship to improve. However, they were perhaps as intransigent in their views as any couple either of us has treated. What made this case difficult was that they were both poor communicators, but in completely different ways. Their inability to communicate was in part based on and in part exacerbated by extreme tentativeness, mistrust, and an unwillingness to take any risks that would increase their vulnerability. They had both retreated to positions of safety in the relationship, and each was so convinced of his or her innocence and the other's malevolence that they were barely willing to glance at each other.

Space limitations prohibit in-depth psychological profiles of either Carl or Laura, but it is important to note certain aspects of each that fueled the flames of their discord. Carl had grown up to be a timid, retiring man who viewed himself as unworthy of women. At the same time, he was quite angry at most of the important women in his life for making him feel so unworthy. With his mother, his first wife, his two daughters, and now with his current wife, he behaved in a hostile, withdrawn manner but experienced himself as a victim. When he and Laura first met, he fell in love as he never had before. He viewed Laura as a beautiful, enchanting woman who seemed, incredibly, to find him wonderful as well. He came as close as he had ever come to letting his guard down and surrendering to his feelings during their courtship. However, some experiences early in their relationship convinced him that she was no safer than other women, and thus, rather than continuing to let down his guard, he retreated once again—first by becoming intensely angry, and ultimately by withdrawing into chronic hostility. In one of these experiences, she had refused to make love with him one night because her son had just come to town and was staying with them. In the second experience, she left town to spend time with relatives and did not want him to come along. In both instances, he experienced her behavior as uncharacteristically distancing: she appeared to be, suddenly and for

no apparent reason, withdrawing from him in a cold manner, with minimal explanation and no apparent ambivalence. It was experiences like these, later confirmed in his mind by other sudden mood swings, that led him to hypothesize that she had a multiple personality. Once he had formulated this hypothesis to explain her behavior, he urged her to seek therapy, insisting that she had serious emotional problems. He described many bizarre incidents to the therapist with respect to their past relationship, incidents that, if true, would have suggested that Laura had had severe dissociative problems at the very least.

Laura, on the other hand, categorically denied that any of these incidents had ever occurred, and her version of the events on those days made Carl seem like someone with either a very poor memory or, even worse, a paranoid streak. Laura had been quite happily married previously, and, until her husband died, had been wife and mother in an all-American family. She expended a great deal of energy maintaining "appearances." Most of the time, she was highly controlled and formal. In contrast to Carl, who was practically a psychotherapy junkie, she mistrusted therapy and therapists and was reluctant to enter into marital therapy again. Despite her controlled demeanor, her intense bitterness toward Carl manifested itself whenever she was asked to give her view of the relationship problems. She would immediately become highly emotional: sarcastic, teary, and adamant about her victimization. She depicted Carl as someone who claimed to want a close relationship but who "unconsciously" sought distance at every opportunity. He spent his evenings reading books about military history and responded to her only when she initiated it; invariably, she insisted, his responses were full of hostility.

Carl and Laura were treated for a total of 56 sessions, an unusually long term for BMT. Initially, they had been referred by their previous marital therapist, who had been doing an insight-oriented type of marital therapy with them but was moving to a different city. Carl had positive feelings about this previous therapy while Laura felt that it had been a waste of time. Carl had somehow received the impression that the therapist based his approach on "family-of-origin work." He was disappointed to hear about the treatment model described in this chapter, but was willing to try it.

Initially, considerable progress was made using behavior-exchange strategies. This couple had so little in the way of positive experiences together that they felt uplifted by the enhanced quality of their day-to-day lives that the structure induced. But therapy was unsuccessful in making much of a dent in their communication. Even during the therapy sessions, in which couples are usually on their best behavior, each was so reactive to the other that collaboration was easily disrupted, and within five minutes of any conversation, they were furious at each other. Carl attacked Laura for virtually everything she said or did, and then denied that he had been attacking her. When she teased him, he viewed it as hostile, and accused her of being defensive or naïve, whereas she insisted that she had not intended hostility. She would eventually explode with anger, and they would quickly escalate into very destructive, reciprocal verbal abuse of each other. From the therapist's point of view, Carl was a poor communicator who was quite difficult to understand. Moreover, the hostility and mind reading to which Laura reacted were very real. On the other hand, she was also quite provocative in her hostile defensiveness and her categorical denial of ever being wrong or imperfect in any way would have made her difficult for any partner.

As time went on, they began to retreat toward a comfortable withdrawal. They continued with some of the low-cost behavior-exchange exercises that made life more pleasant at home but would not venture into dangerous territory, which meant that almost any kind of communication was taboo. Despite a couple of satisfying sexual encounters, their retreat included an implicit ban on sex, since any initiation by either of them required communication and communication was dangerous. His initiations were tentative and ambiguous, as were her responses. By the time they entered the bedroom, he was convinced that she was not interested and she was convinced that he had decided against it. In the end, nothing happened.

In addition to the lack of further progress, the ultimate impact of therapy was jeopardized by the difficulty in maintaining a therapeutic alliance with both spouses simultaneously. As time went on and it became apparent that the therapist was not going to insist that Laura was emotionally disturbed and needed long-term psychotherapy, she became more favorably disposed toward the therapist and toward therapy. Her major complaint about previous therapists had been that they "just talked about things and nothing happened." She liked BMT. Carl, on the other hand, blamed the lack of progress on the behavioral emphasis and felt that intensive, insight-oriented work was needed. Of course, what he meant was that Laura needed such work.

After 22 sessions of BMT, the therapist decided to split the couple up and alternate individual sessions with them every other week. This turned out to be the turning point in the therapy. During these individual sessions, he was able to provide a degree of support to each of them that would have been impossible in the conjoint sessions. In the conjoint sessions, any support he provided for Carl would interfere with his alliance with Laura, and vice versa. Moreover, when only one of them was present, he was able to recommend ways of breaking through their communicative impasses that would not have been accepted in the presence of the partner, since each was afraid of losing face by acknowledging any role in the problem. By suggesting ways of reversing negative and facilitating positive communication at home in a context of validation and emotional support, the therapist was able to chip away at the overlearned patterns involving defensiveness, hostility, and withdrawal.

The individual sessions also provided the therapist with an opportunity to present a more sympathetic view of the absent partner to the one who was present. In both cases, the absent partner was depicted as a well-intentioned person who wanted to be close but was desperately afraid of taking risks and making himself or herself vulnerable to rejection. These presentations were largely accurate, but would have been denied by the absent spouse had she or he been present while the remarks were being made. In fact, however, Carl did want a close relationship with Laura, but had "learned" from the early experiences with her that he could not depend on her. In order to be safe, he had to keep a healthy distance between them. These learning experiences in the relationship confirmed his previous experience of himself with women. Yet his sense of betrayal for her initial "misleading" presentation of herself as different from other women was acute, and thus his withdrawal was tinged with chronic hostility. She also experienced him as unsafe and dangerous, since he would say he wanted to be close but at the same time would respond to her with anger and avoidance.

Essentially, the strategy was to engage in troubleshooting and thematic work with each of them individually, while providing suggestions to each as to how to improve communication. For example, she tried out some new ways of responding to him when he seemed impatient with her for not understanding him. Her new, relatively nondefensive questions were a great deal more successful than were her previous responses.

After six or seven sessions with each of them, they came together for further conjoint work, focusing on communication and problem-solving training. The process went much more smoothly this time. At the time that Carl and Laura stopped therapy, they had greatly increased their conversational repertoire. They had a comfortable relationship in which they were taking vacations together for the first time in three or four years, engaging in sexual relations about once a week, and spending their evenings together rather than in isolation. There were still things the couple could not talk about. For example, discussing the "early incidents" that shaped their mistrust of each other was still taboo. Is this a relationship we would have wanted for ourselves? Probably not. Were these people considerably better off than they had been before entering therapy? Most definitely.

Carl and Laura were not a textbook case by any means, but in reality few cases are. They were more difficult to treat than the average couple, but, despite their hostility and mistrust of one another, they had one thing in common that made successful therapy a realistic possibility—they both wanted a close relationship.

REFERENCES

Ables, B.S., & Brandsma, J.M. (1977). *Therapy for couples*. San Francisco: Jossey-Bass.

Baucom, D.H., & Epstein, N. (1990). *Cognitive-behavioral marital therapy*. New York: Brunner/Mazel.

Baucom, D.H., Epstein, N., Sayers, S., & Sher, T.G. (1989). The role of cognitions in marital relationships: Definitional, methodological and conceptual issues. *Journal of Consulting and Clinical Psychology, 57*, 31–38.

Baucom, D.H., & Hoffman, J.A. (1986). The effectiveness of marital therapy: Current status and application to the clinical setting. In N.S. Jacobson & A.S. Gurman (Eds.), *Clinical handbook of marital therapy* (pp. 597–620). New York: Guilford Press.

Baucom, D.H., & Mehlman, S.K. (1984). Predicting marital status following behavioral marital therapy: A comparison of models of marital relationships. In K. Hahlweg & N.S. Jacobson (Eds.), *Marital interaction: Analysis and modification* (pp. 89–104). New York: Guilford Press.

Birchler, G.R., Weiss, R.L., & Vincent, J.P. (1975). A multimethod analysis of social reinforcement exchange between maritally distressed and nondistressed spouse and stranger dyads. *Journal of Personality and Social Psychology, 31*, 349–360.

Bradbury, T., & Fincham, F. (1990). Attributions in marriage: Review and critique. *Psychological Bulletin, 107*, 3–33.

Christensen, A. (1988a). Detection of conflict patterns in couples. In K. Hahlweg & M.J. Goldstein (Eds.), *Understanding major mental disorder: The contribution of family interaction research*. New York: Family Process Press.

Christensen, A. (1988b). Dysfunctional interaction patterns in couples. In P. Noller & M.A. Fitzpatrick (Eds.), *Perspectives on marital interaction*. Clevedon, England: Multilingual Matters.

Floyd, J.F., & Markman, H.J. (1983). Observational biases in spouse observation: Toward a cognitive/behavioral model of marriage. *Journal of Consulting and Clinical Psychology, 51*, 450–457.

Fruzzetti, A.E., & Jacobson, N.S. (1990). Predicting depressed mood following relationship dissolution: A more naturalistic test of the hopelessness theory of depression. Submitted for publication.

Gottman, J.M. (1979). *Marital interaction: Experimental investigations*. New York: Academic Press.

Gottman, J.M., & Krokoff, L. (1989). Marital interaction and marital satisfaction: A longitudinal view. *Journal of Consulting and Clinical Psychology, 57*, 47–52.

Gottman, J.M., & Levenson, R.W. (1985). A valid procedure for obtaining self-report of affect in marital interaction. *Journal of Consulting and Clinical Psychology, 53*, 151–160.

Gottman, J.M., & Levenson, R.W. (1988). The social psychophysiology of marriage. In P. Noller & M.A. Fitzpatrick (Eds.), *Perspectives on marital interaction*. Clevedon, England: Multilingual Matters.

Gottman, J., Markman, H., & Notarius, C. (1977). The topography of marital conflict: A sequential analysis of verbal and nonverbal behavior. *Journal of Marriage and the Family, 39*, 461–477.

Gottman, J., Notarius, C., Markman, H., Bank, S., Yoppi, B., & Rubin, M.E. (1976). Behavior exchange theory and marital decision making. *Journal of Personality and Social Psychology, 34*, 14–23.

Greenberg, L.S., & Johnson, S.M. (1988). *Emotion-focused marital therapy*. New York: Brunner/Mazel.

Guerney, B. (1977). *Relationship enhancement*. San Francisco: Jossey-Bass.

Gurman, A.S., Kniskern, D.P., & Pinsof, W.M. (1986). Research on the process and outcome of marital and family therapy. In S.L. Garfield & A.E. Bergin (Eds.), *Handbook of psychotherapy and behavior change* (3rd ed.). New York: Wiley.

Gurman, A.S., & Knudson, R.M. (1978). Behavioral marriage therapy: I. A psychodynamic-systems analysis and critique. *Family Process, 17*, 121–138.

Hahlweg, K., & Markman, H.J. (1988). The effectiveness of behavioral marital therapy: Empirical status of behavioral techniques in preventing and alleviating marital distress. *Journal of Consulting and Clinical Psychology, 56*, 440–447.

Hahlweg, K., Revenstorf, D., & Schindler, L. (1984). Effects of behavioral marital therapy on couples, communication and problem-solving skills. *Journal of Consulting and Clinical Psychology, 52,* 553–566.

Haley, J. (1963). *Strategies of psychotherapy.* New York: Grune & Stratton.

Holtzworth-Munroe, A., Jacobson, N.S., DeKlyen, M., & Whisman, M. (1989). Relationship between behavioral marital therapy outcome and process variables. *Journal of Consulting and Clinical Psychology, 57,* 658–662.

Jacobson, N.S. (1978a). A review of the research on the effectiveness of marital therapy. In T.J. Paolino & B.S. McCrady (Eds.), *Marriage and marital therapy: Psychoanalytic, behavioral, and systems theory perspectives.* New York: Brunner/Mazel.

Jacobson, N.S. (1978b). Specific and nonspecific factors in the effectiveness of a behavioral approach to the treatment of marital discord. *Journal of Consulting and Clinical Psychology, 46,* 442–452.

Jacobson, N.S. (1979). Behavioral treatments for marital discord: A critical appraisal. In M. Hersen, R.M. Eisler, & P.M. Miller (Eds.), *Progress in behavior modification.* New York: Academic Press.

Jacobson, N.S. (1983). Beyond empiricism: The politics of marital therapy. *American Journal of Family Therapy, 11,* 11–24.

Jacobson, N.S. (1984). A component analysis of behavioral marital therapy: The relative effectiveness of behavior exchange and problem solving training. *Journal of Consulting and Clinical Psychology, 52,* 295–305.

Jacobson, N.S. (1989a). The maintenance of treatment gains following social learning-based marital therapy. *Behavior Therapy, 20,* 325–336.

Jacobson, N.S. (1989b). The politics of intimacy. *Behavior Therapist, 12,* 29–32.

Jacobson, N.S. (in press). Contributions from psychology to an understanding of marriage. In F. Fincham & T. Bradbury (Eds.), *The psychology of marriage: Basic issues and applications.* New York: Guilford Press.

Jacobson, N.S., & Anderson, E.A. (1980). The effects of behavior rehearsal and feedback on the acquisition of problem solving skills in distressed and nondistressed couples. *Behavior Research and Therapy, 18,* 25–36.

Jacobson, N.S., Dobson, K., Fruzzetti, A., Schmaling, K.B., & Salusky, S. (1990). Marital therapy as a treatment for depression. Submitted for publication.

Jacobson, N.S., & Follette, W.C. (1985). Clinical significance of improvement resulting from two behavioral marital therapy components. *Behavior Therapy, 16,* 249–262.

Jacobson, N.S., Follette, W.C., & McDonald, D.W. (1982). Reactivity to positive and negative behavior in distressed and nondistressed married couples. *Journal of Consulting and Clinical Psychology, 50,* 706–714.

Jacobson, N.S., Follette, W.C., & Pagel, M. (1986). Predicting who will benefit from behavioral marital therapy. *Journal of Consulting and Clinical Psychology, 54,* 518–522.

Jacobson, N.S., Follette, W.C., Revenstorf, D., Baucom, D.H., Hahlweg, K., & Margolin, G. (1984). Variability in outcome and clinical significance of behavioral marital therapy: A reanalysis of outcome data. *Journal of Consulting and Clinical Psychology, 52,* 497–504.

Jacobson, N.S., & Holtzworth-Munroe, A. (1986). Marital therapy: A social learning/cognitive perspective. In N.S. Jacobson & A.S. Gurman (Eds.), *Clinical handbook of marital therapy* (pp. 29–70). New York: Guilford Press.

Jacobson, N.S., Holtzworth-Munroe, A., & Schmaling, K.B. (1989). Marital therapy and spouse involvement in the treatment of depression, agoraphobia, and alcoholism. *Journal of Consulting and Clinical Psychology, 57,* 5–10.

Jacobson, N.S., & Margolin, G. (1979). *Marital therapy: Strategies based on social learning and behavior exchange principles.* New York: Brunner/Mazel.

Jacobson, N.S., & Moore, D. (1981). Spouses as observers of the events in their relationship. *Journal of Consulting and Clinical Psychology, 49,* 269–277.

Jacobson, N.S., Schmaling, K.B., & Holtzworth-Munroe, A. (1987). Component analysis of behavioral marital therapy: Two-year follow-up and prediction of relapse. *Journal of Marital and Family Therapy, 13,* 187–195.

Jacobson, N.S., Schmaling, K.B., Holtzworth-Munroe, A., Katt, J.L., Wood, L.F., & Follette, V.M. (1989). Research-structured versus clinically flexible versions of social learning-based marital therapy. *Behaviour Research and Therapy, 27,* 173–180.

Jacobson, N.S., Waldron, H., & Moore, D. (1980). Toward a behavioral profile of marital distress. *Journal of Consulting and Clinical Psychology, 48,* 696–703.

Johnson, S.M., & Greenberg, L.S. (1985). Differential effects of experiential and problem-solving interventions in resolving marital conflict. *Journal of Consulting and Clinical Psychology, 53,* 175–184.

Lederer, W.J., & Jackson, D.D. (1968). *The mirages of marriage.* New York: Norton.

Levenson, R.W., & Gottman, J.M. (1983). Marital interaction: Physiological linkage and affective exchange. *Journal of Personality and Social Psychology, 45,* 587–597.

Margolin, G., Talovic, S., & Weinstein, C.D. (1983). Areas-of-change questionnaire: A practical approach to marital assessment. *Journal of Consulting and Clinical Psychology, 51,* 920–931.

Margolin, G., & Wampold, B.E. (1981). Sequential analysis of conflict and accord in distressed and nondistressed marital partners. *Journal of Consulting and Clinical Psychology, 49,* 554–567.

Markman, H.J. (1981). Prediction of marital distress: A 5-year follow-up. *Journal of Consulting and Clinical Psychology, 49,* 760–762.

Markman, H.J., & Kroft, S.A. (1989). Men and women in marriage: Dealing with gender differences in marital therapy. *The Behavior Therapist, 12,* 51–56.

Masters, W.H., & Johnson, V.E. (1970). *Human sexual inadequacy.* Boston: Little, Brown.

Novaco, R.W. (1976). Treatment of chronic anger through cognitive and relaxation controls. *Journal of Consulting and Clinical Psychology, 44,* 681.

Patterson, G.R. (1974). Interventions for boys with conduct problems: Multiple settings, treatments, and criteria. *Journal of Consulting and Clinical Psychology, 42,* 471–481.

Patterson, G.R., & Hops, H. (1972). Coercion, a game for two: Intervention techniques for marital conflict. In R.E. Ulrich & P. Mounjoy (Eds.), *The experimental analysis of social behavior.* New York: Appleton.

Patterson, G.R., & Reid, J.B. (1970). Reciprocity and coercion: Two facets of social systems. In C. Neuringer & J.L. Michael (Eds.), *Behavior modification in clinical psychology.* New York: Appleton.

Robinson, E.A., & Price, M.G. (1980). Pleasurable behavior in marital interaction: An observational study. *Journal of Consulting and Clinical Psychology, 48,* 117–118.

Satir, V. (1967). *Conjoint family therapy.* Palo Alto, CA: Science & Behavior Books.

Skinner, B.F. (1974). *About behaviorism.* New York: Vintage Books.

Snyder, D.K. (1979). Multidimensional assessment of marital satisfaction. *Journal of Marriage and the Family, 41,* 813–823.

Snyder, D.K., & Wills, R.M. (1989). Behavioral vs. insight oriented marital therapy: A controlled comparative outcome study. *Journal of Consulting and Clinical Psychology.*

Spanier, G.B. (1976). Measuring dyadic adjustment: New scales for assessing the quality of marriage and similar dyads. *Journal of Marriage and the Family, 38,* 15–28.

Stuart, R.B. (1969). Operant-interpersonal treatment for marital discord. *Journal of Consulting and Clinical Psychology, 33,* 675–682.

Stuart, R.B. (1980). *Helping couples change: A social learning approach to marital therapy.* New York: Guilford Press.

Thibaut, J.W., & Kelley, H.H. (1959). *The social psychology of groups.* New York: Wiley.

Vincent, J.P., Freidman, L.L., Nugent, J., & Messerly, L. (1979). Demand characteristics in observations of marital interaction. *Journal of Consulting and Clinical Psychology, 47,* 557–566.

Vincent, J.P., Weiss, R.L., & Birchler, G.R. (1975). A behavioral analysis of problem-solving in distressed and nondistressed married and stranger dyads. *Behavior Therapy, 6,* 475–487.

Weiss, R.L. (1978). The conceptualization of marriage from a behavioral perspective. In T.J. Paolino & B.S. McCrady (Eds.), *Marriage and marital therapy: Psychoanalytic, behavioral, and systems perspectives.* New York: Brunner/Mazel.

Weiss, R.L., & Birchler, G.R. (1978). Adults with marital dysfunction. In M. Hersen & A.S. Bellack (Eds.), *Behavior therapy in the psychiatric setting.* Baltimore: Williams & Wilkins.

Weiss, R.L., Birchler, G.R., & Vincent, J.P. (1974). Contractual models for negotiation training in marital dyads. *Journal of Marriage and the Family, 36,* 321–331.

Weiss, R.L., Hops, H., & Patterson, G.R. (1973). A framework for conceptualizing marital conflict, technology for altering it, some data for evaluating it. In L.A. Hamerlynck, L.C. Handy, & E.J. Mash (Eds.), *Behavior change: Methodology, concepts, and practice* (pp. 309–342). Champaign, IL: Research Press.

Wile, D.B. (1981). *Couples therapy: A nontraditional approach.* New York: Wiley.

Wills, T.A., Weiss, R.L., & Patterson, G.R. (1974). A behavioral analysis of the determinants of marital satisfaction. *Journal of Consulting and Clinical Psychology, 42,* 802–811.

EDITORS' REFERENCE

Budman, S., & Gurman, A.S. (1988). *Theory and practice of brief therapy.* New York: Guilford Press.

CHAPTER 5

Bowen Theory and Therapy

Edwin H. Friedman, D.D.

It would be difficult to do justice to the depth and complexities of Bowen theory within the framework of an entire book, no less the confines of a single chapter. This is so, in part, because many of its basic concepts are interdependent and require a constant circularity of exposition. It is also true because Bowen theory is really not about families per se, but about life. The task of explaining Bowen theory is something like being given the assignment, "Write a history of protoplasm (and other natural systems) in 30 pages." Rather than trying to "explain" it, therefore, this chapter will be *about* it. I will focus on what I perceive to be the uniqueness of Bowen theory within the late-20th-century social and philosophical phenomenon that we have come to call "family therapy," and on what "the Bowen approach" has in common with pre–21st-century thinking in other fields of scientific endeavor. Such a perspective may lead the reader to conclude that Bowen theory has more to do with cosmology, astronomy, or immunology than with "fixing" families, but, at the least, it will help differentiate differentiation. As both the family movement and his theory have evolved since Bowen published his first papers over 30 years ago, "the Bowen approach" may

now stand as more different from all other approaches to family therapy than family therapy is itself different from individual model thinking. But those differences can serve as a framework for clarifying his thinking.

Limiting the focus of this chapter in this way has been made possible by the publication in the past few years of several volumes and essays devoted to the theory and its application. *Family Evaluation* by Michael Kerr (Kerr & Bowen, 1988) is the most comprehensive work on the theory, *Bowen Family Systems Theory* by Daniel Papero (1990) gives more emphasis to the application, and, of course, there is Bowen's own (1978) collection of essays, *Family Therapy in Clinical Practice*. Several other recent books that focus on one particular aspect of family life from the perspective of Bowen theory are *The Evaluation and Treatment of Marital Conflict* (Guerin, Fay, Burden, & Kautto, 1987); *Adult Children of Divorce* (Beal & Hochman, in press); *Biofeedback Frontiers* (Rosenbaum, 1989); *The Therapist's Own Family* (Titelman, 1987); *Genograms in Family Assessment* (McGoldrick, 1985); and *Generation to Generation: Family Process in Church and Synagogue* (Friedman, 1985), which applies Bowen theory to work systems and the interconnection between work systems and family systems. In addition, three collections of selected early Georgetown Family Center symposia papers exist, and the Family Center has a library of videotapes of Bowen conducting interviews or discussing various aspects of his theory. The Family Center also maintains a bibliography of other important papers written by members of the faculty, and publishes a quarterly with articles and reviews of presentations on Bowen theory and natural systems concepts.

One caveat is in order before proceeding, however. Precisely because Bowen theory is so tied up with the most fundamental issues of life, it is open to different understandings. What is about to be presented, therefore, is not meant to be the definitive view of Bowen theory. Rather, it is how one disciple who has spent two decades trying to apply it to families, institutions, and his own life has come to see it.

First, I will provide an overview of several characteristics of Bowen theory that set it apart from almost all other theories of family therapy. I will then discuss the theoretical significance for both his own theory, and for the conceptualization of human life generally, of four of Bowen's basic constructs, followed by an exposition of three principles that underlie the application of Bowen theory. As befits the Bowen approach, this chapter will be weighted more in the direction of theory than practice, with discussion of practice serving to elucidate the theory further, rather than the theory being a prelude to learning technique. The chapter will conclude with some thoughts designed to show that Bowen theory has the potential for being a true paradigm shift that challenges thinking in all the social sciences because of the way in which it reformats traditional dichotomies in the field, particularly with respect to culture, gender, pathology, and the process of healing.

FUNDAMENTAL CHARACTERISTICS OF BOWEN THEORY

The Breadth of Its Perspective

As already stated, Bowen theory is not fundamentally about families, but about life. The fact that it can be applied to families is almost incidental to the wider focus that Bowen has tended to refer to as "the human phenomenon." But that wider focus extends beyond the human dimension to all of protoplasm, if not all of creation. Bowen has constantly emphasized over the years that we have more in common with other forms of protoplasm than we differ from them, and that the traditional social science efforts to emphasize the differences, almost to the exclusion of the similarities, have decreased our objectivity about, and perhaps increased our denial of, what really makes us tick. Underpinning and infusing his ideas is the assumption that the human animal is part of evolutionary *emotional* processes that go back to the beginning of time, or at least to that propitious moment when the first eukaryotic cell, the first cell to develop a nucleus, appeared. It promptly separated itself from the hitherto only available process of reproduction (cloning), thus giving differentiation new meaning, and, possibly for the first time, giving rise to the existential, and perhaps biological, category of *self*. Therefore, what we observe in families today—the opposing forces for togetherness and self, the perpetual reactivity that undulates through any emotional system, the chronic anxiety that is transmitted from generation to generation, as well as the myriad of symptomatic labels that the social sciences have proliferated to describe these phenomena—are all a kind of background radiation that goes back to that "biological big bang." It is thus not really possible to comprehend the thrust of the Bowen approach to human families without also considering the nature of our entire species and its relationship to all existing life, and indeed to all previous life (and other natural systems) on this planet, if not throughout the cosmos.[1]

During the last decade, for example, there has been an increased emphasis at the annual Georgetown Family Center symposia on papers that relate family life to other natural systems, or even that are about other natural systems but do not make the explicit effort to relate them to

---

[1] *Editors' Note.* In this, the Bowen approach certainly stands in marked contrast to most of the rest of the field of family therapy, and of psychotherapy more generally, wherein the contemporary thrust is toward more midlevel and at times even minitheory development.

human families. More than 25 years ago when these symposia began, they consisted almost exclusively of papers by residents and others attracted to the family movement who focused on the application of Bowen theory to a variety of family problems or their own families of origin, and the guest speakers were almost all well-known figures in the family-therapy field. Today, the major speakers are experts on whales, monkeys, ethology, sociobiology, slime molds, and so on. But, *and this is crucial, it is not simply comparisons of behavior that are being sought, but rather what is common to all "emotional," that is, natural systems.* Similarly, in various parts of this chapter, parallels will be shown between cellular processes and families. From a natural systems point of view, these comparisons may be seen as homologies rather than analogies. Analogies are comparisons; homologies are parallel evolutionary pathways. Bowen theory strongly suggests that humans, being colonies of cells, colonize like their cells. But if this is true, it is not because cells are the basic components to which humans can be reduced, but because humans develop the same kind of emotional fields (see especially Calhoun, 1963).

If it is characteristic of all family therapists to widen their focus from the individual to the family, then in Bowen's thinking, making the nuclear family the unit of observation is only a way station in that outward migration of perspective. Focus on the family is a way to maintain a direction that leads toward understanding the more encompassing natural systems that families mirror, and of which they are a part; that knowledge can then reciprocally help us to understand families. (Developing this evolutionary perspective is a large part of what "family of origin" work is about.) Bowen theory thus is very much a thinking therapist's therapy. That is not to say that it denies emotions—quite the contrary. The term emotional—as in emotional system, emotional triangle, or emotional cutoff—is constantly used in order to avoid a dichotomy between the psychological and the physical, and the emphasis on thinking is not to deny feeling but to emphasize the importance of self-regulation in the process of differentiation. Bowen theory will always appeal more, however, to those therapists who tend to think in universals than to those whose primary concern is the immediacy of symptom relief. And the clients who

seem to do best with it are those who both want to take responsibility for their selves and have the capacity to think beyond their own condition. From a Bowenian perspective, the capacity to think about "the human phenomenon" from a Bowenian (that is, a natural systems) perspective is itself an essential part of the therapeutic process. At the very least, the protoplasmic–cosmological context means that, on the one hand, all of life is germane to understanding families, and, on the other, that the future of the human family is bound up with the evolution not only of our species, but of all life on this planet, and perhaps beyond. For the family therapist, as will be seen, this orientation leads to a "unified field theory" of family symptomatology, and a connection between one's work with families and the ultimate course of one's own destiny. And, if ethologists are correct, then such commitment to the survival of one's species is also what we have in common with other forms of animal life. In this respect, Bowen's effort to apply his theory to the "human family" in his work on "societal regression" is a logical outcome of the breadth of his perspective.

A Perspective of Universals

A second major characteristic of Bowen's thinking that sets it apart from almost all other theories in the field is its tendency to conceptualize in terms of universal continua rather than discrete categories (e.g., nature/nurture, marital problems/child problems, male/female, patient/therapist, physical illness/emotional illness). Bowen theory constantly strives to make continuous what other theories dichotomize. Encapsulated best in one of his favorite comments, "Schizophrenia is in all of us," its emphasis on the emotional forces common to all of protoplasm reduces the significance of the conventional divisions associated with culture, gender, pathology, and therapy, and changes radically what information a therapist should consider important. His concept that the family should be the "unit of observation (or treatment)," on the one hand, puts emphasis on the emotional forces common to all families, and, on the other, reduces greatly the significance of which family member bears the symptom.

From the other direction, the general tendency in the helping professions to catalogue existence according to traditional social science and psychiatric categories can throw people off regarding the understanding of Bowen theory. At various times, Bowen's ideas have been pigeonholed as behavioristic, holistic, biologically determined, learning theory, cognitive therapy, a throwback to psychoanalysis, or just plain cold—and, at times, Bowen theory will appear to belong less to therapy than to the disciplines of sociology, ethology, or anthropology. Actually, the natural systems aspect of Bowen theory suggests that dividing the subject matter of those three disciplines separately is artificial. Similarly, with regard to conventional divisions in psychiatry itself between, say, the humanistic (insight) and the biological (medicine), Bowen theory does not fit in one camp or the other. While it is rooted in biology and biological metaphor, the central Bowenian concept of *differentiation* is about integrity, not the administration of drugs. Still another conventional dichotomy in the helping professions that can skew an understanding of Bowen theory is that between research and practice. As will be shown below, "re-search" is part and parcel of Bowen therapy.

Unless one understands that striving to comprehend the unity of life's forces is the intrinsic principle that gives all of Bowen theory its coherence, then viewing any particular aspect of the theory in isolation will give it the wrong slant. Thus, Bowen therapy is often thought of simplistically as the family-of-origin approach by those who are primarily concerned with technique. Ironically, systems thinking is all about understanding components in terms of their structures. It is vital not to confuse mode with melody. Many Bowenian concepts will sound similar to ideas in other theories, and one can easily be misled about their meaning, unless they are heard within the creative matrix of his own central concepts, particularly natural systems and differentiation.

One important technical ramification of the theory's striving for unity, the way it streamlines the approaches to change, should also be mentioned in this context, and will be elaborated below. The unity of perspective turns the therapeutic endeavor of promoting differentiation into a broad-spectrum antibiotic that may be applied to any family no matter what its nature

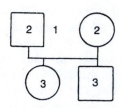

or the nature of its "dis-ease." For those who mistake complexity for depth, this may appear oversimplified, but streamlined formulations ($E = MC^2$, for example) also satisfy other time-honored criteria for the acceptance of a scientific theory, such as parsimony and aesthetic elegance.[2]

An example of how Bowen has expressed this unity can be shown with the aid of the above diagram.

According to Bowen, symptoms can show up in one of three locations: (1) in the marital relationship (as conflict, distance, or divorce), (2) in the health of one of the partners (physical or "mental"), or (3) in one of the children (though this last could also be placed in the space between parent and child). The same multigenerational forces create symptoms at any of these three locations. The Bowenian concept that the family is the unit of observation (or treatment) means that what is important is not the location, or even the form, of the symptom that has surfaced at any of these sites, but getting to the systemic forces, both those within the nuclear family and those that are being transmitted from previous generations. An example of the power for different ways of thinking that Bowen theory offers is the different criterion that this focus on the nuclear family sets up for successful marriage. Instead of dividing marriages into two basic categories, those that last and those that do not, or those that are happy and those that are not, the new criterion based on the above model is that marriages are successful to the extent that the nuclear family is symptom-free in all three locations (with the understanding that no marriage achieves a grade better than 70 percent).

For a Bowenian-trained therapist, therefore,

---

[2] *Editors' Note.* Again, the approach is extraordinary in its differentness from so much of the field, which seems increasingly to believe that there probably does not exist a near-universal antidote for family (among other) difficulties.

the question of specialties ("Do you see couples? Individuals? Families with alcoholism, substance abuse, violence?") has no meaning. The "specialty" is always the same: skinning cats—in one way or another. This same focus on systemic emotional factors rather than specific problems or their location also characterizes Bowenian consultation with work systems. Thus, differentiation in the leader becomes a more important goal than specific administrative solutions or improved managerial techniques, no matter what the type of organization. (This leads to another continuity where others dichotomize. Family systems and work systems are both emotional systems.)

There are two major ways in which this way of thinking is contrary to prevailing methods of conceptualization. The first is that it diminishes the importance of becoming expert in specific symptomatologies, or their location, as well as finding specific techniques for a broad array of issues; the second is that it is a principle that transcends culture. To appreciate how really different that is, it is only necessary to look through a year's supply of any family-therapy (or other social science) journals, or to read the list of workshop topics at any helping-profession conference, and see that 90–100 percent of the presentations are on subject matter that Bowen theory says is irrelevant to understanding and modifying family process—not false, not inaccurate, but simply "not the information that counts." Similarly, most mental health programs and institutions organize themselves around foci that Bowen theory says should be defocused.

One small example that will serve both to illustrate and to metaphorize how Bowen theory constantly comes in at a tangent to accepted dichotomies in the field is his view of what is essential in the functioning of the human brain. Most discussion of the brain in psychological circles today splits it longitudinally by hemispheres, "right brain" and "left brain," and there is much emphasis on their separate functions, as well as on the categorizing of people in terms of which hemisphere seems to be more influential in their mental processes. The brain division that Bowen has emphasized, however, is on a horizontal plane. Using McLean's theories of "the triune brain" (McLean, 1985), Bowen theory sees the right-brain/left-brain distinctions as subsets of the far more crucial distinction

between the cortex and the limbic system. The view is that a person's *method* of perceiving, conceptualizing, or expressing ideas is far less significant than, and is always a function of, a more continuous fundamental process: one's ability to regulate one's reactivity, that is, differentiation.

The Emotional Being of the Therapist

A third characteristic of the Bowen approach that distinguishes it from other family theories is its emphasis on the self-development of the therapist. Bowen has consistently maintained that it is hard for the patient to mature beyond the maturity level of the therapist, no matter how good his or her technique. In Bowen theory, the *differentiation of the therapist is technique.* As will be seen below, the capacity of a therapist to apply Bowen theory is a function of the therapist's own differentiation. According to Bowen theory, therefore, maintaining a nonanxious presence, or being objective, or even promoting differentiation in others, is connected to the *being* of the therapist, not to his or her know-how. Here, Bowen theory again makes continuous what other theories would categorize separately, that is, the distinction between a therapist's supervision and his or her own "therapy," as an essential part of training in the Bowen school involves the therapist's working on his or her own differentiation. From the point of view of a Bowenian supervisor, the therapist can bring in situations either from client families or from his or her own family of origin. Indeed, if the differentiation of the therapist *is* technique, bringing cases of *other* families to one's supervisor may not even be the optimal way to receive supervision. (The extent to which this idea can be viewed as radical in some quarters is evidenced by the fact that Bowen-trained therapists have sometimes had difficulty receiving certification from some professional accreditation boards on the grounds that seeing the same person for supervision and therapy is unethical or unhealthy.)

There is another, perhaps more essential, way in which "the being of the therapist" is related to the functioning or at least the thinking of the therapist in Bowen theory. Kerr (1981) has stated that it may not be possible to comprehend

Bowen theory merely by reading about it or attending workshops. He has suggested that the therapist must first go through an emotional change. While such a notion smacks of cultism and "true believers" and can lead to the dangerous ad hominem position that if you disagree with the concepts, you are not differentiated (how do you distinguish those who disagree from those who cannot hear it?), to the extent that Kerr's observation is accurate, then Bowen theory may belong to that method of inquiry that can only be learned by apprenticing to the master or the master's disciples. While to some that characteristic may be enough to invalidate such thinking as more befitting the occult, the master–disciple relationship has always been an acceptable method of passing on a learned tradition in our civilization, sometimes with spectacular results. It is not possible, for example, to understand the Talmud simply by reading translations, or even a book on how the talmudists reasoned, or the meaning of their technical terms and pet phrases. One must study for some time with those who know the process. Similarly, a thorough grasp of Bowen theory is probably only achievable by studying the concepts over some period in the context of encountering one's own experience of life while maintaining some type of disciple relationship with someone who has already gone through the process. For those who might consider such teaching processes as more befitting religion than science, it should be noted that there exists evidence that Nobel prize winners in the hard sciences have frequently been part of multigenerational traditions of teachers who were Nobel laureates (Zuckerman, 1967), suggesting, among other things, that a successful way of thinking had been passed down through apprenticeship.

To the extent that Kerr's comment is accurate, the notion that an emotional change is as crucial to the training process as to the treatment process is unique to Bowen theory among family therapies, and it has a curious parallel in its application. That parallel has to do with patients who do everything "right" according to the Bowenian prescriptions and still do not make progress. They, too, must first go through some emotional change analogous to what the therapist had experienced in his or her training before *their* "technique" will work—and if the therapist

did not experience that shift, the client is not likely to do so.

BOWEN THEORY

Four Seminal Constructs

Here are four major interlocking concepts in Bowen theory that underpin all other Bowenian ideas and that "differentiate" Bowen theory from other family theories. As stated earlier, they will be presented not to explain them, but to show their theoretical significance both for the theory itself and for theorizing about families generally. Those constructs are *differentiation, emotional system, multigenerational transmission,* and *emotional triangle.* In the original formulation of his theory, Bowen referred to eight basic concepts. The other four are *nuclear family, family projection process, sibling position* (see also Toman, 1961), and *societal regression.* In addition, he later began to add, but never finished developing, a ninth, *spirituality.* Because of space limitations, only four have been selected for discussion here—those deemed to best elucidate the thrust of this chapter, the uniqueness of Bowen theory. The others are referred to in passing, and *societal regression* is discussed specifically in the conclusion. A fuller explanation of all of them can be found in Kerr (1981) or Bowen (1978).

Bowen's major constructs are interdependent. None is fully understandable without some comprehension of the other three, and all are held together by a premise that subsumes the entire theory, that there is a *chronic anxiety* in all of life that comes with the territory of living. It may manifest itself differently in different species, families, or cultures, and different families will vary in the intensity of chronic anxiety they exhibit, depending on such other variables as basic levels of differentiation and the position a given nuclear unit occupies on their own extended-family tree, but it is essentially the same phenomenon.

Chronic Anxiety

What Bowen refers to as "chronic anxiety" is not to be confused with worries about a specific problem of living, nor is it reducible to a phobia or a compulsion. "Chronic anxiety" is a far more pervasive, natural systems phenomenon of which the specific foci of personal anxiety are only the tracers. In psychoanalytic theory, anxiety is distinguished from fear as being a fear that is unfounded. Bowen's concept of chronic anxiety includes that notion, but a natural systems context suggests it is less something that is unnatural (that is, neurotic) than the exaggeration of a basic rhythm of life: the instinctual, nonthinking response necessary for wilderness survival as well as the habits required for playing sports. At times, the role of chronic anxiety in Bowen theory may seem to have something in common with the part played by *angst* in existential philosophical systems, but Bowen has taught it less as a quality of the human mind than as a biological phenomenon that humans have in common with all forms of life. Sometimes chronic anxiety appears to play the same theoretical role as Freud's "libido," an energizing force. It cannot be equated with angst or libido, however, and must be considered in terms that are universal to all creatures on this planet.

For Bowen, chronic anxiety is the emotional and physical reactivity shared by all protoplasm, the responses that are automatic rather than mediated by the cortex. It is transmitted from previous generations by families both cumulatively and idiosyncratically, and it is experienced and expressed more intensely by various individual members of our species because of the way previous generations in their families have channeled the transmission of their own. But the transmission does not begin with our own families; it is a natural systems phenomenon that goes back to the beginning of life on this planet (in this universe?). "Aha," you say, "but lower forms of life do not have a cortex, so the comparison is of apples and oranges." That is just the point. The cortex is not always as dominant as homo sapiens would like to believe. When our anxiety is low, our unencumbered thought processes enable us to differentiate from other forms of life, from previous generations, and from one another, but when our anxiety is high,

what we think is thinking is merely mental activity. Cerebration also can be reactivity, that is, in the service of chronic anxiety, and you can be as reactive with your left brain as with your right. Another way of putting this is to say that cerebration can only be considered thinking, according to Bowen theory, when it is in the service of, or is the result of, differentiating processes. Thus, clearheadedness (and, therefore, differentiation), while solely a human attribute, is achievable only by dealing with the same emotional forces that affect all other species. It is this connection between our emotional beings and the functioning of our cortex that has led the Family Center to study all forms of colonized life. And, as we will see below regarding Bowen therapy, the omnipresence of chronic anxiety in all human systems lays the groundwork for striving for objectivity in the functioning of any Bowen-trained therapist. In all events, *chronic anxiety is understood to be the primary promoter of all symptoms, from schizophrenia to cancer from anorexia to birth defects. The antidote, and the preventive medicine, always is differentiation.*[3]

Differentiation

Differentiation is the lifelong process of striving to keep one's being in balance through the reciprocal external and internal processes of self-definition and self-regulation. It is a concept that sometimes can be difficult to focus on objectively. As the emotional system of family therapists has evolved over the past quarter century, the term has almost become a buzzword that identifies its user as a follower of Bowen. No one trained in any other major family-therapy school would ever use the word any more, even in passing, lest he or she be defined as belonging to the wrong school. For their part, of course, Bowen's disciples never use the term "enmeshed" (a buzzword of the "structuralists") for the opposite of differentiation, what they call

---

[3] *Editors' Note.* It is impossible to underscore that, like differentiation, chronic anxiety is probably also not a single variable that "causes" things to happen, but rather, a multivariate concept. The subcomponents of both differentiation and chronic anxiety need to be better differentiated through empirical work.

"fusion." Ironically, a term that was coined in the service of objectivity has become emotion-laden and a source of much reactivity. Nothing, of course, shows less differentiation, since *differentiation* means the capacity to become oneself out of one's self with minimum reactivity to the positions or reactivity of others. Differentiation is charting one's own way by means of one's own internal guidance system, rather than perpetually eyeing the "scope" to see where others are at.

Differentiation as used by Bowen refers more to a process than to a goal that can ever be achieved. (When people say, "I differentiated from my wife, my child, my parent, etc.," that proves they do not understand the concept.) It refers to a direction in life rather than a state of being, to the capacity to take a stand in an intense emotional system, to saying "I" when others are demanding "we," to containing one's reactivity to the reactivity of others (which includes the ability to avoid being polarized), to maintaining a nonanxious presence in the face of anxious others. It refers, as well, to knowing where one ends and another begins, to being able to cease automatically being one of the system's emotional dominoes, to being clear about one's own personal values and goals, to taking maximum responsibility for one's own emotional being and destiny rather than blaming others or the context: culture, gender, or environmental forces. It is an emotional concept not a cerebral one, but it does require clearheadedness. And it has enormous consequence for new ways of thinking about leadership. But it is, as Bowen liked to say, a lifetime project, with no one ever getting more than 70 percent of the way to the goal.

Differentiation is not to be equated, however, with similar-sounding ideas such as individuation, autonomy, or independence. First of all, it has less to do with a person's behavior than, as mentioned, with his or her emotional being. Second, there is a sense of connectedness to the concept that prevents the mere gaining of distance or leaving, no less cutting off, from being the way to achieve it. Third, as stated above, it has to do with the fabric of one's existence, one's integrity. Obviously, differentiation has its origin in the biological notion that cells can have no identity, purpose, or distinctiveness until they have separated from—that is, left—their

progenitors (differentiation is a prerequisite to specialization even if one is ultimately going to fuse to accomplish one's purpose). But also implicit in this biological metaphor or homologue is the idea that such self has little meaning if the cell cannot connect. In its simplest terms, therefore, differentiation is the capacity to be one's own integrated aggregate-of-cells person while still belonging to, or being able to relate to, a larger colony. As already indicated, such a biological metaphor also has ramifications for thinking and the conduct of therapy, since the incapacity to achieve some balance in the self–togetherness struggle will tend to create a style of thinking that shows up in either/or, all-or-nothing, black-and-white conceptualizations and, eventually, family cutoffs. Conversely, the capacity to think systemically and avoid the polarizations characteristic of reactivity seems to go along with the emotional growth associated with differentiation. The major theoretical significance of differentiation for the overall development of Bowen theory, and for theorizing in the social sciences generally, is as follows: A problem common to all social science theorizing is that the more accurately any system of thought can make predictions, the less room it allows for free will. It is one thing to develop a theory about subatomic particles, plate tectonics, or black holes and, without any conflict at all, use as a criterion of the theory's validity its power for prediction. When the subject matter is the human animal, however, then the more elegant the theory, the less dignity is left for the human. It is, after all, precisely because the human is not a soulless star or particle that social science theory always fails to gain the same measure of certainty found in the "hard" sciences. It may be the awareness of this dilemma that has led many family therapists to try to synthesize family and individual model thinking.

Bowen's way of handling the problem has been to develop his systems theory consistent with natural systemic concepts despite the uncontrollable or unknowable implicit in the human animal having *animus*, but to leave room for a variable that could account for the differences, the inconsistencies, and the otherwise unexplainable that result from human will. What the Bowenian concept of differentiation does is to supply a variable that allows the rest of the theory to be developed in a systematic, consistent manner. But it keeps the theory honest by allowing for exceptions. In addition, the variable provided by differentiation helps Bowen theory deal with a problem common to all systems theory: how to account for change at all if systems are perpetually kept in balance by their own homeostatic forces. Why, for example, do some identified patients improve despite the system, or why, despite the impeccable logic of systemic thinking, do things sometimes just not turn out the way they are supposed to? And why do the elements that we assume have caused pathology in one system not have pathogenic effects in another?

It is perhaps in this context that Bowen's scale of differentiation (Kerr, 1981) can best be understood. The scale is an effort to say that despite the universality of systems concepts, people are different. But, the scale suggests, the differences that count are not to be found in the categories of information that are traditional sociological classifications nor can those differences be understood in the conventions of psychodynamics. What counts, according to the scale, is a person's capacity to function in a differentiated manner, as that term was defined above. And that is more a function of sibling position, triangles, and multigenerational processes than of gender, culture, or environmental conditioning.

Bowen's scale of differentiation is connected to Bowen theory's striving for unity. It is a lens for looking at the breadth of humanity in a manner that is continuous, not an effort to create a Brave New World of "alpha pluses" and "delta minuses." When Bowen first published his "scale," he was astounded to see how many missed the significance of continuity and began to use the scale against itself by employing it in their research to create discrete categories. That is precisely *not* what the scale is about.[4]

Carried to its logical conclusion, the scale has problems. For example, if you were to reach 100 on the scale, would you have all friends (since you could presumably then relate to anybody) or no friends, since at 100 who could relate to you? On the other hand, Liebnitz' theory of

---

[4] *Editors' Note.* Thus, the "scale" is not a "scale" in the usual sense of having certain psychometric properties (cf. Gurman, 1978).

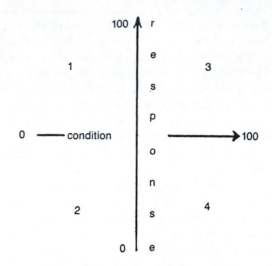

Figure 5–1. Condition and response

limits in calculus also breaks down at infinity. The usefulness of a theoretical concept is not necessarily destroyed by inconsistencies within it. What counts is its *power* to engender new thinking and glean observations that other models do not permit.

One way of demonstrating the power of Bowen's scale of differentiation to create a different perspective is with the bipolar figure shown in Figure 5-1.

In this figure, the horizontal axis, marked "condition," is the intensity of the family symptom, crisis, or anxiety attendant upon the crisis. The vertical axis, labeled "response," is the degree of differentiation in a person or a family, and is always inversely proportional to the amount of chronic anxiety transmitted to the system from previous generations. If you were to plot families or individuals along both axes, you would find that they would distribute themselves in all four quadrants. Those in quadrant 1 would not be likely to become dysfunctional, either because, objectively, they were not in crisis (scoring low on the horizontal scale), or because the crises that they were experiencing were not overwhelming since their level of differentiation (their position on the vertical scale) was high. Those in quadrant 2 also score low in the objective intensity of their crises (the horizontal scale), but more of them will develop symptoms because their level of differentiation (their capacity to deal with the crises they do experience) is also low on the vertical scale. In other words, such families may be lucky and not experience many critical events, but when they do, those crises will be magnified by their low level of differentiation. It will simply take less to throw them. Because, however, the normal tendency is to chart our existential position in life only on the horizontal scale (leaving out the differentiation variable), families in this quadrant (and often their therapists) will perceive themselves (unobjectively) to be further along the horizontal axis than they actually are.

This is brought sharply into relief by the fact that families in quadrant 3 are actually experiencing a higher degree of crises (horizontal scale), but because they are less reactive and handle their crises better (also high on the differentiation scale), they will, owing to the relative lack of symptoms, appear to be lower on the horizontal scale than they are. They are also less stressed because they handle their stress better. Again, however, by observing these families from a single-pole perspective, one might assume that they simply have fewer problems. It would be more accurate to say that these families have a greater likelihood of recuperation because their degree of resiliency of response is high. Also implicit here is the notion that symptoms have more to do with a family's position on the vertical axis than on the horizontal axis. In other words, symptoms are less related to strain (external pressure) than to stress (response). Thinking about stress as a vertical-axis phenomenon rather than a horizontal "condition" has, of course, major ramifications for taking responsibility for stress, as the term is normally used.

By contrast, the families most likely to dysfunction are those in quadrant 4, who score high on the horizontal scale and low on the vertical scale of differentiation, which, after all, really concerns their capacity to handle life's problems. They are the families least likely to heal. From a single-variable point of view, they will be viewed as dysfunctional simply because of the objective nature of their condition (disease, environment, existential dilemmas, family crises, etc.), whereas the bipolar perspective enables one to see that with the same amount of objective crisis (condition) in their lives, they still might have been less dysfunctional had their level of differentiation placed them in quadrant 3.

The most useful way to express the relationship between condition and response illustrated by this bipolar graph is as follows (keeping in mind that the differentiation level has a great deal to do with the amount of chronic anxiety transmitted from previous generations): given the same objective circumstances, families or individuals are more likely to dysfunction or develop symptoms *to the extent that* their differentiation is low, and to tolerate more intense symptoms, or rebound better from intense crises, *to the extent that* their differentiation is high. The bipolar graph also illustrates Bowenian methods of conceptualization because it emphasizes continuity rather than discrete categories. (Graphs make things more "graphic" than is true about any spectrum of humanity.) As stated above, the very capacity to think in terms of *to the extent that* rather than *either/or* is essential to Bowenian theory conceptualization.

Elsewhere (Friedman, 1985), I have tried to express the continuous quality of this relationship between condition and response by using the concept of a "hostile environment." In normal, linear conceptualizations of a hostile environment, only the horizontal axis is considered. The toxic quality of a hostile environment (HE) is usually understood to be simply equal to the strength (S) times the number (N) of toxic agents or pathogens (viruses or people) in it: $HE = S \times N$. A nonlinear understanding of the toxic quality of any hostile environment that includes Bowen's variable of differentiation would indicate that its potentially damaging effects are proportional to the response of the organism (RO), or HE/RO. According to this formula, the values on the vertical (response) scale (found in the denominator) can always dilute the power of the values in the horizontal (condition) scale (expressed by the numerator). No matter how large the numerator is, even a small increase in the denominator reduces its power considerably. More striking, as the denominator approaches zero, which would occur when the organism is being passive, taking a victim stance, or nullifying its own efforts with a high degree of reactivity, then no matter how small the numerator (how slight the objective damaging potential of the environment), the toxicity takes on infinite proportions.

Finally, there is one clinical aspect of the concept of differentiation that should be highlighted here because it also helps illustrate how different Bowen theory can be. The concept of differentiation is a focus on strength rather than pathology. It comes up fully on the side of personal responsibility rather than faulting the stars, society, the environment, or one's parents, for that matter. Despite the tinge of predestination associated with multigenerational transmission, differentiation is inherently an antivictim, antiblaming focus. Just as it is a variable that prevents systemic concepts from "blowing away" individual dignity, so too, when it comes to change, precisely because differentiation is a focus on the individual's response, it refuses to allow the system to take all the responsibility. And that is why, as will be seen below, Bowen therapy focuses on the vertical axis for both client and therapist.

Emotional System

A second basic construct in Bowen theory is the concept of an emotional system. It is interdependent with the aforementioned concept of differentiation and the concept of multigenerational transmission (to be explored next). It is, in fact, the context that joins them.

The term "emotional system" refers to any group of people or other colonized forms of protoplasm (herds, flocks, troops, packs, schools, swarms, and aggregates) that have developed emotional interdependencies to the point where the resulting system through which the parts are connected (administratively, physically, or emotionally) has evolved its own principles of organization. The structure, or resulting field, therefore, tends to influence the functioning of the various members more than any of the components tend to influence the functioning of the system. A family emotional system includes the members' thoughts, feelings, emotions, fantasies, associations, and past connections, individually and together. It includes their physical makeup, genetic heritage, and current metabolic states. It involves their sibling position and their parents' sibling positions. It rotates on the axes of their respective paths within the multigenerational processes transmitted from their own families of origin, including the fusion and the cutoffs. It includes the emotional history of the system itself, particularly the conditions under which it originally took shape; the effect upon it of larger emotional and physical forces; how it has dealt with transitions, particularly loss; and the quality of differentiation in the system, both now and in the past, particularly of those at the top. In effect, it includes all the information that can be put on a family's genogram.

Bowen has come to use the term "family" as synonymous with "emotional system," so defined. An emotional system is not to be equated, however, with a "relationship system" or a "communication system," though it includes them. In fact, Bowen has gone out of his way to avoid the terminology of information theory, general systems theory, or cybernetics when describing an "emotional system," because "self" from a natural systems' point of view is not a concept; it is a dynamic reality capable of maturation. Cybernetics is for cyborgs. It is also Bowen theory's rootedness in the evolutionary processes of all natural systems that makes the concept of an emotional system equally valid for an organ or an organization.

There are two aspects of Bowen's concept of a family as an emotional system that help bring out the distinctiveness of Bowen theory. One is the criterion that this concept establishes for what information is important; the second is how this method of conceptualization is similar to the antireductionist, field-theory models emerging in other scientific disciplines.

Regarding criteria for information, family therapy currently is in an informational bind. Every family will produce an encyclopedia of information about itself. Is the therapist simply to write down dutifully every fact he or she hears? Not only is that impossible, but such a focus on the content of what is heard is likely to fuse ("enmesh") the therapist in the emotional processes of the family. Many facts reported by family members, particularly cultural and environmental explanations for their functioning, while appearing to be helpful, often are really efforts to deny personal responsibility or to obfuscate emotional process. Objective observation is eroded if the therapist is trying to observe everything. The problem of data gathering is intensified by the fact that every therapist today regularly receives notices of books or conferences on literally hundreds of symptoms and new approaches. Since information generally increases at an exponential rate, the problem can only get worse. For example, if we go back in history by a factor of ten to the year 199, the amount of information that existed then would fit on one shelf in our libraries today. If we think forward in history by a factor of ten to the year 19990, however, we have to assume that the amount of information in existence then will be beyond the capacity of even the most sophisticated optical memory banks of today. One can never catch up. Not only is it impossible in such an atmosphere to be objective, but to the extent that members of the helping professions moor their sense of confidence in their knowledge of pathology or technique, they are doomed always to feeling inadequate. The way out of this bind is not to specialize, which only sends the avalanche of information in the opposite direction, but to find criteria for what information is important.

This is precisely the function of Bowen's concept of an emotional system. It concentrates the focus of what to take note of (primarily, levels of differentiation, interlocking triangles, and chronic anxiety), and it reduces greatly the importance of the data that many other approaches to family therapy consider significant, if not vital, by seeing such information as the content rather than the driving force of emotional process. For example, from the perspective of an emotional system, culture does not "cause" family process. It stains it (that is, makes it visible). Culture, rather than being the formative process, is the medium through which family process works its art. Elsewhere (Friedman, 1985) I have tried to show that, using Bowen theory, it is possible to develop laws of family process regarding such factors as loss replacement, cutoffs, pain thresholds, the similarity of opposite extremes, secrets, triangles, chronic conditions, and the like that have the same relevance for all families irrespective of culture. And to the extent that there is divergence between two families with respect to these laws, those differences cannot be traced back to cultural, environmental, or gender differences, but to factors that involve levels of chronic anxiety and differentiation. Another way of putting this is as follows: The concept of an emotional system suggests that if you knew all of the cultural and environmental factors in a family's background, but

knew nothing about the family members' emotional processes as defined by Bowen theory, you could not make very accurate predictions about how they will fare in the future. On the other hand, if you knew all the emotional process factors as defined by Bowen theory, you would not need to know any of the background cultural factors in order to make very accurate predictions about that family's future. From the perspective of an emotional system, cultural and environmental factors are far less important than is the timing of significant changes; the kind of people they are (their personalities) and their backgrounds are less important than the positions they occupy in the triangles of their contemporary systems and the paths of multigenerational transmission.

The second aspect of the emotional-system concept that helps sharpen the distinctiveness of Bowen theory is its similarity to what has come to be called field theory in other sciences (Sheldrake, 1988), particularly physics, astronomy, and biology. In recent years, within all of these areas of inquiry there has been some movement away from the notion that structures can be understood in terms of their components (matter) alone. In physics, together with the tradition of progressively narrowing the focus to smaller and smaller particles in an effort to try to find the elementary components of matter (from atom—which means uncuttable—to electron to lepton to quark), another approach has been developing that defocuses that infinitely regressive search. It tries to understand all matter not as particles, but as waves in a *field*. One of the reasons for going in this direction, besides the bottomless pit found in the search for elementary particles, is a striving for unity, an effort to understand the four major forces of the universe with one theory. Parallel thinking has gone on in astronomy with models called "string theory" that suggest that matter and energy are laid out across the heavens in patterns established by the original big bang and function dynamically in patterns that are still evolving from (and, therefore, are still in touch with) those initiating events.

In biology, a similar effort to get away from explaining protoplasm purely in terms of genetic programs has received new impetus. There has always been some awareness that certain biological phenomena are not explainable, and, indeed, seem to go against, the notion of genetic determinism alone, but the new technologies of microbiology have provided more evidence for the fact that genes no more may be the basic constituents of protoplasm than atoms are the basic constituents of matter (Webster & Goodwin, 1982). Actually, from this perspective, what has been given up is the importance of the notion of basic constituents. For what is now realized in both physics and biology is that the way constituent particles function is not necessarily according to their own nature alone, but often is due to their position within force fields that encompass them. In other words, change their position and they will function differently; change the forces and they will appear to have different natures. Genes, for example, can function differently depending on their position on a chromosome. The rotation of the axis of symmetry of an amphibious embryo can result in its producing twins. The transplantation of cells to another location on a chick embryo can result in the cells developing partly according to their nature and partly according to their position on the embryo. One can cut away parts of certain embryos in an early-enough stage and they will still produce a complete creature, though smaller. Here is a description in terms of field theory from astronomy of the relationship of Jupiter and her moons that might just as easily be a description of schizophrenia within the relationship system of a family:

Gases from Jupiter's moons are transported to Jupiter by the magnetic field between them, thus providing atmosphere to their host's planet—it is reasonable to consider the field as the operative entity, with planet and satellites as nodes within it.

What the Bowen concept of an emotional system has in common with field theory in biology and physics is, first of all, a striving for the unity of all forces; second, a veering away from materialistic reductionism (explaining structures in terms of their components); and third, an emphasis, instead, on the forces in the field and the position of various members within the field (thus, the emphasis on triangles, multigenerational transmission, sibling position, and "I" position). Indeed, Bowen has, at times, used the phrase "emotional field" rather than emotional system. So used, a field may be defined as an environment of influence that is not material in itself (a magnetic or gravitational field, for example), but comes into existence because of the proximity of matter to matter. However, once the field does come into being, it has more power to influence the discrete particles within it than any of those pieces of matter can continue to influence the field they have, by their presence, "caused" to exist.

Bowen's emphasis on emotional rather than environmental or cultural factors can be understood as an effort to stay focused on the field. And *differentiation*, within this context, becomes making oneself aware of the encompassing fields, as well as one's position in them, so that one can make choices.

One application of the concept of emotional systems that will help illustrate field theory is an approach to leadership I have been calling "leadership through self-differentiation" (Friedman, 1985). Early in my experience as a supervisor, I noticed that whenever a member of the helping professions was having difficulty functioning creatively, imaginatively, or in a well-defined manner in any institution (hospital, clinic, or partnership), the person leading his or her organization was poorly defined: a person who rarely took stands, a peace-monger, someone without vision, someone who was more a reactor than an initiator. Later, I learned that this was true for all organizations—military, religious, educational, business, and families.

As a result, in supervising leaders of any kind of institution, including the family, I have taught that if the person at the top will focus primarily on his or her own differentiation (i.e., providing vision, defining self, working at being a non-anxious presence, while taking care to remain connected), then such functioning will have a systemic effect on the rest of the individuals in the organization, that is, the organizational field. (Often a person who can do this will tend to become the one "at the top" even if he or she does not have the title.) When the "head" of any institution moves in a better differentiated direction, not only will everyone become more productive, but their relationships with one another also will improve. What distinguishes this basically Bowenian notion of leadership as a field theory concept is that it is not saying that the leader (or parent) becomes a model to emulate. Rather than serving as a primary copy to be replicated, what leadership through self-differentiation affects is the field, which then affects the components within it. It is not a matter of specific behavior by a leader leading to similar specific behavior by a follower. Direct connection or observation between the head and the other components around specific issues is not involved. The components are not influenced because they learn to do by observing or through "identification." Leadership through self-differentiation, is based on an organic concept: it is the nature of organic fields (the human body or a body politic) that when one of the components (an organ or an organism) can evolve to the position of "head" and then differentiate itself, the systemic ramification of that connectedness through the entire emotional system (field) is what influences the functioning of the other components and the nature of their relationships with one another.

Other evidence for the field theory aspect of this process is that when leaders (heads), or parents, can be taught to function in this way, chronic ailments in the system that appear to be unconnected often seem to go quietly away, though usually no clear cause-and-effect chain is visible. And the principle seems to transcend the size of the following. The head of an elephant, after all, has as much influence on its body as does the head of a chinchilla on its body. The process seems similar to the uncanny self-regulation processes found in successful biofeedback where, through information loops, thinking can change cellular and, hitherto considered involuntary, glandular responses. It is also similar to any situation in which a person suffers from a variety of chronic conditions for which there are a myriad of appropriate specialists, and then finds that a change in central metabolic processes, and sometimes in his or her vision about life's goals, affects all symptoms at once.

Finally, it should be mentioned here that the Bowenian emotional systems or field concept produces one more example of continuity where there has traditionally been dichotomy. Through the basicness of its biological metaphor, the concept of an emotional system breaks down the usual distinctions among different types of institutional life (sports, business, health care, religion, etc.) and unifies that which promotes the health of institutions with that which promotes personal physical well-being. All this, in turn, feeds back to the notion mentioned above that in Bowen theory, thinking is an emotional phenomenon—and so, then, also must be leadership. If that is so, then management consultants will have no more luck changing corporations or partnerships fundamentally than therapists are able to bring essential change to families as long as they focus on technical, managerial, and administrative solutions rather than on promoting differentiation (an emotional change) at the top.

Multigenerational Transmission

Of all the central Bowenian concepts, it may be the multigenerational perspective that gives the others their Bowenian dimension. At first, the concept sounds similar to what all social science research would accept, that the past influences the present. There is a difference, however. For Bowen, it is not simply the influence of the past, but it is, to use Rupert Sheldrake's phrase, "the presence of the past." Basically, the concept states that emotional responses, both their nature and the degree of their intensity, are passed down from "generation to generation," a triple entendre that means not only (1) parents to children, but also (2) the replication from any consecutive stages of reproduction, and (3) the overall process itself. Such transmission is conducted through all the conduits of an emotional system as defined above. In addition, while families differ in the way they do this, differences between families have less to do with cultural or environmental characteristics of the family (which, as stated, supply the medium of expression rather than the driving process) than with the position of those families as weak or strong limbs on their larger extended-family tree, and, ultimately, the position of those extended families as limbs on the human family tree. What most defines where any nuclear family grouping (or any member within a family) is situated on those trees is the basic level of chronic anxiety or its reciprocal, the basic level of differentiation of self, that multigenerational processes have formatted and reinforced over the generations. The same phenomenon seems to apply to "branches" of an organization.

More is involved here, however, than the

conditioning of the past, or something we have inherited or *introjected* from our ancestors. Bowen's multigenerational-transmission concept is rooted in the notion that all generations are part of a *continuous natural process*, with each generation pressing up against the next, so that past and present almost become a false dichotomy. (Even with "time," Bowen theory makes continuous what is conventionally categorized separately.) It is this warping of time, so to speak, that gives Bowen's theory of transmission its special dimension and differentiates it from other theories that emphasize the "influence" of the past. Not only does it suggest you "can go home again," the intimation is that you never left.

As mystical as this sounds, it has some extraordinary similarity to the aforementioned effort to understand the cosmos known as "string theory." (The fact that you tear off a page from the calendar does not mean that that unit of time has actually ceased to exist.) Thus, not only can the future be predicted on the basis of the past, but the past can be reconstructed on the basis of the ever-evolving present.

"Working on one's family of origin," therefore, as the phrase has come to be used, is far more than a matter of scaring up one's ancestors like Gilbert and Sullivan's *Duke of Rudigore*. And it is even more than learning to "understand" one's parents or to reconnect with theirs. The connection that is important is with the natural processes that are formatting one's destiny, processes that not only go back for generations, but ultimately to all life's processes since creation. The specifics, therefore, of researching cutoffs; finding long lost relatives; correlating dates of change; delineating interlocking triangles; noting similarities of symptoms, issues, and the positions of those who become symptomatic over the generations; or changing one's responses to habitual family interactions, while useful in their own right for obtaining distance from, and (one would hope) gaining more objectivity about, one's present emotional state, have a far more fundamental purpose. *They are angles of entry into the universal, if not cosmic, processes that have formed our being.* It is the capacity to get in touch with that process, to know it and experience it, to be affected by it all over again, and then not to be reactive to it, that, according to Bowen theory, is the source of self-

differentiation. And, says Bowen theory, to the extent that individuals can accomplish that, they will find an immediate carryover to functioning in all their relationships. It is here that we can see the raison d'être for family-of-origin focus as a form of supervision of therapists. Not only does it increase self-differentiation, an essential factor in dealing with anxiety, but it also gives the therapist first-hand "familiarity" with the basic life processes—which, according to Bowen theory, are what we are really dealing with anyway, no matter what the family problem.

Bowen first became aware of the latter ramifications of the multigenerational transmission process while working with medical residents. He noticed that they became better physicians when, in the course of their working on their own marriages, they were induced to go back to their families of origin. In recent years, I have had a similar experience with members of the clergy. Every minister, no matter what his or her denomination, who has come in for help with a crisis in faith has found that the crisis atrophied when he or she used the conflict as an entrée back into the emotional processes of his or her family of origin. In other words, their religious commitment became clearer and more self-affirmed when the ministers came into contact with, and were able to differentiate themselves from, the same emotional processes that contributed to their originally joining the clergy. Such increased differentiation has almost never led to their leaving their profession. What happens seems more akin to their acquiring it for their own.

The significance of Bowen's multigenerational transmission concept for his own theory is, as already stated, that it puts the entire theory into the framework of natural systems, that is, life in this cosmos. The significance for family therapy, and theory generally, is its deemphasis on symptoms in the process of obtaining change, and the setting of different criteria for judging the severity of a problem. In ascertaining the degree of illness in a given family tree, it focuses more on the structure of the root system than on the immediate fruitfulness or barrenness of its boughs.

One clinical example will illustrate this. A therapist has two families come in who are in apparently similar situations. In both, say, there are anorexic girls of about the same age, from similar socioeconomic backgrounds, and with similar sibling positions, similar weights, similar petulance, similar conflicts of will with their parents, a similar degree of anxiety in their parents about the symptom, and so on. Family diagrams, however, show that in one system there is evidence everywhere of failure to cope—early death, lack of reproduction, a great deal of divorce and marital conflict, other members of the patient's generation (cousins) often focused or dysfunctional—whereas in the genogram of the other girl; the evidence everywhere is of strength and resiliency. On the basis of that multigenerational comparison, one can make a far better prediction of which child has the better chance of recuperation than one could based on information about the present state of things.

The most significant ramification of the way in which multigenerational transmission deemphasizes the focus on specific symptomatology is as follows. Much, if not most, of the change that occurs in families and other institutions does not last. And much of what we thought was change often recycles either in a different form or in a different location. Much change is merely transformation. In true change, something remains the same. The illusions of change and the recycling of symptoms are attributable to what may be called "the myth of the primary site," which is the assumption that disease or dysfunction originates in the place in which it first surfaces or to which it can be traced back. The alternative to that way of thinking, however, is not to say that it began in a different location, but to assume that what is *primary* is not a site but the coming together of necessary and sufficient processes at a particular moment. In other words, the onset is not caused by something natural to the specific *location* where it "began," but by the fact that it was at a propitious moment in a multigenerational emotional transmission process. Bowen has analogized this process to a tornado that can only come into being when all the right conditions of temperature, pressure, and humidity are met simultaneously. If only two are satisfied, you do not get two thirds of a tornado. He has applied this way of thinking to physical illness, for example, suggesting that both emotional and physical conditions must be satisfied simultaneously. However, it can really be applied to the formation

of any symptom or dysfunction, in a person, a family, or an organization.

Problem-afflicted churches and synagogues illustrate the primary-site paradox well, though it can be found in all institutions to the extent that they become involved in the family process. Every religious hierarchy has institutions that are known as "pills" or as "plums," and the members of the clergy in any denomination know well which they are. The plums tend to have three clergy in a century; the pills tend to spit them out every other year, if not twice a year. The failures of all hierarchies, no matter what the denomination, to change these institutions are identical, and their overall batting average is about the same as that in the war on cancer. The usual response is to put in new, better, healthier, younger clergy. But as with cancer, malignant processes are not changed by "new blood." Similarly, the clergy in congregations that tend to the pill end of the spectrum often become engaged in long, bitter battles to get rid of a few dissidents; sometimes they are successful, but often, even after such excision, they find the problem resurfacing several years later in "cells" that had never had contact with the "cells" that left. It is as when a surgeon says, "We found a small malignancy, but don't worry, we got it all." "Getting it all" assumes that the disease process *began* in the primary site. Still another way of asking the question that will show we are always dealing with processes rather than location or specific amounts of matter is: Where does something go when it is said to have gone into remission?

Not only does Bowen's concept of the multigenerational transmission process avoid the will-o'-the-wisp of the primary site, but it also offers new ways for understanding institutional character. Again, using churches and synagogues as models for any institution, one might begin by asking what was present in their early development that allows some to recuperate faster or with less trauma. It is not that they do not face the same issues. Many religious institutions are thrown off track when the separation (divorce) from some minister was poorly handled. The origins of many "pills" begin in a split from another congregational colony. Still another possibility worth researching is that all institutions "institutionalize" the emotional processes (and the pathology) of the founding families. Since law firms, professional sports teams, businesses, professional partnerships, and many health-care institutions replicate similar phenomena, Bowen's concept of multigenerational transmission suggests different approaches to curing their ills than focusing on managerial techniques or administrative solutions. It may be that only well-differentiated leadership, supported by the hierarchy of stockholders, can reformat multigenerational influence. This is in stark contrast to the concept of "know-how." As with therapists, because of all the books and workshops now available on managerial and administrative techniques, everyone "knows how." Yet there are still only a very few really successful organizations in any field of endeavor. If the problem were know-how, we should see more successful institutions. Related here is the fact that the Bowenian concept of transmission suggests a different classification principle for consulting with work systems. All institutions can be regrouped, and then compared, more significantly, according to longitudinal principles of differentiation and the multigenerational transmission of chronic anxiety, rather than separated into conventional sociological categories of function or product.

Finally, here is one small example of great illustrative consequence: In reviewing the family budget, a husband was showing his wife how he had several sources of income, and how he allocated funds from these various sources for different family expenses. The wife responded, "Why do you break it up that way? It's all one pot. There is no reason why this source should pay for that expense. You've made things unnecessarily complicated, and hidden the overall strength in that dichotomous approach." She suggested unifying procedures, and he resisted strongly, though he could give no logical reason why he insisted on maintaining the present pattern. Finally he said, "Things just evolved this way. As this source developed, I was able to justify this expense, and they just kind of 'grew up together.'" The principle that emerges from this illustration, and it is a principle that is equally applicable to all institutions, work, or family, is that *evolutionary flow has more power to format the structure of relationships than the logic of their contemporary connections.*

Emotional Triangle

A fourth, essential Bowenian concept is the idea of an emotional triangle. This refers to any three parts of an emotional system, either three individuals or two persons and an issue. Bowen has referred to triangles as the "molecules" of families, the basic building blocks. While the term is often shortened to "triangle," the concept is more complex than a triad. Emotional triangles have specific rules that govern their emotional processes, such as the idea that you cannot change a relationship between two others or between another person and his or her habit. They function perversely; the more you try to change the relationship of two others (again, either two other people or a person and his or her habit), the more likely it is that you will reinforce the very aspects of the relationship you want to change.

Kerr (1981) has suggested that triangles are natural phenomena, and certainly their universality would hint of that. They are not more prone to form in one culture than another, or in one century than another, nor are the rules they follow gender-specific in any way. He has also tried to show evidence of emotional triangles in other species. Bowen has suggested that triangles form out of the anxiety of two-person systems, that it is impossible for any two persons to maintain the level of differentiation necessary to retain a stable relationship, and that one way of stabilizing a relationship, therefore, is to draw a third party into it, either directly or by discussion. (How long can two people talk to each other without beginning to talk about a third?)

While the concept of an emotional triangle may not appear to have the theoretical weightiness of the three concepts discussed previously, it goes a long way toward supplying a method for linking and operationalizing the others. It has enormous clinical and administrative significance. For example, the concept of a triangle can help explain why systems do not change despite reorganization (e.g., centralization or decentralization) if that change fails to affect the relevant triangles. Similarly, the concept of an emotional triangle can go far toward explaining why change does not occur when new people enter an old system. What any newcomer to a family or a work system really enters is a set of previously established interlocking triangles, with all the emotional process that conveys. (The fact that triangles do not change when one of the parties leaves also explains why neither death, divorce, nor leaving home usually change family triangles.)

With regard to therapy, this central concept supplies a strategy in itself. It is that if you, as a therapist, allow a couple to create a triangle with you, but take care not to get caught up in the emotional process of that triangle either by overfunctioning or being emotionally reactive, *then, by trying to remain a nonanxious presence in that triangle, you can induce a change in the relationship of the other two that would not occur if they said the same things in your absence.* This procedure can work equally well in a work system, in therapy, or in one's own family.

Another major theoretical ramification of the concept of an emotional triangle is that it offers a different perspective on stress. One of the universal rules of triangles is that, to the extent that you become responsible for, or try to change the relationship of, two others—two people or a person and a habit—you will experience the stress for their relationship. The idea that *stress is positional rather than quantitative* has enormous consequence for the way people function in all their emotional systems. Just explaining this notion can often help highly stressed individuals to see changes they have to make far more easily than do efforts to have them understand personal qualities that are motivating them to remain in stressful dilemmas. It is, once again, a focus on the (vertical) response axis rather than on the (horizontal) condition axis. Because the concept of an emotional triangle emphasizes position rather than personality, it is a concept that belongs to field theory, and when one can see how various triangles interlock, sometimes one can almost see the entire field. Indeed, the opposite may also be true, that the failure to see the network of triangles, or how one is caught in a given triangle, results in more either/or thinking and blaming.

The concept of an emotional triangle, particularly of interlocking triangles, also helps plot the path of multigenerational transmission when viewing genograms, and can help us see things as similar that we might otherwise treat as different. For example, far fewer mothers die in childbirth today, and that is certainly due in part to advances in medicine. But even at its worst point in recorded history, the majority of mothers did not die in childbirth. If the higher mortality rate years ago can be explained in terms of poor medicine alone, why were there not more deaths? On the other hand, the concept of an emotional triangle suggests the possibility that the same family position most conducive to postpartum depression today (which may have taken up the slack of many of those deaths) as well as to many modern birth-giving mortalities, namely, an emotional triangle between a passive or critical husband and a distant or critically dependent mother (of the new mother), was a major variable that influenced which mothers died and which mothers recovered from childbirth complications years ago. (There is implicit here an assumption that any patient's response to "complications" from any medical procedure, if not the manifestation of the complications themselves, is related to his or her differentiation.) Thus, the concept of an emotional triangle can identify similarities over the generations that one might otherwise not see if one focused on conventional sociological distinctions such as the age in which an event occurred.

The major clinical significance of the concept of an emotional triangle is that it focuses on phenomenology rather than interpretation. When Bowen left the psychoanalytic movement, one aspect of psychoanalysis that troubled him was its unverifiability. (See below regarding his concern for objectivity.) Interpretation of others' motivations is slippery stuff. The very process invites projection. In addition, motivation is irrelevant to determining the validity of an action, so there is the ever-present danger of ad hominem reasoning, that is, evaluating the worth of an action or an idea on the basis of an attribute or the situation of the person making the statement or the psychological reason why it is performed.

Clinically, the concept of an emotional triangle frees one from having to read minds. It keeps one focused on factors that are describable and veridical. And it enables one to gauge change in a manner that is less affected by the psyche of the observer. In short, the concept of an emotional triangle is tied up with the objectivity of the observer, and, as will be seen shortly, that is a major principle in the application of Bowen theory.

BOWEN THERAPY

As in the previous section on theory, the following discussion of "Bowen therapy" will focus primarily on what I perceive to be most characteristic and different—though what may be most characteristic and different is that Bowen theory tries not to emphasize any distinction between theory and therapy in the first place! This is precisely why supervision is aimed at the thinking and differentiation of the therapist rather than at teaching him or her a set of techniques. The assumption is that the therapist will be able to promote differentiation in a family (the ultimate aim of all Bowen therapy) to the extent that the therapist has promoted his or her own. Another way of saying this is, from the perspective of Bowen theory, that any technique has the potential to "work," and the same technique (reframing, restructuring, reconstruction, rituals, paradox, family of origin, use of gender issues, etc.) will have different results, depending less on its appropriateness for a given family situation, how it is employed, or the background, personality, gender, and style of the therapist, than on the degree of differentiation in the therapist employing it. As mentioned above, it is the "being" of the therapist, the therapist's presence rather than any specific behavior, that is the agent of change. That presence includes engaging without being reactive, stimulating without rescuing, and teaching a way of thinking and observing without willing the other's head to change. The power of the therapist is based more on the nature of the connectedness that comes with being human, that is, the nature of emotional systems, than on specific skills at fixing families. It is almost as though the verb "to be" were transitive, and one could, by the nature of one's being, "*be*"—that is, have an effect on—someone else.[5]

Within the therapeutic encounter itself, there are not actually a lot of specific techniques to be taught. Coaching couples to be more self-defined, teaching people to be more objective about themselves in relation to their environment, tutoring about the principles of triangles, encouraging people to learn about their multigenerational emotional histories and to go back and face issues they have fled, reworking family cutoffs, and teasing out, and challenging or encouraging the emergence of self are the basic pathways, and any that is promoted by a nonreactive therapist who is continuing to work on his or her own maturity is in the service of differentiation. Over the years, a body of specific ways to go about this has evolved and can be learned from any Bowen-trained therapist through example, supervision, or videotapes.

More important for this chapter on differentiating differentiation than showing how to apply Bowen theory are some of the principles that underpin the application. As stated earlier, by the nature of the case, this entire chapter has been weighted toward theory, not practice. *The theory was not prelude to the practice; thinking it is the practice!* The discussion of application that follows, therefore, is for the purpose of further clarifying the theory, rather than some culmination that describes how to do it. And the various clinical examples cited, therefore, should be understood as having this illustrative purpose rather than as instructions on the proper, no less the only, way to deal with that particular situation.

Three principles about the conduct of therapy that Bowen has tried to teach his disciples will be discussed. They have to do with (1) the objectivity of the therapist, (2) the effect of proximity on protoplasm, and (3) a natural-systems-based view of healing as a self-regenerative process. All fit logically within the framework of the major characteristics and theoretical constructs discussed above—though because of the emphasis on the being of the therapist, the concept of differentiation will be seen to occupy a position of increasingly central importance, unifying theory and therapy, therapeutic functioning and client functioning, and the three underlying principles themselves. As the major constructs, all three are interdependent so that none can be fully understood without some understanding of the other two. It will also be seen that Bowen therapy's construction of the therapeutic encounter forces a reframing of traditional questions about treatment strategies,

---

[5] *Editors' Note.* The empirical question implied by this position, of course, involves the relative contribution to outcome of the therapist's way of thinking vs. technical factors, an area of Bowen therapy certainly in need of systematic research because of the strength of Bowenian assertions on the matter.

therapeutic failure, and termination, and establishes different criteria for evaluating change.

Objectivity

Shortly after Bowen joined the Georgetown Medical School faculty, a story circulating in the wake of his pioneering studies with hospitalized families at National Institute of Mental Health (NIMH) was of a woman who had come to him for a pass to go home. According to the tale, she also asked for a prescription for sleeping pills, and as Bowen was writing out the prescription, she added that when she got home, she was going to use them to kill herself. As the story was told, Bowen just went on writing the prescription, and without even looking up, asked, "Well just how many do you think you'll need?" In one version, she went home, took them out, immediately became nauseated, and flushed them down the toilet.

The story of that event, which occurred about 30 years ago, would be heard today as an early precursor of what has come to be called paradox, or what Bowen came to call a "reversal." His response was far more than an effort to affect the client, however. It was a manifestation of Bowen's own lifelong effort to maintain objectivity (a scientific attitude), which he has always seen as crucial to effective change. Indeed, he winds up in the position that whatever promotes objectivity also promotes change, and was led to this connection from the realization years after NIMH that "I did my best work with my research families."

Almost all schools of therapy have been concerned about objectivity, of course. What has been special about Bowen's approach to this universal quest is that he has seen the problem of objectivity as an emotional phenomenon and not as a cerebral or a sensory issue. The Bowenian guideline is: *Objectivity is inversely proportional to reactivity.* As mentioned above regarding chronic anxiety, clearheadedness is an emotional state, and is maximized when the therapist works on his or her own self-regulation, which is partly a function of differentiation and partly a function of staying detriangled. This way of thinking, which makes the achieving of objectivity dependent on the emotional being of the therapist rather than on his

or her acuity of perception, or "powers of observation," is what unifies the factors that promote objectivity with those that promote healing.

To understand Bowen's response to the woman's provocative statement, one has to realize that within the perspective of Bowen theory, the major thrust of paradoxical or any other "technique" in the application of the theory is less toward changing the head of the client than toward maintaining the differentiation (i.e., reducing the anxiety) of the therapist. Paradox is aimed at the paradoxer, to help keep him or her out of that pernicious triangle that subverts all well-intentioned therapeutic efforts: the triangle in which the therapist winds up stuck with the responsibility for the client's problem or destiny. It is here that objectivity and therapeusis become one. As was shown above, remaining in a triangle (here it is Bowen, the woman, and the responsibility for her life), but staying untriangled, is in itself a therapeutic stance. It follows, therefore, that *all detriangling procedures designed to maintain objectivity (differentiation) in the therapist automatically contribute to differentiation in the client. In other words, the change process does not center on the behavioral functioning of the client, but on the same emotional functioning in the therapist that optimizes his or her objectivity. This also means that when a family appears to be stuck, the therapist should focus primarily on changing his or her own input into the therapeutic triangle.* In addition, since most efforts on the part of a triangled therapist to will change in a client increase or stem from anxiety in either client or therapist, by remaining focused on issues in the therapeutic triangle, the therapist also promotes healing and objectivity simultaneously.

Bowen's reconceptualization of the problem of objectivity in terms of emotional triangles is also worth noting because it was, in some ways, his own effort to remain objective about the field of psychotherapy, as well as to stay out of one of its major (emotional) triangles. It is one more example of what is so often characteristic of his own thinking processes: his tendency to come in at a tangent to conventional dichotomies. In the 1950s, the range of therapeutic modalities was much narrower than it is today. Psychoanalysis and behaviorism were almost the only choices. They were not only different schools, but also different establishments. Psychoanalysis saw the objectivity problem in terms of transference: the tendency of the patient to reproduce in the relationship with the therapist the same system of responses, expectations, and fantasies that had been programmed (habituated) by his or her parents, and the countertransference, the phenomenon where the therapist either does likewise or falls into the trap of responding as the patient's parent had. Behaviorism tried to avoid the issues of "freedom and dignity" completely by treating the human animal as a laboratory animal (Skinner, 1971). Psychodynamics (and insight), the therapeutic relationship, and motivation were irrelevant; "contingencies of reinforcement," or conditioning, was the name of the game. Bowen avoided getting caught in that either/or by, on the one hand, honoring the concept of transference, while, on the other, trying to approach it from a laboratory—that is, a research—observer position.

Instead of considering the interpretation of the transference to be the key to change, which meant encouraging one to form, Bowen thought the therapist should try to *stay out* of the transference as much as possible by functioning in a detriangled manner that kept it fulminating within the family, in front of him. He was shifting the therapy setting, as he put it in an early presentation, "from couch to coach" (Bowen, 1978). And his guideline to the therapist who became too active, itself often a manifestation of anxiety, was, "Make yourself as small as possible in the session." As will be seen in the next section on proximity and protoplasm, "make yourself small" can have fundamentally significant consequences, not only for the objectivity of the therapist, but also for the very survival of a client.

With regard to the present matter of objectivity, "make yourself small" was a guideline to help the therapist adopt a "nonparticipant" vantage point outside the emotional field that would enable him or her to observe more objectively, that is, to distinguish process from content. In addition, the logic of the theory suggested that it would, at the same time, actually promote change faster than encouraging the transference, because the therapist would be less likely to absorb, or to be absorbed into, the family emotional system. The therapist was, of course, participating, but as a catalyst. And catalyst means, by definition, something that by its presence fosters a reaction between other elements that cannot occur in its absence but which maintains its own integrity by not becoming lost in the process. This is also, of course, the perfect detriangled involvement.

To appreciate how radically different the idea of staying out of the transference was in its day, one might compare it to the position of Reinman and other 19th-century geometricians who broke with Euclid's fundamental ideas on parallel lines, saying, "If space is curved, there are no such things as parallel lines." In other words, a basic postulate was not discarded as much as it was turned on its head. And, just as in geometry, where that simple-appearing, non-Euclidian change in a basic premise led to viewing things in a new dimension (and, down the line, to relativity and a guide for interplanetary travel), so the concept of staying out of the transference led Bowen to seeing the client in a new dimension and to an entirely new adventure in comprehending the human condition: systemic family therapy. (Bowen has described part of his own intellectual odyssey in his epilogue to Kerr's [1988] *Family Evaluation.*)

As in so much of Bowen theory, precisely because it is a basic shift in conceptualizing, the idea of "staying out of the transference" cannot be easily classified by the standard conventions of psychotherapy. The position is akin neither to that of insight nor to that of behaviorism. It preserves the power inherent in the therapeutic presence, but emphasizes the factors that will make that presence objective. What also makes the concept of staying out of the transference difficult to comprehend is that it can sound like a prescription for doing nothing. But, as already mentioned, the truth is quite the contrary. The art is to remain a part of the triangle without getting "triangled," that is, without becoming either a focus of the others' displacement, a conduit for their connection, or reactive to their relationship. That requires a kind of balance and self-regulation similar to walking a tightrope—while someone is standing there shaking it. It must be added, however, that a detriangling maneuver after one has been caught for a while, wittingly or unwittingly, in a family system seems to have freeing effects similar to what follows in the resolution of a transference.

There are a variety of methods that Bowenian therapists have learned to use to foster an objective state: mischievous, paradoxical responses; avoiding interpretations; diagramming the family on a blackboard; telling (disguised) stories about other clients as projective techniques; and making clear one's own positions. But the major "technique" that Bowen and his disciples have taught as *the way to maintain such an objectivity- and differentiation-promoting position is simply to ask questions*. One might even say that the major "intervention" in Bowenian therapy is a question. Questions are a marvelous way of staying in touch with someone without becoming responsible for the person or the person's dilemmas. Also, as long as you are the one asking the questions, you cannot be the overfunctioning expert giving all the answers. After a while, you learn that questions are quite subversive of mind sets and often have more staying power than suggestions for new behavior. For example, one might ask a single woman who says she does not date because her family taught her that men were weak and she does not want to hurt them: "Would you be willing to take a month and see how many men you could destroy?" Or, to an overfunctioning, perpetually deadline-giving father who has just given his son six weeks to shape up: "Why not five?" Then you come to realize that sometimes you can ask the "wrong" person a question (a three-cornered shot, so to speak), so that the one you really want to hear (be objective about) the informational content of the sentence will overhear it (louder) because his or her defenses have been outflanked. For example, to a married woman in front of her frustrating, passive-aggressive husband, the question might be: "What gets stirred up in you when your husband acts like such a wimp?" Or to a father in front of his arguing wife and son: "Can your son seduce his mother into an argument any time he wants?"

Questions, obviously, can also be a form of challenge, as in the question to any family member who is acting helpless in the face of a relative's initiatives: "What would it take for you to become less vulnerable to his/her remarks (actions)?" And challenge is a way of promoting growth without increasing dependency and subjectivity. In other words, questions are inherently detriangling maneuvers. Sometimes the question in "reversal" form can sharpen awareness by paradoxing the whole therapeutic encounter, as when clients report in a self-satisfied manner that they are doing better and the Bowen-oriented therapist responds in a calm, inquisitive manner, "Could you make it go back to the way it was? How would you go about it?" Pursuing the subject diligently, the therapist thus gets the clients to think out the problem carefully and respond searchingly, and with thoughtful deliberation, to one another's suggestions for regression, and why they think "that" would no longer work. Talk about staying out of the transference! Who ever had a parent nonanxious enough to invite planning for making things worse?

Other schools have emphasized the use of questions, of course, but rarely because of their effect on the emotional field between therapist and client or because of the objectivity-promoting stance and self-regulation they promote in the poser! This is not to say that the information obtained by asking these questions is unimportant—quite the contrary. As Bowen has emphasized, "the more I learn about the family, the more they learn." This attitude fits the basic research orientation he has tried to recapture since the pioneering days at NIMH. But how information, the "message," is perceived by the therapist, or the family, depends on the emotional system, the *medium* in which it is transmitted. And that depends on the degree of differentiation (or the opposite, the degree of anxiety) in the field, which, in turn, depends primarily on the emotional being of the therapist. From the perspective of Bowen theory, therefore, *when it comes to promoting change, clarity may be more important than empathy, not only because helping people to be objective about their position in life automatically contributes to their healing, but also because it is only when a therapist's orientation is concerned with clarity that he or she may distinguish empathy from anxiety.*

Proximity and Protoplasm

Around 1970, Bowen was seeing a family once a month and recording the interviews for training. The wife was given to serious breakdowns in her functioning and had been hospitalized several times. During one of these interviews, the husband, a very concerned and sensitive (if also somewhat passive) man, was describing how no amount of effort on his part to understand his wife seemed to make any difference. At this point, Bowen responded that he did not think it would ever again be possible for husbands and wives to understand one another. The next tape showed the couple six months later. The woman was no longer depressed, and was going about her daily business bright and cheerful as if she had been relieved from shouldering some tremendous burden. As Bowen asked the couple questions designed to find out how the change had come about, the husband volunteered, "I've stopped trying to understand her."

At about that same time, a research project was taking place that was concerned with very similar emotional phenomena and that ultimately may prove to have more significance for the application of Bowen theory than will his own work at NIMH. It was not research with human families, however, but with a much smaller form of protoplasm. In 1970, the results were published of an extremely sophisticated experiment in which organisms from a species that had not evolved immune systems (*gorganzoa*) were moved toward one another in increasingly greater degrees of proximity (Theodore, 1970). It was known that creatures of the same species that do not have immune systems will fuse upon contact and become one organism since the immune system is basically the capacity to distinguish self from non-self. Indeed, without immunologic systems, there would be no existential category of self (Thomas, 1974). We need them not only to ward off enemies, but also in order to love, that is, touch. The other side of transplant rejection is the capacity for self-differentiation. In this experiment, what was observed was that at a certain distance, the smaller organism began to disintegrate, and within 24 hours had lost the principles of its organization completely. Careful controls proved that the larger one had done nothing to do the other in, either through the secretion of substances or through any form of frontal attack. The disintegration of the smaller organism was purely the result of its own metabolic mechanisms functioning reactively to the *proximity* of the other. *The experimenters had "induced autodestruction" by moving the creatures closer to*

a member of their own species. While one might be tempted to blame the larger for not giving its partner enough distance, that misses the most important dimension of this (emotional) phenomenon. Had the disintegrating partner been able to develop more capacity to discriminate self from non-self (worked on its own vulnerability to the other), it might have been able to tolerate more proximity.

The ramifications of this finding for human protoplasm are extraordinary. They suggest that the major problem of families may not be to get members to be closer, but to enable them to be clearer about where they end and others in their life begin. Most of the helping professions seem to be largely concerned with promoting proximity rather than differentiation, despite the fact that the natural movement of protoplasm seems to be toward other protoplasm. In other words, *the basic problem in families may not be to maintain relationships but to maintain the self that permits nondisintegrative relationships.*

Two different comments from women clients reflect the opposite ends of this emotional phenomenon. One, thinking back on how she had lost the self that was now reemerging, said, "The day I got married, I disappeared." The other, upon finally seeing some evidence that her partner's self was emerging, said, "When my husband said, 'I,' suddenly there were two of us."

This is more than an issue of "boundaries," as some like to put it. It is *existential* in the deepest sense of the term. It gets to the very essence of protoplasm and the essential nature of anxiety. Of course, with human organisms we are dealing with a far more complex understanding of space and size. The issue of the smaller or larger organism gets played out in families not in terms of avoirdupois, but rather in categories of over- and underfunctioning. *Nothing fuses people like one overfunctioning in the other's space, whereas nothing creates emotional space like self-definition.* It is here, by the way, that we can distinguish more clearly the concept of *fusion* as used by Bowen and *enmeshment* as used by the structural school. *All fusion involves enmeshment, but there is in the biological concept of fusion the additional sense of the loss of the organism's integrity*, the principles that give it coherence. Thus, fusion can have a positive valence or a negative one (homey togetherness or perpetually reactive argumentativeness). Similarly, we gain another way of comprehending differentiation. Autonomy or individuation can be conceived of as an external spatial phenomenon, in which case it can be accomplished without concern for the inner coherence provided by integrity; differentiation cannot.

An enormous number of "individual" symptoms, both physical and "psychological," take on new meaning when viewed in the context of the loss of self in a relationship. The notion that proximity can induce autodestruction in one partner to a relationship when there is no capacity for an immunologic response (either because of the degree of fusion between them or because there was not enough self to permit it) opens the door to viewing all chronic conditions that manifest themselves in one relative as by-products of the fusion that characterizes their relationship with each other. This perspective on "individual" symptoms ultimately sets the groundwork for (1) making the promotion of differentiation (that is, the capacity for an immunologic response) the basic healing strategy for any symptomatic person no matter what the nature of the symptom (with cancer patients, it almost may be conceptualized as a holistic approach to imagery), and (2) working with the nonsymptomatic spouse (or parent or child) when the symptomatic family member is the underfunctioner. For, as Bowen has taught, it is very difficult to get the underfunctioner to move until the overfunctioner (who luckily also tends to be the more motivated one) can reduce his or her overfunctioning, that is, can "make himself or herself smaller."

These notions about proximity, protoplasm, and anxiety also have fundamentally significant ramifications for the therapeutic relationship. They suggest that responses from helping professionals such as rescuing and supporting not only may be counterproductive, "enabling," or codependent, but may, if the helper overfunctions enough, actually induce autodestruction, that is, dis-"integr"-ation in the client. It is in this context that we can fully appreciate the fundamental significance of Bowen's admonition to the therapist to "make yourself small." And it is here that we can see how essentially connected are the differentiating processes that promote objectivity and those that promote well-being.

Overall, the proximity/protoplasm perspec-

tive suggests that *fusion with a client has more toxic potential than lack of empathy*, and that *anxiety in the helper can be more damaging than even sexual contact* (which sin we would all prefer to focus on).[6] All this brings us back to the idea that the health of the client begins with, and cannot go beyond, the level of differentiation achieved by the helper.

Translated into practice, the proximity/protoplasm factor means that the therapist, instead of trying to will togetherness directly, might promote it more effectively by encouraging the self (differentiation) of the individual members, because, as Bowen once put it, "A self is more attractive than a no-self." (Another Bowenism that captures the same paradox of togetherness is that in any relationship the one doing the *least* amount of thinking about the other tends to be the one who is more attractive to the other.) In other words, people do not have to be taught how to get closer. Moving toward others is natural. Anything, therefore, that a therapist can do on the side of differentiation—challenging self, reducing anxiety, encouraging reconnection with one's own family of origin, and the like—is not opposed to togetherness, even if it is initially perceived in that way by others who have temporarily lost a part of their selves in their relative's progress, but is really in its cause. The issue is far deeper than effectiveness, of course. It relates, rather, to how togetherness can be promoted in a manner that minimizes the sacrifice of integrity of all family members and the consequent recycling of symptomatology within the family that accompanies such loss. As the diagram illustrating the unified field theory of all family symptoms suggests, the issue of integrity is not merely a matter of compromise or ethics, but probably a condition that minimizes carcinogenesis, or any other dis-"integr"-ative process. The bottom line is that whenever you increase togetherness without also increasing self-differentiation, you run the risk of losing that togetherness through the autodestruction of one of the partners.

Here is an example of one way I have found to convey the connection between proximity and self in a clinical situation familiar to any family

---

[6] *Editors' Note.* Another eminently testable, and important, hypothesis.

therapist, the one in which an overfunctioning woman is on the verge of burnout, or worse, because she has allowed herself to become triangled into taking responsibility for every relationship in her family. She is usually thinking of separation, perhaps even of abandoning her children. Both options run contrary to her values of family togetherness, yet she also can no longer carry the burden and the frustration of the togetherness they have. She may be perceived as controlling in her effort to preserve the family, but her perceived controllingness is really an adaptation in which she has sacrificed enormous amounts of her own self to the mindless control of her family's emotional processes. (It is amazing how little control people have over the way they control others.)

I begin by drawing a large circle representing her with the other members of her family as intersecting figures. "This is the family," I say.

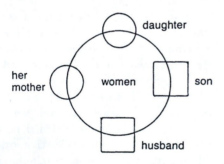

Then I erase those parts of the smaller circles and squares that have crossed over her line, and add, "This is the outline of yourself." (One woman with uncommon perceptiveness said, "They look like lesions.")

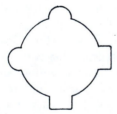

Next, I ask, "Would you be willing to try to move your circle outside the intersections and complete the outline of yourself over there, away from them, but keep relating to them from outside their space?" She is warned, however, that all of the other creatures in her life will immediately feel her pullout from the fusion as taking

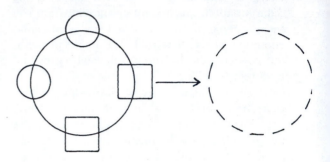

some of their cells along with her. Predictably, they will react characteristically to their gaping wound, responding automatically to glob her back into the togetherness according to the way they have been wont to do in the past. They will, in short, have symptoms for togetherness. Most people can tell you exactly what that symptom in their partner, child, or parent will be (drinking, spending, getting sick, having an affair, having an accident, becoming hypercritical, running away from home, etc.). But, this woman is told, if she can contain her anxiety and learn how to be nonreactive to the sabotage (the reactivity of others), which means staying on course for her own differentiation without cutting off (often by maintaining a mischievous-response mode), there is a more than likely chance that the others will succeed in closing their own wounds, and then everyone can relate to one another as better-defined individuals from outside one another's space. (The nonreactive stance is often best maintained through a mischievous-response mode: "Honey, there's a sale on your favorite Scotch across town." "Why are you telling me that?" "Well, remember that job that you said if I took it, you'd leave? I took it.")

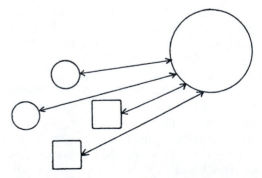

This is really a form of leadership (the same diagrams can be drawn for the burdened, frustrated leader of any organization), and it can be a very powerful form of medicine, but not for those who prefer peace to progress. Actually, once a Bowenian-coached client begins to move into a differentiating mode, more time is probably spent, at first, in learning how to deal with the sabotage than in learning how to differentiate. Interestingly, *the major variable in the outcome (cutoff, reglobbing, or a more differentiated togetherness) seems to be the adroitness and persistence of the differentiating partner, not the degree of reactivity or severity of the symptom in the family member wanting to dedifferentiate the relationship.* What can be said with some surety is this: the togetherness that results from an approach that emphasizes self-differentiation rather than "cooperation" usually tends to be more lasting, to be less vulnerable to future changes or regressions in either partner, and to be characterized by healthier (noncritical) interchanges. This is probably true because the togetherness that results is not based on increasing the emotional dependencies and is not an adaptation to the symptom, but evolves out of the increasing self-reliance and strengths of the partners. And the same can be true for parents differentiating from their children, or from their own parents.

Finally, as this coaching example illustrates, the understanding of proximity and protoplasm being presented here is consistent with the previously mentioned emphasis throughout Bowen theory on focusing on the strength in a family. This idea will now be further reinforced by the notion that healing is a natural (that is, a self-regenerative) process.

Healing as a Self-Regenerative Phenomenon

The most crucial concept in understanding and practicing Bowen therapy is his view that healing is a self-regenerative process. Self-regenerative means not only self-responsible, but also self-actualizing. The act of taking responsibility for one's own emotional being and destiny is not only the key to survival, but that very attitude creates the self that is the necessary resource for that end.

I began to appreciate the centrality of this notion to all of Bowen's thinking from the very beginning of my association with him (1967) as a result of two events that occurred in consecutive supervision sessions. The context of one was the relationship between therapist and patient and the context of the other was the relationship between supervisor and therapist, but the concepts were essentially the same.

In the first situation, a colleague suddenly interrupted our session with a call from a mental hospital. She had gotten herself institutionalized by sending the anxiety of her internist through the roof with her outlandish fantasies. She was now complaining that they were trying to get her with gas fumes sent through the ventilators. Avoiding the content of her fears, whether or not they were true or she was crazy, Bowen responded, "Maryanne, you have a right to think as crazy as you want, but if you don't shut up about it, they're going to commit you." She was out the next day.

At the time, I simply focused on his foxiness. In one masterful stroke, Bowen had stayed out of the triangle with her craziness, declined the gambit of her perversity, reframed the entire issue into a category that she could do something about, and made her responsible for her own condition, if not her destiny.

The following week, I saw that something much deeper was involved than Bowen's adroitness. This time the issue was my own concerns. I was worried about the fact that I could not be covered by malpractice insurance until I was eligible to join one of the recognized therapy associations. This time his response was, "Malpractice is most likely to occur when the professional gives too much promise." As I considered the novelty of thinking about malpractice litigation as a breach-of-promise suit, I suddenly realized that he was asking me to deal with my anxieties in the same manner as he had dealt with his patient, to focus on my own input and, in the process, to behave toward the problem in a manner that was self-regulatory. Eventually, I came to realize that this focus on responsibility for self, and *his confidence that in promoting its actualization he was optimizing the conditions for healing processes to do their work*, was the logical bottom line of a natural systems orientation to both healing and pathology. "Natural" means that both are driven by the same universal forces that describe life everywhere, and "systems" means they are part of one another. This self-regenerative perspective changes the entire thrust of therapy; crisis or illness, instead of being "merely" an anxious occasion to be fixed, now becomes an opportunity for the growth of the client as well as the evolution of the species. And it changes the criterion for deciding which member of a family to work with from who has the symptom to who is most motivated to continue the pursuit of differentiation. The logic of the paradigm is as follows.

A Natural Systems View of Pathology

The characteristic that all pathogens have in common is the absence of a factor that regulates their own growth and behavior. While this is most obviously true in malignancy where, unlike "normal" cells, malignant cells fail to differentiate, specialize, or limit their proliferation, it is the same with families, organizations, and civilization itself. Whether one is considering an acting-out child, an obstreperous, given-to-tantrums, or tyrannical family member; whether one is considering members of an organization who persistently try to bend everyone to their will; or whether one is observing a totalitarian nation; what is always true about such forces is that they never will say "no" to themselves. They, of course, have no self apart from their behavior to say "no" to. It is precisely this inability to differentiate that gives to viruses, abusers, and totalitarian states their infectious, invasive, or malignant quality.

This same inability to regulate self not only contributes to unregulated growth, but it also prevents the growth we call maturity. Bowen has, in fact, often substituted the word *immaturity* for *pathology*. After all, creatures without the capacity to regulate their own behavior cannot learn from their experience. This is why reasoning with (immature) human troublemakers is as effective as reasoning with a virus. It is also this lack of a self-regulatory factor that makes it natural for pathogens to pass their own functioning on, unmodified, from generation to generation. An interesting natural systems parallel exists between multigenerational transmission of pathology (that is, immaturity) in cancerous processes and in families with acting-out children. In vitro studies of leukemic cells have shown that where the missing growth (regulatory) protein can be reinserted into the malig-

nant cells, the transmission of their malignant characteristic to the next generation immediately ceases (Sachs, 1986). Bowen-trained therapists tend not to see children but to work with the parents *instead*. This is a very similar form of intervention, as there is no such thing as acting-out children with mature parents, and when the parents can learn to be better differentiated (and in that process to be more self-regulative), the transmission of immaturity to the next generation often ceases. More than that, interfering with the transmission from one generation to the next in this way stops metastasis into society.

Pathogens, however, never do it alone. There is always another self-regulation issue involved in the creation of pathology, the failure on the part of the host. This brings us to a second natural characteristic of all pathological processes. Pathology is less the result of the presence of the pathogen than the product of its replication. To a very large extent, pathological processes (physical or relational) that continue are simply those that are tolerated by the surrounding "cells." Oncogenesis does not have to result in the disease we call cancer. Indeed, the development of all life may have as much to do with relationships as with essence, since recent studies have shown that cells develop, particularly in the embryonic stage, not only according to their own DNA, but also according to what adjacent cells will permit them to do.

Churchill's comment that World War II got started because "the malice of the wicked was reinforced by the weakness of the virtuous," could just as easily be applied to any troublemaking process in any body or body politic. He was talking about immunologic failure.

Bowen therapy is about the immunologic response. It is a focus on strength rather than weakness, on the evolution of self that is necessary for its expression and on the self-regulation that keeps the opposite extreme auto-immunity (reactivity) in check.

The concept is just as applicable to work systems. I have found that the leader of any organization functions as its immunologic system; to the extent that he or she is well-defined (meaning, primarily, clear and nonreactive), the pathogens, though present, are far less likely to replicate. And, once again, there is a natural-systems parallel. Recently, it was discovered that our nerves communicate not only electrically to that which is contiguous, but also chemically to other, relatively distant parts of the body through the release of substances called neurotransmitters that dock at appropriate receptor sites. With this discovery has come the awareness that the brain is the largest organ of secretion in the body, and that its main function might be to preserve the health of the organism (thinking may be a bonus). For every neurotransmitter thus far discovered that is released by the brain, the appropriate receptor site exists in the immunologic system, and vice versa (Pert, 1986). And this ties back to the previously mentioned concept of leadership through self-differentiation, that the functioning of the "head" has a systemic effect on the body (politic) that can be far more influential than what the "head" actually says to its followers.

A Natural Systems View of Healing

Implicating the good guys in the course of pathological processes brings us around to the other side of self-regulation. If the essence of pathology is its absence, the process that leads to health is its development, *not in the pathogenic force, however, but in the organism's response.* (This is a focus on the vertical axis rather than the horizontal one in the bipolar graph.) Bowen's views of the way to promote such self-regulation have also been influenced by two natural-systems processes. One is that life moves toward life. In other words, life does not have to be taught how to do it. The second is that the processes of maturation have their own time frame. Not only can they often not be speeded up, but sometimes it is necessary, as with fermentation or embryonic development, to slow processes down in order to gain the best results. Both of these views have significant technical ramifications for the conduct of therapy and are joined around the issue of anxiety, since it requires lowering one's anxiety to allow these processes to go their natural way, yet faith in their capacity to know their job can also lower one's anxiety about having to do something about it oneself.

Bowen's confidence in the natural order of things is similar to Einstein's. He almost seems to be making a statement about life's forces sim-ilar to that which Einstein made about physical forces, "I don't believe God plays dice with the Universe." The healer, in other words, does not have to take responsibility for making health happen, but for discovering the universal forces that make life tick, and then lining up the client's thinking and functioning with those life-sustaining forces that have continuously evolved since Creation. One may, therefore, have "faith" in natural processes. You can trust them, and having the confidence to rely on them, can free any healer to defocus the symptom and the attending anxiety, and refocus his or her own efforts on becoming a healing presence, that is, one who tries to promote healing rather than to will it.

This commitment to natural processes, by the way, was probably one of the factors that kept Bowen from joining those in the early days of the family movement who kept inveighing against the "medical model" because of its diagnosis of individuals. From Bowen's perspective, it was more likely psychiatry that had broken with the medical model, which, as he understood it, was a model that sought to describe life with the facts of nature rather than the subjectivity of metaphor.

From a natural systems perspective, the healing presence functions primarily in two ways: it inhibits the inhibitors and it stimulates the resources. The physician, for example, does not sew your cells together; he or she works primarily in two directions, to inhibit that which prevents them from doing what comes naturally (reducing inflammation, for example) or to initiate processes that need a jump start, for example, by injecting a weak form of the very virus that is the enemy in order to flag the T cells. Carried over to therapeutic functioning, what that means is (1) reducing the chronic anxiety that inhibits healing in emotional illness in exactly the same manner that inflammation inhibits physical healing, primarily by *being* a well-differentiated, nonanxious presence; and (2) stimulating the organism's own resources, which means guiding or challenging the self of the client to emerge. (Bowen has taught that what makes any paradoxical or challenging remark a weak or strong form of the live virus is the investment and anxiety in the healer.)

This focus on aiding the release of natural processes and on healers applying their will primarily to their own self-regulation, rather than to the regulation of others, has important ramifications for the major therapeutic problem of resistance. A natural systems orientation to healing helps minimize that inflammatory, sabotaging reactivity.

It does not take much experience in the field to see that the most intense forms of family symptomatology (anorexia, suicide, schizophrenia, abuse, violence, and many chronic physical diseases, not to mention a whole catalogue of marital and parent–child issues) tend to occur in families characterized by extreme will conflict, by which I mean that members of the family are constantly trying to will one another to adapt to their will rather than applying their will to their own self-differentiation. Willing others to change is, by definition, loss of self in the relationship. What often happens is that family will struggles become extended, like some huge hydrocarbon chain, into the therapeutic encounter where therapists get into willing their clients to stop willing other family members. And supervisors try willing their supervisees to stop willing their clients. All willing of others immediately creates an emotional triangle, of course, since it puts the willer between the willed one and that person's own will or habit. That is enough reason to understand its ineffectiveness. But willing others is also generally a reactive phenomenon. Willing clients to change, therefore, is not only usually ineffective, but it tends to excite the very inflammatory processes that prevent natural healing processes from doing their work.

Conversely, issues of resistance in therapy tend to fall away when therapists focus their will on their own self-differentiation, and when their focus on natural-systems processes disengages them from that struggle. One of Bowen's guidelines for staying out of will conflict, which is related to overfunctioning responsibility and anxiety, has been that he takes responsibility for what happens in his office but not for what happens between sessions. My own way of putting it to therapists has been, "All healing that depends on the functioning of the healer rather than of the client is faith healing."

The second natural process basic to what Bowen has taught about therapy is that the process of maturation takes time. It cannot be willed or even speeded up beyond its own time frame. This notion also ties back in a similiar way to the basic issue of anxiety, both the client's and the healer's.

The relationship between time and healing has two important consequences for therapeutic functioning. One has to do with the frequency and length of the therapeutic encounter, and the other with criteria for evaluating change. Since Bowen theory does not equate change with symptom relief or feeling better, but with an increase in the differentiation level of the family, it has a long-range perspective. Bowen-trained therapists, therefore, tend to be less concerned about the frequency of sessions than about the length of time a family stays in the process. Thus, families are rarely seen more frequently than biweekly, and as they increase the management of their own anxiety and self-directedness, often every third or fourth week, or, eventually, even several times a year. Longevity in the therapeutic contact promotes deeper involvement with multigenerational processes, and the emotional change discussed above that seems to be a prerequisite to any new patterns of thinking or behavior having the capacity to maintain a differentiating effect is just not something that fits into a timetable. That kind of emotional shift requires that some member of the family be committed to the process of differentiation for several years. From a conventional perspective, this approach may appear to encourage dependency, but Bowen theory again comes in at a tangent. Dependency may be more connected to frequency than to longevity, because if there is too little time between sessions, the therapist's presence cannot be differentiated from the change process. Dependency on the therapist, therefore, may be less a function of how long one goes to the "doctor" than of whether or not such visits are continuing to promote further differentiation, for example, by helping the client stay in touch with a particular way of thinking. Theoretically, this also means that "terminating therapy," as the phrase is usually used, makes little sense in this context. Dependency that continues to promote differentiation is, after all, by nature not dependency as that term normally connotes. A coach can be helpful even with decreasingly frequent contact as long as one plays the game.

However, the key to the dependency issue may really have very little to do with time intervals and much more to do with a shift in the differentiation of the client. When clients start wondering whether or not to continue, I draw an arrow on the board that has a zero in the middle.

"This is the arrow of progress," I say. "When clients first come in, they are way over to the right, meaning that they are highly anxious, constantly reactive with little self-regulation of their direction in life. When they wonder whether to continue, they have finally reached zero. Zero is characterized by the loss of the pain that originally motivated them to come in, but also the loss of that same stimulus for continuing to work on themselves." If they wish to continue to try to move their progress past zero, and I always suggest cutting the frequency of the sessions at that point, then two gains are probable. One is less likelihood of regression, and the second is, if regression does occur, that one can usually get it back to the furthest point one had previously reached.

Actually, much larger questions are raised by this emphasis on longevity rather than frequency. The notion of weekly visits to a therapist is, of course, simply convention, as is the notion that therapy should be outside the context of learning. For the past several years, I have been conducting a seminar in family emotional process for ordained clergy that has forced my faculty and me to question both assumptions. The "training" program meets three times a year for three consecutive days. (It is based on a similar program Bowen conducts on a four-times-a-year basis for therapists.) One day is devoted to the parishioner family, one day to the congregation as a family, and one day to the members of clergy's own families of origin. The mornings are theoretical and the afternoons clinical. Only half of one day is actually devoted to what might conventionally be called "therapy," the afternoon of the third day, when we subdivide into family-of-origin groups. Yet the changes in emotional functioning that we have been seeing in the people attending are certainly equal to those

we have observed in clients who are seen biweekly for a year or more. The only way we have been able to explain the depth of the changes we are observing (aside from the fact that by selection we are dealing with a very motivated group) is that the three perspectives when projected simultaneously seem to have a holographic effect, with the result that those in the training programs find every aspect of their emotional lives perceivable in greater depth throughout the year (not just during the nine days) because of the added dimensions. But it is Bowen theory that makes this possible by putting all three systems on the same "wavelength."[7]

The second practical therapeutic ramification of allowing natural processes to develop in their own time is the time frame that should be used for evaluating change. Bowen has taught that it takes four years to change a family, that is, to modify its emotional processes to the point that the multigenerational transmission will not automatically continue into the next generation—and four years is not a guarantee. The multigenerational-transmission perspective also probably means that evaluation of change requires a perspective of several generations. Since one obviously cannot wait that long, Bowen theory's emphasis on differentiation suggests two criteria for making predictions about how fundamental any change in a family may be that is outside the criterion of time. First, to the extent that any change in a nuclear family goes along with a change one of the partners made with his or her own family or origin, it is *more* likely to be a fundamental change. Second, any change that occurs because family members have become more adaptive to the symptom or the symptom

---

[7] *Editors' Note.* We believe it understates the matter to refer to the factor of patient motivation as an "aside," in that it is so widely acknowledged that such motivation has an important influence on both the process and outcome of (probably all) psychotherapy.

+

← ————————————————— 0 ————————————————— Client begins here

Client considers
terminating here

bearer is *less* likely to last than if the symptom goes away because the family has become less fused into it.

All of this brings us full circle to the differentiation of the therapist because for the therapist to be willing to go along for that long requires a commitment to the same fundamental processes that are a premise of Bowen theory to begin with: self-differentiation and the evolution of our species. In other words, unless therapists are committed to the ongoing process of their own growth, they are not likely to have the emotional stamina to endure. The power of self-differentiation for promoting natural healing processes cannot be underestimated. The track record of many healers, marriage counselors, or oncologists shows too much willingness to quit when the going gets rough. Sometimes, it appears to be a lack of persistence, sometimes a failure to realize that one has the most power in a relationship precisely when one is ready to quit, and sometimes it just seems to be a morbid fatalism (disguising anxiety). For years I wondered what it was that differentiated the more motivated. Then one day I realized that it was something more essential to self, something Bowen had always taught more by the example of his life than through any specific lesson. I had been discussing with a client who had worked through some very difficult problems what distinguished those who succeed in changing their life course. Since he was a former boxer, I used an analogy from his sport, and said that I thought it was the capacity to "take a punch." To my surprise and enlightenment, he responded, "You've got it wrong. It's not the *capacity* to take a punch; it's loving it." This is also what Bowen has taught: loving the struggle, being challenged by life to hang in there and find new ways to think about and approach its problems.

To recapitulate: Family therapy from a Bowenian perspective emphasizes a way of thinking rather than a set of techniques. This emphasis is equally appropriate for the training of therapists, the conduct of therapy, or the coaching of clients regarding their functioning in their own emotional systems (family or work). Supervision, therapy, leadership, and growth thus become one. The approach is rooted in a natural-systems concept of disease and healing that gives the theory an internal consistency. Thus, if personality, psychodynamics, and cultural background are not important in understanding family emotional process, neither are they the determining factors in the functioning of the therapist. The transcendent notion always is self-differentiation, which is understood to be the decisive variable in the etiology and cure of all emotional problems and the conduct of successful therapy (or supervision), and, in the end, the key to the evolution of our species (from a natural systems perspective, the ultimate purpose of all family therapy). In addition, the focus on the differentiation of the therapist as the key to therapeutic technique unifies objectivity and healing. When all is said and done, however, how you want your client to function in his or her relationships with others must characterize your own functioning in your relationship with your client—not because the client will learn to copy you, but because the emotional field in which you both operate must be conducive to further differentiation.

CONCLUSION

There is one more part to Bowen theory—its application to society and society's way of understanding itself. Indeed, the most significant aspect of Bowen theory may not lie in its therapeutic potential for a given family, but rather in its power to reformat the knowledge conventions of the social sciences and so influence what therapists see. And this may be still one more example of Bowen theory's uniqueness, the lens it supplies for looking at its own field.

In these concluding remarks, I shall describe briefly Bowen's concept of *societal regression*, its relevance for the field of family therapy (actually for all the helping professions), and the shift in social-science thinking Bowen theory says is necessary before change artists can have an effect on society's own emotional processes. As will be seen, his views on this matter have influenced his functioning in the field.

Societal Regression

If Bowen used universal concepts of life to understand families, he also reversed that perspective and asked what we can learn about society at large from what our concentrated focus on the family has reciprocally elucidated about life. It is not that society can be reduced to its molecular components (families), but rather that the same emotional forces are at work in both fields. Applying his major concepts to civilization, Bowen developed a concept he called "societal regression." Through this concept he has viewed society as a family, that is, as an emotional system, complete with its own multi-generational transmission, chronic anxiety, emotional triangles, cutoffs, projection processes, and fusion/differentiation struggles.

Bowen's concept of societal regression states that all of civilization goes through peaks and valleys in the curve of its own anxiety. Once again, the anxiety that is important is the chronic anxiety transmitted through the generations rather than its specific foci in a given age. As Kerr has put it, it is what exists between people rather than in them. In this view, phenomena such as increasing divorce rates, cults, the drug culture, inflation, and rampant diseases (plagues, tuberculosis, influenza, cancer, AIDS), and perhaps also the increase in homosexuality, can be viewed as symptoms of more anxious periods. In addition, as with any emotional system, "the family of man" also has its pet foci around which its free-floating anxiety will tend to crystalize: communists in one age, carcinogens in another; recombinant DNA in one generation, nuclear war in another; and so on through cholesterol, conservation issues, and ozone holes. Bowen's view regarding these crises in the human family was the same as with any family: try to minimize reactivity and maximize objectivity. Take care not to get caught up in the world's emotional system; these problems, too, will go their way if handled objectively—sometimes because we find solutions, but often because they simply seem to spend themselves or disappear from view when we get focused elsewhere. Above all, stay grounded in your own continued self-differentiation. This is precisely what Bowen has tried to practice with regard to the family of family therapists.

While annual conferences of some major family-therapy associations have grown from 500 to 5,000, Georgetown family-therapy symposia went from 1,500 in the late 1970s to one tenth that number in the 1990s. But it is not simply the variety or the competition that has decreased

Georgetown attendance. *Bowen wanted it that way.* He feared that much of family therapy's popularity is a fad, itself symptomatic of societal anxiety. Since it is the nature of symptoms to recycle, Bowen did not want his theory to vanish in the next transformation. As a result, Bowen practiced the same effort at self-differentiation with regard to the family of family therapists that he recommended to any therapist or family member. He tried to maintain a separateness from the rest of the field that would enable him to continue the development of his own thinking. He, therefore, became more concerned with the development of his theory than with its relevance to any specific, contemporary problem.

Family Therapy and Societal Anxiety

From the perspective of Bowen theory, family therapy has failed to differentiate itself sufficiently from the very anxiety that produces the problems it seeks to cure. Societal regression, therefore, far from being ameliorated by the field of family therapy, is reflected in its own emotional system. According to this view, the anxiety shows up (1) in the way family therapy has aped consultation methods everywhere, focusing on administrative and managerial techniques and pursuing data indiscriminately rather than focusing on emotional processes and the self-regulation and growth of the therapist; and (2) more importantly, as I shall elaborate below, in family therapy's unquestioning acceptance of the paradigm of either/or dichotomies that characterizes all social-science conceptualization.

An example of the former, again from the perspective of Bowen theory, is the manner in which new issues (or symptoms) constantly come into view, occupy center stage for a while, and then exit to the wings of some archive. In the 1970s, almost no family-therapy conference was without a speaker on sexual dysfunction. Then, in rather rapid succession, the foci switched to cults, divorce, anorexia, gender issues, violence, substance abuse, and so on. Another example is the way in which therapeutic orientations also rapidly shift; for a while, it was epistemology, then in succession, paradox, circularity, family of origin, ethnicity, feminism, rituals, object relations, and constructionism. Today, approaches proliferate, and family-therapy training institutes cross-pollinate them in major cities across the country. There is little focus on the emotional being of the therapist. Indeed, Bowen theory might say that the pursuit of data and technique through books and conferences resembles a form of substance abuse, binding the anxiety that will never really be reduced until the field focuses more on its own differentiation.

There is, however, a second, more important way in which Bowen theory would see family therapy as fused into society's anxiety: the tendency toward dichotomy rather than continuity in its thinking processes. This is a more fundamental issue because it is related to the structure of Bowen theory itself and its grounding in natural systems, and it illustrates how the theory could affect the emotional system of society on the deepest level—for, as mentioned, discontinuous classification is not confined to therapy but is found throughout the social sciences. Thus, from the perspective of Bowen theory, family therapy's fusion with society's anxiety does not begin "out in the field" when therapists start engaging with families, but is transmitted during our professional training and coded in the very methods of conceptualization employed by our institutions of learning. Or, to put it another way, the problem of reducing societal anxiety may lie less in changing "the family's construction of reality" (Reiss, 1981) than in reframing the therapist's (or therapy's) construction of reality—chiefly, the tendency in the social sciences to frame issues in terms of dichotomous, discontinuous either/or categories that often become the basis of polarization, rather than in terms of continuous, natural systems, emotional processes that link all symptoms, all people, and all generations. (And, since the structures of society are isomorphic to its anxiety, Bowen theory would link all academic disciplines, professional specialties, and their journals.)

The reason the conventional dichotomies in the social sciences reflect societal anxiety, according to Bowen theory, is that as thinking in any emotional system moves toward the either/or, all-or-nothing black-or-white dichotomization of life, it begins to take on the characteristics of rigidity, concreteness, and lack of imagination that are found to be so blatant in the most anxiety-impaired members of our species. As mentioned above, there is a curious connection

between the tendency to think in terms of either/or, all-or-nothing categories and the lack of resiliency of response in relationships. What schizophrenics are totally incapable of doing is thinking in terms of continua. And when societal anxiety becomes elevated, fundamentalism—that is, seeking certainty through reductionistic answers—increases.

This emphasis on the continuity of all emotional processes may be Bowen theory's most characteristic feature. It is what ultimately differentiates it from almost all other thinking in the social sciences. It is also what gives the theory the power to reframe the way questions have been traditionally posed. Bowen theory, therefore, is not simply a new set of answers, but is perhaps best understood as a new paradigm, that is, a new way of seeing. It pursues a different level of inquiry. It surrenders the promise of certainty on elementary cause-and-effect levels in order to obtain a broader (more objective) perspective. While an approach to change that questions the relevance of relevance may not stimulate avid political involvement, Bowen theory does contain the seeds of an upheaval potentially far more radical than the most status-quo-disturbing social action. It is a revolution in what information is considered relevant to the process of change, and in the way problems are to be conceptualized.

I have tried to foreshadow this vital aspect of Bowen theory by highlighting throughout this chapter some of the ways in which the theory makes continuous what other ways of thinking tend to dichotomize. It was shown, for example, that with regard to the human brain, Bowen saw degrees of reactivity as far more influential in human relationships or self-expression than right or left "brainedness." It was shown that a way of thinking about leadership that is far less given to polarization arises when leader and follower are seen as parts of an organic unit rather than as separate categories of a hierarchy. Similarly, it was shown how Bowen's focus on the nuclear-family unit as the unit for treatment or observation blurred the distinctions among child problems, marriage problems and individual health problems. With regard to therapy itself, it was shown how Bowen theory's emphasis on the differentiation of the therapist (his or her emotional being) diminished the significance normally accorded to different therapeutic techniques or distinctions between therapy and supervision. Similarly, it was shown how the focus on objectivity made the clinician and the researcher one.

To show the power for different conceptualizations that flows from Bowen's nondichotomous approach I will begin with four of the most influential, automatically accepted dichotomies in the social sciences: nature/nurture, body/mind, this culture/that culture, and male/female, and describe how Bowen theory would reformat all of these divisions in terms of continuous natural systems processes with the result that new questions arise about the structure and strategies of the helping professions. Then I will list many of the major dichotomies and polarizations characteristic of social science thinking and, next to each, also show the alternative, continuous level of inquiry that Bowen theory would focus on instead.

Some Generally Accepted Dichotomies

Nature/Nurture

The assumption that nature (genes) and nurture (environment) are separate, discontinuous elements in the development of humans fractionates thinking on many issues in both the mental and physical health fields. In some ways, this dichotomy almost organizes the helping establishment. The Bowenian notion of multigenerational transmission in an emotional field and of the nuclear family as an emotional unit suggest the possibility that emphasis on birth as a dividing line skews the reciprocal influences of this conventionally dichotomized pair. From the perspective of Bowen theory, family emotional factors could influence a child both mentally and physically either before or after the child emerges from the womb. Such conceptualization even reframes the untouchable issue of acquired characteristics.

Body/Mind

While more and more attention has been given to psychosomatic medicine, both directly as well as through biofeedback and guided im-

agery, as the term "psychosomatic" conveys, most in the field still see the mind and the body as two discrete entities that affect one another rather than as elements that function as parts of each other within a broader field. The Bowenian concept of differentiation and family emotional system rooted in natural evolutionary processes would conceptualize both body and mind as part of self, and relate all disease to problems of differentiation—what Kerr has referred to as "uni-disease." Focus on nuclear-family emotional processes rather than on specific clinical entities unifies both ends of the body/mind dichotomy by establishing a different level of inquiry: an individual's position in his or her family emotional field. The body/mind dichotomy influences profoundly the way the helping professions are currently structured (It is the starting point for the division into specialties), and it establishes the criteria for the choice of a healer, but Bowen theory would force us to ask to what extent the professional specialties that have evolved in our society reflect the range of dysfunction human organisms experience, and to what extent we think about ourselves the way we do because of the Yellow Page listings. More fundamentally, the continuous connection between mind and body that position in one's family emotional field establishes raises an even more disturbing question. If it is true that a very specific category of people become burdened with most of civilization's ills (if they do not get one thing, they will get another), how much progress will we really have made when we have cured cancer if we do not at the same time make progress in affecting multigenerational transmission? After all, homologously it may be the same thing.

This Culture/That Culture

As mentioned earlier, Bowen theory's focus on emotional process as a natural systems phenomenon rooted in and common to all protoplasm turns culture into the medium of expression rather than the driving force of family pathology. It suggests that when families hold their cultural background responsible for the way they function, not only is that not important information to jot down, but it is at that very moment *denial*, denial of personal responsibility (and avoidance of efforts at differentiation), as well as denial of the multigenerational transmission unique to that family. Focus on emotional processes rather than on culture also suggests that the differentiation of the therapist is far more critical in clinical outcomes than is his or her understanding of the client's background.

Male/Female

From the point of view of Bowen theory, all of the above would also hold true for the dichotomy of male/female. While this dichotomy is based on an obvious natural distinction, and has been sharpened by the political concerns of the women's movement, when it comes to understanding families, or for that matter the "human phenomenon," Bowen theory would say that maturity (that is, differentiation or reactivity) is more significant than gender. Bowen theory would not deny the distinction between male and female or the sociological differences that have developed around it, but the theory would question whether information based on the gender dichotomy is the most significant information on which to base the process of changing emotional systems. It would say, rather, that nothing stated in this chapter about triangles, differentiation, multigenerational transmission, or a person's position in his or her family emotional system is more accurate about one gender than about another—and that any given female person's vulnerability to dysfunction or capacity for recuperation can be predicted and promoted far better from information obtained from the bipolar graph than from data, accurate as such data may be, about physical or sociological differences between the sexes. This way of thinking also suggests that, when choosing a healer, the differentiation of the professional (his or her capacity for self-regulation, nonreactivity, etc.) is a better criterion than his or her gender.

Bowen Theory and Social Science

In order to bring out more clearly the differences between Bowen theory and conventional

Conventional Dichotomy	Bowen Formulation
nature/nurture	multigenerational emotional processes
body/mind	family emotional field
this symptom/that symptom	nuclear family's level of chonic anxiety
one culture/another culture	family's own emotional process
male/female	maturity of response
right brain/left brain	reactivity
thinking/feeling	degree of self-differentiation
leader/follower	organizational emotional field
present/past	multigenerational transmission
supervision/therapy	self-regulation
research/practice	pursuit of objectivity
psychiatrist/psychologist (discipline)	capacity-to-think systems
this technique/that technique	differentiation of the healer
support/challenge	anxiety of the professional
insight/behavior	promoting differentiation
quit/adapt	sustain a nonreactive presence
independence/dependence	resiliency of the bond
toxic/nontoxic condition	response of the organism
cause/effect	change in the balance of the field
one age/another age	relational triangles
happy marriage/divorce	degree of nuclear-family dysfunction
family system/work system	emotional process
a work system/a different industry	differentiation of the leader
one decision (choice)/another decision	maximizing objectivity

social-science formulations, particularly its overall characteristic of emphasis on continuity, here are some of the more common dichotomies found in the social sciences or family therapy listed side by side with how Bowen theory would reframe that issue. Many have been mentioned separately in various parts of this chapter; collectively, however, they show how far-reaching the continuity principle can be. In each case, the dichotomy listed on the left represents either a division basic to the thinking processes in the social sciences or a polarization around which choices are often made in therapy. The Bowen formulation, listed on the right, in each case creates a different level of inquiry that turns the poles of the corresponding dichotomy into nodes within a continuous, natural systems process.

When a family is chronically polarized around specific issues, we know that the polarization is really an emotional phenomenon and is not due to the content of the dichotomy. Could the same be said about polarizations in the social sciences? Could the dichotomies listed above be emotional barriers that hinder our horizons and imaginative capacity, much as the equator did geographically for centuries? To continue the analogy, are the social sciences so bound up with certain unquestioned ways of organizing our minds that other information can never even be conceived of, no less recognized, until we can get past these barriers? Might the source of this way of conceptualizing be societal regression? Is it an anxious flight from responsibility that tends to support those forms of thinking that focus us on pathology (which has infinite capacity to spawn data) rather than on strength, which would then force us to focus on self, that is, differentiation? Is this the schizophrenia that Bowen says is in all of us? And, if that is so, as is often the case with severely impaired families, is our tendency toward dichotomous thinking the result of an emotional cutoff from previous generations? Bowen theory might suggest that the cutoff here is the primary discontinuity. It is the emotional cutoff that the social sciences have made with our natural-systems link to our protoplasmic past, and it has had the same effect that cutoffs have in any family: we emphasize how we are different rather than how we are the same. Ultimately, from the point of view of Bowen theory, dichotomous formulations in the social sciences are not only discontinuous in their conception, but the very act of conceiving human problems in that mode discontinues us.

The journey of human thought constantly comes to crossroads, and the path chosen by the person leading the safari at that moment not only will describe (a view of) reality, but will also shape the reality of future generations by influencing what people see.

An interesting retrospective is provided by a long lost paper by Freud published for the first time in English in 1987. In 1915, Freud wrote a paper entitled "A Phylogenetic Fantasy" in which he suggested that modern anxiety is a form of reactivity transmitted by protoplasm from generation to generation since the trauma of the Ice Age. When the paper was rediscovered 70 years later, the psychoanalytic estab-

lishment went out of its way to show that it was wildly speculative. The major ideas—which come perilously close to Bowen's natural systems orientation, his theoretical grounding in evolutionary theory, and his notion of an emotional system—were not, they said, a part of the mainstream of Freud's thought. But they might have been. He wrote the paper during a period of great upheaval in traditional concepts of reality. The year 1915 was a decade past the year when Einstein published his special theory of relativity and the year before he published his general theory of relativity. It was also 15 years after Max Planck put forth his quantum theory that revolutionized conventional concepts of cause and effect, and for which he received a Nobel prize in 1918, three years after Freud wrote this monograph. For whatever reason, Freud continued down a mechanistic path of cause and effect. Had he continued to think out the ramifications of his Ice Age fantasy for the intergenerational links of human anxiety, not only might psychotherapy as the 20th century has known it have taken a far different turn, but so might much of literature, education, the administration of court systems, and the manner in which the news media frame issues. Bowen theory may have a similar capacity to affect all dimensions of society.

There are, of course, problems with Bowen theory. No effort to encompass all of life's processes will ever be totally consistent. There will always be exceptions. Another problem is the tautological relationship between chronic anxiety and differentiation: levels of differentiation in a family both determine and are determined by the levels of chronic anxiety. As mentioned earlier, it is difficult to come up with criteria to show how one can disagree with, or not buy, Bowen theory and still claim to be differentiated. Do you have to think like Murray Bowen in order to understand his theory? The biggest problem with the theory is that it cannot be disproved. Basic to the acceptance of any theory for discussion is that it must set up the grounds for its own refutation, cf. solipsism or revelation. What kind of research project could prove it wrong? At the very least that fact lends credence to the previously stated view that Bowen theory and its therapeutic ramifications cannot be understood or evaluated through criteria drawn from another paradigm. It is, for better or for worse, its own paradigm.[8]

Perhaps the best way to capture the complexities of Bowen theory's depth is to point out what many of us who have spent more than two decades in trying to grasp its range and thrust repeat every few years, "I think I'm beginning to really understand it."

REFERENCES AND BIBLIOGRAPHY

Beal, E., & Hochman, G. (1991). *Adult children of divorce.* New York: Delacorte Press.

Bowen, M. (1978). *Family therapy in clinical practice.* New York: Jason Aronson.

Calhoun, J.B. (1963). *The ecology and sciology of the norway rat.* U.S. Department of Health, Education and Welfare/Public Health Service Publication Number 1008, Washington D.C.: U.S. Government Printing Office.

Freud, S. (1987). *A phylogenetic fantasy* (translated by A. Hoffer & P. Hoffer). Cambridge, MA: Harvard University Press.

Friedman, E. (1982). *The myth of the shiksa.* In M. McGoldrick & B. Carter (Eds.), *Ethnicity and family therapy.* New York: Guilford Press.

Friedman, E. (1985). *Generation to generation: Family process in church and synagogue.* New York: Guilford Press.

Guerin, P.J., Fay, L., Burden, S.L., & Kauggo, J.G. (1987). *The evaluation and treatment of marital conflict.* New York: Basic Books.

Kerr, M. (1981). Family systems theory and therapy. In A.S. Gurman & D.P. Kniskern (Eds.), *Handbook of family therapy.* New York: Brunner/Mazel.

Kerr, M. & Bowen, M. (1988). *Family evaluation.* New York: Norton.

McGoldrick, M. & Gerson, R. (1985). *Genograms in family assessment.* New York: Norton.

McLean, P. (1985). Brain evolution related to family, play and the isolation call. *Archives of General Psychiatry. 42,* 405–417.

Papero, D. (1990). *Bowen family systems theory.* Needham Heights, MA: Allyn & Bacon, division of Simon & Schuster.

Pert, C.B. (1986). Wisdom of the receptors: Neuropeptides, the emotions and bodymind. *Advances, Institute for the Advancement of Health, 3,* 3.

Reiss, D. (1981). *The family's construction of reality.* Cambridge, MA: Harvard University Press.

Rosenbaum, L. (1989). *Biofeedback frontiers.* New York: AMS Press.

Sachs, L. (1986, January). Growth, differentiation and the reversal of malignancy. *Scientific American.*

Sheldrake, R. (1988). *The presence of the past.* New York: Times Books.

Skinner, B.F. (1971). *Beyond freedom and dignity.* New York: A.A. Knopf.

Theodore, J. (1970, August 15). Distinction between "self" and "not-self" in lower invertebrates. *Nature, 227.*

Thomas, L. (1974). *Lives of a cell.* New York: Viking Press.

Titelman, P. (1987). *The therapist's own family. Toward the differentiation of self.* Northvale, NJ: Jason Aronson.

Toman, W. (1961). *Family constellation.* New York: Springer.

Webster, G., & Goodwin, B.C. (1982). The origin of species: A structural approach. *Journal of Biological Structure, 5,* 15–47.

Zuckerman, H. (1967, November). The sciology of Nobel prize winners. *Scientific American.*

---

[8] *Editors' Note.* As illustrated by some of our earlier notes, we do not agree that the theory cannot be disproved or, at least, that certain of its tenets cannot be stated as hypotheses that are testable. Nonetheless, it may be the *belief* on the part of Bowen theorists that the theory cannot be refuted (i.e., subjected to testing by standard research methods) that has colored the theory's attractiveness to some in the family field and, thereby, unnecessarily limited the range of its potential audience and adherents.

EDITORS' REFERENCE

Gurman, A.S. (1978). Contemporary marital therapies: A critique and comparative analysis of psychoanalytic, behavioral and systems theory approaches. In T. Paolino & B.S. McCrady (Eds.), *Marriage and marital therapy.* New York: Brunner/Mazel.

CHAPTER 6

Brief Therapy: The MRI Approach*

Lynn Segal, L.C.S.W.

This chapter describes and explains brief therapy, a 10-session, generic model of problem formation and problem resolution developed at the Mental Research Institute (MRI) in Palo Alto, Calif. In the spring of 1967, MRI's Brief Therapy Project began with three goals: (1) to find a quick and efficient means for resolving complaints that clients bring to psychotherapists and counselors; (2) to tranform therapy from an art into a craft that could be more easily taught to others; and (3) to study change in human systems.

Brief Therapy can be used to treat individual, couple, and family problems. Its broad applicability is based on its view that the client's complaint is the problem, not a symptom of something else. Furthermore, rather than believing that human behavior is caused by the intrapsychic workings of an individual, Brief Therapy views behavior, especially a client's problematic behavior, as a function of interaction with other people, especially significant others—family, friends, co-workers, supervisors, and other professional helpers. Thus, as a gen-

eral rule of thumb, the Brief Therapist assumes that the primary determinant of a person's behavior—that is, that which perpetuates the behavior—is other people's behavior.

This somewhat controversial position on human behavior stems from Brief Therapy's having incorporated a cybernetic model with persistence and change as its cornerstone. When a Brief Therapist confronts an individual or family entrapped in a pattern of persistent and sometimes destructive behavior, two questions come to mind: What makes this behavior persist? What is needed to change it? (See Watzlawick, Weakland, & Fisch, 1974, p. 2.)

BACKGROUND OF THE APPROACH

Cybernetics arose from a series of interdisciplinary conferences begun in 1940 and sponsored by Josiah Macy, owner of Macy's department stores. Their purpose was to investigate circular feedback mechanisms and circular causal systems in biological and social systems. In short, cybernetics is the study of self-regulation as it occurs in both natural systems (e.g., homeostatic

---

* Although this article discusses MRI's Brief Therapy, the author is solely responsible for its presentation.

regulation of the body) and manufactured systems (e.g., the heating system in one's home). Conference participants included such luminaries as Gregory Bateson, Margaret Mead, Warren McCulloch, Willam Pitts, Lawrence Kubie, Norbert Weiner, and Heinz von Foerster.

Gregory Bateson

Gregory Bateson, the cultural anthroplogist, borrowed many ideas from the Macy conferences—goal-directed machines, neurocomputation, formal logic and mathematics—and applied them to the study of communication. Since the 1930s, Bateson had searched for schema to describe and explain social systems as something more than the sum of their parts. For instance, he wished to avoid explaining a sadomasochistic relationship as the interaction of a sadist and a masochist, a type of explanation that is described as additive rather than systemic.

Bateson continued to formalize his ideas in a book he wrote with Jurgen Ruesch titled *Communication: The Social Matrix of Psychiatry* (Ruesch & Bateson, 1951), setting the stage for a grant he received from the Rockefeller Foundation to study paradoxes of abstraction in communication. Together with Jay Haley, Don Jackson, William Fry, and John Weakland, Bateson and his colleagues studied communication and paradox in a variety of contexts, including animal behavior, fictional films, humor, hypnosis, and psychotherapy. As their work progressed, they found that systemic thinking provided a powerful tool for explaining behavior without having to resort to the internal workings of mind or instinct.

Housed in the Veterans Administration Hospital in Menlo Park, Calif., it seemed almost inevitable that they would soon turn their attention to psychiatric patients and their families. Their fascination with mental illness and families led to the group's seminal paper, "The Double Bind Theory of Schizophrenia" (Bateson, Jackson, Haley, and Weakland, 1971). In it, they redefined schizophrenia as an attempt to cope with ongoing family communication characterized by recurring double binds.

Schizophrenic families, said the Bateson group, communicated in a contradictory manner, but the contradictions were not obvious because they took place at different levels of abstraction, particularly between the verbal and nonverbal levels. These families forbade metacommunication, blocking any discussion that might resolve the contradictions. And since most identified patients were children or adolescents, they were unlikely to leave home.

The following example illustrates the type of communicational patterns that may repeatedly occur in these families. A mother visiting her son at the hospital might ask him for a hug. As he approaches, to comply with her request, she becomes uncomfortable and tense. If the son then withdraws, she accuses him of not loving her. If he continues to approach her but in a stiff or wooden manner, she accuses him of rejecting her. If he comments on her behavior, she accuses him of disrespect. Finally, his condition prohibits his becoming independent of the family. The reader should not take this example to mean that the son is victimized by his mother. Those family members diagnosed as schizophrenic would also respond to other family members with double binds of their own.

The identified patient's schizophrenic ramblings were explained as an attempt to escape the double binds by trying not to communicate, a logical impossibility if one views all behavior as communication. If one cannot not behave, one cannot not communicate. In attempting to do so, these patients double-bind other family members. For example, one patient sent his mother a Mother's Day card that read, "For someone who has been like a mother to me."

Although a novel explanation of schizophrenia, the paper's true importance rests on the argument that distrubed behavior is a function of an interpersonal system rather than an intrapsychic one, wedding cybernetic epistemology to psychiatry.

Milton Erickson

Bateson, however, did more than unite the founder and first members of MRI to study interpersonal communication and epistemology. He introduced them to Milton H. Erickson, a world-class Brief Therapist. (In the late 1930s, Bateson had consulted with Erickson about the Balinese use of trance.) While directing his research project, Bateson introduced Erickson to his project members and arranged for Haley and Weakland to visit Erickson at his Phoenix home to study his work. In later years, Haley's writing played a large role in making Erickson's work public (Haley, 1967, 1971, 1985a, 1985b). Erickson was the prototypical Brief Therapist. Using a variety of directives and hypnotic techniques, he tailored the treatment to each patient, breaking the rules constraining most traditional therapists, and in doing so, quickly resolved the patient's presenting complaint. All the members of the Brief Therapy Project were students of Erickson.[1]

Heinz von Foerster

No account of Brief Therapy would be complete without mentioning Heinz von Foerster. A physicist and mathematician by training, he joined the Macy conference in the late 1940s before becoming the director of the biocomputer laboratory at the University of Illinois. He first came to the attention of the family-therapy community in 1978 when Paul Watzlawick invited him to be the keynote speaker at an MRI conference.

It was an ideal time for von Foerster to become known to the therapeutic community. Family-systems theory and MRI both needed a theoretical "shot in the arm." On a parallel but separate track, he had spent the last 30 years studying cognition and developing an observer-based science he called the "second cybernetics," or the cybernetics of the observer. A leading proponent of an experimental epistemology called constructivism, his work provides an epistemological basis for Brief Therapy.

The MRI

When the Bateson project disbanded, Don Jackson founded the Mental Research Institute. Its first members included Jay Haley, Jules Riskin, Virgia Satir, and John Weakland. MRI's goal was to use the cybernetic ideas from the Macy conference and the Bateson project as a basis for family therapy.

About 10 years later, in 1967, several MRI research associates had become disillusioned with family therapy and increasingly interested in the brief hypnotic therapy of Milton Erickson. These factors led Jackson to establish the Brief Therapy Project under the direction of Richard Fisch. The original members included Arthur Bodin, Jay Haley, Paul Watzlawick, and John Weakland.

The project is now in its third decade of operation and interest in Brief Therapy continues to grow.[2] MRI-sponsored Brief Therapy workshops have been given in major cities of the United States, Europe, and South America.

The project's first book, *Change: Principles of Problem Formation and Problem Resolution* (Watzlawick et al., 1974), has been translated into nine languages. This was followed by a "how to" book entitled *Tactics of Change: Doing Therapy Briefly* (Fisch, Weakland, & Segal, 1982), which has been published in several languages. Additionally, project members have published 10 other books related to MRI's interactional view.

WHAT IS A PROBLEM?

How a therapist conceptualizes "problems" determines the therapeutic process—who is seen, what questions are asked, how the data are analyzed, what goals are set, what techniques are used, and how outcome is evaluated.

The psychotherapy literature, however, uses the term *problem* freely, as if reader and author agree on its definition. But do they? When clinicians are asked, "What is a problem?" many are hard put to give a conceptual answer. Some clinicians describe a particular dimension of the term, "It has to do with suffering," or, "It is something someone wants to change." Others offer examples of diagnostic categories from the

---

[1] *Editors' Note.* And "Ericksonian psychotherapy" now includes many variations, as Lankton, Lankton, and Matthews (Chapter 8) point out.

[2] *Editors' Note.* It is essential to keep in mind the distinction between the MRI's Brief Therapy and "brief therapy" as a much more general reference to a style of practice that includes such diverse forms as brief psychodynamic therapy and brief cognitive therapy (Budman & Gurman, 1989).

Diagnostic and Statistical Manual of Mental Disorders (revised third edition) (DSM-R-III): depression, chemical addiction, anxiety.

Most therapists would probably agree that there are now two general definitions that capture the meaning of the term in clinical work. Either it refers to the patient's presenting complaint or it refers to something that causes the complaint, in which case the complaint will be labeled the symptom. When the problem is viewed as a cause of the patient's complaint, it may be located inside an individual or between individuals, that is, a family-systems problem.

The problem may be viewed as either psychopathology or a deficiency. In simpler terms, either something is broken or something is missing. Depending on how a therapist accounts for the patient's problem, attempts will be made to repair or patch up the damage or supply what is lacking.

To understand Brief Therapy, the reader must understand how the brief therapist defines problem and how this definition affects treatment. It should also be noted that the following definition is not offered as the true or proper way to define "problems," but rather as the definition the members of the MRI Brief Therapy group invented when they built their short-term, generic model of problem solving.

Definition of a Problem

The Brief Therapist uses four criteria to define a problem, beginning with one or more clients, who say:

1. I am in pain or distress;
2. I attribute my pain to the behavior of others or myself;
3. I have been trying to change this behavior; and
4. I have been unsuccessful.

Therapeutic Distinction and Implications

First, to carry out treatment, someone other than the therapist must believe that a problem exists.

Second, a client's problem can be connected to someone else's behavior. Since many identified patients—teenagers, small children, psychotics, and spouses—are unmotivated for treatment, this definition supports the therapist's working with other family members to change the identified patient's behavior.

Third, the complaint is the problem, not a symptom of an underlying disorder.

Fourth, problem behavior is inextricably tied to problem-solving behavior, a key point in understanding "how" problems persist.

Fifth, the definition transcends psychiatric contexts, applying to a wide variety of complaints.

Sixth, the definition shifts the therapist's focus from understanding the particulars of each diagnosis to developing skill in changing behavior, thoughts, and feelings.

Seventh, the definition is nonnormative. The client's distress defines the existence of a problem, not the client's behavior. Normative models define normal behavior and then attempt to account for deviance. To determine whether the client has a problem, the normative therapist matches the client's with the model's norms. If the therapist finds a problem but the client does not accept the diagnosis, the client is labeled resistant, which may then be used as further evidence to confirm the therapist's findings. In normative psychotherapy, either the therapist or the client can declare that a problem exists. Thus, in a nonnormative model such as Brief Therapy, someone other than the therapist must "feel" or "own" the problem.

Eighth, Brief Therapy's goal is to reduce or eliminate the client's distress. Either of two factors can bring this about: the behavior has changed, or the client is no longer distressed by it. Usually, both conditions are met, but if the client's distress decreases although the behavior remains unchanged, this would also be considered a success.

This position on goal setting usually raises the question of limit setting. Clinicians will frequently ask, "Do the therapist's personal and professional values determine what the Brief Therapist will accept as the client's goal of treatment?" The answer is a simple "yes." This author will not help a client achieve a goal that runs counter to the client's values and beliefs. For example, clients may ask the therapist to help them to engage in asocial behavior in the belief that to do so will reduce their distress—"Help me not to feel nervous or remorseful about stealing so I can support my drug habit, or help me not to feel guilty about abusing my child."

In the final analysis, the Brief Therapist always sets the goal of treatment. In most cases, the client's and therapist's goals will overlap or be similar. The responsibility for setting goals, however, rests with the therapist, not the model. The Brief Therapy model is nonnormative. It does not contain a list of what constitutes the right or correct way for people to behave. Therefore, the Brief Therapist must take personal responsibility for what he or she believes to be useful or helpful to the client rather than claim to be only a spokesperson for some seemingly "objective" or scientific model of human behavior.

Ninth, Brief Therapy's definition of a problem does not require the therapist to interview the entire family when treating a family problem or to interview both spouses when treating a marital problem. Given the client's permission, the therapist will work with anyone who is motivated to resolve the problem.

HOW PROBLEMS ARISE AND PERSIST

Problems develop and persist through the *mishandling* of normal life difficulties—predictable occurrences that arise in most people's lives. These would include accidents, such as loss of work, and transitions in the family life cycle, from courtship to marriage, the birth of a child, children beginning school, children leaving home, and loss of a spouse through death or divorce. This proposition does not exclude the view that biochemical or neurological events may play a role in problematic behavior. Rather, the proposition suggests that despite what goes on inside a person, in the overwhelming majority of cases, the interpersonal events become the primary focus for diagnosis and intervention. Obviously, if one suspects that an organic problem is causing the patient's acute pain, this must be checked by an internist or neurologist. But for most of the everyday complaints presented

to the working therapist, this view of problem formation provides a sufficient basis on which to proceed.[3]

The original difficulty becomes a problem when mishandling leads clients to use more of the same "solution." A vicious circle is set in motion, producing a problem whose severity and nature may have little similarity to the original difficulty.

People, including therapists, mishandle problems because they are making an error in problem solving. They use solutions that seem logical, necessary, or the "only thing to do." Usually, these solutions are consistent with their culture, their frame of reference, and their view of reality. In the Western culture, we believe in attacking problems head on. "If you don't succeed, try, try again"; "When the going gets tough, the tough get going." Thus, someone who has a problem is like the proverbial man caught in the quicksand. The more he struggles, the more he sinks; the more he sinks, the more he struggles.

ATTEMPTED SOLUTIONS

Though people may develop ingenious ways to mishandle problems, four major patterns have been observed: (1) demanding that self or others be deliberately spontaneous; (2) seeking a no-risk method when some risk is inevitable; (3) attempting to reach accord through opposition; and (4) confirming the accuser's suspicions by defending oneself (Fisch et al., 1982).

Attempting To Be Deliberately Spontaneous

Clients use this solution with sleep disorders, sexual difficulties, substance abuse, writing blocks, the inability to create, and whenever

---

[3] *Editors' Note.* While Segal could not be clearer or more explicit here, we wish to underscore what he is saying because we believe that many family therapists have failed to appreciate the MRI stance on this matter.

they try to force themselves or others to "feel" an emotion or to want something.

Most people occasionally will wrestle with uncomfortable feelings or have difficulty with a bodily function or performance. Viewing them as normal life difficulties that will pass with time usually ensures their spontaneous self-correction. Once one begins to force their correction, however, one becomes caught in the trap of forcing spontaneous behavior, setting the stage for a full-fledged problem.

Although one might expect clients to use this solution with themselves (self-talk), it often occurs at the interpersonal level. One or more family members ask, demand, or suggest that another family member be spontaneous—"Cheer up," or "You should want to go to school."

In the following example, a woman describes how she and her husband deliberately tried to make her orgasmic.

PATIENT: Before I married, I don't think I ever had an orgasm, but I never thought about it. You know, I tried sex, and it was fine. The trouble started just before I got married. I was with some girlfriends and we got to talking about sex. They told me that I had never had an orgasm.

THERAPIST: They told you?

PATIENT: From our discussion, I realized that I'd never had one. And then it became a problem. And sex was no longer just enjoyable. I kept, you know, waiting for it to happen. Sex became work. There was no pleasure.

THERAPIST: In the first conversation, what made you think that you were not orgasmic?

PATIENT: What I felt when I made love didn't fit what they were describing. No firecrackers went off; there was no big release. And after it happened, you were supposed to feel, I don't know, a series of peaks. You would peak and then come down and your body would do something. And I knew that never happened to me. One time I was very close.

THERAPIST: After you found out that you didn't have orgasms, what did you try?

PATIENT: First we tried examining my body and figuring out where everything was. Then what to manipulate, the clitoris . . . and when that didn't work. I was so preoccupied with having an orgasm and what we were doing, step by step, that sex was just a pain. I mean, there was no spontaneity. There was no fun in it at all. It was just a process we went through. The next thing we did was to talk with friends, another couple we were close to. They told us about different positions, things like that.

The client enjoyed sex until her friends suggested that something was missing. This led to her understandable but unfortunate solution—trying to be orgasmic. She might have become orgasmic during the marriage if sex had not become deliberate and self-conscious.

Seeking a No-Risk Method Where Some Risk Is Inevitable

This solution is often found with regard to problems that arise from life difficulties associated with work, dating, or making a major decision. The problem solver, attempting to avoid a mistake or the risk of failure, creates what he or she wants to avoid, that is, more doubt and indecision. For example, consider a shy, single man who wants to meet women but fears rejection. When approaching a woman, he anxiously seeks the perfect opening gambit, only to find himself tongue-tied. Such clients frequently complain that when they meet a woman for the first time, their minds go blank. People who try too hard to close a sale or obtain a job have similar complaints. The following illustrates how one man tried to solve the problem of failing job interviews.

THERAPIST: What do you do immediately before, during, and after an interview to maximize your chances of being hired?

PATIENT: Ok. I do something very few people ever do. I prepare a presentation about the company.

THERAPIST: Based on knowledge of . . . ?

PATIENT: Based on my knowledge. It is about a 12-page presentation. I outline what my approach to managing information systems would be. In the report I also analyze the company's weaknesses and strengths.

Attempting to increase his chances of landing the job, in seeking certainty, the client tries to impress the company. In this example, he prepares a 12-page report that explains what is wrong with the company, a solution that is likely to alienate the person who might hire him.

Attempting To Reach Interpersonal Accord Through Opposition

This solution arises from the belief that all problems can be solved by talking. Frequently used in marital and parent–child conflicts, this solution often degenerates into criticism and nagging. The following example illustrates how family members used this solution to deal with the father's depression after he had had two strokes.

SON 1: You have to work harder if you want to improve your physical well-being, and I think that . . .

SON 2: Only in improving your physical well-being are you going to improve your mental well-being, and I think you can do it. I don't know what it's like to feel what you have in your hands and in your leg.

SON 1: I realize that I don't have the physical limitations that you do, but you look at television and you see people who are painting with the brush held in their teeth. You may not be able to work in your shop anymore, but I think that if you really wanted to, you could do a heck of a lot of things right now. I think it's a matter of saying, "Damn it, I'm going to do this for myself because I want to."

FATHER: Well, it started out—the question of me and the trouble that I was having with everybody and everything. I still think there is a hell of a lot wrong with me physically that none of you give me credit for.

MOTHER: You're looking at me.

FATHER: I mean you.

MOTHER: Well . . .

FATHER: It seems to me that everybody—the way I walk . . .

MOTHER: Well . . .

FATHER: I don't walk and drag my leg because it feels good. It feels like hell to drag that fucking leg, and that's no good. I try [crying].

MOTHER: Well, when I tell you to lift your leg and stop dragging your foot, hon, I'm only telling you for your own good. I think that if you concentrate on lifting your leg, you will

be able to do it. You only started dragging it during the last three weeks, and I don't think it's physical; I think it's a little bit of laziness.

FATHER: It is not. It happens. That leg will not lift.

MOTHER: Well, it will lift if you try to lift it.

FATHER: Then you walk around behind me and lift the damn thing.

Confirming the Accuser's Suspicions by Defending Oneself

Many problems associated with paranoia arise from this solution (see Fraser, 1983). It begins when person A defines person B's comment or directive as insidious or intrusive. Person A becomes defensive or withdraws. Person B then takes a greater interest in person A, and the cycle continues.

This solution is frequently used with parent–teenage problems. The typical teenager wants to spend less times with parents and siblings, preferring to be with friends or to spend time alone. Sometimes, the parents, fearing that something is wrong or feeling shunned, make a greater effort to talk with the teenager or to encourage the teenager to join in family activities. The teen, in turn, experiences the parents as intrusive and becomes even more reclusive or stays away from home more. Given the increase in teenage suicides and the media's amplifying of parents' fears with publicity about the threat of copycat suicide, one can expect a significant increase in this pattern of interaction.

The following example illustrates two patterns: too much discussion, and drawing attention to oneself by attempting to be left alone. The client describes how he dealt with his ex-wife's request to accompany him to France on his vacation.

PATIENT: She asked how come I'm going to France. I said, "What do you mean, how come?" She replied, "I want to go with you!" I told her, "You can buy your own ticket, but you also have to validate your passport." But she kept on insisting. Finally, I said, "You cannot go with me!" But she kept on insisting. Does this make sense? I couldn't reason with her, so I hung up.

THERAPIST: She called you to ask if you would take her to France?

PATIENT: Yes.

THERAPIST: You didn't want her to go with you?

PATIENT: I was going alone. I had made up my mind.

THERAPIST: You gave her all the reasons why she could go alone?

PATIENT: Yes. She had the money! She could do the same thing.

THERAPIST: What stopped you from saying, "Look, Mary, I don't want you to go with me"?

PATIENT: I did. I told her, "You know, I'm not stopping you from going, but you're not going with me."

THERAPIST: You're not going with me, that's what you told her?

PATIENT: That's what I told her.

THERAPIST: Did you tell her why?

PATIENT: No I didn't. . . . It's not only why, I did not want to have any association with her. I'm finished.

THERAPIST: Did you tell her that?

PATIENT: Many times.

THERAPIST: This is a crucial point. It has to do with your wording. How did you tell her you didn't want her to go to France with you?

PATIENT: I didn't stop her. I didn't tell she couldn't go.

THERAPIST: I don't follow.

PATIENT: I told her that I had my ticket and she could not go with me. I told her she could get another flight.

THERAPIST: Did you ever tell her that even if you could change your plans and arrange your schedule to fit with hers, you wouldn't want to go with her?

PATIENT: No. I did not want to express any resentment. I was afraid it would only make matters worse. I never express anger or resentment to her.

The more the client attempted to be left alone by hiding his true feelings, his resentment and anger, the more his ex-wife pursued him. He might have been better off telling her, "I don't want you to join me on my vacation. I can't stop you from going to France. That's up to you, but I do not want to be with you."

In summary, the theory and techniques of Brief Therapy rest on two assumptions: "Regardless of their origins and etiology—if, indeed, these can ever be reliably determined—the problems people bring to psychotherapists persist only if they are maintained by ongoing current behavior of the client and others with whom he interacts. Correspondingly, if such problem-maintaining behavior is appropriately changed or eliminated, the problem will be resolved or vanish, regardless of its nature, or origin, or duration" (Weakland, Fisch, Watzlawick, & Bodin, 1974, p. 144).[4] This summary also applies to the problems therapists have with their clients and the solutions therapists use for these problems.

THE TECHNIQUES OF BRIEF THERAPY

Brief Therapy may be operationalized as a set of tasks designed to (1) identify which family members are motivated for treatment and arrange for them to attend the initial interview(s); (2) collect clear and specific data about the problem and its attempted solutions; (3) set a specific goal; (4) formulate a case plan to promote benevolent change; (5) implement interventions to interrupt the attempted solution; (6) assess the efficacy of treatment; and (7) terminate treatment.

Setting the Stage for Treatment

Treatment begins when the therapist talks with a potential client who is calling for an appointment. This statement is made to underscore that many treatment models conceptualize treatment as beginning with the first interview. How the therapist handles this initial contact depends on the understanding of two concepts—client position and therapist maneuverability.

Client Position

The term *position* denotes a verbal or written statement a person makes regarding what he or

---

[4] *Editors' Note.* It is striking how much more stridently univariate leading MRI proponents were on this matter two decades ago, in comparison with Segal's noticeably more moderate position, highlighted earlier, on the influence of biological factors on problems brought to psychotherapists.

she thinks and feels about an issue. In a treatment context, a person "takes" a position when expressing his or her views about the problem or treatment to another person, such as the therapist or a family member. The term is often used in political discussions and in-depth news reports but it is rarely found in clinical discussions.

The term position is also found in the writings of Eastern religions. Students are taught to give up their worldly positions if they wish the world to be perfect. This is no easy feat to accomplish. If most of us started the day with this goal (a paradox in and of itself), we would find that we had positions about the quality of our night's sleep, our breakfast, the weather, the traffic, and so on. "Position" can be used to describe a person's sense of self. If someone consistently expresses positions on a myriad of subjects, clinicians are inclined to say, "The person has a good sense of self," or, "There's somebody home there." Conversely, people who take no positions might be described as having "little sense of self." They might be diagnosed as schizoid or borderline.

The Brief Therapist makes use of several client positions to change how a client views the problem and to gain his or her compliance when making therapeutic directives. *First, is the client a customer for treatment?* A customer is a person seeking treatment, who, in effect, says (takes the position), "I am distressed about the behavior of myself or another. I have been unable to change it, and I am asking for your help." Customers are distinguished from "window-shoppers," those people who appear to want help but are just biding their time until the person who has pressured them into treatment backs off. A typical window-shopper might be the male alcoholic whose only motivation for treatment is to appease his wife and regain entry to the family home. Couples ordered by the court to seek marital therapy are another example of window-shoppers. A window-shopper may become a customer, but for this to happen, the therapist must address directly the lack of an apparent motivation to work on the presenting complaint. For example, the alcoholic might admit that his wife is a problem to him. Thus, if no one in the family is a customer, no treatment can take place. Therapist and client can have a conversation that looks like psychotherapy, but it is a charade and a waste of time.

Second, what is the client's position on the problem? What does the client think is causing the trouble? For instance, a mother might believe that her son's problematic behavior is due to either a chemical deficiency, an emotional problem, or parental mishandling. To gain her compliance in carrying out a therapeutic directive, it might be framed as either a means of assessing the extent of her son's chemical inbalance, a mechanism to develop the son's ego strength, or a tool to make her parenting more effective.

Third, what is the client's position on treatment? What does the client expect the therapist to do? Is he or she seeking insight or advice, or does he or she want the therapist to use hypnosis to solve the problem. The client's position on the problem and treatment can be viewed as directives from the client, instructing the therapist as to which directives would be most useful and how to frame them.

Maneuverability

The term *therapist maneuverability* denotes the therapist's freedom to use his or her best judgment. This would include the freedom to see different family members, to ask questions, and to determine the timing and pace of treatment.

Although somewhat absurd, the following example illustrates this concept. Prior to his operation, a patient makes several requests of his surgeon. He wants the bright lights turned off during the operation; he is superstitious about people who wear glasses and requests that the surgeon remove her glasses during the operation; finally, uncomfortable with people standing too close to him, he asks that only the surgeon stand within three feet of his person. To comply with these ridiculous demands would severely reduce the surgeon's maneuverability and jeopardize the operation.

Now consider the client who does not want his wife to know that he fears she is mentally ill. He wants the therapist to come to dinner, pose as an old friend, and secretly assess his wife's mental status. These circumstances would severely restrict the gathering of needed data. One's maneuverability is also restricted by clients who claim that they cannot talk about what is bothering them because they are embarrassed to discuss their problems with another person.

The therapist's maneuverability is reduced when clients answer questions in a vague or contradictory manner, leaving the therapist on shaky ground when it comes time to make an intervention. The client can say, "I think you misunderstood me." For example, the therapist, about to make a directive, restates the husband's position about his wife's lack of sexual interest. She wants to make sure that he confirms that she understood him correctly since the directive was predicated on how he saw the problem. The husband, not to be pinned down, replies, "That's not what I really meant. You can't believe everything I say about sex. I'm Catholic and Catholics always lie about sex." With this statement he informs the therapist that he will not make his position clear.

Maintaining one's maneuverability also depends on taking one's time. Like most psychotherapies, the steps of treatment are sequential; one cannot make a case plan before collecting data. Therapists often give up their maneuverability by making directives prematurely.

In the final analysis, maintaining one's therapeutic maneuverability depends on an inner attitude rather than on a set of techniques—the therapist's willingness to fire the client. Rarely, if ever, does this happen, but if therapists cannot even imagine doing so, they are likely to give up their maneuverability. Bruno Bettelheim, a noted psychoanalyst, warned analysts in private practice never to become financially dependent on too few patients. If one cannot afford to lose the patient, treatment is compromised.

The First Telephone Contact

Treatment begins with the first telephone contact. The therapist must try to determine which family members are customers and arrange to see them for the first visit. In most instances, the customer is the person who calls for the first appointment. Additionally, the therapist must take steps to preserve his or her maneuverability.

Customers, acting out of their anxiety and concern, often try to determine who will be seen for the first interview. For example, a mother,

calling about her son's problem, may insist that the child be seen alone. This request might be handled by asking, "How eager is your son to come in for treatment?" When the mother makes the usual reply, "He's not really eager, but he promised me last night that he would go. And he knows that if he tries to get out of it, Ill drag him in," the therapist can suggest that the mother attend the first interview for the purpose of giving information and helping the therapist plan how to get the boy to see him. The same technique can be used with a man or woman who is ready to drag an unwilling spouse to counseling.

During the intial telephone contact, some clients will ask the therapist to take a position about his or her expertise. They might ask if the therapist specializes in marital therapy. The Brief Therapist would reply "no." Claiming to be a marital therapist would be to take a position about one's expertise when nothing is known about the case. The Brief Therapist would say, "I work with marital problems, but I'm not a marital therapist. I can explain this difference when you come in." This statement leaves open the option for telling the client that one also works with individual or family problems.

Clients may ask the therapist to contact their previous therapist before the first meeting. Although this request would appear to be a time-saving measure, it can reduce the client's efforts to provide clear and specific data since since it can be assumed that the previous therapist has supplied all the important information. Even more troublesome, it can imply that the Brief Therapist will continue the previous therapist's treatment. This request might be handled by saying, "I would prefer to see you once or twice before I talk with your previous therapist so I can be clearer on my own impressions of you and your trouble." This response would also be used if the therapist were asked to read the previous therapist's case notes.

Data Collection

When collecting data, the therapist directs clients to talk to him or her rather than to each other. Answers should be specific and concrete. Descriptions of interaction should read like a script. If the client says, "I really let her have it," the therapist will need to ask, "What did you say? Then what did she say or do?"

Joining, the emotional connection between therapist and client, arises from the therapist's interest in the client's problem and how the therapist attempts to deal with it. The bond can be strengthened if the therapist avoids challenges and confrontations when there is a need for greater clarity. Clients can be motivated to work harder in the interview if the therapist takes a *one-down position*. For instance, when needing more clarification with a client whose tone implies, "I have told you everything I can at least twice," the therapist might say, "Please bear with me, I'm not myself today. Would you mind going over that again?" Or, "In all fairness to you, I must let you know that in all my years as a therapist I have never worked with your kind of problem. So I will need to go over this very carefully."

Most therapists are trained to take the one-up position by presenting themselves as the expert. They fear that taking a one-down position will destroy their credibility. However, if clients really want to do business, if they truly are "customers" for treatment, they will work extra hard to explain their problems or elaborate on almost anything else one needs to know.

Defining the Problem

The first interview begins by asking the client, "What is the problem that brings you here today?" A minority of clients will give concrete and specific answers. They might reply, "Our 15-year-old daughter is cutting classes, staying out late, refusing to do things with the rest of the family, and making constant demands for money and clothing." Usually, however, clients' answers are more ambigious—"We don't communicate," or, "I'm depressed." The therapist now must find out what these remarks mean.

Some clients will begin by giving a long, detailed personal history and will need coaxing to get them to address the question: What is the problem right now? Using a one-down strategy, they might be told, "Please let me interrupt you for a second. I need to let you know something. I have a hard time digesting information when I don't know where a history is leading. It would really help me if you could begin by giving me a picture of the trouble you are having right now. Then we could go over your history."

Next, clients are asked how the complaint is a problem. What does it stop the client from doing or make the client do unwillingly? For instance, parents frequently answer that they have no life of their own because they are afraid to leave their child or teenager unsupervised. Or a couple's continual disagreements lead to unwanted fights. The employees in conflict with their manager frequently complain of stress, difficulty in sleeping and unwanted self-absorption, which put a strain on the marital relationship.

Answering this question has several uses. First, it acts as a useful barometer of the client's distress. Second, it helps distinguish the complaint from what the client thinks is causing it. When the therapist asks what trouble or problem brings them in, many clients assume they are being asked about the cause of the trouble. For instance, when spouses state, "We don't communicate," they might mean that they cannot make agreements, that their marriage lacks intimacy, or that one spouse finds the other boring. Their answer, "We can't communicate," is an explanation for the complaint, their position on the problem. Third, explaining how a complaint is a problem often suggests what might be a goal of treatment. For example, the parents who are afaid to leave their child alone might be ready to terminate treatment when they feel that their child's behavior has improved sufficiently for them to go off for a weekend or take in a movie.

Finally, clients are asked why they sought treatment when they did. Asking this question also helps assess customership, uncovering those factors that led to making the initial phone contact. It gives the therapist a picture of the straw that broke the camel's back.[5]

The Attempted Solution

Next, the therapist must determine who is trying to solve the problem, what solutions have

---

[5] *Editors' Note.* Indeed, the "Why now?" question provides the central organizing principle for an entire method of brief psychotherapy, which one of us (A.G.) has written about at length (Budman & Gurman, 1989).

been tried and discarded, and what solutions are still being used. For example, parents may report: "We have done everything to reach her. We have tried to reason with her, we have grounded her, we have taken away her allowance, etc." What questions are asked will depend on the particular problem. If the identified patient performs the problematic behavior in the presence of others, it will be important to learn how these other people respond to or handle the problem.

There are also times when people deal with a problem but do not consider it an attempt to solve it. However, from the Brief Therapist's perspective, all behavior is communication and all communication is potentially a means of influence. For example, consider the mother who, in response to her child's misbehaving, says, "I don't know what I did to deserve this." She does not report making these statements as an attempted solution, but if she frequently does so within the child's hearing, it is part of the problem–solution cycle.

Setting a Goal

After a description of the problem and the solutions that will be attempted has been obtained, the therapist should establish a goal for treatment. The Brief Therapist will ask, "Since we only have 10 sessions, we need to define a goal of treatment that would tell us you are beginning to solve the problem. You're not completely out of the woods, so to speak, but you'll have found the trail and can find your way on your own. So, what would be the smallest, concrete, significant indicator of this?"

Several benefits accrue from setting a small, concrete goal of treatment. First, if the client has been feeling hopeless about solving what feels like a monolithic life problem, setting a small, attainable goal can increase his or her hope and motivation for treatment. Second, while suggesting that change is possible, setting a small, concrete goal also provides a measure of success for the client and the therapist. Thus, reaching the goal increases the probability of continued positive change because it "relaxes" the client, reducing his or her use of the problem-perpetuating solutions.

Goals should be formulated as increases in positive behavior rather than reduction or elimination of negative behavior. For example, a couple seeking to reduce its fighting says the goal of treatment is "to stop these awful fights!" The therapist should then reply, "When you reduce your fighting, what might be the smallest thing that would take place, of a positive nature, something that you do together, that would tell us that things have improved?"

Case Planning

After these data have been collected, the therapist must plan how to interrupt the attempted solutions that perpetuate the problem. The therapist must decide who should be seen for the remaining interviews, what directives should be used, and how the directives should be framed. As Haley noted (1963, p. 45), "One of the difficulties involved in telling people to do something is that psychiatric clients are noted for their hesitation to do what they are told." Thus, as case planners, therapists must decide what they want clients to do and how to get them to do it.

The therapist can determine if the necessary data have been collected for case planning by answering the following questions:

What is the complaint?

What is the attempted solution?

What is the client's goal?

What are the client's positions on the problem and treatment?

If these questions cannot be answered, the missing data can be obtained during the next interview. If all the data have been collected, the following five questions should be answered:

1. What is the attemped solution?
2. What would be a 180-degree shift from the attempted solution?
3. What specific behavior would operationalize the shift?
4. Given the client's positions, how can the therapist sell the behavior?
5. What might the client report that would signal that the intervention has been successful and the case is ready for termination?

The therapist must now find the rule or common thread in the client's solutions. Assuming that every speech act, verbal and nonverbal, carries a command, the question can be posed, "What command is common to the solutions used by the client and anyone else involved with the problem?"

More on Report and Command

Gregory Bateson conceptualized every communicative act as having both a report and a command. Usually, adults do not command (give orders to) other people unless they are military personnel or children. Most people only focus on the report of every communication. A report is usually a declarative statement, such as, "It is raining," or "You are reading a chapter about Brief Therapy," or "I feel hungry." However, clinicians know that many spouses, sensitive to control issues, focus on the commands of each other's speech acts rather than on the report. For instance, a husband might ask his wife, "Is there anything good to eat?" His wife hears the command, "Make me something to eat!" Couples caught in "power struggles" lose sight of the report (content) in each other's communication, perceiving only the commands. Each interprets the other's behavior as an attempt to define the relationship and to tell the person what to do.

Commands are not always obvious. Untrained observers, which includes most clinicians, are not likely to perceive them. This is partly due to commands being implied rather than explicitly observable. Some communicative acts seem more like commands than reports. One example is a request. Given a certain verbal tone, the question, "Will you take out the garbage?" would be heard as an outright order. The therapist can ask, and at times must guess, what command the recipient of the attempted solutions experiences.

To illustrate how the concept of command is applied to the attempted solution, consider a hypothetical client complaining of insomnia. She has tried several solutions to induce sleep. She has read dull books, hoping to bore herself asleep; exercised to tire herself out; drunk milk because she has heard that calcium biochemically induces sleep; and practiced relaxation exercises to rid herself of the tension she believes to be keeping her awake. Each solution was different, but all carried the same command— sleep! Thus, command is determined by context, that is, the problem. Under different circumstances, drinking milk might carry the command, "Take away my hunger or thirst." A student studying for a test might experience the command associated with his or her assigned reading as, "Memorize the facts."

As another example, consider a father who has been trying to get his teenage son to behave differently. One evening, tired of fighting, he tells the boy a story about his own childhood, hoping to let the boy know he understands because he once was a teenager himself. The son, however, perceives the command rather than the report, and experiences his father's sudden urge to share as simply another attempt to change him. The father ends up feeling frustrated and misunderstood; the boy feels as though the father never gets off his back.

The Mine Field

Determining the basic solution indicates what class of behaviors will interrupt the attempted solution. Equally, if not more, important, it tells the therapist how to avoid the "mine field"— those remarks or directives that are "more of the same" attempted solutions. For instance, to intervene with the insomniac described in the example, the mine field would include any directive that commands sleep.

To avoid the mine field and determine an effective intervention, the therapist can ask himself or herself what directive would shift the client's basic solution 180 degrees. For example, if an obese client has attempted to lose weight with diets, exercise, and self-hypnosis, all her solutions carry the command, "Lose weight!" A 180-degree shift would occur if she were instructed to gain weight. She might be told, "I don't know why this is true, and I'm sure it will sound crazy to you, but recent research shows that in cases where someone has tried all the diets like you have and none of them have worked, there is one thing that will break the cycle." If the client is eager to learn more, she is then told, "What you have to do is break your upper limit by 10 pounds. We don't know why this is true, but it does seem to work." Family members' attempted solutions can be interrupted by instructing them to encourage the client to eat more or avoid exercise. The mine field would be any suggestion or directive aimed at losing weight.

The insomniac can be instructed not to sleep. One patient with a psychoanalytic bent was told that there were important clues to the cause of his insomnia. What he needed to do was take a pad and pencil to bed and write down all his thoughts when unable to sleep. The therapist implied that it is beneficial to stay awake. The longer a patient remains awake, the more data he or she can collect. Milton Erickson instructed many of his insomniacs to perform distasteful but useful tasks during the hours they could not sleep. A client who is waxing the kitchen floor cannot also be lying in bed attempting to force sleep. Parents who demand compliance from their teenager can make a 180-degree shift by apologizing to the child for expecting too much from the child academically. After apologizing, they refrain from asking questions about the child's school work. If the child voluntarily complains that school is difficult, they tell the child that he or she is doing the best possible given his or her limitations.

Reframing

Clients will need help with performing directives that appear counterintuitive; for example, "When sitting on a nervous horse, it is not easy to follow the instructor's orders to let go of the reins. One *knows* the horse will run away, even though it is really the pull on the reins that is making him jump" (Weakland et al., 1974, p. 289). Thus, we come to the second main task of case planning—how to frame directives. The technique for changing the client's view is called reframing, which means "to change the conceptual and/or emotional setting or viewpoint in relation to which a situation is experienced and to place it in another frame which fits the 'facts' of the same situation equally or even better, and thereby changes its entire meaning" (Watzlawick et al., 1974, p. 95).

Shakespeare demonstrated a keen understanding of reframing when he wrote, "There is nothing good or bad, but thinking makes it so."

In many cases, reframing consists of verbally turning the bad into the good, and vice versa. Rumor even has it that Virginia Satir convinced a couple that the husband's chasing his wife around the house with a large steak knife was really his primitive way of establishing emotional contact.

The following example of reframing was done by Richard Fisch of the MRI when working with the anxious parents of a young boy. The parents were trying to control their son's behavior with a series of escalating rules and regulations. A key "position" was the parents' belief, particularly the mother's, that they could "intuit" when the boy was getting into trouble. Based on their intuitions, they would take corrective action—more of the attempted solution.

THERAPIST: We have one sonar and one radar. You [to father] have something that picks up sound, and you [to mother] have something like radar.

MOTHER: I guess this is how we have been able to keep the lid on as long as we did.

THERAPIST: I'll tell you the thought that I had. It's far-fetched, so I don't want to push it at all, but let me mention it for whatever it's worth. I'd say that it's probably fairly reliable that the two of you have different styles, but are perceptive in picking up what this kid is doing or even is about to do. In a sense, the two of you are describing that each of you has well-tuned, well-trained, receiving equipment. It would be nice, although it sounds far-fetched, if those abilities could now be trained as sending sets. Not only would you be able to use your powers of intuition to tell how the wind is blowing, but also to determine how the wind will blow. Now the interesting thing is that your intuition sounds like a much more powerful tool than the one you usually use with Robby, which is words.

MOTHER: Words don't work.

THERAPIST: You have a fabulous receiving mechanism of communication. But it's not the mechanism you use in trying to help control him.

MOTHER: I guess that's because I don't know how.

THERAPIST: Yes, but you don't know how you receive. The only reason I want to mention it is that I would not want to exclude the possibility of using your intuition, not just simply to receive, but to send. It would be a shame for it not to be used. Then you would not have to be verbally explicit with Robby, who, no matter how explicit you are, is going to do any damn thing he pleases.

MOTHER: That's true.

By giving her intuition a try, the mother agrees to try a different method of controlling her children, extrasensory perception (ESP). Using ESP is mutually exclusive with her attempted solution—nagging, threatening, and limit setting.

Any situation or problem can be reframed. For example, an angry and frustrated father can be given assignments that allow him to vent his feelings harmlessly and therapeutically, and caretakers can be instructed to be even more helpful and sacrificing. Curious and insight-oriented people can be motivated to try novel ideas, to see what new things they can learn, while the resistant client might be encouraged not to change. Obviously, the technique of reframing is value-free. It is the reframer, the therapist, who must operate according to what he or she believes to be correct, helpful, or useful to the family. Reframing is not unique to psychotherapy. It occurs in many walks of life— politics, sales, international diplomacy, and everyday family relations. Like many powerful change techniques, reframing has the power to harm as well as the power to heal.[6]

INTERVENTIONS

The ultimate goal of Brief Therapy is to reduce or eliminate the client's suffering. To this end, interventions seek to alter the patient's view of the problem and to interdict the problem-maintaining behavior used by the client and/or significant others.

---

[6] *Editors' Note.* And, as Doherty and Boss (Chapter 20) emphasize, it is the intention of the therapist using paradoxical methods (or any other type of method) more than the content of the intervention that establishes the therapist's trustworthiness.

Paradox

Sometimes the Brief Therapist will instruct the client to increase a behavior that traditionalists call a symptom. This technique is commonly referred to as *symptom prescription* or *paradoxical injunction*. Many clinicians first learning about Brief Therapy erroneously assume that the use of paradox or symptom prescription is the essence of the model. Nothing could be further from the truth. Thinking in terms of paradox is neither necessary nor useful. If a depressed client has been fighting the depression, telling the client to increase it for 10 minutes a day is asking him or her to do something different (i.e., stop fighting it), making a 180-degree shift in the attempted solution. Whether or not the intervention can be called a therapeutic paradox is not only irrelevant, but also dilutes the clarity and simplicity that were designed into the model, that is, as a technique to change the attempted solution.

Do Something Different or Do More of the Same

Therapists have two classes of directives at their disposal to change attempted solutions. Either they tell the client to do something different or they tell the client to do more of the same.

Asking the client to do more of the same is usually based on the prediction that the client will not comply with the therapist's directives. Thus, change is the result of resistance. For example, a noncompliant client might be told, "I'm beginning to understand how hurt you have been by your daughter's behavior and I can see why you would want to see her suffer. But I also know that to acknowledge your wish for revenge is unacceptable to you. You have found an ingenious way of making her suffer while looking like you are only trying to help. Now, the only suggestion that I have is to stop playing around and really get her. I would predict that, if you really work at it, you will have her begging to return to the hospital in about three weeks."

Or a teenager might be told to keep up his or her rowdy behavior and poor school performance in order to help his or her parents avoid facing a marital problem. The teenager is commended for making a loyal sacrifice, ruining his or her own life to protect the parents. In both examples, the behavior is framed with the aim of making it ego dystonic while encouraging the client to continue doing it.

Interventions and Patterns of Attempted Solutions

As stated previously, five problematic problem-solving solution patterns have been observed: (1) demanding that self or others be deliberately spontaneous; (2) seeking a nonrisk method when some risk is inevitable; (3) attempting to reach accord through opposition; (4) confirming the accuser's suspicions by defending oneself; and (5) attempting to master a feared event by avoiding it. The following describes some of the interventions commonly used with each of these patterns.

Demanding That Self or Others Be Deliberately Spontaneous

The therapist can instruct the client to maintain or intensify complaints correlated with this solution for diagnostic purposes. For example, a client's premature ejaculation was resolved by instructing him and his wife to time the speed of his ejaculation with a stopwatch. The assignment was framed as a requirement for diagnosis. Instructing the husband to perform his symptom while instructing his wife to time it mutually excludes their attempted solutions. Neither could use any measure designed to forestall ejaculation.

One subgroup of problems associated with this category of solutions arises from demanding compliance through voluntary action. Examples would include the wife who wants her husband to bring her flowers but would consider the act invalid if she asked him to do it and the parent who wants a child "to want" to go to school. The primary intervention in these cases is to get the client to ask for or require behavior of the other that is under the person's voluntary control. For instance, the parent can be instructed to tell the child to go to school. If the child protests, "I don't want to," rather than entering into a dia-

logue about it, the parent can reply, "You don't have to *want* to, you just have to go." A child can control going to school, but cannot make himself or herself want to go. The wife who wants her husband to bring her flowers might be told about conditioning theory and how her husband must have a positive experience. The bottom line, of course, is that she ask for the flowers and receive them in an appreciative and gracious manner.

Seeking a Nonrisk Method When Some Risk Is Inevitable

The strategy used with this solution is to expose clients to the feared event while restraining them from sucessfully completing it. Clients with a writing block can be instructed to sit at their desks with their materials for only 10 minutes each day. No matter how little or how much they write, they must stop at the end of 10 minutes. No further writing is permitted for 24 hours. Students who become anxious when taking exams can be encouraged purposely to miss one or two questions. Sometimes, clients can be induced to follow these assignments with an intervention called a "devil's pact." The pact circumvents framing the intervention and instead the therapist and client make a bargain. It is presented as follows: "I believe I have a way I can help you with your problem, but it will take some doing on your part. What I will ask you to do will not be illegal or immoral and it will be within your capacity to do it. However, I will not tell you what it is until you promise me that you will do it, no matter what you think or feel about my suggestions. Now, take a week to think this over and next week when we meet, you can give me your decision."

Attempting to Reach Accord Through Opposition

Clients using this solution are usually struggling with another person—child, spouse, elderly parent, or lover—who is demanding to be treated with care, respect, or deference. Although the client experiences himself or herself as reasonable and the other as uncooperative, the recipient of the attempted solutions is likely to experience the client as bossy, controlling, pushy, or intrusive.

The primary strategy with these complainants is to get the complainant to take a one-down position. This shift requires careful framing to gain compliance. For instance, parents who were angry with their daughter's unwillingness to attend school and her sullen moods alternated their attempted solutions between demanding that she attend school and trying to engage her in conversations about what was troubling her. The primary aim of treatment was to stop these solutions. First, the parents were told that their daughter was struggling with problems of self-esteem that caused her to withdraw from friends and school. Additionally, she was experiencing an adolescent identity crisis. Typically, like many adolescents, she was trying to define her identity by becoming the opposite of everything the parents stood for, and so was unlikely to take their advice or to listen to them.

Once the parents accepted this framing, it was a small step for them to understand that pushing her to do things would provoke her to do the opposite. They were told that the daughter needed time alone to have an important inner dialogue with herself, so she could reflect on her own behavior. However, the parents could not simply stop pushing since the daughter was likely to interpret their silence or lack of interest as silent nagging or an attempt to make her feel guilty. Therefore, they were instructed to return home and apologize to her for being bad parents. They were to tell her that they had gone to counseling to learn what they could do about her and had learned something very disconcerting—they were using her to avoid attending to their own marital problems.

This last statement is intended to reframe the parents' new behavior as something other than an attempt to change the daughter. Then, if they let her alone, the daugher is less likely to interpret it as a ploy to get her out of the house. In this particular case, the parents were instructed to do things as a couple, telling the daughter that they could not invite her as usual because the outings were assignments designed by the therapist to improve their marriage. This left the daughter home alone with no one to fight with or to keep her company.

Confirming the Accuser's Suspicions by Defending Oneself

This pattern of problem and attempted solution can be interrupted when the defendant agrees with the accuser. For example, a couple seen at MRI had been caught in this pattern for over 30 years. The wife had accused her husband of "not being any fun" and of providing mediocre financial support. He defended himself by replying that he had sacrificed much to give her what he could. In his early 20s, he had followed her from Europe, giving up a law career to work for the rest of his life as a tailor.

At the completion of the second interview, the husband was asked to come to the next session by himself. His wife was told that he had the problem, which was why the individual session was needed; that is, he was coming to treatment so we could try to fix him. During the third visit, the husband said he was willing to "do anything within his power that would bring these never-ending arguments to a close." He agreed to carry out the directive, and that evening he told his wife what he had learned in treatment: (1) that she was right, he was no fun; and (2) that he was too old to change. By taking this one-down position and agreeing with her, he brought their arguments (i.e., her complaint) to an end.

Sometimes the loop between accuser and defendant can be broken with an intervention called *jamming*. One way of evaluating the informational value of a message is to equate it with its probability. If a message is highly probable, it is likely to carry little new information. For example, one would not watch the weather report on television if the weather or the report never varied. Similarly, the perfunctory kiss of couples that occurs every morning or evening usually loses its informational value for communicating affection.

A young woman seen at the MRI Brief Therapy Center complained that her mother was intruding into her life. The mother was concerned that the client would never settle down and form a lasting relationship with a man. Although the mother lived halfway across the country, she would often call and question the client about her current dating behavior. The client defended her behavior, leading her mother to accuse her of being overly critical of men. If the client refused to talk about men, the mother accused her of hiding bad news. The mother had heard about the MRI's Brief Therapy Project and encouraged her daughter to see us for treatment.

The primary intervention with the daugher was to "jam" the loop between herself and her mother. During treatment, she was instructed to call her mother and deliver the following message: "I am going to MRI and receiving Brief Therapy. One of the things I have learned is that I am too picky about men." Her mother replied, "I knew I was right. I am so relieved to hear you are going to treatment." The daughter continued, "They also told me that from now on, every time we communicate—by letter, phone, or face to face—I am always to tell you that things are bad whenever you ask me about dating. And they said you would understand why I was instructed to do this." The mother replied, "Well, things are bad with you 90 percent of the time." Her daughter answered, "Well, now they will be bad 100 percent of the time."

This intervention coincided with a reduction in the mother's telephone calls and questions about the client's social life, resulting in less tension and a more positive feeling between them. When the mother visited the client several weeks later, she told her daughter, "You've changed. You seem less angry."

Attempting to Master a Feared Event by Avoiding It

This solution is most clearly associated with phobias, writing blocks and public speaking anxiety. Generally clients attempt to solve this problem by either endlessly preparing only to find the more they prepare (try to be perfect or free of anxiety), the more unprepared they feel, or they procrastinate, avoiding the dreaded event.

Clients who overprepare can be instructed to perform the act and deliberately make a mistake. This works extremely well with people who have test anxiety. They are instructed to deliberately answer one question incorrectly. Similarly, clients who fear public speaking can be instructed to say they lost their train of thought and ask the audience for help.

Other problems lend themselves to slightly different solutions, but are based on the same theme—interrupting the avoidance. Clients with writer's block can be instructed to work only 10 minutes a day. They must sit at their desks with all their materials and after 10 minutes they must stop, even if they feel unblocked and are writing freely.

All these interventions interdict the avoidance and the demands for high performance. Hopefully, clients will return the following week sheepishly reporting they carried out the assignment and went further—that they wrote for an hour instead of 10 minutes or introduced themselves to someone when they were instructed to only watch how others socialize at a gathering and to avoid conversing. Now the therapist is in the position to amplify this positive change by urging them to slow down the rate of change!

General Interventions

In addition to these specific interventions, the Brief Therapist may use some general-purpose interventions, individualizing them to the particular client or case.

Dangers of Improvement

This intervention consists of asking clients what new problems might or will arise when the presenting difficulty is resolved. If clients cannot come up with any on their own, the therapist, using a little logic and imagination, can always invent a few. To help the client understand the logic of dangers of improvement, the therapist might say, "You know, everyone likes to think that if they just got rid of the problem, everything else would be fine. But life does not work that way. There is no free lunch. Take something like winning the lottery. What could be better? But even with something so apparently positive, there are dangers of improvement. Once you have your millions, how will you deal with your friends? Will you give them money or pay their way? They might resent it. Or, if you don't share your money with them, they may resent that too. You don't know these things. What about your job? Will you continue to work? If not, what will you do? Everyone you know works. You could find people who don't work, but would you be comfortable with them? They would either be indigent or affluent. They have different values. Then, there will be all the people who want to sell you things, offer you deals, and try to become your friend. Now I'm not saying it wouldn't be great to win the money, but it would have its problems. So let's get back to your problem. What might happen once you get rid of it?"

Once the therapist and client have invented some possible dangers of improvement, the therapist can use the findings as a basis for another general-purpose intervention—go slowly.

Go Slowly

The injunction to "go slowly" can be used either to slow down or to speed up a client's progress. Sometimes, the therapist needs leverage to slow the client down. The client's anxiety and impatience encourage the rushing of assignments and not allowing enough time for an intervention to take effect. If the client sees improvement as a mixture of positives and negatives, he or she will be more relaxed and will tend to carry out assignments more carefully. The client is also less inclined to be thrown by the ups and downs that accompany changing behavior.

Conversely, the instruction to "go slowly" can also be used to speed up or simply to support a positive change. Many clients become enthusiastic when things begin to change, but they are just as likely to feel defeated when they backslide. Telling the client to go slowly can be tied to predictions of slippage and of the client's disappointment. Predicting some responses may prohibit them or alter their importance if they do occur.

Telling the client to go slowly also suggests that the therapist does not feel an urgent need to change the client, and that the client needs to cooperate with any suggestions the therapist may give.

U-Turn

Sometimes, the intervention and/or framing used in a previous session missed the client's

position or left the client feeling misunderstood or angry. When this occurs, the therapist must make a correction, a "U-turn," and proceed in another direction.

When taking a one-down postion, the therapist might tell the client, "I did a lot of thinking about your problem after our last session. As a matter of fact, I saw Dr. X., an expert on this kind of problem. He helped me to see that I had things all wrong. He suggested that you might try the following . . ."

TERMINATION

The brevity of contact, and emphasis on action rather than affect, makes termination a natural, simple process.

There are three criteria in the patient's report that indicate that the patient is ready to terminate: (1) a small, but significant, change has been made in the problem; (2) the change appears to be durable; and (3) the patient implies or states an ability to handle things without the therapist.

When terminating, the therapist will attempt to extend his or her therapeutic influence. Clients are usually given credit for positive change, but cautioned against believing that the problem is solved forever. If the client is hesitant about ending, termination might be framed as a necessary vacation from treatment during which therapeutic gains can be incorporated into one's daily life. The resistant or negative client can be told that his or her improvement is inconsequential, or at best temporary. The therapist might then predict that the client's situation will get worse.

CASE EXAMPLE

Presenting Problem

Mr. and Mrs. Jones sought treatment because their 15-year-old daughter, Jan, was cutting classes and failing in school, staying out beyond her curfew, refusing to help around the house, and constantly demanding money, clothing, and more freedom. Both parents agreed that "she had a knack for breaking you down" with her constant nagging.

Attempted Solutions

The parents had dealt with Jan's misbehavior in several ways. First, they tried to reason with her. Second, they grounded her. When these methods failed, they sent her to an uncle "who was good with kids," but he could not tolerate Jan's behavior and sent her home. One night, the police picked her up for breaking the town's curfew. The parents let her spend the night in juvenile hall, hoping it would teach her a lesson.

Positions

Both parents were customers for treatment. Their problem was Jan's misbehavior, which was a problem to them in two ways: (1) they were concerned that she was ruining her life, and (2) she was difficult to deal with and be around. Their position on the problem was that Jan was misbehaving. Their position on treatment was: "counsel us, teach us how to handle our daughter." Their attempted solution was to try to gain compliance through opposition.

Session 1

Since the parents were obvious customers for treatment and gave such clear information, the therapist intervened quickly. He ended the session by suggesting that they might "give her some of her own medicine" by acting unreasonably when she began to nag them. Wanting to test their compliance, the therapist told them they were only to *think* about how they might respond differently when she nagged them during the coming week, but they were not to act differently.

The interview ended with the parents' agreeing that their attempted solution, primarily the use of reason, was not working. Additionally, the homework assignment reinforced this conclusion by asking them to continue using nonproductive solutions while thinking about how to make an unreasonable response to Jan's nagging. Just thinking about this assignment was

likely to change how they would respond to her during a future struggle. Additionally, the assignment would test their compliance with therapeutic directives.

Session 2

Jan was seen alone during the first half of the second session. The therapist concluded his talk with her by explaining that she had discovered a "sure-fire" method for getting what she wanted from her parents. She would simply nag them until they gave in to her demands. It would be foolish to give this up, even if it meant walking around "in a chronic state of rage or taking an occasional trip to juvenile hall. You'll get used to this." She was sent to the waiting room with the understanding that the therapist's only remaining work was to teach her parents that they could not change her and must learn to live with her.

The aversive interventions with Jan encouraged her to misbehave despite the costs. Complaining about this suggestion to her parents would only serve to reinforce the belief that the therapist was aligned with the parents.

The therapist spent the remainder of the interview with the parents. He learned that while the mother had reduced her attempts to reason with or threaten Jan, she still wanted to deal with her from a position of power that she did not have.

She was told that she needed to teach Jan a most important lesson—that one hand washes the other. If Jan could not learn this in the next year, she would probably go throught life expecting to take without giving, setting herself up for disappointment and frustration. To teach this lesson now, however, the mother would have to give up her usual methods, using words, and take some nonverbal action that would create some mild discomfort in Jan.

Given the parents' frustration with her, this suggestion had great appeal, setting the stage for an intervention called *benevolent sabotage*, which allows the parents to vent their frustration harmlessly while reversing their attempted solution.

The parents were instructed to make all requests to Jan as follows: "There is something I would like you to do. I can't make you do it but

I wish you would." The request was to be made only once. If there was no compliance, then the parents would employ benevolent sabotage to teach Jan that one hand washes the other. For example, the mother might arrive late when picking Jan up for an important appointment or carelessly wash her favorite white blouse with the colored clothes. If Jan complained about her behavior, the mother was simply to apologize. To make the mother's mindless mistakes more believable, she was instructed to tell Jan that during the remainder of the interview she learned some personally disturbing things about herself. This was essentially a cover story, providing a reason for the mother's self-absorption, a reason that it was hoped would disconnect the parents' behavior from Jan's.

Session 3

The parents reported that Jan "was in tears all week because no one would fight with her." The mother made one request in the precribed manner and Jan complied, so there was no need for benevolent sabotage. However, the assignment had made both parents realize that they were making life easy for Jan on a noncontingency basis. They asked for advice. Should they buy Jan a $35 pair of leather boots for her birthday? The therapist had remembered that Jan refused to wash her bras by hand, creating an additional expense for bras ruined by the washing machine.

The parents were instructed to buy and gift-wrap four bras and present them to her on her birthday. If Jan balked at the present, the mother was to say, "Oh, I'm sorry Jan. I thought you would like them."

The next topic discussed was Jan's nagging. Although the nagging was on the decline, her mother still tried to reason with Jan. The parents were given a second assignment—to collude to confuse her when she started to nag them. The aim of this intervention was to block the mother's attempt to reason with Jan. They were given the following instructions. The next time the father heard his wife and their daughter arguing (Jan's attempt to break her mother down), he was to enter the room and hand her a nickel. If Jan asked why he did this, he was to reply, "I don't know. I just felt like it." Both parents were

then to leave the room. Collusion, like benevolent sabotage, distracts the parents from their usual verbal solutions, which only perpetuate the problem.

Session 4

The parents continued to report improvement. The father laughingly described how his handing Jan a nickel when she started to nag her mother left her bewildered. Jan's mother gave her the bras for her birthday. Upon opening the present, she said, in a faint voice, "Four bras. They cost as much as the boots I wanted!" The parents immediately apologized, explaining that they thought she would like four bras because she would not have to wash them by hand. Jan quietly said, "Thank you," and left the room.

The parents reported that during the remainder of the week, Jan appeared much more relaxed. She took her time at the dinner table and joined the family to watch television. They were pleasantly surprised when she used part of her allowance to buy her mother candy for Mother's Day.

The therapist warned them not to become too enthusiastic about Jan's progress. The more she improved, the harder it would be to see her leave home, which was inevitable within the next few years. He suggested that they have a planned relapse to slow things down. They were to accomplish this by occasionally using their old attempted solutions, reasoning and threats, to deal with her.

Session 5

The parents found it difficult to bring about a relapse. Jan's behavior and attitude continued to improve. She spent more time at home, showed a renewed interest in her sewing, and, as her mother stated, "She's a much happier person."

Three-Month Follow-up

Jan's parents reported that her behavior continued to improve. There was much less fighting with her siblings and she was complying with simple requests. The parents felt confident about taking a weekend trip by themselves, trusting Jan and her siblings to stay at home without supervision. The mother had not found it necessary to act helpless or to use benevolent sabotage. There was no further treatment.

Twelve-Month Follow-up

Jan's behavor continued to improve. She became more considerate of other people. When relatives visited a few months earlier, she volunteered to give them her room. She was showing more respect and care for her siblings, occasionally doing small favors for them. Her grades had improved from Ds and Fs to Bs and Cs. Her parents continued to spend more time as a couple, and there was no further treatment.

WHY IS BRIEF THERAPY DIFFICULT TO PRACTICE?

Brief Therapy radically departs from traditional models of treatment. It does not distinguish between "healthy" or "unhealthy" families or functional or dysfunctional marriages, nor does it diagnose clients according to the DSM-III-R. It rejects the notions that people are mentally ill or that their complaints serve a purpose or function. Thus, clinicians who want to practice Brief Therapy must give up or suspend their usual ways of conceptualizing and treating problems.[7]

A minority of clinicians find this easy. They are purists rather than eclectics. During their clinical careers, they will totally embrace two or three models of treatment. So, when learning Brief Therapy, they make no attempt to integrate it with their previous training. For a variety of reasons, they experience no difficulty suspending or giving up their traditional notions about normality, psychopathology, and diagnostic catagories.

Most clinicians, however, are eclectic. They

may want to learn Brief Therapy, but struggle to integrate it with their previous training. Unfortunately, the two will not integrate. This is a frustrating experience for them. Many complain that they cannot forget everything they learned or deny what is staring them in the face, that is, the "reality" of the patient's or family's pathology. The root of this integration problem is epistemological.

Epistemology

Brief Therapy will not integrate with traditional therapies because it rests on a different epistemology. Most psychotherapies share an epistemology referred to as "linear," "monadic," "Newtonian," or "traditional." Gregory Bateson referred to it as the epistemology of forces and impacts. Sharing the same epistemology is what permits eclectics to embrace and integrate several models of treatment. That is why one can often find therapists originally trained in a Freudian model also using ideas and techniques from Gestalt psychology, models emphasizing personal responsibility and self-esteem, and Rolfing. Although these models differ from one another, all share important epistemological assumptions: (1) the determinants of a person's behavior lie inside the person, within the boundary of a person's skin; (2) human behavior operates according to the laws of efficient causality, that is, where the cause precedes the effect; (3) the causality is energy based; (4) a person's behavior, particularly what is called symptomatic behavior, is purposeful and adaptive; and (5) most basically, they all assume that an "objective" reality exists than can be discovered, that is, clinicians believe they discover what "really" makes people think, feel, and act as they do.

Enter Family Therapy—the Paradigmatic Shift Begins

When family therapists assert that a client's problem is a function of family rather than individual pathology, they depart from the belief that the causes of human behavior lie inside a person. They are also implying that laws of efficient causality are no longer useful in under-

---

[7] *Editors' Note.* Of course, one does not have to believe that all who seek psychotherapy are mentally ill in order to believe that some are, e.g., most schizophrenics of the sort treated most helpfully by psychoeducational methods (McFarlane, Chapter 11).

standing what takes place in a family. The family therapist has shifted epistemologies.

"Since approximately the end of World War II," writes MRI senior research associate Paul Watzlawick (Watzlawick & Weakland, 1977), "a very different epistemology has gained increasing acceptance. Rather than basing itself on the concept of energy and unidirectional causality, it is founded on the concept of information, that is, on order, pattern, negentropy, and in a sense the second law of thermodynamics. Its principles are cybernetic, its causality is of a circular, feedback nature, and with information as its core element, it is concerned with the processes of communication in the widest sense—and therefore also with human systems, e.g., families, large organizations and even international relations" (p. xii).

Embracing the systemic view changes the meaning of familiar psychiatric terms. Thus, for example, "Symptoms, defenses, character structure and personality can be seen as terms describing an individual's typical interactions which occur in response to a particular interpersonal context" (Jackson, 1965, p. 1). As a result, descriptions of a behavior that formerly was viewed as a function of "intrapsychic" relations are now conceptualized as a function of "interpersonal" relations, shifting the therapeutic domain of study and intervention from the individual to the family. This does not mean to imply that the interpersonal view of behavior is "correct" or "true" and that intrapsychic explanations are false, but rather that the interpersonal view offers the clinician a totally new and equally valid way of understanding and dealing with problematic behavior.[8]

Family Systems: A Closer Look at the New Epistemology

A family is a skinless system. It has no physical boundaries as do the walls of a cell or physical connections between its elements as do the parts of our bodies. An energy-based causality, useful when accounting for intrapsychic dynamics, is not useful for explaining skinless systems. Clearly, people do not cause each other to behave like billiard balls ricocheting into one another on a slate table. Watzlawick, Beavin, and Jackson (1967) have emphasized:

There is a crucial difference between the psychodynamic (psychoanalytic) model on the one hand and any conceptualization of organism-environment on the other, and this difference may become clear in the light of the following analogy. If the foot of a walking man hits a pebble, the energy is transferred from the foot to the stone; the latter will be displaced and will eventually come to rest again in a position which is fully determined by such factors as the amount of energy transferred, the shape and weight of the stone, and the nature of the surface on which it rolls. If, on the other hand, the man kicks a dog instead of a pebble, the dog may jump up and bite him. In this case, the relation between the kick and the bite is of a very different order. It is obvious that the dog takes his energy for his reaction from his own metabolism and not from the kick. What is transferred, therefore, is no longer energy, but information. In other words, the kick is one piece of behavior that communicates something to the dog, and to this communication the dog reacts with another piece of communication—behavior. This is essentially the difference between Freudian psychodynamics and the theory of communication as explanatory principles of behavior.

When Watzlawick and his colleagues refer to communication, they are referring to all verbal and nonverbal behavior occurring in an ongoing interpersonal context. Family systems are said to be *rule governed*. A rule is defined as a redundant pattern of circular or interdependent interactions. People are mutually causing each other to behave. Circular patterns of behavior are like all circles: they have no beginning and no end. Furthermore, the shift from linear to circular causality shifts the primary clinical question from "Why does this person behave in a certain manner?" to "What is necessary for this behavior to persist?" These differences are manifestations of the underlying epistemologies. They are reflected in how we explain a person's behavior, particularly "disturbed" behavior. Do we view behavior as a solution to an internal problem, which is only secondarily affected by other people, or do we view the behavior as an

---

[8] *Editors' Note.* As with Segal's earlier clarification of the role of biochemical/neurophysiological aspects of clinical problems in the MRI view, the preceding two sentences should make clear that the interactional approach does not deny the existence of an inner (mental) life, as some of the approach's critics argue at times.

integral and inseparable part of a social system whose meaning can only be understood in a social context? The behavior can be explained either way, but not both ways simultaneously!

Although nontrivial, this distinction is often overlooked or misunderstood. Hoffman (1981) notes:

Using the phrase "metaphysics of pattern" psychologist Paul Dell has recently called attention to a profound difference between the transactional model of family research on families of schizophrenics and the etiological one. Studies that try to establish an etiology are different from the traditional individually oriented ones that have assumed a causal link between family structure and psychotic behavior. But to say that a particular condition is contingent on a given type of family organization, or to think that there is a direct connection, is to make the mistake of linear thinking.

The transactional view, according to Dell, is not concerned with etiology but amounts to a redefinition of what schizophrenia is. Transactional researchers take the position that behaviors labeled schizophrenic are part and parcel of the pattern of family relationships in which the behaviors are embedded, and that neither family nor afflicted individual can be singled out as the "location" of the disorder. (pp. 86–87)

Frustrated by the problem of discontinuity, many therapists become either "family" or "individual" therapists. But why must one choose? Both formats can be used, but they must be used separately. To move freely between them, however, usually requires some understanding of why one wants to choose in the first place.

The desire to choose arises from our beliefs about knowledge. In the West, most educated people ascribe to a "correspondence theory" of knowledge. Knowledge is treated like a photograph: it represents a copy of something else. We call that something else "reality." People unquestionably assume that reality exists and we can discover it. Heinz von Foerster's constructivism offers an alternative way to treat knowledge.[9]

Constructivism

Like all epistemologies, constructivism asks, "What can we know?" However, rather than assuming that reality exists and asking how we can discover it, constructivism asks: "What is an observer that he or she may have cognition and know?" Thus, it shifts attention from "observed systems" (i.e., the world of reality) to "observing systems" (i.e., each one of us).

Observers are human beings, and thus living systems. Notes Maturana (1983), "Everything that can be said is said to another observer who may be his- or herself." Thus, observers communicate with themselves and other observers about their experience.

Constructivists argue that observers invent reality rather than discover it. Although an outrageous claim, constructivists are not solipsists who suggest that everything is merely a figment of the imagination. Rather, constructivism challenges the belief that an observer, whether a layperson or a scientist, can be "objective."

Objectivity, the cornerstone of the scientific method, links knowledge to observation. Scientific knowledge is obtained with the senses rather than through reasoning. One must perform and observe experiments whose results are independent of the scientist—that is, they are objective. To say something has an objective existence is to claim that it exists independently of observation. But how can we *know* something exists without observing it?

Scientists are not objective; they are consensual. They make agreements about their experience among a community of qualified observers. Acquiring knowledge with the senses has its problems. Sensory data can be unreliable.[10] You can experience this for yourself. If you close your eyes, cross your index and middle finger, and touch the two to the tip of your nose, you experience two nose tips. How do you determine how many you "really" have? You look in the mirror. You use another sensory modality for verification. Similar experiments show that

---

[9] For a more complete description of constructivism, see Segal (1986).

[10] *Editors' Note.* Of course, the scientific method also provides various means for empirically assessing the degree of unreliability involved in any set of measurements. Unreliability in empirical measurement is not a sign of the weakness of the scientific method, but rather a source of information.

the same problem arises with all the senses. No matter how many sensory inputs or observers we use, we still cannot be objective. Upon reflection, however, it becomes quite clear that we cannot use one sense modality to confirm another or to confirm that something exists independently of our experience. The eye cannot hear; the ear cannot see. We can only correlate one sensory experience with another. As Segal (1986) points out:

Confirming reality by matching two sensory inputs is dramatically demonstrated in the screen version of Alexander Dumas' classic tale, *The Count of Monte Christo*. After many years of unjust, solitary confinement, Edmund Dantes, the story's hero, agonizes for the company of another person. One day a large stone in his prison cell begins to move and out crawls an old, bedraggled-looking man. Dumbfounded and speechless, Dantes cannot believe his eyes. Initially, his visitor stands motionless. Dantes must find out if he is hallucinating. He walks toward his perceived visitor, wide-eyed, holding his breath. Then, when in half an arm's distance of him, he stops and slowly touches the man's hair and face. Having made this tactile connection, the expression on Dantes' face undergoes a metamorphosis. Wrapping his arms around the visitor, he heartily embraces him, and begins crying tears of joy. "I was afraid you weren't real," cries Dantes. By correlating his senses of touch and vision, Dantes believed he confirmed his reality. (p. 16)

To assume that the senses are a window on the world has additional problems. The nervous system is undifferentially encoded, meaning that the body's sensors only encode how much stimulation they receive and not what makes them fire. The electric energy coming from any of the body's sensors is the same voltage, about 80 millivolts. The frequency that a neuron fires depends on how much stimulation it receives. But the strength of its pulse is always the same. How do we have such a rich experience of sight, sound, and color from this collection of 80-millivolt pulses?

The problems with objectivity are foreign to most traditionally trained psychologists trying to understand perception. When studying vision, they might ask a subject to look at colored blocks when doing experiments in color or shape perception. A constructivist offers a unique criticism of these studies, pointing out that the

experimental design begs the question. The experimenter, like most of his or her colleagues, begins by assuming that the blocks exist independently of observers, and then tries to account for how the subject perceives them. How does the experimenter know that the blocks exist independently of observation? The experimenter who makes such a claim then must account for his or her own capacity to perceive them.

This is a knotty problem for traditionalists or realists who adhere to the scientific method when studying perception. They are caught in a "game without end." Assuming that objectivity is attainable, they must not study their own perception because this is self-referential, and philosophers and logicians have clearly shown that this leads to paradox.

Paradox contaminates our formal logic and reason. A paradoxical conclusion is false when it is true and true when it is false, for example, "I am lying." To avoid self-reference and paradox, experimenters must never study their own experiences. Thus, the logical loop is closed. The experimenter's experience remains unaccounted for. This leaves no choice but to treat the blocks as existing independently of observers. That is, they exist in reality, and knowledge is believed to correspond to that reality, to match it.

As for the issue of Brief Therapy's incompatibility with traditional models of treatment, we see that it centers on letting go of or suspending one's thinking about people and their problems. But how one views knowledge will have a great deal to do with how one handles it. Most of us assume that knowledge represents some truths about reality. As such, asking a person to suspend his or her traditional thinking is like asking that person to deny the truth or deny reality. Herein lies the root of the problem. Constructivism may have a solution.

Constructivism offers an alternative to the assumption that knowledge corresponds to or "matches" reality, like matching the paint on one's kitchen wall. Constructivists suggest that knowledge "fits" reality (Von Glasserfeld, 1981):

If . . . we say that something "fits," we have in mind a different relationship. A key fits if it opens a lock. The fit describes a capacity of the key, not the lock. Thanks to professional burglars, we know only too well that there are many keys that are shaped quite differently from our own but which nevertheless unlock our doors. The metaphor is crude, but it serves quite well to bring into relief the difference I want to explicate. From a radical constructivist point of view, all of us—scientists, philosophers, laymen, school children, animals and indeed, any kind of living organism—face our environment as the burglar faces the lock that he has to unlock in order to get to the loot. (pp. 20–21)

The Newtonian Revolution

The belief that we can discover reality with the scientific method is about 300 years old. Before the 16th century, most people believed that God had made human beings in his own image and placed them on the stationary planet earth, the center of God's living, spiritual universe. Reality started "with God at the top and descending through the angels, human beings, the animals to the ever lower life forms" (Capra, 1982, p. 71). All human action was explained in terms of teleology, a form of causality in which the effect *precedes* the cause. Thus, everything took place for the greater glory of God.

In 1543, the medieval view of reality began to unravel. Nicolas Copernicus dared to assert that the earth spun on its axis and revolved around the sun, ushering in the overthrow of Ptolemy's 1,600-year-old geocentric universe. Man had been evicted from the center of the universe.

Philosophers and scientists began to claim that nature's true language was mathematical rather than biblical. Galileo's theories swept away beliefs in scholastic substances and teleological explanations. Physical entities are composed of indestructible atoms, moving in an infinite homogeneous space and time, whose process can be formulated mathematically. In short, all that mattered was matter.

Sir Isaac Newton, crown prince of the scientific revolution, reduced this new materialistic universe to the three laws of motion and the law of gravity. Comprised of souless, purposeless, lumps of matter, Newton's material world moved in a coordinate system of absolute time and space.

The mathematics of classical science, culminating in Newton's calculus, gave physics a powerful tool with which to understand nature. It was immensely successful because it provided a common denominator to explain such apparently diverse phenomena as heat, light, sound, magnetism, and electricity. Naturally, it was seen to "match" an objective reality rather than to fit an invented one.

Newton's mechanistic world view permeated Western consciousness, touching every branch of human learning. Popularizers by the hundreds brought Newtonian wisdom to the masses. The philosopher and mathematician d'Alembert (1964) summarizes:

Natural science from day to day accumulates new riches . . . The true system of the world has been recognized . . . In short, from the earth to Saturn, from the history of the heavens to that of insects, natural philosophy has been revolutionized; and nearly all other fields of knowledge have assumed new forms. . . . Spreading throughout nature in all directions, this fermentation has swept with a sort of violence everything before it which stood in its way, like a river which has burst its dams . . . Thus, from the principles of secular science to the foundations of the religious revelations, from metaphysics to matters of taste, from music to morals, from the scholastic disputes of theologians to matters of commerce, from natural law to the arbitrary law of nations . . . everything had been discussed, analyzed or at least mentioned. (p. 28)

One of the products of this 17th-century scientific revolution is our love affair with efficient causality. D'Abro (1951) notes that "Newton gave the world the first rigorous doctrine of causality. Most simply, the doctrine asserts that the same causes generate the same effects" (p. 45). The causal doctrine asserts, "The evolution of every physical system is controlled by rigorous laws. These, taken with the initial state of the system (assumed to be isolated), determine without ambiguity all future states and also all past states. The entire history of the system throughout time is thus determined by the laws and by the initial state" (p. 45). Scientific theories could predict as well as explain.

The doctrine of causality appeared to fulfill the perennial search for certainty. No longer inhabited by spirit(s), nature operated without will or purpose like a giant clockwork, independently of human beings and God. As Robert J. Oppenheimer (1954) explains, "The giant machine [the Newtonian universe] was objective in the sense that no human act or intervention qualified its behavior" (p. 13). Using one's intelligence, one could *discover* nature's secrets. Thus, it comes as no surprise that when emperor Napoleon asked Laplace, a French mathematician and astronomer, how God fit into his system, Laplace stated that he had no need of that hypothesis.

The shift to a secular–scientific view of reality permeates our language, our logic, and our thinking. We are all Newtonians at heart. We believe in science, and in causality, and unwittingly assume that knowledge *matches* reality.

In the next section, two constructivists, Gregory Bateson and Heinz von Foerster, take a fresh look at our secular–scientific thinking.

Von Foerster Examines Bateson Examining Newton[11]

Gregory Bateson spent the last 30 years of his life studying human communication. When writing and lecturing, he often described how language blurs the distinction between descriptions and explanations. Occasionally, he presented his ideas in a written form called a metalogue—a fictitious conversation between a father and his daughter.

Von Foerster is particularly fond of Bateson's metalogue entitled, "What Is an Instinct?" (Bateson, 1971, pp. 38–39), for two reasons. First, Bateson shows how the laws of nature are an invention. Second, he shows that a hypothesis is a statement linking two sets of descriptions, not two sets of facts.

VON FOERSTER: Here is a Batesonion metalogue that is particularly pertinent to today's discussion entitled "What is an instinct?" Bateson always begins his metalogues with his daughter Catherine asking him an awkward question.

DAUGHTER: Daddy, what is an instinct?

VON FOERSTER: Now, if my son or daughter asked me, "What is an instinct?" I would, of course, proudly give a lexical definition, e.g. "An instinct, my dear, is the innate aspect of

complex behavior which is. . . ." Bateson avoids this trap.

FATHER: An instinct is an explanatory principle.

VON FOERSTER: So, instead of addressing himself to the semantic significance of her question, he immediately shifts the focus of their talk to its *dialogical* significance. What is the political significance of language? What happens when someone uses the *word* "instinct" in a dialogue? What consequences does language have for our thinking and behavior?

DAUGHTER: But what does it explain?

FATHER: Anything, almost anything at all. Anything you want it to explain.

VON FOERSTER: Please note that something that explains everything explains nothing. Also, the daughter suspects that. She says:

DAUGHTER: Don't be silly. This doesn't explain gravity.

FATHER: No, but this is because nobody wants to explain gravity. If they did, it would explain it! We could simply say that the moon has an instinct whose strength varies inversely as the square of the distance. . . .

DAUGHTER: But Daddy, that's nonsense.

FATHER: Of course this is nonsense, but it was *you* who mentioned instinct—not I.

DAUGHTER: All right—but then, what does explain gravity?

FATHER: Nothing, my dear. Because gravity is an explanatory principle.

DAUGHTER: Oh, do you mean that you cannot use one explanatory principle to explain another? Never?

FATHER: Hardly ever. That is what Newton meant when he said, "Hypotheses non-*fingo*."

DAUGHTER: And what does that mean, please?

FATHER: Well, you know what hypotheses are. If you *say* there was a full moon on February 1 and another on March 1, and then you link these two observations together in any way, the statement that links them is a hypothesis.

VON FOERSTER: Bateson defines a hypothesis as a statement linking two "descriptive statements." A hypothesis does not link two *facts*. We must investigate how we make descriptions.

DAUGHTER: Yes. And now, what "non" means I know. But what's *fingo*?

FATHER: Well, *fingo* is the Latin word for "make." It forms a verbal noun, *fictio*, from which we get the word "fiction."

[11] This excerpt taken from Segal (1986, pp. 56–57).

DAUGHTER: Daddy, do you mean that Sir Isaac Newton thought that all hypotheses were just made up like stories?

FATHER: Yes, precisely that.

DAUGHTER: Didn't he discover gravity with the apple?

FATHER: No. He *invented* it.

DAUGHTER: Oh.

Bateson suggests that even something as seemingly inviolate as a "law of nature" can be questioned and that we should carefully distinguish a *law* from *a law of nature*. One is a rule of law and the other is an explanatory principle. People mistakenly assume both have the same logical structure. The game of law has three sets of players: the lawmakers, the police, and the people who must obey the law. If you break the law, you go to jail. At least, this is how the law is supposed to work.

In science, we may say that planets obey Newton's "law of gravitation." Mercury, however, disobeys Newton's law of gravitation. It does not move around the sun as Newton's law predicts. Is Mercury punished? No. It is the lawmaker, Sir Isaac Newton, who is punished: his law is replaced by Albert Einstein's law.

CLOSURE

If the reader has comprehended this last section, he or she will understand that the first time they read this chapter, its meaning was most likely derived using a traditional epistemology. If the chapter is now reread from a constructivist perspective, the reader will understand that the Brief Therapy model is only one of many keys to unlock (e.g., solve) the kinds of human problems people bring to counselors and psychotherapists. But, it is hoped, the reader will also realize that the model invents the problem to be unlocked. The next logical step is more difficult to take—to see that all models of psychotherapy are systems invented by observers, systems that invent problems or classes of problems such as mental illness, and what is necessary to resolve them.

REFERENCES

Bateson, G. (1971). Metalogue: What is an instinct? In *Steps to an ecology of mind*. New York: Ballentine.

Bateson, G., Jackson, J., Haley, J., & Weakland, J. (1971). Toward a theory of schizophrenia. In *Steps to an ecology of mind*. New York: Ballentine.

Capra, F. (1982). *The turning point: Science, society and the rising culture*. New York: Bantam Books.

D'Abro, A. (1951). *The rise of the new physics* (Vol. I) (p. 45). New York: Dover Press.

D'Alembert, J.L. (1964). Elements de philosophie. Quoted in F.W. Matson, *The broken image: Man, science and society*. New York: George Braziller.

Dell, P. (1981). Quoted in L. Hoffman, *Foundations of family therapy*. New York: Basic Books.

Fisch, R., Weakland, J., & Segal, L. (1982). *The tactics of change: Doing therapy briefly*. San Francisco: Jossey-Bass.

Fraser, J.S. (1983). Paranoia: Interactional views on evolution and intervention. *Journal of Marital and Family Therapy, 9*, 383–392.

Haley, J. (1963). *Strategies of psychotherapy*. New York: Grune & Stratton.

Haley, J. (1967). *Advanced techniques of hypnosis and therapy: Selected papers of Milton H. Erickson, M. D.* New York: Grune & Stratton.

Haley, J. (1971). *Uncommon therapy*. New York: Norton.

Haley, J. (Ed.). (1985a). *Conversations with Milton H. Erickson: Vol. 1. Changing individuals*. New York: Triangle Press, distributed by Norton Books.

Haley, J. (Ed.). (1985b). *Conversations with Milton H. Erickson: Vol. 2. Changing couples*. New York: Triangle Press, distributed by Norton Books.

Haley, J. (Ed.). (1985c). *Conversations with Milton H. Erickson: Vol. 3. Changing families*. New York: Triangle Press, distributed by Norton Books.

Hoffman, L. (1981). *Foundations of family therapy*. New York: Basic Books.

Jackson, D.D. (1965). The study of the family. *Family Process, 4*, 1–20.

Maturana, H. (1983). Lecture, "The biology of social systems," presented by the Family Therapy Program, Department of Psychiatry, University of Calgary, Canada; sponsored by the Alberta Heritage Foundation for Medical Research.

Oppenheimer, R.J. (1954). *Science and the common understanding*. New York: Simon & Schuster.

Ruesch, J., & Bateson, G. (1951). *Communication: The social matrix of psychiatry*. New York: Norton.

Segal, L. (1986). *The dream of reality: Heinz von Foerster's constructivism*. New York: Norton.

Segal, L., & Moley, V. (1982). Brief treatment of sexual dysfunction: Case study of couples therapy. In L.R. Wolberg & M.L. Aronson (Eds.), *Group and family therapy*. New York: Brunner/Mazel.

Von Glasserfeld, E. (1981). In P. Watzlawick (Ed.), *The invented reality. How do we know what we believe we know? (Contributions to constructivism)*. New York: Norton.

Watzlawick, P. (1978). *The language of change*. New York: Basic Books.

Watzlawick, P. (Ed.). (1984). *The invented reality. How do we know what we believe we know? (Contributions to constructivism)*. New York: Norton.

Watzlawick, P., Beavin, J., & Jackson, D.D. (1967). *Pragmatics of human communication*. New York: Norton.

Watzlawick, P., & Weakland, J. (Eds.). (1977). *The interactional view*. New York: Norton.

Watzlawick, P., Weakland, J., & Fisch, R. (1974). *Change: Principles of problem formation and problem resolution* (p. 95). New York: Norton.

Weakland, J., Fisch, R., Watzlawick, P., & Bodin, A. (1974). Brief therapy: Focused problem resolution. *Family Process, 13,* 141–168.

EDITORS' REFERENCE

Budman, S.H., & Gurman, A.S. (1989). *Theory and practice of brief therapy.* New York: Guilford Press.

CHAPTER 7

Contextual Therapy[*]

Ivan Boszormenyi-Nagy, M.D., Judith Grunebaum, L.I.C.S.W., B.C.D., and David Ulrich, Ph.D.

BACKGROUND OF THE APPROACH

Current Evolution of Contextual Therapy

Contextual therapy is a comprehensive relational and individual therapeutic approach; it is an effective preventive design based on our understanding of basic relational structures and processes. At present, the field of psychotherapy is characterized by wide divergences in conceptual points of view about goals and methods and philosophical debate about the basis of the therapist's interventions. Criteria such as measurable effectiveness or narrative meaningfulness and commitments to epistemologies of "preexisting reality" versus constructed "truth" are proposed as the significant parameters of therapeutic meaning and effectiveness. These debates divide the entire domain of psychotherapy and are not limited to family-therapy discourse.

A goal of contextual therapy is to provide a conceptual schema that allows the inclusion of many significant aspects of other approaches to psychotherapy, provided that they are ethically concerned and contractually responsible. We suggest that a multilateral contractual approach provides an overarching conceptual framework that can eventually integrate these divergent perspectives. In this sense, "contextual" means the total range of persons who are potentially affected by the therapeutic effort; ethical concern regarding the impact on them of the therapeutic intervention constitutes the essence of the "multilateral contract."

The contextual orientation assumes that the leverages of all psychotherapeutic interventions are anchored in relational determinants, and

* This chapter was coauthored by Ivan Boszormenyi-Nagy and Judith Grunebaum. However, since David Ulrich was coauthor with Dr. Nagy of the original version published in 1981, he remains a source of inspiration, an important contributor to, and coauthor of the present chapter.

The authors wish to thank Catherine Ducommun-Nagy and Henry Grunebaum for their generous editorial and moral support.

that a comprehensive approach addresses these determinants in terms of the four interlocking dimensions of (1) facts, (2) individual psychology, (3) behavioral transactions, and (4) relational ethics. While we speak of relational determinants for therapy, the contextual approach never loses sight of the goal of benefiting persons, as well as promoting change within systems. The entry point and purpose of interventions are to provide healing for an individual's pain or symptoms, as well as to address relational problems.[1]

Development of the Approach

Psychotherapy, in part, originated as a medical specialty and its scientific premises were based on the logical positivism and "work machine" metaphor of the then-prevailing scientific philosophy. Consistent with this model was a hope for a complete and "objective" understanding of the mind, and with it a scientific method for "curing" specific pathologies. The basic assumption came to be that mental symptoms originated within the mind of the individual. But with Freud's implicit theory of the "object-relatedness" of human instinctual drives, a turn toward the relational occurred. This shift became explicit in the writings of Ferenczi (1931, 1932), who, according to Guntrip (1961, p. 390) and Balint (1952, 1968), postulated a *primary object love* for the mother" as underlying all later development. According to Guntrip, Ferenczi's notions both disturbed Freud and influenced Klein (1932), Fairbairn (1954), Winnicott (1964), and Guntrip himself. Sullivan's interpersonal psychiatry was another stimulus in Boszormenyi-Nagy's early development as a therapist, as was Kalman Gyarfas as a mentor. In philosophy, major progress toward the "relational" as a fundamental category of reality was secured with the publication of Martin Buber's dialogic philosophy and philosophical anthropology. Buber's radical philosophy of "the interhuman" converged with and provided inspiration for a growing conviction about the relational essence of life (Buber, 1958, 1965; Friedman, 1988).

During the 1950s, a small number of clinicians (Bell, Boszormenyi-Nagy, Bowen, Fleck, Jackson, Lidz, Satir, Wynne) gradually recognized the limitations of individual therapy, particularly with children and with psychotic adults. They began to explore conjoint therapy, initially for the nuclear family. In 1957, Boszormenyi-Nagy and his co-workers introduced family therapy as a research project at the Eastern Pennsylvania Psychiatric Institute in Philadelphia. This project explored intensive psychotherapy of hospitalized psychotic patients. It was influenced by the psychoanalytically oriented therapy of schizophrenia, primarily the object relations theory of Fairbairn (1954), in addition to the interpersonal theories of Fromm-Reichman (1950), Searles (1955), and Sullivan (1953). Early contextual speculations relied on a Hegelian dialectical integration of existential and object relational insights toward a more explicitly relational model. The inseparability of the self (individuation) from relatedness was one of the early working hypotheses (Boszormenyi-Nagy, 1965). This dialectical model is different from both linear and circular principles of change.

Synergistic with a phase of classical, systemic family therapy, an increasingly dialectical, contextual understanding of depth relational dynamics developed. Methodologically, emphasis shifted to total attendance, communications, and behavior patterns. In conjoint family therapy, treatment was not restricted to the diagnosed member. The work was rapidly expanded to people with a wide spectrum of nonpsychotic symptoms and their family members.

Intrinsic to this new paradigm was a commitment to a multilateral therapeutic contract. Although unrecognized as pivotal to conjoint family therapy, an implicit ethical reorientation was under way. However, the ethical implications of this pluralistic contract were obscured by enthusiasm for the new causal clues, as in the work of Bateson (1951) and his co-workers, who were applying his systematic studies of communication within families (1956) to new therapeutic interventions. Initially, the explorative and technical innovations attracted more enthusiasm than the contractual implications of the simultaneous care of several persons, often in conflict with one another. Although there

---

[1] *Editors' Note.* While not alone in this regard, contextual therapy certainly is among a rather small group of (family) therapy approaches that is as explicitly concerned about individual functioning, experiencing, and relating as about interactional and transactional matters.

have been numerous trenchant critiques, the cybernetic metaphor (Weiner, 1961) and systems theory (von Bertalanffy, 1968) continue to be powerful theoretical models for the field, despite some recent new directions (Anderson, 1987; Goolishian & Anderson, 1987; Hoffman, 1990). During the 1960s, a number of family therapists began to discover that work should not be limited to the nuclear family or to transactions in the here and now; multigenerational patterns of connection began to find their way into conceptual frameworks and clinical methodologies (Boszormenyi-Nagy, 1966; Boszormenyi-Nagy & Spark, 1973). In the early 1960s, Boszormenyi-Nagy and his associates, including Spark and Framo, increasingly aware of depth relational processes, began to explore the therapeutic leverages to be found in the ethics of transgenerational relationships, for example, "loyalty" and "rewarding allegiance" (Boszormenyi-Nagy, 1966, p. 71; Boszormenyi-Nagy, 1972), and in the *multilateral therapeutic contract* itself. "Loyalty," for instance, referred to the implicit ethical demand of filial indebtedness that life places on each new generation. Parallel with this, Bowen was also developing a multigenerational approach, culminating in his collected works published in 1978.

The evolution of the contextual approach since 1958 has been an organic process. The impetus has been the societal background of overburdened, isolated, and fragmented nuclear families. Contextual therapy is a discourse that has evolved in direct response to social, political, and economic realities. It is the family approach that is most immediately resonant to the news in the daily papers and sociodemographic statistics. The conditions under which the family as a social institution is trying to survive are visible to everyone. Divorce statistics document that families are trying to exist in the vacuum that was left when the connection between viable relationships and intergenerational rootedness broke down and the ethical implications of that connection were lost. In this social context, such ethical dynamics as family loyalty and other imperatives that stem from common roots were severely tested. In our current social context, the family has become even more fragmented, and there are growing numbers of women and children unable to maintain themselves above the poverty line. Ethical issues,

both within the family and between the family and the larger society, have never been more urgent. In making these concerns primary, contextual therapy departs from a primary emphasis on abstract hypotheses such as "structural" abnormalities or "rigid rules" of communication. The significant burdens for today's nuclear family are complex, but they cannot be reduced simply to sequences of interactions occurring within the nuclear, or even extended, family itself.

Multilateral concern is not limited to intergenerational connections as such. Whether one person or several are present at the session, the goal of contextual therapy is to achieve a responsible orientation to intermember issues of trust and fairness. The very use of the term "patient" or "symptom" has to be questioned when the multilateral ethics of relationships becomes the guiding principle. In contrast with some other models, the contextual approach always retained interest in each individual's subjectivity, not just psychologically, but also in terms of the inherent ethical properties of claim, obligation, rights, entitlement, and relational merit. Contextual therapy tends to avoid both the dehumanizing effects of techniques based on an overly simplistic understanding of systems philosophy and the inadvertent blaming of the "family" system.

The development of a multilateral perspective challenges the reductionistic application of psychological or transactional explanations of human behavior and emphasizes the risk of their use in clinical situations, especially those involving clear-cut and dangerous abdication of adult responsibilities and abuse of power and trust. Moreover, a distinction can be drawn between those therapies that propose strategies within substitutive relational contexts (e.g., mainly through the utilization of therapeutic transference in individual and group settings) and those that offer assistance within the participants' original or current relational context.[2] We agree with other family therapists that the latter avenue offers many therapeutic possibil-

---

[2] *Editors' Note.* Behavior therapy also emphasizes the importance of treating behavior in its natural environment, when possible, in order to promote generalization of treatment effects.

ities that are unethical and clinically inefficient to ignore.

THE HEALTHY OR WELL-FUNCTIONING MARRIAGE OR FAMILY

Four Dimensions of Relationships

Four distinguishable but interlocking dimensions of relationships must be considered in order to describe what we regard as a "healthy" family. These dimensions make up the relational context and dynamics of family functioning (Boszormenyi-Nagy, 1979; Boszormenyi-Nagy & Krasner, 1986).

Facts

The first dimension of a comprehensive approach to assessment and treatment planning has to do with facts, with what is provided by destiny. For example, ethnic identity, gender, physical handicap, illness, adoption, and survivorship are all given facts; they are parts of a configuration of destiny. Some facts are unavoidable—a distribution of chance and fate. Other facts are avoidable—a created reality, constructed by human understanding, agency, and choice. These actualities also become facts. For instance, the contingent historical context that one "inherits" and that influenced the lives of one's parents and other predecessors becomes a set of facts or realities with consequences for future persons. The social context—especially injustices committed against one's family or group, but also the priorities, definitions, and practices available at any given time in history or culture—is an actuality with which every person or family must contend (Boszormenyi-Nagy, 1973; Grunebaum, 1987, 1990). These factual, historic injustices (dimension 1) become part of the legacy imperatives (dimension 4) for future offspring.

The same holds true within the family; for instance, unresolved marital conflict between mistrustful parents becomes a fateful fact, implying a "split-loyalty" situation for a child. The requirement to consider the welfare interests of others also has factual implications. For example, if one generation does not consider the consequences of damage to the environment, that failure becomes a fact for future generations. At this level, an obligation cannot be reduced to a value judgment as the outcome has survival implications. *Here, "ethics" and factual consequences merge.*

Psychology

The second, strictly individually based dimension may be given the general heading of psychology, or what happens within the person. A significant characteristic of psychological phenomena is that symbolic meanings can be transferred between persons. In this domain, one relationship may be substituted for another. Theoretical parsimony is not served by invalidating the significance of drives, psychic development, and subjective experience. On the contrary, the intensive, in-depth relational implications of psychoanalytic and cognitive theories need to be explored, expanded, and integrated with the other contextual dimensions. This dimension includes all phenomena based on psychic or mental functions, such as cognitive and emotional development, fantasy, dreams, and other symbolic processes.

Transactions

The third contextual dimension may be characterized as the domain of transactions and is based on the patterns of organization within the family. Structure, power alignments, roles, and communication sequences are different ways of describing observable aspects of the interactions occurring in the present and how such interactions contribute to or prevent both change and stability, or adaptation. The goal that a family therapist tries to foster is progressive interaction. At this level, lack of sufficient "self-delineation" or differentiation of individuals leads to dysfunctional forms of reciprocity, whereby members protect one another from having to define boundaries, to make choices, and to function as whole, independent agents (Boszormenyi-Nagy, 1965; Boszormenyi-Nagy & Krasner, 1986). Self-delineation is a dialogic process; in the context of a meaningful relationship, each person strives for identity, boundaries, and need complementarity (Bozsormenyi-Nagy, 1960). The family is viewed as an "organism" like other organisms, and the steering mechanisms by which it evolves are its relevant dynamics. Most of the family-therapy literature, and even social science, pertains to this dimension.

Relational Ethics: The Balance of Fairness

The fourth dimension, which we regard as the cornerstone of contextual therapy, is concerned with relational ethics. We consider relational ethics to be a fundamental dynamic force, holding family and societal relationships together through reliability and trustworthiness. According to multilateral logic, the balance of fairness among people is the most profound and inclusive "cluster" of relationship phenomena. This is the context to which the term "contextual therapy" applies.

Here, "ethics" carries no implication of a specific set of moral precepts or criteria of right versus wrong. It is concerned with the uniquely human process of achieving an equitable balance of fairness among people. By "fairness" we mean neither the mechanistic rigidity of giving all three children bicycles for Christmas, *nor a barter system in which each item is exchanged for an immediate trade-off*. Rather, the preservation of a long-term, oscillating balance among family members, whereby the *basic life interests* of each are taken into account by the others, is the criterion of "healthy functioning." This is not a self-denying ethic; it leads to benefits on both sides of the relationship. Furthermore, what one person experiences is not the criterion of fairness. To gauge the balance, it is necessary to employ a multilateral process, by which we mean consideration by each family member of the interests of all family members, including his or her own interests—and a reciprocal exchange of these considerations. Relational ethics are founded on the principle of equitability, that is, that everyone is entitled to have his or her welfare interests considered by other family members. Multidirected partiality is the principle that balanced consideration be extended to the interests of those persons who

will be affected by clinical intervention (Boszormenyi-Nagy, 1967, 1986). In addition, therapeutic recognition of the *multilateral* nature of relationships is a central goal of contextual therapy, and suggests fundamental implications for autonomy and health.

Entitlement and indebtedness vis-à-vis others are existentially given or earned, whether or not they are acknowledged or mutually validated. Trust is the fundamental property of relationships. It can be depleted or restored. Relationships become trustworthy to the degree that they permit dialogue concerning issues of valid claims and mutual obligation. Such issues cannot be reduced to a subcategory of the psychological dimension; basic trust and spontaneous concern may be a potential of all human beings, but the realization of trustworthiness is an ethical achievement (Erikson, 1964; Winnicott, 1971). It is the consequential outcome of a relationship and does not originate primarily in the individual's mind or mental state. Thus, satisfaction from relationships is determined not only by the fulfillment of one's own needs, but also by the capacity for giving concern and gratitude (Erikson, 1964; Winnicott, 1963, 1971). Merited trust and accountability lead to participation in progressive interactions, as contrasted with repetitive sequences that eventually deplete human resources. The capacity to recognize and act upon indebtedness is an important criterion of functional adaptation and the continuing evolution of life. Receiving through giving is an important potential resource of all close relationships. Entitlement earned through giving due concern and giving becomes an enabler of action. The motivational theory of contextual therapy postulates *entitlement* as a comotivator, along with needs and the biological and mental adaptations expressed by evolution. Together they codetermine the direction, form, and freedom of action.

Unlike symbolic or transactional phenomena, the "credit" earned or inherited within the domain of relational ethics allows no valid substitution. Merit earned by a mother through her actions can be repaid only to the mother. Contextual therapy differs radically from therapy based solely on psychological or transactional premises. Action or consideration of actions toward acknowledgment of a debt, or toward realization of one's entitlement, is seen as a fundamental move toward building trust and health.

The Basic Relational Context

The Multigenerational Perspective

It is inadequate to assume that all of the variables crucial to a child's development or family functioning could be found within the parents or within the parental relationship. Instead, it is necessary to use a framework of at least three generations, including the historic, social context of each generation. At any point in time, at least three generations overlap. Even if the grandparents are absent or dead, their influence continues and has consequences for their descendants. Psychological, transactional, and ethical dynamics lose crucial meanings and therapeutic usefulness if they are not seen in this perspective.

Legacy and the Ledger of Merit and Indebtedness

The term "legacy" has been introduced to denote a configuration of expectations that originate from rootedness and impinge on the offspring (Boszormenyi-Nagy, 1976). Certain basic contextual expectations convey an intrinsic imperative stemming not from the merit of the parents, but from the universal implication of being born of parents and other ancestors. At the current stage in the evolution of contextual therapy, the term "legacy" is used to denote the universal injunction of parental accountability, including the human mandate to reverse the injustices of the past for the benefit of the next generation and posterity. This has also been called "the parental imperative" (Grunebaum, 1987). Thus, the roots of the individual's very existence become a source of mandates that affect his or her personal entitlements and indebtedness. The origins of legacy mandates are multigenerational; there is a chain of destiny anchored in every generative relatonship and these chains determine the facts and the quality of the survival of descendants.

The Ledger

In referring to personal entitlements and indebtedness, we use the concept of the *ledger*. In the contextual approach, the ledger has to do with an implicit "accounting" of what has been given and what is owed in return. It is hard to imagine a first interview, or even an ordinary conversation, that does not refer to premises about reciprocity. Ledger issues permeate our daily lives and relationships. Our efforts at scientific theory building have alienated us from the language of fairness and merit, and the practices of care and connection. We are not dealing with ledger in the sense of barter, balancing of power alignments, or behavioral contracts that specify something for her and something for him. Here, ledger is a statement about the equilibrium between two ethical components. The first has to do with the debts and entitlements dictated by legacy and its counterpart, *filial loyalty*. These may vary greatly even between two siblings; for instance, it may be imperative for one to become a success and for the other to become ill. Stierlin (1974) has called these specific intergenerational expectations role "delegations." Delegations stemming from one's origins may place unfair burdens on the offspring, such as the consequences of alcoholism in the preceding generation. But whatever the specific terms, they derive their weight from the fact that the children were born of particular parents. Destructive "delegation" is not what we mean by legacy. Children are ethically bound to accommodate their lives somehow to their legacies, and to pass on the constructive possibilities within their inherited predicaments.

The other ethical component of ledger has to do with accumulation of merit through contributions to the welfare of the other. In this sense, giving is the "right" of the giver. Thus, "entitlement" may combine what is inherently due as a parent or child and what one has come to merit. One who contributes to a balance of fairness by supporting the interests and regarding the vulnerabilities of the others may be said to acquire *merit* and *entitlement*. In terms of relational ethics, merit is the unit that counts. A natural mother who abandons her child may have *earned* no merit, yet the legacy of filial loyalty puts the child into a special ledger position vis-à-vis the parents, who still retain some entitlement stemming from their reproductive roles. Therefore, it becomes inevitable that the child's loyalty will be split between the natural and substitute parents. Adoption studies have demonstrated this.

The family is strengthened by moves toward trustworthiness and weakened by moves away from it. Moves toward trustworthy relatedness we call *rejunctive*; moves away from such relatedness we call *disjunctive*. A family context is never enhanced by moves away from merited trust. A spouse, for instance, will not improve his or her marital relationship by trying to destroy the partner's residual trust in his or her parents. The descriptive term "relational stagnation" (Boszormenyi-Nagy & Spark, 1973) is used for any instance of familial disengagement from concern about fairness. In a stagnating family, moves toward rejunction are blocked or canceled out. In a healthy family, conflict, position taking, negotiation toward mutual understanding, and recognition of mutual investments are accepted and valued. Major damage to trustworthiness enters the family through the phenomenon of *"destructive entitlement,"* entitlement earned through *actually suffered past injustice.*

Asymmetry of the Parent–Child Relationship

A deep context of relational ethics exists in relationships stemming from intergenerational rootedness. Such rootedness provides an inherent synergism. Those who are linked by membership in successive generations have an intrinsic convergence of loyalty that engenders profound consequences.

We consider the anchor point of multigenerational trustworthiness to be the responsibility for parenting, which is a structure basic to the lives of all higher animals. A central principle of intergenerational relationships is what we call "equitable *asymmetry*," which recognizes that most of the giving flows from *parent to young child* (Boszormenyi-Nagy & Krasner, 1986; Grunebaum, 1990). Even if a person has no children, the "care-giving" imperative can be expressed through the commitment to relieve one's own parents' difficulties and to contribute to posterity in many other ways. Parental ac-

countability will affect the basic potential for trust in future generations. Here the ethics of accountability meets the ethics of "the right to give." Parental responsibility can include the decision not to have children.

Marital Relationships

An ethical dimension exists in all relationships. For marital partners, the criterion of "health" is linked to a *symmetry* of rights and responsibilities. Depending on their integrity and on the complementarity of their needs (Boszormenyi-Nagy, 1965), marital partners can develop trustworthy convergence and symmetry of give and take. But if their welfare interests clash, negotiation and compromise are known to be necessary and fair.

Couples are usually members of the adult generation, and, therefore, are potentially capable of the equality and reciprocity necessary for viable long-term, adult relationships. However, many variables intervene, such as external events or social and political inequalities, that drastically alter the capacity for symmetrical give and take, and necessarily lead to a search for balance. There are also inherent *asymmetries*, such as a man's and a woman's different relationship to and accountability for biological reproduction (Boszormenyi-Nagy, 1976; Grunebaum, 1987, 1988). However, it is within the social domain that equitable rebalancing can occur, and thus the social ideology and practice that structure the allocation of responsibility for child care and breadwinning, the division of labor, must be considered an ethical dynamic on the societal level that fatefully influences the assignment of "roles" within the family. To a large extent, adaptive functioning depends on the partners' ability to negotiate role allocations and definitions to suit their own personal relationship and circumstances, and to redefine the dictates of social practice when necessary. In health, each couple chooses its own set of practices based on complementarities at the transactional level, which are chosen and negotiated. In this sense, there is a continual interplay among individuals, relationships, ideas, values, and social practices within the larger societal context (Grunebaum, 1990).

Loyalty

"Loyalty" is one of the earliest concepts in the development of contextual therapy. Originally, the concept emphasized the merited "allegiance" earned through due caring or generative contribution. Parental responsibility has a reciprocal imperative in the child's loyalty to its roots. Loyalty is a factual, relational dynamic, central to the child's functioning even into adulthood. The child has a reservoir of trust out of which he or she can initiate advancements of trust toward the parents. This reserve of trust derives from the legacy of intergenerational relatedness. Additionally, it derives from the human concern for the fairness of giving and receiving. To the degree that the parents are able to maintain a balance of fairness, they acquire a merit that personalizes and validates the child's basic loyalty commitment. Ultimately, however, the child's *right to give* is a factor that codetermines the child's loyalty to the parent, along with the *obligations* arising from filial indebtedness. This current view expands the original obligation-based notion of the origins of filial loyalty.

The fact that common rootedness creates an interlocking of vital interests is often obscured by divergence at the level of attitudes. Violent conflict can erupt when an adolescent's behavior challenges his or her parents' view of how fast the adolescent should grow up. Yet, except in the most pathological instance, all three concur that growing up is one of the child's basic welfare interests. As an essential part of this process, both parental accountability and filial loyalty are renegotiated and given new meaning at each new phase of family evolution.

However, since the "self" evolves through transactions with others, each phase of the life cycle offers opportunities for dialogue; family members may react to individuation in a member with a growth-inhibiting or growth-validating response. But developmental transitions afford the opportunity for relational enrichment and mutual growth (Shapiro, 1988). Important markers are the separation of children from the home, the marriage of children, the birth of grandchildren, and the sickness and aging of grandparents. Each of these phases requires a redefinition of loyalty, and a shift in the direction and distribution of accountability. The core ethical dynamic of fairness requires that the vulnerable person deserves consideration; the one giving consideration deserves acknowledgment.

A Relational Definition of the Self: "Self-delineation" and "Self-validation"

Individuation is a desirable goal. But our definition of individuation strongly emphasizes a "both/and" as oppposed to an either/or orientation. Autonomy is measured by both the capacity for *self-object delineation* and the capacity for responsible engagement within relationships, or *"self-validation."* Self-validation is both a condition for and a benefit of the mature relational dialogue. Self-validation expresses the goal of multilaterality; it refers to the observation that the "self" benefits both as a functional entity and in terms of increased value, when engaged in relating to others mutually and reciprocally. It is well expressed in the Talmudic saying, "If I am not for myself, who am I? If I am not for others, what am I? If not now, when?" Noble or self-sacrificial actions that are costly to the self are not considered healthy.

Contextual Therapy and Feminist Values

The contextual orientation (Boszormenyi-Nagy, 1965, 1967) anticipated the notion of the "relational self" currently being elaborated by contemporary feminists (Gilligan, 1982) and many other researchers concerned with understanding "prosocial" behavior (see Grunebaum, 1987, 1990). Bowen (1978) implies that "differentiation of self" can occur only in a context of engagement with and responsibility to others. The notion of health, which is basic to the contextual approach, is that of interdependence and differentiation based on considerations of each person's needs and rights. Synergistic with feminism, the multilateral perspective and goals of contextual therapy extend into the social realm. The dynamics of the healing process are inseparable from the recognition of social injustice, and thus of social responsibility and social change. Moreover, its concern about fairness makes contextual therapy part of a broad-based concern for humankind's survival. The multigenerational mandates and concern for the quality of human relationships, made explicit by contextual therapy, can be conceived of as a "transgenerational tribunal" concerning the survival of humankind (Bozsormenyi-Nagy, 1987a).

Conflicts of Interest

Problems are considered ubiquitous in human life and often involve conflicts of existential interests, or conflicts among many desirable goals. In contextual therapy, there is no assumption that the interests of individuals will be identical, or even that there are no conflicting goals of the family as a whole (Ruddick, 1990). The process of facing conflicts of interests, often underplayed in other family-therapy approaches, is central to the contextual definition of relationships. Well-functioning families emphasize their own relational resources for solving problems, rather than viewing life's problems as shameful and pathological events to be avoided.

Intimacy

Shared affection and sexuality are great resources of relationships. They are the valued rewards of risking intimacy. The search for intimacy is a deep motive of human beings—the desire to be known, understood, and confirmed as a person on one's own terms, a relational "entitlement." In our current era, it is not fashionable to perceive sexuality and intimacy as contingent on a context of trustworthiness and fairness. Yet clinical and human experiences demonstrate that interpersonal injustice eventually will erode closeness and sexual attraction.

Levels of intimacy and separateness are seen in terms of investedness in relationships. Behavioral expressions of mutual investment indicate concrete availability for the sharing of burdens and emotional accessibility. However, investedness is not reducible to these behavioral expressions. Parent and child have a shared existential interest in each other's lives and welfare even if there is an emotional "cutoff," or even if there has been adoption of the child by others. Parents have a shared interest in their children's lives even if the commitment between them has ended.

Relationships with extended family offer op-portunites for ongoing concern and periodic assessment of the multilateral requirements of caring relationships. Traditional extended-family patterns were arenas of a variety of modes of giving, taking, and receiving. Loyal belonging to a family is synonymous with the members' needs and rights to give and receive. We consider the delicately balanced nuclear family as impoverished with regard to such opportunities. However, the so-called normative nuclear family fortunately is more myth and ideology than reality, as documented by research that demonstrates an uninterrupted flow of resources in both directions between adult child and grandparent generations (Walsh, 1983).

The Social Context

Although we believe that the desire for interhuman fairness is basic and universal, it is also observable that ethnic, socioeconomic, gender, and other "differences" bring out special forms of fairness, reliability, exploitation, and distributions of benefits and burdens. It is possible to say that some cultural practices are more fair than others. For instance, it cannot be considered "just" when a culture prescribes such human mutilation as wife burning or sacrifice, infanticide, or harsh and abusive child-rearing practices. Nevertheless, the persistence of such practices must be viewed in the context of the culture as a whole and in terms of the material contraints of its factual, contingent historical evolution, spiritual values, and the demands of reality with which the culture or community had to contend. Societies differ with regard to their respect for human rights.

The specific definition of group belonging and loyalty varies from family to family. Although loyalty is a resource, adversity and injustice toward one's group reinforces loyalty and may lead members to be prejudiced and fearful of outsiders. In healthy families, solidarity and intimacy within nonkin relationships are desirable and are not based on the reactive need to be *disloyal* to one's kinship group. The resources of relating to nonfamily members depend on shifting gears to a different level. However, relationships with friends, colleagues, subordinates, students, and business partners also have to be governed by the guidelines of due consideration. They are complementary to a healthy family and enrich family life. Prejudice toward outsiders is not considered healthy or desirable.

Relationship with Posterity

A key feature of the contextual approach is the consideration of the interests of posterity. This transgenerational aspect of family relationships is as crucial as are interactions with existing partners. The reason why this becomes an imperative is that members of future generations cannot defend their own survival interests. They are entirely vulnerable to the consequences of the priorities and actions of past generations. Responsibility for posterity can become visible in family decisions about parenthood in cases of genetic or congenital damage threatening the offspring. How fair is it to have a child if its parents cannot secure its healthy growth? How fair is it to existing offspring, in terms of the realistic appraisal of family resources? Nevertheless, even in cases of severe handicap, families often rise to the challenge and develop enriching resources for facing such circumstances of destiny. An unfair burden can lead to a triumph for the whole family and for each member. The criterion of health is how equitably and realistically such a burden is shared.

THE DYSFUNCTIONAL FAMILY

Contextual therapy deemphasizes pathology as its rationale and guideline; instead, it focuses on relational resources as leverages for change. Since resources are conceptualized as interhuman and dialogical (Boszormenyi-Nagy, 1966, 1973, 1986), descriptions of families in terms of their systemic patterns of organization or as clusters of "conversing" individuals each with his or own "construction of reality" are inadequate from our point of view (Goolishian & Anderson, 1987). The first model, based on an abstract description of the family, discounts the factor of human agency. The second model makes all points of view equally valid and ignores both the social context of the family and the relative desirability of different perspectives. On the other hand, family descriptions emphasizing the symptom of an individual member are also misleading. The family of the school-phobic child is, at the same time, the family of the depressed mother and the alienated father. Pathologizing the family as the cause of individual difficulties is the tragic mistake of many family-therapy schools, even if this covert blaming is couched in technical language. We are referring to the pathologizing use of such terms as "schizophrenogenic mother," which was a phrase much used and abused, but had the aura of legitimacy because it was stated in scientific language and fit with many cultural biases about women in their role as mothers.

In our view, the family is the source of the most fundamental resources and relational options, even if there are seriously shocking inadequacies in the behavior of some members, and even if the family as a social institution has been the location of flagrant injustices inflicted upon women, children, and men, as well. Inequitable allocation of reponsibility and lack of acknowledgment of the parenting role of mothers (Grunebaum, 1987) do not diminish the value and crucial importance of *caring relationships*. Yet these very injustices, as feminists have pointed out, must be implicated in any discussion of the causation of dysfunction. Contextual therapy has the resources to join with other critiques of the contemporary family because it views long-standing interpersonal injustice, especially within the family, as pathogenic in and of itself. The history of social injustice must be given a central place in the review of debts and entitlements, so as to overcome the implicit assumption that the family, especially mothers, can compensate for any form of societal injustice and other historic hardships (Grunebaum, 1987, 1988, 1990).

Regarding a rationale for any kind of therapy, we are far from a scientific formulation of the causes of family problems. As science has progressed, explanations of how symptoms develop have become increasingly complex and sophisticated. In the medical sciences, it is increasingly accepted that symptoms must be approached as a failure of resistance to disease processes. Disease is considered to be a process of the relations between host and environment. Environmental assaults on the immune system are one of the exciting frontiers in medical research. Contextual therapy converges with advances in the fields of immunology, in the sense that its ultimate goal is prevention of dysfunction and the rehabilitation and strengthening of the family's own "immune system"—the resources of care, concern, and connection.

Distributive justice in the allocation of a family's resources, as well, and the process of negotiation by which such decisions are made are crucial determinants of health—and pathology. Beyond the family, the community's priorities regarding the distribution of health and social resources are an important determinant of who develops symptoms and which symptoms develop. While it may be difficult to claim a direct causal relationship between any two variables, the consequences of certain human choices are often not difficult to predict; for instance, community decisions regarding how much to invest in breast-cancer research affect the daily lives of thousands of women and their families. Neither biological nor social science encompasses all the values necessarily inherent in social decision making.

Family Description Via the Concept of Stagnation

Despair maintains family dysfunction. The type of despair is related to the loss of hope and trust in the world that results from ethical *stagnation* (Boszormenyi-Nagy & Spark, 1973). It is maintained by a form of "justification" that we call *destructive entitlement* (Boszormenyi-Nagy, 1981, 1986, 1989), a form of ethical credit based on actually suffered past injustice. Destructive entitlement may lead people to relate vindictively to innocent others because something is actually "owed" to them from the past; it then seems justified to be callous concerning the rights of other people with whom they now live. It is a self-sustaining, cumulative social process, which, if enacted, leads to unfairness in new relationships. The concept of destructive entitlement captures well the self-defeating "spiral" that leads to depletion of the trust and reciprocity that sustain individuals and communities through periods of personal, familial, social, and environmental change. Destructive entitlement may also turn to self-destructiveness.

Stagnation is the world of ethically invalid attempts at solving life's problems. It tells us that

"the only one to whom you owe anything is yourself," as if self-realization could occur without responsibility and interdependence. The concept of relational stagnation challenges the dichotomy of the "identified patient" and "the well sibling," and questions the notion of "well" members in "pathological" systems. In this sense, contextual therapy is a "systems theory"—albeit, we believe, a more differentiated one than those based on the cybernetic metaphor alone. Wellness is a relative concept; from the contextual vantage point, the identified patient may be the most resourceful member.

Neither individual suffering nor good functioning and personal enjoyment are discounted. However, the relevant criteria for good family functioning are relational balances—for instance, whether the suffering member is suffering on behalf of other family members and whether the "well" individual or "functional relationship" is thriving at the expense of others or other relationships. Individual functioning or good role performance does not indicate anything per se about the "balance of fairness" within families. Trustworthy relating must be based on the awareness and consideration of the basic life interests of all members. A sick person may be advancing trust and hope by giving others a chance to help; the well member may be overfunctioning to the point of depletion. Overgiving, martyrlike attitudes undermine family relationships and can create destructive guilt for others.

Detrimental Relationship Configurations

The contextual approach distinguishes specific relationship structures and configurations as keys to the family's functioning. We are guided by these principles and consider them to be the basic structures of relationships within families. We have already discussed these structuring principles in the previous section on the "well-functioning family," but will provide a framework in this section for identifying some "miscarriages" of these basic principles and resources. In describing these typically encountered family problems, we in no way intend to convey that they are not also potential resources.

In the broadest sense, the term "exploitation" may cover most of what is ethically stagnant or "pathological" between people. If people's actions lack merit, there is an inequitability of give and take; then trustworthiness of relationships breaks down, interactions become ethically stagnant or "pathological," and there is no support left for future acts of merit. When trust has deteriorated, intention is diverted from the effort to balance the ledger in universal terms of human decency and concern. Some forms of exploitation are transient interactions; others warp the growth prospects of the family and sap its health.

Split Loyalty

One of the most salient points of connection between individual and relational theory, and the point of greatest relational tension, occurs when one person becomes involved in the predicament of *split filial loyalty*; that is, when the parents express deep mistrust of each other and the child can offer loyalty to one parent only at the cost of his or her loyalty to the other. Whereas the term *loyalty conflict* indicates a breach between a trustworthy primary filial loyalty and a competing peer loyalty, "split loyalty" connotes a fragmented primary loyalty or trust base. The child is torn between mistrustful parents or other *essential* caretaking adults.

A split between parents is not in itself the issue. The fact that a child seems closer to one parent or the other does not have to cause concern. The issue is the *unconditional* nature of the child's involvement in the split. The clinical clues may be subtle, for example, the mother "explains" the father to the children. Or they may be more blatant. One parent confides to the children about the other. The mother and father engage in angry outbursts and the child takes on the job of calming them. But the child cannot calm them. It does not work, so what remains for the child is a more and more desperate use of symptoms to bring them together. An anorexic girl reported a dream in which her parents were lying near death on adjoining gravesites. In the time it would take her to feed one, the other would die.

A heavy impact on the child occurs when, for instance, the mother and her parents are aligned against the father, and the child is expected to join this alignment. Thus, the child is charged with being loyal to one parent at the cost of his or her loyalty to the other. But the child cannot give up the commitment to Father's side. "I can and have to side with my father." (The dilemma for the child would be the same, of course, if the alignment were against the mother.) This impact becomes greater because the child's commitment includes not only the father, but also the excluded grandparents. Therapeutic leverage is invoked not by highlighting the ambivalence toward each parent, but by making the split in loyalties central. In concrete terms, a therapist might say, "When you have to stand up for your father against your mother, what do you do with that? That is a terrible dilemma." It is emotionally costly for the young child to play the rejunctive role: "If you are going to take me away, then I am going to stay with Mommy; if she is going to take me away, then I am going to stay with you." The therapist will at least attempt to acknowledge the child's desperate predicament. Instead of inviting the child to be "disloyal" to either parent, the therapist adopts an action plan based on an alliance in the best interests of the family as a whole. However, by "the family as a whole" we do not imply the sacrifice of individual member's interests in behalf of total family solidarity; rather, we mean a balancing of each member's best interests with the needs and valid claims of other family members.

Invisible Loyalty

We conceive of filial loyalty as a universal and central relational dynamic, originating from rootedness and parental merit, on the one hand, and from the offspring's right to give, on the other. Filial loyalty can take either overt or covert forms. One of its overt forms is the sometimes deeply anguished efforts of adults to keep their lines of caring open to aging and difficult parents. In its covert forms, it may provide a far more powerful determinant of pathology and resistance to health than has yet been fully realized.

Laing (1965) and Stierlin (1974) have described the "mystification" of the child that is seen when the child has no way of getting access to direct knowledge of the multigenerational ledger terms to which his or her own life has been subordinated. In developmental terms, the child is vulnerable. He or she may "buy into" the expectation that the debt to the parents is endless and that its payment takes priority over every other human concern. The parent's unwillingness to accept "installment" payments on the indebtedness can make the obligations boundless. Or a nonreceiving parent can violate the other pole of the child's loyalty, the need and right to be spontaneously giving. The covert connections may be infinite, though unconsciously perpetuated. If, for instance, the father scorns weakness, the son's fear of weakness may repeatedly immobilize his efforts. Or if the mother is an obsessive housekeeper, the grown daughter, following a rupture with her parents, may go on a house-cleaning binge that alienates her husband. Indirect loyalty to the more distant parent can be expressed in disloyalty to one's spouse. Here, the intrapsychic process could be one of unconscious displacement; the ethical dynamic is that of *invisible loyalty*. Neither of these dynamics excludes the other or can be reduced to the other.

The "Revolving Slate" and "Destructive Entitlement"

Plays, novels, professional discourse, and daily experience all call attention to an extraordinary aspect of the human condition. This is the fateful mandate that patterns shall be repeated, against unavailing struggle, from one generation to the next. For instance, a young man decides against parenthood because, "I see too much of my father in myself, and I don't want to pass it on," protecting against the possibility of having such children, but depriving himself of being a father. Conversely, the destructively entitled parent repeats a damaging pattern both as an expression of invisible loyalty and as a lack of remorse. An ambivalent father abandons his wife, who, in turn, abandons their son. The father rescues the child, then abandons his second wife, and the child along with her. The stepmother is the only one with whom the child can have a relationship of trust. To exonerate his mother, the son can only put his father down: "You are no better than she is." To exonerate either the father or mother, he can only put his stepmother down: "You are no better

than they are." To exonerate her, he can only put down his therapist: "You are no better than any of us." Much more is involved here than an unconscious displacement of hostility. The child is caught in a vicious self-destructive chain reaction. He tries to balance the ledger by substituting his father as a monster instead of his mother, and so on. As the child gets older, his vindictive behavior may extend to his own spouse and children. This intergenerational linkage of substitutive balancing is ethically invalid. Moreover, it blocks the possibility for self-healing remorse. All generations are caught on a revolving slate of vindictive behavior.

To behave otherwise would require the grown son to step out of the context of his generative rootedness. Consciously, he may struggle to give his children a better life. But the unconscious, ethically binding premise is: "How can I treat my children better than my father treated me, without being disloyal to my father?" So, while there are grounds for existential guilt, the child turned parent may actually feel little guilt over his unfairness to his own children.

We hold that *this "revolving slate" aspect of invisible filial loyalties reinforced by earned "destructive entitlement" is the chief factor in family and marital dysfunction.* It is important to recognize that while destructive entitlement is valid in its past context, it becomes unjust when the person begins to act on it. Therapy can never undo the extent of earned destructive entitlement. However, therapy aims to help the person rely less upon it. Life cannot be lived over again. The grown offspring who acts on destructive entitlement will be disengaged from the ongoing task of weighing what is fair in his or her relationships with spouse, children, and significant others. The disjunction may take symptomatic forms, such as contempt, hatred, avoidance, coldness, indifference, or cruelty. Liberation from the revolving cycle of destructive action can take place only through the discovery of resources of direct loyalty and trustworthiness. If they are to achieve freedom, individuals must discover rejunctive ways of preserving loyalty and exonerating the generations before.

Interlocking-Need Templates: The Psychological/Interpersonal Dimension

A husband and wife may be joined in collusive arrangements through their "interlocking-need templates" (Boszormenyi-Nagy, 1962, 1965). Psychoanalytic object relations theory provides a psychological framework for this pattern of relating (Fairbairn, 1954; Guntrip, 1961; Dicks, 1964). For instance, a spouse's complaints about a partner's coldness or anger enable him or her to disown his or her own needs for distance. The two may be locked into a tightly overutilized relationship in which each serves as the monstrous and denied part of the other. They can act out this substitutive victimization for years. One may then become symptomatic. They may try to salvage the relationship by drawing on their child, whose burden may then become enormous. The interweaving of dimensions 2 and 4 can be seen in the the "bad object" attributions of people in the process of substitutive vindication. Preferences dictated by loyalty may determine the choice of projective identifications. However, object relations theories do not fully address the dynamics of the choice of the target of projections.

Exploitation

While providing a reservoir of trust, the child is vulnerable to the family's definition of what is fair. This gives the parents a wide margin for exploitation, much of which can go unnoticed by outsiders. The most neatly tended suburban house can contain a jungle. The one who appears to the world as the "good sibling," meeting all outward criteria of health, may be the most exploited and the most vulnerable. When social agencies do become involved with a family, they may collude in the scapegoating of the "bad" child, whose "badness" may be the desperate move of any family member to secure resolution of some relational imbalance. We collude with a culturally biased "ideal" to the extent that we regard as "normal" the pattern of the commuting father who believes he is "living his life by the book," doing what is expected of a man and keeping his accounts in balance when he goes out into an untrustworthy competitive world and spends himself earning money. In turn, he may expect his wife and children to offer him trust and emotions. Such a father may be acutely uncomfortable with any attempt to hold him accountable in human terms.

Parentification

It is in the child's interest to have a good parent. If the parent falls short, the child will try to make up the deficit. Thus, the legacy of filial loyalty tends to make the child *parentified*. In a healthy family, to the extent that a child supplements the parents' resources, this can be an avenue of growth and enrichment, for example, the child who comforts the mother when she has suffered a loss. Yet, when parents begin to draw heavily on a child's resources, the child can become captive to devoting his or her life to being a parental figure. There is not much chance for normal growth. The damaging feature is not the transactional role reversal between the parent and child, but the unilateral depletion of the child's resources and natural tendency to develop the capacity for trust.

To an outsider, the overresponsible, parentified child might appear narcissistic, unwilling to yield his or her place at center stage. To the child, however, being in the center may represent an intrinsic command to which he or she loyally responds. Or the child's oedipal strivings may mask the underlying care. As one 6-year-old put it, "I am an overconcerned child." Abrupt collapse during adolescence may terminate the effort. At the other pole of "parentification" is the "black sheep," a psychotic, delinquent, or otherwise failing member without whom the parents could not survive. Or a son may drive himself to win glittering but empty successes to dispel the gloom of his parents. One result is predictable: unless the pattern can be overcome, the parentified child will not be able to give freely to spouse or children.

Upon leaving the family as a result of selecting a partner or engaging in an activity that falls far short of one's own intellectual and interpersonal capacities and is unacceptable according to family standards, disloyalty to the family is only temporarily offset by sacrificial giving to the mate. A married couple may collusively share a denial of the importance of ties with the two families of origin. In a mixed-religion marriage, the spouses may promise unusually stable loyalty commitments to each other, as though both parties, by becoming outcasts from their loyalty groups, could form a new in-group. Such promises, however, may mask the partners' lack of individuation within their families of origin, and the new commitment may be to a commonly shared "cause" rather than to each other. The more passionately the family of origin rejects the traitorous member, the more likely it is that he or she will remain tied to the early loyalty system, albeit in this negative form. By remaining tightly bound in the posture of opposition, the person dramatizes an example of that which is unacceptable to the family. Through this action, the defiant member may hold the rest of the family together at his or her expense, consolidating the family's values through "loyal opposition" while appearing to be "disloyal."

Long-suppressed anger about being given up for adoption or abandoned in other ways by parents may erupt through displacement upon adoptive parents or a mate. Unresolved marital arguing, sexual dysfunction, and the like may represent a functional attitude of rejection of the mate in order to bolster invisible loyalties to the family of origin. Even when other dynamics are operating in marital conflict, we believe that this ethical dynamic influences the outcome.

Finally, the "well sibling," who, it appears, has successfully escaped the pathogenic system, may often be caught in a guilt-laden commitment to overavailability. He or she may be commissioned to take care of the entire family's needs for manifest reason and organization, thus allowing the others to enjoy their regressive gratifications in safety.

In therapy, one of the first steps toward deparentification consists of helping the family to acknowledge the trust advances drawn from the parentified child. Acknowledgment helps to remove the binding force that keeps the offspring captive.

ASSESSMENT OF SYSTEM FUNCTIONING AND DYSFUNCTION

The concept of "family diagnosis" can easily be misleading and can limit the openness of the therapist to true understanding. The locus of a family's resources lies in the success or failure of dialogue between people and not in boundaries between "subsystems" or other abstract schema for describing ongoing relating. Nevertheless, observations of family relationships suggest hypotheses that do include all four dimensions—the factual context, individual psychology, observable transactions, and the dimension of relational ethics. In reality, all aspects of relationships are inseparable and ever-present. While we distinguish these dimensions for the purpose of choosing a therapeutic method, for a contextual therapist, goals have to be consistent with each person's options for discovering the resources in his or her significant relationships and for self-validation.

The observations that are emphasized for assessment purposes are the qualitative aspects of family relationships. From the first moments of contact, the therapist gathers impressions about the climate of trust within the family. Are people capable of listening and hearing one another and committing themselves to statements about their needs, desires, and rights? Are they free to make requests of others and to state grievances and express gratitude? The contextual therapist will ask specific questions about the concrete availability of family members to one another and the degree to which they can share both the benefits and the existential problems of life. Even blaming and accusatory discourse is valued because it reveals the longing of people for acknowledgment and fairness. Complaints are valued as a resource because they indicate a continuing reservoir of hope in relatedness. In contrast, if family members avoid issues of fairness, even vis-à-vis the therapist, it is not a good "prognostic" sign.

For a contextual therapist, emotional "cutoffs" (Bowen, 1978) from the family of origin are viewed as clues to invisible loyalties and relational stagnation. Severed relationships are also seen as indicators of psychological "freezing" of the self, emotional and cognitive dissociations, and a tendency to "polarized fusion" (Boszormenyi-Nagy, 1965) within new relationships. Dimension 2 character development often serves as a vehicle for the transmission of destructive entitlement, and destructive entitlement fuels repetitive and mutually damaging interactions in the present. Clinically, what matters is not the degree of destructive entitlement, but the extent to which a person relies on it.

In a family with small children, a thorough evaluation of an individual symptomatic child may be invaluable to determine, for example, the degree of learning deficit, the usefulness of medication for attention-deficit disorder, or even the likelihood of abuse occurring in the home. From the vantage point of contextual therapy, however, these evaluative devices can be destructive when they are used in such a way as to place the child in a position of disloyalty to his or her family. When careful attention is given to validating the child's crucial interests in maintaining a positive image of and ties to the family, these tools can be invaluable resources for determining which issues need to be addressed first. If a child is setting fires, protection of the child and the family would be everyone's right. Therefore, multidirected partiality would guide the therapist in making use of hospitalization, residential treatment, or other community services that would be of benefit to the child and the family. To deprive a family member of any effective treatment because of any type of theoretical reductionism would be unfair and, therefore, contraindicated by the contextual approach. In working with community agencies or other therapists, however, the key to a contextual intervention would be to avoid a competitive struggle for the family's loyalties.

Similarly, for symptomatic members, biological treatments, specifically designed psychotherapy for post-traumatic stress disorder, detoxification for addiction, and so on are utilized when appropriate. However, they are not a substitute for helping the family to sustain, repair, and heal relationships over the long term. If conducted in collaboration with a contextual therapist, such individual or specific treatments may facilitate the readiness of members to reengage in reparative efforts and dialogue.

The relationship between assessment and treatment is dialectical. From the first moments of assessment, the therapist is engaged in trust building with the family. On the other hand, assessment is an ongoing process and reassessment may be necessary in the midst of treatment. The response of the family to the courage of the therapist in raising issues of relational ethics is part of both evaluation and treatment and should guide the therapist's future behavior.

The therapist seriously regards the convictions of people based both on their stage of development and their particular group and family loyalties. The evolution and integrity of particular solidarity groups over time have important implications for assessing the ethical dynamics operating within the family. Therefore, the contextual therapist makes use of genograms and verbal reports to inquire about the ethnic, social-class, racial, and political contexts of the family members' history. Migration experiences are of particular importance. Certain aspects of a person's legacy are located in the specifics of his or her group's identity and solidarity.

Family resources are the main focus of assessment. They are seen as potentially self-validating—an ethically fruitful aspect of relating inseparable from mutuality. "The grandmother was a resource" is not a contextual statement. "Grandmother became less depressed when her daughter accepted her offer of help" would be a contextual statement about resources. The family members' capacity for expressing their "truths" and convictions about fairness is an important indicator of prognosis for treatment. Initial resistance or honest disagreement is a more favorable sign than overcompliance with the therapist's ideas.

GOALS AND GOAL SETTING

Legacy-Based Treatment Goals

There are fundamental, universal treatment goals that do not depend on the specific characteristics of families or family members. These fundamental goals are basic to the contextual approach. However, the manner in which the method is applied varies greatly depending on the particular psychology, history, interests, and resources discovered within each family member and among family members. The fundamental goal of contextual therapy is prevention: "The efforts of the therapist are aimed at developing a preventive plan for both current and future generations" (Bernal, 1982, p. 1). Consistent with this overall goal is the goal of benefiting all persons who have an interest in the outcome of therapy. Thus, multidirected partiality determines the goal as well as the contract with each family member and the method of working toward that goal with the family. The existential facts provide a basic orientation for the therapist in understanding the context of the family's presenting problems. The reduction of distress and symptomatology is also an important goal, but a fundamental change in the family members' capacity for relatedness is the overriding aim.

Self-validation

It is the claim of the contextual approach that in extending due consideration, there is a dynamic link between the benefits for the receiver and the benefits for the giver. The term "*self-validation*" describes the universal principle of receiving through giving or caring. Its essence is in the enhancement of self-worth, derived from the "give and take" of relationships. The concept implies the most important relational resource, the roots of true individuation. It is the core of an action-oriented therapeutic design. We believe that these goals converge with the family members' desires for hope, trust, and commitment. Thus, self-validation represents an option for bilateral benefits (Boszormenyi-Nagy & Krasner, 1986).

It follows, then, that the basic goal is rejunctive effort, that is, finding options for giving and receiving among family members. This is fostered by (1) encouraging open negotiation of ledger issues; (2) exploration of loyalty and legacy impasses, especially sources of destructive entitlement; (3) "deparentification" (Bernal, 1982; Boszormenyi-Nagy & Krasner, 1986) through acknowledgement; and (4) actions that address inequities. The ultimate rejunctive goal of (5) self-validation provides leverage for any intermediate goals.

Each member of the couple or family is made accountable for his or her own unique and specific relational position with insistent encouragement from and creative assistance by the therapist. The intermediate goals are action designs, trial actions, and shifts of attitude and intention. As sources of members' destructive entitlement are discovered, their capacity for dialogue and self-validation increases, not primarily through insight, but in mutually crediting exchanges with other family members.

No claim is intended that the goals of contextual therapy are so esoteric that they have nothing in common with other approaches. On the contrary, the contextual approach seeks to utilize all useful therapeutic knowledge. As in "uncovering" therapies, we do consider the importance of ego strength in planning attempts at improved relationships. We share the assumption that growth and relief from pain, depression, and other symptoms occur through facing avoided emotional processes. We consider the therapeutic implications of responsibility for imposing one's "projections" or other defensive tactics on others. But the consideration of avoided aspects of the self often necessitates, and also frequently makes possible, the courageous renegotiation of avoided relationships.

We attempt to enable family members to face and forgo irrational, unproductive guilt and to earn, claim, and recognize their own entitlements. Facing realistic, existential guilt—based on actual harm done to others either deliberately or inadvertently—is seen as a valuable relational resource and guideline for expanding the accountability within families that will diminish guilt feelings and lead to increased trustworthiness. As members work on this mutuality, each extends his or her own entitlement and, thus, self-worth. This is a different way of asserting oneself than simply to claim one's rights. It acknowledges each person's "right to give" and the nonentitlement and depletion that result from not having or not utilizing that option. We have found that this rationale is especially effective with persons whose ego functions show arrested development as a result of traumatic experience, deprivation, and especially exploitation by essential parenting figures. The added leverage of caring about the ethical implications of relationships may help to strengthen a weak ego (see also Winnicott, 1963).

Thus, psychological development is only one criterion for determining how to prioritize goals. If it is indicated, one may choose to engage in "intrapsychic work" with individuals. In fact, this may be a necessary first step. But in other instances, the therapist may be called upon to urge a person to take a rejunctive step, such as visiting a sick parent before it is too late. Without taking this step, the person might have to face guilt feelings, often expressed in ways that are dysfunctional, and may further complicate emotional development, especially if he or she has obtained the blessing of the therapist. At best, the individual often achieves a great benefit in terms of individuation. Thus, the psychological unreadiness of either partner is not necessarily a contraindication to reengagement, but the therapist must be careful to assess pain or the illusion of benefit that may result from such an attempt and to "coach" the person about disappointments and possible gains. Benefit for the person comes from increased agency, not primarily from the parent's response.

As in transactional approaches, we aim for an age-appropriate, fair power and role structure in the family, as well as for complementary male–female contributions based on choice and negotiation. While gender and generation (Goldner, 1988; Grunebaum, 1987, 1990) are viewed as primary organizing principles of family life, there is no a priori conviction regarding "natural" or "given" and fixed social roles for members distinguished by gender. However, historically determined role allocations of rights and responsibilities must be addressed as part of the review of inherited legacy and loyalty configurations. The goal is to achieve a balance of fairness in the distribution of the burdens and benefits of adult life, and to take into account "differences" that have led to past injustice and to acknowledge and redress them. Discovering these and other sources of destructive entitlement will help free people from resistances to this task, and help with the willingness to engage in problem solving and to improve communication skills.

Therapeutic skill and timing are essential to determining the choices people have on their paths toward self-delineation and self-validation. These are openly discussed. Timing in all therapy is inseparable from correct assessment of where people are on the continuum from live motivation to desperate stagnation. Much of what occurs in therapy is understanding the signals that people are ready (or not) to end reliance on destructive entitlement and to seek and explore self-validating modes of redress and giving.

Questions of goals should be discussed periodically with the family. Such discussions are always fruitful and ethically sound therapeutic practice. The responsibility for defining goals leads to more efficient use of therapy and greater responsibility and control in the family members' own lives.

THE STRUCTURE OF THE THERAPY PROCESS

Theoretical premises and clinical method are closely interwoven in contextual therapy, and rely for their effectiveness on the commitment of the therapist to the *multilateral contract*. This orientation has little to do with how many people are seen at once. Whether the arrangements are individual, conjoint, concurrent, or three-generational depends on their *optimal resource potential* for expanding mutual trustworthiness and self-validation. For the purposes of family therapy, we consider it desirable in most, but not all, situations to begin with as many family members as are interested and are willing to come. We would seldom insist that a meeting of the full family is absolutely required. The decision about whom to see belongs to the therapist based on information shared by the family and, of course, to some degree will reflect the personal style of the therapist. "Optimal resource potential" means bringing together as many people as can really work with one another toward mutual benefit. Such decisions are made according to the uniqueness of each family. For example, in the early stages of therapy, the legitimate privacy of an adolescent may require consideration. If there is shame associated with one's origins, this should not be disclosed in the presence of an adversarially inclined spouse. In such situations, individual sessions are desirable.

On the other hand, a young child should not be encouraged to talk about family problems in individual sessions without assurance of respect for his or her loyalty and attachment to the family (Boszormenyi-Nagy, 1972). This guideline is particularly crucial in instances of suspected child abuse or violence between parents. It is, of course, an absolute requirement that everyone's safety be preserved, but it would also be naive to expect that "disclosure" of serious family problems by a child would lead simply or primarily to relief. With the disclosure of serious lapses of parental reliability by a child in individual therapy sessions comes the real likelihood of suicidal behavior, retraction under threats, and denial or meaningless apologies extracted by the therapist from the offender. However, at minimum, acknowledgment of the facts by the parents must be a prelude to any real work in conjoint therapy. Such a family crisis demands the utmost sensitivity, care, and skill, and it cannot be said too strongly that decisions must be made on a case-by-case basis. In such situations, individual sessions with everyone at first may be the only possible and safe avenue for beginning a multilateral process.

At any time, any family member may be seen alone if there is something that requires discussion in private. Through negotiation and the discretion of the therapist, the privacy of what was discussed may be preserved. It is not our intention as family therapists to dissolve all privacies, and we no longer push for the unconditional disclosure of all "secrets." Automatic confidentiality of everything addressed in separate sessions, however, is seen as inconsistent with the multilateral contractual context of therapy (see Karpel [1981] for a somewhat different perspective on the handling of "secrets").

Couple treatment is not considered a separate modality. When parenting is an essential component of marriage, the therapist will make it clear at the outset that he or she expects to include the children in the treatment contract, if not the process, because the work of the couple therapy will have direct consequences for the children. If there are no children, the work is done in the context of responsibility for potential parenting and consideration of the spouses' legacies of filial loyalty. Whether the couple does or does not intend to have children, the partners' responsibility toward their own parents and all those who invest them with trust is an important issue.

Similarly, if an individual asks for treatment and has not yet given any consideration to involving the family, we do not see this as a separate treatment modality. Even if the therapist is working with individuals, new explanations for individual symptoms and their recurrence will emerge as the symptoms are placed in their relational context. But far more is involved than history taking or a cognitive understanding of the connections between symptoms and context. If the therapist is committed to the multilateral approach, the essence of the implicit and explicit therapeutic contract is to benefit not only the person in treatment, but also the others to whom that individual is linked through interlocking basic welfare interests. Some people immediately and intuitively appreciate this approach. For those who want to know why they are being asked to talk about their families, the therapist can state the conviction that consideration of one another's interests is integral to the therapist's approach. In the examination of legacy and relational balances, the issue is not just "what is good for you," but, "What beneficial effect can your actions have on the welfare of those with whom you have deep relational ties?" In addition to its clinical and ethical validity, the multilateral contract is "prudent" from the perspective of possible legal damages resulting from "alienated affection," violence, and other causes of damage to a patient's relatives.

Thus, multigenerational contractual ethics are not simply a set of cognitive guidelines. They engage every individual at the level of action, emotion, and concern for the interests of other members, while for the therapist, they provide the master plan for all therapeutic interventions and the basic leverage for mobilizing resources. From this vantage point, to suggest a combination of "individual psychotherapy plus family therapy" would be simply a contradiction in terms, since individual work is defined by the same context as when many family members actively participate.

Since we regard mutual accountability and individuation as corollaries, there is no attempt to separate family members, except as part of a temporary "moratorium" and as required to insure the appreciation of valid needs for privacy or safety. Family members connected through shared rootedness eventually will be considered as potential resources for one another in their attempts to repair and reconstruct relationships.

The multilateral perspective requires a single therapeutic contract for the family. This indicates either one therapist or cotherapists who can function collaboratively, sharing the same basic convictions but with respect for differences of interpretation and style of application. The principal advantage of cotherapists is that one can learn from the vantage point of the other, especially if they are of opposite genders. In this sense, the cotherapy team has the opportunity to model multilaterality, equality, and mutuality. The decision to use cotherapists may also turn on practical considerations, as when one family member needs separate sessions. The possible disadvantage is that, unless the cotherapists respect each other, they may mirror or reinforce the mistrustful behavior of family members, such as competing for members' loyalty or gratitude. In this event, they will place the family in both a historically familiar and a *real* split-loyalty predicament. In optimal circumstances, cotherapists may be able to help one another with inclusive partiality toward all members, especially when therapy begins in crisis situations of intense conflict and mistrust.

Since contextual therapy is not concerned primarily with transactional sequences occurring in the present, spatial arrangements within the therapy room are regarded as relatively insignificant. However, they are sometimes important clues to the degree of alienation or stagnation between members; for instance, at the end of a brief therapy of seven sessions, a teenage daughter and her mother were able to sit close together, affectionately touching each other after months of mutual withdrawal and of vindictive blaming on the part of the mother. However, this development occurred spontaneously after many "deparentifying" interventions by the therapist in which the mother was asked to acknowledge the daughter's caring. The mother also was acknowledged by the therapist with regard to her parenting difficulties in a "blended family" and as a person who, as an adolescent, had been treated unfairly herself.

Therapy may be helpful even if limited to a single session. The therapist takes no rigid position about how far the family members can go, or how fast, toward their multilateral goals. Once reengagement in the fundamental dynamics of trust and self-validation has occurred, they may have reached their initial goal. The point of termination that is most desirable is the point at which the family members have restored enough trustworthiness so that they are motivated to undertake further dialogue on their own (Bernal, 1990). The family members and the therapist may arrive more or less simultaneously at a sense that enough work has been done.

In practice, families sometimes terminate as soon as they have achieved symptom relief. This could be a "bad" termination in the sense that disjunctive implications for this and future generations remain unaltered. But honestly facing that family members want to stop is preferable to the therapist's assuming responsibility and setting unilateral goals for the family's progress. Even a vigorous early refusal to continue treatment could be a "good" termination if it means that family members have recognized the issues and acknowledged their ethical implications.

There is no "typical" length of treatment. It can vary from one or two sessions to two or three years, or more. It is usually weekly or biweekly, but it can be less frequent and may become less or more frequent depending on the goals and resources of the family members. Sometimes an individual or couple will continue after the others have accomplished their goals. In private practice, the therapist makes recommendations and the family members must then decide how much they can afford to pay or how easily they can get away from school, work, or other significant commitments.

THE ROLE OF THE THERAPIST

The role of a contextual therapist is one of active personal engagement in the common situation of the therapist and family members mutually invested in their work together. Right from the start, the engagement requires the courage to raise issues of relational balances. The therapist's goal is to be a catalyst of resources already potentially present when the family comes for help. He or she encourages the partners to undertake a multilateral process of position taking by helping each person to formulate his or her own perspectives and claims and then to begin to hear and respond to the vantage points of others. As each new thread of the fabric of family relationships is identified and discussed, the therapist may ask, "When that happened, how did you see your father acting? How would he explain it? How would he think about what you did? How would your sister think about it? How would you have wanted it to be different?"

The therapist guides and makes connections by being interested and curious. The focus, however, is not only on cognitive exploration, affective discharge, or insight. From the outset, regardless of symptom or problem, family developmental stage, treatment motivation, and so forth, the goal is always one of helping all partners to shift their intentions in the direction of rejunctive effort. In this sense, their first struggle is to overcome their destructive entitlement and to become free to consider another perspective. At this point, active therapeutic engagement has begun.

One can conceive of rejunctive actions as following a gradient. At the beginning, there may be only the shift of intention, the beginnings of a willingness to imagine what the other persons might think. Further along, if the significant other is not available to share the therapeutic process, there might be a letter, a telephone call, a visit with the intention of beginning to reopen a relational exploration. Later, there might be more substantive exchanges. The therapist has such a gradient in mind when he or she asks the person to consider: "I do wonder what more you can do at that point. Your mother calls you, but she doesn't hear what you are saying. What do you think about this? What else can you do?" As the person responds to this encouragement, the therapist acknowledges the response. Although it may sometimes be the therapist's task to point out the risks of inaction, it is not necessary to criticize people for what they so far have been unable to do. As therapy progresses, each person's reliance on destructive entitlement, the callous disregard for others, will diminish.

The gradient may never reach as high as the therapist would wish. Family members sometimes report that it was years since they had tried to have an open conversation with a parent, and the result then was a disaster. The parent would only lay blame, stir guilt, or withdraw. The person may ask; "What can be accomplished now? How can I change such a parent? Why should I hurt myself again?" The goal can be spelled out, not in terms of how to change the parent, but in terms of what the person is willing to invest in making the attempt to change the relationship, whether this attempt is successful or not. As a wife said, after her husband's parents had rejected his offer to go to their home for Passover for the first time in years, "At least now he can live with himself." Self-validation has

started to show its liberating and security-engendering effects.

In some respects, this therapeutic approach may appear similar to the ego-supportive work of individual psychotherapy. The distinction is that the therapist offers support to the patient not only for insight, but for actions that, through consideration of relational merit, will elicit the remaining resources of trust and concern in their significant relations with others. This, in turn, will lead to a self-sustaining spiral of self-validating effort and and spontaneous concern, and thus an expansion of ego strength (see also Winnicott, 1963).

The therapist may use self-disclosure to the degree that this facilitates movement toward trust building. It is limited to what is appropriate in the sense that it does not arouse anxiety or embarrassment or create new and unfair burdens for the members. Since the therapeutic relationship is one of asymmetrical power and vulnerability, the responsibility for maintaining boundaries is always the therapist's. From the outset, the therapeutic task is established as belonging to the family members. As past and present items come up for review, it is the son or daughter, for instance, who has to figure out how the father would explain what he did, or else actually ask him about it. It is, on the other hand, the father's option to earn entitlement and self-validation by caring about the injustice suffered by his daughter or son. Thus, instead of prescribing transactions, the therapist holds everyone selectively accountable for a multilateral perspective. This is, in effect, a "practice in accountability" for self and others, culminating in the responsibility for dealing with the vicissitudes in the person's total life situation, including the future interests of his or her offspring.

As one person learns the perspectives of the various family members whose lives have impinged on his or her life, the therapist can build and revise an understanding of the legacies, invisible loyalties, destructive entitlement, and ledger balances. The therapist will guide all partners toward those rejunctive tasks that are needed and available for the restoration of balance. This job becomes quite specific. An analogy might sometimes be finding the "window in the sky" through which a space shot must pass if it is to attain a stable orbit. The question is: *How can any person design a way to relate to the other as a human being, on terms that may for the first time in his or her life be acceptable to the self and carry value for the other?* If such a point of ethical engagement or *relational resource* is found, there will be, of course, later departures from it and disappointment. But as long as there is a possibility of finding this point of convergence, hope has been generated for restoring a degree of trustworthiness. If the attempt fails, the therapist will have to help people find reserves of strength to weather the failure. The therapist needs a solid conviction of the value of trying again with better plans for action. It may not be long before the efforts with family members will begin to accumulate outside the therapy sessions, so that the therapist becomes aware that he or she is, in fact, treating an extended family.

Based on his or her conviction about the principles of contextual therapy, the therapist is an active guide from the beginning. As trust deepens, the therapist can be more openly confronting. Once the family members have experienced the benefit of the goals of self-validation and mutual confirmation, the need arises to explore concrete, new behavioral options for achieving them. Since the participants' roles from the outset have involved exercising responsibility, the therapist need make no major shift in roles as termination approaches.

Multidirected partiality implies the dialectical process of empathic siding, crediting of past injustices and contributions, and holding people accountable for being "fair" to others. The fairness of a person's action or viewpoint can seldom be judged from the vantage point of one individual, but must be the outcome of dialogue and negotiation. The therapist actively structures the process at the beginning. Later, his or her influence is one of support, consultation, and tracking the coherence and consequential significance of the conversation. All of this requires courage, accountability, and much self-reflection on the part of the therapist. By being partial to one person, the therapist creates a dialectic between that person as "figure" and the other members as "ground" or context surrounding and caring about "the one." Then the therapist will move on to siding with someone else. In this way, he or she evokes an intermember dialogue that gradually intensifies spontaneously.

TECHNIQUES OF CONTEXTUAL THERAPY

What We Don't Do; What We Do Instead

Pointing out the inherent imbalances of fairness has inherent risks, because a person may either reject the idea or wait for the therapist to work on it. Nor is it the therapist's task to decide the ultimate justice of the issue of why the mother, father, or grandparent behaved as he or she did. The therapist makes the members accountable for asserting the merits of their own positions regarding the fairness of each side. There is no relabeling; it is not the therapist's task to try to deny a person's initial reality, but to explore it and use it as a starting point. If a person feels acknowledged, there is less need for resistance and defensiveness. Even blaming is understood as a statement of hope, and the role of the therapist is to discover its meaning, extend acknowledgment, and try to transform it into a justifiable request or claim. The aim is to elicit the family members' thinking about and recognition of unused trust resources.

The therapist guides but does not take a rigid position on any issue. If the therapist is inflexible or moralistic, the family members can leave him or her "holding the bag." Instead, the task is to apply a flexible, sequential taking of sides that recognizes each person's entitlements and also each person's obligations. However, the contextual therapist will need to be persistent about the basic principle of multilateral consideration, even as he or she allows for a "moratorium" as needed by the family members.

We do not prescribe tasks on a transactional or power basis. While recognizing much that is "systemic," we do not follow the premise that the therapist's restructuring of the transactional or communicational system, without effort by individuals to be accountable for themselves and for their relationships, will bring lasting change. If the person cannot discover what to do, the therapist may suggest that the person consider an action, or may encourage action, for example, "Is there any way I can help you to get this done?" The underlying assumption is that the essence of therapy is action leading to a balance of self-validation and fair accountability. The more experienced and skillful the therapist, the more he or she can help with options for personal action.

If a parent's failure to help a child results from a lack of knowledge, there is nothing to prevent the therapist from instructing the parent. Advice given sympathetically will often be accepted, contrary to what some schools of therapy believe. Yet we do believe that there are often more powerful obstacles to progress, with the greatest being the reliance on historically valid, earned destructive entitlement. Its management is based on the process of *exoneration* in a three-generational, therapeutic context.

It should be clear at this point that the goal of therapy is not to explore pathology. If one person appears to have done something sadistic, the focus is not on the affect or motive per se, but on how this action affected the balances among people and where the resources are for reparation and for rebuilding trust. The therapist will explore the sources of destructive entitlement that provide the context for understanding and enabling the perpetrator of unfair actions to regain credibility and respect and to shift to self-validating modes of relating.

Generally speaking, the conventional kind of intrapsychically directed interpretation is not sufficient. *Making accountable is different from making aware.* At best, unilateral interpretations may only interrupt the momentum of the dialogue. Since the focus is on real relationships, there is no primary need to deal with derivative or symbolic materials. The focus is not primarily on "What are your needs?"—although this may be a crucial starting point. Instead, it is, "What do you want, what do you want to do about it, what should you do about it?" Nor is there any implication that once people have achieved insight, they are on their own with it outside the therapist's office. Instead, what they intend to do about it is the issue that generates therapeutic leverage. This approach introduces relational accountability as a leverage for psychological therapy.

Seldom is the focus on "why?" in individual terms. Nothing could be more stagnant than two parents drawing on their own expertise to interrogate a child as to why she stole a sweater from a shop. The focus needs to be broadened to the relational context of the event. If the child's act was an effort to end the parents' alienation, the therapist does not condone the theft, but the stagnation becomes the focus of treatment. As the partners' destructive entitlements confront each other, a formidable impasse is created that cannot be understood in terms of individual psychopathology or transactional patterns.

As for transference, the therapist ignores it at his or her peril, as when a family colludes to leave the therapist stranded, or one spouse expects the therapist to be a benevolent parent who makes the other spouse seem inadequate. In such instances, the therapist moves not to interpret the action, but to offset it, as by calling on the husband or wife to adopt a parenting role, or by showing that he or she does not side against the spouse. The more the therapist is coercive, the greater is the risk of being cast as the bad parent. But sometimes this risk has to be balanced against the risk of stagnation.

Thus, the therapist's awareness of transference, projection, and so on, serves as a guide to intervention, but these phenomena are not viewed simply as "intrapsychic phenomena." It is advisable, for instance, to examine how, within the transference, for each person the therapist may become a competitor for loyalty vis-à-vis the person's family of origin (Boszormenyi-Nagy, 1972). The contextual relevance of emotions is that they are often indicators of the ethical balances in the family. The degree to which neurotic defensiveness burdens other family members may also come to have clinical importance as an ethical issue.

Major Aspects of the Therapeutic Method

Multidirectional Partiality

The therapist becomes an advocate for all within the basic relational context, that is, the multigenerational extended family, including the dead. This position seems simplistic. However, openness to multilaterality is one of the sources of the greatest resistance. All human beings are inclined to see the world in terms of prejudicial, implicitly scapegoating attitudes. It is never easy for a therapist to exonerate a seeming monster such as an abusive parent. To earn the position of multidirectional advocate, the therapist offers his or her commitment to finding and utilizing the resources of trust in the family. The commitment is not made in words; it is made by acting from the first moment with this rejunctive goal in mind and by refraining from any action that would preclude it. To accomplish this end, the contextual therapist does not proceed primarily on the basis of his or her intuition or own values or any single technical guideline. Instead, consideration is given to the interests of all involved in all their dimensions—factual, psychological, transactional and ethical. This requires systematic formulation in the therapist's own mind of hypotheses on each level of "relational reality" (Boszormenyi-Nagy, 1981).

Toward the participants, the therapist does not adopt a stance of impartial contemplation of all the competing interests. We hold that "impartiality" or "neutrality," if it can actually be achieved, is an undesirable goal, and its pursuit can be deadening and dangerous. The therapist is multidirectionally partial, empathic, acknowledging, and endorsing, listening to one person and then turning to another person. This reinforces the multilaterality that exists between them, but from the therapist's point of view, it is an ongoing choice of direction, a sequence of sidings to which the term "multidirectional partiality" has been applied (Boszormenyi-Nagy, 1966).

The therapist has little investment in family controversy. Time is not allotted to vague, chaotic exchanges; the therapist does not join in collusive battles from which he or she may emerge only as the target. Of course, the family may erupt in controversy, and the therapist may briefly get thrown off balance. The return to solid ground comes with the demand, "Wait a minute. I first want *you* to make a clear point, and then *you*." When an honest statement of position from one person becomes ammunition for his or her victimization, the therapist moves at once to block its destructive impact.

The therapist sets the family members the task of defining the issues that have depleted trust among them. At the outset, it is not a matter of saying, "Now, let's see what's fair about this," because the word "fair" can trigger resistance and polarize attitudes. To elicit articulate, authentic positions (i.e., to get positions subjectively defined as clearly as possible), we start with one member's complaint, treat it as something deserving of respect, and develop it by

asking for specific concrete descriptions. Even the act of restating one's position in the presence of the therapist can enhance trust. Once the statement is made, the therapist invites the other person to respond. As the process unfolds, the therapist puts increasing demands on each to state his or her viewpoint. If the therapist allows anyone to water the statement down or laugh it off, this is condescending. If the therapist allows people to obscure their own points or those of others in a flurry of recriminations and counterattacks, the attempt has failed. The thrust is toward requiring each to become accountable to the other. Helping each member clarify something may prevent the dialogue from breaking down. If the therapist steps in to make a point for a person, however, the therapist may feel relief but the work stops.

As the context deepens, the first clues as to multigenerational, dynamic linkages may emerge. When this happens, the therapist expresses interest and curiosity and thus brings the connections to the surface. An important perspective is the parents' or members' to explore experiences of past injustice. Acknowledgment by the therapist establishes the basis of an alliance with the parents for further exploration of the children's problems. The issues on which family members are able to take a position may at first be derivative. The wife may question her husband's commitment to finding a better job, when the implicit issue is whether he will leave his mother. Or the husband may allege that the wife does not care what happens to the children at school. The therapist may move by stages to the central issue: "Are you saying that your wife lacks sensitivity to the children's experience, or even suffering?" Later, "Are you two struggling with what you give to and receive from each other, but talking about the children instead?"

As this kind of dialogue builds among the family members regarding their valid entitlements, it acquires a momentum of its own. Any moralistic imposition of the therapist's own values is countertherapeutic. Within this context, affect usually surges spontaneously. What emerges is more pointed and more intense than if the therapist were to invite diffuse expressions of affect. At the end of such a session, there may be a mood of quiet elation among people who have advanced enough trust both to speak and to hear one another. This cannot happen if the therapist is afraid or unable to permit significant issues to be joined. If the same issue exists in his or her family and it remains unfaced, the therapist may not be ready to allow others to deal with it.

How Partiality Is Applied

By advocating for the principle of fairness, the therapist earns trustworthiness; family members learn that partiality to one person will be followed by an attempt to elicit a different, often opposing, position from other family members, with each position representing the person's experience of reciprocity in the relational context being explored. This includes both justified claims and indebtedness, to which acknowledgment or reparative action is the trust-building response. We consider the therapist free to relate actively to each family member, as long as the therapist is alert to the risks of transference and countertransference. Offering partiality to one family member after another, or to several simultaneously, is not the same as "joining" the family for restructuring or strategic purposes. The therapist balances the siding with the demand for accountability from that person. This is, first, the demand to define one's own point of view as responsibly as possible. "You made a point, it probably has some truth in it or you wouldn't have said it. So let's look at this now. When you say your husband has put his work ahead of you from the beginning, what is the meaning of this? How do you measure it?" In the extreme case, "I have the feeling that if I were your wife, in this regard I would feel that you were unfair. Can you account for that?" If the mother holds back and allows her daughter to defend her from the father at the cost of incurring the father's rage, the therapist asks the mother to comment. The essence of the question is, "How do you account for your part here?" Next, the demand is to listen to and consider the interests of the other. "You have heard what she said—now I would like you to consider it." The goal of this process is a clearer definition of individual positions and responsibilities rather than a "circular" diffusion of different points of view.

The effort requires a high degree of sensitivity to the immediate status of each person's relational ledger. Does he or she state or imply that his or her side is being overlooked? If it is, the reaction will be swift and predictable. The person is still too deeply hurt to be able to consider someone else's interests and legitimate claims. The therapist may need first to engage in deeper siding. If the issue involves a parent, the therapist says, "You haven't told me much about how you were hurt or treated unfairly." Or, "When your parents brought you into this problem between them, you were in the most burdensome situation for any child." In making such statements, the therapist is not leading the offspring into either simple dependency or a loyalty conflict, because it has already been made clear that the therapist will act as the parents' advocate as well.

As partiality moves apace with the demand for accountability, whatever ambivalence there is will erupt. Some aspects of disloyalty or hostility will emerge as negative items on the ledger. From moment to moment, the therapist may be siding with someone who is under stress, and then with another. He or she may make statements to the effect: "I feel you're protecting your mother. As a loyal daughter, you should. That's the big burden—being a child who's trying to make allowances, extending extra credit, giving payment in advance, like most children do. You are an overgiving daughter who's angry because you've given so much."

If the siding becomes undemanding of effort, then the therapeutic progress stops. On the other hand, the therapist who is overly confrontational may evoke the experience of previous injustice too closely to move the therapeutic process forward. Even the therapist's acknowledgment may be heard through the filter of the person's earned destructive entitlement and, therefore, be rejected. In such instances, a moratorium is in order: "If you can't make a clear point now, we'll come to it later." Carefully balanced partiality may make it possible for the individual with personality deficits to progress in treatment, despite the possible historic injustices the person may have endured.

Effective partiality requires discrimination about ledger balances. A daughter may provoke an insult from her father. At the transactional level, her annoyance at the insult may seem out of place; after all, she may have provoked it. But both the provocation and the annoyance may be related to a deeper context of parentification. *If the therapist attempts to deal only with the immediate transactions, the daughter will lose hope that she can be understood by the therapist.* Despair may provoke her to circumvent the therapist's efforts. Sometimes unconscious associations, or expressions of strong feeling at moments of intense arousal, may be a better guide to the true state of the ledger than observing interactional sequences. However, all information available to the therapist should be utilized as a guide to understanding and intervention.

The therapist who sides strongly with a child by acknowledging the child's efforts to hold the family together may appear to side against a mother whose attitude toward the child is one of complaint. But at a deeper relational level, the therapist is also offering partiality to the mother by congratulating her on the contributions of her child. This attitude is based on deep convictions about how important it is to recognize the convergence of people's interests in preserving and improving the quality of their vital relationships. A shift of perspective, or "reframe," may be an intermediate step, but it is not a *goal* of intervention.

At some point, the momentum of multidirectional partiality may collapse. A spouse who has clearly stated his or her distress at the other spouse's coldness may, every time he or she shows genuine warmth, manifest a lack of trust by disqualifying or not recognizing it. Then the therapist will restore leverage by deepening the concern for what is happening between them and turn toward the sources of each spouse's destructive entitlement that led to the current impasse.

An important, more recent consideration is the relational impact of "distributive injustice," such as genetic disease or mental retardation. Unlike "retributive" unfairness, distributive injustice involves no perpetrator; the unfairness is between the person and his or her destiny. Yet it is simply human for such a person to be and/or act "destructively entitled" toward others. Multidirected partiality has to address both the person's "contract" with the "justice of existence" and the human justice of how the burdens were distributed. The concepts of "transgenerational solidarity" and "invisible relational tribunal" are pertinent here for therapeutic planning (Boszormenyi-Nagy, 1987a).

The Loyalty Context of Therapy

It is empirically founded[3] that apparent therapy gains based on disloyalty to one's family are unreliable. From the first moment of contact, especially when working with children, the therapist frames the work as a process in which family loyalty will be respected. Self-sacrifice based on the willingness to be exploited will also be challenged. The therapist listens to but does not enter into the process of blaming. Instead, the preferred stance is conveyed by such remarks as, "I have never seen a family in which people were born to be monsters. What could you do? What is good in this family?" In a bad situation, "What is best to do? If it doesn't work now, did it ever?" And, "If you can't relate to her, could your children?"

When a parent lodges a complaint against a child, the therapist asks the child, "Tell us what you have tried to do to help yourself and your family. I am sure you can think of having tried to be helpful." When the parents complain about each other, the therapist may address the child: "Are you worried about your parents? Do you think this family needs help? How have you been trying to help them?" Such questions are based on our clinical experience that in any family the child's loyalty leads to helping efforts. Almost invariably, these can be openly elicited. A process of dialectical exploration is persistently applied. If the parent says the child is bad, the therapist listens, and may acknowledge the seriousness of the behavior, but then asks what is also good about the child.

When this loyalty framework has been firmly established, the exploration of grievances can be safely undertaken. The child is not asked to report on what is going on in the family or to denounce the parents in the presence of a therapist who is a stranger and a potential adversary

---

[3] *Editors' Note.* We assume that the authors are using the word "empirical" in the sense of something being based on practical experience, and not in the sense of being derived from methodologically sound scientific research; we would be most pleased to see such a basic hypothesis tested by valid research methods.

of the parents. If the child brings a dramatic accusation against the parents, it becomes their task to show what concern they have about the child's complaint. But the therapist's inclusive partiality reduces the child's guilt and anxiety caused by the therapist's necessary questioning of the parents.

In the ultimate case, when the child says, "You don't love me," and the parents' reply shows that the child is right, the therapist can ask the child, "Do you think your parents are happy about this?" And to the parents, "Now where do you go from here?" But also, "Tell me how was it when you were your child's age."

When the therapist is engaged in being partial to one person, "Tell me more about how you were hurt," this is always within an established loyalty framework. The goal is not, "I am going to teach you how to redirect hate from your husband and children and put it back where it belongs." Instead, the context is one of working to understand and *exonerate* the other. If the therapist acknowledges that the person's life was indeed a tragedy, it does not have to follow that the parents deserve all the blame. Most likely, they were at least as much victims as victimizers themselves.[4]

Loyalty considerations are based on the conviction that to leave the person in a condition of unresolved hate or resentment toward a parent is damaging to the offspring's capacity to chart their own course toward individuation and commitment to the their own families of procreation. We have encountered some people whose therapists taught or allowed them to believe that the end goal of therapy is to learn about their feelings by focusing their hatred on their parents. The client will not discover new freedom if this is the goal. Such a move goes against people's most deeply sensed loyalty, destroys what may be valuable resources if not for them, then for their children, and provides them with a malignant projection of responsibility for taking charge of their own lives. It drives invisible loyalties underground, where their symptomatic effects will be all the more pernicious. And it leads the offspring to an unbearable conclusion: "If

they were inhuman, I can't be any better, or I have no right to a better life, or to any life at all."

The therapist can give the screw another turn by implying that he or she would be the better parent. Some child psychiatrists make the comparison explicit, when they suggest that the therapists' reliability might be redemptive evidence to the patients that their parents were not the only kind of people in the world. On the other hand, loyalty conflicts engendered by therapy must be openly addressed because it is just here that healing may take place. If the therapist is more trustworthy in some ways than the original family, the client can also come to accept the "good" aspects of his or her parents. Most important, it is a major principle of this therapeutic model that loyalty is not simply an obligation, but an opportunity for and a right to reciprocity and giving that, if denied, deplete self-esteem and self-worth and lead to despair and character distortions. This conviction, based on clinical experience, is the reason we consider the expression of a child's loyalty and spontaneous generosity to be as much a *right* as an obligation.

Exoneration

The most consistent predictor of improvement is the readiness of a parent to engage in the process of *exoneration* of his or her own parents. The task for the offspring is to begin to dispel the cloud of shame, blame, and implicit contempt that hangs over their lives and envelops the entire family. If this sounds like a ponderous or unpalatable therapeutic task, it might be worth considering that everybody is engaging in it anyway. The offspring who demands that the therapist accept himself or herself as a monster is also insisting that it cannot be one's parents who are the monsters. A newlywed who will not be diverted from a narrative of all the partner's unfairness is saying, in effect, "Compared with this, my mother or father was not so bad." These are all expressions of an indirect form of loyalty based on the *revolving slate*. Such attempts to be loyal or protective usually benefit no one and lead to new unfairness and, thus, an accumulation of *destructive entitlement*. The challenge for the therapist is to help family mem-

---

[4] *Editors' Note.* See Madanes (Chapter 12) for a rather different view of how exoneration and multilateral exculpation may be addressed in such cases.

bers to find better ways to "exonerate" a parent, ways that will not destroy the prospects for decent relationships.

Thus, information about a client's parents is gathered in the spirit of fair exoneration. The goal is not merely to obtain information, to achieve better cognitive understanding, or even to find more closeness and warmth, although all these are worth having. The goal has less to do with insight than with conscious intention and commitment. But invisible loyalties are often unconscious, and character resistances to making this dynamic conscious may have to be addressed. It is essential, however, that the therapist does not view the undoing of denial or displacement as the primary or only goal. Rejunctive efforts often lead to a lessening of the need for these defenses; therefore, profound "character change" may come about as the consequence of such efforts, which are the result of a dialectic among insight, intention, and action.

At first, a person may say, "I don't want to live in the past. My father and I let it alone and that's the way we both like it." Here, the intent is only to preserve stagnation and invisible loyalties and to postpone debts whose pressure may be felt only after the chance for acknowledgment has irrevocably passed. The therapist encourages the person to face all aspects of his or her ambivalence and move on to consider the long-term significance for enhancing everyone's deliverance from lasting resentment. The action can begin with a willingness to examine why he or she does not want to think about it. Such an examination may reveal curious discoveries, for example, "Aunt Molly would turn over in her grave if I should take sides with Mother against Father." From there, "What do *you* think about it? How do *you* really feel about it? Then, what more can *you* do about it?" This leads to, "What would be important for you to know to convince you that there might have been some good things about their lives? Could you find out more? What do you imagine could happen if you began to talk to them about it?" Later, "Could you ask them about never seeming to care how well you did? How would you do this?"

Either way, the exonerative effort is carried out with due regard for the person's ambivalence, the rage or resentment, shame or guilt, and grief or mourning that are a necessary aspect of healing. For parents and grandparents, the essential task is to try to think about what the events of their lives meant to them and so to experience how it came about that they did what they did, and thereby to see their actions in a human context. However, an important principle guides the sequencing of the therapist's partiality, the principle of *equitable asymmetry* in the parent–children relationship. The children's destructive entitlement must be fully acknowledged and discussed before they are asked to "exonerate" their parents. The nature of the process, of course, will be determined by the ages of the "offspring" and the intensity of hurt.

Giving to the parent can also be a move toward exoneration. "If I can give, I am not so shameful, dangerous, or helpless after all. If I am not so weak, then perhaps I was not so deprived after all, or perhaps I am capable of developing resources of my own." The new approach might consist of finding something the person can say on his or her own terms that the parent will be willing to hear.

The task of exoneration can be accomplished even if the parent never responds to it. The goal of rejunction concerns learning to accept prior intergenerational imbalances and the responsibility for one's own relational integrity, whatever actions that may entail. This may seem very difficult to the offspring who has been abandoned or abused; it may also be very hard for the therapist when parents do not respond to great efforts on the part of their children to sustain and renew dialogue. Yet even the most injured person is helped to turn a self-commiserative or self-abnegating attitude into an active stance. Even if people cannot change their parents, they do not have to remain passive victims. They can learn to rely on the integrity of their own actions for emotional and relational sustenance and self-validation. At least their "right to give" is restored.

Bringing Children Into Treatment

The introduction of children into any therapeutic setting requires sensitivity to a major pitfall. The very fact that the therapist shows adult concern for the child creates a situation in which there is some implicit disloyalty for the child. This cannot be avoided; therefore, an effort is needed to avoid its consequences as far as possible.

The hazard is greater if the child is being seen alone. In the traditional child-guidance approach, the child therapist and caseworker sometimes took sides with their respective clients. Their arguments with each other would neatly parallel the conflict in the client family. Another aspect of the split approach was that the therapist's effort to build a relationship with the child might set up a loyalty conflict with the parents. It was also considered good technique to assure the child that, in this setting, whatever he or she said about the parents would reflect no disloyalty. If the parents tried to draw on the child's loyalty, they were accused of "undermining" treatment. Thus, the child was "bound" (Stierlin, 1974) and "double-bound" (Bateson, Jackson, Haley, & Weakland, 1956) unless the therapist had the resources to offer a multilateral definition of the treatment context.

We may ask the question: What is a child therapist? Clearly, the therapist can protect the child's interest only by taking into account the interests of that child's parents. We know of cases where family members have been parceled out to as many as four independent therapists. In doing this, there is no allowance for a multilateral view of anybody's interests. In working with the child, this means meticulous attention to the process of framing the contract as one of helping the child *and* the family as a whole. Nothing less will be in the interests of the child.

How To Include the Children

Work with children is an integral part of the contextual approach. Even when the spouses present with a marital problem, the therapist makes it clear from the outset that he or she expects to see the children at a very early stage of the treatment, if only for a few sessions. This puts the marital problem into an intergenerational context. Parenting is an essential and inseparable part of marital considerations, and it is ethically the weightiest issue in its demands for human concern. The future life prospects of young and even yet-unborn children represent the highest ethical priority, and, therefore, the greatest therapeutic leverage.

Asking the parents to report on their chil-

dren's status yields only an outside view. The therapist cannot bring life into the children's standpoint, or get a direct sense of relational balances. As time goes by, the children are developing, and they, as well as the parents, may need help. If there is severe marital difficulty, the therapist needs to see how the burden of this situation leads to the children's parentification. How the parents are taking unilaterally from the children, and how the children struggle and suffer with this, especially without any acknowledgment, are of great import to the therapist. When the children speak up from the vantage point of their position in life, the therapist can ask the parents to respond to the children. This challenges parents to put what they are saying about the children together with what the children are saying to them.

Even if the focus is on the marital situation, the greatest therapeutic leverage comes through consequences for the children. This is leverage in the ethical realm, stressing the children's entitlements to a trustworthy climate for growth and the parents' accountability for seeing that the children's entitlements are examined in a fair light. This is the core of trustworthiness in relationships and the formation of basic trust in a dependent child. As a mother remarked of her son, "When he saw that his children were being hurt, he started doing something about his marriage." This holds equally true if there is a divorce pending. What happens to the children then becomes even more a focus of concern.

Parental refusal to bring children into treatment is seen in terms of disengagement from ethical considerations. The therapist is persistent: "I really want you to be accountable for doing the best possible work. I will help you if I can. But let me tell you, your parenting is an inseparable part of your marriage. I want to know more about the children. Let's see if you can do better by them. Every day counts in their development, and they may urgently need help now. You have a parental duty to look at this." Even if the parents strongly deny that the children need to come in, the therapist does not compromise regarding this principle. The matter is one in which there can be no minimizing of consequences. Meanwhile, the therapist may be considering what factors give the parents an immunity from guilt and concern for their children.

Introduction of the children is on the basis of a therapeutic contract with the parents. The therapist is not bringing the children in so that the parents can sit back as judges while the therapist does child therapy. Instead, the therapist prepares the way by asking, "How will you handle it with the children while they are here?" If the therapist takes over from the parents, they are no longer accountable and the therapist is implicitly acting as the better parent.

Once the parents have brought out an item in relation to the child, whether it has to do with the effect of their marital dispute on the child or with an issue between them and the child, this opens the way for the therapist to ask for a response to the parents from the child within a loyalty framework. "How are you trying to help?" If before this context has been established the child erupts with accusations, this discussion is better postponed. Once the parents have given permission, the child is freer to speak, and it becomes the parents' task to respond.

Almost without exception, the child will advance enough trust to respond with some openness about what is going on in the family and what the child has tried to do about it. Almost invariably, the parents are shocked at the degree of the child's awareness and pain. At this point, the therapist moves to acknowledge the child's contribution and to urge the parents to acknowledge it. The format is one of enabling and trust building. The focus is not on the child's burden, but on the fact that the child is trying to do something about it. This is a profoundly positive event, and the therapist ensures that the child is not left to congratulate himself or herself. Whatever acknowledgment the parents can give the child at this point is a first step toward the balancing of accounts. It is a step toward deparentification, because the parents are receiving help, and this diminishes the pressure on the child to preserve the marriage, as well as relieving whatever blame or responsibility the child has taken on. The parents are also encouraged to clarify for the child what they intend to do to make things better. If the therapist can exercise enough leadership to establish this kind of context, there is little risk that the introduction of the children into the sessions will be an act of exploitation. The very fact that the child

can witness the concern of the adult world diminishes the risk of further parentification.

Resistance

There is no less resistance encountered here than in psychoanalytic or systemic approaches. Avoidance, denial, repression, disassociation, distancing, triangulation, fusion, evasiveness, disengagement, failing to face the truth or make connections, escape from accountability—by whatever label they are called, these old, familiar processes are active forces in the process of exploring relational balances. In addition, as people are encouraged to begin an examination of their respective positions in the presence of significant partners, resistances are revealed even more quickly.

The therapeutic approach is neither to interpret such resistance nor to try to bypass it. Instead, the participants are encouraged to face, in their real relationships rather than in the substitutive context of therapeutic transference, the ethical issues from which their resistance derives, to define their distinctive positions regarding these issues, and to move toward a multilateral consideration of each other's interests. The multidirectional partiality of the therapist both supports and directs this. This device is not available in traditional individual therapy or in approaches that exclude people's deepest motivations or view all perspectives as equally valid.

Such an approach generates anxiety. Stirring up anxiety is not the goal; neither is it the immediate goal to reduce anxiety. The objective is to lead everyone through the anxiety to considerations that will begin to restore trust. In this process, of course, timing must be taken carefully into account. If the therapist forces premature confrontations between people, if family members are held accountable or pushed into taking stands too soon, the ongoing dynamic of the treatment process can collapse. Demands for exoneration that come too rapidly can undermine people's defenses and lead to further resistance. Rather than taking a rigid position, the therapist can take an unyielding interest in the possibility of progress. Finally, if there is no movement, the therapist can suggest the option: "You decide if you can work this way, looking at all sides. Not everyone can. If not, there are other ways to seek help." Even if this stage is reached, the participants are still given the task of facing the issue and making a responsible choice.

Summary

The attitudes of caring, due acknowledgement, courage to face the depth of conflict, and confrontation of responsibility and other painful issues of life lead to respect for the therapist. These attitudes will encourage family members to make an increasingly trust-based commitment to the treatment and to forge the alliance. If genuine caring and attentiveness were techniques, they would lose their meaning. Attention and caring translate into action, but they are based on mutually sought sequences of spontaneous speaking and responding. Live relationship is an important aspect of therapy. Homework and other techniques are often used, such as writing letters, making phone calls, and visiting, but one of the most serious errors is to mistake these suggestions for action as the goals of therapy themselves. What matters are the intentions of the family members. Homework is always designed with a relational goal in mind.

Techniques

The application of multidirected partiality, a disciplined method, cannot be reduced to specific techniques.* However, many techniques that endorse and generate authenticity, empathy, and reciprocity may be useful. For example, Chasin and Roth's (1990) dramatic enactments

---

* However, we wish to report a series of studies conducted by our co-workers Guillermo Bernal et al. (1990) that indicates how the method of multidirected partiality may be studied for research purposes—a contribution that can be useful for training purposes as well. The current authors were among the "subjects" in this study as "experts" who were asked to identify classes of "actions" that they believed characterized *Contextual* family therapy. This part of the study led to the development of an instrument that was used to test the validity of intended treatment and rater reliability in an outcome study of "brief CFT" with heroin addicts. And as the authors say, "We have used a method that can be easily replicated and applied with other modalities of family therapy" (p. 330).

of the ideal future and the disappointing past are uniquely helpful in evoking the partners' destructive entitlement and hopes for rebalancing, and often liberate the couple's own resources for negotiating a more "just," present-oriented relationship and for a courageous renewal of dialogue with the previous generation. Papp's structured fantasy technique (1990) evokes many themes of longing for connection and trustworthiness, as well as of conflicts of interest and commitment. While these techniques were created for work with couples, there is no inherent reason why they cannot be adapted for use with intergenerational relationships (Grunebaum, 1990). Techniques that mystify, are coercive, assume total responsibility for change, or are disrespectful should not be used because they erode the basis of the therapeutic relationship. In practice, the method of multidirected partiality structures the turning to and siding with each partner, and, therefore, no special techniques are necessary.

CURATIVE FACTORS IN CONTEXTUAL THERAPY AND MECHANISMS OF CHANGE

We have already discussed how "insight" may be one component of the healing process. Since invisible loyalties and destructive entitlement are often partly unconscious, the contextual therapist will be engaged in the task of enabling all relating partners to achieve clarity and awareness of historic factors that are having an impact on current relationships. However, this form of insight is encouraged primarily via the multilateral process of dialogical relating induced by the therapist, not by "interpretation" in the classical sense of the term. The growth of understanding of one's own and one's partner's actions, attitudes, and vulnerabilities goes far beyond insight in the psychoanalytic sense. The understanding that is sought through this dialectic process is not primarily psychological understanding, although psychological and interpersonal understanding are part of both the method and the goal. It is, rather, a deepened apprehension of "relational reality" (Boszormenyi-Nagy, 1979) that is neither a "construction," a metaphor, nor a realtiy that is "given," but a dialogical reality that cannot be reduced to one person's viewpoint.

The therapist's goal is to determine historic truths about relationships when possible, to take into account the various shared or conflicting meanings of those truths. The idea of "truth" or "reality" and its meaning to any individual is treated with respect and not taken lightly; multiple perspectives are viewed as equally worthy of being heard, even if not equally valid when viewed as statements about interhuman issues.

The therapist does not construct new, pragmatic realities, but encourages family members to increase their options by expanding the trust basis of their own relationships. Contextual therapists attempt to increase the responding capacity of family members. Such capacities are not thought of as instrumental skills. The potentials for *response and responsibility* (Buber, 1965) are viewed as closely related and available to anyone who is open to these human possibilities. Relational growth occurs when the therapist is able to help the family members give up their reliance on destructive entitlement, even though the ethical credit based on actual past injustices cannot be altered, and begin to risk trust and trustworthiness; the key therapeutic movement does not take place by learning specific skills, but by learning that everyone benefits from mutually rewarding, reciprocal exchanges. We believe that these forces are "liberated" naturalistically in the treatment process because the human longing for trustworthiness and trust is an essential fact of human existence.

The therapist's personal maturity plays a crucial role in therapy. Since every person is to some extent destructively entitled, his or her effectiveness will be determined by the degree to which he or she has been able to come to terms with this. The therapist will respond unavoidably when his or her own sense of justice is activated or offended. The therapist should trust his or her own ethical intuitions, but reflect on their sources in his or her own familial or cultural contexts. Again, it is crucial to remember that the therapist's values and definitions of fairness will inevitably become part of the treatment situation; ordinarily, the therapist welcomes being challenged by family members (Grunebaum, 1990, 1991). The requirements of multidirectional partiality place a heavy demand on the therapist who has a need for finding a

culprit in either a person or the "dysfunctional system."

The concept of "countertransfernce" is now understood quite differently from its original, classical Freudian meaning by many schools of therapy (e.g., Racker, 1968; Searles, 1959, 1961). From our perspective, the therapist's "countertransference" always has its source in prior relational contexts. It can be utilized as a resource for deepening one's capacity for engagement in the multilateral process. Therapists who seek rapid evidence of symptom change, who fear being drawn into the system, who are suspicious of the resources inherent in the therapeutic relationship, or who need to be active in an instrumental way probably should adopt another approach to family treatment.[5]

Other Approaches

Within its four-dimensional framework, contextual therapy is open to all therapy modalities (Boszormenyi-Nagy, 1987b). The intergenerational approaches of Bowen (1978), Paul (1990), and Framo (1990) are compatible with and very helpful to contextual therapists. However, since they focus primarily on interpersonal psychological processes, from our perspective, they may at times not provide a broad enough methodological framework or set of goals for understanding or promoting healing through rejunctive dialogue. Paul does focus on the consequences for children of their parents' failure to mourn their own parents' death, and establishes a three-generational context for dialogue regarding unresolved grief, fears, and other vulnerabilities. Each family member is approached with deep respect for his or her unacknowledged suffering. However, the emphases of these approaches on "differentiation," or "affect," or "anachronistic images of parents" are limited goals that do not encompass issues of actual abuse and other injustice or that seem to provide room for dialogue about these *real* events. Often a context

---

[5] *Editors' Note.* It is rare, and to us refreshing, to read such an explicit statement of the "contraindications," so to speak, for a therapist's selection of a particular approach to family therapy. By way of contrast, read Colapinto's (Chapter 13) detailed description of the profile of the ideal structural family therapist.

of real familial or social injustice leads to the necessity for the denial of rage, grief, and vulnerability. The connections between "feelings" and the factual human and social context must be explored or the dangerous kind of reductionism that has characterized all of psychotherapy may occur. Nonetheless, all the intergenerational approaches are seminal in our thinking and refer to different aspects of a typical contextual therapy process.

Contextual therapy utilizes the systemic concepts of progressive interaction and adaptation. We believe that the pluralistic contract with several persons is characteristic of all family-therapy approaches, even though its ethical implications often are not highlighted. But many clinical interventions based on systemic thinking can be helpful when employed within the methodological framework of multidirectional partiality.

SPECIAL ISSUES IN MARITAL TREATMENT

We do not consider marital treatment to be a modality distinct from family therapy. Yet, as we have discussed, the marital relationship has specific characteristics that are different from those of intergenerational relationships. The ethical principle that is unique to such dyads is the principle of *equitable symmetry*; since couples are members of the adult generation, each partner is potentially capable of the equality and reciprocity required for long-term relationships. This criterion of "fairness" is, thus, the opposite of the "fairness" in parent–child relationships. Moreover, since adults are often members of the same generation, the time span for "rebalancing" ledger issues is shorter, and so the process is often more intense. Because couples often share the same political, social, or ideological contexts, membership in the same generation often engenders loyalties that, to some extent, mitigate the loyalty conflicts of early marriage (Grunebaum, 1990). It is extremely important to explore these dynamics, especially with elderly couples in long-term marriages. The health risk to the surviving spouse after bereavement documents the ethical, interpersonal, and emotional importance of horizontal peer relationships.

A couple relationship reflects the dialectical interconnectedness of vertical and horizontal family relationships. Often, split-loyalty configurations, a pattern of relating that impinges on the offspring in the new family of procreation, originate in an unresolved loyalty conflict between the spouses and their families of origin. Furthermore, the *extent to which a couple has been able to achieve symmetry* or parity in its own relationship will have consequences for all future generations. In our society, which values the two-generation nuclear family, the marital dyad is pivotal. The couple dyad is actually crucial in maintaining intergenerational continuity and transmitting the new "culture of procreation," an alchemy of each partner's familial legacies.

Both the structure of the therapy process and the method used when a couple relationship is the presenting problem vary only in emphasis and in the sequencing of partiality. The couple's *commensurate potential for giving and receiving* will be the focus both of assessment and of treatment. Since we have already said that children and parents are often included at some point in the treatment of couples, we will not elaborate further on either the reasons for or the goals of these interventions. Furthermore, we believe that the members of a couple, as adults, are entitled to freedom for intimacy, companionship, sexuality, recreation, and physical contact—possibilities of connectedness that are enhanced when the distribution of adult benefits and responsibilities is open to choice and negotiation (see also Acker, 1988).

TREATMENT APPLICABILITY

We consider the contextual approach relevant to most human problems, especially as it utilizes the pertinent knowledge of other approaches. However, we can find no contraindication for *any* thoughtful, integratively informed and responsible therapeutic approach, if therapy is indicated at all. Therapists must be aware of the limits of what therapy can accomplish. One session might be enough to meet the family's own goals, regardless of what the therapist might ideally wish for that family. On the other hand, a number of specific treatment modalities may be indicated simultaneously or employed sequentially. It would be unethical not to refer a member for an established and effective treatment for individual symptoms, such as medication for depression. Complex multimodal treatment programs require careful planning, sequencing, and collaboration with other treatment providers. Perhaps, however, the most distinctive feature of contextual therapy is its clear conviction that relatedness, accountability, and caring are valuable goals to be sought beyond impersonal "change" for its own sake.

The application of multidirectional partiality is entirely determined by the unique needs of the family or couple seeking help. Therefore, referral for another type of treatment or collaborative treatment with specialists in the fields of addiction, child placement, or hospitalization, or treatment for the post-traumatic stress disorder for victims of abuse, may be what is indicated by the principle of equitability. However, what is unique about the contextual approach is the emphasis on the multilaterality of relationships, the options for the bilateral benefits of giving and receiving as suggested by the concept of *self-validation*, and the insistence on concern for the consequences of clinical interventions for all those potentially affected and, in particular, for future generations. These are unique ethical considerations not elaborated on or explored by other approaches.

CASE ILLUSTRATION: THE S. FAMILY

Presenting Problem and Family Description

The S. family is a "blended" nuclear family composed of two parents and three children, and was referred to therapy by the school. Both parents are of Italian-American, middle-class origins, and both are divorced. The mother has two children from her previous marriage—Nina, age 13, and Joey, age 10. She also has a daughter, Ellen, age 7, with her present husband. The couple has been married for 10 years. Mr. S.'s father left when Mr. S. was 10 and had not been heard from since. Mrs. S. described herself as "the black sheep" of her family, her sister being "the favored" daughter. She said that her ex-husband visited his two children and paid child support, but with frequent delays, and often disappointed the children by being late to pick them up. The latter circumstance has been a source of great irritation to Mrs. S. and of tension in the family. The presenting problem was described by the parents as follows: "Nina has a mind of her own."

Clinical Assessment

From a developmental perspective (Dimension 2), the parents' description of Nina would seem to describe a normal developmental crisis of adolescence in relation to her needs for increased autonomy. The other children appeared to be doing well, except for Joey's somewhat sad appearance. The parents also complained about chronic fighting among the children, especially between Joey and Ellen, the parents' common child, who seemed the least burdened and the most spontaneous of the children. The parents appeared hurt and puzzled by Nina's attitude and viewed her as deliberately defiant and unwilling to be helpful; in the earliest moments of the first session, the mother stated that Nina's unhelpfulness around the house was "unfair," especially since she recently had had to increase her own hours at work for financial reasons. Yet the parents seemed genuinely concerned and eager to help solve "Nina's problem" and wondered what they could do. The family had taken other steps to deal with their problems, such as attending church discussion groups about family issues, and had attempted to have regular family meetings on their own. These efforts were viewed as indicating the many resources already present in this family.

From a transactional perspective (Dimension 3), we hypothesized that Nina's behavior and the fighting between her and her mother might deflect attention from unresolved parental or marital problems. Another possibility was that the mother was "triangulated" between her own children from her former marriage and her new husband, potentially involving her third child as well, and also between her children and her former husband, with resentment and unresolved issues still being enacted through the children. At this point in the therapy, there was almost no communication between Mrs. S. and her ex-husband.

From the perspective of Dimension 4, which highlights relational factors, it appeared that the family members were basically committed to one another's welfare and had taken many sincere steps to get help. These were seen as major resources that could be a starting point for further work. A contextual assessment would emphasize such *relational* determinants as the parents' own "destructive entitlement," factors that would be obstacles to treating their children "fairly," depending on their developmental and relational needs. Destructive entitlement and invisible loyalties would also interfere with the mother's capacity to have a good relationship with her second husband and a collaborative co-parenting relationship with her former husband. In fact, in attempting to resolve issues of filial loyalty with their family of origin, people often make marital choices that are unsuitable or doomed to failure. The first failed marriage then takes on a "precious culprit" function in order to ensure immunity from the disloyalty of the second marriage. The mother's experience of having been parentified and treated unfairly by her father seemed to indicate her own experience of injustice and, therefore, destructive entitlement. Some statements from the first interview offered clues as to the issues a contextual therapist would regard as crucial. Joey, in describing his current behavior, said, "I used to be the best child to my mother, but now I do things that I know I'll be punished for and I do them anyhow." (The therapist wondered whether this might be Joey's attempt to bring together the two different sets of expectations in the two very different households of which he is a member.)

Demonstrating a "parentifying" and "parentified" attitude, Mr. S. complained in the first interview that Nina did not "care enough" to be helpful, expressing profound hurt and puzzlement. He thus offered the therapist a sense of his vulnerability and previous hurts, perhaps as a consequence of having been abandoned by his own father. His relationship with his two stepchildren seemed tentative. Nina looked isolated and anxious, and her mother seemed overburdened, angry, and estranged from Nina.

Formulation

The fact that this is a remarried family determines many aspects of the family's life. The mother finds it difficult to represent her former husband positively to their joint children, especially in view of how she is burdened by his irresponsibility toward her, and the children as well. This places both Nina and Joey in a split-loyalty predicament. They are parentified by being unable to complain, for instance, about not getting their allowance on time because, from their vantage point, that would amount to siding with their mother against their father. Based on the first session, it became clear that there was added tension because Joey and Nina's father had stated his intention to remarry and the children had been the messengers of this news. Although Mr. and Mrs. S. had been together since Nina and Joey were small, the children seemed to find it confusing and disturbing that they were expected to call both their stepfather and their biological father "Dad," indicating an intense split-loyalty situation. Nina's adolescent behavior was described as a betrayal of caretaking and belonging. These misinterpretations are the hallmarks of parentification.

Unresolved resentment toward families of origin seemed to be currently active and were obstacles to the couple's having a more harmonious and intimate relationship. For instance, in a later couple session, it was learned that Mrs. S.'s mother (the maternal grandmother) had recently criticized Mr. S. for being "cold toward his stepchildren." The anxious manner in which Mrs. S. handled this added further weight to the "working hypothesis" regarding her invisible loyalties and destructive entitlement. In addition, Nina's willing acceptance of the role of scapegoat seemed to reflect a form of invisible loyalty to her mother, and there was evidence that Joey was beginning to join Nina in her sullen and defiant behavior.

Goals and Goal Setting

The family responded actively to the therapist's initial attempts at multidirected partiality. The therapist's first impression that the family would make use of therapy seemed correct. Each family member had something to contribute and each seemed to listen while the other spoke, with the possible exception of Nina, who appeared anxious and distracted. Most of the members seemed to agree that they would like to work on their goals of less "fighting" among the siblings, of the mother's being less overburdened and being able to secure the children's help, from which they would all benefit, and of the family's generally being "more cooperative." Joey, in particular, seemed very anxious for the family to get help. Nina seemed almost eager to accept her "bad girl" role, but agreed to come for more sessions with the family.

The therapist's "intermediate" goals were to (1) deparentify the two older children, especially Nina; (2) explore and restore some trustworthiness within the inevitable split-loyalty dilemma; (3) offer partiality to both parents and explore and acknowledge sources of their own destructive entitlement; and (4) help Mrs. S. negotiate more directly with her former husband regarding their children and not involve the children as intermediaries. It was hoped that this dialogue would enable the parents to be more open to their children's distress, and to make requests of them that were fair and realistic. Goals were discussed with the family members in their own terms, but since they already used the language of intergenerational injustice and distributive justice within the family, the "discourses" of the family and of the therapist were not widely divergent.

The Course of Therapy

Therapy with this family lasted seven sessions.

First Session

All five members were present at the first session. The parents were asked to speak first. This is not primarily a structural intervention based on an organizational hypothesis, but an invitation to the parents to give permission to their children to speak openly about family problems. This minimizes the risk of disloyalty and creates a climate in which it is safe for the children *not* to be overprotective of their parents, and thus to make individuating statements. The therapist asked the parents how they handled

Nina's behavior *as a team*. There was evidence that Mr. S. was reluctant to make demands of his stepchildren and anxiety on the mother's part regarding the effect of *her* two children's behavior on her marriage. At one point, the mother said, "I just feel it's my responsibility to get *my son* up in the morning." The therapist actively elicited everyone's perspective and, in particular, asked Nina if she could tell what she was doing that might show how she was trying to help. Mrs. S. was asked if she could think of anything that showed concern on Nina's part, but she described Nina as completely devoid of caring. Nina was only too willing to agree with her mother's description. The family's initial resistance, which this interaction reflects, was respected by the therapist as it represents the family's misguided attempts to remedy long-term unfairness. In this session, the mother almost immediately introduced a three-generational perspective when she spontaneously offered to tell a story about how harshly her father had treated her when she once "got drunk" as a teenager.

By the end of the first session, the therapist's multidirected partiality had begun to shape the therapist's relationship with each family member. The mother's increased openness demonstrated the effectiveness of the therapist's multilateral advocacy and was an expression of giving to her children. This began the process of a shift away from blaming and scapegoating and toward self-delineating and self-validating modes of relating.

Sessions 2, 3, and 4

The next three sessions were conducted with the couple alone. The purpose of offering the parents this opportunity was to explore areas of adult intimacy and to explore in more depth how invisible loyalties and destructive entitlement might be obstacles to marital commitment and effective parenting. By offering partiality to each partner for his or her unique set of difficulties, the therapist catalyzed an implicit dialogue between them regarding their asymmetrical relationship with the children. Mr. S.'s acknowledgment that he could offer "stepfatherly," as compared with "fatherly," love to Joey, if painful, opened up an unfaced issue between the couple and was a necessary first step toward building trust and managing the predicament in a more resourceful way. Actually, Mr. S. revealed a great deal of empathy and affection for Joey when he said: "He's hanging in there pretty good, so far!"

The parents' relationship with their own families was explored in the third session. It revealed that Mr. S. had almost no ongoing relations with his family of origin and had "adopted" his wife's family as his own. Mrs. S. has continued to have somewhat conflictual relations with her parents. In the third session, a serious covert, unresolved loyalty conflict emerged. Mrs. S. brought up the fact that on a recent trip with her to the doctor, her mother had said, "The main problem you are having with your children is Dave!" [Mrs. S.'s husband and the children's stepfather]. "He hates Nina and Joey and they hate him because they know he hates them." Mrs. S. described how profoundly shocked she had been by her mother's remarks, and her husband described to the therapist how devastated he was and that he had become deeply depressed for several weeks. He added, "For one dumb remark, I didn't deserve that!"—for the first time expressing some genuine anger. At the fourth session, this discussion was continued. The therapist invited Mrs. S. to ask her mother to come in for some direct discussion of this issue, but neither parent was open to this suggestion at that time. The therapist was ready to accept a moratorium on the issue for the moment, but insisted that Mrs. S. would have to be more open and more *directly* giving to her mother in the future. The question of whether the couple made time to spend together privately was also explored in this session, and it was learned that they did not, but wanted to find ways to have more fun together.

Session 5

The whole family returned for the fifth session. Nina seemed a little less willing to point the finger of blame at herself, but Joey was visibly upset. As the mother tried to "find out" more about his feelings, with the therapist's encouragement, she rather insensitively asked Joey if he was "going through menopause." Joey then reported the painfulness to him of his sis-

ter's claim that she considered him to be "two-faced." This led the therapist to wonder whether this might be an implicit reference to the trials of getting along in two different families, and decided to explore this issue with everyone. Joey described, with exquisite poignancy, how, in each household, he had to listen to negative remarks about the other parent. And with great sadness and grief, he did acknowledge that his mother was "right" about how much his father disappointed him when he was late in picking him up. The therapist promised to explore in the next session whether the parents could find better ways to manage this situation.

Session 6

In this session, the therapist confronted the parents by holding them accountable for improving their management of the situation. At the same time, he acknowledged the difficulty of doing so and their legitimate grievances. The most potent therapeutic element here was the partiality offered to the parents through the possibility of doing better for their children's sake. The therapist's attitude was free of judgment and blame, but was insistent on the possibility of progress. He also recruited the children's opinions on how things could be improved, believing that children's contributions to their family's welfare are uniquely valuable. Joey wished that "his father would do what he promises" and that "his mother would find a way to get along with him." The mother was visibly moved.

Session 7

At this session, the last of the sessions with the S. family, Mr. S., the stepfather, was not present. Perhaps this absence was related to the recent discussion of the children's need for a good opinion of their real father. However, there was much to be hopeful about in this session. Nina sat close to her mother, shoulders touching, and looked much more relaxed. Mrs. S. appeared less angry. The therapist met alone with Nina for a few minutes, and in this discussion, Nina revealed that she had understood her mother's message that she really loved her and had been trying "to give more affection and understanding to me [Nina] than Mother had received from her parents." And later, when the whole family came together, the therapist used the opportunity to be a "benevolent go-between," in reporting to her mother the essence of Nina's remarks. In response, the mother stated that she had begun to talk to Joey openly about his problems with his father. She also reported that, regarding Nina, she herself had "changed," and had decided to "give more, even if *Nina* doesn't" and "to let her know that she loves her despite her troublesome behavior." The mother and daughter seemed to have begun a conversation that would continue for many years, indicating that an intergenerational impasse has been breached. The therapist welcomed and endorsed the significant change in the mother's attitude and demeanor, and offered partiality to her for her efforts to relinquish her parentifying search for validation from the children. The family did not return for further sessions.

CONCLUSION

In concluding this exposition of contextual therapy, we wish to challenge the reader to struggle with the concepts we have put forth, as they go "against the grain" of many of our most deeply held cultural values. In addition, we also wish to emphasize that the interpretation and application of any theory of therapy to human situations will be determined by the unique, emerging relationship between the therapist and family members.

Endnote. For an excellent *demonstration* of Contextual Therapy, see videotape "From Symptom to Dialogue: A Consultation with Ivan Boszormenyi-Nagy" with detailed clinical analysis and commentary. (see references)

REFERENCES

Acker, J. (1988). Class, gender, and the relations of distribution. *Signs, 13*, 473–497.

Anderson, T. (1987). The reflecting team: Dialogue and meta-dialogue in clinical work. *Family Process, 26*, 4.

Balint, M. (1952). *Primary love and psychoanalytic technique.* London: Hogarth.

Balint, M. (1968). *The basic fault: Therapeutic aspects of regression.* London: Tavistock Publications.

Bateson, G., Jackson, D., Haley, J., & Weakland, J. (1956). Toward a theory of schizophrenia. *Behavior Science, 1*, 251–264.

Bateson, G., & Ruesch, J. (1951/1968). *Communication: The social matrix of psychiatry.* New York: Norton.

Bernal, G. Guidelines for conducting intergenerational family therapy. Project Proposal for Grant 5-RO1-DA03543. *National Institute of Drug Abuse.*

Bernal, G. (1982). Parentification and deparentification in family therapy. In A.S. Gurman (Ed.), *Questions and answers in family therapy, volume II.* New York: Brunner/Mazel.

Bernal, G., Flores-Ortiz, Y., Rodriguez, C., Sorenson, J., & Diamond, G. (March, 1990b). Development of a contextual family therapy therapist action index. *Journal of Family Psychology, 3:3*, 332–331.

Bernal, G., Rodriguez, C., & Diamond, G. (1990). Contextual therapy: Brief treatment of an addict and spouse. *Family Process, 29*, 1.

Boszormenyi-Nagy, I. (1965/1985). A theory of relationships: Experience and transaction. In I. Boszormenyi-Nagy & J. Framo (Eds.), *Intensive family therapy: Theoretical and practical aspects.* New York: Brunner/Mazel (First edition, New York: Harper & Row).

Boszormenyi-Nagy, I. (1966). From family therapy to a psychology of relationships: Fictions of the individual and fictions of the family. *Comprehensive Psychiatry, 7*, 408–423.

Boszormenyi-Nagy, I. (1972/1987). Loyalty implications of the transference model in psychotherapy. *Archives of General Psychiatry, 27*, 374–380. Reprinted in *Foundations of contextual therapy: Collected papers.* New York: Brunner/Mazel.

Boszormenyi-Nagy, I. (1976). Mann and Frau (Man and woman). Familiendynamik (Stuttgart, Germany).

Boszormenyi-Nagy, I. (1979/1981). Contextual therapy: Therapeutic leverages for mobilizing trust. Report 2, Unit 4. *The American family.* Philadelphia: The Continuing Education Series of Smith, Kline & French Laboratories. Reprinted in R. Green & J. Framo (Eds.), *Family therapy: Major contributions* (pp. 393–416). New York: International Universities Press.

Boszormenyi-Nagy, I. (1987a). Transgenerational solidarity: The expanding context of therapy and prevention. In I. Boszormenyi-Nagy (Ed.), *Foundations of contextual therapy: Collected papers* (pp. 292–318). New York: Brunner/Mazel.

Boszormenyi-Nagy, I. (1987b). Contextual therapy and the unity of therapies. In I. Boszormenyi-Nagy (Ed.), *Foundations of contextual therapy: Collected papers* (pp. 319–330). New York: Brunner/Mazel.

Boszormenyi-Nagy, I., & Krasner, B. (1986). *Between give and take: A clinical guide to contextual therapy.* New York: Brunner/Mazel.

Boszormenyi-Nagy, I., & Spark, G. (1973/1984). *Invisible loyalties: Reciprocity in intergenerational family therapy.* New York: Harper & Row. (Second edition, New York: Brunner/Mazel).

Boszormenyi-Nagy, I., & Ulrich, D. (1981). Contextual family therapy. In A. Gurman & D. Kniskern (Eds.), *Handbook of family therapy.* New York: Brunner/Mazel.

Bowen, M. (1966). The use of family theory in clinical practice. *Comprehensive Psychiatry, 7*, 345–374.

Bowen, M. (1978). *Family therapy in clinical practice.* New York: Jason Aronson.

Buber, M. (1958). *I and thou.* New York: Charles Scribner's Sons.

Buber, M. (1965). *The knowledge of man: A philosophy of the interhuman.* New York: Harper & Row.

Chasin, R., & Roth, S. (1990). Future perfect, past perfect: A positive approach to opening couple therapy. In R. Chasin, H. Grunebaum, & M. Hersig (Eds.), *One couple, four realities: Multiple perspectives on couples therapy.* New York: Guilford Press.

Erikson, E. (1964). *Insight and responsibility: Lectures on the ethical implications of psychoanalytic insight.* New York: Norton.

Fairbairn, W.R.D. (1954). *An object-relatedness theory of personality.* New York: Basic Books.

Friedman, M. (1985). *The healing dialogue in psychotherapy.* New York: Jason Aronson.

Friedman, M. (1989). Martin Buber and Ivan Boszormenyi-Nagy: The role of dialogue in contextual therapy. *Psychotherapy, 26,* 3.

Fromm-Reichman, F. (1950). *Principles of intensive psychotherapy.* Chicago: University of Chicago Press.

Gilligan, C. (1982). *In a different voice: Psychological theory and women's development.* Cambridge, MA: Harvard University Press.

Goldner, V. (1988). Generation and gender: Normative and covert hierarchies. *Family Process, 27,* 1.

Goolishian, H., & Anderson, H. (1988). Human systems as linguistic systems: Preliminary and evolving ideas about the implications of clinical theory. *Family Process, 27.*

Grunebaum, J. (1987). Multidirected partiality and the parental imperative: An answer to the feminist critique of systems theory. *Psychotherapy, 24,* 35.

Grunebaum, J. (1988). Contextual therapy, child abuse, and feminism. Paper presented in the Workshop on Contextual Therapy: Applications with Abusive Families. American Association of Marital and Family Therapy, New Orleans.

Grunebaum, J. (1990a). From discourse to dialogue: The power of fairness in therapy with couples. In R. Chasin, H. Grunebaum, & M. Hersig (Eds.), *One couple, four realities: Multiple perspectives on couple therapy,* New York: Guilford Press.

Grunebaum, J. (1990b). Contextual therapy with elderly couples. Paper presented at Workshop on Working With the Elderly. American Psychological Association, Boston.

Grunebaum, J., & Boszormenyi-Nagy, I. (1991). Videotape. *From symptom to dialogue.* Consultant and Founder of the Contextual Approach: Ivan Boszormenyi-Nagy. Editor: Judith Grunebaum. Available G-N Productions; 37 Gray Gardens East; Cambridge, Mass.

Guntrip, H. (1961). *Personality structure and human interaction.* New York: International Universities Press.

Hoffman, L. (1990). Constructing realities: An art of lenses. *Family Process, 29,* 1.

Jonas, H. (1984). *The imperative of responsibility: In search of an ethics for the technological age.* Chicago: University of Chicago Press.

Karpel, M. (1980). Family secrets: I. Conceptual and ethical issues in the relational context. II. Ethical and practical considerations in therapeutic management. *Family Process, 19,* 3.

Klein, M. (1932). *The Psychoanalysis of children.* New York: Grove Press.

Laing, R.D. (1965/1986). Mystification, confusion, and conflict. In I. Boszormenyi-Nagy & J. Framo (Eds.), *Intensive family therapy: Theoretical and practical aspects.* New York: Brunner/Mazel. (First edition, New York: Harper & Row).

Papp. P. (1990). The use of structured fantasy in couple therapy. In R. Chasin, H. Grunebaum, & M. Hersig. *One couple, four realities: multiple perspectives on couple therapy.* New York: Guilford Press.

Paul, N. with Paul, B. (1990). Enhancing empathy in couples. In: R. Chasin, H. Grunebaum, & M. Hersig, *One couple, four realities: multiple perspectives on couple therapy.* New York: Guilford Press.

Ruddick, S. (1982). Maternal thinking. In B. Thorne & M. Yalom (Eds.), *Rethinking the family: Some feminist questions.* New York: Longman.

Searles, H. (1955). Oedipal love in the countertransference. In *Collected Papers on Schizophrenia and Related Subjects.* New York: International Universities Press.

Shapiro, E. (1988). Individual change and family development: Individuation as a family process. In Celia Falicov (Ed.), *Family transitions: Continuity and change over the life cycle.* New York: Guilford Press.

Stierlin, H. (1974). *Separating parents and adolescents, A perspective on running away, schizophrenia, and waywardness.* New York: Quadrangle.

Sullivan, H. S. (1953). *The interpersonal theory of psychiatry.* New York: Norton.

Van Heusden, A., & van den Eerenbeemt, E. (1987). *Balance in motion: Ivan Boszormenyi-Nagy and his vision of individual and family therapy.* New York: Brunner/Mazel.

Walsh, F. (1983). Normal family ideologies: Myths and realities. In C. Falicov (Ed.), *Cultural perspectives in family therapy.* Rockville, MD: Aspen Publication.

Weiner, N. (1961). *Cybernetics* (2nd ed.) Cambridge, MA: MIT Press.

Winnicott, D. W. (1963). *Maturational processes and the facilitating environment: Studies in the theory of emotional development.* New York: International Universities Press.

Winnicott, D. W. (1971). *Playing and reality.* New York: Basic Books.

CHAPTER 8

Ericksonian Family Therapy

Stephen R. Lankton, M.S.W.,
Carol H. Lankton, M.A.,
and William J. Matthews, Ph.D.

Milton H. Erickson, M.D., is known for his creative and pioneering contributions to family therapy as reported in works by Bateson (1972, 1979); Haley (1973, 1985a, 1985b, 1985c); Watzlawick (1976); Bandler, Grinder, and Satir (1976); Fisch, Weakland, and Segal (1982); Madanes (1983); Ritterman (1983); Lankton and Lankton (1986); and others. Erickson himself, however, never offered a family-systems formulation of his work. There are no entries entitled "family" or "systems" in the indexes of Erickson's collected writings (Rossi, 1980), in Erickson's collected lectures and seminars (Rossi & Ryan, 1985; Rossi, Ryan, & Sharp, 1983), or in any book written by him (Cooper & Erickson, 1954; Erickson, Hershman, & Secter, 1961; Erickson & Rossi, 1979, 1981; Erickson, Rossi, & Rossi, 1976). This is primarily due to Erickson's desire to avoid structural theories for individuals and families. As he did not promote attention to these features, many writers and editors also failed to attend to the broader, systemic aspects of his work. Nevertheless, his approach and in-

tervention strategies did, in fact, utilize an implicit ecosystems orientation. Aspects of his influence and contributions to family therapy are far reaching and profound (Fisch, 1990).

Three volumes by Jay Haley—*Uncommon Therapy* (1973) *Conversations with Milton H. Erickson: Vol. 2, Changing Couples* (1985b), and volume 3, *Changing Children and Families* (1985c)—are family-therapy–oriented books containing verbatim transcriptions of Erickson work and conversations. *Uncommon Therapy* is noteworthy as an attempt to clarify Erickson's influence on family therapy and his reliance on a health-oriented developmental framework. While this book makes an extensive reference to various aspects of the family by means of the cases presented, this is possibly reflective of the editor's intention. Erickson's work has often functioned as a projection screen for theorists and provided the data they framed in varying conceptual formulations. Certainly this is true regarding his highly distinctive approaches to families that others have attempted to clarify and discuss in terms of specific systemic factors (Araoz, 1988; Czech, 1988; Dammann, 1982; Haley, 1984; Lankton & Lankton, 1983, 1986; Leveton, 1985; Loriedo, 1985; Malarewicz, 1988; Ritterman, 1983; Schmidt & Trenkle, 1985).

Haley is often cited as the chief expositor of Erickson's work because of his extensive exposure to him over almost two decades (Broderick & Schrader, 1981, p. 25). He, in fact, coined the term "strategic" to describe therapy wherein the therapist is active and assumes the responsibility for initiative movement toward change. His interpretation of Erickson influenced the above writings as well as the intense attention focused on Erickson's work by a wide range of therapists internationally. The International Congresses on Ericksonian Approaches to Therapy sponsored by the Milton H. Erickson Foundation in Phoenix, Arizona, have provided further dissemination of Erickson's material worldwide, as have an increasing number of therapist-trainers. Recognizing such a broad range of impact, it is the purpose of this chapter to provide an understanding of Erickson's influence on the practice of family therapy and to examine relevant aspects of current methods of Ericksonian family therapy.

The Ericksonian–strategic approach is a method of working with clients that emphasizes common, even unconscious, natural abilities and talents. This is in distinct contrast to traditional individually oriented approaches that place an emphasis on dysfunctional aspects of clients in an attempt to analyze, interpret, or develop insight for them during therapy sessions. Instead, it works to frame change in ways that reduce resistance, reduce dependence on therapy, bypass the need for insight, and expand creative adjustment to developmental demands, while removing the presenting problem and allowing families to take full credit for changes achieved in therapy.

There does not seem to be any singular or identifiable influence in the development of Erickson's thinking—certainly not in the way that he has become an identifiable influence for so many of his students. Early in his life, he had expressed an interest in medicine, and as a college student, he was quite intrigued by a stage show he once witnessed using hypnosis. He later studied hypnosis with Clark Hull at the University of Wisconsin, although it may have been

Erickson who influenced Hull to study this area (Elizabeth Erickson, personal communication, May 23, 1990). During the mid-1930s, Erickson was interested in Freud's notion of the unconscious and its influence on behavior. Erickson's early research focused on tracing a client's symptomatic presentation or neurosis to its origin in the past. Later in his development, Erickson was to shift his focus from historical causes of symptoms to the present functioning and day-to-day interactions of clients. During his medical studies at the University of Wisconsin, as a psychiatric resident in Colorado, and, of course, in his later professional life, Erickson seemed to have been drawn to eclectic thinking (Elizabeth Erickson, personal communication, May 23, 1990). Eclecticism and pragmatism could be considered the major influences on Erickson's development.

RATIONALE AND PHILOSOPHY

Strategic therapy credits Milton Erickson (1901-1980) as its source and inspiration. Erickson's work spanned 50 years and 30,000 people. (Lankton and Lankton, 1983, p. xiii) who came from a broad background; rich, poor; single, married; adult, children; "neurotic," "psychotic"; inpatient, outpatient; urban, rural; and educated, illiterate. Derived from and used with this rich diversity, there are several tenets that affect the practice of therapy as well as the way in which problems and people are viewed.

Since problems are not thought to be "inside" a person's head, there is a depathologizing of people (Fisch, 1990). Problems are thought to be the result of trying to move toward a more normal state in an unfolding life cycle (Haley, 1973, p. 150). Consequently, assessment is an activity that frames the presenting problem in terms of the developmental and interpersonal climate experienced by all the individuals in the family. Likewise, therapy is directed toward helping family members contribute to a creative rearrangement of their relationships so that developmental growth is maximized. Accompanying the reduction of the pathology-oriented assessment is a corresponding reduction in so-called resistance.

Additionally, in Ericksonian family therapy,

the therapist is active and shares responsibility for initiating therapeutic movement and "creating a context in which change can take place" (Dammann, 1982). This is often facilitated by introducing conversational material into the therapy session and by the use of extramural assignments. That is, a therapist may not wait until clients spontaneously bring up material, but may invite or challenge clients to grow and change by creating a context in which it can occur.

Ericksonian family therapy is interested in getting clients active and moving (Zeig, 1980). This movement must be in their lives outside the office. Assignments are given in order to have clients carry out agreed-upon behaviors between the sessions. Hypnotherapy and the use of anecdotes, therapeutic metaphors, and indirect suggestions are ways of conversing with clients to help create the impetus during sessions to carry out new relational behaviors or congruently engage in the homework assignments. It is from the learning brought by new actions and not from insight or understanding that change develops. It may be, in fact, that "change leads to insight" (Dammann, 1985, p. 195). Consequently, clients' understanding of or insight about a problem is not of central importance. The matters of central importance are the clients' participation in new experiences and transactions in which they congeal developmentally appropriate relational patterns.

Utilization is a term that Erickson used to depict his approach in two important areas. One is the here-and-now use of material presented by the client. If a family member demonstrates relaxation, tension, talkativeness, silence, questioning, passivity, movement, stillness, fear, confidence, and so on, it is to be accepted and used to further the therapeutic movement in a natural way. Tension and "resistance" are not seen as or labeled as such, but are accepted and in some manner used to facilitate a context for change. If a mother, father, and child cling closely to one another, rather than attempting to separate them spatially and calling their resultant hesitation or anxiety "resistance," the therapist may ask them to let the child hold them even closer together with each arm as the interview takes place. This is using the here-and-now behavior to increase the joining and the comfort of the client as well as to reduce the

discomfort or anxiety that any other intervention would create.

The second manner in which utilization is intended to be understood applies to using the potential abilities each client brings to the session.[1] Using the latent resources of each person will allow for a rich diversity in a "typical" family-therapy session. Each person, for instance, can fantasize, recall, regress, anticipate, relax, forget, imagine, alter consciousness, and so on, and, using these natural abilities, the client and therapist can cooperate in developing a wide range of helpful contexts for change. It follows from the utilization approach that therapists must "speak the clients' own experiential language" and "meet them at their model of the world" (Lankton & Lankton, 1983, p. 5).

Indirection is an orientation to offering ideas that Erickson developed in the last few decades of his career. It became a well-known principle of his approach (Rossi, 1980a; Haley, 1963, 1973, 1976; Watzlawick, Weakland, & Fisch, 1974; Fisch et al., 1982; Lankton & Lankton, 1983). One aspect of indirection is the latitude it provides for each family member's own experience and thinking. The ambiguity can give rise to a degree of pleasant mental excitement or curiosity about change. Rather than detracting from communication, ambiguity enhances it. This applies not only to hypnosis, but also to normal communication conducted with families in waking-state conversation.

Ericksonian therapy is future oriented and is centered on an integration of family and hypnotherapy, though these areas are often seen as extremes with very little convergence. Erickson's approach grew in these two areas independently as it provided examples for the philosophical work of Bateson and other epistemological thinkers who emphasized the need to depart from a model of linear causality associated with the medical model of therapy.[2]

---

[1] *Editors' Note.* As will later become clear, the Ericksonian therapist facilitates clients' use of their change abilities *indirectly*. In this, they certainly differ from behavioral family therapists' emphasis on explicit and direct coaching and instruction, and yet they share the same kind of optimism about people's capacities to change.

[2] *Editors' Note.* Indeed, Ericksonian family therapy is an example par excellence of the untapped possibilities for conceptually and technically integrating "individual" and "systemic" treatment methods.

BACKGROUND

In 1952, Bateson's research project on communication elected to investigate Erickson's work since he, more than any other therapist known to the team, was concerned with how people change (Haley, 1985a). Erickson's pragmatic contributions were appreciated by the aesthetically oriented Bateson (Keeney, 1983) and the other members of the research project—John Weakland, Jay Haley, Don Jackson, and William Fry. The group recognized this in the important 1956 paper, "Toward a Theory of Schizophrenia" (Jackson, 1968a), wherein Bateson, Jackson, Haley, and Weakland discussed examples of Erickson's work. Subsequently, members of the clinically oriented Mental Research Institute (MRI) continued to cite Erickson for several years (Bateson, 1972; Haley, 1963, 1967; Jackson, 1968a, 1968b; Satir, 1964) as they developed family therapy. Under the later direction of Watzlawick, Weakland, and Fisch, MRI continued to provide robust models for ideas and techniques from Erickson's work throughout the 1970s, especially as they related to change in human systems and brief strategic therapy. Much of Erickson's work was simultaneously attended to by hypnotherapists, as he was the founder of the American Society of Clinical Hypnosis, in 1957, and editor for 10 years of the *American Journal of Clinical Hypnosis.*

As the Bateson team attempted to articulate a transactional approach to therapy, Haley (1963) published a remarkable work elucidating many examples of Erickson's "strategic therapy" work with both individuals and couples. It seems clear in retrospect that Erickson's work contained some of the sparks of inspiration regarding an emerging approach and an emerging language in therapy. It will be useful to summarize some aspects of the traditional approach as it offers a background against which Erickson's contributions will be contrasted (Dell, 1985; Keeney, 1983; Maturana & Varela, 1987). In this way, we can provide a better understanding of the importance of family-therapy work derived from his influence.

The traditional approach follows thinking that gave rise to Cartesian thought and Newtonian physics. Bateson (1972) once attempted to clarify this: "The difference between the Newtonian world and the world of communication is simply this: that the Newtonian world ascribes reality to objects and achieves its simplicity by excluding the context . . . In contrast, the theorist of communication insists upon examining the metarelationships while achieving its simplicity by excluding all objects" (p. 250). In several essays throughout his last decade of life, Bateson (1972) wrestled with the illusive problems of epistemology and ontology and their relationship to then-conventional therapy.

Conventional therapy was based on an assumption that there is an objective truth that might be attained by observation, separate from any influence on the observed persons. It includes belief in an observable and objective reality that is thought to be independent of our efforts to observe it. This line of thinking is in keeping with the contributions of Descartes (the universe is a great machine we can know by observing it) and by his student Newton.

A leading thinker of the age of enlightenment was Immanuel Kant. In 1781, he published *Critique of Pure Reason*, which supplied one of the most comprehensive treatises that suggested that people, by observing, create order in the universe. Order may not be present until one observes, and certainly reasoning about that which was presumably observed offers no further certainty. Kant's treatise preceded Freud's *Studies on Hysteria* by 115 years but Freud (1938, 1966) was not favorably influenced by it. In 1923, Freud (1966) took exception to Kant's premise: "There is nothing in the id that could be compared with negation; and we perceive with surprise an exception to the philosophical theorem that space and time are necessary forms of our mental acts" (p. 538).

With this emphasis, the entire profession of therapy was to be influenced by the belief, common to psychoanalysis, that we could know the truth of a separate reality and that acts of observation did not alter this external reality. The posture toward reality was separation from it—studying it by reduction. The simple act of reducing and labeling seems innocent enough, but it does not credit the "observer" with the action of inventing the label that is applied. Consequently, traditional therapy, in its attempts to search for problems rooted in the past, has developed a rich language to describe the intrapsychic domain of single individuals. This description often pathologizes the individual and typically excludes his or her present life context.

The therapeutic stance of "separateness," pathology orientation, and search for problems may result in an adversarial position being taken.[3] The language of therapy reflects this adversarial position with metaphors of resistance, conflict, defense, hidden motive, suppression, power, and so on. No one has spoken more eloquently than Szasz (1961) and Laing (1967, 1972) about the individual and social injuries that are the by-products of attempting to help within such a framework. Placed in an adversarial position, purposefully or inadvertently, labeled individuals will easily demonstrate more behavior that will reinforce a therapist's conviction about the independent existence of an internal pathology. It was this very trend that Erickson wished to avoid throughout his career (Erickson, 1985).

Erickson suggested that traditional therapy made clients lie in the proverbial "Procrustean bed" of theory by cutting off their legs or stretching them on the racks to make clients fit. He frustrated his students from time to time by stating that he did not have a theory of human personality (Lankton & Lankton, 1983). His approach has demanded that therapists rethink their adherence to such structural models. We find instead that he alerted us to ideas about how to interact to help people change. The Ericksonian approach aims at being scrupulously unique with each client. Each question, silence, discussion, metaphor, paradoxical directive, and the like, must be delivered with an ongoing sensitivity to the special needs of the listener. For example, a therapeutic metaphor may elicit a grief reaction from one individual while the same story at another time or to another individual may not have the same result. Likewise, interventions are changed slightly for each individual and each goal, and it is in the uniqueness rather than in the commonality that the therapeutic bond is forged. Therapies built upon

traditional paradigms are built upon generalizations about individuals and the most successful Ericksonian approaches are built upon a recognition of the uniqueness of individuals.

THE HEALTHY, WELL-FUNCTIONING MARRIAGE AND FAMILY

Functional roles are distinguished from gender roles in that they pertain to "who does what" rather than "who is what." One of the common understandings among Ericksonian family therapists is based on a pragmatic sense that "getting a job done" is more important than "who is supposed to do the job." That is, there is no such thing as "men's work" and "women's work"; instead, there is "our work." Each person in the family is expected to contribute to the jobs of family maintenance, of course, but perhaps more important, each person is encouraged to recognize the contributions, whether unique or not, of all other persons. Minor problems are solved through the pragmatic negotiation of "what needs to be done and who can do it most appropriately."

How Problems Are Solved

As each developmental stage introduces a need to adjust aspects of life-style, it may be that each day introduces a need to make small changes in behavior. These adjustments can be major problems in families—although they are seldom the problems recognized by their conscious dialogues. Each of these changes, in our model, is problem-solving behavior or can be a "resource" in general. Major problems are solved by the acquisition and automatization of the skills and resources required for these daily and developmental adaptations.

The concept of *automatization* correctly suggests that these skills will become unconscious. For instance, the newly married couple needs to be able to use thousands of experiences and communications that were not demanded by the previous environment. These include various kinds of caring, expressing hope, visualizing a positive future, confiding certain insecurities, keeping secrets, and so on. All of these skills,

---

[3] *Editors' Note.* We disagree with the authors on this; that is, contrary to the view, often in our opinion overstated, that such a "separateness" position destines the therapist–patient relationship to become an adversarial one, we see that, not infrequently, it facilitates therapeutic joining, empathy, and mutual goal setting in that patients themselves often have such a "pathology orientation."

while not defined by institutions of socialization, themselves comprise numerous processes of perception, cognition, and visceral experience. Given this situation, there must be thousands of such intimacy-building experiences and transactions that the system will demand of each member of the couple in the early stage of marital development (and of each family member at all stages of development). It is assumed that since the environment is likely to demand these behaviors and transactions, each person attempts to learn and use these skills in a relevant and unique way. Learning methods are unique in each family. Most of these skills are acquired without conscious awareness mediating the process. Involvement in daily socialization processes builds these constellations of experience without much examination or deliberation.

Each person, then, relies on internal resources (experience, urges, memory, fantasy, ideas, etc.) as he or she attempts to adjust to life's daily demands. Simultaneously, each person is part of the environment that makes demands on the others in the family (along with family of origin, work, school, neighborhood contacts, bills, etc.). Thus, creative problem solving comes from maintaining relations that allow for flexibility in stimulating one another's personal resources. Rigidity or redundancy is not likely to be as useful in providing the creative mix needed for developmental transitions. However, many sorts of continuance and redundancy will be essential. For example, ongoing nurture and support from a parent of an infant and redundant joining behaviors (e.g., smiling, eye contact, and touching) contribute to the secure atmosphere needed to engage in problem solving.

Growth of an Adaptive, Functioning Family

To illustrate the process of growth and development, Erickson once described his son's first date. Summarizing, he said that his son told him they had stopped at the malt shop for a milk shake. Erickson added, "And some mucous-membrane stimulation." Then the son and his date went to the skating rink. Erickson added, "And some rhythmical physical activity." Then back to the malt shop for a hamburger with all the relishes and "some more mucous-membrane stimulation." He said that when his son came home, he reported that he had been to the malt shop and skating rink, "but I knew what he had really been doing; he had been looking at that girl, touching her, and having mucous-membrane stimulation and rhythmical physical activity" (Erickson, personal communication, 1975)!

While this is a humorous anecdote, it also illustrates human development as including accomplishments that are usually outside of normal awareness. Yet, witnessing this unconscious level of skill acquisition provides an informative facet to socialization and ultimately to developmental growth.

From this perspective, we see that people continually organize ever-more-complex constellations of visceral, perceptual, and cognitive processes. While consciously each individual family member may be under the impression that a certain problem is the focus of concern, we may see that, at the unconscious level, a rather different purpose is being served.

Growth and change at the unconscious level are accomplished by one of two general processes. People stimulate one another (1) to organize still more complex and appropriate ways of adapting or (2) to disorganize and reorganize new constellations of experience and transactions. The former especially applies to the learning paradigm of children and the latter especially to individuals who have learned limits that inhibit their experience (Rossi, 1980b, p. 100). This learning may take place at unconscious levels or at conscious levels. Children learn the expression of aggressive and affectionate behaviors from parents through modeling, for instance (Bandura, 1969). Conscious learning includes such behavior as deliberate acts of memorization, imitation, and rehearsal. Both levels of learning are continual in families and may reinforce or inhibit one another, depending on unique circumstances.

Affection and sexuality in a family are expressed according to the convention and norms of the time (Erickson, 1978, personal communication). Of course, a generational boundary will separate subgroups of parents and children and determine differences for the expression of affection and sexual desire accordingly. Intimacy and separateness among family members would also change over time as the developmental requirements and cultural expectancies change in the family. Levels of emotional openness among members could be intense and would be modulated according to social convention and developmental sophistication—just as in every ethical model of family functioning.

Boundaries and Alliances in Organization of the Family

Although Ericksonians do not normally speak of boundaries in the family as Salvador Minuchin would, we do speak about the more tangible process that includes experiences kept private to the individual, those kept between the marital dyad, and those that are kept among members of the child subsystem. Certain behaviors will be allowable or positively sanctioned between some family members and will be punished or discouraged between others. The family as a unit is also seen as entitled to set rules and to keep private information that is not made available to members of the extended family and the families of origin. Contact between any dyadic pair ought to be permissible. In general, there is nothing different or outstanding in the Ericksonian model of family interaction other than that which is legal, ethical, and permissible in each cultural subgroup found in America.

WHEN FAMILIES HAVE PROBLEMS

Interactional Nature of Problems

The major influence of Erickson's work was, as mentioned, to take people out of the pathology-oriented framework. Behavior may be identified as undesirable by family members or as "pathological" by mental health personnel, but this is only a label affixed to a strip of behavior in a particular context. While it may be easier to converse about behavior by referring to it as "healthy" or "pathological," these terms carry a certain "baggage" that includes a heavy price. It is our belief that placing a pejorative label on individuals or families does not contribute to the effectiveness of therapy and may actually inhibit possibilities for change. We will instead attempt to approach the question of how people in families adapt to and solve problems in general; that is, how they act whether or not someone considers the process problematic or pathological.

Perhaps the most appropriate way to decide whether problems exist in the family is to ask the family. The consciously defined purpose or goals for each person's behavior may be narrow compared with the potential and creative adaptation that is possible. A simple example is found in those families who present a child as problematic and who narrowly define the appropriate and available roles for each child according to gender—such as girls are nurses, not doctors. Creating the idea of expanded roles may have a significant effect on the presenting problem.

In another example, a wife sought therapy, complaining that her husband was not close and withheld security from her. She agreed that, in turn, she withheld sexual contact from him. When the husband responded to her sorrow and tears with a pledge to be close and to show his emotional self to her as she desired, she said she did not believe him. In conversing with the couple on only this one feature in their relationship, we can realize that each spouse's perceptions and thoughts about the other formed a self-fulfilling prophecy.

If the husband wishes to be close to his wife for the various pleasures and rewards of intimacy (smiles, supportive statements, empathy, eye contact, joy, sexual contact, etc.), he can see that his efforts will probably not pay off. She essentially rebuffs and punishes his overtures. Although it is possible that he might continually attempt to convince her of his attention until she is convinced, it is more likely that he will simply stop trying: a punishing atmosphere is not a fertile soil in which to grow the seeds of emotional expression and intimacy.

As a contributory part of this vicious circle, she learned not to reach out to another person, especially when she feels sad or unacceptable. The husband had learned to show affection by joking and to handle his general anxieties by keeping them to himself, while he quietly watched television. When his wife sensed that he had anxieties but withdrew from her, she concluded that she somehow was not worthy or was unacceptable to him. In turn, she attempted to solve that problem by feeling a sadness and not reaching out to him. One might say, metaphorically, that she appeared to be a sad child, sulking and waiting for her parents to notice her and make amends. Ironically, her husband did not notice such behavior as a plea for attention. He took quiet withdrawal as a suitable way to solve problems and, in a sense, he appreciated her lack of neediness. He did not like the lack of sexual contact that came as a result, but he could not understand or respond to the wife's sulking as she would have liked. Of course, as long as he complained about the lack of sexual contact and continued not to "open up" to her when she sulked, she gathered further evidence that she was unloved and unwanted—she felt insecure and she reported that he was withholding security.

With this couple, we could conclude that the enormous range of problem-solving resources that might be used is being reduced by conscious mind limitations of perceptual "filters," beliefs, and the redundancy that comes from using the same behavioral expressions, mannerisms, and words. There are so many ways that each of them could change the scenario: the husband could release his tensions as tears, the wife could ask for attention for her sadness, the wife could reach out and hug him when she feels distant, the husband could "smother" her with nurturing when he sees her sulk for attention. Some of these solutions may be better than others in the sense that they open up doorways for future growth, and others, while they are solutions, only solve the immediate problem but do nothing to change the frame in which the problem occurs.

The complexity of unconscious resources that could come together to create one of the above solutions is more diverse still. Consider the wife's choosing to ask for attention when she is sad and feeling unaccepted. This choice could be motivated by memories of herself being ignored by her father (she could tell her husband how sad she was as a child and elicit his sympathy and support in this metaphoric solution); she could motivate herself with encouraging self-talk (stating something about how she deserved to reach out, that she was worth it and she would

give it a try); she could conclude that her husband really wants her to be active when he is quiet and withdrawn (that is his way of telling her that he wants her to approach him); or she could nurture the husband and help shape his behavior into a more emotionally expressive mode; and so on.

Each of these solutions takes a different set of visceral, cognitive, memory, behavioral, and perceptual resources. Her previous learning most likely contains the bits and pieces of unconscious experience that would make up any one of these possible ways of solving the problem. Likewise, the husband could solve the problem by changes in any number of regrouping of unconscious tools in just the same manner as that detailed for the wife. Better still, each might attempt to reorganize his or her experience so that the spouses gain mutually reinforcing changes at the levels of unconscious urge, perception, cognition, behavior, expectation, role, and, finally, family organization.

For our purposes, resources are all those previous experiences, behaviors, feelings, beliefs, and perceptions that have contributed to the client's adaptability, some of which may be known to the client and some of which may not be immediately obvious. Erickson would often use whatever the client presented as a potential resource for change. For example, with a woman who perceived the space between her front teeth to be a horrible disfigurement, Erickson had her learn to spit water between her teeth, which he later used as a basis for an important social interaction (Haley, 1973). Her initially percieved "disfigurement" became a resource.

The assumption that clients have bits and pieces of experiences (resources) needed to solve a present problem is based on our assessment of clients (discussed in greater detail under "Assessment"). In our clinical experience, we have observed that while many clients may not have, or perceive that they do not have, all the resources to resolve an immediate issue, such as nurturance in the aforementioned couple, they typically have subsets of related resources, such as friendly behavior to co-workers, tenderness toward a sibling or friend, or feeling comforted by a parent. With these existing experiences as a positive foundation, we seek to develop the specific and sometimes larger resources needed for problem resolution in the marital or family system.[4]

How Problems Can Develop

There are four interrelated processes that occur at all times:

1. People have various unique resources to use in all situations.
2. Resources form the behaviors by which we communicate.
3. As people communicate, they evoke various resources and behaviors in others, who simultaneously evoke various resources and behaviors in them.
4. This interactive process continues on a moment-by-moment basis and changes the resources and communication as it does.

For example, as a teenager, one of our clients was not allowed to communicate in affiliative and tender ways with either parent. He remembered his mother as superficial and his father as cold, rigid, and strong. He feared his father and the result was that he did not allow himself to express sexual behaviors. His parents may have communicated this apprehension to the child in any one of a number of ways, including outright noxious stimulus (shouting) or punishment (withholding privileges), or it may have been defined by the parent as outside of the acceptable role for children in the family (role limiting) or the parent may have expressed a belief that any sexual conduct is reprehensible (cognitive framing). Behavior by the client attempting to gain sanction from either parent required that he somehow inhibit sexual urges, or the perceptions of tenderness, or thoughts about the

need for either experience, as well as sexually expressive behaviors, affects, and the integration of this total package of sexual experiences (or all of the above) into a role. It is not the role definitions, behaviors, or beliefs per se that are the causes of the conflict, but the existence of the whole package—the inhibiting communication, the biological and social demands, and the available experiential resources for a solution.

Although this history was actually shared by the young man and his father, it is, in a way, a hypothetical example. It is a reconstruction of the past filtered through their available memories and needs. The situation may serve to illustrate unsatisfying growth. *Growth is accomplished by associating conscious and unconscious experiences in ever-more-complex constellations.* These complex associations become "experiential building blocks" that provide the foundation upon which we maximize social, biological, and subjective satisfaction and communicate with others.

Certain adjustments may seem to furnish the building blocks for one phase of life but adversely influence the choices we make at another phase. One major reason for this adverse influence is that certain creative adjustments can be difficult or impossible without the earlier "experiential building blocks" or without the proper environmental stimuli to evoke needed resources.

Thus, the young man's adjustment that seemed most appropriate in childhood may be characterized as depression in adolescence—a suppressing of developing age-appropriate erotic and sexual perceptions (personal needs) in favor of attending to the sanctions or needs of others (parents). This particular adjustment however, contributed remarkably to a problem that threatened the existence of his new family a decade later when his wife complained of his lack of intimacy. The easy and creative adjustment of intimacy between the spouses was limited since it needed to be built upon certain earlier experiences or evoked by communication the wife had not learned to express. The lack of emotional openness and intimacy was not only the husband's "problem." Certainly, the behavior used by each spouse to build this intimacy with each other helped or limited each person's use of the set of experiential building blocks he

---

[4] *Editors' Note.* It fascinates us to see how (and how often) linguistic differences between therapists can lead to the impression of actual differences in clinical conceptualization. Here, for example, when the authors speak of the "resources" patients have, but which are not being used, we believe they are referring *precisely* to the distinction behavior therapists make between problems of "response acquisition" (roughly, not knowing how to do something) and "response performance," (which implies that the person "knows"/has learned the response, but that it is under such stimulus control that it does not appear (often enough) under specific (often, environmental/interpersonal) conditions of concern.

or she had. The wife took his lack of approach as indifference and said she did not like it; the husband construed her complaints as criticism and kept at a distance from her.

These two ways of looking at how a problem can develop (from limited use of personal experience or from communication that evokes behavior that was not wanted) are really just two sides of the same coin, but together they may help clarify the interplay of personal resources and social elicitation, personal response to elicitation, personal response influencing subsequent elicitation, and so on. Ultimately, no particular adjustment ought to be seen as final since environmental demands for creativity in later years may be far more complex, sophisticated, and subtle than could have ever been anticipated in one's earlier life.

This is not just a cross-generational transmission of a problem. Consider, too, that the father and the son were deprived of certain learnings and joys due to the son's adjustment with depression. It is impossible to measure the effect such loss had on the family of origin at the time it was occurring. And, too, it is hard to measure the impact of this loss of learning by all members on others in the social network in the years that follow: The father did not substantially alter the way he acted with the next four boys who were born. The depressed boy, as a teen, took to frightening his younger brother several times a week in the presence of his peers. The boy who was frightened never learned to ask for assistance in solving the myriad of life's little problems. He subsequently was convicted of a felony and served a prison sentence.

The work with this family was unusual in that this session lasted for more than four hours. During this time, the family members invited the first author to be blunt in his assessment of them, which he was. The therapist suggested to them that they had not developed the resources to be connected and affiliative (e.g., tender, caring, gentle) with each other. He then offered direct and indirect suggestions and metaphors focusing on the feelings and behaviors associated with affiliation. Each person was instructed to practice specific affiliative behaviors in the session. As a result of this work with all four grown brothers and their father, all but one of them embraced each other, cried, and stated that they had never said, "I love you," to any other family member before that day. One can only wonder how every member of that family might have grown up differently if the father and the first son had solved their intimacy problem before the other sons were born. There is no simple and linear connection that traces the etiology of a problem. Rather, the nuclear family is more like a nuclear reaction, with each experience and transaction stimulating the other. In total, each person brings a set of resources to the next developmental task and the interplay continues.

Symptom Formation and Identified Patients

We have come to think of a presenting problem as representing one of two possibilities: (1) as metaphoric, that is, an attempt to solve a class of problems of which it is itself a member; or (2) as a problem that stands for itself. A simple example of the latter is the client who develops a snake phobia as a result of some unpleasant interaction with a snake. In the case of the former, symptoms can develop from attempts to solve developmental problems with skills that will not do the job in an environment that is not helping people use the tools and potentials they have most efficiently. In this instance, "symptoms are forms of communication. As such, symptoms are frequently important signs or cues of developmental problems that are in the process of becoming conscious" (Erickson & Rossi, 1979, p. 143). That is, a husband may repeatedly insist that the family organization allow him the luxury of being unquestioned. During courtship, this arrangement may have seemed attractive to his wife-to-be, but after marriage and during childbearing stages of development, such an arrangement is unlikely to be suited to the wife. However, the rule of family organization may prescribe the continuance of this mode of problem solving. If environmental situations require attention to needs the wife has, the family's style of interaction is not sensitive to that requirement. Perhaps at this time the overcompliance of the wife will become an anxiety symptom that is brought to therapy. Alternatively, a child may begin an exaggerated and extended crying episode or perhaps experience encopresis. A husband may develop a presenting problem of "blackouts" or a bridge phobia. In a manner of speaking, any of these symptoms may serve to indicate that the behaviors that have customarily been used to solve familial problems are not working and someone is overusing an inappropriate tool for the job. How one determines the difference between a presenting problem as a symptom and as a problem that stands for itself is a result of the assessment of the history of the problem, the attempted solutions, and the problem's function within the family system.[5]

Factors Influencing the Type of Symptom

Communication in the family and the larger ecosystem provides each individual with the necessary clues on how to develop a symptom. The actual selection of a symptom is a complex and mysterious matter. It would be an extreme oversimplification to say that the symptom is "caused" by a given behavior or sequence of behaviors. Instead, we must remember that all experience (or at least most experience) in a family is negotiated as in the above scenario: a symptomatic display is determined by a complex interaction of communication, historical use, physical health, and perhaps serendipity or random change. It may be the overuse of a problem-solving behavior (since other resources are underdeveloped or prohibited) or it may be the system's reaction to the underuse of other resources. All the while, family members continue to communicate and inadvertently shape experience.

Berne (1972) has discussed and documented a phenomenon of communication that may contribute to the rise of specific symptoms. In a family where "colorful" metaphors for solving problems were centered around the anal sphincter (e.g., "he's tight," "this is a pain in the ass," "kick in the butt," etc.), it might be expected that problems related to the anal sphincter would arise (encopresis, spastic colon, diverticulosis, etc.).[6] We think of the communication

in a family as continually framing events, focusing awareness, and evoking experience. In these ways, it parallels the intense aspect of hypnotic communication. Berne and Laing share Erickson's more pervasive definition of hypnosis, and actually state that important limitations on using certain problem-solving behavior are attributable to the hypnotic effect of the family of origin. Berne (1972) states, "The child is, in effect, hypnotized by his parent into carrying out a certain life pattern" (p. 343), while Laing (1967), writing extensively about how we learn to place limits on our problem solving, states, "One is likely to find that the child is being induced to behavior as he is by tactile-kinetic-olfactory-visual signals: and that this is part of a 'secret' communications network, dissociated from the official verbal communiques." Laing (1972) concludes by saying, "The clinical hypnotist knows what he is doing; the family hypnotist almost never" (p. 80).

What Laing attributes exclusively to the family of origin, he might have extended to all current socializing institutions, which, of course, includes the current family unit. Indeed, the behavior, both physical and social, of experimental subjects who have been instructed to carry out posthypnotic tasks seems closely to resemble many of the behaviors seen in family members at times when compulsive symptomatic behavior is being carried out (Rossi, 1980a, p. 390).

Although it seems reasonable that all members of a system who know of a problem share it in some way, it is also likely that some people in a family are functioning with fewer limits on their experience than are others. Therefore, some individuals will appear healthier than others even though all members may be said to share the problem.

The individual who is obviously symptomatic may have chosen, or may seem to have been chosen in this way, to operate beyond the allowed behavioral and experiential limits (as defined by himself or herself or others). Some symptoms we see in family therapy are beyond the range normally considered voluntary, whereas others involve actions normally thought to be voluntary (for instance, panic attacks are usually considered involuntary while extramarital affairs are usually considered voluntary). However, the issue of free will is not really the

---

[5] *Editors' Note.* To use an old refrain, sometimes a cigar is just a cigar. Sometimes, we think that too many family therapists too often have difficulty recognizing cigars.

[6] *Editors' Note.* Note also that the presence of some problems that "stand for themselves," of which certain physiological dysfunctions may be examples, can *lead to* the use of such metaphors, as well as mirror them.

point. The issue, in the Ericksonian approach, is helping families delimit the problem solving used at each developmental stage. Consequently, the "truth" of how symptoms arise is far less important than how creative adaptation can arise.

ASSESSMENT OF SYSTEM FUNCTIONING

Unit Levels of Assessment

Assessment must, to some degree, involve a family-system context even when an individual seeks therapy for a symptom that he or she considers separate from any family influence. An interpersonal-developmental framework is the lens through which all problems presented for therapy are examined. Within this framework, individual, dyadic, triadic, family-system, and extended-system units of influence are considered. A family, an individual, or an organization of any size can be viewed as going through continuous cycles of stability and instability in traversing stages of interpersonal development. For example, at the family level, the birth of a child or the relocation of a home marks a period of noticeable instability when contrasted with times that are characterized by homogenous routines and a relative redundancy of daily-living patterns. For the individual, graduation from college, a new job, and physical illness are examples of such unstable periods. Even here, however, the larger context of family-of-origin or extended-system influences must be assessed.

The family cycle of stability/instability is most often initiated by the changes brought on by requirements of particular developmental stages. At each new stage of development, novel experiences or alterations in the usual types of experiences and transactions must be learned. For instance, when the birth of a baby signals a change in the family to the child-raising stage of development, hundreds of new experiences, transactions, and behaviors must be learned: postponing one's gratifications for the sake of the child's needs, learning to ask for help with the child, being able to experience joy in the child's

growth, acquiring a vast array of caretaking skills, and so forth.

If these experiences are readily available as resources resulting from previous learnings, the disorganization within the family system is relatively short and the transition to new organization is relatively easy. Conversely, to the extent that the resources are not available, the disorganization becomes more debilitating. Resolutions to the disorganization will come eventually with the implementation of problem-solving mechanisms and techniques used individually and collectively by the members of the family.

Although Ericksonian family therapists do not rigidly require a specific grouping of family members for diagnosis, most therapists prefer that they participate in conversations and displays of the "problem" behaviors or presenting complaints. This allows first-hand knowledge to be acquired about how members punctuate ongoing experience, how it is labeled, and how it is altered by each person's view of reality. It gives an immediate display of the flexibility or limits used by each family member to solve the situation he or she perceives to be "a situation." Most logically, then, the members of the primary marital dyad ought to be present and communicating with each other about the goals during assessment phases. Also, they need to be present to communicate with any of the "identified patients" about goals and "problems" during this same period.

Psychological Levels of Assessment

When we meet an individual, couple, or family, we set assessment goals that will facilitate our understanding of that system on at least four arbitrary levels of functioning. As shown in Figure 8-1, these levels include family organization, social roles, communication and behavior (including emotional), and beliefs as they define and limit the use of unconscious resources. Each of these interactive dynamics can be seen as influencing the others, with the highest level of complexity being represented by the level of family structure. Thus, such an assessment helps to organize our thinking about the complexity of experiences and transactions in the family that can maintain the problem. The *family organi-*

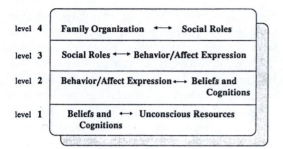

level **4**	Family Organization ⟷ Social Roles
level **3**	Social Roles ⟷ Behavior/Affect Expression
level **2**	Behavior/Affect Expression ⟷ Beliefs and Cognitions
level **1**	Beliefs and Cognitions ⟷ Unconscious Resources

Figure 8-1. Problem-solving levels

zation delineates the degree of role diversity that is possible for its members. In assessing a family system, we look at the various roles being played and listen for the type of role-defining transactions that have, of course, occurred countless times and in a multitude of ways prior to these roles becoming typical. These transactions can occur as verbally stated beliefs, perceptual predispositions, behavioral modeling, physical abuse, and so on.

The *social roles* that have been defined for each member can be seen as limiting and influencing the communications of individuals within the system. We use the term "communication" to refer to verbal, nonverbal, emotional, and behavioral aspects of transacting. If family structure does not allow or encourage a particular member to develop a role for being assertive, aggressive, or angry, for example, that member will not be able to generate communications congruent with solving problems in that manner. To the extent that not playing this role is a firmly engraved expectation and learning, then even an occasional transaction of demanding anything from anyone, even in response to blatant wrongdoing, will not be an acceptable option. Members learn to play particular roles and their communications can be seen to be congruent only in these roles.

Such communications are assessed as the interface between roles allowed by the family and the level of *beliefs and unconscious resources.* The kinds of communications that members are allowed, that which they rehearse to themselves and for which they are reinforced for delivering, determine the kinds of belief systems they then formulate. Self-images are consolidated, often rigidly depicting family members in terms of the selected roles ("That's just the way I am!"). Once this belief system has been formulated, uncon-

scious resources that could mediate contrary experiences will not impinge on the normal waking states of the individuals. Or if they do, they are considered a conflict or an indication that therapy is needed. If a person who believes she is not the kind of person who can have aggressive impulses should become aware of that experience, she will deny those urges. In the same way, a person who believes he cannot be confident in front of a group spends all of his time noticing his lack of confidence when he is in front of groups. A belief is a way of saying, in effect, "This range of experience is the only range of stimuli I can notice."

If we conceptualize family complexity in this way, specific problems presented for therapy are usually described in terms of conflicts taking place among these coexisting elements of these interactive dynamics. For example, conflicts between family organization and role limits might be worded as, "Johnny is not fitting into the family—his school behavior is disruptive." Problems between role limits and available communications might be expressed as, "I am so ashamed of my conduct," or, "Johnny has not been himself lately since he's been running with these older boys." Problems of incongruence between allowed communication/behavior and held beliefs might be expressed as, "I don't know how to be happy," "I'm anxious all the time," "It's just my nerves," and so on. Conflict at this level also includes the absence or presence of communication/behaviors (including emotional behaviors) that are not in keeping with the conscious belief system. An example is someone who believes he or she should perform better (absence of behavior) or a person who shows every sign of strongly suppressed emotional reactions (presence of behavior). Still another way of expressing such a conflict is, "I don't cry—I can't cry." In these statements, we see the recurrence or absence of a behavior that, in turn, reinforces a belief and shapes a perceptual predisposition.

One of the most important aspects of assessment is the interpersonal impact of communications. Since each person's selection of communication is largely outside of awareness, careful therapist attention to these behaviors is very informative and includes more than interpersonal skills. For instance, a person who greets others with a warm smile and is also capable of releasing the smile demonstrates a skill of taking information from external sources. But the person who cannot release the smile suggests difficulty and communicates in such a way as negatively to influence problem solving and the use of personal resources within the dyad. In this example, the facility of memory, external orientation, and anticipated difficulty all have an important bearing on problem solving, one well beyond the strict interpersonal dimension in which they were detected. Yet, they could be ascertained by the family members' interpersonal postures with one another and with the therapist.

Testing Tools and Typical Observations

In some cases, an extensive assessment phase necessarily may be preceded by such pragmatic activities as establishing sufficient rapport, determining how to communicate with a client in a way that we understand, reducing a crisis, and recognizing clients' motivation for therapy. It is our desire, however, to develop a useful framework in which to think about clients as soon as possible. We can make some generalizations about what we consider a useful framework.

For us, although not representative of all Ericksonian family therapists, an assessment phase includes an intake interview (or, in some cases, even a prior written summary from clients) in which we address four areas: First, the *presenting problem*, as well as the preliminary goals they wish to reach in therapy, is determined. Second, *family organization* is assessed, including a conceptualization of the current stage of development (and related demands), as well as the demands of the next logical stage of development the family will be entering. An understanding is developed of the family's way of explaining typical time structuring, the family's involvement with extended career and social networks, and each person's involvement with the symptom. Particularly, we are interested in how engaging in the symptom represents an adaptive response or "best choice" (Lankton & Lankton, 1983) for the interpersonal and developmental demands currently being encountered.

The third area of the initial assessment involves gathering *background information about the problem itself*. This includes gathering from our conversations with the family a sense of who knows about the problem, how each person in the family responds to the problem, what is being accomplished by having the problem, and what might be accomplished if the problem were not present. We also seek a history of the problem's occurrence and previous treatment received for it. Finally, we acquire cogent *information about the family of origin of each spouse*—we may do this even if it might initially seem unrelated to the specific presenting problem.

The fourth area involves an *analysis of the interactive dynamics* discussed in the previous section. In order to assess the interpersonal orientations as well as perceptive, cognitive, behavioral, and emotional flexibility of each family member with some sense of uniformity, we often ask each person to complete the interpersonal checklist (ICL) (LaForge et al., 1954; Leary, 1957). We ask them to characterize the self as well as the spouse and involved children. Most professionals will assess the interpersonal dimension by various intuitive means. We prefer to fortify our intuition and clinical acumen with the use of the ICL in those cases in which it will not hinder our relationship with the family. While this is not a tool ever used by Erickson (Erickson, E., 1988), we find its problem-solving orientation to be compatible with Erickson's approach.

This checklist consists of 128 adjectives, which are checked as they are considered to be generally characteristic of the self, spouse, or child in at least some situations. Results or raw scores are used to suggest each person's typical interpersonal postures (we do not use the standardized scores). This is discussed in depth elsewhere (Lankton & Lankton, 1986), but we will summarize it here since it will contribute to a better understanding of the interpersonal dimension. The solicited self-report is divided across two axes (or four quadrants), with the vertical axis designating dominant/submissive behaviors (and, we would add, feelings and beliefs) and the horizontal axis denoting affiliative/disaffiliative behavior.

We discuss the graphs with clients only if they are interested. For our information, we compare the completed graphs with each other (e.g., self seen by self vs. self described by spouse) as well as with our own perceptions of the actual people with whom we are interacting. We have found as much agreement between clients' self-reports and how they are seen by others (i.e., family members) as we have found disagreement. Sometimes, although the parents' reports of themselves and each other may be consistent, both of their reports may disagree with the child's report on himself or herself. We may also observe behaviors consistent with a role that a family member is using quite adequately and yet find that, according to this member's subjective self-report, he or she does not identify with adjectives that are often used to describe those role behaviors. In such a case as this, we would be alerted to possible attitudes and beliefs that may prevent a person from acknowledging the interpersonal flexibility that he or she has developed even though it is not consistent with a self-image that has been described by the adjectives.

Rather than being a liability, the range of interpretation afforded by this device provides considerable assessment ideas, regardless of whether family members accurately perceive themselves or not. We are not looking for an absolute "truth," label, or personality type. We are interested in a summary of typical or most preferred interpersonal resources and alternative resources members can use. Conversely, we are also interested in behaviors related to ICL areas (sometimes entire quadrants such as friendly/submissive or dominant/disaffiliative) that, for whatever reason, are largely avoided by the individual. We always consider how the ability to engage in avoided behaviors might contribute to a more satisfactory response to developmental demands and a reduction of the symptoms or complaints.

Information derived from the writing, interview, and self-observed reports contributes to tentative assessment about how it is to live in this particular family structure, with its available roles, behaviors, emotional resources, communication skills, and beliefs. However, these are only hypotheses, and to fill in our initial sense of being in this family, we rely on a structured form of communication among family members to create a context for experiencing some family dynamics in action. Typically, we ask the dyad representing the greatest conflict, distance, or misunderstanding in the system to engage in a

carefully directed sequence of sharing a single short statement and feeling (about their desire, goal, problem, or so on) with the other family member. The second member is asked to repeat accurately both the thought and the feeling conveyed by the partner before engaging in the sharing. That is, the second person responds with another thought and feeling, which the first member must then repeat accurately. In a very short time within the first session, it is usually possible to "track" the typical way in which each member uses communication tools to solve a problem. Members will display how, in this context, they make available communications and behaviors or supporting attitudes, or limit themselves and others with inflexibility—whether perceptual, cognitive, or emotional–behavioral. We refer to this procedure as an "A-B, A-B calibration loop."

Assessment and Treatment Are Inseparable

The initial phase of assessment occurs before the end of the first interview. The calibration procedure just described often creates segues into treatment, which makes the former indistinguishable from the latter. As it clarifies the existence of agreed-upon goals and frames the situation so that it attributes motivation to the clients, the assessment phase *is* also treatment. With some families, of course, accomplishing these assessment goals continues over several sessions. But typically, conversation with the family about these tentative hypotheses has resulted in several specific goals being clarified and other goals being communicated but not verbally clarified within the first session and the phase of treatment dictated by those goals begins.

Assessment is an ongoing process in Ericksonian therapy, however, and as such, it continues to be a consideration throughout therapy in addition to its concentrated emphasis at the outset. It is, therefore an integral part of an Ericksonian therapist's participation with a family. Family members' use of or reaction to each intervention introduced by the therapist yields new and valuable information that influences the setting of additional goals. Furthermore, these reactions may help guide therapy by informing therapists what types of dialogues and assignments might further facilitate change if focused on or introduced into the session.

The Role of the Verbal Interview

A therapist with an ongoing assessment orientation will discover new information about a family in a constantly changing variety of ways, including simple observation–participation, structured interaction, protective responses to metaphor and ambiguous function assignments or skill-building assignments, and home visits, as well as the conventional verbal interview. We do not often utilize home visits, though assessment in social or work settings sometimes takes place and enhances understanding. With some families, we structure a particular activity as an assessment context and sometimes personally accompany or guide clients through it (such as the shy married students whom we accompanied to the library, asking them to research romantic poetry they might wish to read to each other). More often, we outline a task for clients or suggest a context in which they might complete some activity between sessions and ask them to report their problems, accomplishments, or understandings during our subsequent meetings. In this way, assessment of both needed and available resources is often accomplished. It is within the verbal interview that information becomes available to therapists, but a structured interaction serves as the stimulus for the learning. Similarly, a structured interaction task, such as that described above as a calibration loop, can be seen as a component of a verbal interview, with the resulting information being more immediately available to the therapist.

Assessing Family Strengths and Resources

When a symptom or a problem has developed in response to encountering demands that the family seemingly has no better way to resolve, we ask ourselves and the family what resources would be needed to create a more desirable resolution and what prevents the family from using those resources in such a manner. Often, needed resources (experiential and/or transactional) are available, but simply are not orga-nized or associated with the context in which they seem to be needed. A hallmark of Erick-sonian approaches to therapy has been that it is solution–strength–resources oriented. Erickson's work demonstrated that, at the core, most people are capable of almost all necessary abilities, despite whatever seemingly limited behaviors and beliefs might have been developed (as a best choice) in response to traumatic or difficult developmental experiences. In all of our assessments, whether in the context of participation, conversation, verbal interview, reports from clients engaged in structured interaction tasks, or other interventions, we make conclusions about perceptual, cognitive, and emotional–behavioral strengths and flexibility—the choices to which family members have to respond in their environment.

GOAL SETTING

General Treatment Goals

Assessment as just described is that part of treatment during which specific goals are communicated by the family. It does not result in any diagnostic category for individuals or dysfunctional labels for the family. Goal setting does not focus on the absence of an undesirable state in the family, but rather on the presence of a desirable state.

While the uniqueness of families and the variety of challenges they face are understood, we still assume a basic commonality of people, regardless of gender, ethnicity, or stage of development, such that similar treatment goals are likely to apply in many cases, modified somewhat with regard to presenting problems and between-family differences. For example, basic affective experiences such as the ability to feel angry, sad, tender, loving, afraid, or confident are routinely relevant as treatment goals, with the determination of which specific one(s) to retrieve depending on the roles being taken in a particular family. Similarly, certain problem-solving behaviors, such as the ability to express feelings, delegate authority, cooperate, set limits on calls from a parent, be friendly to peers, nurture others in the family, ask for help, or even rebel, compete, or otherwise disaffiliate, can be routinely applied when these skills have been unavailable or avoided for whatever reason. Goals related to attitude or change in cognitive beliefs can be of the greatest variety since there may be many reasons or beliefs why it is unacceptable to feel or behave in particular ways. Thus, interventions focusing on larger goals of attitude and belief changes will typically be offered over the course of treatment (e.g., metaphors with a theme that challenges a particular belief or attitude) while clients have the ongoing experiences of changes in smaller, more defined behaviors and concomitant feelings that will challenge and erode those limiting attitudes and beliefs.

In other words, all people, regardless of their gender or the roles allowed by or taken within their family structure, are entitled to have all of their emotions, to have behavioral flexibility to both ask for and give help, to get close and set boundaries, to nurture, to be firm, and so on. Any belief that limits clients' ability to act and feel in these ways provides the basis for the therapeutic contract. In doing this, *the goal is to help clients develop new beliefs that will allow a greater flexibility and expression of self and the development–evolution of the family. This is true regardless of their differences or the problems that have brought them to therapy.*

Cocreation in Goal Setting

There is a cocreation of goals that involves a moment-to-moment process wherein the therapist is stimulated by the clients' behavior and reacts. At the same time, the therapist's behavior stimulates the clients' subsequent behavior. Within this recursive process, goals for each member can be shared or identified and addressed in a logical or pragmatic sequence that is derived from assessment of which members are most receptive, rigid, flexible, or distressed. The process of setting goals, like that of assessment, is ongoing throughout treatment until the decisive goal of symptom or problem resolution is accomplished and new relational patterns are established. Although goal setting is a major concern in the first few sessions, therapists and clients are continually cocreating and modifying goals for therapy. Sometimes it is the ultimate or decisive goal that changes, but more typically

this goal is expanded in accordance with a vast array of component parts or subgoals that may not have appeared to be related as the problems were first presented.

We always ask each member what he or she would like to have changed in the family and how, and even if members contradict each other, each input becomes the basis of a goal. Rarely, however, are families in the pain of seeking therapy able to formulate solid, "go-to" or future-oriented (Rossi, 1980d, p. 171) goals and congruently express them. So, each member expresses wishes in accordance with his or her own flexibility of communication, understanding of the problem, belief of what is possible, and so forth. Typically, clients underrate their current resources as well as what they would be capable of achieving. Rather, they focus on their limitations, the difficulty of the symptom or problem, and only aspire to the merest relief from the intensity of pain. In other words, they do not usually think to set as goals the possibility of their fondest dreams coming true in terms of relating ideally within their family and social network.

Therapists, too, participate in the setting of goals by assessing everything said by all members, both verbally and nonverbally; discussing the symptom and its apparent function; and then asking rhetorically, "What experiences and transactions does it seem that this family really needs in order not only to resolve this symptom, but to move creatively into and through the current stage of development in such a way as to lay the groundwork for comfortably entering the next logical stage and its inherent demands?" The answer to this question may not come all at once. Occasionally, the "answers" that come to mind prove to be wrong; that is, the goals that might appear to be relevant to the clients are eventually discovered to be irrelevant after all, in which case they are abandoned as new understanding comes and new goals are set.

It is not unusual for different family members to have different or contradictory goals. For example, the father who wants his 18-year-old daughter to obey the same family rules as her younger siblings—to stay at home more and to participate in the same family events that she did as a younger child—may be in direct opposition to the adolescent, who is striving for independence and separation from her family.

This difference becomes part of the therapeutic conversation and is discussed by all the participants. Such interventions as developmental reframing of the issue may be offered by the therapist, and tasks marking differences between different-aged siblings and/or tasks that may allow the father and daughter to connect in a new way may be introduced, depending on the context.

Therapists cannot separate themselves from personal values in the process of either assessing or setting goals with a family, although every effort is made to be as neutral as possible. However, it is reassuring to realize that clients will only follow suggestions or benefit from interventions that are relevant to accomplishing goals consistent with their values and the therapist will have the opportunity to discover how a goal that had appeared to be relevant did not prove to be relevant for that family after all, and it can then be abandoned or modified to fit. We may become blameworthy for wasting a family's time when we fail to be relevant, but it is not possible to force values or to install them in a passive family. Perhaps, in a "value clash," attitudes are challenged and thinking is stimulated in such a way that new values come to be held by both clients and therapist.

Discussing Treatment Goals with the Family

In the initial phase of therapy, a great deal of discussion is devoted to spelling out and clarifying just what the ultimate goal or treatment contract is to include, even leaving it at a "stop doing something" if that is the current frame that makes the most sense to the family. Also, each member will have contributed his or her ideas about what will be needed or desired in order to accomplish that goal, and many of these ideas are translated directly and explicitly into treatment goals. As therapy continues at this point, we want to show our support and our belief in the family's ability to accomplish these goals (when we do hold such a belief) by implying that the family members will develop through the life cycle in desirable ways, usually far beyond the scope of simply correcting the immediate symptoms of their imbalance or distress.

By implying the eventual achievement of the family's desired goals at some point in the future, we believe that a contract has been created between the therapist and family for the development of specific goals leading to this desired future. For example, let us imagine a couple in which both spouses have made it obvious that they want more intimacy, connection, and trust in their relationship but have been somewhat vague as to what this would entail specifically. We can ask them to picture themselves several months in the future at a time when they will have resolved certain difficulties and will be able to see things they may not have previously seen clearly. By presupposing that they will succeed, we provide emotional support and an opportunity to speculate about what they might be seeing in this future time when they will be interacting differently. We can speculate abstractly at first, watching for ideomotor communication back to us from each client confirming or disagreeing with our views. All the while, we then speculate more specifically in areas that have been confirmed as relevant by the couple's reaction. For example, "What I think you're going to see are people who have grown and matured. There will be pride in what you've done yourself. You will have accomplished being comfortable asking about and hearing the feelings of the partner and you won't feel frightened to respond with kindness and love. I see more laughter and a future where you will be sharing sadness and increasingly touching. Maybe you see something more or maybe you need to think about it longer." In response to a speculation like this by the therapist, both members have the option to indicate their agreement or disagreement or to "search" inwardly for how this possibility has personal meaning and relevance. As each partner signals nonverbal or vocal identification or confirmation, an unconscious contract emerges that has as much significance as the conscious treatment contract.

These somewhat specific goals are then transformed by the therapist into specific terms as much as possible—specific changes in affect, behavior, belief, self-image, and family structure for each member. Then, clients may be aided in the process of reaching the goals by any number of interventions the therapist may select, often having received clues from a family about how its members can be motivated. When therapeutic metaphor is applied, as is often the case in our framework, we design the metaphor around the specific goal and then tell the story to the family. Since it is in a metaphoric package, we do not state ideas about the explicit goal itself. In this way, we only stimulate thinking and experiencing related to the goal but clients are simultaneously free to respond in ways that are relevant for them, even if that means "tuning out" the therapist or modifying the story to "mean" something uniquely different and more personally relevant than the therapist originally intended. In this way, we proceed indirectly, that is, by not giving orders or voicing expectations that clients change as we would select, but in unique ways that fit for them.

THE STRUCTURE OF THE THERAPY PROCESS

The Question of Standard Structure

A consistent hallmark of Ericksonian approaches to therapy is that there is little consistency with regard to a standard way of structuring therapy. We sometimes see, as Erickson did (Haley, 1973; Erickson & Rossi, 1979), all family members, sometimes only the identified patient, sometimes everyone except the identified patient. At times, this decision is based on a strategic rationale and at other times it is made because of pragmatic considerations. While therapy might proceed most ideally when all involved members can be present and motivated, we are willing and able to operate in less than these ideal conditions. Nonetheless, therapy is conceived with utmost regard for the larger context. Even when we are only working directly with one member of a family, we would describe the process as family therapy because of the interpersonal–developmental framework for the therapy. In these cases, clients' changes are considered in light of the indirect influence they will exert on all absentees with whom the one member is involved.

The Role of Psychotropic Medications

Psychotropic medications are often of greater concern in the therapy of more dysfunctional life-styles, such as with individuals labeled as psychotic. However, there are families that may be referred in which one or more members are taking some form of prescribed medication, whether antidepressant, antianxiety, or antipsychotic. In these cases, it is usually a goal of therapy to facilitate a learning process such that this member(s) can function in a creative way in response to interpersonal and developmental challenges so that medication will not be required as a means for containing depressive, anxious, or psychotic feelings, behaviors, and beliefs. Rather than mask feelings and subdue impulses that form symptoms, we prefer to understand the positive intention or the function of the symptom and help members cocreate a better symptom and drug-free option for accomplishing that function. Therapists without medical degrees need, therefore, to work in harmony with a psychiatrist or physician toward that end.[7]

While in our personal practices, concurrent psychotropic medication is uncommon, there are certainly other contexts in which practitioners of Ericksonian approaches must frequently grapple with this issue. Many therapists work with inpatients, families in which one member is hospitalized, or outpatient populations who seem to be dependent on some psychotropic medication in order to maintain their outpatient or minimally functional status. Erickson, although a psychiatrist himself, preferred to avoid the prescription and use of psychotropic medications when possible, even for his psychotic clients. Though recognizing its benefit in certain cases, he usually worked to teach alternative choices and methods of functioning to this population, as well as to others who would have normally been maintained with medication by most other professionals. Erickson, as chief psychiatrist at inpatient units, demonstrated how

---

[7] *Editors' Note.* While we loudly applaud the authors' collaborative stance in their relationships with psychiatry and medicine, we also question the assumption here that many of the very kinds of clinical problems for which referral to a psychiatrist may be appropriate, in fact, are created by such repression-driven processes.

effectively communication and strategic interaction techniques of intervention could be used
with many clients who had long since been abandoned as "hopeless" by others. He was able to
be effective with these people due to an abun-
dance of patience, persistence, and creativity on
his part. Unfortunately, these characteristics are
hard to come by. Mental health workers are
short of time (and sometimes energy) and med-
icating the symptom is often seen as an easier
choice.

Duration of Therapy

Therapy time is unlimited and varies, depending on the motivation of the family, the
amount of pain, the severity of the symptom,
the rigidity of the family, the resources available, and the therapist's ability to communicate
with the family and to understand how the family
is stuck or the function of the symptom, motivation for entering into therapy, and so on.
While a "comprehensive" or holistic approach
is valued, Ericksonian therapists simultaneously
seek to help families accomplish as much as possible in the shortest possible time. Ideally, a
therapist will seek to intervene at all relevant
levels in a significant way in one session such
that the symptom and its supporting family organization begin to be reorganized, new relational patterns can develop, and further therapy
is unnecessary. This actually does happen from
time to time, but more often, in the first session
we come to understand what will need to be
accomplished in the second and then the third
and then the fourth session.

Therapy is a discontinuous process that can
continue intermittently for years with different
therapists in response to changing circumstances
or weekly for years with the same therapist ham-
mering away at one continuing problem. Ericksonian therapists attempt to communicate that
clients have the resources they need and are in
control of their lives. One powerful way to give
this message is not to require a mandatory "next"
session. Only in those cases where clients need
to have the security of a regular visit are regular
visits suggested. Depending on the severity of
the problem, we urge some clients who are seen
in this manner to continue an ongoing therapy
in their geographical location as a condition for

this additional, alternative therapy. But other
highly functional clients, who nonetheless have
suffered from an ongoing problem for years, are
sometimes able to make a new arrangement or
"reassociation of experiential life" in one of these
intensive sessions so that no additional therapy
is ever sought (Rossi, 1980d, p. 38; Erickson &
Rossi, 1979, p. 9).

More typically, however, we see local clients
at least twice, often for four to eight sessions,
and very occasionally for up to two years. Some
families are not amenable to any therapy contact
beyond the first or second session. In a family
in which roles are rigidly upheld by redundant
communication, symptoms seem to be a highly
symbolic manner of expression. Perhaps this is
the case in all families but it is not obvious or
noticeable except in certain families. With such
families, we must put aside any idea of negotiating a broader treatment contract in favor of
doing whatever small amount of therapy the
family will tolerate and accept. This may be the
merest disruptive intervention, such as a paradoxical prescription (Lankton & Lankton, 1986),
an ordeal assignment (Haley, 1984), or a strategic reframing of an existing communication
that helps the family nudge past a developmental snag it is encountering and change the
way the family members currently come together around the symptom.

Time Between Sessions and
Decisions about Structure

Each case can be handled differently, both as
to the length of a session and to the length of
time between sessions. Some clients may be
seen twice a week or until a crisis is surmounted
and then switch to being seen once a month for
a few months more. Other clients may be seen
once every two weeks or once a month, while
others are seen on a regular weekly basis. Sessions are usually held every week or every two
weeks for an hour to an hour and a half—we may
see out-of-town and other "long distance
clients," or clients who benefit from an intermittent, discontinuous therapy once every several months for several years.

The decision to set the duration of therapy is
a joint decision. Most often, the therapist will
simply accept the clients' desires in this area.

However, some clients, in a childlike manner, may request a duration that seems to reinforce the self-view that they are powerless and the therapist may veto the choice. Other clients may be poorly motivated and set a long time between sessions as a way to be certain that nothing useful really comes from the meetings. In these cases, the therapist may again veto the decision. It is entirely arbitrary and improper to demand that each client be able to use the same format for therapy. All members of every family have a unique sense of urgency, timing, desire, and motivation, and a unique speed of experiencing and learning. Therapists who are sensitive to that will find that such a utilization approach increases the cooperativeness of clients, reduces the work of therapy, and shortens the time needed to accomplish goals.

THE ROLE OF THE THERAPIST

Who Talks to Whom

As in all other areas of this therapy, there is no set rule to determine the correct ratio of therapist–family talking. Initially, clients may do considerably more talking as they describe their problems, their connection to the problems, their goals, and their current situation to the therapist. The therapist may initially do nothing more than introduce directives into the conversation so that family members will talk to one another. Having the family members talk to each other creates an implicit suggestion that they are the experts and will solve the problem with their own efforts and from their own experience. It displays much of their problem-solving communication and thereby provides process data about the flexibility and perceptiveness in communicating with one another (at least in the context of the therapist's office).

Later, if treatment includes hypnotherapy and therapeutic metaphor, clients may not talk to each other or to the therapist as much; they are busy attending to their own thoughts and experiences when the therapist is speaking. And there are times when it will be most useful for one member to talk primarily to the therapist while the other members are given an opportunity to understand that member differently.

It is important to remember, however, that while a client is quiet at the overt verbal level, communication continually takes place between the client and therapist. Much of the client's communication will be by means of ideomotor response when the therapist is talking. Therapists continue to observe and employ this unconscious communication throughout the therapy (Erickson & Rossi, 1981, p. 121; Lankton & Lankton, 1983).

Self-Disclosure

Ericksonian therapists use self-disclosure as they do other interpersonal stances that might seem beneficial in each unique situation. Self-disclosure about the past takes the form of therapeutic stories. The story may be about the therapist or the therapist's acquaintances. At other times, the therapist will be a peripheral character in stories that feature former clients (disguised for confidentiality). In many of the therapeutic stories we design, we borrow extensively from a personal experience but ascribe that experience to another character about whom we can speak in the third person (Lankton & Lankton, 1989). This allows us to regulate appropriate interpersonal distance and lessens the possibility that the story will introduce countertransference elements connected with being too personally revealing. However, sometimes the nature of the experience is such that there is no need to alter it in this manner. Therapists need to understand how people respond to and learn from the experience elicited by stories (Gordon, 1978; Lankton & Lankton, 1983, 1986, 1989; Rossi, 1980).

Outside the context of therapeutic metaphor, there are frequent opportunities for the therapist's personal reactions and perceptions to be offered as grist for the therapeutic mill. We continue to be aware that what we say and do stimulates the family at several levels. Therapists must be thoughtful about how and what they say to clients and what conscious and out-of-awareness reactions are elicited from clients. In this way, self-disclosure must be considered a special case of focusing attitude, behavior, and affect—and as such is an intervention that will stimulate family members.

Joining the Family

The Ericksonian model is built on the understanding that joining is crucial to enhancing communication and change. This is a part of the utilization approach and entails acceptance of the client's world and the rapid development of rapport. To this end, we attempt to speak the experiential language of each client system, "to include the patient's own style of speech, whether abrupt, impolite, or even outrageously profane" (although such profanity is soon discarded) (Rossi, 1980d, p. 336). One observable feature of this is taking on the actual language, sentence structure, phrasing, and body posture of clients as we speak to each of them. This often requires a large departure from conventional speech, as in the case of a family with a hospitalized son who only spoke by mumbling sounds. In speaking with him throughout the first session, the first author placed explanations within a predominantly mumbled style of speaking. While progress was slow by ordinary standards, the young man shook the therapist's hand at the end of the session and clearly verbalized that everything that was said "added up." Previously, this man would not attend to his former therapist for an entire session but preferred to speak to angels whom he claimed to see near the ceiling. In contrast, his father was very articulate and precise in speaking. Hence, he was spoken to in a manner similar to his own preferred style. By comparison with the previous therapy, communication with this family was very rapid because the joining was accomplished by speaking each person's language. In this way, we help clients understand and respond by using their own capacities for packaging information.

The Therapist's Changing Role

Making a strategic and therapeutic difference without exerting or imposing control is a balance the therapist maintains throughout therapy. The Ericksonian therapist attempts to be somewhat peripheral at all times, minimizing the importance of the therapist and emphasizing the power and the credit for change to the family. This balance is as important at termination as at other times. As the conversation will introduce memories, ideas, understanding, and so on, it is kept foremost in mind that the suggestions must be "in accord with the subject's understandings and desires" as these have been communicated by the family members (Rossi, 1980c, p. 16). In this role, there is no deviation from the beginning to the end of therapy.

Clinical Skills and Therapist's Responsibility

Observational skills are one of the most basic requirements for a therapist to be successful in this approach. Erickson's own children report that "observe, observe, observe" was one of their father's most consistent pieces of advice. This observing is not designed to derive the "truth" about a client or family, but rather to be certain to receive as much communication from clients as possible. Erickson's contention that all behavior is ideomotor communication (Erickson & Rossi, 1981) suggests that the more the therapist is open to observing, the more communication will be received and the more meaningful communication from therapists can be for each client. It is essential that an Ericksonian therapist be able to observe the family members and experience the dynamics or characteristics of the family system with externally directed sensory awareness (without subvocalization or imagination). Ericksonian therapists work to notice and, by responding in kind, respect all messages family members send, both verbal and nonverbal.

In addition to such essential therapist skills as observation, flexibility, self-disclosure, active participation, and speaking each client's experiential language, we also recognize the value of more conventional therapist qualities, such as intelligence, courage, patience, caring, warmth, genuineness, and honesty. There is sometimes an ethical concern about the honesty of strategic approaches in that interventions may not always appear to be straightforward or may be better understood and articulated by therapists than by clients. However, Booth (1988) has clarified that Erickson's influence was that of honest participation in therapy. A paradoxical prescription, for instance, though it recommends continuing a symptom or interpersonal pattern, has as its ultimate purpose helping clients to reach their goals by trying in a different manner. Indirect suggestions and binds that are designed with regard to overloading, confusing, or bypassing the conscious mind are not designed to be manipulative or dishonest but to offer a choice and multiplicity of ways in which a goal can be understood or accomplished. Figure 8-2 indicates the types of indirect suggestions that might be used in family therapy.

Yet, if a problem is framed as positive when the family has believed that it is troublesome, one can again question how truly honest such an approach can claim to be. Our response to this is that positive framing as the basis of the approach must be entirely honest and congruent in order for it to have any desired effect. If a positive frame does not make sense to the therapist, none will be offered for consideration to the family. Important to note here is that any positive frame offered by therapists must be consistent with the therapist's beliefs, not just something to "sell" to families. We have stressed that clients will only follow those suggestions that are in their best interest and relevant for them to follow. At worst, it is possible for us to inadvertently to waste clients' time, but it is not possible for us to manipulate them to do something irrelevant or against their will. All positive labeling is founded on the premise that people are attempting to make the best choices available to them at all times and that it is (probably) always possible to frame the problem as having some positive, adaptive purpose for which the family can be, in a manner, complimented.

Perhaps it follows, then, that the therapist, in addition to honest optimism, must have the inclination to look for the good in people, to believe in their innate worth and the availability of resources and potentials, and to look for how their "stuckness" is their best effort at satisfying developmental demands.

TECHNIQUES OF ERICKSONIAN MARITAL AND FAMILY THERAPY

Variety in Therapy Sessions

A study of Erickson's own practice reveals a wide variety of typical sessions. This is due, in part, to the fact that his professional work spanned five decades and also to the fact that he was an innovative practitioner, experimenting

with and revising his therapy throughout his life. Consequently, it is difficult to make generalizations about his therapy conduct without finding several exceptions to every observed pattern. Since he emphasized the need to treat each case uniquely, it is common to find a wide variance, too, in the work of his students. Each person or group influenced by Erickson tends to emphasize one or several of his contributions and to minimize others, depending on personal styles and preferences of working. Some practitioners tend to emphasize homework assignments, others emphasize paradoxical directives, and still others may emphasize metaphor or hypnosis. There is some commonality or consensus, however, about specific techniques and strategies that are considered to be "Ericksonian" even though these will be disproportionately used by individual practitioners (Lankton, 1985b). It is certainly true that Erickson's influence is closely associated with a variety of unique and distinctive interventions, but he was also known for his practical, commonsense connection with people through such time-honored traditions as empathy, understanding, and "down-to-earth" advice.

Utilization: Creating a Treatment Alliance with Joining Techniques

With regard to joining a family to create a treatment alliance, Erickson was perhaps best known for his willingness and ability to utilize anything and everything offered by his clients. This tendency seemed to be based on his conviction that people were making the best choices they were currently able to make and that even "undesirable" behaviors were, nonetheless, valuable communications that could be used to understand clients and propel them toward desired changes.

Erickson was skilled at building rapport and putting a positive frame around experiences others took to be only negative. Meeting people at their model of the world (Lankton & Lankton, 1983) appeared to be natural and reflexive for him. Because of the wide range of given models, interpersonal flexibility is perhaps the greatest therapeutic technique an Ericksonian therapist can have.

The most striking example applies to empa-

1. Open-ended suggestions

Beginning therapy: "You can learn in many ways."

Gathering history: "There are a number of ways of drawing together facts and information to help us direct our actions in any quest."

Making contract: "Formal ways of agreeing on the direction of conduct have been a foundation of social gatherings that enhance the way people make a productive use of time."

Bringing spouse: "Some creative methods of motivating others to participate in things that influence their lives always result from necessity and desire."

Learn from experience: "You can develop a line of thought for your own use."

Use learning at home: "And keep your learnings and memorize them and use them in your own family in various places in your home."

2. Implication

Beginning therapy: "Since you began when you arrived in my office . . ."

Gathering history: "The first thing people do when they explain their past . . ."

Making contract: "Since you want to use your time here for certain gains . . . please tell me when you'd like to begin."

Bringing spouse: "While you think about getting your spouse in therapy, let's talk about what you can do."

Learn from experience: "Which lesson do you imagine you will learn first?"

Use learning at home: "The more you find ways to use the learnings now, the more you're likely to use them with each other."

3. Questions or statements that focus or reinforce awareness

Beginning therapy: "I wonder if you experience yourself ready to begin."

Gathering history: "You probably couldn't say what part of your history is the most important facet of this current problem."

Making contract: "I just wonder what you'll eventually decide to work on in the therapy."

Bringing spouse: "I doubt that you currently know how you will best go about getting your spouse to join us next week."

Learn from experience: "What can a person learn from an experience?"

Use learning at home: "Have you decided when you'll use this learning?"

4. Truisms

Beginning therapy: "Chairs were intended to be comfortable and serve a function."

Gathering history: "Everyone knows that we understand things best when those things are placed in their rightful historical context."

Making contract: "Sooner or later you decide what you wish to change."

Bringing spouse: "Everybody knows how two heads are better than one."

Learn from experience: "Experience is a great teacher."

Use learning at home: "Everyone knows the importance of doing some homework."

5. Suggestions that cover all possible alternatives

Beginning therapy: "You might be able to get right to work or you might warm up to it gradually; perhaps you will suddenly find yourself in the midst of therapy or maybe you will pinpoint a starting date; possibly your start will be entirely different."

Gathering history: "You can go into your history slowly, gradually, quickly, with feeling or with a sort of detachment or not at all."

Making contact: "You can either work on something that comes up or you can think it through carefully, or you might let it change each week or you could identify something that is important and stick to it; maybe you'll have a unique way to go about it."

Bringing spouse: "A time to bring your spouse may be selected, or it may be prescribed; it may come to your mind or only intuitively occur to you; you may not know at all how you'll bring it up."

Learn from experience: "You may learn some or all of the material, and you may know what you learn or not know what you learn, and you might learn nothing at all."

Use learning at home: "You may not use this or you might use this learning; you might modify it when you use it; and you can use all of it or only part of it; or you might mix the distinction between what you learn and what you invent."

6. Apposition of opposites

Beginning therapy: "It's fine to take a long time beginning as we may get to the solution with less waste."

Gathering history: "The less you notice the immediate situation, the more you have a capacity to concentrate on the important part of your past."

Making contract: "The more things you can think about being up in the air, the easier it may seem to get down to earth as you decide where to start."

Bringing spouse: "The more you feel alone in this matter, the more you'll feel like bringing your partner."

Learn from experience: "The more you have been in the dark, the more enlightening a learning may be."

Use learning at home: "Since you waited so long for relief from the problem, you are entitled to use it throughout your vast future."

7. Binds of comparable alternatives

Beginning therapy: "Would you prefer to have me begin talking or would you prefer to begin talking?"

Gathering history: "You may go into your past immediately or gradually get to it."

Making contract: "You might decide on what to work for in therapy or you may just want to explore many issues."

Bringing spouse: "I don't know if you will want all of your family present or if you will only want your spouse here."

Learn from experience: "You may learn from the experience or merely use the experience."

Use learning at home: "You can select the way you will use this after therapy or discover the way you will use this at home."

8. Conscious–unconscious double binds

Beginning therapy: "The conscious mind may not notice when the unconscious mind is beginning to work toward a solution."

Gathering history: "Your conscious mind may think you need to share some part of your past while your unconscious mind desires to share some other portion of your past."

Making contract: "Your conscious mind may not notice how your unconscious will single out something you want to start changing."

Bringing spouse: "Your conscious mind may be doubtful of how your unconscious mind can figure out how to get your spouse to come to the therapy."

Learn from experience: "An unconscious learning from the experience may be developed in the conscious mind as well."

Use learning at home: "Your conscious mind might already have some ideas of where you will use this while your unconscious handles doing it correctly."

9. Double dissociative conscious–unconscious double binds

Beginning therapy: "Your conscious mind may have begun with the aid of your unconscious or perhaps your unconscious is ready to begin with any aid you can offer consciously."

Gathering history: "Would you prefer to let your conscious mind lead your unconscious into the history related to your problem or let your unconscious lead your conscious mind into a recounting of important information?"

Making contract: "Your conscious mind didn't know that your unconscious would choose the right thing to begin therapy, but your conscious mind could wonder which topic your unconscious would choose."

Bringing spouse: "Your unconscious may let your conscious mind know how you will get your spouse into therapy or your unconscious may not even know what your conscious mind is coming up with."

Learn from experience: "Your conscious mind can be interested in what you learn from the experience and your unconscious mind can take care of really learning from it, or perhaps your unconscious mind only allows you to develop interest as your conscious mind develops a learning."

Use learning at home: "And one might let the conscious mind select the site for using the learning while the unconscious is trusted to carry it out, or one may allow the conscious mind to carry out a learning and let the unconscious select the location, and time."

10. Non-sequitur double bind

Beginning therapy: "Let's begin now or use the time constructively."

Gathering history: "You will be able to either tell about your past or else you'll just go into the relevant part of your personal history."

Making contract: "Your unconscious will come up with what you want out of therapy or you will consciously decide what to work on."

Bringing spouse: "You'll probably want to get someone close to you into therapy or you'll want to bring in your spouse."

Learn from experience: "You can either learn from this experience or teach it to your children."

Use learning at home: "Will you use these learnings at home or change your maladaptive behavior?"

Figure 8-2. Indirect suggestions and binds in family therapy (From Lankton & Lankton, 1986, pp. 247–249)

thy. For some families, appropriate empathy that meets them at their model of the world will include such conventional elements as reflective and active listening, positive regard, and self-disclosure. However, for other families, meeting them at their model of the world may instead require the temporary use of challenge, admonition, confrontation, or apparent alliance with one family member against another. And with others, Erickson demonstrated successful joining by the use of unexplainable ambiguity, humor, confusion, metaphor, or other types of fascination. But all of these different techniques are used with the belief that *symptomatic or destructive behaviors were learned for some adaptive purpose and offer valuable information about the demands upon and resources within the family system.*

Empathy, positive framing, utilization, and paradoxical prescription, then, are the related techniques primarily used during the joining phase of therapy. They are related to such an extent that when all four occur, they are an orchestration and it is appropriate to consider them a single, four-part intervention. Empathy and the resulting rapport are prerequisite to trust and therapeutic alliance. Such rapport is essential when other interaction circumvents limiting expectations or conscious understanding. This often occurs when the conversation in therapy becomes a paradoxical symptom prescription.

For a behavior to be utilized or therapeutically prescribed, it must first be framed positively with the belief that it exists for some good reason. It will, therefore, not be a "psychoanalytic" reason. At the very least, there is some positive intention even though the behavior itself may accomplish little except to increase problems within the family. We typically employ paradoxical prescription to some extent with almost every family, even when no obvious symptom is presented. There are always interpersonal orientations or typical roles or characteristics that are part of any family constellation. Since these dynamics are part of the current model of the world for that family, we can meet them at that model by positively framing and recommending, suggesting, or prescribing that each continue to do exactly what each is doing as it provides a way to accomplish what each wants. Even with a destructive behavior, it is

possible to frame positively the intention behind it and to recommend that the person continue to work toward accomplishing that intention. However, we will help clients develop experiences that create nondestructive alternatives to reach that intended goal.

The greater the rigidity of a family's model of the world (whether acting like a united front family, a chaotic family, or whatever), the more likely we are to find that the family has a narrow and set role for the therapist to take. In these cases, we find that prescribing a paradox speaks to the ambivalence of the family. This ambivalence essentially states that the family members want to change, but not if it involves doing anything differently. Here, then, paradoxical prescription is not even rightly called paradoxical. The family is instructed and asked to continue with the problematic behavior just as in the past. An understanding of the positive intention for the existence of the problematic behavior is as essential as rapport.

Once clients acknowledge their agreement to the paradoxical assignment the role expectations placed on the therapist will be gone. They will no longer insist that the therapist be available for the sole purpose of, say, finding out if Johnny is crazy or sane. Thus, the therapist becomes far more useful to the family and yet the limited conscious mind set of the family members has not been challenged or antagonized.

Selection of Particular Techniques for Specific Goals

Techniques used with an Ericksonian approach vary depending on the case being treated, but several unique interventions are associated with the approach and had their origin in Erickson's practice. These include, but are not limited to, paradoxical assignments, ambiguous function assignments, skill-building assignments, therapeutic ordeals, therapeutic metaphors, anecdotes, conscious–unconscious dissociation, hypnotic induction in family therapy, therapeutic binds, indirect suggestion, relabeling, and reframing. These interventions are always considered in relationship to our assessment of the family system and the resulting treatment goals that are developed and, as shown in Figure 8-3, then applied to the relevant level(s) of that system. Specific protocols for some of the above interventions will be presented in a following section.

Having assessed family dynamics at four levels of related complexity, unique interventions can be designed and applied to help clients effect each level. Figure 8-3 groups interventions according to their typical goal target. While many approaches to therapy emphasize one specific level of goals, the preferable approach would be for therapy to help clients to stimulate or guide changes on all levels in a coordinated manner. However, with some families, this comprehensive, or holistic, approach may not be possible or desirable. Ultimately, the decision to use a particular technique or strategy depends on the family's disposition toward therapy, the rigidity of family organization, and how much therapy will be tolerated. Generally, the more rigid the family structure, the more it is likely to be symbolized by a very specific symptom, and even though such a family ideally might benefit from systemwide interventions, this may be unrealistic and impossible. In such a case, the decision as to what interventions are to be included is dictated by practicality, and perhaps a reliance on simple disruption of a problematic routine with positive framing, symptom prescription with alteration, and minimal therapeutic input and structured interaction. This is especially true when ethical and legal concerns demand that one intervene to aid the victims of family violence.

In more receptive families, we set about designing the indicated variety of interventions that should help guide changes at all levels in a coordinated manner. Treatment plans must constantly be subject to revision, however, as when interventions are designed and delivered but new relational patterns do not develop and symptoms fail to vanish. In these instances, there are several possibilities to consider. Were the goals relevant or are there additional goals that had not been recognized? If no new goals emerge and the existing ones continue to appear relevant, then we have a choice of applying the same interventions again more effectively (perhaps shaped by learning from client feedback) or selecting different interventions targeted at the same goal. Ericksonian family therapy works to maintain flexibility with regard to a wide array of possible interventions and tries to see each family and each problem as unique and to avoid any temptation to create a set of interventions that are routinely applied to apparently similar problem categories.

As there are some guidelines as to whether to ask clients to perform skill-building tasks outside the session or to go into trance during a session, so, too, there are a few influencing factors that contribute to intervention decisions. With regard to the intervention of hypnotic induction, for instance, we reserve the right to use

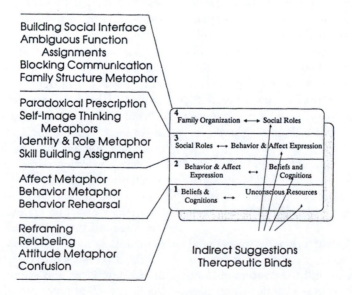

Figure 8-3. System-wide interventions

hypnosis only with those families whose members we trust or whose actions we can predict. We do not want inadvertently to add an intervention as controversial as hypnosis into an equation where it is likely to do more harm than good. Though hypnosis cannot actually harm anyone, its reputation can be further damaged if it is used carelessly in a context in which family members in a crisis might excuse inappropriate actions based on the fact that, according to their misconception, they "were hypnotized" and so, in their view, were not accountable or able to control themselves. For this reason, we make certain to introduce hypnosis only after we have assessed a family as stable, functional, and oriented as to the naturalness of trance as something they already do for and to themselves. They understand that they are not oblivious or "under" our, or anyone else's, control. Similarly, we find that ambiguous function assignments are best used by clients who may be rigidly adhering to a specific world view but from a consciously organized perspective. We do not advocate this intervention with psychotic or borderline members as it may add unnecessarily to their confusion in a way that does not promote eventual clarification.

Creating Changes in Family Experience

Therapy is often framed as a somewhat paradoxical situation in which the family agrees to continue, with certain experimental (therapeutic) alterations, their positively framed "problem" behaviors inasmuch as these now are believed to represent a means of accomplishing desired changes to which all have agreed. With these contracts and this framework in operation, a variety of techniques can be and are employed toward attaining the goal of helping clients retrieve their own resources and stimulate their own thinking, feeling, and behaviors that can be brought to bear on the developmental problems. This will facilitate the family's finding alternative ways of responding to current interpersonal demands.

Changes in family structure and transactional patterns are sought to the extent that members indicate a readiness to shift the context of their rules for relating as well as changes in or alleviation of a specific symptom. Among the commonly used techniques associated with Ericksonian family therapy at this phase are task assignments and ambiguous function assignments, structured interactions, blocking communication, behavior rehearsal, and therapeutic metaphor in the context of hypnotherapy with one or several family members.

Using Hypnosis as a Modality for Communication

Hypnotherapy with several family members present was introduced by Erickson at least as early as 1945 (Haley, 1973, p. 179). However, not all of the family-therapy models that developed as a result of Erickson's influence have included hypnotherapy. Other practitioners of Ericksonian-style family therapy emphasize strategic assignments, therapeutic ordeals, paradoxical directives, behavior rehearsal, structured interactions, direct suggestion, and so on, with the usual exclusion of hypnotherapy and hypnotic indirection.

It is certainly possible simply to have therapeutic "conversations" that do not in any way resemble a formal trance or dramatic metaphor. While we typically use all of these techniques in our practice, we find hypnosis to be a very convenient way to accomplish interview management, continue diagnostic assessment, and stimulate a great deal of thinking, feeling, and resource retrieval within the session. There are a variety of opportunities to introduce hypnosis in family therapy, one of which is simply to notice and encourage naturally occurring altered states of consciousness that family members will automatically experience. Whether or not formally to label the experience as a "trance" is arbitrary. Experiences of searching for meaning in response to an ambiguous or cryptic suggestion or communication can lead to what we call "therapeutic receptivity," or that condition in which one or more family members eagerly welcome continued input that promises to help them discover their relevant life experiences and facilitate the "answers" for which they are searching.

When hypnosis is to be used as a modality for exchanging ideas and stimulating thinking with a family, we find several guidelines to be helpful. First, we rarely hypnotize the identified patient because we do not wish to reinforce the family myth that this member is so "sick" as to require such a "formidable" intervention as hypnosis. In addition to protecting the identified patient from further exposure to this kind of discrimination within the family, this policy allows the therapist to avoid playing the role that a rigid family might be assigning; for example, "fixing the problem in the 'sick' member." We do, however, tend to introduce hypnosis for the purpose of facilitating relief to the person currently experiencing or communicating the most pain. This person is likely to be especially receptive.

Also, we sometimes introduce hypnosis in the family session to help the member who is the problematic interrupter in the session. Benefits include the obvious removal of this member from the role of interrupter and helping this person to provide us with even more information about his or her reaction in the family. These individuals are usually experiencing some urgency to do something, such as to be helpful, to protect themselves, or even to do something angry. Therapists can offer the heightened concentration of trance as a means for them to use additional personal resources to better accomplish the beneficial aspects they may have in mind. Often, this person, having been complimented on the intention behind the interrupting (positive framing), is urged to continue that observation and understanding (paradoxical prescription), but in an altered way that will allow a greater appreciation of the perceptions involved. Not only does the interrupter alter the customary interrupting, but he or she often accomplishes meaningful and atypical results and understandings while in trance.

If the identified patient also happens to be the family member who is in the most pain as well as the problematic interrupter, then we make an exception to the first guideline and offer to hypnotize the identified patient along with the "healthiest" member of the family. In this way, we dilute any conclusions that might otherwise be drawn by the family as to who is "all good and innocent" versus who is "all bad and wrong." Hypnosis of the two individuals simultaneously provides a context for building rapport if they are struggling and failing to build it for various reasons. And if they are overinvolved or over-identified with one another and struggling to disaffiliate, they can often use hypnosis to facil-

itate the building of a separation. Reasons for becoming involved with the induction of these chosen members need to be ascertained from interaction with the unique clients.

In some cases, we hypnotize all adults in the family. This can be done for the purpose of a shared goal or, alternatively, for individual goals that are unique in each case. It is usually beneficial to provide the conscious minds of clients with a reason or reasons for launching themselves into trance in any of the various combinations just described. A variety of possible reasons could be derived from the motives and difficulties of the family members. But again, these reasons are worded in a positive, goal-directed, choice-enhancing framework. These may vary from obvious suggestions that the reason for hypnosis is to assist them in reducing pain to suggestions that the reason for introducing hypnosis is somewhat unrelated to the concerns they originally wished to address. Of course, the variation in this range must be determined by an assessment of each family member.

Occasionally, we will also facilitate a trance experience with selected children in the family who are old enough to be able to communicate verbally, concentrate attention, and recognize that hypnosis is just a way of becoming familiar with oneself and attending to thoughts and beliefs and feelings in a completely natural and safe way. A shared hypnotic experience almost always stimulates an enhanced sense of rapport within the entire family, even for those who simply observe.

With regard to inducing trance, we have mentioned that it is possible simply to notice the naturally occurring altered states of inwardly focused attention and suggest that this experience be intensified. This is not very different from the often routine suggestion to someone experiencing a particular emotion to "go with that feeling." Though this directive is not usually associated with hypnosis per se, formal hypnotic induction need not sound any more unusual than this, though it may include additional focusing-inward suggestions such as, "You can close your eyes as you allow yourself to go deeper with that feeling and perhaps notice that things outside you can seem irrelevant for the moment, the more you just go with that feeling and focus all of your attention on discovering where it might lead you." The word "trance" need never be used at all, especially when it would unduly arouse fearful reactions. In other instances, however, trance can be suggested to one or all members by using its formal label but doing so in such a way that it sounds no more menacing or mysterious than simply asking family members to "turn to your spouse and say . . ." After all, it is just another intervention. In and of itself, it cures nothing. It is simply a modality for exchanging ideas as are other more commonly accepted interventions. Figure 8-4 outlines a typical induction sequence, and Figure 8-5 provides protocols for the construction of therapeutic metaphors in the context of hypnotherapy.

Therapists use different methods of inducing hypnosis but the two most common are internal fixation and external fixation. The *internal-fixation method* we prefer involves an elicitation of the unconscious contract that accompanies the conscious contract developed and shared with the therapist and usually supported by the clients' initial request for treatment. This was addressed in goal setting as a rationale and will here be detailed as a technique. With clients who are prepared to become absorbed in a contemplation of their possible gains from therapeutic work, one can ask the subjects, often the members of the marital dyad, to close their eyes and consider what their family interaction will look like to them in a prescribed period of time— that is, what changes they will see or expect to find. It is recommended that therapists estimate and suggest a period of three to six months, or, in some cases, to select a longer period of up to 18 months. Most couples can notice important changes within such a frame. Subjects should actually be expected to envision scenes in which they view themselves and one another. Therapists, in this situation, can offer ideas and make suggestions, positively frame behaviors, and imply a successful development of needed and de-

---

1. Orient the client to trance.
This step involves making certain that the clients are physically and psychologically prepared for the trance.

2. Fixate attention and rapport.
Most frequently clients' attention is fixated on a story, on their body sensations, or on an external object.

3. Establish a conscious–unconscious dissociation.
Therapists use "conscious–unconscious dissociation language," including the possible use of anecdote and education about unconscious processes to assist clients in the development of dissociated and polarized attention.

4. Ratify and deepen the trance.
Ratification of the client's processes of unconscious search is easily accomplished by helping focus client awareness on the many alterations that occur in their face muscles, reflexes, respiration, and skin coloration. Deepening may be facilitated by several means, including confusion, offering small incremental steps, or indirect suggestions and binds.

5. Utilize trance to elicit experiences and associate experiences.
Therapeutic use of trance includes using those unconscious processes stimulated by induction. Metaphor provides an altered frame of reference that allows clients to entertain novel experience. The experiences needed are determined by the diagnostic assessment and contracted therapy goals. Experience may be facilitated by the use of indirect suggestion and anecdotes, and binds. Finally, therapists help clients arrange elicited experiences into a network of associations that will help them form a perceptually and behaviorally based map of conduct.

6. Reorient the client to waking state.
Reorientation may be rapid or gradual. At this stage, the therapist has a final opportunity to assist clients in developing amnesia, posthypnotic behavior, and/or other trance phenomena that are part of the treatment plan. The techniques of metaphor, indirect suggestion, binds, confusion, and paradox may also be used at this stage.

Figure 8-4. Induction-sequence outline

1. **Family-structure metaphor**
   1. Illustrate how a protagonist's discomfort (which is obviously different from the identified patient's problem) relates to a family structure (similar to that of the client-system).
   2. Illustrate how the protagonist's family organization changes as a result of interacting differently (a model of reorganization suitable for the client-system's desired developmental goal).
   3. Show how the discomfort (still entirely different than any in the actual family) was resolved by changing the family and do not provide sufficient logical connection between the disappearance of the symptom and the reorganization of the family in the story).

2. **Self-image thinking protocol**
   Central self-image (CSI) construction:
   1. Describe a protagonist who is seeing a reflection or picturing himself or herself accurately.
   2. Explain how the protagonist recalls and experiences several desired qualities (which may be resources retrieved earlier in the session).
   3. Describe how the original visual image of the self is altered in behaviorally specific ways consistent with each quality being experienced.

   Self-image scenarios process:
   4. Using the story of the protagonist imaging his or her "CSI" as a device, describe imagined background details as follows.
   5. Introduce a positive, non–anxiety-producing scene and people and describe the protagonist experiencing and thinking through behaviors in that scene (keeping the desired resources constant).
   6. Introduce other backgrounds and people in gradual successive approximations from the previous scenes to, eventually, the most difficult and contracted therapeutic goal.

3. **Affect and emotion protocol**
   1. Establish a relationship between the protagonist and a person, place, or thing that involves emotion or affect (e.g., tenderness, anxiety, mastery, confusion, love, longing, etc.).
   2. Detail *movement* in the relationship (e.g., moving with, moving toward, moving away, orbiting, etc.).
   3. Focus on some of the physiological changes that coincide with the protagonist's emotion (be sure to overlap with the client's facial behavior and other identifiable bodily changes).

4. **Behavior-change protocol**
   1. Illustrate the protagonist's observable behavior similar to the desired behavior to be acquired by the client. There is no need to mention motives. List about six specific observable behaviors.
   2. Detail the protagonist's internal attention or nonobservable behavior that shows the protagonist to be congruent with his or her observable behavior.
   3. Change the setting within the story so as to provide an opportunity for repeating all the behavioral descriptions several (three) times.

5. **Attitude-change protocol**
   1. Describe a protagonist's behavior or perception so it exemplifies the maladaptive attitude. Bias this belief to appear positive or desirable.
   2. Describe another protagonist's behavior or perception so that it exemplifies the *adaptive* attitude (the goal). Bias this belief to appear negative or undesirable.
   3. Reveal the *unexpected* outcome achieved by both protagonists that resulted from the beliefs they held and their related actions. Be sure the payoff received by the second protagonist is of value to the client.

Figure 8-5. Metaphor-construction protocols

sired behaviors and experiences. Most often, however, the therapist ought merely to inquire from the standpoint of a curious-inquirer role, being certain not to show interest in the meaning of the answer. The members might be asked, for instance, to consider whether or not they expect certain specific gains (in the three to six

months) that the therapist has been led to expect to occur.

In such a context, clients will demonstrate three types of responses to the specific named experiences and behaviors enumerated by the therapist. Each person will either shake or nod his or her head or exhibit ideomotor trance forms of identification and internal search phenomena. Head nods almost always indicate that the words spoken by the therapist are acceptable to the client's frame of reference and that they have identified a meaningful and desirable personal experience. Head shakes do not necessarily mean the ideas introduced by the therapist are undesirable. More investigation and unconscious communicating will determine whether the ideas did not fit with the client's sense of direction or simply did not fit because of unacceptable wording. *Search phenomena*, seen in light trance, indicate that clients sense a fit between what the therapist implied and their own internal frame of reference. But it further demonstrates that clients are not altogether certain that the resources they need are available. Hence, they are searching for connections between the goals they value and the tools they know they have. In other words, the search phenomena indicate the client's willingness and perceived need to move in the implied direction at the present time.

This nonverbal dialogue with therapists constitutes the unconscious contract. Again, it takes place by means of *ideomotor response* to ideas surveyed by therapists who imply successful developmental gains. Clients can also answer verbally, of course. In so doing, they will often indicate a further elaboration of the presenting conscious contract. Subsequent to such a dialogue, therapists can proceed to introduce hypnotic induction, suggestions, metaphors, assignments, and other interventions to help clients find a way to begin movement toward these contracted areas. This form of gentle induction of hypnosis illustrates that hypnosis is a natural response to communication and problem solving. It demystifies hypnosis and furthers the notion that it has a rightful place in the realm of natural and ordinary interventions from which therapists can choose.

The procedure for *external-fixation methods* is very similar to that used in a typical ritualistic induction. The subjects are asked to focus their attention on some close external object so that they might become more absorbed in the processes of concentration. As they do this, therapists proceed with any one of a variety of inductions most suited for the particular clients before them: conscious–unconscious dissociation induction, systematic relaxation and deep-

ening, naturalistic, conversational, traditional, guided imagery, and so on. However, therapists trained in the Ericksonian approaches are most likely to use a conscious–unconscious dissociation or a conversational induction (Rossi, 1980e). Such an induction does not rule out a procedure such as the previous one for assessing unconscious motives and unconscious contracting.

Hypnotherapeutic interventions strictly aimed toward the verbally shared contract will be understood as relevant by most clients. A clear contract reduces a client's surprise or possible sense of having been tricked by the introduction of a hypnotic trance. With some clients, this is of concern and ought to be given serious attention. With other clients, it is less of a concern because of their understanding that they are seeking the therapist's professional skill regardless of the specific forms it takes.

Regardless of the method of induction chosen, what happens before and after the trance need to be considered carefully. After the trance experience is terminated, it is useful once again to ask clients to engage in the problem-solving communications that had preceded the trance. In this way, resources retrieved during the trance will be associated immediately with relevant concerns and the course of problem solving will (it is hoped) be enhanced. Even if no immediate solutions are forthcoming, simply the altered trancelike experiences of comfortable dissociation and increased understanding and objectivity or closeness and rapport are likely to be of benefit in the general process of working on solutions together. Additionally, the entire trance experience is logically embedded in the middle of a structured interaction that is designed to bolster changing family structure and transactional patterns.

ERICKSONIAN FAMILY THERAPY

Homework and Out-of-Session Tasks

As mentioned in the previous section, skill building, paradoxical prescription, and ambiguous function assignments are among our most frequently relied-upon interventions, both in and, particularly, as an adjunct to therapy sessions. We distinguish among these three types

1. Identify clients' developmental stage and tasks related to their contracted goals.
2. Isolate or identify some of the missing experiences and transactions from that developmental stage which clients could use to achieve their desired outcome.
3. Find an activity that is a component part of the needed skills or invent a context in which a portion of those skills are learned.
4. Help motivate clients by appealing to a strength or resource and assign the use of that resource in the homework task.
5. Help clients distract the limiting aspects of their conscious mind from the opinion that their homework is related to the family developmental task.
6. After homework is completed, use further assignments, metaphors, and suggestions to help clients integrate their skills and use them appropriately for the developmental tasks.

Figure 8-6. Skill-building assignments (Adapted from Lankton & Lankton, 1986, p. 132)

of assignments (Lankton, C., 1988) and find all three useful, though not necessarily with all clients. *Skill-building assignments* tend to be reserved for those clients who are particularly impoverished with regard to a specific set of skills, with whom we cannot communicate efficiently, and with whom we can have an extended therapy relationship. Many clients fit into this category who have been diagnosed as "psychotic" or "borderline" and families whose needed skills have been limited, and whose communication abilities are impaired, but whose willingness and availability for therapy are unrestricted. Figure 8-6 provides specific guidelines for skill-building assignments.

With almost all clients, however, we make use of the other kind of assignments out of the session. Paradoxical prescriptions, as mentioned before, involve continuing to do something that perhaps had been considered to be the symptom or part of the problem, but doing it with positive labeling for the intention behind it, encouragement to do the behavior voluntarily (as opposed to involuntarily), and doing it in a manner that alters or disrupts the usual routine of the behavior. The particular version of alteration usually has been elaborated upon in great detail within the course of hypnotic induction and therapeutic metaphor in the session. Typical family structure is disrupted (Lankton & Lankton, 1986).

Ambiguous function assignments have consistently proved to be worthy therapeutic interventions, both for eliciting otherwise unknown assessment information and for satisfying the family members' need to become involved in therapy. The increased involvement seems to come from stimulating a variety of thinking, feeling, understanding, and disruption of rigid conscious sets. In this capacity, it can act as a catalyst that promotes an active and personal integration of concepts that might have been elicited or emphasized within the session in a more philosophical, abstract, or irrational manner. Family organization that has already been somewhat disrupted with paradoxical prescriptions is further challenged with this process. Family members carrying out an ambiguous assignment no longer can apply the usual power hierarchy to solve the ambiguity. Indeed, no one knows what the purpose of the assignment is. While engaged in these extramural assignments, clients will, at some level, be reworking and rethinking the experiences they were examining in trance. Thus, the assignment becomes a way to help clients utilize the learning from the session to become active in the home.

Creating ambiguous function assignments is a process that is limited only by the therapist's creativity and considerations that the assignment must, of course, be legal, safe, possible, and ethical. It does not, however, involve a particular skill to be acquired or the continuation, albeit altered, of an existing behavior. The guidelines for constructing such assignments are very general. As can be seen in Figure 8-7, we design a specific activity in which clients do something they would not normally do, and the activity usually involves an object of some sort that may or may not have symbolic significance. The purpose of the assignment is intentionally left quite vague (thus the term "ambiguous function") and the clients are usually asked to speculate as to what the purpose might be or what they have concluded regarding a reason for the activity or the reason the therapist might have had for asking them to do such a thing. This questioning is usually concentrated during the session following the completion of the assignment. It is a process of looking at progressively deeper levels of interpretation by the client in response to the question, "Yes, but what did you *really* learn?" In this way, clients become the therapist and, at the same time, help ther-

---

Initial assignment construction

1. Help stimulate clients' pleasant mental arousal, thinking, and imagination with indirect suggestion and dramatic holding methods.
2. Deliver the assignment with compelling expectancy.
3. Imply that a therapeutic value and learning come from the activity.
4. Assign a specific task (time, place, act) but do not reveal its purpose.
5. Make use of an actual physical object.
6. Make sure the client is behaviorally involved in active homework.
7. Place binds of comparable alternatives on the client's performance.

After the assignment is completed

1. Ask what client(s) thought was to be learned from it.
2. Maintain "therapeutic leverage" while utilizing the client's responses.
3. Empathize and reinforce each learning.
4. Identify and accelerate the client's motivation.
5. Do not accept the client's initial thinking as complete.
6. Continue expectancy and imply the existence of more information.
7. Challenge or stimulate the client to do the continued thinking.
8. Continue the above until therapeutic receptivity is maximized.

Figure 8-7. Ambiguous function assignments (Adapted from Lankton & Lankton, 1986, p. 137)

apists better understand what they desire but have had difficulty communicating.

Dealing with Times When Change Does Not Happen

"Resistance" is a term we rarely use except to say that it is an upside-down and backward way of cooperating. We recognize that it has long been part of the official language of therapy, but the practice of therapy is evolving and slowly abandoning its adversarial metaphors about conflict, defense, attack, and resistance. We note that people only use suggestions that are relevant for them to follow. When clients do not respond in the manner the therapist has anticipated, there is some good reason why this is so and additional understanding can be gained by examining the responses that did occur.

We do not find our clients resisting us because we do not attempt to impose anything on them. By contrast, we once reviewed a tape of a family in which the therapist had explained to us that "their resistance lies in the fact that they do not use their insight to change." That therapist seemed to believe that the client was wrong and the therapist was right—yet therapeutic change had not happened! *Change is a matter of getting in contact with experiential resources, organizing them, and associating them in such a way that new relational patterns make the symptom obsolete.* Perhaps insight was not what was needed to help accomplish this.

What is too often casually labeled as client resistance is actually an indication that clients are attempting personal growth into areas where they have "doubt," lack experiential and transactional tools, or are fearful to proceed. For instance, standing up for one's own needs in the face of an intrusive parent, while necessary, might seem easy to the therapist to carry out but be met by much anxiety because of the client's conditioned visceral reaction or inexperience using selective memories to create a feeling of confidence. Still, this might be termed resistance. Our way of dealing with and responding to hesitation involving this kind of doubt or anxiety is to rethink the situation, reassess resources, facilitate a strengthening of both the experience of the desired resources and the association to the specific context, engage in additional and different interventions designed to help the client reach the same goal or goals from a different angle, and so on. We label neither ourselves nor the family as failing or resisting.

Common and Serious Technical Errors

There are three common mistakes that are closely related to the use of the techniques and an understanding of the basic approach. Therapists often confuse a technique with an approach. It is easier to discuss Erickson's techniques than to find appropriate words to convey the subtle but important difference embodied in his contribution and approach. Since Erickson's approach, therefore, has been frequently associated with his distinctive techniques, novices will attempt to apply a technique without an adequate sense of how to let the techniques develop out of a natural interaction with clients. In other words, the utilization approach (Rossi, 1980e) and the cooperation principle (Gilligan, 1986) with families ought to give rise to the formulation of interventions. However, lacking such understanding, flexibility, and security in oneself, a therapist can arbitrarily choose an intervention that may satisfy the therapist's need to be active or "uncommon" but does not come from an understanding of the family.

Therapists learning to incorporate the approach often have difficulty taking a stance based outside of the traditional approach in which they were trained. In short, a therapist can try to treat a label. The common mistake surfaces in training and supervision and reflects a total misunderstanding of the importance of Erickson's overall contribution. A revealing question such as, "What metaphor could I use with a borderline client?" speaks to this problem. The questioner has revealed the typical problem of attempting to salvage a therapeutic relationship built on the epistemological errors of a traditional approach by the use of new and flashy techniques from an entirely different approach. It must be similar to inquiring how one plays rock-and-roll chords on the frets of a sitar designed to approach the sound of music from an entirely different framework than the one that gave birth to rock and roll.

The third and final problem is one that is probably common to most therapies. That is, therapists may attempt to intervene when they merely hear of complaints or problems that are presented. They will apply techniques such as hypnosis to dig up further historical material in an attempt to better "reveal the problem." However, they fail to engage clients in conversations regarding goals and solutions that are being sought. The Ericksonian approach and the techniques developed out of it are designed to get clients moving toward goals. Beginning with that purpose in mind, and keeping it in the foreground, is often hard for therapists who wish to have the security that comes from talking about problems and unpleasant feelings and early childhood traumas. While there may be a place for these things in any particular family-therapy session, these are not the major focus. Therapists who are not goal directed and future directed will misdirect clients with the techniques that arise from Ericksonian family therapy and will misuse the approach.

CURATIVE FACTORS IN MARITAL–FAMILY THERAPY

The primary factors that lead to change in Ericksonian family therapy are the new relational patterns. Whether or not the family members happen to take the time to gain what therapists like to call "insight" is irrelevant. This is analogous to a child's learning to ride a bicycle. Learning to articulate the manner in which balance is maintained and pedals are pushed is secondary to the actual occurrence of balancing and pedaling.

Interpretations, when used, are not considered a means of conveying the objective truth. Rather, they are used to punctuate an event or experience and provide it with a verbal "handle." It is clear that this act of labeling makes it possible for clients more easily to identify or disidentify with an experience depending on the perceived desirability of the label. For example, a husband who attempts not to display sadness in the marriage might be able to identify with the act of holding back this tenderness if it is interpreted to him as his means of reducing tensions in the family as it did when he was a child. Yet, he might be able to distance himself from the withholding if it is interpreted as his means to further the emotional distance from his wife as his parents had done with him. While either of the interpretations may be a reasonably accurate shorthand means of describing the complexity of such behavior, the effect of accepting one or the other is therapeutically different. In the Ericksonian approach, this multiple level of association is something a therapist is expected to be sensitive to and manage. Since Erickson was interested in the process of change, it is possible to use many of his own words in this section to illustrate how he conceived of the process.

Acquiring Experiential and Interpersonal Skills

The advice provided from Erickson's view is that "mental disease is the breaking down of communication between people" (Rossi, 1980d, p. 75.). He added, "Problems exist precisely because the conscious mind does not know how to initiate psychological experience and behavior change to the degree that one would like" (Erickson & Rossi, 1979, p. 18). Consequently, therapy is a learning process in which communication from the therapist is needed to "facilitate the emergence of untapped potentials and response systems that the patient's own ego has not been able to utilize in a voluntary and intentional way" (Erickson & Rossi, 1980d, p. 97).

The acquisition of experiences and transactional resources is a process of learning from one's self. Personal involvement of each family member is important in facilitating such learning. Indirect suggestion, metaphor, puzzles, and so on are employed in the conversations with clients to help them make better use of their capacities for experiential learning. "Erickson has shown that by creating a similar confusion through the use of vague, ambiguous, and puzzling statements, the hypnotic subject is very likely to invest the first concrete, understandable piece of information he is given with an unusual degree of importance and validity" (Watzlawick, 1976, p. 29). There is no gain for family members if they comply with the direction of the therapist. "It is true that direct suggestion can effect an alteration in the patient's behavior and result in a symptomatic cure at least temporarily. However, such a 'cure' is simply a response to the suggestion and does not entail that reassociation and reorganization of ideas, understandings and memories so essential for an actual cure" (Erickson & Rossi, 1979, p. 9).

Learning to have and use new responses in the family requires that members do, in fact, use the novel associations outside of the office. Indeed, it may be only in the extramural setting that a full personal involvement of resources is effected. Since the approach is based on the use of naturalistically occurring experiences insofar as these can be expected in the home, assignments and daily living routines can help play a part in the acquisition of such skills and experiences. The skills we are talking about are not merely gross motor skills, but are the plethora of perceptual, cognitive, visceral, and emotional skills that are often too subtle to have become labeled in psychology. Obviously, then, interpretation of the actual mechanism of change is not feasible and technique is less important than interpersonal understanding and client involvement.

Transference

As so much of the interpersonal posture fosters internal search, there is often a hypnotic quality, or we could argue that there is a hypnoticlike relationship, to much of therapy. Therapists must be sensitive to and carefully manage the factors of rapport. Erickson has noted that hypnosis does not harm anyone but hypnotists sometimes do. He clearly notes the importance of managing one's own countertransference aspects so as not to direct therapy in a manner that serves the personal needs of the therapist rather than the needs of the clients.

Important Qualities of the Therapist

Since the "personality" of the therapist is a reification and an abstraction, it is not at all clear that this entity exists outside of a broader context. But as there is a characterizable set of communications and a redundancy in the frequency of behaviors and experiences found in the repertoire of each person, we can make some generalizations about two major qualities of the therapist that are important variables in therapy. The first is that it is desirable that therapists have great pragmatic understanding of people and of coping with life's exigencies. The second quality is an ability to step outside of oneself into the world of another person while at the same time retaining an awareness of that pragmatic understanding of coping with life. These two qualities are the operational aspects of what is usually called empathy and sympathy. An excitement about learning is visible in the most successful therapists. And finally, the ability to articulate, especially the differences between one's own experience and that of the client, is highly valuable.

While the actual and total psychological health of the therapist may not be necessary to the therapist's doing a fine job, it is likely that these factors will be present in an individual who would be labeled as "healthy" and "mature." Therapists must be sufficiently mature that they can satisfy their personal and social needs without manipulating and using others. Only in this way can we expect that therapy will be uncluttered by the machinations that give rise to iatrogenic illness. Therefore, Ericksonian techniques of therapy are only taught to people who are well founded in medicine, psychiatry, psychology, social work, or dentistry. Qualification for admission to training seminars is the possession of a proper academic degree. Although the holding of such a degree does not assure the maturity, mental stability, or general experience level of the professional, it does, at the least, ensure that the person has been exposed to peer-review boards, professional knowledge, and academic grounding.

Other nontangible qualities may influence the fitness of one therapist for a certain family. Such factors as warmth, grooming, style of speech, and other variables such as favored gestures that unconsciously communicate information about background may all be important in various cases. Certainly, some therapists and some clients cannot easily, and ought not, continue to try to work together.

The Importance of Technique

As previously mentioned, the techniques of Ericksonian family therapy are secondary to the therapist's conception of people and problems. The latter is the real contribution of his approach—a concept that is nonpathologizing, utilitarian, future oriented, action oriented, client centered, experience evoking, and developmentally framed. Rossi (1980d) may have had this point of view when he wrote:

Human experience is far more replete with examples of psychotherapeutically effective interpersonal relationships that have corrected maladaptive behavior than all the combined efforts of organized psychotherapy. There are as yet no scientific measurements of the kindly word, the challenging note, the whispered doubt, the anguished gasp, the threatening tone, the mocking noise, the contented murmur, the encouraging sound, the expectant silence. Upon such forces as these can rest the success or failure of psychotherapy. The potency of the therapy derives from the therapist's capacity for sympathetic and empathic response rather than from years of familiarization with the tenets and precepts upon which

many of our current schools of analysis and psychotherapy are founded. (p. xvii)

TREATMENT APPLICABILITY

Ethics of Approach

The use of an Ericksonian approach in family therapy depends on input from the therapist and receptivity by the therapist for stimulation of clients' life experiences. It is altogether possible, then, to expect that any type of family, disorder, or socioeconomic background would be suitable to the approach, providing it was in the range of expertise of the therapist. The results are often achieved for goals broader than the original presenting problem and much learning will take place without being strained through the conscious mind filters of each family member. While this is true in all therapies, Ericksonian approaches are perhaps more sensitive to the psychological level or unconscious influences occurring in therapy.

This brings us to a potential criticism of the approach. While it is easy to intellectualize about a different epistemological approach, in the moment-by-moment pragmatics of therapy we must be effective and accountable. Often, effective intervention is done when there is openness to new ideas—a situation that occurs when the limitations of conscious mind biases and beliefs are bypassed by means of indirect interventions.

Effective intervention with a choking person does not (cannot) require informed consent. In therapy, however, requiring prior conscious consent before eliciting motivations for actions may effectively stop therapy and block progress toward a more specific presenting problem (e.g., stopping nightmares). In these situations, the Ericksonian approach frequently works from the knowledge that clients follow suggestions that are most relevant for them and that prove to be in their best interest. Hence, an unconscious contract based on tacit or implicit approval can be obtained from a client. But once again, this may raise the question of ethics and informed consent as it has been viewed historically (Edgette, 1989; Zeig, 1985d).

Related to this issue is the need for good training and supervision for therapists and the importance of developing a research methodology that measures the effectiveness of training and therapist performance. Therapists in training must learn to be comfortable and confident, often with less verbal feedback than in other approaches. They must learn to rely on highly trained and developed observation to a greater extent. And although no two interventions are alike, accountability is accomplished by its emphasis on pragmatic and reality-based goals with clients. Furthermore, despite the uniqueness of each intervention, well-specified protocols or intervention patterns exist, are becoming more widely known, and may provide the basis for further refinements of effectiveness and therapy outcome.

Much excellent quantitative research on the effects of Ericksonian techniques is being done and published (Godin, 1988; Hollander, Holland, & Atthowe, 1988; Matthews, Bennett, Bean & Gallagher, 1985; Matthews, Kirsch, & Allen, 1984; Matthews & Langdell, 1989; Matthews & Mosher, 1988; Murphy, 1988; Nugent, 1989a, 1989b; Omer et al., 1988; Otani, 1989). These studies, while an important contribution to the understanding of Ericksonian techniques, tend to be laboratory analog studies rather than treatment studies, and tend to be based on small samples. More outcome research comparing the effectiveness of Ericksonian techniques (e.g., metaphor, ambiguous function assignments, and paradoxical prescription) with other treatment approaches needs to be done. Finally, as the profession continues to grow through the current trends created by the changing therapeutic paradigm, it is expected that the influence of the Ericksonian–strategic approach will continue to grow and flourish among researchers as well as clinicians.

CASE ILLUSTRATION

This case illustrates a typical course of therapy for a family that was experiencing significant stress despite all members being basically functional. They were seen for four sessions and accomplished changes considered desirable by both members of the couple.

Initiation and Background

Jill Norton checked the Yellow Pages under "Family Therapists" and called for an appointment. She was unsure as to whether her husband would be willing to attend. Jill and Jack were a high-school-educated couple who had been married for five years. Jack worked as a produce manager in a grocery store and Jill was a dental assistant. They had one son, 2 years of age. Jill described communication problems of such severity and duration that she was certain she would be divorcing Jack within the month if he did not change. Therapy was her last resort.

Both had come from southern homes in which children were taught stereotypical sex roles and trained to rely on these roles for a certain security. However, Jill had been exposed to professionals and paraprofessionals in the course of her dental assistanceship and had developed a model of career advancement beyond that which either she or her husband had brought to the marriage.

Assessing the Family Organization as a Problem-Solving Unit

Their family organization displayed a stereotypical power hierarchy that used social-role ascriptions to validate the husband's overt power position. His primacy in the relationship guaranteed that his decisions would have priority, and, in fact, his wife's needs and feelings would be secondary in almost every case. Her development of power had resulted in an incongruent power arrangement (Madanes, 1983) in which she reclaimed some of her centrality in the relationship by withholding attention and sexual contact from her husband. She came to this position after months of theatrical emotional expression and complaints of various dissatisfactions.

They frequently quarreled about the care of their child. Jack wanted Jill to stay home and raise their son "properly" and resented the fact that she placed the boy with a sitter so she could go to work. Even worse, according to him, she sometimes used day-care arrangements just so she could go off on her own and do something recreational rather than stay home to do traditional mothering. Although he enjoyed the extra money she brought to the household, official use of the money had also turned into a battleground parallel to their sexual situation. That is, she felt that she had some claim on this money that she had earned and that it should be spent in some ways she wanted and that his authority regarding this was not ultimate. She threatened and withheld affection (sex) when he did not allow her some discretion in spending the money.

She did not want to spend her money on a pickup truck but on dresses. She did not want to spend it on a stereo but on a romantic night on the town together. He insisted that she had no place to wear the dresses anyway and that a truck was obviously appropriate as a practical purchase; a night on the town was a frivolous expenditure whereas a stereo would last for years. In short, her ideas were of little value and his ideas were superior. Needless to say, they were not having sexual relations—when he advanced, she refused.

Use of Social Roles to Solve Problems in the Family System

Jill's ability to negotiate for her needs to be met in this family was inhibited from the beginning of their courtship. In fact, it was a pattern that had been established long before she entered courtship. Jack's role as the omnipotent authority had been perfectly appropriate during courtship and the early stages of their marriage. At that time, he rescued her from the (seeming) tyranny of her parents. During courtship, he seemed to embody all that a young woman could ask for: he was decisive, opinionated, and made all the right decisions about dating. After eight months, they were married.

Jill continued to follow him, somewhat less contentedly, into the period of childbearing. He had wanted a child and she had not really formulated a better or alternative idea. Consequently, she became pregnant. Her social role(s) had not included the prerogative for her to speak out for her needs. She did not think about her needs much and did not know how to talk about them well, at the time. All of her training, of course, required that problem solving be done with only peripheral perception of her needs and no integrated understanding of how she could represent them to others. The only exceptions

to this pattern were those needs that were congruent with the passive, compliant, relatively dependent role of the stereotypical young southern woman.

Jill and Jack lacked certain reciprocal behaviors. He was unaware and unable to nurture and she was oblivious to the possibility that she could make a straightforward expression of her needs. The presenting problem as stated closely related to this lacking set of behaviors. She had resorted to subterfuge to get her needs met because she did not know any other way to do it. He clung to his authoritarian "old ways" of solving problems and even exaggerated them because he knew nothing else. Furthermore, these old ways had worked in the past and even had been the very basis of their original attraction and relationship.

Use of Cognition and Belief to Solve Problems in the Family System

Jill did not comprehend the possibility of getting her needs acknowledged. She did not think about solving some problems by becoming angry and standing firmly for what she reasoned was correct. That is, she did not think to do so unless, as in this case, it was to threaten to end the relationship. It had not occurred to Jack that they should put themselves in an egalitarian relationship or to sit down and talk through their difficulties. He clung, rather blindly, to the idea that his expectations and interpersonal needs would be met by his wife. This was true for him even when he had not spoken about those needs. He did not think that the type of praise and reassurance that he requested was something that he, too, should give to his wife. He did not think that he should need to ask for the support he desired and was being denied.

Unconscious Resources Available for Problem Solving

Both Jack and Jill were bright, attractive people who seemed genuinely to care for each other despite their conflict. In the course of the sessions, they both demonstrated an ability to laugh, cry, show concern for the feelings of the other, and honestly to self-disclose a variety of information, beliefs, and emotion. When asked,[8] Jack described a background in which he had almost no appropriate model for how a man relates lovingly to a woman. His mother had been involved in numerous unsatisfactory relationships, and his only model had been his grandfather, who, although caring toward Jack, had behaved very authoritatively with his own wife. Jack had loved and respected his grandfather, and he internalized this model of behavior as a map that guided his use of unconscious resources. This model had worked for his grandfather two generations earlier, but it was not being similarly appreciated by Jill. Jack and Jill both demonstrated potential and motivation for learning to use themselves differently.

Jill was incongruent. She seemed saddened and self-critical about the fact that she did not please her husband according to custom. Yet, she was also curious, eager, and seeking attention for the wider view of the world she was gaining since she began to work. We might say that she was, at some level, attempting to reconcile her disappointment and sadness and her excitement about a possible future.

Developmental View of the Situation

Developmentally, this family had entered into a new stage of demands and sanctions. That is, they now had a child reaching the 2-year-old age of independence, intelligence, and verbal demandingness. These changes in the child actually seemed to parallel or echo the changes occurring in the marital dyad. Now, more than before, they had become aware of the need to use new abilities and to make and use limited free time beneficially. Their child presented them with constant opportunities to agree or dispute values that arose with each decision concerning his management and instruction. Their unified role as parents was complicated by their

diverse expectations and social roles. Also, their relating to each other was severely restricted and personal gratifications were being delayed. Both felt this to be unfair. We can see how the social, familial, and biological demands on this family, just as on the child, were calling for a change in the use of personal resources, roles, and family organization.

As Jill entered this stage, her growth and responsiveness had resulted in an ability to use more problem-solving skills than she had used in previous developmental stages. She also had an additional set of role models and career options available to her. But she was experiencing role conflict. She could go to junior college and beyond. She could approach the examples provided by the other women in the dental office where she worked. She was beginning to flirt with the idea that she might enjoy more gratification than that which comes from staying home and having another baby. Jack, of course, hoped that Jill would somehow continue to supplement the family income while also relieving him of the increased demands of their one child. He hoped she would take a traditional role— having another child, nurturing the child, and arguing less with Jack's authority. Jack and Jill communicated in one way or another that they wished to learn to do similar behaviors although each was seeing it through the lens of his or her own age and level of understanding: negotiating for needs to be met, being firm in stating needs, using disaffiliation as a problem-solving behavior, being more alone with free time, trusting that support and attention can be found when it is asked for, and showing affection or appreciation for differences between them that are noticed and trust that they are accepted by others.

Treatment and Interventions

The specific goals of treatment proceed differently in each case—but in each case, intervention at each level of the system is desired. A systemwide set of interventions, therefore, will most efficiently and responsibly assist the family members in a readjustment for changing both the consciously stated goal and the myriad of unspoken desired and related concerns. This allows for a greater range of problem-solving

---

[8] *Editors' Note*: It is interesting to note that while the treatment approaches of both the MRI's Brief Therapy and strategic therapy have well-cemented foundations in Ericksonian thinking, the Ericksonian style of family therapy described in this chapter includes a good deal more attention to the individual developmental histories of family members than do the other two, as this unfolding case illustration shows.

skills on their part. We will examine the treatment interventions as they relate to these dimensions.

Treatment was actually initiated during Jill's first phone call when we told her that we would like to see her and her husband. That same day, Jill came to the authors' (S. and C. Lankton's) office and picked up our intake forms. In this brief meeting, she wept as she spoke. It was possible for her to reduce her anxiety and we had the opportunity to make some early observations. She seemed both frightened that her marriage would end and angry at her husband for the ongoing difficulty between them. She communicated easily but we avoided listening to a one-sided story. She informed us that, after her phone call to us, she had secured her husband's agreement to participate.

They delivered their completed forms to us the next day, prior to the first session. Both agreed in their views of Jack as excessively dominant. Jack viewed Jill as behaving very much the same as he saw himself, whereas Jill's self-report revealed her to be excessively dependent. This suggested that Jill was not communicating the way she felt or that Jack was deaf and blind to her communications about these aspects of herself. Indeed, Jack's presenting complaint was that Jill wanted to be the boss. Her concern was that Jack wanted to "run" her like a machine.

Both entered the first session well groomed and polite. We spoke about the checklist they had completed prior to the meeting and how they reported perceiving each other and themselves. In brief, their checklist reports matched the stories they had told us. They both saw Jack as predominantly using dominant and friendly behavior to solve problems. Jill's self-view compared with Jack's view of her, on the other hand, differed greatly. As one might expect, Jack saw her as trying to use friendly dominating behaviors while she still saw herself as using friendly and dependent behaviors. We asked them to tell us how they thought out or came to use these ways of acting and expecting as they did. Jack spoke of his grandfather's influence in his life, which amounted to a "when men were men and women were women" type of influence.

After talking with them regarding some of the above information, we told four stories to illustrate several points. For instance, we told of Erickson's work with a couple in which the husband had promised to take regular turns with his wife in cooking gourmet meals but never did take his turn. Erickson instructed the wife to tell her husband that his week to cook had finally arrived. She was to bring home gourmet meals for herself and the children for the duration of his week since she correctly anticipated that he would only "boil potatoes and fry hamburgers." Of course, the husband in the story was very interested in why his gourmet food did not come. Within a short time, the husband decided to cook the gourmet meals he promised. Three other stories dealt with the importance of and the consequence related to checking out assumptions that were held about a spouse before acting upon them.

At the second session, they revealed that during the week Jack had actually been cooking for Jill for the first time. There had been a bit of improvement but still much of the communication was conflicted. In fact, Jill came in crying about mismatched communication and expectations about money and dinner and compliments that had occurred just minutes prior to the session.

We told them three additional stories concerning how, though he might be surprised to hear it, women can actually be thought of as "life forms" and how they, like other life forms, are unpredictable, and, furthermore, how it often is best that they can be unpredictable. We modeled how a woman (C. L.) can actually disagree with or correct a man (S. L.) in the session, and also how a man can respect both the woman and himself as he responds.

A paradoxical assignment was then given: They were asked to continue to avoid having sex but in a different (paradoxical) way. We asked Jill to make the advances four times a week and Jack to refuse sex. Reasons for this assignment were provided and their agreement was secured.

Finally, they were given specific instructions for an ambiguous function assignment: They were to rearrange five of the pictures on their walls each night. They were to do it together without speaking and always in a new random pattern. Then they were to discuss their speculations about why we had asked them to participate in this assignment and what they might learn from the activity. At the end of the session, we charged them one half the fee of the previous session because, we said, they had made such progress and we were proud of them and the work they had done. Reducing the fee, while not typical in our practice, seemed to fit in this situation. The couple did not have much money and was concerned that the treatment, which was showing success, might end. Our reducing the fee increased their motivation to change and demonstrated our genuine interest in them.

In the third session, they reported having been far happier with each other during the past week. They had many thoughts about the picture-rearranging assignment, especially related to the notion that each should (1) be comfortable with the changes made by the other, (2) not make assumptions about the other's behavior, and (3) work with the other as a team. As a result of the paradoxical "sexual" assignment, Jill empathized about how hard it must have been for Jack always to be in the role of initiating sex. She did not think the assignment was to teach this but it had occurred to her repeatedly during the week. Following each revelation by either spouse, time in the session was used to build a solid and accurate communication between them about whichever experience had been learned (the A-B, B-A communication activity).

Finally, hypnosis with metaphoric intervention was used to help stimulate learning for behavior and attitude changes. The specific behaviors illustrated in the trance included, for instance, how to ask for needs to be met. Several attitudes were also discussed and highlighted, in the trance, including the appropriateness of men and women becoming more powerful and how men and women both benefit from this in different ways. Metaphoric examples illustrating sexual conduct and satisfaction, similar to the kind about which they had spoken, were shared. Their fee was again reduced by half of what was paid the last session.

In the fourth and last session, hypnosis was again used as the primary modality for exchanging information and stimulating thinking. Metaphoric interventions were employed, which we expected would help the husband clarify his ideas about women who have power not posing a threat to a man. Emotions of joy and courage were also elicited by means of other metaphors. Finally, the couple once again was charged half the amount paid at the last session. This amount

was now $7. Jill and Jack reported that they were getting along very well. They were enjoying doing things for each other and were having sexual contact four times a week. Both of them were initiating it. The husband was taking renewed interest in the child and the wife was making plans with her husband to take a few more evening courses at the junior college. She was smiling again.

Discussion and Case Summary

The interventions described here were designed to help stimulate change on all levels of the family system. The ambiguous function assignment perturbed the level of family organization by entering ambiguity into the decision making, communication, and rules of interactions. When Jill and Jack played equal roles in rearranging the pictures, neither could know how much the other understood the meaning of the task and they could not use the habitual channels or power plays to resolve the ambiguity.

The paradoxical directive disrupted their usual sex roles by giving them an excuse for not expressing their needs and for not listening to each other. This paradoxical conduct freed them from the necessity of developing new roles while providing them with a suspension of their normal framework such that they did indeed develop roles that integrated desired behavior, attitudes, and emotions related to their unique marriage, personal needs, and stage of development. Simultaneously, it became nearly impossible for either member to continue to blame the other for the immature roles to which they had become accustomed.

Therapeutic metaphors for behavioral and emotional change helped stimulate the use of problem-solving resources at the level of behavioral and emotional communication. These stories were delivered both in and out of trance and always in a manner that included indirect suggestions. Thus, the therapy offered gentle guidance to ways in which they might implement their desires but provided a wide latitude for them to discern their own unique synthesis and outcome. Helping them carefully communicate and give feedback to each other about their learning ensured that they were building new channels of perception, understanding, and intimacy, and finding new ways to solve problems.

Finally, therapist modeling as well as therapeutic metaphors for challenging and stimulating attitude changes provided input at the level of attitude and beliefs. Hypnosis, confusion, indirect suggestions, and therapeutic binds, as well as humor and the general novelty of the sessions, further helped alert the couple to unconscious resources and broadened perceptions of possibilities of experience.

Therapy was officially concluded after the four sessions discussed here but follow-up contacts continued on a monthly basis for one year and both consistently reported that the problems they had complained about were gone. They explained that they had some communication problems early in the marriage but they felt they had matured and that whatever had caused the problems lay in the past. They said they listened to and enjoyed each other with no complaints about who is bossing whom. In fact, they added that they welcomed divergent ideas from each other and felt that they had learned to appreciate the differences that each brought to the marriage and child rearing. Recently, a three-year follow-up revealed that Jill and Jack were still very happy with their marriage. She has retained her job and he has been promoted. They have a second child and Jill has been attending junior-college classes intermittently.

CONCLUSION

It has been 10 years since Erickson's death. Numerous articles, books, and research studies about his approach have been published in that time. There have been two Evolution of Psychotherapy Conferences at which practitioners of Ericksonian and other major psychotherapy approaches have met to discuss their similarities and differences. Erickson's ideas and techniques are being taught in a number of colleges and universities at both the master's and doctoral level. Clearly, a clinical space has evolved for Erickson's work.

It is in this space that Ericksonian ideas can grow and develop. It is also in this space that the fruits of his efforts can suffer the effects of a "killing frost." This frost can occur when therapists who seek to use Ericksonian techniques (e.g., paradox, symptom prescription, metaphor, and hypnosis) do so in the absence of a systemically organized treatment plan. To intervene without consideration of the larger system could result in no change in the presenting problem or, in the worst of scenarios, a deterioration of the client's situation.

In order for practitioners of this approach to refine and develop its techniques, research that seeks systematically to measure the importance of such variables as indirect suggestion, utilization, metaphor, and ambiguous function assignments in both laboratory and clinical settings is needed. Are these techniques necessary for therapeutic change? What do they contribute to the potency of change? How effective are these methods in comparison with other methods of change? Qualitative and quantitative methodologies need to be developed to address these questions. In the absence of research that informs practice, the growth and development of the Ericksonian approach will be inhibited.

Milton Erickson's legacy was his creative approach to problem solving in therapy and his ability genuinely to connect with his clients. While there was only one of him, each of us is also unique. That the initial seeds Erickson has left in the form of his ideas and interventions should develop is essential for continued change. How they develop is purely dependent on our own unique creativity, a very Ericksonian notion.

REFERENCES

Araoz, D. (1988). *The new hypnosis in family therapy.* New York: Brunner/Mazel.

Bandler, R., Grinder, J., & Satir, V. (1976). *Changing with families.* Portland: Meta Publications.

Bandura, A. (1969). *Principles of behavior modification.* New York: Holt, Rinehart & Winston.

Bateson, G. (1972). *Steps to an ecology of mind.* New York: Ballantine Books.

Bateson, G. (1979). *Mind and nature.* New York: Dutton.

Berne, E. (1972). *What do you say after you say hello?: The psychology of human destiny.* New York: Grove Press.

Booth, P. (1988). Strategic therapy revisited. In J. Zeig & S. Lankton (Eds.), *Developing Ericksonian psychotherapy: State of the arts. Proceedings of the Third International Congress on Ericksonian Psychotherapy* (pp. 39–58). New York: Brunner/Mazel.

Broderick, C., & Schrader, S. (1981). The history of professional marriage and family therapy. In S. Gurman & D. Kniskern

(Eds.), *Handbook of family therapy* (pp. 3–56). New York: Brunner/Mazel.

Cooper, L., & Erickson, M. (1954). *Time distortion on hypnosis.* Baltimore: Williams & Wilkins.

Czech, N. (1988). Family therapy with adolescent sex offenders. In J. Zeig & S. Lankton (Eds.), *Developing Ericksonian psychotherapy: State of the arts. Proceedings of the Third International Congress on Ericksonian Psychotherapy.* New York: Brunner/Mazel.

Dammann, C. (1982). Family therapy: Erickson's contribution. In J. Zeig (Ed.), *Ericksonian approaches to hypnosis and psychotherapy* (pp. 193–200). New York: Brunner/Mazel.

Dell, P. (1985). Understanding Bateson and Maturana. *Journal of Marital and Family Therapy, 11,* 1–20.

Edgette, J. (1988). Dangerous to self and others: The management of acute psychosis: Using Ericksonian techniques of hypnosis and hypnotherapy. In S. Lankton & J. Zeig (Eds.), *The Ericksonian monographs, No. 3: Treatment of special populations with Ericksonian approaches* (pp. 96–103). New York: Brunner/Mazel.

Edgette, J. S. (1989). Tempest in a teapot: Ethics and Ericksonian approaches. In S. Lankton (Ed.), *The Ericksonian monographs, No. 5: Ericksonian hypnosis: Application, preparation and research* (pp. 105–116). New York: Brunner/Mazel.

Erickson, E. (1988). Letter discussing Dr. Erickson and the ICL, personal communication.

Erickson, M. (1975). Personal communication, Phoenix, Ariz.

Erickson, M. (1983). In E. L. Rossi, M. O. Ryan, & F. A. Sharp (Eds.). *Healing in hypnosis: The seminars, workshops, and lectures of Milton H. Erickson; Vol. 1.* New York: Irvington.

Erickson, M. (1985). In E. L. Rossi, M. O. Ryan, & F. A. Sharp (Eds.) *Life reframing in hypnosis: The seminars, workshops, and lectures of Milton H. Erickson; Vol. 2.* New York: Irvington.

Erickson, M., Hershman, S., & Secter, I. (1961). *The practical application of medical and dental hypnosis.* New York: Julian Press.

Erickson, M., & Rossi, E. (1979). *Hypnotherapy: An exploratory casebook.* New York: Irvington.

Erickson, M., & Rossi, E. (1981). *Experiencing hypnosis: Therapeutic approaches to altered state.* New York: Irvington.

Erickson, M. H., Rossi, E. L., & Rossi, S. I. (1976). *Hypnotic realities: The induction of clinical hypnosis and forms of indirect suggestion.* New York: Irvington.

Fisch, R. (1990). The broader interpretation of Milton H. Erickson's work. In S. Lankton (Ed.), *The Ericksonian monographs, No. 7: The issue of broader implications of Ericksonian therapy.* (pp. 1–5.) New York: Brunner Mazel.

Fisch, R., Weakland, J., & Segal, L. (1982). *The tactics of change: Doing therapy briefly.* San Francisco: Jossey-Bass.

Freud, S. (1938). *The basic writings of Sigmund Freud.* New York: Random House.

Freud, S. (1966). *The complete introductory lectures on psychoanalysis* (James Strachey, Trans.). New York: Norton.

Gilligan, S. (1986). *Therapeutic trances: The cooperation principle in Ericksonian hypnotherapy.* New York: Brunner/Mazel.

Godin, J. (1988). Evocation and indirect suggestion in the communication patterns of Milton H. Erickson. In S. Lankton & J. Zeig (Eds.), *The Ericksonian monographs, No. 4: Research, comparisons and medical applications of Ericksonian techniques* (pp. 5–11). New York: Brunner/Mazel.

Gordon, D. (1978). *Therapeutic metaphors: Helping others through the looking glass.* Cupertino, CA: Meta Publications.

Haley, J. (1963). *Strategies of psychotherapy.* New York: Grune & Stratton.

Haley, J. (Ed.) (1967). *Advanced techniques of hypnosis and therapy: Selected papers of Milton H. Erickson, M.D.* New York: Grune & Stratton.

Haley, J. (1973). *Uncommon therapy: The psychiatric techniques of Milton H. Erickson, M.D.* New York: Norton.

Haley, J. (1976). *Problem solving therapy.* San Francisco: Jossey-Bass.

Haley, J. (1984). *Ordeal therapy.* San Francisco: Jossey Bass.

Haley, J. (1985a). *Conversations with Milton H. Erickson, M.D.: Changing Individuals.* New York: Norton.

Haley, J. (1985b). *Conversations with Milton H. Erickson, M.D.: Vol. 2: Changing couples.* New York: Norton.

Haley, J. (1985c). *Conversations with Milton H. Erickson, M.D.: Vol. 3: Changing children and families.* New York: Norton.

Havens, R. (1985). *The wisdom of Milton H. Erickson,* New York: Irvington.

Hollander, H., Holland, L., & Atthowe, J. (1988). Hypnosis: Innate ability of learned skills? In S. Lankton, & J. Zeig (Eds.), *The Ericksonian monographs, No. 4: Research, comparisons and medical applications of Ericksonian techniques* (pp. 37–56). New York: Brunner/Mazel.

Jackson, D. (Ed.) (1968a). *Communication, family, and marriage: 1.* Palo Alto, CA: Science & Behavior Books.

Jackson, D. (Ed.) (1968b). *Therapy, communication, and change: 2.* Palo Alto, CA: Science & Behavior Books.

Keeney, B. (1983). *The aesthetics of change.* New York: Guilford Press.

Kershaw, C. (in press). *Dancing with dragons: Hypnosis in couples therapy.* New York: Brunner/Mazel.

LaForge, R., Leary T. F., Naboisek, H., Coffey, H.S., & Freedman, M. B. The interpersonal dimension of personality: II. An objective study of repression. *Journal of Personality, 23,* 129–153.

Laing, R.D. (1967). *The politics of experience.* New York: Ballantine Books.

Laing, R.D. (1972). *The politics of the family.* New York: Ballantine Books.

Lankton, C. (1985a). Generative change: Beyond symptomatic relief. In J. Zeig (Ed.), *Ericksonian psychotherapy. Vol. 1: Structures* (pp. 137–170). New York: Brunner/Mazel.

Lankton, C. (1985b). Elements of an Ericksonian Approach. In S. Lankton (Ed.), *Ericksonian monographs, No. 1* (pp. 61–75). New York: Brunner/Mazel.

Lankton, C. (1988). Task assignments: Logical and otherwise. In S. Lankton, & J. Zeig (Eds.), *Ericksonian psychotherapy: state of the arts. Proceedings of the Third International Congress on Ericksonian Approaches to Psychotherapy* (pp. 257–279). New York: Brunner/Mazel.

Lankton, C., & Lankton, S. (1989). *Tales of enchantment: Goal-oriented metaphors for adults and children in therapy.* New York: Brunner/Mazel.

Lankton, S. (1988). Ericksonian systemic approach. In S. Lankton & J. Zeig (Eds.), *Ericksonian psychotherapy: state of the arts. Proceedings of the Third International Congress on Ericksonian Approaches to Psychotherapy* (pp. 417–437). New York: Brunner/Mazel.

Lankton, S., & Lankton, C. (1983). *The answer within: A clinical framework of Ericksonian hypnotherapy.* New York: Brunner/Mazel.

Lankton, S., & Lankton, C. (1985). Ericksonian styles of paradoxical therapy. In G. Weeks (Ed.), *Promoting change through paradoxical therapy* (pp. 134–186). Homewood, IL: Dorsey Press.

Lankton, S., & Lankton, C. (1986). *Enchantment and intervention in family therapy: Training in Ericksonian approaches.* New York: Brunner/Mazel.

Leary, T. (1957). *Interpersonal diagnosis of personality: A functional theory and methodology for personality evaluation.* New York: Ronald Press.

Loriedo, C. (1985). Tailoring suggestions in family therapy. In J. Zeig (Ed.), *Ericksonian psychotherapy. Vol. 2: Clinical Applications* (pp. 155–162). New York: Brunner/Mazel.

Lustig, H. (1975). *The artistry of Milton H. Erickson, M.D., Part I and Part II* (videotape). Haverford, PA: Herbert S. Lustig, M.D., Ltd.

Madanes, C. (1983). *Strategic family therapy*. San Francisco: Jossey-Bass.

Malarewicz, J. (1988). Ericksonian techniques in family therapy. In J. Zeig & S. Lankton (Eds.), *Developing Ericksonian psychotherapy: State of the arts. Proceedings of the Third International Congress on Ericksonian Psychotherapy* (pp. 446–451). New York: Brunner/Mazel.

Matthews, W. (1985). A cybernetic model of Ericksonian hypnotherapy: One hand draws the other. In S. Lankton (Ed.), *The Ericksonian monographs, No. 1* (pp. 42–60). New York: Brunner/Mazel.

Matthews, W., Bennett, H., Bean, W., & Gallagher, M. (1985). Indirect versus direct hypnotic suggestions—an initial investigation: A brief communication. *International Journal of Clinical and Experimental Hypnosis, 32* (3), 219–223.

Matthews, W., Kirsch, I., & Allen, G. (1984). Posthypnotic conflict and psychopathology: Controlling for the effects of posthypnotic suggestion: A brief communication. *International Journal of Clinical and Experimental Hypnosis, 32* (4), 362–365.

Matthews, W., Kirsch, I., & Mosher, D. (1985). Double hypnotic induction: An initial empirical test. *Journal of Abnormal Psychology, 94* (1), 92–95.

Matthews, W., & Langdell, S. (1989). What do clients think about the metaphors they receive? *American Journal of Clinical Hypnosis, 31*, (1), 242–251.

Matthews, W., & Mosher, D. (1988). Direct and indirect hypnotic suggestion in a laboratory setting. *British Journal of Experimental and Clinical Hypnosis, 5* (2), 63–71.

Maturana, H., & Varela, F. (1987). *The tree of knowledge*. Boston: New Science Library, Shambhala.

Murphy, M. (1988). A linguistic-structural model for the investigation of indirect suggestion. In S. Lankton & J. Zeig (Eds.), *The Ericksonian monographs, No. 4: Research comparisons and medical applications of Ericksonian techniques* (pp. 12–27). New York: Brunner/Mazel.

Nugent, W. (1989a) Evidence concerning the causal effect of an Ericksonian hypnotic intervention. In S. Lankton (Ed.), *The Ericksonian monographs, No. 5: Ericksonian hypnosis: Application, preparation and research* (pp. 23–34). New York: Brunner/Mazel.

Nugent, W. (1989b). A multiple baseline investigation of an Ericksonian hypnotic approach. In S. Lankton (Ed.), *The Ericksonian monographs, No. 5: Ericksonian hypnosis: Application, preparation and research* (pp. 69–84). New York: Brunner/Mazel.

O'Hanlon, W. (1987). *Taproots*. New York: Norton.

Omer, H., Darnel, A., Silberman, N., Shuval, D., & Palti, T. (1988). The use of hypnotic-relaxation cassettes in a gynecological-obstetric ward. In S. Lankton & J. Zeig (Eds.), *The Ericksonian monographs, No. 4: Research, comparisons and medical applications of Ericksonian techniques.* (pp. 5–11). New York: Brunner/Mazel.

Otani, A. (1989). An empirical investigation of Milton H. Erickson's approach to trance induction: A Markov chain analysis of two published cases. In S. Lankton (Ed.), *The Ericksonian monographs, No. 5: Ericksonian hypnosis: Application, preparation and research* (pp. 35–54). New York: Brunner/Mazel.

Ritterman, M. (1983). *Using hypnosis in family therapy*. San Francisco: Jossey-Bass.

Rosen, S. (1980). *My voice will go with you*. New York: Norton.

Rossi, E. L. (Ed.). (1980a). *The collected papers of Milton H. Erickson on hypnosis: Vol. 1. The nature of hypnosis and suggestion*. New York: Irvington.

Rossi, E. L. (Ed.) (1980b). *The collected papers of Milton H. Erickson on hypnosis: Vol. 2. Hypnotic alteration of sensory, perceptual and psychophysical processes*. New York: Irvington.

Rossi, E. L. (Ed.) (1980c). *The collected papers of Milton H. Erickson on hypnosis: Vol. 3. Hypnotic investigation of psychodynamic processes*. New York: Irvington.

Rossi, E. L. (Ed.) (1980d). *The collected papers of Milton H. Erickson on hypnosis: Vol. 4. Innovative hypnotherapy*. New York: Irvington.

Satir, V. (1964). *Conjoint family therapy*. Palo Alto, CA: Science & Behavior Books.

Schmidt, G., & Trenkle, B. (1985). An integration of Ericksonian techniques with concepts of family therapy. In J. Zeig (Ed.), *Ericksonian psychotherapy. Vol. 2: Clinical applications* (pp. 132–154). New York: Brunner/Mazel.

Szasz, T. (1961). *The myth of mental illness, foundations of a theory of personal conduct*. New York: Hoeber-Harper.

Watzlawick, P. (1976). *How real is real? Confusion, disinformation, communication*. New York: Vintage Books.

Watzlawick, P., Beavin, J., & Jackson, D. (1967). *Pragmatics of human communication*. New York: Norton.

Watzlawick, P., Weakland, J., & Fisch R. (1974). *Change*. New York: Norton.

Weakland, J., Fisch, R., Watzlawick, P., & Bodin, A. (1974). Brief therapy: Focused problem resolution. *Family Process, 13*, 141–168.

Yapko, M. (1990). *Trance work*. New York: Brunner/Mazel.

Zeig, J. (Ed.). (1980). *A teaching seminar with Milton H. Erickson*. New York: Brunner/Mazel.

Zeig, J. (Ed.). (1982). *Ericksonian approaches to hypnosis and psychotherapy*. New York: Brunner/Mazel.

Zeig, J. (Ed.). (1985a). *Ericksonian Psychotherapy, Vol. 1: Structures*. New York: Brunner/Mazel.

Zeig, J. (Ed.). (1985b). *Ericksonian Psychotherapy, Vol. 2: Clinical applications*. New York: Brunner/Mazel.

Zeig, J. (1985c). *Experiencing Erickson: An introduction to the man and his work*. New York: Brunner/Mazel.

Zeig, J. (1985d). Ethical issues in Ericksonian hypnosis: Informed consent and training standards. In J. Zeig (Ed.), *Ericksonian Psychotherapy. Vol. 1: Structures* (pp. 459–474). New York: Brunner/Mazel.

Zeig, J., & Lankton, S. (Eds.). (1988). *Developing Ericksonian psychotherapy: State of the art. Proceedings of the Third International Congress on Ericksonian Psychotherapy*. New York: Brunner/Mazel.

CHAPTER 9

Focal Family Therapy: Joining Systems Theory with Psychodynamic Understanding

Arnon Bentovim, F.R.C. Psych., and Warren Kinston, M.R.C. Psych.

HISTORICAL PERSPECTIVE

Psychoanalytic Origins of Family Therapy

Family therapy arose out of psychoanalysis and psychoanalytically informed thinking. The early pioneers were either psychoanalysts themselves (e.g., Ackerman [1958], Wynne [1965], Lidz [1963], Stierlin [1977]), or were closely involved with psychoanalysis (e.g., Dicks [1967], Skynner [1976], Boszormenyi-Nagy & Framo [1965]). Some of the pioneers continued to practice an approach that was clearly allied with psychoanalytic work, whereas others repudiated their origins.

In the United Kingdom, the emergence of psychoanalytic theories of individual emotional development created a context in which it was easier for family therapy to maintain links with the psychoanalytic tradition. The "controversial discussions" in the 1940s were generated by Melanie Klein's (Klein, 1949) work on primitive object relations, and those led to a gap between the United Kingdom and the United States with regard to psychoanalytic conceptions. Psychoanalytic schools of thought in the United Kingdom emphasized the role of the emotional environment and the importance of relationships with the mother and the family (Bowlby, 1949; Winnicott, 1964).

The awareness of the traumatic impact of World War II and the Holocaust on individuals and families also proved to be an important influence on psychoanalytic thinking. In addition, work in the United States at this time by Bettelheim (1950) and Erikson (1963) emphasized the influential role of the family and social environment, but their contribution never became part of the American mainstream of psycho-analytic theorizing. Early American family therapists such as Jackson (1959), even while breaking with the American version of psychoanalytic theory, recognized that British reformulations such as that provided by Fairbairn (1949) could be seen as a bridge between intrapsychic therapy and family therapy. Further developments and applications of object relations theory in the United Kingdom proved successful in the field of marital work (Dicks, 1967), general practice (Balint, 1964), and hospital practice (Main, 1957). In each case, it was noted that disturbance in a person is invariably linked to relationship problems with key others in the immediate social context.

Balint and colleagues (Balint, Balint, & Ornstein, 1972), in a piece of brief therapeutic work, predicted correctly that the patient's partner would come in with the patient as the therapy progressed, and the therapist then worked with the couple as part of the psychotherapeutic work with the individual. Group analysis in the United Kingdom was a product of psychoanalysis, and was dominated in the early years by psychoanalysts (Foulkes, 1973). The application of object relations theory to group psychotherapy by Ezriel (1956), Bion (1961), and Turquet (1975) also paved the way to a move from an approach that saw a therapeutic group taking up various family roles to one that saw those same roles in the family itself. Skynner (1976) developed family therapy in this way. Skynner initially worked with the family as a special form of group, a family group as distinct from a stranger group, but soon came to see the family as a unique institution. The eventual move from seeing the family rather than the individual as the focus of work was then a small step.

Our own development began in psychoanalysis and hospital psychiatry, included the use of group therapy, and then moved to a deep and ongoing involvement in family therapy. We continue to work in all three fields.

Recent theoretical developments have brought psychoanalytic thinking even closer to the concerns of family therapists, and vice versa. A prime theoretic issue within psychoanalysis in recent decades has been that of narcissism and observations, concepts, and modes of intervention that arise from narcissistic pathology.

Early psychoanalytic writers, following Freud, had established that narcissism referred both to a person's sense of self and to a form of relationship in which that self was determined by or lost within the other (Andreas-Salome, 1962). These two notions led to the development of two separate streams of theory and technique. Kleinian writers saw narcissism as a self-protective mode of relating in which separateness is denied, the object is destroyed, and the emotional, dependent, needy part of the person is deprived of support and emotional nourishment (Rosenfeld, 1964; Kernberg, 1975). More classical analysts saw narcissism as concerned with the self-representation and its integration, continuity, and valuation (Stolorow, 1975). Such an approach to narcissism was further developed by Kohut (1971).

These psychoanalytic ideas have been taken up by one of us in associated research that has been much influenced by our study of the family. The relation between the classical self-orientated approach to narcissism ("self-narcissism") and the Kleinian object-orientated approach ("object narcissism") was clarified by Kinston (1982, 1983a, 1983b), and the relation of narcissism to repression and trauma has been clarified by Kinston and Cohen (1984, 1986, 1988). This work demonstrated that traumatic handling of the child in the family leads both to a negative valuation of the self owing to the associated nonrecognition or rejection of the child's inner core and to the development of an object-narcissistic shell to ensure physical and psychic survival. Trauma, therefore, imprints an identity on the individual and is the basis for the repetition of relationships in social life and for the occurrence of catastrophic events in life and therapy (Cohen & Kinston, 1989a).[1]

Object-narcissism manifests in three forms: as collusive pseudorelatedness (noted as the "false self" in Winnicott's writings), as apparent nonrelatedness (the "stone wall" of narcissism), or

---

[1] *Editors' Note.* The discussion that precedes and follows is extremely significant, as it represents one of the few considerations of the role of trauma to appear in "mainstream" family-therapy literature. In this way, this chapter, while grounded, in part, in psychodynamic thought, reflects a genuine effort at theoretical and clinical integration, bringing together, as it does, the intrapsychic, the interpersonal, and the transactional.

as need-driven malrelatedness (i.e., scripts or games) (Kinston & Cohen, 1988). In other words, its features are as overtly relational as intrapsychic. When the relationships are modified and object-narcissism abandoned, then the underlying trauma presents and physical, psychological, and social deterioration result (Cohen & Kinston, 1989a).

This psychoanalytic research, complementing our family research, has focused more and more on the therapist–patient relationship as a new health-promoting endeavor. A new relationship is needed to repair the trauma that persists as a "hole in the mind," and that is the source of defenses and pathological relating. The role of trauma, although emphasized by Freud, frequently has been bypassed by modern psychoanalysts, by many psychiatrists, by most family therapists, and by society as a whole. The upsurge of traumatic stress disorders in association with the Vietnam war and civil disasters, however, has increased the awareness and attention of psychiatrists (Kinston & Rosser, 1974). Physical and sexual abuse of children and marital violence are also starting to make family therapists aware of the long-term consequences of traumatic events for thinking and behavior patterns (Bentovim, 1990).

It is worth noting that the role of trauma was recognized in the early days of family therapy (Jackson, 1957), but appears to have been ignored in subsequent theories and techniques. The reason for this may lie in the fact that trauma is a one-way event and not alterable via punctuation. It brings to the fore issues of responsibility, power, inequalities among family members, and the place of social reality—all notions alien to much family therapy (as well as psychoanalytic) thinking.

Psychoanalysis and Family Therapy Today

When we look at the role of psychoanalysis in family therapy today, a variety of pictures are identifiable. One approach is to involve all family members in individual psychotherapy or psychoanalysis. Another approach involves seeing the whole family together and giving interpretations to it as an entity with the main stress being placed on transference and countertransference experiences and fantasies. In this approach, the flow of the material in sessions and the issues to be tackled may be left to the family to bring up spontaneously, reminiscent of the method of free association (Box, Copley, Magagna, & Moustaki, 1981; Zinner & Shapiro, 1974). Various approaches have been developed by therapists whose practice no longer can be designated "psychoanalytic" but who have picked out a major area of family–emotional life on which to focus, and whose psychoanalytic origin is unmistakable. For example, Bowen (1976) and Framo (1976) are particularly concerned with intergenerational issues and individuation, and Boszormenyi-Nagy and Spark (1973) with the issues of family loyalties, justice, and fairness.

In contrast to these various approaches, but perhaps closest to the last group, it is our stance to continue to draw on the knowledge and spirit of psychoanalysis while remaining true to our understanding of the nature of family functioning and pathology and the distinctive interventions that flow from these. Our work, therefore, aims to contribute to the development of both family theory and psychoanalytic theory.

Our initial foray into the family field was stimulated by the brief focal therapy with individuals as developed by Balint and Malan at the Tavistock Clinic (Malan, 1963, 1976). Their approach was based on the view that if one understood the individual's core conflict, it would be unnecessary to do prolonged intensive work. Winnicott (1971) had shown that brief intensive consultations with children could provide a therapeutic encounter with the patient that often unlocked long-standing obstacles to change. These findings ran counter to the dogmatically held belief that change could only occur as the result of long-term work.

The essence of these therapeutic developments was the abandonment of slavish adherence to prescriptions as to what constituted a proper method of intervention. The early family therapists in the United States also noted that a wide variety of methods appeared to be effective when applied to families. Ferber and associates (Ferber, Mendelsohn, & Napier, 1973) commented that the theories legitimizing such new methods appeared to be little more than a rationalization for the interventions. Madanes and Haley (1979) made the useful distinction between therapies oriented to methods—such as the structured approach to anorexia nervosa that should always include a family meal, definition of roles, and so on—and approaches catering to the needs of a particular case. The Mental Research Institute's Brief Therapy approach is one in which the nature of the intervention is not known in advance.

In a similar fashion, rather than expecting theory to legitimize methods, we expect the needs of the family to legitimize what we do. In other words, we have taken a pragmatic approach and have assimilated virtually all methods that have emerged in family therapy over the past 20 years. The needs of the family are defined by the theory we develop for each family. Without knowing it at the time, we had stumbled on a genuinely systemic conception (Kinston & Algie, 1989). Haley (1977) made the important observation that a formulation must precede intervention because it was possible to make a formulation—for example, of an "irresolvable symbiotic tie between child and mother"—that defined intervention as impossible. Our psychoanalytically oriented view similarly assumed that a suitable formulation of family life would point the way to therapeutic action. An important task, therefore, was to conceptualize the general nature of such a formulation.

Although many concrete aspects of psychoanalytic treatment could not be transferred to working with the family, certain broader principles were. Indeed, nonanalytic family therapists in many cases have been rediscovering the wheel. Intense opposition to change is a long-standing psychodynamic principle. Another is deterioration in functioning once the core disturbance is approached. Just as verbal or intellectual insight in psychoanalysis is meaningless or of limited value, we would expect the same to apply in family therapy. However, the therapeutic focus on altering patterns of action and meaning fixed by past trauma is generally a new idea for family therapists.

Development of Our Approach

Whereas a good deal of the early development of family therapy in the United States focused on schizophrenia, the development of family work in the United Kingdom began almost exclusively in child-guidance and child psychiatric clinics.[2] The emotional and behavioral disturbances in a child psychiatric practice are amenable to a psychoanalytic approach, in contrast to schizophrenia, which is relatively inaccessible. In order to apply psychodynamic thinking to family work in this service context, we set up research that had three main objectives:

1. To develop our capacity to see the family as an entity with its own life and meanings.
2. To discover ways of eliciting family interaction clinically and systematically.
3. To learn how to describe and assess family interactions in terms that are clinically meaningful and not entirely based on descriptions of individuals.

We established a workshop in 1973 to apply Malan's method of brief focal psychotherapy to families, and this work was reviewed and written up after two years (Bentovim & Kinston, 1978; Kinston & Bentovim, 1978). We became aware from that review that our methods of diagnostic interviewing and of formulating family dysfunction required improvement. Our ways of assessing process and evaluating change also required attention. Further workshops then followed, and are still ongoing, to examine these problems with clinicians and develop the methods. The methods have also been applied to specific target groups, such as families with a child who needs to go into care (Bentovim & Gilmour, 1981) or with a child who has suffered physical or sexual abuse (Bentovim, 1990).

Methods of systematic description and assessment were pursued simultaneously (Kinston, Loader, & Stratford, 1979; Loader, Burck, Kinston, & Bentovim, 1981; Miller, Loader, & Kinston, 1984). Ways of eliciting clinically relevant interaction other than in the therapeutic context were also required. A standardized method of clinical interviewing was devised (Kinston & Loader, 1984, 1986) and the task-interview approach introduced by others was improved (Kinston, Loader, & Miller, 1988a; Kinston, Loader, Miller, & Rein, 1988b). These

---

[2] *Editors' Note.* While the origins of American family therapy certainly did involve the treatment of schizophrenia, a separate generative thread in the early clinical scene also involved the child-guidance movement.

methods have also been applied to specific target groups, including obese children (Kinston, Loader, & Miller, 1987a, 1987b; Kinston et al., 1988a, 1988b) and school refusers (Huffinton & Sevitt, 1989).

Throughout this period, we have shared our approach with colleagues using videotaped material to show that it is possible to describe and assess family functioning through the approaches developed and to create an appropriate theory of the core disturbance in relationship to a particular family. We have worked to demonstrate that it can be done reliably. As we have already indicated, we regard it as a matter of principle (and a fundamental postulate of the systems approach) that methods of intervention are secondary to an understanding of the family. In confirmation, we have found that, in general, the increasing sophistication of interventions in the family-therapy field over the past decade has been integrated into our daily therapeutic work without difficulty.

Describing the Family

We now must turn to the question of how to describe the family in its context and how to describe the family itself. The family attends because its members perceive a problem either with one of them, or occasionally with family functioning, or because someone else perceives a difficulty and makes a referral. Our approach refuses to focus on the problem as perceived by the family alone, or by the referrer, but attempts to put the problem into its appropriate context. The assessment of any family provides a cross-sectional snapshot that must be placed in the context of the phase of its life cycle and of its social and general historical situation.

We have developed a general theory of symptom formulation from family research into childhood obesity (Kinston, 1987), which is based on a simple social-systems model (see Figure 9-1). The social system comprises the individual, the family, and society as its key elements, each of which is a system. The experiences that define society, families, and individuals are distinct but dependent on each other. Society's experiences are defined in terms of attitudes, norms, rights, and values. These persist largely through the

family, which serves as the agent that transmits and reproduces culture. The family depends on the societal context for support and legitimization and for its own sense of value. The family's experiences are defined in terms of its own interactions and meanings and it is itself reproduced by individuals in the family, since individuals are nurtured and socialized by the family. At the same time, individuals create and regulate the interactions and meanings within the family. The circle is completed as individuals confirm or react to (or, rarely, transform) society. At the same time, society recognizes and assigns value to individuals through their activities and achievements.

This is a completely systemic view. Despite claims to the contrary, the majority of family therapists largely ignore society and concern themselves with interactions between the family and individual members, with varying degree of emphasis on the family as a whole, or on the individual member, or on the interaction between the two.[3] Those who note the role of society tend to gravitate to political action rather than to therapy. At this stage, we, too, have taken a limited view of societal experience and will not be reporting on our steps to include this component. Because we treat families within the U.K. National Health Service, our work is legitimized through social structures and so involves certain societal statutory responsibilities. This becomes particularly evident when we work with families that have transgressed societal boundaries, for example, with respect to violence or where failure to care for a child requires the child's removal from the family.

A SEVEN-LEVEL DESCRIPTION OF FAMILY FUNCTIONING

When we came to evaluate our initial attempts to work with families (Kinston & Bentovim, 1978), we soon discovered that the family field

---

[3] *Editors' Note.* We agree fully with this observation, and we believe it is accurate because, in the end, the place in the lives of families where family therapists have the greatest therapeutic (i.e., change-inducing) leverage is within the family, not between the family and its society or culture.

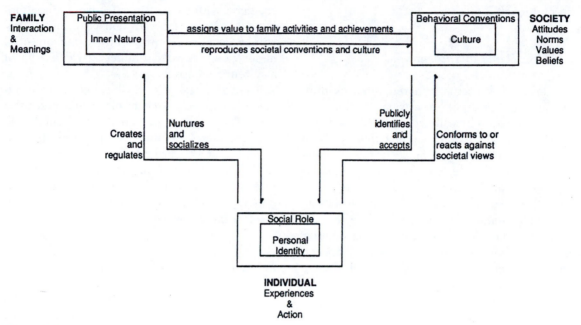

Figure 9-1.

lacked a coherent system for describing families. We found ourselves using many concepts, but we realized that we used these in a somewhat arbitary and unsystematic way. It has now become clear to us (Kinston & Bentovim, 1990) that family functioning requires description on seven distinct levels, hierarchally arranged.

Level 1. Concepts of Interaction

Level 1 descriptions are the concepts or ideas about family interaction and family life without which the simplest objective description, let alone the necessary complex account required for therapy, is utterly impossible. Without concepts to organize observation, a family interview is a complex jumble of phenomena and the observer feels lost and unable to know how and where to direct his or her attention.

Concepts applicable to the description of families may be either elemental or global. An elemental concept might be "interruption," "laughter," or "direct agreement." Examples of global concepts are "boundaries" and "parenting." Both forms are taken to be self-evident and assumed to be enduring features of family interaction. Such concepts can be ordered in

terms of levels or aggregated with others, so that, for example, "interruption" is part of "continuity," which could be aggregated with "clarity" and "responsiveness" and other qualities to form the conceptual domain of communication. It is possible to analyze communication in other ways, for example, into subdomains of pragmatics, semantics, and syntactics (Watzlawick et al., 1967).

Domains used in the family-therapy field have been identified and analyzed. For instance, Loader and co-workers (Loader et al., 1981) and Kinston and co-workers (Kinston et al., 1987a, 1987b) list the main domains as the affective life of the family, communication, boundaries, alliances, adaptability and stability of family organization, and competence for family tasks, and they subdivided each into subdomains. We later describe these concepts in more detail.

Concepts become part of the expert's specialized language and are important for any comparison of families. Therapists must, however, apply them to particular families and must validate their constructs empirically to the satisfaction of their colleagues as well as of outsiders. In any case, therapy requires realities to alter, and to appreciate realities it is necessary to focus on actual events in detail. This takes us to the second level.

Level 2. Items of Interaction

These are the actual concrete items of inter-action and the simplest account of things or events that are clinically recognizable in a particular case. The event may be either verbal or nonverbal—for example, an actual interruption, a particular hostile gesture, an identifiable agreement or disagreement, a given promise. As with concepts, these descriptions are not simple or elemental in any absolute sense. For example, the hostile gesture would be made up of a vast number of bodily movements. Clinicians require descriptions at a certain level of complexity that is sufficient to contain a basic quantum of clinical meaning.

Items can be evaluated as good or bad according to prejudice or social convention, but no judgment can be made as to whether an item taken on its own is functional or dysfunctional in the total family context. Indeed, when stripped of context, items make little sense.

Level 3. Episodes of Interaction

Level 3 descriptions are necessary because, although elements are the fundamental clinical building blocks of description, both concepts and items need to be organized into episodes that involve the whole family. An episode is an actual combination that has an inherent completeness and a coherence in time. For example, an episode might consist of all the elemental interactions (and the associated underlying concepts) required to describe a family meeting to plan an outing. An episode in the Z. family in therapy could be specified as follows: the father starts talking to the mother, who withdraws into silence; the father then criticizes their infant daughter; the mother joins in criticizing; and the father becomes silent before once again addressing the mother.

This level of description is referred to by Keeney and Ross (1985) as the "political frame of reference." Episodes have also been termed cycles or sequences. Dysfunction cannot be assessed from a single episode, but the identifi-cation and description of an episode are pregnant with implications for family functioning. This level of description is so universally emphasized that it is frequently (but incorrectly, in our view) regarded as inherently definitive of a systemic approach.

From a clinical point of view, episodes are sufficiently contextualized to make sense on their own. They link into the realities of family life and, therefore, communicate in a way that descriptions at a lower level do not. However, clinicians feel the urge to put any given episode into the context of other episodes, similar or different; in other words, to move up one more level in the framework.

Level 4. Patterns of Meaning

Level 4 descriptions produce patterns of meaning by placing family episodes in context. This level of description is referred to by Keeney and Ross (1985) as the "semantic frame of reference."

A clear judgment about the existence of dysfunction can now be made from a single account. For example, the family referred to above may plan an outing in a way that seems competent and reasonable. However, if such plans routinely are made and never carried out, or if the outings typically end in disaster, then the episode in the family is seen in a larger perspective and would be properly judged to be evidence of dysfunction.

Episodes may be reflexively put into their own context and family therapists focus particularly on episodes that regularly repeat or recycle. Such dysfunctional episodes feed back on themselves, occur without provocation, and become the primary preoccupation in family life (Kinston & Bentovim, 1981).

The salient context at level 4 is general and has no predefined limit. As the context of a relevant event or episode enlarges, deeper and more complex meanings emerge. For example, the repeated pattern of criticizing a child to generate togetherness in the Z. family would take on a different meaning if the mother had suffered physical abuse as a child than it would if the parents had had a lengthy separation following the birth of their child.

In principle, therefore, any and all perspectives can be brought to bear to bring out the fullest possible meaning of any actual episode. Very often, the meaning of any reality is to be found in the opposites that constitute it. Therefore, appreciating or reconciling such opposites is necessary. For example, if a particular episode is identified by the family or therapist as "disruptive," it is possible for it to be simultaneously identified as "cohesive." Such a way of deriving meaning long has been recognized by family therapists with labels such as "reframing" and "positive connotation."

Therapists, however, have a responsibility to intervene for the benefit of the family, and they must go beyond patterns of meanings to synthesize a model of the family as a whole, using all descriptions so far obtained. This leads to the next level.

Level 5. Holistic Formulation

Level 5 is a holistic formulation that provides a single complete account of the family as it is now. We see this as a systemic account of the family because it integrates lower-level descriptions, especially episodes (level 3) and their dysfunctional meanings (level 4). This account takes note of all relevant factors in generating a model of how the family works and can be used for intervention. Many family therapists extend or restrict the definition of relevant factors to a greater or lesser degree, while still claiming to use a family-systems approach.

To give a coherent explanation or a model of the way the Z. family works, we need to extend our inquiry. Having established that the parents come together through criticizing the child, and that the meaning pattern relates to the abuse of the mother as a child, we would need to bring these and other factors into play. Thus, we would consider interlocking patterns that draw a woman who has been abused in childhood to a particular marital partner, and vice versa; the stage in the marital relationship; the age of the child who triggered a particular response; the reasons why the case came to professional notice at a particular time; and so on. Examples of holistic formulation will be described in a number of different clinical contexts.

These five levels make up the actual levels, with the lower three relatively concrete and spe-

cific and the upper two more abstract and general. Two further levels of description exist that describe "ideal" or "theoretical" families. In one, the ideal is a type of family to which the actual family conforms to a greater or lesser degree. In the other, the ideal is a potential description the family may actualize.

Level 6. Type Formulation

Level 6 refers to the typing or categorization of the family based on one or more of its features that are considered characteristic. The aim of typing is to group together different families and to use this grouping for predictive purposes. This is required for a number of systematic activities, such as clinical policies, service planning, and adapting differentially to the needs of different groups. Such systematization may be required to enhance a therapeutic process, minimize costs, or support or orient the staff. Type description is appropriately regarded as "higher" because it encompasses and puts into perspective all descriptions at lower levels, and because it puts a family into the wider context of all families (Fisher, 1977). However, a family type requires substantial validation to be used by therapists, whose natural preference is for unique actual descriptions. At times, a type may become established by clinical lore—observations being distorted to fit postulated type characteristics.

Straightforward empirical approaches have used overt symptoms as a basis for type, for example, schizophrenic, delinquent, or multiproblem families. Olson and co-workers (Olson, Sprenkel, & Russell, 1979) have tried to use two dimensions, adaptability and cohesion, to classify families. Psychodynamic conceptions have also been applied, such as obsessional, phobic, or hysterical families. A more relevant attempt by Reiss (1981) based on paradigmatic forms of interaction of families with their environment has not penetrated clinical work substantially. Attempts have been made to test whether there is such an entity as the psychosomatic family (Minuchin, Rosman, & Baker, 1978). We have tried to base a clinical typology on the handling of traumatic events (Kinston & Bentovim, 1981). This will be presented later in the chapter.

Level 7. Requisite Formulation

Level 7 is an idealistic formulation. It is a conception of the family as it might be in the future if therapy is successful. All intervention has, by definition, some conception of a future for the family, even though this may be left indefinite or implicit. Level 1 and level 4 assessments of dysfunction, for example, are based on the violation of certain ideas of healthy interaction. In making such an assessment, an implicit description of appropriate function is being assumed. Deliberately thinking sytemically about what is possible for the family may lead to a useful consideration of the constructive contribution of other agencies, networks, or treatments, even if such issues have not emerged in descriptions prior to this level.

For a holistic–systemic approach, the level 7 description is an ideal future scenario that takes all relevant realities, including family and therapist values, into account. In order to make such an assessment without blocking a family or setting themselves and the family an impossible task, therapists need to have the widest possible imaginative and theoretical access to the family, to themselves, and to conceptions of family operation.

We have found that our focal family-therapy model requires satisfactory descriptions on all lower levels in order to derive a satisfactory level 7 description. Other family-therapy approaches do not take the same view (Kinston & Bentovim, 1990). For example, behavior therapists concentrate on concrete items (level 2) and observation of episodes (level 3) while ignoring patterns of meaning (level 4) and a holistic account (level 5). The Milan approach emphasizes the need for a holistic account (level 5), but denies the value of a requisite formulation (level 7) or typologies (level 6).

We have also found it necessary to appreciate the variety of different dimensions (level 1), rather than being locked into any single one of them. It is necessary, as well, to find ways of appreciating the immediate and longer-term historical contexts to enable us to make sense of family behavior at level 3. It was, of course, essential to be able to recognize items of interaction (level 2) and to combine them into episodes or cycles (level 3). The higher levels (levels 6 and 7) have also proved necessary for rational

therapy and for our clinical research. We will look at the various levels in more detail.

THE CONCEPTS AND ITEMS OF FAMILY LIFE

To help us describe families, we developed formats and procedures. Concepts of interaction were examined in early work (Kinston et al., 1979) and these were later organized and elaborated using dimensions of family functioning in the Family Health Scales (see Figure 9-2 and Kinston et al., 1987a) and the Summary Format of Family Functioning (Loader et al., 1981; Miller et al., 1984).

Concepts of family health were invariably seen to vary as dimensions from optimal through adequate to dysfunctional and then breakdown (Kinston et al., 1987a, 1987b; Lewis, Beavers, Gossett, & Phillips, 1976), and this occurred because values had been built in at level 3. We will now give a brief description of interactions described under each of the conceptual-domain headings. Each domain has the aspects best described in family cultural terms, in relationship terms, and in individual terms.

The Family Health Scales

Affective Life

Emotional aspects of family life include family atmosphere as a cultural feature, the nature and quality of emotional relationships within the family, and the degree and quality of emotional involvement, affective expression, and mood of family members. Family atmosphere may be described in such terms as comfort, warmth, harmony, safety, and humor, or, at the other extreme, as cold, uncomfortable, excited, dead, poisonous, panicky, chaotic, or claustrophobic. Relationships can be seen as perverse, attacking, unsupported, and inconsistent, or as facilitating, appreciative, and supportive. We can see emotional involvement as detached or overresponsive, emotionally intrusive or securely attached, and with or without understanding. Affective expression can be adequate, spontaneous, and

	Breakdown	Dysfunctional	Adequate	Optimal
FAMILY ATMOSPHERE	Dead, chaotic, sense of panic, intense discomfort, claustrophobic.	Uncomfortable, cold, tense, unsafe, overexcited.	Basic sense of safety, but with some tensions.	Comfortable, vital, warm, harmonious, sense of safety, humor available.
NATURE OF RELATIONSHIPS	Perverse, attacking rejecting, devaluing, over-dependent.	Unsupportive, un-appreciative, in-consistent, undermining.	Relationships supportive but with some inconsistencies.	Affiliative, supportive, valuing, appreciative.
EMOTIONAL INVOLVEMENT	Absence of involvement or intense overinvolvement—positive or negative.	Detachment, over-responsiveness; emotional intrusiveness.	Attachment with marginal over- or underinvolvement.	Empathic relations: understanding without intrusion.
AFFECTIVE EXPRESSION	Feelings concealed or used manipulatively; expression of affect is overwhelming or absent.	Restricted range of emotions; impoverished, confusing, or inconsistent expression.	Adequate expression of feelings with some difficulties.	Clear, open, direct, spontaneous and sensitive; full range of emotions available.
INDIVIDUAL MOOD	Inappropriate affect and/or painful or negative emotions predominate.	Members are ill at ease, flat, depressed, over-excited.	Family members reasonably at ease with themselves and their family.	Prevailing mood of members is appropriate to the situation, sense of well-being.

Figure 9-2. Descriptors from the "affective life main scale" of the family health scales, which considers the emotional life of family members (From Kinston et al., 1987a)

sensitive, or feelings can be impoverished or concealed or used manipulatively. Emotions can also be confusing or inconsistent. Individual family members can be at ease with themselves, and experience a sense of well-being or be ill at ease, with dysphoric experiences and negative pessimistic imagery. (See Figure 9-2.)

Communication

The communication dimension includes the continuity of topics, the involvement of members of the family, and how messages are expressed and received. Communication can be severely fragmented and chaotic, there can be occasional disruption and blocks, or the family can share the focus of attention, with topics and themes developing naturally. All members may participate in conversations or a particular family member may dominate, or be withdrawn, or be excluded or ignored. Messages can be clear or confused and indistinct. There may be incon-

gruence between verbal and nonverbal messages or indirect masked messages. Clarity may be mechanical or inhibited or messages may be delivered naturally and spontaneously. Messages may be heard with appropriate acknowledgment and response, or there may be lack of attentiveness or failure to acknowledge, or responses may be bizarre. (See Figure 9-3.)

Boundaries

In this dimension, we are concerned with the family's relationship to the environment, and with family cohesion, intergenerational boundaries, and individual autonomy. Families with a distinct identity and yet integrated with the outside world contrast with families that are suspicious and threatened, uninvolved, and overly self-sufficient, or cut off and insular. An optimal stage of individuation will be balanced with closeness, but family members may be generally isolated from one another or grossly overin-

	Breakdown	Dysfunctional	Adequate	Optimal
CONTINUITY	Severe disruption, fragmented, chaotic communication, fixation on a topic.	Mechanical, disjointed, stuck; topics poorly sustained.	Occasional loss of continuity, but little disruption.	Ability to share a focus of attention; natural development of topics and themes.
INVOLVEMENT	Marked domination, severe withdrawal, active exclusion.	One or more members attempt to dominate or have difficulty in participating.	Minor degree of inequality of participation.	All members participate fully, as appropriate.
EXPRESSION OF MESSAGES	Indirect or masked messages; verbal/nonverbal incongruence; minimal verbal interchange.	Clarity impaired; expression is mechanical, inhibited, or confused.	Messages are generally clear, but sometimes meaning is uncertain or ambiguous.	Clear direct messages delivered naturally and spontaneously.
RECEPTION OF MESSAGES	Failure to listen, acknowledge, and respond, or bizarre responses.	Lack of attentiveness; inappropriate responsiveness.	Listening and acknowledgment are adequate with occasional lapses.	Members listen, acknowledge, and respond appropriately to one another.

Figure 9-3. Descriptors from the "communication main scale" of the family health scales, which considers verbal and nonverbal interchange among family members (From Kinston et al., 1987a)

volved. Instead of a well-defined but flexible and age-appropriate parent–child distinction, there may be a rigid boundary between the generations or so much blurring that there is little to distinguish between the roles of parents and children. The individual members may have a sense of self-awareness and be responsible for their own behavior or may evidence difficulties with self-assertion, with a poor sense of self and problems in belonging in the family. (See Figure 9-4.)

Alliances

The dimension of alliances refers to the pattern of relationships—the marital relationship, the parental relationship, and parent–child relationship(s). Parent–child interaction may be based on care and concern, appropriate attention to the children and participation in the children's activities, a strong parental coalition, agreement on child rearing, sharing of pleasure, and a mature, supportive, affectionate relationship in the marriage. We may, alternatively, find needless disagreement between parents, evident marital dissatisfaction or distance, serious discord between children, or exclusive or shift-

ing alignment with parental conflict repeatedly being detoured through a child. The parents may be predominantly unsupportive of the children and show poor understanding of them. Parent–child relationships may be rejecting or based on exploitation, and children may be ignored or disqualified; the children may relate to their parents in a cooperative spontaneous way or one or more of the children may exhibit oppositional, withdrawn, or domineering behavior while others may avoid, reject, or cling to parents. Siblings may interact freely with shared enjoyment, affection, and concern, and differences that can be easily resolved, or they may show extreme rivalry or permanent discord. (See Figure 9-5.)

Family Adaptability and Stability

Family adaptability and stability refer to the family's capacity to function as a continuing group with commitment on the part of members. In some families, there is a lack of safety within the group and family members do not stand up to each other. There may be an imminent sense of breakup or a sense that family stability is only maintained at the cost of severe

	Breakdown	Dysfunctional	Adequate	Optimal
RELATIONSHIP TO THE ENVIRONMENT	Family is cut off, insular, threatened, fragmented; very weak family identity.	Family is overly self-sufficient; helping agencies involved in family disturbance.	Family unit is somewhat over- or underinvolved with its social environment.	Family has a strong, distinct identity and is integrated with its social environment.
COHESION	Extreme isolation of family members, or gross overinvolvement	Members over-react to one another; or are intrusive and/or detached and uninterested.	Minimal over- or underinvolvement between members.	Family is close, but members show appropriate individuation.
INTERGENERATIONAL BOUNDARY	Overly rigid boundary or little distinction between roles of parents and children.	Parents or children disrupt generational boundaries; confusion in parent/child roles, or some role reversal.	Parent/child distinctions generally clear with occasional uncertainty or inflexibility in role behaviors.	Well-defined and appropriate parent/child distinctions.
INDIVIDUAL AUTONOMY	Members show poor sense of self, overdependence; or pseudo-independence, isolation.	Problems of separation and individuation are evident in members.	Self-assertion occurs but problems in autonomy or self-development in some areas or in a member.	Self-awareness and awareness of others; each member shows a sense of responsibility and belonging.

Figure 9-4. Descriptors from the "boundaries main scale" of the family health scales, which considers separateness and connectedness between family members and the outside world (From Kinston et al., 1987a)

and pervasive pathological interaction. The family may be overwhelmed by even minor environmental demands or it may deal with these in a constructive manner. Family organization may be flexible, with roles and relationships that adapt to meet individual needs; alternatively, it may be inflexible, rigid, or unadaptable. (See Figure 9-6.)

Family Competence

Competence deals with family conflicts, decisions, and problems. Differences between family members may need to be acknowledged and resolved using negotiation and compromise. Alternatively, conflicts remain unresolved, and there is repeated displacement, triangulation, or denial of conflict. Continuous futile arguments may develop, leading to withdrawal and the breakdown of communication. Similarly, decision-making processes may be clear and involve the appropriate family members, or they may

be disruptive and ineffective and the family may not recognize the need to make decisions. Problems also may not be recognized or may be responded to in a delayed and inadequate fashion. Alternatively, the family may perceive problems accurately and tackle them with flexibility and in a spirit of mutual cooperation. Management of children is one of the key areas in which competence must be assessed. Child care may ensure appropriate behavioral control, consistency, and flexibility, or expectations of children may be inappropriate or confusing, with insufficient behavioral control. (See Figure 9-7.)

THE DERIVATION OF MEANING

Using the above concepts or dimensions, we have indicated the variety of interactional elements and episodes that can be observed when viewing the family or can be heard in reports of family life. We have already described the dis-

	Breakdown	*Dysfunctional*	*Adequate*	*Optimal*
PATTERN OF RELATIONSHIPS	Serious deficiencies: marked splits, scapegoating, severe triangulation, or isolation of all family members.	Serious discord or distance between members, or shifting or exclusive alignments. Children repeatedly detour parental tension or conflicts.	Satisfactory relationships but with greater closeness or distance between some family members than others.	The nature and strength of relationships between family members is constructive and appropriate to their respective ages and roles.
MARITAL RELATIONSHIP	Destructive relationship, e.g., couple fused, at war, or isolated from one another.	Overt marital difficulties; or both partners dissatisfied.	Basically satisfactory with some areas of discontent.	Mature relationship; warm, supportive, affectionate, empathic, compatible; spouses work together well.
PARENTAL RELATIONSHIP	Parents not working together at all, or extremely weak, divisive, or conflicted relationship.	Parents repeatedly disagree, act without reference to one another, or one parent repeatedly takes over or opts out.	Basic agreement on child rearing but with some deficiencies in support and/or working together.	Strong parental coalition; agreement and cooperation in child rearing; sharing of pleasure and mutual support.
PARENT–CHILD RELATIONSHIP	Both parents reject, ignore, exploit, continuously attack, or disqualify a child.	Parental attitudes and behaviors are clearly unsupportive or harmful; poor understanding of the children.	Parents support children and enjoy being with them but with minor or occasional problems in relating to the children.	Parents show care and concern; understand and pay attention to children appropriately; and are ready to participate in their activities.
CHILD–PARENT RELATIONSHIP	Children avoid, reject, continually oppose, or cling to parent(s); or show marked differentiation in their attitudes toward each parent.	One or more children show oppositional, withdrawn, overdependent, or domineering behavior toward parent(s).	Child–parent relationships are secure, but with mild difficulties in some areas or between particular dyads.	Children relate to both parents; are cooperative yet spontaneous; feel safe and show appropriate dependence.
SIBLING RELATIONSHIPS	Sibs fight continuously or ignore each other; extreme rivalry and competition for the parents' attention.	Obvious discord or distance between the sibs.	Sibs affiliate with some limited rivalry, quarreling, or lack of contact.	Sibs interact freely with shared enjoyment, affection, concern; differences can be resolved.

Figure 9-5. Descriptors from the "alliances main scale" of the family health scales, which considers the relationships and coalitions among family members (From Kinston et al., 1987a)

tinction between the simple elements and episodes of family interaction (levels 1 and 2) and the systems of meaning and dimensions of family life (levels 3 and 4). We must now turn our attention to the way in which we make sense of the particular interactions. An understanding of meaning is required to make the connections that enable us to create a total picture of how a given family works at present (level 5).

We have indicated that meaning is derived from a context-based interpretation of observable interaction. The aim is to provide an account

	Breakdown	*Dysfunctional*	*Adequate*	*Optimal*
FAMILY STABILITY	Sense of imminent family breakup; stability is only maintained at the cost of severely dysfunctional interaction.	Feeling of insecurity within the family; lack of commitment to the family.	Family has a secure identity, but some evidence of fragility or instability.	Family is secure as a continuing group with high commitment from its members.
RESPONSE TO CHALLENGE	Family ignores or is overwhelmed by demands or its own needs; relates poorly or destructively to its environment.	Family relates to environmental demands or needs of members in a paranoid, confused, or stereotyped way.	Family responds fairly well to problems and challenges but with some inconsistencies or difficulties.	Family deals with internal and external demands constructively; and takes opportunities to develop itself.
ORGANIZATIONAL ADAPTABILITY	Family is so rigid or so chaotic that severe disruption and minimal adaptation follow stress.	Roles and arrangements are inflexible and often inappropriate to family needs or to particular circumstances.	Family organization is flexible, but with blocks or rigidity in some areas.	The family is able to adapt rapidly and appropriately to meet individual needs and changing circumstances.

Figure 9-6. Descriptors from the "adaptability and stability main scale" of the family health scales, which considers the capacity to alter to meet changing needs and circumstances while remaining the same (From Kinston et al., 1987a)

that can be said to make sense of the interaction, which is the object of study. Such an approach is usually described as a hermeneutic one, and it is an essential part of the needed psychoanalytic tradition (Ricoeur, 1970), and, some would say, of all social science (Steele, 1979). Interpretations or systems of meaning can be seen as the depth structure of a family in contrast to interactions, which are surface manifestations. Meanings structure confusion and obscurity and are validated by a community of like-minded interpreters. Interpretations, therefore, can be used as a basis for deductions and nonclinical investigative efforts (e.g., Kinston et al., 1987a, 1987b, 1988a, 1988b). In other words, we are putting forward a view that family interaction occurs within a coherent meaning field, a view that, broadly speaking, family therapists share.

To be a human being is to experience one's situation in terms of meaning, and family interactions that occur against a background of desire, feelings, and expectations are inevitably charged with meaning. *There is no one-to-one correspondence between surface action and depth meaning.* A particular interaction pattern may relate to a variety of different meanings, and a

particular meaning (and its associated actions) constitute a family reality. We have found it helpful to distinguish between common meanings and intersubjective meanings.

Common Meanings

Common meanings are rooted in the psychic life of the individual family members. Each member has his or her own unique experience, much of which remains unconscious or private and not directly relevant to the concerns of other family members or the family therapist. There are certain common meanings that, however, are shared at the time of marriage and develop in common afterwards. When children appear, they assimilate and contribute to these. Common meanings are exchanged and shared, unconsciously and by example and instruction, and include beliefs, views, guiding principles, fears, and expectations. They are the basis for belonging, loyalty, and cohesion within the family. Common meanings are essential for comfortable communication, pleasurable participation in interests, and tolerance of each other's pain. They

	Breakdown	Dysfunctional	Adequate	Optimal
CONFLICT RESOLUTION	Conflicts are denied or ignored, lead to continuous futile arguments, or to withdrawal and breakdown of communication.	Poorly handled conflicts disrupt completion of tasks. Members become embroiled in the conflicts of others.	Conflicts generally acknowledged and resolved, but occasional overreaction, denial, or lack of resolution.	Conflicts acknowledged and resolved by negotiation and compromise between the relevant participants.
DECISION MAKING	Decision making is severely impaired: no recognition of need for decisions; lack of acceptance of result; no action on decisions.	Making decisions is a problem for the family. The process is often disrupted or ineffective.	Decisions are generally taken and acted upon where necessary, but with occasional difficulties or dissatisfaction.	Decision processes are clear, involve members appropriately, produce satisfaction, and outcomes are accepted.
PROBLEM SOLVING	Lack of capacity for solving problems in an effective way.	Problems often not recognized, or response is delayed, inadequate, uncoordinated, or impulsive.	Problems are tackled but somewhat inflexibly, inefficiently, or simplistically.	Problems accurately perceived, tackled with flexibility and good sense; spirit of cooperation.
CHILD MANAGEMENT	Behavioral control is absent, chaotic, bizarre, or ruthless.	Overt problems managing children; unrealistic or inconsistent expectations.	Children handled fairly well, but some difficulties or inappropriate expectations.	Expectations of the children are realistic and control is flexible yet consistent.

Figure 9-7. Descriptors from the "family competence main scale" of the family health scales, which considers the skills required to carry out the family tasks of nurturance and socialization (From Kinston et al., 1987a)

are the basis of consensus, easy conflict resolution, and a coherent response by the family to the environment and to developmental changes. When a member leaves the family, he or she can take these meanings without disrupting the family and can use them in the creation of a new family.

Intersubjective Meanings

Intersubjective meanings, by contrast, are not the property of any single member, but instead are rooted in the interactions that constitute family life. They are, therefore, part of the self-definition of the family as a whole. Intersubjective meanings are created by different members taking up complementary roles. Should a member leave, he or she can only perpetuate the meaning by finding others who relate in a particular way or coercing them to do so.

In a psychoanalytic theory, complementarity is understood by use of object relations theory.

An individual is described as projecting an aspect of himself or herself or interjecting aspects of others. Such activities result in the individuals involved being locked together. If one departs, a substitute must be found.

Powerful common meanings lead to the development of a web of intersubjective meanings. This notion is not a new one in family theory and has been referred to by a number of labels, including "family matrix," "family identity," and "family myth." These terms clearly express the notion that the family has its own reality, which members serve. It has been noted that members of healthy families appear weaker when seen separately at interviews, whereas in poorly functioning families, a separate individual interview reveals strength in members (Lewis et al., 1976). This is so because the family's emotional and cultural reality has an obscuring effect on its members' psychic reality.

Stress and the Development of Dysfunction

We have already commented on past traumatic events as a critical factor in the presentation of a family for therapy. The experience of an event as stressful and potentially traumatic depends on existing meaning systems based on urges for survival, well-being, and attachment. Meaning systems are required for the psychological handling of stress and the activation of any frequent, and possibly continuous, experiences that are mainly unconscious. Systems of meaning developed during childhood ordinarily can subsequently undergo relatively minor modifications, but there may be major alterations in adults following massive trauma (Kinston & Rosser, 1974). Psychoanalysis aims at a major revision of meaning.

In family therapy, we refer to the parents and children who present for help as the "family of procreation" and the previous generation (that is, grandparents, parents, and siblings of parents) as the two "families of origin." In the families of origin, the parents obtained personal experiences and family life experiences that resulted in unique systems of meaning. Marital choice then depends on both similarities (common meanings) and complementarity (intersubjective meanings). Children are born into this marital reality and immediately alter it. Events that occur in the family of procreation have minimal adverse effects on the children if the parents can contain their mental impact and can connect them positively. Children usually cannot be completely shielded from traumatic events, as most are unconsciously produced by the parent. However, parents and others can assist in repairing the damage. The health-promoting processes of acceptance, integration, and resolution and working through of meanings associated with traumatic events are often incomplete in childhood and are the basis of vulnerability to stress in adulthood.

Healthy families adequately nurture and socialize their children and provide psychosocial protection and support for all members. Functioning in the main dimensions may not be optimal but is adequate. Underlying and enabling this is a functional web of common and intersubjective meanings. Dysfunctional families that show inadequacies on the main dimensions reveal certain characteristics in their episodes of interaction, which need to be noted in a clinical assessment. The characteristics are as follows:

1. *Repetition.* Certain interactions are extremely repetitive, often to the point of characterizing the family.
2. *Irrelevance.* Pathological interaction appears to be independent of external events and irrelevant to the needs of the situation. Cycles of interaction often appear to be set off randomly or haphazardly.
3. *Vicious circles.* Dysfunctional patterns of interaction exist that are self-maintaining.[4] Each element leads to the next and finally back to itself (hence we refer to the episodes as "cycles.")
4. *Compulsiveness.* A simple request to the family to stop behaving in this way cannot be complied with for any significant length of time, and often not at all.
5. *Urgency.* The cycle has a dominating and urgent quality that overrides apparently destructive consequences.
6. *The symptom (or presenting problem) is part of the cycle.*

Looking at cycles in terms of common and intersubjective meanings reveals clinically important differences among families. For instance, pathological common meanings may predominate or constructive meanings may be lacking, or intersubjective meanings may excessively influence the role assigned to a particular family member. The following example illustrates these points.

In Kinston and Bentovim (1981), we described the K. family, an enmeshed family in which common meanings were pathological. Thirteen-year-old Sheila presented medically with life-threatening obesity and was admitted for rapid weight loss and psychological management. Family members believed in the importance of mothering in the family to the degree that all members expected the mother's complete availability. If the mother was absent, the father took

---

[4] *Editors' Note.* Of course, functional patterns of interaction exist that are self-maintaining in healthy families. It is not the circularity of causality that distinguishes health from pathology, but our labeling of given patterns as desirable or otherwise.

her place and followed the same rules, which included the prescription that family members should speak whenever they wanted, members should ignore any other family member's discourse, and members should eat whenever they wanted. The meaning of these rules, which were held by each individual as well as being part of the family culture, was that "separation or any threat of separation is equivalent to total abandonment and death." This meaning was associated with complete avoidance of the awareness that severe obesity was itself life-threatening.

In another family described in the same chapter, there was absolute disagreement as to whether or not the family would have another child. It emerged that there was a lack of common meanings where they were required. The first child had been adopted and the second child was born with a variety of physical abnormalities. The father, in his family of origin, had a sibling born with severe mental retardation, and following the birth of his own child with minor physical problems, he felt he could not take the risk of a further child being born impaired. He was convinced the child would be severely handicapped like his sibling. The mother, on the other hand, experienced her own upbringing as one occurring in a state of blissful warmth and care, due to the attention paid to her minor asthmatic problem. For her, a further child represented a welcome addition to the family and she felt no concern about a possible handicap. Indeed, for her, a degree of handicap was an additional welcoming feature. A lack of common meanings with respect to another child thus led to interpersonal distance and a failure in conflict resolution.

As an example of pathological intersubjective meanings, we described a family where a father and his young adult son constantly quarreled and competed, activating each other into dangerous and risky behavior, such as driving recklessly while drinking and taking drugs. The mother found herself shifting in her alliances, supporting her husband and her son in turn. This repetitive pattern of interaction acquired meaning in the context of the family's histories. Both parents had fathers in special roles, yet these roles were diametrically opposed. The father's father had died early and was greatly idealized by his mother. The mother's father had left the family at an early age and was as greatly denigrated.

Both parents had never mourned their own fathers, but instead preserved them intact in the family despite their totally opposite characters. The relationships with dead fathers were involved in the intersubjective reality of the current life. On the one hand, the father found himself having impossibly ideal expectations for his own son, much as he had felt from his own father, and this led to merciless criticism. At the next moment, the father found himself criticized and denigrated by his wife when she offered maternal support to her son. Thus, a classical triangling situation based on complementary roles expressed powerfully held intersubjective meanings concerning father–child relationships.

When families are in the grip of such intensely held meanings, they cannot respond effectively to actual current events and experiences. Meeting the stresses of family life and fostering the development of individuals require a variety of flexible responses. But overpreoccupation with intense fears and historical concerns led, in the examples given, to such actions as overeating, conflict between parents, and dangerous life-threatening activities, which are, in effect, avoidance maneuvers. Such avoidance maneuvers may be deployed to prevent a family from facing any aspect of the whole gamut of human experiences, whether this be mutuality, commitment, intimacy, loss, separation, individuation, personal change, disappointments, or even historical reality. Pathological cycles of surface action with their dominating urgent quality result in the emotional implications of many different aspects of life being ignored.

A Proposed Typology

Level 6 refers to a classification of families. Any classification depends on the form of lower-level description. We have proposed, but not yet validated, a typology that emerges from our descriptive approach.

In the families that come to our clinic, it is possible to distinguish those where the primary stress that gave rise to pathological meanings and dysfunctional cycles occurred in the family of origin from those where attendance is due to stressful events in the family of procreation. In other cases, the presentation implies severe stresses in both the family of origin and the family of procreation, either because events in the previous generation had so affected matters that stresses in the family of procreation are precipitated, or because family-of-procreation events have activated buried, but not inactive, family-of-origin traumas.

We have distinguished the following three mechanisms for the handling of meaningfulness. These explain the formal characteristics of the operative meaning system in the family. The mechanisms apply to events in either the family of origin or the family of procreation, although with the final result differing in each.

1. *Denial, nonassimilation, or ignoring.* For example, the obese family showed a complete lack of appreciation of the life-threatening nature of obesity.
2. *Repetition without resolution or working through.* For example, in the family with father–son quarrels, there was a straightforward re-creation of attitudes toward fathers.
3. *Depositing or reversal,* that is to say, attempts by a family to turn experiences into their opposites. For example, parents who lived in foster care themselves as children may become absolutely determined that, whatever the consequences, their child will not go into foster care.

Although these mechanisms are not independent of each other, they do seem to be applicable independently and to make sense when applied clinically. Byng-Hall (1989), for example, describes replicative and corrective scripts in families corresponding to types 2 and 3 above. We suspect that particular characteristics and forms of family interaction in the presenting family (that is, the family of procreation) can be linked with each of the categories in Figure 9-8, which summarizes our clinical findings. If there is no trauma, this means that stressful events have been accepted and worked through to form functional, common, and intersubjective meanings (category A). Categories B and C indicate the differential effects on meaning, depending on whether the site of stress is the family of origin or at procreation and according to the mechanism used for handing meaningfulness. Category D refers to those families where stress is to be found in both generations. We are currently studying this classification using our key

method of description, the focal formulation and focal hypothesis, and it is to this that we now turn.

THE HOLISTIC FORMULATION

A holistic view of the family has been built into our approach by requiring the therapist to develop a focal hypothesis to explain *all* known disturbances in light of the family history. To assist the therapist in gathering and laying out the information required for creating a focal hypothesis in a systematic way, we have developed a focal sheet (its details and a case example will be provided later). Its essence is captured in a focal hypothesis. There are four logical steps in the construction of a focal hypothesis, or holistic formulation.

Step 1. How Is the Symptom a Part of the Interaction?

The first step in making a focal hypothesis is to restate the symptoms in family interactional form or as an expression of a family meaning. In other words, it is necessary to clarify the features of the symptom or problem presented and appreciate how it fits into the family (or sometimes into the family-and-agency context). That is, we ask ourselves, "How does the family interact around the symptom, and how does the family interaction affect the symptom?"

Example 1 (from Kinston & Bentovim, 1982) is the difficult L. family with Richard, a 6-year-old boy with behavior difficulties. He was unresponsive and defiant and had frequent temper tantrums. These problems, combined with his lack of friends and his poor school progress, were recognized as getting him excluded from the family, drawing his parents together.

Example 2 (from Furniss, Bentovim, & Kinston, 1984) is the J. family, which was referred for help with Nikos, a 10-year-old, mentally handicapped boy. He was well adjusted in his present school, but disinhibited, hyperactive, and uncontrollably aggressive in the family. The symptoms were especially prominent in public and with his father. The symptom in the family context was found to be an expression of the

Site of Stressful Events	Handling of Meaningfulness of Events by Family Members Involved	Characteristic of Operative Meaning System in Presenting Family
A. Family of origin and family of procreation	Accepted, integrated, resolved, worked through	Functional web of common and intersubjective meanings
B. Family of origin: • Events that have affected both parents as children and hence their ways of being and systems of meaning	Denied, ignored, not assimilated	No meaning, loss of meaning, artificial meaning
	Repeated, accepted, not resolved, not worked through	Shared pathological common meanings and repetition of intersubjective meaning
	Deposited, reversed	Reversal of past intersubjective meanings
C. Family of procreation: • Events that affect the mother and father as adults and require integration within already operating systems of meaning	Denied, ignored, not assimilated	Displacement of meaning, falsity of meaning
		Lack of shared common meaning
	Repeated, recreated	
	Deposited, reversed	Shared common meaning that x is bad or contains all bad things
• Events, including the parental response, that affect the next generation • Or current (e.g., handicap, accident, stage in family life cycle)		
D. Family of origin and family of procreation: • Events in the former, including the resulting systems of meaning that lead to events in the latter • Events in the latter that activate undealt-with issues in the former	(Combinations from the above)	

Figure 9-8. Classification of family pathology.

family belief (meaning) that nobody should control any child.

Example 3 (from Jacobs, 1986) is the D. family, consisting of two parents and four young adults. This was an unusual situation where the only daughter, who was 21, was involved in an ongoing incestuous relationship with her father. We concluded that the symptom was not the incest per se but its public announcement.

Drawing the rest of the family's and professionals' attention to the ongoing incest kept the family together, and, in particular, increased parental concern and marital closeness despite the discomfort.

Example 4 is the Q. family, an Orthodox Jewish family in which the 16-year-old daughter presented with weight loss, cessation of periods, and school failure. The therapist concluded that her attitude toward these problems focused parental attention on her exclusively, and meant that other children in the family were ignored.

Step 2. What Is the Function of the Current Interaction?

Having established the way that the symptom is a part of family life, the next step is to determine the function of the symptom-interaction complex. The therapist has to infer from a variety of clues what the current interaction (in which the symptom is embedded) would be were it not present.[5]

In the L. family, we suspected that if the parents did not draw together and exclude their son, the result would be severe conflict between the parents.

In the J. family, with the uncontrollable handicapped child, we concluded that taking control of the children would mean viewing Nikos as handicapped rather than as naughty.

In the D. family, containing an incestuous relationship, we concluded that the incest controlled emotional closeness between the parents: too much might lead to actual physical violence between them, and too little, or complete marital separation, would result in the father's becoming overtly psychiatrically ill.

In the Q. family, with the failing elder daughter with anorexia nervosa, we concluded that removal of attention would make the family face problems in the other children—the 13-year-old son with early autistic symptoms and the 9-year-old son who was also failing markedly at school.

Step 3. What Is the Disaster Feared by the Family?

The third step is to ask what the disaster is that is so feared by the family that the interactional consequences clarified in step 2 cannot be

---

[5] *Editors' Note*. We believe it is essential that the therapist not overlook the distinction between the *function* of symptoms and interactions and the *consequences* thereof. Consequences require systematic descriptive *observation* to be determined, while functions require systematic *inference and attribution* to be arrived at.

faced and dealt with sensibly. Why, for instance, in the L. family is marital conflict avoided? Why in the J. family is recognition of the child's handicap avoided? Why in the D. family are the acceptance and handling of marital violence or psychiatric illness avoided? Why in the Q. family are the sons not being helped?

In the L. family, the feared disaster was that marital conflict would inevitably lead to marital breakdown. In the J. family, recognizing the handicap would mean taking the blame for it. In the D. family, there was a conviction that violence would lead to murder and psychiatric illness would lead to suicide. In the Q. family, there existed a fear that if the daughter were not the center of the mother's life, she (the daughter) in effect would be abandoned, and an intolerable recognition of the boy's chronic autistic handicap would be forced on them.

Step 4. How Is the Current Situation Linked to Past Trauma?

It could be argued that anxieties such as those listed are present in many families and that their selection is arbitrary and nonspecific. However, following our theoretical principles, a fourth step is essential. A plausible link between formulations developed in the previous steps and salient traumatic events in the past family life must be demonstrated using available evidence and psychodynamic principles.

In the L. family, we speculated that the most salient historical event was the mother's incestuous relationship with her own father, the discovery of which eventually led to his imprisonment and to marital breakdown. The link between this family-of-origin trauma and the current family dysfunction appeared to be that if parental relationships with children compete with the marital relationship, the end result will be the breakdown of the marriage. Only complete exclusion of the child can prevent this. This is the reverse of the exclusion of the parent as occurred in the family of origin.

In the J. family, what appeared most salient was that at the time of the mother's pregnancy with Nikos, there was a period of intense marital conflict and the therapist discovered that a conviction had developed that this conflict had actually caused the handicap. Facing the handicap now would mean facing this guilty knowledge. The trauma here lay in the family of procreation.

In the D. family, the prime salient events were identified in the father's family of origin. The father had been beaten as a child, which was justified by moral strictures, and his brother had attempted suicide after being abandoned by a girlfriend. These traumatic experiences provided the conviction that violent action is possible and permissible and that death follows abandonment or separation. Each of the parents had an isolated young adulthood and each clung to the other. This clinging led to an inability to deal with conflicts and to sexual failure. Incest maintained the parents' marital relationship, but at a safe distance.

In the Q. family, the salient trauma lay in the mother's family of origin. The mother was a Holocaust survivor. Her own mother, the maternal grandmother, was her only surviving relative, and they clung together. The maternal grandmother had to support the family and so could give only limited attention to her daughter, who felt abandoned. Also salient in the history of the father of the family was a younger brother who had been hospitalized with a psychotic illness, and the father himself had had a psychiatric illness when he was in his 20s. Thus, the context was established for feared recreations of environmental disaster, chronic psychiatric illness, absence and weakness of fathers, and mothers and daughters distant from each other.

Step 5. Summarizing the Focal Hypothesis

It is necessary to summarize the focal hypothesis to produce a short memorable statement, which the therapist can keep in his or her mind in working with the family.

First case: "The L. family is excluding the child so as to overcome a marital breakup as occurred in the family of origin due to a competing parent–child relationship."

Second case: "The person who takes control of Nikos turns him from a naughty boy into a handicapped boy, and so has to take responsibility and blame for the handicap, which the J. family believes was caused by marital conflict at

the time of the mother's pregnancy with him."

Third case: "Incest between the father and his young adult daughter keeps the parents and other members of the D. family together, but at a safe distance apart because closeness would lead to violence and possibly murder, while separation would cause worsening of psychiatric illness and suicide, based on what occurred in the family of origin."

Fourth case: "Rachel's symptoms focus parental attention on her, thus helping them to avoid repeating a family situation, where a daughter is abandoned. In addition, it diverts them from the major handicaps of their sons because such damage is intolerable given the past disasters in both parents' lives."

Requisite Changes

Having developed a holistic integration of the relevant aspects of family life, we can now turn to level 7, an ideal potential scenario of what the family could be like. This is what is requisite for the family. It is necessary for the therapist to specify required changes that would be meaningful for the family and possibly achievable through the therapist's own work. Requisite changes can be specified before the institution of therapy and can be used by "blind" assessors at follow-up. As well as these system changes, symptomatic alteration is always required. On its own, symptom loss is insufficient. We noted in our earliest paper (Kinston & Bentovim, 1978) that symptomatic change alone may be a "false" indicator—for example, the disturbance may move from one child to the other, or to the marriage.

Requisite family-system changes should specify actual alterations in interaction and not depend on vague or abstract notions. While criteria do need to be essentially objective (that is to say, socially sharable events), they must not be based on excessively subtle shades of intuition. Hence, carefully specified criteria can lead to stringent and convincing evidence of therapeutic effect. Still, it may be difficult to decide whether the change in interaction following therapy actually meets the criteria for successful outcome. It is not always possible to give explicit details of targets for change because of the open-system nature of the family. A variety of forms of surface interaction may contain and express the therapeutically achieved resolution.[6] Changes in meanings are recognized by alterations in interaction or expressed beliefs or in the ability of the family to discuss previously unmentionable subjects.

Since there are many ways to achieve a desirable outcome, the criteria themselves (though not the way they are decided) need to be concrete and independent of the modality of treatment or the theoretical stance. For example, references to "ego strength" or "absence of double binds" are not satisfactory.[7] The family itself may initially not be aware of or not value some material, unlike the symptom or conventional goal-attainment scales or change targets. For example, acknowledgment of the traumatic experience judged to be the origin of the disturbance is not meaningful to most families at the onset of treatment. We will discuss a case later in detail to demonstrate the therapy process, but in the four cases we have already mentioned, descriptions of the requisite level were as follows:

1. In an improved L. family, the parents would speak directly and openly to each other and face up to and resolve their conflicts. Richard would be perceived reasonably accurately as both good and bad and would not be triangulated into the parental relationship. Richard's behavior would improve so that he would invite rejection less often. The 4-year-old boy in the family would be described and related to by the parents realistically and not treated as special and ideal. Richard and John would relate more closely in an age-appropriate fashion.

2. In the improved J. family, the parents would take control over the children. Nikos would not be allowed to be destructive and would stop swearing, and the provocative and difficult behavior of the other children would also be dealt with firmly. Appropriate generational boundaries would be established; for example, the parents would be able to talk to each other without a child's stopping them. Each parent would acknowledge achievements of the other and would not undermine the other. The parents would be able to talk about their feelings of responsibility for the handicap, and would cease seeing Nikos as the "bad one." Nikos' potential and degree of handicap would be realistically acknowledged.

3. In the improved D. family, a decision would be taken to stop the incestuous relationship. The parents either would decide to separate or would find a way of living together harmoniously. Mental health issues would not predominate in family discussions. All the adult children would move off to create their own lives and families in an independent way.

4. In the improved Q. family, the oldest daughter's periods would return and uncertainty about her weight would stop. The oldest daughter would also be less jealous and undermining. The parents would let her pursue her own career and would cease being overconcerned. The parents would be able to talk together about their handicapped son. All family members would stop interrupting and talking for each other. The younger son would work up to his potential.

ASSESSMENT FOR THERAPY

In the previous section, we described how we conceptualize the problem presented by the family or by the referring agency. We have also described the way in which we form a focal hypothesis and decide what would be requisite for a family in terms of a possible useful outcome of therapy. We now need to turn to the practical task of assessment so that we can describe in some detail how this goal is reached. From the

---

[6] *Editors' Note.* Of course, for research purposes, one would, nonetheless, need to offer rules regarding how one would decide what types of change constituted "resolution," lest all manner of "evidence" qualify as supporting the efficacy of a particular method of treatment.

[7] *Editors' Note.* We disagree with this assertion. While, for example, vague references to "ego strength" are inadequate as outcome criteria ("required formulation"), there is real value in assessing the effectiveness of a given therapeutic method in terms that are theoretically specific to, and meaningful within, that way of thinking. Whether a particular method *also* yields significant clinical changes that are outside or beyond the tenets of that way of thinking is a very important, but very different, matter.

earlier sections, it can be seen that developing a holistic formulation requires appreciation of many factors: cycles of dysfunctional interaction, stressful events and experiences in families of origin and during the life of the current family, meanings and themes that were prominent, and the quality of family life on various quasi-holistic dimensions. We need to be able to gain information in all of these areas as part of the assessment, and we do this principally through a family diagnostic interview.

The Family Diagnostic Interview

Conceptually, we separate the assessment process from treatment, but in practice, effective work with a family demands that the therapist join therapeutically with the family from the very beginning. The initial contact with a referred family usually involves tasks, such as contact with the referrer, convening the initial meeting, and conducting the interview, all of which need attention if the assessment process is to be carried through properly. As far as the family is concerned, contact should be experienced as therapeutic from the very outset and not merely as a routine event prior to going on a waiting list. In the initial one or two sessions, the therapist needs to answer the question of what the family is about and be clear that simple responses, such as referral to a remedial teacher or a basic medical diagnosis or advice on handling crises, are not all that is appropriate. Generally speaking, we favor inviting the whole family from the outset. In addition, professionals who play a major role in family life are invited—for example, social workers from a welfare agency, a probation officer appointed by a court, or a community nurse involved in ongoing health care. In the hospital setting, the pediatric specialist would also participate. Subsequent individual marital interviewing may be required for the assessment. Contact with other professionals in the network, such as the family physician, may also be indicated.[8]

The interviewing method varies greatly depending on the orientation and style of the therapist. Like most pragmatic research, the issue is not what questions are being asked, but whether enough questions are being asked to provide the information the interviewer needs in order to carry out the assessment that we have indicated is needed.

We have found it helpful to use a number of techniques, including circular questioning, triadic questioning, the "gossiping" technique, structural techniques, and communication tasks (e.g., the "discuss this among yourselves" tactic). There may be times when specific tests are necessary, as in the individual assessment of the intellect of a child or parent. When family disturbance appears to be absent, it may be helpful to use a family task interview. Our research with this interview confirms that the therapist's presence and participation obscure the very interaction he or she needs to identify (Stratford, Burck, & Kinston, 1982). Instead of carrying out the whole interview, one or two of the formal tasks may be carried out by a family with or without the therapist present, such as planning an outing, building a tower of bricks, discussing how family names were derived, or discussing likes and dislikes of members. There are also a number of more clinically oriented tasks, including asking a family to construct a genogram together while the therapist observes them via closed-circuit television or a one-way screen. Tasks like this give the family a simple and relatively unstressful experience within the assessment process and may assist the therapist in joining with them.

When referrals are made from other agencies, there may be legal requirements to be handled. For example, in our work with sexually abused or physically abused children, it is often useful to ask the family to discuss with the social worker the reasons for referral during the diagnostic interview. This task can help reveal the interactional process between the family and the care environment.

Although our approach is pathology oriented, the formulation of requisite change demands that the therapist appreciate family strengths. The approach of the family to tasks given during the therapy provides an indication of the re-

---

[8] *Editors' Note.* See Imber-Black's (Chapter 19) discussion of a systematic approach to dealing with clinical issues of the family's relationship to larger social systems, especially to systems of professional helpers.

sources of the family, as well as dysfunctional patterns.

The Focal (Family) Therapy Assessment Sheet

To gather the mass of information that can arise from a meeting with the family, and then to derive a focal hypothesis and a statement of the requisite change, we have found it essential to have a format we call the Focal (Family) Therapy Assessment Sheet. It consists of a front sheet to record actual key details and a number of columns to record various aspects of the family context, complaints, and family description.

Front Sheet

The front sheet is used to record key factual details that set the scheme for the assessment interview(s): the name of the family, the referral agent, and the date of the interview. A family tree bringing in as much of the extended family as is relevant can also be inserted here (see Figure 9-9).

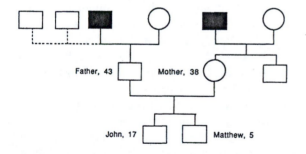

Father, 43   Mother, 38

John, 17   Matthew, 5

Figure 9-9.

Column I—Family Composition and Professional Network

The first column contains facts about the family and its members, including their names, ages, family status (e.g., step-relative, foster or adoptive child), country of origin, and occupation or school. Names are noted in age order spaced out down the column and that of the index patient is underlined or asterisked. All

family members and active members of the household, such as lodgers, are included. The permanent absence of family members from interviews is noted. In the lower part of the column, members of the professional (e.g., general practitioner, social worker) and paraprofessional (e.g., priest, helpful neighbor) network who are involved with the family are noted.

Column II—Current Complaint

Information about the complaints that have brought the family to treatment is recorded in this column. Details of the onset, nature, and duration of the complaints are inserted adjacent to the name of the relevant family members, using their own words. The definition of the current complaint as presented by the referrers and others in the helping network is recorded in the lower part of the column, if this differs from that of the family.

Column III—Reported Past Events, States, and Relationships in Previous and Current Family Systems

This column contains past events, states, and relationships chosen because they are considered to be salient or significant to the family as traumas or stresses that are likely to have had sufficient impact in shaping family life. Some events that the therapist feels still have a bearing on present-day family life may not be seen as relevant by the family. Clinical judgment is used, therefore, in deciding salience. The events are recorded in chronological order, approximately in line with the family member(s) to which they refer.

It is necessary to distinguish between events in previous family systems (i.e., the families of origin or other families in which the family members have been involved, such as previous marriages) from events in the current family system.

Column IV—Surface Action

This column allows recording of both reported and observed overt interactions. Reported material about current family life and relationships may be obtained from the family itself or from outsiders. The observed surface action refers to dysfunctional cycles within the family, including family–therapist interactions, which are judged to be characteristic. It is best to adhere to the present tense here and it may be useful to include a structural map of the family.

Column V—Meanings Active in the Family

Meanings, beliefs, or values that are active and alive consciously and unconsciously in the family, and that underlie and drive surface action, are detailed in this column. It should be possible to illustrate the meanings by reference to interaction and to statements from family members. Meanings should be identified in a short, pithy form highly specific to the family concerned.

Column VI—Handling of Stressful Events

In this column, the information in columns III, IV and V must be linked. The therapist records his or her speculation about the way in which the family has handled the key stressful events and which meanings have been attached to them. In other words, the therapist develops a theory of how past experiences have become part of the family's characteristic culture and behavior in the present time.

Column VII—Requisite Changes

This final column contains the changes in the family that the therapist decides have to take place if the therapy is to be considered successful. These changes are delineated in concrete, behavioral, and visible terms as far as possible. All dysfunctional meanings in column V should have been resolved by the end of therapy, and the family should be able to talk about them. The salient traumas should also be open to acknowledgment and free discussion by the family. Changes may need either to be observed by the therapist or, in some matters, to be reported by the family.

Using the Assessment Sheet

Making a focal assessment, creating a focal hypothesis, and determining requisite change require the therapist to stand back from the family and take a comprehensive and holistic view of it. It is, therefore, positively undesirable to attempt to use the Focal Therapy Assessment Sheet as a recording tool during a diagnostic interview.

We have developed an individual and a team approach to deal with the complexity of assessment. If a team is used, members of the team should divide up the various recording tasks; for example, one member of the team can note cycles of interaction while another listens for the salient events and the meanings of these for the family and a third gathers the factual information. It is also usually helpful to have one team member keep a running process record of the interview as a whole. In addition, a video recording of the family session may be useful to check the information that the group has derived. The sheet can then be completed by the team as a whole during a break or as an entirely separate operation on a later occasion. The therapist's work with the family involves the therapist in observing the family, acting or intervening in various ways, and evaluating his or her own responses as well as those of the family. This normally is an implicit process but for training purposes it can be done explicitly. What is required is a level 1 description of interaction from the videotape, in which all significant elements, comments, actions, and expressions are noted and divided into natural level 2 segments or episodes. The therapist then has to make a level 3 description, that is, must attribute meanings to the interactions observed. All this needs to be done in the light of the therapeutic purpose, which is to derive a focal hypothesis.

To illustrate this process, a part of the initial assessment of the G. family[9] containing two boys—John, aged 17, and Matthew, aged 5—is provided in Table 9-1. Matthew was referred at the age of 5 years by a pediatrician because of his worsening overweight, disruptive high levels of activity, and aggressive behavior, particularly at school. On the left-hand side of Table 9-1 is a description of what was happening in the interview based on a videotape recording, and on the right-hand side are the comments of the therapist about her aims, in response to attempts by a supervision group to clarify and specify the meaning of the interaction. The final focal formulation and focal hypothesis that were derived from this particular case are shown in Figures 9-10 and 9-11.

THE THERAPY PROCESS

The major goal of therapeutic work is the resolution of the trauma embedded in the family and captured by the focal hypothesis. This applies to every family. Trauma has a damaging effect on the relationships and the feelings and behaviors of family members and it is these with which the requisite changes are concerned. What in other therapy models would be seen as goals of treatment (e.g., a parent taking control of a child's behavioral difficulties) in our approach is an expected by-product of the resolution of the traumatic issues that spill over into all aspects of the family's life. This goal, articulated to suit the particular family, needs to be shared with the family at some suitable point in the therapy. Some families may grasp the issues very quickly whereas with others this awareness occurs far later in the process. The language of the focal hypothesis is simple and rooted in family life, so the level of comprehension or thinking within the family is not an issue. We do expect to have our hypothesis of the family dysfunction discussed explicitly at some point in the therapeutic work, and we also expect the results of

[9] We wish to thank Anne Elton, principal psychiatric social worker at the Hospital for Sick Children, Great Ormond Street, London, for permission to use this case and for her detailed assistance in preparing the material for publication.

effective therapy to be seen in individuals as well as in the family as a whole.

The Mechanism of Change

We have emphasized that in our approach we regard cure as dependent on the resolution of trauma, which is recognized by the family's developing a number of prespecified requisite changes. To achieve this goal, it is appropriate to employ any technique at the appropriate tactical and strategic junctures in the therapy, using the guidance of the focal hypothesis (or systems model). Although all family therapists are concerned with interaction, our hierarchy of description points to a contrast between those therapeutic approaches that center primarily on a particular problem or mode of interaction of the family and those that aim primarily to restructure patterns of relationships within the family (i.e., regard the family as a whole as the object of assessment and change). Although our approach belongs unequivocally to the latter group, families are frequently more than content with limited change. The distinction between narrow and broad aims for change is a source of conflict among different family-therapy schools and produces confusion in outcome studies.

The broad approach demands a breakdown of existing patterns and the reconstruction of a different family culture, identity, or theme. Restructuring must be stable and should assist the family and its members to evolve in a constructive fashion after therapy. The more a therapeutic approach is oriented toward restructuring, the greater will be the need to take a historic–genetic approach and so provide interventions that contribute to the creation of a new psychological reality. The approach developed by Chasin (Chasin, Roth, & Bagrad, 1989) is naturally incorporated as describing techniques of creating new future and past realities. Where a more limited goal for change is accepted, interpretation or reframing can be used, but it is provided pragmatically or opportunistically to impart impetus. In holistic change, the therapist's personality and psychological health may also play an important part. Intense feelings and thoughts in the therapist–family relationship—that is, transference and countertransference—are then more likely to develop.

TABLE 9-1.
Detailed Analysis of an Initial Assessment of the G. Family

In the early part of the session, the therapist "joined with" the family—the parents, and sons John, 17, and Matthew, aged 5. In observing the problem the parents had in controlling Matthew's noisy, disruptive behavior, she established the parents " 'fear of violence' and 'loss,' " and their difficulties in establishing control of him. She joined with John, the adolescent in the family, and brought both parents into the session. Shared areas of dislike were clarified (e.g., of "work" for all family members) and their personal concerns and difficulties were determed (e.g., John's obesity at the same age as Matthew). Previous marital problems were identified.

Account of Interview—Section of First Interview	Comments of the Therapist
1. Therapist now asks why the family is here and what the biggest worry is. John thinks the reason is that his mother is especially worried about Matthew being very active but then adds that she is worried about both he and Matthew fighting. The mother says these two things are linked and goes on to describe how worried she is that Matthew does not know his own strength and might really damage a small child in a fight. Meanwhile Matthew, sitting beside the mother, is carolling and singing away in a totally nonchalant and somewhat contemptuous manner, indicating his total lack of concern for his mother's anxiety.	1. The therapist wanted to discover what problems, experiences, and concerns there were. She concluded that the family was greedy, confused, and overwhelmed by a host of difficulties and could not focus on the most important problems. It was noted that the family members were undermining each other, talking across each other. Matthew's behavior was totally ignored.
2. The mother thinks that the father worries about Matthew. This is said in a rather meaningful way, with the emphasis on "worries." She adds that she thinks the father may also worry about Matthew's effect on her and her way of coping with him, which has not been very successful, especially when he is more active and potentially dangerous. In her description of Matthew's behavior, she shows a mixture of some admiration at his cleverness and exasperation at his demands.	2. During this description of Matthew's very difficult behavior, the therapist was wondering whether she should ask the parents to control Matthew and, if so, when.
3. The father agrees that he is worried about the effect on the whole family. He thinks that there is a problem because he does not get on with, or is not very close to, his son John. He then says that he does not have very much patience and smacks Matthew fairly quickly if he does not obey. In this way, like the others, he is giving thought to the family's problems. In being asked about the reasons for the lack of closeness with John, the father brings in the fact that his mother-in-law has always lived with them and has intruded on them, stopping them from being a family.	3. The force of family response in relation to the issue of the grandmother indicated this to be of major emotional importance and a salient aspect of both current family life and of the conflict within this family. There was a suggestion that the grandmother's role may be important in relation to the problems of controlling each of the children successively. The therapist picked up the mother's statement of the family being a "four-generational" one and felt that this may be perceived as a major problem in the family—because of the difference in age.
4. The mother enlarges on this and describes the grandmother as "the missing person" who has always lived there. The family lives in her house and are all quite involved with her. The mother described how Matthew will go upstairs with his grandmother when he has been chastized by his mother. Meanwhile, Matthew is roaming around the room and shouts hello at this point as if to an unseen person. In a very lively way, the mother proceeds to describe, backed up by the family, the problems of sharing space with the grandmother, who has more space for herself in the house than the four of them have. It is a shared house but the grandmother regards it as all her own.	4. Space is clearly a central issue, and is illustrated by Matthew's wandering about the room.

Account of Interview—Section of First Interview	*Comments of the Therapist*
5. The mother described the problem of living with "four generations," and when therapist asks what this means, the mother lists Matthew at 5, John at 17, themselves, and the grandmother at 75. Matthew has really been hitting and provoking John for some time. John playfully fights back and at this point the father interrupts and tells John to stop.	5. Although Matthew had been the obvious provoker, it is John who was reprimanded, which says something about who controls and whose behavior gets controlled. The children seemed to ignore the parent's expectations by using the relationship to the grandmother as an alternative and perhaps more powerful parental figure. Matthew used the opportunity created by criticism of John to try to push him out in order to get close to his parents and to make John into the bad one.
6. The mother then goes on to illustrate how the grandmother holds the family for ransom by suggesting they are trying to get rid of her whenever they suggest any minor changes within the house, for example, of furniture. Periodically, Matthew stops his running around and lies across his mother's lap.	6. Matthew is perhaps trying to comfort his parents and to respond to their frustrations.
7. The therapist then asks the father what he thinks the grandmother might worry about and he agrees with his wife, adding that he feels under a particular obligation not to move the grandmother out or to ask her to move because he bought the house from her. At this, the mother adds, rather angrily, that her mother has the biggest rooms in the house. Matthew makes faces at the camera.	7. The therapist ignores Matthew's running around the room. This is accepted as a model by the family, which likewise ignores Matthew. The urgency in the mother's voice is responded to by the therapist, who gives reassurance. The therapist keeps a balance of contributions by turning the mother's questions to the father.
	The session continues in further exploration of the relationship with the grandmother and of the father's family until the therapist brings the first part of the consultation to a conclusion.

The therapist needs to review these phenomena as information, to maintain self-command, and to so shape interventions as to handle them either directly or indirectly. Flexible integration of all the therapist's experiences into the therapy process remains the guiding principle. By contrast, the narrower approach lends itself to reliance on the therapist, perfecting a limited range of interpersonal skills and interventions that deflect or protect against deep involvement.

Structuring the Therapy

The primary aim of therapy is to meet the needs of the family. This aim must be put into the context of the therapist's capabilities, his or her interest in the family, and the techniques that he or she uses habitually or needs to develop (if still in training). The focal approach demands consideration of the system being treated, the system giving treatment, and the way these interact. As far as the system being treated is concerned, it is important to bring in any agent that has a direct accessible interacting role with the family in relationship to the problem being presented. For example, in the G. family alluded to, in the problem of the 5-year-old presenting with obesity, overactivity, and aggressive behavior, the grandmother was a key actor; in cases of family breakdown, a child-care professional or a foster family may need to be included. In other cases, of course, the presence of a grandparent in the home or involvement of other professionals may be irrelevant to the family's problem and these individuals would not be included in therapy.[10]

Sometimes a part of the family system may be worked with, for example, the marital couple alone or an individual. In the case of Richard in

[10] *Editors' Note.* We wish to underscore that it is quite possible for the family therapist to work with a broad network of "patients" or others in the family's life and yet still maintain attention to the dynamic (psychodynamic) meanings of symptoms and of interaction. Rather often of late, we think, family therapists have seemingly come to believe that using a wide-angle lens on the family precludes high resolution.

I Family and Professional Network Composition (Age, status, occupation, presence/absence)	II Current Complaint (Duration, nature, complainant)	III Reported Past Events, States, and Relationships in:	
		(a) Previous family system	(b) Current family system
Hans, 42 German parents. Supervisor on railroad.	Feels he is not close enough to his eldest son, John, because maternal grandmother intrudes between them.	Considerable secrecy about father's family. His father (PGF) was a prisoner of war who died in a shooting accident but father was told he died in the war. His mother (PGM) then married a Russian, who adopted him and PGM divorced him and remarried. There was an older brother, who died.	Parenting has been shared between parents and MGM.

Before Matthew's birth, there were marital problems between the parents. MGM did not expect another child because of mother's gynecological problems. The parents, in fact, planned him. Relationships between parents and MGM then deteriorated. Mother tries but fails to stop MGM's giving Matthew fattening food. |
Margaret, 38 Housewife	Tension with maternal grandmother because of her intrusiveness.	Mother's father (MGF) died when she was 15. He was easy-going and her mother (MGM) was dominant. Quarrels ensued if MGF tried to challenge MGM. He was the only one who could. It was only possible for mother to cope with MGM by passivity. Mother had one brother with whom she did not get on.	
John, 17 Working	Unhappy at work.		John had similar weight problems until he started using a bicycle at 10. He has also had learning problems and needed remedial help. He has been an anxious boy.
Matthew, 5 At school	Obese, excitable, overactive: the mother is afraid he will hurt someone at school because of his size. School finds handling him a problem. Family cannot control his behavior or his eating.		
Maternal grandmother, 75 Shares the family home

(All family members are English-born) | | Maternal great-grandmother lived in the house when mother was growing up. Sacrifice by children was called for without complaint in that household. | The family bought their home from MGM 13 years previously and she continues to live there. She has retained as much space as the rest of the family put together. |

IV Surface Action		V Meanings Active in the Family	VI Handling Meanings, and Past Events	VII Requisite Changes
Reported (Current family life and relationships)	Observed (Explicit, typical behavior)			
	Father is also overweight.	Major secrets are present and there is no way of discovering them.	Matthew's activity may represent the family's wish to be active in relationship to MGM and to pursue the family's desire for space.	1. Matthew's overweight to be reduced, eating to be controlled.
All the family enjoys eating. Father feels he and his wife are now too far apart. Father and John are disappointed with their jobs. Mother is helpless and tries uselessly to control Matthew by shouting and smacking. He persistently interrupts his parents.	Both parents seem depressed and hopeless. The family atmosphere is rigid and flat. Matthew's lively, provocative behavior contrasts with the rest of the family's unhappiness.	Assertive activity, like control, can be violent and lead to a painful loss. There is no great pleasure in work or school. Overeating is the tip of the iceberg.	Compliance may be necessary now because assertiveness in the family of origin was associated with violence and loss.	2. Parents to be able to (a) manage Matthew's behavior and (b) enjoy activities with him. 3. Father and John to enjoy more activities together. 4. Parents to be in charge of children and MGM to be noninterfering.
The boys share a room and irritate each other. However, John has taken a younger boy under his wing and Matthew likes older children. Matthew can be good with John.	Matthew claims he is older than his age. Matthew fights John when loss is discussed. Matthew is intrusive, uninhibited, and talks over the therapist. The parents respond passively to this.	Children cause separation of parents. It feels as if there are four generations in the family. Daughters who have marital problems look after their mothers.	Secrecy is maintained and disasters (e.g., shooting) are not revealed. History repeats itself in that mothers and daughters must live together even when they marry. But mother attempts to reverse it by seeking help.	5. More satisfactory living conditions to be negotiated with MGM. 6. Parents to enjoy joint activities. 7. All members to be appropriately assertive.
Maternal grandmother fears that she will be moved to a house for the elderly. She allows Matthew to eat with her, as John used to. John still goes to her to avoid household chores.	Family expresses sadness at the absence of MGF, because 'he would control MGM.'	Grandmother feels that she will be got rid of and so takes a hard attitude.		

Figure 9-10. Focal formulation of the G. family

1. *How do symptoms fit into family interaction?*

   Parents can control neither their children nor their dependent grandmother and turn to outside professionals.

2. *How would the family interact without the symptoms?*

   Without outside help, there would be violent confrontation across generations and between the parents.

3. *Why is the speculated interaction avoided?*

   Loss by death due to violence or suicide, or by extrusion.

4. *How is this linked to past events?*

   Both parents lost fathers and as children had to look after their parents without being able to complain or confront them.

Summary

Inability to control or complain to dependent relations requires outside help to avoid confrontations that would otherwise lead to violence and loss.

Figure 9-11. Focal hypothesis for the G. family

the L. family, the mother was offered some individual therapy simultaneously with the family work because the pervasive traumatic experiences of her childhood and early adolescence appeared to dominate the family. In most such cases, a single therapist is generally sufficient. However, cotherapy is useful in cases with major legal or extensive societal involvement, such as child physical or sexual abuse, because of their complexity and the emotional pressure that develops during therapy.

A therapy supervision team is useful, and is essential during the training of therapists where the forms, documentation, descriptions, and development of interventions require discussion and explication. Other therapeutic approaches use a team regularly, and we, too, believe that teamwork remains useful whatever the experience and ability of the therapists. There are several methods of observation: sitting behind a one-way screen, sitting in as a noninvolved observer, watching by closed-circuit television, or viewing videotape subsequently.

Our approach derived from those methods developed because of the shortage of time available for individual psychotherapy, and because family work was believed to be more economic. We have observed over the years that, unlike in individual therapy, there is little inherent tendency for family therapy to persist without purpose. The effort of organizing the family to come to therapy, and the fact that attendance leads to venting stresses in a public way, usually means that once sufficient change has occurred, there is a desire to terminate. It has, therefore, not been necessary to regard formal time limitation as an inherent aspect of the approach. Typically, cases may be seen at three- to four-week intervals over six to nine months. However, there may be factors in a particular case that call for a time limit to be set, as in testing the rehabilitational potential of an abused child. Family circumstances, such as travel abroad or a parent whose occupation causes extensive absences, may also dictate the time available. The natural long-term development of the focal family approach is that one (or more) individuals within a family become aware of personal traumatic experiences and circumstances that may lead them to choose to have a period of individual treatment to assist in their longer-term personal growth. Emotional growth in the case of a child may require separation from the family or attendance at a special school. Sometimes, other treatments are part of the context of family therapy. For instance, marital partners may each be in separate group treatment and need to do some family work on their shared problems.

The time gap between sessions often fluctuates, depending in part on the techniques being employed. For instance, if a structural technique such as setting tasks at home is used, then frequent sessions may be necessary, possibly at weekly intervals. At the other extreme, a strategic–systemic intervention that focuses on the impossibility or inadvisability of change may require a longer interval between sessions.

In academic and educational centers, technical issues may not be dictated by the needs of the family alone. Our view is that the fully trained therapist needs to be able to use a variety of techniques and to administer many different forms of intervention. Hence, there may be periods during training when a therapist deliberately practices structural techniques and sees families at shorter intervals.

The Role of the Therapist

Our approach contrasts with some therapeutic approaches where the role of the therapist is clearly defined. For example, a structural family therapist automatically assumes a role as the leader of the family system, clarifying goals and taking control of the session. The therapist does have to take a highly active role in the early stages in order to make an assessment and later may do so when testing whether criteria for improvement have been met. However, during therapy, the therapist's behavior may vary enormously. He or she may overtly control sessions on some occasions and be highly active and directive, even explicitly taking responsibility for bringing about changes. At other times, however, the therapist may appear to abdicate responsibility and allow the family to be in control. On occasion, the therapist makes himself or herself the center of a communication system and at other times facilitates and encourages family members to talk with one another. There may be occasions when self-disclosure is an important intervention; on other occasions, he or she may maintain an attitude of secrecy or neutrality in terms of his or her own views. The therapist's role may evolve as therapy progresses, or there may be radical changes from session to session.

Since our approach emphasizes response to the family's need rather than adherence to the therapist's technical theories, the prime goal in training is to develop flexibility in dealing with the family. A therapist must value and use a variety of skills and techniques and must value and appreciate other (nonfamily) modalities of treatment.

An ability to develop and articulate an imaginative theory of the family, the focal hypothesis, is primary. The focal hypothesis needs to be maintained (or specifically modified) throughout the process of therapy, as it acts as the terms of reference for all activity and for evaluation of results. In order to keep therapy on track and to enable clinical research, we have developed a specific process instrument called the Focal Therapy Record Sheet.

The Focal Therapy Record Sheet

We have repeatedly emphasized that our approach is to separate assessment from the therapeutic process itself. This is true not only when instituting therapy, but also on a session-by-session basis throughout therapy. With the focal formulation and hypothesis as a frame of reference, it is necessary to identify the main priorities for attention and intervention from session to session and to develop a strategy for action with the family (Kinston, 1986). In the session itself, the therapist needs to handle whatever the family presents with sensitivity and needs to respond to it naturally, while still pursuing his or her strategic aims. Tactics, therefore, should be flexible. Occasionally, a strategy may have to be abandoned. However, if the therapist is repeatedly deflected from his or her strategy, then something is missing from the focal hypothesis, or alternatively, the competence of the therapist in this case needs to be questioned. At the completion of each session, it is necessary to assess what has happened, what new has emerged about the family to elaborate or disconfirm the focal hypothesis, and which of the requisite changes have been made.

To facilitate this rational approach to the therapeutic process, we devised the Focal Therapy Record Sheet (FTRS) for completion by therapists. It is laid out in seven columns, as shown in Figure 9-12.

1. Therapist's Aims

This column should be completed just prior to the session or immediately after the end of the previous session. The therapist records his or her aims and plans for the sessions and any key thoughts. For example, in the initial stages, aims may include gathering information about the family, further conceptualization of family dysfunction, clarification of practical points about the setting of therapy, and so on. Later, the aims may be to test the focal hypothesis or to produce a particular change in family interaction or in family meanings. The therapist also notes here any technique he or she intends to use. Aims may be described in the form appropriate for this technique.

Therapy will be neither brief nor focused if

the therapist does not make preparatory plans for each session. Unfortunately, in busy clinics, it is only too easy for this essential discipline to be omitted.

2. Family Feedback and Intersession Events

Feedback from the family about previous interventions and reports of intersession events can give important information about change, difficulties in changing, new problem areas that have arisen, or the appropriateness of the therapist's intervention in the previous session. Family feedback coupled with the therapist's preset aims for the session form the combined, basic starting point for each new session.

If the feedback is unexpected and does not fit with the preset aims, the therapist may have to readjust these aims immediately. Such incongruity may be due to family factors or therapist factors. Family factors include new information about salient events that change the direction of therapy and apparently randomly intervening events such as sudden illness, unexpected redundancy, or an accident. Therapist factors generating incongruity include insufficient assessment and conceptualization and inappropriate or unskillful application of techniques.

3. Content Related to Focal Formulation

This column should document the unfolding of the session and include the main details of the family interaction and information reported in the session. The material under this heading serves as a brief clinical summary of the process of the session. Inferences about the effect of intervention do not belong here.

4. Information Relevant to the Focal Formulation.

As the therapist's comprehensive understanding of the family deepens, his or her aim and plans and methods of intervention will alter. It is, therefore, important at each session for the therapist to note explicitly the emergence of new data relevant to the focal hypothesis. This is part of a continuous reassessment of the family dysfunction and fine-tuning of the system model that is being used.

In this column two types of information are distinguished:

a. New information that enlarges an already-known problem area. This may add to the understanding of the mechanisms or rules the family or family members use, or it may have implications for tactics and techniques to be used.
b. Any new information that demands a qualitative alteration in the focal formulation.

5. Area of Focal Formulation Worked On

This column reflects the fact that in any session there will be many areas of the focal formulation on which the therapist could potentially work. Explicitness about the area of the focal formulation actually being dealt with in the session allows the therapist the check whether:

a. Work in the session is still in line with the focal formulation.
b. The problem areas judged to be relevant are indeed tackled in the session.
c. The criteria for improvement in the area on which the therapist has worked in the session have been met.

6. Therapists' Strategies and Interventions

The therapist records here the strategy and main techniques and tactics used during the session together with the family's response. Any tasks for the family to complete between sessions are also recorded. It is possible to use this column to check that the therapist is intervening in a consistent, persistent, and therapeutically logical fashion in successive sessions. Comparison with prespecified aims (column 1) checks whether the therapist's direction has been maintained within a session.

7. Criteria for Improvement Met

Improvement in the family requires symptom loss and a variety of changes in interaction as laid down in the focal formulation. The therapist notes here any improvements that have occurred according to these preset criteria. Successful therapy demands maintenance and consolidation of change, so the same or similar but progressively greater achievements may be recorded over several sessions. This column, therefore, provides a form of continuous outcome evaluation, which has proved to be far more satisfactory than conventional snapshot assessment.

At the end of each session, the improvements made can be compared with the aims (column 1) and with improvements noted in column 7 for previous sessions. This enables a check on the course of therapy and assists in the choice of aims for the subsequent session.

The use of the FTRS was illustrated in detail by Furniss, Bentovim, and Kinston (1984). This paper used the case of Nikos in the J. family, referred to earlier, to lay out the entire process of therapy. The early phases of the therapy used structural techniques that aimed to deal with Nikos' disruptive behavior, calm him down, and assist the parents to gain control. We had concluded that taking control in this family meant taking responsibility for the handicap and that Nikos' role was to ensure that the parents would be protected from this. In sessions 9, 10, and 11, therefore, the therapeutic goal moved to reframing Nikos' disruption to the family as helpful rather than as a hindrance. The therapist informed the family that "Nikos thinks he has to help them by creating a minor disruption so his parents will not have to talk about painful matters." The focal hypothesis also specified that the parents felt the handicap was due to their marital conflict.[11]

Details of two important sessions, 13 and 14, are given in Figure 9-12. As well as illustrating the use of the FTRS, the material also demonstrates two key aspects of our approach. Session 13 describes the deterioration in family functioning that accompanied the emergence of the trauma and preceded the final working through of the focal hypothesis. In session 14, the therapist decided to see the parents alone, illustrating that work can move to a part of the family. After this watershed, the therapy was terminated at session 16, with the therapist able to record that most of the criteria for improvement had been met.

The FTRS is also an educational and research tool. As an educational tool, it provides the necessary discipline for development, thinking, and reflection. As a research tool, it enables meaningful clinical studies, for example, into the basis for using particular techniques or strategies.

We have noted, for instance, that clinical practice and techniques used in marital cases follow a different course from those used in child-sexual-abuse cases. The opening phase in the former typically involves problem definition and the exploration of the family of origin through genograms, and sculpting to release emotion and begin the creation of a new reality (Bentovim, 1990). The opening phase in sexual abuse typically involves establishing the reality and extent of abuse, encouraging acceptance of responsibilities for acts, and strengthening the relationships between the nonabusing parent and the children (Bentovim et al., 1988).

An Illustrated Case—The G. Family

[See Figures 9-10 and 9-12 for the Focal Therapy Assessment Sheet]

Following the diagnostic interview with the G. family, six family sessions were held, the final session occurring eight months after the first. The long intervals between sessions were due to the family's repeatedly canceling appointments, ostensibly for reasons of ill health. However, on at least two occasions, it was clear from phone conversations that there was resistance to attending. Although, in some situations, regular attendance by all or some subset of members might be compulsory (e.g., in abuse or major breakdown work), in others, such as this one, any attendance at all was regarded as an achievement. John, the older boy, did not attend any session after the first. Both parents came with

---

[11] *Editors' Note.* While all this recording may at first strike the reader as cumbersome and burdensome, note that these entries are typically very brief and would appear to require no more time than what is ordinarily needed for the entry of typical "process" or "progress" notes in a family's clinical charting record.

1. Therapist's Aims	2. Family Feedback and Intersession Events	3. Content Related to Focal Formulation
SESSION No. 13, Week 26		
Explain that the discussion about blame and guilt had to be avoided because of the parental belief that the handicap was caused through marital conflict before the boy's birth.	Parents did speak with each other at home about problems with the children. (Task set in session 10 now accomplished.)	The parents talk about Nicos' future and their hopes of a 'miracle drug' for his hyperactivity. Nicos is very tiring for the parents; only the parents or Kate can look after him and they fear that this will always be so.
		Parents say they have been coming to therapy for too long.
SESSION No. 14, Week 29		
(Parents only)		
Find out what first made the parents see that Nicos was handicapped.	Father reports that the parents communicate much better and that Nicos is still the problem.	Mother first blames herself for not having done enough for Nicos concerning school and medical care. She feels guilty about his handicap.
Reassess Nicos' handicap.		Father blocks the subject of guilt and diverts the talk to drugs, then to schooling and the value of a boarding school. All problems are projected into the future.
		Then the parents start talking of the time around Nicos' birth and mother breaks into tears. She feels that he would be different if there had not been the conflict between her and her husband.
		Mother expresses pain about realizing that Nicos is handicapped. Parents share pain. Lack of communication acknowledged as reason for insecurity in the marriage.

Matthew to the second, third, and fourth; the mother and Matthew came alone to the fifth and sixth. Despite considerable effort, including letters from the therapist, the maternal grandmother did not attend.

The aim in presenting this case is to demonstrate a typical conventionally documented therapy from our clinic (although the FTRS is omitted here).

Second Session

The main aim was to strengthen the bond with the family to continue exploration of family patterns of behavior, and in particular to elucidate implicit rules that governed interactions. In pursuing this, further family history was also obtained. Both parents talked more of their own experience of emotional deprivation, in particular, their shared experience of having had little positive demonstration of affection from the parent of the same sex. The therapist specifically empathized with their past pain. The parents were then able to talk of the deprivation expe-

4. Further Information Relevant to Focal Formulation	5. Area of Focal Formulation Worked On	6. Therapist's Strategy and Interventions	7. Criteria for Improvement Met
Parents were very reluctant to continue to talk with each other about marital problems. The attempt to bring back Nicos as the only problem is indicative of the great anxiety about opening up marital conflicts.	Parents' unrealistic views of Nicos' handicap. Parents' reluctance to think about the time of Nicos' birth.	*Structural:* Therapist accepts parents' reluctance to talk. Therapist suggests that the parents should come on their own to discuss help for them as parents of a handicapped child.	Definite deterioration: parents less able to talk about their problems than expected.
Father gets blamed not only for the parental conflict around the time Nicos was born, but also for the handicap.	*Active meaning:* Marital conflict prior to birth of a handicapped son as the original precipitating stressful experience reflected in the parents' dysfunctional interaction.	*Dynamic:* Therapist's interpretation of the wish for a "wonder drug" to make Nicos normal leads the parents to refer to his birth. The therapist then explores original conflict around this time.	Commencement of shared mourning for the handicap.

Figure 9-12. Example of part of a focal therapy process record in the J. family

rienced by the grandparents, in particular, the childhood hardships of the maternal grandmother, hitherto presented in a predominantly unsympathetic and negative light. The repetition of the pattern of daughters caring for their mothers emerged and was explicitly identified by the mother as "falling into the daughter–mother pattern."

In both families of origin, inconsistent discipline was described and also difficulties in dealing with conflict between the grandparents. In addition, there was a strong prohibition in both families on direct criticism or any expression of anger. Negative feelings had to be suppressed. In the mother's words, "I had to draw a cocoon round myself and swallow feelings." The father was also inhibited, perhaps because of the mysterious violent death of his father. He could hardly bear to discuss the possibility of feeling angry with members of his family. Not surprisingly, both parents were unable to be explicitly aware of their anger at the maternal grandmother. Significantly, Matthew's only spontaneous interjections occurred when the family spoke about family tensions and described minor arguments.

The factual information about past experience was gained directly, whereas information about the rule of not expressing anger was gained by circular questioning, for example, "Who would be most angry with grandmother for feeding cake to the boys?" Matthew's resistance and refusal to speak were not challenged but were accepted by the therapist as a reasonable option, and were then ignored. The purpose here was in part to model for the parents a refusal to get drawn into conflict and in part to connote his behavior as appropriate.

At the end of the session, the final therapeutic intervention was to connote the family rules positively. In swallowing their feelings and sacrificing their own needs to care for those in other generations, the family members were praised as protective and able to deal with their conflicts.

Intersession Contact

The mother phoned twice to cancel sessions because of illness. She vividly described worrying behavior by Matthew, such as climbing on roofs, running about dangerously, and striking other children. She conveyed a sense that he was almost beyond his parents' control. At one point, the therapist asked the mother if she was expressing her own fears of Matthew's coming to harm if he stayed in his family. After an initial furious response, the mother calmed down and acknowledged the reality of the dangers she was describing, although she said she was sure that she wanted Matthew to stay in the family. In one conversation, the therapist emphasized that Matthew's safety and physical health depended on ensuring that he did not overeat.

Third Session

In this session, the first strand of the hypothesis was actively worked on, namely, not feeling in control. At the start of the third session, the parents described their success in getting the grandmother to stop feeding Matthew. They attributed this change to the grandmother's feeling threatened by the invitation to attend family therapy. The therapist wondered whether the mother might not have been firmer with her following the phone conversations. The potential self-destructiveness of Matthew's behavior

was further discussed. The parents were asked to discuss what realistic expectations they would have of a 6-year-old in relation to tidying up at bedtime, this being a particularly difficult time for the family. With great difficulty, the parents agreed on some expectations and on ways of managing this period in the future. The therapist encouraged the parents to spend time in enjoyable activities as a reward for Matthew's compliance. This was advised particularly to assist the father, who had talked at the initial interview of his feeling of loss because of not having a close relationship with the older boy. Some tasks and rewards were explicitly set for the family to carry out at home to support the work of the session. Charts and diaries were to be used to check compliance. The therapist used predominantly structural and behavioral techniques in this session.

Fourth Session

This session was held three months after the third. The family members did not bring their star charts and diaries with them. Matthew, as before, separated himself and sat quietly writing. The parents initially gave positive feedback, describing Matthew's bedtime behavior as much improved with their new management. However, it soon emerged that this improvement had lasted for several weeks but had not been sustained, largely because the parental management had not been consistently continued. In addition, the mother had been physically ill for much of this period.

As the therapist explored the events of the more recent weeks, the interactions in the family became increasingly dysfunctional. Tension between the parents rose, partly over their management of Matthew, but more because of their concern as to how to manage when the mother was ill.

These phenomena (disorganization, rising tension, illness) suggest that the trauma is being reached. The father insisted that the mother had to look after herself, as well as the house and the children, because of his long working hours. However, he clearly felt guilty about this, and his wife felt uncared for, despite her awareness of his work pressures. At this point, Matthew came to their rescue, interrupting and seeking attention in a variety of disruptive ways. The parents were inconsistent; for example, the mother complained verbally of his general behavior but hugged him during the session and appeared to encourage it. The therapist used the interaction to help the parents to contain and manage Matthew. For example, he got them to agree to how they wanted Matthew to behave and pressed them to enforce it. At this point, the father became angry about being "psychoanalyzed" and walked out of the session, taking Matthew with him. Left alone, the mother claimed that her husband had left because he felt upset and guilty about not being able to care for her when she was ill. She wished to continue coming to therapy and thought she could persuade her husband to come with her.

The therapeutic tactic had again been predominantly structural and confronting. This is not usually appropriate to facilitate the reworking of a trauma. The family had strongly resisted this approach and the consequence of confrontation was enacted. The family split up. The family had mentioned a neighboring family whose children were taken into foster care because of inadequate parenting, and it might have been more helpful to approach the family psychodynamically, talking more of the needs, the past, and secondary fears rather than trying to restructure. This issue of children being abused and poorly cared for was felt to be too sensitive to link directly to the parents' fears. The therapist agreed with the mother's opinion that the father had been more upset by describing what he felt as noncaring in the marriage than by a failure to control his son. In view of the history of broken or unsupportive marriages, this is not surprising. The known trauma and disasters were losses within marriage and not loss of children.

Fifth Session

The mother and Matthew came alone to this session. The need for psychodynamic intervention with respect to the third element of the hypothesis was now clear. However, to set the scene, Matthew required controlling without excessive confrontation. The therapist set up a structured task in which the mother was helped to get Matthew playing without interrupting for

five minutes and then a reward was provided. In the course of doing this, and discussing its use at home, the mother's style of communication was noted and fed back to her. She and her husband avoided asserting their own wishes and instead talked in a way that deferred to Matthew's opinion or invited comment or disagreement. The mother then described her past sadness at not being able to mother Matthew closely as a baby because of her hospitalizations for serious illnesses. She expressed her mixed feelings at the loss of her own independent working life as a result of late pregnancy. Her ambivalence and her sense of loss and of failure at mothering were linked to her current difficulty in being appropriately firm with Matthew. The interventions appeared to relieve her guilt and self-blame.

Sixth Session

The mother and Matthew again came to the session without the father. In this session, there was a marked difference in Matthew's behavior. For the first time, he was positively friendly to the therapist and the mother reported improvements in her management of him and in his behavior. She disagreed with the therapist on some points in a healthy and self-assertive way. She had shared the tasks set by the therapist with her husband and also had involved him in helping her to develop a clearer way of conversing. She noted that his speech was also inconsistent, and the therapist had also noted this in the sessions. She conveyed the impression that she had actually wanted the sessions for herself alone. As the caregiver to two other generations, she was in touch with her own need for care. The therapist, therefore, offered a short period in an intensive day unit using the excuse of giving her more time to practice her new ways. However, she refused. She ended the treatment by saying that she knew that she could request further help if she wanted to in the future. She felt that Matthew was much improved and reported that the older boy's work and social life were more satisfactory. Her husband had the possibility of changing jobs, which might enable to family to move and so redefine the amount of space to be set aside for the grandmother.

Requisite Changes

As regards the requisite changes, Matthew's obesity had progressively reduced over the last six months and the grandmother had stopped interfering in his handling. We had both reported and direct evidence that the parents were able to manage Matthew more effectively and to enjoy some activities with him. However, the father was still doing this infrequently and inconsistently, and little change was reported in the relationship between the father and John. John himself had probably improved somewhat. There were no changes in the living arrangements, but there was less tension among the three generations and more acceptance of separate needs. A potential change of housing was on the horizon. There was no change in the time spent together by the spouses, but the bond between them had real strength in that they supported each other in times of stress and had been able to work together on some of the parenting problems.

CONCLUSION

The principles of our approach may be summarized as follows:

1. The approach is developmentally oriented and considers the health of the family in the context of its life cycle within and across generations.
2. The approach is rooted in the explicit offer of therapy and is, therefore, oriented to detecting possible family disturbance.
3. The family is viewed as a system that has human beings as its components and that is embedded in a social context. Therefore, purposes, feelings, and meanings are critical factors in any formulation of a family's situation, and culture is a critical constraint.
4. Traumatic events are the prime originator of disturbances that lead to families' seeking professional help. Traumatic events on individual, family, or social levels are events associated with intense anxiety and helplessness. They cannot be talked about and are represented by repetitive patterns of action that are dysfunctional.
5. Therapeutic work has to change patterns of action as well as meanings. In other words, the family both has to change its way of being and has to gain an understanding of how the dysfunction arose.
6. The therapist needs to be maximally flexible in the use of techniques and decision rules as he or she pursues a strategy that will release the family from its habitual dysfunction and enable it to create a new reality.
7. In carrying out therapy, psychoanalytic understanding of mental life is invaluable and therapist self-awareness is essential.
8. The detailed model involving focal hypothesis and formulation and the mode of recording described are generally applicable. (However, notwithstanding this claim, in certain cases, assessment will reveal that a simple response to the complaint may be all that is required.)

REFERENCES

Ackerman, N.W. (1958). *The psychodynamics of family life*. New York: Basic Books.

Andreas-Salome, L. (1962). The dual orientation of narcissism. *Psychoanalytic Quarterly, 31*, 1–30. (Translated by S. Leavy from Narzissmus als Doppelrichtung, *Imago, VII*, 361–386, 1921).

Balint, M. (1964). *The doctor, his patient and the illness* (2nd ed.). London: Pittman.

Balint, M., Balint, E., & Ornstein, P.H. (1972). *Focal psychotherapy: An example of applied psychoanalysis*. London: Mind & Medicine.

Bentovim, A. (1979). Family interaction and techniques of intervention. *Journal of Family Therapy, 1*, 321–343.

Bentovim, A. (1990). Physical violence in the family. In R. Bluegass & P. Bowden (Eds.), *Forensic psychiatry*, London: Livingstone.

Bentovim, A., Elton, A., Hildebrand, J., Tranter, M., & Vizard, E. (1988). *Sexual abuse within the family*. Bristol, England: John Wright.

Bentovim, A., & Gilmour, L.A. (1981). A family therapy interactional approach to decision making in child care, access and custody cases. *Journal of Family Therapy, 3*, 65–78.

Bentovim, A., & Kinston, W. (1978). Brief focal family therapy where the child is the referred patient. 1. Clinical. *Journal of Child Psychology, Psychiatry and Allied Disciplines, 19*, 1–12.

Bettelheim, B. (1950). *Love is not enough—the treatment of emotionally disturbed children*. New York: Free Press.

Bion, W. (1961). *Experience in groups*. London: Tavistock.

Boszormenyi-Nagy, I., & Framo, J.L. (Eds.) (1963). *Intensive family therapy*. New York: Harper & Row.

Boszormenyi-Nagy, I., & Spark, G.M. (1973). *Invisible royalties*. New York: Harper & Row.

Bowen, M. (1976). Theory in the practice of psychotherapy. In P. J. Guerin (Ed.), *Family therapy*. New York: Gardner Press.

Bowlby, J. (1949). The study and reduction of group tension in the family. *Human Relations, 2*, 123–128.

Box, S., Copley, B., Magagna, I., & Moustaki, E. (1981). *Psycho-

therapy with families: An analytic approach. London: Routledge & Kegan Paul.

Byng-Hall, J. (1989). Replicative and corrective scripts (Presentation to Institute of Family Therapy, London).

Chasin, R., Roth, S., & Bograd, M. (1989). Action methods in systemic therapy: Dramatizing ideal futures and reformed pasts with couples. *Family Process, 28*, 121–136.

Cohen, J., & Kinston, W. (1984). Repression: A new look at the cornerstone. *International Journal of Psychoanalysis, 65*, 411–422.

Cohen, J., & Kinston, W. (1989a). Understanding failures and catastrophes in psychoanalysis. *Discussion Document*, SIGMA Centre, Brunel University.

Cohen, J., & Kinston, W. (1989b). Cycles of growth during psychoanalytic therapy. *Discussion Document*, SIGMA Center, Brunel University.

Dicks, H. (1967). *Marital tensions*. London: Tavistock.

Erikson, E.H. (1963). *Childhood and society*. New York: Norton.

Ezriel, H. (1956). Experimentation with the psychoanalytic session. *British Journal of Philosophy of Science, 7*, 25–41.

Fairbairn, R. (1949). *Psychoanalytic studies of the personality*. London: Tavistock.

Ferber, A., Mendelsohn, M., & Napier, A. (1973). *The book of family therapy*. Boston: Houghton Mifflin.

Fisher, L. (1977). On the classification of families: A progress report. *Archives of General Psychiatry, 34*, 424–433.

Foulkes, S.H. (1973). The group as matrix of the individual's mental life. In L.R. Wolberg & E.K. Schwartz (Eds.), *Group therapy: An overview*. New York: Intercontinental Medical Books.

Framo, J.L. (1965). *Rationale and techniques of intensive family therapy*. New York: Harper & Row.

Framo, J.L. (1976). Family of origin as a therapeutic resource for adults in marital and family therapy: You can and should go home again. *Family Process, 15*, 193–210.

Furniss, T., Bentovim, A., & Kinston, W. (1984). Clinical process recording in focal family therapy. *Journal of Marital and Family Therapy, 9*, 147–176.

Glaser, D., Furniss, T., & Bingley, L. (1984). Focal family therapy: The assessment stage. *Journal of Family Therapy, 6*, 265–274.

Haley, J. (1977). *Problem solving therapy*. San Francisco: Jossey-Bass.

Huffington, C., & Sevitt, M.A. (1989). Family interaction in adolescent school phobia. *Journal of Family Therapy, 11*, 353–376.

Jackson, D.D. (1957). A note on the importance of trauma in the genesis of schizophrenia. *Psychiatry, 20*, 181–184.

Jackson, D.D. (1958). Guilt and control of pleasure in schizoid personalities. *British Journal of Medical Psychology, 31*, 124–130.

Jackson, D.D. (1959). Family interactions, family homeostasis and some implications for conjoint family therapy. In J. Masserman (Ed.), *Individual and family dynamics*. New York: Grune & Stratton.

Jacobs, B. (1986). *Incest: The relationship between ethics and family therapy in a nonstatutory agency*. Doctoral dissertation, Institute of Family Therapy, London.

Keeney, B., & Ross, J.M. (1985). *Mind in therapy: Constructing systemic family therapies*. New York: Basic Books.

Kernberg, O. (1975). *Borderline conditions and pathological narcissism*. New York: Aronson.

Kinston, W. (1980). Theoretical and technical approach to narcissistic disturbance. *International Journal of Psychoanalysis, 61*, 385–394.

Kinston, W. (1982). An intrapsychic schema for narcissistic disturbance. *International Review of Psychoanalysis, 9*, 253–261.

Kinston, W. (1983a). A theoretic context for shame. *International Journal of Psychoanalysis, 64*, 213–226.

Kinston, W. (1983b). The positive therapeutic reaction. *Scandinavian Psychoanalytical Review, 6*, 111–127.

Kinston, W. (1986). Purposes and the translation of values into action. *Systems Research, 3*, 147–160.

Kinston, W. (1987). A general theory of symptom formation (discussion paper). Family Research Programme, Brunel University, London.

Kinston, W., & Algie, J. (1989). Seven distinctive paths of decision and action. *Systems Research, 6*, 117–132.

Kinston, W., & Bentovim, A. (1978). Brief focal family therapy where the child is the referred patient. 2. Methodology and results. *Journal of Child Psychology, Psychiatry and Allied Disciplines, 19*, 119–143.

Kinston, W., & Bentovim, A. (1980). Creating a focus for brief marital and family therapy. In S.H. Budman (Ed.), *Forms of brief therapy*. New York: Guilford Press.

Kinston, W., & Bentovim, A. (1982). Constructing a focal formulation and hypothesis in family therapy. *Australian Journal of Family Therapy, 4*, 37–50.

Kinston, W., & Bentovim, A. (1990). A framework for family description. *Journal of Contemporary Family Therapy, 12*, 279–297.

Kinston, W., & Cohen, J. (1986). Primal repression: Clinical and theoretical aspects. *International Journal of Psychoanalysis, 67*, 337–355.

Kinston, W., & Cohen, J. (1988). Primal repression and other states of mind. *Scandinavian Psychoanalytic Review, 11*, 81–105.

Kinston, W., & Loader, P. (1984). Eliciting whole family interaction with a standardized clinical interview. *Journal of Family Therapy, 6*, 347–363.

Kinston, W., & Loader, P. (1988). The family task interview: A tool for clinical research in family interaction. *Journal of Marital and Family Therapy, 13*, 67–88.

Kinston, W., Loader, P., & Miller, L. (1987a). Quantifying the clinical assessment of family health. *Journal of Marital and Family Therapy, 13*, 49–67.

Kinston, W., Loader, P., & Miller, L. (1987b). Emotional health of families and their members where a child is obese. *Journal of Psychosomatic Research, 31*, 583–599.

Kinston, W., Loader, P., & Miller, L. (1988a). Talking to families about obesity: A controlled study. *International Journal of Eating Disorders, 7*, 261–275.

Kinston, W., Loader, P., Miller, L., & Rein, L. (1988b). Interaction in families with obese children. *Journal of Psychosomatic Research, 32*, 513–532.

Kinston, W., Loader, P., & Stratford, J. (1979). Clinical assessment of family interaction. *Journal of Family Therapy, 1*, 291–312.

Kinston, W., & Rosser, R. (1974). Disaster: Effects on mental and physical state. *Journal of Psychosomatic Research, 18*, 437–456.

Klein, M. (1948). *Contributions to psychoanalysis*. London: Hogarth Press.

Kohut, H. (1971). *The analysis of self*. New York: International Universities Press.

Lewis, J.M., Beavers, W.R., Gossett, J.T., & Phillips, V.A. (1976). *No single thread: Psychological health in family systems*. New York: Brunner/Mazel.

Lidz, T. (1963). *The family and human adaptation*. London: Hogarth Press and Institute of Psychoanalysis.

Lidz, T., Cornelison, A., Fleck, S., & Terry, D. (1957). The intrafamilial environment of schizophrenic patients: II. Marital schism and marital skew. *American Journal of Psychiatry. 114*, 241–248.

Loader, P., Burck, C., Kinston, W., & Bentovim, A. (1981). Method for organising the clinical description of family interaction: The family interactions format. *Australian Journal of Family Therapy, 2*, 131–141.

Madanes, C., & Haley, J. (1979). Dimensions of family therapy. *Journal of Nervous and Mental Disease, 165*, 88–98.

Main, T. (1957). The ailment. *British Journal of Medical Psychology, 30*, 129–145.

Malan, D.H. (1963). *A study of brief psychotherapy*. New York: Plenum.

Malan, D. (1976). *The frontier of brief psychotherapy.* New York: Plenum.

Miller, L.B., Loader, P., & Kinston, W. (1984). Further development of the format for family description. *Australian Journal of Family Therapy, 5,* 215–218.

Minuchin, S., & Fishman, C. (1981). *Family therapy techniques.* Cambridge, MA: Harvard University Press.

Minuchin, S., Rosman, B.L., & Baker, L. (1978). *Psychosomatic families: Anorexia nervosa in context.* Cambridge, MA: Harvard University Press.

Olson, D.H., Sprenkel, D.H., & Russell, C.S. (1979). Circumplex model of marital and family systems. *Family Process, 18,* 3–28.

Papp, P. (1982). The Greek chorus and other techniques of paradoxical therapy. *Family Process, 19,* 45–58.

Reiss, D. (1971). *The family's construction of reality.* Cambridge, MA: Harvard University Press.

Ricoeur, P. (1970). *Freud and philosophy: An essay in interpretation.* New Haven, CT: Yale University Press.

Rosenfeld, H. (1964). On the psychopathology of narcissism: A clinical approach. *International Journal of Psychoanalysis, 45,* 332–337.

Selvini Palazzoli, M., Boscolo, L., Cecchin, G.F., & Prata, G. (1978). *Paradox and counterparadox.* New York: Aronson.

Skynner, A.C.R. (1976). *One flesh: Separate persons: Principles of family and marital psychotherapy.* London: Constable.

Steele, R.S. (1979). Psychoanalysis and hermeneutics. *International Review of Psychoanalysis, 6,* 389–412.

Stierlin, H. (1977). *Psychoanalysis and family therapy.* New York: Aronson.

Stolorow, R.D. (1975). Toward a functional definition of narcissism. *International Journal of Psychoanalysis, 56,* 179–186.

Stratford, J., Burck, C., & Kinston, W. (1982). Influence of content on the assessment of family interaction: A clinical study. *Journal of Family Therapy, 4,* 359–370.

Turquet, P. (1975). Large group processes. In L.C. Kreeger (Ed.), *The large group: Dynamics and therapy.* London: Constable.

Weakland, J.H., Fisch, R., Watzlawick, P., & Bodin, A. (1974). Brief therapy focused problem resolution. *Family Process, 13,* 141–168.

Winnicott, D.W. (1964). *The child, the family and the outside world.* Harmondsworth, England: Penguin.

Winnicott, D.W. (1971). *Therapeutic consultations in child psychiatry.* London: Hogarth Press and the Institute of Psychoanalysis.

Wynne, L.C. (1965). Some indications and contraindications for exploratory family therapy. In I. Boszormenyi-Nagy & J.L. Framo (Eds.), *Intensive family therapy.* New York: Harper & Row.

Zinner, J., & Shapiro, R. (1972). Projective identification as a mode of perception and behaviour in families of adolescents. *International Journal of Psychoanalysis, 43,* 523–530.

Zinner, J., & Shapiro, R. (1974). The family group as a single psychic entity: Implications for acting out in adolescence. *International Review of Psychoanalysis, 1,* 179–186.

CHAPTER 10

The Milan Systemic Approach
to Family Therapy

David Campbell, Ph.D.,
Rosalind Draper, A.A.P.S.W.,
and Elaine Crutchley, M.R.C. Psych.

BACKGROUND OF THE APPROACH

Several years ago, we were taken to the small coffee bar on a side street in Milan, Italy, where Mara Selvini Palazzoli, Luigi Boscolo, Gianfranco Cecchin, and Giuliana Prata had devised much of the Milan approach from hours of discussion, argument, and persuasion. We believe the approach could have been created in no other way. As a method of family therapy, it mirrors the scene in the coffee bar in that it is essentially about creating a context in which new ways of thinking about behavior may emerge.

The development of the Milan approach has been a complicated process of continuous change as therapists develop new ways of thinking about and practicing family therapy in response to feedback from families, colleagues, and trainees. This makes the task of describing

the approach difficult. We have divided its development into six stages: (1) the birth of the Milan approach (1967–1975); (2) development of the basic principles: hypothesizing, circularity, and neutrality (1975–1979); (3) splitting into two teams (1979–1982); (4) dissemination and clarification of the approach (1979–present); (5) application of the approach to other settings (1979–present); (6) new systemic approaches (1983–present).

The Birth of the Milan Approach (1967–1975)

In 1967, Mara Selvini Palazzoli completed her journey from internal medicine through individual therapy and psychoanalysis to family therapy by founding the Milan Center for the Study of the Family. This journey is described in *Self*

Starvation (1974), which tells of her 20-year struggle to cure patients suffering from anorexia nervosa. The story is remarkable as an account of a therapist so challenged by the mysteries of the illness that she was prepared to change her own basic assumptions about the therapeutic process. She invited three other psychoanalysts—Boscolo, Cecchin, and Prata—to form a study group at the center. For several years, they met one day a week, without pay, seeing families and reading and discussing the works of Don Jackson, Jay Haley, Paul Watzlawick, and Gregory Bateson. In order to root their thinking in one model of family therapy, they limited their readings to the Palo Alto group and declined invitations to present or publish their ideas in the therapeutic community until their own model could be supported by case studies. They were spurred in their efforts by several consultations with Watzlawick, who visited them in Italy during this period.

The emergence from their chrysalis was marked by the publication of their first article in English, "The Treatment of Children Through Brief Therapy of Their Parents." (Selvini Palazzoli, Boscolo, Cecchin, & Prata, 1974) This paper introduced the major early themes of the Milan approach: the importance of the referral, the use of the team during therapy, positive connotation, and rituals, all of which would be developed in later publications. Above all, it was the description of rituals, such as a funeral rite, which were powerful interventions designed to change the interaction of the family as a whole, that captured the imagination of many people in the therapy field.

Four years later, their keenly awaited book *Paradox and Counterparadox* (Selvini Palazzoli, Boscolo, Cecchin, & Prata, 1978b) was published in English. In this fuller account of their work with anorexic and psychotic families at the center, they articulated a theoretical framework based on several important concepts. From Watzlawick, Beavin, and Jackson's (1967) *Pragmatics of Human Communication*, they adopted the notion that the family was a system in which symptomatic behavior was maintained by transactional patterns governed by rules. They described the equilibrium of the system between homeostasis and the capacity for transformation. In psychotic families, it was *hubris* that drove

individuals in a symmetrical struggle against one another for the ability to define family relationships. Yet the power to define relationships does not reside within the individual, but is only in the rules of the game. This idea that "the behavior and attitudes of the family members in schizophrenic transaction were mere moves whose sole purpose was to perpetuate the family game" (Watzlawick et al., 1967, p. 27) is one of the most powerful and enduring ideas from this period.

They described for the first time the structure of their family-therapy sessions. It consisted of five parts: *the presession*, during which the therapists gather information for the session; *the session*, which lasts about an hour, consists of questions, and may be interrupted by observing team members; *the discussion of the session*, in which the therapists meet apart from the family to discuss ways in which to conclude the session; *the conclusion of the session*, during which the therapists rejoin the family and present their comments or prescription; and *discussion of the family's reaction to the comment or prescription*, which takes place after the family has left. The structure of the sessions in the Milan approach has also been discussed by other therapists (Campbell, Reder, Draper, & Pollard, 1983; Campbell, Draper, & Huffington, 1989b; Hoffman, 1981; Tomm, 1984a, 1984b).

Having used a new theoretical formulation to identify the family "game" in schizophrenic families, the members of the Milan group applied their thinking to the development of the intervention. Based on the notion that symptomatic behavior helps to maintain the "homeostatic tendency" in the family system, the therapy team offers a counterparadoxical intervention that prescribes no change and thereby supports the homeostatic tendency. The Milan group adapted the basic principles of paradoxical injunction, which had been developed by the Palo Alto group (see Watzlawick, Weakland, & Fisch, 1974), by combining them with systemic formulations and rituals. At this time, this approach was innovative, although paradoxical prescriptions now are seen less as "things in themselves" and more as incorporated into the way in which therapists think about change in family systems.

In order to be able logically to prescribe no change in the symptomatic behavior, the team coined a phrase for one of its basic therapeutic principles: *the positive connotation*. This refers to the therapist's attempts to qualify not only the symptomatic behavior, but all observable behavior, as being "positive" or "good" since it was "inspired by the common goal of preserving the cohesion of the family group" (Selvini Palazzoli et al., 1974). This helps the therapist to avoid being influenced by the powerful labeling and blaming so characteristic of disturbed families, thereby getting closer to a truly systemic view of the family system. In this way, the therapist becomes more acceptable to the family since the therapist is seen as accepting the family as it is. Another function of the positive connotation is that it leads the family to question why the cohesion of the group that the therapists describe as being so good and desirable should be gained at the price of needing a "patient," and such a paradox may trigger the capacity for transformation.

In *Paradox and Counterparadox*, the Milan team described interventions based on the formulation of specific repetitive patterns of family interaction, which the team referred to as "games," such as the secret coalitions between family members and their original families, the way the behavior of one sibling may serve to keep another sibling in the family, and the adolescent's attempt to reform the parents' marriage at the time of leaving home.

Many of the interventions described in the book are based on family rituals. The purpose of the ritual is to address the conflict between the family rules operating at the verbal level and those operating at the analogic level by a prescription to change behavior rather than an interpretation to provide insight. The team believes that the development of insight takes place after change occurs. The value of "ritualizing" the prescribed behavior is that the ritual itself may become a new context, one of a higher order than a direct prescription from a therapist, and because of that, the ritual is often more likely to be carried out by the family.

The development of the Milan team's thinking is described in an important paper from this period, "A Ritualized Prescription in Family Therapy: Odd Days and Even Days" (Selvini Palazzoli et al., 1978a). There, they clarified the distinction between a ritual and a ritualized prescription, which specifies formal aspects of the prescription but no content. Rituals specify both formal aspects and content and, therefore, cannot be repeated. A ritualized prescription, on the other hand, provides a formal structure that can be used with many families in many different circumstances. The article describes a powerful prescription in which, on alternate days of the week, one parent decides alone how to deal with a troublesome child while the other parent acts as if he or she were not there. This may have the effect of creating a new pattern of transaction among family members, thereby blocking their traditional ways of behaving. Selvini Palazzoli and colleagues also suggested that such a prescription exploits a possible competition between parents, such that each will try to become "the best" in the eyes of the therapist and attention may be directed away from the problem behavior.

The second half of *Paradox and Counterparadox* presents interventions with different foci and suggests areas in which the new thinking of the group may develop. The focus shifts toward the role of the therapist in the family's struggle to maintain homeostasis and to resist change. During the middle and later stages of family therapy, the family may become more resistant as the members experience things beginning to change, and when this happens, the family may repudiate any further attempts by the therapy team. The Milan group specified interventions that they employed to help them through such impasses, such as the following message to the family: "We have to try to change the past for Matilde. . . . We have to try to be what her parents were not . . . it's difficult, and we still don't know how to accomplish it. But we will try as best we can" (p. 160). Another example consisted of the therapist's declaring impotence by saying that, in spite of the cooperation of the family, "we find ourselves confused and incapable of forming clear ideas, of helping them . . ." (p. 148). This message was followed by the confirmation of the next session, which creates a paradoxical situation in the mind of family members, in that the therapists are not able to help and yet offer to set up further appointments.[1]

---

[1] *Editors' Note.* Perhaps this is not a big issue, but we do not find this message to be paradoxical.

The Second Stage: Hypothesizing, Circularity, Neutrality (1975–1979)

"But how did you hit upon that particular intervention?" (Selvini Palazzoli et al., 1980b, p. 3). This question, which was put to the Milan group by interested correspondents, led the team to elaborate the fundamental principles of conducting the interview, which could then be used as a methodology for other therapists. The three indispensable principles were presented in the landmark paper "Hypothesizing—Circularity—Neutrality: Three Guidelines for the Conductor of the Session" (Selvini Palazzoli et al., 1980b).

The hypothesis is described as a means of organizing the information available to the therapist in order to provide a guide to his or her activity in conducting a systemic interview. It is "neither true nor false, but rather more or less useful" (Selvini Palazzoli et al., 1980b, p. 3). A hypothesis allows the therapist to search out new information, identify the connecting patterns, and move toward a systemic formulation of the family's behavior. In addition, an interview that is conducted from the basis of a systemic hypothesis allows the therapist to hold on to a view of the family's behavior that is different from the family's simply by being "a difference." The hypothesis, as it guides the interview, will introduce information and structure (or negentropy) into the family system, which tends toward repetitive patterns of behavior and diminishing appreciation of differences. Various writers have described their application of this principle in their own work (Campbell et al., 1983, 1989; Tomm, 1984a, 1984b) and this topic will be discussed later in this chapter.

Of all the features of the Milan approach, none has caught the imagination or aroused the interest of therapists more than *circularity*. Because of its widespread use, and misuse, it is worth reminding ourselves of the Milan group's original definition of the concept. "By circularity we mean the capacity of the therapist to conduct his investigation on the basis of feedback from the family in response to the information he solicits about relationships and, therefore, about difference and change" (Selvini Palazzoli et al., 1980b, p. 6). The therapist is trying to construct a map of the family as an interconnected set of relationships (the relations of both ideas and be-

havior), and the most effective way of creating such a map is to ask questions about differences—particularly questions that are derived from the feedback from previous questions of difference.

In particular, this means that a question such as, "Have you or your wife been more worried about this problem?" will produce a reply such as, "My wife," which the therapist interprets as information about relationships, say, between the husband and wife or husband and problem or wife and problem. The way in which the therapist uses that information to construct a map will depend largely on the hypothesis that guides the therapist toward making certain connections and not others. For example, the therapist may use the feedback "My wife" to develop a hypothesis of a wife who is distant from her husband and close to an identified patient. If this were the case, then on the basis of circularity, the therapist might ask another question, such as, "Are there other areas in which your wife has different interests than yours?" or, "How does this affect the relationship between your wife and your child?"

The article goes on to describe types of questions the group found helpful in eliciting differences during the family interview, such as triadic questioning, in which one person is asked to comment on the relationship of two other family members; difference in behavior rather than qualities intrinsic to the person; changes in behavior before or after a specific event; hypothetical circumstances; and ranking family members for a specific behavior or interaction.

Although these "questions of difference" have been adopted and described in the field as circular questions, the term "circular question" was never used in this original paper. It is important to remember that it is not simply a matter of asking a question of difference, but it is the attention paid to the development of a systemic hypothesis and the use of feedback that characterize circularity or the "circular question."

If circularity is the favored child, *neutrality* is often the scapegoat—a concept that is easily misunderstood. The original presentation of the principle of neutrality, although brief, is very clear. The Milan group refers to neutrality as the "specific pragmatic effect which the therapist's behavior exerts on the family (and not his intrapsychic disposition)" (Selvini Palazzoli et al., 1980b, p. 11). They provide a helpful hypothetical example in which each family member, when asked, was puzzled and uncertain as to whom the therapist was siding with during the session. This clearly places neutrality in the realm of a strategic stance taken by a therapist.

However, other authors (Campbell et al., 1983, 1989; Tomm, 1984a, 1984b) have broadened the principle to include the therapist's position vis-à-vis change and therapeutic outcome. For example, Tomm (1984) writes, "Some of the most serious difficulties in therapy arise when therapists become committed too strongly to the idea that a patient or family must change, or even worse, when they as therapists believe that they must somehow effect this change. The therapist's goal is meta change, that is, a change in the family's ability to change. The therapist avoids taking a clear position for or against any specific behavioral outcome" (p. 263).[2]

The final feature of the Milan approach that was developed during this period was the importance placed on the referring person and the referral process. The paper entitled "The Problem of the Referring Person" (Selvini Palazzoli et al., 1980a) was, in typical Selvini Palazzoli fashion, the result of several years' research prompted by a review of cases that had gone wrong.[3] In these cases, they had created their systemic map of the family while unknowingly excluding "one of its members who occupied a nodal heomeostatic position in that family, the referring person" (p. 1). The team presented helpful suggestions about how to avoid falling into this trap; for example, discussing the referrer's role over the telephone before the first session. In some cases, the referrer is invited to the initial session so that his or her relationship to the family and the presenting problem can be explored with the family. When the team members have confirmed their hypothesis about the referring person, this may lead to an intervention in which the homeostatic function of the

referrer is recognized and supported. In the example in the paper, the team told the family that it would not offer family therapy because to do so would jeopardize the close relationship between the referring doctor and the family.

In clarifying the fundamental principles of conducting the interview, the Milan group's thinking about the family as a system began to shift from the Palo Alto view that the problem helps the system maintain its homeostasis toward the Batesonian view that family problems are the inevitable result of family beliefs that do not fit reality. Tomm (1984) has written: "They began to see systems predominantly as evolving rather than as homeostatic. The family only appeared to be stuck; in actuality, it was always changing. The patterns of behavior that yielded the impression of stuckness or homeostasis were the result of epistemological errors made by the family."

This changing view is reflected in the way in which the group members understood the meaning of the intervention. In the first stage (1967–1975), they discussed the intervention as a means of bringing about a transformation in the pattern of behavior that maintained the homeostasis of the system. In the second stage (1975–1979), they described therapy as a means of introducing difference into the belief system of the family. If the family is an evolving system, then the therapist will have endless opportunities to introduce differences through the interview and the circular questioning technique. The intervention ceases to be an all-or-nothing assault on a static system. In fact, they concluded their "Hypothesizing—Circularity—Neutrality" (1980b) paper with the intriguing question, "Can family therapy produce changes solely through the negentropic effect of our present method of conducting the interview without the necessity of making a final intervention?" (p. 12).

With the publication of these two major papers, "Hypothesizing—Circularity—Neutrality" and "The Problem of the Referring Person," all of the main features of the work done by the team of four had been presented to the outside world. These features were: (1) the use of a team, (2) family rituals as interventions, (3) positive connotation, (4) hypothesizing, (5) circularity, (6) neutrality, (7) the referring person, and (8) a complete method of conducting family therapy based solidly on systemic ideas. Ironically, the

---

[2] *Editors' Note.* While the therapist may not favor any *particular* outcome, he or she must have a way to assess/measure/evaluate "metachange." We would be eager to learn how Milan-style therapists might reliably and validly assess such change, but to date they do not seem to have offered a methodology by which to do so.

[3] *Editors' Note.* We note that some observers (Anderson, 1986) do not agree that Selvini's work constitutes "research" in most traditionally accepted senses.

arrival of these stimulating ideas and the excitement they created in the family-therapy field coincided with the breakup of the group that produced them.

The Third Stage: Splitting Into Two Teams (1979–1982)

"The team is dead, long live the team." We think of the splitting up of the original Milan team as a step each of the individuals found necessary to take to ensure the continued development of their ideas. After finishing the task of clarifying their method, it seems that each must have considered the kind of feedback that would be most helpful in enabling them to move on to their next stage of thinking and practice. Selvini and Prata are researchers. The control of variables is important; constancy is a term that crops up again and again in Selvini's work. They clearly develop their ideas from the feedback acquired from analyzing family behavior in relation to a controlled variable such as an intervention or a telephone questionnaire (Selvini Palazzoli, 1986; Di Blasio, Fischer, & Prata, 1986). On the other hand, Boscolo and Cecchin have developed their work as a result of consultations to families and agencies throughout the world and from the feedback from trainees within their own multilevel family-therapy training. They are not researchers, nor has Selvini, by her own claim, trained anyone in family therapy.

Selvini's research is based on a lifelong, passionate quest to understand and treat psychotic individuals and their families. She reports (Selvini Palazzoli, 1986) the hit-and-miss frustration of making a new intervention for each family in each session, and when, in 1979, she struck upon an intervention that produced dramatic changes, she decided to repeat the same intervention with a number of families with psychotic members, an "invariant prescription" (Selvini Palazzoli, 1983, 1986; Selvini Palazzoli & Viaro, 1988). This became the basis of her research and signaled a new direction, which led to the splitting up of the original team several years later. She was joined in her research by Guiliana Prata from the original team and several former trainees, including Maurizio Viaro. Interesting accounts of the development of Selvini's research

and some of the differences between the two Milan teams can be found in Selvini Palazzoli, (1983, 1986), Barrows (1982), Di Nicola (1984), Pirrotta (1984), and Tomm (1984a, 1984b).

(However, it has been Selvini's work with the invariant prescription that has occupied her research since 1979, and it is beginning to bear fruit (Selvini Palazzoli, 1983, 1986).) The invariant prescription requires that parents of psychotic children spend increasingly longer periods of time away from their children without telling anyone where they are. The method for conducting this type of therapy consists of separating the parents from the rest of the family in a series of carefully described stages over a number of therapy sessions and then reuniting them with their family at the end of treatment.

While the prescription appears to be a powerful intervention in bringing about change in the pattern of the family game, it has also provided the constant variable against which each family member reacts slightly differently. This allows the researchers to focus carefully on each individual and to assess his or her contribution to the complex family game.

Yet perhaps the most significant and lasting discovery from this vein of research will prove to be the description of the process by which psychotic behavior takes place in families. The child becomes involved in the symmetrical struggle between the parents and does something unusual in an attempt to challenge the power of the person who seems to be winning the struggle. The person who is seen as losing does not understand the intentions of the child, turns hostile, and even sides with the winner, but rather than give up the child, continues by acting crazier and crazier.

The development of the team's thinking from the invariant prescription to a general model for psychotic processes occurring in families is described in their recent book *Family Games* (Selvini Palazzoli, Cirillo, Selvini, & Sorrentino, 1989). Selvini has also written about how this model can be used when working with individuals, an indication of their increasing awareness of the individual within the family system, and that there will always be families that are not amenable to a family-treatment approach (Selvini Palazzoli & Vialo, 1988).

The research that Selvini and her colleagues have completed makes a powerful and convincing case for therapists to use the invariant pre-scription with the appropriate families, and we think her work will have a significant impact on the family-therapy field. In the end, however, it may be the therapists' aesthetic preference for conducting therapy that determines the extent to which these ideas are incorporated into the practice of family therapists.

Boscolo and Cecchin, who refer to themselves as the Milan associates, initiated a three-year family-training course at the original center in 1977, the details of which are described in a jointly written article (Boscolo & Cecchin, 1982). When the team split up, they continued to run the training program and they began to travel abroad, giving workshops, presenting papers at conferences, and eventually participating in training courses organized in other countries. They worked with Helm Stierlin's team in Hei-delberg and their early forays to the English-speaking world took them to the Charles Burns Clinic in Birmingham, England, the Ackerman Institute in New York, and the University of Calgary in Canada. In 1981, they also launched two-week summer residential courses, one for English-speaking participants and another for Italians.

It is difficult to summarize the effect that Bos-colo and Cecchin's teaching and training events have had on the family-therapy field, but it seems to us that they have enabled others to appreciate what Keeney (1983) calls the cyber-netic epistemology through the way they use the feedback from the system around them to define the context for their actions.

Boscolo and Cecchin have described the way in which their own thinking has been trans-formed by feedback from trainees (Boscolo & Cecchin, 1982; Boscolo, Cecchin, Campbell, & Draper, 1985). In one example, they found that when the early generation of trainees went back to their agencies armed with new ideas to enable them to change the system, the other members of the system experienced this as a negative con-notation and resisted any attempts to change. By now, this thinking is intrinsic in their work, and they have developed many interventions to deal with this pattern.

These experiences have influenced the way in which they conduct therapy. While they con-tinue, like the original team of four, to use the five-part structure for their sessions and utilize

hypotheses and circular questioning, they prefer to adapt new interventions to each session for each family. In some cases, when appropriate, they might give no intervention, and they have been exploring the possibility of conducting the interview in such a way that it is sufficient to trigger transformations in the family's belief sys-tem without a final intervention.

Boscolo and Cecchin's ideas have been further explored in a book written in collaboration with Lynn Hoffman and Peggy Penn called *Milan Systemic Family Therapy* (1987). Penn and Hoff-man interview Boscolo and Cecchin using the transcripts of four consultations with which they were involved. In reading the book, one be-comes engaged by the recursive process that the therapists create with the families they are in-terviewing and with the wider system created by the questioning of Penn and Hoffman. The book demonstrates the principles of hypothe-sizing, circularity, and neutrality in action, but more important, it highlights how Boscolo and Cecchin are constantly evaluating the context within which the request for consultation is oc-curring, constructing hypotheses about mean-ings and premises that organize the family's actions and relationships.

Sergio Pirrotta (1984) has made an interesting comparison of the work of Boscolo and Cecchin with that of Selvini by observing family-therapy sessions conducted at the two centers. He con-cludes: "Boscolo and Cecchin concentrate on teaching an epistemology . . . that is different from what the students are used to rather than attempting to teach a clinical method. Their therapeutic activities can be seen as . . . attempts to introduce new ideas, new patterns of thinking to the family members." On the other hand, he sees that in the Nuovo Centre of Selvini and her colleagues, "The focus of the research is to find similarities in the games that 'crazy' families play and consequently what countermoves a clinician can make to interrupt these games and force the family to behave differently" (p. 12).

Pirotta describes the Milan associates' stance of neutrality as "effective in softening the hold that the family has on their perception of the problem and thus quietly challenging their epis-temology." Selvini works with a direct, nonneu-tral style, often with parents alone to alter their behavior in a prescribed fashion. This nonneu-tral stance appears to have the powerful effect of providing a point of clarity, albeit artificially, in an otherwise chaotic interactional system. She is seen as "holding one part of the system 'still' while the rest of the members and the rules revolve around it and readjust to the new point of fixture" (p. 13).

The metaphor that best describes Boscolo and Cecchin's approach, according to Pirotta, is that "therapy is the intersection of two systems, the therapy team and the family, to temporarily form one family-in-treatment system . . . and the mutual influence on one another is seen as bringing about change in and of itself" (p. 13). Selvini's work is characterized by the metaphor of a "contest or game." The power of the therapist not only is recognized, but it is also wielded with great effectiveness. The aim is to use such power to engage the family members to follow the prescription. If they do not, the therapy sessions may be terminated.[4] The aim of therapy is to "interrupt the family's rigid game and force them to invent a new one where the players have more flexibility of choice in how they behave" (p. 14). The split of the team has clearly led to distinct models of conducting therapy that nevertheless enhance each other through comparison.

The Fourth Stage: Clarification and Dissemination of Ideas (1979–Present)

During the period immediately following the breakup of the team, Selvini and Prata quietly continued their research, and although they did some teaching in Europe, they did not travel as widely as Cecchin and Boscolo, who created pockets of interest in various centers throughout the world.

Hoffman (1981) was the first person to pull the components of the Milan approach together and place them in their historical perspective as the systemic model. Her analysis makes fascinating reading because she demonstrates the way in which the Milan approach evolved from the history of ideas in family therapy, and she later identifies some of the areas of cross-fertilization between the Milan approach and others in the field.

We would like to focus on three areas in which interaction with ideas put forward by other practitioners and writers helped to clarify some of the basic tenets of the Milan approach as it was being developed by Boscolo and Cecchin.

1. Much of Keeney's work seems to have given verbal expression to aspects of the Milan approach that had not been fully articulated (Keeney, 1983; Keeney & Sprenkle, 1982). The notion of an *ecosystemic epistemology* suggests that a therapist must recognize the connection, the recursive relationships, among all aspects of his or her perceiving, thinking, and behaving. It is not sufficient to call oneself a systemic thinker since linear thinking is also a part of our "ecology." Cecchin echoed this point when he said, "If you think all intervention should be systemic family therapy, then you miss opportunities to make other kinds of interventions at other levels, such as home visits, meeting teachers, etc. All these techniques are part of the ecological pattern" (Boscolo et al., 1985, p. 280).

The next logical step is to include the observer as part of the system being observed. The therapist must explain the effect the family has on his or her view of the family. Keeney (1983) says the appropriate term "cybernetics of cybernetics" was first coined by Margaret Mead, however, this concept begins to pull into focus much of the recent work of Boscolo and Cecchin, particularly their consultations to therapists who are stuck with particular cases.

An ecosystem, according to Keeney, is capable of "ecological self-correction" (p. 135), and in family-therapy terms, this means the family has the capacity for self-healing when the ecosystem becomes "appropriately responsive to symptomatic behavior" (Keeney, 1983, p. 165). We find this notion supported in some of the most exciting recent work of the Milan associates, which is their attempt to leave the therapist-plus-family system in such a way that the family's own self-healing capacity is activated.

2. The work of the original Milan team relied heavily on the idea that much mental illness was

---

[4] *Editors' Note.* Note the contrast here with other methods of therapy, in which such resistant behavior would be *worked with* rather than perhaps taken as a signal to stop treatment. Interestingly, Holtzworth-Munroe and Jacobson (Chapter 4), while operating out of an extraordinarily different behavioral model of therapy, take a very similar stance regarding patient noncompliance with extratherapy prescriptions and directives, although they would first consider the possibility that a treatment planning error on the therapist's part may have occurred.

the result of confusion among different levels of meaning. Good behavior in one context might be bad behavior in another. Tomm has tried for several years to analyze the way in which beliefs affect behavior and the way meaning in different contexts leads to confusion. He has been aided in his quest by the work of two communication therapists from the University of Massachusetts, Cronen and Pearce (Cronen, Pearce, & Tomm, 1985; Cronen & Pearce, 1985). Together, they clarified a hierarchy of levels of meaning that create contexts that give meaning to behavior, but since meaning (or beliefs) and actions are recursively connected, the actions can create an upward or implicative force to change the beliefs. Two levels of context may be organized so that each is equally the context for and within the context of the other. Then, if no change in understanding arises when one context is momentarily seen as higher than the other, the two contexts are mutually confirming, but if treating it as higher leads to contradictory interpretations, the connection between them is called a paradox or a "strange loop."

This work has helped family therapists understand and negotiate their way through the quagmire of paradoxical behavior that is described by the Milan group. The notion of higher levels of meaning creating a context for lower levels of behavior has been taken on by Boscolo and Cecchin in their current work. For example, they have described their approach in these terms, "The Milan approach tries to change the world view, the premises. You can operate at the higher level of premises even while you change behavior at a lower level, if you have in mind the higher premises" (Boscolo et al., 1985, p. 278).

3. The physicist Ilya Prigogine's concept of *evolutionary feedback* (Prigogine & Stengers, 1977) helped shift Boscolo and Cecchin from a model of homeostasis in which change was a process of intervening in a pathological or redundant homeostatic pattern toward a view of the family as a system characterized by nonequilibrium. The family can be considered as a system vulnerable to change, when any small, random instability amplifies through a process of oscillation and pushes the system beyond its present organization to a new state. Evolutionary feedback refers to the natural process of feedback among the components of any evolving

system, and it is through this process that a random event may create an instability. Boscolo adds, "In terms of family therapy the oscillation can start in relation to a behavior that the therapist is not very much aware of. And this can be the beginning of a change. So, Prigogine says, the therapist is just a facilitator" (Boscolo et al., 1985, p. 287).

The notion of an oscillating system implies that events will occur consecutively and, therefore, exist in time. Boscolo and Cecchin have utilized this concept to great effect to help clarify the bind workers get into when they have different roles to fulfill. Cecchin has said, "In systemic theory you are not 'something,' you are 'someone in this moment' in relation to the context, who has acted in time. So if you introduce the concept of time you can say, 'I am the therapist now but tomorrow I will be the social controller'" (Boscolo et al., 1985, p. 288).

Along with the theoretical development, other therapists have been challenged by the Milan approach to develop various aspects of method. Penn (1982) at the Ackerman Institute in New York City has been very creative in her efforts to unravel the mysteries of circular questioning. She identifies this method as a means of creating a "corrective loop" consisting of the therapist, family, symptom, and intervention as one interconnected system. This loop becomes what Keeney (1983, p. 77) calls a "unit of mind" made from a sequence of events that are connected through feedback and that only changes its structure as a result of new information or differences. Therefore, when circular questioning is used to join these components into a loop, "there is a potential for everything inside the loops to change or restructure itself when information is introduced" (p. 171). Penn goes on to identify nine categories of "circular" questions. In a later paper (Penn, 1985), she explores the effect of using the hypothetical question as a circular question. Such questions, she proposes, lead the family to a process of "feed forward," in which the evolutionary potential for change is evoked. The family members gain a sense of their own potential to imagine new solutions, and once this potential is evoked, it is more difficult to return to their old solutions.

Karl Tomm (1984a, 1984b) has the rare ability to explain and categorize some of the elusive features of this method so they can be grasped by those of us who have to work hard for our inspirations. Tomm's collaboration with Cronen and Pearce (Cronen et al., 1985) fueled his interest in the recursive relationships among the different levels of meaning that organize behavior, and he identified two different types of questions being asked in a circular interview. One type of question was aimed at *information gathering*, while the intention of the other type was to effect a change in the different levels of meaning (Tomm, 1985). He calls these *reflexive questions* because the ability of such questions to create changes in the hierarchy of meanings depends on the reflexive effect that one level of meaning has on another. But, he points out, the important distinction in a reflexive question is the intentionality of the therapist in wanting to bring about change (see also Tomm, 1987b, 1988).

The application of the "cybernetics of cybernetics" and the work of Maturana (which will be discussed later) to family therapy has led Tomm and others to consider the presence of the therapist in a therapist–family system as a continuous "intervention" for the autonomous system of the family. Thus, Tomm coined the phrase "interventive interviewing" as a generic term referring to the activity of the therapist (Tomm, 1987a). This perspective enables the therapist to look more closely at all of his or her behavior during a therapeutic interview—and not to consider just the final statement as an intervention. As therapists look more closely at their own behavior, at their intentionality, Tomm argues, they need a new guideline for conducting the session that allows them to evaluate their own processes of evaluation. In order to postulate a new guideline, Tomm has, with audacious modesty, cracked the holy triumvirate to add "strategizing" to hypothesizing, circularity, and neutrality. The elegant formulation broadens the scope of the Milan approach, adding, for example, strategizing that is based on "what ought to be" to the traditional notion of neutrality, founded on acceptance of "what is." This distinction will help therapists to maintain a systemic view of their position in the system by giving them tools to see that whatever they are doing or thinking (or whatever they are told to do or think) may be considered merely a "posture" that is adopted as a particular systemic response at a particular time.

We have already alluded to the difficulties in understanding the concept of neutrality. Cecchin (1987), in a paper entitled "Hypothesizing, Circularity and Neutrality Revisited: An Invitation to Curiosity," reframed neutrality as a "state of curiosity." This reframing has been a liberating experience for therapists using a constructivist approach as neutrality is no longer seen as a stance assumed by the therapist to keep "meta" to the family. Using concepts derived from Maturana (1978), Maturana and Varela (1980), Keeney (1983), and Bateson (1973, 1979), Cecchin demonstrates how systemic therapy creates a language using context in which multiple descriptions and patterns are drawn forth within a coevolving therapeutic process. The therapist's curiosity makes him or her interested in many possible descriptions and the pattern that connects these descriptions, rather than in searching out the "true" explanation for the problem. Cecchin describes this "alternative perspective as one which celebrates the complexity of interaction and invites a polyphonic orientation to the description and explanation of interaction" (p. 406).

The Fifth Stage: Application of the Milan Approach to Different Settings (1979–Present)

Cecchin has told an interesting story about the way a group of trainees was applying the training in their own work settings. The trainees had come back to the center a year after completing their training. "They said they felt pretty good about their work and they discovered that everything they learned during the training was totally useless" (Boscolo et al., 1985, p. 292). This seemingly paradoxical statement conveys two important levels of meaning about applying the Milan approach: some of what is learned in a training course can never transfer to nontraining contexts, but at another level, training in systemic thinking may enable therapists to find new solutions to perennial problems in their own workplaces. This section is about some of those solutions the second generation has had to fashion from experience.

The issue that seems to unite all these workers is the struggle to facilitate a kind of interaction between their own subsystem and the larger system around it, which will enable the whole system to continue solving new problems. For example, in 1978, the closure of the mental hospitals in Italy forced mental health workers to find new approaches to the treatment and rehabilitation of their patients. One group in Bologna set up an "experimental" house on the grounds of a large mental hospital to rehabilitate 30 chronic patients into the community (Castellucci, Frurggeri, & Marzari, 1985). Their aim was to interact with the wider system beyond the hospital in such a way that the rehabilitation of individual patients would be possible. To do this, they utilized Prigogine's ideas about instability and fluctuation (Prigogine & Stengers, 1977), which had been a part of their training in Milan. They created instabilities for each patient by presenting new information in the form of projects aimed at the departure of the patient. However, this instability will only trigger a fluctuation if the team is also able to offer some constancy to balance the instability. In this case, the constancy is represented by respect for the time frame in which the individual can tolerate change and by intense optimism on the part of the staff. By vigorously presenting constancy and instability to the patient, both the workers and the wider system were able to continue progressing toward integration within the larger system.

Alexander Blount in Massachusetts (Blount, 1985) used a different conceptual base to organize a mental health center with a similar goal of rehabilitation. He creates a context in which the clients' previous learning patterns based on blame are not supported by the staff, thereby allowing the clients to experience some flexibility in their way of thinking, which represents new learning for the client that leads to a new view of relationships. Like many workers in such positions, Blount is accountable to the larger system—the state authorities—to show results for his work, and he has devised an ingenious method for meeting a "linear" demand with a systemic solution. He creates with each client a treatment contract in which problems, goals, and methods can be spelled out and monitored, and this form is given to the authorities as well as to the client to measure progress. But some questions in the form—such as, "In which ways do identified problems impair day-to-day functioning of those people affected?"—also introduce systemic thinking into the definition of the problem.

Another creative means of introducing systemic thinking while respecting the "reality" of the larger system is described in the work of Fruggeri and co-workers (Fruggeri, Dotti, Ferrari, & Matteini, 1985; Cecchin & Fruggeri, 1986). They worked from a district-based mental health service that offered a range of services from pharmacology to psychotherapy. Reflecting the Milan associates' vigor in clarifying the different contexts in which one is working, they first separated the patient's requests for help into the two levels of command and report; then they devised responses for the two levels and finally a framework for recombining the two levels as they are originally presented to the workers. For example, if a patient requests drugs to help with anxiety, the team offers feedback that it calls *acceptance–redefinition*, which accepts the content of the patient's request (the drug) "but at the same time redefines drugs as only a partial instrument of intervention ('They will help you to feel a little better') and delimits their function in respect to the therapy ('They won't change you'). The team's redefinition of the therapeutic context is therefore maintained" (p. 140).

The Milan approach also provides the conceptual framework for one worker to offer a consultation to others. Inevitably, the consultant is part of that system as the participant-observer, but the difference here is that a consultant responds to feedback from a position of broader neutrality. Anderson and Goolishian (1986) describe their work in consulting to agencies involved in treating domestic violence. Their experiences are relevant to many situations in which the consultant becomes a participant in many mutually conflicting meaning systems that have paralyzed the worker's sense of effectiveness. The consultant must work from a base of interest in all the views of those involved without becoming attached to any one view of reality, so that he or she can maximize the possibility of new information entering the system and the sense of "stuckness" being overcome.

The principles of systemic consultation have been extended to organizations in the work described by Campbell and colleagues (1989a). They use the concept of an organizational life cycle and hypothesize that problems arise within organizations when (1) individual needs conflict with the stage of development in the organization, and (2) significant relationships may be threatened by change. They use the principles of systemic interviewing combined with experiential exercises to allow new information to enter the system so that change can occur.

Other types of consultation have been described in Campbell (1985), Campbell, Draper, and Huffington (1989a), Van Trommel (1984), Imber-Coppersmith (1985), and Nitzberg, Patten, Spielman, & Brown (1985).

The Sixth Stage: New Systemic Approaches (1983–Present)

The latest stage in the evolution of the Milan approach is one in which many groups that built theoretical foundations on the work of the Milan group, particularly the teaching and training of Boscolo and Cecchin, are beginning to differentiate their work from that of their teachers and to develop their own variations of systemic family therapy. They are all united in their attempts to understand the implications of second-order cybernetics (the cybernetics of cybernetics) and to build them into family therapy; the variations appear in the way these groups draw the implications and apply them in different settings and with different client groups.

The basic premise of second-order cybernetics is that the observer is a part of the thing he or she is observing, and by implication, the therapist is a part of the system to which he or she is offering therapy. If therapists step inside the boundary around a family being observed, then they become part of a closed, autonomous system. Their observations are influenced by what they observe and what they observe is influenced by their observations. The circle is complete and there is no outside reality. The question then arises: From this self-reflexive position, how does the therapist conduct therapy? Here the work of Maturana and Varela has proved invaluable to questing family therapists.

We have chosen to date this final stage from 1983 because in April of that year Tomm organized a conference in Calgary that united Maturana, Von Foerster, Boscolo, and Cecchin. Although many people had read Maturana's work, that conference seemed to be the first step in bringing his ideas into the fold of systemic family therapy. He has since lectured and traveled throughout Europe and America, leaving behind groups of therapists intent on putting his ideas into practice. The reader who wants a full discussion of Maturana's ideas should refer to his original work (Maturana, 1978; Maturana & Varela, 1980; Mendez, Coddou, & Maturana, 1988).

Several of his ideas have been adopted by therapists who are struggling to solve the problems posed by second-order cybernetics. He and Varela (Maturana, 1978) coined the term *autopoeisis* to refer to a process whereby component parts interact only with each other and only with the components that are necessary to realize the unity or organization of the whole. An autopoeitic system, then, is informationally closed to the outside environment. Its behavior is determined by the structure of the system, not by the properties of the entities that perturb the system. This concept of *structure-determined systems* has been very influential in recent family-therapy thinking. It has led therapists to appreciate that they cannot change families through therapeutic interventions but can merely coexist in a therapeutic domain in which they may perturb the system through interaction but that will only lead to therapeutic change if the structure of the family system allows the perturbation to have an effect on its own organization.

When two or more such structure-determined systems interact, they create a *consensual domain* in which reality is defined through language. Therapists have found this concept helpful in their attempts to create a new reality with a family. Language is a process of consensual agreement between people and is, therefore, the basis of one's view of reality. This idea has much in common with the view of radical constructivists that we invent reality (Von Glasersfeld, 1984). If reality is no longer something that exists "out there," then the act of creating reality is the act of a person observing, then making distinctions about these observations, and, finally, sharing with another person through language.

Two of Maturana's colleagues in Chile, Carmen Mendez and Fernando Coddou, have discussed the therapeutic implications of maintaining the view of an objective reality (Mendez et al., 1988). They argue that what we call reality is not the grasping of an objective reality but the acceptance of a certain type of evidence as the criteria for validating our own reality. These criteria for accepting evidence are established in agreement with other people through the phenomenon of language. When there is disagreement about the criteria for validation, an argument may ensue in which each side tries to convince the other that he or she has a true picture of reality whereas the other does not. Then if the disagreement persists, it is only a small step before each assesses the other as "mistaken, bad (morally bad), resistant, or ill (crazy)." One can easily imagine the effects of this process in society when certain groups are empowered to diagnose and categorize others on the basis that those in authority have mastered an objective knowledge.

"The only way out of this trap is to accept that constitutively we as biological entities do not have access to an objective independent reality." In its place, the authors suggest the concept of *objectivity in parentheses* to denote that the comparisons we make to define our reality are specified by the operation of distinction that brings forth that which is distinguished. When these ideas are carried into clinical practice, the therapist aims not to change the family, but to create a "domain of interaction" that allows the family members to see they are creating their own reality.

Andersen (1984) is one of the clinicians who is building these ideas into his practice. He has used a systemic model, influenced by the Milan group, for some years, to consult to general practitioners and other professionals working with physical illness. His latest work is described in Andersen (1987). To create a truly coevolving therapeutic domain with the family, one team from northern Norway takes great care to listen to the family's explanation of the referral and the attempts to solve the problem, taking particular notice of the family's style, language and rhythm, and modes of exchanges in order to copy them as much as possible. The therapist and family are regarded as an autonomous system and, therefore, are not interrupted by the observers behind the screen. In fact, they have modified the original Milan technique and prefer to work without a hypothesis since it restricts the therapist's ability to understand the family's own construction of reality. As the interview draws to a close and the observers individually prepare their own thoughts about the family, the lights are turned down and the one-way viewing mirror is literally reversed. The family then observes the team "reflecting" on the conversation that has just taken place with the family. Andersen's approach is based on the idea of the family–therapist system as an autonomous, structure-determined system, and through the interviewing style also allows the family and therapist to appreciate each other's views not as "objectivities" but as "objectivities in parentheses."

Varela (1979) is also interested in the way reality is created through agreement among people. He expands Maturana's idea that our understanding of reality is based on our position as observers and offers the concept of the observer community. That is, the understanding of reality is the result of shared observations, and when taken together, they create what he calls an "epistemology of participation" (p. 276). "The act of understanding is basically beyond our will because the autonomy of the social and biological systems we are in goes beyond our skull because our evolution makes us part of a social aggregate and a natural aggregate which have autonomy compatible with but not reducible to our autonomy as biological individuals . . . The knower is not the biological individual" (Varela, 1979, p. 276).

Among those who are developing these ideas further is Hoffman (1985), who discusses the way she sees these ideas incorporated in the Milan approach. She is particularly interested in therapists' shifting from the "observed system" framework to the "observer system" framework, which puts the therapist in touch with the premises or shared views of reality that are held by the family. She goes on to say, "If one is looking for a premise that would explain the presence of a problem, one has to be clear about the nonobjectivity not only of the family's perceptions but of the observers' constructions of those perceptions" (p. 33).

If the therapist, then, moves toward the view that the focus of therapy is not an observable interaction or dysfunctional family structure, but is, instead, the various premises that people hold about a problem, it is logical to conceive of what Anderson and colleagues (Anderson,

Goolishian, & Windermand, 1987) have called *problem-determined systems*. This is an exciting new development in the field because as a concept it incorporates the ideas of structure determinism and the nonobjective view of reality and it is highly operational for the therapist whose job it is to address problems in many different contexts. "A problem determined system may be an individual, a couple, a family, a work group, an organization, or any combination of individuals that is communicatively interactive and organized around a shared languaged problem. If we substitute the concept of problem determined systems as the appropriate descriptor for the target of treatment, it follows then that we would drop such concepts as individual therapy, couples therapy, family therapy or larger systems therapy. The definition of the problem marks the context, and therefore the boundaries of the system to be treated" (Anderson et al., 1987, p. 7).

They have now taken these ideas further and renamed the problem-determined system a "problem-organizing system", (Anderson & Goolishian, in press) to emphasize that through language we are constantly evolving new meanings and that problems are not fixed entities. A problem having been created through language also dissolves as alternative meanings and descriptions emerge. The therapeutic system is thus a "problem-organizing, problem dis-solving system" in which the therapist is the "participant-observer and participant-manager" of the therapeutic conversation. The juxtaposition of these two ideas—the therapist's intimate involvement with this coevolving language system and the responsibility to create the space for a meaningful dialogue to emerge—challenges practitioners to be constantly aware of their position within the therapeutic system.

The Milan approach to family therapy has now been established on the family-therapy scene for over 10 years. It has reached a point in its development at which practitioners no longer adopt defensive postures about the tenets of the approach, but are seeking to address some of the dilemmas that critics have highlighted. One of the core issues here is how to equate a circular, systemic paradigm with a concept of power that, according to Bateson (1973, p. 463), is a "myth . . . which is still epistemological lunacy." Critics with a feminist perspective have seen this denial

of the reality of power as one of the means whereby family therapy can maintain the status quo. MacKinnon and Miller (1987) have been more specific in their criticisms by recognizing the difference between a first- and second-order cybernetic approach. This perspective has challenged ideas about therapeutic objectivity and created an awareness of social context rather than punctuating the boundary around the family and artificially locating pathology within that system. However, despite its potential, they see the Milan approach as developing in a conservative direction.

Dell (1989) has tackled the apparent clash between Bateson's view of the myth of power and our human experience of power and its abuses by suggesting that when Bateson was discussing power, he was "speaking in the domain of scientific explanation, whereas the rest of us, when we believe in 'power,' are speaking in the domain of experience and the domain of description" (p. 8). Fish (1990) has gone further and challenges Bateson's dictums on power and control, which he sees as preventing a greater integration between a systemic paradigm and the needs of individuals. He suggests that such an integration might be better achieved if Ashby's views on cybernetics are taken into account.

The introduction of the epistemology of second-order cybernetics and constructivism has led to a major shift in thinking and practice within the Milan approach. It will be interesting to observe whether those working in this field will continue to be as open to new challenges to systemic thinking. If such openness continues, perhaps a greater integration of our understanding of the complexity of human systems will be achieved.

THE HEALTHY OR WELL-FUNCTIONING FAMILY

As systemic therapists, we cannot define health in a family or marriage without behaving in a nonsystemic way. To define "health" or "normality," we would be acting as if we could see an objective reality distinct from ourselves and abandoning the hard-won position of second-order cybernetics, whereby the observer is included in the total arc of reality and is not an outside agent acting therapeutically upon a unit (the family or marriage) that is separate from himself or herself.

The effect of establishing certain standards for healthy functioning is to put the therapist into a context that leads to a way of thinking about problem solving, based on first-order cybernetics, in which the therapist is seen as someone who fixes and cures a problem residing in a separate system. Instead of the system creating the problem, "we see the new epistemology implies that the problem creates the system. The problem is whatever the original distress consisted of, thus whatever the original distress on its merry way through the world has managed to stick to itself. . . . The problem is the meaning system created by the distress and the treatment unit is everyone who is contributing to that meaning system" (Hoffman, 1985). Thus, the systemic therapist is part of that meaning system, which will include the family's definitions about what is considered healthy, as soon as the family walks through the door. The therapist will seek to understand what "health" means for the family and how ideas about health connect with other beliefs and actions for the family. There are times when the family's definition of health could result in a child's being abused or being put at risk of suicide. This dilemma is considered elsewhere in this chapter; it requires a recognition that the therapist is operating within a different context—that of social control.

We would agree with Jackson (1977) that there is no such thing as a normal family, marriage, or individual. We see families and marriages as complex sets of relationships where the beliefs and actions of the members of the system fit or do not fit comfortably for them. For example, in one army or navy marriage, the fact that the husband is frequently away for long periods may cause a problem because the wife becomes depressed when he is absent. But in another marriage where the same circumstances apply and similar amounts of time are spent together and apart, the wife does not get depressed while the husband is away and both husband and wife find the relationship satisfying.

It is important that the idea of healthy family functioning not be divorced from the meaning system that creates it, in this instance, the problem-organizing system. We need to ask how our views about health can help or hinder the creation of a therapeutic context. Concepts of health may be applied on a pragmatic basis if this is helpful within such a context, but without coming to believe that they constitute an objective reality.

Thus, what is normal or healthy is what works for the individuals involved or when behavior and beliefs in the system over time do not lead to any members of the system defining a problem or behaving symptomatically. When problems are defined from within or from outside the system, as systemic therapists we see our work as looking for explanations for the meaning of the behaviors and relationships that surround and support the complained-of problem behavior.

We seek to understand how, as the system moves through time and relationships have to change as life-cycle events occur, individuals feel close relationships to be under threat and seek to preserve them as they were, thus creating tension for the system. Family members will seek to resolve such tension by renegotiating and redefining relationships such that a comfortable fit between the action–belief ecology of the individual and that of the other family member is regained. Because human systems are constantly "languaging" together (Anderson & Goolishian, in press), there is a continuous process in which actions and beliefs are being reassessed in the context of redefined relationships, which then allows alternative actions and beliefs to emerge, thus recursively affecting relationships.

It is a fundamental premise of a systemic therapist that all behavior has meaning in the context of certain relationships at a given moment and that the family is the expert about itself. Appreciating this meaning, and that family members may do the wrong things for the right reasons, is the beginning of a systemic understanding of how discrepancies between beliefs and actions in a family or marriage occur and lead to the development of symptomatic behavior.

Accommodating, adjusting to, and accepting new information, ideas, beliefs, and actions are necessary for the family to feel intact and to evolve over time. That is, the family is not stuck in repetitive sequences of behavior that Tomm (1984a) says are the result of "epistemological errors made by the family, when the family appears to be following an outdated or erroneous belief or 'map' of their reality." Our view is that when relationships are experienced by family members as defined and declared, they are usually experienced as acceptable and tension-free; however, ambiguity leads to uncomfortable discrepancies between behaviors and beliefs in the family or marital system.

Yet family members belong to many more systems than their nuclear or extended family, and this multisystem membership increases the complexity and variety of possible relationships. Every family member is constrained by the needs of other members of the system to support certain relationships as well as to develop satisfying relationships for himself or herself.

Some family members become symptomatic but others do not because they become part of a problem-defining pattern of behavior. The reasons that this pattern develops are enormously complex. Essentially, one person must exhibit behavior that an observing person defines as "different," difficult, or symptomatic. The initial behavior can be part of random fluctuation, biologically or psychologically determined, but only comes alive as a symptom when someone else describes it as such or acts in a way to exacerbate the original behavior beyond acceptable units. When this individual behaves in an uncharacteristic or different way, the rest of the system works in such a way as to try and make the previously expected and familiar behavior occur.

Patterns of interaction that become expected and familiar generate family maps that guide subsequent interaction. Maps make it difficult for new patterns of interaction to occur, and thus the family or couple appears to be stuck and unable to evolve new patterns of interaction to fit the demand of new events. The capacity of a coevolving system to respond to challenges to established patterns of interaction as events that precede change is another important premise in systemic thinking about functional families.

THE DYSFUNCTIONAL FAMILY

For a systemic therapist, dysfunction occurs within a context where a relationship is defined between the therapist and the family or couple.

Within a coevolutionary framework for thinking about family and marital systems, the decision to seek outside help is an indication that one or more family members view the system as not functioning well enough for such members to maintain the kinds of relationships they want in terms of closeness to or distance from other family members. This view may lead to behaviors that involve either therapists or social controllers with the family system.

The traditional process by which families are diagnosed or typed tends to describe the family as though it exists "out there" apart from the context in which it is being observed. While we sometimes use shorthand family labels such as "enmeshed," "centripetal," or "rigid," we try to describe the wider context that includes the beliefs and expectations about the problem and the solution that are held by the referrer, various family members, the therapist, and the agency he or she comes from. Inevitably, we find that when we are pursuing such a systemic formulation, diagnostic labels for family behavior limit our view and prove unhelpful.[5]

In order to understand the way certain behaviors come to be labeled as dysfunctional, it may be helpful to trace the process by which the family responds to certain selected behaviors. Each family member carries inside him or her a hierarchically organized set of beliefs, premises, or constructs. They derive from the different levels of feedback from the environment. The highest, most inclusive beliefs are those that come from interaction with cultural values: "protect one's family," "respect the rights of others." Lower-level beliefs, such as "be successful" or "avoid conflict," derive from feedback from the community, family, workplace, dyadic relationships, and the like. These beliefs combine to exert a contextual force to guide people toward specific action. These actions provide the data by which people support or reject the belief that guided that particular

---

[5] *Editors' Note.* Such diagnostic labels may be unhelpful since there exists no valid family diagnostic system to guide the choice of treatment interventions. At the same time, there *is* some relevant research on the differential effectiveness of different family treatment methods with families containing a member with individually diagnosable psychiatric disorders.

action. Thus, belief and action are joined in a recursive relationship and are experienced by the individual as a "good-enough fit" to allow the appropriate development of the individual or as a "bad fit," in which case the individual's relationship with the environment is threatened.

In the context of a family group, actions or behaviors create relationships among family members. The actions of one person impinge on the belief–action "fit" of another. If, for example, a mother becomes withdrawn from her daughter, the daughter will "fit" this behavior to her own set of beliefs, and through this process, her beliefs will guide her toward some action in response to her mother. If the fit between the mother's behavior and the daughter's own beliefs is a good-enough one, the daughter's behavior will contribute to the evolution of the ecology of her ideas and actions, but if it does not fit, the daughter will not know which possible action will maintain the ecology. The daughter may resort to behavior to reestablish a good-enough fit.

These behaviors may then come to be labeled as mad or bad. In some families, this is the first step in a painful, escalating drama. Attempts to eradicate behavior are often seen by the individual perpetrator as yet another example of behavior that does not fit or is not understood, and, therefore, the individual tries harder to make this new behavior fit. Symptomatic behavior is a secondary phenomenon that follows initial changes in beliefs and actions that did not fit and thereby were experienced as a threat to relationships maintained by the prevailing ecological balance.

In order to experience such a threat, the individual must construct a reality in which one discrete event, such as a mother's withdrawal, is separate from another event, such as the mother's attention; it must compare unfavorably with the previous event; and such a comparison must be recognized as a bad fit.

Von Glaserfeld (1984) has written that the reality we create from experience supposes "that the future will resemble the past"; consequently, if individuals compare two events unfavorably, they will assume that the future will resemble the unfavorable comparison. In fact, the future may *become* the past in the experience of a family under threat. But it is our beliefs or constructs that determine the way we break the flow to create a sense of time and the way we make comparisons that leads to the experience of fit. Beer (1981) reminds us that human beings invent time to support their beliefs.

Our approach stems from the view that individuals, whether they be family members or therapists, construct their own sense of reality and time. These basic constructs determine what behavior is acceptable in order to maintain a comfortable relationship between ideas and behavior. When new or strange ideas or events intrude, the individuals who observe the behavior may attempt to preserve their own ecological balance by repeating old behaviors and in the process label certain differences as unacceptable and eventually "symptomatic." In the language of Maturana and his colleagues, dysfunction or pathology is "brought forth" by an observer who is part of a larger observer-and-observed system (Mendez et al., 1988).

The appearance of one symptom rather than another is determined by the way individuals select or "bring forth" certain features of the behavioral landscape for special attention. Some families select behavior that is based on physical illness; other families are interested in achievement, loyalty, or competition. Over time, these themes become part of the pattern of behavior that represents the family's belief–action ecology. Beliefs about relationships may become based on beliefs about illness or loyalty, and when these themes arise in the normal course of events, the family members react strongly as though relationships are threatened. Similarly, the family may respond quite differently to one child's being ill than to the illness of another child. Individuals fit into the pattern in the same way that specific behaviors do.

Gender, birth order, physical characteristics, and so on, acquire meaning over many generations and fit into the family's sense of fit among beliefs and actions. When one particular child does not fit expectations, the sense of fit and family relationships may be threatened; individuals then respond to particular behaviors in particular individuals in ways that protect relationships or beliefs from the threat of change, and this response may set off an escalating pattern that eventually becomes labeled as "symptomatic."

THE ASSESSMENT OF SYSTEM FUNCTIONING AND DYSFUNCTION

We are aware that any group of therapists will develop their own ideas, which inevitably depart from the original source—in this case, the Milan approach. In the following sections, we refer to the way in which we have adapted the Milan approach to our own work.

In our work, we have tried to shift the focus of assessment from the family to the therapist–family system. We look at the fit between the therapist and the therapist's questions and the family members and their replies. We then assess whether or not the fit is creating a therapeutic context—that is, a context in which the family members are able to take in new information, increase their awareness of the connectedness of their beliefs and behaviors, and solve their own problems.

Through the interviewing process, the therapist is continually assessing the "therapeuticness" of the context that is created through the interaction between therapist and family. In order to be therapeutic, the context must allow for several things to occur:

1. Family members must feel that their point of view is being heard and appreciated, that they can trust the relationship with the therapist and allow him or her to explore their meaning system.
2. The family and therapist must feel that there is some risk of change as they engage in the therapeutic interview.
3. The therapist must feel that the family's responses stimulate his or her curiosity to learn more about the connectedness of the beliefs and behaviors of the family and suggest directions in which the interview may go. We try not to attribute "stuckness" to the family's reluctance to give information. Instead, we assume that the therapist is not asking the right questions, ones that will allow the family to give a response that stimulates further questioning.
4. Both therapist and family must feel that new

information is being exchanged and new territory is being explored. One of the aims of the interview is to counteract the patterns of redundant behavior that maintain the problem behavior. This is done by the introduction of new information in various forms.
5. Both therapist and family should feel that through the interview the problem behavior and attempts to solve it are being connected to the wider beliefs in the system. In this way, both family and therapist experience greater systemic awareness.

The process by which the therapeutic context is assessed is one of matching the family's response to our expectations of what responses we think will fulfill the criteria mentioned above. Specifically, our own expectations derive from two sources: (1) an amalgam of all the therapeutic relationships we have experienced in the past, which underpins (2) the construction of a hypothesis about the way beliefs and behavior are connected for this particular family.

Part of the process of constructing a hypothesis also involves making continual ongoing assessments about which of the family beliefs and relationships offer the greatest possibility for introducing new information. That is, some beliefs organize more of the behavior connected to the problem and others are more peripheral, and these beliefs can be placed in a hierarchy or "prioritized" (see Cronen & Pearce, 1985) for the benefit of the therapist. For example, a family may initially present the therapist with a range of beliefs from various sources, such as ethnic background, cultural or religious influences, gender issues, life-cycle stages, and family constellation, but the prioritizing of these beliefs in terms of their influence on the problem behavior can only be accurately done by observing (and assessing) the feedback the family gives to the therapist's questions.

The feedback is used to construct a hypothesis that guides the interview, and the tools by which the assessment process is carried out are the circular questions that stimulate responses for the therapist's hypothesis. There are many types of questions that explore the different levels of organization within the family's meaning system (see Tomm, 1985, 1987b).

GOAL SETTING

As systemic therapists, we begin our work with families or couples by defining the context in which a problem has been identified and in which a family seeks (or is sent for) help. Defining the therapeutic context includes understanding the therapist's relationship to the problem behavior. If the therapist has some interest in protecting people from harm or preventing behavior from occurring, or has a responsibility to do so, he or she will work with the family in a particular way. The therapist clearly has a goal that is defined by the context and may choose to articulate this goal for himself or herself and/or the family as they begin working together. Certain situations lead the therapist to having to take control—a move from the domain of autonomy to that of constraint. It is important for the therapist to clarify with the family in which domain they are engaged.

On the other hand, if the therapist has no responsibility for the problem behavior, he or she may define a different context in which to work. In this case, we believe the therapist's position that is most helpful to families is one in which the responsibility for change is left with the family members. Here, the goal of therapy is different. While the therapist may have a goal of being available, helping to create a therapeutic context, and maintaining a systemic view of the process, the specific goals of what the family members want to achieve and how they want to do it are left to them. The therapist is responsible for creating a context in which change can occur, as therapists are also part of a wider context that defines their role. However, how the family changes is the responsibility of the family, which we see as having the capacity to find its own solution. It is possible that the direction the family takes in the change process may not always be what we would want.[6] We would re-

spect the choice as long as the context allows that autonomy. If the context is different (for example, one of child protection), we would have to take control of the direction of change.

If setting goals is required as part of an evaluation of therapy in which the therapist might wish to comply, such an evaluation creates a different context—research. This should not be confused with the context of protecting people or of remaining neutral, as defined above.

Families usually have their own goals for treatment and we find it very helpful to explore these during the interview, not to establish jointly held goals for treatment, but rather to understand goals as aspects of the family's belief system that will have a great bearing on the way the family attempts to organize the relationship with the therapist. The therapist's goals are generally to maintain a therapeutic context in which the family's belief system can be explored and new ideas put forward for the family to consider.

THE STRUCTURE OF THE THERAPY PROCESS

The process of therapy starts with a referral when someone contacts the clinic with a concern. The referral process is in itself an important source of information on the beliefs that have arisen within the system about the presenting problem; we are interested not just in the content of the referral, but in what may have led the referrer to ask for help at this time. Our usual practice is to ask for all family members living at home to attend the first interview. There are times, however, when information we receive causes us to request a meeting with the professionals involved prior to meeting the family. A family member's failure to attend would be regarded as information and the therapist would develop hypotheses arising from his or her curiosity about the fact that the family organizes itself in this way.

There are no rules about who should be involved in such meetings. Based on feedback we receive from the family, we might ask for members of the extended family, or a professional who has a key role with the family, to be invited to the session. The fact that a member of the family is in individual therapy would not prevent

---

[6] *Editors' Note.* While we certainly agree that the therapist should not impose his or her values in the selection of treatment goals, we think that there are times when "what the family wants" is not a sufficient, or perhaps even appropriate, criterion for deciding on treatment aims, for example, when the family desires change that is impossible or highly improbable, by virtue of individual constitution, disability, and so on.

us from offering to meet with the family. We would recognize that the individual therapy is an important part of the relationships that have become organized around the problem.

Therapists work in many different contexts—often in institutions in which therapy is only a small part of their work. They may be responsible for social welfare, teaching, or controlling symptoms. Are these roles compatible with the position of the systemic therapist? We would say yes, but that it is important, however, that the therapist be clear about the context in which he or she is working. For instance, in one context it may be necessary to prescribe medication to alleviate distressing symptoms. Fruggeri (Fruggeri et al., 1985) describes how a request for medication needs to be redefined as, "This medication may make you feel better for a while but will not change you."

An essential part of the original Milan team's philosophy was the emphasis on teamwork as the means to achieving a systemic perspective of the problem. The team remains important in our work, although we would now recognize that when one is working on one's own, the systemic perspective can be maintained by constantly reflecting on one's own position within the system. However, the team facilitates the development of a systemic perspective as each member will contribute different emphases and viewpoints, which guards against the danger of the solo therapist's accepting the family's view of reality and so losing his or her curiosity.

The responsibility of therapists is to provide a context in which a therapeutic conversation can be facilitated. They will want to make the room comfortable but will not tell the family members where they should sit. They will provide the means to enlist children in the conversation by making physical materials available and asking questions that are appropriate to the developmental stage of the child. Therapists are interested in how the environment is used by the family, as they are involved in every bit of analogic communication, and use the information to hypothesize about the problem-organizing system.

Sessions typically take place about every four weeks. This allows new ideas introduced within the session to perturb the family's belief system so that new possibilities in the way in which the family relates can begin to emerge. Time must

pass for this process to occur and become something the family owns, rather than merely a response to what the therapist told them. At the beginning of therapy, however, it may be important to see the family at shorter intervals to engage with the family, but later the interval between sessions will be longer. If a family member called to say that an earlier appointment was required, we would be interested in the information that this request represented. Is the person someone who might experience losses if changes occurred?

THE ROLE OF THE THERAPIST

The effect on the role of the therapist of a co-evolutionary epistemology is that, on the one hand, we try to conduct the session in a way that controls the flow of information, and, on the other hand, we remind ourselves that the therapist in the room becomes part of the therapist-and-family system and that the outcome of that interaction cannot be perfectly controlled.

Systemic therapists are very active in attempts to maintain the guidelines for a session, as described in "Hypothesizing—Circularity—Neutrality" (Selvini Palazzoli et al., 1980b). A systemic therapist is directive to the extent that he or she asks family members questions. However, the tone of the interview is that of the therapist being a naïve inquirer needing information from family members in order to come to some understanding of the family's organizational predicament.

The therapist does not alter this role of inquirer throughout the therapy. He or she will, for example, begin a session by inquiring as to what problem the family has that day or what they expect from the session. Influenced by the premise that the system of family and therapist is different each time they meet, the therapist does not assume that the preoccupations of session 1 will also be the family's preoccupation in session 2, and so on throughout the therapy. This stance is also in keeping with the therapist's wish to act unpredictably by supporting the goal of acting in a way that prevents the family from expecting predictable patterns of interaction. The therapist continues to challenge the family with new information.

Being directive as a systemic therapist is, therefore, not aimed at changing family members' behavior in the here-and-now or even in the immediate future. Rather, the therapist asks questions in order to introduce differences into the family's belief system that may, in turn, affect the family's behavior.

The way the therapist acts offers the family members opportunities to develop a different perspective on family relationships and to experience some other connectedness as they give the therapist information. But any changes in the family's behavior are, in the therapist's view, the result of how family members choose to act or interact in response to new information. Thus, the responsibility for change is left with the family.

At times, when the therapist has to assume responsibility for changing the way family relationships are organized (e.g., when a child is removed from home in the interests of health or safety or when a mad or bad parent has to be forcibly separated from the family to protect all in the system from physical harm), then the therapist is responsible for change as a social controller and not as a systemic therapist. Many aspects of the limits of the therapist's responsibility depend on the context in which the therapist is working. Thus, when preventing suicide or protecting children, the therapist is clear about his or her responsibility as an agent of social control.

Tomm (1984) also suggests that therapists using the Milan approach assume greater responsibility than those using other family-therapy approaches because such therapists accept that the reality they present to the family is their own construction rather than something that belongs to the external world.

The aim of the interview is to use feedback and introduce new information. New information usually emerges as the therapist tracks the family's beliefs as shown in language introduced by family members as they answer the therapist's (circular) questions. In order to facilitate the circular interviewing process, the therapist aims to be active in creating feedback loops with the family members. Individuals in the family talk mainly to the therapist, with the effect that family members listen rather than talk to each other.

The use of the family's ideas and language, which represent the family's epistemology, is a powerful way of joining with the family. The relationship between the therapist and family members is secured as the therapist shows to the family members, through the use of their feedback to inform the therapist's questions, that he or she is trying to understand the way the family sees itself. The therapist also asks questions that challenge the family but are congruent enough with family beliefs to be of interest to the family.

For example, if a brother introduces the idea of a catastrophe as he answers the therapist's question, the therapist will find out what catastrophes other family members perceive. The therapist thus remains connected to the family and, at the same time, enables the family members to be connected in different ways with one another as well as creating new information in the system. It seems that this often is irresistibly fascinating to the family members, who are also making new disclosures to one another.

Therapists tend to use self-disclosure as they reflect on the family's information and try to introduce differences to the family's perceptions by sharing how they think their own experiences can fit with the family's experience to create a new view of reality. As systemic therapists, we listen to the family and try to introduce differences to the family's perceptions by connecting family members' experiences to other beliefs and experiences within the family.

A therapist who begins to feel less in charge at some point in therapy may disclose a view as to how he or she thinks the family sees him or her as a therapist. For example, we have asked family members to comment on how they think we have been doing as therapists. When inviting family members to disclose a personal opinion, we try to connect the family's request for personal information to the wider context of its relationship to therapy. For example, a mother might ask the therapist, "Do you have any teenage children yourself?"—to which the therapist might reply, "Would you have more confidence in me as a therapist if you knew I, too, had teenage children?" or, "Are there some things you would particularly like me to understand about teenage children?"

During the interview, the therapist needs to work at two levels at the same time in order to translate content into process. Thus, while creating feedback by using the answer to one question to influence the content and structure of the next question, the therapist must also create a context for the family in which the interview releases new information hitherto not shared by family members. The ability to understand the way in which the family expresses process through content is an important skill to be developed, as is the capacity to imagine connections between apparently disparate events and beliefs as they are described by the family members, and thus use feedback to facilitate the process of the cocreation of a new reality. Crucial to this process is the therapist's ability to monitor his or her own position in the system. Appreciating the relationship between neutrality and the capacity to continue to facilitate the flow of information is a necessary skill.

As a therapy-team member, the therapist in the room also needs to be able to see his or her own perceptions and points of view about the family system as only one set of perceptions that contribute to a larger, evolving reality.

TECHNIQUES OF MARITAL–FAMILY THERAPY

We have maintained and developed the structure for therapeutic work that was outlined in *Guidelines to Conducting Therapy* (Selvini Palazzoli et al., 1980b). The therapist is responsible for creating the context in which a therapeutic conversation can proceed. He or she joins with the family or couple to form the therapeutic system about which the therapist maintains a curiosity that allows him or her to form hypotheses and ask questions from which feedback is elicited from a stance of neutrality. In this way, connections between the problem and the relationships and beliefs that are affected by the problem are explored without any element of blame for the family's problems.

The structure of the sessions broadly follows that outlined in the original paper (Selvini Palazzoli et al., 1980b). There is a presession discussion during which, with the information available, some working hypotheses are constructed. These hypotheses are intended to guide the therapist in questioning so that the therapist can begin to understand the connec-

tions among behaviors, beliefs, and the relationships organized around the problem. There follows the interview with the family, which may be interrupted at any point for team discussion. The intervention is no longer delivered in a rigid formula at the end of the session. Rather, the whole interview is seen as offering possibilities for interventions (see below). However, the end-of-session discussion is seen as important in reflecting on the feedback within the therapist–family–team system. The therapist, with or without the team, takes charge of the therapeutic conversation—he or she is the "participant manager and participant observer" (Anderson & Goolishian, 1987, p. 3)—by defining a context in which new meanings about beliefs and behaviors can evolve.

The joining process is clearly a vital function of the participant-manager of the therapeutic conversation. It is important that hypotheses are used to give direction to the questioning of the therapist, but as these questions elicit feedback from the family, the therapist should be monitoring this in relation to his or her own ideas. There is a real danger of becoming married to the hypothesis so that feedback from the family is ignored. We believe families feel joined in the therapy process when questions begin to connect the content to important beliefs and relationships that are affected by the problem. We also emphasize the importance of using the family's language not just as a joining technique, but also because it is through language that the family creates its own reality.

Circular questioning is seen as one of the fundamental techniques of systemic therapy, although this was not the phrase used in the original paper. These are questions that are constantly making connections among actions, beliefs, and relationships of individuals within the system. As such, they can have an impact on family members in that they allow them to become more aware of their own systemic process. A family entering therapy often comes in with the premise that the problem is in one person or possibly within a dyadic relationship. Questioning can make explicit the contradictions in the belief systems of each person that have organized the relationships around the problem. Apart from questions about behavior, beliefs, and relationships, questions can also introduce the element of time, which is often experienced as being frozen when a family has a problem. By being asked hypothetical questions about the future, the family can start to consider alternative possibilities that can affect present relationships. Questions that introduce new possibilities into the system have been called reflexive questions (Tomm, 1987) because they facilitate a process of reflection within family members that perturbs the system. It is important that questions stay connected to the feedback that the family is giving if such questions are not to be summarily dismissed as irrelevant by the family.

The intervention is not, therefore, confined to the end of the interview, but occurs throughout the session. The final message is a punctuation of the therapeutic conversation in which the team members share their ideas with the family. Having used working hypotheses throughout the session, the team will talk around the issues raised within the session. Gradually, each individual's contribution, which often starts as a linear statement, will connect to others so that a systemic formulation emerges, which is the basis for the final intervention. The intervention aims to describe the system through the material that has emerged within the session so that alternative realities that may have been introduced through interventive questioning are highlighted. Symptomatic behavior is positively connoted, as is the behavior of all family members in terms of preserving relationships within the family. The conflicting belief systems that have led to the badness of fit are framed in terms of a dilemma that the family members are facing. It is often important to introduce the element of time into the intervention as this allows the family to recognize that alternative actions will be possible. We also address the family's relationship to therapy as part of the system that may have become organized around the problem.

Part of the intervention may include a task the family members are requested to try out in the form of an experiment to help us understand the family better. How the family responds to such a request is seen as information that helps us to understand where the action–belief misfits are occurring. We would suggest a task where words may have become too predictable and, therefore, are failing to introduce new information into the system. If certain behaviors are prohibited because of a belief within the family, a task

might be suggested that would incorporate that behavior but in a different context. Sometimes a family may be giving two or even more contradictory messages as if they were one. The task used here is often a variant of the "odd days and even days" prescription (Selvini Palazzoli et al., 1978a), in which the contradictory injunctions are separated out so that alternative behaviors become a possibility. In some situations, differences are acknowledged and the task can be to spend time looking at common themes. It is not the specific behavior that is seen as bringing about change, but rather the family's experiencing alternative connections between beliefs and actions, such that "new" ways of relating can emerge. Tasks, as with other aspects of an intervention, should always address the relationship to therapy.

We do not find the concept of resistance a helpful one in that it implies that there is some quality that resides within the family that opposes any change that therapy might bring about. When therapists talk about a "resistant family," they are referring to the family–therapist relationship in which there is a lack of fit between the action and beliefs of the therapist and those of the family. Having taken this position, we can then ask (1) whether we are asking the questions that can introduce new information into the system, that is, what other areas we should be curious about; and (2) whether we need to develop a hypothesis that considers how our relationship with the family affects the wider network of significant relationships.

The therapist must try to maintain a balance between following feedback, thereby staying connected to the family, and challenging the family with questions that may perturb the system. A trainee learning this approach may be so preoccupied with asking circular questions that he or she fails to follow the feedback from the family. Probably the most common error for an interviewer is continuing to ask questions that no longer make a difference to the system, often questions on a content level that are not linked to a higher-order process. Questioning should be addressing tension within the family's belief system and so there should be an element of challenge. Questions about content need to connect to the higher-order process and answers to process questions should then become content for a higher-order process so that there is a constant swinging to and fro between content and process.

Another difficulty arises when the therapist loses the ability to be curious about the family. The therapist has accepted a view of how this family should be that may be either the family's view or, more seriously, the therapist's own view. If it is the former, the therapist will no longer be intrigued by how this family tells its story in this manner. If the latter, he or she may want to impose his or her understanding of how the family should act on the family members. There are times when this may be necessary, as, when the therapist is aware that a child is being abused. It is important that the therapist recognize that he or she has moved from a domain where the family is autonomous into the domain of constraint in which he or she must act as a social controller rather than as a therapist.

The point at which therapy should be terminated when using this approach is not always clear as it may be with some other approaches. This is so because the therapist is not looking for some predetermined behavioral change. Within the family–therapist system, as it develops over time, both family and therapist will be making new connections between beliefs and actions. This may lead to the symptomatic behavior's changing or, possibly more commonly, to the family's perception of the behavior as changing so that it is no longer regarded as a problem. In this case, the purpose for which this system came together is no longer present and the family and therapist arrive at a mutual decision that there is nothing further to talk about at this time. The therapist may offer a review session after a longer interval that is, therefore, a different punctuation for this system and underlines our belief that the family has the capacity for change within itself.

There are situations that arise from the belief systems of therapist, family, and referring agency that lead to the therapy's terminating other than by mutual agreement. The family may find that the therapist has not become sufficiently connected to its belief system and may choose to leave therapy. We would respect the family's decision that at this time we were unable to introduce difference into their ecology of beliefs and actions in a way that was helpful to them. After all, there are other ways to resolve

the stuckness that the family is experiencing other than that offered by conversations with us, for example, by rehousing or using other helping services.

The therapist also has a belief system about therapy's coming to an end that includes considerations about time available, ethical issues in relation to outcome, and the importance of not holding onto a family and thus preventing it from developing a belief that it can develop its own solutions. We are constantly aware of the position we hold within this system in maintaining the family's belief system. This may result in the therapist's ending therapy although the family may say it still has problems. Boscolo and Cecchin (Boscolo et al., 1987) tell the family that they are terminating therapy because although there may still be problems, they no longer are psychiatric problems. A new meaning is thus attached to problems that does not include the presence of a therapist.

When a family has had to come to therapy, it may be the beliefs of the referring agency as to whether or not there has been an improvement that will be important in the ending of therapy. If it seems that improvement has taken place, then therapy within this context may stop, although the family may wish to continue with a new context of its own. On the other hand, if the agency has seen no improvement in behavior, then help may be sought elsewhere.

In our approach, we are constantly aiming to provide a context in which new meaning systems can emerge. The family that presents with a problem that has organized relationships, actions, and beliefs, through conversations with the therapist, will begin to make new connections between the beliefs so that the problem can be redefined. This may mean that the problem behavior will stop or, more frequently, that it no longer will be seen as problematic.

MECHANISMS OF CHANGE

As one of many approaches to family therapy, the Milan approach shares with others some common characteristics, such as respect and empathy for the clients, acknowledgment of the need to engage the family in therapy, an appreciation of the interconnectedness of family behavior, an attempt to offer alternative models of thinking or behaving, and recognition of the importance of providing a suitable context for therapy. But this approach is also characterized by some features that are not common to every family therapist. They include the emphasis placed on the referring context as part of the problem, an appreciation of the repetitiveness and interconnectedness of family behavior, the questioning technique based on a systemic hypothesis, the neutrality of the therapist, the observation of verbal and analogic levels of communication, the attempt to follow closely the feedback loops between the therapist and the family, and the inclusion of the therapist's view as a part of the system that may maintain the problem. In addition, the theoretical underpinning of this approach has some distinctive features.

We are interested in the way family members attribute meaning to various life events. The cumulative effect of many meanings attributed to many events creates a hierarchical meaning system that defines our view of reality, identifies problem areas, and designates which problem-solving behaviors are available to us. This world view is a pattern of connections between the events and the meanings attached to them that has been established in a way that is most adaptive and helpful to the individual at the time the pattern was being established, but is experienced in the present as not being able to resolve some problem.

As a pattern of connection becomes helpful, certain experiences or meanings are rejected because they do not fit the most helpful pattern. But while some experiences are rejected, they do not disappear, but remain as shadows, usually retreating from consciousness, that further validate the connections that are becoming established. Thus, while rebellious behavior may be rejected in an individual meaning system, the concept remains to define the concept of loyal behavior within the same meaning system.

In general, the aim of therapy is to interview the family in such a way that allows individuals to make new connections between events and meanings and thereby to create a new meaning system from which alternative behaviors may emerge. Specifically, the questioning process achieves this by loosening some of the present connections and suggesting new connections for the family members to consider.

Therapy does not aim to provide a cure, but rather is seen as a stage in an evolutionary process in which the family is struggling to adapt to its environment. It is a special stage, however, in the sense that a therapist infiltrates the family ranks and tries to introduce new ways of thinking to enable the family to move on without the therapist's help.

While we are interested in meaning, the mechanisms of change are not based on an insight model. The individual does not change as a result of making conscious decisions following a cognitive reworking of his or her experience; rather, in the context of a systemic-family-therapy interview, the individual finds himself or herself in the midst of a new pattern of connections that is created as other family members share their views about relationships. All family members participate in a process in which a new pattern is being created around the individual. The individual's cognitive efforts only contribute one small slice of the new systemic pie, and by definition, understanding of the pattern is beyond the realm of any individual consciousness. Our experience with families whose members have reported a change in the symptomatic behavior is that they do not make connections between the changes and any understanding or insight about their behavior. They talk as though the changes have occurred incidentally and without any obvious cause.

The family's interpretation of its own history is a part of the complicated matrix that makes up its hierarchical meaning system, and for this reason the place of history in the family's meaning system is important for the therapist to understand. Accounts of history are pursued as information about the way the family construes reality rather than as a therapeutic exercise in itself. We believe that the past is contained in the present and that, like Selvini (Selvini Palazzoli, 1986), if we make our interventions in the more complex system of the present, we have more powerful therapeutic results.

Interpretations are not used in the model. The interview consists of questions, some of which are more exploratory and some more focused, and very rarely would we offer a direct comment of our own. Some people have described our interventions as similar to interpretations, but the aim of an intervention is not to inform or direct people to a particular thought, but to change the context by reorganizing information to create a different perspective on relationships. As a result of making new connections, the family members may change their ways of relating to one another. However, that is not the aim of the therapy, but is seen as one of many possible solutions the family may find for the problem.

The therapist's personality is a crucial element in the therapist–family system, but only in so far as it enables the therapist to relate attentively to the family while making multileveled connections in his or her own mind at the same time. Inevitably, the personality of the therapist affects the family, but in this model, it is not promoted within the session as a means of enhancing the therapy. In order to ensure that the family members direct their attention to their own participation in the circular questioning process, the therapist adopts a neutral stance. The Milan approach, like any kind of psychological therapy, requires therapists to be sensitive to their own and others' reactions to what goes on around them. However, these reactions are used by the therapist to decide what question to ask next in order to make a connection that will make a difference. The therapist is continuously observing the space between himself or herself and the family and making judgments about where to move in that space. When conducting a systemic interview, any feelings that inevitably arise in the therapist, such as, "That woman makes me feel aggressive," should be used as clues to the beliefs about "aggressiveness" in the family and the way in which such beliefs affect behavior among all the relationships. The therapist would then include ideas about the family's beliefs about aggressiveness in the next stage of the hypothesis.[7]

As we look at our systemic colleagues, it seems to us that there are some important features of the Milan approach that attract some therapists and not others. The "feeling" of conducting a Milan-style interview is one of excitement about being connected to a larger-than-oneself process

from a slight distance that protects one from being engulfed, but a process nevertheless in which one is a cocreator of reality. We would suggest that somewhere within the psyche of such therapists, these experiences strike a resonant chord. Another feature, also mentioned by Hoffman (1986), is the "shedding of power," and we have found that this approach interests people who prefer to approach conflict from a complementary rather than a symmetrical position.

The efforts of the therapist are directed toward systemic change in the family. That is, while the Milan therapist respects the symptoms of the individual and assumes that this is the ticket that will allow access into the family meaning system, he or she also attempts to formulate this behavior as a feature of the patterns of belief and behavior that affect everyone in the family—the whole system. The therapist, through the interview, follows the lead presented by the symptom and makes new connections that connect the symptom to other parts of the family system. For example, after inquiring about a child's stealing, the therapist might then ask whether other members of the family feel they are not getting as much as they deserve.

The intervention of the therapist is aimed at the level of the family meaning system that then affects behavior. As the beliefs that are connected to the symptom, such as stealing, become loosened or placed in a new context, the stealing no longer will be necessary to provide the fit with the corresponding belief. Although it is possible to conceptualize that change to beliefs can occur at the behavioral level, we find that working primarily at the level of beliefs gives the therapist a broader view and greater therapeutic potential.

The coevolutionary model suggests that therapy works when there is a good fit between family and therapists. A good fit takes place when the family can allow the therapist to explore its meaning system and the therapist is able to use feedback in a way that both respects and challenges the family.

Rather than identify characteristics of the family or the therapist that might be counterindicative of therapy, then, it is more consistent, within this model, to assume problems of fit. For example, a therapeutic failure might be de-

---

[7] *Editors' Note.* While terms such as "countertransference" are rarely found in the literature of Milan systemic therapists, this is from the perspective of the psychodynamics of the therapy process. From this construction of reality, the therapist would be seen as containing the split-off and projected aggressiveness that exists within the family.

scribed in this way, "This therapist working within the constraint of this agency at this time was not able to respond to the feedback from the family in such a way that therapy could develop." We assume that both therapist and family are constrained by the values and beliefs of other systems to which they are connected, and an examination of those constraints is the only means of understanding the way therapist and family fit together to create a therapeutic context.

Making judgments about the success or failure of therapy raises an interesting issue for the Milan approach. It highlights the fact that the work of the Milan therapist who may be working from a neutral posture is only one approach to family work among a vast number of alternatives. Each of these alternatives, such as structural family therapy, behavior modification, or social casework, can be seen as an integrated system of theories and practice, each of which will establish its own criteria for judging successful treatment based on its theories about treatment and outcome. At the same time, each of these alternatives is also a part of a much larger system that is organized to address the recognition and acceptance of therapy—all kinds of therapy—by society. The type of evaluation that is useful feedback for this larger system (e.g., criterion-based measures of symptomatic behavior) may not be such helpful feedback to subsystems organized to offer family consultations with a neutral position with regard to whether or in what direction families change.

This means that evaluation, like other aspects of work in this model, is clearly context dependent. In the context of providing information for a government agency, the Milan therapist, like any other, would want to know what percentage of family-therapy cases showed diminished symptomatic behavior. Also, if the therapist were in a context of outcome research in which a therapist's opinion was used as a criterion for successful outcome, an opinion could be given, but that is different from the *doing* of therapy in which the therapist does not form such an opinion. But in the context of creating feedback to inform the Milan therapist about the success or failure of his or her own work, the therapist would use different criteria. For example, the therapist would be interested in whether or not

the family members viewed themselves as having a problem.

The larger system is organized to set external standards by which therapy is judged; Milan therapists who do not have the legal responsibilities of the larger system are organized to respond to the family's own definition of whether it has a problem.

Evaluations that have been done, such as the follow-up study by Prata (see Speed, 1985), have been based on the family's self-report to such questions as: "Do you still have the problem you came to us about? Do you have any other problems? Have you sought help from any other sources?" Bennun (1986) completed the first systematic comparison of families treated with a problem-solving approach and families treated with the Milan approach using a self-report questionnaire and found that both groups showed significant symptom reduction but that families treated with the Milan approach showed a wider systemic perspective about problem behavior in the family.

SPECIAL ISSUES IN MARITAL THERAPY

There are some specific issues that distinguish work with couples from work with a larger family group. We have already discussed the concept of "fit" between members of a family group and how problems arise when the action–belief schema of one person no longer fits with the schemata of other members. When working with couples, the same concept of fit applies, but becomes the focus of the work more overtly than it does with families. Members of families can be likened to a pile of golf balls. Each ball has a multifaceted surface, so that the area that one ball shares with another is relatively small. However, the large number of facets creates the potential for contacts with many balls. In contrast, a couple is like two toy building blocks that share a large, flat surface when they are fitted together—a fit that can become solid and stable.

For us, the most obvious feature of the couple's presentation to the therapist is the fit or the complementarity between the two individuals. The therapist becomes part of a coevolving system with the couple the better to understand aspects of this fit within the couple's relationship, and the meaning the symmetrical, complementary, or parallel behavior has for this relationship. The therapist establishes a process whereby the partners describe what they do and how each is affected by the other person's behavior, thus helping each to monitor feedback from the other. The therapist is interested in explanations for behaviors and how these might connect to beliefs that may have provided a good-enough fit within the family of origin, but are less helpful within the marital dyad. The therapist's curiosity about the meaning of the fit between the partners will include challenging them to reflect and comment on possible losses and gains in the relationship in giving up certain beliefs and behaviors: What would be the implications of change for the individuals and the relationship?

The therapist seeks to create a therapeutic context that enables the partners to become observers of their own relationship; in other words, to look at the construction created by the two building blocks and not at the separate blocks. He or she may use metaphors to facilitate them in this process. One such example we have found useful for a couple in an acute crisis is to liken the relationship to a situation in which one of the children of the couple is in an intensive-care unit. All resources are pooled to aid recovery regardless of the effect it will have on the relationship between them. When a couple has been chronically estranged, the metaphor is more that of the patient on a life-support machine where effort is focused on preventing further deterioration and avoiding any increase in stress. The effect of a "no change" prescription is to create a context for the couple in which alternative fits between the partners can be explored.

In attempting to understand the meaning of the fit for a couple, there are other characteristics of a two-person system that present challenges to the therapist:

1. *A two-person system initially appears to generate less information* in terms of differences that emerge from the questioning of the therapist as there are fewer people present to comment on relationships among other members of the family. With a couple, the therapist must map the wider system of which the couple is a part.[8] This can be done by (a) introducing the dimension of time, by asking questions to find out when the relationship was not as it is now, and more important, by asking questions about the future that can allow the couple to speculate on the possibility of alternative solutions to the dilemmas in the relationship; and (b) asking questions that bring the wider system into the interview, for example, to each partner: "What would you like your children to get from the other parent?" "How would your in-laws react if your wife/husband were to start taking your position more often?" "What would your parents/in-laws believe about how you should act in this situation?"

2. *Process is more easily identified but more difficult to deal with effectively.* There is a greater danger of the therapist's being drawn into an alliance with one partner. Each member of a couple in a symmetrical relationship may want to enlist the therapist as his or her supporter, because, in contrast to a family group, no one else is available; in a complementary relationship, the therapist may become preoccupied with content, and identify one partner as a victim. The therapist must always be aware of being a participant in the process of the co-evolving system but use the position as observer of the process to remain curious about what his or her part in the process means in the fit between the couple. The therapist might use such questions as the following:

"How would your relationship change if I were seen to favor one point of view?"
"What would your husband have to do for me to favor his side of the story?"
"How do you think your wife expects me to respond to what she has just said?"

It is of even greater importance than with families to share the questioning equally between the partners, so that each has an opportunity to

---

[8] *Editors' Note.* The wider system must be mapped from within *this* clinical perspective. It is not universally the case, however, that this wider mapping occur in order for effective therapy to occur (cf. Holtzworth-Munroe & Jacobson, Chapter 4; Segal, Chapter 6).

talk on a certain theme. It is essential that the therapist monitor his or her own response to the couple so that he or she can continue to draw forth alternative possibilities rather than believing either partner's view of the reality. If the therapist is addressing more to one partner, then he or she needs to consider what questions would lead to becoming as interested in the other partner's story.

The therapist should use content to ask questions about process, and as process emerges, the therapist pulls out dilemmas or difficult stalemates that are presented to the couple during the session. How the couple responds to these dilemmas provides content for further exploration of process.

For instance, in a session in which a wife has told the therapist how she has had periodic bouts of depression that coincide with the time of year when she was abused as a child and lead to estrangement from her husband, the therapist is asking the couple what each partner might lose if the wife were to "give up" her depressions.

WIFE: He'd lose his role.
THERAPIST: What does the role mean to him?
HUSBAND: It's been a habit and a duty for me. I looked after my mother when I was a boy and she developed cancer. I loved her but as I got older, it got to feel like a duty.
THERAPIST: It sounds as if both of you chose people who were potentially strong but had a vulnerable bit similar to your own vulnerable bit. At this point in the relationship, can you risk just having a stronger person to relate to, and allowing one another to be vulnerable without seeing vulnerability as a weakness or handicap?

As when working with families, systemic therapists would never impose their goals for change in a relationship. Instead, they will seek to understand the goals each partner may have within the relationship and will be hypothesizing about how such goals are linked to beliefs each partner has about intimate personal relationships. The therapists will want to make such beliefs and premises explicit so that they can ask questions about how these beliefs contribute to the stuckness within the relationship.

Therapists in these cases may choose to develop such premises once they have been made explicit. Within a session, they may ask each partner to talk for several minutes on how he or she would view the relationship if the context established by this premise were to change. In the couple described above, the therapist spent time asking the couple what the losses would be to each of them and to their relationship if the wife were to give up her episodes of depression.

Therapists working with couples, therefore, appear to be more directive in that they will want to understand the meanings of the symmetrical, complementary, or parallel behaviors in relation to the fit between the couple. The role of the participant-observer is of crucial importance in the coevolving therapist–couple system. As a result of the recursive process between couple and therapist, a fit is established that can allow the partners to become more objective about their own relationship and, therefore, will open up new possibilities of actions and beliefs. One final comment is on the issue of gender, which is crucial for many therapists working in this field. We would see this as one aspect of the different beliefs and experiences that each partner brings to the relationship that organizes the fit between them.

TREATMENT APPLICABILITY

The Milan approach was originally developed as a method of treating families with anorectic and psychotic patients. MacKinnon and colleagues, (MacKinnon, Parry, & Black, 1984) analyzed the presenting problems of the 32 cases the Milan group describes in the literature and found that 97 percent presented either severe psychosomatic or psychotic symptoms. MacKinnon suggested that the Milan approach is ideally suited to families whose beliefs maintain the unit as a tightly organized system that is often closed to information from the outside world. While we would agree with MacKinnon, we have also seen that the impact of systemic thinking and the Milan approach is such that we see therapists in many different settings using these ideas with many different client groups (see Campbell & Draper, 1985).

We would apply our approach to any family in which the attempted solution to the problem has, over time, become entwined with the family's meaning system, so that alternative solutions are constrained by beliefs and relationships at one remove from the problem behavior. Conversely, this approach would not be necessary for cases in which the feedback from the problem has not created a second-order meaning system. For example, we assume that some feedback will create conflict about people's beliefs and relationships. When this happens, an individual becomes preoccupied with the context of the message and the relationship to the giver of the message, and the *content* of the message is lost. The result of this loss is that the conflict is incorporated into the family's meaning system. But with some problems, such as a child's sleeping problem, the attempts to solve the problem may *not* have created a confusion between the attempted solution and the relationship between the people involved in the solution, and, therefore, ideas and suggestions from a therapist, which are given directly, can be accepted because they are not seen as a threat to any relationships or beliefs.[9]

Time is another important factor in considering the applications of this treatment approach, because behavior must create sufficient feedback within the meaning system to be noticed and compared and finally registered as a "problem." Behavior that is short-lived and not fully established may also change as a result of more directive or suggestive methods of treatment.

We see ourselves as part of a large system consisting of many professionals with many types of interventions. Likewise, a family can be seen as a system consisting of many needs and desires. We try to use our systemic thinking to create a map of the fit between the needs of the family and the possible interventions in the professional network. We are clear that *we* can offer family therapy that aims to create a context

in which family members use new information to solve their own problems, and so we would refer a family for another type of treatment when the expectations of the family or the professional system are too discrepant from what we can offer—for example, to specialist services such as for hospital-based work, legal problems, child abuse, or suicidal behavior in which there are strong expectations for individuals to be protected, assessed, legally controlled, or treated with drugs.

We always consider the fit between the family and the wider context. If the family members had a fixed belief that they wanted one type of treatment, such as hypnosis, and felt our way of working was too discrepant to fit their expectations of what would be helpful, then we would support their view that they should pursue an alternative treatment. Situations such as this often arise when we are feeling stuck with a family. We often discover that the family's beliefs about family therapy or about a "talking cure" are of a lower order in the hierarchy than beliefs about medication (see Cronen & Pearce, 1985). In such a case, we might say, "At this time, we recommend that the family pursue a treatment based on medication," or, "For the time being, we suggest chemotherapy together with family therapy."

When a family presents for therapy but makes it clear to us that the members do not want to participate, then we assume that the problem exists within the relationship between the family and the referring person or the wider network (see Selvini Palazzoli et al., 1980a). In such cases, it is appropriate to recommend no treatment to the family. If a problem within the network can be identified, it may be more appropriate to offer a consultation to the referrers in order to clarify how the referral is experienced by the family and the way the referral may preserve beliefs and relationships within the network.

There are certain ethical issues that arise for people struggling to learn and practice the Milan approach. The most common ethical objections that have been presented to us are that (1) you cannot be a neutral therapist if you have legal responsibility; (2) if you care for your clients, you cannot honestly be a neutral therapist; and (3) the use of paradox is manipulative. We be-

---

[9] *Editors' Note.* We believe this to be an extraordinary assertion, or at least a unique one, in the writing on the Milan approach. In other words, if the family has not fundamentally become organized around a symptom (presumably due to its recency or its being peripheral to the family's experience?), then *direct* intervention is preferred.

lieve that these are not ethical conflicts but instead reflect the failure of the therapist to appreciate systemic thinking and to formulate a clear definition of context. For example, to apply systemic thinking to the first statement would mean that a doctor or social worker can carry *both* legal *and* "therapeutic" responsibility simultaneously. A social worker may be working therapeutically and then discover that some abuse has occurred. At that moment, the context immediately changes to one of legal responsibility and the social worker takes the necessary action within that context (Boscolo et al., 1987). Neutrality should not be a stance of aloof detachment, but one of respectful curiosity by which the therapist communicates concern for the problems he or she is drawing forth from the family.

Similarly, with regard to the third statement, using a positive connotation or prescribing no change may seem unreal or manipulative when one is considering the family's desire to be rid of the problem, but since these problems are also part of a larger context in which the behavior has evolved within a coherent meaning system, it can be appropriate and "systemic" to connect the problem behavior to the meaning it has for the whole system. For example, with families we often say, "Johnny may be doing the wrong things for the right reasons."

CASE ILLUSTRATION

We have chosen to describe a case with an unusual presenting problem that nonetheless presents a range of conceptualizations and techniques. It is not an everyday sort of case, but the reader should find that it highlights many of the important features of our work.

We were asked to see a 56-year-old barrister and his wife because he had recently been disbarred for bringing the legal profession into disrepute through persistently running up bills that he could not pay. (In Great Britain, a barrister is a lawyer who specializes in courtroom work; in this case, in criminal proceedings.) Mr. B. had accumulated large debts, had serious marital problems, and had begun drinking heavily, all of which culminated in a suicide attempt a few days before his hearing. At the hearing, the evidence was heard and Mr. B. was disbarred. He was also told that he could apply for reinstatement at some time in the future provided he received treatment and could produce medical evidence that would support his claim for reinstatement.

Mr. B. had been examined by a psychiatrist, Dr. P., who concluded that he was a man with depressive symptoms and a deep-rooted personality disorder based on his relationship with an authoritarian father figure. Although various types of treatment were considered, it was felt that he was not motivated for intensive psychotherapy, and since Mr. and Mrs. B. had two accomplished and sympathetic daughters (aged 25 and 21), that perhaps marital or family treatment would be most helpful, and they were referred to us.

The referral letter was accompanied by a thorough family history. Mr. B. was the eldest of three siblings. His sister, 49, an archeologist, was divorced and had had a number of psychiatric-hospital admissions throughout her life. His brother, 44, a salesman, was reported to have problems with alcohol and with drifting from job to job. At the head of the family were a stern, aloof, self-made, successful businessman who gave little support to Mr. B. and a vague, withdrawn mother who believed in ghosts and psychic powers. Mrs. B. was born in Australia, but when both of her parents died when she was 8 years old, she was separated from her sister and sent to live with an unmarried aunt in England. Little was known about her background and it seemed she had adopted Mr. B.'s powerful, problematic family. He was successful as a barrister and claimed that he lived for his work and so neglected his personal life. Finally, after a series of financial problems, his colleagues in the law chambers came to his rescue and monitored his affairs by holding his earnings and paying him a weekly salary.

As we prepared for the first interview, we were particularly interested in the process by which the referral was made and that by which the problem was defined. Mr. B. had been sent by the tribunal, and his return to the bar was dependent on his being able to obtain a good report from us. Since the context for getting a report was also the context for therapy, this created confusion among different levels of meaning. If, for example, Mr. B. found that therapy was helpful, did this mean he was creating the experience that would help him get a good report, or that he was genuinely changing his views of his behavior, or both? The second issue was that there were several ideas about what problem needed to be tackled in therapy. The tribunal wanted him to manage his financial affairs and deferred to the psychiatrist, who said Mr. B. had a psychological defect but would not be motivated for individual psychotherapy, and since many problems seemed connected to his marital relationship, marital and family therapy were indicated. Since problems were being defined by these higher authorities, it was difficult to ascertain what Mr. and Mrs. B. felt their problems were and what they wanted to do about them.

The aim of our first session was to clarify the position of therapy in these different contexts. We felt we needed to understand the different meanings that our behavior as therapists would have and how our behavior might be seen as an opportunity for some parts of the system to change and for others to continue as they were. We conducted the therapy in our usual manner, with one of us (D.C.) interviewing the family and the other (R.D.) working behind a one-way screen. There were several breaks for discussion, and for most sessions an intervention was prepared and given to the family at the end of the session. Only Mr. and Mrs. B. came to the first session. Mr. B. looked the part of a down-on-his-luck barrister: overweight; wearing a slightly crumpled, dark, three-piece suit; and with a rather sad, downtrodden manner. Mrs. B. was careful and composed and seemed like a woman who had put a cheerful face on much adversity. After discussing the results of the tribunal and some of the family background, the therapist tried to clarify how the problem was seen by various members of the system.

D.C.: What's Dr. P.'s view of your coming here?

MR. B.: He's very anxious for me to come. He's always taken the view that it's between my wife and me, and if we are more frank with each other . . .

MRS. B.: It's hard to know. He has always been the master in the house, and I've done every-thing he asked to please him. You haven't shielded us. Dr. P. studied all the reports and then he said, 95 percent of him is completely normal and 5 percent is abnormal.

MR. B.: I would have thought that was a rather good proportion [laughs].

D.C.: [to Mrs. B.] Do you agree that something in your relationship has to be looked at?

MRS. B.: I don't know, how do you shield a family?

MR. B.: That's not what I meant. . . . I've been able to talk to Dr. P. and lately to people in chambers. Since setting up chambers a few years ago, I've had a close relationship with my clerk, who is 20 years younger . . . also people whom my wife doesn't like, who are younger. I have helped them and I've told them my problems.

MRS. B.: I think you put too much trust in them.

MR. B.: I never had close friends until the last few years.

D.C.: How do you explain that?

MR. B.: I was always shy and frightened of older men. Didn't enjoy things like drinking, cards, etc., and I was anxious to get home to the home atmosphere.

D.C.: Who's most concerned about him?

MRS. B.: Me, his mother, then the children.

D.C.: Who outside the family?

MRS. B.: He puts too much trust in them. Me . . . his mother . . . then the children.

D.C.: Who outside the family?

MRS. B.: He puts too much trust in them.

We understood this exchange to mean that there was disagreement among members of the system. It seemed that Mr. B. was allied with the psychiatrist and his colleagues in chambers by having a problem, but the definition of the problem lay blame on his wife, who shifted the problem, but as she did so, she pushed her husband further toward his colleagues. At a later part of the session, the therapist explored the dilemma created by Mr. B.'s being sent for therapy.

MR. B.: The judge asked Dr. P. what the outcome was likely to be, and Dr. P. said that unless a psychological or personality defect in me could be attended to, it would happen over and over again, and with treatment it could probably be put right in one to four years, and I was disbarred. But if I can present a report from whomever is treating me, in due course I can apply for recall to the bar.

D.C.: What kind of treatment did Dr. P. think you needed?

MR. B.: He always said we should be treated together.

D.C.: What is his view of what needs to be done between you?

MRS. B.: I think it's communication, but his sister had a great deal of mental illness. His early family background is complicated.

MR. B.: I don't think that has anything to do with it.

D.C.: Do you agree with Dr. P.?

MR. B.: Dr. P. is probably a little confused. I told him what my relationship with Jackie is. Then I made the suicide attempt. Following that, everything came out. He met my wife and my elder daughter and his views changed rapidly.

D.C.: What do you think would have to happen before you could be reinstated?

MR. B.: I know what the bar wants. It wants a medical report on the lines of somebody recovering from a physical illness, to say he's better now. I personally think it's going to be virtually impossible to produce such a report in my case. But I hope somebody will be able to produce one . . . I've tried to explain what is wrong . . . my own weaknesses . . .

D.C.: Do you see the problem as primarily your own weakness or as lack of communication with your wife?

MR. B.: It's not a simple question . . . principally my weakness.

MRS. B.: You were *too* strong.

D.C.: Which do you think is the problem?

MRS. B.: There *has* been communication between us.

D.C.: If it weren't for being disbarred, would you have sought help?

MRS. B.: No, we've had a good marriage, everyone has problems.

MR. B.: I went for help. . . .

D.C.: Who most wants you to be here today?

MR. B.: Me.

D.C.: Then who?

MR. B.: If you mean who most wants me to get rid of whatever is wrong, I'd say four to five friends in chambers.

D.C.: What do they think needs to be done?

MR. B.: Difficult to speak frankly in front of my wife because it will upset things at home. Their [friends in chambers] view is that Jackie puts too much pressure on me to do things I shouldn't do. Their view is that whatever is wrong with me is wrong with us.

D.C.: Do you agree?

MR. B.: Yes. [Mrs. B shakes her head.]

D.C.: Do you not agree?

MRS. B.: No.

D.C.: [to Mrs. B] How do you explain that you disagree?

MRS. B.: I don't know . . . he has always told me things that weren't right; about his pension, his savings. . . . A lot of the problem is that you don't tell the truth.

D.C.: What did you hope would come from this meeting?

MRS. B.: To see the way clear to manage his own affairs. He has asked for no help and I hope he can manage.

MR. B.: What I hoped for was a course of treatment. I recognize I don't manage. I hoped to make a beginning and then see.

Mr. and Mrs. B. were invited to the second session. After trying to define the context of the therapy in the first session, we felt more comfortable about looking at the marital relationship they were clearly offering for exploration. We hypothesized that their marital discord projected blame onto each other and thereby protected the relationship with the families of origin and their own children. The pattern we observed was one of Mrs. B. criticizing her husband because his parents were so difficult. This enabled him to defend his parents. He replied by defending his parents, or shouting at his wife for leaving the field in a sulk. We did not give an intervention in this session, but clarified and positively connoted the bickering because of the opportunity it provided finally to get a correct picture of Mr. B.'s parents.

In order to develop hypotheses about the wider network of relationships, we invited the daughters and also the clerk from chambers, who looked after Mr. B.'s financial affairs. Although one daughter was out of the country, seeing Mr. B. in this context had a powerful effect on us. People around him seemed in awe and at the same time pitying and patronizing. The daughter who was present was bright and articulate, but the compassion she showed for her father seemed distant and businesslike, and both she and the clerk seemed to resent professional intrusion as much as her father seemed to relish it. This led us to hypothesize that Mr. B.'s problems created a network of helpers who enjoyed feeling helpful but inevitably became competitive about who had the most power to affect the goings-on in this diverse and interesting group. We gave an intervention that suggested that Mr. B. might have decided he could not manage his affairs in order to endear himself in the three worlds in which he lived (his work, his marriage, his family), and that if the people in these three worlds were to feel that someone else could be more effective in helping Mr. B., they might begin to feel that they themselves were redundant or they might look for some other cause in which to become interested.

Although we worked to understand the connections in the helping network, each of those involved shared the view that the relationship between Mr. B. and his father was the key to open the lock. We began to explore this further in the fourth session, which was attended by Mr. and Mrs. B. and their two daughters. Much of the content of the session confirmed the view that Mr. B. spent much of his life trying to win his father's love and that Jackie supported him in this effort but also seemed to resent her husband's filial loyalty. This information seemed to be given easily and was probably not new for the family. In order to create a context in which the family could make some new systemic connections, the therapist asked a number of "circular questions" that linked these themes to their daughters.

D.C.: Mrs. B., do you think your husband wants your daughters to have the same feelings for him that he had for his father?

MRS. B.: I should think not.

D.C.: How would he like their experience to be different?

MRS. B.: I don't know. . . . He would probably want them to be able to come to him for advice or support . . .

And another question later:

D.C.: [to Gillian] Do you think your father is worried that his troubles will affect you in any way?

GILLIAN: No, he can see that we're busily getting on with our own lives.

D.C.: [to Mrs. B.] Which of your daughters do you think is more upset about what's happened to your husband?

MRS. B.: They're both very concerned.

These replies suggested to the therapist that the family members may have wished to preserve the father's counselor role and to protect the daughters from too much distress. At the end of this session, we felt we had sufficient information to make a formulation that connected the presenting problem to the themes and relationships across three generations. We took 30–40 minutes to discuss our formulation and then delivered a more formal intervention to the family. We decided the therapist would read it, giving it the weight and importance of a family history.

Mr. B. grew up in a powerful family. He was loyal to his parents. He did not want to disappoint either of them. He knew that if he challenged, it would have disappointed his mother and father. His father had to remain in a one-up position. He was caring and one person was clearly seen to be the head of the family. Mr. B. took the challenging part of himself into court, where he could succeed and his father could be proud of him. . . . Mrs. B. grew up without a family and wanted to be part of a family. They met and became a very effective team in the way Mr. B. provided the failure and Mrs. B. translated that into a need. This allowed the grandparents to care for Mr. and Mrs. B. by settling the problems and the grandfather was able to remain in a one-up position. Now in his own family, Mr. B., by not being seen as the powerful head of the family, relieves Cathy and Gillian (daughters) of the burden of supporting their father in the way their father supported his own father. He has held back until he was sure the girls were through their adolescence and on their own feet. . . . We are concerned that as he becomes more competent in managing his own affairs, the daughters may feel he is being the competent head of family. Then they may get the feeling they need to support him as he supported his father.

We realized that if we had suggested that Mr. B. were himself in a dilemma, we would have perpetuated a pattern whereby other people are placed in a position to comment or pass judgment on Mr. B.'s life. But by placing ourselves in a dilemma, Mr. B. was able to step back and pass judgment on us while at the same time being aware that if we had a dilemma, we might not be able to produce a good report and that, therefore, he had a dilemma as well.

Mr. B.'s interesting reply to the intervention suggested that he felt there was nothing he could do to influence events, and that in such a context in which he was being judged, he could only call on the higher authorities to help us help him.

Following this session, Mr. B. and his legal colleagues made the decision to reapply to the bar.

We had two more sessions, which seemed like after-the-fact interviews as in view of their decision and the fact that the cases were being prepared. One was another session with Mr. and Mrs. B. and the clerk, and then a final one without the clerk, but they seemed like "lame-duck" interviews, since it was very important for Mr. B. to maintain the position that he had been "straightened out." Our view was that he believed that in order to secure the best possible report from therapy, he needed to be seen as having sorted out his problems, but he also needed to be seen as a cooperative patient who would willingly submit himself to therapy. The bind created by the referral to therapy continued to the very end.

The content of these sessions continued to focus on the marital relationship and the conflict between Mr. B.'s family and his colleagues at work. At the end of the final session, we felt that it was most appropriate to offer a statement about the therapeutic bind created by his referral and the therapist ended the session with the following message:

In most cases, we see families that recognize when they can cope on their own and when they have had enough therapy, but we see that this will never happen with the B. family because Mr. B. is in the position where other people always decide for him whether he needs support . . . such as the tribunal, his clerk, Dr. P., and his wife. But we are confused as to whether he is in this position because he has

decided to be generous to us as therapists, as he has said many times how helpful therapy has been, . . . or whether he genuinely cannot judge his own growth and development, when he is so able to assess other people; . . . or whether he feels Jackie needs reassurance that from time to time *she* will be needed to provide the cocoon and support he needs when he is not being successful. This is very hard to understand.

A few weeks after the final session, we prepared a report, which was sent to the psychiatrist and which he, in turn, sent on to the tribunal. The report included a brief summary of the therapy and the changes the B.'s claimed had taken place. We recognized his dilemma of having no way to prove he had changed unless given the opportunity, yet as therapists, we could not predict how he would behave in the future. He had said he felt more mature and competent, partly as a result of rallying many people around him to understand and support him, yet as long as he felt his competence depended on these relationships, it was difficult to know what he was capable of doing.

Several months later, the therapist received a telephone call reporting that Mr. B.'s application to the tribunal had been successful and he was able to rejoin the bar and begin working.

This case demonstrates a number of important theoretical and technical issues:

1. By paying attention to the referral process, the therapy team begins to understand something of the way in which the context of therapy could be more constraining than helpful for work with this client. The client is in therapy because someone else says this should be so. This perspective is typical and is useful in creating a context for change in this approach to therapy. The effect on the therapy team and the client of the therapy team's saying, "Wait a minute, we need clarification and explanation about the referral," is to connect the therapy team and the client as they seek to understand the meaning of the referral, and more important, this search becomes an intervention that begins to move the client to an observer position.

2. The exchange between Mr. and Mrs. B. and the therapist about trust shows how the therapist's commitment to following feedback and the therapist's naïve curiosity allow dif-

ferent and contradictory levels of belief held by the client to emerge, and by asking for clarification, the therapist challenges the client's belief system at the same time that he clarifies their mutual contract for work.

3. The therapist's questions about Jackie and reinstatement that initially seemed unconnected become, in the dialogue about the effect of these matters on relationships, a unifying theme regarding the quality of family members' experience of relationships.

4. The reader might ask what the outcome would have been if the question of reinstatement had remained the central theme of therapy at a content level. Using this approach, the view is that the therapist avoided an escalating symmetry with the client family involving the clients in loss of face. By broadening the context of the inquiry, Mr. B. was able to allow reinstatement to become less than central and to look at other themes that connected reinstatement with broader aspects of his life.

5. The spirit of inquiry and curiosity demonstrated by the therapist in his relationship with the clients enabled the client family members to look at themselves and discover different points of view, which, we believe, herald behavior change.

REFERENCES

Andersen, T. (1984). Consultation: Would you like co-evolution instead of referral? *Family Systems Medicine, 2*, 370–379.

Andersen, T. (1987). The reflecting team. Dialogue and meta-dialogue in clinical work. *Family Process, 26*, 415–428.

Anderson, H., & Goolishian, H. (1987). Systems consultation with agencies dealing with domestic violence. In L. Wynne, S. McDaniel, & T. Weber (Eds.), *Systems consultation*. New York: Guilford Press.

Anderson, H., & Goolishian, H. (1988). A view of human systems as linguistic systems: Some preliminary and evolving ideas about the implications for clinical theory. *Family Process, 27*, 371–393.

Anderson, H., Goolishian, H., & Windermand, L. (1987). Problem determined systems: Towards transformation in family therapy. *Journal of Strategic and Systemic Therapies, 5*, 1–13.

Barrows, S. (1982). Interview with Mara Selvini Palazzoli and Guliana Prata. *American Journal of Family Therapy, 10*, 60–69.

Bateson, G. (1973). *Steps to an ecology of mind*. St. Albans: Paladin.

Bateson, G. (1979). *Mind and nature: A necessary unity*. New York: E.P. Dutton.

Beer, S. (1981). *Brain of the firm* (2nd ed.). Chichester, U.K.: Wiley.

Bennun, I. (1986). Evaluating family therapy: A comparison of the Milan and problem solving approaches. *Journal of Family Therapy, 8*, 235–242.

Blount, A. (1985). Towards a "systemically" organized mental health centre. In D. Campbell & R. Draper (Eds.), *Applications of systemic family therapy: The Milan approach*. London: Grune & Stratton.

Boscolo, L. (1985). Personal communication.

Boscolo, L., & Cecchin, G. (1981). Personal communication. Montisola, Italy.

Boscolo, L., & Cecchin, G. (1982). Training in systemic therapy at the Milan Centre. In R. Whiffen & J. Byng-Hall (Eds.), *Family therapy supervision: Recent developments in practice*. London: Academic Press.

Boscolo, L., Cecchin, G., Campbell, D., & Draper, R. (1985). Twenty more questions—Selections from a discussion between the Milan associates and the editors. In D. Campbell & R. Draper (Eds.), *Applications of systemic family therapy: The Milan approach*. London: Grune & Stratton.

Boscolo, L., Cecchin, G., Hoffman, L., & Penn, P. (1987). *Milan systemic family therapy*. New York: Basic Books.

Burbatti, G., & Formenti, L. (1988). *The Milan approach to family therapy*. New York: Aronson.

Campbell, D. (1985). The consultation interview. In D. Campbell & R. Draper (Eds.), *Applications of systemic family therapy: The Milan approach*. London: Grune & Stratton.

Campbell, D., & Draper, R. (Eds) (1985). *Application of systemic family therapy: The Milan approach*. London: Grune & Stratton.

Campbell, D., Draper, R., & Huffington, C. (1988). *Teaching systemic thinking*. London: Karnac Books.

Campbell, D., Draper, R., & Huffington, C. (1989a). *A systemic approach to consultation*. London: Karnac Books.

Campbell, D., Draper, R., & Huffington, C. (1989b). *Second thoughts on the theory and practice of the Milan approach*. London: Karnac Books.

Campbell, D., Reder, P., Draper, R., & Pollard, D. (1983). *Working with the Milan method: Twenty questions*. Occasional Paper, Institute of Family Therapy, London.

Castellucci, A., Fruggeri, L., & Marzari, M. (1985). Instability and evolutionary change in a psychiatric community. In D. Campbell & R. Draper (Eds.), *Applications of systemic family therapy: The Milan approach*. London: Grune & Stratton.

Cecchin, G. (1987). Hypothesizing, circularity and neutrality revisited: An invitation to curiosity. *Family Process, 26*, 405–413.

Cecchin, G., & Fruggeri, L. (1986). Consultation with mental health system teams in Italy. In L. Wynne, S. McDaniel, & T. Weber (Eds.), *Systems consultation*. New York: Guilford Press.

Cronen, V., Johnson, K., & Lannemann, J. (1982). Paradoxes, double binds and reflexive loops: An alternative theoretical perspective. *Family Process, 20*, 91–112.

Cronen, V., & Pearce, W. (1985). Toward an explanation of how the Milan method works: An invitation to a systemic epistemology and the evolution of family systems. In D. Campbell & R. Draper (Eds.), *Applications of systemic family therapy: The Milan approach*. London: Grune & Stratton.

Cronen, V., Pearce, W., & Tomm, K. (1985). A dialectical view of personal change. In K. Gergen & K. Davis (Eds.), *The social construction of the person*. New York: Springer-Verlag.

Dell, P. (1989). Violence and the systemic view. *Family Process, 28*, 1–14.

Di Blasio, P., Fischer, J., & Prata, G. (1986). The telephone chart: A cornerstone of the first interview with the family. *Journal of Strategic and Systemic Therapies, 5*.

Di Nicola, V. (1984). Road map to schizo-land: Mara Selvini Palazzoli and the Milan model of systemic family therapy. *Journal of Strategic and Systemic Therapies, 3*, 50–62.

Fish, V. (1990). Introducing causality and power onto family therapy theory: A correction to the systemic paradigm. *Journal of Marital and Family Therapy, 16*, 21–37.

Fruggeri, L., Dotti, D., Ferrari, R., & Matteini, M. (1985). The systemic approach in a mental health service. In D. Campbell

& R. Draper (Eds.), *Applications of systemic family therapy: The Milan approach*. London: Grune & Stratton.

Golann, S. (1988). On second-order family therapy. *Family Process, 27*, 51–65.

Harris, Q., & Burnham, J. (1985). A training programme in systemic therapy: The problem of the institutional context. In D. Campbell & R. Draper (Eds.), *Applications of systemic family therapy: The Milan approach*. London: Grune & Stratton.

Hoffman, L. (1981). *Foundations of family therapy*. New York: Basic Books.

Hoffman, L. (1985). Beyond power and control: Toward a "second-order" family systems therapy. *Family Systems Medicine, 3*, 381–396.

Hoffman, L. (1988). A constructivist position for family therapy. *Irish Journal of Psychology, 9*, 110–129.

Imber-Coppersmith, E. (1985). Families and multiple helpers: A systemic perspective. In D. Campbell & R. Draper (Eds.), *Applications of systemic family therapy: The Milan approach*. London: Grune & Stratton.

Jackson, D. (1977). The myth of normalcy. In P. Watzlawick & J.H. Weakland (Eds.), *Studies at the Mental Research Institute, Palo Alto 1965–1974*. New York: Norton.

Keeney, B. (1983). *Aesthetics of change*. New York: Guilford Press.

Keeney, B., & Sprenkle, D. (1982). Ecosystemic epistemology: Critical implications of the aesthetics and pragmatics of family therapy. *Family Process, 21*, 1–19.

Lane, G., & Russell, T. (1987). Neutrality versus social control. *Family Therapy Networker*, May–June, 52–56.

Lederer, W. (1968). *The mirages of marriage*. London: Norton.

Levin, S., Raser, J., Niles, C., & Reese, A. (1987). Beyond family systems—forward problem systems: Some clinical implications. *Journal of Strategic and Systemic Therapies, 5*, 62–69.

MacKinnon, L., & Miller, D. (1987). The new epistemology and the Milan approach: Feminist and sociopolitical considerations. *Journal of Marital and Family Therapy, 13*, 139–155.

MacKinnon, L., Parry, A., & Black, R. (1984). Strategies of family therapy: The relationship to styles of family functioning. *Journal of Strategic and Systemic Therapies, 3*, 6–22.

Mashal, M., Feldman, R., & Sigal, J. (1989). The unravelling of a treatment paradigm: A follow-up study of the Milan approach. *Family Process, 28*, 457–470.

Maturana, H. (1978). Biology of language: The epistemology of reality. In G. A. Miller & E. Lennenberg (Eds.), *Psychology and biology of language and thought*. New York: Academic Press.

Maturana, H., & Varela, F. (1980). *Autopoiesis and cognition: The realization of the living*. Holland: Reidel.

Mendez, C.L., Coddou, F., & Maturana, H. (1988). The bringing forth of pathology. *Irish Journal of Psychology, 91*, 144–172.

Nitzberg, L., Patten, J., Spielman, M., & Brown, R. (1985). Inpatient hospital systemic consultation: Providing team systemic consultation in in-patient settings where the team is part of the system. In D. Campbell & R. Draper (Eds.), *Applications of systemic family therapy: The Milan approach*. London: Grune & Stratton.

Penn, P. (1982). Circular questioning. *Family Process, 21*, 267–280.

Penn, P. (1985). Feed-forward: Future questions, future maps. *Family Process, 24*, 299–310.

Pirrotta, S. (1984). Milan revisited: A comparison of the two Milan schools. *Journal of Strategic and Systemic Therapies, 3*, 3–15.

Prigogine, I., & Stengers, I. (1977). New alliance, 2. Extended dynamics—towards a human science of nature. *Scientia, 112*, 617–653.

Ricci, C., & Selvini Palazzoli, M. (1984). Interactional complexity and communication. *Family Process, 23*, 169–176.

Selvini, M. (Ed.) (1988). *The work of Mara Selvini Palazzoli*. New York: Aronson.

Selvini, M., & Selvini Palazzoli, M. (in press). Team work: An indispensable tool for clinical research in family therapy. Ways of fostering and promoting its creative potential.

Selvini Palazzoli, M. (1974). *Self starvation*. London: Human Context Books.

Selvini Palazzoli, M. (1983). The emergence of a comprehensive systems approach. *Journal of Family Therapy, 5*, 165–177.

Selvini Palazzoli, M. (1984). Behind the scenes of the organization: Some guidelines for the expert in human relations. *Journal of Family Therapy, 6*, 299–307.

Selvini Palazzoli, M. (1985a). The emergence of a comprehensive systems approach: Supervisor and team problems in a district psychiatric centre. *Journal of Family Therapy, 7*, 135–146.

Selvini Palazzoli, M. (1985b). The problem of the sibling as the referring person. *Journal of Marital and Family Therapy, 11*, 21–34.

Selvini Palazzoli, M. (1986). Towards a general model of psychotic family games. *Journal of Marital and Family Therapy, 12*, 339–344.

Selvini Palazzoli, M., Boscolo, L., Cecchin, G., & Prata, G. (1974). The treatment of children through brief therapy of their parents. *Family Process, 13*, 429–442.

Selvini Palazzoli, M., Boscolo, L., Cecchin, G., & Prata, G. (1977). Family rituals: A powerful tool in family therapy. *Family Process, 16*, 445–453.

Selvini Palazzoli, M., Boscolo, L., Cecchin, G., & Prata, G. (1978a). A ritualized prescription in family therapy: Odd days and even days. *Journal of Marriage and Family Counseling, 4*, 3–8.

Selvini Palazzoli, M., Boscolo, L., Cecchin, G., & Prata, G. (1978b). *Paradox and counterparadox*. New York: Aronson.

Selvini Palazzoli, M., Boscolo, L., Cecchin, G., & Prata, G. (1980a). The problem of the referring person. *Journal of Marital and Family Therapy, 6*, 3–9 (b).

Selvini Palazzoli, M., Boscolo, L., Cecchin, G., & Prata, G. (1980b). Hypothesizing—circularity—neutrality: Three guidelines for the conductor of the session. *Family Process, 19*, 3–12 (a).

Selvini Palazzoli, M., Cirillo, S., Selvini, M., & Sorrentino, A.M. (1989). *Family games: General models of psychotic processes in the family*. New York: W.W. Norton.

Selvini Palazzoli, M., & Prata, G. (1983). A new method for therapy and research in the treatment of schizophrenic families. In H. Stierlin, L.C. Wynne, & M. Wirsching (Eds.), *Psychosocial intervention in schizophrenia: An international view*. Berlin: Springer.

Selvini Palazzoli, M., & Viaro, M. (1988). The anoreche process in the family. A six stage model as a guide for individual therapy. *Family Process, 27*, 2, 129–148.

Speed, B. (1985). Evaluating the Milan approach. In D. Campbell & R. Draper (Eds.), *Applications of systemic family therapy: The Milan approach*. London: Grune & Stratton.

Tomm, K. (1984a). One perspective on the Milan systemic approach: Part I. Overview of development, theory and practice. *Journal of Marital and Family Therapy, 10*, 113–125.

Tomm, K. (1984b). One perspective on the Milan systemic approach: Part II. Description of session format, interviewing style and interventions. *Journal of Marital and Family Therapy, 10*, 253–271.

Tomm, K. (1985). Circular interviewing: A multifaceted clinical tool. In D. Campbell & R. Draper (Eds.), *Applications of systemic family therapy: The Milan approach*. London: Grune & Stratton.

Tomm, K. (1987a). Interventive interviewing: Part I. Strategizing as a fourth guideline for the therapist. *Family Process, 26*, 3–13.

Tomm, K. (1987b). Interventive interviewing: Part II. Reflexive questioning as a means to enable self healing. *Family Process, 26*, 167–183.

Tomm, K. (1988). Interventive interviewing: Part III. Intending to ask lineal, circular, strategic or reflexive questions? *Family Process, 27*, 1–15.

Tomm, K., & Wright, L. (1982). Multilevel training and supervision in an out-patient service programme. In R. Whiffen & J. Byng-

Hall (Eds.), *Family therapy supervision: Recent developments in practice*. London: Academic Press.

Ugazio, V. (1985). Hypothesis making: The Milan approach revisited. In D. Campbell & R. Draper (Eds.), *Applications of systemic family therapy: The Milan approach*. London: Grune & Stratton.

Van Trommel, M. (1984). A consultation method addressing the therapist–family system. *Family Process, 23,* 469–480.

Varela, F. (1979). *Principles of biological autonomy*. New York: North Holland Press.

Viaro, M., & Leonardo, P. (1982). Getting and giving information: Analysis of a particular interview strategy. *Family Process, 22,* 27–42.

Viaro, M., & Leonardo, P. (1986). The evolution of the interview technique: A comparison between former and present strategy. *Journal of Strategic and Systemic Therapies, 5,* 14–30.

Von Glasersfeld, E. (1984). An introduction to radical constructivism. In P. Watzlawick (Ed.), *The invented reality*. New York: Norton.

Watzlawick, P., Beavin, J., & Jackson, D. (1967). *Pragmatics of human communication*. New York: Norton.

Watzlawick, P., Weakland, J.H., & Fisch, R. (1974). *Change: Principles of problem formation and problem resolution*. New York: Norton.

EDITORS' REFERENCE

Anderson, C.M. (1986). The all-too-short trip from positive to negative connotation. *Journal of Marital and Family Therapy, 12,* 351–354.

CHAPTER 11

Family Psychoeducational Treatment

William R. McFarlane, M.D.

BACKGROUND OF THE APPROACH

At present, the psychoeducational approach is in use most extensively with families of patients with schizophrenia. As will be evident, its development grows directly out of the long and tortuous search for an effective treatment for schizophrenia, a problem that continues to defy adequate, let alone simple, explanation and to evade widely varying attempts to ameliorate its impact. While new applications by the originators of the approach developed by Anderson, Hogarty, and Reiss (1986) and by others are being tested, the focus of the most refined forms of the method relate to schizophrenia. For that reason, the present chapter will deal primarily with theoretical issues and clinical techniques primarily relevant to that disorder.[1]

The rationale for developing a new therapy for schizophrenia needs little explanation. In spite of the widespread use of antipsychotic medication, the progressive deinstitutionalization reforms of the last decade, and expanding treatment, residential, and rehabilitation services, the prognosis for patients with this illness has changed remarkably little. Between 1 and 2 percent of the population is afflicted; only 25 percent of first-episode patients recover, while the rest often appear consigned to a life of increasing mental dysfunction, emotional deadness, social isolation and rejection and major disabilities in work and relationships (Yolles & Kramer, 1969). Patients who take medication regularly can still expect to have a 40 percent chance of relapsing during the first year after any given episode, so that for many, life consists of two alternating states and contexts: being psychotic and hospitalized and being marginally stable and living dependently with the support of others, especially the family of origin (Schooler et al., 1980).

What has not been so apparent to clinicians, including many family therapists, is that for families of persons afflicted with schizophrenic illness, life is drastically different and in most respects more stressful and more demoralizing than is the case in most psychiatric disorders and in nonpsychotic family dysfunction. This cu-

---

[1] Note that these approaches are based almost entirely on the attempt to develop practical interventions based on research findings, rather than adventures in the application of cherished theoretical constructs. It is to emphasize that point that so much background literature is presented here; the author begs the patience of those readers who are already comfortable with this conceptual orientation.

rious absence is largely the result of the dominance of the poorly substantiated belief that family and parental dysfunction are the sole or predominant source of the symptoms and disability of the "identified patient." We have been preoccupied with ferreting out the causal transaction patterns, while, to a large degree, ignoring the devastating impact of watching one's child deteriorate into someone who is all but a stranger, and a most incapacitated one. To roughly the same degree, many clinicians have ignored the fact that families have become the *de facto* caretakers of individuals with schizophrenia, without the required knowledge, training, resources, or support.

Family psychoeducation can be most simply understood as an attempt to deal simultaneously with both of these realities: the disappointing record of antipsychotic drugs used alone and the complex burdens imposed on families by this illness. It should be stated at the outset that, in many significant ways, family psychoeducation (PE) is not a family therapy at all, but rather a strategy for treating a bona fide disabling and chronic illness that is best defined as a functional impairment of the brain. In fact, a general definition of PE should include the central notion that families and other natural social groups can be trained to create an interactional environment that compensates for, and may partially correct, functional disability in one member of the group. Recognizing that some readers may be puzzled, if not outraged, by the concept that family intervention might proceed successfully with the assumption that the patient is suffering from something other than dysfunctional family process, what is presented here will attempt to trace the conceptual and empirical development of this approach and its rationale.[2]

Early Theories and Practice

The family has been a focus in the study and treatment of schizophrenia since the advent of psychoanalysis. However, family therapists and theorists began intensive work in this area during the late 1950s. From hindsight, it appears that the early efforts to understand the family's role were influenced by psychoanalytic thinking, especially that of Fromm-Reichmann (1948) and Laing and Esterson (1970), who viewed parent–child interaction as radically destructive and causal of the disorder itself. With that concept as a foundation, Bateson and associates (Bateson, Jackson, Haley, & Weakland, 1956) developed the double-bind hypothesis, Lidz, Fleck, and Cornelison (1965) described schismatic and skewed family structures, Bowen (1960) traced increasing immaturity through three generations, and, more recently, Selvini Palazzoli, Boscolo, Cecchin, & Prata (1978) posited schizophrenic transaction. These theories share a number of characteristics that make their acceptance questionable. First, none allows the possibility that symptoms might be determined primarily by deficits in brain function and integrity. Second, they do not lead, or at least have not led, to empirical validation. Third, to qualify as specific etiologic factors they would have to be ubiquitous in all families with a schizophrenic member and uniquely present only in those families; there are no studies that demonstrate such associations. Fourth, if one theory were correct, the others would be incorrect; to date, none of these concepts has shown more validity than the others. Fifth, and perhaps most telling, they have not been the basis for an effective family therapy that ameliorates symptoms and prevents their recurrence.[3]

---

[2] *Editors' Note.* Within this *Handbook,* and the field at large, those "schools" of family therapy whose views are most divergent from those presented in this chapter are Bowen theory (Friedman, Chapter 5), the MRI approach (Segal, Chapter 6), the Milan approach (Campbell, Draper, & Crutchley, Chapter 10); the strategic approach (Madanes, Chapter 12); and the symbolic-experiential approach (Giat Roberto, Chapter 14). Given this range and number of anticipated "outraged readers," we concluded that a chapter on family psychoeducational treatment was a *sine qua non* for the second edition of the *Handbook,* even though it is not, in McFarlane's view, "a family therapy at all."

[3] *Editors' Note.* Speaking of outraged readers, we more than suspect that many of the advocates of the Bowen, Milan, and the Mental Research Institute approaches just alluded to would argue that their methods are effective in this clinical context. We believe that McFarlane means to refer to empirical documentation of effectiveness and prevention, which may mute the outrage somewhat.

Effects of Deinstitutionalization

It is somewhat ironic, but true nevertheless, that during the very period—the mid-1970s—in which family therapy was being abandoned for treating psychotic disorders, the effects of deinstitutionalization were beginning to be felt by two groups: community-based clinicians and families. While the original architects of the mass discharge of patients from psychiatric hospitals intended that a range of services would be provided to enhance community adjustment, budget restrictions often have precluded all but the discharge process itself. Since then, families in increasing numbers have found themselves replacing most of the functions of the state hospital: providing food, clothing, and shelter; monitoring symptoms; managing medication compliance; instituting rehabilitation efforts; and controlling dangerous and bizarre behavior. They have received some help from publicly supported clinical services, but this has been notoriously inadequate.

Multiple-Family Therapy

One relatively obscure response to the question of the relation between families and schizophrenia was the advent of multiple-family groups, in which several patients and their respective families meet together on a regular basis. Beginning in about 1960, two innovators of multiple-family therapy (MFT), Laqueur (Laqueur, LaBurt, & Morong, 1964) and Detre (Detre, Sayer, Norton, & Lewis, 1961), assembled their groups to solve ward-management problems—rather than from a theoretical family-systems perspective—and both described immediate and surprising benefits to patients, with reference to symptoms and sociability, and to family members, with reference to morale and communication. A number of clinicians began using this approach, primarily because of its practical advantages and early results that seemed unexpectedly promising.

In retrospect, one major difference between single- and multifamily approaches was that, in the latter, families were sufficiently joined to each other that messages of blame coming from therapists were usually neutralized, while direct emotional support and opportunities for trading successful techniques for managing illness-related behavior often dominated the discussions. With time, the emphasis in multifamily groups centered on balancing the needs of patients with those of families, rather than on families being converted from theoretically dysfunctional interaction patterns.

MFT was an approach that lacked the conceptual elegance of family-systems ideas, but it compensated by delivering clinical results. Because that efficacy was not rigorously demonstrated, MFT remained an esoteric practice used in scattered clinics and hospitals serving the chronic mental patient. However, a few observers thought that social support for families may be a crucial variable in determining outcome, because, as we shall see, the social processes surrounding the relentless course of mental disability tend to leave families at least isolated, if not abandoned and rejected. This was a compelling idea, given the growing evidence that social isolation appears to be associated with morbidity in many conditions, including depression, heart disease, and schizophrenia (Beels, 1981).

Drug Therapy and Biological Research

A major blow to pure family-systems beliefs and a major clue to the nature of schizophrenia was the emerging evidence from double-blind experiments that antipsychotics reduced or eliminated symptoms of acute episodes in the vast majority of patients treated.[4] Further, maintenance medication was shown repeatedly to foster a continuation of remission at roughly twice the effectiveness of placebo. Drug effects on survival in the community are so substantial that the effects of social therapy can barely be discerned in some studies (Hogarty & Goldberg, 1973).

At first conceived as tranquilizers, further research has shown that these drugs have a much more specific effect: they block dopamine at the synapse between neurons and thereby block in-

---

[4] *Editors' Note.* This is quite accurate if "pure family-systems beliefs" is taken to mean "interactional/transactional." But note that such research is entirely concordant with *general* systems theory, which in no way precludes the relevance of biological factors to family life.

terneuronal propagation of electrical activity in key pathways in the brain. The association between this effect and the reduction of symptoms is quite strong and has been replicated many times (Snyder, Banerjee, Yamamura, & Greenberg, 1974; Meltzer, 1979; Crow et al., 1979). While there are many uncertainties remaining as to the role of dopamine regulation in schizophrenia, the role of antipsychotics in blocking symptoms and improving control over attention and arousal is well established (Spohn, Lacoursiere, Thompson, & Coyne, 1977).

From the foundation established by the dopamine hypothesis, research has proceeded to document a number of major alterations in brain function and even structure. Recent advances in brain-imaging techniques have revealed that ventricular enlargement occurs in roughly one third of all schizophrenic patients (Weinberger, Wagner, & Wyatt, 1983). Because gliosis (i.e., cerebral scarring) has been observed in the areas adjacent to the ventricles, it is possible that the common factor explaining both phenomena is infection or trauma that occurred earlier in life (Stevens, 1982). Regardless of cause, many patients have actually lost a significant portion of neuronal tissue by the time of the first episode and have a much poorer course (DeLisi et al., 1983).

Furthermore, other techniques that allow in vivo observation of cerebral blood flow and regional brain metabolism disclose that there are abnormally low levels of blood circulation and glucose metabolism in patients' frontal lobes—an area most directly associated with higher-level cognition, initiative, and integration of affect and thought (Weinberger et al., 1986)—and in some studies, abnormally high levels of activity in temporal and occipital lobes, which are areas in which auditory and visual sensations are registered and processed (Ingvar & Franzen, 1974). More specifically, metabolism does not respond to mental tasks that require activation of the frontal lobes (Weinberger et al., 1986), leaving the patient powerless to perform crucial, higher-level cognitive functions.

As further corroboration of a significant biological contribution to onset and course, more refined genetic studies have made it clear that inheritance of a predisposition proceeds independently of family interactional effects. Studies of identical twins continue to find that there is roughly 40 percent concordance, even when the twins are reared apart in adopting families (Kendler, 1986). Of great interest are two studies that suggest that offspring of affected parents are more vulnerable to schizophrenia when the adopting family is measurably dysfunctional (Wynne, Singer, & Toohey, 1976; Tienari et al., 1987). These findings strongly suggest an interaction effect: an inherited or perinatally acquired vulnerability being exacerbated to the point of manifest symptomatology by environmental stresses.

Psychosocial Factors and Course of Illness

By shifting the focus of attention from etiology to determinants of the course of illness, one group of researchers has reliably and usefully clarified how social processes, including but not limited to family interaction, might influence what happens in a psychotic illness once it is established. In addition, we now have a much broader perspective on what happens to families as they attempt to cope with a member who is mentally ill.

The most influential and persuasive work in this area has emerged from the Institute for Social Psychiatry in London. Initiated by George Brown and his colleagues, hypothesizing that affective factors might account for relapse, they created a factor they called "expressed emotion" (EE) (Brown, Monck, Carstairs, & Wing, 1962). Having assessed its presence or absence in key relatives, they followed patients for nine months and found that when EE was higher, relapse occurred much more frequently. When this study was replicated by Vaughn and Leff (1976), medication emerged as a major influence on relapse only when EE was high in one relative: 53 percent of patients who remained in daily contact relapsed while taking medication, while 92 percent of those without medication relapsed. In low-EE homes, the comparable figures were 12 percent and 15 percent.

Here, then, was a phenomenon that bridged the social and biological conundrums, because a minority of families seemed to have a negative influence on the same, presumably biological, processes that medication seemed to affect.[5] At the same time, it was clear that some families were as protective against relapse as medication, because in "low-EE" households no medication effect was observable. Expressed emotion consists of an attitudinal aspect—highly critical views of the patient—and a behavioral component—a tendency to be "overinvolved"; that is, highly protective, attentive, or reactive in relation to the patient. Finally, Brown and Birley (1968) and Leff (Leff, Hirsch, Gaind, Rhode, & Stevens, 1973) had found that life events had exactly the same kind of effect as EE, regardless of the EE status of family members.

The background for PE family approaches includes two other research areas. One emphasizes the effects on the family of having an ill member and the other the social network of the patient and family. A sizable body of literature now exists that documents nearly devastating effects on families when faced with a mentally ill member in their midst over long periods of time. These burdens include chronic tension and fear, sleep disruption, financial drain, confusion, limitation of social contacts, interference with daily routine, deprivation of attention for siblings, marital conflict, overt depression, and exacerbation of medical conditions (Kreisman & Joy, 1974; Johnson, 1986). Furthermore, many families complain that being blamed by professionals and friends for the illness induces guilt, confusion, anger, and, eventually, demoralization and rejection of the patient.

The social networks and social supports of schizophrenic patients and their families have been studied extensively, with a singularly consistent finding: patients particularly—and to a lesser extent, families—are more isolated than their peers, even those with other psychiatric disorders. Pattison (Pattison, Lama, & Hurd, 1979), Hammer (1963), and Garrison (1978) noted smaller network size, as did Brown (Brown, Birley, & Wing, 1972), who also found an association between family isolation and high EE. Patient social networks are constricted and more family-based at first admission (Tolsdorf,

1976), while the entire network decreases in size after the illness has taken hold (Lipton, Cohen, Fischer, & Katz, 1981). The explanation for this process is complex, but probably includes withdrawal of contact and support by friends and extended kin and reduced social initiative by family members secondary to shame and/or preoccupation with the patient. It seems likely that attenuated social support leads to the loss of adaptive coping capacity for family members and exacerbates the effects of caretaking burdens.

A Core Psychological Deficit: The Attention-Arousal Hypothesis

The studies reviewed above led Anderson, Hogarty, and Reiss (1986) to develop a family-based treatment that had as its principal goal the prevention of symptomatic relapse. Hogarty and Ulrich (1977) had found that the risk for relapse declined appreciably over two years, such that at the end of that period, the risk was one third that at the point of hospital discharge, assuming maintenance medication throughout. Combined with data from emerging long-term studies, this finding suggested that there may be a slow, natural restitution process that can occur, but only when relapse does not intervene (Harding, Brooks, Ashikaga, Strauss, & Breier, 1987).

Psychophysiological research on schizophrenia provided a model that linked more specifically the emerging biological and drug studies with the psychosocial literature, suggesting a possible clinical strategy. Beginning with Kraepelin, it has been argued that schizophrenics are impaired in their capacity to control attention: they select irrelevant stimuli, shift attentional set inappropriately and have difficulty remaining alert to cognitive tasks.[6] Further, many studies have found that the regulation of arousal is impaired in this disorder, leaving patients vulnerable either to nearly disabling levels of autonomic hyperactivity under conditions of mild stress or to underresponsivity when arousal

---

[5] *Editors' Note.* And, again, it is such a bridging that is consistent with general systems theory, if not with "pure family-systems" theory.

[6] For a comprehensive review of this complex subject, Neuchterlein and Dawson's (1984) review is highly recommended.

is appropriate. Attention appears to be subject to influence by arousal, such that at moderate levels of arousal, attention is improved, but at higher levels, it begins to deteriorate rapidly. Further, Tecce and Cole (1976) found that distraction of attention produced increases in arousal. Two methods are known to assist in the regulation of arousal and attention: antipsychotic medication and the reduction of the intensity, negativity, quantity, and complexity of stimuli from the environment. It was the latter alternative that suggested a mechanism for relapse in high-EE homes. Sturgeon and associates (Sturgeon, Kuipers, Berkowitz, Turpin, & Leff, 1981) and Tarrier and co-workers (Tarrier, Vaughn, Lader, & Leff, 1979) had found that, in fact, high EE *was* associated with high levels of psychophysiological arousal in the patients.

This concept suggested a clinical approach: combine antipsychotic medication with a program for families that helped them to reduce the level of intensity and complexity in their household and relapse conceivably could be delayed, reduced in severity, or perhaps eliminated entirely for the less severely ill patient. Two major components of such an approach would be the education of family members about the details of the disorder and the provision of support and guidance over a fairly prolonged period after an episode. Previous experiments in that direction seemed to be successful (Beels, 1975; Goldstein, Rodnick, Evans, May, & Steenberg, 1978, Langsley, Machotka, & Flomenhaft, 1971), so that the likelihood of a more ambitious program's succeeding seemed high enough to warrant the attempt. The PE program described in the following is the result, while the multiple-family-group method also outlined here has developed as a natural extension of the author's work on MFT.

THE HEALTHY OR WELL-FUNCTIONING FAMILY

Because all psychoeducational approaches developed to date are designed to address specific major psychiatric disorders, they proceed with an unusual assumption for a family therapy. That is, it is assumed that the family is within the normal range of functioning, until clearly proved

otherwise, and that a better outcome for the ill member is most likely when the family makes compensatory adjustments to its daily life that are dictated by the specific characteristics of the disorder itself. It is also assumed that these disorders often tend to elicit in family members responses that are self-defeating, though understandable. Thus, the approach described here helps families to adopt effective, though somewhat *abnormal*, styles of relating to the affected individual. It is also assumed that, until further research clarifies the issue, general family dysfunction varies independently of the presence of schizophrenia or other mental disorders, so that the clinician practicing family PE can expect to encounter well-functioning *and* highly dysfunctional families.

Based heavily on research summarized in the previous section, it is possible to describe the optimal functioning of a family afflicted with schizophrenia along a number of dimensions.

Boundaries

Because of the peculiar sensitivity of the schizophrenic patient to overstimulation, the structure of the family needs to provide a flexible but enhanced set of barriers between the patient and other members of the family. That is, family members may continue to try to involve the patient in family activities, but respect his or her need to regulate stimulation by allowing for withdrawal when it seems necessary. Anderson (Anderson et al., 1986) has described this concept as "erecting barriers to overstimulation" and it is an extension of conventional ideas about the value of interpersonal boundaries in normal family functioning. There is a phasic aspect here as well: the need for increased interpersonal distance is greatest in the immediate postpsychosis period and diminishes with time and with the natural course of recovery from an acute episode. The family needs to create appropriate boundaries in a benign fashion, because rejection and abandonment lead to increased symptoms as well. Finally, parents especially are encouraged to direct their attention and concern to well siblings, who are at risk of being ignored, to their detriment, if the illness becomes the overriding focus of the entire family.

Parents faced with schizophrenia in a child

will tend to rank marital needs well below what appear to be the more pressing needs of their ill child. The family in which the patient does relatively better is usually characterized by a balance such that parents attend to their needs as marital partners, to the maximum extent possible, if only to avoid being exhausted and overwhelmed over the course of a chronic illness. The maintenance of generational boundaries also reduces anxiety in the patient by avoiding guilt-inducing restriction of parental activities and by communicating a clear, consistent sense of structure. The result of a strong marital alliance is a system in which the occasional reemergence of symptoms does not generate high levels of anxiety in other family members and, thereby, provides the greatest chance that the symptoms will be manageable.[7]

To enhance interpersonal and intergenerational boundaries, it is essential that the family's outer boundary be open to support, information, guidance, recreation, and simple social contact. It appears that without outside sources of pleasure, distraction, constructive criticism, and opportunities for gratifying work, most families will tend to drift into isolation and be at risk for high levels of EE. Given the tendency of more peripheral members of the family's network to avoid what they may interpret as a fearful or repulsive individual, in most cases, the family members will have to make special efforts to retain the contact that they and the patient will need, albeit in different amounts. It is the need for social support that seems to make many families prefer the multifamily-group format.

Communication

There are two levels at which family communication is important when facing the problems of a mentally ill relative. First, some significant accommodations have to be made to the cognitive impairments of the schizophrenic patient. Communication, especially in the early posthospital period, will need to be clear, straightforward, concrete, and moderately specific. There is abundant evidence from the EE literature that positive comments and a calm, supportive tone are crucial in getting through to, and helping stabilize, an ill relative. Requests need to be made directly and simply. The low-EE families in the author's studies have tended to be markedly low key, tentative, and nonpressuring in their communications to the patient, often waiting for the patient to take the initiative in conversation. Anderson has recommended a Bowen-like approach, acknowledging the statements of others directly and taking responsibility for one's own statements, purely from a practical point of view: individuals with attentional dysfunction will find it easier to track conversations if it is clear who is saying what and why. Clearly, all the general rules for communication apply here as in other families, but the need is more acute.

The other area of communication relates to interaction among well members of the family. Schizophrenia induces severe strains in all areas of family life and readily precipitates disagreements about what to do that can escalate to outright conflict, especially between spouses and between parents and well children. Avoiding blame, making clear requests for changes in behavior, admitting vulnerability, staying on the topic, getting consensus on resolution of conflict and problems, and simple sharing of information are essential to surviving with a schizophrenic member in one's midst.

Structure

The well-functioning family with a mentally ill member tends to have a hierarchy that is sufficiently clear that necessary rules can be established and respected and that the caretaking functions of the well members of the family can be carried out without being countered by the dysfunctional behavior of the ill member. Such a clear structure tends to allay tension; reduce the possibility for nagging, criticism, and excessive interaction; and induce clarity and predictability into family life. The family in which the

---

[7] *Editors' Note.* Perhaps this amounts to pointing out the too-obvious, nonetheless, we note here the great relevance of structural family theory (Colapinto, Chapter 13) for psychoeducational treatment. Interestingly, both models are very explicit about what generally constitutes healthy or well-functioning families, in contrast to some other family-therapy approaches, which eschew such discussions (e.g., MRI, Chapter 6; Milan, Chapter 10; Strategic, Chapter 12).

parents are clearly in charge is the calmer, more therapeutic family.

Structure and limit setting become very important around medication compliance: in some instances, parents may decide that the patient's using medication as prescribed is necessary for the *family's* well-being and require its continuation, even if the patient does not agree. The same is true for dealing with violence and bizarre behavior: setting limits will often be the only way to extinguish these behaviors and to preserve a semblance of normality in the home.

Knowledge and Coping Skills

Living with schizophrenia is at least as difficult and confusing as treating it. Thus, the truly well-functioning family has to possess (1) the available knowledge about the illness itself, and (2) coping skills specific to this or other psychiatric disorders, skills that are counterintuitive and are still being developed. It is a core principle in psychoeducational work that it is unrealistic to expect families to understand such a mystifying condition and to know what to do about it. Given that perspective, the healthier family is one that has access to information, with the implication that the treatment system is a crucial source of that information. As to coping skills, many families have developed, through painful trial and error, methods of dealing with positive and negative symptoms, functional disabilities, and the desperation of their ill relatives. These successes, however, are few and far between. So, a critical need is that families have access to each other—via multifamily-group contact and indirectly through professionals and leaders of the family self-help movement. In sum, to define the overall functioning of a given family, one must consider the informational, treatment, guidance, and peer-support resources that are accessible to its members.

THE DYSFUNCTIONAL FAMILY

There are two levels at which family dysfunction relates to symptom development: etiology and course of illness. The question of causality in schizophrenia is at present so poorly understood that the researchers who have developed new family intervention strategies have preferred—wisely—to beg the issue entirely. Regardless of the data or lack of data, family therapists must be fully aware that the assertion that families may play a role in the disease's onset is an extraordinarily sensitive issue for families themselves and for members of the family-advocacy movement.

As is apparent in the background material, the association between family interaction and *course* of illness is somewhat clearer and highly relevant clinically. We can summarize that body of literature by stating that families in which there is a high level of intensity and complexity, especially if negative in tone, will be more likely to induce arousal, and ultimately symptoms, in the schizophrenic member of the family, if there is extensive contact. Further, actual outcome depends heavily on the type and severity of the impairment of the patient per se, with a wide range of variability.

A careful review of the EE literature[8] reveals that this construct represents a very different dimension than is usually connoted by family pathology. Vaughn and Leff (1976) found that low-EE relatives were "cool, controlled and concerned but not overly anxious *in their response to the patient's illness*" (authors' italics). They were more distant and seemed to understand the patient's desire/need for psychological space. They saw that what was wrong represented a disease of the mind, not misbehavior or indolence; that is, they were not ashamed of their own parenting. Characterologically, they were more tolerant and patient. Finally, it is important that the high-EE relatives made two thirds of their critical comments about negative symptoms,[9] not understanding their basis in cognitive deficits and/or medication side effects.

To further qualify the notion that EE is synonymous with dysfunction, consider the following findings:

---

[8] See Leff and Vaughn (1985) for a useful summary of this work.

[9] These include anergia, loss of initiative, flat affect, poverty of thought, and anhedonia.

- Brown (Brown et al., 1972) found that EE decreased spontaneously if the patient improved over nine months.
- Miklowitz, Goldstein, and Falloon (1983) found that overinvolvement correlates with poor premorbid adjustment, which increasingly appears to be an indicator of subtle, but now measurable, brain damage.
- Wig and co-workers (1987) and others have found wide variations in levels of EE in different cultures, with the highest levels seen in California and the lowest in India, correlating inversely with cultural expectations for sociovocational performance and psychological mindedness.
- Brown's and the author's data reveal an association among high EE, social isolation, and stigma experienced by the family.

Taken together, these findings suggest that family EE is best conceived as a failure of adaptation to a "chronic disaster" or perhaps as efforts to gain control over a relative's illness (Hooley, 1985), rather than as signifying primary family dysfunction.

It needs to be added that clinicians working with a general population of families can expect to find a percentage that are pathological in a family-systems sense. At a minimum, this is predictable as a function of the genetics of schizophrenia: estimates of schizophrenia-spectrum disorder in parents of schizophrenic adults run as high as 25 percent (Singer, Wynne, & Toohey, 1978). There is increasing evidence that suggests minor degrees of cognitive and psychophysiological impairment in this same subgroup (Wagener, Hogarty, Goldstein, Asarnow, & Browne, 1986). It is possible that this underlies the consistent observation that a significant proportion of relatives manifest "communication deviance," a subtle process that remains elusive in terms of its clinical significance (Singer et al., 1978). In any case, some families may manifest difficulty in maintaining a focus of attention and, therefore, will have varying degrees of difficulty in problem solving. In an occasional case, outright symptoms of residual psychosis or paranoid disorder may be present. Finally, if one accepts that family functioning varies independently, then it would be expected that a few families with "ordinary" structural or communicational dysfunction will appear.

The experience of Anderson and the author is that those problems are usually surmountable and that such families ultimately benefit from the PE approaches. The working assumption is that the great preponderance of apparent dysfunction seen during an intake–engagement process is secondary to the effect of the psychosis and disability on the family. Because so much of that effect is attenuated by education, support, and interfamily contact, it increasingly has seemed wise to hold final judgment on the extent of individual or family psychopathology until these treatment elements have been offered and allowed to have a therapeutic impact.

THE ASSESSMENT OF SYSTEM FUNCTIONING

In the remainder of this chapter, we will explore the concrete technical tasks that make up family psychoeducation. Techniques for two distinct formats—single-family PE (SFPE) and multiple-family PE (MFPE)—will be described separately when necessary. However, the emphasis is on a core set of phased interventions that are common to both. Anderson, Hogarty, and Reiss (1986) have described the single-family approach comprehensively in a recent volume, while the author has developed and recently completed an extensive trial of the multifamily version. These approaches consist of four sequential phases: (1) engagement with the family, usually at the time of an acute psychotic decompensation; (2) an educational workshop, in which the clinicians present information and describe key behavioral guidelines didactically; (3) a reentry period, when biweekly sessions focus on stabilizing the patient out of the hospital; and (4) a rehabilitation phase, when sessions emphasize the slow and careful raising of the patient's level of functioning. In the multifamily version, phases 2, 3, and 4 are carried out in a group of five or six families, as is phase 2 in the single-family version. A clinician meets with one family during phase 1 in MFPE and in phases 1, 3, and 4 in the single-family method. Patients are present only in phases 3 and 4 in both modalities.

Psychoeducational assessment is distinct from other family-therapy approaches in several key aspects. The primary one is the centrality of building an alliance with the significant relatives in the patient's life. The focus of assessment should include being genuinely interested in the family's experiences and reactions to them. To the extent that the assessment process communicates to family members the clinician's desire to help them and the patient, it should accomplish one major goal: the creation of a collaborative treatment system in which family members become engaged as partners and experts on the daily life of their schizophrenic relative.[10]

The format for the assessment process is the same as that for the "joining" phase (see "Structure of the Therapy Process" section). The clinician contacts all family members with whom the patient has frequent contact and invites them to meet at a convenient time. If the family is small, or if contact is infrequent, with only one or two relatives, special efforts are made to involve them. Before meeting, the clinician makes sure that he or she has met or communicated with the staff treating the patient and is aware of the latest clinical status of the patient. The patient is, however, not included in these sessions unless he or she is well compensated and capable of tolerating a discussion of his or her condition as an illness. Since the greatest advantages for successful family engagement seem to exist in the early days of an acute hospitalization, it is rare that patients participate in these meetings.

The assessment process can be conceived as a triad: (1) crisis assessment, (2) eliciting of the family's reactions to the illness and the treatment system, and (3) a brief evaluation of the family as family. Each will be described in turn.

Evaluating the Present Crisis

The initial task is to determine the present state of affairs. This includes getting a clear picture from each family member of what he or she has observed of the patient's decompensation, what the person thinks might trigger the relapse, and what early prodromal signs of decompensation are. Further, the clinician gathers information about coincidental events that are stressful to the family members and how these affect their coping with the psychosis. The contracting process begins at this point by asking what kinds of help the relatives would like to receive from the treatment team.

Eliciting Family Reactions to the Illness and Treatment System

This part of the evaluation involves taking a kind of emotional history of the specific effects that the patient's illness has had on each family member. The technique is straightforward empathic inquiry: usually, families find great relief in unburdening themselves about the toll in fear, anxiety, confusion, and sense of loss that this condition exacts. It is important to be aware of the way in which each individual has attempted to cope with these stresses, while also assessing the personal resources in the family. The variety of responses is great: the most common include centering of attention on the patient, denial of severity, suppression of grief, sacrifice of personal pleasures and ambitions to provide protection and control, and anger and frustration with the patient and treatment system. Because of the last of these negative reactions, it is important to communicate to family members that the program described here will avoid dealing with family members in anything other than a respectful, supportive, and collaborative manner.

Evaluation of the Family and Social System

To prepare the way for reducing ambient stress for the patient and family members, the family clinician needs to have a general sense of the interactional style, structural alliances, spe-

---

[10] *Editors' Note.* While the purposes and organization of much of what occurs in PE assessment *are* quite distinct from those of other approaches, building working alliances and conveying genuine interest in the family certainly are universal requirements of the early phase of all psychotherapy and family therapy.

cific communication patterns, coping strategies, and extended-family and social-network resources of the family as a whole. This will involve taking a brief genogram; asking about who spends time, or tends to interact, with whom; watching for difficulties or strengths in communication (especially clarity of content, ability to listen, and acknowledgment of others' comments and feelings); asking about contacts with friends, relatives, and outside social or community groups; finding out about sources of enjoyment and distraction; and ascertaining recent life events and changes in household membership, even if these represent desirable outcomes. Pains must be taken to avoid any implication that the family's functioning is what triggers the patient's episodes.

Finally, if the intent is that the family join a multiple-family group (MFG), a brief inquiry should be made into feelings about this format. At a time of crisis, some families will not tend to view sharing experiences with others with enthusiasm. Also, it is useful to know about any previous group experiences (especially if they were negative) or aspects of family life—other than the illness itself—of which the members might feel ashamed and any concurrent or past participation in self-help groups. The picture that emerges can then guide the clinician in deciding how best to frame the MFG as useful to the specific needs of a given family.

GOAL SETTING

A salient feature of the psychoeducational model of treatment is that the goals of treatment are explicit and openly negotiated with all participants.[11] In the treatment of schizophrenia, Anderson's single-family and the author's multiple-family approaches have two overriding goals: the prevention of relapse and the gradual integration

of the patient into the highest possible degree of community participation. For a given case, these goals are the starting point for negotiating specific goals with the patient and family. They are sequential in their implementation, but also circularly interdependent: improved functioning is impossible without first establishing symptomatic stability and "stress resilience," which appears only gradually with the passage of time in remission.

There are several secondary goals that apply in almost all cases:

1. Establishing a treatment team that includes key family members and that addresses the clinical goals stated above.
2. Managing the family's interaction and impinging stresses in a way that keeps family burden to a minimum.
3. Providing information about the psychiatric disorder of concern and laying out a set of clear, workable guidelines for family members to follow, to achieve the main goals.
4. Providing continuity of care for patient and family.
5. Developing an enduring social network that supports the family and clinical goals, either through resurrection or expansion of the family's natural network (in SFPE) or through the organization of a network of affected families by the clinical team (in MFPE).

Having established some general objectives, there is another process of goal setting that follows from the goal of establishing the treatment team: the clinician gathers from all family members, patient included, what they hope to achieve by exerting themselves on behalf of the treatment effort. Because some family goals— that the patient resume working immediately, that he or she become independent of all support, that the patient be without symptoms— may be unrealistic, a respectful negotiation between the clinician and family members will be required to set more realistic versions of the family's goals. Fortunately, for most families, agreement about goals is readily achieved, because what they want is usually what the approach is designed to do: prolong remission and enhance day-to-day functioning. Goals that do not relate directly to patient remission and rehabilitation are usually postponed until the pa-

---

[11] *Editors' Note.* While PE is not, per se, a form of behavioral treatment, in the sense of being steeped in the views of learning theory, PE probably does have more explicit commonalities with behavior therapy than with any other family approach: in addition to the ways in which treatment goals are negotiated, both approaches place a heavy emphasis on the empirical research base for their interventions (cf. Falloon, Chapter 3; Holtzworth-Munroe & Jacobson, Chapter 4).

tient has found a functional niche in the community.

From the goal-setting process, a contract emerges that sets conditions for the patient's discharge from the hospital, agreements about frequency of sessions and participation in the meetings, an approximate length of treatment, and the agreed-upon treatment goals. In most applications of the approach, the clinician needs to make clear that he or she will be available to the family for crisis intervention as necessary, and to represent the family's interests and concerns to the treatment system. This includes a commitment to act as the patient's case manager, especially in making decisions about, and arranging for, ancillary services.

Problems that interfere with any member's being able to help or participate can be the focus of intermediate goals. Of concern are practical obstacles, especially transportation, baby-sitting, scheduling, medical illness, and the like. For those going into an MFG, the contract should include a commitment (1) to give the group format a fair trial, (2) to attend regularly, (3) to communicate any problems about group attendance to the leaders, and (4) to try to give and receive help from other families and patients.

THE STRUCTURE OF THE THERAPY PROCESS

Format and Social Structure of Sessions

A fundamental tenet of this model follows from the research on schizophrenia that implicates interpersonal and environmental stress—here translated as emotional intensity and rapid change—as the principal risks predisposing to relapse. Each phase of the approach has different optimal arrangements, depending on the specific needs of the patient and the treatment goals that apply during that phase.

Joining Phase

During the joining phase, which typically occurs during an acute episode and hospitalization, the goal is quickly to develop a supportive and informed alliance with all the relevant members of the family. Meetings, usually without the patient present, should occur frequently and be flexible in duration, averaging an hour in length. These often help to allay the family's anxiety and, by diminishing the intensity of communication from family to patient, contribute to more rapid recompensation of the patient. If the clinicians, usually two in number, have decided to conduct a PEMFG, the usual procedure is that each engages roughly half the families, on a single-family basis, until the educational workshop occurs. Also, it is desirable to have one single-family joint session with both clinicians during this phase. During this phase, as well, the family clinician holds short and less frequent sessions with the patient alone to foster an alliance and acceptance of the intent and direction of treatment; these sessions are supportive and empathic, and definitely *not* actively psychodynamic or exploratory.

Educational Workshop

The family clinicians, after engaging a small number of families, conduct an educational workshop for them, preferably as a multifamily meeting, usually lasting most of a day, and usually on a weekend. (See "Techniques in Psychoeducation" for a full description.) The workshop is specifically for family members and friends of the patient; patients are not usually invited, unless they are exceptionally well compensated and are not delusional or denying illness. The clinicians working with the families conduct the workshop, assisted by the psychiatrist(s) treating the patients. Experience suggests that the optimal size is from four to seven families, which seems to be the ideal range for an ongoing PEMFG.

The format for these workshops differs dramatically from that of therapy sessions. They proceed in an informal lecture-and-discussion fashion, with a classroom-type seating arrangement. Audiovisual aids are used extensively, particularly to illustrate concepts of brain function, medication effects, and symptoms and signs. In the author's workshops, the biological information is presented via a professional-quality videotape with frequent breaks for questions and discussion. The family clinicians then present a number of guidelines for the management of schizophrenia—"survival skills," as Anderson (1983) calls them— followed by an open-ended discussion (see Figure 11-1). During breaks and over lunch, there is ample opportunity for informal social contact between families and between families and clinicians.

While some teams have elected to have the educational function carried out by "specialists in family education," the author's experience suggests that having the actual treating clinicians conduct the workshop has enormous clinical benefits. The main advantage is that the clinicians have ample opportunity to demonstrate their authority as experts and, because each MFPE clinician has had joining contact with but a few of the families attending, all group members have a chance to begin to make an alliance with the other clinician. Similarly, the value of having the treating physicians involved cannot be overemphasized, because families rightly continue to see them as crucial to the management of illnesses.

Reentry and Social-Vocational Rehabilitation Phases

Session structure in the phases after the workshop is more familiar to family therapists. In SFPE, one clinician meets with the family, now including the patient whenever possible, while in MFPE, the same families who attended the workshop together, again with the important addition of patients, begin meeting with both clinicians on a regular basis. Single-family sessions are usually an hour in duration; MFG sessions are usually 1-½ hours, and sometimes longer. In both formats, meetings take place two weeks apart, although some PEMFGs will need to meet weekly for four to six weeks to establish cohesion. These basic formats are continued for at least 12 months. Frequently, once the rehabilitation phase has reached a plateau, usually after 18–24 months, it becomes possible to reduce the frequency of sessions to three- or four-week intervals.

The decision to reduce the frequency of sessions is linked closely to the issue of termination. It depends on family preference, degree of patient improvement, and, in PEMFGs, the sense of the group about continuation for social and personal support purposes. Most families, particularly those in PEMFGs, seem to want to continue at a low level of intensity for extended periods. Many PEMFGs evolve into quasi-natural social networks; "real" interpersonal relationships develop and continue through and outside the group. Increasingly, the author has seen as a central goal of the PE approach the

---

Here is a list of things everyone can do to make things run more smoothly:

1. *Go slow.* Recovery takes time. Rest is important. Things will get better in their own time.

2. *Keep it cool.* Enthusiasm is normal. Tone it down. Disagreement is normal. Tone it down, too.

3. *Give 'em space.* Time out is important for everyone. It's okay to offer. It's okay to refuse.

4. *Set limits.* Everyone needs to know what the rules are. A few good rules keep things calmer.

5. *Ignore what you can't change.* Let some things slide. Don't ignore violence or use of street drugs.

6. *Keep it simple.* Say what you have to say clearly, calmly, and positively.

7. *Follow doctor's orders.* Take medications as they are prescribed. Take *only* medications that are prescribed.

8. *Carry on business as usual.* Reestablish family routines as quickly as possible. Stay in touch with family and friends.

9. *No street drugs or alcohol.* They make symptoms worse.

10. *Pick up on early signs.* Note changes. Consult with your family clinician.

11. *Solve problems step by step.* Make changes gradually. Work on one thing at a time.

12. *Lower expectations, temporarily.* Use a personal yardstick. Compare this month with last month rather than with last year or next year.

Figure 11-1. Family guidelines

establishment of such support networks, because they may be essential to preserving and enhancing the gains made during the active therapeutic phases.

Structure of Sessions

The internal structure of sessions in both formats has evolved in the light of experience. In general, most psychoeducational sessions proceed fairly strictly according to Figure 11-2. This approach is surprisingly effective in either a single-family or multiple-family context. It has become clear that a rather standardized, predictable structure is beneficial, especially during the acute episode and immediate posthospital discharge phases, as a means for the clinician to maintain benign control over sessions. Families and patients are usually anxious and uncertain and often desperate for quick solutions to nearly overwhelming contextual and psychiatric difficulties. To the extent that patients and family members have difficulty controlling affect or tracking a conversation, the problem-solving approach provides an acceptable rationale for bringing errant participants back to the topic.

While the therapeutic core of this sequence consists of *steps 4–10*, *steps 1–3* are essential. In essence, the clinician makes an emphatic attempt to avoid beginning the session with laments from anyone about any negative events or feelings. To do this, it is often necessary for the clinician to inquire specifically about enjoyable or novel events in the family's life, even if they seem trivial. Further, the clinician may take the lead by describing similar kinds of events in his or her own life. In single- and multifamily formats, it is important to hear from everyone, even if a given patient or family member can make only a brief or superficial contribution. The emphasis is on setting an optimistic, accepting, warm, and inclusive tone as preparation for what follows—direct, and sometimes more stressful, attention to illness-induced problems.

The *second and third steps* involve reviewing the success or shortcomings of the task assigned in the previous meeting. In addition, it is helpful to inquire about other intervening events to assess unforeseen stresses on the family or patient. In the PEMFG, each family should have an opportunity to report progress or untoward occurrences, so that the clinician can make an informed decision about which family may need

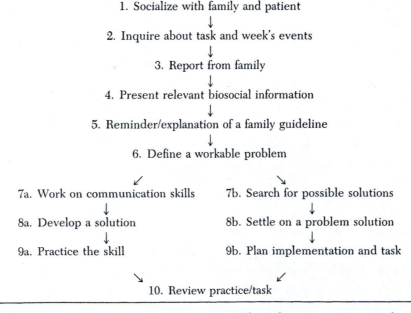

Structure of the average session

1. Socialize with family and patient
↓
2. Inquire about task and week's events
↓
3. Report from family
↓
4. Present relevant biosocial information
↓
5. Reminder/explanation of a family guideline
↓
6. Define a workable problem

7a. Work on communication skills   7b. Search for possible solutions
↓   ↓
8a. Develop a solution   8b. Settle on a problem solution
↓   ↓
9a. Practice the skill   9b. Plan implementation and task

10. Review practice/task

Figure 11-2. Psychoeducation in schizophrenia— core paradigm for treatment in single- and multifamily contexts

problem-solving efforts during the present group session.

Step 4 involves placing the problem implicit in the report in a perspective that relates it to the realities of schizophrenia as an illness. It depends on the clinician's knowledge of effective strategies for managing various aspects of the recovery and rehabilitation process. In general, this involves relating psychosocial phenomena to their likely consequences for an individual with schizophrenia. Most clinicians focus on attention and arousal or the effects of symptoms and medication on cognition and behavior. (See the section on "Techniques" for a fuller explanation of the rationale and technique for these interventions.)

Step 5 follows directly from *step 4*. If a problem is present because of symptomatic or disability aspects of a disorder, then the general approach to a solution is suggested by one or more of the guidelines put forth in the educational workshop. In other words, *steps 4 and 5* are closely linked: most problems occur as a result of more or less obvious effects of the disorder and can be addressed through one or two of a number of clinically reliable methods. In PEMFGs, with time clinicians will find that they can ask other family members to suggest which guideline is likely to be relevant. The attempt here is to induce a sense of control and clarity that sets an optimal tone for the specific problem solving that follows.

Steps 6–10 follow well-tested problem-solving and communication-skills approaches refined by Falloon and Anderson. Because these are the technical core of the PE approach, their implementation in single- and multifamily formats is described in the section on "Psychoeducational Techniques."

Medication Issues

The role of antipsychotic medication is central to the PE approach to schizophrenia and mood disorder. The assumption is made and reinforced consistently throughout the course of therapy that maintenance medication is a cornerstone of recovery and successful rehabilitation. More specifically, resistance to environmental overstimulation is greatly enhanced by antipsychotics and, except in unusually calm, friendly, simple, and unpressured contexts, most patients require that protection to lead any semblance of a normal life.

The PE approach depends on, or strives to create, a collaborative working relationship among patient, family, psychiatrist, and family clinician(s). In every phase of treatment, channels of communication must remain open between all members of the therapeutic team. For that reason, the psychiatrist should be familiar with the fundamental precepts of PE, especially the emphasis on a slow, gradual recovery and the need to monitor environmental stresses and symptom level, adjusting drug dosage to prevent reactive resurgence of symptoms. The family clinician assumes an intermediary role, evaluating patient status on the basis of the wealth of information available from family members and ancillary therapists and relaying it to the physician. This process is enhanced if the psychiatrist joins the session periodically, particularly if it is a PEMFG, to use the naturalistic aspect of the therapy context to better gauge dosage needs.

Because noncompliance with medication is a major cause of relapse and yet so common, a great deal of the educational material in PE methods focuses on the rationale for drug treatment, while the ongoing work involves defining compliance as facilitating specific goals of the patient and family. The clinician must first convince family members to accept the value of medication and then to support the prescribed regimen. For particularly noncompliant patients, this can even take the form of requiring medication as a condition for being allowed to be discharged from the hospital and to return to the family household. More commonly, supporting the family members to reinforce their requests that the patient continue the regimen is sufficient.

THE ROLE OF THE THERAPIST

In PE work with families, the clinician is generally active in setting the agenda for sessions and directly providing most of the guidance for the family's handling of the major illness-related problems. In this approach, it is assumed that, on the one hand, the clinician knows more about generic methods for managing mental illness than the family or patient, while, on the other hand, the family and patient know more about what they have been through, what works for them, and how to solve problems creatively. Thus, the meta assumption is that the combination of the patient's hopes, the family's experience and creativity, and the clinicians' expertise and skills are the irreducible amalgam necessary to manage a major mental illness. The MFPE modality adds the unique contribution of other families and patients as additional resources for support and ideas.

In practical terms, the clinician's role changes with the phase of recovery. During the acute episode, the task is to reach out actively to family members and the patient to begin the creation of a collaborative team. In the educational phase, the clinicians are teachers and experts, while in less obvious ways they enhance their connection with family members and, in MFPE, the connection between members of different families. In the reentry phase, the single-family clinician takes charge of helping family members to understand and apply family guidelines and then to guide them and act as an idea resource during problem-solving efforts. When indicated, the clinician also may choose to intervene actively to change communication patterns when the existing process precludes problem solving. Also, this phase requires a more conventional clinical role as the monitor of the level of symptoms in the service of relapse prevention.

MFPE clinicians during the reentry phase have a more complex task: to create cohesion in the MFG and, once achieved, to use multifamily problem-solving and communication-skills techniques to achieve relapse prevention and clinical stability. Further, they must decide when to intervene on a single-family basis to deal with a crisis, impending dropout, special issues that a family feels it cannot discuss in the MFG, or especially complex case-management and entitlement problems. To do all this requires active intervention in the problem-solving process while also promoting the highest possible degree of interfamily activity. What makes it feasible is the division of labor between the two clinicians: usually, one concentrates on tracking the process of the problem-solving efforts and the other on alternative solutions for the problem at hand.

The clinician's role in the rehabilitation phase is similar to that for reentry. The focus is on setting tasks that carefully increase the patient's responsibilities and social activity in carefully graduated steps. Simultaneously, the clinician monitors the patient for reemergence of symptoms that may herald a stimulus overload situation. Here, responsibility is shared more equally between clinician and family: the clinician structures the session while the patient and family carry out the task between sessions. In MFGs the clinicians share the problem-solving process with other families, often making the sequencing and tracking of problem-solving activity their only therapeutic focus—the specifics are left to the families to work out, with occasional input as indicated or as requested by family members and patients. As patients gradually achieve functional goals, the MFPE clinicians shift actively to promoting social network development among the families in the group.

At the emotional level, the role of PE clinicians is distinct from that in other family therapies. Because the family is defined as a collaborator in the treatment of the patient, the natural relationship between its members and the clinician(s) is one of collegiality, friendliness, sharing, negotiation, and openness. To the extent that the clinician also must address the emotional reactions of families to the illness and the loss of the ill relative's potential, the proper emotional stance is one of empathy and validation. Socially, the clinician must remain on the side of the family and patient, even when that means having to advocate for their interests within the mental health and social welfare systems.[12] Finally, throughout the problem-solving and task-assignment processes, the clinicians assume full responsibility, overtly and explicitly, whenever the outcome is less than what was intended. This may help to save family and patient from feeling guilty or demoralized.

A word on tone seems needed. To the extent possible, the clinician should adopt the low-key, unflappable, and warm style that is advocated

---

[12] *Editors' Note.* Fulfilling this less-than-traditional role for a family clinician can certainly be enhanced by the perspective on dealing with families at the interface of larger social systems set forth by Imber-Black (Chapter 19), significant differences between many assumptions in the two points of view notwithstanding.

for families in their dealings with the patient. The goal is to reduce the level of stimulation for the patient to the optimal point, including during sessions.

TECHNIQUES IN PSYCHOEDUCATION

Compared with family therapies, the techniques used in psychoeducation are deliberately simple and applied openly, with a full explanation.[13] To the extent possible, the goals of treatment are established by the patient and family, the methods of illness management are presented by the therapist elaborately and explicitly at the outset of treatment, and the primary techniques leading to change are education, problem solving, and task assignment. For that reason, psychoeducation is perhaps the most linear of family therapies, and is intentionally so. The assumption is that, given information and advice, families will attempt to apply them to aid in the patient's recovery and rehabilitation. The PE approach assumes that resistance is the result of clinician error, usually from inadequate joining or from setting treatment goals or tasks that are ill advised or at least premature. The rest of this chapter describes the salient methods commonly used to carry out the treatment goals, especially to build a treatment alliance and put in practice the family guidelines. The techniques are organized by phase, although those used in each phase overlap extensively.

Joining

Previous sections on assessment and the role of the clinician have described the most important aspects of the joining phase. Beyond the supportive and engaging effects of active listening, the approach depends heavily on two technical points. The first involves eliciting from each family member his or her own particular responses to the illness. For most families, this invitation to disclose what are sometimes seen as shameful feelings is the first they will have had from a professional. The effect is often to reexperience emotions that relatives have suppressed for a long time and that often distort both individual and family functioning.

The task for the clinician is primarily to listen to these expressions, accept them nonjudgmentally, and validate their reasonableness and power. Many PE clinicians have found it useful to share some of their own frustrations with the illness, without suggesting that they relate to the patient in question. It will prove useful to gain a sense of which specific symptoms or behaviors are most troubling to a particular relative. Tactically, it is especially important to allow family members to express anger and exasperation, toward both the patient and the treatment system. Doing so during joining sessions will reduce the likelihood that such feelings will emerge later when the patient is present.

The other crucial intervention in the joining phase is to allow family members to express their sense of loss, to begin or further the mourning of their ill relative's unfulfilled potential. Families vary widely in the degree to which they have accepted the extent of the illness and its effects on the qualities or abilities they most admired in the patient. Using straightforward and sensitive inquiry, the clinicians encourage each member to recount his or her favorite memories of the patient in the premorbid period or as a child. Then, they validate as real and painful the difference that relatives see between the present state and those more positive memories. Usually, this leads to expressions of sadness and something analogous to mourning. While it is unlikely that a completion of mourning will occur during the joining phase, validating the family's sense of loss will help families to continue, and often complete, the mourning process in later sessions.

Other important interventions in the joining phase that clinicians might employ are:

1. To state specifically and explicitly that the rationale for meeting with the family is their concern for the patient's welfare, their expertise on the specifics of the patient's situation, and their power to assist the recovery process, and not because family interaction is a cause of the disorder.

2. To explore and validate family strengths, es-

---

[13] *Editors' Note.* Again, note the similarities in this paragraph between psychoeducational and behavioral marital and family treatment approaches.

pecially the family members' continuing hope and concern, stamina, tolerance, and cooperation in meeting with the clinical team. Further, if the family has developed effective coping strategies, to congratulate the family members in their creativity and to offer to help to reinforce them in the reentry phase.

3. To build a sense of hope and optimism by communicating (a) the clinician's commitment to work with them over an extended period and (b) information about the efficacy of family psychoeducational approaches and long-term-outcome research findings.

Educational Workshop

A few technical recommendations have emerged for conducting an educational program for families. The leaders should take frequent breaks during the presentation of material to answer questions from family members and to ask them if they understand the information presented, whether they have had similar experiences, and whether the rationale for the family guidelines make sense to them. Further, if the intent is to use the workshop as the first meeting for a PEMFG, eliciting responses common to several families' members will begin to reduce social isolation and build group cohesion, making overt the shared realities implicit in the group.

For best results, the workshop should be held on one day, rather than in separate meetings, to build intensity and assure that all information is conveyed to all the participants. That format makes possible a lunch break that the clinicians should use as an opportunity to solidify their social relationships with families and to encourage social linkages among the various families attending. The latter is especially important as the first step in a PEMFG.

The information conveyed in the workshop is a powerful intervention; it empowers families, reduces guilt, lays a conceptual foundation for work on recovery and rehabilitation, and affects the level of expressed emotion. Figure 11-1 provided a list of guidelines presented to family members to use in fostering treatment goals. What follows is a brief explication of the guidelines themselves. In essence, they are designed

to interrupt the attention-arousal cycle by lowering the stimulus load the patient receives from the family and home environment and from outside the family, derived from life events.

1. *"Go slow."* By reducing the family's expectations for a rapid return of full functioning, the stimulation inherent in excessive pressure will be eliminated or reduced. This takes the practical form of letting patients rest extensively, if needed, after returning home, until they spontaneously take an interest in increasing their level of activity and responsibility, as in the gradual recovery from any severe illness.

2. *"Keep it cool."* The attention-arousal model implies that families should try to take a relaxed, low-key stance in relating to the patient, especially during the recovery phase. This guideline warns against too much criticism about things over which the patient may have little control, whether that be agitation or extreme lethargy and withdrawal. Conversely, excessive enthusiasm is possibly detrimental, because of its stimulation potential and because patients may perceive it as condescension.

3. *"Give them space."* This point emphasizes that to reduce stimulation and prevent relapse, the environment must be kept simple and calm. So, up to a point, patients may need to withdraw from contact for several hours, or even days, if they feel vulnerable to overload. Families should continue offering contact and joint activity, but should not expect it if the patient seems unable to tolerate it.

4. *"Set limits."* The clinicians set forth the principle that families should proscribe violence, suicidal gestures, and disruptively bizarre behavior and should follow through. The intent is to clarify boundaries and reduce the level of uncertainty and struggle at home, usually reinforcing the parents' and siblings' role as caretakers who need and deserve a minimum of peace and quiet to survive in the long run. It is important to link clear family structure with a lower level of ambient stress and with societal expectations that will apply once the patient begins to reenter the outside world.

5. *"Ignore what you can't change."* Because

many family members become excessively preoccupied with symptoms and their daily fluctuations, increasing interaction and stress for everyone, the clinicians suggest that family members ignore them unless they are increasing rapidly or are reappearing after a long absence. Delusions are of special interest. Families should avoid discussion of delusional content and focus on the emotional effects the delusions have on the patient—fear, anxiety, and the like; that is, they should be sympathetic but not instructional.

6. *"Keep it simple."* Because even highly intelligent but partially recovered patients have marked impairments of attention and cognition, family members need to keep communication clear, straightforward, and at a moderate level of specificity. Arousing topics—such as religion, politics, and sex—should be avoided. Requests should be made clearly, using the "I" statement format, rather than as criticisms of present or past behavior. Whenever possible, the tone should be positive and friendly.

7. *"Follow the doctor's orders."* The workshop emphasizes the idea that recovery depends on medication to reduce vulnerability to relapse. For those families ambivalent about medication, the clinicians reinforce the importance of family support for the medication program and their potential role as sources of information about the patient's clinical status.

8. *"Carry on business as usual."* To counteract the tendency for families to become exhausted, demoralized, or rejecting, this point emphasizes the need for them to maintain social contacts, hobbies, work interests, and marital enjoyment as antidotes. This links conceptually to reducing attention directed toward the patient, thereby further fostering recovery.

9. *"No street drugs or alcohol."* Though it may seem self-evident, this point needs to be made explicit, because families differ in their tolerance for substance abuse. Some may elect to permit relapse-inducing chemical ingestion rather than to set limits and cooperate with the team in convincing the patients of the dangers of illicit drugs and alcohol. Others may simply be unaware

of the psychosis-inducing effects of these agents.

10. *"Pick up on early signs."* The possibility of heading off a relapse in its earliest stages is far greater than when actual psychotic symptoms have recurred. Once the family has clarified what the specific signs of impending relapse are in a given patient, the clinician encourages them to report their reemergence quickly as a major bulwark in the relapse-prevention component of the approach.

Community Reentry

Given that the goal for this phase of treatment is the prevention of relapse of psychotic symptoms and rehospitalization, its objectives follow directly from the guidelines and their underlying principles: to succeed, reduce the stimulus load presented to the patient and foster a slow, gradual recovery of functioning. The result will usually be enhanced resilience in the face of stress.

This phase continues until those objectives seem securely achieved, usually heralded by the return of "spontaneous signs of life," as Anderson describes them (personal communication). What usually happens is that the PE approach is able to prevent relapse, especially when the patient can recuperate for several months with minimal pressures and expectations. Then, he or she will begin to seem interested in taking on a new role, seeing a friend, attending a social event, and so on. If this new behavior is not overly ambitious and occurs without the reemergence of symptoms, the clinician can assume that the reentry process has been successfully completed. There is wide variation in the length of time this process may take, ranging from two months to 18 months, depending on the severity and duration of illness, previous functioning, medication response and compliance, and how well the family is able to apply the guidelines.

Themes that come into focus during this phase include (1) recognizing early signs of relapse, (2) bolstering interpersonal and intergenerational boundaries, (3) setting limits on intolerable behavior, (4) finding methods to assure medication compliance, (5) attempting in-home and, later, out-of-home trials of increased responsibility and social activity, and (6) dealing with dangerous and suicidal behavior. The techniques used in dealing with each of these issues are similar— each is linked to the biological or contextual aspect that may be problematic, and the clinician invokes the appropriate guideline and leads a problem-solving process. The latter is described in detail in this *Handbook* in Chapter 3 on behavioral family therapy and will not be repeated here. The major modification required for the PEMFG approach involves getting as much input from other families as possible, especially in the "problem-solution-proposal" portion of the process.

Social and Vocational Rehabilitation

After roughly one year of slow, gradual, and stepwise recovery, if relapse has not intervened and the patient appears to be more interested in reengaging in community life, the treatment shifts to a rehabilitation mode.[14] This phase is roughly similar in its execution to the previous phase, except that the roles of the clinician and family members are rather different. Whereas the general rule was to avoid relapse at all costs and the family attempted to reduce its performance expectations, the emphasis here is on applying carefully modulated pressure to increase the patient's responsibilities and to foster a more active social life.

In the vocational arena, the PE approach builds on the small tasks mastered previously to begin the patient's search for a job or an appropriate sheltered work opportunity and a wider-ranging social life. Here, patients play a more active role in the sessions, because one needs to capitalize on their natural interests and abilities. Initially, family members may help by offering part-time work in their own places of employment or those of friends. Gradually, however, more and more initiative is left to the patient. The family members increasingly play the roles of coaches and cheerleaders, though at times they may also need to apply direct pres-

sure to get the patient moving. Throughout, new levels of function are entered with careful planning and patients are monitored for any signs of symptom recurrence or general agitation or withdrawal. If these are increasing rapidly, the plans are abandoned and a month or so allowed to pass before trying again, perhaps at a temporarily lower level of expectation.

The same general approach applies to the effort to expand the patient's social network, confidence, and skills. Because social contacts will be stressful, it is crucial that they be undertaken gradually. After patients have been able to visit relatives at some distance from home, the next step is usually to contact other patients they may have met in treatment programs or workshops. Some will have reliable friends whom they knew before they became ill; these friends will be invaluable because they have a sense of the person in the well state and often are less disturbed by the present deficits. Throughout this phase, problem solving and task assignment can help to move the process along carefully and yet steadily. Nevertheless, progress is often slow and may have to be interspersed with therapeutic work on vocational issues. Finally, only one area—work or social activity—is slated for increasing functioning during this phase.

Specific Techniques in Psychoeducational Multiple-Family Groups

Community Reentry

Leading a PEMFG requires a number of techniques specific to the format itself. Those that have appeared to be most useful are included here.

Throughout the course of the therapy, a degree of latitude should be allowed for family members to engage in small talk or more intense discussion of topics unrelated to the official therapy procedure. Interaction not closely controlled by the therapists should be fostered, rather than inhibited, for up to one quarter of the time in a given group meeting, especially at the beginning of the session. The clinicians should engage in this small talk as freely as possible without dominating it.

MFGs with a relatively stable membership

---

[14] *Editors' Note.* It is interesting that a self-described "linear" approach to therapy aims to bring about such significant second-order (Guttman, Chapter 2) changes.

that are conducted over long periods typically go through phases, much as do all persistent social networks. Preferably, a PEMFG assumes a long-term, closed-membership group format, the form that has consistently shown the highest degree of efficacy. The fundamental reason is that much of a PEMFG's effectiveness depends on the formation of a closely knit social network among the families in the group. That takes time, and a minimum degree of consistency of membership, to evolve.

An effective PEMFG moves from one extreme (leader centered) to the other (group centered) over a two-year course. That process is inherent in the MFG, but experience suggests that it is more effective to exaggerate these extremes in groups for schizophrenic patients and their families. In the beginning, the group is markedly dependent on the therapists, with respect to both process and content. By the last phase, the leaders become almost optional and, therefore, must be comfortable with an unusually peripheral role.

Technique in the early months of the first phase involves beginning with predominately leader–group-member interactions. The style of the clinicians here is a gradual alteration of the lecture-discussion format of the educational sessions. Only when spontaneous interfamily interaction begins to take place should the orientation become more group centered. Group members' dissatisfaction with the leader-centered style, manifested by directing comments to one another or openly initiating more group discussion of the workshop content and/or guidelines, is a good indication that the group is sufficiently cohesive that a more intensive interfamily process is apt to be therapeutic.

Then, the process gradually shifts to implementation of the family guidelines, using a more task-oriented and group-centered leadership style. The leaders use whatever issues are of concern as a vehicle for teaching the problem-solving approach, which increasingly is focused on one or another family in the PEMFG. Other families' members contribute possible solutions and "pros and cons" to the problem-solving process. Repeated discussion of the key family guidelines occurs in relation to almost all problems raised by families. The activity of the leaders shifts from initiation of the therapeutic work to facilitating and guiding or tracking it. Increas-

ingly, the patients contribute as equal partners in socializing and problem solving, especially when the clinicians model seeking their input. This stage should include the use of cross-family linkage techniques. For example, the leaders may ask a specific mother how she reacted to her son's psychosis, then ask another, then ask the two to compare notes, and then generalize to other mothers, asking them similar questions. Specific kinds of interactions can be encouraged as subgroups form. For instance, facilitating discussions of relatives' reactions to the patients' illnesses, followed by the patients' describing their own subjective experiences, is usually deeply moving, while it begins to break down the barriers between families and between patients and their own relatives.

Relaxing boundaries during the subgroup phase can usually be fostered deliberately by emphasizing cross-parenting interventions, which will tend to increase the emergence of family members as individuals in their own right. In this process, parents in one family take an interest in the patient in another family. Gradually, however, these contacts take on the quality of real relationships, like other senior-to-junior–adult bonds, increasingly focusing on healthier aspects of the patient and on his or her functional progress. During the later sessions of this phase, the leaders should begin to take a less central position, using cross-family linkage and group-interpretative techniques to achieve a process transitional between being leader and being fully group centered.

Social and Vocational Rehabilitation

As in the comparable phase of SFPE family work, the second major postworkshop phase, beginning at about 12 months and lasting from six to eight months, focuses on the gradual resumption of responsibility by the patients in the PEMFG, with their own families and the other families in the group collaborating in the effort to enhance the schizophrenic members' psychosocial functioning. The leaders clearly frame this as the task for the group, but should gradually turn over much of the actual implementation of this process to the group, so that family members work with each other across family boundaries.

The dominant technique to be used throughout this phase is cross-family linkage within a problem-solving format. Emphasis is on cross-parenting interaction to enhance the sense of maturity and competence in the patients. The goal is that the family and the PEMFG serve as a bridge of support and encouragement as the patient gradually emerges from the family environment into the more pressured nonfamily world of work and social activity.

A specific function that the PEMFG can serve is to reduce overinvolvement, especially as manifested by excessive protectiveness or overfunctioning on the part of family members. The means for achieving this are relationship substitution, in which relatives' emotional preoccupation with the patient is attenuated by increasing interest in members of other PEMFG families. Occasionally, other families may directly encourage a given family member to be more emphatic in supporting rehabilitation interventions.

Building a Social Network

Again, it is difficult to draw a clear distinction between the second and third postworkshop phases, but after one to two years, the PEMFG gradually begins to take a different direction in terms of both process and content. When the families have achieved significantly more adaptive coping skills and relapses have become rare, the group should require less and less of the leaders, while the members take a genuine interest in each other as friends or quasi-neighbors. The content of discussions may move gradually from issues concerning the patients to general problems facing the mentally ill in the community or marital and personal issues of the nonpatient members. A common theme that emerges is what the parents are going to do with themselves if they need to pay less attention to their schizophrenic offspring. One easy solution should be suggested—to socialize with one another. Thus, the PEMFG is directed to become a social network in which "therapeutic" relationships become "real."

It is at this stage that the leaders can begin increasingly to turn the process over to the group members, while encouraging the development of social connections. The real hallmark of this phase is the beginning of spontaneous outside socializing, both by the whole group and by various (usually unpredictable) combinations of group members. Thus, the clinicians should (1) encourage outside contact of family members; (2) make some sessions, especially at holidays, social occasions; and (3) honor requests for occasional separate subgroup meetings (such as parents' meeting alone) or for meetings in members' homes. One way to handle the later phase is to encourage the group to become allied with one of the national self-help organizations, perhaps even to become the nucleus of a local branch.

MECHANISMS OF CHANGE

Levels of Change

It is not clear from experience to date what the exact process is by which improvement occurs in psychoeducational approaches. That change does take place seems now beyond question, however. In the reported studies of its use for relapsing schizophrenic patients, the one-year relapse rates range from 9 to 19 percent, using similar selection and relapse criteria, random assignment designs involving family PE, and individual supportive therapy and antipsychotic medication in both treatment conditions (Falloon et al., 1985; Goldstein et al., 1978; Hogarty et al., 1986; Leff et al., 1982). Two-year relapse rates vary from 15 to 30 percent. The outcome of MFPE is in the same range, in the studies being conducted by the author, in which the SFPE outcome is less favorable than for MFPE when the former lacks any formalized contact between affected families—that is, the effect of interfamily social support seems to play a role in enhancing efficacy. These rates compare very favorably with those in studies of medication maintenance or medication and individual supportive therapy. In the family studies cited, two-year rates ranged from 69 to 90 percent; a major drug study found a one-year rate of 40 percent, using injectable medication (Hogarty et al., 1979).

These results and clinical experience suggest that change occurs at three levels: for the patient, for the family, and for the family's social network. Outcome appears to be determined by a complex interplay of all three levels. The simplest model has the family influencing the patient and being influenced by the larger social context, including the treatment system and the community. Second, improvement in the patient's condition tends to provide cues for further development of the family's and patient's coping capacity and alterations in the treatment approach, in a classic positive-feedback-loop interaction. In the rest of this section, we will review the principal candidates for factors that seem to produce improvement within this model of treatment.

Variables Affecting Change

Clinical experience provides a short list of factors that appear to correlate with change or rate of change. First, patients who have been ill longer will respond more slowly and probably less dramatically than will younger, less disabled patients, as will those who had a poorer premorbid adjustment and who respond poorly to medication. In our experience, the use of illicit street drugs in significant quantities, even if not producing dependence, will dramatically interfere with achieving a good result, especially in concert with medication noncompliance.

Second, families that (1) lack resources (money, decent and uncrowded housing, and employment opportunities); (2) are small in number (especially single parents); (3) find themselves in stigmatizing, rejecting social networks; and (4) are experiencing many and frequent external stresses will, in general, progress more slowly. The reason is simple. All of these factors must be addressed therapeutically to achieve the treatment goals and doing so consumes the clinicians' time and energy. Families with previous exposure to intensive family therapy are somewhat slower to change, because they tend to view the clinician with suspicion, so that joining proceeds more slowly.

Actual measurements of change in Hogarty and Anderson's studies, as in those conducted by Leff and Falloon, have documented a clear association between change in levels of expressed emotion and remission and social/vocational improvements in the study patients. Further, in Falloon's and Goldstein's projects

there was an even stronger association between the families' mastering of the target coping skills and relapse rates of patients. In another analysis, Falloon noted a significant decrease in the level of reported burden experienced by the family after his behavioral family-management program. (See Chapter 3.)

Third, because schizophrenia and other disorders for which PE models have been tested are usually treated in institutional contexts, the level of support from the allied components of the treatment system will determine outcome. Schizophrenic patients, especially, need other services beyond PE; in fact, in the later phases of the treatment, they become essential as rehabilitation resources for the patient. The solo practitioner working with families as advocated here will need to make special efforts to learn about the resources available for this population in the community and spend a fair amount of effort on developing contacts with them. This is not a model that is usually effective when applied as the only intervention.[15] Finally, at the community level, a high level of stigma and rejection of patients and their families is associated with familial overinvolvement and a poorer outcome (McFarlane, unpublished).

Reducing Ambient Stress and Stimulation

As noted in the section on goals, success in the PE treatment of schizophrenia depends on relapse prevention. Several processes contribute to achieving that end. Perhaps the sine qua non is successful joining with individual families. The validation and reassurance that should be seen in this process greatly relieve anxiety, guilt, anger, and demoralization, simplifying and deintensifying the interaction of patients and their relatives. Consequently, therapists who find they cannot empathize with the emotional agony of the family should consider treating other conditions with other approaches. This phase of treatment is so crucial to outcome that mastering

---

[15] *Editors' Note.* We agree with McFarlane's views on the use of PE in solo practice, and while we would not expect solo practitioners to be as effective as institutional practitioners of PE, we think there is still great value in the individual clinician's adoption of PE principles in dealing with a variety of psychiatric disorders.

it may often require supervision by experienced PE clinicians. Perhaps it goes without saying, but this approach does not rely on neurotic transference or transference interpretations for its success: in fact, the latter are to be avoided altogether.

Education of the Family

It appears that retention of specific information about the illness itself is usually limited and, therefore, unlikely to affect outcome significantly. On the other hand, the metacommunication—that the family does not *cause* it—has a great effect on family guilt, confusion, and tendencies to criticize or push the patient beyond his or her capacities. Instruction about specific coping strategies is also appreciated and often put into action almost immediately, with a positive effect on patient arousal and general clinical status. In MFPE, the workshop format is crucial as a low-stress method for beginning to build group cohesion, which in itself further reduces family isolation, stigma, and self-blame. It tends to allow the PEMFG to begin in a calmer and more focused manner, making patient attendance less stressful and more therapeutic. In both treatment formats, the completion of mourning the loss of the patient's mental health seems to prepare the way for interfamily relationships and effective problem solving.

Effects of Ongoing Family Intervention

Alterations of Family Interaction

In MFPE and SFPE, it is possible to identify the crucial interventions that appear to prevent relapse. Directly coaching relatives in lowering the level of intensity, frequency, and complexity of their interactions with the patient, even if only partially successful, has visible effects on clinical symptoms and rate of recovery. The same can be said of limit setting, especially when it is part of a general effort to put the parents in charge of the ill offspring. In those families in which communication tends toward fragmentation or blame, basic training in communication skills

usually contributes to the outcome by lowering criticism and raising clarity and warmth.

In MFPE, relaxation of family boundaries in the PEMFG effectively reduces intrusiveness and excessive involvement by gradually fostering replacement of intrafamily, patient-focused interaction with interfamily relationships. While it evolves slowly, this process proceeds smoothly, at a pace that is comfortable for the participants. When interaction involves a patient in one family and well members of another family, the effects on the patient's social functioning and the relatives' morale are usually impressive.

Controlling the Rate of Change

Central to the effectiveness of the PE approach to schizophrenia is the effort to control the rate of change experienced by the patient. The first element that seems to be necessary is convincing the family to decrease its expectations for the patient. A period of rest after an acute episode induces a natural recovery process that is hastened at great risk. While many relatives balk at this approach, most become convinced by the results. After several months, most patients do indeed begin to seek a higher level of activity, which the family and clinician can direct into constructive channels. Thus, the one-step-at-time technique, gradual increases in responsibilities and socialization, the anticipation and handling of effects of life events, and the use of carefully monitored pressure by family and clinician all contribute to the effort to promote a modulated rate of change and the optimal balance of stimulation.

Social-Network Formation

Beginning with the educational workshop and its potential as the beginning of group cohesion and ending with the conversion of the PEMFG to a self-help/advocacy group, the multifamily format allows for the maximum degree of retention of gains made in the active treatment phase. Central to this effort are the encouragement of social contacts between participating families, the validation of group social and problem-solving interactions during PEMFG sessions and, when indicated, the gradual replacement of problem solving by socialization. An approximation can be achieved in the SF approach by a strong effort to restore the family's natural social network, but there appear to be limits to the effectiveness of that approach (Anderson, 1983).

Termination Issues

It is probably too early in the development of this general approach to be clear about what constitutes an appropriate termination, especially given the chronicity of most cases of schizophrenia. It seems that many families fully learn the guidelines and move on to other interests, often into advocacy for the mentally ill. Some drop out prematurely, often when the clinicians agree that they have failed to effect an optimal outcome. Between these extremes are the great majority of families who, in conjunction with the clinicians, decide that continued but infrequent contact—monthly or bimonthly—is sufficient. On the other hand, because of their generally pleasant social aspects, many families in PEMFGs appear to want to continue participation indefinitely. The author has found that long-term outcome is greatly enhanced by the continuation of families in PEMFGs for at least two years, and preferably three.

SPECIAL ISSUES IN MARITAL THERAPY

Theoretical Considerations

For those conditions that seem amenable to treatment with PE approaches, most of the theoretical rationale and techniques will apply in a general way to married couples. Particularly as related to joining with the well spouse, providing information and guidelines, and developing an ongoing collaborative treatment program, there are many benefits to be expected, whether or not the couple is in conflict.

At the practical level, however, a number of complications present themselves. First, most schizophrenic patients are not married, by virtue of the usual age of onset of the illness and its devastating effects on social skills and the tolerance for intimacy. Second, male married patients tend to be paranoid and often uncooperative in treatment and suspicious of the intention of clinicians. Third, female married patients are usually separated from their husbands, because of the effects of the illness on both relatedness and role performance. Thus, for the application most suited to PE—in schizophrenia—there are few cases where a marital format is likely to be relevant. Anderson's experience has been that in the few cases where the approach was practicable, the results were promising (personal communication, 1985).

The general issue is the intersection between marital problems engendered by the spouse's illness and those that are inherent to the couple's previous relationship. Given the episodic and often deteriorating course of schizophrenia, there is a high likelihood that an unequal, caretaking relationship evolves once a major mental illness begins. In PE, there is a strong tendency to reinforce that complementarity until recovery is sufficient to begin establishing a more equal functional balance. This is particularly difficult for some spouses, for whom the prolonged loss of affect and spontaneity, as well as the inability to contribute financially and instrumentally, represents a direct deprivation. Consequently, the tendency to pressure the patient, either emotionally or functionally, is strong. Add to that the inherent ill effects of conflict and emotional intensity and the risks for relapse in the ill spouse, and for deep dissatisfaction and confusion in the well spouse, are great.

Assessment

The areas to review in evaluating a couple in which one member is mentally ill include the style and functional status of the marriage previous to the initial episode, the aspects of the relationship in which the well spouse feels especially deprived and resentful, the functional effects of the illness on the marriage and parenting, and the willingness of the well spouse to forestall full functioning in favor of a gradual return to maximum possible functioning. Clearly, a review of conflicts, sexual dysfunction, and communication problems is necessary, both because these may interfere with the treatment program and because they may have to be addressed at a later phase.

Goals

The goals of PE for a married couple often involve more flexibility on the part of the clinician. Usually, the demands on the ill spouse have an irreducible quality that has to be respected and worked around. Therefore, "going slow" may mean going back to work, but doing everything possible to insulate the patient from any other pressures or stimulation. The same may apply where the well spouse wants more companionship: partial satisfaction of this desire may become a treatment goal as a means of maintaining the optimum atmosphere at home, even though this may present a degree of stimulus overload. Thus, the couple's goals are more likely to be accepted at face value than in a family-of-origin case. Fortunately, many married schizophrenic patients are less disabled than their unmarried counterparts and can often withstand the pursuit of a more ambitious set of goals.

Technical Differences

As implied above, the primary difference is the management of marital conflict—primarily by mediation—in the course of recovery, balancing deprivation of the well spouse with the stimulus load experienced by the ill spouse as both evolve during the recovery process. The stepwise progression of functional expectation and performance is crucial in this work, because it gives the well spouse the sense that there may be less frustration in the future. More specifically, a full discussion is required as to which areas are most important to a given couple, especially intimacy and the ability to work, so that priorities can be set. Usually, other areas have to be sacrificed to those with the greatest importance. The other principal recommendation is that more focused discussion of marital conflict or other problems that predate the illness should be postponed until a modicum of stability has been present for several months.

There are two other specific technical considerations that bear inclusion here. One is that the usual structural arrangement—that parents be in charge of the patient offspring—cannot apply in most marital cases. Therefore, where coercion seems to be required, it has to be replaced by persuasion, education, and direct request; in the extreme situation, separation may have to be posed as the consequence of truly intolerable behavior. Second, in PEMFGs, it is preferable to form groups composed exclusively of couples. The issues faced by them are sufficiently different from those in two-generation families that group process is somewhat impaired by mixing the two family structures. In our own experience, we have made a strong request, bordering on a requirement, that the spouse *and* parents participate wherever feasible.

TREATMENT APPLICABILITY

Diagnosis

As is evident from the preceding, the principal application for PE has been in treating schizophrenic patients. The great majority of reported experiences have concerned research studies in which recently admitted inpatients, usually in their late 20s and living with the family of origin, are treated for a period extending well beyond discharge and through the outpatient phase. In addition, Glick and his colleagues at Cornell University have developed an adaptation of Goldstein's (Goldstein et al., 1978) brief psychoeducational approach for use during the inpatient phase (Haas et al., 1988). They found that there were significantly superior outcomes in the family-based treatment for well-functioning schizophrenic patients, but not for patients with mood disorders or for poorly functioning patients with schizophrenia. The sicker schizophrenic patients may be more likely to respond to the Anderson model of long-term PE treatment.

The question of applicability in mood disorder is partly answered by another study by Anderson and her colleagues at the University of Pittsburgh (Anderson et al., 1986). They developed and tested a one-session educational group for relatives of patients with mood disorders during an acute inpatient admission; 62 percent of the families were conjugal. Analysis of the data dis-

closed few differences in clinical outcome between the educational group and a process-
oriented MFG. Both groups seemed to induce
more dyadic satisfaction in the patients than a
comparison group that was denied any family
involvement, while the spouses reported *less*
marital satisfaction. The main difference was
that the PE-group attendees reported more satisfaction with the treatment program, regardless
of clinical outcome. Thus, at present, there is
some evidence that the PE model will induce
clinical change in mood disorder; at the very
least, the recipients of education apparently appreciate having the information.

Many other diagnoses seem amenable to PE
methods. These have included sexual dysfunction (Kuriansky, Sharpe, & O'Conner, 1982), attention-deficit disorders of childhood (Dulcan,
1985), bulimia (Conners, Johnson, & Stuckey,
1984), rheumatoid arthritis (Schwartz, Marcus,
& Condon, 1978), myocardial infarct (Frank,
Heller, & Kornfeld, 1979), breast cancer (Spiegel & Yalom, 1978), senile dementia (Zarit &
Zarit, 1982), childhood asthma (Abramson &
Peshkin, 1979), essential hypertension (Eaustaugh & Hatcher, 1982), seizure disorders
(Flora, 1977), cystic fibrosis (Johnson, 1974), and
juvenile diabetes (Koukal & Parham, 1978).
Note that in all such conditions, the common
denominators are (1) major, chronic biological
dysfunction that induces changes in social and
family interaction and (2) some evidence that
targeted intervention to alter that social interaction in a manner specific to the disorder will
influence the biological and behavioral processes
favorably.

Family Characteristics

In schizophrenia, probably the main characteristic that recommends PE treatment is the
family members' availability. In the author's and
Anderson's experience, nearly every family that
attends a PE workshop continues for an extended period in working on the stabilization
and rehabilitation phases. In the author's pilot
and large-scale outcome studies of MFPE and
SFPE, at least two thirds of all families offered
the program participated significantly. However, from that experience, it is also possible to
suggest relative indications.

1. Patients who relapse frequently after achieving symptomatic remission in the hospital
   and while compliant with a medication
   regimen;
2. Family members who react to the illness with
   high levels of distress, especially when expressed as anger at the patient and intolerance of residual symptoms;
3. Families that are by their nature intense and
   expect much from their members socially and
   vocationally;
4. First-episode patients in whom the diagnosis
   is certain;
5. Families in which there are multiple external
   stresses, whether economic or simply a confluence of difficult life circumstances or
   events; and
6. Families that appear "highly dysfunctional"
   from a systems perspective.

The last indication arises from the frequent
observation that severe mental illness *induces* a
surprising degree of behavioral and communicational "pseudodysfunction" that responds remarkably quickly to education, reassurance, and
outside supportive guidance.

The author has evolved a set of indications for
MFGs in the treatment of severe psychiatric disorders, the principal among them being family
isolation. This relates to the set of findings linking isolation to poor outcome in a wide variety
of maladies. The more specific indication is a
severe degree of overinvolvement that predates
the onset of the manifest illness. It is here that
the disenmeshment potential of the PEMFG is
highly effective and low in risk. Beyond that,
the general recommendations for PEMFGs are
their economy and therapist gratification. Thus,
they are most useful where resources are short
and clinician exhaustion and demoralization are
likely. Finally, the MFG format, with its power
to induce conformity with therapeutic social
norms, is highly useful for adolescent and/or
drug-abusing patients and their families.

Indications for Ancillary Treatments

It is hoped that the reader understands that
for major psychiatric disorders, family PE should
be carried out in the context of a full range of
therapeutic and rehabilitative treatments. Thus,

medication, day hospital, sheltered work, vocational rehabilitation and training, alternative residential options, psychosocial clubs, and family self-help groups are all used as indicated.

The failure of PE usually calls for a thorough pharmacological evaluation and possibly an inpatient admission to achieve as full a symptomatic remission as seems possible. Sometimes, failure only means that the process has not continued long enough to have the full effect. In rare instances, the family truly does not cooperate and seems consistently to undermine treatment. Here, judicious use of systemic methods, especially positive connotation, can establish a workable therapeutic system. However, our present estimate is that such families represent less than 2–3 percent of all cases.

Ethical Issues

The ethics of PE are nearly unassailable. Given the repeated demand by families that they be given information and guidance (Hatfield, 1983), the general model does what few psychiatric treatments can do: meet the customers' expectations. Nevertheless, there are a few ethical traps. The primary one is the necessity for an accurate diagnosis. The main risk in PE is consigning a patient to an officially sanctioned disability status, when, in fact, he or she is suffering from a drug-induced psychosis, mood disorder, or transient atypical psychosis. The clinician needs to present these possibilities when they exist and be ready to change the diagnosis and therapeutic direction whenever an error becomes clear. Second, families need to know what is currently understood about positive long-term outcome (Harding et al., 1987) so that they and the rest of the clinical team do not set up excessively *low* expectations (Harding et al., 1987). Finally, families and patients should be informed of the risks as well as the likely benefits of maintenance medication.

Outcome Evaluation

The assessment of outcome in PE treatments is usually narrowly clinical. In schizophrenic patients, remission and improved social and vocational functioning and quality of life are the goals and expected outcomes. Happily, they are usually achieved. Also, the model assumes that therapy is successful when the family reports reduced burden, has decreased its level of criticism and preoccupation with the patient, has gained some knowledge about the illness, has developed key coping skills, and has expanded its social network. Perhaps the most important and gratifying outcome is that clinician, patient, and family have achieved a significant margin of improved morale and hope.

CASE ILLUSTRATION

In order to flesh out the reader's general understanding of the PE approach to treatment, it seems useful to present a description of a case—in this instance, a young man who was treated in an MFG. This case was selected partly because it is not entirely typical: the patient was not living at home and the family problem was that the family members had distanced themselves somewhat from the patient rather quickly after the onset of the schizophrenic illness. Thus, his parents, unlike those described as high in expressed emotion, were only critical by implication in that they tended to avoid their son, seemingly because of his condition and the disruptive behavior that accompanied it; also, they were anything but enmeshed.

Present Illness

John, a 20-year-old, single, white man, was admitted to the state hospital in a middle-sized city. He was in an acutely psychotic state. This was his fourth admission in two years. He had been insomniac for several days, spending most of the nights laughing and singing. He also was suspicious of the other patients in his group home, had paranoid delusions about his finger, which had been bitten off at a party about a year earlier, and was markedly withdrawn. He was preoccupied with sexual thoughts, had been disruptive in the home, was agitated, and had "a wild look in his eyes."

He reported that the other patients in the

group home were driving him crazy, especially his roommate, who masturbated openly and frequently. He admitted to using a great deal of marijuana and alcohol to control his anxieties, which were not relieved by antipsychotic medication. From the history, it seemed that he had deteriorated rapidly over the course of two weeks. His parents were somewhat taken aback by his readmission, because they had believed that he was well, but had not been in close contact during that period.

During his hospitalization, he recompensated rather quickly on a higher dose of medication. However, he remained agitated and preoccupied with retaliatory thoughts about the person who bit off his finger and with sexual material. He was discharged, with a diagnosis of schizoaffective disorder, back to the same group home, but was given another roommate. Because of the intervention of the PE family clinician, a special arrangement was worked out whereby he would have to attend the day program for only two days a week until she advised that he could attempt a more active schedule.

Previous History

John was born anoxic, so much so that his parents were not allowed to see him for 24 hours. Although his development was apparently normal, it became clear during elementary school that he was dyslexic and hyperactive, and he was treated successfully for many years with Ritalin. However, because he read so poorly, he dropped out of high school, having taken up with a group of friends who abused drugs. Wisely, it seemed at the time, he joined the Navy, hoping to find a more productive niche and a less dissolute social network. Though well intentioned, this plan ended after five weeks with John psychotic and medically discharged. He was hospitalized and reconstituted well on medication. However, after that and two other admissions, he was unable to tolerate community life, especially when it included the use of readily available street drugs and alcohol. His parents were so upset by the turn of events that they refused to have him at home after the second admission and he remained in a series of group homes until the index admission.

Family History

John's father was a long-distance truck driver and his mother owned and operated a successful florist shop. John was the middle child of three, having an older sister and a younger brother, both of whom refused to accept that John was ill and with whom he had had serious conflicts since midadolescence; they were both developing and functioning well. Both parents were notably torn by John and his illness, feeling extreme guilt on the one hand and extreme embarrassment and confusion on the other. Not surprisingly, these feelings were shared by the siblings.

Course of Treatment

The clinician who accepted the case was John's inpatient-service social worker. She met with the parents early during the acute admission and established a collaborative relationship with them. They quickly set up a contract and a consensus on treatment goals: to help John stabilize in the community, to wean him off drugs and alcohol, to intervene to tone down the enthusiasm of the group-home and day-program staff members who were working with John, and to attempt slowly to get him established in a work setting. In this case, the clinician and supervisor agreed that the long-term outcome would be improved by reconciling John and his family, that is, by *decreasing* the interpersonal distance in this particular family.

Almost immediately, a crisis arose that required a readjustment of treatment goals and procedure. John's father, after watching a documentary television special on mental illness, became acutely depressed and nearly shot himself, having become convinced that John's case was both serious and hopeless. He was admitted and given antidepressant medication, but was unable to attend the educational workshop and the initial sessions of the PEMFG. He recovered quickly enough, but his wife insisted that he not attend the group for fear that more information might bring on another depression. Thus, the treatment proceeded without him.

For his part, John resumed his previous lifestyle: drinking excessively, going to parties, abusing marijuana, and staying up most of the night. He continued seeing a woman he had met in the hospital. In the MFG, he was difficult to contain, but made a good connection to two of the other male patients in the group. The clinicians began to educate John and the other patients about the connection between drug abuse and relapse. His mother became concerned about another male patient who abused drugs even more than John, and urged John to attend a day program to get out of the house and away from drugs. In one of the early sessions, John said he wanted to go fishing and at the next session reported that he and his father and brother had done so, apparently at the urging of the mother. At another group session, the mother described her fear and shame about John's first episode and was generally supported and validated by the other parents. John seemed not to be troubled by this confession, perhaps because it was somewhat relieving to hear it said aloud. From then on, the mother's attendance and activity level in the group increased steadily, in spite of her retiring interpersonal style. She became very good at supporting other mothers who had difficulty with setting limits.

After six months in treatment, John had calmed down considerably, but remained obsessed with somatic complaints, especially gastric distress and vomiting secondary to an ulcer, which he treated by drinking too much coffee. He had decreased his drinking and drug use, seemingly because his mother had begun to join with the other parents in the group and the clinicians in urging him to abstain. He was open about his disappointment concerning his father's absence, but saw no response. As part of the treatment-inspired gradual increase in social activity, he began spending more time at his parents' house on weekends and at his uncle's house periodically. He reported that he felt more comfortable there than at the group home. He received much confirmation from the clinicians and the other parents for his success in seeking out less destructive social contacts.

His condition deteriorated from that point, apparently secondary to growing conflicts involving members of the group-home staff, John, and the family clinicians, who continued to insist that he phase into a full program gradually. The group-home staff grudgingly agreed but, in classic institutional style, deflected its displeasure onto John. He looked increasingly depressed, went to the program even less, and seemed prepsychotic. The clinicians worked out a truce with the group-home staff members, who agreed to a stepwise increase in expectations for John in return for promising not to hound him about his occasional refusals to attend. He seemed to respond well to this intervention. He then went on a vacation with his family.

When they returned, he seemed markedly improved. From that point on, he remained in a good mood, was almost completely appropriate in the PEMFG, and spontaneously requested advice on, and a referral to, the state vocational rehabilitation service. He continued to complain about the group home, but without the previous degree of affect. He stayed home on Halloween night specifically to avoid drugs and frightening experiences, a decision that seemed wise to everyone in the MFG. He selected an automobile mechanics program through the vocational rehabilitation service. The PEMFG worked out a plan whereby he would practice on an old car, which belonged to one of the other parents, that needed a minor tune-up. His success at this task proved to be a victory for both John and the entire PEMFG.

As John continued to make slow progress—for example, he turned down an offer of some mescaline—his mother seemed to become more active in the group sessions, primarily with regard to other patients. However, she also became more vocal in her approval of John's small achievements, conforming to the positive view that most of the other parents seemed to have of him. He spent more time at home, which gave the clinicians a chance to use that setting as an arena for more vocationally oriented assignments: he began washing the dishes after dinner and helping his father and brother make household repairs. In the group, John and his mother were given the task of reengaging a family that seemed to be dropping out—John talked to the patient and the mother visited his mother. They eventually succeeded.

By one year, John was nearly asymptomatic and seemed to have forgotten about his somatic problems. As plans proceeded for his workshop placement, he began to become interested in moving to a subsidized and supervised apartment, about which he had learned at the group home. In the group, he began to be a useful participant in group problem solving around other patients' problems. Interestingly, by 15 months, John's mother was sitting next to him during some sessions, without any suggestions to that effect; in the same group, the parents who started out as overly close to their ill offspring had begun sitting apart. At the time of this writing, John appeared completely compensated, well motivated, and somewhat optimistic about and interested in his future. His drug and alcohol abuse had all but ceased and he seemed a likely candidate for vocational training and rehabilitation.

What was remarkable about this case, and about most cases treated successfully within this paradigm, was the major contribution made to the clinical outcome by seemingly trivial therapeutic events and maneuvers. The influence of other parents, both in urging abstinence and in providing appreciation for his success; the cross-family relationships of his mother with other parents and patients; the gentle, noncoercive, but persistent shaping of the behavior of John; the reengagement of his parents; and focused problem solving were the elements that fostered the recovery process.

AFTERWORD

The psychoeducational multifamily-group approach described here represents the wedding of two powerful and well-established models of treatment, both uniquely developed and suitable for alleviating the psychiatric and personal catastrophe that is schizophrenia. For better or for worse, PEMFGs rarely make for great theater, but they are quietly and gradually effective in promoting the restitution and rehabilitation of the afflicted person, the relief of family burden and suffering, and the rebalancing of family relationships. The outcome data available and continuing to emerge suggest that this eminently teachable and practical approach is the most cost-effective psychosocial treatment yet developed for chronic psychiatric disorders. Ultimately, however, the most persuasive recommendation for this type of work is that it allows the family and patient to move this devastating illness off to a corner of their lives and to proceed to live a bit more as their neighbors

and friends do, something that until now has been all but impossible for most of these families.

REFERENCES

Abramson, H.A., & Peshkin, H.M. (1979). Psychosomatic group therapy with parents of children with intractable asthma: The Peters family. *Journal of Asthma Research, 16*, 103–117.

Anderson, C.M. (1983). A psychoeducational program for families of patients with schizophrenia. In W.R. McFarlane (Ed.), *Family therapy in schizophrenia*, (pp 99–116). New York: Guilford Press.

Anderson, C.M., Griffin, S., Rossi, A., Pagonis, I., Holder, D.P., & Treiber, R. (1986). A comparative study of the impact of education vs process groups for families of patients with affective disorders. *Family Process, 25*, 185–206.

Anderson, C.M., Hogarty, G.E., & Reiss, D.J. (1986). *Schizophrenia and the family*. New York: Guilford Press.

Bateson, G., Jackson, D.D., Haley, J., & Weakland, J. (1956). Toward a theory of schizophrenia. *Behavioral Science, 1*, 251–264.

Beels, C.C. (1975). Family and social management of schizophrenia. *Schizophrenia Bulletin, 13*, 97–118.

Beels, C.C. (1981). Social support and schizophrenia. *Schizophrenia Bulletin, 7*, 58–72.

Bowen, M. (1960). A family concept of schizophrenia. In D.D. Jackson (Ed.), *The etiology of schizophrenia*. New York: Basic Books.

Brown, G.W., & Birley, J.L.T. (1968). Crises and life change and the onset of schizophrenia. *Journal of Health and Social Behavior, 9*, 203–214.

Brown, G.W., Birley, J.L.T., & Wing, J.K. (1972). The influences of family life on schizophrenic disorders: A replication. *British Journal of Psychiatry, 121*, 241–258.

Brown, G.W., Monck, E.M., Carstairs, G.M., & Wing, J.K. (1962). Influence of family life on the course of schizophrenic illness. *British Journal of Psychiatry, 16*, 55–68.

Connors, M.E., Johnson, C.L., & Stuckey, M. (1984). Treatment of bulimia with brief psychoeducational group therapy. *American Journal of Psychiatry, 141*, 1512–1516.

Crow, T.J., Baker, H.F., Cross, A.J., et al. (1979). Monoamine mechanisms in chronic schizophrenia: Post-mortem neurochemical findings. *British Journal of Psychiatry, 134*, 249–256.

DeLisi, L.E., Schwartz, C.C., Targum, S.D., et al. (1983). Ventricular brain enlargement and outcome of acute schizophrenic disorder. *Journal of Psychiatric Research, 9*, 169–171.

Detre, T., Sayer, J., Norton, A., & Lewis, H. (1961). An experimental approach to the treatment of the acutely ill psychiatric patient in the general hospital. *Connecticut Medicine, 25*, 613–619.

Dulcan, M. (1985). Psychoeducational therapy with families of severely impaired children. NIMH Clinical Training Human Resource Development Grant.

Eaustaugh, S.R., & Hatcher, M.E. (1982). Improving compliance among hypertensives: A triage criterion with cost benefit implications. *Medical Care, 20*, 1001–1017.

Falloon, I.R.H., Boyd, J.L., McGill, C.W., Williamson, M., Razani, J., Moss, H.B., Gilderman, A.M., & Simpson, G.M. (1985). Family management in the prevention of morbidity of schizophrenia. *Archives of General Psychiatry, 42*, 887–896.

Flora, G.G. (1977). Problem solving in diagnostics and therapeutics of neurology: The treatment of seizure disorders. *South Dakota Journal of Medicine, 30*, 15–16.

Frank, K.A., Heller, S.S., & Kornfeld, D.S. (1979). Psychological intervention in coronary heart disease: A review. *General Hospital Psychiatry, 1,* 18–23.

Fromm-Reichmann, F. (1948). Notes on the development of treatment of schizophrenics by psychoanalytic psychotherapy. *Psychiatry, 11,* 263–273.

Garrison, V. (1978). Support systems of schizophrenic and nonschizophrenic Puerto Rican women in New York City. *Schizophrenia Bulletin, 4,* 561–596.

Goldstein, M.J., Rodnick, E.H., Evans, J.R., May, P.R.A., & Steinberg, M.R. (1978). Drug and family therapy in the aftercare of acute schizophrenics. *Archives of General Psychiatry, 35,* 1169–1177.

Haas, G.L., Glick, I.D., et al. (1988). Inpatient family intervention: A randomized clinical trial. II. Results at hospital discharge. *Archives of General Psychiatry, 45,* 217–224.

Hammer, M. (1963). "Influence of small social networks as factors on mental hospital admission. *Human Organization, 22,* 243–251.

Harding, C.M., Brooks, G.W., Ashikaga, T., Strauss, J.S., & Breier, A. (1987). The Vermont longitudinal study of persons with severe mental illness. I: Methodology, study sample, and overall status 32 years later. *American Journal of Psychiatry, 144,* 718–726.

Hatfield, A.B. (1983). What families want of family therapists. In W.R. McFarlane (Ed.), *Family therapy in schizophrenia* (pp. 41–68). New York: Guilford Press.

Hogarty, G.E., Anderson, C.M., Reiss, D.J., Kornblith, S.J., Greenwald, D.P., Javna, C.D., & Madonia, M.J. (1986). Family psychoeducation, social skills training and maintenance chemotherapy in the aftercare treatment of schizophrenia. *Archives of General Psychiatry, 43,* 633–642.

Hogarty, G.E., & Goldberg, S.C. (1973). Drug and social therapy in the aftercare of schizophrenic patients. *Archives of General Psychiatry, 28,* 54–64.

Hogarty, G.E., & Ulrich, R.F. (1977). Temporal effects of drug and placebo in delaying relapse in schizophrenic outpatients. *Archives of General Psychiatry, 34,* 297–301.

Hogarty, G.E., et al. (1979). Fluphenazine and social therapy in the aftercare of schizophrenic patients. *Archives of General Psychiatry, 36,* 1283–1294.

Hooley, J.M. (1985). Expressed emotion: A review of the critical literature. *Clinical Psychology Review, 5,* 119–139.

Ingvar, D.H., & Franzen, G. (1974). Abnormalities of cerebral blood flow distribution in patients with chronic schizophrenia. *Acta Psychiatria Scandinavia, 50,* 425–462.

Johnson, B.H. (1974). Before hospitalization: A preparation program for the child and his family. *Child Today, 3,* 18–21.

Johnson, D. (1986). The family's experience of living with mental illness. Paper presented at National Alliance of the Mentally Ill, National Institute of Mental Health Colloquium, Rockville, MD.

Kendler, K.S. (1986). Genetics of schizophrenia. In A.J. Francis & R.E. Hales (Eds.), *American Psychiatric Association Annual Review, Vol. 5.* Washington, DC: American Psychiatric Press.

Koukal, S.M., & Parham, E.S. (1978). A family learning experience to serve the juvenile patient with diabetes. *Journal of the American Diabetes Association, 72,* 411–413.

Kreisman, D.E., & Joy, V.D. (1974). Family response to the mental illness of a relative: A review of the literature. *Schizophrenia Bulletin, 10,* 35–57.

Kuriansky, J.B., Sharpe, L., & O'Connor, D. (1982). The treatment of anorgasmia: Long term effectiveness of a short term behavioral group therapy. *Journal of Sexual and Marital Therapy, 8,* 29–43.

Laing, R.D., & Esterson, A. (1970). *Sanity, madness and the family.* Middlesex, England: Penguin, 1960. (Originally published 1964.)

Langsley, D., Machotka, R., & Flomenhaft, K. (1971). Avoiding mental hospital admission: A follow-up study. *American Journal of Psychiatry, 127,* 1391–1394.

Laqueur, H.P., LaBurt, H.A., & Morong, E. (1964). Multiple family therapy: Further developments. *International Journal of Social Psychiatry, 10,* 69–80.

Leff, J.P., Hirsch, S.R., Gaind, R., Rhode, P.D., & Stevens, B.C. (1973). Life events and maintenance therapy in schizophrenic relapse. *British Journal of Psychiatry, 123,* 657–660.

Leff, J.P., Kuipers, L., Berkowitz, R., & Sturgeon, D. (1982). A controlled trial of social intervention in the families of schizophrenic patients: Two year follow up. *British Journal of Psychiatry, 146,* 594–600.

Leff, J., & Vaughn, C. (1985). *Expressed emotion in families.* New York: Guilford Press.

Lidz, T., Fleck, S., & Cornelison, A.R. (1965). *Schizophrenia and the family.* New York: International Universities Press.

Lipton, F.R., Cohen, C.I., Fischer, E., & Katz, S.E. (1981). Schizophrenia: A network crisis. *Schizophrenia Bulletin, 7,* 144–151.

Meltzer, H.Y. (1979). Biochemical studies in schizophrenia. In L. Bellak (Ed.), *Disorders of the schizophrenic syndrome* (pp. 45–135). New York: Basic Books.

Miklowitz, D.J., Goldstein, M.J., & Falloon, I.R.H. (1983). Premorbid and symptomatic characteristics of schizophrenics from families with high and low levels of expressed emotion. *Journal of Abnormal Psychology, 92,* 359–367.

Neuchterlein, K.H., & Dawson, M.E. (1984). A heuristic vulnerability/stress model for schizophrenic episodes. *Schizophrenia Bulletin, 10,* 300–312.

Pattison, E.M., Llama, R., & Hurd, G. (1979). Social network mediation of anxiety. *Psychiatric Annals, 9,* 56–67.

Schooler, N.R., Levine, J., Severe, J.B., et al. (1980). Prevention of relapse in schizophrenia: An evaluation of fluphenazine decanoate. *Archives of General Psychiatry, 37,* 16–24.

Schwartz, L.H., Marcus, R., & Condon, R. (1978). Multidisciplinary group therapy for rheumatoid arthritis. *Psychosomatics, 19,* 289–293.

Selvini Palazzoli, M., Boscolo, L., Cecchin, G., & Prata, G. (1978). *Paradox and counterparadox.* New York: Aronson.

Singer, M.T., Wynne, L.C., & Toohey, M.C. (1978). Communication disorders and the families of schizophrenics. In L.C. Wynne, R.L. Cromwell, & S. Matthysse (Eds.), *The nature of schizophrenia.* New York: Wiley.

Snyder, S.H., Banerjee, S.P., Yamamura, H.I., & Greenberg, D. (1974). Drugs, neurotransmitters and schizophrenia. *Science, 184,* 1243–1253.

Spiegel, D., & Yalom, I.D. (1978). A support group for dying patients. *International Journal of Group Psychotherapy, 28,* 233–245.

Spohn, H.E., Lacoursiere, R.B., Thompson, K., & Coyne, L. (1977). Phenothiazine effects on psychological and psychophysiological dysfunction in chronic schizophrenics. *Archives of General Psychiatry, 34,* 633–644.

Stevens, J.R. (1982). Neuropathology of schizophrenia. *Archives of General Psychiatry, 39,* 1131–1139.

Sturgeon, D., Kuipers, L., Berkowitz, R., Turpin, G., & Leff, J.P. (1981). Psychophysiological responses of schizophrenic patients to high and low expressed emotion relatives. *British Journal of Psychiatry, 138,* 40–45.

Tarrier, N., Vaughn, C., Lader, M.H., & Leff, J.P. (1979). Bodily responses to people and events in schizophrenics. *Archives of General Psychiatry, 36,* 311–315.

Tecce, J.J., & Cole, J.O. (1976). The distraction-arousal hypothesis, CNV and schizophrenia. In D.I. Mostofsky (Ed.), *Behavior control and modification of psychological activity.* Englewood Cliffs, NJ: Prentice-Hall.

Tienari, P., Sorri, A., Lahti, I., Naarala, M., Wahlberg, K.E., Moring, J., Pohjola, J., & Wynne, L.C. (1987). Interaction of genetic and psychosocial factors in schizophrenia. The Finnish adoptive family study: A longitudinal combination of the adoptive family strategy and the risk research strategy. *Schizophrenia Bulletin, 13,* 477–484.

Tolsdorf, C.C. (1976). Social networks, support and coping: An exploratory study. *Family Process, 15,* 407–417.

Vaughn, C.E., & Leff, J.P. (1976). The influence of family and social factors on the course of psychiatric illness: A comparison of schizophrenic and depressed neurotic patients. *British Journal of Psychiatry, 129,* 125–137.

Wagener, D.K., Hogarty, G.E., Goldstein, M.J., Asarnow, R.F., & Browne, A. (1986). Information processing and communication deviance in schizophrenic patients and their mothers. *Psychiatry Research, 18,* 365–377.

Weinberger, D.R., Jeste, D.V., Teychenne, P.F., et al. (1986). Physiologic dysfunction of dorsolateral pre-frontal cortex in schizophrenia. *Archives of General Psychiatry, 43,* 114–135.

Weinberger, D.R., Wagner, R.L., & Wyatt, R.J. (1983). Neuro-pathological studies of schizophrenia: A selective review. *Schizophrenia Bulletin, 9,* 193–212.

Wig, N.N., Menon, K., Bedi, H., Leff, J., Kuipers, L., Ghosh, A., Day, R., Korten, A., Ernberg, G., Sartorius, N., & Jablensky, A. (1987). Distribution of expressed emotion components among relatives of schizophrenic patients in Aarhus and Chandigarh. *British Journal of Psychiatry, 151,* 160–165.

Wynne, L.C., Singer, M.T., & Toohey, M.L. (1976). Communication of the adoptive parents of schizophrenics. In J. Jorstad & E. Ugelstad (Eds.), *Schizophrenia 75: Psychotherapy, family studies, research.* Oslo: Universitetsforlaget.

Yolles, S.F., & Kramer, M. (1969). Vital statistics. In L. Bellack & L. Loeb. (Eds.), *The schizophrenic syndrome* (pp. 66–113). New York: Grune & Stratton.

Zarit, J.M., & Zarit, S.H. (1982). Families under stress: Interventions for caregivers of senile dementia patients. *Psychotherapy: Theory, Research and Practice, 19,* 461–471.

CHAPTER 12

Strategic Family Therapy*

Cloé Madanes

Strategic family therapy is a development that stems from the strategic therapy of Milton Erickson (Haley, 1967a, 1973). A primary feature is that the responsibility is on the therapist to plan a strategy for solving the client's problems (Haley, 1963, 1967a, 1976; Herr & Weakland, 1979; Montalvo, 1973; Montalvo & Haley, 1973; Papp, 1980; Rabkin, 1977; Watzlawick, Weakland, & Fisch, 1974). The therapist sets clear goals, which always include solving the presenting problem. The emphasis is not on a method to be applied to all cases, but on designing a strategy for each specific problem. Since the therapy focuses on the social context of human dilemmas, the therapist's task is to design an intervention in the client's social situation.

Erickson's emphasis was on the idiosyncrasies of the individual. Refusing to label anyone as pathological, he believed that there were many different ways of living and many different kinds of people, and his method of therapy developed from this point of view.

Strategic therapy developed at a time in the field of therapy when everyone was interested in why people behaved the way they did. The development of the approach marks a shift from explaining to people why they behave the way they do to telling them how they could behave differently or what they could potentially do. Erickson was interested in personality, but not with a focus on how or why it develops in a particular way. When he gave an explanation, it was not in terms of how a person developed; instead, he would say something like, "He's the kind of person who is interested in insects"— but he would not be thinking about how the man developed this interest in insects. His idea was that the therapist uses this interest in insects to get the man to do something else that is important to him. He accepted idiosyncrasies and individual differences as if they were given naturally and are simply something that makes the world interesting and that makes change possible. Erickson's emphasis on tolerance is a hallmark of strategic therapy.[1]

---

* Portions of this chapter have appeared in different form in Madanes (1981, 1984, and 1990).

[1] *Editors' Note.* Erickson's tolerance for individual differences is discussed in greater detail in Chapter 8 by Lankton, Lankton, and Matthews.

One set of goals for strategic family therapy is to help people past a crisis to the next stage of family life. These stages have been described by Haley (1973), who defined a problem as "a type of behavior that is part of a sequence of acts between several people" (Haley, 1976b, p. 2). The strategic approach emphasizes a distinction between (1) identifying a problem presented in therapy and (2) creating a problem by applying a diagnosis or by characterizing an individual or a family in a certain way. Psychiatric and psychological diagnostic criteria are seldom used, and *the first task of the therapist is to define a presenting problem in such a way that it can be solved.* The approach is sensitive to and includes a social network wider than the family, particularly involving professionals who have power over the person with the presenting problem (Laing, 1967, 1969).

Interventions usually take the form of directives about something that the family members are to do, both inside and outside of the interview. These directives are designed to change the ways in which people relate to each other and to the therapist. Directives may be straightforward or paradoxical, simple and involving one or two people, or complex and involving the whole family. *The directive is to strategic therapy what the interpretation is to psychoanalysis. It is the basic tool of the approach.*

Since in strategic family therapy a specific therapeutic plan is designed for each problem, there are no contraindications in terms of patient selection and suitability.[2] The approach has been used with persons of all ages and all socioeconomic classes with presenting problems of various kinds. In each case, the therapist designs a strategy; if this strategy is not successful in accomplishing the goals of the therapy, a new strategy is formulated. This is not an approach in which the therapist continues to do more of the same when he or she is failing. The approach allows the therapist to borrow in turn

from all other models of therapy any techniques that might be useful in solving a presenting problem.[3]

What makes a therapist choose a particular strategy is how he or she conceptualizes a problem brought to therapy as well as the specific characteristics of the problem itself or of the people who present it. These characteristics are mostly in the head of the therapist. That is, the way a therapist thinks about a problem and the way that problem touches him or her is what determines what strategy will be used to solve it. For example, an adolescent son who refuses to go to school may be thought of as being disobedient and out of the control of the parents; or he may be thought of as misunderstood and mistreated by rejecting parents; or he may be thought of as a pawn in a struggle between the parents, in which one parent takes revenge on the other by arranging that the son fail; or he may be thought of as being concerned about and protective of the parents, sacrificing himself to keep the mother company and so replacing the father and freeing him for other endeavors; or he might be thought of as the victim of an oppressive school system that is not geared to his sensitivity and talents. All of these hypotheses may fit the situation equally well. *The hypothesis that is chosen* from among the many different ways to think about a problem is the one that appeals most to the therapist at a particular time; it *is the one that elicits his or her sympathy and interest in the family.*

The many different ways of thinking about a problem tend to cluster around a set of concepts that are most frequently used in strategic therapy. Each concept tends to encompass a range or continuum that goes from one extreme to another. For example, a therapist might think about relationships in a family in terms of hostility or love, with a range of mixed or ambivalent emotions between the two extremes. But whether a therapist thinks at all in terms of hostility and love instead of, for example, in terms

---

[2] *Editors' Note.* That each course of strategic therapy is custom-tailored to the clients at hand does not necessarily imply (in our view) that all problems brought to therapists are solvable—by strategic or *any other* method of treatment. The implication of Madanes' view, as we see it, is not that therapists should expect to be 100 percent successful, but that they should challenge their own creativity and ingenuity and not *assume* that given problems are not solvable.

[3] *Editors' Note.* The essential pragmatism and outcome orientation of strategic therapy should not be mistaken for unsystematic, incoherent technical eclecticism; while Madanes' description of her suggested interventions certainly does draw upon a wide variety of ideas and sources, it is very firmly grounded in a consistent and clear position about the nature of families and of therapeutic change.

of equality and hierarchy, determines what strategy for therapy will be chosen.

In human relations, nothing is ever all black or all white—where there is love, there is hate; power is always associated with dependence; behavior is never totally either voluntary or involuntary. As soon as one seems to have defined a situation and understood it without ambiguities, the opposite definition comes to mind and appears equally feasible. It may be that *what is characteristic of a good therapist's thought processes is a particular tolerance for ambiguity.*

CONCEPTUALIZING A PROBLEM

The following are six dimensions for conceptualizing a problem brought to strategic therapy.

Involuntary Versus Voluntary Behavior

Characteristically, the problems presented to therapy are introduced as involuntary behavior by the symptomatic person. The relatives sometimes share this view, or they may prefer to think of the problem as voluntary and under the control of the patient. For example, headaches are often considered involuntary by everyone involved, while stealing cars tends to be considered deliberate, voluntary behavior. Of course, there are exceptions; husbands have been known to argue that their wives deliberately bring on a headache to reject them, and certain parents of delinquents have gone so far as to propose that there must be a specific brain damage associated with stealing mopeds.

A strategic therapist generally prefers to think of all symptoms (except for organic illness) as voluntary and under the control of the patient, although this thought may or may not be shared with the clients. Even with organic illness, often the extent of the handicap is related to this issue of voluntary or involuntary behavior. Sometimes a first step in resolving the presenting problem is to redefine it as involving voluntary rather than involuntary behavior. This may be the only intervention that is necessary, as the client may solve the problem once the client accepts the idea that it is under his or her control. At other times, the request deliberately to produce in-

voluntary behavior has a paradoxical effect and the unwanted behavior disappears. In some situations, a client may present a problem as involving voluntary behavior on his or her part, and the therapist may choose to redefine it as involuntary and out of the client's control.

The issue of whether a behavior is voluntary or involuntary is crucial to some cases and to some strategies and quite irrelevant to others. For example, defining drug addiction as voluntary rather than involuntary behavior is usually crucial to the therapy. However, whether a couple's bickering is voluntary or involuntary is not necessarily relevant to change.

Helplessness Versus Power

A symptomatic person tends to appear helpless in that he or she presents unfortunate and/or involuntary behavior that is out of his or her control; the person cannot change even though he or she wants to. However, this very helplessness is a source of power in relation to significant others whose lives are often limited and dominated by the unreasonable demands, fears, and needs of the symptomatic person. The nonsymptomatic members of the family appear to be in a position of power in that their own behavior is under their control, but they are helpless to influence the symptomatic person, who, in fact, has a great deal of power over them. Those in power are always dependent on the powerless, and the helpless have power over the powerful. For example, a baby can be seen as being more powerful than the mother and a servant as more dominating than the master.

A therapist can think in different ways about the power and helplessness of various family members. The therapist may choose to view the helpless symptomatic child as powerful or as victimized, and the parents may be seen as tyrannical or exploited. The therapist may or may not choose to share these thoughts with the family. A therapist thinking within the dimension of power and helplessness also may choose to redistribute power and the responsibility that goes with it. Children may become agents of change, or parents may become therapists to their children. *How a therapist thinks about power, and whether he or she thinks about power and help-*

lessness at all, will determine how the therapist designs a strategy for change.

Metaphorical Versus Literal Sequences

A child who refuses to go to school may be thought of as being a disobedient child, and the problem may be understood as how to get the child back in school. In contrast, the refusal to go to school may be considered an allusion to another situation in the family; the therapist may connect it, for example, to the mother's depression and difficulty in finding a job. The child's behavior in relation to the parents may be considered similar to the mother's behavior in relation to the father. The child's refusal to go to school in spite of the parents' efforts may be considered an allusion to and a metaphor for the mother's refusal to go to work in spite of the father's efforts to convince her. The parents' struggle with the child may have replaced the struggle between the mother and father in the family. The idea that a symptom may be a metaphor for the problems of another person may lead a therapist to focus on resolving those problems instead of focusing directly on the symptomatic person. The therapist who thinks of the presenting problem as part of a sequence that is metaphorical for another sequence may think that a change introduced in one sequence of interaction may have repercussions in other relationships in the family (Madanes, 1984).

These ideas about metaphor in families led to a second concept: the idea of planning ahead (Madanes, 1981). Even though this is a simple idea, it has developed only recently as a result of a change in focus on past causes of current behavior to anticipated consequences of that behavior. The sequence is this: A father comes home from work upset and worried that he might be fired. His wife tries to help him and reassure him. Their son develops a symptom, and the father pulls himself together and behaves like a competent parent, giving his child medication, comfort, and caring. At that point, he is no longer a man afraid of losing his job. He has become a concerned father and a mature adult in relation to his child.

Is it possible that the child has planned this behavior to help his father pull himself together? Could the child have developed a symptom to

free the mother from having to try to help the father? Is it possible that the child could plan ahead in this way? The question is not merely theoretical. If a therapist can develop such a hypothesis when interviewing a family, he or she can begin to understand the child's plan. To understand this plan, it is best to focus on the helpfulness and protectiveness of the child. In what way is the child's plan helpful, and what is unfortunate about this mode of helpfulness? The child's plan to help the parents often creates a worse problem than the one the child is intending to solve. The unfortunate nature of this helpfulness is what must be changed. This helpfulness causes the power of the child over the parents to be exaggerated. The child exerts power and influence inappropriate to his situation as a child in the family. Through problem behavior, the child can change a parent from a helpless, upset person into a competent, helpful parent.

When the child's plan is known, the strategy for solving the problem becomes immediately apparent: to arrange for a new sequence of interaction by which the same end can be achieved without the symptom.[4] Then the child no longer need exhibit the symptom. It is difficult to think that a child has the intelligence to plan such a sequence. Yet, it is difficult to think that a child does *not* have that intelligence. Children are intelligent in ways that are more complex than that. It is rather simple, for example, for a child to anticipate how the father will respond to his or her behavior; curiously, however, it has taken quite a long time to develop the idea that children do plan ahead in these ways. The issue arises: If the child plans, is such planning done consciously? Is it deliberate? At times it is. Children have been known to explain how and why they plan symptomatic behavior. For example: "If I am sick, then my father will not drink that day," or, "If I am sick, he will not go away," or, "If I am sick, my mother will not go out with her girlfriend." But the question arises as to whether the child really plans or whether it is the father who elicits this kind of behavior from

---

[4] *Editors' Note.* The position of the strategic therapist here is very clear: symptoms (invariably?) serve interpersonal functions. Note that the notion of interpersonal *functions* is decidedly different from a notion with which it is often confused, that of interpersonal *consequences.*

the child so that he can pull himself together and think of himself as a caring father rather than as a failing adult. Or, does the mother elicit the behavior in the child so she can be free from having to support her husband in his difficulties? *What is the truth is really not the question. The important consideration is the kind of punctuation of the events that will best lead to designing a strategy for change.* Some therapists prefer to think of the child as the initiator of sequences and some prefer to think of the parents in this way. Probably all are involved, although this is not necessarily the case. The question is, what kind of thinking will help the therapist develop a strategy to solve the problem? It is important to remember that a therapist is only seeking a workable hypothesis, one that will help to develop a plan to interfere with the unfortunate plan of the family or the child.

Hierarchy Versus Equality

Related to issues of power and helplessness are issues of hierarchy and equality. Some therapists think that a well-functioning family is an organization of equals, while others prefer to think that hierarchy is essential to the effectiveness of a family system. Deciding whether to shift from hierarchy to equality or vice versa, and when to make that shift, also may be at issue in the conceptualization of a problem.

When problem behavior is metaphorical of other problem behavior, or when a sequence of interaction is metaphorical of another sequence, or when a child plans to be helpful to the parents in indirect ways, there is an incongruity in the hierarchical organization of the family (Madanes, 1981). That is, when the child carries out a plan to help the parents in indirect ways with issues that are important to them, the child takes a position of leadership in the family; this is incongruous with the fact that the parents support the child, care for the child, provide the child with guidance, and so on. There is a dual hierarchy in the family: In one, the child is in charge; in the other, the parents are in charge of the child. The task of the therapist is to correct this hierarchy and reorganize the family so that the parents are in a superior position and help and support the child and the child does not take care of the parents in unfortunate ways.

When it is a spouse who develops symptomatic or problem behavior, two incongruous hierarchies are simultaneously defined in the marriage. In one, the symptomatic person is in an inferior position because of helpless and disturbed behavior, and the other spouse is in the superior position of helper. Yet, at the same time, the symptomatic spouse is in a superior position by not being influenced and helped, while the nonsymptomatic spouse is in the inferior position of being an unsuccessful helper whose efforts fail and whose life can be organized around the symptomatic spouse's needs and problems (Madanes, 1981).

Hostility Versus Love

People can be seen as being motivated mainly by hostility or by love; the same action can be interpreted or motivated by either emotion. A man may reject a woman because he does not like her, or because he considers himself unworthy of her and fears that she will not be happy with him. Parents' disciplining of their children can be seen as acts of love or of punitiveness. Some therapists prefer to think in terms of rejection, revenge, punitiveness, aggression, envy, jealousy, hate, and other unsavory motivations. Others go to extreme lengths to see everyone as being concerned about others, benevolently motivated, and compassionate. The issue has to do with both the attribution of meaning and the question of redefinition as a therapeutic tool. Once a therapist understands a problem in a certain way, he or she has attributed meaning to the motivations of the people involved. This particular meaning constitutes an important consideration with respect to the therapist's choice of strategy. Even more important, however, is whether the therapist's conceptualization of the problem coincides with the view that is presented or whether he or she will choose to redefine and change this view. That is, a rebellious adolescent boy may present himself as being motivated by hostility and the desire for independence and the parents may see him in the same way. The therapist, however, may think that the young person is benevolently concerned about his parents and distracts them from their other difficulties by providing them with a focus for their concern. The issue then is whether the therapist will choose to explain this view to the family and will base a strategy on this redefinition of the situation or will not explicitly address the issue at all. Strategic therapists tend to think of and redefine people as being benevolently motivated, probably because this view is more conducive to sympathy and interest in the human dramas brought to therapy.[5]

Personal Gain Versus Altruism

A symptomatic person may be motivated by personal gain or by altruism. If the symptomatic person is seen as being hostile, his motivation is always thought to be personal gain. However, if the symptomatic person is seen as being motivated by love, the therapist may view the person as being concerned either with helping others or with receiving more affection. For example, a symptomatic child may be seen as being concerned about and loving toward parents and siblings. The symptom then may be seen as related to an attempt to receive more affection from them or as an effort to help them by becoming, for example, a communication vehicle between them. The two motivations are not necessarily exclusive. If the therapist accurately perceives whether the child is motivated by personal gain or by altruism, then the strategy of the therapy is laid out. All he or she has to do is to arrange for the same consequences of the symptom to take place without the symptom, and the problem behavior should disappear. For instance, if a boy has fears because he wants demonstrations of love from his father, the therapist need only arrange for these demonstrations of love to take place without the fears and the fears will be gone.[6]

Issues of personal gain and altruism are more important in relation to the symptomatic person than to other relatives because a correct understanding of the symptomatic person's wishes can lead quickly to a strategy for change. However, if one considers the possibility that other family members are involved in the problem and are instrumental to maintaining or resolving it, the issue of whether they are motivated by personal gain or by altruism is equally important.

THE GOALS OF THERAPY

Therapists need shared values to sustain them through changing times. In a complex and constantly changing society, new problems constantly develop, old problems are given new priorities, and therapists work in always changing situations. A set of goals that applies to all therapy would sustain their integrity and help them through these times.

Different varieties of therapy, counseling, and social assistance have become so commonplace today that some form of therapeutic intervention has probably touched the lives of every family in the United States. The same is probably true for most of the economically developed world. Therapists are influencing millions of people not only through their clients and their students, but also through the mass media. Magazines, newspapers, radio, television, and the movies are influenced in major ways by the field and provide continual psychological recommendations. If therapists were clear about their values, they could be clear about how they want to exert their influence on these media. Clear goals can also help therapists do no harm, and not harming is the first consideration of a therapist.

A central question in therapy has been whether there is a basic dilemma that human beings face and from which all other human dilemmas stem. Philosophy, literature, and religion have asked the same question. Various themes have been proposed and have organized our thinking about the human drama. Different schools of thought have proposed that we are doomed to sexual frustration, that we ultimately seek self-destruction, that we can never overcome the trauma of birth, that we are motivated by pure selfishness, that we are overwhelmed

---

[5] *Editors' Note.* But seeing people as also motivated by such feelings as anger, envy, and the like does not inherently block the therapist from being sympathetic or empathic, or concerned and interested. See, by way of contrast, Chapter 7 by Boszormenyi-Nagy, Grunebaum, and Ulrich.

[6] *Editors' Note.* This is a concrete example of the issue (actually, a variation thereof) we raised two notes ago: We believe there is more than ample evidence from the behavioral literature that numerous fears (of both children and adults) have little to do with family dynamics, and are maintained by sets of contingencies apart from the family.

Author's Note. I agree with Editors' Note 6. For instance, I have a fear of spiders that has nothing to do with anyone in my family.

by the meaninglessness of life, that we are caught in a web of paradoxical communications, and that all attempts to change bring about more of the same. These are some of the concepts that have been used to explain not only the behavior of people in therapy, but also family relations, work difficulties, and social conflicts. In a strategic approach, all problems brought to therapy can be thought of as stemming from the dilemma between love and violence (Madanes, 1990). The main issue for human beings is whether to love, protect and help each other, or to intrude, dominate, and control, doing harm to and using violence on others. The problem is compounded because love involves intrusion, domination, control, and violence, and because violence can be done in the name of love, protection, and helpfulness. The more intense the love, the closer it is to violence in the sense of intrusive possessiveness. Similarly, the more attached to and dependent we are on the object of our violence, the more intense is the violence. How does a therapist steer people toward love and away from violence when there is so often such a fine line between the two?

There are four dimensions of family interaction that correspond to different kinds of emotional and spiritual development. Each dimension corresponds to specific types of problems brought to therapy, and for each dimension there are specific strategies of choice to solve the problems.[7]

1. To Dominate and Control

One dimension involves people struggling for control and power over their own lives and over the lives of others. Family members oppose each other in antagonistic ways, so that the presenting problem can best be understood as an attempt to gain power over significant others. Power is used for personal advantage, people are mainly motivated by the wish to satisfy selfish needs, and relationships are mostly exploitative. Each individual's goal seems to be to dominate for his

or her own benefit. The main emotion of family members is fear. The therapist needs to redistribute power among family members and change how the power is used, moving people away from selfish desires and toward the wish to be loved. Typical problems are delinquency, some forms of drug abuse, behavioral difficulties, and bizarre behavior. The strategies of choice involve changing the involvement of parents and other relatives, negotiating privileges and obligations between family members, changing who benefits from the symptom, and using rituals and ordeals (Madanes, 1981; Haley, 1973, 1980, 1984, 1987).

Correcting the Hierarchy

This strategy basically consists of organizing the parents to take charge of the family. When adolescents or young adults are antisocial or out of control (delinquent, drug addicted, or violent), and the parents are reasonably benevolent, they can be put in charge of establishing control over their offspring by agreeing on rules for them and consequences if the rules are not followed. Likewise, grandparents and other relatives can be put in charge of the children. The idea is that the older relatives will provide the necessary kindly guidance to reorient the young person to socially acceptable behavior. In so doing, the older relatives will come together in agreement and resolve conflicts that may have initially caused the young person's outrage. The therapist introduces metaphors of the rules and regulations that insure truce, peace, and survival, and of fair punishment and compensation (Haley, 1980; Madanes, 1981).

Sometimes, in order to restore the parents' protectiveness, it is necessary to take power away from professionals. A protective-services worker may be intruding into a family and causing strife and violence, a probation officer may be divesting parents of authority, or school teachers may oppress or discriminate against a child. The therapist needs to defend the family's rights—for example, by transferring power from a protective-services worker to a grandmother or from a probation officer to a father—and to organize parents to protect a child and defend his or her integrity against the court system or the school system.

---

[7] *Editors' Note.* What follows is an eminently testable series of strategic hypotheses linking dominant family interaction styles with both categories of presenting problems *and* preferred therapeutic interventions.

Negotiations and Contracts

When people are trying to dominate and control, the therapist needs to help them negotiate and reach agreements. Negotiations about money, children, relatives, leisure time, and sex are part of every marital and family therapy. The therapist helps family members express their preferences and compromise with each other. These negotiations are often written as contracts between family members. All the work of the therapy may consist of negotiating a contract and encouraging the family to respect the terms.

Changing Benefits

Sometimes, a family rewards hostile acts with attention and concern. In these cases, it is useful to reverse the situation so that hostility by one family member results in gratification rather than suffering for others.

Rituals and Ordeals

Rituals are useful in marking the transition from one stage of family life to another or to indicate a transition in a relationship. The drama of the ritual should be commensurate with the severity of the problem presented to therapy. For minor problems, a birthday party or a trip to visit relatives may be appropriate. A serious transition may require, for example, a ceremony of renewal of marital vows.

Rituals are particularly indicated when people have to overcome very bad things they have done to each other. The ritual signifies that the past is over and that this is a new beginning.

The ordeal is a strategy devised by Milton Erickson to make it more difficult for a person to have a symptom than not to have it (Haley, 1984). Interactional ordeals are particularly interesting. An ordeal could be for a symptomatic husband to give his wife—or better yet, his mother-in-law—a present every time the undesirable behavior occurs, or to give money to his wife's children from a previous marriage. The ordeal is something that the person dislikes but that would improve his or her relationship with significant others. The therapist sets up a win/win situation. If the symptom does not occur,

the problem is solved; if the symptom occurs, the penalty improves relationships with the family (Madanes, 1990).

2. *To Be Loved*

The second dimension involves the difficulties resulting from a desire to be loved. Family members are involved in a struggle to be cared for that often leads to self-inflicted violence. A child may seek punishment as a way of obtaining attention. A spouse may develop an incapacitating symptom in the hope of eliciting concern from the other spouse. Rivalry, discrimination, antagonism, and disagreements are often based on a desire to be specially favored. The wish to be loved and appreciated can bring out the best qualities in people, but it can also result in irrationality, selfishness, and harm. The main emotion among family members is desire. Needs never seem to be fulfilled and there is always frustration and discomfort. The therapist needs to redistribute love among family members and to change how love is used, changing the wish to be loved to the desire to love and protect others. Typical problems are psychosomatic symptoms, depression, anxiety, phobias, eating disorders, and loneliness. Interactions are characterized by excessive demands and criticism. The strategies of choice are changing the way parents are involved with their children, prescribing the symptom or some aspect of the symptom, prescribing a symbolic act, and prescribing the pretending of the symptom.

Changing a Parent's Involvement

A therapist may observe that a child's disturbing behavior has the function of involving an otherwise distant parent, who interacts with the child by punishing him or her. The strategy is to engage the parent with the child in positive ways, such as playing together, so that the child need not misbehave to maintain a relationship with the parent (Haley, 1976; Minuchin, 1974).

Instead of being distant, a parent may be overinvolved with a child's symptom, but not around other areas of a child's life. A strategy is to keep parent and child intensely involved with each other around other issues (Madanes, 1990).

A related strategy (Madanes, 1990) is to change the memory of an adult's involvement with his or her parents in the past. This strategy is useful with people who are tormented with low self-esteem because of memories of being victimized by their parents. The strategy is to say that there must have been someone kindly in the person's childhood who perhaps has been forgotten but who must have existed and whose influence explains the good qualities that the person presents today. Perhaps it was a grandmother, an uncle or an aunt, even a teacher. When a new memory of a kindly person is retrieved, the therapist can say that, if one or two kindly actions are remembered, there must have been many more. The therapist can also suggest that every time a bad memory comes to mind, it should be counteracted with the newfound memories of the kindly grandmother, for example, so that the person will carry inside the image of the good grandmother to counteract the image of the cruel parent.

Prescribing the Symptom

Prescribing the symptom was the first paradoxical strategy described in the therapy literature (Frankl, 1960). If a person came to therapy to get over a symptom, the therapist asked him or her to have more of the symptom. For example, a person who had stomach aches was asked to have more stomach aches, to have them at a certain time, in a certain place, and so on. A natural development of this strategy is to have parents prescribe the symptom to a child. If a boy is a fire-setter, the father will make him set fires under the father's supervision several times a day, so that setting fires becomes an obligation, like homework.

Another variation of this strategy is to prescribe where, when, and how the symptom will take place. A depressed man can be asked to get up early in the morning to sit in a special chair and be depressed. A couple is instructed that every day at a specified time the spouses are to take turns criticizing each other for seven minutes. At the end of each seven minutes, the other spouse is only to answer, "I'm sorry, dear," and nothing more. Then it is the other one's turn to complain. Under the guise of improving communication, communication is in fact blocked and negative sequences are discouraged (Madanes, 1984).

Another possibility (Madanes, 1990) is to provide a script to be carefully followed so that communication is predictable, precise, and positive. The script can be prescribed to a couple, to siblings, or to parents and children. A therapist can instruct spouses on what to say to each other so that communication will be satisfying for both. Most people just want to hear their spouse say, "Thank you, dear," and, "I'm sorry, dear." When these lines are spoken with sufficient frequency, most spouses will report good communication and great improvement in their relationship.

Prescribing a Symbolic Act

When people are involved in compulsive self-destructive behaviors, an effective strategy is to ask them to perform repetitively an act that is symbolic of the self-destructive act but which lacks the self-destructive consequences. Self-destructive behaviors are usually a misguided attempt to punish someone who does not provide enough love and attention. So the symbolic act should involve a certain punitiveness toward those whom the person is symbolically punishing. This strategy is particularly useful with bulimics and with people who engage in such acts as pulling out their hair or sticking pins in themselves.

In the case of a bulimic, for example, the therapist can organize the family members to buy all the junk food that she prefers for binge eating (fried chicken, cookies, cheap ice cream, french fries, etc.) and set it out on the kitchen counter. In the presence of the family, the bulimic is to mash up all the food with her hands, symbolizing what goes on in the stomach when it digests the food. When it is all mashed, she is to throw it into the toilet. If the toilet clogs, the family member the bulimic loves or resents most (for example, the father) is the only one allowed to unclog the toilet. The act symbolizes not only what the bulimic does to herself, but also what she puts her family through (Madanes, 1981).

Prescribing the Pretending of the Symptom

A child may have stomach aches to obtain love and dedication from the parents. A husband may become depressed so that his wife will comfort him. In these cases, the function of the symptom is a personal gain for the symptomatic person and the benefit consists of receiving love. The therapist can arrange for the child to pretend to have the stomach ache and for the parents to comfort him or her as if it were a real stomach ache. The depressed husband can be asked to pretend to be depressed and the wife to take care of him as if his depression were real. When the benefit is obtained for the pretended symptom, then the real symptom is no longer necessary (Madanes, 1981).

3. *To Love and Protect*

The third dimension involves the desire to love and protect others. The wish to love and protect can bring out our highest qualities of compassion, devotion, generosity, and kindness. It may also elicit intrusiveness, possessiveness, domination, and violence. Intrusion and violence are often justified in the name of love. The parent who punishes for the child's "own good," the lover who dominates to protect, and the teacher who criticizes to enlighten are all examples of love that may lead to violence. A family member powerless to take care of a loved one resorts to indirect means of caring. A child distracts a parent from his or her problems by developing unreasonable fears or by ruthlessly attacking those around him. The parent, concerned, may temporarily take respite from her or his own problems to take care of the child. By arranging this respite, the child is offering love and protection to the parent, but this love is at the cost of the child's sacrifice and compromises the child's own desires, accomplishments, and fulfillment. This love is also violent in its manipulation.

The main emotion among family members involved at this level is despair. The wish to love and protect others is the highest human inclination, yet the seeds of violence are contained within that desire. The therapist needs to change how family members protect and love

each other and who takes care of whom, introducing the wish to repent for the violence inflicted in the context of a loving relationship. Typical problems presented to therapy are suicide threats and attempts, abuse and neglect, guilt, obsessions, temper tantrums, and thought disorders.

The strategies of choice are to reunite family members, orienting them toward the future and arranging deeds of reparation; to change who is helpful to whom; and to empower children to be appropriately helpful to their parents.

Reuniting Family Members

When a problem brought to therapy is related to the pain of separation and exclusion from a loved person, the task of the therapist is to reconcile and reunite family members and to heal old wounds so that separation is no longer necessary. If parents and children have become estranged from each other, particularly mothers and children, no matter what the age, no matter what the presenting problem, one must assume that the symptom is related to the estrangement. The main effort of the therapy must be to bring people together again.

Sometimes, parents want to expel their children literally or emotionally. In these cases, containment is part of the strategy of reuniting family members. In fact, often, before one can do anything else in therapy, one has to arrange for the family to contain the children without expulsion. It is important to understand that in the parents' minds, expulsion may not be contradictory to wanting to love and protect their children. Parents with very low self-esteem may love their children, and precisely because they love them, want to give them away to others, that is, to people they think will be better parents.

Sometimes, one spouse loves the other and wants to stay in the marriage while the other is rejecting and resentful and refuses to come to therapy. In these cases, the best strategy may be to coach the loving spouse on how to win the other one back, how to understand the other spouse, how to respect his or her freedom, how to give the kind of love that the other one wants, and so on. Similarly, sometimes it is necessary to coach a parent on how to deal with a child, and sometimes it is necessary to coach a child on how to put up with, sympathize with, and take care of a parent.

When a young person is so alienated that self-inflicted violence has reached the point of a suicide threat, and the therapist judges that the relatives truly want the young person to live (rather than secretly desiring the person's death), hospitalization can be prevented by organizing a suicide watch in the home. All dangerous instruments, such as knives and scissors, are removed from the house and family members take turns watching the suicidal young person 24 hours a day. The suicidal person, moved by all this love and concern, eventually abandons the suicide threats. The relatives are encouraged to be loving and kindly and to sacrifice themselves in providing this watch. In some cases, the suicide threats are just that and the person has no intention of committing suicide. The suicide watch acts as a deterrent because it limits the person's freedom to an intolerable degree.

In establishing a suicide watch, the therapist should not put one spouse in charge of the other. The suicide threat is often an attempt to escape an unfortunate marriage. The suicide watch may increase the feeling of intrusiveness and subjugation and escalate the violence. When an adult, married or not, threatens suicide, it is best to organize the family of origin rather than the spouse to conduct the suicide watch.

Changing Who Is Helpful to Whom

Sometimes, the function of the symptom is to help someone else and the benefit for the symptomatic person is altruism. For example, the daughter of a depressed mother may make a suicide attempt; the mother is then forced to come out of her depression to help her daughter. The girl's suicide attempt is helpful to the mother in that it makes her pull herself together and behave like a mother to a daughter who needs her. The strategy here is to ask the mother to pretend to be depressed and the daughter to pretend to help the mother in age-appropriate ways, for example, by saying reassuring things, entertaining her with games, and expressing love directly. The hypothesis is that the depressed mother is covertly asking the daughter

for help and the daughter is covertly helping the mother by attempting suicide. The pretending makes the mother's covert request overt and provides the daughter with appropriate ways of helping her mother that are not self-destructive (Madanes, 1981).

Another strategy is to change who has the symptom. This is an idea based on an important value of American culture: taking turns. In America, people take turns at speaking and do not interrupt each other; they stand in line; they take turns at playing, at chores, in love, and in sex. When a family presents with an adolescent or adult child who is very bad and other children who are very good, it is natural to suggest to the siblings that it is not fair. Why should only one be bad and ruin his or her life? Why should this sibling get all the attention and take on the task of providing thrills or a purpose in life for the rest of the family? If the other children took their turns, the bad one could be good sometimes and get on with life. The therapist appeals to the love between siblings and to their sense of fair play. This makes explicit an implicit family rule in a way that moves the good siblings to change so that the bad one need no longer be bad (Madanes, 1984).

Empowering Children To Be Appropriately Helpful

This strategy is useful when parents present as incompetent, helpless, physically ill, addicted to drugs or alcohol, abusive, or neglectful. The children love and protect the parents, but the parents are not giving love and protection to the children. Nothing is asked of the parent or parents. The children are put in charge of one aspect of the parents' life—their happiness. The therapist asks the children, "How could your parents organize their lives so that they would be happier? Should they go out more often? To a movie? To a restaurant? Perhaps they could go away for a weekend or have a candlelight dinner at home. Maybe the children could cook and serve the dinner." As the discussion proceeds, the therapist encourages the children to make concrete suggestions, for example, as what movie the parents should see or what restaurant they might choose. Children may be put in charge of taking care of themselves, of organizing the parents to get along better with each other so that they can be happier, or of organizing the household and the family's good times. All this is done in age-appropriate and playful ways so that there is no burden to the children; on the contrary, they are relieved to be able to express their love and to take care of their parents. The children are not really in charge. The whole organization is play, more in fantasy than in reality. The parents are moved as they experience their children's love for them and they respond in kind, correcting the hierarchy and taking responsibility for themselves and for their children (Madanes, 1984).

It might seem that expecting children to initiate change and be helpful to their parents is an excessive burden. But the fact is that in these families the children are already in that situation. All that the therapist is doing is organizing them to be more effective helpers with less personal sacrifice. In fact, it gives children great satisfaction to have a function that is overtly recognized and appreciated as helpful to the parents.

Orienting Toward the Future and Deeds of Reparation

People sometimes come to therapy with feelings of depression, worthlessness, and guilt. They are obsessed with their failure and the lack of meaning in their lives. Instead of arguing with them, the therapist can agree that they may be worthless and guilty; however, since they themselves are not important, they might give more of themselves to others for whom life *is* important (Madanes, 1990). They might select a group of people, preferably those somehow related to their guilt feelings, and do anonymous good deeds for them. For example, a Vietnam war veteran haunted by visions of atrocities witnessed or committed could be sent to donate money, time, and work to organizations that care for Vietnamese orphans. Or an army commander, depressed and obsessed with guilt over his errors in judgment, that may have led to the loss of his soldiers, can be told to do reparation by donating money and effort to the support and guidance of the widows and children of his men lost in battle. Preferably, the good deed will be anonymous, so that it is unquestionably done

not for reward or recognition, but purely for reparation and out of altruism.

The strategy of doing good deeds is especially useful for those who are mourning the death of a family member. The therapist can ask the parents, children, and/or siblings to collect funds and make a special donation once a year, for example, in the name of the deceased. Another variation is for the family to work to fulfill the dreams of the member who has died (Eddy, 1986).

Often, a therapist needs to change the clients' version of the past so that the present and the future may change. The central issue in many therapies is the struggle to arrive at an acceptable version of one's life. Sometimes, the therapist needs to offer a major rewriting of the clients' story (Keim, Lentine, Keim, & Madanes, 1988).

Just as it is useful to bring out the best from the past to remind people of their original love and good intentions toward each other, so it is helpful to project people into the future, suggesting that in 10 or 20 years, this day, this week, or this month may or may not be remembered. It is in everyone's power to create good memories of love, caring, playfulness, and humor that can be remembered many years from now (Madanes, 1990).

4. *To Repent and To Forgive*

In the fourth dimension, the main issue between family members is to repent and to forgive. When individuals have inflicted trauma on each other and have suffered injustices and violence, interactions are characterized by grief, resentment, lies, secrecy, deceit, self-deprecation, isolation, and dissociation. The main emotion is shame because of what one has done, because of what one has refrained from doing, or because one cannot forgive. If family members are to continue to relate to one another, the therapist needs to reapportion the shame. Often, the victims are blamed, and that must change. As the therapist clarifies who did what to whom, the wish to avoid responsibility and blame must change to the desire to become compassionate and to develop a sense of unity with others. Typical problems are incest, sexual abuse, attempted murder, and sadistic acts. The strategies of choice are to create an atmosphere of higher emotions, to find protectors for the victims, and to elicit repentance, forgiveness, compassion, and a sense of unity with others.

Creating a Positive Framework

This strategy includes improving the quality of life and creating an atmosphere of higher emotions. The therapist makes an effort to improve communication, assertiveness, and the ability to give and receive love.

Often, a therapist needs to raise people from the grimness of their situation into a better way of being. It is useful to start every session by pointing out to clients, as well as to remind them during the session, that they have come to therapy out of love and concern for each other and that they are seeking a better way of being and of relating to each other. These comments by the therapist prevent angry interactions and petty hostilities among family members.

Humor and the use of the absurd are an important part of this strategy. When people are irrationally grim, the introduction of playfulness can elicit new behaviors and bring about new alternatives. What makes change possible is the therapist's ability to be optimistic and to see what is funny or appealing in a grim situation.

Finding Protectors

In cases of abuse and neglect, the very existence of the family unit is threatened. The therapist needs to look for strong, responsible people in the extended family or in the community and transfer responsibility to them and away from professional helpers. The transfer needs to take place gradually and in stages so that ultimately, under the care of the protector, family members will be able to forgive each other. For example, if an adolescent has been abused by a father, a responsible uncle or grandmother can be put in charge of supervising the family to make sure that this will not happen again. At first, the family will be supervised by both the protective-services worker and, say, the uncle; then only by the uncle, who will report to the protective-services worker; and finally by the uncle alone

with the worker remaining available to reopen the case if necessary.

Sometimes, a therapist needs to support a spouse in leaving a marriage and in finding protection and support with extended family or friends. A therapist might also encourage a spouse to press charges against the other spouse or to seek a court injunction against any further contact. A therapist might want to recommend only a temporary or limited separation to prevent violence while resolving conflicts. In certain cases, a therapist may want to bring in a grandparent or another relative to live with the couple temporarily. Often, the presence of a third person, a witness, prevents violence.

Clarity about when to recommend a separation is even more important in cases of violence against children. It is usually better to expel a parent than to remove a child. If a child must be removed from the home, it is usually preferable to find a placement with relatives rather than with strangers. Keeping a child within the natural network with a caring grandmother or aunt is always better than placing the child with strangers.

Compassion and Unity

Eliciting compassion and a sense of unity is useful when working with individuals who have been the victims of trauma and injustice and are obsessed with trying to remember and to understand why this happened to them. After spending the necessary time helping the person to recover and understand childhood memories, it is important to reach closure and end the subject. The therapist says that, even though it was very painful, what really happened to that particular person is not so important. For example, whether or not a particular woman was sexually molested as a child is not as important as the fact that so many millions of women have been abused through the centuries. Each one carries within her the memory of all those women who suffered, and her pain is each woman's pain. If a man was abandoned by his mother, what matters is that so many children suffer terrible injustice and torment without reason or explanation. It is important for each person to make some contribution toward ending that pain. The adult has more in common with the therapist or with a friend than with the abused child he once was. This appeal to separate from the past while at the same time developing a sense of unity with the rest of humanity helps people to disengage from past traumas and get on with their lives.

Repentance and Reparation

There is a method consisting of 16 steps for working with sex offenders and their victims (Madanes, 1990) that is therapeutic for both the victim and the victimizer. The method is presented here in some detail for a situation in which the offender is an older brother, and some guidelines are given for using the steps in other circumstances.

This method is unique within the strategic approach and within the field of therapy, in that it was developed not only because it is therapeutic for the victim as well as the victimizer, but also because it is the morally correct thing to do (Madanes, 1990).

16 Steps to Reparation

In the case of an older brother who molests a younger sister or brother, the first step is to obtain an account of the sexual offense. The therapist gathers the family together and asks everyone to describe exactly what happened. The therapist can encourage the victim to talk, but there should be no pressure. There is tremendous group pressure on the offender when everybody explains all they know and all they knew. It is very difficult for the offender to deny what he did.

The guiding principle for the therapist is that there can be no secrets in these families. Incest is possible because it is secret, so in these families all secrets must be violated. In a normal family, people keep secrets from each other without severe consequences. In families where sexual abuse occurs, people characteristically try to keep secrets from each other and from the therapist. When there has been incest, one cannot allow any more secrets, because a secret can deteriorate into another incestuous relationship.

Step 2 involves the therapist's asking each family member, starting with the offender, why

what the offender did to the victim was wrong. The offender usually has trouble explaining why it was wrong. He will say that it is against religion, that it was wrong because he was caught, that it is against the law, and so on. Then the therapist asks the parents to explain other reasons why it was wrong. The parents will say that it was wrong because it was painful, violent, an intrusion on the person.

In step 3, the therapist agrees that it was wrong for all those reasons, and then points out that it was wrong for one more, very important reason—that it caused the victim spiritual pain. Depending on the religious and cultural background of the family, the therapist uses the expression "spiritual pain" or "pain in the heart." Sexuality and spirituality are related. A sexual violation is a violation of the person's spirit, and that is why it is particularly wrong. It is more hurtful than a physical attack, like hitting someone over the head. Families never disagree with this view.

The fourth step consists of the therapist saying that a sexual attack also causes a spiritual pain in the victimizer. It is horrible to do something like that to somebody else, particularly to a sibling one loves. The therapist expresses feeling for the pain of the offender.

Step 5 usually takes place spontaneously. Someone in the family tells the therapist that the victimizer, and perhaps other family members, was also sexually molested by relatives, by strangers, or by friends of the family. Usually, there has been incest in several generations. There are rarely just one victim and one victimizer.

The therapist sympathizes with this, and in step 6 says that the acts of the offender caused spiritual pain not only to the victim and the victimizer, but also to the mother and to other family members. In attacking the victim, the offender was attacking his mother, his father, and everybody else in the family, because he was doing this to the child they love.

Step 7 is to ask the offender to get on his knees in front of the victim and express sorrow and repentance for what he did. He must do this on his knees and in such a way that it is apparent to everyone in the room that he is sincere and truly penitent. The offender often objects, and sometimes the parents support his objections. The offender wants to say that he is sorry but he does not want to get on his knees because it is humiliating. The therapist needs to say that that is exactly why he should get on his knees. If the offender refuses, the therapist says that the therapy cannot proceed until he gets on his knees and that, in fact, the therapist must report to the court that the offender is not truly repentful and so perhaps therapy is not indicated. The alternative is usually institutionalization.

It may be necessary to have the offender express sorrow and repentance on his knees again and again, until the therapist and family are satisfied that he is sincere. The victim can forgive him if she or he wants to, but does not have to forgive.

In step 8, the therapist asks the other family members to get on their knees in front of the victim and express repentance and sorrow for not having protected the victim. If the offender is resistant to getting on his knees one might do step 8 first, and then go back to step 7. It is important to have a humiliating apology as soon as possible, preferably by the end of the first or second session. This is therapeutic for the offender and very therapeutic for the victim. It establishes publicly, in front of the whole family, that the victim was a victim, that she or he does not have to apologize, that nobody is interested in what the victim contributed to the situation, and that she or he does not even have to forgive. One of the problems of victims is that they tend to define their whole personality as that of a victim. Now the victim can leave the session with a feeling of not being accused and not having to be punished. This is the beginning of not having to think of herself or himself always and only as a victim.

Step 9 involves discussing with the parents what the consequences will be if something like this happens again. The therapist encourages the parents to settle for the harshest consequence: expulsion from the family, which usually means institutionalization.

In step 10, the therapist sees the victim alone and encourages her or him to talk about the abuse, to express her or his feelings, fears, and pain. The therapist expresses sympathy but emphasizes that when very bad things happen to people, they develop a special quality of compassion that raises them to a higher level of being. They can empathize more deeply with the pain of others. The therapist can also say that, even though this seems so terrible now, what happened is just one very small part of the child's life. It is useful to give a time frame, saying that the offense probably took just a few minutes in a day that had 24 hours, in a year that had 365 days, out of all the days of her or his life. While this was happening, other important things were happening. She or he had friends. Perhaps the child liked to dance or liked music or art. The therapist orients the victim toward beautiful things in life and begins to put the offense in that context. It is an unfortunate thing that eventually will be forgotten.

In step 11, the therapist begins to find a protector for the victim. It is a mistake to think of the mother in this role. Usually the mother in these families is very weak and cannot protect the victim. As an ultimate result of the therapy, the mother should be stronger and able to protect the victim, but at this stage in the therapy she is not. It is best to look for another relative, somebody in the extended family. A respectable, responsible uncle or two grandmothers might be very good protectors.

Step 12 is reparation. The therapist asks the parents to think about what the offender could do as an act of reparation, even if the reparation is somewhat symbolic because there is really nothing he can do to compensate for sexual violence. This should be an act involving a long-term sacrifice, beneficial to the victim.

In step 13, the therapist discusses activities for the offender in order to orient him toward a normal life. The therapist talks about school, sports, relationships with friends, and what is sexually normal. It is best to spend some time with the father and son alone, encouraging the father to talk frankly with the son about sex, sexual impulses, normal sexual outlets, and what to do when an inappropriate sexual impulse arises.

Step 14 is restoration of love. One cannot end these therapies without restoring the mother's love for the offender as much as possible. There are two types of mothers in these cases—those who turn against the offender and those who turn against the victim. In both cases, one has to restore the mother's love, and this can be very difficult. The therapist can help the mother recall how she loved her child when he or she was a baby and how available she was to help him or her grow and develop, emphasizing how she can continue to do so. Positive identification can be encouraged by pointing out similarities between the mother and the child. The child can be encouraged to demonstrate love to the mother, hoping that she will respond in kind.

Step 15 involves restoring the victimizer's position in the family as protector of the younger siblings—not as *the* main protector, but in a protective relationship in the way an older sibling should behave toward a younger. One might have the offender advise the younger children on how not to get into trouble, how to avoid strangers in the street, how not to talk to bad people, or how to refuse drugs.

In step 16, the therapist helps the offender to forgive himself. This is sometimes very difficult. Here one might use the strategy of doing good deeds. The therapist can say that whenever the offender becomes obsessed with thoughts about what he did, he should do a good deed for others. For example, there are organizations for abused women to which they can donate their time or their money.

Sexual perversion and sexual abuse may happen only sporadically. The consequences, however, are devastating for the victim. Because of this danger, it is best not to end therapy, but to continue scheduling sessions for a long time, even if only every four or six weeks, to keep an eye on the family and detect any signs of trouble that could lead to another offense.

When the Offender Is the Father—and Other Circumstances

In cases where the offender is the father, the same steps are followed, including having the father get on his knees and express sorrow and repentance to the victim. The members of the family also get on their knees in front of the victim to express sorrow and repentance for not having protected her. When the offender is an older sibling, it is usually the offender who resists getting down on his knees. When the offender is the father, he often gets down on his knees without argument and cries and repents. It is the mother who refuses. The mother will say that she did not know anything about the offense, that there was no way that she could have known, that she has no responsibility, that she does not appreciate the implication that she

was somehow involved, and so on. The therapist can say that at least she could have had open communication with her child, so that the child would have come to her. She should express sorrow and repentance on her knees for not having had that type of communication with the child. One might even include the grandmother, and have her on her knees for not having had the kind of communication with her grandchild that would have allowed the grandchild to go to her for protection. These steps are very important, because the therapist must give the victim the sense of being righted.

When the offender is the father, it is necessary to add a marital stage that consists of discussing and finding solutions to the marital and sexual problems that are always pervasive in these cases.

In some cases, the offense happened in the past and the victim comes to a therapist wanting not only to remember, but also to clarify the situation with the parents. The parents are brought in and all the steps are followed in the same way. If the father is dead, all the steps that are possible are carried out with the rest of the family.

CASE STUDY: THE FATHER WITH A PAIN IN HIS MARRIAGE[8]

A man in his early 50s was referred for court-ordered therapy. He was addicted to painkillers and, over a period of 11 years, had forged numerous prescriptions to obtain drugs. He had worked for 20 years as a printer, and during the last nine of those years he had forged prescription forms, to which he had easy access because of his job. He was not fired because his work was appreciated, but he had appeared in court numerous times, had suffered various penalties, and had a trial pending and the possibility of a jail sentence. His attempts to overcome his addiction had failed, and so had previous therapy. The man was married and had four children, three sons and one daughter. The second son

---

[8] The therapist was Penny Purcell, M.A., and the supervisor was Cloé Madanes. This case study was published in somewhat different form in Madanes (1984).

was away at a seminary, studying to become a priest. The three other children, ranging in age from 14 to 22, were living at home.

The therapist and the supervisor decided to see only the man and his wife in the first interview and to approach the problem as a marital one; the idea was to solve whatever marital problems were related to the addiction and delinquency and to arrange for the wife to help the husband in changing his behavior. When the couple came to the first interview, the husband immediately presented himself as an addict and took the blame for the family's problems. The wife said that for 10 years she had done everything she could, that she was tired of her husband's promises, had too many resentments, and was unwilling to do more. Both spouses appeared indifferent to the therapist, and it was clear that they were complying with the court order for compulsory therapy, but did not think anything would come of it; they had been through this before.

In an attempt to define the problem as an interactional one, the therapist suggested that the husband was addicted to painkillers because he had pain and that someone in the family must be giving him the pain. The couple denied this, saying that only he was to blame; but finally the husband said that the children irritated him with their untidiness. The wife immediately jumped on the husband, defending the children with such intensity and anger that it was clear that she was in a powerful coalition with the children against him. As husband and wife talked about their lives, it became evident that the wife also derived power from holding a superior position in practically all areas. She had had more education than her husband, held a job that was artistic and intellectual, was a competent housewife and mother, led a rich spiritual life (she went to Mass every day), and felt that she was a superior person in every way. She constantly put down her husband, but he never criticized her. She accused the husband not only of being a bad husband, but also of being a bad father, irritable, insensitive, demanding, and cruel to the children.

The therapist attempted to bring the spouses together in various ways, emphasizing their successes and their love for each other, and suggested that the husband invite the wife to do something with him outside the house; this was

to be something he would like to do, even though it might not be the wife's favorite activity. The husband had great trouble deciding what to ask the wife to do with him, but he finally came up with going to a restaurant where he would like to have dinner and to a show that he would like to see.

At the second session, the spouses reported that things between them were better. The oldest son had provoked the father, and the father had refused to quarrel with him; as a result, the young man apologized. The father related that this son used drugs and that neither of the boys did any chores. The therapist attempted to bring the couple together in agreement as parents, but the father pointed out that it was difficult for him to enforce anything, since he himself was an addict. The mother blamed the father for all difficulties and reasserted her coalition with the children against him.

It was clear that, although there had been improvement since the first session, the therapy would be slow and painful if it continued to focus on direct attempts to bring the couple together as spouses and as parents. The wife's coalition with the children against the husband would prevail over the therapist's attempts to bring the spouses together. An indirect strategy of approaching the parents through their children might succeed in a shorter time and with less pain for all involved. The therapist asked the couple to bring the children to the next interview.

The two younger children (the couple's 14-year-old daughter and 17-year-old son) came to the next appointment, and the therapist took them into the therapy room, leaving the parents in the waiting room. She told the children that the father took medication because he had a pain in his marriage. She said that she had tried to help the parents to be happy together but had failed because they had forgotten how to be happy and so she needed the children's help. They would be in charge of the parents' happiness, and from then on it would be their responsibility to see that their parents had a happy marriage. She asked the children if they would agree to assume this responsibility, and help their parents to be happy. The children timidly said Yes. Both children appeared shy and worried, and the daughter seemed particularly depressed. They had obviously come to the session with some trepidation.

The therapist gave paper and a pencil to the boy and asked the children to start making a list of the things they could arrange in the next two weeks so that the parents would experience happiness. For example, would it be possible to arrange a special dinner for the parents in the home, for which the children would set the table, cook, and serve, and which the parents could enjoy without having to prepare anything or wash the dishes afterward? The children said that that would be possible, and the therapist began to discuss with them how the table should be set to create a special atmosphere that would make the parents happy and that would bring them together. They were to use the good tableware and tablecloth and cloth napkins instead of paper, and they were to provide candlelight to create a more romantic ambiance. The children agreed to all this and wrote it down. Then they discussed with the therapist what they could cook. It turned out that they only knew how to make hamburgers, so hamburgers and salad would be the menu. The children and the therapist chose the day and time for the meal and decided how to give instructions to the older brother so that he would cooperate with the preparations. The children would serve the parents, and then they would eat in the kitchen after the parents were finished. As this conversation progressed, the children became more vivacious, and the son enthusiastically wrote down their decisions.

The son suggested that the parents should go out one evening to dinner and a movie. There was some discussion about which movie they should see, and the children agreed on one that both parents might like. The daughter volunteered to sit with the elderly grandmother who lived with them so that the parents could go out with peace of mind. The children also planned to stay out of the living room a couple of evenings that week so that the parents could watch television alone together.

Once the children finished their plan for the parents for the next week and it was all down in writing, the therapist brought the parents into the therapy room. She told them that she had explained to the children that the father's pain was a pain in his marriage and that the parents had forgotten how to be happy together, and so she had put the children in charge of the parents' happiness. From then on, the parents were to follow the children's instructions, and the children would tell them what to do so they could be happy again. She said that the children had prepared a list of the things the parents were to do in the next week, and would now read it and explain it to the parents. The parents began to laugh as soon as the dinner was explained to them and, as the plan developed, they were clearly moved by their children's concern for them. The mother did not object since it was a plan devised not by the therapist, but by her wonderful children. The parents promised to follow all the instructions, and the session ended with the therapist's congratulating them for having such wonderful children.

The family came back one week later, and the therapist once more asked the children into the interview room alone. They reported on how the plans had been carried out. The dinner had not gone quite as planned because they had neglected properly to explain the situation to their older brother, who had come home unexpectedly and eaten half of the hamburgers they had prepared for the parents. They also had not set the table as nicely as they might have, so it was decided to repeat the dinner but to do it better and with the collaboration of the brother, to whom the therapist wrote a letter explaining the plan. Everything else had gone well. The children made a similar plan for the next two weeks, encouraged by the positive changes that had occurred in the parents' mood and in the way they got along together. This time, they added a plan for the parents to spend a couple of evenings out together. The parents were called in, and they confirmed the children's report and listened to their instructions for the next two weeks. They were amused, and the mood between them was better than in previous sessions. Then the children were asked to go to the waiting room so that the therapist could talk with the parents for a few minutes. The parents reported improvement in their feelings for each other. They also discussed with the therapist the father's decreased use of drugs. (He had been undergoing court-ordered urine testing every day, which was reported to the therapist; his urine had been found to be clear of drugs since the beginning of the therapy—for the first time in many years.)

The session two weeks later proceeded in a similar manner. The children reported first and made another plan for the parents; then the parents confirmed the children's report, listened to the new plan, agreed to follow it, and finally talked for a few minutes alone with the therapist. The older brother sent word to the therapist that he would follow his younger siblings' instructions, but that he now had a full-time job and could not come to the sessions. The children's new planned activities for the parents included a trip to a beach and casino resort, birthday and anniversary celebrations, social gatherings, and outings to the theater. When the parents went to the casino, the mother discovered that she enjoyed gambling a great deal; this was a good sign because it implied that she could also develop a vice. This was the first indication that she had an inclination to indulge in an activity that is not quite proper. The father was no longer the only one of the two who had such inclinations.

In the third month of therapy, the couple reported that they were quite happy together, but the wife said that she was still suspicious and that she could not forget the past. She was always looking for signs of the husband's previous addiction, searching the old places where he used to hide his medication with the idea that she might find it again. The therapist suggested to the father that he leave love notes in those old hiding places so that, when the wife looked there, not only would she not find the medicine, but she would be reassured by the messages that her husband loved her.[9] The husband did this, and the wife's suspicions disappeared. She reported that she was pleased because the husband's behavior toward the children—and particularly toward the oldest son, with whom he had clashed most—had changed greatly. The father had had a long, fatherly talk with this son and had become more involved with him; the young man had quit using drugs, was saving his money, and had been accepted back into the Navy to complete his training.

The therapy proceeded in the same way for approximately six months. The father's urine remained clear, and he faced his charges, paid his fines, and did not have to serve a jail sentence.

During this period, the middle son came to the session one day while he was on a visit home from the seminary. The therapist reported to him what the family had been doing and explained that now his younger brother and sister were in charge of the parents' happiness. This son had been the child most involved in helping the parents in the past, and the therapist had to ease him out of this position and ascertain that he would not interfere with the plans of his younger siblings. Also during this time, the daughter turned 15 and blossomed into a very attractive young woman. To the surprise of the therapist and supervisor, who had not noticed, the mother explained that the daughter had been born with a clubfoot and although she had had an operation, she had remained clumsy and physically unsure of herself. She was also dyslexic and had always been afraid and ashamed of writing. Being in charge of the parents had raised her confidence, and now she was doing well in school, had a boyfriend, and was happy with herself physically and intellectually.

The therapy proceeded in the same manner until the last session, when the parents said that they now knew how to be happy together and no longer needed such close supervision from the children.

To summarize, the marital problems were solved by the children, who were put in charge of the parents' happiness. The children's authority was expressed through very concrete plans for what the parents were to do. The parents' relationship improved as a result of the children's instructions, and also as the parents mirrored the good relationship and the competent interaction between brother and sister. The cross-generation coalition between the mother and children against the father was broken as the children were put in charge of both parents, bringing them together at the same level. The father's addiction and delinquency were never addressed directly; they disappeared as his marital and family situation improved. He became a more competent father and was able to give his children and wife the guidance and support they needed. Moved by the children's concern and caring, the wife became more tolerant and understanding. The behavior of the two problem children improved, one as a result of the change in the father, the other as a result of the authority vested in her by the therapist.

---

[9] This intervention was suggested by Judith Mazza.

THE GOALS OF THERAPY, REVISITED

There are some goals common to all therapies (Madanes, 1990):

1. *To control action.* Most people come to therapy because they want to change their own behavior or that of significant others. They are concerned because they cannot help behaving in ways that are harmful to themselves or to others. Therapists want to promote the deliberate control of behavior by the person engaging in the behavior, rather than by others or by uncontrollable impulses.

2. *To control mind.* When people come to therapy disinterested in changing their behavior, they usually come because they want to change the way they think or feel. They are bothered by anxiety, fears, delusions, obsessive thoughts, sadness, and the like. It is important for a therapist to encourage the discipline of controlled emoting and thinking, to control the mind so that negative thoughts can be replaced by positive ones and so that people do not waste time, miserably obsessed with unpleasant or unproductive ideation.

3. *To control violence and anger.* Of all the actions and feelings to be controlled, these are the most important. No one comes to therapy to be hurtful and mean. People come to therapy to bring out the best in themselves. Therapists of all schools struggle to bring out what is good in a person, and none intends to promote violence and anger.

In the past, therapists used to think that there was an anger within that needed to come out and be expressed and so eliminated. It was thought that unexpressed anger would be harmful to the person containing the anger. Today, it is known that the expression of anger is the anger, just as the expression of violence is the violence. Therapists need to transform anger into positive actions and to encourage the patience and tolerance necessary to survive in our families and in society.

It might be argued that some problems brought to therapy could be solved through the expression of violence and anger. For example, a man who beats his wife could be encouraged to attack his son instead; a school counselor could encourage a frustrated teacher to express his or her anger toward a child who is not learning. These are examples of common approaches to life's difficulties, but they are not examples of therapeutic interventions. To encourage anger and violence is not therapeutic.

4. *To encourage empathy.* It is impossible to be a therapist without a heightened sense of empathy for the situation of others. It is the ability to put oneself in the other's place and sympathize with the other's misfortunes that makes therapy possible. It is also this ability that enables us to live in a family and in society. All therapists encourage empathy toward others as a part of a well-adjusted and emotionally satisfying life. To feel for others develops intelligence and a sense of justice.

In the past, therapists promoted empathy only within the nuclear family. Later, they began to include the extended family. Some began to promote feelings of empathy toward all who share the same ethnic background. Today, therapists tend to minimize the importance of family of origin or ethnicity as compared with what the whole human race has in common. When one's forebears are the whole of humankind, one carries within oneself unlimited potential.

5. *To encourage hope and humor.* Only death is unsolvable. In therapy there is always the possibility that a problem will be solved. No one is incurable and no situation is hopeless. If the therapist is hopeful, then the clients can be hopeful about their own lives.

A situation can be hopeless or hopeful depending on the point of view. For example, a retarded person will not become president of the United States, but can lead a productive life and take care of himself or herself; in that sense, he or she is not hopeless. It is the therapist's task to create a framework in which goals can be attained and hope is possible.

Humor, together with intelligence and empathy, is what makes the human condition bearable. Often, the problem in therapy is how to raise people from the grimness of their situation to a higher level of being. In this regard, humor is invaluable. It enables us to come out of ourselves and laugh at our own predicament. The realization that suffering is inevitable and death comes in the end can only be countered with a sense of the absurd.

6. *To promote tolerance and compassion.* Therapists today agree on the importance of promoting tolerance of individual differences and

desires. The explicit encouragement of tolerance promotes good relationships among parents and children, husbands and wives, and friends, neighbors, and co-workers, blocking the intrusiveness that is often at the root of anxiety, fears, and emotional disturbance.

Tolerance and compassion constitute a protective environment in which young persons can grow and develop in their own particular ways. Intolerance and intrusiveness lead to expulsion, punishment, and control by others. When families do not contain and protect their members, agents of social control and total institutions take over and often violate human rights.

7. *To encourage forgiveness and kindness.* The only way we can survive from day to day without emotional breakdown is by forgiving and forgetting. We must forgive our parents, our children, our friends, our teachers. We must also forgive ourselves for our mistakes. If family members are to continue to relate to each other, they must forgive.

Related to the concept of altruism is the idea of reparation and restitution. Therapists often encourage deeds of reparation toward those whom one has deliberately or unwittingly hurt. To perform unselfish acts that involve sacrifice is more therapeutic than talking to a therapist about guilt and depression.

8. *To promote harmony and balance.* A goal of therapy is to bring harmony and balance into people's lives. To love and to be loved, to find fulfillment in work, to play and enjoy—all are part of a necessary balance. An important goal for all clients is to lead a balanced life in harmony and not in conflict.

REFERENCES

Eddy, D. (1986). Completing Brad's dreams. *Family Therapy Networker, 10,* 32–33.

Frankl, V. (1960). Paradoxical intention: A logotherapeutic technique. *American Journal of Psychotherapy, 14,* 520–535.

Haley, J. (1963). *Strategies of psychotherapy.* New York: Grune & Stratton.

Haley, J. (Ed.) (1967a). *Advanced techniques of hypnosis and therapy: The selected papers of Milton H. Erickson.* New York: Grune & Stratton.

Haley, J. (1967b). Toward a theory of pathological systems. In G. Zuk & I. Boszormenyi-Nagy (Eds.), *Family therapy and disturbed families.* Palo Alto, CA: Science & Behavior Books.

Haley, J. (1973). *Uncommon therapy: The psychiatric techniques of Milton H. Erickson.* New York: Norton.

Haley, J. (1976). *Problem-solving therapy: New strategies for effective family therapy.* San Francisco: Jossey-Bass.

Haley, J. (1980). *Leaving home.* New York: McGraw-Hill.

Haley, J. (1984). *Ordeal therapy.* San Francisco: Jossey-Bass.

Herr, J., & Weakland, J. (1979). *Counseling elders and their families.* New York: Springer.

Keim, I., Lentine, G., Keim, J., & Madanes, C. (1988). Strategies for changing the past. *Journal of Strategic and Systemic Therapies:, 6,* 2–17.

Laing, R. (1967). *The politics of experience.* New York: Pantheon Books.

Laing, R. (1969). *The politics of the family.* New York: Random House.

Madanes, C. (1981). *Strategic family therapy.* San Francisco: Jossey Bass.

Madanes, C. (1984). *Behind the one-way mirror: Advances in the practice of strategic therapy.* San Francisco: Jossey-Bass.

Madanes, C. (1987). Advances in strategic family therapy. In J. Zeig (Ed.), *The evolution of psychotherapy.* New York: Brunner Mazel.

Madanes, C. (1989). The goals of therapy. *British Journal of Family Therapy, 2.*

Madanes, C. (1990). *Sex, love, and violence.* New York: Norton.

Madanes, C., Dukes, J., & Harbin, H. (1980). Family ties of heroin addicts. *Archives of General Psychiatry, 37,* 889–984.

Minuchin, S. (1974). *Families and family therapy.* Cambridge, MA: Harvard University Press.

Montalvo, B. (1973). Aspects of live supervision. *Family Process, 12,* 343–359.

Montalvo, B., & Haley, J. (1973). In defense of child therapy. *Family Process, 12,* 227–244.

Papp, P. (1980). The Greek chorus and other techniques of family therapy. *Family Process, 19,* 45–57.

Rabkin, R. (1977). *Strategic psychotherapy.* New York: Basic Books.

Watzlawick, P., Weakland, J., & Fisch, R. (1974). *Change.* New York: Norton.

CHAPTER 13

Structural Family Therapy

Jorge Colapinto

DEVELOPMENT OF THE MODEL

Structural family therapy is a method of conducting therapy that is predicated on a set of assumptions about the organization and dynamics of families, about how they relate to individual problems, and about the processes that effect change in families and individuals. The model shares with other family-systems approaches a preference for a contextual rather than an individual focus on problems and solutions. Distinctive of structural family therapy, on the other hand, are the use of spatial and organizational metaphors, both in describing problems and in identifying avenues for solutions, and the active role assigned to the therapist as an instrument of change.

Like the individuals and families that it has endeavored to understand and help, the structural model grew and changed as a function of context. First the Wiltwyck School for Boys and then the Philadelphia Child Guidance Clinic, both devoted to children's needs, but each serving a different population, provided Salvador Minuchin and his co-workers with the sources

of challenge and inspiration for his development of a distinctive approach to clients—and left their marks in the process.

First Approximations: Wiltwyck

In the early 1960s, Salvador Minuchin was a psychiatrist at the Wiltwyck School for Boys, a correctional facility for young delinquents in the state of New York. There, he assembled a team of therapists and researchers[1] interested in transforming the institutional setting of the school into a family-oriented treatment program. Among others, the group included Braulio Montalvo, who after many years of productive association would be credited by Minuchin with having been "my most influential teacher" (Minuchin, 1974). Their rationale for embracing a family focus was typical of the then-fledging field of family therapy: gains obtained through con-

---

[1] *Editors' Note.* Among the various family therapies, structural therapy has been especially distinguished by its long-time connection with empirical research on basic family interaction processes and treatment outcome.

ventional treatment of the youngsters tended to evaporate once they were returned to their families (Minuchin, 1961).

The Need for Action Techniques

The predicament of the Wiltwyck group, however, was unique: while family therapists so far knew mostly of middle-class, verbally articulate, insight-oriented clients, the typical Wiltwyck client was "the ghetto-living, urban, minority group member who is experiencing poverty, discrimination, fear, crowdedness, and street-living" (Minuchin, Montalvo, Guerney, Rosman, & Schumer, 1967, p. 22). Because the style of interaction in these families tended to be concrete and action-oriented, rather than abstract and verbal, the team looked into alternative, "more doing than talking" therapies. Action techniques, role playings, home-based modalities of treatment, and other nontraditional forms served as inspiration for the development of diagnostic and treatment techniques tailored to poor families (Minuchin & Montalvo, 1966, 1967). A remarkable example—because it quickly became a distinctive feature of the emerging model—was the technique of "enactive formulation" (or, as it is now known, *enactment*), whose name was derived from Bruner's (1964) classification of experiential modes:

The therapist can *say* something or *do* something that expresses the same meaning, or preferably, he can do both. For instance, in one family session a therapist found himself under heavy attack. He then changed his seat and sat among the family members. Pointing to the empty chair, he said, "It was very difficult to be there being attacked by you. It makes me feel left out." The therapist might have described in words alone that he felt left out of the family; instead, he changed his seat to be among the family members and then commented on his feelings. He sensed that although his verbal statement would pass unnoticed by all but the most verbal members of the family, his "movement language" would be attended to by everyone. (Minuchin et al., 1967, p. 247; italics in the original)

Context as Explanation

The Wiltwyck atmosphere not only posed a demand for new techniques, but colored the development of new concepts as well. In a 1978 interview, Minuchin reminisced: "We didn't know anything. And since we didn't know anything, we invented everything. We broke through a wall in our treatment room and put in a one-way mirror and began to observe one another and to build a theory out of nothing" (Malcolm, 1978, p. 84).

The theory started at the opposite end of its psychodynamic counterparts—with a sociological analysis of the impact of social context on poor families. In *Families of the Slums*, after reviewing sociological and anthropological reports on the life of the poor in various cultures, Minuchin's team adopted the view that "an action-excitement orientation, special styles of communication, limited number of usable roles, etc., seem to characterize low-income groups in a wide variety of social settings, and there is every reason to believe that ethnic and racial factors do not account for these characteristics but that social class variables do" (Minuchin et al., 1967, p. 24).

Minuchin and his co-workers went on to note that low-income groups differentiate into two subgroups: a more stable one, whose members enjoy at least the benefits of a support network; and the more unstable, disorganized, isolated group, plagued with various forms of social pathology (alcoholism, disease, mental illness, addiction, delinquency), from where the Wiltwyck residents typically came. Families from this most disadvantaged group provide a peculiarly dysfunctional context for child rearing, as vividly described in a 1965 report quoted in *Families of the Slums* (p. 26):

The outstanding characteristic in these homes was that activities were impulse-determined; consistency was totally absent. The mother might stay in bed until noon while the children also were kept in bed or ran around unsupervised. . . . The parents often failed to discriminate between the children. A parent, incensed by the behavior of one child, was seen dealing a blow to another child who was closer. . . . Directions were indefinite or hung unfinished in mid-air. . . . As the children outgrew babyhood, the parents differentiated very little between the parent and child role. . . . (Pavenstedt, 1965, pp. 94–95)

The negative effects of this kind of context on the behavior of children had previously been documented in a study by Malone (1963), showing that preschool children from disorganized families exhibited low frustration tolerance, dominant use of motor action over language, concrete thinking, need-satisfying object relations, and other predictors of chronic acting out and impulse disorders (Minuchin et al., 1967).

The premise that social context is a most powerful organizer (or disorganizer) of families, and that family context is similarly powerful in organizing (or disorganizing) individuals, seemed to call for therapeutic interventions aimed at context rather than at an isolated problem—and indeed this would become a cornerstone of the structural model throughout its various phases of development. In the case of the Wiltwyck population, the "context of the problem" was of such dimension as to invite hopelessness; indeed, Minuchin has in retrospect regarded the experience as a reminder that therapy—individual or family—cannot provide the answer to poverty (Malcolm, 1978). This limitation notwithstanding, the knowledge gained at Wiltwyck inspired the development of structuring strategies for helping underorganized families through the mobilization of extended family and social network resources (Aponte, 1976a). More recently, Minuchin himself has led an application of structural thinking to the understanding and changing of the large systems of service delivery that make up the relevant context of poor families.

Function and Structure

In an attempt to understand the disorganized family better, the Wiltwyck group used as a background Talcott Parsons' model of the nuclear family (Parsons & Bales, 1955), where, by contrast, family members are neatly organized in a structure of roles or functions, along the axes of hierarchy (representing the differences in power between parents and children) and instrumental versus expressive functions (representing what Parsons considered to be the "normal" division of labor among father, mother, son, and daughter).

Parsons' paradigm helped to highlight, by comparison, the structure and distribution of functions typical of the Wiltwyck population: spouses who tended to interact not as such but only as parents, or single-parent families in which the mother provided continuity while men were transient; parents who oscillated between autocratic power and helpless relinquishment of executive functions; sibling subsystems that became primary socializing agents. The child growing up within these structures "seldom finds enough moments of a 'cooperative collective,' and must, in general, settle for whatever sense of protection he can derive from people generally absorbed in the intrusive and conflicting aspects of living collectively" (Minuchin et al., 1967, p. 242).

The early connection between Parsons' gender-role paradigm and the structural model has attracted criticism from feminist writers (Luepnitz, 1989). In reading *Families of the Slums*, however, one does not get the impression that Minuchin and his co-workers regarded Parsons' stereotypical division of instrumental and expressive roles as the ideal solution for their disorganized clients. What one can see is how the Wiltwyck experience nurtured the conviction that families need *some* kind of structure, *some* form of hierarchy, and *some* degree of differentiation between subsystems.

Forging the Model: Philadelphia

While wrestling with the specifics of the Wiltwyck families, Minuchin maintained an interest in the universal. His discussion of the structure and processes typical of disorganized families opens with a famous quote from Harry Stack Sullivan: "Everyone and anyone is much more simply human than otherwise, more like everyone else than different" (Sullivan, 1962; quoted in Minuchin et al., 1967, p. 193).

The opportunity to test Sullivan's assertion came in 1965, when Minuchin was appointed director of the Philadelphia Child Guidance Clinic, and his developing model of family therapy came into contact with a more heterogeneous client population, which included both working-class and middle-class families.

A Training Context

Determined to turn the clinic into a family-oriented facility, Minuchin brought Braulio Montalvo from Wiltwyck and Jay Haley from California to help in training the staff. Teaching as they continued to learn, and benefiting from the systematic use of live supervision and videotape review (Montalvo, 1973), the three men generated an intensive and fruitful mutual exchange of observations and ideas on family dynamics and strategies for change. Years later, in his preface to *Families and Family Therapy*, Minuchin (1974) would credit the contributions of Montalvo and Haley to his thinking.

The needs of training-on-the-job, and Haley's own preference for focusing the training on change-eliciting skills rather than theoretical understanding, contributed to imbuing the developing model with a teachable, concrete, step-by-step quality. The focus was on showing the "steps of the dance," on teaching specific skills "without burdening the student with a load of theory that would slow him down at moments of therapeutic immediacy" (Minuchin & Fishman, 1981, p. 9). The trend was accentuated in the late 1960s, when the clinic obtained a grant to train "lay therapists"—minority paraprofessionals with no previous psychotherapeutic experience or formal education (Montalvo, 1973) —and culminated in the late 1970s, when one of the most popular workshops offered by the clinic was titled, "An Alphabet of Skills."

A New Challenge: Overorganized Families

At the same time, the clinic's association with the Children's Hospital of Philadelphia provided Minuchin with an opportunity to apply his vision of the family as a powerful organizing context to the understanding of psychosomatic conditions. In the early 1970s, he formed a research and treatment team at which core were Minuchin himself, the pediatrician Lester Baker, the psychiatrist Ronald Liebman, and research psychologist Bernice Rosman—a former collaborator at Wiltwyck and coauthor of *Families of the Slums*. The clinical and research findings of the team were later summarized in *Psychosomatic Families* (Minuchin, Rosman, & Baker, 1978).

The first patients to be approached were diabetic children with unusually frequent, medically unexplained emergency hospitalizations for acidosis. When conventional psychotherapy aimed at enhancing the patient's stress-handling abilities did not improve the condition, family intervention did (Baker, Minuchin, Milman, Liebman, & Todd, 1975). Minuchin and his co-workers began collecting data that showed a correlation between certain family traits (enmeshment, overprotectiveness, rigidity, absence of conflict resolution) and the special vulnerability of the diabetic patients. Similar connections were established for psychosomatic asthma, where children suffered recurrent attacks or depended heavily on steroids (Liebman, Minuchin, & Baker, 1974c; Minuchin, Baker, Rosman, Liebman, Milman, & Todd, 1975; Liebman, Minuchin, Baker, & Rosman, 1976, 1977), and for anorexia nervosa (Liebman, Minuchin, & Baker, 1974a, 1974b; Minuchin, Baker, Liebman, Milman, Rosman, & Todd, 1973; Rosman, Minuchin, & Liebman, 1975, 1977; Rosman, Minuchin, Liebman, & Baker, 1976, 1977).[2]

Most of the interactional traits identified by Minuchin and his co-workers in these largely middle-class, "intact" families had already been pointed out in the Wiltwyck families. There was a crucial difference, however: far from exhibiting disorganization and instability, the families of psychosomatic children appeared to be too tightly organized and, if anything, excessively stable. They called for a therapeutic strategy focused on *de*structuring the family's rigid patterns, and *re*structuring them according to more functional parameters: clearer boundaries, increased flexibility in transactions, conflict negotiation, and detriangulation of the identified patient. *Enactments*, first implemented at Wiltwyck for the purpose of effective communication with nonverbal clients, were now used deliberately to provoke destabilizing crises among

---

[2] *Editors' Note.* But note that the data of structuralists believed quite widely to support their theoretical stance about the "psychosomatic" family have not received universal acceptance (cf. Coyne & Anderson, 1988, 1989).

clients who talked too much (Minuchin & Barcai, 1969).[3]

Of the three syndromes treated by Minuchin and his team, anorexia nervosa was the best suited to a family-focused approach. Unlike asthma and diabetes, in which the dysfunctional context plays just an exacerbating role on a primarily physiological condition, anorexia has no demonstrated physiological basis, which opens the possibility for a well-designed family intervention to bring about a "cure," not just an amelioration of an otherwise chronic condition. Indeed, Minuchin's success in the treatment of anorexia nervosa was a major factor in attracting therapists to the structural model. Clinical experience with cases of anorexia nervosa also played an important role in clarifying the tenets of structural family therapy; an early "prototype" of the model (Minuchin, 1970) utilized one such case as an illustration.

A Comprehensive Model

Minuchin's first systematic formulation of his model was published in 1972, in an article entitled, precisely, "Structural Family Therapy." Some of the tenets presented there, like the displacement of the locus of pathology from the individual to the transactional context, the emphasis on present reality rather than history, and the notion of constructed realities, were held in common with other contributors to the field of family therapy; others, like the special attention paid to the diverse points of entry that different families offer to the therapist, and the characterization of therapy as a realignment of the family's structure of transactions, were more specific to the approach.

Further expansion and refinement of the model were the natural consequences of the wide range of clinical experiences being gathered in the clinic, which was gradually becoming a major service agency with sizable outpatient and inpatient components, and of Minuchin's

intellectual association with Haley and Montalvo. This phase culminated in the publication of the classic *Families and Family Therapy*, a fully developed account of the structural way of understanding and treating families (Minuchin, 1974).

In 1976, Minuchin stepped down from the politics of directorship and concentrated on the training of family therapists. The continued effort to break down structural family therapy into discrete skill components that the trainee could rehearse is reflected in Minuchin's latest rendition of his therapeutic approach, *Family Therapy Techniques* (Minuchin & Fishman, 1981), in which most chapters are named after techniques. Running parallel to such effort, however, was the growing recognition that the effectiveness of structural family therapy depended on its being learned as a therapeutic stance rather than as an aggregate of useful tools (Colapinto, 1983, 1988). The dilemma, yet to be satisfactorily resolved, is also reflected in *Family Therapy Techniques*, whose "technical" chapters are preceded and followed by conceptual frameworks that attempt to put techniques in their place. Minuchin's preference for biosocial over physical models of systems is evident in those frameworks, which draw metaphors from Lewis Thomas' essays on animal life, Arthur Koestler's efforts at capturing in language the relationship between whole and part, and Ilya Prigogine's theory of change in living systems.

THE FUNCTIONAL FAMILY

A quotation from Lewis Thomas opens the chapter on families in *Family Therapy Techniques*: "There is a tendency for living things to join up, establish linkages, live inside each other, return to earlier arrangements, get along whenever possible. This is the way of the world" (Thomas, 1974, p. 147).

Structural family therapy sees the family as a living organism, constantly developing and adapting to a changing environment—"an open sociocultural system in transformation" (Minuchin, 1974, p. 51). One implication of the organismic view of families is a sense of acceptance of and respect for different forms of family life,

---

[3] *Editors' Note.* Such destabilizing enactments remind us of Roberto's (Chapter 14) description of some symbolic-experiential family therapy techniques that are designed to "destroy crystallized forms" of family patterns.

and a wide definition of normality. "Freud," wrote Minuchin, "pointed out that therapy changes neurotic patterns into the normal miseries of life. His comment is just as true for family therapy" (Minuchin, 1974, p. 51). A well-functioning family is not defined by the absence of stress, conflict, and problems, but by how effectively it handles them in the course of fulfilling its functions. This, in turn, depends on the structure and adaptability of the family.

Family Function and the Individual

The function of the family in society is the "support, regulation, nurturance, and socialization of its members" (Minuchin, 1974, p. 14).

A fundamental premise of structural family therapy is the inextricable association of family and individual: the family exists for the individual, the individual exists within the family, to which he or she must adapt. The family context has the power "to organize the data and to maintain definitions of self and others" (Minuchin & Fishman, 1981, pp. 144–145); the position of the individual in the family conditions his or her experience.

Adaptation to one's family, far from being a surrender of individual identity, is its main condition. Unlike Laing (1976), who saw in the family an enemy of individual differentiation, Minuchin sees the family as the matrix of identity: the individual becomes such as a result of participating in multivariated family transactions. One differentiates within, rather than against, the family group; individual and family are not contraries, but different cuts of reality.

Structure

How well a family fulfills its function vis-à-vis its members depends on the family structure and on its adaptability. Like other adapting organisms, families need some form of internal organization that dictates how, when, and to whom to relate. These *transactional patterns* make up the structure of the family.

Generic and Idiosyncratic Constraints

The structure of transactional patterns operates as a set of rules that constrain the family members' freedom of behavior. Some of these constraints are generic: for instance, no family could function as such unless its members accept some degree of interdependency (as between husband and wife) and some form of hierarchy (as between parents and children). Other constraints or rules are mutual expectations that develop idiosyncratically within each family:

The origin of these expectations is buried in years of explicit and implicit negotiations among family members, often around small daily events. Frequently the nature of the original contracts has been forgotten, and they may never have even been explicit. But the patterns remain—on automatic pilot, as it were—as a matter of mutual accommodation and functional effectiveness. (Minuchin, 1974, p. 52)

Family rules may not be readily apparent to an observer. A therapist interviewing a family whose children get up and down from their chairs and leave the rooms unexpectedly (in the therapist's view) may conclude that the family is chaotically dysfunctional; a closer observation, however, may reveal that family members can predict which child will be leaving the room, how far the child will go, and when he or she will return, and that the entire dance has an adaptive purpose.

Complementarity

Family rules develop primarily through a process of correlated differentiation: the behaviors of any two family members mutually accommodate in such a way that one develops selective aspects of himself or herself, while the other develops a complementary trait. Typical examples are the harsh and the soft parent, the active and the passive spouse, the left-brain and the right-brain siblings. When all the members of the family are considered, the resulting image is like a jigsaw puzzle, where the irregular borders of the various pieces fit—complement—each other. Carrying the metaphor further, the salient borders of each piece represent the traits expected from each member (harshness, passivity, left brain), while the concave sections represent traits not expected. In well-functioning families, complementarity takes the form of effective teamwork.

Although the notion of complementarity may appear to be identical to that of circular causality—they both underscore the mutual determination of behavior within a family system—there is a difference. Circular causality designates a *sequential* two-way interaction (A's *behavior* causes B's *behavior*, and vice versa), represented by arrowed lines connecting A and B (thus, A⇌B). Complementarity, on the other hand, designates a *spatial* configuration (A's and B's *shapes* fit), represented by the interlocking pieces of the puzzle. This semantic difference is not trivial, but is consistent with the structural therapist's preference for tackling spatial arrangements (literal and metaphorical) among family members, rather than sequences of behavior.

Subsystems and Boundaries

The structural model discerns various subgroupings within the family, defined by their function. Individual members of a family participate in several subsystems.

Thus, a husband and a wife form the spouse subsystem, which serves as a powerful context for mutual support (or for disqualification), and they also participate with their children in the parental subsystem, which is organized around issues of nurturance, guidance, and discipline. The children, in turn, are also members of the sibling subsystem—their first peer group and a laboratory for supporting, enjoying, attacking, scapegoating, and generally learning from one another.

Rules that prescribe who should be in contact with whom about what are called *boundaries*. They can be depicted graphically as encircling lines that surround a subsystem or an individual and separate that subsystem or individual from the rest. Examples of boundaries are the rules prescribing that children should not participate in arguments between spouses, or that parents should knock at the door of a teenager's room before entering.

Like the membrane of a cell, boundaries need to be strong enough to protect the healthy development of subsystems—and, therefore, individual growth. The siblings' subsystem needs to enjoy some autonomy vis-à-vis the parents if the siblings are to learn to accommodate to each other. A father and a son can only get to know each other if they abstain from using the mother as a mediator. A diabetic adolescent needs to be more alert than her parents to the signs of dehydration if she is to own her body.

Excessively rigid and impermeable boundaries, on the other hand, would impinge on the effectiveness of the family, and even its viability as an organism: "If the boundary around the spouses is too rigid," for instance, "the system can be stressed by their isolation" (Minuchin & Fishman, 1981, p. 57).

Permeability of boundaries is necessary not only for the viability of the family, but for the healthy growth of the individual as well. The tendency of many therapists to regard "strong boundaries" as an absolute positive from the point of view of the differentiation of the individual is the expression of a cultural bias that extols the virtues of independence and privacy. Structural family therapy adopts in this respect the "countercultural" position that individual differentiation is achieved through multiple dependency—through participation in multiple subsystems, beginning with the family's. What to some other therapists looks like mastery of autonomy, to the structuralist may look like isolation.

Frustrated by the linguistic difficulties in communicating his ideas on the interdependency of individual and family, of part and whole, Minuchin resorted to Koestler's coining of the term *holon* as a synonym for "subsystem."

Every holon—the individual, the nuclear family, the extended family, and the community—is both a whole and a part, not more one than the other, not one rejecting or conflicting with the other. A holon exerts competitive energy for autonomy and self-preservation as a whole. It also carries integrative energy as a part. The nuclear family is a holon of the extended family, the extended family of the community, and so on. Each whole contains the part, and each part also contains the "program" that the whole imposes. Part and whole contain each other in a continuing, current, and ongoing process of communication and interrelationship. (Minuchin & Fishman, 1981, p. 13)

It is through the individual's adaptation to various subsystems—being a holon in holons, entering into a variety of complementary relationships—that his or her identity is forged. In healthy families, subsystem boundaries are "defined well enough to allow subsystem members to carry out their functions without undue interference," but at the same time, flexible enough to "allow contact between the members of the subsystem and others." Clarity of boundaries is more crucial than the specific composition of each subsystem: "A parental subsystem that includes a grandmother or a parental child can function quite well, so long as lines of responsibility and authority are clearly drawn" (Minuchin, 1974, p. 54).

Hierarchy

The hierarchical arrangement of a family is expressed by rules that prescribe differential degrees of decision-making power for various individuals and subsystems. While some form of hierarchical arrangement is a condition of family functioning, families can function with many different kinds of hierarchy. Generally, in a well-functioning family, the parents are hierarchically positioned above their children—they are "in charge," not in the sense of arbitrary authoritarianism, but in the sense of leadership and protection. In single-parent families, a functional hierarchical arrangement may include the role of a parental child, when his or her clearly defined responsibilities contribute to the overall coping capabilities of the family.

In clinical practice, it may be difficult for the therapist to differentiate between the concepts of "boundaries" and "hierarchy." Wood (1985) and Wood and Talmon (1983) have provided a useful clarification of the relation between the two.

Adaptation and Development

The structure of a healthy family changes over time, as it accommodates to changing needs generated by its own evolution: children are born, grow up, and leave; adults get older, develop new interests, or lose strengths. In the process,

boundaries are redrawn, subsystems regroup, and hierarchical arrangements shift.

A simplified model consisting of four broadly defined developmental stages, each requiring some form of restructuring, is offered by Minuchin and Fishman (1981). In the first stage, *couple formation*, a new system is formed through mutual accommodation; the new spouses need to give up part of their respective ideas and preferences, develop new rules, negotiate a different relationship with relatives and friends. In the second stage, *families with young children*, the arrival of each new member forces a rearrangement of closeness and distances in the family, a new differentiation of functions among the spouses, and a renegotiation of their patterns of relationship with the extrafamiliar—relatives, friends, work. The third stage, *families with school-age or adolescent children*, is dominated by the need to relate to powerful extrafamiliar systems—first, the school itself, then other children's families, and finally the peer group. In the fourth stage, *families with grown children*, parents and children once again renegotiate their relationship, this time as adults, while the parents themselves become again a twosome.

The model has value only as an illustration of the fact that structures need to evolve:

This developmental schema describes only the middle-class family, with husband, wife, and 2.2 children. More and more, it is likely that the family will also form some sort of extended network or will experience divorce, desertion, or remarriage. In moving through such stages, people also face very complicated challenges. But whatever the circumstances, the basic flow remains: a family has to go through certain stages of growth and aging. It must cope with periods of crisis and transition. (Minuchin & Fishman, 1981, p. 26)

Demands for structural transformation do not originate only in the family's developmental needs. They may also be forced upon the family by idiosyncratic changes in its social environment—a move to a new town, a change of jobs, a major shift in the family's financial situation. The family's ability to transform itself in response to internal and external demands depends on its ability to plumb and mobilize individual resources, potential coping behaviors that may have remained underutilized by virtue of the dynamics of complementarity. Some families manage better than others to access those resources.

Maintenance and Change

Structure and adaptability are complementary features. In its pursuit of its function, a family needs both to maintain a stable structure and to change it. On the one hand, the family's continued viability requires that members develop a mutual accommodation to each other's preferences, strengths, and weaknesses; transactional patterns of distance and hierarchy need to be formed and maintained. On the other hand, existing structures may need to be challenged in response to new circumstances inside or outside the family: conflict may need to be raised and dealt with, hidden resources may need to be actualized.

Well-functioning families manage to survive without sacrificing differences and enrichment; they have the capacity alternatively to establish and challenge transactional patterns. For instance, a close protective relationship between a parent and a handicapped child may serve an important maintenance function over a relatively extended period, and then change as the child begins to show evidence of competence that might be hampered by overprotection.

Hierarchical arrangements in healthy families also change over time in response to changing contexts; the hierarchical position of a child, for instance, varies according to his or her age, order of birth within the sibling subsystem, whether the parents are two or one, and so on. When the child is an increasingly competent adolescent and the influence of the peer group grows, issues of autonomy and control need to be renegotiated. Fluid structural arrangements may emerge at these transitional junctures that may appear dysfunctional to an observer who assesses them in the abstract; however, they may represent a healthy way of dealing with the transition. Similarly, a 14-year-old girl may assume a parental role when her mother temporarily succumbs to physical illness or depression, and thus she prevents the dismemberment of the family that might result if her siblings and herself were placed in foster care.

The dialectics of maintenance and change can be synthesized in the notion of steady growth. A healthy family is in a continuous process of structural growth. It has the capacity to become increasingly complex, to develop an ever-increasing availability of alternatives—which, in turn, favors the growth, development, and complexity of its individual members.

The emphasis that structural family therapy places on structural growth and complexity as a marker of health is evident in two statements published 14 years apart. The first one is that fathers should play a role in the family—not because of the "need for a male role model," but because "we feel that the family has more possibility for change as the complexity of its system increases. When a man participates in the family in the role of an adult male, he adds differentiation and specialiation to the family's manner of approaching life; therefore, the possibility of mobilizing resources for change within the family increases" (Minuchin et al., 1967, p. 316).

The second statement is a reference to Prigogine's dissipative structures:

For years family therapy emphasized the power of systems to maintain themselves. Now the work of Prigogine and others has shown that if a system is partially open to the inflow of energy or information, the ensuing instabilities do not lead to random behavior . . . instead, they tend to drive the system to a new dynamic regime which corresponds to a new state of complexity. (Minuchin & Fishman, 1981, p. 21)

THE DYSFUNCTIONAL FAMILY

A dysfunctional family is one that cannot fulfill its function of nurturing the growth of its members. The structural theory of family dysfunction includes (1) a description of dysfunctional family structures, (2) an explanation of family dysfunction, and (3) a description of the relationship between family dysfunction and individual symptoms.

Description of Dysfunctional Structures

The first observations of structural dysfunction in families go back to the early recognition of five patterns among the Wiltwyck families: the "disengaged family," the "enmeshed family," the "family with the peripheral male," the "family with noninvolved parents," and the "family with juvenile parents" (Minuchin et al., 1967, p. 352). In *Families of the Slums*, Minuchin and his co-workers describe how their original focus on disorganized families evolved into the now-familiar *disengagement/enmeshment typology*:

Our simple concern . . . with the relinquishment of executive functions on the part of the parents gave way to the realization that *some* families apparently functioned as if the parents (the mothers in particular) were *overly* concerned with executive functions. This led us to the further realization that actually there seemed to be an axis of disengagement-enmeshment along which our research families were oriented, mostly toward either extreme. (Minuchin et al., 1967, p. 350)

In the disengaged family, boundaries among family members are overly rigid, emotional distance is excessive. The "syndrome" of disengagement includes failure to mobilize mutual support, underdevelopment of nurturant and protective functions, and excessive tolerance to deviation.

Observing this family, one gets the general impression that the actions of its members do not lead to vivid repercussions. Reactions from the others come very slowly and seem to fall into a vacuum. The overall impression is one of an atomistic field; family members have long moments in which they move as in isolated orbits, unrelated to each other. They act as parts of a system so loosely interlocked that it challenges the clinician's notions that a change in one part of a system will be followed by a complementary change in other parts. (Minuchin et al., 1967, p. 354)

More concrete descriptions of interaction in disengaged families include delayed responses and a paucity of contacts.

There are situations in which the children and their mother are involved in parallel play or in activities devoid of any contact among them; at other moments the children activate themselves in ways that are seemingly designed to activate their mother into making a relating response. But even when there is an increase in acting-out, the activities of the children do not seem to be related to a need for contacting others. One notices little attentiveness from member to member and few attempts to engage in reciprocal interplay . . . (Minuchin et al., 1967, p. 355)

In enmeshed families, on the other hand, boundaries are excessively weak and there is excessive proximity among members. The family appears to turn upon itself; there is a low level of individual differentiation and autonomy, and the response of the group to any "deviant" behavior is very intense. Indicators of enmeshment include an increase in the rate of communication, exaggerated concern and protectiveness, mutual demands for loyalty, narrow perceptions of self, and paralysis at times of transition when different responses are needed. "This family system is characterized by a 'tight interlocking' of its members. Their quality of connectedness is such that attempts on the part of one member to change elicit fast complementary resistance on the part of others" (Minuchin et al., 1967, p. 358).

Enmeshed and disengaged families are "ideal" types; most or all families include enmeshed and disengaged areas of transaction. Typical examples of enmeshment are the absence or fragility of individual boundaries (for instance, the parents of a diabetic adolescent know better than she does when she needs insulin), and the intrusion (or the recruitment) of one family member in the subsystem of two others (for instance, a father and son always have their differences mediated by the mother, or a brother and sister always have their fights interrupted by their parents).

Hierarchies can also become excessively weak and ineffective, or excessively rigid and arbitrary. In the first case, the younger members of the family may find themselves unprotected because of a lack of guidance; in the second case, their growth as autonomous individuals may be impaired, or power struggles may ensue. A special case of hierarchical dysfunction is the *cross-generational coalition*, in which the spouses argue their conflict through a child, and each tries to enlist the support of the child against the other. Chronic cross-generational coalitions have been structurally associated with psychosomatic illness (Minuchin et al., 1978) and with addiction (Stanton & Todd, 1982).

Explanation of Family Dysfunction

Dysfunctional family structures result from a combination of stressors impinging on the family and the failure of the family to cope with them. Stressors may be external (the family faces financial hardship or lives in a violent neighborhood) or internal (children reach adolescence, a parent dies). They may be universal, as in the case of developmental transitions in the lives of family members, or idiosyncratic, such as having an accident, suffering from chronic or catastrophic illnesses, or losing a job.

Structural family therapy's sensitivity to the role of external stressors in family dysfunction originated with the Wiltwyck experience. Disengaged structures were seen there as a response to apathetic, overwhelmed, self-derogatory single mothers who experienced themselves as exploited, often presented with psychosomatic and depressive symptoms, and could not establish control or guidance over their children (Minuchin et al., 1967). The mother's predicament, in turn, was explained by her social context—which has obviously not changed much in 25 years:

A prominent feature of disengaged families is the isolation of the mother, who seems unable to contact the external world and to draw on extrafamilial sources. In the most extreme forms of this profile one must look beyond the chronicity of incompetence in mothering to a family history usually lacking in anchorage points such as stable work patterns and stable relationships to a male, friends, or other social groups. . . . Though the family may have contacted many social agencies, the mother's relationship to them is characterized by extreme passivity and dependency. . . . As a group . . . disengaged families are seldom contacted or "reached." Even if they are, however, they soon become dropouts from community programs.

Enmeshed structures were also explained as a response to the hardships of single parenthood—this time under the shape of an overcontrolling reaction to the sense of helplessness:

We are impressed by the constant engagement maneuvers in these families, most of which reflect or are in response to controlling operations on the part of the mother. These include fast interchanges around her controlling responses and the children's rebellious activities. . . . In the enmeshed family profile any evidence of loss of control over her children makes the mother anxious. The predominant fear is that of becoming helpless, rather than of becoming "mean . . .". She has an overwhelming need for a continued hold on the children. These families usually do not include an adult male, but if there is one, his power is clearly restricted and controlled by the woman.

While the socioeconomic makeup of the client population at Wiltwyck helped to highlight the role of social context as stressor, the working- and middle-class families served by the Philadelphia Child Guidance Clinic—comparatively better sheltered from the vicissitudes of the social environment and more autonomous in their functioning—called Minuchin's attention to the other component of the dysfunctional equation, the internal variables that account for a family's inadequate, stereotypical response to stress.

The most basic of those variables is defined in the negative. The family *lacks* the capacity to challenge and modify patterns of transaction that have ceased to satisfy the needs of its members; instead, it exhibits an inertialike tendency to stick to obsolete patterns. For instance, young spouses who have developed a tightly interdependent complementary relationship, with limited occasions for open conflict or for developing relations outside the couple itself, fail to review the rules of their implicit contract following the birth of their first child, or a family with older children who require increasing autonomy continues to deal with them as if they were younger children, needing only nurturance and discipline.

Explanations for structural inertia range from unawareness (where dysfunctional patterns are perpetuated because family members simply cannot think of alternative ways of dealing with each other, or see the need for them) to fear (where dysfunctional patterns are perpetuated because family members are afraid of the consequences of experimenting with such alternatives). In either case, the underlying mechanism is complementarity: in the course of their transacting, family members shape each other's behaviors and mutual expectations, and gradually make each other unaware and/or fearful of the possibility of behaving in ways that depart from established patterns. Joe does not expect Sue to be able to handle the baby while he is working; Sue is afraid that Joe will explode if she demands more cooperation from him.

The most common transactional expression of "fear of change" is the mechanism of *conflict avoidance*, by which two parties shy away from inflicting upon themselves and each other the pains inherent in conflict resolution. Disengagement and enmeshment represent different strategies for avoiding conflict—in one case by curtailing contact and in the other by denying difference and disagreement. Even the constant bickering in which some couples engage serves the purpose of conflict avoidance, inasmuch as it allows for the chronic expression of each party's hostility without pressing for either to change or for a resolution of the conflict. When a third party, such as a child, is present, cross-generational coalitions serve a similar function in covertly channeling conflict.

While there is a universal capacity for conflict avoidance in human groups, some families may have more of a reason to use it. The study of the enmeshed two-parent, middle-class families of psychosomatic children provided a rich observational field for the exploration of the dynamics of overprotection, showing how the involvement of the whole family with the sick child, the heightened concerns regarding the physical welfare of the child, and the constant eliciting and supplying of protective responses helped to submerge potential conflicts (Minuchin & Fishman, 1981).

Relationship Between Structure and Symptom

The structural model describes various types of relationships between family structure and symptoms.

Family Context as Ineffectual Challenger

The family may support the symptom in a *passive* way, just by failing to challenge its continuous display. In this case, the family contrib-

utes to the problem "by default": the other members adapt complementarily to the symptomatic one, and structural inertia hinders the emergence of events that might challenge the symptomatic behavior. For instance, a pattern of overprotection and heightened loyalty makes it impossible for anybody in the family to challenge one member's drug habit.

Family Context as a "Shaper" of the Individual

From a historical perspective, the family's structure contributes a more *active*, if generic, role in the development of symptoms: family context shapes the individual's experience and behaviors—and this includes *problem* behaviors. The handicapping effect of dysfunctional family structures on individual experience has been a basic premise of structural thinking ever since the Wiltwyck days.

Thus, a family may foster dysfunctionality just by hindering the development of the more mature forms of behavior. In families of anorexics, for instance, the excessive parental involvement with the daughter and the family's devaluation of womanhood discourage a developmentally appropriate feeling of autonomy and an inner sense of worth, encouraging by default an excessive reliance on external achievement and control maneuvers. More generally, children from enmeshed families learn to depend exclusively on their families for a sense of support and loyal belonging, at the expense of their ability to respond differentially to various social settings. Disengaged families, on the other hand, instill in their children a skewed sense of independence.

Family Context as a "Beneficiary" of the Symptom

Some families go beyond the passive acceptance of dysfunctional behaviors or the creation of a context that facilitates them: they *encourage* the recurrent display of a specific symptom. In these families, the symptom performs a regulatory function. The origins of the symptomatic behavior may lie in the family dynamics itself, or in biological or social circumstances of the individual family member; in either case, the behavior is now serving the purpose of protecting the stability of the whole system.[4] Thus, in a *detouring-attacking triad*, a delinquent boy may offer an opportunity for the parents to join in *anger* against him, while in a *detouring-protecting triad*, a diabetic girl may allow the parents to focus their joint *concern* on her. In either case, parental conflict is sidetracked. For the sake of system maintenance, parents and child appear alternatively to request the symptom and volunteer it.

The Symptom Bearer

Family dynamics contributes to determining *who* becomes symptomatic: the structure of alliances and coalitions developed over years of spousal negotiation and child rearing renders some people more vulnerable than others to the label of deviance. Other factors, however, may play an equal or stronger role; examples are organic conditions such as asthma, a mild learning disability, or a chemical imbalance in the brain, and circumstantial events originated in the extrafamilial, for example, a bad year in school.

Specific Correlations Between Structures and Symptoms

The most comprehensive attempt to correlate specific family structures with specific categories of symptoms came from the psychosomatic project. As mentioned before, a cluster of traits—enmeshment, overprotectiveness, rigidity, and absence of conflict resolution—was consistently identified in families of psychosomatic children. However, many elements of those traits have been found in clinical practice among other dysfunctional families that do not present psychosomatic problems, and there are no comparative studies demonstrating that the cluster itself is specific to psychosomatic families. In the area of antisocial behaviors, the Wiltwyck experience has shown that a juvenile delinquent may come

from an enmeshed family where there is too much control and little room for experimentation, or from a disengaged family where there is little guidance.

In fact, the terms "enmeshed family" and "disengaged family," while convenient as shorthand, are misleading. Most families include elements of both enmeshment and disengagement, and the current emphasis of structural family therapy is on identifying functional and dysfunctional areas of the family structure, rather than on categorizing pathological structures as such. Minuchin has celebrated the absence of a taxonomy of families: "Fortunately for family therapy, therapists have not been able to develop diagnostic categories for families that can pigeonhole some family forms as normal and others as deviant; with any luck, we never will develop them" (Minuchin & Fishman, 1981, p. 263).

ASSESSMENT

Structural family therapy focuses on change more than on diagnosis. It subscribes to the concern that the demands of a comprehensive diagnosis may draw the therapist into a disheartening obsession with pathology. Assessment does not precede intervention, but is an inextricable part of it.

Focus of Assessment

Assessment is inseparable from joining because it is conducted as the *therapeutic system* (see below) is being formed. It is also inseparable from the challenge to the system because it is conducted with an eye on change. Its purpose is not to render a detailed account of everything that is wrong with the family, but to be a map that will guide the therapeutic intervention.

Family Shape

The map offers an overall view of the family and some specific features of the terrain. The overall view is a picture of the more easily recognizable features of a family: How many people are in the family? How are they related? How

---

[4] *Editors' Note.* Structuralists share with strategic therapists (e.g., Madanes, Chapter 12) a belief in the interpersonal functions of psychological symptoms.

old are they? The picture may be titled, "A three-generation family," "A blended family," "A single-child family," and so on, which convey some impressionistic information of how the family is shaped—something akin to the gestalt impression of a puzzle.

Some shapes are named for the developmental stage that the family is negotiating: families with babies, families with adolescents, families that include elderly parents. Other names are more reflective of the therapist's idiosyncratic response to the first bits of information about the family. Minuchin, for instance, talks about "accordion," "shoe," and "fluctuating" families (Minuchin & Fishman, 1981, pp. 53–55). These shapes have an anthropognomic rather than a pathognomic flavor, reminiscent of the structuralist's preference for normalizing over stigmatizing labels. Other shapes may be more indicative of a specific area of trouble, like the "out-of-control families" and the "families with a ghost."

Points of Entry

Within the overall picture of the family, the therapist focuses specifically on two areas of detail. One is the set of family characteristics to which he or she will need to adjust: the family's preferred style of communication and problem solving, accepted range of distance/proximity for interpersonal exchanges, stance regarding issues of autonomy and control, distribution of functions, ways of dealing with conflict, beliefs, attitude toward outsiders, hierarchical arrangement, leaders of change and resistance.

Structural Strengths and Weaknesses

The other specific focus of assessment is on transactional patterns that may be supporting the problem and/or can contribute to its solution:

The family map indicates the position of family members vis-à-vis one another. It reveals coalitions, affiliations, explicit and implicit conflicts, and the ways family members group themselves in conflict resolution. It identifies family members who operate as detourers of conflict and family members who func-

tion as switchboards. The map charts the nurturers, healers, and scapegoaters. Its delineation of the boundaries between subsystems indicates what movement there is and suggests possible areas of strength or dysfunction. (Minuchin & Fishman, 1981, p. 69)

Structural Assessment and the Individual

Minuchin has criticized the error of "denying the individual while enthroning the system" (Minuchin et al., 1978, p. 91). This does not imply an endorsement of traditional individual assessment, but rather the recognition that individuals hold the key to systemic change. A change in the system consists of individuals changing each other, and, therefore, requires the detection and mobilization of untapped individual resources.[5]

The structural assessment of individual members does not look for what the individual *is*, but for the many different ways of being that the individual may actualize within a variety of different contexts: What kind of a husband is he to his wife? Of a father to his son? Of a son to his mother? And how else could he be, were it not for the idiosyncratic constraints of his family structure? It is an assessment predicated on the premise that family members mutually activate, reinforce, trigger, and sustain, and, therefore, selectively develop, certain aspects of each member's self, while other potential aspects are suppressed or remain underdeveloped. Umbarger (1983) has noted that although the notion of reciprocal influence is common among system thinkers and other behavioral scientists, "the structuralists have made it more emphatic than others have through the persistent reevaluation of individual psychology as bound to the interpersonal context. The special theoretical contribution of this model is to return consistently to these interactional structures, showing how they constrain and shape the individuals within the system" (pp. 21–22).

The structural therapist wants to access the latent aspects of the individual's self, not on the

---

[5] *Editors' Note.* This comment reminds us of Duhl and Duhl's (1981) notion that "You can't kiss a system," i.e., that therapists do not change family systems per se, i.e., at the level of systemic organization.

assumption that they are hiding under the individual's defenses, but on the assumption that they are being discouraged by context. A 12-year-old girl may behave more maturely when she is treated as the oldest daughter than when she is treated as a fragile child. A 34-year-old woman may appear incompetent as a mother when her husband is around, but manage nicely when he is away on a business trip. A man may be tentative and wimpy at home, but a respected leader at work.

Unit of Assessment

Structural family therapy allows for flexibility in selecting the unit of assessment. Of course, at least two people are required, because the model's reliance on observation of interaction for diagnostic purposes renders individual verbal accounts of family dynamics largely useless. *Three* people are required for the therapist to be able to observe coalitions, protection or invasion of subsystem boundaries, and detours, without having to become the third member.

Naturally, the ideal assessment unit would include "everybody who is relevant" in the case. But this admits at least two interpretations: (1) those who are a part of the *problem*—without them, the therapist cannot obtain a comprehensive understanding of the underlying dynamics; or (2) those who will play an important part in opening certain avenues for *change* and/or obstructing others—without them, the therapist cannot access potentially valuable resources and crucial roadblocks.

The two criteria do not necessarily overlap. In the case of a child who is failing in school, for example, where transactional patterns enacted in the school setting are most probably "a part of the problem," the first criterion would call for always involving the school in the process of assessment (and treatment). The second criterion, on the other hand, provides a choice. The therapist may choose to assess only the family, according to the rationale that the investment of the family in the child is enough for the project of therapeutic change; or the therapist may still choose to assess the system of family–school—but now on the grounds that the school can be made to play a part in bringing about change (Aponte, 1976b; Eno, 1985).

Because they are more interested in change than in diagnosis, structural therapists tend to think about the unit of assessment in terms of the second criterion. Of course, it is impossible, for any given family, to know a priori which of the two criteria harbors the best promise—and, in any case, who will be relevant. Paradoxically, the definition of the appropriate unit of assessment depends on assessment, and it may vary as assessment progresses. A sensible guideline is to begin with the group of people who, because of their regular transactions with the identified patient, could hardly be ignored in terms either of understanding the problem or of exploring avenues for change; in practical terms, this usually means the household. As the formation of the therapeutic system progresses and the therapist collects additional information, other members of the extended family—or even the extrafamilial, such as school personnel—may be involved in the process of assessment.

Assessment Procedure

Preplanning

Assessment begins with the information gathered during an initial telephone call or by reading an intake sheet. On the basis of simple, concrete information, such as the composition of the family and the ages of its members, as well as more subtle data, such as who makes the initial call and how that person describes the family problems, the therapist generates his or her first impressions about the family's "shape" and some of the possible strengths and weaknesses. These initial hypotheses are invaluable in guiding the first contacts of the therapist with the family, even if they may have to be discarded quickly at that point.

Tracking

Following the content and the process of the family interaction, like the needle of a record player follows a groove, is the basic structural procedure to collect information on the family map. As the therapist listens to and encourages the contributions of family members, observes their mutual dance, and asks for clarifications and expansions, he or she begins to draft first answers to structural questions: whether family members can converse without being interrupted, whether they tend to interact in age-appropriate ways, how they organize each other's behaviors, how they deal with or avoid conflict, what alliances they tend to form.

On the assumption that structure is expressed through action, the structural therapist tracks actual transactions more than verbal accounts; "When a family member is talking, the therapist notices who interrupts or completes information, who supplies confirmation, and who gives help" (Minuchin & Fishman, 1981, p. 146).

Staging Enactments

In addition to the observation of spontaneously enacted transactions, structural assessment requires the active creation of scenarios to probe further the strengths and weaknesses of the family. If a parent and child dyad exhibits what appears to be a healthy relationship, the therapist may introduce a more difficult subject to test whether they can handle the additional stress. If, on the contrary, the subsystem appears to be floundering, the therapist may change the subject, or modify the seating arrangement, to explore whether the quality of the transaction improves under different conditions.

The therapist can then intervene in the process by increasing its intensity, prolonging the time of transaction, involving other family members, indicating alternative transactions, and introducing experimental probes that will give both the therapist and the family information about the nature of the problem, the flexibility of the family's transactions in the search for solutions, and the possibility of alternative modalities for coping within the therapeutic framework. (Minuchin & Fishman, 1981, p. 79)

Search for Strength

Staging enactments is particularly useful for assessing individual strengths that may lie concealed under the weight of the family structure. The therapist needs to resist the pull to focus on pathology and be drawn into a pessimistic view of the family. He or she needs to take the initiative in bringing to the foreground the "more competent ways." He or she may direct family members to behave unusually ("Could you talk to him as if he is your brother, not a mental patient?"), or briefly occupy the stage himself or herself ("Right now, with me, you were able to be 15 years old"). In the opening moments of a consultation with the family of an "uncontrollable" 5-year-old girl, even before people take their seats, Minuchin addresses the identified patient, who is already showing signs of agitation, and asks her a question about her younger sister. In response, the patient shows that she can act like a normal 5-year-old (Minuchin & Colapinto, 1980).

The technique of searching for strength sometimes consists of eliciting competent behaviors, as in the example above, and at other times of translating apparently "obvious" or even negative descriptions into evidences of competence. This requires from the therapist a disciplined way of looking and listening. Says a mother, famous for her negativistic descriptions of her children: "I've always had a problem with them. . . . Miranda is outgoing and tomboyish. She used to be very tomboyish. Ruby used to be more domesticated . . ." Reflects the therapist: "The mother's description is highly differentiated; she is clearly a sensitive person who is observant of the children's individual developmental processes" (Minuchin & Fishman, 1981, p. 106).

Reframing the Problem

Tracking and staging enactments is a collaborative form of assessment. Information does not only proceed from the family to the therapist, but also proceeds the other way around, as the therapist selectively chooses to highlight certain transactions and contents and ignore or downplay others. The technique of *punctuation* is used by the therapist to feed back to the family members a transactional version of their sayings and doings in the session: "You are a close family." "You are protective of your daughter." "It's easier for you to talk to your mother than to your father." Because these statements are comments on transactions, they challenge the notion that individual behaviors are a straightforward expression of individual motivation. They help the family members to see their behaviors as part of a larger whole, and prepare the ground for a change in their perceptions of the problem—from an individual-based problem, requiring exploration and "rewiring" of the individual's inner life, to an interaction-embedded problem, requiring exploration and rewiring of the family's ways.

The reframing of problems requires from the therapist the ability to capture the family's reality with "transactional lenses" that highlight the complementarity of behaviors. In another moment of the consultation quoted above, Minuchin observed the mother's futile attempts to control the behavior of the girl in the room. Eventually, he asked, "Is this how the two of you run your lives together?" Had he asked if that was the usual behavior *of the girl*, he would have confirmed the family's perception that the problem was, indeed, owned by the girl; as it was, the consultant exposed the transactional nature of the problem.

TREATMENT GOALS

Goals of treatment are negotiated between the therapist and the family. In one sense, goals are relatively simple to negotiate. If the family does not have one specific complaint, but a general sense of *malaise*, the agreed-upon goal might be an equally generic exploration of the family's patterns. Usually, however, there is a specific complaint, and in that case the agreed-upon goal would be to eliminate the source of the complaint—to get Johnny to improve his performance in school, Annie to start eating, Pete not to run away, Betty to stop shoplifting. Of course, concern with the original complaint may or may not be shared by all family members. While Johnny might agree with the rest that school improvement is a good idea, Pete might not see anything wrong with his spending a few nights out of the home—maybe even Pete's stepfather does not think it is as bad as the mother feels. So the therapist listens, invites a discussion with other family members, explores what it is that each one wants, establishes congruences and oppositions between the respective goals, helps

the family formulate common goals when this is possible, and recognizes the areas of dispute when it is not. Since all of this also provides information about the shape of the family, the possible points of entry, and especially the possible ways of reframing the problem, goal setting does not need to be thought of as a separate activity.

Family's Goals and Therapist's Goals

In another sense, however, the family and the therapist necessarily disagree on goals. The family's goal includes not only some kind of formulation of the desired outcome, but also the members' expectations of the kind of service they will get from the therapist. Often, what the family expects is a focus on the identified patient.

The family's expectations of therapy are consistent with dominant cultural myths about psychopathology and the role of therapy—myths to which therapists themselves have contributed:

> Though we pay lip service to the strengths of the family, and talk about it as the matrix of development and healing, we are trained as psychological sleuths. Our instincts are to "search and destroy": pinpoint the psychological disorder, label it, and eradicate it. . . . We are the specialized personnel who have earned our credentials to defend the normal by developing and maintaining a typology that frames deviancy as mental illness. (Minuchin & Fishman, 1981, p. 263)

The goal of the structural therapist, on the other hand, is to help the family change so that the individual changes, because he or she sees individual problems as parts of patterns and potential solutions as parts of structural realignments. To help the family, the therapist needs to challenge the family's ideas of where the problem is located and how it should be solved, which amounts to challenging the family's expectations of the role of the therapist. "The word *challenge* highlights the nature of the dialectic struggle between family and therapist within the therapeutic system" (Minuchin & Fishman, 1981, p. 67).

The disagreement between family and therapist at this level of goals is inherent in the process of structural family therapy. The family's goal is elimination of the complaint *with maintenance* of the family's structure; the therapist's goal is elimination of the complaint *through transformation* of the structure.

Connectedness and Differentiation

The pursuit of family transformation involves a dialectic interweaving of the themes of connectedness and differentiation. In the early Wiltwyck days, developing a sense of connectedness was the major goal in the treatment of disengaged families:

The therapist aims at providing to all members some sense of "re-echoing"—some evidence of contributions to the interpersonal field and of interpersonal causality. By organizing different situations, he demonstrates repeatedly the phenomenon of complementarity or reciprocity, which the family has difficulty experiencing. (Minuchin et al., 1967, p. 355)

With enmeshed families, on the other hand, the goal was to help the family members differentiate:

In this profile the therapist must focus on decelerating the basic tempo and intensity of reverberations within the field. (If not) responses by one member continue to merge with the counterresponses of others, and the experience of the distinctness of one's own actions and the feeling of responsibility for one's actions are blurred. (Minuchin et al., 1967, p. 359)

While the emphasis on family typologies diminished as the structural model developed, the polarity of connectedness and differentiation as treatment goals has remained. The pursuit of differentiation within the family is at the core of the characteristic boundary-making interventions of the structural therapist, while "challenging the world view" of the families that cannot recognize the interconnectedness of their reality is the main thrust of structural reframings (Minuchin & Fishman, 1981, pp. 64–72).

The goal of individual change is pursued simultaneously with pursuit of the structural goal. A change in family structure implies a change in the positions occupied by the individual members; their experience changes accordingly. Re-

ciprocally, it is through changes in individual behaviors that the structure is made to change.[6]

STRUCTURE OF TREATMENT

It makes ecological sense to regard the family as the overall framework for therapy. "The family is the natural context for both growth and healing, and it is the context that the family therapist will depend on for the actualization of therapeutic goals" (Minuchin & Fishman, 1981, p. 11).

Clients

Within this overall framework, the structural model allows for flexibility in the configuration of treatment sessions. While most may be attended by the whole family (typically including parents and children, and sometimes grandparents who live in the same household or participate actively in transactions), others may be reserved for selected members, depending on the need to concentrate on the development of specific subsystems. The children, and sometimes the parents, may be excused from specific sessions, "since not everything will happen at once and not every family member need be involved each step of the way" (Umbarger, 1983, p. 56).

Therapist

Structural[7] family therapy is more appropriate for a "solo" therapist, because of its reliance on *joining, tracking*, and the therapist's *use of self*, none of which lends itself to easy coordination with another person. When a second therapist or a team is available, they are more effective

---

[6] *Editors' Note.* Unfortunately, in our view, data are hard to come by that support strongly the view that symptom change (in the individual) in the absence of structural change is less enduring. It is not that there are contradictory data, but that there are few bearing on the matter.

[7] *Editors' Note.* But the therapist's use of self *may* lend itself to very useful, if not easy, coordination in at least some types of family therapy, e.g., Symbolic-Experiential Therapy (cf. Roberto, Chapter 14).

as observers—preferably placed behind a one-way mirror—who can monitor the therapist and periodically feed back their observations to him or her, without introducing an element of distraction in the joining of therapist and family.

Time and Space Parameters

The structural model does not prescribe standards regarding length of treatment, number of sessions, or duration of each session; they are subject to negotiation between therapist and client. Actual experience in the application of the model has proved that it varies widely along all these parameters, reflecting the variety of therapists' preferences and styles, cultural backgrounds of the client families, presenting problems, and institutional settings. When it comes to length of treatment, for instance, some therapists simply are faster than others at challenging family patterns and pushing for transformation; some may limit their intervention to facilitating a difficult transition, while others may stay connected to the family for a more ambitious project. Some families use the therapist as a catalyzer and neither expect nor become interested in a prolonged relationship; other families may appreciate the thrill of a continued challenge. Similarly, the duration and frequency of sessions may depend on the therapist's own preferences, on the families' availability of time, or on the bureaucratic structure of any given agency.

While the model itself does not set standards concerning time variables, the structural therapist may use them to the advantage of the therapeutic process—for instance, by designating a special session to be longer, allowing for more time between sessions when prescribing a certain task, or cutting a session short as a way of intensifying the effect of an enactment. The various roles and techniques available to the therapist may also be structured in a sequence of stages, adapted to the needs of specific clinical environments (Karrer & Schartzman, 1985; Lappin, 1988).

Structural family therapy is more prescriptive regarding the *spatial* arrangement within the therapy room, which needs to be flexible enough to accommodate the therapist's restructuring maneuvers. A standard recommendation is a combination of individual chairs and a two-person sofa, no obtrusive furniture, and toys appropriate to the family's children.

ROLE OF THE THERAPIST

Structural family therapy assigns a decisive role to the therapist as an instrument of change. It is the therapist's behavior, rather than the intrinsic efficacy of techniques or prescriptions or the appropriateness of interpretations, that helps families change.

As noted earlier, the structural therapist's distinctively active stance was initially justified by the specific characteristics of the population at Wiltwyck, which limited the value of the "talking therapies" and required more concrete forms of communication. Subsequently, the experience in Philadelphia demonstrated the power of action to bypass abstract verbalization and effect substantial organizational change in other, more "verbal" families.

The structural therapist is expected to engage the family in the therapeutic project, introduce challenges that force adaptive changes, and support and coach the family members as they cope with the fallout. Over the course of treatment, the therapist needs to vary the level and intensity of his or her involvement with the family; there is even some (although not much) room for quiet reflection and neutrality.

The primary injunction from the model to the therapist can be summarized in three words: "Make it happen." This requires the performance of a variety of roles.

The Therapist as Producer

One of these roles is production of the conditions that will make therapy possible—the "formation of the therapeutic system." It involves the techniques of *joining*, in which the therapist gains the family's acceptance of him or her as a special, nonpermanent, but influential member, with the capacity to challenge the system from within: a *search for strength*, the localization of family resources that will be used by the family and therapist as "building blocks" in the construction of alternative patterns, and the *reframing of the problem* as a family rather than an individual one, so as to encourage the participation of the family in the healing endeavor.

The Therapist as Stage Director

A second role of the structural therapist is to create situations that challenge the existing structure and push the family toward more functional patterns. Here, the therapist takes advantage of his or her position as a temporary member of the system. As a stage director, the therapist sets up scenarios for enactments, where he or she can then have an impact on the complementary patterns—monitoring the flow of transactions and directing the family members to interact in novel ways.

The Therapist as Protagonist: Use of Self

From the role of director, the structural therapist may shift to the role of protagonist, intervening directly in family transactions—interrupting, pushing, challenging, supporting family members selectively. By using himself or herself as an additional participant in family transactions, the therapist effectively unbalances the family organization.

As an instrument of change, the use of self should not be confused with self-disclosure of the therapist's personal experiences, which the structural model discourages because it attracts attention to the therapist and distracts from family process. In the structural model, stories from the therapist's own life are only justified as instruments of joining ("I have two sons of the same ages").

The Therapist as Narrator

The structural therapist is also a coauthor, with the family, of a revised "script" for family transactions. The therapist's challenge to the family's belief structure—the assumptions that family members hold about the motivations, preferences, capabilities, and limitations of one another—proceeds hand in hand with the chal-

lenge to the transactional structure. By commenting on observed transactions, old and new, the therapist questions the family members' attribution of meaning to each other's behavior, and assists in the development of new meanings.

Therapist's Profile

The structural model requires from the therapist a respectful curiosity about diverse forms of family experience and strengths, a commitment to help families change, a preference for concrete behavioral changes over talk about changed feelings, a disposition to construct hypotheses on the basis of scanty data and to have them corrected through a close encounter with clients, the ability to set clear goals and to express them frankly, a willingness to direct, a directedness of expression, a tolerance for intensity in human transactions, and the courage to raise intensity when necessary.[8]

Minuchin is powerful, but his intensity is not a function of his personality; it reflects his clarity of purpose. Knowledge of family structure and a serious commitment to help families change make powerful interventions possible. Families will usually respond to messages delivered with the kind of intensity that comes from being clear about the goal. . . . Therapists too often dilute their interventions by overqualifying, apologizing, or rambling. (Nichols, pp. 495–496)

TECHNIQUES OF STRUCTURAL THERAPY

The structural therapist utilizes a variety of techniques in the pursuit of structural change. Their use is selectively dictated by the vicissitudes of the therapeutic process as continually assessed by the therapist; the structural model does not

---

[8] *Editors' Note.* We agree with Colapinto's implicit message here, that not every therapist can effectively practice every type of family therapy, and that it is extremely important that the match between therapists-as-persons and the requirements of adopting a given therapeutic style or model be given its due consideration. This position obviously has significant implications for education and training.

prescribe specific matches between a given technique and a given problem.

Techniques can be classified in two broad groups, depending on whether their primary application is to the formation of the therapeutic system or to a change in family patterns.

The Formation of the Therapeutic System

The first order of business for the structural therapist is to be accepted *in* the family; that is, to be accepted not just as somebody to meet once a week, but as a regular, if temporary, participant in family transactions, with the right to engage family members and, eventually, challenge them.

Joining

The therapist gains such a position through a series of movements generically called "joining." They include simple rules of etiquette, such as making friendly contact with all family members, and deliberate techniques such as *confirmation*, in which the therapist responds sympathetically to family members' expressions of concern, sadness, anger, fear, even rejection of therapy, and *maintenance*, in which the therapist is mindful and respectful of the rules that govern distances and hierarchies within the family system—for instance, by addressing the parents before addressing the children. Confirmation may also take the form of a nonjudgmental description of a transaction among family members, such as when the therapist comments, "You seem to be engaged in a continuous struggle."

Selective Joining

Structural joining is not the same as being nice to people. While needing to be accepted, the therapist does not want to accommodate to the point of being "inducted" into the system and, thereby, rendered impotent. One way of introducing an element of challenge in the very process of joining is to emphasize the affiliation with one member more than with others. In some cases, the therapist may want to position himself or herself closer to the most peripheral member of a family; the therapist may then select his or her wording carefully to indicate special affiliation with that member, or enact a nonverbal *mimesis* of the member's mood, tone of voice, posture, or behavior.

Joining as an Attitude

The skill of joining requires more than the application of a technique:

Joining a family is more an attitude than a technique, and it is the umbrella under which all therapeutic transactions occur. Joining is letting the family know that the therapist understands them and is working with and for them. Only under this protection can the family have the security to explore alternatives, try the unusual, and change. Joining is the glue that holds the therapeutic system together. (Minuchin & Fishman, 1981, pp. 31–32)

The attitude that joining requires combines elements of proximity and affiliation (respectful curiosity, acceptance, the ability to put oneself in the other's shoes, sensitivity to corrective feedback) with elements of distance and differentiation (questioning the family's ways, hinting that there are others, encouraging dissent). Good *tracking* of process, as discussed in the section on "Assessment," may help put the therapist's effort to join the family on "automatic pilot."

Other Techniques

The techniques involved in searching for strength and reframing the problem were discussed in the section on "Assessment."

While the focus on the formation of the therapeutic system is more obvious during the initial encounter with the family, the need to maintain the viability of the system is a continuous one. The techniques of joining, searching for strength, and reframing continue to be used throughout treatment, as the therapist protects his or her gained position within the family, and regains it whenever he or she claims the right to challenge the family structure.

Changing Family Structure

The structural approach to changing the family relies on the challenge to current patterns of transaction. Here, the word "challenge" does not necessarily connote a harsh confrontation. Although some challenges may take the form of confrontation—for instance, in the technique of unbalancing—the word has a more generic meaning, designating any therapeutic intervention that makes it difficult for the family to engage in its usual modes of transaction. The challenge is to the dysfunctional pattern, not to the motivation of those who participate in the pattern.

Challenging techniques especially developed by the structural model are aimed at directly affecting the family's structure of transactions by creating an alternative pattern in the room.

Enactment, the actualization of transactional patterns under the control of the therapist, is usually regarded as the most distinctive structural technique, because it best expresses the premise that more change comes from dealing with problems than from talking about them. If the family claims that the mother does not have any control over her children and depends on the father for law and order, the therapist may create a situation in the therapy room that requires the mother to organize the children's play, and then block the rescuing attempts of the father until the mother succeeds.

The purpose of enactment is to offer a context in which the family can experience the substitution of functional for dysfunctional transactions. The therapist "makes it happen" by monitoring the transaction in progress—one moment supporting it with a suggestion, and the next moment pulling back to leave room for the family members to transact, occasionally refocusing them. At the same time, the therapist also intensifies the family's experience by commenting on stumbling blocks and successes: "He gave you that look again and you stopped dead in your tracks." "Now you are talking to your father like a real 16-year-old."

Enactments rarely beget instant change. The family needs to repeat the experience of possible alternatives in many different forms before new patterns can be maintained. Each successful enactment contributes a bit to enlarging the experience of the possible, showing that change is possible and what it might look like. The therapist may prescribe "homework" as a way of extending an enactment beyond the boundaries of the session. For instance, the sibling subsystem may be instructed to prepare a pleasant surprise for the parents, as a way of both reinforcing the boundaries of that subsystem and promoting internal negotiation. Naturally, homework cannot be monitored by the therapist with the same immediacy as an in-session enactment, but it has the advantage of taking place in the natural environment and over an extended period.

Boundary making is a special form of enactment in which the therapist modifies patterns of over- and underinvolvement by allowing some members, but not others, to participate in a transaction. Examples of boundary making are the prescription of a physical movement that results in the formation of a group of people facing each other, with their backs toward the rest; asking a family member to watch in silence from one corner of the room or from behind a one-way mirror; prolonging a dyadic interchange; using phrases that convey the desirability of separation ("You talk for him," "Do you need to check every answer with her?"); and using physical gestures aimed at blocking interruptions or distracting visual contacts (raising a hand, standing between people).

Boundary making disrupts the operation of detouring mechanisms and other conflict-avoidance patterns, and encourages the emergence of underutilized skills within the subsystem in question—such as a couple that is being protected from interruption by the children, or children who are being protected from interruption by the parents. New skills sometimes emerge spontaneously (the siblings, for instance, develop their own way of solving their differences without parental arbitration), but more often they are identified through the therapist's intervention in the bounded subsystem—pointing out the ways in which subsystem members shape each other's behaviors, highlighting their complementarity, and encouraging experimentation with new shapes. To a father locked in a hopeless contest of recriminations with his daughter, the therapist may say: "You keep saying that you have no influence over your daughter, but right now she is asking for your help. She is giving you power. Accept her request." This modality of intervention, known as *working on complementarity*, is the main contribution of the structural therapist to an enactment, once it has been initiated.

Intensity is a quality that the structural therapist attaches to some of his or her interventions to increase the level of challenge to the family system. Intensity can be achieved through numerous repetitions of the same message, through tone of voice, or through a dramatic statement or intervention. Examples of particularly intense techniques are unbalancing and crisis induction.

In *unbalancing*, the therapist capitalizes on the expertise that the family has allocated to him or her to challenge a rigid family hierarchy. The therapist, for instance, may purposefully ignore a domineering family "switchboard." While this "goes against the grain of the therapist's cultural imprinting, because it requires the capacity to speak and act as if certain people are invisible" (Minuchin & Fishman, 1981, p. 173), it may force a realignment of family hierarchy, for example when the ignored member attempts to draw the other members into a coalition against the therapist.

In a more active form of unbalancing, the therapist becomes a protagonist of family transaction, entering into a coalition with a family member. For instance, the therapist may support a devalued family member against another member, in which case, "the family member who changes position in the family by affiliation with the therapist does not recognize, or does not respond to, the family signals. He operates in unaccustomed ways, daring to explore unfamiliar areas of personal and interpersonal functioning, highlighting possibilities that were previously unrecognized" (Minuchin & Fishman, 1981, p. 162).

Crisis induction is the creation of a situation that leaves the family no choice but to face a chronically avoided conflict. An example is the lunchtime session in anorexia cases, in which the symptom literally is brought into the room and the family is asked to deal with it.

Unbalancing and crisis induction are risky operations that may threaten the continuation of treatment. They require from the therapist clarity of purpose and a difficult balancing of commitment to change and sensitivity to corrective feedback from the family.

Challenge to the Family's World View

In addition to techniques that directly alter the transactional structure of the family, the structural therapist utilizes others that affect the structure indirectly by challenging the family's world view. Universal truths, moral imperatives, cultural traditions, folkloric common sense, invoked expertise, and the family's own preferred metaphors can be used by the therapist as vantage points from which to challenge the premises that underlie family rules, provide alternative explanations, and suggest directions of change.

In the West family, who came to therapy because the father, a minister was having difficulties controlling his two adolescent daughters, Mr. West refers to his wife and daughters as "the three girls." The therapist rises, "stopping the clock," and points up a moral: "You must have difficulties in your relationship with God, since you don't understand that He created hierarchy in the family. There is a right place for the parents and a right place for the children." (Minuchin & Fishman, 1981, p. 215)

Some Common Technical Errors

Most of the technical errors that a structural family therapist can make are generically gathered under the rubric of *induction*, a phenomenon in which the therapist inadvertently becomes organized by the rules of the family. Induction should not be confused with the accommodating moves of the therapist who intentionally adopts the rules of the system as a part of his or her joining.

Centrality is a variety of induction in which the therapist accepts the family's enticing for him or her to become the central figure of treatment, which inhibits family transaction. The therapist may fall into constantly asking questions, responding to requests for advice, or always being at one end of a power struggle. Or the therapist may unwittingly respond to family clues and rush to the protection of a member who appears to be at the losing end of a transaction—an induction known as the *rescuing maneuver*; for instance, an adolescent is being verbally abused by her parent and the therapist anxiously interrupts the transaction or admonishes the parent.

Another common error is *overfocusing on content* at the expense of visible structural patterns. "If family members are avidly telling their story, the therapist's attention may be locked into content. Sometimes a therapist tracks the communication of the most verbal family members, unaware of the family life being enacted before his unseeing eyes" (Minuchin & Fishman, 1981, p. 34).

The power of family rules to induct therapists is complementarily reinforced by traditional clinical training, which encourages therapists to be central, helpful, and focused on content.

On the other hand, structural therapists may also err in the opposite direction—by not allowing themselves to be inducted enough. When this happens, the therapist does not pay enough attention to the family rules, fails to accommodate to them, and "loses touch" with the family. He or she then operates at a distance that is not appropriate for the structural model, relying excessively on the free-standing value of the techniques and unable to register feedback from the family. It is the error of *overtechnicism* (Colapinto, 1983, 1988). The therapist may, for instance, set up an enactment and expect the process to take care of itself ("You two talk about this"), or grossly miscalculate the consequences of an unbalancing.

DYNAMICS OF CHANGE

Structural family therapy operates on the basis of a set of assumptions about change, derived from the structural understanding of family dynamics.

1. Change and resistance to change. Change, in families and individuals, is a natural process of growth that can be arrested. When that happens, the potential for change and a resumption of growth is still inherent in the family itself, and, more specifically, in areas of its individual members' selves that have so far been suppressed by virtue of complementarity. Family members "are always functioning with a portion of their possibilities. There are many possibilities, only some of which are elicited or contained by the contextual structure. Therefore, breaking or expanding contexts can allow new possibilities to emerge" (Minuchin & Fishman, 1981, p. 14).

A family may change spontaneously when it realigns its structure to cope with a changed environment. On the other hand, the family may resist spontaneous change and reinforce its current structure. Resistance to change is then expressed through the predominant adhesion to existing family rules, with individual members countering others' movements toward change.

2. Family change and individual change. The family, as a powerful organizer of its individual members' behaviors, is a major influence in shaping the individuals, and whether and how that shape can change. The family is the natural context for change, and even though individual members can initiate change without the help or the "permission" of the family, such change necessarily brings about reverberations in the family, some of them in the form of resistance. Harnessing the power of the family on behalf of the individual, and attending in vivo to the reverberations of change in the family, are the two major advantages of family therapy.[9]

3. Therapeutic change. Individuals and families who fail to change spontaneously may change with the assistance of a therapist who opens for them the possibility of experiencing alternative patterns. Resistance to change is either circumvented (typically through the use of enactments) or directly challenged (for instance, through a crisis induction).

4. Behavioral change and cognitive change. Changes may be initiated at the level of behavioral interaction or at the level of cognitive or emotional experience. The way family members experience each other changes when their interaction changes, and the way they interact changes when their experience of each other

---

[9] *Editors' Note.* We wish to underline that Colapinto is speaking here of family therapy-in-general, not just of Structural Therapy. These two characteristic advantages of family therapy may constitute a good deal of the potency of family methods that is attributable to so-called "nonspecific" factors that are common to all family-therapy approaches.

changes. Therefore, both a disruption of actual transactions and a challenge to the clients' mutual experience can initiate change.

However, even when choosing the latter route, the therapist uses actual transactions in the room as referents. Changes in clients' experiences are brought about not by the therapist's long explanations, but by his or her brief punctuation and reframing of enacted transactions. The same applies to cognitive processes that contribute to therapeutic change, such as the understanding of the phenomenon of complementarity: they need to be anchored in concrete experience.

WORKING WITH COUPLES

The structural model has not developed a separate set of concepts or techniques for the treatment of couples. The couple is conceptualized as a subsystem that may become one of the foci in the treatment of a family, or that may itself take the initiative of requesting treatment. In either case, assessment and treatment of the couple subsystem follow the same guidelines that apply to the family.

There are some differences in emphasis in the choice and application of techniques. For instance, it may not be necessary to reframe the problem as an interactional one, because couples requesting therapy are comparatively closer to perceiving their problems as interactional anyway; on the other hand, reframing may be needed to change the definition of what kind of interactional problem it is. Similarly, the consistent focus on an already identified subsystem offers comparatively more opportunities to apply techniques for working "inside" the subsystem—such as enactment and working on complementarity—than to use techniques for differentiating subsystems, such as making boundaries. However, the structural approach also pays attention to the context of the couple and its relationship to other subsystems; for instance, how being a father and mother affects the relationship of husband and wife. Stanton (1981) has developed a model for couple therapy that combines elements of the structural and the strategic approaches.

TREATMENT APPLICABILITY

Structural family therapy has been primarily developed and applied in clinical settings, both agency-based and private, where children, including adolescents, are the identified target of intervention. There is comparatively little documented experience on the application of the model to the treatment of adults; existing reports suggest that the model applies when there is a strong involvement of the family in the life of the individual adult (Fishman, 1979; Stanton & Todd, 1982).

The model applies to all shapes of families, from the disengaged to the enmeshed end of the continuum. Naturally, the extremes pose a higher level of challenge. An extremely disengaged family may make it difficult for the structural therapist to reframe the problem and recruit the necessary resources. An extremely enmeshed family may present too rigid a front against the therapist's attempts at restructuring. But these obstacles to applicability are not absolute; they can be overcome by the therapist's determined joining or intensity. It is fair to say that limits to the applicability of the model to families are determined by the therapist's style rather than the family's.

A more complex issue, because it interfaces with the controversy about the validity of the psychiatric diagnosis, is the applicability of the model to specific individual syndromes, such as character disorders. Again, the less a problem lends itself to an interactional reframe (whether the result of family rigidity or of the weight of a diagnosis), the less are the chances for a successful application of the structural model. Again, these obstacles are not absolute, but are relative to the therapist's ability to reframe and challenge. Depression can be seen as an interactional phenomenon (Minuchin, 1974).

There are problems to which the model definitely does not apply. The organic substrata of some psychotic phenomena do not respond to structural family therapy, any more than the organic substratum of diabetes does. However, just as structural family therapy can be effective in reducing the number of acidosis crises (Minuchin et al., 1978), it is also applicable to the interactional fallout of organic psychoses. At the other end of the explanatory continuum, while the model cannot cure the social context of poor, underorganized families, it can help them develop the interactional skills that help other poor families cope better.

REFERENCES

Aponte, H.J. (1976a). Underorganization and the poor family. In P. Guerin (Ed.), *Family therapy: Theory and practice*. New York: Gardner Press.

Aponte, H.J. (1976b). The family school interview. *Family Process*, 15, 303–310.

Baker, L., Minuchin, S., Milman, L., Liebman, R., & Todd, T. (1975). Psychosomatic aspects of juvenile diabetes mellitus: A progress report. In *Modern problems in pediatrics* (Vol. 12), White Plains, NY: S. Karger.

Bruner, J.S. (1964). The course of cognitive growth. *American Psychologist*, 19, 1–15.

Colapinto, J. (1983). Beyond technique: Teaching how to think structurally. *Journal of Strategic and Systemic Therapies*, 2, 12–21.

Colapinto, J. (1988). The structural way. In H.A. Liddle, D.C. Breunlin, & R.C. Schwartz (Eds.), *Handbook of family therapy training and supervision*. New York: Guilford Press.

Eno, M.M. (1985). Children with school problems: A family therapy perspective. In R.L. Ziffer (Ed.), *Adjunctive techniques in family therapy*. Orlando, FL: Grune & Stratton.

Fishman, H.C. (1979). Family considerations in liaison psychiatry. *Psychiatric Clinics of North America*, 2 (2).

Karrer, B.M., & Schwartzman, J. (1985). The stages of structural family therapy. In D. Breunlin (Ed.), *Stages: Patterns of change over time*. Rockville, MD: Aspen.

Laing, R.D. (1976). *Facts of life*. New York: Ballantine Books.

Lappin, J. (1988). Family therapy: A structural approach. In R. Dorfman (Ed.), *Paradigms of clinical social work*. New York: Brunner/Mazel.

Liebman, R., Minuchin, S., & Baker, L. (1974a). An integrated treatment program for anorexia nervosa. *American Journal of Psychiatry*, 131, 432–436.

Liebman, R., Minuchin, S., & Baker, L. (1974b). The role of the family in the treatment of anorexia nervosa. *Journal of the American Academy of Child Psychiatry*, 13, 264–272.

Liebman, R., Minuchin, S., & Baker, L. (1974c). The use of structural family therapy in the treatment of intractable asthma. *American Journal of Psychiatry*, 131, 535–540.

Liebman, R., Minuchin, S., Baker, L., & Rosman, B. (1976). The role of the family in the treatment of chronic asthma. In P. Guerin (Ed.), *Family therapy: Theory and practice*: New York: Gardner Press.

Liebman, R., Minuchin, S., Baker, L., & Rosman, B. (1977). Chronic asthma: A new approach in treatment. In M. F. McMillan & S. Henao (Eds.), *Child psychiatry treatment and research*. New York: Brunner/Mazel.

Luepnitz, D. A. (1988). *The family interpreted: Feminist theory in clinical practice*. New York: Basic Books.

Malcolm, J. (1978, May 15). A reporter at large: The one-way mirror. *The New Yorker*, pp. 39–114.

Malone, C.A. (1963). Some observations on children of disorganized families and problems of acting out. *Journal of Child Psychiatry*, 2, 22–49.

Minuchin, S. (1961). The acting-out child and his family: An approach to family therapy. Paper presented at the William Alanson White Institute, New York.

Minuchin, S. (1970). The use of an ecological framework in the treatment of a child. In *International yearbook of child psychiatry* (Vol. 1). New York: Wiley.

Minuchin, S. (1972). Structural family therapy. In G. Caplan (Ed.), *American handbook of psychiatry* (Vol. 2). New York: Basic Books.

Minuchin, S. (1974). *Families and family therapy*. Cambridge, MA: Harvard University Press.

Minuchin, S. (1974). "I think it's me" (videotape). Philadelphia Child Guidance Clinic.

Minuchin, S., Baker, L., Liebman, R., Milman, L., Rosman, B., & Todd, T. (1973). Anorexia nervosa: Successful application of a family approach. *Pediatric Research*, 7, 294.

Minuchin, S., Baker, L., Rosman, B., Liebman, R., Milman, L., & Todd, T. (1975). A conceptual model of psychosomatic illness in children. *Archives of General Psychiatry*, 32, 1031–1038.

Minuchin, S., & Barcai, A. (1969). Therapeutically induced crisis. In J.H. Masserman (Ed.), *Science and psychoanalysis* (Vol. 14). New York: Grune & Stratton.

Minuchin, S., & Colapinto, J. (Eds.) (1980). "Taming monsters" (videotape). Philadelphia Child Guidance Clinic.

Minuchin, S., & Fishman, H.C. (1979). The psychosomatic family in child psychiatry. *Journal of the American Academy of Child Psychiatry*, 18 (1), 76–90.

Minuchin, S., & Fishman, H.C. (1981). *Family therapy techniques*. Cambridge, MA: Harvard University Press.

Minuchin, S., & Montalvo, B. (1966). An approach for diagnosis of the low socioeconomic family. *American Psychiatric Research Report*, 20.

Minuchin, S., & Montalvo, B. (1967). Techniques for working with disorganized low socioeconomic families. *American Journal of Orthopsychiatry*, 37, 380–387.

Minuchin, S., Montalvo, B., Guerney, B.G., Rosman, B.L., & Schumer, F. (1967). *Families of the slums*. New York: Basic Books.

Minuchin, S., Rosman, B., & Baker, L. (1978). *Psychosomatic families: Anorexia nervosa in context*. Cambridge, MA: Harvard University Press.

Montalvo, B. (1973). Aspects of live supervision. *Family Process*, 12, 343–359.

Parsons, T., & Bales, R.F. (1955). *Family, socialization and interaction process*. Glencoe, IL: Free Press.

Pavenstedt, E. (1965). A comparison of the child-rearing environment of upper-lower and very low-lower class families. *American Journal of Orthopsychiatry*, 35, 89–98.

Rosman, B.L., Minuchin, S., & Liebman, R. (1975). Family lunch session: An introduction to family therapy in anorexia nervosa. *American Journal of Orthopsychiatry*, 45, 846–853.

Rosman, B.L., Minuchin, S., & Liebman, R. (1977). Treating anorexia by the family lunch session. In C.E. Scaefer & H. L. Millman (Eds.), *Therapies for children: A handbook of effective treatments for problem behavior*. San Francisco: Jossey-Bass.

Rosman, B.L., Minuchin, S., Liebman, R., & Baker, L. (1976). Input and outcome of family therapy in anorexia nervosa. In J.C. Claghorn (Ed.), *Successful psychotherapy*. New York: Brunner/Mazel.

Rosman, B.L., Minuchin, S., Liebman, R., & Baker, L. (1977). A family approach to anorexia nervosa: Study, treatment, outcome. In R.A. Vigersky (Ed.), *Anorexia nervosa*. New York: Raven Press.

Rosman, B.L., Minuchin, S., Liebman, R., & Baker, L. (1978). Family therapy for psychosomatic children. Paper presented at the annual meeting of the American Academy of Psychosomatic Medicine, Atlanta.

Stanton, M.D. (1981). Marital therapy from a structural/strategic viewpoint. In G.P. Sholevar (Ed.), *Handbook of marriage and marital therapy*. Jamaica, NY: Spectrum.

Stanton, M.D., & Todd, T.C. (Eds.) (1982). *The family therapy of drug abuse and addiction*. New York: Guilford Press. American Journal of Drug and Alcohol Abuse, 1978, 5, 125–150.

Sullivan, H.S. (1962). *Schizophrenia as a human process*. New York: Norton.

Thomas, L. (1974). *The lives of a cell: Notes of a biology watcher*. New York: Bantam Books.

Umbarger, C.C. (1983). *Structural family therapy*. New York: Grune & Stratton.

Wood, B. (1985) Proximity and hierarchy: Orthogonal dimensions of family interconnectedness. *Family Process, 24*, 487–507.

Wood, B., & Talmon, M. (1983). Family boundaries in transition: A search for alternatives. *Family Process 22*, 347–357.

EDITORS' REFERENCES

Coyne, J., & Anderson, B. (1988). The "psychosomatic family" revisited reconsidered: Diabetes in context. *Journal of Marital and Family Therapy, 14*, 113–123.

Coyne, J., & Anderson, B. (1989). The "psychosomatic family" reconsidered II: Recalling a defective model and looking ahead. *Journal of Marital and Family Therapy, 15*, 139–148.

Duhl, B.S., & Duhl, F.J. (1981). Integrative family therapy. In A. Gurman & D. Kniskern (Eds.), *Handbook of family therapy*. New York: Brunner/Mazel.

CHAPTER 14

Symbolic-Experiential Family Therapy

Laura Giat Roberto, Psy.D.

BACKGROUND OF THE APPROACH

Symbolic-experiential family therapy is a model for family and marital therapy pioneered by Carl Whitaker beginning in the 1940s. It is a model based in its inception on treatment of psychotic persons and their families, and of families intolerably stressed by severe environmental trauma (e.g., wartime). In the five decades since its inception, symbolic-experiential therapy has been applied to a wide range of presenting family complaints in many populations and areas of the world.

Whitaker first experimented, along with Thomas Malone and John Warkentin, with *seeing* disturbed relationships in their (familial) context and *using* therapeutic relationships (in cotherapy dyads) in the early 1940s, at a time when other pioneering theorists also began observing family systems. At this time, Murray Bowen, Lyman Wynne, Gregory Bateson, Ivan Boszormenyi-Nagy, and Nathan Ackerman, at different medical and Veterans' Administration centers, all independently engaged in the study of the families of hospitalized psychotic individuals. These scientists were advancing psychoanalytic theory, with its emphases on internal conflict, arrested individual development, and mother–child enmeshment, by examining whether such symptoms in psychotics might be reinforced by dysfunctional family interaction patterns and beliefs. Whitaker's first book, *The Roots of Psychotherapy* (1953), was later published with Thomas Malone while they were on the psychiatry faculty at Emory University. In it, their epistemological shift from internal conflict to interactional dysfunction was first discussed.

It must be noted that the techniques developed within the symbolic-experiential model were not simply aimed at psychotic symptoms. Whitaker, for example, trained in child psychiatry at the Child Guidance Clinic in Louisville, Ky., and at nearby Ormsby Village (Neill & Kniskern, 1982; Whitaker & Ryan, 1989). This exposure to play therapy and to children's metaphorical, nonanalytical emotional processes began to create a dimension to interventions that is uniquely experiential and "here-and-now" (Roberto, Keith, & Kramer, 1987). In this vein, symbolic-experiential therapy shares a common ancestry with structural family therapy, which also addresses the ongoing emotional dynamics of the therapy session in progress.

The techniques of intervention that Whitaker and Warkentin developed to address affective problems were modified in the treatment of what appeared to be psychotic reactions in the scientists in residence at the Oak Ridge atomic research installation in Tennessee during World War II (Whitaker & Ryan, 1989). The scientists, and war veterans returning from Europe, were bound by secrecy and the experience of ambiguous and traumatic experiences (for example, the nuclear testing at Los Alamos). In retrospect, it appears that these civilian scientists and the soldiers were probably showing posttraumatic stress disorder. Whitaker and Warkentin, a child therapist trained at Brown University, were forced to develop methods for handling intense transference reactions and regressive behavior. Such symptoms require the ability to respond affectively to clients in a more proximal, rather than distant, therapeutic posture, in order to provide emotional structuring and reassurance.

This piece of history in the development of symbolic-experiential therapy influenced heavily the role of the therapist (or cotherapists), and distinguishes this method from strategic and systemic models that utilize therapist distance and neutrality (Roberto, in press). From an initial grounding in the treatment of children and psychotics, early applications to anguished individuals living in traumatic war circumstances influenced the early theorists to focus on the fact that developmental events, the "original symbolic [emotional] experiences, stem from realizing the uniqueness of one's own perceptions, one's own vulnerabilities, and one's limits . . ." within specific social and cultural contexts and times (Whitaker, 1985a). If symbolic (emotional) experiences are such fundamentally formative events in transient adult as well as child and psychotic problems, then they must be crucial factors in the process of all individual change and of therapeutic change.

This central role for emotional experience also requires that the therapist or cotherapy team be affectively engaged with the couple or family in therapy. In other words, while the original orientation of symbolic-experiential therapy was psychoanalytic, based on the work of Melanie Klein, August Aichorn, and Otto Rank (Neill & Kniskern, 1982), later applications led the theorists to modify their approach. While Whitaker had already been particularly interested in Rank's concept of the therapist as an ally rather than as a blank screen for client projections, the nature of alliance itself began to shift to interpersonal process in the therapy room. The "second period" of investigation, terminating at the Oak Ridge atomic facility, focused on the use of an affectively focused, here-and-now, ecologically oriented view of emotional symptoms rather than on the previous analytic wish-defense theory of symptom formation (Roberto, in press).

A "third period" of experimentation with symbolic-experiential methods occurred when Whitaker became chair of the Department of Psychiatry at Emory University in Atlanta, where he and Malone began the use of dual cotherapy (which they called "multiple therapy"). Again treating psychotic (schizophrenic) clients, the central question was whether psychotic symptoms might be an attempt to gain competence with, or mastery over, distorted perceptions and familial disruption. The use of cotherapy at this time resembled the later systemic method of providing an observing team in which one member could track interactional process while the other actively made therapeutic interventions. Both experiments—using a therapeutic team and framing psychotic symptoms as an attempt to adapt or to achieve mastery—were unique and represented radically different views of the nature of schizophrenia and of the role of the therapist, at a time when schizophrenia was seen as constitutional and deteriorative.

Interestingly, during this period of experimentation, the use of cotherapy and team intervention was not restricted to hospitalized psychotic clients. Richard Felder, from the Grady Hospital, joined the team during this time. The faculty set up a didactic structure for the Emory medical students that included process groups with the faculty and cotherapy interviews for the students with their own clients (Whitaker & Ryan, 1989). Periodical case conferences for the faculty culminated in the 1955 Sea Island conference (the 10th Emory-sponsored conference), which is considered historically to be the first conference that truly focused on family process per se. It included family researchers from Philadelphia, such as John Rosen, and from California, such as Donald Jackson and Gregory Bateson.

While the Emory University faculty later split up, diverging into private practice of individuals and of families, Whitaker carried his model to the University of Wisconsin School of Medicine in 1964. Over the decades of the 1960s and 1970s, a postgraduate specialization in marital and family therapy was developed with the participation of David Keith, another child psychiatrist. The specialty was housed in the child psychiatry division of the Department of Psychiatry's residency program and trained psychiatry and psychology residents until the mid-1980s. The training program included beginning and advanced theory seminars and cotherapy practica with live and videotaped supervision, both individually and in groups. The edited training videotapes produced at the University of Wisconsin are among the classic didactic videotapes in the marriage and family field (Roberto, in press).

It can be appreciated that the siting of the second training program for symbolic-experiential theory, also a university department of psychiatry, influenced teaching techniques heavily. There has been great emphasis on the use of cotherapy with faculty as a training tool, in addition simply to pairing beginning clinicians with each other. In the tradition of medical school education, trainees are encouraged to undergo their own experience of marital or family therapy, which, we believe, has profound effects on personal maturation as well as on the ability to form more effective alliances with the families that come to us in distress. Finally, the postgraduate academic training context allows for team experimentation, consultation, supervision, and publication in an atmosphere less pressured by the business of private practice, an atmosphere increasingly rare for training programs in the private sector.

HEALTHY OR WELL-FUNCTIONING MARRIAGE AND FAMILY

It is a myth that functioning marriages and families are free of difficult problems. As Weakland (1983) once pointed out, "When you have a problem, life is just the same damned thing over and over. After the problem is solved, life is just one damned thing after another." From the symbolic-experiential view, every couple and family has a unique organization that serves both to aid adaptation and to block needed change. It is only persistent problems that interfere with healthy functioning.

Symbolic-experiential theory distinguishes a family's *structural organization* from its interpersonal and affective *process*. Structure pertains to relational boundaries, subgroup membership, roles, and allocation of privileges and responsibilities. Process pertains to emotional dynamics, including the presence of intimacy and separation, attachment and empathy, sexuality, and conflict tolerance.

From a structural perspective, permeable boundaries (both internal and external) characterize the healthy family. There is an external boundary that defines extended and nuclear families, as well as internal boundaries that separate generations and subgroups (Whitaker & Keith, 1981). With nonfamily members, there is allowance of outside relationships. Members may have access to friends and outside interests without this being perceived as threatening to others. This access is volitional and is not a response to family conflict, as in running away. With extended-family members, there is a three- to four-generation family identity that is transmitted to the offspring. Characteristics of the maternal and paternal families of origin are replicated, clash, and become integrated into a novel gestalt in the nuclear family. Commitments to both extended families are secondary to nuclear-family commitments; however, permeability here means that under unusual circumstances, the family of origin is attended to first (e.g., hospitalization, crisis) without creating competition or anxiety in spouse or children. Ideally, the families of origin can be on friendly terms, so that married offspring do not perceive a need to "choose" one set of relatives over the other or to defend one to the other.

Dyadic alliances and flexible coalitions are available for problem solving. When one member is symptomatic, others can ally to advise, encourage, or confront. One member may confide in another without creating fear of exclusion and without permanent pairing. Several members may interact around a stressful problem, with participants changing during the next problem. The most enduring alliances function best within parental and sibling groups. A common symbolic-experiential metaphor is that of the "generation gap," in which family members are encouraged to recognize the different motivations of parents and children even while they cooperate across generational lines—for example, "grandparents and grandchildren have a common enemy—parents." It is also important for children to be available to each other as allies, even if it means transcending age differences.

Flexibility in alliances and coalitions also means that the member identified with a problem can change. Whitaker (1985a) has called this phenomenon the "rotating scapegoat." Essentially, the healthy family allows each member to admit to problems as well as to define competencies. Identified problems are not reified into monolithic inadequacies (Whitaker & Keith, 1981), but are viewed as transient complications.

Role flexibility allows individuals to express differences and to change behavior or beliefs without disqualification, making use of their own life experiences, familial legacies, and developing preferences. These roles are not real, but products of interactions and perceptions of the parents, grandparents, siblings, and children.

There are transgenerational mandates that shape individual behavior on the basis of past events, losses, and belief systems that combine to create roles for each family member (Boszormenyi-Nagy & Krasner, 1986; Roberto, 1987; Whitaker & Keith, 1981). However, in the healthy family, these can be examined, negotiated, and adapted to as individuals advance in their own life cycles. This does not mean that such negotiations always take place gracefully. At times, sudden individual change produces tremendous confusion, anger, and/or conflict. However, well-functioning families experience these disruptions without hopelessness or perceptions of failure. To put it differently: "The secret of being a good parent is in the enjoyment of being hated at times, rather than fearing it" (Whitaker, cited in Neill & Kniskern, 1982, p. 367).

Gender-role flexibility requires specific attention in symbolic-experiential theory. Although most American families still demonstrate sex stereotyping, well-functioning families have the capacity to resist the pressure of our masculine-oriented culture. In such families, a married woman with children is able to focus on herself without punitive consequences. A father may attend to his marriage or family without questioning his adequacy as an adult male. Here, our definition of familial health clearly deviates from norms in the 1980s. Other models of family therapy also attempt to address "alpha" prejudice (Hare-Mustin, 1987), or sex stereotyping, by agreeing that flexible gender roles are healthy. However, we feel that unless a proactive stance is taken regarding the role of women, systemic therapies are all at risk for "beta" prejudice or lack of intervention, leading to actual enabling of repressive family behavior.[1]

In the "Cartesian" stress model described by Carter and McGoldrick (1980), life-cycle stress is contrasted with transgenerational stress impinging on the family. Symbolic-experiential therapy incorporates and utilizes freely family life-cycle theory, assessing nodal events and transition periods (birth, death, marriage, adolescence, leaving home). However, unlike other schools of family therapy, we examine closely the ways in which pressures and organizational patterns are transmitted *across generations, as well as across the life cycle.* Essentially, transgenerational patterns occur in a different, much longer time frame than transactions in the nuclear family. Usually covert, the beliefs and or-

---

[1] *Editors' Note.* In this chapter, Roberto explodes a number of myths, misrepresentations, and misperceptions of symbolic-experiential family therapy (S-EFT), which we believe are rather widespread in the field, although she does not herself identify these as such. Therefore, we will call attention to them. The first of these is the notion that S-EFT is at least insensitive to the unique concerns of women, and may even operate in such a conservative fashion as to work against women's needs.

ganizational structures of previous generations produce a unique type of stress by guiding and constraining the nuclear family to reproduce earlier patterns. The healthy family finds creative ways to reconcile present needs with the past traditions and values that cycle slowly through current living.

Process characteristics of the healthy family, in contrast to structural characteristics, involve how its members negotiate and respond to nonverbal, emotional imperatives such as intimacy needs, bonding with children, differentiating from each other, maintaining commitment to each other, and expressing/resolving conflict. Bonding and intimacy exist between parent and child, between marital partners, and between siblings. Although attachment is not necessarily expressed verbally or with displays of affection, members of a healthy family report with confidence that they are special to each other. There is a sense of trust that implies that one's parent or sibling can be emotionally responsive. With infants and young children, bonding is shown in cuddling and monitoring the child. Expressed sentiment is not the sole, or even primary, indicator of bonding. In a couple, intimacy can be seen in the way a husband looks at his wife when she addresses him.

Differentiation and individuation in functioning families distinguish members from one another. Each member is able to hold his or her individual perceptions without being "spoken for" or interpreted by others. The children are not lumped together anonymously, nor are the parents seen as a global "they." This state of differentiation requires that the two adult partners have separated to a degree from their own families of origin, so that they can tolerate separation in partner and children.

The healthy family shows tolerance for conflict and allows disagreement to become overt and explicit. However, overt conflict is sustained in such a manner that resolution is possible, through either new framing of the problem, agreement, or compromise. The resolution may not be couched in formal ways, but rather may evolve as differences are maintained and acknowledged. Along with tolerance for disagreement, healthy families possess a degree of empathy among members. Despite their differences, a parent can understand a teenager's frustration, a spouse can have compassion, and a child can comfort an adult.

Sexuality is contained or "bottled up" in functioning families within generational lines. Capacity for sexual intimacy continues between the adult partners even after children are born and require care. The children can engage in peer sexual play and flirting without turning to siblings or friends for early sexual gratification. Parents can also play and joke with children about sexuality—for example, a mother can tease husband and son about who is her "best guy."

Abundant interconnections (identification) among family members can produce intense affect and perceptions of attachment. Whitaker and Keith (1981) have differentiated "passion," including both positive and negative affect, from experiences such as affection in the deeply interconnected family. This distinction again implies the presence of sexuality among family members, which is constrained by functioning subsystem boundaries but not repressed in children or adults. This affect can be discharged in play and ritual, not in destructive ways, and is visible in a continual process of disorganization and reintegration.

Autonomy in healthy families does not threaten well-being and satisfaction. If the parents plan to be away, their absence does not provoke acting out by the teenagers. Conversely, independent behavior in a child of school age does not precipitate parental depression. Autonomous behavior is one aspect of the individuation process and is seen in the capacity to take action without obtaining permission and without guilt.

Loyalty and commitment are not usually discussed as part of healthy-family process. However, in order for a family to experience the sense of a whole, or group, identity, some degree of mutual commitment must exist. Boszormenyi-Nagy and Krasner (1986) view emotional commitment as a bedrock upon which relational permanence is founded and maintained despite conflict and misfortune. We agree that this invisible process is a powerful buffer against dissolution in healthy families.

Capacity for problem solving is another indicator of family functioning. Since every family experiences normative developmental and transgenerational stress, the essential determinant of health is its potential to generate solutions.[2] Again, this potential does not obviate periods of disruption. Rather, such families can generate alternatives freely until a feasible resolution evolves. Alternatives may arise from past traditions, familial values, new roles, fantasies, family support networks, or random searching (Whitaker & Keith, 1981).

Along with the capacity for problem solving, healthy families can maintain playfulness and humor (Keith, 1987). There are surprises, and everyone can mock his or her own and each other's assumptions. Humor produces drama, adding excitement to ordinary life.

In well-functioning families, a sense of cultural adaptation is achieved by balancing cultural and familial mandates. Many families of the 1980s have experienced migration within three generations, which adds an ethnic dimension to family organizational patterns. Present culture exerts a powerful influence on family processes, such as autonomy, intimacy, and authority—witness the explosion in the frequency of eating disorders as the American feminine ideal became emaciated. Yet each extended family also carries transgenerational values and roles from distant cultures, for example, a child focus in Italian families. The two forces of present culture and family organization combine, clash, and ultimately blend to form present-day adaptation.

Finally, creativity emerges from family interest in studying itself. As in the family that keeps a photograph album, healthy functioning includes the capacity for reflexive observation, or metaperspective. This reflexivity does not mean ongoing critical analysis, but rather an awareness and appreciation for the family's ongoing concerns and well-being.

PATHOLOGICAL OR DYSFUNCTIONAL MARRIAGE OR FAMILY

As in the healthy family, characteristics of the dysfunctional family include both structural and process aspects. Structurally, families that come to the clinic often show problems of overly rigid or overly fused internal boundaries. For example, a daughter is unable to address her father directly and will only confide in her mother. Or a couple may be locked into an enmeshed folie-à-deux, in which the husband is grieving over his wife's abuse by her mother. For this reason, Haley (1977) commented, from his problem-solving model, that a sine qua non of the dysfunctional triad is the presence of poorly functioning hierarchies with inadequate boundaries.

With overly rigid external boundaries, clinical families report isolation and tend toward secrecy regarding their problems. Offspring may be forbidden to separate from the parents and become involved "outside." Overly permeable external boundaries lead to overdependency on helping professionals, inclusion of outsiders in familial problem solving, and triangulation (e.g., affairs).[3] Whitaker states, "A delinquent is a person who has his feelings in a low-voltage situation, for example, in the community rather than at home" (cited in Neill & Kniskern, 1982, p. 370).

Nonfunctional subsystems result from these disorganized boundaries. Spouses cannot attend to marital issues, children are parentified or infantilized, generational markers are lost with failure of individuation, siblings are divided onto family "teams" and alienated, and extended families are drawn in or cut off. In some families, it becomes difficult for the adults to acknowledge that they have a marriage. They may be more attentive to the needs of the children or of the grandparents than they are to each other. Conversely, a couple united against the world (rigid external boundaries) may abuse the children. Children in a family with enmeshed internal boundaries may live for their parents and let

---

[2] *Editors' Note.* Here is common S-EFT myth number two, that S-E therapists are only concerned about in-therapy process and experience and ignore the need of couples and families to be able to generate action alternatives. How S-E therapists deal with helping families to generate alternatives is, of course, quite different from many other approaches to therapy, most notably behavioral approaches (cf. Fallon, Chapter 3, and Holtzworth-Munroe and Jacobson, Chapter 4).

[3] *Editors' Note.* While the intervention principles and methods of S-EFT are among the most nontraditional in the field, it is interesting to note that the language of S-EFT conveys a good deal of borrowing of concepts (e.g., "boundaries," "triangulation") from other family-therapy approaches.

their sibling relationships stagnate. Or, in a family with rigid internal boundaries, they may withdraw into individual substance abuse, depression, or anger. Children in families with disorganized boundaries are easily exploited in order to comfort the adults, to substitute for missing partners or grandparents, or to channel tension away from symptomatic marriages. Although they adapt readily to their family belief system and emotional milieu, such children frequently lose their sibling alliances and become distant or deidentified (Roberto, in press).

Coalitions result from disorganized boundaries and nonfunctioning subsystems. If a mother and father cannot make decisions together, then perhaps the father turns to his mother. Coalitions do not always take the form of "pathological triads" (Hoffman, 1981). An alternative form of coalition consists of two individuals in a state of tension, each of whom acquires an ally rather than the two joining forces against a third party. This form is called a "tetrad" (Schachter, 1982). Examples of the tetrad appear in families where the father favors the eldest daughter, the mother is closest to the middle son, and the parents avoid each other.

Role rigidity, including sex stereotyping, is another structural characteristic of dysfunctional families. We believe that this problem occurs on a transgenerational level, where mandates from a parent's family of origin keep him or her from remaining flexible and open to adaptation. Under these conditions, the nuclear family adopts a rigid and constricted set of solutions to the problem of whom to be and how to act. For example, in a wealthy family, the young adult daughter would like to attend art school, but instead is studying international banking and drinks too much.

Overly rich or sparse interconnections (identifications) result from this mixture of poorly defined boundaries and rigid role expectations. Family members either may feel "overconnected" to each other, experiencing distress whenever the others act in unusual ways, or they may feel "underconnected," as when a father complains that he "is not close enough" to his youngest son.

Dysfunctional processes differ from dysfunctional structure, and have to do with the ways in which certain relational needs are dealt with. As in healthy families, there are nonverbal, emotional imperatives that require attention in assessing family dysfunction. In a family with rigidly maintained internal boundaries, relationships become disengaged or distant (Minuchin, 1974). Members may respond to this with a "nice" veneer of pseudomutuality, or they may withdraw their interest in coexisting and drift into a state of overt, even hostile, emotional cutoff.

In the dysfunctional family with overly fused or enmeshed internal boundaries, members have difficulty with separation and change because these cause disruption in others. Such families tend to instill a sense of obligation in offspring by unspoken delegations in which the offspring are pressured to behave in certain ways that maintain the family organization (Boszormenyi-Nagy & Krasner, 1986; Roberto, 1986). Family "delegates" can become scapegoats if they develop symptoms, or remain as "white knights" if their symptoms are culturally invisible, as in the type A personality (Whitaker & Keith, 1981). Self-sacrifice and codependency behaviors are another type of dysfunctional family process. An atmosphere of self-denial is characteristic of psychosomatic families (Roberto, 1986; White, 1983). Codependency behavior is seen in psychosomatic and addictive families. Self-sacrificial behavior in families is frequently related to emotional maltreatment or physical/sexual abuse in the family of origin. Although many family-therapy models define self-sacrifice as a problem and intervene to alleviate it, there is typically a blatant disregard for the transgenerational (family-of-origin) events that have produced it and maintain it (as in the case of a woman whose father had molested her and who now lives with her husband and children across town so she can take care of Dad).

Failure of parental empathy is a process dysfunction that is highly resistant to present-focused interventions. Parents who have been abused or neglected as children have difficulty seeing their children's point of view or protecting children's needs (Boszormenyi-Nagy & Spark, 1973/1984; Boszormenyi-Nagy & Krasner, 1986). Where this lack of commitment is seen, the remaining emotional investment (if any) has to be carefully nurtured in therapy and heavily promoted.

Conflict is perceived as dangerous and unwelcome in dysfunctional families. Because there is chronic tension, and symptoms in one or more family members, each individual is vulnerable to fears that tension will escalate. In families in which there is fusion, the central concern is that fusion will increase as the symptomatic member gets worse and needs further care. Where there is distance, everyone shows sensitivity about alienating each other further. Although there can be explosiveness, such an impasse can produce conflict avoidance as well. Conflict avoidance is seen in the way that spouses declare that their marriage is "wonderful" when their 15-year-old daughter is addicted to cocaine, or when a father and son have no disagreements and yet the son is delinquent. It is possible for a family to have repeated arguments over the same symptoms without being able to sustain the fights long enough to clarify the problem or resolve it. For example, the mother lectures and the bulimic daughter makes snide comments; the mother scolds the daughter for insolence and the daughter goes off to purge. This pattern of premature closure is also a type of conflict avoidance (Roberto, 1986).

We assume that symptoms develop when dysfunctional structures and processes persist over time and interfere with a family's life tasks. Although healthy families show transient problems in structure or process, in dysfunctional families these conditions become rigidified and acquire a "high voltage"—creating intense emotionality or behavioral disorganization (Whitaker & Keith, 1981). There are three sources of stress to a family: those from the outside environment (e.g., job loss); developmental stresses within the family (e.g., an adolescent who will not leave home); and transgenerational stresses within the family (e.g., the early death of a grandfather). Stresses in any of these three areas become impasses through a dynamic, circular interchange between situational upheaval, developmental pressures, and transgenerational forces (Roberto, Keith, & Kramer, 1987).

Whitaker believes that transgenerational stress results from the presence of myths, or family legacies, that bind offspring to respond to needs and losses in previous generations (Whitaker, 1976b; Whitaker & Keith, 1981). The emotional pressure is to be loyal to the experiences of the past rather than to adapt one's perceptions of the world and oneself to changing conditions and times. As he puts it: "How to stay dead: Just keep telling anyone who will listen about the good old days" (cited in Neill & Kniskern, 1982, p. 365). In dysfunctional families, offspring labor under preset roles from their families of origin, repeating the positions they occupy there in their marriages and child rearing. These positions continue to be important in maintaining a kind of balance in the family of origin—for example, being mother's defender, grandfather's nurse, or father's business partner.

Symptoms, according to the symbolic-experiential model, occur in three different contexts. An individual can be "driven crazy" in an interpersonal context where he or she is repeatedly disqualified or belittled. Or a person can feel as if he or she is "going crazy," meaning that the person is in a state of temporary disorganization or confusion. Finally, symptom bearers placed under intolerable stress can "act crazy," as in the case of a schizophrenic son who begins making bizarre gestures during a family argument.

One example of a disqualifying context with the capacity to "drive one crazy" is the parentification of a child. It is produced by an intense child focus, so that the child comes to feel responsible for the well-being of the parent(s). This singling out of a child can be accompanied by pressure and control of allowed life choices by the family, leading to a variety of self-destructive and exploitative behaviors, such as psychosomatic behavior, violence, sexual or physical abuse, self-mutilation, addictions, depression, or suicide. However, any discussion of self-destructive behavior would be incomplete without including "culturally invisible pathologies," symptoms that carry approval and are socially acceptable; these include a drive for achievement, perfectionism, excessive work orientation, self-absorption to the detriment of family and marital commitments, intellectualization, and specific addictions such as tobacco dependence, caffeinism, and compulsive overeating or dieting.

In this model, the identified patient or symptom carrier siphons off tension from the dysfunctional family without creating overt conflict about its organization and belief system. We do not trivialize this by reframing it or positively connoting it as misguided "helping" behavior. Rather, it represents a convergence of prescribed familial roles and legacies, biological predispositions in the symptomatic member, previous attempts by the family to solve its problems, and perhaps random misfortune, as well.

The role of diagnosis in symbolic-experiential family therapy is to expand the family's view of the identified patient into more relational terms. Since dysfunction exists from reification of chronic interpersonal problems and rigidifying of mutual expectations, transgenerational diagnosis combats reification by translating back from symptoms to interactions. Significant family events are not only in the present, but also in the history of the three-plus-generation family. Diagnostic assessment is the first step to reacquainting a family with its own covert rules of operation.

ASSESSMENT OF FAMILY FUNCTIONING AND DYSFUNCTION

In symbolic-experiential therapy, families are assessed using an explicit theory of healthy functioning. Therefore, we measure symptomatic structure and process in the context of *intact competencies and resources for change*. It is a competency-based, rather than problem-focused, model of assessment and treatment. Whitaker has commented in numerous papers on the danger of reifying family symptoms on the part of diagnosticians and therapists. Locating symptoms within a nuclear family apart from the larger familial and social contexts leads to a type of stigmatization. As he playfully stated, "We put people in the hospital because they have delusions. [But] if I have a delusion, they call it a theory." Although questions are formulated in initial sessions to elicit perspectives on current problems, these current problems must always be viewed against the twin templates of the family's stage in the life cycle and its own transgenerational belief system.

Assessment is meant to capture successively smaller "shells" of context, moving the unit of diagnosis from macroscopic (the extended-family system) to microscopic (the identified patient). In between, we move to the level of the nuclear-family system and its overall emotional climate. Is it a family of individualistic achievers? Or does it live in an empty home where the members practice phobic avoidance? Has the group become passive and helpless in the face of prolonged distress? The next lower level of fixed triangles and tetrads is explored. Accordingly, levels of assessment move from large familial beliefs and relational legacies, through complex problems of cultural or religious conflicts, to the level of circular interactions, and finally to the unitary level of psychological, somatic, and fantasy symptoms in the individual.

Assessment methodology is based on the live interview, using information from both verbal and nonverbal interaction. It is not necessary that all parties agree on an explicitly verbalized problem, such as that there are too many marital arguments per week. We assume that each family member has a unique construction of the current problem, as when a husband thinks that his wife is not interested in him sexually and the wife feels overburdened with family obligations and expectations. Further, if these reactions are superimposed on longer-term attempts to cope with intolerable relational stress, family members may lack the language verbally to describe their experience of the problem over time. Important nonverbal cues include positioning in the therapy room, pregnant silence, presence or absence of play and humor, speaking volume, eye contact, and body language. Diagnostic sessions are structured as a task interview for the extended family, with an emphasis on history taking, three-generation genogramming, and identification of "ghosts" or living extended relatives who are involved in cross-generational stress. At the same time that information gathering proceeds, the initial sessions themselves become a "trial of labor" (Whitaker & Keith, 1981), in which the cotherapists may observe the family's response to outside intervention and the process of consultation. For example, the author called in both the biological and adoptive families of a bulimic young woman for extended-family consultation. Although family members readily gave information about the problems leading to her adoption out as a toddler, there was a nonverbal quality of tension, literalness, and pseudomutuality in the conversation. Later, the adoptive mother acknowledged that members of both families, who were closely involved, feared exposure of severe parenting problems to an outsider. This family anxiety was expressed throughout midphase therapy in the young woman's fantasy that she should choose between family advice and consultation with the therapist.

Assessment is positioned in the course of consultation in the earliest sessions, usually in one to three interviews. During this "trial of labor," the cotherapists work toward a personal understanding of each family's preferred roles, dominant beliefs about the outside world, relational values, developmental history, and interactional patterns. Two covert "battles" take place during assessment—an effort to enter into the family system with a diagnostic and therapeutic agenda, and an effort to receive from the family an ongoing willingness to examine themselves. The "battle for structure" and "battle for initiative" are described later as early-stage techniques. Participation in these inevitable battles results in the second track of diagnostic information: the family's response to confusion, anxiety, and the disruption of established patterns. As one example of the battle for initiative, a professor's family gave a severely problematic history in the paternal family of origin, reporting that the father had been left for the first eight years of his life in the care of cousins because his father and mother were working abroad as covert military advisors. Although he was allowed to rejoin them, he was unable to attach and later hovered constantly over his own teenagers. When the cotherapists remarked on his lack of parents, the father immediately protested that his family had "gotten over it and was extremely close." This denial of real loss and deprivation boded poorly for the therapy, which was protracted and in which change occurred very slowly.

Finally, assessment is positioned to create maximum disorganization as quickly as possible in clinical families. Our commentary is likely to be dramatic, metaphorical, humorous, and stepped up in intensity from the information given to us. This escalation is a deliberate attempt to increase complexity, challenge fixed perceptions, and create a therapeutic context that includes the elements of curiosity and surprise. For this reason, Whitaker has been referred to as "a destroyer of crystallized forms" (Minuchin, cited in Hoffman, 1981).[4]

Diagnostic findings are communicated to the family in an ongoing way rather than as a self-contained procedure. Increasingly, the cotherapists focus on dysfunctional process rather than discrete symptoms. We emphasize and comment on each member's affect and fantasy activity, not simply behavior. The diagnosis we give is essentially a systemic reframing of the current problem, in which the contribution of the identified patient is reformulated as a segment of a larger familial pattern that involves three generations. The diagnosis is offered empathically, but also as a challenge for the family to create a more livable alternative should they desire to do so.

SETTING AND MODIFYING THERAPEUTIC GOALS

The symbolic-experiential model contains several broad treatment goals that apply to most dysfunctional couples and families, as well as problem-specific goals. The two broadest goals are (1) to increase the sense of cohesion and belonging within a couple or family so that the members perceive themselves as a nurturing and problem-solving unit, encouraging cohesion not only within the nuclear family, but in its connections with the extended family composed of the parental families of origin; and (2) to enhance a couple's or family's ability to support the completion of developmental tasks for each individual member (that is, the healthy individuation of each family member) (Roberto, in press; Whitaker & Keith, 1981). Symbolic-experiential therapy holds these two broad goals in common with other transgenerational family therapies, reflecting its emphasis on promoting effective mastery of life-cycle tasks for individuals so that, over the life span, these skills can be brought to marriage and the rearing of children and thus strengthen the family unit.

Each couple or family requests consultation because of specific interactional and relational impasses that create distress and ineffective problem solving. We assume that after a prolonged period of impasse, a family no longer is able to provide the cohesiveness and intermember support that is basic to long-term health. In addition, the impasses themselves can lead to chronic conflict or distancing problems, poor de-

---

[4] *Editors' Note.* The ways in which S-EF therapists "destroy" such "forms" are not infrequently seen as being random, haphazard, and incoherent. Roberto's explication of the systematic integrity of S-EFT should help to correct this misperception.

cision making, mood disturbance, appetitive or chemical-dependency problems, sexual dysfunction, and social or work tensions.

The *central goals selected for a couple or family begin with identification of the predominant areas of distress*. It is a common misconception that transgenerational techniques avoid a problem focus and immediately reframe presenting symptoms as by-products of long-term familial dysfunction. While this formulation is part of overall treatment planning, initial goals are set in collaboration with distressed family members who seek relief from immediate disturbances. If there are several overt problems during the same time in a couple or family, they are prioritized, keeping in mind both family distress and the bias of transgenerational therapy toward promoting life-cycle transitions.

Chris and Sandra, both of whom had been previously married, sought consultation for severe conflict in their three-year-old marriage. Sandra felt that Chris was too accommodating with his demanding ex-wife and distant from his teenage children, and consequently expected a great deal of her. Chris viewed his second wife as self-critical and overanxious about his children, oversensitive to his ex-wife's hostility, and pessimistic. One of the teenage daughters was quite volatile and physically violent, which had resulted in an out-of-school suspension at the time of the first interview.

The therapist chose to support this fragile remarriage, reflecting each spouse's concern for the tension and negativity in the relationship. Initial meetings were held with the couple to help the spouses overcome resentments from past marriages and build a sense that "things can be better this time." After the spousal relationship had been strengthened considerably, family sessions were held with the children present and some participation by their mother to create more intimacy between them and their noncustodial father.

There is a great difference in symbolic-experiential family therapy between *mediating goals* and *ultimate goals*. Mediating goals have to do with creating a new therapeutic environment, or "conversation" as cyberneticians note, in which familial interaction is altered to produce a different affective experience of important family relationships. These mediating goals include:

1. *Disorganizing rigid, repetitive cycling of interaction* in order to create a space for alternative responses to distressing behavior. Heavy emphasis is placed on interrupting chronic relational patterns in the process of the therapy session. This includes encouraging family members to experiment with different roles within the group, with an attitude of "play" or openness to discovery (Whitaker & Keith, 1981).

2. *Activating and allowing constructive anxiety*, or confusion, in family members other than the symptom bearer. Whitaker (Whitaker & Ryan, 1989) distinguishes between "negative anxiety," or *fear of harm*, and "positive anxiety," or *fear of failure to accomplish all one is capable of*. Symbolic-experiential therapy tends to focus more on "positive anxiety" by positively reframing symptoms as efforts toward competence and by overtly addressing the life-cycle transitions each family member is facing.

3. *Expanding the presenting problem* to examine the participation of each member in systemic tensions. In this way, the integrity of the larger family unit is preserved, scapegoating is bypassed, and a group solution focus can be constructed (Roberto, in press; Whitaker & Keith, 1981). This mediating goal is not unique to symbolic-experiential therapy, but is true of all family systems therapies.

4. *Encouraging and supporting any new decisions* that are consistent with each extended family's dominant beliefs, values, and traditions. Each family consists of its own unique culture, compounded of heritages of maternal and paternal families of origin as well as the adaptations that have taken place while residing in different communities (or countries) and different times.

5. *Creating transgenerational boundaries*, including a boundary around the extended family, so that its members are aware of their mutual interconnection. Intergenerational boundaries are considered necessary precursors to adequate decision making in parental, grandparental, sibling, and offspring subgroups.

6. *Creating a "therapeutic suprasystem"* (Roberto, in press) in which the family and the cotherapy team, although separate in some

ways, develop a shared meaning system and intermember alliances. It is the dynamic interaction of each cotherapist with each family member, along with the cotherapists' ability to separate, that will allow the couple or family to evolve new positions and renegotiate intimacy and authority.

In distinction from mediating goals, ultimate goals are developed between a couple or family and the cotherapy team, specific to their own unique organization and relational tensions. These goals are selected from an enormous array of potential changes, such as a couple's desire for greater mutual disclosure and intimacy, parental concern over violence toward children, spouse abuse, chronic conflict between spouses, greater accountability for children toward parents and elders, and control of substance abuse. Other goals include the need for stronger boundaries between parents and children or grandparents and children in an enmeshed family, the development of greater connection between a family and the community or larger culture, and increasing work productivity and interest. It must be noted that relational tensions and symptoms in marriages and families often appear around the axes of intimacy, authority, and autonomy (individuation). Thus, ultimate goals for a couple or family in therapy frequently involve attempting to renegotiate the degree of intimacy and interdependency, effectiveness of parental authority, and maintenance of some autonomy for each member.

Several theorists have stated that the ultimate goals of treatment, as opposed to mediating goals, are codeveloped by the therapy team and the clinical family. Whitaker (Whitaker & Keith, 1981) has noted that, in some cases, ultimate goals are unclear or "unconscious" during the process of therapy and become clearer in retrospect. Mediating goals, since they involve deliberately induced experiences led by the cotherapy team, are also not explicitly discussed. However, they are more unilateral, based on the therapy team's understanding of family systems theory and our model of dysfunction. In the case of ultimate therapy goals, one reason that familial goals are often out of awareness is that individuals are not necessarily cognitively oriented toward the source of their distress. Frequently, a family member may enter therapy

because of recurrent emotional upset with very little intellectual understanding of the relational dysfunction producing the upset. In these situations, a family member at times can articulate only, "We want to get along better," or, "I want this marriage to survive." It may be only later in therapy, or even after substantive changes occur, that this member can articulate, "We needed more separation and were overly close," or, "I needed to express myself in my marriage instead of following my husband's direction all the time."

When there is disagreement within a couple or family over ultimate goals, it is our position that *families do not fail, therapists do* (Whitaker & Ryan, 1989).[5] That is, a family must be offered the understanding and expertise necessary to help it accomplish its goals. If the parents wish to steer their eldest son into the family business, and strongly value family commitment and loyalty, it is the therapy team's role to examine with them the cost to the family if the son should refuse, and the cost to the son should he flout his family's traditions. If the therapy team is unable or unwilling to offer understanding to the family, there is often a countertransference problem that needs to be addressed. It is the family's right—in fact, its nature—to develop a vision for survival into the future and for the values, roles, mandates, and beliefs that will preserve the family's integrity.

However, therapists often disagree with couples or families about specific planned solutions to accomplish their ultimate goals. We believe that this is the area in which the therapist's values are most likely to come into play. It is true that, at times, therapist values also contradict a family's ultimate goals. For example, if a father wishes to beat or torture his children, a therapist who values protection of the young must disagree. Similarly, the abuse of wives or the elderly, sexual exploitation of children, and economic exploitation of children (e.g., using them as drug couriers), if viewed as ultimate goals by a family member, must be opposed.

---

[5] *Editors' Note.* This is reminiscent of Haley's dictum that there are no incurable families, only inept therapists. The difference on this matter, however, is that S-EF therapists do not view therapist failures as being as significant as do strategic therapists (cf. Madanes, Chapter 12; Keith & Whitaker, 1985).

Theoretically, we believe that such behaviors are rarely ultimate goals, but attempted solutions to obtain a wished-for relationship. The abusive husband may be fighting off memories of abandonment by his own father, and looking to his wife to bolster his poor self-image. The exploitive parent, who expects a child to enter a magnet school to enhance family status, is often reacting to feelings of shame regarding past events in the family of origin. When viewed in this way, the therapist is freed to disagree with the methods being used to achieve a desired relational goal. The therapy team is able to engage in an ongoing debate with the couple or family over the assumptions in the current strategies for getting needs met, and to suggest alternatives and explore them.

A husband and wife brought in their 13-year-old daughter, Kathy, for therapy when she began to starve and became anorexic. The father, an Arabic teacher, agreed with her Asian mother and aunt (both homemakers) that she was a stubborn and uncooperative child. The father, who had been ejected from his own family, enjoyed female deference and punished his daughter's assertiveness. The mother and aunt, Cambodian refugees, believed strongly in family (particularly sororal) loyalty and were hurt by Kathy's negativity. The therapy team learned that the mother's family had been executed by Communist insurgents. They suggested that the mother might better obtain Kathy's loyalties by sharing with her the grief she had hidden, rather than by berating her while the father punished her.

Ultimate goals, as they evolve between a family and the cotherapy team, are modified into a language that speaks metaphorically to each family. In the case described above, the metaphor of grieving with the daughter captured the mother's and aunt's devotion to their family of origin, while opening a way for them to bring Kathy closer instead of adding to the father's harsh discipline. The metaphor of grief, while it was not immediately sensible to this cut-off and demanding father, later bore emotionally relevant meanings when he became ready to face his rejection by his offended parents (who, it emerged, were opposed to his marriage outside their faith). Over time, the "therapeutic supra-system" of family-plus-team creates shared meanings as well, which bolster the process of renegotiating family roles. For example, in the case under discussion, the team continued over a period of several weeks to emphasize the theme of mothers bringing their daughters close, a theme valuable to the two therapists (parents of daughters) as well as to the Cambodian mother and aunt.

As goals are established between family and cotherapy team, they often emerge in affective and even motoric terms. For the reasons described earlier, family members in distress may articulate their symptoms in affective terms or psychosomatic terms rather than intellectual formulations. While the therapist could "jump to another level" and make these formulations and goals cognitive, we prefer to match the level of experience presented by the family. Thus, if initially spouses state that they "want to get along better" (a somewhat affective statement), the cotherapists will explore the emotional atmosphere of the marriage and the connection between the two sets of in-laws in order to match their experience. If a family presents with psychosomatic symptoms, such as persistent colitis or nausea, the cotherapists will initially explore with them what conditions would create more physical comfort and less stress and physical anxiety.

STRUCTURE OF THE THERAPY PROCESS

Couples or families are seen in an office setting at a variable frequency, typically weekly to biweekly. It is not unusual for families to come for monthly sessions in the late phase of therapy when they are experimenting actively at home with their own solutions. While continuity is important in this model, it is also desirable to avoid the impasses that can arise from time-unlimited weekly meetings. At times, it can appear that "the best way to avoid psychotherapy [read 'change'] is to have regular interviews with a therapist" (Whitaker, cited in Neill & Kniskern, 1982, p. 373).

Whether pharmacological interventions are used depends on the nature of the presenting problem. Although this model emphasizes the interactional aspects of psychological symptoms, that does not preclude concurrent use of medications for stabilization during psychotic episodes or hypomanic breaks. Where medications are used, they are framed as simple aids to crisis management or stabilization—not as a means of problem resolution. The dominant danger in the use of psychotropic medication, aside from the physiological side effects, is the self-reinforcing nature of medication use; if medication decreases distress, then the problem must be a need for medication. Medication may also be used for acute psychotic-level depression; however, the use of antidepressants is rare since symbolic-experiential family therapy emphasizes the explicit use of affect.[6] Family sessions can become quite affectively intense, and keeping suicidal family members out of physical danger is desirable. The author, for example, prefers to use hospitalization before medication in cases of suicidality, in order to convey the need for safety rather than the need for emotional suppression through drugs.

Symbolic-experiential therapy utilizes a *therapeutic suprasystem* constructed of the treatment family (couple) plus cotherapists or a therapist and consultant. The subsystem of the family includes the symptomatic member(s) for whom help is sought, the nuclear family that lives with and attempts to adapt to the symptomatic member(s), the two extended families represented in the marital dyad or parent, and the friendship or collegial networks surrounding the symptomatic member(s). All of the individuals just described may be included in family interviews for the purpose of mobilizing concern, increasing resources, and bringing about change.

A three-generation diagram guides the sessions, regardless of who attends each interview. We work from a carefully constructed genogram throughout therapy, reminding us recurrently of vital connections between family members and of recursive transgenerational patterns or legacies. This transgenerational framework extends the therapist's understanding of the developmental life cycle over extremely long time spans, a factor that allows us to treat adult individuals, childless couples, and established families with children using the same theoretical language. However, the therapist makes choices regarding whether and when sessions will include the marital dyad, sibling subgroups, or extended-family reunions. Typically, careful discussion takes place during the first telephone contact to suggest that beginning interviews include as many extended-family members as possible, at least for diagnostic purposes. Marital dyads are selected where the children are considered nonsymptomatic by the parent(s), although they may be brought back later if the therapist considers the offspring to be emotionally bound by the therapeutic problem being treated. Siblings and other subgroups are likely to be selected out later in therapy for the purpose of strengthening children's alliances and separating them from the parents.[7]

The subsystem of the treatment team in this "therapeutic suprasystem" optimally includes a cotherapy team of two. When two therapists are consistently present, a tetradic or four-way interaction process is created as opposed to the triadic interaction of multiple family members plus therapist. The use of cotherapy has been reported since the 1920s and practiced by family therapists since the 1940s (Hoffman & Hoffman, 1981). Numerous documented advantages have included facility in training; mutual complementarity and support; continuity of care; modeling of intimacy, autonomy, and healthy conflict; division of roles in the session; construction of a "binocular" systemic view; and increased creativity on the parts of both therapists (Russell & Russell, 1979–1980; Dowling, 1979; Ferrier, 1984; Dick, Lessler, & Whiteside, 1980; Silber & Bogado, 1983; Mueller & Orfanidis, 1976; Hannum, 1980; Latham, 1982).

We regard the cotherapy dyad as a special case of the systemic treatment team, able to perform a number of unique functions and flexibly to

---

[6] *Editors' Note.* We do not agree with the implication that prescribing medication per se runs a high risk of implicitly labeling, or reinforcing the label, of one family member as "the" problem (biologically). Sophisticated clinical psychopharmacologists are always aware of the patient attributions that may follow their prescribing, and make efforts to keep their prescribing in context or perspective. Even more important, we believe it is not on target to suggest that medication taking dampens affect in a way that constrains the process of psychotherapy. Indeed, a great deal of research has demonstrated that, for large numbers of patients, medication and psychotherapy are synergistically beneficial.

---

[7] *Editors' Note.* A fourth S-EFT myth, in our view, has been that S-E therapists only work with large groups, refuse to see individuals, etc.

interchange these functions as necessary from moment to moment. Unlike larger systemic teams, the dyad allows for increased intimacy and, indeed, is often described with the metaphor of marriage (Dick, Lessler, & Whiteside, 1980). The similarities include the need for a strong friendship, open communication and problem solving, a balance between autonomy and closeness, a desire to learn, and acceptance and integration of individual differences. Cotherapy teams can also be said to proceed through developmental stages, as does a marriage.

From a structural rather than a process point of view, the presence of a two-person team creates a tetrad. Tetrads have been found to function in a more stable manner than therapeutic triangles, since at no time is any individual excluded from an alliance (Roberto, in press). In the event that a cotherapist is not available, a common alternative form is the use of a solo therapist plus consultant or peer supervision (consultation group). This alternative has few of the process advantages of a cotherapist, but does provide several similar functions—support, division of roles in a session, construction of a binocular view, and stimulation of creativity. Special consultants have been used for pharmacology, religious problems, and social and community problems. Symbolic-experiential therapists may utilize members of the clergy (Whitaker & Keith, 1981), pediatricians (Silber & Bogado, 1983), cotherapists of different ethnic backgrounds (Hightower, Rodriguez, & Adams, 1983), psychopharmacologists (Mueller & Orfanidis, 1976), and agency caseworkers as cotherapists or consultants.

Finally, frequently a family is seen by a solo therapist who unconsciously turns to someone else without deliberate planning. From our viewpoint, spouses and families of origin are often consulted indirectly by a frustrated therapist caught in a therapeutic impasse. This consultation can take the form of irritability at home, preoccupation, taking positions with one's own family that one does not dare to do in therapy, and the like.

As mentioned previously, the purpose of the cotherapy team and mechanisms of the team are diverse. The object of symbolic-experiential interventions is not strictly symptom relief, but also change of the transgenerational patterns that are producing symptoms. In dysfunctional families, these patterns have become rigidified, depersonalized, and devoid of anxiety. Therefore, a primary goal for the cotherapists is to reintroduce the intimate disclosure and anxiety that mobilize individuation and change. These affective states will produce unpredictable behaviors that can disorganize symptom cycles. For example, an ambitious businessman and father becomes aware that he stays at the office out of fear that his wife loves his paycheck and not him. His increased anxiety may produce an unexpected Saturday at home or a much-needed and intimate quarrel.

Cotherapists behave unpredictably in front of the family in many ways and, therefore, model individuation and change. They may suddenly distance themselves and withdraw from a heated conflict to talk with each other instead of the family. They may change the subject and introduce a fantasy about the family session. They may side unpredictably with different members, reverse roles with one member and engage in his or her symptoms *for* him or her. They may bring in unannounced consultants, or share teaching stories. This deliberate unpredictability is what Whitaker refers to as "therapeutic craziness." It forms a backdrop of process underlying specific intervention techniques.

Essentially, the therapeutic suprasystem of family-plus-cotherapists is unbalanced, in that the cotherapy subsystem is more flexible than the family subsystem. The cotherapy-team members join and separate more easily, maintain a less rigid boundary with others, and show other characteristics of a healthy family. This live demonstration of flexibility creates *experiential alternatives* for family members, while the therapists actively interfere with their rigid, pseudomutual, closed, or ritualistic organization by means of challenge, humor, interactional observations, reframing, and other techniques.

Although the cotherapy team demonstrates flexibility, unpredictability, and shifts in intimacy/distance throughout therapy, they must take different positions at different points in therapy. In early sessions, they must convey that they are in charge of the therapy's structure. The early "battle for structure" involves setting the format of sessions, deciding who will attend and how long the sessions will be (typically, an hour to an hour and a half), and setting boundaries around the cotherapy team (e.g., that neither will meet with the family alone or with an individual alone). In other words, although the team is now part of a suprastructure, certain decisions about the ground rules of the therapy are unilateral. In the midphase of family therapy, the cotherapists must capitalize on their acceptance by the family and move to reorganize the family members by avoiding instruction, withholding immediate solutions, and forcing the family to generate experiments cooperatively. In late-stage therapy, the team can become more disclosive and educational, since the family is more self-sufficient and less destructive or closed within itself.

The length of symbolic-experiential family or marital therapy is time-unlimited, and could best be described as growth-oriented and intermediate in term. Sessions are not limited to a brief solution-focused intervention, which is commonly a two- to three-month procedure. However, they do not have a psychoanalytic structure, which can extend to three, four, or more years in which successive regressions are induced and analyzed in relation to a central therapist. We see most couples and families in a range of six months to two years, depending on the severity of relational symptoms and the extent of psychological damage to individual members.

THE ROLE OF THE THERAPIST

The therapeutic position of the cotherapy team is as a consultant, or advocate for change, on behalf of the distressed individual or family. Rather than appearing to be in charge of treatment, the cotherapist is instead a "coach" who observes and suggests change. He or she is not positioned as an expert consultant who directs content and sets goals of treatment for the family, but as an experienced consultant who facilitates desired change via use of self, perspectives on the family life cycle, knowledge of transgenerational family process, and indirect techniques. Active but not directive, symbolic-experiential family therapists inquire overtly into early-phase symptoms, pursue anxiety-arousing issues in the family, and follow up consequences of previous attempts to make change.

Included in this definition of activity is the deliberate use of silence in the session, which will be discussed further as a technique. Silence is used to demarcate events in the session, redirect a focus, or dramatize an intervention.[8]

Strict adherence to patient initiative is preserved. "Efforts to be regarded as magic" (Whitaker & Keith, 1981) are invitations to counterpressures from the family to slow down or even prevent change, becoming a game of strategy (Selvini Palazzoli, Boscolo, Cecchin, & Prata, 1978). We find it more productive to track the progress of each session very closely, refusing to move ahead toward stated goals any faster than the clients do. This stance, over the course of therapy, effectively forces families to develop a new organization that is their own and that they can (and must) feel responsible for themselves. To put it differently, "Whenever the therapist steps off his throne he [or she, and the family,] is apt to grow" (Whitaker, 1982b). Theoretically, it is the combination of the cotherapists' creative power, the family's own investments in the therapy, and the increasing "sweatbox" of progressive therapeutic sessions that will trigger the leap into a new organization by the family members themselves.

Frequent intervention in family interaction distinguishes this form of therapy from systemic forms. Beginning in the first session, the cotherapy team creates a tetrad that enables each therapist selectively to assume a transient partiality or alliance with specific members when useful. A series of interchanges are set up between individual therapists and family members or subgroups, so that each uses his or her own personality and style to a great extent. This does not minimize the primary teaming of the cotherapists; indeed, one significant mistake in cotherapy is to join with a clinical family in the absence of (or in defiance of) one's cotherapist to form a coalition. In a strong and properly functioning cotherapy team, however, each

---

[8] *Editors' Note.* We agree that the S-E therapist *is* a "coach" in the sense that he or she is not a "player" on the "field" of the family's life. Still, the coaching metaphor does not adequately capture the S-E therapist's "position," in that coaches (in athletics, for example) *are* defined as experts; they *do* direct the content of and set goals for the training of those with whom they work, and they do not merely "suggest" change, but, in fact, regularly demand it.

therapist can be as available to family members as to his or her partner, if necessary.

Each therapist's use of self, or participation using personal responses, is a method of remaining differentiated from the therapeutic system while working with affectively loaded material. This personal participation increases after the initial phase of family therapy is begun, and is intended to disrupt the idealized "honeymoon state" of the early therapist–patient relationship to allow for individual differences and healthy conflict. At the same time, the whole self of the therapist is not shared in the sense of bringing in unresolved familial problems of one's own, or uncontrolled regression. Most productive in the use of self are fragments of therapeutic experience, personal reflections, teaching stories, or countertransference responses that highlight family dysfunction. Helm Stierlin has called this behavior "healing by encounter," in which therapists induce change not by restructuring, but by a kind of participant observation.

This emphasis on participant observation ultimately preserves the family's responsibility for change even while the therapist or therapists are responsible for making intervention. The cotherapists are responsible for controlling the structure of therapy, including how they will intervene, whom they believe should come for sessions, and how they choose to perceive the family problems. They are responsible for mastering technique and transcending it enough to maintain creativity and flexibility.[9] The family is responsible for maintaining initiative, or motivation to make change, and for wading through potential impasses. The cotherapists are responsible for breaking impasses, since we define impasse not as "resistance," but as induction of the therapists into the family's dysfunction. Breaking impasses is achieved normally through bilateral consultation, peer supervision, or a change in therapeutic position. Refusing responsibility for initiative helps family members to examine their own areas of influence and limitations, such as telling an ambivalent husband, "I'm certainly staying with my wife, but I really couldn't advise you on whether to stay with yours."

Symbolic-experiential family therapy, in keeping with the use of self, utilizes a high degree of self-disclosure that is deliberate and thoughtful. The purpose of using personal communication is partly to provide a model for the family of intermittent separating and joining, a problem of boundaries. Second, self-disclosure accentuates therapeutic observations by adding affect. This accentuation can help create shifts in the family's existing range of stability, and lead the therapeutic suprasystem into a new dynamic range of functioning as a result. In demonstrating the use of unpredictable, individual responses as they arise, the therapists teach the family to individuate as individual members, as subgroups, and as separate from the cotherapy team. Finally, by speaking intimately and subjectively at times, the therapists induce family members to allow their own subjectivity (even irrationality) to emerge for examination. This nontechnical mode of intervening grants the therapist freedom to not demand or push for change. Everyone can become involved in the current atmosphere of the therapy at each stage. The therapists can even expose their own dilemmas regarding each stage of work and then resume autonomous functioning later. As Whitaker writes, "They [family members] don't really want to stay out of the family. They *do* want to be free to go in and out as they choose."

Self-disclosure need not be literal, but metaphorical, pointed, and dramatic. The forms of self-disclosure change with the stage of therapy, with teaching stories in early phase, fragmentary fantasies or reflections in midphase, and spontaneous interpersonal messages in the late phase. There are two types of self-disclosure— disclosure to family members and disclosure to the cotherapist. Disclosure to family increases proximity and pressure; disclosure to the cotherapist draws a generational boundary, separates, and provides feedback that is less direct and challenging.

As a therapeutic technique, therapist proximity in symbolic-experiential family therapy is

---

[9] *Editors' Note.* We believe there is often an inherent tension here in the training of S-E therapists who are neophytes in their overall experience as family therapists (as opposed to those who bring at least a moderate amount of family therapy background to their S-E training), in that it is difficult to transcend technique one has not yet mastered. Perhaps this is why a number of people have suggested that training in S-EFT is better offered as an advanced learning experience, rather than an introductory one.

varied. Initial "joining" with a new family is not seen as volitional, but rather as an inevitable part of the evolving treatment suprasystem of cotherapists plus family. Both proximity and distance have their technical uses. Proximity exposes interactional alternatives between specific family members and each therapist, which can later be used by the family members with each other if they wish. Distance reinforces subsystem boundaries when they are overly weak or vulnerable to outside forces. For example, the cotherapy-team members may distance themselves if approached as substitutes for intimacy by a husband or wife. We do not dictate a fixed proximity or distance from treatment families in practice or training.

TECHNIQUES OF MARITAL AND FAMILY THERAPY

Symbolic-experiential family therapy utilizes a specific set of goals, which include increasing the family's sense of cohesiveness as a whole while at the same time increasing the individuation of its members. As a second goal, we seek to make a person's irrational, "crazy," or affective side more available since it is this irrational side that promotes change.

In terms of symptom control, alleviation of presenting symptoms has a high value. However, we assume that just because dysfunctional patterns maintain symptoms, removing a symptom through ritual, persuasion, or punishment (ordeal) will not magically erase dysfunctional family patterns. Thus, we expand the goals of symbolic-experiential family therapy to include the broader goals of personal growth and capacity for change (morphogenesis).

The type of change in family pattern resulting from symbolic-experiential therapy is not controlled. There is no definition of the values a healthy family must have, or the way in which members must live out their roles in the family. We assume that each family has its own culture or belief system. The aim of symbolic-experiential family therapy is to aid the family to develop its own customs more freely, without being bound to carry values or goals set in the past or to make up for the past. Thus, "it is like teach-

ing tennis to an advanced player" (Whitaker & Keith, 1981, p. 208).[10]

The process techniques we will describe later are intended to disorganize rigid patterns of behavior, to activate anxiety and confusion surrounding the identified patient, and to support decisions by family members involving how to make change within the family's unique belief system.

Symbolic-experiential family therapy uses a staged model of treatment. The structure of therapy moves from high to low; the position of the cotherapist moves from central to peripheral; directiveness decreases; use of self-disclosure increases; and personal responsivity to each individual within the family increases. For this reason, we divide our discussion of techniques into early-phase, midphase, and late-phase/termination strategies.

In early-phase marital or family therapy, the therapists move rapidly to build up considerable influence within the new family–cotherapist suprasystem (Whitaker & Keith, 1981; Whitaker, 1976a). Several "battles" are fought before any family can invest enough emotionally to depend on the cotherapy team while the family reorganizes to cure the scapegoat or work on further differentiation or give up time-honored symptoms. However, this does not imply any kind of direct confrontation with a new family. We assume that it is necessary to care about one's clinical families openly and warmly, in contrast to a blank-screen or uniformly neutral stance (Napier, 1983). Even though it may not be verbalized, "the caring is the anesthesia" for the operation (Whitaker, 1975). Joining is seen in the cotherapists' interest in the family's perceptions, in their personal interchange with each member, in use of self (e.g., shared stories), in humor, and in play activity with children.

The first interventions in early-phase sessions involve an attempt to begin with three generations of family representation, since this tends to increase complexity and disorganization. We

---

[10] *Editors' Note.* Paralleling our previous note, we would add here that some tennis players, or would-be players, do not even know the proper grip of the racket, the difference between "love" and "fault," etc. Symbolic-experiential therapists do not see it as part of their "teaching" role to provide such basic instruction.

definitively arrange for an entire household to be present. Early interventions move toward defining the whole (family) through each member, defusing scapegoats by avoiding heavy focus on their symptoms, separating generations via genogramming, identifying subgroups in the family, and describing the structure of therapy. Defining the family through each member yields a systemic reconstruction of the presenting problem. Initial questions by the cotherapy team focus on process, since usually clinical families have lost the capacity to observe their own interchanges in the course of reacting to events. Our questions are reflexive in that they contain parts of a systemic understanding and are particularly oriented around the interpersonal nature of symptoms. For example, a depressed wife might be asked, "If you got fed up and left him, would your parents be surprised or say, 'I told you so'?"

Two "battles" take place in early-phase therapy: the battle for structure and the battle for initiative (Whitaker & Napier, 1977). Essentially, the *battle for structure* establishes the cotherapists' position in the therapeutic metasystem as consultants for change. At this stage, we tell the family that in order to be helpful, we must be given access to all extended-family relationships directly or indirectly (e.g., information, interviews). It is the equivalent of asking a medical patient with a painful arm to show and discuss the arm. Without access, intervention is interesting and perhaps fun, but not necessarily helpful. This is conveyed honestly without pressure or anger. The battle for structure also involves a family's willingness to allow the therapist to "restructure" its definition of the problem by investigating the interpersonal nature of the symptoms (Keith, 1974).

The second battle is the *battle for initiative*. This conflict is demonstrated when a family attends a second session and inquires what the members are to do or talk about next, usually while avoiding the differences that emerged in the first session. The cotherapists are called upon to direct family attention to relational disturbances (both structure and process). In some families, a "fencing match" takes place in which members vie for a judgment as to whose perception of the problem is correct. We convey that each member's position is a reflection of the family problem, and that couple or family decisions will evolve through group negotiation rather than through therapist preferences. Question: "Should I change my career?" Answer: "We're both happy with ours, we can't tell. Do you think you'd do that much better with another job?" Put differently, this model of therapy does not attempt to advocate one lifestyle (college, marriage, children) over another.

Cotherapy techniques in early-phase treatment include modeling dyadic intimacy and separation, modeling parenting, allying with different persons and subsystems or taking on their style, shifting the focus when one therapist is off-track, alternating joining with observing, and alternating active/passive involvement (Hannum, 1980).

In the middle phase of therapy, the cotherapy team operates differently in order to facilitate *reorganization around the interpersonally expanded symptom*. The emphasis is on the therapist–family suprasystem as a working, cohesive team. The cotherapists move toward the family affectively to activate caring. Use of self begins to include sharing personal responses and associations. Family members are then free to reciprocate. This process of "use of self" creates an existential concern, replacing early-stage symptom focusing and automatic responses (e.g., "I know what he's going to say, I've heard it 20 times before"). For example, a distant eldest son may be told that it looks as if he is trying to get away from his family. He may be advised, "If I were you, I'd probably want to pack a suitcase and head for Paris." As members strengthen their involvement with the cotherapists, their interrelationships must shift, since they become more autonomous while still attached to each other. The cotherapists mirror this process by separating at times from each other and focusing individually on specific family members.

There are four central strategies in the midphase of therapy: *creating alternative interactions, replacing key players in certain conflicts with oneself, increasing the focus on others besides the scapegoat*, and *avoiding blame of the caretaking parent (or spouse)*. These strategies serve to increase the family's experiential understanding of the systemic nature of the problem. For example, symbolic-experiential theory was among the first to highlight the role of the spouse in maintaining alcoholism.

Midphase techniques include the following:

1. *Redefining symptoms as efforts for growth.* A variant of positive connotation, this redefinition links symptomatic behavior to the family's need for change. For example, a depressed 9-year-old's social withdrawal may be redefined as an effort to avoid getting rejected any more.

2. *Highlighting covert family conflict.* Whenever there is indirect evidence of disagreement, the cotherapists move to uncover it. For example, when a teenager glares at her mother, a therapist may comment, "And I thought only your husband was angry at you!"

3. *Replacing roles of individual members to alter problem interactions.* For example, a therapist may ask the wife to step out of a marital fight, saying, "Wait a minute, let me show you how to really go after your husband."

4. *Modeling fantasy alternatives to real stress.* This technique involves creation and deliberate use of absurdity to increase flexible problem solving. The cotherapists create fantasy "solutions" that would not work for the real family. For example, a father may be told, "Maybe if you took your son's clothes, he couldn't go out and buy drugs." Or an anorexic daughter might be told, "Why don't you just go ahead and yell at your mom instead of killing yourself?" In the face of such extreme suggestions, smaller shifts in behavior appear less threatening and foreign.

5. *Separating interpersonal stress from internal stress.* Real relational problems can be constructively distinguished from individual reactivity to such problems. In one couple therapy, the husband and wife were told that their differences seemed quite workable, if only they would get over being terrified that their partner would be as disappointing as their opposite-sexed parent.

6. *Augmenting family despair.* Family members frequently will present themselves as irretrievably damaged by their problems. Such ultimatums are meant to coerce the symptomatic member to change and are rarely useful. We prefer to increase despair

as a way of removing covert ultimatums. For example, an anxious young man may be told that his critical father will probably never change, and will likely continue to run him down in new ways, and maybe even become chronically ill and move in with him.

7. *Using self.* This includes sharing dreams, primitive thoughts, and even touch. In one family, a father with a history of abusing his children and dissociative tendencies was reluctant to cuddle his children for fear that he would attack them. His depressed wife was afraid that if she told him to, he would feel criticized and blow up. The therapist put the 3-year-old on her lap while listening to the father's fears, and both parents visibly relaxed.

8. *Setting up extended-family reunions.* These reunions provide a type of consultation in middle-phase therapy. By adding members from multiple generations, they provide demonstrations of longer-term family patterns. For example, a young adult who suspected that her adoptive family looked down on her brought in her biological family for a consultation. The biological and adoptive mothers, who were cousins, described how the biological mother had been systematically infantilized by their grandmother and later diagnosed as psychotic. The daughter became aware in a new way how she allowed herself to be infantilized as well.

9. *Reversing roles.* Role reversal allows cotherapists to take the position of various individuals in the family, forcing that individual to shift into another position for a period of time. The procedure of the "Greek chorus" (Papp, 1980) and the recent variant of "triadic consultation" (Hoffman, 1981) are really examples of this type of role reversal. The cotherapists make predictions and comments and disagree from the points of view of opposing members. Family members can agree or disagree with these predictions and comments, and create new viewpoints for themselves.

In the midphase, the cotherapy team adds other alternatives to the earlier modes of teaming. The therapists can join together to mirror family patterns—that is, join the family on different sides of an issue, engage in conflict with each other, and then suspend or resolve the issue. They can move to block communication, where one therapist supportively draws away a highly active member with him or her to let the others face each other. Finally, they can alternate supporting and confronting family patterns. This is similar to a common systemic-team intervention, where observers behind a mirror challenge while the interviewer supports. One cotherapist can issue a challenge, while the other softens it and supports the family (Mueller & Orfanidis, 1976).

In the late phase of therapy, the family operates as a mobile milieu therapy unit within the family–cotherapist suprasystem (Whitaker & Napier, 1977). Family cohesion is higher than in early sessions, and subgroups have been mobilized around problem areas. This commitment and activity allow the family therapist to take a more peripheral role since the family can reflexively observe itself. The task of the cotherapists is to intervene only as needed. Often in late-phase therapy, central problems are redefined as new identified patients are activated (e.g., a distant father). As the couple or family gains familiarity and creativity in generating alternatives, the therapeutic suprasystem begins to separate into its component subsystems of cotherapy team and family. The subsystems are related, however, in a different context—that of bilateral competence rather than consultant and patient. This shift of context is brought about by the cotherapists, using several techniques:

1. *Use of self with spontaneous disclosure.* Present-focused disclosure creates a transparency that connotes equality and peer status.
2. *Requests for feedback regarding therapeutic events.* The cotherapists can survey family members for their perception of events in therapy and their level of satisfaction regarding changes already made and yet to be made.
3. *Overt grieving over approaching termination.* The therapists explicitly refer to termination, making it more salient, and suggest that they are connected to the family rather than vice versa. For example, one might say, "You'll probably be thinking of firing us soon."

Critical interventions in symbolic-experiential family therapy are utilized to highlight affect, augment disorganization, and create drama to focus on interactions that pose problems. One of the more renowned interventions is teaching stories and dreams. Teaching stories are a unique mixture of direct (educative) and indirect ("paradoxical") communication, which have the characteristic of producing successive meanings as the story is contemplated. They are highly metaphorical messages which, by their indirectness, protect the teller from ready extrusion or simple rejection (Fellner, 1976). The teller is also excused from committing himself or herself to the position taken in the story.

Universals are allusions to events and social experiences that are relevant to any person. They are intended to be culture-free observations that underscore a problematic interaction and increase family tolerance for discussing implications. Nodal events are universals, such as common experiences during birth, marriage, death, and divorce. Other universals include social patterns that are ubiquitous: grouping, hierarchies, inclusion and rejection, cooperation and opposition.

Humor and joking are processes in healthy families that, for some reason, are rarely utilized in family therapy in a predetermined manner. Symbolic-experiential therapy relies on humor to buffer therapeutic challenge and preserve the perception of support when therapists are confrontative. Joking adds symbolic value to humor by creating a point (education) while maintaining proximity and alliance (support).

The extended-family reunion is a recent procedure (Whitaker, 1979) that creates a ritual around three-generational content. Reunions involve planning and setting up a one-time gathering of an entire extended family for a period of one day to a week, with the family therapist present. This gathering is not structured into therapeutic tasks, but rather is utilized to make intergenerational connections concrete and to generate therapeutic material.

A precursor to the extended-family reunion, and an alternative to it, is the therapeutic task called, "Before I Was Born." Clients in therapy who experience difficulty gathering information regarding their families, or who experience intense anxiety during interactions with their families, are encouraged to request more personal data in the form of a narrative from parents and grandparents describing their lives up until the identified patient was born. This time constraint removes the identified patient from the frame of reference, decreasing symptomatic behavior. The data, usually in letter or audiotape format, most commonly explicate events previously hidden by families of origin or "punctuated" in such a way that the data could not be used. A frequent finding is an episode of loss or traumatic conflict that has been suppressed and that yielded compensatory patterns in the family with little explanation.

Symbolic-experiential family therapy uses few out-of-session assignments aside from the specialized interventions listed. Theoretically, if a main goal of intervention is to disorganize established symptom cycles and allow the family to generate new alternatives, structured assignments carry the risk of premature closure. Several process-oriented assignments are reserved for impasses and escalations. After a particularly disruptive session, we may advise a couple or family to refrain from further discussion for 48 hours. Of course, this is done with the understanding that an oppositional group will maintain its position by continuing discussion. This leaves the cotherapists with the option of countering that they were attempting to forestall further unpleasantness, should things become more explosive. A common restraint, used when a family appears reluctant to take action about a problem, is to advise no action—a prescription. This restraint, when used, is only applied when the therapists actually believe that action will cause further upheaval, and they wish to heighten tension about the impasse rather than break the impasse. The restraint does not originate in a hope that the family will "defy" the therapists, in contrast to strategic models.

Resistance, in the symbolic-experiential model, *can best be defined as maintaining an organization under intolerable stress.* In the face of mounting pressure to make change, by helping professionals or by demands of the family's life cycle or environment, it is a basic law of human behavior to return to previous patterns. We do not interpret this resistant behavior as deliberate scheming or game playing, nor does this model treat resistance as a cybernetic property of social organizations. Rather, it is seen as a human event reflecting the failure of previous relational patterns to contend with changing family needs and expectations. This failure, over time, creates increasing stress and anxiety in family members. In the face of failure, we try harder, using the only tools and perceptions we have. Symbolic-experiential theory holds that resistance is an inevitable part of change, just as "battles" are an inevitable part of therapy. Therefore, it is to be managed with a combination of challenge, support, and humor.

CURATIVE FACTORS IN MARITAL AND FAMILY THERAPY

Symbolic-experiential therapists take the position that in family therapy, the chief source of change stems from changing one's position with significant others and experiencing oneself differently as a consequence. This experience is immediate and affect laden, not conceptual as is intellectual insight. A family member who can communicate differently, take a new stance relationally, or view his or her partners in a more open-ended way will receive new information about himself or herself. Newness creates a sense of change, of potential, and of excitement and increased self-esteem. This process is not a primarily intellectual one; the cognitive realization of change is secondary. As Whitaker wrote, "Insight is a by-product of growth or change rather than a precursor or a cause of growth or change" (cited in Neill & Kniskern, 1982, p. 366). For example, an anorexic teenager and her family were in therapy for one year. Toward the end of that period, with her anorexia in remission and the entire family treating her as a young adult, the cotherapists asked the family members what they thought had helped. The mother commented that it was hard to say—that the daughter had somehow learned to tell them differently what pained her, and the parents had somehow learned in what ways she did and did not need them at the age of 16. Although the mother knew experientially that they had changed, she could not articulate cognitively what precisely was different.

A secondary level of change, less immediate, involves cognitive mastery—a type of insight. Cognitive mastery can be historical or interactional in transgenerational family therapy. Historical "insight" or mastery evolves as past events in the extended family are explicated and discussed in the context of present-day symptoms. For example, as a dependent, self-effacing wife explores her willingness to cater to a demanding husband, she may recognize that her own self-sacrificing mother passed down a legacy of nurturance to others. This type of historical mastery is a hallmark of Bowenian family therapy. Kerr (1981) and Friedman (1987) have commented on the clarifying effect of historical insight, and on the maneuverability granted to the family therapist who encourages such clarification rather than prescribing or "willing" change. Historical mastery also carries a certain appeal for individuals and families that are organized around rich relational interconnections. For such families, the importance of familial belief systems and intergenerational mandates regarding life choices is experienced actively and "makes sense" emotionally (Roberto, 1986, 1987). A problem with historical insight is that one can "learn a lot but not change much" (Keith & Whitaker, 1980) in the sense of taking different actions in the present.

Interactional insight, which is present- rather than past-oriented, evolves as current relational patterns emerge in family sessions and are commented on or challenged by the cotherapy team. Interactional insight is more highly stressed in symbolic-experiential therapy than in other transgenerational models such as Bowenian therapy or contextual therapy. We believe that it is interactional insight that carries the weight of therapeutic reframings and makes them "real" to a clinical family. For example, a trainee cotherapy team was treating a severely depressed obese woman, who had been sexually abused in childhood, and her equally depressed social-isolate husband. For them, "reality" was that the outside world is dangerous, even lethal, and that they should turn (desperately) only to each other. After weeks of impasse in which every marital interaction produced bilateral disappointment and frustration, the cotherapists were advised to point out to the husband and wife that they treated each other as adversaries in addition to mistrusting outsiders. In the words of the Quaker saying, "Everyone is crazy except me and thee, and sometimes I have doubts about thee." After this observation, the husband began to respond to the cotherapists' present focus by holding a bit more optimism about the marriage; the wife began to notice her profound mistrust and victim stance in the marriage.

Insight—both historical and interactional forms—are utilized by all forms of transgenerational family therapy. We believe that the process of gaining insight is a powerful source of change because commenting on family processes calls forth the symbolic function of language. Essentially, symptomatic patterns that were covert, and even denied, become overt and open to scrutiny. By becoming overt in discussion, dysfunctional beliefs and roles in the family are harder to ignore and to escalate. Thus, commentary by the therapist (and, later in therapy, by family members themselves) changes the meaning of symptoms by changing their symbolic value. The chief methods of commenting on family process, to produce insight, include the use of reframing, metaphor, and systemic messages that link present symptoms to extended-family values and needs.

Whitaker has discussed various forms of metaphor in detail, including "as if" play, in which cotherapists joke and tease family members about their roles in the family problem. For example, an overburdened mother can be likened to a war-weary veteran with battle fatigue while the youngest child is labeled the family court jester. Other forms of metaphor include fantasies about the family, allegories (nicknaming an adolescent daughter Divine Wrath), and allusions to significant events (comparing two warring families of origin to the Hatfields and the McCoys).

Reframing is a universal procedure that has been elaborated in its most sophisticated form through the work of strategic therapists. From a transgenerational perspective, we can only add that reframes are quite effective when they include specific information about extended familial events. For example, a grimly harsh and unavailable divorced father entered therapy with his two young sons, insisting that the therapist coerce his eldest child (who was electively mute) to account for his hostility. After discovering that the paternal grandfather was equally harsh with the father, the therapist commented that the eldest son was not so much hostile as "on strike" against the family boot-camp atmosphere. The father softened markedly as he began to recall the loneliness in his childhood home.

Systemic messages are utilized heavily in systemic family therapy, particularly in the Milan group (Selvini Palazzoli et al., 1978) and at the Ackerman Institute (Papp, 1980). Of particular relevance here is the high frequency of transgenerational information in systemic messages used by the Milan group. Although a message may include any specifics about family behavior as long as all members are included in it, Selvini Palazzoli almost invariably refers to behavior over two to three generations in the messages she utilizes. We have found that messages to the family that include three generations of information appear to carry great power in challenging our families to create a different alternative. One offshoot of our experiments has been the technique of the *family legacy* (Roberto, 1986, 1987) in which the therapist formulates his or her version of how the family has organized over time, and the fact that they will not be able to stay loyal to their traditions and structures if changes are made now.

Symbolic-experiential family therapy is concerned with moving beyond behavioral change to the fostering of maturational growth (Keith & Whitaker, 1980). It could be argued that symptom relief and behavioral change indicate maturational growth, but the two are by no means equivalent. For example, it is common for an alcoholic parent to become dry by participating in Alcoholics Anonymous, but this change yields a "dry alcoholic" with intimacy and self-esteem problems rather than a recovered alcoholic per se. Maturational growth calls for experiential change beyond symptom relief, and even beyond historical and interactional insight. Experiential change is the key curative factor in symbolic-experiential therapy, and is produced in circular interaction between the family and the person (or self) of the therapist. Understanding and inducing experiential change is a difficult task since it involves the paradoxical procedure of utilizing rational or theoretical thought to explore an irrational or nontheoretical shift. As Whitaker put it, "Part of the problem is the theoretical delusion that *science is curative*— that enough . . . information . . . will bring about the resolution . . . of distress" [italics added] (Whitaker, 1976a).

In his classic paper "Psychotherapy of the Ab-

surd" (1975), Whitaker broached the concept of augmenting symptoms through deliberate expansion of a family's irrational themes or complaints. These complaints are often irrational, or logically absurd, in the sense of constituting self-defeating, emotional-laden impasses. Whitaker proposed "using" the absurdity to push the underlying conflicts to their limit. This engagement with their irrationality, and the "pushing" of it, activates the unspoken attachments and commitments that people have to the healthy parts of their relationships. It is a procedure equivalent to the positive feedback loop in systemic language, but is carried out by the therapist's working "in close" and personally engaged with the family. Faced with the family's impasse, the therapist can provisionally accept the beliefs at face value and extend the implications, bringing out the true needs and values underlying the absurd self-defeating situation.

For example, a wife plagued with psychosomatic symptoms and intractable migraines commented in marital therapy, "Every time my husband touches me in bed, I hate it so much I want to open the bedroom window and scream down the block. I hold it in and freeze up. Then he leaves me alone." The author commented that she knew that touch had been frightening for this wife, who, as a child, had been repeatedly fondled sexually by an older cousin and verbally terrorized by her father. The therapist had the fantasy, not in the realm of logic, that perhaps the next time the couple was in bed the wife should phone her mother (who had supported her terrorization and treated her with daily enemas for 12 years) and scream incoherently. The wife immediately responded that it was not that aversive in bed, not half as much worth screaming about as her abuse had been. She had experienced the absurd fantasy and had reorganized around it.

The deliberate use of, and participation in, absurdity, or irrationality, brings experiential change also through a gradual reorienting of the family to the fact that therapists are human, that emotional life is inevitable and not disposable, and that one simply tries to do the best one can to manage conflict and make decisions, but that there is no "magic bullet." Such reorienting can also elicit a more compassionate stance between family members and on the part of individuals. The more that the therapist allows irrationality, converses in it, responds to it, and avoids structuring it with prescriptions and advice, the more that the family members can accept it in themselves without defensiveness and an overlay of symptoms.

Another road to experiential change lies in the expression of affect in therapy. Paul states (1987) that sharing emotional pain with others who have participated functions to short-circuit pathological guilt, denial, and other defenses. We believe that it also short-circuits isolation, shame, and the loss of pride associated with symptoms and being a patient. Again, this affective sharing is better induced not by prescriptions from a neutral or distant therapist, but from a partial and emotive therapist who can ally with a family member's affect. A side effect of working with affect is that it also increases family cohesion, a much-needed commodity in these families. In addition to maintaining a stance of partiality or empathy, two other elements foster experiential change. One is the therapist's access to his or her own responses to the family (in psychoanalytic treatment, this is called "countertransference") and the ability to integrate them into the process of therapy. A second element is the use of affect in conversation between cotherapists, which models for the family that emotionality can be a constructive aid to intimacy.

We define success as the family's ability to report that it has the resources to solve remaining problems without the participation of outsiders. Additionally, in the successfully terminating family, members have self-confidence regarding their strengths and a high level of trust regarding a mutual commitment to solving their problems together. We also look for increased tolerance of life stress without reifying it into one member's problem, and without despair or hopelessness.

Last, when examining curative factors in family therapy, there is a metalevel above interactional shifts within the family and above the circular interface between the family and the therapist or cotherapy team. That is the level of the therapist's own position within his or her own family of origin and marriage, influencing which moves the therapist can make and how he or she relates to the cotherapist. Therefore, symbolic-experiential family therapists place high value on family therapy for the family therapist while in training. In the Bowenian model, an insight-based coaching procedure is used (Carter & Orfanidis, 1976). Consistent with our emphasis on experiential change, symbolic-experiential therapists in training are encouraged to enter therapy with their spouse or partner, children, parents, and grandparents if possible. Part of this emphasis comes from the idea that emotional growth involves being able to use as much of our own creativity as possible (Keith, 1987), and that good personal psychotherapy increases creativity. If "I become the patient [i.e., the locus of change] rather than the therapist. . . . I get excited and discover new components of *my* self" (Whitaker, 1985b).

A second aspect of this idea comes from the emphasis in transgenerational approaches on what Bowen calls "the human condition" and what Boszormenyi-Nagy calls "the dialogue": the concept that, as individuals within family systems within social systems within ecosystems, we and our families are more fundamentally alike than different. Napier (1983) alluded to this when he pointed out that in order to have a constructive understanding of the process of change, therapists must be able to connect with the process "from the inside out," experientially, from a position in which pain, confusion, and frustration are acceptable and potentially positive. In order to make change, one must first be willing and able to acknowledge relational stress without panic or despair. Further, even if the family therapist is motivated by caring and good intentions, it is doubtful if he or she can provide a path through early-phase anxiety if he or she is not familiar with how to handle personal relational stress. The notion of family therapy for the family therapist or trainee is controversial in an era that stresses uniform, solution-focused, skeleton-key interventions. The fostering of experiential change has profound implications for the therapist's role in family therapy. Demystification of the therapeutic process and of the person of the therapist is a most important curative factor.

Finally, the role of experiential change as a curative factor must not be underrated lest, as in brief strategic therapies, we begin to exclude many basic problems from treatment—such as the narcissistically vulnerable marriage, recovery from divorce, disagreement over childbearing, or violence.

SPECIAL ISSUES IN MARITAL THERAPY

The symbolic-experiential model considers marital couples to be, in effect, a subgroup of two extended families that are united by the marriage. Each spouse brings to the marriage the unique cultural and relational history, legacies, mandated roles, beliefs about the world, and values that characterize his or her family of origin. Thus, in looking at a married couple, the symbolic-experiential therapist is looking at a "cross section" of the two families of origin, as expressed in their two adult offspring, at the time of the consultation. This orientation is noted in Carl Whitaker's now-classic comment, "I don't believe in marriage. . . . It's really just two scapegoats sent out by two families to reproduce each other. . . . The battle is which one it will be" (Whitaker, cited in Neill & Kniskern, 1982, p. 368).

Despite this somewhat cynical description of the cybernetics of marriage, this model also regards marriage as the testing ground for personal individuation from the family of origin and for renegotiation of intimacy and autonomy in one's first equally influential adult–adult relationship (one's marriage). Thus, paradoxically, Whitaker also noted, "The greatest ordeal in life is marriage—it is the central focus for enlightenment and the natural therapeutic process in the culture" (cited in Neill & Kniskern, 1982, p. 366). This heavy emphasis on marriage as one arena in which to rework one's self-views and one's relational options outside the family of origin is a primary distinction between the symbolic-experiential model and the natural systems (Bowenian) model of therapy.

Technically, there are several special issues in the treatment of couples that stem from our view of the influence and "therapeuticness" of marriage. In the initial assessment, the cotherapy team focuses on many specific aspects of marital intimacy and allocations of tasks and power to see how they have been negotiated up until the present. The spouses are asked about their sexual relationship, amount of marital time together, and their ability to discuss controversial problems that are emotionally loaded. They are asked who performs what tasks for the couple and any children, how this was decided, and how decisions are generally made in such crucial

areas as finances, job commitments, and social commitments. These questions are much less pertinent to an extended-family interview, where the discussion is not as focused on bilateral peer negotiation. We view young married people as in a more complex phase of separation from their families than are never-married individuals, struggling overtly or covertly to balance their desire for belonging and love with their first taste of individual freedom and adulthood.

In the process of setting mediating goals, there are several that are specific to the needs of couples in conflict. Rather than downplaying spousal tensions and refocusing their individual distress upon the two families of origin, spousal tensions are augmented. The underlying message to spouses is that the marriage is a crucial vehicle for self-expression and differentiation from one's family, and that its future welfare cannot be taken for granted or discarded lightly. In some cases, where there is so much conflict that one or both spouses consider marital separation, the cotherapy team may encourage a trial separation—as much to highlight the importance of facing and resolving marital distress as to accommodate dissatisfied partners.

The structure of marital psychotherapy does not differ from the structure of family sessions, nor do the cotherapists play a different role. If there are children, they will be included in some marital sessions in order to examine the boundaries between the couple and the children and to strengthen the marital boundary if necessary. In the midphase of treatment, there are extended-family meetings, including one family of origin at a time, to examine the unresolved problems with family members that have interfered with a spouse's skills and interest in marital problem solving. With nontraditional partnerships, such as gay or lesbian couples, the inclusion of some family-of-origin meetings can be an important part of helping each partner to take more authority with his or her family and solidify the "coming out" process. This experience, when possible, adds strength to the partnership by firming its boundaries as a commitment "different from but equal to" that previously made to the family.

A special issue that has to be taken into consideration in couples therapy is the effort to address adequately the needs of remarried people.

Early formulations in symbolic-experiential therapy, as in other models, did not attend to the unique dilemmas posed by partnerships in which one or both may have one, two, or more ex-spouses, ex-in-laws, noncustodial biological children, and stepchildren. In couples treatment, the cotherapy team is often faced with the fallout from previous divorces that have produced bitterness, cynicism about the future, and mistrust of commitments. Stated differently,

Once the delusion that marriage was sacred was fragmented, the process of developing a life of isolation became one of the substitutes for marriage as enslavement. The marriage was broken up. . . . Unfortunately . . . the affectional investments they [the spouses] had made in each other were not cancelable, and their freedom to invest themselves in another partner was hedged with suspicion and paranoid feelings about any marital relationship. (Whitaker, 1989, pp. 97–98)

Couples in remarriage do need more support and aid in reconstructing complicated family lives that include coparents, steprelations, limited legal authority over children, and mourning the loss of previous marital traditions, hopes, and dreams. Symbolic-experiential therapy does not contain a specific protocol for this work. Couples struggling in a remarriage are deserving candidates for stepfamily support groups and associations, in addition to the marital psychotherapy they are seeking for specific tensions in the current marriage.

TREATMENT APPLICABILITY

Symbolic-experiential psychotherapy, like other transgenerational therapies, is at its most powerful when members of an extended family are available for participation. This does not imply that the members are immediately willing to participate, nor must they be available locally for consultation. Because of the possibilities for conference calling and for extended-family consultations during the process of therapy, family members need not reside together or even in the same town. However, in order to utilize many of the techniques of symbolic-experiential therapy, particularly those that are affectively focused, there must be some active psycholog-

ical or biological bond between family members in treatment. For example, parents who are ambivalent about their commitment to an adopted child may find it difficult to relate to their own familial tensions as expressed in the child's problems. This happens because, in some adoptive families, the child is seen as a "conditional" member who does not have the full loyalty of the parents unless he or she behaves in certain expected ways.

Similarly, there are other structural and dynamic problems in families that may make this approach more difficult initially. An individual who is chronically antisocial or narcissistic, such as a cut-off father who is minimally committed to marriage and family, will tend to recoil from the intimacy of family psychotherapy. While this model allows for addressing this problem and allying with narcissistic individuals, such individuals may respond more slowly unless the rest of the family is sufficiently strong to confront that person with the consequences of his or her distance. In this kind of case, it may be preferable to initiate individual psychotherapy for the distressed spouse, or child, focusing on family-of-origin work until he or she is differentiated enough to confront the narcissistic partner or parent.

Immediate posttraumatic conditions which have affected a couple or entire family, may make this form of psychotherapy emotionally difficult. For example, immediately postdivorce, some parental pairs may find it too aversive to face each other in family sessions (Whitaker & Keith, 1989). This is also true in some families where sexual or physical abuse has occurred, the psychological wounds are not yet contained, and interaction with the hurtful member would open the wound. Again, in such circumstances, it might be advisable to utilize individual family-of-origin work, drawing on the intact relationships available to the wounded member, to strengthen his or her coping skills before instituting family or marital sessions.

There are circumstances when a referral to individual psychotherapy is made after a course of family psychotherapy has been completed. For example, a couple addresses a sexual dysfunction in marital therapy and achieves resolution of the dysfunction and increased intimacy. One partner then wishes to explore chronic work problems that hinder her achievement in her professional field. One of the cotherapists chooses with her to continue on a one-to-one basis for several weeks to explore further her fears of achievement and success.

Referral is made for the use of medications, for hospital care, and for medical testing when symptoms may have an organic origin. For example, anorexic or bulimic people will need frequent blood work during their family treatment, in order to ensure that their heart function will not suddenly fail. An alliance with the family physician, gynecologist, or specialist (such as a neurologist or orthopedist) may be necessary. In areas of educational failure, referral may be made for tutoring, educational testing, or special classroom placement for children with learning difficulties. None of these referrals replaces marital or family psychotherapy, but augments it through physiological intervention. If medication is indicated for chronic psychotic symptoms, hyperactivity or attention deficit, or thought disorders that are difficult to control, a primary-care physician or consulting psychiatrist may be contacted for this reason.

One of the chief strengths of symbolic-experiential marital and family therapy, which utilizes the cotherapy team, is that if it is difficult to form an alliance at the outset, a cotherapist can be chosen accordingly. This option creates a number of therapeutic alternatives within this model that make it applicable to a wide variety of marital and family problems. For example, in a multicultural family where one parent is Asian, an Asian cotherapist will add considerable power to the cotherapy team. For couples' work, a dual-sex cotherapy team will help achieve the gender balance that may be missing in the marriage. In working with psychosomatic families, utilizing a nurse practitioner or family physician as cotherapist can refocus somatized tensions quite rapidly.

Because of the three-generational emphasis of symbolic-experiential therapy, this model contains tremendous potential for intervention with specific difficult-to-treat populations. Clients who are cut off from their families of origin, such as those who are depressed, socially isolated, agoraphobic, or socially phobic, can master their anxiety when they begin to examine the nature of their family connections in this treatment. Conversely, families that show enmeshment and overly rich interaction between members can achieve a comfortable degree of separation with this treatment while their need for group loyalty is preserved.

Families that have become fragmented as a result of community intervention, political upheaval, or catastrophe (war, immigration, or environmental disaster) are strengthened by a three-generational approach. Couples and families in which one member is severely dysfunctional and has become the "scapegoat" experience substantial improvement in the "ill" member when symbolic-experiential methods are used (Whitaker & Keith, 1989). Finally, this model of therapy is well suited to families with minor children, since children are curious about their parents' emotional experiences and enjoy a subjective approach to relating.

There are several circumstances in which we may choose not to recommend marital or family treatment, or recommend no treatment. One of these circumstances is a family's ongoing involvement with a different therapeutic experience. When a couple or family is experiencing dissatisfaction with an ongoing individual or family therapy elsewhere, we recommend that the dissatisfaction be discussed with the therapist and resolved mutually before any contact with us begins. If the ongoing therapy is marital or family therapy, we will offer ourselves as consultants to the primary therapist, rather than supersede the work that is ongoing. We assume that in these situations, family member(s) are having difficulty negotiating differences with their therapist and are initiating a potential triangle to avoid negotiations.

A second situation in which we may recommend no treatment is that in which a couple or family has completed psychotherapy and experiences an acute disruption or symptom later. If the family members have retained their skills for coping with disagreement and distress, they are seen for an interview and encouraged to utilize their new strengths to address the problem themselves. The cotherapy team will remain available, but only if the family's own attempted solutions are not effective.

Effectiveness of the Approach

In clinical practice, one is dependent on subjective rather than empirical, double-blind experimentation to test the effectiveness of an intervention. Outcome is assessed in terms of client satisfaction, amelioration of the presenting symptom, increased facility at individual and family problem solving, and evidence of improved functioning socially and vocationally.

When a family has come for consultation with somatic symptoms (e.g., ulcerative colitis, esophageal spasm, low weight, psychogenic or bulimic vomiting, hypertension), we examine the frequency of the symptom and confirm our observations with the family physician as one measure of success. For families with a psychotic member, the number of subsequent hospitalizations is also a criterion for success. Since hospitalization means that the couple or family feels inadequate to handle a relational crisis unaided, decreased hospitalization means to us that the family members perceive themselves as more competent at intervention.

The proliferation of transgenerational approaches to marital and family intervention and the increased size of the sociological and gerontology literature on the importance of multigenerational alliance serve as consensual support for the importance of these interventions. Like a Delphi study, in which a clinical method is deconstructed and examined by a panel of expert practitioners who must agree on cental criteria, the growing literature on extended familial support as an underpinning for elderly care, chronic care, and healthy rearing of the young points to the potential effectiveness of transgenerational theory.

CASE STUDY

Gwendolyn contacted the family-therapy institute to request help for unremitting problems with binge eating and laxative abuse that she has had for six years. Aged 23, she was an artist and a homemaker caring for two preschool children in her marital home. Rene, her 27-year-old husband, was in his family's nursery business and was not aware of the bulimic symptoms. Her therapist saw her two times alone at her insistence, then clarified that no changes were likely without the inclusion of her husband. Marital sessions were begun and the therapist brought in his longtime cotherapist as well. The children,

who were to be included in many later sessions, were not routinely involved at this point as Gwendolyn had indicated that the marriage might soon end at her request. Indeed, it seemed questionable whether the marriage had "taken" at all since the wedding four years earlier.

The battle for structure had been enjoined when the first therapist linked marital sessions to any future success. The couple responded by choosing marital therapy, but immediately began to manifest a struggle over initiative—demonstrated by Rene's obvious reluctance to acknowledge any concern over his wife's symptoms and marital dissatisfaction. Passive and flat, he listened quietly to the cotherapists' questions and deferred most discussion to his wife. They interacted like a teenage couple who were "going together" but had little investment in real intimacy; Gwendolyn was shy and secretive and Rene was reserved and defensively distant. The young wife began a flirtation with the male cotherapist, bringing him a present and a poem. She complained about Rene's friends. The couple hesitantly told the cotherapists about an early separation in the marriage during which Rene turned to his family (not friends) for support and Gwendolyn turned to her artist friends. They revealed that for the first two years of their marriage, Rene had insisted upon living with his large, close family, until Gwendolyn forced him to choose between them by demanding a separation. Finally, Gwendolyn noted that the couple had decided to marry only after she became pregnant at the age of 18, an event treated as shameful by her family of origin in Alabama.

The marital therapy, in its second month, was showing signs of surviving the battle for initiative. As this crucial information came out, Gwendolyn and Rene were increasingly committing themselves to a bilateral exploration of their chronic disappointments in the marriage. The cotherapists challenged, supported, teased, and empathized with each spouse in his or her ambivalence about stoking the marital fires. At the same time, they spoke frequently to each other as a way of demarcating themselves as a team and avoiding the invitation to enter into a marital triangle. Not surprisingly, as the next order of business, Rene bitterly announced that his wife had had an ongoing affair during their early separation, which showed signs of continuing after Gwendolyn returned home. He missed several meetings, as if to dare her to turn to the male cotherapist as a substitute. The cotherapists rescheduled, urging her not to settle for another affair. Rene returned, complaining of overwork but willing to move from twice-monthly meetings to weekly meetings. They were wholly invested now and arguing explosively rather than drifting quietly apart. Gwendolyn admitted that she was vomiting as well as abusing laxatives, frightened of Rene's anger and eager for sympathy from the cotherapists. The sympathy was there, accompanied by a firm conviction that the conflicts would not kill the marriage, and a great deal of cotherapist discussion regarding the frightening aspects of marriage and intimacy. A few therapeutic jokes eased some of her fear and his stoniness; the couple began to play spontaneously with each other as the cotherapists had, and even began to exchange affection shyly.

At this time, Gwendolyn revealed that her father had mysteriously vanished one day after her parents had quarreled and that a younger brother had renounced heterosexuality completely. The cotherapists interpreted this as a sign that the wife, and perhaps the husband, was ready to expand the definition of the marital problems past early-stage focusing on her purging and his distance. Discussion of Gwendolyn's genogram, taken in the first session, showed that she was one of eight children in her family, born to parents just out of their teens who were religiously opposed to birth control. The parental marriage appeared never to have absorbed either parent's dependency needs, and the young father had kept an on-the-road job in sales. Gwendolyn's mother looked to two older sons for support, as her own older brother had disappeared and her father had died during her engagement, leaving a bitter widow who did not help out with the eight grandchildren. After Gwendolyn's father's disappearance, her mother was sufficiently bitter in her own right to annul her 20-year marriage as if it had never been. Rita, her mother, forbade them to search for the missing father or to mention his name in the family home. A nurse, she turned to the writing of children's fairy stories for pleasure, and responded to letters from her now-grown daughter, Gwendolyn, only with fairy tales and allegories.

Rene's family, in contrast, was determinedly intact, if one considers chronic conflict "intact." Husbands were powerful, notoriously promiscuous, and uninvolved with their wives, saving their loyalties for the family business. Also a large family, the three sons vied for favor with their father by competing over who spent the longest hours at the business and in visiting the parental home. One son intermittently cut the family off for long periods and the youngest daughter had anorexia nervosa. Gwendolyn "fit" well into Rene's family since she kept her opinions to herself and stayed home with the children while Rene worked. However, as the youngest son and his mother's confidante, Rene was considered a bit "soft" and so he worked especially hard to appear as callous as his brothers.

The cotherapists remarked on the effectiveness of the two families' antimarital education, wondering aloud what kind of in-laws they made. Gwendolyn's mother had never publicly recognized Rene's existence, declining to attend the wedding by pleading intense depression. After the wedding, Gwendolyn was taken to live in Rene's parents' home, but they cautioned Rene during the early separation that a woman from such an unhappy home probably would not make a good wife and mother. Predictably, after Gwendolyn forced Rene to move out of his parents' home by separating from him, he continued to defend his father to her while she made it her job angrily to fight their overinvolvement.

Discussion of the two extended families put many of the spouses' symptoms in context: Gwendolyn's chronic resentment and wishes to flee into an affair, her secretive use of binge eating and purging to vent affect indirectly, and the adolescent, "playing-house" quality of their marital interactions. Similarly, Rene's self-doubt and fear of ridicule had become meaningful, illuminating his choice to avoid his angry wife even at the expense of her marital fidelity. The early phase of marital therapy was ending, and the marriage was now wide open to review. As if to underscore this new open quality, Gwendolyn agreed to a physical examination by the internal-medicine specialist to assess any damage from laxative abuse. Fortunately, there was no tissue damage as yet.

By now, Gwendolyn was binge-free and purge-free, trying hard to focus on her marriage instead of her friends and her angry mother. However, Rene became deeply depressed, as if he was noticing for the first time how empty and superficial their marriage had been for four years. As if to distract him from his emptiness, Gwendolyn revealed that she had been physically abused throughout her childhood by her mother, who whipped her with sticks and broom handles. Rene had been told about the abuse early in the marriage, but in such a way that it was understood that neither should examine the abuse or its effects on Gwendolyn's pervasive sense of rejection and resentment. The cotherapists encouraged the spouses to take seriously their families' failure to launch them and support the marriage. Rene began to claim that he also was holding secrets and was harboring intense negative feelings and fantasies he had not disclosed to anyone. In the 12th month of meetings, he admitted to having had a lawyer draw up divorce papers after "discovering" his wife's diary accounts of her affair. Rene truly began to despair, claiming that he and his wife had "been living a lie." As if to push him over the edge, Gwendolyn asked him for permission to continue extramarital relationships as long as she did not actually become sexually involved without telling him. Rene agreed. His main concern remained a terror of disapproval by his father or uncle if he should neglect the family business. It was time for the first extended-family consultation—with Rene's family.

Everyone attended except the eldest son, Tom, Jr., who at the time was cutting off his parents again. In the flesh, there was little forbidding about this family as the father introduced his wife and four other adult offspring, including the anorexic daughter. It was clear that Rene was seen as the "good" son who made no demands. In fact, each time he and his father began to converse, the women (notably the mother and eldest daughter) intervened to make sure that nothing unpleasant was said. Betty, Rene's mother, confessed to crying a great deal over the years over the frequent conflicts between Tom, Sr., and the children. "What hurts one," she felt, "hurts everybody"—especially when Tom was hurt. The eldest daughter added that she had moved 1,000 miles away to get away from "such a strong family." The spouses brought into the family were generally considered outsiders, according to the married younger daughter, although her husband "jumped right in" because he got close to Tom. Tom allowed as how he and Betty might be possessive, but pointed out that the homes of his parents and in-laws were no different. The grandfather, who was from Sicily, demanded respect; Tom also wanted respect for his guidance, as well as gratitude. He wanted to take any blame that might come up for conflicts in his family. The female cotherapist chided him for being greedy in taking all the blame especially because it made Tom mad. She liked this overwhelming father and announced that he could only claim one-eighth of the blame. Tom didn't buy it. He wanted someone to take all the blame, if not himself, then perhaps his middle son, Rick, who had broken the "closeness" rule by divorcing his own wife after a year of marriage. In fact, only married Marie had no marital problems—and she was still on her honeymoon.

Rene's first meeting with his family of origin was quite emotion-laden as he and Tom repeatedly squared off and were persuaded to desist by the mother and older sister. Rene pushed hard for recognition from his father for his hard work and his family loyalty; Tom pushed back, scolding him for not going to law school and for his loyalty "to the damned business." The cotherapists, determined not to let these overresponsible parents and guilt-prone offspring create a failure, kept congratulating them on their "delightful" confrontations and cheering on the men.

Following this challenge to his father, the first he had ever made, Rene began to find Gwendolyn interesting. Turned on by his increasing vulnerability, she began confiding in him about her chronic anxiety, food obsessions, and resentment toward her mother. It was in this middle phase of marital therapy, almost a year into the process, that Gwendolyn mastered her own fear and alienation enough to inform her mother that she had bulimia. A flurry of letters, phone calls, and an offer to visit followed from Rita. Although the cotherapists suggested that her entire family come, Gwendolyn temporized by asking an older and a younger sister, who immediately flew in from Arizona.

The aim of the cotherapy team with Gwendolyn's family was far different than with Rene's family. Rene's enmeshed, intensely connected clan required prying apart and the vigorous (joyful) support of conflict to help desensitize them. Gwendolyn's family was a far different matter. Abandoned by the father, left to be raised by a lonely mother, alienated from one another and physically/verbally abused, these young women had a fragile connection to sisterhood. Both cotherapists had strong countertransference responses, especially to the parentified older sister, who was obese and seemed resigned to life as a loner. The male cotherapist in particular was quite tender. He encouraged Gwendolyn to tell both sisters that she had been beaten, and to hear out the story of the elder woman (who had not protected Gwendolyn). This first meeting became, simply, a divulging of terrible secrets between them. Because of the fragile underbelly in the family, three more meetings were held before the sisters departed again.

With both spouses now actively enjoined in separating from their families, the marriage became much hotter. Rene, as if he finally felt Gwendolyn was strong enough to "take it," vented his rage and humiliation at her having an extramarital affair. His assertiveness gained him a partnership in the family business but angered Gwendolyn. Both spouses initiated brief affairs, and the wife moved for a second separation. This time, Rene did not ask her to come back. He ran his own home for the first time, and even nurtured the children, who remained with him. Gwendolyn found this fascinating and frightening. Rene would not cave in! They upped the ante: she asked to return, and Rene said no.

Through this "late-stage" period of marital therapy, the cotherapists knew that the issue at hand was the willingness of each spouse to make a real commitment to an intimate, living marriage. Rene and Gwendolyn seemed to be doing a fine job of testing each other, jockeying for concessions, and getting called on manipulative behavior. A little advice was allowable now: they seemed more married than they had been, conflicts and all. Eighteen months into marital therapy, Gwendolyn returned to their home and the separation ended. The impasse was over. The female cotherapist, moved by her recognition of the hard road they had travelled, shared with them her admiration and respect for the mutual commitment and courage each had shown in facing themselves, their pasts, and their visions for the future. Both therapists, over the next several weeks, bade the couple goodbye.

REFERENCES

Bateson, G. (1972). *Steps to an ecology of mind: Collected essays in anthropology, psychiatry, evolution, and epistemology.* San Francisco: Chandler.

Bernard, H.S., Babineau, R., & Schwartz, A. (1980). Supervisor–trainee cotherapy as a method for individual psychotherapy training. *Psychiatry, 43,* 138–145.

Boszormenyi-Nagy, I., & Krasner, B.R. (1986). *Between give and take: A clinical guide to contextual therapy.* New York: Brunner/Mazel.

Boszormenyi-Nagy, I., & Spark, G.M. (1973/1984). *Invisible loyalties.* New York: Harper & Row; Brunner/Mazel.

Bowers, W.A., & Gauron, E.F. (1981). Potential hazards of the cotherapy relationship. *Psychotherapy: Theory, Research and Practice, 18,* 225–228.

Carter, E.A., & McGoldrick, M. (1980). *The family life cycle: A framework for family therapy.* New York: Gardner Press.

Carter, E.A., & Orfanidis, M.M. (1976). Family therapy with one person and the therapist's own family of origin. In P.J. Guerin (Ed.), *Family therapy: Theory and practice.* New York: Gardner Press, pp. 193–218.

Dick, B., Lessler, K., & Whiteside, J. (1980). A developmental framework for cotherapy. *International Journal of Group Psychotherapy, 30,* 273–285.

Dowling, E. (1979). Co-therapy: A clinical researcher's view. In S. Walrond-Skinner (Ed.), *Family and marital psychotherapy: A critical approach.* London: Routledge & Kegan Paul, pp. 173–199.

Dunn, M.E., & Dickes, R. (1977). Erotic issues in cotherapy. *Journal of Sex and Marital Therapy, 3,* 205–211.

Epstein, N., Jayne-Lazarus, C., & DeGiovanni, I.S. (1979). Co-trainers as models of relationships: Effects of the outcome of couples therapy. *Journal of Marital and Family Therapy, 5,* 53–59.

Fellner, C. (1976). The use of teaching stories in conjoint family therapy. *Family Process, 15,* 427–431.

Ferrier, M. (1984). Teamwork: Process, problems and perspectives. *Journal of Strategic and Systemic Therapies, 3,* 17–23.

Friedman, E. (1987). How to succeed in therapy without really trying. *Family Therapy Networker, 11,* 26–31.

Gurman, A.S. (1985). Plenary Session presented to Annual Meetings of the American Association for Marriage and Family Therapy, San Diego, Calif.

Haley, J. (1977). Toward a theory of pathological systems. In P. Watzlawick & J. Weakland (Eds.), *The interactional view.* New York: Norton Press, pp. 31–56.

Hannum, J.W. (1980). Some cotherapy techniques with families. *Family Process, 19,* 161–168.

Hare-Mustin, R.T. (1987). The problem of gender in family therapy theory. *Family Process, 26,* 15–33.

Hightower, N.A., Rodriguez, S., & Adams, J. (1983). Ethnically mixed co-therapy with families. *Journal of Family Therapy, 10,* 105–110.

Hoffman, L. (1981). *Foundations of family therapy.* New York: Basic Books.

Hoffman, L.W., & Hoffman, H.J. (1981). Husband–wife cotherapy team: Exploration of its development. *Psychotherapy: Theory, Research and Practice, 18,* 217–224.

Keith, D.V. (1974). Use of self: A brief report. *Family Process, 13,* 201–206.

Keith, D. (1987). The healthy family. Unpublished manuscript.

Keith. D.V., & Whitaker, C.A. (1980). Add craziness and stir: Psychotherapy with a psychoticogenic family. In M. Andolfi & I. Zwerling (Eds.), *Dimensions of Family Therapy*. New York: Guilford Press, pp. 139–160.

Kerr, M.E. (1981). Family systems theory and therapy. In A.S. Gurman & D.P. Kniskern (Eds.), *Handbook of family therapy*. New York: Brunner/Mazel, pp. 226–264.

Latham, T. (1982). The use of co-working (co-therapy) as a training method. *Journal of Family Therapy, 4*, 257–269.

LoPiccolo, J., Heiman, J.R., Hogan, D.R., & Roberts, C.W. Effectiveness of single therapists versus cotherapy teams in sex therapy. *Journal of Consulting and Clinical Psychology, 53*, 287–294.

McMahon, N., & Links, P.S. (1984). Cotherapy: The need for positive pairing. *Canadian Journal of Psychiatry, 29*, 385–389.

Mehlman, S.K., Baucom, D.H., & Anderson, D. (1983). Effectiveness of cotherapists versus single therapists and immediate versus delayed treatment in behavioral marital therapy. *Journal of Consulting and Clinical Psychology, 51*, 258–266.

Minuchin, S. (1974). *Families and family therapy*. Cambridge, Mass.: Harvard University Press.

Minuchin, S., Rosman, B.L., & Baker, L. (1978). *Psychosomatic families: Anorexia nervosa in context*. Cambridge, Mass.: Harvard University Press.

Mueller, P., & Orfanidis, M.M. (1976). A method of co-therapy for schizophrenic families. *Family Process, 15*, 179–191.

Napier, A.Y. (1983). Keynote address presented to the Annual Meetings of American Association for Marriage and Family Therapy, Washington, D.C.

Neill, J.R., & Kniskern, D.P. (Eds.). (1982). *From psyche to system: The evolving therapy of Carl Whitaker*. New York: Guilford Press.

Papp, P. (1980). The Greek chorus and other techniques of paradoxical therapy. *Family Process, 19*, 45–57.

Paul, N. (1987). Personal communication.

Roberto. L. Giat (1986). Bulimia: The transgenerational view. *Journal of Marital and Family Therapy, 12*, 231–240.

Roberto. L. Giat (1987). Bulimia: Transgenerational family therapy. In J.A. Harkaway (Ed.), *Eating disorders*. New York: Aspen, pp. 1–11.

Roberto. L. Giat (1988). The vortex: Sibling relationships in the eating disordered family. In M. Kahn & K.G. Lewis (Eds.), *Sibling therapy*. New York: Norton Press, pp. 297–313.

Roberto. L. Giat (in press). *The tree of life: Models of transgenerational family therapy*. New York: Guilford Press.

Roberto. L. Giat, Keith, D.V., & Kramer, D. (1987). Breaking the family crucible: Symbolic-experiential family therapy. Workshop presented to Annual Meetings of American Association for Marriage and Family Therapy, Orlando, Fl.

Russell. A., & Russell, L. (1988). The uses and abuses of co-therapy. In J.G. Howells (Ed.), *Advances in family psychiatry, vol. II*. New York: International Universities Press, pp. 401–410.

Schachter, F.F. (1982). Sibling deidentification and split-parent identification: A family tetrad. In M.E. Lamb & B. Sutton-Smith (Eds.), *Sibling relationships: Their nature and significance across the lifespan*. Hillsdale, N.J.: Erlbaum, pp. 123–151.

Selvini Palazzoli, M., Boscolo, L., Cecchin, G., & Prata, G. (1978). *Paradox and counterparadox: A new model in the therapy of the family in schizophrenic transaction*. New York: Jason Aronson.

Silber, T.J., & Bogado, P. (1983). Pediatrician and psychiatrist as co-therapists. *Adolescence, 18*, 331–337.

Simon, R. (1985). Take it or leave it: An interview with Carl Whitaker. *Family Therapy Networker, 9*, 35–75.

Weakland, J. (1981). Personal communication.

Weinstein, I.P. (1971). Guidelines on the choice of a co-therapist. *Psychotherapy: Theory, Research and Practice, 8*, 301–303.

Whitaker, C.A. (1975). Psychotherapy of the absurd: With a special emphasis on the psychotherapy of aggression. *Family Process, 14*, 1–15.

Whitaker, C.A. (1976a). The hindrance of theory in clinical work. In P.J. Guerin (Ed.), *Family therapy: Theory and practice*. New York: Gardner Press, pp. 154–164.

Whitaker, C.A. (1976b). A family is a four-dimensional relationship. In P.J. Guerin (Ed.), *Family therapy: Theory and practice*. New York: Gardner Press, pp. 182–192.

Whitaker, C.A. (1979). Personal communication.

Whitaker, C.A. (1982a). My philosophy of psychotherapy. In J.R. Neill & D.P. Kniskern (Eds.), *From psyche to system: The evolving therapy of Carl Whitaker*. New York: Guilford Press, pp. 31–36.

Whitaker, C.A. (1982b). The ongoing training of the psychotherapist. In J.R. Neill & D.P. Kniskern (Eds.), *From psyche to system: The evolving therapy of Carl Whitaker*. New York: Guilford Press, pp. 121–138.

Whitaker, C.A. (1985a). The normal family. Unpublished manuscript.

Whitaker, C.A. (1985b). Symbolic-experiential family therapy. Invited workshop presented to: Eastern Virginia Family Therapy Institute, Norfolk, Va.

Whitaker, C.A., & Keith, D.V. (1981). Symbolic-experiential family therapy. In A.S. Gurman & D.P. Kniskern (Eds.), *Handbook of family therapy*. New York: Brunner/Mazel, pp. 187–224.

Whitaker, C.A., & Keith, D.V. (1986). Conversation hour on co-therapy. Annual Meetings of Association for Marriage and Family Therapy, Orlando, Fl.

Whitaker, C.A., & Malone, T.P. (1953). The roots of psychotherapy. New York: Blakiston.

Whitaker, C.A., & Malone, T.P. (1987). The roots of psychotherapy. New York: Brunner/Mazel.

Whitaker, C.A., & Napier, A.Y. (1977). Process techniques of family therapy. *Interaction, 1*, 4–19.

Whitaker, C.A., & Ryan, M.C. (1989). *Midnight musings of a family therapist*. New York: Norton.

White, M. (1983). Anorexia nervosa: A transgenerational system perspective. *Family Process, 22*, 255–273.

EDITORS' REFERENCE

Keith, D.V., & Whitaker, C.A. (1985). Failure: Our bold companion. In S.B. Coleman (Ed.), *Failures in family therapy*. New York: Guilford Press.

PART III

Special Issues and Applications

CHAPTER 15

Family Therapy as the Emerging Context for Sex Therapy

Marilyn J. Mason, Ph.D.

Most contemporary observers would probably agree that a significant gap exists between sex therapy and marriage and family therapy. Some therapists have even stated that, all too often, the only time they hear the pairing of the words "sexuality" and "family" it means incest! This, indeed, is a sad commentary on, yet perhaps an apt reflection of, the polarization of sex therapy and family therapy. This chapter attempts to address this void by focusing on the connecting threads that weave family-systems issues and sexual issues.

The lack of comfortable language also has been a serious stumbling block to discussing this value-laden issue. And this deficiency is often compounded by the therapists' own "no talk" family rules. That is, many family therapists, still loyal to their family of origin's discomfort with discussing sexuality openly, create a conspiracy of silence around sexual concerns. Further pointing up the need to close the gap between family and sex therapies is the current acquired immune deficiency syndrome (AIDS) epidemic;

families and therapists are being forced to talk openly about sexuality.

Sex therapists and family therapists agree that sex is symbolic; it can be the metaphor for the dynamics of a relationship. Too often, we have assumed that treating the "metaphor" was automatically treating the sexual dysfunction, only to learn later that the dysfunction often continued. Information, education, cognitive restructuring, and behavioral skills can be essential. Sex *is* metaphor, but much more. For example, the issue of sexual power had not been brought into this arena. Researchers Schwartz and Blumstein (1986), in examining power in sexual relationships, concluded that feminism has redefined sex, taking away some of the woman's power (in traditional relationships, sex had been seen as a "gift"). Feminism and its influence on sexual behaviors continue to challenge us to examine our assumptions about sexuality. Recent research forces us to reexamine our educational materials and clinical practice.

This chapter begins with the clinical evolution

of family therapy as the context for sex therapy and continues with the context in which sexual issues are presented in family therapy (seldom are they the presenting issue). The next section focuses on clinical sexual concerns in family therapy. The following section discusses assessment and models for clinical decision making; the conduct of therapy concludes the chapter.

EVOLUTION OF FAMILY THERAPY AS THE CONTEXT FOR SEX THERAPY

How have we reached this stage in our history of sex therapy? A review of prominent approaches to the meaning of sexual dysfunction reflects their historical–cultural context. According to LoPiccolo (1981), five approaches to sexual dysfunction preceded our current thinking. The earliest understanding (1880s) of sexual dysfunction was as "moral degeneracy," with abstinence and moderation as therapy, and stemmed from the work of Krafft-Ebing (cited in Masters, Johnson, & Kolodny, 1986). The second understanding of sexual dysfunction focused on "psychosexual immaturity" with psychoanalysis as the treatment, as reflected in the work of Freud (1962) and Havelock Ellis (cited in Masters et al., 1986). In the 1930s and 1940s, we saw sexual dysfunction defined as "anxiety" and treated with approaches ranging from systematic desensitization and behavioral techniques to sex therapy (Lazarus, 1965; Salter, 1949; Wolpe, 1969). Another understanding of sexual dysfunction was that dysfunctional ideas were the cause of sexual dysfunction and that cognitive therapy was the most appropriate treatment method. Cognitive approaches were addressed in rational-emotive therapy with education and skills training applied (Ellis, 1962). In the 1970s, Masters and Johnson led the next interpretation, with fear of failure combined with sex as a learned skill; behavioral treatment was the preferred mode. At that time, Kaplan (1974), Hartman and Fithian (1972), and LoPiccolo (1973) added quasi-behavioral approaches.

In the 1970s, sex therapy flourished; sexual skills were taught and a general openness developed as individuals gave themselves the permission to be sexual in ways their families and churches had not allowed. Many positive changes occurred with the sexual revolution as more families discussed sexuality more openly. However, these behavioral changes often did not address systemic issues, issues that were often the root of the dysfunction with its accompanying "emotional homeostasis" (LoPiccolo, 1986).

The current perspective on sexual dysfunction, which views sex therapy systemically, leads to treating the underlying dynamics of the symptoms (unresolved family-of-origin issues, power, control, etc.), while concurrently focusing on attitudes, belief systems, information, and behavioral skills.

We have progressed to the point at which we can agree that sexuality always involves much more than what we do with our genitals (Nelson, 1988). The sexual revolution, however, spawned a moral confusion regarding sexuality. A *Time* magazine survey in 1977 found that 61 percent of the people interviewed thought it was "harder and harder to know what's right and what's wrong these days" (Tannehill, 1980, p. 423). In this study, 74 percent wanted the government to crack down on pornography in movies and books, yet 70 percent said that "there should be no laws, federal or state, regulating sexual practice." These findings support the ambiguity we face as professionals.

Sexuality should be acknowledged in history taking; the therapist and client(s) can contract whether to work specifically on sexual issues. One move toward resolving ambiguity is through clinicians' intake forms that today include questions about sexuality. Some therapists, however, state that their theoretical biases call for the client to bring up any discussions of sexual concerns. They will not initiate questioning concerning clients' sexual relationships. Still others believe they should include sexuality in their interviews. Recently, in one training session, several professionals stated that they "just never hear any sexual concerns." When they returned to participate in their second day of training, two members of the group excitedly exclaimed (in very similar styles), "Why, I heard two clients talk about sexual problems last night!" In training health professionals regarding sexuality issues, we have learned that once the therapists break their own "no talk" rules, their clients do also.

In addition to family messages about sexuality

are those of the client's church or religious training, often the nurturing ground for many irrational beliefs, unclear attitudes, and sexual myths. The sexual revolution of the 1970s drew attention to religious messages about sexuality. No previous period in history has produced a comparable amount of books, ecclesiastical studies, caucuses, and movements on sexual issues of various religious groups (Nelson, 1983).

Ethnicity also influences the kinds of messages that people learn, for example, Scandinavian patterns for expressions of intimacy may differ greatly from Italian and Greek messages. As one couple stated wisely, "Our marriage has seemed to be a cross-cultural anthropological field trip." These inherited messages shape behavioral patterns and attitudes. We need to respect clients' points of view and not assume that our own "openness" toward sexuality will be the same goal for our clients.

This chapter is written for family therapists and therapists in training who most often will be doing sex therapy in the context of marriage, couples, and family therapy. Family therapists do not have to be "sex therapists"; we are responsible, however, for acknowledging that sexuality is an organizing principle in every family.

CONTEXTS FOR SEXUAL ISSUES IN FAMILY THERAPY

Perhaps one of the strongest reasons sexual issues are often not identified in family therapy is that the context in which the sexual concern is expressed is not typically the presenting complaint. Sexual dysfunctions and concerns do not arise in a vacuum. Just as a sexual issue affects a marital or family relationship, so does a marital relationship, as well as other factors, affect how sexual issues are dealt with. Evaluation of the marital and family relationship will be discussed later; here, we will present the five major contexts in which sexual concerns are presented in family therapy: presenting complaints, relationship issues, couples' issues, developmental concerns, and medical concerns. It is in these contexts that family therapists often read the client cues (individual and interactional) to aid the clients to talk openly about their sexual concerns. Although some clinicians state that they

deal only with what is presented in the here-and-now therapy session, many clinicians take the responsibility for being directive, giving clients permission to talk about sex in their interview hour.[1]

Presenting Complaints

Because of the dearth of sexual-health clinics and clients' guilt and shame about approaching sexual therapy, most individuals and couples wanting to work on sexual issues will enter clinics specializing in marriage and family therapy. But most people do not present their sexual issues immediately; when they do, the therapist must assess whether the contract being sought is for sex therapy or for related relationship work.

Judy and Ted entered therapy seeking help because of Ted's problem with premature ejaculation; another therapist had referred them for sex therapy. They had completed therapy on the dynamics of their relationship and disclosed that they thought that family therapy was going to change their sexual dysfunction. Both were well motivated; goals were easily set and brief therapy was successful. Judy and Ted were quick to refer their best friends to the clinic, assuring them of an "almost 90 percent" success rate.

George and Mary, too, at first seemed to be candidates for brief therapy. Their presenting concern was George's inhibited sexual desire. After history taking, goal setting, and identifying and reframing the function in their relationship, we contracted with them to begin the sex therapy. After their first homework assignment, with sensate focus as the first phase, Mary and George returned to therapy expressing anger and frustration toward each other. "I thought he was in charge of initiating," Mary exclaimed. "Why, I was almost dead asleep when he came in and asked, 'Do you suppose it's too late for our homework?' I was furious," said Mary, whereupon George glowered at her and said, "There you go again, putting me down. Is that all you can ever do?"

We were rather surprised to see this change in the couple. As their stories unfolded, we

---

[1] *Editors' Note.* We think that this observation is entirely accurate, although at major variance from the impression one might have by reading many of the most influential books and journals in the field and by attending many of its most popular workshops.

learned that George remained furious because Mary had returned to school and could no longer take care of him as she previously had in her traditional wife role. George explained that he was afraid that she would divorce him; many of their friends recently had divorced. After inquiring about their family histories, including George's own previous divorce story, we decided to interrupt the contract to do relationship work and enhance the couple's communication skills work before returning to the more behavioral aspects of the sex therapy. Both were disappointed that they could not "do it all" as quickly as their friends had, but made the commitment to work through their unresolved relationship issues before proceeding with sex therapy.

Although the presenting complaint can be a help to the therapist when clients can talk about their concerns, it can also be a call for some other form of therapy. A seasoned therapist or a sensitive beginning therapist will talk openly with the partners about their contract setting and, if necessary, change the contract.

May and Tom, who described themselves as "children of the '60s," had no difficulty with sexual functioning. They agreed that they had developed excellent sexual skills but that they still did not trust each other to be an intimate emotional partner. They were surprised that their positive sexual relationship did not automatically guarantee their intimacy. As they examined their history, they discovered that they had ignored the friendship in their marriage and realized that it was their friendship that needed attention.

Therapists can best help their clients to integrate their sexuality into their relationship when they weave together sexual and relationship concerns.

Relationship Issues

It is not unusual for sexual concerns to be embedded in relationship struggles. Often, when clients work through problems of trust, fear, anger, and resentment, and we sense that these issues have a deeper history, we may find a sexual concern at the root of the relationship issue. Often, the layer immediately under the relationship issue as enacted in the clients' struggles in their relationships is an internalized experience that has not yet been revealed and often is not resolved. Among these relationship barriers are (1) body image (old image of a former overweight or too-thin self, under- or over-developed sexual self); (2) resentment over buried sexual hurts; (3) distorted interpretations about the meaning of sexuality from early religious training or family messages; or (4) sexual shame stemming from unresolved sexual abuse. Any of these issues can cause difficulties in a relationship and create barriers to intimacy.

Lila entered therapy because of her inability to maintain relationships with men. Because she thought her "biological time clock" was running out, she wanted to have children in a marriage. Lila blamed herself for what happened in relationships with men—she internalized all their responses to her to mean that she should have done something differently. Her lack of a sense of separateness gave us a clue to look for shame and boundary violation (Fossum & Mason, 1986). We learned that Lila had been sexually molested by a "close" cousin at age 10 and raped during her last year of college. She thought she had resolved her hurts from these experiences. Although she had never revealed the childhood sexual abuse, she had talked with a college counselor about the rape. But she had buried both stories in secrecy and shame. In a women's group, during the course of therapy, she learned how fearful she was of closeness with males; she also learned the importance of sharing her story and that these assaults were not her fault. As she worked through the old feelings, she developed a stronger boundary between herself and others. She no longer internalized messages and cues as her former "shameful self" had. Lila soon was able to forgive herself and, with support, face her fears. Lila did go on to develop a lasting relationship with a man.

Other relationship issues arise during behavioral sex therapy. Family therapists recognize that sexual dysfunctions have "purposive" functions in relationships, and this function must be examined and worked with, often in a multigenerational context. But once a family therapist has worked with the relationship issues, he or she must return to the sex therapy and reintegrate the work on relationship issues with the specific sexual problem at issue. This is the bedrock of many clinical errors in marital and family therapy.[2]

John and Katy reported that they had been to three previous family therapists, and that each time they began to address the sexual issues in their relationship, the therapy shifted to some other concern and they soon terminated therapy without working through their sexual difficulties. They entered therapy reporting that they now recognized this pattern (or was it the therapists' pattern?) and once again asked for help with their sexual relationship. Katy said she was apprehensive about bringing it up again. I promised them I would focus on their sexual relationship. In taking sex histories with each of them individually, I learned that John was bitter because he had learned of Katy's genital herpes after their marriage and was "punishing" her with his withdrawal. Katy had become the pursuer. Their "dance" pattern became fixed, both feeling resigned to their misery. As I introduced some preliminary touch homework assignments, John's resistance increased.

I soon learned that John was still furious with his mother, who had solicited his partnership when his father left after his parents' divorce. John revealed that he feared that Katy might "consume" him and saw that his anger insulated his fears. For her part, Katy revealed that, as she was growing up in an alcoholic family, she had learned to be seductive to get what she wanted from her father. She had used those approaches with John when they began dating. They then both focused on their unfinished business in their families of origin. As they listened to each other's stories, they deepened their compassion for each other. While working with their family issues, I also wove in analogies to the present sexual barrenness, keeping the sexual issue alive in the therapy. As they were able to see each other more clearly, I was able to set a specific contract for sex therapy. The result was a combination of information, education, and behavioral approaches in the context of intra-

psychic, interpersonal, and intergenerational issues.

Couples Issues

Just as a couple's relationship difficulties might be translated into the partners' sexual relationship (e.g., sex as revenge or sexual withholding as punishment), we find that in many couples the relationship issues may mask sexual concerns.

Patty and John entered therapy with an apparent power struggle, stating they were equally upset with each other about how "loose" they felt in their marriage. Patty had been excited when Mike returned from treatment for alcoholism, and both looked forward to a new start in their marriage of 17 years. In their couples group, they had had some very tender moments and were delighted about rebuilding their relationship. However, Patty, bursting into tears, said that Mike seemed not to be interested in her sexually when he was sober. She also said she had been afraid to bring the subject up; she thought that if she had to "demand" sex, it wasn't really worthwhile. Mike said he had been less attentive to Patty because he was having erectile problems, and he knew it increased the hurt for Patty if he approached her and nothing happened sexually. Mike admitted he had been gradually withdrawing from Patty; he had turned to his 12-step recovery program with Alcoholics Anonymous (AA) for his closeness. We gave Mike and Patty the brief educational message they needed—that the androgen level in Mike's blood could take up to 13 weeks or so to become established (Alouf, 1975). Mike said he had not been informed in treatment about the chemical rebalancing. Both were relieved to receive this needed information. In addition, we gave them an intercourse "ban" and told them to come together in whatever ways they chose *without intercourse.* We also directed them to talk daily with each other about their feelings and thoughts and to listen to one another. Over time, both Patty and Mike stated they were truly enjoying the newly found "play" in their relationship and could also talk more openly about what they wanted and how they felt. Mike regained this erectile competency after approximately 14 weeks.

Nora and Debra had been in a relationship for six years, and when they entered therapy, Nora complained that she felt suffocated by their closeness and resented Debra's lack of interest in the lesbian community in their town. As we explored their depen-

---

[2] *Editors' Note.* We fully agree. Lankton, Lankton, and Matthews (Chapter 8) distinguish between problems/symptoms that "stand for something else" and those that "stand for themselves." Very often, sexual dysfunctions stand for *both,* and the "reintegration" that Mason calls for is, therefore, essential.

dency issues, we learned that before Debra met Nora, she had been in several serial relationships following the breakup of a long-term relationship with her first lover. Debra informed us that she was afraid that if she became involved with the outside community, she might become promiscuous and ruin their relationship. Debra needed to learn that it is common for people ending relationships not only to grieve, but also to reestablish a sexual identity—often through dating a variety of people. We assured her that this pattern did not mean that she would become promiscuous; we reframed her feeling of "promiscuity" to "transitional coping." Nora and Debra did expand their friendship network into the lesbian community. They came back for one additional interview to share their joyful story. Debra and Nora laughed about their delight in discovering that the duration of their therapy was two sessions.

When couples can relate their therapy to their marital contract and are experiencing moderate, rather than severe, marital stress, the sex therapy often facilitates resolving other marriage problems (Sager, 1976).

Developmental Concerns

The family life cycle is a central concept for family therapists (Carter & McGoldrick, 1988). In addition to structural changes in family systems, therapists also need to be aware of the qualitative changes in relational processes (Wynne, 1986). Superimposed on the life cycle are the developmental sexual concerns in family life, including the birth of a baby and protection against sexual abuse of children and so on (Gadpaille, 1975; Money, 1981; Pertras, 1980). Recently, writers have been integrating the influence of psychosexual development of family members into the stages of the family life cycle (Maddock, 1983). Several developmental sexual concerns are of special importance to family therapists, as discussed in the following.

Parent Education

The family's responsibility for sex education has long been controversial. The rhetoric of sex education has been the rhetoric of avoidance. Family sociologist R. Hill (1980) stated that perhaps we cannot count on the family for adequate sex education; indeed, schools and churches have become highly involved in the sex education of young children. Parents find it difficult to talk to their children about all sexual topics, stating that they lack the vocabulary, knowledge, and experience.

When we add to that difficulty the high numbers of cases of sexual abuse of young children (9 percent of parents in a random sample said one of their children had been a victim of attempted or completed sexual abuse), we see the need for programs to aid parents in preventing child sexual abuse (Finkelhor, 1984). These prevention programs help parents teach their children about "good" and "bad" touch (Kent, 1979). However, parents still are a long way from providing the needed information for children in accurate and useful ways (Finkelhor, 1984), partially owing to differences in sexual values among people as well as lack of clarity about their own sexual values. Therapists can help timid parents by giving them permission to discuss sexual issues by breaking the family no-talk rule. Some family therapists break the rule by asking, "How does your family talk about sexuality?"—including the question with other family-assessment questions.

Ken and Debra were concerned that their children's questions be answered honestly. Both felt awkward about discussing sexuality and told us that they had planned to ask a sex-therapist friend to talk about sexuality with their children. Their therapist encouraged them to be their children's own sex educators; they could let their children know how difficult sex was to talk about, but that they would do it anyway. In this way, they would give their children permission to come to them when the children had questions, and if they did not know the answers, they would promise to find them.

Birth Control

The discussion of birth control can arise at various stages in the family life cycle. For the newly divorced single person, it is a sensitive issue. An example is a person coming out of a long-term paired relationship with a partner who had had a tubal ligation or vasectomy. The therapist can validate the client as a sexual being by asking, "What are you choosing to do with regard to birth control now that you are single?"

This question also addresses the need for birth control when family structural changes occur.

Another area for birth-control sensitivity is information for adolescent children. More than half of all high-school students will have had sexual intercourse before graduation (Boyer, 1987). The teen-age pregnancy rate has been increasing; the rate in the United States is approximately 96 per 1,000 for 15- to 19-year-olds (Gutmacher Institute, 1985). In addition, two million new cases of sexually transmitted diseases occur annually among those under 25 (Kantner & Zelnick, 1973). With the increase in AIDS, we can only speculate about what will happen with the adolescent population. Parents need support and encouragement to discuss their values with their children; they have the responsibility to guide their children in their sexual development. Today, perhaps more than at any other time in our history, parents need to teach children about "safe sex."

Safe-sex guidelines include six practical guidelines—"be informed; be observant; be selective; be honest; be cautious; and be promptly tested and treated" (Masters et al., 1986).

Fertility Issues

Infertility is considered by many to be a major life crisis (Menning, 1976) and is estimated to affect 17 percent of the U.S. population of childbearing age (approximately 3.5 million people) (American Fertility Society, 1980). Its medical definition refers to the inability to conceive a child after at least one year of regular, unprotected sexual intercourse or the inability to carry a pregnancy to live birth (Mahlstedt, 1987). Much of the treatment involves diagnosis and treatment of the physiological conditions, yet the psychological stress is often drawn out over the years, because of long-term treatment, loss of self-esteem, sexual-dysfunction issues, and loss of the ability to fantasize or of the biological continuity of the family. Guilt and shame and unresolved past issues often surface with this crisis.

Menopause

The word "menopause" refers specifically to the cessation of a woman's menstruation, the end of fertility; it is typically defined retrospectively (one or two years after the last menstrual period) (Masters et al., 1986). The period immediately before and immediately following the menopause is referred to as the *climacteric*, which often lasts about 15 years. Approximately 80 percent of women have symptoms stemming from their hormonal changes (Masters et al., 1986), with hot flashes ranging in intensity from a feeling of warmth to profuse sweating and in duration from mere seconds to 15 minutes. Other related symptoms during this time of estrogen deficiency include lessened vaginal lubrication during sexual arousal and loss of tissue elasticity, causing pain during intercourse. Women are encouraged to meet with their physicians concerning the advantages and disadvantages of estrogen-replacement therapy.

Often, stress on the family's system during this period in a woman's life can be accentuated as children leave home. With increasingly later starts in childbearing, we are likely to see more stress when parents at this stage are more liberal (Reiss, 1971). Women often face depression at this time. The skilled clinician will gather information about the overlap between the climacteric and the life-cycle issue of adult children leaving home. Many women recognize the need to grieve their "empty nests." During this postchildbearing stage, marital partners often renegotiate intimacy patterns (Cleveland, 1976).

Findings on menopausal difficulties vary. Some find no evidence for an "increased rate of depression or major psychiatric disorders following the menopause" (Ballinger, 1981); others state that the interpretations of the female experience have been based on reports of "sexist male physicians" (Alington-MacKinnon & Troll, 1981); still others believe that much of the menopause research is methodologically flawed, especially concerning the psychological aspects (Bart & Grossman, 1978). There is active disagreement regarding the effects of menopause on female sexuality, with some studies showing a decline in sexual interest and capacity for orgasm.

Sex and Aging

Although age alone does not diminish sexual interest or potential, some specific changes in both men and women can surface in individual or couples therapy (Butler & Lewis, 1976). These are in addition to the cultural prejudices about sex in the older years (ageism). Both men and women need information about male and female changes with aging. While we are discussing aging here from clinical experiences of heterosexual couples, clinicians need to be aware that ageism also affects the gay and lesbian communities (Berger, 1982; Wolf, 1982).

Women and Aging

Because of women's hormonal changes and/or aging, changes occur in vaginal functioning through reduced elasticity in vaginal walls and lessened vaginal lubrication (Butler & Lewis, 1976). For many women, the arousal time is slower and can be affected by medications, such as Valium, Librium, antidepressant drugs, and major tranquilizers (Heiman & LoPiccolo, 1988). Sexually active postmenopausal women apparently have less shrinkage of the vagina (Leiblum, 1983).

Treatment often includes the recommendation for sexual activity, yet of 12 million widowed persons in the United States, 10 million are women and three out of four elderly men are married. Treatment recommendations typically include physical exercise, masturbation, sexual activity where possible, and Kegel exercises for maintaining vaginal-muscle tone.

Kegel exercises (pelvic-floor-muscle exercises) are helpful for the conditioning of the pubococcygeus muscle. They are done by contracting the pelvic muscles that support the vagina.

These same muscles are used when a woman stops the flow of urine or tightens the vagina against an inserted object, such as a tampon, a finger, or an erect penis. The muscles are contracted firmly for one or two seconds and then released; this is repeated in a series of 10 contractions several times a day for maximum results (Masters et al., 1986, p. 35). Although it is not certain whether Kegels improve sexual res-

ponsivity, we do recommend their use for maintaining sexual self-awareness.

Men and Aging

Since no definite ending to male fertility occurs, the aging experience is different for men, who, unless body-changing illness strikes, do not experience cyclical bodily changes. In addition, patriarchal domination behind male socialization makes it difficult for men to become vulnerable, with them often denying the need for adaptation to aging (Nelson, 1988).

Although men experience a slowing down in sperm production after the age of 40, production does continue until age 80 or 90 (Masters et al., 1986). No major shift in hormone levels occurs in men as it does in women; the testosterone production diminishes gradually between age 55 and 60. And although only a small percentage of men experience a *male climacteric*, clinicians can be sensitive to the men over 60 (about 5 percent) who do. It is marked by depression, decreased sexual desire, and reduction of potency, sometimes due to lowered testosterone levels (Kolodny, Kahn, Goldstein, & Barnett, 1978; Masters et al., 1986).

What is common for most men over 55 is the longer time and stimulation needed for penile erections, less firm erections, partway elevation of testes, semen reduction, lessening of intensity of ejaculation, and less physical need to ejaculate (Masters et al., 1986). In addition, many aging men experience prostate difficulties, causing pain for some (Stone, 1986). When these changes occur, they cause anxiety not only for the man, but for his sexual partner as well.

Overall activity, rather than chronology, affects sexual functioning, according to most recent clinical findings (Woods, 1979). Longitudinal studies at Duke University have shown that sexual-activity patterns stay quite stable over middle and late adulthood, with only a modest decline in most people (Masters et al., 1986). Although such studies suggest that sexual activity decreases somewhat with age, it is difficult to tell whether the decline is physiologically or culturally correlated. Many researchers have focused only on coital activity (Masters et al., 1986).

One sexually aware 92-year-old man who consented to be interviewed in a sexuality workshop stated, "What formerly had been a means to an end is now an end in itself" (Mason, 1981). Perhaps future research will follow patterns of sexual behavior as it accepts a broader definition of human sexual behavior.

Singles and Sex

During many of their sexual developmental years, people are "single." This includes all those men and women, both heterosexual and gay/lesbian, who are sexual when not in paired or committed relationships. We can expect to be single at different periods in the life cycle. Whether we are young adolescents entering paired relationships, young adults pairing at later ages, separated (in cohabited or marital relationships), divorced, or widowed, it is important for clinicians to recognize their own blind spots and cultural values and the need to assume that all people are sexual beings. We will find a variety of sexual attitudes at these different stages. What everyone shares, however, is an increased awareness and fear of sexually transmitted diseases (STD), ranging from Chlamydia trachomatis to genital herpes to AIDS—whether the person is involved in a nonmarital (including communal), premarital (or prepared), postmarital, or extramarital relationship. Clinicians who often see the outcomes of these diseases can do prevention work by focusing on the rule for "safe sex" (Masters et al., 1986).

Often we see abortion affecting a sexual relationship when the abortion is considered a shameful secret (Mason, 1986). Therapists need to be aware of the context of the abortion, that is: (1) Was it an adolescent pregnancy? (2) What is the quality of the partners' relationship, if and when known? (3) Was it an unplanned marital pregnancy? (4) Was the couple choosing a child-free life-style? (5) What health issues are involved? It is important for therapists also to be aware of their own biases so that they can be most helpful to clients in their decision-making process. In some cases, therapists refer their clients to specific resources for education, religious interpretations, and/or support.

Cancer

Current statistics show that one out of every 11 women will develop breast cancer, the leading cause of cancer death in women. Mastectomy (removal of a breast) often is followed by body-image (nudity) concerns, lowered sexual desire (not feeling "womanly"), and/or depression.

Joyce and Gene discussed in their initial interview their recent history with Joyce's breast cancer and treatment. Joyce wept as she reported how attentive and caring Gene was with her in her cancer recovery, but as soon as Joyce's condition stabilized, he returned to losing himself in his work and cutting himself off from the family. As we proceeded with marital therapy, Joyce angrily burst forth, "I will no longer be sick in order to have some closeness with you." Joyce and Gene disclosed that they had been separated prior to her cancer diagnosis. They agreed that during their separation, they had never resolved their "unfinished business." When Joyce learned of her cancer and called Gene, he moved back home without their working through their previous conflicts. The cancer provided the catalyst to bring them back together initially, and seemingly was highly functional in their marriage. Joyce trembled and Gene wept as they talked openly about their fears of this continuing. During the sessions, they grew more honest with each other and worked on family-of-origin issues. The cancer has now stabilized, and their marital transactions are being completed.

Cervical cancer accounts for slightly more than 60,000 new reports of cancer annually (Masters et al., 1986). Surgery or radiation therapy and pelvic scarring can add to couples' stress in sexual functioning.

Cancer of the uterus lining (endometrial cancer) can occur after age 40. Many women who have had hysterectomies (surgical removal of the uterus) do not have any negative effects on their sexual functioning. However, clinically we see women who have a diminished sense of their sensuality and femininity, which, in turn, affects their desire level.

Ovarian cancer is less common, affecting 17,000 additional women a year in the United States, particularly women working in the electrical, textile, and rubber industries and/or those who have had extensive pelvic radiation. The early signs, including abdominal pain, can cause a withdrawal from sexual activity.

Prostate cancer accounts for 17 percent of cancers in men and the onset is typically after age 40. The surgical removal of the prostate (prostatectomy) may cause erectile dysfunction because of the damage to the nerves supplying the penis. Radiation therapy or hormone therapy may cause psychological concerns.

Cancer of the testes is rare, appearing in younger men (20s and 30s), with about 50 percent being painful (Masters et al., 1986). Many men are infertile after treatment through surgery, drugs, or radiation and can experience guilt, self-blame, and lessened "manliness."

Chemical Dependency and Alcoholism

The correlation of sexual concerns with alcoholism and drug dependency is high (Kaplan, 1974; Mason, 1984; Masters et al., 1986; Meiselman, 1978). Some studies show that almost 50 percent of those seeking sex therapy suffer from drug abuse and alcoholism, either their own or their partner's (Coleman, 1982). Although alcohol does depress behavior in general, it also releases inhibitions, causing an increase in libido. As Shakespeare expressed it, "(Drink) provokes the desire, but it takes away the performance" (*Macbeth*, Act 2, Scene 3, Line 34). Research supports this truism, indicating that both men and women show negative effects physiologically in sexual arousal with alcohol, yet many people think it increases their sexual responsiveness (Masters et al., 1986).

Narcotics such as heroin and morphine produced erectile dysfunction in 48 percent of 162 addicts in a recent study (Masters et al., 1986), retarded ejaculation in 59 percent, and lowered sexual interest in 66 percent; of 85 female addicts, 27 percent had orgasmic dysfunction and 57 percent had lowered sexual interest. Treatment can be difficult since addicts often attempt to cover up sexual difficulties or have used the drugs as a substitute for sex. Because of the heightened sensual experiences for both men and women, narcotics can often lead to other sex-related problems, including prostitution for women, as they attempt to raise money for their drugs.

The barbiturates and other hypnotic drugs af-

fect sexuality similarly, giving, at least temporarily, the permission to be sexually uninhibited. However, behind the behavioral "freedom" lies guilt for many women. Women researchers found that women who were treated for drug abuse in treatment programs did not show any lessening of guilt posttreatment. In fact, a correlation of sex guilt with locus of control for women has been shown (Pinhaus, 1978).

Hallucinogens (LSD and marijuana) often are used in the search for aphrodisiac effects. A high percentage of people using marijuana (83 percent of the men and 81 percent of the women) claimed it improved their sexual experiences (Masters et al., 1986). There have been few studies on the effects of LSD on sexual functioning. Users of amphetamines and cocaine report a heightened interest in sex; yet over time, most amphetamine and "coke" users experience a lessening of their sexual interest and capability. Men can have erectile failure with their use (Kolodny, 1983). The hormone androgen can increase the sexual drive without altering consciousness; it increases the libido and performance of both men and women. In men recovering from alcoholism, androgen requires substantial time to resume its natural levels (up to 13 weeks) (Alouf, 1975).

Whatever the addicting drug is, we find a common clinical pattern in the fears of intimacy in relationships in addicts and their partners (Mason, 1986).

Diabetes

Diabetes, an endocrine disorder, affects approximately 4 percent of the U.S. population. Although retrograde ejaculation occurs in about 1 percent of diabetic men, their sex drive typically is not affected.

About 50 percent of diabetic men have organically caused erectile dysfunction, accounting for several million cases in the United States alone (Masters et al., 1986). Sexual difficulties also have been identified in about one third of diabetic women; secondary anorgasmia takes place four to six years after the disease has been discovered (Masters et al., 1986). In addition, women with diabetes need information about the use of K-Y Jelly when vaginal lubrication is reduced. Untreatable nerve damage and circulatory problems create barriers to sexual activity; the communication of the partners becomes a primary factor in maximizing their sexual relationship.

Heart Disease

Fears and anxiety about sexual activity often are found in heart-attack patients, but studies show that these fears are not substantiated (Wagner, 1975). What therapists have been telling their clients for many years still appears to hold true—that intercourse has about the same cardiovascular stress as climbing two flights of stairs. Yet men particularly fear intercourse to the extent that many cease all sexual activity. Some men have stated that they fear death during intercourse; this is a very low probability, according to several studies. Indeed, when death during intercourse occurs as a result of heart problems, the person typically was already extremely stressed.

Many men find they can reduce cardiovascular stress by changing their intercourse positions. Women with heart disease report fewer sexual concerns (Masters et al., 1986). However, heart-diseased women often express their concerns for their partners' comfort and pleasure. Several books are now available for couples in recovery from heart disease (Levin, 1988).

Drugs can affect sexual response; and physicians give a variety of answers to their cardiac patients, making it even more important for the family therapist to clarify what is physiological and what is psychosocial stress (Renshaw, 1978). Many men beginning antihypertensive medications, especially alpha-methyldopa, report diminished sexual functioning (Kolodny et al., 1978; Laver, 1974; Newman & Salerno, 1974). Treatment here includes reducing the drug and using sex therapy.

Treatment often also includes the reintroduction of safe, pleasurable sex through self-stimulation, masturbation, and gradually reducing the fear of coitus (Wagner, 1975). With all heart-disease concerns, the support of partners and their communication are essential to positive outcomes (Mackey, 1978).

Prostatitis

Inflammation of the prostate can be either acute (sudden) or chronic (long-lasting), causing painful urination or low back pain; it also can interfere with sexual functioning (painful ejaculation) (Masters et al., 1986). Aging men experience such a high degree of prostate difficulty that it can almost be included as a life-cycle phenomenon. Fifty to 75 percent of all men aged 80 or over have benign prostatic hypertrophy; men between 41 and 50 experience it at a rate of about 30 percent (Stone, 1987). The chances of prostatic cancer also increase with aging. Drug treatment is often used for acute prostatitis, with little effect on sexual functioning. However, with some of the surgical procedures for prostatitis and prostatic cancer, an increase in erectile dysfunction can occur.

During this stage of age-related changes, treatment typically includes training in assertiveness and in empathy; penile implants may be recommended for some patients.

Sexually Transmitted Diseases

Formerly referred to as "venereal disease," STDs incorporate a wider category of infections transmitted sexually; this name change relieves some of the stigmatism of the venereal-disease label.

Gonorrhea is the oldest known sexual disease, being described in the *Old Testament* (Leviticus 15) about 1,500 B.C. Hippocrates (400 B.C.) said it resulted from "the excessive indulgence in the pleasures of Venus" (the goddess of love). When Neisser identified the gonococcus in 1879, it was named *Neisseria gonorrhoeae*. During wars, it spread rapidly: an epidemic of gonorrhea took place during World War I and a near-epidemic in World War II. With the advent of penicillin, the disease became less prevalent in the 1950s. Today it has again reached epidemic proportions, with more than a million cases reported annually—a number that it is suspected may represent only one fourth of the actual cases (Masters et al., 1986).

Gonorrhea is transmitted through any form of sexual contact, including fellatio, sexual intercourse, anal intercourse, and, infrequently, cunnilingus. Clients with known or suspected gonorrhea are encouraged to see a gynecologist (for women) or a urologist (for men) for culture tests. Treatment includes the prescription of abstinence; also, the patient must notify any sexual partners who might have been involved in either transmitting or receiving the disease. The therapist may play an important role in encouraging and helping clients to face shame and betrayal issues.

However, gonorrhea is not the primary cause of this inflammation of the male urethra. *Nonspecific urethritis* (NSU) has a high rate among college students, with about 80–90 percent of cases due to causes other than gonorrhea. The organism typically isolated is *C. trachomatis* or *T. mycoplasma*. The symptoms of NSU are similar to those of gonorrhea but usually milder. Treatment with tetracycline generally will clear it up; penicillin usually is not effective. Therapists find that when clients report chlamydia, they may need a reminder to inform their partners. About 30–50 percent of women who are sex partners of men with chlamydia-positive NSU have *C. trachomatis*. For women, it is estimated as five to 10 times more common than gonorrhea in college and middle-class populations. In addition, 30–60 percent of women with gonorrhea also have chlamydia infections (Masters et al., 1986).

Syphilis, another old disease (mentioned near the end of the 15th century), is said to have originated with Columbus' first voyage to the West Indies; but new theories of transmission have developed in recent years (Hyde, 1979). Far less common than gonorrhea, with 2,000 new cases reported in the United States in 1983, the male–female ratio of this disease is two to one. Half of the men infected are homosexual or bisexual (Masters et al., 1986). Syphilis is far more contagious than gonorrhea, with one in two chances of catching it through a single act of intercourse with an infected partner (Fulton, 1974). It also can be transmitted through blood transfusions or from a pregnant woman to her fetus. Primary-stage chancres can heal within four to six weeks, but that does not mean that the disease has disappeared. Secondary syphilis begins from one week to six months after the chancre heals if treatment was not effective. Its danger is in its latency, after symptoms disappear. Fifty to 70 percent of people with un-

treated syphilis stay in this stage, where the disease is no longer contagious but the infecting microorganisms enter into various brain, spinal-cord, and blood-vessel tissues and bones. When pregnant women with syphilis are treated adequately, congenital syphilis can be prevented. The diagnosis is made through a blood test; treatment includes penicillin and/or tetracycline.

Herpes is a highly contagious STD that, in some forms, can be transmitted through nonsexual contacts. Its name comes from the ancient Greek word *herpein*, meaning "to creep," referring to the skin rashes that Roman physicians described in the first and second centuries A.D. Genital herpes affects approximately 15–20 million Americans, with about 500,000 cases reported annually. Transmitted via sexual intercourse, rubbing of genitals, oral–genital contact, and oral–anal or anal intercourse, the herpes virus can live for at least several hours, which raises the possibility of the infection's being further transmitted by nonsexual means. Although it was thought that genital herpes infections were caused by the type 2 virus, this etiology is no longer credited. In the United States, 10–20 percent of cases of genital herpes are caused by the type 1 virus (formerly thought to be limited to cold sores and fever blisters) (Peter, Bryson, & Lovett, 1982). In Japan, 35 percent of first episodes are due to the type 1 virus.

At present, there is no known cure. Infected women are encouraged to have Pap smears and pelvic examinations every six months because of the high correlations of herpes with cervical cancer and cancer of the vulva (Hyde, 1979; Masters et al., 1986). Many people find themselves feeling ashamed and depressed following their discovery of herpes and have faced their responsibility to inform sexual partners of the herpes with great anxiety. Clinicians often can coach clients in asking assertive questions about the possibility of transmission of STDs.

AIDS, a public-health threat without parallel in modern times, is a breakdown of the immune system needed to protect the body against infections. Its victims are subject to infections that are both deadly and rare. More than 40,000 cases of AIDS had been reported in the United States as of 1987, with about 22,000 deaths, and cases have been reported in more than 30 other countries. The number of new cases is doubling or tripling every year; most tragically, AIDS is usually fatal.

Of the first 10,000 cases of AIDS in the United States, 73 percent involved homosexual or bisexual men. Even higher percentages were found among intravenous drug abusers, of whom 94 percent of were men—almost half between the ages of 30 and 40. Now that the disease has surfaced in heterosexual people as well as in the gay community, health clinics have waiting lists many months long to handle what they term the "worried well." It is known that the transmission can also be nonsexual, via intravenous-needle sharing or blood transfusion. Originally, it was stated that the incubation period was up to five years, but new studies show it can be as long as 15 years. It is not difficult for clinicians to see the relevant therapy issues: shame, threat of fatal disease, fear, depression, and anger.

For families of gay men and women, the awareness of AIDS has added another dimension to the sexual-orientation issue. One recent national survey with a somewhat biased sample (from the Federation of Parents and Friends of Lesbians and Gays) showed that the AIDS outbreak reopened old wounds for parents who had come to terms with their child's homosexuality (Robinson, Skeen, & Walters, 1987). Despite their fears, 89 percent of the parents declared that the AIDS outbreak had not made them feel more negative about homosexuals and homosexuality. It did bring out attitudes toward "safe sex," and 40 percent said they felt more concern and compassion for gays. Family therapists can be sensitive to the findings, which include that (1) families are requesting additional information, and (2) a high percentage (50 percent) of families say they would not tell anyone outside the family. With these findings from a more liberal and supported group of families, we can only suspect that those without such support may be having an even harder time in adjusting.

Sex and the Disabled

Pervasive myths about sexuality often are greatly exaggerated with the disabled—those with spinal-cord injuries and persons who are blind, deaf, mentally retarded, or mentally ill. Until recently, this group has been ignored by helping professionals. Cole's (1975) pioneering work developed sex education for the disabled and their advocates. Essential to this education is the reminder that sexuality must not be equated simply with genitality, and not all disabilities directly affect genitality (McKinlay, 1983).

Spinal-cord injuries (SCI) may cause paraplegia (paralysis of legs) or quadriplegia (paralysis of all four limbs) and loss of all sensations in the body below the level of the injury. Bowel and bladder control usually are lost, and there can be loss of sexual function as well. Most SCI males experience a loss of the ability to have normal erections, some loss of ejaculation, and a loss of fertility. Intercourse is often possible for about four out of five men with incomplete SCI. Most SCI women typically have normal fertility and can have children, although many of these women do report a loss of genital sensations and orgasmic responsiveness and of reduced vaginal lubrication. Both men and women report "phantom" (nongenital) orgasms, including psychological feelings of orgasm and physical sensations in some other, unaffected part of the body (Comarr, 1970; Money, 1960). Research on self-concept, self-esteem, and body image has increased (Bogle & Shaul, 1981; Breman & Hadley, 1976; Lovitt, 1970; Singh & Magner, 1975). Bullard & Knight (1981), Rabin (1980), and Triescham (1988) have published books giving overviews related to sexuality and spinal injury. Illustrated self-help books are also available for SCIs (Mooney, Cole, & Chilgren, 1975). Therapists can be helpful in dealing with family and psychosocial needs.

Blindness and deafness can be accompanied by sexual difficulties, but, typically, it is sexual ignorance and lack of social skills that are at the root of such problems. No real physical limitation on the body's sexual responsiveness exists in people who are blind or deaf. Touch exercises with sex-related materials are helpful for the blind; deaf students are enjoying sex-education courses taught through signing.

Mental retardation can present a problem for sex educators, however, such education must be undertaken for mentally retarded persons because they cannot readily gain information from others as the rest of society can (Kempton, 1978). Many people are concerned that sex education will "cause" sexual "acting out" (aggressive sexual acts or these related to poor impulse control), but quite the contrary is true; the *lack* of education causes the problems. Issues of concern to therapists include contraception, privacy, and opportunities for relationships (Masters et al., 1986).

Illness and surgery are often areas of misinformation and feelings of sexual inadequacy, and physicians' and therapists' attitudes play an important role in the recovery process. A physical illness such as multiple sclerosis can disrupt the physical aspects of sexual response, and affect the emotional self as well. Another area therapists face is postsurgery disruption or cessation of sexual activity. For example, clients who have had an ostomy procedure need support to inform potential partners of the surgery before sexual relations begin and need to be comfortable in discussing covering an opening or appliance for aesthetic reasons during lovemaking. For example, when odors are a problem, therapists can suggest bathing and emptying the bag before making love (Pincus et al., 1984).

In all areas of the medical concerns listed here, good communication styles are essential as is a validation of sexuality. Cole (1983, p. 12) reminds us that "sexuality, like other birthrights, cannot be taken away by society; society may channel sexual attitudes and expressions, but it cannot prohibit all the forms and transformations generated by sexual energy." Working with clients with medical problems increases learning opportunities and challenges for the interested clinician.

CLINICAL ISSUES IN FAMILY THERAPY

This section considers the most frequently presented clinical issues for clinicians involving sexuality and sexual functioning. Although group sex therapy is often used for treating these concerns, the trained marriage and family therapist can work quite effectively with these problems and issues.

Anorgasmia

Formerly called "frigidity," anorgasmia refers to a woman's difficulty in attaining orgasm. It is a synonym for the term *orgasmic dysfunction*

created by Kaplan and Masters and Johnson (Masters et al., 1986). Anorgasmia is the primary issue in female sexual dysfunction and accounts for approximately 90 percent of cases in most large studies. Approximately 15–20 percent of those seeking sex therapy are women who have never experienced orgasm (Heiman & LoPiccolo, 1988). It is linked to organic causes in less than 5 percent of cases (Masters et al., 1986). To make therapeutic decisions, it is helpful to identify which of the following diagnostic categories best describes a patient's difficulty.

1. *Primary anorgasmia*—women who have never had an orgasm in reaction to any type of sexual stimulation. It should be noted that a large number of anorgastic women have never been effectively stimulated (Kaplan, 1974). Success rates of therapy are high when orgasm is defined as in self- or partner genital manipulation (85–95 percent) (Heiman, LoPiccolo, & LoPiccolo, 1976; Heiman & LoPiccolo, 1988; Kohlenberg, 1974).

2. *Secondary anorgasmia*—women who are no longer orgasmic, but who were formerly orgasmic on a rather regular basis. Women who have undergone treatment for alcoholism often report this condition and often find that, as they resolve intrapsychic and interpersonal issues, they can become orgasmic. Anger, power, and control issues often are embedded in sexual dynamics. Therapy success rates average about 70–80 percent (LoPiccolo, 1981). Delaying the man's ejaculation by the squeeze technique can be helpful. The couple's nonsexual interaction is a part of the whole picture and needs to be acknowledged.

3. *Situational anorgasmia*—women who have had orgasms on specific occasions, for example, when masturbating or with the use of a vibrator or oral simulation. This often is seen in couples where the man becomes impotent in response to a woman who cannot reach a climax following clitoral stimulation and requires prolonged coitus (Kaplan, 1974). It is difficult to determine success rates here.

4. *Coital anorgasmia*—women who can become orgasmic by various means but do not have orgasms during intercourse. Several studies suggest that about 10 percent of women have never experienced coital orgasm (Masters et al., 1986). Studies also show that about 10 percent have coital orgasms on an infrequent basis. For those

who require *coital* orgasm as proof of "success," the success rates of therapy are between 30 and 50 percent (LoPiccolo, 1981). Kaplan reminds us that not having orgasms during intercourse is within the normal range of sexual response and should not be called dysfunctional. There are no hard data to support the fact that failure to reach a climax during coitus is indicative of either the presence or absence of pathology (Kaplan, 1974).

5. *Random anorgasmia*—women who do experience orgasms in different sexual activities but infrequently. Treatment focuses on examining both intrapsychic and interpersonal issues and then moving into Masters and Johnson's sensate focus exercises or Barbach's (1975) *For Yourself* exercises. Kaplan's (1974) clearly directed treatment plan is also helpful for family therapists, while Heiman and LoPiccolo's (1988) *Becoming Orgasmic* is found useful by many clients.

Dyspareunia

Dyspareunia, or painful intercourse, can be either organic or psychosocial in nature. Poor vaginal lubrication—often caused by "drying" drugs (such as antihistamines, marijuana, and certain tranquilizers), birth-control foam, or insufficient lubrication—can result in discomfort. Also, diabetes, vaginal infections, and estrogen deficiencies can be the cause. It has been difficult to discern "causes" here; it is often an association of psychosocial and physical conditions.

Men can also experience painful intercourse. Typically, the pain is in the penis (inflamed or scratched) but can occur in the testes, urethra, or prostate. It can involve psychosocial factors. Treatment calls for inquiring about relationship difficulties, family history, and family background, as well as about physical problems and the use of drugs.

Vaginismus

Vaginismus is the involuntary tightening or closing of the vaginal introitus, with a spasm of the outer third of the vagina, prohibiting penetration. This conditioned response probably stems from pain or fear associated with vaginal penetration. It has even been seen as a protective reflex for any organically caused female dyspareunia. (In other words, women will shut down rather than experience gross discomfort.) Vaginismus formerly was thought to indicate unresolved "penis envy" and hostility toward men, but clinical experience tells us that it is more often associated with rigid religious strictures, ignorance, rape, or sexual abuse.

Treatment success is high (90–95 percent) when a physical-dilation program accompanies therapy (Fuchs et al., 1973). Therapists can find technical direction in Kaplan's (1974) *The New Sex Therapy* or Masters, Johnson, and Kolodny's (1986) *On Sex and Human Loving*.

Premature Ejaculation

Premature ejaculation, the most common male sexual dysfunction, has been hard to define owing to the difficulty of operationally defining "premature." Does premature mean not accomplishing a specified number of thrusts? Does it mean that a partner is not orgasmic in at least 50 percent of their encounters? Or does it mean that the man does not have total voluntary control over his ejaculations? Kinsey found that 75 percent of men ejaculated within two minutes of vaginal entry (which now seems unlikely), and this length of vaginal containment prior to ejaculation was thought to be a sign of "biological competence" (Masters et al., 1986, p. 466). This view certainly fit with earlier cultural beliefs that sex was primarily for male pleasure. Currently, Masters and Johnson state that about 15–20 percent of American men have at least some degree of difficulty with controlling rapid ejaculation. Clinically, the problem is often identified by women.

Treatment differs, as does the theory here: Kaplan (1974) advocates the use of the Semans stop–start technique (Semans, 1956) while Masters and Johnson (1970) base treatment on the "squeeze procedure," a method consistent with behavioral therapy (from the early work of Wolpe, 1958).

Ejaculatory Incompetence

Ejaculatory incompetence, also known as *retarded ejaculation* (the opposite of premature ejaculation), refers to the specific inhibition of the ejaculatory reflex. Men may respond to sexual stimuli with erotic feelings and have firm erections, and yet be unable to ejaculate even though they desire orgastic release. Common in men under the age of 35, the pattern is either primary (the man never has been able to ejaculate in the vagina) or secondary (the man has lost the ability to ejaculate in the vagina). There is a secondary pleasurable aspect of this condition in that it allows prolonged periods of coitus and suggests a "staying power." Unfortunately, when partners discover that this ability is accompanied by an inability to ejaculate intravaginally, it often disrupts the "pleasure" aspects and evokes tension. Masters and Johnson report that retarded ejaculation is seen in all age groups and is two to three times more common than ejaculatory incompetence. Other factors involved here may be stress, chemical rebalancing in postalcoholism or drug treatment, fatigue, or tension.

Treatment approaches include an integrated combination of psychotherapy and structured sexual experiences. Success rates reported from small samples indicate a range of from 50 to 82 percent (Heiman et al., 1981). Masters, Johnson, and Kolodny (1986) report that in treating primary or secondary ejaculatory incompetence, about 85 percent of their patients become successful with masturbation and 50 percent by noncoital partner stimulation.

Erectile Failure

Erectile failure, also known as erectile dysfunction, refers to the inability to have or maintain an erection firm enough for coitus. Impotence, the formerly common term for erectile failure, has been replaced (as has the term "frigidity" for women) because of its pejorative tone. Men with primary erectile dysfunction have never been able to have intercourse. Secondary erectile dysfunction refers to males who had had intercourse before the onset of the dysfunction and is about 10 times more common than primary dysfunction (Masters et al., 1986). Since almost all men will experience the loss of erection at some time (Kaplan states that approximately half the male population will have occasional episodes), Masters and Johnson

(1970) use the term "secondary erectile dysfunction" only if the erection problems occurred in at least 25 percent of a man's sexual encounters. Causes may be physical, such as diabetes or alcoholism, or psychological, such as unresolved family-of-origin issues or stress reactions. Treatment includes a combined progressive approach. Success rates of treatment for primary erectile dysfunction average between 40 and 60 percent, and for secondary dysfunction, between 60 and 80 percent.

Desire-Phase Concerns

Problems involving desire-phase concerns have become more widely recognized through the work of Chaplain (1979) in her development of a classification system for inhibited sexual desire (ISD). Ziebergeld and Ellison (1982) shifted from the individually focused approach to an interactional approach, referring to ISD as a discrepancy between the partners' levels of desire (Weeks, 1987). The causes can include organic conditions (e.g., hormonal deficiencies, alcoholism, drug abuse, chronic illness), but are primarily psychosocial (e.g., depression, prior sexual trauma, relationship power issues, poor body image (Masters et al., 1986). Treatment (ideally conjoint) is multifaceted, taking both intrapsychic and interpersonal dimensions into consideration and including interpersonal skills training. Therapists typically focus on intimacy, anger, control, and intergenerational factors (e.g., unresolved family-of-origin issues). The incidence of ISD in couples in therapy is reported to be 40 percent and higher (Kaplan, 1979). Outcome research is negligible (LoPiccolo, 1980).

Desire-phase concerns also include sexual aversion, referring to a severe phobia about sexual activity or the thought of it. This terror of sexual contact appears to be caused by severely negative parental sex attitudes, sexual trauma, a partner's sexual pressuring, or, in men, gender-identity confusion. Success rates for resolution of sexual aversion are high. Schover and LoPiccolo (1982) and Masters et al. (1986) report an approximately 80 percent success rate.

Many therapists working with dual-career, child-free couples report a high incidence of lowered sexual desire, and speculate as to what degree the ISD is related to a fear of pregnancy. Family researchers will be challenged with some of the unfolding hypotheses generated by apparent associations among various dimensions of couples' system functioning and sexual functioning.

Sexual Addiction

Sexual addiction, or hypersexuality, refers to compulsive sexual behavior, behavior that seems driven rather than chosen for pleasure or for pain relief. Poor impulse control plays an active part in sexual compulsivity. Although inhibited sexual desire has been identified in the revised third edition of the *Diagnostic and Statistical Manual of Mental Disorders* (DSM-III-R) (American Psychiatric Association, 1987, p. 278), its opposite—exaggerated or excessive sexual desire—has been disregarded. Masters, Johnson, and Kolodny (1986) refer to hypersexuality as "Don Juanism" and "nymphomania." Hypersexuality may be heterosexual or homosexual, oral or genital, and involve a partner or not. This area is perhaps one of the most controversial in sexuality today; some clinicians argue that there is no such thing as sexual compulsivity. Still, Carnes (1984) found that large numbers of men in treatment for chemical dependency (alcoholism) were sexually compulsive and kept secrets and felt shame about their sexual behaviors.

Clients report the "high" associated with the compulsive breakout activity, followed by remorse and shame. After resolving "never to do that again," clients state they had another episode. We see a direct correlation with the borderline personality, narcissism, sociopathy, and hysteria (Goldberg, 1987). Often, the sexual addict is in denial and lives in a private obsessional fantasy world of his or her own, similar to that of the alcoholic. Sexual genograms often reveal intergenerational concerns, with high degrees of sexual inappropriateness. Treatment involves cognitive restructuring, family-of-origin work, and behavioral therapy. Because of the similarity to other addictions, sexual addicts often find a Sex Addicts Anonymous group helpful. These groups focus on the "disease concept" and emphasize the sharing of discussion and mutual support. Although men have surely been socialized to be pursuers, we also see women addicts. Clients have appreciated reading the books *Women, Sex and Addiction* (Kasl, 1989) and *Out from the Shadows* (Carnes, 1986).

Not all self-help groups operate under the same "disease concept" assumptions. Some such groups have different premises and focus on behavior modification. Since the type of group varies from region to region, therapists can check with their local resources to find available group support for clients.

A current controversy exists in the treatment of men (and some women) who have sexually violated young children. Proponents of the sexual-addiction model would treat the behavior through a 12-step recovery model based on the 12 steps of Alcoholics Anonymous (AA); other clinicians would require an inpatient or outpatient sex-offenders program. New behavioral research and therapy show that systematic intervention during masturbation with aversive cognitive controls, managed by the client, is having some positive results (Masters et al., 1986).

Clinicians need to make the distinction between compulsions with victims and those without victims; this is a major factor in recidivism rates. Thorough batteries of psychological tests along with family interviews greatly aid in formulating treatment plans. Couples who request treatment for their relationship and have an underlying sexual addiction will rarely identify it or acknowledge it until it is uncovered and diagnosed by the therapist. Like any addiction, the resolution of other problems makes little progress until the sexual addiction is treated.[3]

---

[3] *Editors' Note.* On this, we certainly disagree. This "treat the addiction first" clinical principle would seem reasonable to us *if* we viewed such sexual behavior patterns as described here as "addictions." We do not view them in this way, and see them as having many more of the characteristics of ritualistic, compulsive anxiety disorders. Thus, we would prefer an approach to therapy based on successful methods developed by (social learning theory) behavior therapists for dealing with obsessions and compulsions, rather than one that is so often based on an acceptance of the reified, disease-oriented metaphor of addictions. For us, the issue is not whether there is "no such thing as sexual compulsivity"; *any* behavior can be engaged in compulsively, but that does not an "addiction" make. Moreover, we are especially troubled by the trendy, bandwagon quality of so much of the treat-compulsive-behavior-as-if-it-were-addictive-behavior movement, and see it offering as much hype as hope.

Posttraumatic Sexual-Assault Syndrome

This term refers to the psychological reaction to rape/sexual coercion that causes problems of sexual avoidance, avoidance of intercourse, fear of touch, and marital discord. Our definition includes forcible rape (either solo or gang), marital (or mate) rape, and coercive "date rape." Nonforcible rape includes statutory rape (intercourse with a girl below the age of consent), homosexual rape and underage-boy rape by a woman. Other examples of sexual coercion are seen in therapist–client sex, professor–student sex, and employer–employee sex, all of which involve power imbalances in the relationship. Clinically, we do not often see the "acute reaction phase" (Burgess & Holmstrom, 1974), which is the initial shock, disbelief, shame, and rage immediately following the assault. More often, we see the posttraumatic response to the crisis with experiences of self-blame, shame, heightened vulnerability, depression, obsessional thinking, and phobias (Nadelson, 1982). Often, the rape either has been kept a secret for many years or has been repressed. Still other clients discover their sexual assault when they are doing family-of-origin work in their therapy. Often, the violations were not termed "rape" because they involved a familiar acquaintance or family member.

With today's clear definitions of what constitutes rape, we see it increasingly being identified by men as well as women. Some studies show that one out of three women will be raped (forced to have sex without her consent) during her lifetime (Boston Women's Health Collective, 1984). Presenting clinical sexual concerns resulting from rape include sexual aversion or vaginismus, lowered sexual desire, and anorgasmia. The sensitive therapist will recognize that frequency of intercourse following rape does not ensure sexual satisfaction. In cases involving a male partner of a rape victim, therapists help the man to work through his shock, rage, sense of guilt, and awkwardness in approaching his partner. Client education about the power dynamics of rape can be helpful here. Treatment includes support groups, conjoint therapy with couples, family therapy where appropriate, the possible exploration of involvement of the perpetrator (in intrafamily rape), and a same-gender therapist. Therapists also find they must give added support to the victim in acknowledging

the sexist attitudes that still persist today—that, in some way, a woman "asked for it." Often, a combination of communication training (Stuart, 1976) and sensate focus exercises (Masters & Johnson, 1970) is used.

Incest

Incest refers to a sexual activity between a person and a close relative, such as a parent, sibling, grandparent, or uncle or aunt. Although brother–sister incest has perhaps been the most common form, the cases reported to authorities usually involve an adult–child relationship (Kinsey, Pomeroy, & Martin, 1948; Masters et al., 1986). For years, clinicians saw incest only in female clients, but now are identifying the male victims of incest, typically of father–son incest (Masters et al., 1986). Mother–son incest is the rarest form of incest, with genital fondling without intercourse its typical manifestation (Meiselman, 1978). Many adult women in psychotherapy reveal childhood incest up to 25 years after the fact. Often, men have not considered their sexual exploitation to have been incestuous. In many cases, children who have been sexually abused have not told their parents and carry guilt and shame into their adult relationships. Brother–sister incest has not been considered to be as damaging (Masters et al., 1986) as cross-generational incest. Experiences are varied; of course, brother–sister incest with a wide age difference and/or physical-size difference could result in severe damage.

According to national statistics on sexual abuse for the general population, it is estimated that one in every five female children and one in every 10 male children will be sexually abused before the age of 18 (Finkelhor, 1979). Clinically, we see a high correlation between incest and prostitution (adolescent and adult). Many incest victims come from alcoholic and drug-abusing families. Few therapists question the psychological damage stemming from childhood sexual abuse; long-term effects in the form of sexual and intimacy problems are commonly found. Also, it is not uncommon to see adult professionals in training experiencing their own posttraumatic stress upon hearing a lecture or reading articles about incest. People guard their history (in secrets and denial) or seem unaware of it and we cannot know when these memories might surface. Incest has become an ethical concern for therapists and others who are professionally involved. With improved reporting laws, we are receiving a great number of reports of sexual intrusiveness, referring to the parent who becomes excessively involved in child care—such as repeatedly giving enemas, bathing 11- to 13-year-old children, failing to observe the need for privacy in the home, and discussing menstruation, bodily changes, or wet dreams in front of other family members. Many programs exist for the treatment and prevention of sexual abuse.

When Lynn and Larry's chemical-dependency counselor called from the hospital's treatment center, he said he wanted a one-time interview with a family therapist before Larry left the treatment program since there had been a brief period of incest during his drinking years and the family had never talked openly about it. In my initial interview with the treatment counselor and the family, it was clear that Larry had had good treatment care. He was able to talk openly about his feelings and share what he had learned with his family, and apparently was humble about his spiritual recovery. Furthermore, he asked his daughters and his wife to forgive him for the incest of his drinking days, assuring them that he now had a new life plan with AA and had changed. Noting the mother's darting glances and the shyness and head-down shame of the 11- and 13-year-old daughters, I suggested that I interview the children separately before we proceeded with the "forgiveness session." During the first 10 minutes of my interview with the daughters, they were protective and naturally withholding. As we talked longer, they revealed, with tears, that the incest was still taking place in the family, having recently recurred on one of their father's visits home. His denial about his alcoholism had indeed been faced, but his denial about his incestuous relationship with his older daughter was still alive. I supported the daughters and told them that it was very important for them to tell their father that they would no longer keep secrets. When they confronted him, he admitted his lies and later said he was relieved at some level to have it known.

What appeared to be a one-time "forgiveness" session became long-term therapy, involving the daughters in their group, the parents in separate same-sex groups, and family therapy on a weekly basis. Family-of-origin sessions included grandparents from both sides (in which Larry's sexual abuse by his father was revealed and Lynn's mother's religiously obsessive family was examined). The family at one point also participated in a multiple-family group for incest families.

The psychological damage resulting from sexual abuse can be very serious and evaluation research needs to focus on the relationship between sexual-abuse prevention and sex education, still a taboo in many places. Treatment includes a supportive environment in which the client can be heard and work through the blocked affect, family-therapy sessions, and sex education. Multiple-family groups, in which the time of the therapy sessions is divided among the families, give additional support to the whole family. Treatment is initially individual, with a same-sex therapist, and then overlaps with therapy, continued individual support, and family therapy, where appropriate.

Treatment of incest, if not done outside the family-therapy clinical setting, presents questions to family therapists. "What is appropriate to talk about openly with the children, and at what ages, and in what context?" "Should the mother and father discuss their sexual relationship in front of the children?" These important questions do not have simple answers. A useful guideline can be the degree of clarity in the family's sexual boundaries. When family boundaries are blurred, a conservative approach is suggested. Often, we find it useful to work with the couple separately and strengthen family generational lines while proceeding with therapy.

Homosexuality or Same-Sex Preference

These terms refer to a preferential sexual attraction to persons of the same sex. It may or may not include sexual experience and it does not preclude heterosexual partners or fantasies. The term "bisexual" refers to those persons who engage in sexual activity with both male and female partners. Masters and colleagues (Masters et al., 1986) report that the rate of bisexuality in our society is probably less than 5 percent if it is defined as sexual activity with both male and female partners during the past year. Antihomosexual laws continue to plague homosexuals of both sexes with regard to their tax status as couples and to questions of child custody, as well as in the workplace and the military services. When this legal status is compounded with antigay family attitudes and church messages, it is not difficult to understand the need for counseling.

The incidence of homosexuality is statistically difficult to measure. Probably the best statistics are from Kinsey, who found that 37 percent of white males had had at least one homosexual experience that led to orgasm and that 10 percent were "more or less" exclusively homosexual for at least three years of their lives between the ages of 16 and 55 (Kinsey et al., 1948). Kinsey's findings showed that, by age 40, 19 percent of females had experienced some same-sex erotic contact (Kinsey, Pomeroy, Marten, & Gebhard, 1953). Many studies have shown differences between males and females regarding the duration of homosexual relationships, with the female relationships tending to be more stable. These differences can be attributed to women's socialization toward monogamous relationships (as opposed to male socialization toward variety), males' disadvantage with intimacy skills, and lack of support for male homosexual relationships (as opposed to indifference to those of women owing to women's "second class" status). With the increase in AIDS cases and increased numbers of years of remission, we are likely to see great changes in relationship patterns. Clinical concerns include decisions to "come out" to both oneself and others, family-acceptance issues, same-sex secrets in marriages, homophobia, relationship rituals (bonding ceremonies), childbearing, and parent–child relationships. Coleman (1981/1982) has written about the difficulty for male homosexuals in learning intimacy skills because of the few role models available. Perhaps one of the most frequent concerns in therapy is the stereotyping by appearance, lifestyle, profession, or personality. It is imperative that therapists examine their own homophobia and attitudes and make appropriate referrals when necessary.

Clyde was a seasoned therapist in his community agency and was quite open about some of his concerns regarding his discomfort with talking openly with gays and/or lesbians in therapy. He sounded quite self-accepting during in-service sexuality training when he stated, "Why, whenever I spot a gay, I handle it— I refer him to John." It took quite some time before Clyde realized that he could not "spot" a gay and that his stereotyping had become his decision-making process.

Heterosexual therapists can work well with homosexual men and lesbian women. Treatment adjuncts often include books, support groups, and family therapy.

Sexual Variations

Sexual variations refer to a minority of nontraditional sexual activities often revealed in therapy, including paraphilia (sexual arousal and gratification dependent on fantasy of unusual sexual experience accompanied by obsessional thinking), fetishism (sexual arousal occurring in response to an inanimate object), transvestism (cross-dressing by heterosexual men), transsexuality (gender crossover), voyeurism and exhibitionism, sadomasochism, bestiality, and pedophilia. Since specific skills are required in the treatment of these variations, we suggest referring the client to a sex therapist or seeking professional consultation from a certified sex therapist.

Although therapists usually find same-issue therapy groups for clients, we have had success in placing a transsexual male in a women's therapy group (on the assumption that more could be learned about the world of women from women). After working through initial discomfort, the entire group worked more deeply on their own gender issues and reported that it had been a rich and rewarding experience.

Extramarital Sex

Extramarital sex (EMS) refers to any form of sexual activity between a married person and someone other than his or her spouse. Although we refer specifically to "extramarital" sex here, we see the same dynamics in many forms of nonmarital relationships, including same-sex relationships. EMS does not have general social approval, but almost 50 percent of clients coming to marital and family therapy have sought help for issues concerning such activities in the part of one or both partners (Humphrey, 1986). EMS affects half of all married couples, according to recent research findings (Humphrey,

1986). It may refer to a range of activities, including having a "one-night stand," being involved in short-term affairs, and utilizing the services of prostitutes. The threat to the marriage increases with the degree of emotional involvement. A range of genital involvement also exists, with some persons participating in "nonpenetrating affairs" (Sarrel, 1984). In addition to time, emotional involvement, and activity level, therapists need to explore secrecy, bilateral involvement, and sexual orientation (Humphrey, 1987). Some distinguish between adultery, the sexual act *outside of marriage*, and infidelity, or sexual dishonesty *inside the marriage* (Pittman, 1989). Treatment must take into consideration the quality of the overall marital relationship, the quality and quantity of the couple's sexual relationship, the presence of any sexual dysfunctions, both spouses' emotional and mental health, and the presence of any unusual circumstances (Weeks, 1987).

It is not uncommon to find persons involved in EMS reporting a poor sexual relationship with a spouse but high satisfaction with another sexual partner. This situation can exist for a variety of reasons; therapists find probing questions here most helpful. Some common reasons for this difference in response are the lack of history in the extramarital relationship; sexual excitement accompanying the "newness"; singular, often romance only, involvement; and lack of outside responsibilities. In other cases, EMS is consensual and part of a life-style. Therapists differ on their approaches; some dictate that the EMS cease in order to proceed with therapy, whereas others do not object to the continuation of the outside relationship. Although many systems therapists state that the third party should be included in a therapy session, such participation seldom takes place.[4] Indeed, the therapist faces may possible difficulties here—secrets, anger and rage, power and control issues, jealousy, and grief. EMS need not be grounds for divorce, and can even ultimately open up a person sexually, which, in turn, can enhance the marriage. With the increase in reported "social diseases," we may soon see a change in research findings on EMS.

---

[4] *Editors' Note.* Another breath of fresh air from an honest author.

CLINICAL DECISION MAKING AND SEXUAL ASSESSMENT

Assessment of sexual concerns is crucial to treatment. Often therapists state that they are uncertain about their competence level when hearing about specific sexual dysfunctions and problems. Although sex histories and attitudinal and behavioral inventories are helpful and often essential, many clinicians feel inadequate to do specific sex therapy in the context of their relationship therapy and would rather refer the person to a certified sex therapist. The dilemma, however, lies in the decision-making process of the therapist, who must decide what level of intervention is appropriate in treating sexual concerns.

P-LI-SS-IT Model

One model of intervention decision making that has proved helpful to therapists is the P-LI-SS-IT model developed by Annon (1975). According to behavioral psychologist Annon, four levels of treatment exist:

- P = permission to talk about sexual issues, reassurance and empathy, and the acknowledgment that we are sexual beings.
- LI = limited information, including sex education, clarification of sexual myths and stereotypes, and bibliotherapy with suggested related books.
- SS = specific suggestions such as Kegel exercises, the squeeze technique, or sensate focus.
- IT = intensive therapy, individual or conjoint, including focus on relationship dynamics and psychological concerns and other complex issues.

Annon suggests that as one moves to greater levels of intervention, more training is required. By using this decision-making model, therapists can decide what they believe themselves qualified to do. Family-therapy training should include adequate training to intervene in the first three levels, through specific suggestion, of the P-LI-SS-IT model. At the fourth level, many family therapists choose to refer individuals and couples to sex therapists.

Sexual Histories

After the therapist gives permission (Annon, 1976) to discuss sexual concerns, clients often contract with the therapist to examine the sexual relationship and proceed with sex therapy. This contracting stage is most important, because clients often state that they originally entered therapy because they wanted a "safe" place in which to discuss their sexual concerns. Others at this time acknowledge that they entered therapy hoping to reach this stage and that it was the motivating force for their doing so. All too often, as family therapists begin talking about sex with clients, other relationship issues surface and therapists proceed to discuss the dynamics of the relationships. Perhaps much of the failure occurs at this stage. When the therapist's no-talk rules meet the clients' no-talk rules, the collusion prevents directive sex therapy from taking place.

Once the contract is set, the therapist introduces an extended sex-history interview with a therapist of the same sex (Kaplan, 1974; Lo-Piccolo & Heiman, 1978; Masters & Johnson, 1970). Often during this long face-to-face interview, deeper relationship issues may surface with secrets revealed from the past. We have found that it can be helpful to refer the couple to another therapist for the sex therapy while the primary therapist can meet with the couple on the relationship issues.[5] The sex-history interview is essential to a good outcome, since it will aid in a diagnosis, or at least a description, of the problem, can identify the etiology, and can indicate appropriate treatment. At this point, the therapy team needs to be aware of any unconscious motivation to sabotage the sex

---

[5] *Editor's Note.* By way of stark contrast, we would almost never make a referral under such conditions, precisely because such a referral may well set up an unfortunate "primary therapy"/"secondary therapy" conflict, in which patients may come to view the former as the "real" therapy. We believe that comprehensively trained family therapists are usually in a perfectly good position to deal with both the behavioral–sexual symptoms *and* the "deeper relationship issues" that are sometimes associated with them.

therapy. If "time out" is taken, it is the therapist's responsibility to reintroduce the contract.

Sexual Genograms

Since the family is where sexual attitudes and behaviors are inherited, it is only natural that a sexual genogram can be instrumental in placing sexuality in its natural context (Berman & Hof, 1986). It is our opinion that the missing dimension in sex therapy has been the family context, the root system from which the current sexual problems grew. Some have traced sexual problems to personalities developed in childhood and treat the dysfunction in the context of personality type (Offit, 1977). This theory would, of course, be difficult to research since the therapy is woven into the psychodynamics of the individual. This approach is not new; while Kaplan has used dynamics of family, she has taken little from major intergenerational therapists such as Bowen (1978), Framo (1976), or McGoldrick and Gerson (1985). At least one writer in the field of sex education has developed the "sexual script" inherited in the family (Gagnon, 1977).

Lynn and Tony entered therapy because of Tony's approaching 50th birthday and his desire to "get his act together" by the end of the year. After working through some of the unresolved grief issues from their families of origin, their relationship dynamics were starting to shift. Lynn then brought up her concern that although they had a good sexual relationship, she was worried that he seemed "far away" during their lovemaking. She also complained that when they ate in restaurants, he liked to face the door so that he could "view the people (women)" as they entered. Lynn had been accommodating this behavior for years and in her budding feminist consciousness was furious that she had colluded in this activity.

In doing their sexual genograms, we learned that Lynn had been loyal to cross-generational intimacy by protecting her father and telling her intimate problems only to older women, on whom she had relied since the death of her mother when Lynn entered college. Tony's emotional cutoffs were due to his inability to have any conflict with a woman. Rather than ask for what he wanted, he would go along with his wife's request and engage in a vivid sexual-fantasy life. Tony soon learned that his rich fantasy life had been his way to cope with differentness. Both had learned to accommodate to each other more easily by smoking marijuana as part of their lovemaking. Their sexual genograms disclosed Lynn's discovery, of when she was 10, of love letters to her mother revealing an extramarital affair, and her loyalty to her mother's secret. Tony was able to remember that his mother had made sarcastic joking comments about his father's sexual functioning in front of the children; Tony never knew what to do with the information. As Lynn and Tony heard one another's stories, they were able to do some brief sex therapy to learn what each other wanted and to communicate their sexual needs and desires in the process.

The use of the sexual genogram with Tony and Lynn shows how a sexual concern can be related to unresolved guilt and loyalty to parents (Boszormenyi-Nagy & Spark, 1979). Each expressed compassion for the other and both were able to change behaviors in a very short time.

Another valuable use of the sexual genogram is with victims of sexual abuse or sexual addiction (hypersexuality). When clients face the shame about their own behaviors and their sexual abuse, they need reassurance that the abuse did not happen in a vacuum (Fossum & Mason, 1986). The sexual genogram is a valuable tool to identify prior abuse in families and to tap the vein of history that may have been repressed. In the short time we have used this instrument, we have found it extremely helpful not only in connecting the sexual experiences to a "family tree," but also in surfacing repressed material.

Sexual-Marital-Adjustment Inventories

In working with couples in therapy, we find that many couples do not know what they want, let alone ask for what they want. It is helpful to use attitude and behavioral inventories to help couples achieve sexual congruence.

A special issue of the *Journal of Sex and Marital Therapy* (Fall 1979) was devoted to the subject and described at least 50 instruments. A related scale, the Locke-Wallace Marriage Inventory, can be a useful adjunct to the assessment. The Sexual Interaction Inventory (LoPiccolo & Steger, 1974) aids couples in describing their enjoyment and frequency of specific sexual acts. We have found it useful as a values-clarification instrument when couples can discuss nondefensively in a supportive environment what behaviors fit with their personal and shared value systems. The therapist can encourage couples to identify their goals in their own sexual activities. This instrument, when used in this way, can bring negative attitudes to the surface, as well as identify areas for improving sexual communication.

Another popular evaluation is that of Kaplan (1983), in which she offers a systematic integration of psychological and biological dimensions of the evaluation process.

Pencil-and-paper self-report instruments do not prove empirically to be helpful owing to social desirability influences that affect patient responses (Beutler et al., 1975; LoPiccolo et al., 1981), yet they can be quite useful clinically. Along with the Sexual Interaction Inventory, the Sexual Arousal Inventory (Hoon, Hoon, & Wincze, 1976) is helpful for women. Social desirability is a factor that often interferes with the usefulness of such inventories. Falsification also must be taken into account. In doing sex therapy in couples groups, we often find that separating the couples into same-sex groups for part of the group time fosters more honest disclosures about sexual behaviors.

Some therapists find the Stuart Marital Precounseling Inventory and Sexual Adjustment Inventory useful for evaluation and data gathering (Stuart, 1980).

Sexological Exams

In addition to sexual-dysfunction interviews and paper-and-pencil tests, another useful area of assessment involves the "sexological" exam (Hartman & Fithian, 1972), in which a direct-observation technique is used. Since this technique has the therapist stimulate the breast and genitals of the opposite-sex patient to determine physiological responsiveness, it raises too many issues for our recommendation. The effects of observation itself or possible transference responses to the therapist are but some of the disadvantages; also, the behaviors are not necessarily transferable to the couples' homes (LoPiccolo, 1986). The codes of ethics for marriage and family therapists would not permit such techniques today. Another observation technique is use of a videotape of the patient couple (Serber, 1974). With the increased awareness today of victimization, this method also seems inappropriate.

What is relevant here is the need for multi-method, multidimensional assessment. Lo-Piccolo (1981) recommends an evaluation of the following factors adequately to assess a sexually dysfunctional couple—and, we would add, individuals: (1) history, (2) current behavior, (3) attitudinal and cognitive factors, (4) psychodynamic and intrapsychic defenses, (5) interpersonal systems, (6) psychiatric status, and (7) biological factors.

SEX THERAPIES

Goal Setting

Both clients and therapists establish goals for the treatment so that therapist and client are clear about the direction and possible length of treatment. Assessment should be thorough so that therapists can discern sexual problem areas. The primary function of goal setting, of course, is that it enables the clients and the therapist to know if they have achieved their treatment aims. A secondary function of goal setting is that it provides the contract to be honored by all parties. Should other issues surface, the contract can be set aside, but it can hold the clients accountable for their stated goals. A related purpose is to give hope to the clients, who may have felt they were "hopeless cases"; brief sex therapy is appealing to clients who previously had spent lengthy hours working on the "metaphor" of their sexual relationship without actually participating in the behavioral aspects. Finally, clients will have gone through a learning-process to which they can refer should they need to address similar problems at another time. Although sex therapy is often seen as first-order change (Watzlawick, 1978), clients who undergo a process that engages them in talking with one another openly about their sexual relationship can experience genuine second-order change (Watzlawick, 1974).[6]

The relationship between therapist and client is crucial to goal setting since the values of the clinician are reflected in longer-term goals. What the therapist defines as "healthy sexual functioning" will be reflected in homework assignments as well as in outcome goals. In the 1970s, sex therapists talked about value-free sex; now, clinicians are much more honest about their biases, and more aware of sexual exploitation in relationships, including that which can occur between therapist and client. The family therapist who is sensitive to families' and couples' values can facilitate sexual congruence. Although the goals for the therapy are known to both client and therapist, it is not uncommon for the clinician to have goals that may or may not be explicit (such as deepening empathy or reducing defensive behaviors).

Besides general goal setting, contract setting often prohibits coitus during the initial stages of sex therapy. In addition, the therapist might suggest reading material about gender socialization and other permission-giving resources.

Structures of Therapy

Although some evidence supports conjoint therapy as more effective than individual therapy (Cooper, 1969; Gurman & Kniskern, 1978; Hogan, 1978; Prochaska & Marzili, 1973), several techniques are effective with individuals (Barbach, 1975; Ellis, 1971; Husted, 1972; Kockott, Dittmar, & Nusselt, 1975). Also, since many more women than men seek therapy, and since many of our clients are single, the marriage and family therapist must be prepared to work with the individual as well as with the couple and the family.[7] Besides the Masters and Johnson co-

---

[6] *Editors' Note.* Perhaps another way of saying this, and one that too many therapists do not acknowledge, is that second-order change (in the rules of the relational system) can come about via direct as well as via indirect clinical methods.

[7] *Editors' Note.* Whether or not the treatment of sexual dysfunction in a patient who lacks an ongoing relationship is maximally helpful could be usefully debated. The even more important point here, we believe, is that family therapists need to be able to deal (and be comfortable with doing so) with individuals as well as couples and families, as Mason argues, for at least practical reasons: (1) some patients have problems that are clearly deserving of professional therapeutic attention, yet they are not involved in a significant intimate relationship; (2) it is not uncommon to find that clinical problems that are defined as relational or interactional respond better to at least some sessions with individual members of the couple/family; and (3) many patients are unwilling to engage in conjoint therapy.

therapy format, with their mixed-gender, dual-therapist approach that includes a physician's medical examination as part of intake, several other formats could be considered. These include those of Hartman and Fithian (1972), who do not require a physician; the Cornell clinic of Helen Kaplan (1974) or the University of Minnesota Clinic in Human Sexuality (1972), in which individual therapists of either gender are used; the University of Washington Clinic of Julia Heiman (1988), and the LoPiccolo group in Missouri (LoPiccolo, 1988). The length of therapy varies from two weeks of daily therapy at the Masters and Johnson clinic to no limit. The type of dysfunction presented and client readiness to change are two variables that affect the duration of therapy (Heiman, LoPiccolo, & LoPiccolo, 1981). The number of sessions per week also varies (Kaplan, 1974). Most therapists agree that when no organic problems are apparent, primary anorgasmic dysfunction, premature ejaculation, and vaginismus can easily be treated with short-term therapy. On the other hand, when there is erectile failure, ejaculatory incompetence, or secondary anorgasmic dysfunction, clients may need more extensive therapy. Psychiatric evaluation varies as well, with a referring therapist evaluation (Masters and Johnson) or psychiatric evaluation (Kaplan).

Individual therapy has been effective in treating orgasmic concerns, and masturbation therapy, systematic desensitization, and cognitive restructuring (Barbach, 1975; Ellis, 1971; Husted, 1972; Kockott, Dittmar, & Nusselt, 1975; Offit, 1977) can be carried out effectively individually. In some individual therapies, it has been possible to use a portion of the therapy hour to work on the sexual issue, such as masturbation for the anorgasmic woman, with progress reports and homework assignments an ongoing part of each session. When contracting for individual therapy with someone in a paired relationship, we often suggest that the partner come in at the beginning and again at the end of the therapy process to discuss shifts in the relationship and to include the partner in the orgasm response.

Whether paired or single, a person often has the need for cognitive restructuring in individual therapy. Clients have restructured irrational beliefs and family and religious distortions through the use of rational-emotive therapy (Ellis & Harper, 1975).

In individual therapies, we suggest a same-sex therapist to support the notion of "gender privilege," the shared socialization expectations of gender.

Couples therapy has been the strength of Masters and Johnson, LoPiccolo, and Heiman and Kaplan. Indeed, many therapies have defined the couple as the ideal unit for therapy, but because of today's high rate of divorce, we often deal with ghosts from the past. This may be the third "couple" a client has formed.

Certainly, the quality of the relationship, as well as the defined problem and goals, is related to whether the couple should have conjoint therapy with a cotherapy team (Hogan, 1978). That marriage and family therapists in private practice often work alone does not preclude their doing effective sex therapy (Mathews et al., 1976; Schmidt, 1977). When conflict exists between therapists, therapy can be more harmful than helpful (Gurman & Kniskern, 1978). Some therapists have found that using educational videotapes that include conjoint therapy with a cotherapy team is helpful for the therapist working alone in private practice.

While cotherapy teams can be advantageous, some disadvantages surface for therapists who may overidentify with one partner's point of view, taking on the battle of the couple. Also, financial constraints can be obvious barriers for couples. At those times when we want to use a cotherapy team and the couple finds having two therapists a financial burden, we suggest seeing the couple every other week rather than weekly. Of course, this procedure does not work with all dysfunctions, nor is there an optimal format for all sexual problems.

Couples therapy provides the context for deepening intimacy skills, while talking openly about sexuality. When couples have difficulty in communication skills, we have sent them to such programs as the Couples Communication Program (Miller, Nunnally, & Wackman, 1976) or the Couples Relationship Enhancement Program (Guerney, 1974) to improve their overall sexual communication skills and make more efficient use of the therapy hour. Since the couple is the focus in these groups, couples often report that they no longer feel so alone with their communication struggles. The therapist trained in methods such as these can facilitate the partners' communication by referring to the skills they have learned there.[8] At other times, we have directed clients to a sexual-attitude-reassessment program, in which the use of media is balanced with didactic information on sexuality to evoke feelings and attitudes toward sexual behaviors and patterns.

The marriage and family therapist is at a distinct advantage in helping couples integrate sexuality into their relationship dynamics, thereby deepening their intimacy (L'Abate & Talmadge, 1987).

Group therapy can be used for women's groups, men's groups, couples groups, and mixed groups. A distinct advantage of group therapy is the support available for specific concerns, such as erectile failure (Lazarus, 1968), primary orgasmic dysfunction (Barbach, 1975; Schneidman & McGuire, 1978), premature ejaculation (Kaplan, 1974), and sexual enhancement (LoPiccolo & Miller, 1975). In addition, group therapy also has proved effective in incest treatment (Justice, 1978) and hypersexuality or sexual addiction (Carnes, 1983), and therapy for male sex offenders and their spouses (Mason, 1976) may be helpful in the group context.

Multiple-family groups have been used in the treatment of family sexual abuse. Although these are not sex-therapy groups per se, the interventions follow the first three levels of the P-LI-SS-IT model (Annon, 1975), thereby meeting many of the requirements of sex therapy. In these groups, family members work together and separately on restructuring the subsystems' sexual boundaries and develop empathy and sexual-assertiveness skills. Sex education is a vital part of the multiple-family-group approach.

---

[8] *Editors' Note.* Except for possible (financial) cost-saving reasons, we would not prefer such an external referral. Note that some methods of couples therapy, such as behavioral marriage therapy (Holtzworth-Munroe & Jacobson, Chapter 4), would not look upon the teaching/learning of communication skills as an ancillary treatment component, but as a core vehicle of change, to be initiated and carried through by the therapist, without collateral change agents. Indeed, we would argue that when the therapist is skilled in such communication training approaches, it is more efficient to include them in the therapy proper.

ETHICAL AND LEGAL DIMENSIONS IN PROFESSIONAL PRACTICE

Legal Dimensions

Today, clinicians must be familiar with the ethical and legal issues related to family therapy and sexuality. We have seen an increase in the reporting of sexual violations—in both the family and the therapeutic context. This may lead to a higher reported incidence of sexual violations. Many clinicians report that they face a dilemma when, after developing trust with a family, they learn about parent–child incest that they are legally required to report to the proper authorities. Even with the client "warnings" that many clinicians give to clients at the time of intake regarding their professional responsibility with "reportable" incidents, many families seem to forget that they were thus advised.

Family therapists and academicians must be astute observers of legal and gender issues as they relate to the ethical dimensions of family therapy. Whether a therapist faces problems of family sexual abuse or of therapist–client abuse, the ethical and legal issues often converge. Often confidentiality and privileged communication can present dilemmas to the therapist (conflict between personal loyalty and legal requirements); many therapists find it essential to seek consultation on such issues.

Clinicians and academicians need to be aware of the family laws in their states and of malpractice and legal liabilities related to their practices. They must be fully cognizant of required reporting. With the increase in reported sexual child abuse, clinicians are often called upon to assess the alleged offender, the child(ren), or others, and need to be aware of the appropriate professional guidelines (Woody, 1986).

Today, many graduate programs in marriage and family therapy are requiring courses in ethics, including legal and professional issues (Piercy & Sprenkle, 1983). Seasoned professionals must rely on professional journals and state organizations to update their information.

Professional liability issues are also being regulated by state law today. Clinic administrators and staff members must know their state laws. Some states are enacting civil laws through legislation to protect clients who have been sexually exploited by counselors or therapists, making it possible for victims to sue both the abusing counselor and the employer of the therapist (Minnesota, Chapter 372, 1986).

In addition, some states have now identified sexual contact in criminal law. For example, Minnesota Statute 609.1356 (revised 1986) not only defines sexual contact, but also identifies what constitutes criminal sexual conduct in the first through fourth degrees, ranging from therapist–client sexual penetration to "willing client" sexual contact (consent by the complainant is not a defense).

In keeping with these changes, some states require that clinics inquire about any previous sexual complaints or charges in initial interviews.

Gender Issues

Gender issues are gaining attention in family therapy (Luepnitz, 1988). Not only are the DSM-III-R (American Psychiatric Association, 1987) sex biases being challenged (Williams & Spitzer, 1983), but gender issues are also being faced in other ways. For example, Hare-Mustin (1978, 1980) states that family therapy may not be in the best interest of women since clinical approaches have grown out of foundations of cybernetics and general systems theory, foundations that did not include how gender has been constructed within families. The Women's Project in Family Therapy (Walters, Carter, Papp & Silverstein, 1988) has supported a feminist perspective, emphasizing the absence of gender in the formulation of systems theory. Their focus on changes in family structure and functioning as a result of women's work outside the home, divorce, and remarriage has affected our theory as well as our clinical approaches and our assumptions about men and women.

When Ben and Maria entered therapy seeking a change in their sexual relationship, they were quite open about Ben's low sexual-desire level and Maria's concern about their lack of sexual intimacy. Rather than encourage Maria to retreat (which we so often do in such cases on the assumption that this would produce an increase in sexual desire along with increased desire for the partner), we did something different. We suggested that Ben enter a men's group

to get support for his change and work on his "feeling acquisition" and communication of affect. Upon his completion of work with the men's group, we did behavioral sex therapy with the couple and both reported satisfaction with their completed goals. With this therapeutic treatment plan, we faced our "old systems shtick"—were we being unfair in suggesting that one person needed to do something while not holding the other person equally accountable for her "half" of the problem? Our former theoretical bias told us that if Ben had a problem, then it was probably partially due to Maria's pursuing him, and that if we could get Maria to withdraw, then Ben would automatically move in. Over the years, we have found this to be only sometimes true. More often than not, Ben would have had the power base, and the system would see only first-order change in that the therapist would help Ben to "get Maria off his back."

An ethical base requires us to examine our inherent sexism and the power imbalances in family theory and family therapy. Although it is, at times, discomforting to both clients and professionals, this is essential.

CONCLUSION

In writing about the family as the context for sex therapy, we realize that this is, in many respects, a working paper. We recognize that we are living in the midst of evolving family theory and evolving family therapy (not to mention research). We have, indeed, been in search of a context for sex therapy. Often, we can only see progress by looking back, and so only need to look back to see the progress family therapy has made over the years since it was a toddler. Now that it is in its adolescence, it is only natural that we as family therapists are exploring sexuality.

REFERENCES

Alouf, F. (1975). ASSECT Midwest Conference. Personal communication.

American Psychiatric Association (1987). *Diagnostic and statistical manual of mental disorders* (3rd ed., rev.). Washington, DC: Author.

Annon, J. (1975). *The behavioral treatment of sexual problems*. Vol. 1. Honolulu: Enabling Systems.

Barbach, L. (1975). *For yourself: The fulfillment of female sexuality*. New York: Doubleday.

Bart, P., & Grossman, M. (1976). Menopause. *Women & Health, 1* (3), 3–11.

Berman, E., LoPiccolo, J., & Madanes, C. (1986). *Sex therapy in search of a context.* Highland, IN: Creative Audio (tape).

Beutler, L., Karacan, I., Anch, A., Salis, P., Scott, F., & Williams, R. (1975). *Journal of Consulting and Clinical Psychology. 43,* 899–903.

Boston Women's Health Book Collective (Eds.). (1984). *The new our bodies, ourselves.* New York: Simon & Schuster.

Boszormenyi-Nagy, I., & Spark, G. (1973). *Invisible loyalties.* New York: Harper & Row.

Bowen, M. (1978). *Family therapy in clinical practice.* New York: Aronson.

Boyer, M.R.P. (1987). Counseling couples to deal with the sexual concerns of their children. In G. Weeks & L. Hof (Eds.), *Integrating sex and marital therapy.* New York: Brunner/Mazel.

Burgess, A., & Holmstrom, L. (1974). *Rape: Victims of crisis.* Bowie, MD: Brady.

Butler, R., & Lewis, M. (1976). *Sex after sixty: A guide for men and women in their later years.* New York: Harper & Row.

Carnes, P. (1983). *The sexual addiction.* Minneapolis MN: CompCare Publications.

Carter, E.A., & McGoldrick, M. (Eds.) (1988). *The changing family life cycle: A framework for family therapy.* New York: Gardner Press.

Cleveland, M. (1976). Sex in marriage: At forty & beyond. *Family Coordinator, 25* (3), 233–240.

Cole, C. (1983). Sexual disorders and the family therapist. In J. Hansen, J. Woody, & R. Woody (Eds.), *Sexual issues in family therapy.* Rockville, MD: Aspen.

Coleman, E. (1981/82). Developmental stages of the coming out process. *Journal of Homosexuality, 7,* 31–43.

Coleman, E. (1982). Family intimacy and chemical abuse: The connection. *Journal of Psychoactive Drugs, 14,* 153–157.

Cooper, A.J. (1969). Disorders of sexual potency in the male: A clinical and statistical study of some factors related to short-term prognosis. *British Journal of Psychiatry, 115,* 709–719.

Ellis, A. (1962). *Reason and emotion in psychotherapy.* New York: Stuart.

Ellis, A. (1971). Rational-emotive treatment of impotence, frigidity, and other sexual problems. *Professional Psychology, 2,* 346–349.

Ellis, A., & Harper, R. (1975). *A new guide to rational living.* Englewood Cliffs, NJ: Prentice-Hall.

Finkelhor, D. (1979). *Sexually victimized children.* New York: Free Press.

Finkelhor, D. (1984). The prevention of child sexual abuse: An overview of needs and problems. *Siecus Report, 13,* 1–5.

Fossum, M., & Mason, M. (1986). *Facing shame: Families in recovery.* New York: Norton.

Framo, J. (1976). Family of origin as a therapeutic resource for adults in marital therapy: You can and should go home again. *Family Process, 15,* 193–210.

Freud, S. (1962). *Three essays on the theory of female sexuality.* New York: Avon.

Gadpaille, W. (1975). *The cycles of sex.* New York: Scribner's.

Gagnon, J. (1977). *Human sexualities.* Glenview, IL: Scott, Foresman.

Goldberg, M. (1987). Understanding hypersexuality in men and women. In G. Weeks & L. Hof (Eds.), *Integrating sex and marital therapy.* New York: Brunner/Mazel.

Gurman, A.S., & Kniskern, D.P. (1978). Research on marital and family therapy: Progress, perspective and prospect. In S. Garfield & A. Bergin (Eds.), *Handbook of psychotherapy and behavior change* (2nd ed.). New York: Wiley.

Gurman, A., & Kniskern, D.P. (Eds.) (1981). *Handbook of family therapy.* New York: Brunner/Mazel.

Guttmacher (Alan) Institute. (1985). *New study of teenage pregnancy in 36 other developed countries suggest reasons why US. teenage pregnancy rates are highest in the western world.* New York: Author.

Hare-Mustin, R. (1978). A feminist approach to family therapy. *Family Process, 17* (2), 181–194.

Hare-Mustin, R. (1980). Family therapy may be dangerous to your health. *Professional Psychology, 11,* 935–938.

Hartman, W.E., & Fithian, M.A. (1972). *Treatment of sexual dysfunction.* Long Beach, CA: Center for Marital and Sexual Studies.

Heiman, J., LoPiccolo, L., & LoPiccolo, J. (1981). The treatment of sexual dysfunction. In A. Gurman & D. Kniskern (Eds.), *Handbook of family therapy.* New York: Brunner/Mazel.

Heiman, J., & LoPiccolo, J. (1986). Historical and current factors discriminating sexually functional from sexually dysfunctional married couples. *Journal of Marital and Family Therapy, 12,* 163–174.

Heiman, J., & LoPiccolo, J. (1988). *Becoming orgasmic.* New York: Prentice-Hall.

Hellerstein, H., & Friedman, E. (1970). Sexual activity and the postcoronary patient. *Archives of Internal Medicine, 125,* 987–999.

Hill, R. (1980). Minnesota Council on Family Relations Annual Meeting, Minneapolis.

Hof, L. (1987). Evaluating the marital relationship of clients with sexual complaints. In G. Weeks & L. Hof (Eds.), *Integrating sex and marital therapy.* New York: Brunner/Mazel.

Hof, L., & Berman, E. (1986). The sexual genogram. *Journal of Marital & Family Therapy, 12* (1), 39–47.

Hof, L., & Miller, W.R. (1986). The sexual genogram. *Journal of Marital and Family Therapy, 12,* 239–247.

Hogan, D.R. (1978). The effectiveness of sex therapy: A review of the literature. In J. LoPiccolo & L. LoPiccolo (Eds.), *Handbook of sex therapy.* New York: Plenum.

Hoon, E.F., Hoon, P.W., & Wincze, J. (1976). The SAT: An Inventory for the measurement of female sexual arousal. *Archives of Sexual Behavior, 5,* 208–215.

Humphrey, F. (1986). Treating extramarital sexual relationships in sex and couples therapy. In G. Weeks & L. Hof (Eds.), *Integrating sex and marital therapy.* New York: Brunner/Mazel.

Hyde, J.H. (1979). *Understanding human sexuality.* New York: McGraw-Hill.

Justice, R. (1978). Evaluating outcome of group therapy for abusing parents. *Corrective & Social Psychiatry & Journal of Applied Behavior Therapy, 24* (1), 45–49.

Kantner, J.F., & Zelnik, M. (1973). Contraception and pregnancy: Experience of young unmarried women in United States. *Family Planning Perspectives, 5* (1), 21–35.

Kaplan, H. (1974). *The new sex therapy.* New York: Brunner/Mazel.

Kaplan, H. (1979). *Disorders of sexual desire.* New York: Brunner/Mazel.

Kasl, C. (1989). *Women, sex and addiction.* New York: Picknor & Fields.

Kempton, W. (1978). Sex education for the mentally handicapped. *Sexuality & Disability, 1* (2), 137–146.

Kinsey, A., Pomeroy, W., & Martin, C. (1948). *Sexual behavior in the human male.* Philadelphia: Saunders.

Kinsey, A.C., Pomeroy, W.B., Martin, C.E., & Gebhard, P.H. (1953). *Sexual behavior in the human female.* Philadelphia: Saunders.

Kolodny, R., Kahn, L., Goldstein, H., & Barnett, D. (1978). Sexual dysfunction in diabetic men. In A. Comfort (Ed.), *Sexual consequences of disability.* Philadelphia: Stickley.

L'Abate, L., & Frey, J. (1983). The E-R-A model: The role of feeling in family therapy reconsidered. In L.L. L'Abate (Ed.), *Family psychology: Theory, therapy, and training.* Washington, DC: University Press of America.

L'Abate, L., & Talmadge, W. (1987). Love, intimacy and sex. In G. Weeks & L. Hof (Eds.), *Integrating sex and marital therapy.* New York: Brunner/Mazel.

Laver, M. (1974). Sexual behavior patterns in male hypertensives. *Australia and New Zealand Journal of Medicine, 4*, 29–31.

Lazarus, A.A. (1965). The treatment of a sexually inadequate man. In L.P. Ullmann & L. Krasner (Eds.), *Case studies in behavior modification*. New York: Holt, Rinehart.

Lazarus, A.A. (1968). Behavior therapy in groups. In G.M. Gazda (Ed.), *Basic approaches to group psychotherapy and group counseling*. Springfield, IL: Thomas.

Levin, R. (1988). *Heartmates*. New York: Simon & Schuster.

Locke, H.J., & Wallace, K.M. (1959). Short marital adjustment and prediction tests: Their reliability and validity. *Marriage and Family Living, 21*, 251–255.

LoPiccolo, J. (1977). From psychotherapy to sex therapy. *Society, 14* (5), 60–68.

LoPiccolo, J. & Lobitz, W.C. (1972). Behavior therapy of sexual dysfunction. In L.A. Hamerlynch, L.C. Handy, & E.J. Mash (Eds.), *Behavior change: Methodology, concepts, and practice*. Champaign, IL.: Research Press.

LoPiccolo, J., & LoPiccolo, L. (Eds.) (1978). *Handbook of sex therapy*. New York: Plenum.

LoPiccolo, J. & Miller, V.H. (1975). Procedural outline for sexual enrichment groups. *Consulting Psychology, 5* (1), 46–49.

LoPiccolo, J., & Steger, J.C. (1974). The sexual interaction inventory: A new instrument for assessment of sexual dysfunction. *Archives of Sexual Behavior, 3*, 585–595.

LoPiccolo, L. (1980). Low sexual desire. In S. Leiblum & L. Pervin (Eds.), *Principles and practice of sex therapy*. New York: Guilford.

LoPiccolo, L., & Heiman, J. (1978). Sexual assessment and history interview. In L. LoPiccolo & J. LoPiccolo (Eds.), *Handbook of sex therapy*. New York: Plenum Press.

Luepnitz, D. (1988). *The family interpreted*. New York: Basic Books.

Mackey, F. (1978). Sexuality and heart disease. In A. Comfot (Ed.), *Sexual consequences of disability*. Philadelphia: Stickley.

Mason, M. (1980). The role of the female co-therapist in the male sex offenders group. In R. Forleo & W. Pacini (Eds.), *Medical sexology*. Littleton, MA: PSG.

Mason, M. (1984). From bodies to beings: Sexuality and spirituality. *Focus on Family*, May/June, 5–6.

Masters, W., & Johnson, V. (1970). *Human sexual inadequacy*. Boston: Little, Brown.

Masters, W., Johnson, V., & Kolodny, R. (1986). *On sex and human loving*. Boston: Little, Brown.

Mathews, A., Bancroft, J., Whitehead, A., Hackman, A., Julier, D., Bancroft, J., Gath, D., & Shaw, P. (1976). The behavioral treatment of sexual inadequacy: A comparative study. *Behavior Research and Therapy, 14*, 427–436.

McGoldrick, M., & Gerson, R. (1985). *Genograms in family assessment*. New York: Norton.

Meiselman, K. (1978). *Incest*. San Francisco: Jossey-Bass.

Miller, S., Nunnally, E., & Wackman, D. (1976). Communication training program for couples. *Social Casework, 5* (1), 9–18.

Mooney, T., Cole, T., & Chilgren, R. (1975). *Sexual options for paraplegics and quadriplegics*. Boston: Little, Brown.

Muney, J. (1981). The future of sex and gender. *Journal of Clinical Psychology, 9* (2), 132–133.

Nadelson, C.C. (1982). A follow-up study of rape victims. *American Journal of Psychiatry, 139*, 1266–1270.

Nelson, J. (1983). *Between two gardens*. New York: Pilgrim Press.

Nelson, J. (1988). *The intimate connection*. New York: Westminster Press.

Offit, A. (1977). *The sexual self*. Philadelphia: Lippincott.

Pincus, J., Swenson, N., & Poor, B. (1984). Pregnancy. In Boston Women's Health Book Collective (Eds.), *The new our bodies, ourselves*. New York: Simon & Schuster.

Pinhaus, V. (1980). An investigation to compare the degree to which alcoholic and non-alcoholic women report sex guilt and sexual control. In R. Forleo & W. Pacini (Eds.), *Medical sexology*. Littleton, MA: PSG.

Pittman, F. (1989). *Private lies: Infidelity and the betrayal of intimacy*. New York: Norton.

Prochaska, J., & Marzill, R. (1973). Modifications of Masters & Johnson approach to sexual problems. *Psychotherapy Theory, Research & Practice, 10* (4), 294–296.

Renshaw, D. (1978). Stroke and sex. In A. Comfort (Ed.), *Sexual consequences of disability*. Philadelphia: Stickley.

Robinson, B., Skeen, P., & Walters, L. (1987). The AIDS epidemic hits home. *Psychology Today, 21*, (4), 48–52.

Sager, C.J. (1976). *Marriage contracts and couple therapy*. New York: Brunner/Mazel.

Salter, A. (1949). *Conditioned reflex therapy*. New York: Creative Age Press.

Schneidman, B., & McGuire, L. (1976). Group therapy for non-orgasmic women: Two age levels. *Archives of Sexual Behaviors, 5* (3), 239–242.

Schover, L.R., & LoPiccolo, J. (1982). Treatment effectiveness for dysfunctions of sexual desire. *Journal of Sex and Marital Therapy, 8*, 179–197.

Semans, J.H. (1956). Premature ejaculation: A new approach. *Southern Medical Journal, 49*, 353–357.

Serber, M. (1974). Videotape feedback in treatment of couples with sexual dysfunction. *Archives of Sexual Behavior, 3* (4). 377–380.

Stuart, R. (1980). *Helping couples change*. New York: Guilford Press.

Tannehill, R. (1980). *Sex in history*. New York: Stein & Day.

Trieschmann, R. (1988). *Spinal cord injuries: Psychological, social & vocational rehabilitation*. New York: Demas.

Walters, M., Carter, B., Papp, P., & Silverstein, O. (1988). *The invisible web*. New York: Guilford Press.

Ward-McKinlay, C. (1983). Sexuality and the disabled. In W. Hansen, J. Woody, & R. Woody (Eds.), *Sexual issues in family therapy*. Rockville, MD: Aspen.

Watzlawick, P., Weakland, J., & Fisch, R. (1974). *Change: Principles of problem formation and problem resolution*. New York: Norton.

Weeks, G. (1987). Systematic treatment of inhibited sexual desire. In G. Weeks & L. Hof (Eds.), *Integrating sex and marital therapy*. New York: Brunner/Mazel.

Wolpe, J. (1958). *Psychotherapy by reciprocal inhibition*. Stanford, CA: Stanford University Press.

Wolpe, J. (1969). *The practice of behavior therapy*. New York: Pergamon.

Woody, J., & Woody, R. (Eds.) (1983). *Sexual issues in family therapy*. Rockville, MD: Aspen.

Wynne, L. (1986). The quest for intimacy. *Journal of Marriage & Family Therapy, 12* (4), 383–394.

Ziebergeld, B. (1978). *Male sexuality*. Boston: Little, Brown.

CHAPTER 16

Treating Divorce in Family-Therapy Practice

Craig A. Everett, Ph.D.,
and Sandra S. Volgy, Ph.D.

The specter of divorce has become an ever-present phenomenon for the American family. Therapists encounter divorce-related clinical issues across a broad range of practices and settings. Similarly, the likelihood that a majority of adults and children will have to deal with the outcome of divorce at some point in their lives is statistically great. Current estimates suggest that nearly 50 percent of all new marriages will end in divorce (U.S. Bureau of the Census, 1984), and that divorce will affect nearly one third of the minor children in this country (Bane, 1979). Other data indicate that 83 percent of these post-divorce single-parent families are headed by women (U.S. Bureau of the Census, 1980) and that these women will become proportionately higher consumers of clinical services (Guttentag, Salasin, & Belle, 1980). It has also been reported that divorce increases the probability of suicide among both males and females (Stack, 1980; Wasserman, 1984). Numerous studies have identified the role of divorce in producing both

adjustment and behavioral problems in children (Hetherington, Cox, & Cox, 1979; Kelly & Wallerstein, 1976, 1977; Wallerstein & Kelly, 1976, 1977, 1980) while Kalter and Rembar (1981) have reported that these children of divorce represent 40 percent of children utilizing the services of mental health clinics.

This prevalence of family dissolution is reflected in recent clinically related literature that has suggested that theoretically the divorce experience should now be viewed as an expectable and normative transitional crisis in our understanding of family-life development (Ahrons & Rodgers, 1987; Kaslow & Schwartz, 1987) rather than as an unpredictable, abnormal crisis for individuals.[1]

With this prevalence of divorce phenomena,

---

[1] *Editors' Note.* Of course, in an increasingly conservative political climate, which we seem to be entering as this *Handbook* goes to press, divorce may, once again, come to be seen as relatively (more) "abnormal."

all clinicians, whether they work predominantly with adults or with children, with couples or with families, will have to learn to treat those who have been affected by the dissolution of their family and its attendant difficulties. The family-therapy field, however, has only touched the surface of understanding the broad impact of divorce across multigenerational family systems. With the limited empirical data available, we cannot yet discern the variety of interactive patterns that occur in the divorce experience to exacerbate and/or create clinical phenomena that appear in presenting clinical syndromes among both individuals and the family system in general.

For example, a family therapist may have difficulty differentiating clinical depression in an individual family member as an expression of object loss and postdivorce adjustment from a syndrome based on endogenous preconditions that were exacerbated specifically by the divorce experience. Or more profoundly, the predivorce depression may be tied to the underlying organizational dysfunctions of the multigenerational system itself, of which divorce was merely a symbolic indicator.

The questions regarding the type of clinical services needed by divorcing clientele and the range of skills and resources required by clinicians to provide these services remain prominent and largely unanswered. In fact, it was tempting simply to entitle this chapter a "Survey of Divorce Therapy" and proceed with reporting an overview of a broad range of associated descriptive and clinical literature. However, we believe that the clinical process of working with divorce requires a systemic reconceptualization that involves both theoretical clarity and therapeutic preparation and resources. Unfortunately, the designation of "divorce therapy" has become something of a nondescript, catch-all category for a variety of clinical interventions and services, which makes the organization of this material a formidable task.

It appears that many clinicians involve themselves in different stages of the divorce process, often with very little awareness of the broad chronology of events, systemic ramifications, criteria for effective restructuring, the nature of transitional crises, or the crucial interface with legal and economic systems engendered by this process. Therapists working in marital therapy may see clients just as they are making a decision to separate or divorce. They will often decide to discontinue conjoint therapy with the spouses as divorce approaches, in favor of working with only one spouse, or perhaps with both spouses individually, to deal with postdivorce adjustment. Other therapists may see only a child who has become depressed or who has begun acting out in school six months after a divorce, without ever involving the parents or inquiring into predivorce clinical patterns and postdivorce attachments. The continuity of the experience for the family as a whole is often lost in the therapist's lack of training and experience in treating this unique family crisis, which can greatly impede the family's progress in its restructuring tasks.

Therapists may also be involved in offering specific divorce-related services, such as mediation or custody evaluations, at certain stages of the divorce process. Others may work with postdivorce blended families, often without ever involving or even assessing the roles of the other natural parent or members of the intergenerational system, such as grandparents. Thus, many clinicians intervene into the divorcing family's life at a singular point in the ongoing process. Few clinicians work with divorcing families from preseparation ambivalence through custody and access planning to postdivorce restructuring into remarriage and stepparenting issues.

It is our position that "divorce therapy" is *not* a discrete or independent clinical discipline, nor is it represented by a clear body of clinical knowledge or specific techniques. Rather, the clinician's role in working with the experiences and outcomes of the divorce process can best be reconceptualized as a stage or task within the broader practice of systemic family therapy.[2] However, what is unavailable to the family therapist at this point is an organized and coherent framework within which to view the family's "everyday" movement through the dissolution process. Such a framework would provide the therapist with a resource to clarify assessment

---

[2] *Editors' Note.* In an era in which every aspect of, or problem in, everyday life seems to have a method, or even a "school," of psychotherapy named after it, it is refreshing to see the authors resist the inevitable temptation to divide up arbitrarily the ecology and fluidity of family experience. We hope others will emulate such a model of rational self-restraint.

and evaluation and to evolve appropriate treatment goals and strategies.

This chapter will offer such a framework. We will consider the systemic interface of certain aspects of the divorce process with the role and resources of the family therapist. The goal of this chapter is to enable the clinician to understand the most salient ingredients of the dissolution process and, therefore, to be able to develop more effective clinical strategies no matter what the presenting circumstances or where in the continuum of the divorce process the family seeks assistance.

DEFINING THE FIELD

As family therapists, it is curious to us that with the substantial growth of family therapy over the prior two decades, the field has not identified significantly the pervasive and critical role that divorce can play in the type of problems presented and the clients who typically present themselves for family treatment. It would be hard to imagine family therapists in any practice or clinical setting for whom the process or outcome of divorce has not affected in some manner a very large proportion of their clients (it is the authors' guess that divorce could affect as high as 70–80 percent of a family therapist's clientele). It is also true that no other discipline, whether it be psychiatry, social work, or psychology, has claimed theoretical or clinical expertise in working with the divorce process.

Although clinicians in many urban settings have identified and marketed themselves as "divorce therapists," it is not clear to the public or to other professionals what services are actually being provided. There are various possibilities: perhaps these therapists will help one avoid the pain of divorce; perhaps they are the only ones willing to wade into the morass of anger and resentment typical of divorcing families; perhaps they possess some special knowledge or training to serve this population better; or perhaps it is simply a marketing ploy to gain more clients for their practice.

We are not aware of any graduate programs, or even postgraduate training centers, that offer specialized or focused training in divorce or "divorce therapy." There do not appear to be any

legislative sanctions in the form of licensure or certification of "divorce therapists." There are certainly courses on working with divorce or "divorce therapy," particularly those offered through programs accredited by the American Association for Marriage and Family Therapy, but probably few exist in traditional clinical-degree curricula.

Some reports in the literature, of course, have attempted to describe issues of "divorce therapy" (e.g., Fisher, 1973, 1974; Brown, 1976; Kressel & Deutsch, 1977; Wallerstein & Kelly, 1977; Kaslow, 1981; Kressel, 1985). Most of this literature, however, does not offer a conceptual clinical framework, nor does it address issues of clinical education and training. Gurman and Kniskern (1978) and Sprenkle and Storm (1983) have reviewed research on the outcomes of divorce therapy but, because of the limited literature available, focus more on comparative and adjunctive matters, such as the practice settings (e.g., conciliation courts), comparative interventions (e.g., groups or services for children), or the role of divorce mediation.

Thus, there appears to be little basis at this time in either the literature or practice to support "divorce therapy" as either a discernible field of practice or as an identifiable body of applied techniques. Of course, this observation addresses explicitly the clinical field and is not intended as a critique of the growing body of literature on divorce that encompasses interdisciplinary studies from sociology, psychology, economics, dispute resolution, and family law (see, for example, the *Journal of Divorce* and the *Journal of Marriage and the Family*).

Perhaps divorce therapy can better be understood not as a distinct discipline or group of techniques, but as a symbolic arena or therapeutic stance in which clinicians have gained knowledge and experience regarding the divorce process and can offer the therapeutic service of shepherding families through the often excruciating experiences of emotional losses, disappointments, and anger that attend the divorce experience.

A secondary but critical question arises with regard to the knowledge and experience useful or necessary to provide adequate training for clinicians working with divorce. There is no literature or any certifying professional organization that has begun to specify criteria regarding either curricula or clinical education for therapists who wish to work with the divorce process, although progress in this direction has been made in the divorce-mediation field.

It is of significant concern that clinicians will practice in areas of divorce-related treatment even though they may be unaware of the complexity of emotional, clinical, and legal issues involved in such treatment. Their naïveté and/or lack of training and experience may potentially do damage to their clients as well as place themselves in both personal and legal jeopardy.[3] It is our observation, with over 30 years of clinical experience between us in working with divorcing families, that the divorce process represents perhaps the most traumatic and far-reaching of transitional events in human experience. Indeed, we would further suggest that divorce carries more incipient and potentially damaging outcomes to human development, personal adjustment, and the continuity of interactional patterns and loyalties than even the experience of the death of a loved one.

While divorce dramatizes the elements of loss and grief (Crosby, Gage, & Raymond, 1983), just as does the experience of death in a close relationship, it occurs not around the explicit loss of an object, but results in the less discernible yet untenable sense of loss around patterns of attachment, interpersonal and structural security, familial identification and bonding, loyalties, and the future of the family experience. All of these issues arise when the actual objects are still present but seemingly unreachable and unavailable in ways that were once comfortable and familiar. Thus, the family members must carry with them the sense of loss while still in the presence of that loving, or formerly loving, object.

Similarly, the ramifications of divorce spread through multiple generational levels of the family as well as the family's social and economic networks. The event of death typically has the influence of increasing support, aid, and even loyalties across family generations and social networks. However, the process of divorce more typically destroys family and cross-generational ties as well as social-network involvements.

In fact, the divorce process, when played out in the adversarial milieu of the legal and judicial systems, turns former lovers and parents into enemies and warriors, and this hostility often spreads to grandparents and other family-network members. Over the years, the most destructive and vengeful custody disputes that we have been involved with professionally have had grandparents or other family members playing economic or emotionally provocative roles in the background. These warring intergenerational factions are often so polarized by the adversarial legal process that children of divorce can end up losing both the stability of their nuclear family and the combined historical continuity of the generations of both families of origin.[4]

A SYSTEMIC CONCEPTUALIZATION OF THE DIVORCE PROCESS

Most theoretical treatments, as well as empirical studies, of the divorce process focus either on the breakup of the marriage, the postdivorce adjustment of the children, or the subsequent reorganization in stepfamilies. These works typically fail to place the divorce experience within the broader developmental life of the family or within the actual interactive process of the family itself. For example, a study may report on the postdivorce adjustment of male children ages 6 and 10 without looking at their relative adjustment in the parent–child subsystem or sibling subsystem prior to the divorce. It may even fail to ask questions about the levels of marital and parental adjustment pre- and postdivorce for the parents. Additional systemic assessment components familiar to the family therapist, such as scapegoating, parentification, and other triangulation patterns within the predivorce system,

---

[3] *Editors' Note.* The authors may appear here to be contradicting their earlier position that divorce therapy is not an "independent clinical discipline" with "a clear body of . . . knowledge or specific techniques." What the authors seem to be pointing to, albeit implicitly, is the all-too-common trend of deriving a *general* theory of human behavior from a *clinical* theory of how to induce change, a trend with which they obviously disagree.

[4] *Editors' Note.* After reading this rich phenomenological outline of several of the major parameters of the complex divorce *process*, we hope that no epidemiologist will ever again refer to divorce as an "event."

are typically ignored, as are intergenerational components that have exacerbated or lessened the impact of the divorce adjustment.

In other words, the clinical literature still persists in examining the smallest possible unit of study without recognizing either broader systemic variables or the ongoing life of the family system. We believe that it is no longer defensible to continue to describe the experiences associated with the event of divorce in terms of individual or even dyadic matters. Divorce occurs as an event in the ongoing history of the family and results in a transitional life crisis, with the potential for both acute and chronic outcomes that will influence individual members, intergenerational and social-network systems, and even unborn members of the new generation of the family. It involves a reorganization of enormous magnitude for the entire family system.

As family therapists, it would seem that our systemic orientation would provide us with enormous resources for understanding the divorce process. The life of a family system is ongoing. It certainly does not cease when an adolescent leaves home to go to college, nor does it cease when a parent dies. In fact, these experiences often serve to enhance family cohesiveness and bonding. In working with the divorce process in family therapy, we can no longer focus solely on the ending of relationships and the adjustment of the children without placing this event in the broader context of the system's life and history.

The family's experience of divorce is much like a pebble thrown into a moving stream, not into a pond that is quiet and self-contained. For a moment, the pebble creates circular ripples that spread out but are then quickly carried off by the current in contorted patterns downstream. The repercussions of the divorce interfere with the ongoing developmental processes and exacerbate embedded dysfunctional patterns of the family, which reverberate in dramatic fashion throughout the intergenerational system. The family will never regain its former contours of structure and organization but must flounder temporarily in order to develop new patterns that will move it toward an uncertain future.

There is an ample early literature that outlines a variety of models and stages descriptive of emotional aspects of the divorce process (e.g., Froiland & Hozman, 1977; Weiss, 1976; Kessler, 1975; Weisman, 1975; Bohannon, 1970). For the most part, these simply identify individual adjustment phenomena borrowed primarily from crisis and grief theory, such as denial, mourning, anger, and disillusionment.

Elsewhere, we have offered a brief model that attempted to capture clinical aspects of the divorce process for the family therapist (Everett & Volgy, 1983): structural decoupling, network coupling, and structural recoupling. The family system's experience of the divorce process can be described across these three stages. The intent of these stages is to identify components of the broad and expectable systemic process rather than simply issues of individual adjustment.

Maturana and Varela (1980) defined a process of "structural coupling" wherein parts of a newly developing system evolve into an organizational whole. This concept can be applied to a divorcing family system where stages of decoupling and network coupling must occur before recoupling produces a newly evolved, organized system. In other words, the family system moves through a period of dysfunction, with or without a display of overt conflict, in which members and their roles gradually disengage from one another. This *structural decoupling* involves the alteration of former roles, both spousal and parental, and the withdrawal of former loyalties to one another and to the system itself.

As this decoupling occurs, the members, both parents and children, begin a process of *network coupling* to establish or renew relationship ties in both the social and extended-family networks. Most individuals do not remain without an intimate social system for very long. Thus, as the loss of the former nuclear system becomes apparent, individuals begin to seek an entry into new systems. This process is ongoing and somewhat meta to the structural decoupling and recoupling tasks. It may be a slow and agonizing process, and is often typified by a parent and/ or subsystem of children relocating near or moving in with their own parents, at least until the transition into a new structure and organization is complete and stable.

The actual dissolution of a family system involves the loss of its former organization. Kee-ney (1982) has observed that it is the underlying organization of a family system that defines its viability and continuity. Thus, in divorce, the organization of the system is lost but, through a process of *structural recoupling*, the former par-ent–child subsystem must redefine and realign initially around issues of custody and parent–child access. This involves explicitly the inter-generational network with grandparents and other extended-family-of-origin members. Over time, recoupling provides a new structure of parents, children, grandparents, and others that will evolve into expectable patterns of interac-tion and circularity. Eventually, this new, quasi-system will face other challenges of integrating replacement spouses (remarriage) and interfac-ing with additional family organizations (step-families).

For the clinician, a family's movement across these stages is never expectably smooth or even predictable. Conflict and dysfunctional patterns may arise at any location throughout the process, and thus delay or even stop the progression. For example, families—parents and occasionally grandparents—that have continued warring in relitigation over custody or property years after the divorce itself was concluded may represent a failure to finalize decoupling. Such unfinished decoupling may lead to ineffective postdivorce recoupling, which effectively blocks the reor-ganization of the system.[5]

This descriptive systemic and developmental model will offer the family therapist a broader perspective of the actual clinical process for the family and aid in a more careful assessment that is not limited to typically observable issues of individual—adult or child—adjustment and be-havior. This perspective will also help in defin-ing for the clinician exactly what place in the ongoing process or around what specific event therapeutic or evaluative services have been re-

TABLE 16-1

Steps in the Divorce Process

1. Heightened ambivalence
2. Distancing
3. Preseparation fantasies and actions
4. Physical separation
5. Pseudoreconciliation
6. Predivorce fantasies
7. Decision to divorce
8. Recurring ambivalence
9a. The potential disputes—mediation
9b. The potential disputes—adversarial
10. Postdivorce coparenting
11. Remarriage
12. Blended-family formation
13. Second remarriage
14. Dual-family functioning

quested. In other words, the clinician need not enter a divorce-related case naïvely, with the risk of becoming unexpectedly snared in the conflict or inextricably trapped in the legal arena of litigation without sufficient resources for assistance.

In an effort to operationalize this continuum from structural decoupling to structural recou-pling, we have identified the major clinical, structural, and legal steps across the divorce pro-cess. These steps represent both issues that the family system must deal with and potential lo-cations for therapeutic intervention and tracking of the family's progress through the divorce ex-perience. Table 16-1 identifies these steps in a developmental sequence. The intervening stage of network coupling parallels these steps and, as we have indicated, continues meta to the on-going structural changes.

The clinician must recognize that in all di-vorce-related cases there exists a history of dys-functional systemic interaction patterns that contain the precursors to the onset of the dis-solution process. Whether these preconditions represent issues ranging from unconscious mate-selection patterns to the presence of depressive spouses, from terminally ill family-of-origin par-ents to scapegoated or parentified children, their presence is embedded in the system's dysfunc-tion and not only will follow, but often will ex-acerbate, the family's movement through the divorce process. Thus, it would be naïve for a family therapist to enter at any point of the di-vorce continuum without an awareness of the

---

[5] *Editors' Note.* We doubt that relitigation is always unde-sirable. Perhaps some unfinalized decouplings are healthy, for example, custodial parent becomes manic and unable to care for his or her children; custodial parent becomes ne-glectful, abusive, or alcoholic, etc. More subtle "healthy" decoupling failures (and relitigation) could include women who, after divorce, become more self-confident, assertive, less depressed, etc., and go back to court for a better deal (financially or custodially).

family's history that has brought it to its present circumstances.

Heightened Ambivalence

If it is possible to describe early-warning signs in the gradual erosion of marital and family relationships, it is around the evidence of ambivalence. All relationships contain certain levels of ambivalence. However, its increasing prominence becomes a clear clinical indicator in the gradual evolution of unsatisfactory and dysfunctional marital relationships. It is observed in increasing doubts about the relationship, in expressions of formerly unverbalized anger, or in fantasies of romantic involvements with others or of leaving the relationship or of the spouse dying or disappearing suddenly. There is always a period of fluctuation in which these feelings alternate between moments of dissatisfaction and the testing of limits, and periods of personal apprehension and renewed involvement with the partner. Generally, this is the period in which the children first become aware of problems between the parents that may have a different and more serious tone than previous problems. The instability and tension in the marital relationship create a sense of caution and dread in those children who are witness to the unpredictable nature of the relationship. They may absent themselves from their parents in order to stave off their own anxiety and to give their parents time to be alone to deal with their difficulties, or they may become more clinging and dependent to reassure themselves of their parents' continuing nurturance.

The therapist must understand such ambivalence both at the level of individual relationship dynamics and as expressed through both parent–child and intergenerational patterns. The therapist must then "read" these reciprocal patterns of ambivalence in order to assess effectively the relative commitment of all family members to the family system. Clinical interventions here may range from labeling the ambivalence to more indirectly or directly perturbing relationship patterns, in an effort to bring the ambivalence into the interactional and therapeutic context in a more focused manner. For example, in certain cases, we may simulate with spouses a mock funeral to dramatize their issues of separation and loss.

Distancing

The behavioral manifestation of heightened ambivalence is observed as family members begin to increase the emotional distance between themselves and spouses, children, or even family-of-origin members. Gradually, this involves the withdrawal of positive affect, which leads to emotional and physical unavailablity. It does not necessarily involve the withdrawal of anger or rage, which may continue at this stage as an indicator of the continuing attachment side of the ambivalence. Much of this is still contained within the nuclear-family system, except when it is acted out through extramarital affairs. The metaprocess of network coupling has not yet really begun. Children are usually aware of the distancing of the more ambivalent parent on a noncognitive level. They are confused by the mixed messages between and from the parents but are afraid to ask what is going on or why everything feels uncomfortable, cool, and tense. This is often a time when children may first ask parents if they are going to get a divorce, a question that usually shocks the parents and is answered with an emphatic, "No, of course not!" This is a response that the child may remember later with anger and mistrust of the parents and the honesty of their answers.

The therapist must recognize that intense conflict is symptomatic of this distancing experience, particularly in the marital relationship in which one spouse is subtly trying to gain some distance while the other spouse responds reciprocally to the unavailablity, and even undefined sense of loss, of the partner. Clinical interventions here need to identify the beginning expressions of homeostatic imbalance observed in even minor alterations in the complementarity of both spousal and parent–child roles.

Preseparation Fantasies and Actions

The metaprocess of network recoupling begins here in a subtle manner as spouses begin to imagine getting their needs met with other partners, of escaping through a return to their own families of origin, or even of living a freer, single life without the responsibilities of spouse, children, or career. Typically, one spouse moves much further beyond the ambivalence and into these fantasies than the other, thus creating further imbalance in the relationship. As these fantasies evolve into actual intentions or behaviors, they carry with them the excruciating experience of how to tell the spouse, one's children, and even one's parents of a decision to separate. In some cases, such an action may be postponed for years because of recurring ambivalence or personal apprehension of loss, anger, fear of failure, or of repercussions from throughout the intergenerational system.

The therapist must identify the growing imbalance within the family as one member begins to pull away and, for the first time, represents an overt threat to the future of the system. This will be responded to with alarm and resentment by the spouse and children, and perhaps across the intergenerational network. However, as one spouse disengages, his or her realignment with social or family ties may actually support the distancing and evolve into an alliance favoring a separation and divorce. The therapist must identify these underlying loyalties and potential efforts either to move away from the children or to engage them in damaging intergenerational alliances and coalitions. As spouses plan for a separation, the therapist will often function in an educative role, discussing issues of how to inform children, parents, and friends, as well as dealing with pragmatic matters of timing, structure, and expectations in planning the separation (see Greene, Lee, & Lustig, 1973; Granvold & Tarrant, 1983).

Physical Separation

The event of one parent moving out of the family household is perhaps the most dramatic and stunning of occurrences throughout the divorce process. Many couples, even those in therapy, precipitously and impulsively make decisions to separate after a major conflict. Most have not thought through issues of their own survival or of the repercussions for their children, family network or financial situation. For the children, this is the first event in the cycle of accepting the reality of their parents' divorce.

Even if separation has been discussed with them during a preliminary period, children typically deny its reality until the actual physical separation has been effected. At that point, they will have various reactions, depending on many factors: age, sex, developmental level, competence, stability, place and role in the family, tension/anger experienced in the family, and family-support systems available to them as resources. Often, the children will appear to be "in shock" and continue to deny that anything is different. Typically, this is the most traumatic time in the divorce process for children. Parents, and therapists, need to allow them to express feelings and to act out to some degree in order to vent their frustrations and fear.

The therapist in this situation must move first to gain some control and structure or the therapy will turn into menial negotiations and reactive threats regarding unplanned everyday issues. Ideally, a therapist working with a couple moving toward separation will have assisted the partners in planning their needs, arrangements, and continuation in therapy. A planned separation can become a constructive period in which to diffuse intense conflict and to test boundaries and personal independence. The therapist needs to clarify in each case that separation can become either a transitional period into divorce or a genuine experimental period to test decoupling and/or to work on dysfunctional issues.

The children should not be neglected therapeutically during this period. Providing information to parents on how to talk to the children, answer their questions, and respond to their fears is important. Identifying patterns of potential side-taking or manipulation of the children by the parents themselves or by grandparents is critical. After the separation and several weeks of experience with it, the children may be invited into therapy, either with the parents or separately in a sibling group. Here, parents can verbalize their intentions in a structured setting with somewhat less anxiety and volatility than at home. The children can pose their questions and express their fears in a context in which the therapist can help the parents to be clear and responsive. The family and/or sibling sessions may continue throughout the separation and into the divorce stage.

Pseudoreconciliation

Many families that have separated experience a sudden sense of loss and apprehension that they are simply not prepared to handle. It triggers their personal fears of being on their own or managing a household by themselves. They will feel a tugging in their gut regarding the absences from their children and guilt regarding a sense of abandonment of their parental responsibilities. Children will create circumstances, events, or problems to bring Mom and Dad back together. Often, they will struggle with a fear of abandonment or rejection by their own extended-family members or friends. The flooding of these feelings, particularly when considerable ambivalence regarding the relationship is present, will cause the former conflicts and problems to appear to be minor. Thus, "moving back in" will be greeted with relief, a new sense of security, and a period (perhaps only briefly homeostatic) of settled interactions. This period is especially difficult for children because it represents a wish fulfillment that encourages them to continue to deny that their parents have serious marital problems. When such a pseudoreconciliation occurs, it often will delay the acceptance of the reality of divorce and will make the hurt and disappointment of the subsequent separation more volatile and painful. For younger children, it will encourage their mechanisms of denial since, "if Mom and Dad got back together once, they can again." This will prevent the children from giving up their fantasy of future reconciliations. Depression in children of all ages is seen more typically after this pseudoreconciliation than following the initial physical separation.

The therapist must recognize that while such a reconciliation only camouflages the underlying dysfunctional patterns, it may also provide the timing and impetus of a transitional crisis to allow potentially second-order therapeutic gains. This event illustrates clearly why a therapist must explore carefully with clients whether they are ready for a separation while being careful never to be caught "recommending" such a decision because, if it fails, the power and ongoing role of the therapist will be diminished. Thus, the therapist must balance a variety of significant therapeutic issues during this stage: identifying the dysfunctional patterns in such a manner that the spouses can continue to recognize them while deciding whether they can deal with them at this point; struggling with a powerful collusion reactivated by fear of separation; managing dramatic interpersonal confusion between parents, children, and family-of-origin members regarding loyalties and the family's future; working through continuing and potentially heightened ambivalence among all system members; and, finally, realizing the potential for either therapeutic change or the discouragement and resultant anger because nothing is really different.

Predivorce Fantasies

For the family that is moving toward dissolution, the underlying conflicts will resurface following the reconciliation, whether it happens in two weeks or 12 months. When these conflicts reoccur, there is often a greater sense of disillusionment and failure related to the fact that trying again has not worked. Here, the spouses, one or both, begin to imagine and plan separate lives and to discuss the possibility of divorce more openly with friends and family-of-origin members. This can create intense reactivity and resentment that will spread throughout the system. For the children, this disillusionment may be observed in expressions of extreme anger and in acting-out behavior directed toward both parents as it becomes clear that the attempted reconciliation is not working. Efforts to diffuse or divert the parents from their marital conflicts may be reflected in the children's behavior as school phobias, academic or behavioral problems, somatic complaints, regressive dependency, or increased sibling rivalry and conflict.

The therapist's role here is to contain the reactivity, assist the family in identifying and working it through, deal with the increasingly unbalanced system, and prepare the family as a whole for the decision to divorce. The therapist must pay particular attention to feelings of rage and depression expressed by both the parents and the children.

Decision to Divorce

As one or both spouses move toward this decision, the probability of returning to earlier stages or therapeutically salvaging the system diminishes. The reality of this decision implies a sense of finality that can be deadening. It also dissolves the prior collusive bonds of the marital relationship that have afforded the couple some underlying protection even in the midst of conflict. Here, the spouses are "on their own," allowing the rage and vengeance associated with intense disappointments and even primitive lost objects to emerge. It is at this point that attorneys are often involved and retaliatory threats regarding custody and property emerge. This is the stage at which the children are most clearly at risk for long-term emotional damage as a result of the behavior of their parents. They may experience their parents as strangers and feel a loss of control over their environment. Their attention begins to wander at school and at home, anger is prevalent, and feelings of comfort and stability are often fleeting. The parents may become so engaged in their own emotional whirlwind that they cannot or will not see the pain and stress experienced by their children as a result of their often immature, manipulative, and irresponsible behavior toward each other. The more the children are made the battleground for competition and retaliation, the greater is the potential for emotional damage.

Therapists working with divorcing couples must have a network of family-law attorneys with which to consult and to whom they may refer. It is at this point that the divorce process begins to move into a new domain, with rules and behaviors unfamiliar to the therapist. The therapist's association with the legal community should identify attorneys who not only are skilled in family law, but who also can remove family and divorce matters from the typical adversarial milieu and respect both the rights of clients to mediate and be conciliatory and the role and skills of the family therapist (see, for example, Steinberg, 1980, 1985).

The therapist will assist the couple in planning for the divorce; explain what to expect when the couple meets with an attorney; make separate referrals of each spouse to known attorneys (unless at an early stage the therapist knows an attorney who will meet informally with both spouses, simply to review with them the legal aspects of divorce); identify the continuing role of family therapy with them, their children, and extended networks as they move through this process; and refer to an experienced divorce mediator if the therapist is not trained explicitly in this area. It is often helpful here to include some sibling and/or individual play therapy for the children to assist them in ventilating their anger, coping with and understanding the complexities of their parents' decisions and behaviors, and learning emotional survival skills to "inoculate" them against the unintended destructiveness of their parents' behavior.

Recurring Ambivalence

This period parallels the pseudoreconciliation following the initial separation and reflects the same issues of uncertainty exacerbated by a new dose of legal reality. It also provides another viable therapeutic window for renewing work on systemic problems. We will often refer clients at the predivorce and divorce stages who are displaying considerable continuing ambivalence to attorneys whom we know will not escalate the clients' state into an adversarial war. This perturbs the continuing relationship ambivalence as well as focuses on issues of loyalty and collusion, so that the forced realities help the couple clarify a direction. The effect on the children of this recurring ambivalence stage is to continue to ignite the wish for parental reconciliation and a return to "normality" as the child perceived the preseparation state. The more children are aware of the ambivalence of their parents, or of either parent, the greater will be their belief that a divorce will not occur and that the parents will reconcile. This state of "limbo" for the child increases anxiety significantly, and the longer it is prolonged, the more likely there will be postdivorce adjustment difficulties.

The therapist's role first is to identify the reemerging ambivalence and bring it into the open so that it becomes accessible to the couple. Second, the therapist must identify potential intergenerational influences that may underlie and trigger the recurring ambivalence. Such factors as parental encouragement or denial of the decision to divorce can be powerful and can sabotage the therapeutic process if they remain unrecognized by the therapist. The therapist's role here may also be to slow the momentum toward divorce somewhat, not in a last-ditch effort to salvage the relationship, but to allow the family members to deal with and work through unspoken issues and disappointments. The therapist needs to assist the parents in not discussing their ambivalence with the children, something parents are prone to do out of the guilt they feel for the disruption in the family. The therapist must also develop strategies for helping the children cope with the increased anxiety that results from confusion and unpredictability in their environment. Such unresolved issues can plague postdivorce families for years in the form of unnecessary emotional resentment and equally unnecessary litigation. The therapist should be aware that a certain proportion of clients at this stage will discontinue the divorce process and renew efforts to gain second-order change in their system.

The Potential Disputes

Mediation

Many divorcing families, particularly those that have arrived at the decision to divorce with similar timing, are able to utilize continuing therapy, and specifically divorce mediation, to work out a self-determined dissolution agreement that may specify everything from custody and parental access to division of estates and pots and pans (see, for example, Everett, 1985; Milne, 1978, 1983). Clearly, the children, as well as the entire family system, are the beneficiaries here. Parents know the needs and circumstances of their children much more intimately than do attorneys or judges. No parents in our experience who have fought each other through the adversarial judicial system can walk away with continuing respect and trust for each other. In most cases, the results are years of distrust and animosity in which the children and finances are utilized in covert or overt power struggles or simply in retaliation for the humiliation engendered by the legal process.

The family therapist has an excellent opportunity and vantage point from which to assist families through this process in a therapeutic structure with a degree of preserved respect and self-determination. We have long advocated adjunctive mediation training for family therapists who, by virtue of their prior education and train-

ing, have considerable resources for both family behavior and conflict management. However, we also caution therapists not to attempt to provide such services without explicit training.

The divorce mediator plays a role in a gray area between the therapeutic and legal arenas, and the potential pitfalls for those who are ignorant or naïve can be devastating to both clients and therapists. The best choice for family therapists is to locate seasoned divorce mediators in their community to whom they can refer divorcing clients and who will respect the therapist's continued therapeutic role with the family. There are, of course, a variety of factors intrinsic to each couple and the couple's legal situation that may indicate the potential for a successful outcome to mediation. These relative indications and contraindications are discussed in the divorce-mediation literature (Irving, 1980; Kressel, 1985; Sprenkle & Storm, 1983).[6]

Adversarial

This alternative route for families through the divorce process is played out clearly within the legal/judicial arena. While we are clearly advocates of mediation, we also recognize that some disputes, for both personal and situational reasons, cannot be worked through therapeutically or mediated successfully. Thus, the role of the adversarial judicial system may be necessary in certain limited circumstances. However, it is our experience that most divorce-related litigation is a result not of genuinely unresolvable disputes, but either of personal pain and often primitive disappointments that result in retaliation or of litigious attorneys who offer their clients grandiose hopes in return for monetary gain or control over the other party. Parents and

---

[6] *Editors' Note.* Sprenkle and Storm (1983) reviewed treatment research on the matter and concluded that *ideal* candidates were those "mediating around a limited number of issues, for whom the level of conflict is moderate, and . . . both spouses feel able to represent themselves in the negotiations. Both accept the divorce and have begun the process of 'letting go.' The mediation occurs early in the dissolution process and before receiving court orders . . . no third parties involved significantly in the dispute. Both parties sense some ability to . . . cooperate with the other. Money is not a major issue . . . and there are adequate resources to carry on as a single person. Finally, the attorneys support the mediation process" (p. 250).

attorneys ignore the potential damage to children and even the loss of the parents' self-respect when they are motivated by pain and revenge. In most cases—except, of course, where there are concerns regarding neglect or abuse—litigation can never be rationalized as in the "best interest of the child." In fact, the emotional intensity that evolves from most divorce litigation often leads family members to lose sight of the explicit issues in dispute.

The therapist has little power, and few resources to provide guidance along this track of the divorce process and faces great potential vulnerability. However, the therapist must develop working relationships with attorneys and the court. Many therapists find the adversarial litigious process so distasteful that they withdraw from active cases at this stage or simply avoid such potential cases altogether. Often, the therapist must be an advocate for the emotional health and functioning of the family in the context of the legal proceedings. This may take the form of identifying emotional vulnerabilities or special needs of family members. It may involve setting firm boundaries with attorneys regarding one's therapeutic and ethical role with a family, or working with both attorneys and judges as a "friend of the court" in recommending postdivorce resources for a family.

In terms of the provision of ongoing therapy, most spouses who are engaged in an adversarial battle are not going to pursue therapy with each other.[7] Even if one could talk the couple into such a pursuit, either spouse or either attorney could easily sabotage the process if he or she were not happy with it. The therapist who agrees to see one spouse individually while the couple is involved in the litigation stage of the divorce process may be able to work on some adjustment issues, but must be very clear at the onset with the client and the attorney in defining his or her position regarding any expected role in litigation. Of course, even clarifying this role does not protect one from the ever-present threat of subpoena.

Some therapists are willing to play the part of an expert witness or custody evaluator during this stage. This is a role that can be useful to attorneys and the court, but, as we have stated elsewhere (Everett & Volgy, 1983), we question both the reliability of such data and the ethical position of therapists, particularly family therapists, who perform such services without requiring stipulations that they have access to all members of the family system. Therapists who have performed such roles by offering evaluations of only one component or member of the family system have rightfully acquired the image of "hired guns." The most viable expert role for a family therapist is to offer an objective assessment of the entire family system, which would involve clinical access to all members, including grandparents and prospective mates. Such an evaluation allows the therapist to address for the court the overall resources and needs of the family, even across several generations, rather than the special interests or adversarial intentions of one party. This role maintains the integrity of the family therapist as serving the family system rather than becoming another pawn in the adversarial process.

Postdivorce Coparenting

The early stages of structural recoupling begin during the final separation when parents, children, and extended-family members struggle to define some basis for interaction and access. Where the separation has occurred impulsively, without therapeutic or legal assistance, these patterns are typically random and lacking in continuity. Following the divorce decree, the "game" of learning to be parents and no longer spouses becomes real. It is a time of uncertainty on everyone's part, involving not only the definition of a new postdivorce parenting structure, but also aspects of personal adjustment and dramatic network recoupling. The children's experience is that of chaos, anger, confusion, bargaining, and alternating periods of depression and beginning adjustment to the two new nuclear-family structures—Mom's and Dad's. The fantasy of reconciliation is still present, but it is being pressed to give way to the reality of the finality of the divorce. The children's adjustment during this period will be linked directly to both the personal postdivorce ad-

---

[7] *Editors' Note.* Except, at times, regarding parenting issues. Rice and Rice (1985) consider in detail the clinical complexities and strategies involved in the therapist's maintaining postseparation alliances with each divorcing spouse.

justment of each parent and their abilities to continue to work with each other as parents. This will be evidenced especially in the parents' ability to let go of their hostility and recriminations and begin to put the children's emotional needs before their own needs to continue their former marital struggles.

Many adult members of postdivorce families enter therapy at this stage either for themselves individually or for their children. While some issues are identified around personal adjustment and resocialization as a single adult, many concerns are focused on the adjustment of the children. These issues often carry an implication that the other parent is not behaving, either personally or parentally, according to the expectations of this parent. The therapist must be very careful here not to become caught in lingering divorce resentments by siding with the presenting client. This can only add unnecessary fuel to a potentially inflammatory struggle.

Following a divorce, it is common for therapy to be offered primarily on an individual basis to the respective postdivorce spouses or the children. However, as family therapists, we would never expect clinical issues to be singularly attached to the behavior of one parent or one child, but rather to be shared reciprocally throughout the system (though one must always keep an eye open for the exception that may represent the potential for abuse, neglect, or destructive use of children in retaliation). Certain levels of emotional support, of course, may be made available in individual sessions. However, for the therapist to attempt serious problem solving regarding dysfunctional behaviors throughout the family system, he or she must seek access to the children, the former spouse, and other extended-family members in order to clarify and diffuse early reactivity.

In many cases, the issues here are not the children but latent or explicit issues of control or retaliation. Family therapy at this stage in the divorce process can be crucial in assisting a family to make a constructive start at structural recoupling. A failure to look beyond the presenting issue to the underlying relationship dynamics can be damaging to the postdivorce adjustment of the family and render the therapist impotent. The parents' need continually to focus on the adjustment issues of the children not only increases the children's sense of guilt

and rage during this period, but also serves to camouflage the left-over relationship issues of the spouses as well as the basic matters of structural recoupling. The degree of continuing antagonism between former spouses during this stage is indicative of a delayed process in what we have described as structural decoupling. It is characterized by the spouses' inability to achieve separation and closure, and is further exacerbated when the spouses experience only limited success in the process of network coupling.

Remarriage

The movement of the first of the former spouses toward remarriage can produce a systemic crisis of cataclysmic proportions. No matter how much stability has been achieved in structural recoupling or how much time has elapsed since the divorce, this event can perturb a dramatic homeostatic imbalance across the dual systems. This seems to occur whether the event takes place six months or six years after the divorce. The entry of a new "player" into the family drama threatens a recoupling system that is, at best, precariously balanced. It can dramatically rekindle latent ambivalence for the other former spouse, who perhaps shared with the children a secret fantasy that the family one day would reunite. It can trigger more primitive issues of early object loss. It can involve grandparents or other extended-family members, who fear that a new "parent" might deprive them of access to the children. It is a signal to the children that their fantasy of reconciliation may have to be given up for all time, and this creates a tremendous resurgence of anger toward both parents, but particularly the less ambivalent spouse, and toward the new player. It often results in alliances or coalitions with the parent who remains "faithful" to the former family. This may lead to the children's refusal to spend time with the other parent.

The therapist must deal with the systemic imbalance and repercussions here as well as be aware of potential rekindling of the legal process (see Kvanli & Jennings, 1986; Sager et al., 1983). A large proportion of postdivorce cases that are referred to us for mediation arise within this stage. Typically, one of the parents, usually the one not entering remarriage, seeks an attorney to reopen litigation. The intent of this action is, at one level, to gain more control through modification of custody, and at the other level, to retaliate for the perceived abandonment. Often, the grandparents are willing to join in and finance this potential litigation. This experience can become even more unpleasant than the actual divorce proceedings. Here, charges of neglect, physical or sexual abuse, and character defamation are thrown back and forth between the parents and directed at the new "parent." This period represents a serious crisis for children and therapeutic intervention is crucial in helping a child understand the contradictory emotions and raging internal anger and hurt that may be present. A therapist who has expertise in treating young children may be necessary to assist with this delicate crisis that could have lifelong repercussions for the child if handled poorly. We have found that concurrent roles of continuing family therapy *and* mediation can be the most productive in preventing escalation toward involving the court. Either of these roles at this stage will require the confidence of control and conflict management because, at some point (and timing is very important), all parties will need to be seen together (i.e., in the same room) in order successfully to diffuse the reactivity and fantasies, and to begin to reconstruct a workable recoupling that integrates this new parent.

Blended-Family Formation

The entry of even just one new parent into this recoupling system creates a new structural shape with associated issues of defining new spousal and parent–child subsystems, new internal and external boundaries, new cross-system (natural parent–stepparent) interactional patterns, and, very clearly, new lines of authority and discipline, as well as potential support and loyalties for the children. It may even involve a new child for the newly remarried couple and thus a new sibling for the children. These events also tend to place more pressure on the nonremarried ex-spouse to heighten his or her networking activities in order to "keep up" with the other and not "look bad" to the children. Often, precipitous new relationships are formed

during this period or the person may withdraw to the family of origin, with resultant periods of depression. Such precipitous actions may create renewed instability for the children and the specter of the complete loss of the remarrying parent if geographical relocation ensues. The potential panic of the "abandoned" ex-spouse will trigger these fears in the children. The entrance of a new parent figure is a new and unique experience for the children, for which they have no models for how to behave. They often take their cues from the angry ex-spouse and displace their anger from the parents to the safer, and at this point less important, stepparent.

The skills of the family therapist are paramount at this stage in his or her being able to recognize the confluence of broad systemic dynamics involving issues of personal attachment and loss, structural complications in shared parenting, intergenerational loyalties, and the developmental needs of the children. This involves dealing with the complex blending of two histories into one shared history while the previous historical persons are still active in the lives of one and all. Again, the treatment of choice when problems are presented at this stage is family therapy, which can involve all dimensions of the recoupling and intergenerational system. This does not necessarily mean seeing everyone together at each session. Rather, the therapist must assess issues of power and coalitions, as well as therapeutic timing and process, in making treatment and intervention plans. This means that the therapist may wish to diffuse the power of a certain coalition by seeing a number of family members rather than the identified members of a problematic triangle. Or the therapist may select one member of the coalition for an individual session in order to create an unexpected imbalance. As family therapy proceeds, the therapist may alternate between seeing the spousal subsystem, the parent–child subsystem, and, occasionally, individual members.

The Second Remarriage

The systemic crisis created when the second former spouse remarries often lacks some of the intensity of the earlier remarriage but can still create disruption and the potential for relitigation. If this occurs a year or two after the first remarriage, a certain power balance has been established and the already remarried spouse may be reluctant to give up some of this perceived power. This second remarriage further complicates the already perplexing juxtaposition of family roles and structures for the child.

The experience of the adjustment following the first remarriage can be utilized by the therapist as a basis for coping with this new complication. At this point in the process, the child may begin to experience a better sense of family balance and harmony when both parents are actually remarried. This stage is often the beginning of a final period of acceptance on the child's part of the endurance of the parental divorce and of letting go of the fantasy of reconciliation. However, children will often cling to a tiny residue of this wish even into adulthood. It also represents a potentially more equally balanced blended system. To assist the families in achieving this balance, the therapist will typically need to work with all aspects of the system.

Dual-Family Functioning

This stage, following the remarriage of the second former spouse, completes the process of the establishment of essentially two intact and structurally balanced nuclear systems. Ahrons (1979) has termed this a "binuclear" family system. At least structurally, there are now two sets of spousal subsystems, two sets of parent–child subsystems, and four sets of intergenerational systems, all linked by the ongoing parenting responsibilities of a shared subsystem of children. The children, as well as the parents, may now be able to reestablish a sense of stability and perhaps normality. The continuing task of structural recoupling now involves all of the actors, with the potential for defining new relationships, continuity, and trust in the future.

The role of the family therapist is enhanced by a broad systemic assessment that can aid the dual-family systems by identifying imbalances and potentially disruptive alliances or coalitions. Therapists must consider the possibility that many individually identified issues can be usefully reframed within the broader task of structural recoupling and as a possible expression of the struggle by all of the intergenerational actors to evolve a new "binuclear" system. At this stage, the family therapist, who has had access to most of the components of the respective subsystems, can play a critical role by predicting potential systemic dysfunctions and by intervening at different locations throughout the broad system to offer structural rebalancing, to mark boundaries, and to diffuse growing reactive disputes.

SUMMARY

The loss that the intergenerational family system experiences in the divorce process is never just of individual objects, but rather of the life and viability of the family system itself. We have said elsewhere that "the 'victim' of the divorce is never simply the children, the loss is of the viability and organization of the family's process. It is perhaps the inadequate rituals of our culture for terminating ineffective family systems, reinforced by an adversarial legal process, that not only creates but often encourages victimization of the family" (Everett & Volgy, 1983, p. 344).

It is this broad thread of loss that the clinician will see displayed in a variety of ways just when the therapist thinks that he or she has a "handle" on the dynamics of the family in treatment. It is displayed not just in the rage and vindictiveness of the spouses, but also in the irrational ability of normally loving parents to use their children to attempt to destroy the former lover. This thread is displayed again not only in the apparent distance and antipathy between separated spouses, but also in their chronic ambivalence and continuing fantasies of reconciliation, or even sexual liaisons, with each other. It can be observed in frightened grandparents who hire attorneys to fight for their children for fear of losing access to their grandchildren. It is seen in parentified children who give up the playfulness of their childhoods to assume a pseudospousal and continuing caretaking role with their residential parent. Or it can be seen in the children who knowingly collude with a parent to substantiate false charges of sexual molestation against the other parent only to protect the vulnerabilities of the former parent. And it is seen in the chronically depressed adult, whose parents divorced 25 years earlier when she was 13, and who has carried irreconcilable loyalty conflicts into her third marriage and relationship with her children because she had to tell a judge in court with which parent she wished to live.

These are some of the threads of systemic loss and problems in decoupling and recoupling that the clinician must be alert to and integrate with other assessment data. Ramifications of these issues may appear at any point throughout the stages of the divorce-process continuum described here. It is hoped that the family therapist will consider "divorce therapy" as a process along the entire continuum with identifiable tasks, strategies, interventions, and goals at each stage along the way. Perhaps as we gain experience and understanding in treating this increasingly expectable life-cycle crisis, the family-therapy field will be able to develop a more informed database from which to treat divorcing family systems with greater competency, leading to more reliably successful outcomes.

REFERENCES

Ahrons, C. (1979). The binuclear family: Two households, one family. *Alternative Lifestyles, 2*, 499–515.

Ahrons, C., & Rodgers, R. (1987). *Divorced families: A multidisciplinary developmental view.* New York: Norton.

Bane, M.J. (1979). Marital disruption in the lives of children. In G. Loevinger & O.C. Moles (Eds.), *Divorce and separation: Context, causes, and consequences.* New York: Basic Books.

Bohannon, P. (1970). The six stations of divorce. In P. Bohannon (Ed.), *Divorce and after: An analysis of the emotional and social problems of divorce* (pp. 29–55). New York: Doubleday.

Brown, E. (1976). Divorce counseling. In D. Olson (Ed.), *Treating relationships* (pp. 399–429). Lake Mills, IA: Graphic.

Crosby, J., Gage, B., & Raymond, M. (1983). The grief resolution process in divorce. *Journal of Divorce, 7*, 3–18.

Everett, C. (Ed.), (1985). *Divorce mediation: Perspectives on the field.* New York: Haworth.

Everett, C., & Volgy, S. (1983). Family assessment in child custody disputes. *Journal of Marital and Family Therapy, 9*, 342–353.

Fisher, E. (1973). A guide to divorce counseling. *Family Coordinator, 22*, 55–61.

Fisher, E. (1974). *Divorce: The new freedom.* New York: Harper & Row.

Froiland, D., & Hozman, T. (1977). Counseling for constructive divorce. *Personnel and Guidance Journal, 55*, 525–529.

Granvold, D., & Tarrant, R. (1983). Structured marital separation

as a marital treatment method. *Journal of Marital and Family Therapy, 9*, 189–198.

Greene, B., Lee, R., & Lustig, N. (1973). Transient structured distance as a maneuver in marital therapy. *Family Coordinator, 22*, 15–22.

Gurman, A., & Kniskern, D. (1978). Research on marital and family therapy: Progress, perspective and prospect. In S. Garfield & A. Bergin (Eds.), *Handbook of psychotherapy and behavior change: An empirical analysis.* New York: Wiley.

Guttentag, M., Salasin, S., & Belle, D. (1980). *The mental health of women.* New York: Academic Press.

Heatherington, E., Cox, M., & Cox, R. (1979). Play and social interaction in children following divorce. *Journal of Social Issues, 35*, 26–49.

Irving, H. (1980). *Divorce mediation.* Toronto: Personal Library.

Kalter, N., & Rembar, J. (1981). The significance of the child's age at the time of parental divorce. *American Journal of Orthopsychiatry, 47*, 40–51.

Kaslow, F. (1981). Divorce and divorce therapy. In A. Gurman & D. Kniskern (Eds.), *Handbook of family therapy.* New York: Brunner/Mazel.

Kaslow, F., & Schwartz, L. (1987). *The dynamics of divorce: A life cycle perspective.* New York: Brunner/Mazel.

Keeney, B. (1982). What is an epistemology of family therapy? *Family Process, 21*, 153–168.

Kessler, S. (1975). *The American way of divorce: Prescription for change.* Chicago: Nelson-Hall.

Kressel, K. (1985). *The process of divorce: How professionals and couples negotiate settlements.* New York: Basic Books.

Kressel, K., & Deutsch, M. (1977). Divorce therapy: An in-depth survey of therapists' views. *Family Process, 16*, 413–433.

Kvanli, J.A., & Jennings, G. (1986). Recoupling: Development and establishment of the spousal subsystem in remarriage. *Journal of Divorce, 10*, 189–204.

Maturana, H., & Varela, R. (1980). *Autopoiesis and cognition: The realization of the living.* Dordrecht, Holland: Reidel.

Milne, A. (1978). Custody of children in a divorce process: A family self-determination model. *Conciliation Courts Review, 16*, 1–10.

Milne, A. (1983). Divorce mediation: The state of the art. *Mediation Quarterly, 1*, 15–31.

Sager, C.J., Brown, H.S., Crohn, H., Engel, T., Rodstein, E., & Walker, L. (1983). *Treating the remarried family.* New York: Brunner/Mazel.

Sprenkle, D., & Storm, C. (1983). Divorce therapy outcome research: A substantive and methodological review. *Journal of Marital and Family Therapy, 9*, 239–258.

Stack, S. (1980). The effects of marital dissolution on suicide. *Journal of Marriage and the Family, 42*, 83–92.

Steinberg, J. (1980). Towards an interdisciplinary commitment: A divorce lawyer proposes attorney–therapist marriages or, at the least, an affair. *Journal of Marriage and Family Therapy, 6*, 259–268.

Steinberg, J. (1985). Through an interdisciplinary mirror: Attorney–therapist similarities. In C. Everett (Ed.), *Divorce mediation: Perspectives on the field.* New York: Haworth Press.

U.S. Bureau of the Census (1980). *Census of population: General social and economic characteristics.* Washington, DC: U.S. Government Printing Office.

U.S. Bureau of the Census (1984). *Census of population: General social and economic characteristics.* Washington, DC: U.S. Government Printing Office.

Wallerstein, J.S., & Kelly, J.B. (1976). The effects of parental divorce: Experiences of the child in later latency. *American Journal of Orthopsychiatry, 46*, 256–269.

Wallerstein, J.S., & Kelly, J.B. (1977). Divorce counseling: A community service for families in the midst of divorce. *American Journal of Orthopsychiatry, 47* (1), 4–22.

Wallerstein, J.S., & Kelly, J.B. (1980). *Surviving the breakup: How children and parents cope with divorce*. New York: Basic Books.

Wasserman, I.M. (1984). A longitudinal analysis of the linkage between suicide, unemployment, and marital dissolution. *Journal of Marriage and the Family, 46*, 853–859.

Weisman, R. (1975). Crisis theory and the process of divorce. *Social Casework, 56*, 205–212.

Weiss, R. (1976). *Marital separation*. New York: Basic Books.

EDITORS' REFERENCE

Rice, J.K., & Rice, D.G. (1985). *Living through divorce: A developmental approach to divorce therapy*. New York: Guilford Press.

CHAPTER 17

Promoting Healthy Functioning in Divorced and Remarried Families

Froma Walsh, Ph.D.

An intriguing ritual has become popular among fifth-grade students at a middle-class school in the Midwest. When a boy and a girl like each other, they formalize their relationship by signing a "marriage contract" in a ceremony witnessed by friends. When a problem erupts, they end their relationship by signing "divorce papers" in a rite again duly witnessed by friends. "Divorces" and "remarriages" are common among these children, as they actually are in their families. Such practices reflect the new realities of contemporary family life, as children attempt to cope with changes around them and as they begin to construct models for their own future couple relationships.

With the rapid social changes of the past two decades, the intact nuclear family is no longer representative of the majority of American families. Half of all couples currently marrying can be expected to divorce (Glick & Lin, 1986). The high divorce rates do not mean that people have given up on marriage. On the contrary, Americans are marrying and remarrying in record numbers. Over 65 percent of women and 70

percent of men are likely to remarry following divorce (Glick & Lin, 1986; Norton & Moorman, 1987). Many others remarry after the death of a spouse, while others live together in second families without legal remarriage. It is estimated that 64 percent of white children and 89 percent of Black children will live in a single-parent household at some time by the age of 17 (Glick, 1984). More than half of the children in divorced families will gain a stepparent in residence, usually a stepfather, since over 90 percent of children are in their mother's custody. Children must also forge relationships with new stepparents (usually stepmothers) marrying noncustodial parents. Many parents with joint custody attempt to construct remarriage family units, with children becoming part-time residents in two households. The tremendous stresses inherent in the transitions through divorce and remarriage and the complexity of relationship networks in remarried-family systems contribute to a divorce rate of up to 60 percent among remarried couples (Glick, 1984).

It would be erroneous, however, to conclude

that the only healthy family form is the intact family in which biological parents remain together. A major task for divorced and remarried families is the construction of new models of "family" in a society that continues to define the intact nuclear family as the norm (Ahrons & Rodgers, 1987).[1] In fact, dissolution of the intact family has always been common. Before the medical advances and lengthening life span of the 20th century, the death of a parent frequently disrupted families and shifted children and widowed parent into a variety of single-parent and stepfamily configurations (Walsh & McGoldrick, 1991).

Clinical theory has long perpetuated the societal myth that any family form that deviates from this ideal model is inherently pathological (Walsh, 1983). Traditional developmental theories have regarded divorce as a sign of pathology in one or both parents and as necessarily damaging to children. Single-parent households have been presumed to be deficient, with therapy commonly aimed at replacing the missing parent by promoting remarriage (Walsh & Scheinkman, 1989). Yet stepfamilies have been regarded as inherently problematic and a poor substitute for the "natural" family unit. As McGoldrick and Carter (1989) note, the "normal" (i.e., typical, expectable) process of forming a remarried family has not been well defined, and new norms are only beginning to emerge (Dahl, Cowgill, & Asmundsson, 1987; Visher & Visher, 1979, 1982, 1987). Our society's persistence in upholding the intact biological nuclear family as the ideal family form leads remarried families to try in vain to emulate an inappropriate standard. Our culture lacks established patterns and rituals to assist families in the reconstruction of these complex relationship networks. The intact family has been used as the standard for assessing family functioning, often with inappropriate measures and norms that do not fit the structure, resources, and challenges of other family arrangements (Walsh, 1989). Clinically biased impressionistic studies (Wallerstein & Kelly, 1980; Wallerstein, 1989) have

been cited widely to reinforce the view that divorce is inevitably destructive to children, if not immediately, then in later development. Such claims fail to take into account the mediating effects of numerous variables, such as the quality of pre- and postdivorce relationships, economic constraints, or the degree of fit between individual and family developmental stages and tasks. A growing body of empirical research has failed to support such a dim view of divorced and remarried families. In fact, emerging research comparing adaptation in divorced and nondivorced families finds that children fare the poorest in dysfunctional families that remain together (Hetherington, 1988). Accumulating evidence suggests that while transitional stresses are likely to generate family turmoil and short-term distress, no family form is inherently either healthier or more dysfunctional than others. Well-functioning families—and dysfunctional families—can be found in each arrangement.

The important issues for research and clinical practice are threefold. First, we need to specify the normative challenges and tasks associated with the establishment and viability of each family form. Second, we need to identify the mediating variables that differentiate successful adaptation and dysfunction in each family form, relative to varying socioeconomic, cultural, and life-cycle imperatives. Third, we need to specify the strategies and methods that are most appropriate for dealing with these issues in clinical practice. Regardless of the dynamics operating in any particular family, divorce and remarriage are major disruptions in the family system. They generate a series of changes in structure and relationships. Each requires a fundamental shift in how the family functions and how members define normal family life in a sociocultural context that regards the biological nuclear family as both typical and ideal.

This chapter addresses the process of reorganization and adaptation in divorced and remarried families with the aim of providing clinical guidelines to depathologize family distress associated with complications in the various transitions and to promote optimal functioning in each family arrangement. Factors found to be relevant to vulnerability and resiliency will be noted. Both immediate and long-term challenges and tasks will be addressed, with recommendations for clinical assessment and inter-

---

[1] *Editors' Note.* Of course, divorced and remarried families are only two types of increasingly common alternative family forms, so that, in many ways, the issues Walsh raises in this chapter pertain to a broader range of families than is implied by the chapter title.

vention. First, a reconsideration of our terms and definitions is needed to sharpen awareness of key issues in divorce and remarriage.

LANGUAGE, BELIEFS, AND PRACTICE

Our language, influenced by our beliefs, in turn influences our vision and our practice with divorced and remarried families. The term "single-parent family" has been applied to quite different family arrangements, resulting in confusion, error, and nonsystemic clinical intervention. The label is used to describe both never-married and divorced one-parent households, usually headed by mothers. Since the term is generally applied to the custodial parent, the noncustodial parent, usually the father, is left without a designation and is rendered invisible. Similarly, the label "unwed mother" contributes to a nonsystemic focus on one parent that ignores the couples relationship and the involvement of fathers—who are rarely referred to as "unwed fathers."

For divorced families with coparenting arrangements, Ahrons (1980; Ahrons & Rodgers, 1987) has coined the term "binuclear family," which better describes and promotes the continuity of relationships between children and parents residing in two separate households when parents share child-rearing responsibilities, particularly in cases of joint custody. Yet even this term poses a dilemma when parents remarry to partners who also have children from previous marriages, creating a family system that may be "trinuclear" or even "quadrinuclear."

Unfortunately, as will be discussed, few ex-spouses are able to collaborate fully in "coparenting." The term "parallel parenting" may be a useful alternative for many families. However, even these terms may not accurately portray the skewed situation in the vast majority of post-divorce families, in which mothers head the primary residence and carry the bulk of responsibilities while father contact and support tend to diminish over time. The term "primary parent" clarifies this arrangement, implying a secondary or backup role for the noncustodial parent, unlike the misnomer "single parent."

The term "single-parent family" is perhaps most appropriate when one parent must carry out all parental obligations and ongoing involvement with the other parent is precluded, as in unwed pregnancy, widowhood, abandonment, or cases of serious abuse. For many families, the term "single parent" reflects the reality of a father's conflictual or cut-off position and his failure to provide ongoing financial and emotional support to his children and their custodial mother. On the one hand, we need to be cautious not to accept the stereotype that single-parent households are inherently dysfunctional without the leadership role of the father. Research on the long-term adaptation of low-income, minority, single-parent families indicates that most do manage to function effectively on their own (Lindblad-Goldberg, 1988). At the same time, we must be careful that use of the label "single parent" does not reinforce a dysfunctional cutoff that may be repairable. Second-hand reports of a father's unwillingness or inability to be involved should not be relied on without evaluating his past, current, and potential future contributions to his family. Clinicians need to check out presumptions that an absent parent is uncaring, destructive, crazy, or hopeless, and attempt to change that situation if appropriate and possible. In order to ameliorate a mother's overburden and to improve the well-being of children, it may be crucial to bring the father from the periphery of the frame into focus for clinical assessment and intervention. Of all research on divorce, the most significant is the clear and consistent finding that children adjust best when both parents can remain involved with them and cooperate in child rearing (Goldsmith, 1982; Isaacs, Montalvo, & Abelsohn, 1986).

Moreover, when referring to a "single-parent household," we need to assess the role of other important members of the household and relational network, especially grandparents, other extended-family members, and a new partner. Such terms as "single-parent family" or "mother-headed household" do not adequately reflect the relational system. We need to be careful that the term "single parent" does not blind us to the important influences and potential resources in other significant relationships in and outside of the primary residence. A systems perspective is essential for assessment and intervention.

Our kinship labels for remarried families also are inadequate and carry negative connotations, especially that of the "wicked stepmother" (Visher & Visher, 1982). Even the prefix "step" implies a more distant and less "natural" relationship. On the other hand, the term "blended family" suggests greater integration than can be realistically expected. Moreover, the inherent ambiguity and changing nature of family boundaries, membership, and roles defy their definition. How does a child refer and relate to a stepparent's family of origin whose members become stepgrandparents, stepaunts/uncles, and stepcousins? How does a remarried mother maintain a relationship with members of her ex-husband's family who are the children's grandparents, aunts, uncles, and cousins, and to whom she may have been very attached? What are a child's relationships to a new stepmother, an ex-stepmother, and their children as a father remarries a second time?

Following McGoldrick and Carter's (1989) preference, the term "remarried family" is recommended "to emphasize that it is the marital bond that forms the basis for the complex arrangement of several families in a new constellation" (p. 400).

A COEVOLUTIONARY, DEVELOPMENTAL PERSPECTIVE

Divorce and remarriage are not simply discrete events. Each is an interactional process that unfolds, over time, in the context of the coevolutionary life-cycle passage of all members in the multigenerational family system. It is important to track the developmental passage of divorced and remarried families. We need to inquire about the history of previous marriages and family units, and the future directions anticipated, in order to understand the problem situation in developmental perspective and in the context of the entire relationship system. The following clinical case illustrates the tunnel vision that can occur.

A father, identifying himself as a "single parent," requested help with the stormy behavior of his daughter. In presenting the case for supervision, the therapist diagramed the family "system" structurally, as follows:

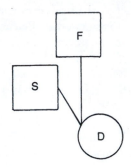

The therapist had assessed the problem as a triangle in which a coalition between the father and the parentified son excluded the daughter, who then sought attention by exhibiting rebellious behavior. Intervention had focused on rebalancing this triangle to improve the father–daughter relationship. Progress was minimal, and the father appeared increasingly depressed.

Outside the frame of assessment were two critical members of this system. The mother had been cut off since the divorce three years earlier because the father viewed her as an "unstable influence." Because the divorce was regarded as a past event, the therapist had not considered relationships with the mother/ex-spouse pertinent. Instead, intervention was narrowly focused within the single-parent household.

The other significant but "invisible" relationship was the father's serious involvement with a woman who had recently begun to press him to marry. The father's unexpressed fears of remarriage, emanating from unresolved issues in his former marriage and divorce, interacted with the daughter's confusion and upset about the loss of her mother, which were intensified by anticipation of remarriage.

A more relevant diagram of the system would include the following, with the arrow showing the flow of time forward, from the past intact family toward the anticipated future remarriage.

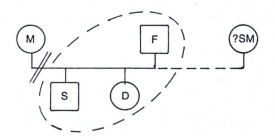

Unfinished business from the past and concerns about the future need to be addressed to facilitate reorganization of the system and to enable members to move ahead in their life-cycle passage. Information about key relationships in the extended families would also be useful in planning intervention.

The inherent complexity and the fragmentation and cutoffs common in divorced- and remarried-family systems make the genogram (McGoldrick & Gerson, 1985) an essential tool for assessment and treatment planning. In constructing the diagram, clinicians and family members can visualize the total family system—including past marriages, unwed parentages, and families of origin—and the positions of various members and subsystems in relation to others. Often, family members, especially children, report that the genogram allows them, for the first time, to "see" how they are all connected. It can assist therapists in sorting out the complicated network of relationships, noting conflictual and cut-off relationships and replication of dysfunctional patterns, identifying potential resources, and determining who should be involved in any intervention plan.

POSTDIVORCE FAMILY REORGANIZATION

Families face a number of challenges and undergo various transitions in the process of adaptation to divorce. The first phase, typically lasting one to two years postdivorce, is a period of high stress and turmoil. Since most families are more distressed after one year than immediately after the divorce, many feel hopeless and discouraged at that time. However, longitudinal research (Hetherington, Cox & Cox, 1981) has found that most families experience a remarkable period of recovery by the end of the second year. They usually restabilize in two years and are functioning well when followed up six years later. Still, many families undergo multiple transitions as residences and custody arrangements change. When remarriage occurs, the complicated process of restructuring old relationships in concert with the new can take as long as four to five years in many families, especially those with children in early adolescence.

It is important for clinicians to normalize the initial postdivorce crisis period as transitional, framing problems as inherent to the process and identifying common issues likely to arise.[2] It is crucial not to overpathologize distress or to assume that long-term treatment is needed before offering information and support, building resources, and promoting restabilization. It is most useful to help families gain a normative developmental perspective, distinguishing both immediate and long-term challenges and expectations.

Economic Distress

Financial strain is the factor contributing most to adjustment problems in single-parent households, especially for lower-income families. National studies have documented that in the first year after divorce, a woman's standard of living declines by 19 percent on average, and in many cases by much more, while a man's increases substantially (Hetherington, 1988). Since 90 percent of postdivorce children live with their mothers, children and their custodial mothers suffer the greatest financial hardship. In fact, half of all children in poverty live in single-parent households headed by women (including never-married parents). The average court-ordered payment of $2,000 per child per year (the minimum requirement in most states) is half of that considered to be at the poverty level. Under economic duress, mothers are forced to work outside the home and often have to move to poorer neighborhoods. The burden is greatest for those who are not well educated; who lack job training, experience, and other resources; and who are unlikely to receive residential property in the divorce settlement. Maternal employment following divorce may be a necessity and may add to a mother's sense of well-being. At the same time, studies suggest that when both parents become less available in the first year postdivorce, children experience a double loss and may show a lag in adjustment. Heth-

---

[2] *Editors' Note.* We agree about the dangers of overpathologizing, but would note that at times the distress of separation and divorce lead to the development of full-blown psychiatric disorders (most often, major depression or chronic severe anxiety), which may be treatable in their own right.

erington (1989a) has recommended that it is more beneficial for children if the custodial parent can wait until the second year to return to, or increase, work outside the home. This would require fathers to follow through with timely child support payments and to sustain an active parenting role.

Several factors contribute to the economic distress of most custodial households. First, inadequate divorce settlements and poor enforcement of support by fathers have been widespread problems (Hewlett, 1986). The shift in divorce laws toward "no-fault" divorce and "equal division" of property was intended to facilitate the divorce process and to compensate women who assumed the primary homemaking and child-rearing responsibilities. However, these legal changes instead have resulted in increased financial hardship for many women and children. Equal division of property is neither equitable nor adequate for women who continue to bear the primary responsibility for child rearing and who are discriminated against in the work force. Consistent with other studies, Hewlett (1986) has found that only 14 percent of divorced women are currently awarded any alimony and only 10 percent actually receive it. Only 60 percent of custodial mothers are awarded any child support, and in most cases the amount awarded is inadequate. Even then, 60 percent of fathers fail to pay *any* child support whatsoever and only one third follow through with the amount decreed by the court.

Another problem concerns the failure of many fathers to share responsibility with mothers for children born out of wedlock, especially in the growing number of adolescent pregnancies. In low-income Black communities, decisions to marry and to assume financial obligations are tied to employment possibilities, which too often are lacking (Wilson, 1987).

Without the support of fathers, custodial mothers confront an inherent conflict in managing financial, homemaking, and child-care responsibilities. Women's jobs are mostly low paying and lack the opportunity for advancement, especially given the necessity of combining child-care and job demands. Adequate child care in most cases is generally unavailable, and unaffordable if it is. Custodial mothers are caught in a bind: If they work, they are likely to be blamed for neglecting their children, whereas if they stay home, they face financial hardship and may have to rely on welfare, with its stigma.

Although many clinicians are familiar with such grim statistics, they often shy away from inquiry about a family's finances.[3] Given the hardships and inequities of divorce, it is crucial to learn how each family's standard of living was affected by the divorce, the level of financial support mandated and actually received, and the attempts by family members to manage economic needs. Empowering and increasing the custodial parent's ability to deal with the financial situation is an important task in therapy. This may involve coaching a mother to obtain needed support from a father or contacting him directly to achieve a more workable agreement and follow-through for support. Since financial support is usually related to the degree of involvement, a family therapist may have to work to interrupt a vicious circle in which fathers withhold support as mothers withhold visitation, each in reaction to the other, using the leverage in their power. Moreover, since economic viability and child-care supports involve work systems and larger social policies, clinicians need to become more active in promoting such changes as flexible work schedules and parental leave to care for a sick child.

Physical Upheaval

With separation and divorce, the shift in residences generates a sense of dislocation for all members. The custodial parent is likely to become overburdened by a myriad of practical problems. Task overload is experienced when one parent is trying to accomplish what two usually do. At least some household disorganization and erratic life schedule can be expected. Typically, family roles, rituals, and pleasurable interactions start breaking down. One predictor of later scores for child adjustment is the *degree*

---

[3] *Editors' Note.* When we first read these findings, we thought that surely the author's sample must have been not very representative of divorced families, or that Walsh had misquoted the figures, etc. Walsh assures us that we were wrong on both counts. We assume, unfortunately, that probably many therapists are ignorant of such data, as we were, and that our collective awareness of how bad life can get economically for divorced mothers is often quite limited by virtue of our exposure in our own clinical practices.

of household disorganization (Hetherington, 1989a). At the other extreme, some families may rigidly hold on to old patterns of living in an attempt to preserve a sense of stability and continuity with the past, as if the family was still an intact unit. Families need guidance in redefinition of roles and reallocation of responsibilities. Given limited resources, children and extended-family members may be called upon to assume a larger share, compatible with their own developmental needs. The predictability of transitional upheaval underscores the importance of early interventions aimed at parental support, pragmatic problem solving, and household reorganization.

Loss of an ex-spouse's extended family and other social support further strains adjustment. Dislocation from home, neighborhood or community, and family and friendship networks compounds the upheaval. Family assessments need to evaluate the changes that have occurred for family members in transition from the former intact family to the present situation. It is especially crucial to assess the loss of former resources, both psychosocial and financial, and to find ways to reclaim or replenish them.

Kin and Social Support

Following divorce, parents tend to turn to their families of origin for help and solace. It is especially important to help a custodial mother to develop supports, by drawing on extended-family members, friends, and neighbors, or sharing a household with another custodial parent. Family conflicts or cutoffs may need repair in order to build a more supportive network. Economic and cultural factors influence intergenerational patterns of support. In white middle-class families, custodial mothers tend to prefer living near, but separately from, their parents, whereas low-income Black and other ethnic families are more likely to share a residence and resources. Living together can bring conflicts, especially between a mother and maternal grandmother.

Structural interventions may be especially useful to address problems of generational hierarchy. When a custodial mother moves back into her own mother's house, there may be struggles over power and control issues, and

conflict over who is the head of the household, the "boss," and the primary parent. The mother, treated as a daughter, may feel a loss of her adult self and sense of competence. Commonly, a dysfunctional triangle can develop if the grandmother and child form a strong coalition while the grandmother criticizes her daughter's parenting or her life-style and the child shows greater preference for and deference to the grandmother. In an increasing number of families, grandmothers are becoming overburdened as they are being called upon to assume primary child-rearing functions after they have already raised their own family. Clinicians can be helpful by bringing in other kin to share responsibilities. Grandfathers, who may have been more peripheral in the rearing of their own children, offer potential resources for the care of their grandchildren. Where finances permit, a housekeeper/baby-sitter arrangement can allow a parent to remain in charge as an employer, delegating authority and responsibility, and drawing on family members for backup support.

Social relationships also change with divorce and single parents are likely to confront issues of social isolation (Hetherington et al., 1981; Isaacs et al., 1986). Former friends of the couple may distance, take sides, or extend invitations only for child-focused events. Women in traditional marriages lose a vital social network connected to their husband's work. A custodial parent may feel too depleted or uncomfortable to socialize alone or initiate contact, and child-care coverage is an ever-present dilemma.

While extramarital affairs are common at the time of divorce, only 15 percent of such transitional relationships go on to marriage (Hetherington, 1988). After divorce, Hetherington found, men commonly initiate a frenetic phase of socializing or casual sexual activity, but by one year are seeking a more serious relationship. Most divorced women do not find casual sexual encounters satisfying, and feel depressed, controlled, and bad about themselves afterwards. Even more than men, they yearn for a mutually caring relationship. The formation of an intimate relationship was the best predictor of happiness for both men and women. However, being a custodial parent interfered with this aim. Also, for many the prospect of intimacy holds fears of unlovability or of attachment that could replicate unresolvable conflict and loss. Fears of coping and remaining alone, combined with concerns about financial survival, propel some into premature remarriage (Norton & Glick, 1986).

Emotional Turmoil

With all the pressures and changes, it is not surprising that the early phase of separation involves considerable emotional turmoil. Divorce has a profound impact on an individual's sense of self. It can be most devastating for women in traditional marriages who lose their identities, as well as their financial security, with the loss of a husband. For men, the loss of their helpmate and emotional caretaker contributes to a high rate of illness, depression, and suicide following divorce (McGoldrick, 1989). For both men and women, changes in self-concept have been found to be pervasive and enduring at six years postdivorce. They are most marked in the first year, when individuals commonly report "not me" experiences and behavior different from the past, discordant with their self-image. Many make striking, but often shortlived, changes in their images. Commonly, they take active steps to improve themselves. It should be kept in mind that children have an added challenge when relating to parents who are changing in physical appearance, emotions, and self-image during the early phase of postdivorce adjustment (Heatherington, 1988).

While a good coparenting relationship is desirable after divorce, in reality, interactional conflict between former spouses is the norm. Hetherington found that in the first year, only 15 percent of ex-spouses had both good relationships and good coparenting collaboration. Only one in four families managed "just reasonable" coparenting. Conflict was more likely to persist with continued attachment and to diminish as those bonds started to weaken.

An emotional divorce may lag behind the legal divorce, especially when continuing involvement around children requires collaboration and restimulates old attachments and conflicts. Father–child involvement often ceases because ongoing contact between the former spouses is too painful for either or both. Parents commonly experience extreme fluctuations in emotions. Such lability may be expressed in waves of intense emotion, ranging from crashing depressions, outbursts of rage, or even death wishes toward the ex-spouse, to relief from the former marital tension and momentary surges of euphoria. The partner who initiated the divorce is prone to lingering guilt while a spouse who did not want the dissolution is likely to carry feelings of abandonment or exploitation and may seek retaliation through custody battles or by later withholding child visitation or financial support. The polarization of positions into victim and villain, too often intensified by the legal process, impedes emotional resolution of the divorce. The greater the ambiguity and ambivalence in the divorce process, the more difficult it is to make sense of the situation and to grieve the loss. One of the most disturbing feelings for many is persisting attachment and nostalgic thoughts of the ex-spouse or the intact family unit. At one year postdivorce, many wonder if the divorce was the right thing and whether they had worked hard enough to make it work, and they view the alternatives less optimistically. Such doubts tend to fade with time.

Clinicians can be most helpful by encouraging divorced clients to review their courtship, marriage, and divorce process. It is useful to coach them to gather clarifying information and perspectives from the ex-spouse, other important family members, and friends, and to examine the factors involved in the breakdown of the marriage. Helping clients to make sense of the process, to take ownership of their part in it, and to accept what was beyond their control can greatly facilitate the emotional resolution of the divorce that is necessary in order to move on with life.

Family Belief System

Divorce, like other major life transitions, disrupts a family's paradigm, the world view and basic premises that underlie the family identity and guide its actions. The parents' sense of mastery and competence is shaken. When family members share unrealistic expectations that the family should function "normally" (i.e., like an intact two-parent family), there is disappointment and a sense of deficiency when those fantasies cannot be realized. Even for well-intentioned family therapists, in the context of societal norms, the implicit standard of comparison is likely to be an intact family, with two adults to carry out responsibilities and provide mutual support.

Similarly, while most divorced adults do eventually remarry, it is crucial that clinicians view single-parent households not merely as way stations in transition to remarriage, but as viable family structures in their own right (Herz, 1989). A third or more of custodial mothers will never remarry. Many fathers rush into remarriage to acquire replacements to carry out the functions of their ex-wives. In any case, the therapeutic goal should not be to help members to endure a waiting period or to seek a replacement to fill a gap, implying that a single-parent household is inherently deficient. Such a frame perpetuates the belief that a new husband/father (or wife/ mother) is needed to rescue the single parent, and children, who cannot function or live a satisfying life without the leadership of a man (or the caretaking of a woman). Herz emphasizes that such premises intensify feelings of being overwhelmed and powerless in coping with the real overload that single parents experience. Therapy should not be guided by the intact family model and attempt to replicate a two-parent household.[4] Instead, parents and children need help in creating a new model for meeting socioemotional and economic needs and reorganizing relationship patterns, responsibilities, and expectations (Lindblad-Goldberg, 1988).

As a divorced family initially attempts to adjust to the loss of the intact unit and to establish new patterns of family life, members are likely to experience a sense of disorientation in a transitional living situation lacking in structure and definition. Daily patterns and rituals, such as dinnertime, are disrupted as attention is demanded for immediate tasks of reordering a household or setting up a new home. This reorganization requires the negotiation of new relationship rules for each member's part in the family unit and for expectations of one another. Added to the lack of behavioral guidelines and ambivalent feelings is the ambiguity of the sep-

aration itself (Ahrons & Rodgers, 1987). Role definitions are unclear for members of divorced families. Norms are in flux regarding living arrangements and the degree of involvement between former spouses, between parents and children, and with new partners. Helping families to negotiate and clarify new relationship rules and expectations will greatly facilitate the transition.

Since marital disruption calls into question many core values and fantasies associated with the intact family, it is important to review the beliefs held by family members and to promote transformation to fit new family requisites. Helping families to reconstruct beliefs and practices to find new expression can preserve a vital sense of meaning in the face of so much loss and upheaval. Divorce and remarriage rituals are especially valuable in sharing the realities of loss and change, in marking the structural shifts, and in facilitating movement forward in the family life course (Imber-Black, 1988; Whiteside, 1988).

Child-Custody Arrangements

Over the past 150 years, child-custody laws have changed from a "parental rights" premise, regarding children as property of the father, to a "tender years" doctrine, entrusting the care of young children to mothers. By 1960, mothers were being given custody in over 90 percent of contested cases, a rate that still prevails (Leupnitz, 1982).

Following divorce, a large number of children grow up without the continuing involvement of their biological father. Weitzman's (1985) investigation of divorce in California revealed that despite changes in divorce laws to promote no-fault divorce and joint custody, 23 percent of fathers did not see their children *at all* after divorce. Moreover, several studies of father–child contact document that even when fathers are involved initially, in most cases, their involvement declines steadily over time, along with child support (Hetherington et al., 1981; Ihinger-Tallman & Pasley, 1987). In a national study, 50 percent of the children had not seen their nonresidential father in the past five years. Of the 50 percent who had contact, 20 percent had not seen him in the past year. Only 16 per-

---

[4] *Editors' Note.* We would generally agree with this, but would note that some ex-wife/mothers themselves strongly value traditional models of the family, including double parenthood. Challenging the family values of such women, especially early in therapy, will often backfire and severely weaken the therapeutic alliance.

cent of all children saw their father weekly (Furstenberg, 1983). Studies also show that visits decrease dramatically when remarriage occurs, especially when the former wife remarries (Furstenberg & Spanier, 1984).

Little research has focused on father custody arrangements since they are so uncommon, but some differences have been noted. In father custody cases, visitation by noncustodial mothers tends to be much more regular and frequent. Furstenberg and Spanier (1984) found that 86 percent of nonresidential mothers had contact in the past year, in contrast to 48 percent of nonresidential fathers. One third of the mothers saw children weekly, compared with only 16 percent of fathers.

A number of factors contribute to the general decline in nonresidential father contact (Weiss, 1979). Geographical closeness facilitates contact, but does not determine it. Transitions around the visit are often awkward and difficult. Visits can be painful and guilt-provoking when contact is brief, intense, and insufficient. Contact between former spouses may stir up old affections, angers, or disappointments that lead them to avoid such contact. As one father expressed it, "It is deeply upsetting to keep returning to the scene of emotional turmoil and failure."

Residential mothers also report numerous dissatisfactions: fathers fail to enforce rules, but instead only offer "good times"; children return drained and unruly; and conflicts persist over differing values and practices. Financial support is the major issue associated with declining father involvement. In most cases, the pattern of withholding support and decreasing or blocking contact escalates over time.

More recently, an equal-rights doctrine, by which parent gender is not a factor in custody decisions, has been expressed in legal joint custody, giving both parents equal rights and authority. Although joint custody has been heralded by advocates for assuring involvement of both parents and it enlarges fathers' rights, the most recent research raises questions about its actual practice and effects. Legal joint custody has been attempted by only a small percentage of families, with mixed results. For many families, what has occurred is merely a change in labels from what, under the old law, would have been termed "liberal visitation." A chief effect may be a psychological boost for fa-

thers who can define themselves as joint parents after divorce. The impetus of the movement has centered on equalizing fathers' *rights*, but has not rebalanced the disproportionate responsibilities shouldered by mothers for the day-to-day care of most children (Weitzman, 1985).

In most cases, joint custody refers to the practice of joint *physical* custody, since the vast majority of divorcing mothers still retain sole legal custody. With either joint or sole *legal* custody, couples can work out any of a variety of coparenting and residential arrangements. In some situations, children split the day or spend varying amounts of time during the week, or else alternate weeks between two homes. In other cases, couples share custody by splitting the year, usually school terms/vacations, or by alternating years children spend in each home. Each arrangement carries both costs and benefits for children and their families.

In general, joint-physical-custody arrangements facilitate more regular contact between children and their fathers, which is preferable to the Sunday "zoo daddy" common in traditional visitation decrees. However, researchers are now qualifying initial optimism about joint custody. Long-term follow-up studies (Hetherington, 1988; Isaacs et al., 1988; Wallerstein, 1989) indicate that when divorce is amicable and both parents remain involved with the children, there is little if any difference in a child's development whether there is joint or sole custody. Earlier reports of positive effects of joint custody came from small samples of couples who had amicable divorces and chose the arrangement. More recent experience with court-mandated joint custody indicates that children's development is impaired when parents are unable or unwilling to cooperate and share responsibility in coparenting. Researchers caution that where parental conflict persists, joint custody is likely to be harmful to children, who are caught in the middle of hostilities.

Joint custody is also contraindicated when a parent cannot be relied upon to maintain a responsible role, as in cases of severe mental illness, addiction, or a history of physical or sexual abuse and neglect. A case-by-case evaluation is needed to determine the appropriate nature and degree of contact with that parent. To ensure children's safety, visits should be well planned and structured, with the collaboration and presence of extended-family members or other responsible adults. Telephone calls, letters, and photographs can also be important means of contact, especially when the noncustodial parent lives far away or visits are not workable.

The benefits of joint custody may be outweighed by the disruptive impact on the child. While split residence does maximize involvement with both parents, it places a heavy burden of adjustment on children, who must shuttle back and forth. Practical problems and frustrations arise constantly, such as having certain clothing, possessions, important school notices, and homework when and where they are needed. More seriously, children who shift back and forth experience a sense of discontinuity and risk not developing feelings of fully belonging in any home or family unit. The shuttle arrangement also makes it hard for a child to maintain daily peer contacts when parents do not live in the same neighborhood. In addition, children are pained by the stigmatizing reactions of peers. One girl was teased by classmates, who called her a "bag lady" because she had to carry her belongings to school on transition days. The mechanics of transporting a child back and forth from one home to the other and covering school functions and medical appointments take considerable energy and require continual coordination. Arrangements demand a high level of mutual trust, cooperation, and communication that few ex-spouses can manage together. When those attributes were lacking in a marriage or severe conflict persists, a joint-custody arrangement is likely to be detrimental to a child's well-being.

Added complications arise over time in most families when renegotiation is required to accommodate to changes in children's developmental needs or parents' living situations. Most joint-custody arrangements are altered or break down altogether when one parent remarries or moves from the neighborhood or community. Since most parents do remarry, initial plans should be viewed as modifiable and parents should be encouraged to envision possible future scenarios and contingency plans.

Thus, successful adaptation depends less on where children live and more on the ability of the parents to collaborate in coparenting without serious, chronic conflict. Emerging research suggests that when this is not possible, children

fare better in sole custody and a primary residence, with predictable, structured visits with the noncustodial parent. The most important key to child adjustment is reliable, nonconflictual *access* to both parents.

An important consideration in all custody arrangements is each child's developmental stage and related needs and tasks. Younger children are more likely to need the security and stability of one primary home. They tend to experience confusion and upset at frequent shuffles between two residences. A child may feel that he or she is always just arriving and leaving again, without a sense of settling in. The frequent separations can bring tearful, clinging responses. As one child sobbed, "I'm always saying goodbye, and wherever I am, I'm always missing someone." For many children, adjustment to the split-household arrangement does not improve with time. After two years of shuttling, one 7-year-old boy said that going back and forth felt "like a roller coaster that broke and can't stop" (Isaacs, personal communication).

The custody situation is further complicated by the fact that siblings may be split up; also, many children eventually experience residential shifts, especially at adolescence (Grief, 1986). Boys are often transferred to their fathers' custody when mothers become unable to handle mounting behavior problems. Shifts may take place when a mother is depleted and without sufficient emotional and financial support, or when parental energies are redirected to educational or career pursuits or into a new marriage. Clinicians need to track the course of family development and custody arrangements and to evaluate whether current plans or proposed shifts are in the best interests of the children and their parents. Consider the following clinical case.

A mother sought help with her 12-year-old son who had become unruly and was repeatedly truant. The therapy initially focused on the single-parent household, aiming to help the mother better control the son's behavior. Since the family had functioned as a single-parent household for eight years, the therapist had not explored the role of the father in current problems. The consultant took a developmental tracking of the family system. The son and his two sisters had lived with their mother since the father "deserted them" when the children were very young. A few years later, the father reinitiated contact and began support payments, but within a year again "disappeared" from their lives. Recently he had reappeared, newly remarried, and he announced his intention to take custody of the son, who was named for him. After an initial upset, the mother and the children had not discussed the situation further, waiting to see what would happen. The son's truancy began.

Therapy was redirected to explore all family members' feelings about the proposed shift and to help them work out a solution to their dilemma. The mother's initial response was anger and confusion about what to do. She did not want to give up her son but had always felt intimidated by her former husband's demands. She was enraged that he had not contributed to child support over the years and now wanted his son for his own needs after she had carried all responsibility in raising the boy to adolescence. Yet her son's recent misbehavior and her inability to control it made her think that the son might be more responsive to his father's discipline and that her increasing burden would be relieved. The daughters were glad not to be forced to leave their mother, but also hurt that their father did not want them. The son wanted contact with his father, but did not want to leave his mother and sisters and did not trust that he could rely on his father. The therapist arranged a separate meeting with the father to clarify his position and to involve him in the process of recontracting his future role, along with his new wife, with all of his children. Follow-up meetings were scheduled to track and support the process. It was most crucial not to undermine the mother's role as the long-standing primary parent or to neglect her needs as solutions were worked out.

A legal complication concerning custody arises for lesbian and gay couples, who are increasingly raising children together, either through adoption or when one is the biological parent by insemination or from a previous marriage. Lacking the legal status of marriages, when these relationships end through death or separation, nonbiological parents lack the protection of divorce and custody laws, leaving their relationships with children ambiguous, at best, or cut off, at worst.

Many of the long-term complications related to custody, visitation, and financial support stem from the adversarial legal system in divorce settlements or from rigid adherence to decisions that prove to be inequitable or are no longer workable (Johnston, 1988). Mediation can be extremely useful, not only at the time of divorce, but also when the need for review and change arises.

Child Adjustment

With any custody arrangement, distress is common for children during the first year postdivorce. Most often, it is externalized in aggressive, noncompliant, antisocial behavior and inflexibility. When overloaded with coping demands, a distressed parent often is unable to support and set appropriate limits for a confused, anxious, or demanding child. The child's upset exacerbates parental distress. As pressures mount, the custodial mother may become more punitive, less affectionate, and more erratic in discipline, while the noncustodial father typically assumes a social role during visits, leaving instrumental leadership to the mother upon the children's return (Weiss, 1979).

Striking gender differences in child adjustment in different phases of divorce have been found (Hetherington, 1987). By two years postdivorce, girls show no differences in emotional, cognitive, or social development from girls in intact families. In contrast, boys evidence more problems in school and at home and express their distress through aggressive and rebellious behavior. Custodial mothers and sons tend to become involved in coercive cycles in which the mother, overwhelmed by multiple stresses, is unable to control the son's misbehavior, which worsens as her sense of failure and incompetence increases. Family life can become dominated by the misbehavior and the boy's constant harassment of and conflict with the mother. A mother who is finally exasperated and depleted may see no recourse but to send the child to his father or another relative. The threat of rejection or abandonment may reinforce a child's belief that his or her badness or unlovability had caused the earlier marital breakup and the loss of the noncustodial parent. In an escalating interactional spiral, a child fearing further rejection may misbehave all the more, provoking a residential shift. Such shifts are not uncommon for boys as they approach adolescence and become more unmanageable. In other cases, a custodial parent who is attempting to establish a new relationship may fear losing that relationship unless the problem child is removed.

Parenting issues in one-parent households concern the inherent difficulty in providing nurturing and discipline for children while meeting other demands, especially when a full-time job is added to household responsibilities. A custodial mother must establish herself as the sole daily manager of the children and the household. To function effectively, she needs essential emotional reserves and confidence in her own abilities. The therapeutic task is to build both actual and perceived competence (Herz, 1989). Clinicians can be most effective by helping a mother with practical problems. Psychoeducational, structural, and behavioral approaches, with concrete directives and support, may be successful in reducing behavior problems and improving parent–child relationships. As mothers are helped to feel more competent and able to control their family situation, their self-esteem is enhanced.

A broad systems perspective is also required to appreciate the circular impact of a child's initial upset and the response of the school and peer network. Hetherington (1988) found that when children, most often boys, expressed distress in the first year of divorce, their aggressive and noncompliant behavior led them into conflict with or bullying of other children. Despite reduced upset and improved behavior by the second year, the bad reputation they had acquired resulted in their exclusion from peer groups, often also generating distress at home. Of note, if they moved to a new neighborhood and school in the second year, they tended to do better and were more easily accepted by peers who had not experienced their earlier upset. These findings suggest that while stability is important, a move may be beneficial.

After six years, with the approach of a boy's adolescence, Hetherington (1987) found that mother–son relationships are still problematic and conflictual. Boys also continue to have more problems at school. Mother–daughter relationships are more likely to be characterized by closeness. There is often a companionate rela-

tionship between a child and a mother who is not remarried. However, it can become dysfunctional when generational boundaries become blurred, as when a parent relates as a peer (Glenwick & Mowerey, 1986) or if roles are reversed, as in a child's monitoring of a parent's dating.

In early adolescence, issues of control and power in decision making become problems, but this was also found true for adolescents in intact families. There was a cluster of drug use, sexual activity, and pregnancy for some. Whereas normal conflicts at puberty tend to diminish at launching in nondivorced families, conflicts especially persist for girls with nonremarried mothers. Good contact with the noncustodial father was found to be helpful when the conflict between the ex-spouses was not great (Hetherington, 1987).[5]

Herz (1989) offers a clinically useful framework for understanding the complexities in the process of reorganization in single-parent households. She offers useful guidelines for successive phases of adjustment focused on three interrelated challenges in establishing a viable unit: financial pressures, parenting, and social relationships.

In the early phase of adjustment, clinicians can help clients see the possibility of many options that are potentially viable and yet help them to take things a step at a time so they will not be overwhelmed by the inherent unclarity and complexities of the postdivorce situation. Given the lack of models for divorced families in our society, it is important to offer information and to be aware of available community resources for support and practical assistance in developing such competencies as basic financial and legal knowledge. Single-parent groups and community drop-in centers may be more helpful in promoting and sustaining long-term adjustment than traditional long-term therapies.

Family therapists can also counter the tendency in clinical assessment to overpathologize mothers heading single-parent households. Diagnostic labels such as "borderline personality"

---

[5] *Editors' Note.* This finding may mean that girls with nonremarried mothers do not launch as well as those with remarried mothers. Some of these girls may have difficulty in forming relationships with men, the process by which many girls traditionally launch.

are often misapplied to unsupported mothers whose current functioning is severely impaired. Such a diagnosis, with assumptions of underlying psychopathology, may lead to blaming the "failure" to marry, to stay married, or to remarry on the woman's character deficits (Walsh & Scheinkman, 1989). "Single-parent" mothers are frequently stereotyped as "chaotic," "excessively needy," "neglectful of their children," and "deficient in exerting executive leadership and controls." The assignment of further tasks to an already-overwhelmed mother generally fails and leaves her feeling more pressured, unsupported, and inadequate. Too often, such a response is mistaken as a sign of a client's resistance and untreatable pathology. Clinicians need to be careful not to overload a mother with expectations and tasks without appreciating her overburdened situation and the constraints imposed by limited resources.

Similarly, clinicians need to counter the tendency to ignore or negatively prejudge a father's potential contributions and motivations based on reports of his past behavior or his "absence." Many fathers are able to develop better relationships with their children after divorce than they had during the marriage. It is important to contact the noncustodial parent directly and to meet to assess and work toward new possibilities for parent–child involvement and for more adequate support of the children and the custodial parent. But it is essential first to gain the custodial parent's agreement for such contact and to reach an understanding as to how it will be in her interests as well as in those of the children. It must be made explicit that the aims of intervention, through either conjoint or separate individual sessions, are not to reunite the former couple or to work on marital problems, but rather to promote better parenting and the well-being of all family members.

REMARRIED-FAMILY ADAPTATION

Remarriage most often takes place within three to five years of a divorce. Men tend to remarry sooner than women and to choose second wives, on the average, who are six years younger than they are. The higher a man's education and income, the more likely he is to remarry, while the reverse is true for women. Over half of remarrying adults have children from previous marriages. Whereas marital satisfaction in nondivorced families is associated with better parent–child relationships, in early remarriage, high marital satisfaction is often accompanied by parent–child conflict (Hetherington, 1987), associated, as will be discussed below, with the various triangles inherent in the structure of remarried families. Remarried couples with children are twice as likely to redivorce (White & Booth, 1985), as a result of child-related problems and despite congenial marital relations.

Remarriage of either biological parent is also accompanied by a further decline in frequency of contact between noncustodial fathers and their children (Furstenberg, Nord, Petersen, & Zill, 1983). One representative study (Anderson & White, 1986) found that 69 percent of children in stepfamilies had contact with their fathers less than five times a year.

Because of the complexity of the adaptational process for all members involved, McGoldrick and Carter (1989) regard remarriage as an additional phase in the family life cycle. They observe, "As a first marriage signifies the joining of two families, so a second marriage involves the interweaving of three, four, or more families, whose previous family life cycle course has been disrupted by death or divorce" (p. 399).

A number of emotional and organizational issues are predictable in remarriage. The following discussion highlights the most important clinical issues in work with remarried families, drawing especially on the longitudinal studies of Hetherington and her colleagues (Hetherington et al., 1981; Hetherington, 1987, 1989a, 1989b) and on the family life cycle perspective and clinical insights of McGoldrick and Carter (1989). For more detailed analyses, readers are also referred to the annotated bibliography of Bergquist (1984) and research reviews by Chilman (1983), Ihinger-Tolman and Pasley (1987), and Pasley and Ihinger-Tolman (1988). Clinicians, and remarried families themselves, will find practical guidance in books by Visher and Visher (1979, 1987), those by Sager and colleagues (Sager et al., 1983), and Wald (1981). Increasingly, the literature is advancing beyond the deficit view of remarriage to examine its potential strengths and resources (as in

Bradt & Moynihan, 1986; Knaub, Hanna, & Sinnet, 1984; and Whiteside, 1982).

Family Paradigms, Myths, and Realities

The model of an intact first family does not fit the complexity and challenges of remarried-family integration. Remarriage thrusts all participants into instant multiple roles and child-rearing responsibilities, without the stepwise progression of the first marriage. Confusion abounds concerning kinship labels, different names, interactional rules, and guidelines for functioning. Members must navigate complex and ambiguous boundaries of the system involving such basic issues as: membership (Who are the "real" family members?); space and time (Where do children really belong? How much time is spent where, when, with whom?); authority (Who is in charge and who should a child obey?). This cluster of issues must continually be renegotiated. Enormous flexibility is required to enable the new family to expand and contract boundaries, to include visiting children and then let them go while also establishing a stable family unit.

Many problems stem from an attempt to replicate the intact family or its ideal image, using inappropriate roles and rules as guidelines. McGoldrick and Carter note several resulting complications. First, a tight loyalty boundary may be drawn around the new household, cutting off biological parents, noncustodial children, and extended family. Second, because the parent–child bond predates the marital bond and is likely to be strong, stepparents and stepchildren may compete for primacy with the spouse/parent, blurring the generational differences in the relationships. Third, traditional gender-role expectations place pressure on women to take responsibility for the emotional well-being of the family and generate adversarial relations with stepdaughters and the ex-wife/mother.

The transition into remarriage is especially difficult because of the wish for instant family unity. Therapists need to help families to counteract tendencies toward fusion and conflict avoidance stemming from their past pain, vulnerability, and fear of failing in the new marriage. It is useful to examine and alter fantasies that can foster denial of normal adjustment problems or lead to a sense of failure when unrealistic expectations are not quickly met. Families gain a more realistic perspective when clinicians normalize the process, offering information about common transitional dilemmas (Whiteside, 1982). It is important for them to take the process a step at a time and to realize that successful remarried-family integration can require from three to five years to accomplish (Dahl et al., 1987). While this news may not be comforting initially, the level of family integration is likely to be higher the longer the new family is together.

Rituals are powerful shared experiences in the integration of the remarried-family system (Imber-Black, 1988; Whiteside, 1988). The celebration of a remarriage ceremony, with the active participation of children and extended-family members, is most valuable in marking the launching of the new family unit. Weaving together practices from previous family traditions and creating new patterns, from dinnertime rituals to celebrations of major holidays, helps to establish a sense of family cohesion. Custody arrangements for holidays that shift children back and forth in alternate years may need to be altered to further a sense of inclusion and continuity. Cross-cultural remarriages require more effort to bridge differences in established traditions (Baptiste, 1984).

Reworking Previous Divorce Issues

As with first marriages, remarriages work best when extended-family members approve or accept the marriage and worst when cutoffs occur. In addition to the family of origin, unresolved issues from past marriages, the process of divorce, and the period between marriages are all carried into remarriage (Wald, 1981). To the extent that each spouse can resolve emotional issues with significant people from the past, the new relationship can proceed on its own merits.

Every remarriage is grounded in loss, whether through widowhood or through divorce (McGoldrick & Walsh, 1991; Walsh & McGoldrick, 1991). When the previous task of mourning the loss of a past marriage and family unit has not been dealt with, the step of remarriage reactivates painful issues. Duberman

(1975) found remarried-family integration to be easier if the previous spouse had died rather than divorced, underscoring the emotional and practical complications posed by divorce. The remarriage of a former spouse is often accompanied by feelings of depression, helplessness, anger, and anxiety. Although men tend to report less emotional upset when ex-wives remarry, they do decrease contact with their children. Financial and custody battles frequently ensue at remarriage (Hetherington et al., 1981). In most remarried families, both spouses prefer distant but cordial relationships with ex-spouses and their new marital partners.

Clinicians may need to further the emotional divorce of former spouses, as they facilitate collaboration in parenting and increasingly involve stepparents. If ex-spouses are not speaking directly to each other or are in continual conflict, the destructive bond maintained by anger and communicated through children needs to be altered so that it will not undermine remarried-family formation.

Children's worries over being the cause of the divorce, of persisting parental conflict, or of a noncustodial parent's cutoff may lead to fears of unlovability or destructive power in the new family. Loyalty conflicts for children are a common source of difficulty, when a child fears that becoming close to a stepparent will hurt or alienate the other parent. Divided loyalties, confusion, and mixed feelings about where a child "belongs" may be expressed in transitional behavior problems or triangulations, as in taking sides or playing one side against the other. One young son repeatedly asked his mother, "Who do you love more, Sam (her new husband) or me?" and, "Who do you love more, Sam or Daddy?"

Any member may have difficulty in forming new attachments, arising from persisting conflict or cutoffs from an ex-spouse, children, or other family members as a result of a bitter divorce. Often a father who has been disengaged from his own children is unable to develop a relationship with stepchildren because of his feelings of disloyalty or guilt (Clingempeel, Brand, & Ievoli, 1984a; Glen, Ievoli, & Brand, 1984b). Other parents may seek to compensate for a sense of failure in the first family by attempting to be a "superparent" in the remarriage family. When, as typically happens, children respond slowly or not at all, the sense of failure may fuel anger and futility. Repairing earlier cutoffs and addressing issues of conflicting loyalty and guilt are therapeutic priorities in such cases.

Children must deal with the permanent loss of the previous intact family. Remarriage shatters lingering fantasies of parents' reuniting. When one 6-year-old was told that her mother planned to remarry to a man whom the child knew and liked, she replied, "Can't you think of anyone else? (long pause) Like how about Dad?"

Parents and stepparents may need help in encouraging and tolerating expression of the range of feelings children are likely to have. The more parents can reassure children that the new stepparent relationship neither replaces nor erases the bond with the biological parent, the less conflictual will be the child's attachments. This requires acceptance of the need for continual involvement with parts of the old family and help for children to maintain relationships with their biological parents.

Stepparent Relationships and Child Adjustment

The different complications of live-in versus visiting arrangements need to be explored (Ambert, 1986). Since households in which the mother has custody account for most remarried-family residences, most research has examined relationships with stepfathers (Hetherington, 1988). Both boys and girls demonstrate initial resistance to a new stepfather, who typically enters the family like a polite stranger. Early attempts to take an active role as a parental authority are commonly rebuffed by children. One child distanced her new stepparent when he attempted to set limits by addressing him as "Mr. Stepfather." Over time, a pattern of disengagement may ensue, with stepfathers assuming a position of uninvolved parenting, with low contact, little warmth, and avoidance of problems.

There are gender differences in child adjustment in remarriage, just as there are in single-parent households. Girls in stepfamilies report more negative stress than do boys in stepfamilies or girls in intact families. Girls, more than boys, tend to give their stepparents a hard time, with noncompliant and often hostile behavior. The longer the time a child has spent in a single-parent household before remarriage, the stronger are feelings of rivalry and fears of loss. When a daughter has occupied a special companionate or parentified position with her mother, she is more likely to view her mother's new husband as an unwelcome intruder. With boys, the development of a good relationship with the stepfather often buffers a previously conflictual one with the mother.

Many stepfathers are able to develop good relationships with their stepchildren. The pattern found to be most successful is for the stepfather first to work at forming a relationship without trying to impose his own authority. Instead, he will fare better if he supports the mother's discipline, and only gradually moves into a more direct authority position. Clinicians can help stepfathers not to take a child's early rebuff personally, but to view it as typical of children's reluctance to be controlled by a stepparent before they have established their own relationship with him. It can take stepfathers almost two years to become comanagers of stepchildren with their wives. They first need to become friends and to strive for mutual courtesy, and not to expect a stepchild's immediate love. Clinicians can be helpful by normalizing this process and facilitating a gradual stepwise progression.

McGoldrick and Carter observe that the most difficult stepparent position is that of stepmothers, who typically are attempting to form relationships with stepchildren who have primary residences with their mothers or shuttle back and forth. With traditional cultural expectations for women in families to assume responsibility for the well-being of all members (McGoldrick, Anderson, & Walsh, 1989), stepmothers tend to find themselves overresponsible for stepfamily integration and harmony and to assume that it is their fault if expectations are not met. Because a woman's identity and self-esteem are so bound up with success in her roles as a mother and wife and with gaining love and approval, she is likely to feel the stepchildren's rebuffs as her inadequacy. Here, too, clinicians need to frame the process as normal and to put the sense of personal failure into its proper context. The stepmother–stepdaughter relationship tends to be most problematic, especially since most step-daughters have maintained close bonds with their mothers. Stepmothers, like stepfathers, fare better with younger children than with teenagers. Interestingly, widows have been found to have better stepparent relationships than divorcees.

The harder a stepparent tries to replace or better a biological parent, the more conflicted a child is likely to be. If a stepparent can back off and can tolerate and respect the bond between the child and biological parent, the child will more readily add on this new relationship and come to value it in its own right. Such factors as the child's age, gender, and primary residence will influence the nature of the steprelationships that develop. They may take a variety of shapes and degrees of attachment. The active role in parenting and the provision of financial support that most stepparents eventually assume need to be recognized by reforming the laws that currently give stepparents no legal standing to continue their relationships with stepchildren in the event of divorce or widowhood.

Family-Life-Cycle Variables

Remarriage joins together the separate life-cycle passages of the two new partners and their families, whose developmental stages are always overlapping. The tasks associated with different family-life-cycle phases and the fit between the joining families will influence the issues they will need to confront. Likewise, the developmental stages of children at the time of remarriage will be a factor in adaptation (Hetherington, 1989b). Younger children tend to adjust to remarriage more readily than do older children. Preteen and adolescent offspring are slower to form close relationships with stepparents and may evidence more behavior problems. Early adolescence appears to be more problematic for remarriage because the task of forming a cohesive family unit is in opposition to the child's developmental thrust toward autonomy and independence. Children may resist expectations for family togetherness and attachment to a new stepparent at a time when they are investing energies in outside relationships and commitments. Since children in divorced families tend to mature faster, they often resent attempts of control by a stepparental authority.

Moreover, with issues of sexuality coming to the fore, adolescents may be uncomfortable with a parent's new sexual relationship. Their own emerging sexuality complicates relationships with stepparents and stepsiblings. Confusion may arise around expressions of affection—or about feelings of attraction and intimacy—between a child and a stepparent or stepsiblings of the opposite sex. With incest taboos and boundaries less clear, sexual abuse does occur more often in steprelationships, usually by stepfathers or stepbrothers.

Since men commonly remarry to considerably younger women, a teenage daughter and a stepmother may experience complicated feelings of rivalry and a blurring of generational boundaries. In later adolescence, as children begin thinking of leaving home, they may be more accepting of the stepparent as someone to take care of their parent in their absence, especially if they had carried out parentified functions in the single-parent household.

Sibling Relationships

Divorce and remarriage pose difficult challenges for sibling relationships, especially when both spouses have children from previous marriages. In single-parent households, boys show more sibling conflict while girls tend to draw closer together, especially when involvement by adults is lacking. In remarried families, sibling rivalry and competition increase, especially when new stepsibling relationships must be worked out and a child's sibling position is altered, particularly that of an only, oldest, or youngest child. Adolescent girls are more likely to become withdrawn and aloof from siblings, while boys may become conflictual. Confusion about sexual issues in sibling relations is also common (Baptiste, 1986). It is useful to clarify boundaries and not to push for more closeness than is comfortable and developmentally compatible.

A further adjustment is required if the remarried couple then has "a child of their own." As our language implies, children from a former marriage may begin to feel that they belong less fully to the remarried-family unit and fear that they will be loved less because of their step status. While it may be hoped that a mutual child will solidify the remarried-family unit, it may, instead, further complicate relationships (Vemer, Coleman, Ganong, & Cooper, 1989). The distinctions between siblings, stepsiblings, and half-siblings may also be confusing for children, who will need to forge their own alliances.

Dysfunctional Triangles

McGoldrick and Carter (1989) describe the most common triangles presented clinically in remarried families. The first involves the two new partners and an ex-spouse. Marital problems center on rivalries and jealousy, or intrusion of the ex-spouse into the marriage. Clinical work is directed at furthering an emotional divorce, while supporting the vulnerable position of the new spouse and solidifying the remarriage unit. Rather than meeting with ex-spouses together, which may stir fantasies of reunion and threaten the new partner, an effective intervention is to coach the pivotal individual, in the presence of the new spouse, to resolve issues with the former spouse.

Other triangles may involve a united-front remarried couple denying even normal difficulties in their relationship but focused on problems with a child/stepchild or joined in conflict with an ex-spouse over children. Here it is helpful to put the biological parent in charge of managing the child and resolving conflict with the ex-spouse, while supporting the new spouse to back off to a neutral position. As the presenting problem subsides, differences and tensions in the new marriage are likely to surface and can be normalized and addressed.

In other cases, conflicts may involve the extended-family members, especially if they have disapproved of the remarriage or are cut off from contact. In some remarried families, conflicts may ensue between stepsiblings or between a child from a former marriage and a child born to the new couple. A flexible intervention plan is required to address various subsystem issues at appropriate phases in therapy. Restructuring of dysfunctional coalitions and repair of cut-off relationships are intervention priorities.

Intervention Guidelines

In work with remarried families, it is recommended that ex-spouses be routinely contacted and invited to meet separately or with the children to hear their views on the presenting problem as it concerns the child and the ex-spouse's role as parent (McGoldrick & Carter, 1989). If remarried, new partners should be involved to structurally reinforce that marital unit and to explore and facilitate that stepparent connection. When informing the primary client family of the intention to make this contact, clinicians are often warned that the ex-spouse is "crazy," "uncaring," and certain to be unresponsive. Nevertheless, a phone call frequently locates a concerned parent who is willing to come in. Ex-spouses are rarely included in joint sessions with the remarried family, and if so, only to deal with specific serious child-focused agendas. Even then, the level of tension creates a climate of high anxiety that may be counterproductive. Such a meeting may have primarily diagnostic value or underscore the seriousness of a situation. For some families, only the passage of time helps them to deal with each other. If a child-focused problem is presented, the therapist should try to involve all parents and stepparents. If joint sessions are held, the focus should be clearly directed to the resolution of specific coparenting issues and cooperation in resolving the child's difficulties. Discussion of unresolved marital issues is not advised at such sessions. The aim is to develop a collaborative parental team that includes stepparents in both households. Whom a therapist sees, and in which configurations, depends largely on the prioritizing of the structural and developmental problems and tasks of the family (Katz & Stein, 1983).[6]

Clinicians need to assist parents in helping children to express the full range of feelings toward all family and stepfamily members and to accept divided loyalties. At the same time, parents should be encouraged to take appropriate responsibility for decisions concerning custody, visitation, and remarriage and not abdicate such authority to the children. Children's opinions and feelings should be considered, and their input should increase with age, yet they should not have the power or be inappropriately expected to make final decisions on such major issues as whether a parent should remarry.

Facilitating Divorce and Remarriage Processes

The processes of divorce and remarriage involve a number of developmental steps and the emotional tasks associated with each (McGoldrick & Carter, 1989). The intense emotions associated with the dissolution of the first marriage are reactivated and must be dealt with at each successive step, including the separation and divorce, the remarriage of either spouse, shifts in custody, changes in residence of either spouse, illness or death of the ex-spouse, and life-cycle transitions of the children (graduations, marriage, illness).

A number of variables must be taken into account in helping a family to achieve a functional postdivorce arrangement. It is not divorce per se but a problem divorce, in which transitional tasks were not accomplished, that poses a particular threat to postdivorce and remarriage adjustment. In fact, the tremendous diversity of postdivorce adjustments should be underscored. Despite some reports to the contrary, emerging research generally finds that, over time, most children and their families do fairly well after divorce, and some demonstrate remarkable resilience. Recent research has begun to identify a broad array of factors that either intensify or buffer transitional stresses and affect immediate and long-term adaptation (Vemer et al., 1989).

In summary, emerging data on different custody and visitation arrangements suggest that successful adaptation depends most of all on active, *reliable involvement* and *responsibility* on the part of both parents and on their *ability to collaborate in coparenting without serious or chronic conflict*. Reports of the negative effects of divorce must be viewed in the context of the fact that 50 percent of fathers have not seen their

---

[6] *Editors' Note.* Note that McGoldrick and Carter's (1989) approach shifts the professional's role from that of psychotherapist to that of go-between, as in divorce mediation. Combining individual and joint sessions brings issues of confidentiality in systems-oriented therapy to the fore. See Doherty and Boss (Chapter 20) for a detailed consideration of the ethical issues involved.

children in the past year and that most do not provide adequate child support. Based on a careful systems assessment, clinicians should make every effort to facilitate contact and support by noncustodial fathers and work through barriers to cooperative parenting wherever appropriate. In cases of destructive conflict or physical or sexual abuse, only limited, supervised contact, if any, may be indicated. A range of extended-family, social, and community resources can be mobilized to support and enable overburdened single-parent heads of households to function most effectively. Children need predictability and structure, as well as warmth and feedback, for optimal functioning.

A general goal for facilitating a viable remarried family is the *establishment of an open, flexible "supra" system with permeable boundaries and clear roles and rules* (Sager et al., 1983). McGoldrick and Carter identify three key "enabling attitudes" that facilitate transition through the steps involved in the formation and stabilization process of remarriage. The first is a reasonable *resolution of the emotional attachment to ex-spouses*. The second is giving up the unrealistic and inappropriate ideal of first-family structure and *forming a new conceptual model of family*. The third is *accepting the amount of time and space necessary for stepfamily organization, as well as the ambivalences and difficulties*. Clinicians need to help families to examine their beliefs and to work out feelings and expectations concerning these aims.

The model for remarried-family functioning proposed by McGoldrick and Carter (1989) identifies tendencies toward dysfunction and serves as a guide for clinical intervention. First, clinicians need to *promote permeable boundaries between the various households to permit children easy access* as agreed on in custody and visitation arrangements. Second, couples need to be helped to *solidify the marital bond*, especially since the presence of children precludes a "honeymoon period." Concomitantly, they need to *understand the difficult position of the stepparent*, who needs to *ease gradually into a role of authority* and to accept and *support the biological parent's attachments to and responsibilities for children*. Third, couples need to reconsider and revise traditional gender roles that are dysfunctional in remarriage so that *each parent takes primary responsibility for his or her own*

children and that financial support is equitably shared.

As future research furthers our understanding of mediating variables that distinguish children and families who do well in different family configurations from those with long-term adverse outcomes, our clinical practice will be better informed and more effective in promoting healthy adaptation in divorced and remarried families.

REFERENCES

Ahrons, C. (1980). Redefining the divorced family: A conceptual framework for postdivorce family systems reorganization. *Social Work, 25,* 437–441.

Ahrons, C., & Rodgers, R. (1987). *Divorced families: A multidisciplinary developmental view.* New York: Norton.

Ambert, A. (1986). Being a stepparent: Live-in and visiting stepchildren. *Journal of Marriage and the Family, 48,* 795–804.

Anderson, J.Z., & White, G.D. (1986). An empirical investigation of interaction and relationship patterns in functional and dysfunctional nuclear families and stepfamilies. *Family Process, 25,* 407–422.

Arendell, T. (1986). *Mothers and divorce: Legal, economic, and social dilemmas.* Berkeley, CA: University of California Press.

Baptiste, D. (1984). Marital and family therapy with racially/culturally intermarried stepfamilies: Issues and guidelines. *Family Relations, 33,* 373–380.

Baptiste, D. (1986). How parents intensify sexual feelings between stepsiblings. *Remarriage, 3,* 5–6.

Bergquist, B. (1984). The remarried family: An annotated bibliography. *Family Process, 23,* 107–119.

Boss, P, & Greenberg, J. (1984). Family boundary ambiguity: A new variable. *Family Process, 23,* 535–546.

Bradt, J.O., & Bradt, C.M. (1986). Resources for remarried families. In M. Karpel (Ed.), *Family resources.* New York: Guilford Press.

Cherlin, A. (1981). *Marriage, divorce, remarriage.* Cambridge, MA: Harvard University Press.

Chilman, C. (1983). Remarriage and stepfamilies: Research results and implications. In E. Macklin & R. Rubin (Eds.), *Contemporary families and alternative lifestyles.* Beverly Hills, CA: Sage.

Clingempeel, W.G., Brand, E., & Ievoli, R. (1984a). Stepparent-stepchild relationships in stepmother and stepfather families: A multimethod study. *Family Relations, 33,* 456–473.

Clingempeel, W.G., Glen, R., Ievoli, R., & Brand, E. (1984b). Structural complexity and the quality of stepfather-stepchild relationships. *Family Process, 23,* 547–560.

Dahl, A.S., Cowgill, K.M., & Asmundsson, R. (1987). Life in remarriage families. *Social Work, 32,* 40–44.

Duberman, L. (1975). *The reconstituted family: A study of remarried couples and their children.* Chicago: Nelson-Hall.

Furstenberg, F., Nord, C.W., Peterson, J.L., & Zill, N. (1983). The life course of children of divorce: Marital disruptions and parental contact. *American Sociological Review, 48,* 656–668.

Furstenberg, F., & Spanier, G. (1984). *Recycling the family: Remarriage after divorce.* Beverly Hills, CA: Sage.

Ganong, L., & Coleman, M. (1986). A comparison of clinical and empirical literature on children in stepfamilies. *Journal of Marriage and the Family, 48,* 309–318.

Ganong, L., & Coleman, M. (1988). Do mutual children cement

bonds in stepfamilies? *Journal of Marriage and the Family, 50,* 687–698.

Glenwick, N., & Mowerey, J. (1986). When parent becomes peer: Loss of intergenerational boundaries in single parent families. *Family Relations, 35,* 57–62.

Glick, P.C. (1984). Marriage, divorce, and living arrangements. *Journal of Family Issues, 5,* 7–26.

Glick, P.C., & Lin, S.L. (1986). Recent changes in divorce and remarriage. *Journal of Marriage and the Family, 48,* 433–441.

Goldsmith, J. (1982). The postdivorce family system. In F. Walsh (Ed.), *Normal family processes.* New York: Guilford Press.

Grief, G. (1986). Mothers without custody and child support. *Family Relations, 35,* 87–93.

Herz, F. (1989). The postdivorce family. In B. Carter & M. McGoldrick (Eds.), *The changing family life cycle: A framework for family therapy* (2nd ed.). Boston: Allyn & Bacon.

Hetherington, E.M. (1987). Family relations six years after divorce. In K. Pasley & M. Ihinger-Tolman (Eds.), *Remarriage and stepparenting today: Current research and theory.* New York: Guilford Press.

Hetherington, E.M. (1988). Presentation at the 46th Annual Meeting, American Association for Marriage and Family Therapy, New Orleans.

Hetherington, E.M. (1989a). Coping with family transitions: Winners, losers, and survivors. *Child Development, 60,* 1–14.

Hetherington, E.M. (1989b). Marital transitions: A child's perspective. *American Psychologist, 44,* 303–312.

Hetherington, E.M., Cox, M., & Cox, R. (1978). The aftermath of divorce. In J.H. Stevens & M. Matthews (Eds.), *Mother/child, father/child relations.* Washington, DC: National Association for the Education of Young Children.

Hewlett, S. (1986). *Family and work.* New York: Ballinger.

Ihinger-Tallman, M., & Pasley, K. (1987). *Remarriage.* Beverly Hills, CA: Sage.

Imber-Black, E. (1988). Normative and therapeutic rituals in couples therapy. In E. Imber-Black, J. Roberts, & R. Whiting (Eds.), *Rituals in families and family therapy.* New York: Norton.

Isaacs, M.B., & Leon, G.H. (1986). Social networks, divorce, and adjustment: A tale of three generations. *Journal of Divorce, 9,* 1–16.

Isaacs, M.B., Montalvo, B., & Abelsohn, D. (1986). *The difficult divorce: Therapy for children and families.* New York: Basic Books.

Johnston, J. (1988). *Impasses of divorce.* New York: Free Press.

Katz, L., & Stein, S. (1983). Treating stepfamilies. In B. Wolman & G. Stricker (Eds.), *Handbook of family and marital therapy.* New York: Plenum.

Knaub, P., Hanna, S., & Stinnett, N. (1984). Strengths of remarried families. *Journal of Divorce, 7,* 41–55.

Lindblad-Goldberg, M. (1989). Successful minority single-parent families. In L. Combrinck-Graham (Ed.), *Children in family contexts.* New York: Guilford Press.

Luepnitz, D. (1982). *Child custody: A study of families after divorce.* Lexington, MA: Heath.

McGoldrick, M. (1989). Women through the family life cycle. In M. McGoldrick, C. Anderson, & F. Walsh (Eds.), *Women in families: A framework for family therapy.* New York: Norton.

McGoldrick, M., Anderson, C., & Walsh, F. (1989). *Women in families: A framework for family therapy.* New York: Norton.

McGoldrick, M., & Carter, B. (1989). Forming a remarried family. In B. Carter & M. McGoldrick (Eds.), *The changing family life cycle: Framework for family therapy* (2nd ed.). Boston: Allyn & Bacon.

McGoldrick, M., & Gerson, R. (1985). *Genograms in family assessment.* New York: Norton.

Messinger, L. (1984). *Remarriage: A family affair.* New York: Plenum.

Miller, D.C. (1987). *Helping the strong: An exploration of the needs of families headed by women.* Silver Springs, MD: NASW Publications.

Norton, A., & Glick, P.C. (1986). One-parent families: A social and economic profile. *Family Relations, 35,* 9–17.

Norton, A.J., & Moorman, J.E. (1987). Current trends in marriage and divorce among American women. *Journal of Marriage and the Family, 49,* 3–14.

Pasley, K., & Ihinger-Tallman, M. (Eds.) (1988). *Remarriage and stepparenting today: Current research and theory.* New York: Guilford Press.

Sager, C., Brown, H.S., Crohn, H., Engel, T., Rodstein, E., & Walker, L. (1983). *Treating the remarried family.* New York: Brunner/Mazel.

Vemer, E., Coleman, M., Ganong, L., & Cooper, H. (1989). Marital satisfaction in remarriage: A meta-analysis. *Journal of Marriage and the Family, 51,* 713–735.

Visher, E.B., & Visher, J.S. (1979). *Stepfamilies: A guide to working with stepparents and stepchildren.* New York: Brunner/Mazel.

Visher, E., & Visher, J. (1982). Stepfamilies and stepparenting. In F. Walsh (Ed.), *Normal family processes.* New York: Guilford Press.

Visher, E., & Visher, J. (1987). *Old loyalties, new ties: Therapeutic strategies with stepfamilies.* New York: Brunner/Mazel.

Wald, E. (1981). *The remarried family: Challenge and promise.* New York: Family Service Association of America.

Walker, K., & Messinger, L. (1979). Remarriage after divorce: Dissolution and construction of family boundaries. *Family Process, 18,* 185–192.

Wallerstein, J. (1989). *Second chances: Men, women, & children after divorce.* New York: Ticknor & Fields.

Wallerstein, J., & Kelly, J. (1980). *Surviving the breakup: How children and parents cope with divorce.* New York: Basic Books.

Walsh, F. (1982). Conceptualizations of normal family functioning. In F. Walsh (Ed.), *Normal family processes.* New York: Guilford Press.

Walsh, F. (1983). Normal family ideologies: Myths and realities. In C. Falicov (Ed.), *Cultural dimensions of family therapy.* Rockville, MD: Aspen.

Walsh, F. (1989). Perceptions of family normality: Refining our lenses. *Journal of family psychology, 2,* 303–306.

Walsh, F., & McGoldrick, M. (1991). Loss and the family: A systemic perspective. In F. Walsh & M. McGoldrick (Eds.), *Living beyond loss: Death in the family.* New York: Norton.

Walsh, F., & Scheinkman, M. (1989). (Fe)male: The hidden gender dimension in models of family therapy. In M. McGoldrick, C. Anderson, & F. Walsh (Eds.), *Women in families: A framework for family therapy.* New York: Norton.

Weiss, R.S. (1979). *Going it alone.* New York: Basic Books.

Weitzman, L. (1985). *The divorce revolution: The unexpected social and economic consequences for women and children in America.* New York: Free Press.

White, L., & Booth, A. (1985). The quality and stability of remarriages: The role of stepchildren. *American Sociological Review, 50,* 689–698.

Whiteside, M.F. (1982). Remarriage: A family developmental process. *Journal of Marital and Family Therapy, 8,* 59–68.

Whiteside, M.F. (1988). Creation of family identity through ritual performance in early remarriage. In E. Imber-Black, J. Roberts & R. Whiting (Eds.), *Rituals in families and family therapy.* New York: Norton.

Wilson, W. (1987). *The truly disadvantaged.* Chicago: University of Chicago Press.

CHAPTER 18

Ethnicity and Family Therapy

Monica McGoldrick, M.S.W.,
Nydia Garcia Preto, M.S.W.,
Paulette Moore Hines, Ph.D.,
and Evelyn Lee, Ed.D.

The United States has had the greatest ethnic diversity of any nation in history, but until recently, public discussion of differences among American ethnic groups has been virtually taboo. We have talked about the melting pot and blinded ourselves to our country's inherent diversity. But ethnicity should be of interest to all family therapists, because cultural norms and values prescribe the "rules" by which families operate, including how family members identify, define, and attempt to solve their problems, and how they seek help. We believe that therapists who appreciate the cultural relativity of family life are in a position to intervene more effectively and that a therapist's own ethnicity influences the helping process. Furthermore, our therapeutic models are themselves reflections of the cultures in which they developed (McGoldrick, Pearce, & Giordano, 1982). Our pilot study of family therapists (McGoldrick & Rohrbaugh, 1987) suggests that ethnic stereo-types are maintained in the minds of family therapists whose families already have been in the United States for several generations.

Common sense tells us that we experience life on the basis of our own cultural values and assumptions, and that, unless confronted by others whose values differ from our own, we inevitably see the world through our own "cultural filters," often persisting in established views despite clear information to the contrary (Watzlawick, 1976).

We see the world through our own cultural filters and we often persist in our established views in spite of clear evidence that contradicts our perceptions. Ethnicity patterns our thinking, feeling, and behavior in both obvious and subtle ways, although generally operating outside of our awareness. It plays a major role in determining what we eat, how we work, how we relate, how we celebrate holidays and rituals, and how we feel about life, death, and illness.

The very definition of human development is culturally based. Eastern cultures tend to define the person as a social being and to define development by the growth in the human capacity for empathy and connection (Plath, 1985). By contrast, many Western cultures begin with the individual as a psychological being and define development as growth in the human capacity for differentiation.

DEFINING ETHNICITY

Our definition of ethnicity refers to a concept of a group's "peoplehood" based on a combination of race, religion, and cultural history, whether or not members realize their commonalities with one another. It describes a commonality transmitted by the family over generations and reinforced by the surrounding community. But it is more than race, religion, or national and geographic origin, which is not to minimize the significance of race or the special problem of racism.[1] It involves conscious and unconscious processes that fulfill a deep psychological need for identity and historical continuity. It unites those who conceive of themselves as alike by virtue of their common ancestry, real or fictitious, and who are so regarded by others.

The consciousness of ethnic identity varies greatly within groups and from one group to another. Families vary in attitude toward their ethnicity from clannishness, regressively holding on to past traditions and fearing any change from cultural norms, on the one hand, to denial of any ethnic values or patterns, on the other. In groups that have experienced serious prejudice and discrimination, such as Jews and Blacks, family attitudes toward allegiance to the group may become quite conflicted, and members may even turn against each other, reflecting prejudices in the outside world. Some groups, if they are close enough in appearance to the characteristics of the dominant groups, have a choice about ethnic identification, whereas oth-

ers, because of their color or other physical characteristics, do not.

Ethnicity intersects with class, religion, politics, geography, the length of time a group has been in this country, the historical cohort, and the degree of discrimination the group has experienced. Generally speaking, Americans tend to move closer to the dominant value system in this country as they move up in social class. People in different geographic locations evolve new cultural norms. Religion also modifies or reinforces certain cultural values. Families that remain within an ethnic neighborhood, whose members work and socialize with members of their group, and whose religion reinforces ethnic values are likely to maintain their ethnicity longer than those who live in heterogeneous settings and have no social reinforcers of their cultural traditions. The degree of ethnic intermarriage in the family also plays a role in cultural patterns (McGoldrick & Garcia Preto, 1984). Nevertheless, there is burgeoning evidence that ethnic values and identifications are retained for many generations after immigration and play a significant role in family life throughout the life cycle. Second-, third-, and even fourth-generation Americans may differ from the dominant culture in values, behavior, and life-cycle patterns.

ETHNICITY AND MENTAL HEALTH

While we are well aware of the problems of stereotyping and generalizing about groups in ways that may lead to prejudice and in no way mean to contribute to this tendency in our culture, we have taken the risk of characterizing differences among groups in order to sensitize clinicians to the range of values held by different people. Of course, each family must be dealt with as unique, and the characterizations used here are meant to broaden the therapist's framework, not to constrict it.

Although human behavior results from the interplay of intrapsychic, interpersonal, familial, socioeconomic, and cultural forces, the mental health field has paid greatest attention to the intrapsychic influences—the personality factors that shape life experiences and behavior. The

---

[1] *Editors' Note.* While ethnicity is phenomenologically more than all these components, there may be times when it is only a single dimension, or a small number of dimensions, of ethnicity that predicts behavior or that allows for reliable distinctions between and among different groups.

study of cultural influences[2] on the emotional functioning of human beings has been left primarily to anthropologists—and even they have preferred to explore these influences in distant and fragile non-Western cultures, rather than the great ethnic diversity among Americans of assumptions about illness and health, normality and pathology. Andrew Greeley (1969), commenting on this tendency, has said:

> I suspect that the historians of the future will be astonished that. . . . (we) could stand in the midst of such an astonishing social phenomenon and take it so much for granted that . . . (we) would not bother to study it. They will find it especially astonishing in light of the fact that ethnic differences, even in the second half of the twentieth century, proved far more important than differences in philosophy or economic system. Men who would not die for a premise or a dogma or a division of labor would more or less cheerfully die for a difference rooted in ethnic origins. (p. 5)

When mental health professionals have considered culture, they have been more absorbed in making international cross-cultural comparisons than in studying the ethnic groups in our own culture (Carpenter & Strauss, 1974; Kiev, 1972). Only recently did we begin to consider ethnic differences in therapists or in client families when developing therapeutic models (McGoldrick, Pearce, & Giordano, 1982).[3]

Ethnicity is deeply tied to the family, through which it is transmitted. As Billingsley (1976) has described the link between ethnicity and family that has enabled Black people to survive in a hostile environment for more than 300 years:

> Ethnicity and family life are two concepts which . . . go hand in hand. They are so intertwined that it is very difficult indeed to observe the one or even to

reflect it seriously without coming to grips with the other. So when we think of Italians and certain other Southern Europeans, we think of large families; we think of the English and certain Northern Europeans in compact nuclear families. When we think of Black families we think of strong extended families, and when we think of Chinese families we must encompass aggregations so large that they often encompass whole communities. (p. 13)

It seems so natural that an interest in families should lead to an interest in ethnicity that it is remarkable that this area has so long been ignored in family therapy. While a few family therapists have recognized the importance of culture, the major models of family therapy make little reference to ethnic differences in the application of their methods. Minuchin and co-workers (Minuchin, Montolvo, Guerney, Rosman, & Schumer, 1967) focused on multiproblem families and developed specific techniques to deal with poor Black and Hispanic families. While the other major models (e.g., Bowen, Haley, and Mental Research Institute strategic, Milan systemic, and the various communications models) emphasize the importance of the family context, they do not make explicit reference to the cultural context within which the family is embedded, and which largely determines its values. The most prominent exceptions are the pioneering work of Papajohn and Spiegel (1975) and, more recently, of McGoldrick and colleagues (McGoldrick et al., 1982). In addition, almost nothing has been written about the cultural determinants of the various models that have been developed and the variability in their application, depending on the cultural fit between the model and the group for which it is used.[4]

In fact, however, a family's culture will determine whether the family will even define a symptom as a problem, and what symptoms develop in which cultural contexts, bringing into question the usefulness of the present diagnostic nomenclature (Fantl & Shiro, 1959; Opler & Singer, 1956; Singer & Opler, 1956; McGoldrick, 1982a). In addition, a patient's "illness" (the experience of being ill) is very different from the course of his or her physio-

---

[2] *Editors' Note.* Cultural influences are ultimately manifest in the actions of individual people, (who interact in families, etc.), so that dissecting a "cultural influence" from a "personality factor" may require an extremely sharp-edged scalpel. This is often a matter of the utmost clinical importance, though not a task easily dealt with.

[3] *Editors' Note.* Ethnic differences probably exert their influence on therapeutic process and outcome in interaction with other factors (including, but not limited to, the therapist's ethnicity) rather than by themselves (as statistical "main effects"). Certainly, empirical study of such patient–therapist interaction effects would be conceptually fascinating and clinically rich.

[4] *Editors' Note.* Another area begging for clinically meaningful research.

logical disease and is strongly influenced by cultural beliefs (Stoeckle, Zola, & Davisdon, 1964). And, naturally, seeking help depends greatly on one's attitude toward the "helper." For example, Italians tend to rely primarily on the family and turn to an outsider for help only as a last resort (Gambino, 1974; Rotunno & McGoldrick, 1982; Zborowski, 1969; Zola, 1966); Black Americans have long mistrusted the help they can receive from traditional middle-class institutions (Hines & Boyd-Franklin, 1982; McAdoo, 1978); and Puerto Ricans (Preto, 1982) and Chinese (Kleinman, 1975) are likely to somatize when they are under stress and may seek medical rather than mental health services. Norwegians, too, often convert emotional tension into physical symptoms, which are more acceptable in their culture than is the overt expression of emotional suffering. As a result, Norwegians are more likely to seek the help of a surgeon than of a psychotherapist (Midelfort & Midelfort, 1982). Likewise, Iranians often view medication and vitamins as a necessary part of treating symptoms, regardless of their origin (Jalali, 1982). Thus, a substantial percentage of potential patients experience troubles and cures somatically and strongly doubt the value of psychotherapy.

Almost all of us have multiple belief systems to which we turn when in need of help. We use not only the official medical or psychotherapeutic system, but also religion, self-help groups, alcohol, yoga, chiropractors, and so on. We utilize remedies our mothers taught us and those suggested by our friends.

These differences can lead to important misunderstandings in therapy. A group whose characteristic response to illness is too different from the dominant culture is likely to be labeled "abnormal." For example, one researcher found that doctors frequently labeled their Italian patients as having psychiatric problems, although there was no evidence that psychosocial problems occurred more frequently among them (Zola, 1966). And Zborowski (1969), in his classic study, found that Italian and Jewish patients complained much more than did Irish or White Anglo-Saxon Protestant (WASP) patients, who considered complaining to be "bad form." Differences in styles of interaction may also be misinterpreted. A high level of interaction is expected in Jewish, Italian, and Greek families, but WASP, Irish, and Scandinavian families

have much less intense interactions and are more likely to deal with problems by distancing. Obviously, therapists need to take these potential differences into account in making an assessment, considering carefully the biases of their own perspective and the particular values of their clients.

For the most part, the ethnic differences that have been described in the family-therapy literature embody common cultural stereotypes. For example, Jewish families are seen as valuing education, success, encouragement of children, democratic principles, verbal expression, shared suffering, guilt, and eating (Herz & Rosen, 1982; Myerhoff, 1978; Zborowski & Herzog, 1952). WASPs are seen as generally valuing control, personal responsibility, independence, individuality, stoicism, keeping up appearances, and moderation in everything (McGill & Pearce, 1982). By contrast, Italian-American families (Giordano, 1986; Rotunno & McGoldrick, 1982) generally are described as valuing the family more than the individual. In these families, food is a major source of emotional as well as physical nourishment, traditional male–female roles are strong, and loyalty flows through personal relationships.

We offer here short sketches of a few ethnic groups to highlight some of the patterns we are suggesting. These characterizations are by no means meant to be comprehensive, but rather to suggest the range of questions that a clinician may need to keep in mind in working with any group, or in understanding himself or herself. The particular insights offered on each group are not presented as the "true truth" about members of that group, but as useful hypotheses, some of which have been suggested in the small research literature that exists on the subject. Our objective is to highlight questions that might be asked by clinicians rather than to attempt to provide the answers, even though in our sketches we have tried to be as detailed as possible, since we believe detail gives more life to the material and helps clinicians think of their own and their clients' experiences in everyday terms. The suggestions we offer to guide clinical practice are based on our own clinical experience and that of our colleagues or other authors, except where research findings are explicitly cited.

The characteristic ethnic patterns we describe

reflect the ethnic origins of the authors, and while they may not be the most frequently researched or written about groups in the clinical literature, they will serve well to exemplify our way of thinking about ethnicity in families and family therapy. For a more comprehensive examination of 17 different American ethnic groups, the reader is referred to *Ethnicity and Family Therapy* (McGoldrick et al., 1982).

IRISH FAMILIES

There are about 16 million Americans of Irish-Catholic background, many of whose families have been in the United States for more than four generations. The culture of this group has remained relatively homogeneous over almost 2,000 years. Irish Catholics began to immigrate in large numbers in the 1840s, primarily because of the potato famine and oppressive conditions in Ireland. Irish Protestants, who are a separate group, have been migrating here since before the American Revolution. Generally, they do not think of themselves as Irish in any meaningful sense, have the lowest rate of endogamous marriage of any American ethnic group, and have tended to lose any sense of their own ethnicity (Fallows, 1979).

Help Seeking

The Irish tend to assume that anything that goes wrong is the result of their sins. Their basic belief is that problems are a private matter between themselves and God, and they are, therefore, unlikely to seek or expect any help when they have trouble (McGoldrick, 1982b; McGoldrick & Pearce, 1981; Sanua, 1960; Zborowski, 1969; Zola, 1966). If they do seek help, they are apt to view therapy as similar to Catholic confession—an occasion on which to relate their "sins" and receive a "penance." They are embarrassed to have to come to therapy, and usually only do so at the suggestion of a third party, such as a school, hospital, or court.

While the Irish rarely seek help for neurotic disorders, they have extremely high rates of psychosis and addiction, primarily alcoholism (Malzberg, 1963; McGoldrick, 1982c; Mc-

Goldrick & Pearce, 1981; Murphy, 1975; Rabkin & Struening, 1976; Roberts & Myers, 1954). In contrast, Jews often view therapy as a "solution" to personal problems, are overrepresented in outpatient psychotherapy, and are underrepresented in psychiatric hospitalizations and treatment for addictions (Malzberg, 1973; Rabkin & Struenning, 1976; Rinder, 1963; Roberts & Myers, 1954).

While in other areas (e.g., literature) the Irish have, perhaps, the most highly developed skill with words of any culture, they may be at a loss to describe their own inner feelings, whether of love, sadness, or anger. They differ markedly in this respect from Jews, who tend to find meaning in articulating all of their feelings. Language and poetry have always been highly valued by the Irish and closely associated with their love of dreaming. Perhaps it's no wonder that they have placed so much emphasis on fantasy. For many centuries, the Irish existed in wretched circumstances, and they used their words to enrich a dismal reality. The poet was always the most highly valued member of their culture, and even today writers are the only members of Irish society exempted from taxes.

Interactional Style

Humor is the greatest resource of the Irish for dealing with life's problems, and wit and satire have long been their most powerful means of attack. Hostility and resentment could (and still can) only be dealt with indirectly in the family, through sarcasm or innuendo. As a result, feelings often build up until, finally, family members silently cut one another off. Hostility is only permitted against the outgroup, and then only for a just and moral cause, such as religion or politics. These values create many difficulties for a therapist trying to understand Irish family patterns. As is reflected in the mystifying character of much Irish literature, the most important things are usually left unspoken or referred to only by allusion. Within the family, feelings are often so hidden that it is hard for anyone to know exactly what is going on. The Irish have been shown to have a much greater tolerance for nonrealistic thinking than do other groups (Wylan & Mintz, 1976). In contrast to WASPs and Jews, for example, who value the pursuit of truth, clarification of feelings does not necessarily make the Irish feel better. Thus, therapy aimed at opening up family feelings will often be unsuccessful. As a general rule, structured therapy, focused specifically on the presenting problem, will be the least threatening and most helpful to Irish clients. Suggestions for opening communication that also preserve the boundaries of individual privacy, such as Bowen therapy, will be preferable to therapy that brings the entire family drama into the therapy session. The strategic techniques of the Palo Alto and Milan groups would also be helpful, since they emphasize change without forcing clients to spell out all their feelings or to make changes in front of the therapist.[5]

Family Structure

Characteristically, the Irish mother has played a strong central role in the family. She has been seen as morally superior to her husband—a more shadowy figure who generally found his companionship in the pub (Diner, 1983). Traditionally, the mother ran things in the home and socialized through the Catholic Church. Children were raised to be respectful and well behaved. Discipline was traditionally strict and enforced with threats, such as, "It's a mortal sin; you'll go to hell." Irish parents have tended not to praise their children for fear of giving them a "swelled head." It was considered important to keep up appearances and not to "make a scene."

Church authority was the major unifier for the Irish, to such an extent that it came before the family (Italians have had the opposite priorities). Irish Catholics have traditionally viewed most things moralistically, following the rules of the Church without question. This, of course, has changed in recent years (Wills, 1971), but the underlying rigidity often remains. It is important in working with the Irish to understand how they feel about religion, since the values of the Church have a strong bearing on their problems.

Even those who have left the Church may have intense feelings about religious issues.

Extended family relationships among the Irish often are not close, in contrast to Jewish, Italian, Black, and Greek families, although Irish families may get together for "duty visits" on holidays and act "clannish." Family members tend not to rely on one another as a source of support, and if they have a problem, they may even see it as an added burden and embarrassment if the family finds out. The sense of emotional isolation in Irish relationships is frequently a factor in symptom development and has important implications for therapy. For example, while large family sessions that draw on the resources of the whole family may be supportive for some groups, for the Irish they may raise the anxiety to a toxic level, leading to denial and the use of embarrassed humor to deal with the sense of humiliation. It is often more fruitful to meet with smaller subgroups of the family, at least in the initial stages of opening up family communication.

Life-Cycle Transitions

For Irish families, death is generally considered the most significant life-cycle transition and family members will do their best not to miss a wake or a funeral. Like Black families in the South who often incur great expense to have a band play and to have flowers and singing and other accompaniments for their funerals, the Irish might delay a funeral for days so that all family members can get there. They spare no expense for drink and arrangements, even if they have very little money. Such customs undoubtedly relate to their belief that life in this world is generally full of suffering and death brings release to a better world. As Shannon (1963) has described it:

Every Irishman was prepared to shake hands with Doom, since that gentleman had been so frequent a visitor in the past. He had no difficulty believing Christianity's doctrines of evil and original sin. These were the most congenial truths of his religion, for they were pertinent in organizing his own experience. It could not be otherwise in a captive, overcrowded society living on the economic ragged edge on an island where the forces of nature met few human

---

[5] *Editors' Note.* In our clinical experience, we have found good cause to add behavior therapy to this list, for these very reasons.

barriers. This was life on the land, hard and lonely. Melancholy in these circumstances was a common cast of mind, death familiar and even looked forward to, and opportunities for social gathering the more dearly prized. Irish social customs accommodated and reflected these needs. The Irish wake, that national institution, expressed death's integral role. (p. 87)

Unlike Blacks, who openly grieve at their funerals, the Irish are much more likely to get drunk, tell stories and jokes, and act as if the wake were a kind of party, with little or no overt expressions of grief. Traditionally, wakes were often far merrier than weddings. There is an old Irish saying, "Sing a song at a wake, and shed a tear when a child is born." (For more specific discussion of how the Irish and other groups handle loss, see McGoldrick et al., [1991].)

Treatment Implications

Trying to talk the Irish out of their sense of guilt and need to suffer is a futile effort. Unlike Jews, for whom the very experience of sharing suffering is meaningful, the Irish believe in suffering alone. Certain strategies may help them limit their guilt and suffering, such as prescribing that it take place within restricted time intervals (see McGoldrick, 1982b; McGoldrick & Pearce, 1981). However, they are unlikely to give up suffering altogether; in fact, to do so would make them feel vulnerable, because they believe that sooner or later they will have to pay for their sins.

Among special areas to include in any assessment of the Irish are the following.

1. A very detailed history of drinking patterns in the family. Heavy drinking is a cultural norm for the Irish and is generally underlabeled as a problem. If an Irish client refers in passing to having two drinks a day, the therapist may well suspect a problem, since it would be highly unlikely for an Irish person even to mention drinking unless it had reached problematic proportions, and "two drinks" may turn out to be more like "six drinks," which then turn out to be "doubles." A useful question, in addition to asking directly about family members' drinking, is to ask whether anyone else in the family ever thought that the client drank too much.

2. The family's relationship to the Roman Catholic Church. If the family members are active Catholics, the church will be a primary factor in their definition of any problems and any solutions. The therapist should beware of getting into a covert triangle involving the church, since the family would be most likely to side with the church, not the therapist, if it came to a choice.

3. Gender imbalance. There is a strong tendency among the Irish for women to be overly central in the family and men to be underinvolved (even more than in many other groups). Mothers may overindulge and overprotect their sons, while underprotecting and expecting too much of their daughters, while fathers act and are treated as irrelevant within the family (McGoldrick et al., in press [a], in press [b]).

4. Ambiguous communication. A therapist needs to be prepared for the likelihood that if one does ask exactly the right question of an Irish person, one will not get the right answer. That is to say, the Irish are masters of ambiguous communication through which they avoid painful issues. The use of humor to distance is an important, though, at times, very troubling tool in Irish communication, which may leave family members frustrated. The Irish cannot be expected to enjoy truth and openness or to feel relieved by having a cathartic heart-to-heart discussion.

The therapist working with an Irish family must be content with limited changes. The Irish may not wish to move beyond the initial presenting problem, and it is important for the therapist not to pressure them into further work. Attempting to get spouses to deal with marital issues after a child-focused problem has been solved, for example, will probably make them feel guilty and incompetent (McGoldrick, Garcia Preto, Hines, & Lee, 1989; McGoldrick et al., in press [b]). It is better to reinforce the change that the family members do make and to let them return for therapy later at their own initiative. Even if the therapist perceives that there are emotional blocks in the family that are still causing pain, it is important not to push the matter. Because of the lack of immediate feedback from the family about therapeutic progress, therapists may be surprised to learn that their Irish families have continued therapeutic work on their own. Their deep sense of personal responsibility is, in fact, their greatest personal resource in therapy. They often continue efforts started in therapy, though they may not openly admit either fault or the resolve to remedy it.

PUERTO RICAN FAMILIES

"Hispanic" is used as an ethnic label only in the United States. Puerto Ricans, Argentinians, Cubans, or Nicaraguans, for example, would never identify themselves as Hispanic in their countries of origin. These countries have in common a language and a certain degree of Spanish heritage, but differ greatly politically, historically, socioeconomically, and geographically. Their cultures are as complex as that of the United States, since they too, were settled by immigrants from Europe and slaves imported from Africa, in addition to native Indians. In some countries, the different races mixed more than in others, creating marked distinctions in physical appearance, beliefs, religious practices, and attitudes toward race. Compared with Spain, Italy, Ireland, and England, these countries are younger, but each has its own distinct culture.

Because the groups are so complex, after a few comparisons, this section will focus primarily on Puerto Ricans. For similar information on two other Hispanic groups, the reader is referred to Bernal (1982) on Cubans and Falicov (1982) on Mexicans.

Hispanics, for the most part, are very nationalistic, and differentiating their national identity is very important. Social class also has great significance in Hispanic countries, especially for those who belong to the upper classes. Some of these countries are political enemies that are in a more or less constant state of war with each other, but even when they are friendly, there is a certain degree of competition that stems from national pride and economic need. In the United States, competition among Hispanic groups is one of the factors that prevents them from becoming a strong political force. Not only are they socioculturally and politically diverse,

but they have different attitudes toward acculturation.

Hispanics from other countries come to the United States for numerous reasons, and gain entry through various channels. Those who come for political reasons may be exiles and do not have the choice of returning to their country of origin, unless a new regime is instituted there that is sympathetic to their beliefs. Many are illegal aliens who live in fear of deportation and under the threat of losing what they have gained. However, most come openly for economic reasons, find work, and try to obtain resident visas. Their goals are to settle here firmly and to become citizens.

In contrast, Puerto Ricans, who are U.S. citizens and can move freely, have developed a unique back-and-forth pattern of migration that depends on economic factors here and on the island, as well as on family needs. This migration pattern and, until recently, the relatively low socioeconomic status of most Puerto Ricans who migrated to the mainland, have affected the way in which the group has adapted to this country. Compared with Mexicans and Cubans, they have not settled here as firmly, and as a group have less political influence. Puerto Ricans in general are viewed as second-class citizens of the United States and, when they come to the mainland, have to deal with prejudices related to their language and color. However, their citizenship does entitle them to various legal and other privileges that other Hispanic groups do not have. Professionally trained Puerto Ricans who can speak English, for instance, have an easier time finding employment because they have American citizenship.

Asking about their national origin and their patterns of migration usually helps in engaging and understanding the family. It also helps to highlight issues of loss, especially for Hispanics who are not able to return home and so lose the support of their extended families. Conflicting cultural values and loss of social status are other issues that become salient and often contribute to the problems that families present in therapy.

Spirituality and Individualism

Although it is important to be aware of differences among Hispanics, they also share unique cultural characteristics that unite them. For example, they tend to emphasize spiritual rather than material values. They work to live, not live to work. In general, they tend to defer to God when life becomes difficult. Most are Roman Catholics, but unlike the Irish, Puerto Ricans, in particular, tend to distrust the Church and its priests, and instead personalize their relationship to God by creating a special relationship with saints. They tend to use the Church primarily to mark rites of transition, such as weddings, baptisms, and funerals.

Family Loyalty

Personalism and respect are other values that most Hispanics share. Personalism emphasizes the inner qualities of people that afford them self-respect and earn the respect of others. Focusing on inner qualities allows a person to experience self-worth regardless of material success or failure. American individualism values achievement, whereas Hispanics value intimate and personal relationships and distrust impersonal structures. Respect refers to certain rules of behavior that acknowledge another individual's social value. The rules of respect are complex and are taught to the children in the family. Raising respectful children is a source of pride for Hispanic parents.

Although personalism and respect are important to most Hispanics, the overriding value that seems to unite these groups is the significance they place on the family's unity, honor, and welfare. Puerto Ricans share with the other Hispanic groups a deep sense of family commitment, obligation, and responsibility. Family ties are strong and relationships intense. Keeping the family together is emphasized to the point that dependence on and sacrifice for the group are often encouraged. Separations are cause for extreme grief and reunions bring extreme joy. Leaving the system implies taking a grave risk (Papajohn & Spiegel, 1975). The family guarantees protection and caretaking for life as long as the person stays in the system. The extended family is relied on to provide support, control, and protection.

Family Structure

Traditionally, Puerto Rican families have been patriarchal. The husband, as the head of the family, is free to make decisions without consulting his wife. The husband's major responsibility is to protect and provide for his family. He is expected to be a dignified, hard-working *macho*. Machismo (maleness, virility), to the Puerto Rican man, is a desirable combination of virtue, courage, romanticism, and fearlessness (Abad, Ramos, & Boyce, 1974). The woman's responsibilities are to care for the home and to keep the family together. The husband is not expected to perform household tasks or to help with child rearing.

This arrangement results in the wife's assuming power behind the scenes, while overtly supporting her husband's authority—which can work as long as she does not challenge him openly. The cultural rule of respect plays an important part in maintaining the marital relationship. Respect in marriage was eloquently defined by a male client who said to his wife, "Respect between husband and wife means that, as a wife, you must be loving, considerate, and never have negative thoughts about me."

Traditionally, the pattern among Puerto Ricans has been to marry young and to have many offspring. Children are seen as the poor man's wealth, the caretakers of the old, and a symbol of fertility. Parents, and mothers in particular, feel obligated to sacrifice for their children. During infancy, the children are loved and enjoyed by all of the adults in the family. Expectations for them are limited prior to age 2, when formal training begins. This training is primarily the responsibility of the mother and the maternal grandmother (Nieves-Falcon, 1972). The mother has the major responsibility for disciplining the children, but the father is expected to be the real enforcer. However, at times the mother plays the role of mediator between the father and children, forming an alliance with the children that tends to isolate the father from the family.

Transferring children during times of crisis from one nuclear family to another within the extended system is a common practice in Puerto Rico. Giving children to a mother, sister, friend, or neighbor for temporary care at such times is not seen as neglect by the child, the natural parents, or the community. It is common for adults to raise children who are not their own, and the cultural expectation is that children should respect all adults. This is not to say that some children may not be adversely affected psychologically or experience feelings of rejection and loss. However, unless the practice is regarded as a problem by the family, it is better for a therapist not to criticize or attempt to alter such arrangements.

The extended family is a source of strength for the couple, and its absence may cause stress and tension in the marriage. For example, women usually depend on other women in the extended family for help with child-rearing and domestic tasks, since the husband is not expected to share these responsibilities. Without the help of the extended family, she may find those tasks unbearable and begin to demand the husband's help. In turn, he may resent her demands and become argumentative and distant, perhaps turning to drink, gambling, and extramarital affairs. The extended family also provides a measure of control for aggression and violence. Without relatives to intervene in arguments and to advise the spouses to respect each other, couples may have serious difficulties.

Life-Cycle Transitions

Marriage, birth, and death are the most important events in the Puerto Rican life cycle. The first two are very happy occasions celebrated by the family and the community. When there is a death, the family members meet together to comfort each other and to pray for the dead. Religious rituals, such as saying masses, rosaries, and novenas (prayers to the saints), are carried out to help the dead and the living. Crying, screaming, and *ataques* (hysterical convulsive reactions), especially for women, are common ways of mourning at a funeral. Despite these visible expressions of grief, there is an underlying acceptance of death in the Puerto Rican culture. Puerto Ricans envision the dead in an invisible world inhabited by spirits who have some influence over the living. People's peace and power are often perceived as being greater in the afterlife.

Extended Family

Puerto Ricans on the mainland quickly find that some of their cultural attitudes are not reinforced by the local society. Culturally, Puerto Ricans learn to depend on the group and the community and are rewarded for submissive and respectful behavior. Conflict and anxiety result when they confront a society that frowns on passivity and expects independent, individualistic behavior. The rules of respect that bind relationships in Puerto Rico are not understood. For instance, the concept of machismo has negative connotations in this society, causing conflicts for the traditional Puerto Rican man. When traditional cultural values are not reinforced by society, they cease to be functional. This culture shock tends to produce significant changes in the Puerto Rican family structure.

The lack of extended family and friends precipitates feelings of loss and isolation. Individuals may feel obligated to fulfill roles and functions that were previously performed by others in the extended system. Consequently, they may undergo extreme anxiety. In Puerto Rico, the nuclear family was never expected to take care of all of their needs. Understandably, they may feel overwhelmed and resentful.

The extended family has always been a source of strength for a Puerto Rican couple, and its absence may cause stress and tensions in the marriage. For example, as pointed out, women usually depend on other women in the extended family for help with child-rearing and domestic tasks, since the husband is not expected to share these responsibilities. In the United States, without the help of the extended family, she may experience those tasks as unbearable and begin to demand the husband's support, especially when she is employed and he stays home without work. This situation is becoming more common because of the racism of the dominant culture as well as the rigidity of male roles in Puerto Rican culture as compared with female roles, which makes males less flexible and women more adaptable to new conditions. The shift in roles does not necessarily become problematic as long as the woman continues to accept the traditional view of family life.

An important point about Puerto Rican family structure in the United States is the increasing number of female-headed households (U.S. Bureau of the Census, 1977), indicating an increase in divorce and separation among Puerto Ricans. This may have come about because, on the mainland, it is easier for women to obtain help from social agencies, thereby lessening their economic dependence on men.

In times of stress, Puerto Ricans turn to their families for help. Their cultural expectation is that when a family member is undergoing a crisis or is having a problem, others in the family are obligated to help, especially those who are in stable positions. Because Puerto Ricans rely on the family and their extended network of personal relationships, it is highly unusual for them to initiate therapy. Those who do are more likely to be acculturated into the American society and to come from higher socioeconomic classes. In contrast, the families who are seen in social-service agencies and mental health facilities are usually referred by a third party and belong to low socioeconomic classes.

Treatment Implications

Most Puerto Ricans who come for help arrive in a state of crisis and expect the same treatment that they receive in a hospital's emergency room. They are generally referred to mental health centers by schools, hospitals, social-service agencies, or the court. Typically, the problems they present are child focused, somatic complaints, or nervousness, or for women, complaints about a husband's drinking, abusive behavior, and general absence from the home. A few may come voluntarily to ask for medication or other concrete services. These families are often isolated and without support systems, and connecting them with community networks such as churches, social clubs, relatives, and spiritists (when these are appropriate) may lessen their isolation and provide natural support.

In therapy, Puerto Rican clients expect a warm and personal relationship with the therapist. They may ask the therapist personal questions in an attempt to feel comfortable and establish trust rather than to be intrusive or to avoid their own problems. A therapist meeting a Hispanic family for the first time will be operating according to their rules of respect by addressing the parents first, using Mr. and Mrs.,

and asking permission before speaking with the children.

The structural approach to family therapy has been used effectively to engage Puerto Rican families in a personal and trusting relationship (Minuchin et al., 1967), primarily because of the emphasis that the approach places on engaging the family in such a relationship. Other reasons for this success, according to Canino and Canino (1980), are that it uses the family and extended family as integral components of the therapy; it considers stressful external life events such as migration, poor housing, and unemployment as part of the family's context and, therefore, as contributors to the development and maintenance of symptomatic behavior; and it is present oriented, concrete, and goal oriented, characteristics that have been found effective in dealing with low-income groups.

A method such as the one developed by Selvini Palazzoli, Boscolo, Cecchin, and Prata (1978), in which the therapist gives the family a brief evaluation of the problem and a prescription at the end of the first session, may be helpful in engaging the family in therapy. Puerto Ricans are likely to respond positively to the group's respectful objective and personal style. Giving a positive connotation to the family's behavior will also aid the engagement. The therapist's assuming of authority in the session will suit Puerto Ricans, who expect the therapist to be the expert and leader.

AFRICAN-AMERICAN FAMILIES

African-American culture is the combined result of African tradition, acculturation to the American mainstream, and varied responses to oppression. In this section, we will discuss Black families whose ancestors were brought from the various tribes of Africa to the United States as slaves.[6]

---

[6] The terms African-American and Blacks will be used interchangeably.

Kinship Bonds

The strong kinship bonds among African-American families can be traced to their historical origins in Africa. There, tribal life provided a sense of bonding between individuals. The dominant value was placed on the collective: "We are, therefore I am." This value was reinforced when the oppressive forces of slavery threatened survival. Unlike any other group, African Americans were brought to the United States not by choice, but by force. Slaves had no human rights; they were stripped of their languages, religions, rituals, names, foods, and customs. Dissension within the group was promoted through slave practices that afforded lighter-skinned Blacks (often children of forced sexual relationships between slave masters and Black female slaves) the "privilege" of working in their masters' homes as opposed to the fields. Also, families were disrupted by slave sales and by deaths related to the horrendous living conditions. Family boundaries were easily relaxed to accept newcomers. However, new family units were also created by the force of slave masters, who mandated procreation to increase their slave holdings.

Today, African Americans constitute 11.2 percent of the U.S. population. (U.S. Bureau of the Census, 1989). Racism and discrimination based on skin color continue to be realities that significantly affect their everyday lives, opportunities, hopes, and expectations regardless of socioeconomic status. Major advances have been made since slavery in income, education, employment, politics, and so on, but Blacks still remain basically at the bottom of the ladder socially, economically, and politically. In 1987, for example, the median income for a Black family was 56 percent ($18,000) of that for a White family ($32,270) (U.S. Bureau of the Census, 1988).

Consequently, it is said within Black communities that a Black person's greatest assets lie not in his or her bank account, but in relationships. The importance of family relationships is intensified by the difficulty that African Americans experience in receiving validation from the larger society and the role that family members play in promoting one another's survival. Family among African Americans is not restricted to nuclear or extended family, but has traditionally included a host of relatives and friends with whom the family members are involved in significant exchanges of resources. Sharing and exchange within the kinship network have allowed Black families not only to survive, but to transcend incredible odds against them. Roles and boundaries between members of the kinship system are not rigidly defined. Since extended-family members tend to live in close proximity to one another, if not in the same household for periods of time, it is not unusual for multiple adults in a kinship system to participate in the rearing of a child.

Parental child and three-generational households (Hines & Boyd-Franklin, 1982) have been particularly valuable adaptations for parents overloaded with too many responsibilities and too few resources. Usually, but not necessarily, the oldest child will assume responsibility for assisting his or her parent(s) with household, financial, and child-care responsibilities. This role can serve as a source of self-esteem and facilitate personal development as long as parental responsibilities are not abdicated and if these responsibilities do not interfere with the youth's own developmental needs. Likewise, a three-generational household can be a supportive structure for all involved if there is consistency among the adults who share executive functions. In this situation, an older family member, usually the grandmother, shares the household and typically provides the necessary child care to enable other adults in the family to work or attend school.

Another common example of role flexibility within African-American families is when children are taken in by a relative because of a crisis or, in some instances, because the relative can provide the child with a more wholesome environment. It is important to understand that many parents have been forced to leave their children and homes to look for work in urban areas that are seen as minefields for children. For these reasons, this process of child keeping or informal adoption is not generally viewed as rejection or neglect. The length of such arrangements is not always predetermined and they may end up being permanent because of the emotional ties that develop.

Economic Factors

Because of their strong spiritual orientation and the constraints that racism has imposed on achievement, African Americans place much more importance on character than on educational or vocational accomplishment. For the average African American, work is highly valued because it allows independence in meeting basic needs and not because it fosters self-expression. Unfortunately, the self-esteem of many Blacks has been lowered by the lack of jobs, by underemployment, by last-hired/first-fired policies, and by discriminatory practices in the workplace. It is becoming increasingly difficult for young Blacks to develop a sense of commitment to the world of work. Though their aspirations may be as high as those of their White counterparts, their expectations for achievement are limited by their realization that, in spite of a lifetime of hard work, many will remain stuck in poverty. Indeed, unemployment remains a serious problem, with a 10 percent rate among Blacks compared with 4 percent for Whites (U.S. Bureau of the Census, 1989); the rates of unemployment for teens have been as high as 70 percent in some urban cities in the last decade. Even those who are highly educated are still afforded fewer opportunities than Whites; for example, African Americans with four or more years of college are more than twice as likely to be unemployed as their White counterparts (U.S. Bureau of the Census, 1989).

Male–Female Relationships

Male–female relationships are increasingly being shaped by economic factors and skewed sex ratios. There are a number of factors that contribute to the low percentage of men in the Black population, including infant mortality rates that are double those of Whites, high rates of substance abuse and death related to hazardous jobs, delays in seeking health care, incarceration, military service, and homicide (U.S. Bureau of the Census, 1989). Because of limited job options and the dismal odds against fulfilling the functions prescribed for adult males in this society, the roles of Black males as fathers and husbands are particularly undermined. Those who fail to meet societal prescriptions face severe pressures on their couple and family relationships. Only 37.7 percent of Black households in 1987 were headed by married couples (U.S. Bureau of the Census, 1989). Far too many Black men find themselves unable to provide for their families' basic needs. Some feel forced to leave their households in order to ensure that their wives and children will receive governmental assistance and medical benefits. This institutional reinforcement of father absence began during the slavery era when Black males were denied the privileges and responsibilities of active fatherhood. It is important to note that the absence of the father/husband from the household does not necessarily mean a lack of contact between marital partners or father and children. Even when this is the case, it is typical for children to maintain contact with their paternal extended family.

Black women have always played active roles in their families and communities. Jobs have been available more often to them than to their spouses, especially in times of high unemployment. Consequently, the economic survival of African-American families has frequently depended on African-American women. Relatedly, racism is viewed as a greater oppressive force than sexism. Black women have been doers by necessity while being penalized for their creativity and strength by the perpetuation of images of them as dominating matriarchs who emasculate males. Relative to other ethnic groups, relationships tend to be egalitarian; however, a husband is likely to be respected privately and publicly as the "head of household" even if he is not working and even when the wife does make more decisions related to the everyday management of the household (McGoldrick et al., 1989).

African-American women tend to place a higher value on the maternal role than on the marital role (McGoldrick et al., in press[b]). Spanier, Roos, and Shockey (1985) found in a population survey of women born during the first half of the century that Blacks tended to be younger at the birth of their first child and to have a shorter wait after marriage before having their first child, a greater likelihood of giving birth outside of marriage, and larger families. There was less of a gap between Blacks and Whites when education was a controlled factor. However, many middle-income as well as poor

Black women are choosing to have children outside of marriage rather than be childless. This decision generally does not represent a devaluation of marriage, but rather an adaptation to the shortage of marriageable mates (Staples, 1985).

The Expression of Feelings

The emphasis in African-American culture is on doing rather than thinking, feeling, or talking. African Americans tend to be nonconstrictive in emotional style. Much is transmitted through nonverbal communication. Given the victimization and relative lack of power that most Blacks experience throughout their lives, it is not surprising that anger is a culturally acceptable emotion. Family members may switch quickly and easily from expression of one type of affect to another. Regardless of race, men generally do not allow themselves the freedom to express their feelings verbally. Black males are particularly likely to adhere to this prescription since a violation, particularly if public, is one more reason to have their masculinity questioned. Many have grown up with the message, reinforced by history, that they must be private and careful in order to stay alive. Their cool exterior can be a smoke screen for disappointment and pain.

Spirituality

The strong spiritual orientation of African Americans has promoted their survival and ability to cherish life in spite of the innumerable odds they have faced over time. Blacks place a strong value on being strong; one is expected to manage life's stresses without buckling under. Pain and suffering are viewed as expected parts of life that strengthen character and test one's faith in a higher being.

Accordingly, the church has been the most significant institution in the Black community (Hines & Boyd-Franklin, 1982). Active church involvement affords an outlet for the expression of feelings; repeated messages are given that reinforce a sense of personal value, personal and social responsibility, hope, and a belief that adversity can be overcome. There are numerous opportunities for individuals to develop and display their talents and develop a social network, as well as gain access to information (e.g., jobs) and a variety of concrete services. The "church family" provides many positive role models as well. Significant life-cycle events such as births, marriages, and deaths are likely to involve church-related rituals even for those who are not active members.

Death and Mourning

The emphasis on the afterlife perhaps accounts for the importance attributed to funerals. Throughout their history in this country, Blacks have had a death rate that has consistently exceeded that of other groups. Frequently, these losses occur without the benefit of anticipatory mourning. Having a good "send-off" at death is important regardless of cost. Funerals typically take place three to seven days following death to permit everyone who wishes to attend the opportunity to make the necessary work and travel arrangements. Attendance symbolizes respect. As a family member, to fail to attend is to open oneself to the suspicion that one has forgotten the importance of one's roots. Thus, much value is placed on community acknowledgment of a death; people begin to visit the family as soon as the death is announced to honor the deceased person's memory and to provide concrete and emotional support to the family. Eulogies often emphasize the desire to be remembered for one's character and commitment to others.

Generally, the cultural values and rituals facilitate healthy resolution of grief. For some, the experience of repeated losses, however, may lead to a general loss of optimism and sense of powerlessness. In these instances, problem solving and family relationships may suffer (McGoldrick et al., in press[a]).

Coping with Poverty

The belief that all Black families are poor and so are inherently dysfunctional is clearly a myth. There are, without doubt, well-functioning poor families. However, when embedded in a context of chronic poverty and discrimination, the healthiest family may be limited in its ability to function at an optimal level. Persistent stress is likely to have adverse effects on individual functioning and family transactions and relationships. Certainly, poor Black families are seen in clinics more often than are middle-income Black families and their ranks are increasing in concordance with a dramatic rise in the number of single-parent households. Approximately 33.1 percent of Blacks in 1987 lived at or below the poverty level (U.S. Bureau of the Census, 1988). These families face the triple jeopardy of being economically poor, politically bankrupt, and discriminated against because of race.

Hines (1989) noted four distinguishing characteristics in the life cycle of poor Black families: (1) Their life-cycle phases seem more truncated than those of middle-class families and transitions are not clearly delineated. (2) Households are frequently headed by women and of the extended-family type. (3) Their life cycle is punctuated by numerous unpredictable events and the associated stress these engender. (4) They have few concrete resources available to assist them in coping with continuous stressors, even meeting basic needs. The demands for flexibility and creativity are endless. Their world view is shaped by their overexposure to tragedy and suffering. Their rage may be directed at society, at members of their own families, or at themselves (Pinderhughes, 1982).

Special Issues of Middle-Income Families

There are an increasing number of middle-income African Americans, with the majority from working-class or poor backgrounds. Within their larger kin system, and even family of origin, there will be great diversity in education, life-styles, jobs, and so on. Although they do not have to struggle to meet basic needs, they, too, are victims of racism, which pervades every aspect of their lives. Most have no or few precedents for dealing with the obstacles they face in living and working in two worlds. Even within families and the same generation, some may prefer to remain isolated while others identify exclusively with the American mainstream; still others attempt to integrate the two. For all, much psychic energy is required to sort out and respond to subtle and obvious racism, which

takes its toll emotionally. For some, the stress encountered results in a lack of connectedness in either the Black or the white world. Others derive from their experience exceptional strength, flexibility, and tolerance for diversity.

The assets of most middle- to upper-middle-income Blacks are tied to their daily work; their hold on any wealth is tenuous, as they remain subject to discrimination based on racism, particularly in their workplaces. Similar to women in general in this society, Blacks are subject to an invisible ceiling above which they are unlikely to be promoted in their careers regardless of their talent. They experience all the benefits and pitfalls of participation in the "reciprocal obligation" process (McAdoo, 1978). More often than not, middle-income parents have struggled to overcome many obstacles. They are likely to demand high achievement from their children. In comparison with their own childhood experiences, their children are seen as living "privileged lives." Many middle-income parents are likely to be recipients (in the workplace) and purveyors (at home) of the message that "to be average and Black is not acceptable to the larger society." They are likely to be concerned about how to reinforce in their children a sense of positive cultural identity, how to teach positive cultural values, and how to educate about racism without creating feelings of undue anxiety or hostility. Typical intergenerational conflicts (e.g., dress, friends) may be doubly complicated as a result of differences in experience with racism. In some instances, children or adolescents from middle-income backgrounds may find it difficult to relate to their more economically disadvantaged relatives and (Black) schoolmates. When these cutoffs occur, the price is, of course, great, as they end up lacking a sense of connectedness and continuity.

Treatment Implications

Effective family therapy always transcends techniques, but this is especially true with African-American families. They are generally ambivalent about involvement in therapy. Talking is not seen as a solution to most problems. When help is needed, they are likely to turn to older relatives or friends. Changes dictated by crises are quickly consolidated into everyday life. They are likely to have little or distorted information about what therapy involves and how it can be helpful to them. History and contemporary experience render them prone to being distrustful of institutions. Most often, when they do come to therapy, they are referred by someone outside of the family and have exhausted all other options. One can generally expect that credibility will have to be earned. Family members will very likely be more concerned about the cultural sensitivity and relevance of a therapist's life experience than about credentials.

Several guidelines for assessment and treatment follow from consideration of the realities of African Americans.

Socialization to Therapy

From the time of the intake, information gathering must be focused and sensitively pursued. Consideration should be given to including in the assessment and treatment process significant "family members" (living both within and outside the household), as well as workers from other agencies who can influence the outcome of therapy. One may lose the participation of those family members who are available if too much pressure is put on them to engage reticent members before those present are personally engaged and convinced that therapy is worthwhile. Therapists are wise to proceed with orienting those who do come about the goals, process, and limitations of family therapy. Concerns and myths should be pursued and addressed. It is essential that the therapist clarify the limits of confidentiality and his or her relationship with the referring agent as well as any other "helping" systems involved in the family's life.

Engagement

Of paramount importance is the primary and ongoing task of engaging families. It is important to demonstrate that therapy can be of value beginning with the first session as families are not likely to commit to lengthy involvements. Since their expectations and fears are that they will be negatively labeled and blamed for the problems they are encountering, it is helpful to identify,

verbalize a genuine appreciation, and employ family strengths. African Americans generally will be concerned about whether the therapist appreciates their history and current societal context. Family members, particularly men, will be more responsive to language that supports their abilities to handle their own problems than language that emphasizes what the therapist can do for them.

Information Gathering

Genograms can be invaluable in working with African-American families. Family members may be reactive to what they see as "prying," particularly when the areas of exploration touch on toxic issues or secrets (e.g., paternity). Therapists should look for an opening to obtain the desired information rather than force an agenda of data gathering.

Empowerment

For poor Black families, options in many instances may be limited as a result of their larger social, economic, and political context. Therapists will earn credibility by acknowledging this reality and can facilitate change by helping family members to recognize and avoid collusion with forces that impede attainment of their goals. One must be sensitive to the practical and emotional impact of ongoing crises on families. It is imperative that therapists help families problem-solve about how to address survival issues, which ultimately detract from their ability to focus on emotional needs and relational processes. However, one also must be cautious not to lose sight of the repetitive processes that render the family vulnerable and likely to be derailed.

The goal of empowerment should be interwoven with every intervention. It is useful to focus on what can be shifted to strengthen families' abilities to be self-sufficient and effective in problem solving and exerting a greater degree of control over their lives. Education about various issues (e.g., parental rights in educational systems) and concrete skills training may enhance their confidence and competence to advocate on their own behalf. The therapist's aim should be to assist (not replace) family members in recognizing and acting on choices, however limited they are. Families can be helped to differentiate between external and personal/transactional barriers to success and to channel their anger and frustration constructively without displacing negative feelings on one another.

Role Clarification/Boundary Setting

Clearly an area for assessment with Black families is the clarity of boundaries and roles. The therapeutic goal, when necessary, is not to encourage "caretakers" to eliminate these roles, but to assist families in realigning in such a way that roles are clarified, responsibilities are distributed, and help can be given in a manner that has the least adverse effect on family members as well as on the "caretakers" (Hines & Boyd-Franklin, 1982). A therapist will earn credibility by acknowledging the adaptive aspects of a helping role, even if shifts in behavior are being advocated.

Parents may also require assistance in avoiding overfunctioning and finding ways to address their individual needs and interests. Metaphors extracted from a client's language can be helpful in making points about balance. Wives and children, in particular, may require coaching to share their concerns with husbands and parents they perceive to be overwhelmed. Therapists can assist them in letting go of caretaking that ultimately promotes distance in relationships and that limits the ability of other family members to act on what is within their means. One cannot underestimate the value of simply slowing down the action so that couples and family members can explore and negotiate unresolved, vaguely defined, or conflictual issues.

Treatment Approaches

Regardless of socioeconomic status or whether or not they come to therapy in crisis, African-American families are likely to be most responsive to time-limited, problem-focused approaches in which the therapist plays an active role (e.g., Minuchin, 1974; Aponte, 1974; Boyd-Franklin, 1989). A family-life-cycle perspective provides a useful framework since it focuses both on the effect of context and external stressors and on how these exacerbate the stressors that accompany normal development and unresolved family issues. Treatment that is truly systems oriented should not only involve an assessment of the problem(s) in relation to the family's structure, functioning, and environmental context, but also examine the problem(s) in relation to the larger systems that interface with the family. Imber Coppersmith (1983) aptly notes that helping systems may give competing messages to a family and may inadvertently sabotage family treatment if ignored in the treatment process. Hines, Richman, Maxim, and Hays (1989) urge a more flexible use of time than is practiced in most traditional settings. Once-a-week sessions ignore the realities of many Black families. The authors describe the multiple-impact family-therapy model (MIFT), which combines (1) an immediate response to a request for service; (2) a brief, problem-oriented treatment approach; (3) the use of a team of therapists who work directly with the family; (4) the involvement of agency representatives connected with the family; and (5) an extended-session format. With the MIFT, within a week of a call for services, a family is seen by a team of therapists for a day-long session. A six-week follow-up visit is scheduled, with interim and subsequent assistance (e.g., systems advocacy) provided by one of the therapists.

CHINESE-AMERICAN FAMILIES

The Chinese-American population in the United States has grown dramatically in recent years. Between 1960 and 1980, this group increased from 240,000 to over 800,000. As of 1980, more than half lived in the western states—with 30 percent in California and 12 percent in Hawaii. In addition, 27 percent lived in the Northeast, with 20 percent living in New York State alone.

Historically, the Chinese constitute the earliest group of immigrants of Asian Americans to the United States. In the 1850s, a large number of Chinese men were brought in as cheap labor to work in the gold mines and on the railroads. They were followed by the Japanese, and later, by Filipinos, Koreans, and others from Asia. As the pioneer Asians, the Chinese suffered the most from racial discrimination. The Chinese Exclusion Act of 1882 and similar restrictions barred them from citizenship, land ownership, and intermarriage, and from bringing their wives to the United States. It was not until 1965 that quotas were eliminated in a new immigration law, thus bringing a new surge of immigrants from Hong Kong, Taiwan, the People's Republic of China, and other Asian countries. In addition, two major national immigration policies helped create the sudden influx of Chinese refugees and immigrants. After the end of the Vietnam war in 1975, about 800,000 Southeast Asian refugees arrived here (Office of Refugee Resettlement, 1985). Most of this second wave of "boat people" were Chinese from Vietnam, a significant number of whom were survivors of hunger, rape, torture, and forced migration. In 1979, after four decades of a "closed door policy," the United States started to admit immigrants from mainland China. Many of these are survivors of the Cultural Revolution (1966–1976).

Family Structure

Although there are similarities among all Chinese Americans, they exhibit unique diversities in spoken dialect, religion, political background, educational background, and socioeconomic level. These complexities are compounded when one considers different generations and the degree of acculturation. Vast differences exist between recent arrivals and those who have been here for decades. As a group, they represent a wide range of cultural values, from very traditional to very "Americanized." Generally speaking, there are four types of Chinese-American families (Lee, 1988).

Type 1. The Traditional Family

Usually, these families consist of family members who all were born and raised in Asian countries. Traditional families include families from agricultural backgrounds, recent arrivals who have had limited contacts with Western culture, immigrants who were older at the time of immigration, and families who live in Chinatowns where they remain isolated from American mainstream society. Family members in such traditional families typically speak their native Chinese dialects and practice traditional Chinese teachings in their daily lives.

Type 2. The Transitional Family

Such families usually are headed by foreign-born parents and grandparents, with strong traditional beliefs, who live with children or grandchildren who were born in the United States or came to this country when they were young. The family system usually experiences a great degree of cultural conflict between the acculturated children and the traditional parents and grandparents. In such families, the parents usually do not speak English well, while the children speak little Chinese or some "broken" version of it.

Type 3. The Bicultural Family

In these families, the parents usually are professionals, English-speaking, and quite "Westernized," like their children. Such families typically came from middle- or upper-class backgrounds, and grew up in urban, cosmopolitan cities such as Hong Kong, Taipei, or Saigon. Family members are well acculturated, bilingual, and bicultural. They have the ability to take advantage of the strengths of both Eastern and Western cultures. They are able to integrate the two contradictory value systems without much confusion.

Type 4. The "Americanized" Family

Such families consist of parents and children who were born and raised in the United States. As generations pass, the roots of Chinese culture begin to disappear slowly, and individual members do not express their interest in or make any effort to maintain their Chinese identity. As in Japanese-American families, interracial marriage is very common. English is the primary language at home.

These four types of Chinese-American families vary a great deal in their value orientations, presenting problems, help-seeking patterns, and treatment expectations, and a family can be classified anywhere on this spectrum. In view of the large number of immigrants in recent years, the majority of the Chinese Americans, like the Korean Americans and other new immigrant groups, will most likely fall into the traditional- or transitional-family categories.

Traditional Chinese culture is influenced by its agricultural background and dominant moral and religious ideas, such as Confucianism, Taoism, and Buddhism. Chinese philosophy emphasizes interdependence, harmonious interpersonal relationships, and mutual obligation or loyalty for achieving a state of psychosocial homeostasis or peaceful coexistence with the family and other human beings (Hsu, 1971). Confucius believed that the family constitutes the most important institution in society. Family socialization practices are marked by a particular emphasis on the cultivation of collective consciousness and responsibilities of the members. Family interactions are determined more by prescribed roles defined by the family hierarchy, obligation, and duties than by a person-oriented process. The very closeness of family relationships may create extraordinary problems involving individual desires versus family obligations.

In most traditional families, the spousal relationship is secondary to the parent–child relationship. Marriage is usually arranged to ensure the family prosperity and to continue the man's family line rather than on a basis of romantic love. Husband and wife do not express love openly, especially in front of children or strangers. Marital conflicts are usually resolved by the in-laws or other adult mediators. Divorce brings shame to the family and is strongly discouraged.

Unlike Black women, Chinese women traditionally do not work outside the home. Many women marry young to have many children. From infancy through early childhood, children maintain a close bond with their mothers. Most parents demand filial piety, respect, and obedience from their children. Physical punishment is acceptable. Psychological punishment—such as guilt and shame—and social controls are also used. Traditionally, sons are more valued than daughters. Older siblings are expected to take care of the younger siblings. Parents usually live with their sons and daughters-in-law until death, and expect to be taken care of in their old age.

In contrast to the Irish family, extended-family relationships among the Chinese are very close. In times of crisis, such as death or war, transferring children from one family to another within the extended-family system is a common practice.

Life-Cycle Transition

Birth, marriage, and death are the most important events in the Chinese family life cycle. Happy occasions, such as a baby's one-month "birthday" (especially for a boy) and a wedding (especially for the oldest son), are celebrated by inviting many extended-family members and friends from the Chinese community to a banquet. When there is a death, the family members gather to comfort each other. Religious or other rituals—such as chanting, burning of paper money and clothing, a "last march through Chinatown," and a large display of food for the dead family member—are all intended to ensure that the deceased gets off to a good start in his or her new "life." The many Chinese who are Buddhists believe that the soul does not perish when one dies, but will reincarnate in another form—a belief that forms the spiritual basis for ancestor worship. In most traditional Chinese households, an ancestral altar is displayed in a prominent place in the main room of the house. The altar is set with incense burners and candlesticks, together with the ancestral tablets and portraits. On the death anniversary of each ancestor, special rites are performed, which consist of making sacrificial offerings, burning incense, and bowing and praying in front of the altar. All family members are expected to participate in these rituals.

For the most part, Chinese traditions are still being practiced (with some modification) by traditional families in Chinese communities in the United States. However, in many bicultural and Americanized families influenced by Anglo-American values and religions, family members adopt a much more individualistic, competitive, and democratic orientation. The power structure of such families has moved from a patriarchal to an egalitarian relationship. "Matchmaker marriage" has been replaced by romantic love and freedom of choice. The marital bond is stronger than the parent–child bond. It is quite common for both husband and wife to work to support the family and to share in household responsibilities.

Treatment Implications

Different types of Chinese-American families may have different presenting problems and help-seeking patterns. The traditional families generally come to agencies with many specific environment and adjustment problems, such as language, housing, or legal difficulties. The transitional families usually need help in resolving intergenerational conflicts, communication and role confusion, marital difficulties, and in-law conflicts. Depression and somatic complaints are common. The bicultural families require little help from counseling agencies and appear to be quite adaptable. The presenting problems of the Americanized families are commonly associated with identity conflict, low self-concept, marital discord, and depression. They are likely to be treated with psychodynamic modalities that focus on self-exploration, while the traditional and transitional families are more likely to be treated with a cognitive–behavioral modality (Murase, 1982).

With the exception of those who are very acculturated, most Chinese-American clients tend to exhibit help-seeking patterns that emphasize self-help and natural community resources as alternatives to mental health counseling. These include family friends, local priests or clergy, herbalists, acupuncturists, primary health-care physicians, and other indigenous healers. It is not within the cultural norm for the Chinese to discuss their emotions or family secrets in public or with strangers. Receiving help from mental health clinics brings "shame" and "loss of face" not only to the individual, but also to the extended-family members. Therefore, it is highly unusual for Chinese clients to initiate therapy. They are generally referred to mental health centers or hospitals by the police, schools, court, or social-service agencies.

The assessment of Chinese families must include information beyond traditional intake data. The therapist must focus not only on the medical or intrapsychic influences, but also on the integration of the physical, psychological, social, cultural, and political factors (Lee, 1982).

In view of the unique Chinese cultural characteristics and immigration history, the therapist should explore the following areas in family assessment:

1. Family migration and relocation history: Who left with whom? When? Why? (How is the family affected by the war experiences?)
2. The effect of migration on individual and family life cycles.
3. "Cultural shock" and adjustment problems.
4. Work and financial stress.
5. Family's place of residence and community influences.
6. Differences in rates of acculturation among individual family members.
7. Physical-health and medical histories of family members.
8. Family problems—role reversal, intergenerational conflict, marital and in-law conflicts, and the like.
9. Family strengths—support from extended-family members, religious community, and so on.
10. Family's concept of emotional problems, help-seeking behavior, and treatment expectation.

Working with Chinese-American families also requires specific, culturally relevant treatment strategies. Chinese Americans, in general, enter treatment with much apprehension, suspicion, and ambivalence. In the initial phase of treatment, the interview sessions should be more structured. The family-therapy approach should be "problem focused," "goal directed," "symptom relieving," and "education oriented." The initial concerns and problems brought in by the family should be accepted graciously and taken seriously, with the recognition that such concerns may be the family's way of entering treatment. In order to engage the family in therapy, it is important for the therapist to (1) acknowledge the identified patient as the problem; (2) assist the family to shift from a "person focus" to a "problem focus"; (3) allow time to discuss the effect of the problem on each family member; (4) verbalize the family pain caused by the difficulties; (5) explore the family's "cultural explanations" of the causes of the symptoms, help-seeking pattern, and treatment expectations;

and (6) reinforce the sense of family obligation and the significant role of the family members in solving the problem together. In explaining the treatment goal, the therapist should focus on the present and the conscious rather than the past and the unconscious, based on relational and interpersonal rather than interaction and intrapersonal factors. Rather than being defined in abstract emotional terms, goals may be best stated in terms of external resolution or symptom reduction, which are easy to understand and measurable (Lee, in press).

Given the Chinese cultural emphasis on interpersonal relationships, the therapist should make an attempt to form a social and cultural alliance with the family during the initial phase of the relationship. It is helpful for the therapist to share some of his or her own personal, cultural, and professional background. In addition, because Chinese families view relationships in terms of a vertical hierarchy, the therapist will need to take a much more authoritative attitude. It is important to convey an air of confidence and understanding. A neutral, nonjudgmental, or relatively passive attitude may be interpreted as noncaring or incompetent. Most Chinese who have sought help in the past from folk healers, such as herb doctors, are accustomed to brief "pulse-touching" diagnostic techniques. Many are also used to receiving "10-minute" medical treatments in crowded public hospitals in Hong Kong or China. Therefore, lengthy questions and extensive evaluation procedures will be viewed as irrelevant and are likely to create distrust and loss of faith. In order to engage the family in treatment, it is important to give the family a brief evaluation of the presenting problems and suggestions on how possibly to deal with it. Interventions that combine diagnostic, teaching, and treatment functions are more acceptable.

Reinforcing culturally sanctioned coping mechanisms and cultural strength is also very important in the treatment of Chinese families. For example, the therapist may discuss religious concepts such as "karma" and fate to help the family deal with losses and unpredictable changes. If appropriate, the use of familiar Chinese philosophical sayings and stories can be very effective to reinforce constructive changes. In addition, cultural strengths—such as support from extended-family members, a strong sense of family obligation, and the focus on educational achievement and the work ethic—should be respected and used creatively in the therapeutic process. Many recent Chinese-American immigrants are the survivors of political turmoil, socioeconomic changes, and cultural transition. The key factor in the establishment of a therapeutic alliance with Chinese families is trust based on mutual respect and the therapist's ability to empathize with compassion.

ETHNIC INTERMARRIAGE

Intermarriage affects every level of a system: the individual, the married couple, the children, the ethnic groups involved, and society as a whole (Heer, 1980). In particular, it increases exponentially the complexities encountered in all marriages during life's transitions, (McGoldrick, 1989). Generally speaking, the greater the cultural difference between the spouses, the more difficulty they will have in understanding each other and adjusting to marriage and the more difficulty their families will have in adjusting to the required changes. However, family emotional process also plays an important role here (McGoldrick et al., 1982). Friedman (1982), who has had many years of experience working with Jewish–Christian intermarriages, concludes that the upset of a family caused by intermarriage most often reflects hidden emotional issues in the family. He calls this process "cultural camouflage": the universal tendency of family members everywhere to avoid responsibility for their feelings, their actions, and their destiny by attributing their cause either to factors in their own background or to aliens (e.g., *shiksas*) from a background that is foreign (e.g., *goyishe*).

Friedman's point is very important. Families may use their ethnic customs or religious values selectively to justify an emotional position within the family or against outsiders (McGoldrick et al., 1982). Friedman believes that people often hide behind their ethnic or cultural identity in order to avoid dealing with emotional issues. In our experience, the opposite problem, failing to appreciate differences that are rooted in ethnicity, is equally difficult. As Pearce (1980) has noted:

Unfortunately, spouses tend to perceive their cultural differences as failings—either badness or madness. With insight, people are able to take some distance from their hurt feelings and stop taking inevitable differences personally. (p. 113)

Intermarriage breaks the old continuity of a system. It disrupts family patterns and connections, but it also opens a system to new patterns, connections, and the possibility of creative transformations. Becoming familiar with a different culture may be an enriching experience that provides new flexibility to a system. Complementary ethnic values, patterns, and attitudes may enhance the potential of a marriage.

Under the best of circumstances, the challenge of differences in a relationship may open the possibility for productive personal changes. For instance, a WASP female who has difficulty expressing anger for fear of losing control and who instead becomes depressed or symptomatic may learn to be more direct and comfortable with her anger by marrying an Italian male, who tends to be confrontative and spontaneous. Or a Jewish husband may teach his WASP wife a new repertoire of emotional expression, freeing her to experience her feelings more fully, while she may teach him that there is a time to stop analyzing feelings and to just get on with things.

Factors Influencing Intermarriage

Although it is said that opposites attract, the tendency is for people to marry others who are similar to themselves and who belong to the same group and race (Ahren, Cole, Johnson, & Wong, 1981). In general, those who marry outside their group are the exceptions. Variables, such as the length of time individuals have lived in this country, as well as race, class, religion, and language, influence the likelihood of intermarriage. Other influential factors are the availability of partners who are suitable in terms of education, economic position, and attractiveness, and the barriers specific groups impose against marrying outside the group. The Anglo-Irish, for example, have had the highest rate of exogamous marriage (Fallows, 1979), whereas Jews, who have always had intense prohibitions against intermarriage, showed a rate of no more than 5 percent between 1920 and 1960. By 1980,

however, the rate for Jewish intermarriage had risen to 35 percent (Crohn, 1986; Barber & Gordon, 1979). Nevertheless, our own studies have indicated that Jews still have one of the lowest rates of intermarriage of all American ethnic groups (McGoldrick & Rohrbaugh, 1987).

In general, the greater the difference between the spouses, the less common will be the pairing and the greater difficulty they will have in adjusting. We have found that the following factors most influence the degree of adjustment required in ethnic intermarriage (McGoldrick & Garcia Preto, 1984).

1. The extent of difference in values between the cultural groups involved. Spouses from similar cultural backgrounds, such as a Puerto Rican and an Italian, will probably experience less disparity than a couple from diverse cultures, such as an Irish–Italian couple.
2. Differences in the degree of acculturation of each spouse. Couples are likely to have more difficulty if one spouse is an immigrant and the other a fourth-generation American.
3. Religious differences in addition to cultural differences. An Irish–Italian marriage will be easier than an Irish–Jewish marriage.
4. Racial differences. Interracial couples are most vulnerable to being alienated from both racial groups and may thus be forced into couple isolation. In addition, their children often experience great difficulty in establishing a clear identity and may be subject to discrimination by both groups.
5. The sex of the spouse from each background. Sex roles intensify certain cultural characteristics. Given that women are generally raised to talk more easily about their feelings, an Irish wife with a Jewish husband will probably have an easier time than will a Jewish wife with an Irish husband. Also, certain pairings seem to be more common than others. Couples consisting of a Jewish male and a WASP female or of a black male and a white female are far more common than the reverse, reflecting, perhaps, the fact that in our culture men have more flexibility to "improve" their status than women do by marrying into groups of greater social standing.

Sex differences also interact with intermarriage in another way. Since most women are raised to be adaptive, a foreign-born woman married to an American man may feel less stressed in adapting to his context than would a foreign-born man, who may feel at a considerable disadvantage in relation to a U.S.-born wife. However, foreign-born males are more likely to be in the United States for work reasons, and thus will have relationships outside the home that may aid adaptation to this culture. Without these work connections, a foreign-born male's adjustment is likely to be problematic and his isolation great. A foreign-born wife who comes from a culture where women do not assert themselves in establishing a social network may also become isolated, especially if she does not work.

6. Socioeconomic differences. As Americans move upward in socioeconomic status, their cultural patterns and values tend toward the mainstream. Partners who come from very different socioeconomic backgrounds or from cultures placing a differential value on socioeconomic status may have added difficulties.

7. Familiarity with each other's cultural context prior to marriage. Presumably, it will be easier for both families to accept a new spouse if they already know people from that cultural group than if this is their first contact. Families that have lived in a heterogeneous neighborhood are probably more prepared for their children to intermarry than those living in a homogeneous neighborhood. Likewise, intermarried couples living in a multiethnic neighborhood will probably experience less pressure to adapt to one set of traditions.

8. The degree of resolution of emotional issues about the intermarriage reached by both families prior to the wedding. All things being equal, families that can hold a wedding that reflects both cultural heritages will probably have a greater chance of success than families in which the children elope or where one side of the family refuses to attend the ceremony. The consequence of the latter situations may be that the recognition or acceptance of the marriage is delayed or never takes place. Falicov (1986) states that a significant percentage of intermarried couples suffer from a covert or overt lack of permission to marry that has serious implications for the marriage.

Patterns of Intermarriage

In many families in which grandparents, parents, and children have all intermarried, intermarriage becomes an accepted pattern. These families tend to emphasize social class, education, and economic status rather than ethnicity. Individuals in these families may marry out in order to improve financial or social status and tend to identify themselves as "American" and to ignore ethnic differences.

A recent survey by Crester and Leon (1982) reaffirms that the literature on ethnic intermarriage is extremely sparse. Of the few studies that have been done, most concern interracial (Barnett, 1963) or interreligious marriages (Bernard, 1980). One notable study of intermarriage in Hawaii indicated that those who do marry cross-ethnically choose partners quite similar to themselves in personality in spite of outward differences (Ahren et al., 1981). They also found that women who marry out are more assertive than those who marry within their own ethnic group. Resnik (1933), in an early study of religious intermarriage, suggests that persons who intermarry are of four types: (1) the emancipated person, (2) the rebel, (3) the detached person, or (4) the adventurer.

Generally, individuals who choose to marry out are seeking a rebalance in the characteristics of their own ethnic background. They may be attempting to move away from certain values and aspects of their cultural identity that they dislike by moving toward others that they admire. As a southern WASP journalist who married a Greek American described it (Haskell, 1982):

"In choosing a life mate of a very different background, I and others like me were probably, without quite knowing it at the time, exempting this person and ourselves from the traditional role associated with the institution of marriage and demanding something else . . . having come from a culture in which everyone holds in their feelings in the interest of social equilibrium, I must have yearned for an explosive element in my life. Andrew, on the other hand, brought up on Mediterranean excess and effusion, retreated to an emotionally cooler place."

Those who marry out may also be seeking to solve a family dilemma. They may be attempting to detriangle from an intense emotional relationship in the family of origin. Crohn (1986) suggests that for Jews, at least, intermarriage may be an attempt to escape, or paradoxically to reaffirm, a sense of Jewish identity. Crester and Leon (1982) found that intermarriage may reflect a high level of emancipation or differentiation from the family of origin, which was also suggested in Resnik's (1933) study. The success of intermarriage will depend to a considerable extent on each partner's ability to establish a degree of independence, but as one intermarried wife suggests (Haskell, 1982): "A modicum of 'success' is assumed in advance, but at the first sign of weakness or failure, the difference in background can become more exasperating than exotic. Then the sense of isolation can be frightening. You're on a high wire without a safety net. You've burned your bridges, forfeited the automatic warmth and protection of the tribe."

Friedman (1982) believes that the person most likely to marry out is the child most important to the balance of the parents' marriage. In his view, the emotional turmoil that surrounds an intermarriage most often reflects a hidden emotional need for fusion on the part of a parent, usually the parent who was most responsible in his or her own family.

I began to realize that Jews who married non-Jews overwhelmingly occupied the sibling position of oldest, or only, with only child defined as an actual single child or any child when there was a gap of five or more years between siblings—the most triangled child, and the more triangled, the more intensely the family reacted and the further the child married out. And the parent who reacts most is the one who occupied a similar position in his or her own family or origin, either during childhood or right then. (McGoldrick et al., 1982)

In Friedman's opinion, this view is supported by the experience that grandparents, who would presumably be more conservative culturally, usually are less upset than the parents about the intermarriage, and that the parents' intensity of feeling reflects the fear that they will be cen-sured by the family for having failed to raise their child correctly.

A couple's accommodation to intermarriage may be easier in the short run if only one side of the extended family is available, since the couple will than have only one set of ongoing in-law relationships to handle. However, partners whose families are distant may experience serious loyalty conflicts about becoming involved in the spouse's family, since they are not available to their own family. At times, of course, people who have no family available or who have extremely negative relationships with their families may seek to gain a new family network through marriage. Although historically marriage was always a family affair (a social and economic arrangement for the two families rather than a love match between the two individuals), in our day the tie to a partner's family is often considered peripheral. It is the rare case, indeed, when in-law relationships are maintained after a divorce, except when there has been a cutoff between the parents and their own child. In those cases in which a person has an intense and close relationship with in-laws, the other spouse often has poor parental relationships.

Couples typically anticipate at the beginning of their relationship that they can overcome all odds in marriage. If their relationship is formed in reaction to family injunctions or in rebellion against family values, they may handle conflicts about the intermarriage by distancing from both extended families. Or one spouse may fuse into the other's family by religious conversion, by taking over the handling of the other's family relationships, or by adopting the accoutrements of the other's culture. Unfortunately, it is rare for intermarried couples to remain open to both extended families and to keep their own cultural traditions, transforming them into new patterns. At times, one set of in-laws may be drawn into collusion with the couple against the other. The extended-family members may also stereotype the new spouse negatively, often as a self-protective maneuver to reassure themselves when they feel that their child is rejecting them and their values by marrying out. It is important to remember that the parents' negative reactions to intermarriage may derive from fears of being abandoned or fears for the survival of their group.

In any case, marrying out of one's group gives

an automatic message to one's family. Choosing a partner from another group may allow a person to bring new possibilities into the family or to avoid interacting with the family by using the spouse as an excuse. Those who intermarry for the latter reason are likely to have difficulty adapting to later life-cycle transitions when most people feel more need for their cultural heritage. The difficulties inherent in these transitions tend to be more stressful when spouses are from different backgrounds, and especially when they are without the support of their families. In our view, working out one's sense of cultural identity is part of differentiating from one's family of origin—which enables the formation of a mature marital relationship.

Attitudes Toward Marriage

Marriage has existed for centuries as an institution that joins a man and a woman in a social and legal relationship for the purpose of maintaining and carrying on the family structure. Probably no other culture in history has ever resembled today's dominant American culture in the value it places on marital togetherness, sharing, open communication between spouses, and keeping the romance going. Even within this culture, however, groups differ greatly in their attitudes toward marriage. For instance, maintaining the family has a very different meaning for WASPs, Germans, and the Irish than for Italians, Hispanics, and Jews. For Hispanics, getting married is more likely to mean adding more relatives to a large, informal family network. Italians have tended to build a marriage on the rules and regulations that have kept the family going for generations. Neither group places much emphasis on marital intimacy. The emphasis, especially for Italians, is on the continuation of the family. For WASPs, Germans, and the Irish, marriage tends to mean the beginning of a new family unit, separate from the extended family. For some Asian groups, marriage means that the wife leaves her family completely to join the husband's family, but closeness between partners is not expected. For example, a Japanese saying holds that a good husband is one who is healthy and absent, and a recent Japanese television commercial states, "Men should keep silent and drink beer" (Cres-

ter & Leon, 1982). Among groups in which marriages are arranged, the emphasis is on the legal contract, guaranteeing the family's economic and social welfare, rather than on the romantic relationship of the spouses.

Although historically, romance has not been considered a prerequisite to marriage, in the United States, this concept is primary. The expectation is that individuals should be in love when they marry and continue to be in love "until death do us part." But the reactions of different ethnic groups to this expectation depend upon attitudes toward marriage and family.

Jews, for instance, tend to view marriage as the continuation of traditions and history. Hispanics may romanticize marriage as the union of love between two families. For the Irish, on the other hand, romance in marriage is not a central concept. In fact, they may even fear romance, considering marriage as the giving of "permission to sin" (McGoldrick et al., 1982).

Male and Female Roles

Historically, most cultural groups have ascribed separate and defined roles to males and females, with the most common being for men to provide and for women to nurture. Nevertheless, cultural groups differ tremendously in the degree of differentiation of sex roles and in the characteristics of the roles themselves. Greeks, for example, tend to be hierarchical in all family roles (Papajohn & Spiegel, 1975), whereas Jews tend to be democratic in family relationships (Herz & Rosen, 1982). There are also vast differences in how power is distributed and exercised among men and women. Although most groups give men more overt authority, in some cultures, women can be very powerful in their roles as caretakers and even decision makers.

Asian women, for example, often become powerful in later life, after the death of their husbands. "Because of the great emotional attachment the oldest son feels toward his devoted mother, the wishes of the mother are frequently respectfully attended to by the son. Thus, although the oldest son is the ruler of the family, it is frequently the mother who rules this son, and therefore the rest of the family" (Shon & Ja, 1982). Irish women, on the other hand, have tended to be openly dominant in family life and to be considered morally superior to men (McGoldrick et al., 1982).

The roles that husband and wife expect to play differ greatly from one culture to another. Spouses may find themselves mystified, if not in serious conflict, when their cultural backgrounds provide a misfit of expectations. As the WASP journalist said of herself and her Greek husband: "Andrew comes from a culture where women do all the work and I come from one where men do all the work, and we're both sitting around waiting for someone to do the work." Greek culture emphasizes hierarchical roles: "Greek men are authoritarian fathers and husbands. They are loving, but particularly to outsiders, appear to be emotionally distant. They are parsimonious with praise and generous with criticism. As the Greek proverb goes, 'A man should love his wife with his heart, but never with his lips' " (Welts, 1982). (This could indicate that Greek men would be a good fit with Japanese women.) Ravich (1969), who studied marital patterns in couples from different backgrounds, said: "Greek men want to dominate the situation and go to great lengths to do so. . . . Their wives know this and follow the male lead" (p. 279). Women are expected not to discuss domestic tensions outside the family. Doing so is considered to be defiance of the husband and risks causing the family shame or criticism (Rodman, 1967). In Puerto Rican culture, by contrast, the wife's sharing of marital issues with extended family, especially with other women, may be an important method of coping with family tensions (Garcia Preto, 1982). Thus, the boundaries around the couple differ from group to group, as does the nature of the marital contract and of the roles expected of each partner.

In contrast to Greeks, WASP males generally play a less authoritative role in the family. Their deepest responsibility is to work. The expectation that they should support their families under any circumstances often leads them to overwork and to being isolated at home. The husband is "reinforced as a workaholic and trained to feel inadequate and irrelevant in child rearing and in maintaining social relationships" (McGill & Pearce, 1982, p. 466). The husband's failure to support his family during a financial crisis is likely to be experienced by both spouses as a breach of contract. This expectation can lead to serious misunderstandings when, for example, a Polish man marries a WASP woman. The following pattern of interaction may ensue. He will probably ask her to go to work during a financial crisis, since Polish men often expect their wives to assume equal responsibility to help the family achieve its goals (Mondykowski, 1982). The WASP wife may react to her Polish husband's request with silent resentment, which he may interpret as a lack of support rather than as her response to his breach of contract. He will probably express his anger verbally, which will only frighten her into becoming more silent and distant, and possibly into refusing his sexual advances. WASPs tend to control their aggression, especially in family situations, by remaining silent and distant and avoiding intimacy (McGill & Pearce, 1982). The wife's silence and sexual avoidance would probably exacerbate the conflict with a Polish husband, who would interpret this behavior as a lack of love and as an affront to his manhood.

In assessing communication problems in intermarried couples, it is important to note particularly the following potential areas of difference:

1. Style of communication: verbal, taciturn, rational, dramatically expressive, and so on.
2. Handling of conflict: argument, reasoning, withdrawal, teasing, indirect response.
3. Attitude toward intimacy and dependence: positive, fearful, assertive, demanding, withholding.
4. Attitude toward grief and sadness: stoic, expressive, emotional, denying, angry.

The Family Context of Marriage

Ethnic groups also differ in their attitudes toward marriage as a subsystem of the larger family context and with regard to the boundaries between the couple and the children, the extended family, and the broader social context. Certain groups view marriage as a union of two working partners, and others as primarily a vehicle for the rearing of children or as an extension of the family network. Jewish families, for example, place tremendous responsibility on marital partners to give attention to child rearing. Other groups, such as the Irish, consider that children should be seen and not heard and they are rarely made the center of adult attention. WASP families fairly readily send their children off to boarding school at an early age if they can afford it, while Italians often find this practice hard to understand because they consider it crucial to keep children close to home.

Different values and attitudes toward rearing children can aggravate the conflicts of intermarried couples. Although loving their children with equal intensity, they may express that love very differently. German parents, for instance, place much more importance on structure, limit spatial exploration, and do not encourage emotional exploration (Winawer-Steiner & Wetzel, 1982). If married to a German, a Jewish parent may have tremendous difficulty with those attitudes, since in Jewish culture children are encouraged to explore, be creative, and express their emotions (Herz & Rosen, 1982). They will both agree, however, on the importance of education and will encourage achievement.

By contrast, Jewish and Italian marital partners are likely to agree on the value they place on the family and on food, but may have conflicts regarding the education of their children. Education is one of the most important goals for Jewish parents. Their children should surpass them in success, even if it means moving away from the family. Italians have had very different attitudes toward education and success. Education has often taken second place to family loyalty, and surpassing the family has not been encouraged, since it implies leaving the family. Hispanics, in this respect, would be complementary to Italians, since they also experience leaving the family as taking a grave risk.

Connectedness to the extended family depends on culture as well. Many groups, such as Greeks, Chinese, and Italians, believe they have a primary obligation to support aging parents, to spend leisure time socializing with them, and not to send them to nursing homes. Other groups consider "duty visits" on holidays and at family funerals sufficient. As one WASP man described it (not ironically): "I am very close to my family. I see them every two or three years." Frequently, a spouse from a group that maintains strong boundaries around the couple or the nuclear family will perceive the partner who is intensely involved with his or her extended fam-

ily as disloyal, when, in fact, the spouse is just responding to a different cultural imperative and set of obligations. One Irish wife sought therapy because she said she was convinced her Greek husband did not love her, since he insisted she accompany him every Sunday and holiday to spend the day with his mother and brothers. He could not understand his wife's complaints. He explained that he often did not even enjoy going, but that he felt obligated and would feel he was "betraying" his mother if he did not. It took the wife some time to realize that her husband's reaction had nothing to do with "love" or "commitment" to her; in Greek culture, loyalty to one's parents is just as intense as loyalty to one's spouse, which it is not for the Irish.

Children of Intermarriage

Children of intermarriage have a built-in problem of how to put together the two different cultures of their parents. They may attempt to resolve the dilemma by identifying primarily with one parent, or in trying to draw from both they may make a creative leap transforming the diversity into new and different perceptions of the world; failing, these children may become symptomatic because they cannot reconcile the diversity[7] (McGoldrick & Garcia Preto, 1984; Schwartzman, 1982).

Recent studies of the ethnic backgrounds of medical students and family therapists have confirmed the impression of others (Heer, 1980) that ethnically mixed couples are more likely to divorce and to have a variety of other problems (McGoldrick & Rohrbaugh, 1987). These studies have shown that their children indicate more personal problems and more relationship problems than children from ethnically homogeneous families. The diversity of intermarriage is thus often problematic for the children as well as for the couple (McGoldrick & Garcia Preto, 1984).

---

[7] *Editors' Note.* In our experience, one way people sometimes attempt to reconcile these differences is by identifying more with (the ethnic background of) one parent than with the other, especially when there is a parental racial difference.

Implications for Therapy:
A Life-Cycle Framework

Our need for a positive sense of cultural identity and continuity with past traditions, far from diminishing, increases over the life cycle (Gelfand, 1979). The sense of ancestral continuity is, of course, much stronger in homogeneous relationships. At the moment of marital choice, however, it is extremely uncommon for couples to have perspective on their later family-life-cycle requirements (McGoldrick, 1988). In our experience, intermarrying couples are particularly likely to abandon cultural rituals, perhaps in an attempt to deny their differentness and their own identity conflicts as well as in an effort at mutual adaptation (Falicov, 1986). This process usually causes a loss of family connectedness and alters the continuity of the family life cycle.

A spouse who marries out reactively and raises children without teaching them his or her native language or cultural traditions may later regret that decision, as the children grow up with little sense of ethnic identity. A spouse who leaves his or her country of origin to marry may later experience a painful longing for homeland and roots. The implications of the decision to "marry out" may only be appreciated many years later, particularly if the need for a supportive and familiar context intensifies. The impact of a decision to intermarry may thus not be appreciated until complex new family structures are in place and full resolution of the loyalty conflicts cannot be achieved.

During courtship, a person may be attracted precisely to the other's differentness, but when entrenched in a marital relationship, the same qualities often annoy. For example, Irish–Italian marriages, which have been very common, may have appeal because the Italian seems warm, affectionate, and sensuous to the Irish spouse, whereas the Irish spouse may seem to the Italian to be lighthearted, independent, and able to handle stress with jokes rather than drama. Once they have married, however, the Irish tendency to resolve a problem by distance may be intolerable for the Italian, who experiences distancing and separation as betrayal. On the other side, the emotional scenes of the Italian spouse are devastating to the Irish spouse, who can never forget the words said in anger or the

loss of control. Often such behavioral patterns, attitudes, and values are not recognized as ethnic attitudes, but are regarded instead as individual psychopathology.

It is rare for such couples to seek premarital counseling. If they do and are motivated to work out family issues, a great deal can be done to prevent problems later on. If couples do come to therapy prior to the wedding, the best advice is to keep open relationships with all family members. Intermarriage requires that each spouse have flexibility to deal with the differences of the other's background. Efforts by one spouse or extended family to ignore or denigrate the other spouse's family will increase the pressure on the couple and may eventually lead to marital breakdown. Therapeutic techniques aimed at helping individuals claim their cultural rituals as part of their own identity often increase their ability to accept differences.

In attempting to understand intermarriage conflicts, it is always important to assess how they interact with life-cycle stresses. The best-written report we have found of the work involved in overcoming an intense cutoff precipitated by an intermarriage is L. Lampiris' (1981) account of his six-year effort to reconnect with his Greek family following a seven-year cutoff that began at the time of his marriage to an Italian woman. His description, complemented by his wife's account (B. S. Lampiris, 1981) (1978) of her own struggles during the same period, conveys the complex way in which the cultural process intersects with life-cycle stresses. It is interesting that in this instance the stillbirth of a child intensified the cutoff, and it was only the failing health of his parents that set the context for the family to shift its patterns and end the estrangement. Lampiris' story seems to confirm Friedman's (1971) hypothesis that parents who go to the extreme of cutting off their children because of intermarriage are primarily reacting to their own difficulty in separating from the child, rather than standing on principle about the intermarriage. Lampiris was born after his parents had lost their first child, and they had no other children. Soon after Lampiris' birth, his father totally cut himself off from two of his own siblings, probably intensifying the son's meaning to the system. The mother, the responsible one in her family, had to deal with an invalid father, a husband who was usually away at sea (which added to the importance her only child had for her), and her son's intermarriage, which may indeed have been an attempt at independence or a striving for emotional elasticity in his family (Friedman, 1971). As Lampiris writes: "I told them that while they thought my wife was the problem, they had focused on the wrong issue. Our problem was so simple we had all missed it. The three of us had never learned to disagree and after the disagreement get on with our relationship. Somehow we had assumed that lack of unanimity meant no relationship" (p. 130).

Lampiris' efforts show, at its best, the attempt of an intermarrying spouse to deal with his own issues regarding the intermarriage, rather than allowing the family or himself to focus on the "differentness" of the spouse. There are many times, however, when spouses react to the real differences between them as if they were personal attacks, rather than differences rooted in ethnicity. Typically, we tolerate differences better when we are not under stress, and indeed find them appealing. When stress is added to a system, our tolerance for difference diminishes, and we become frustrated if we are not understood in ways that fit our wishes and expectations. For example, WASPs tend to withdraw when upset, to move toward stoical isolation in order to mobilize their powers of reason (their major resource in coping with stress). Jews, on the other hand, seek to analyze their experiences together. Italians may seek solace in food, emotional and dramatic expressions of their feelings, and a high degree of human contact. Obviously, these groups may perceive each other's reactions as offensive or insensitive, although within each group's ethnic context, these reactions make excellent sense. In our experience, much of therapy involves helping family members recognize the frame of reference of each other's behavior. Clarifying the differences, however, is not sufficient. As Falicov (1985) maintains, it is necessary to assess the role that cultural differences play in the marital problem and to use cultural issues strategically. Cultural traits in this context are viewed as flexible and valuable resources for change. Spouses may have a sudden and remarkable shift in response to each other when they can come to see the other's behavior as fitting into a larger ethnic context rather than as a personal attack.

Therapy with intermarried couples frequently involves helping them to understand and negotiate their differences in a cultural context, just as one helps other couples to see the roles that sibling constellation, life-cycle stages, and gender play in their perceptions.

Intermarriage requires a degree of flexibility not necessary for those who marry within their own group. Certain differences in values, emotional reaction, and world view may never be bridged, and there will always be dangling ends—aspects of each spouse's heritage that cannot be integrated into the marriage. In our view, awareness that these gaps are natural is crucial for transforming differences in this process successfully. Nothing is more detrimental to the long-term evolution of intermarried families than denying the importance of cultural differences or denying one spouse's heritage as he or she attempts to convert to the other's cultural values. Given that intermarriage is a significant factor in our culture, it is important that we become more flexible in dealing with these complexities so that we are neither rigid in our inability to adapt to these changes nor so thoughtless about our heritage that we lose it unwittingly by trying to change too fast.

ASSESSMENT AND TREATMENT OF RECENT REFUGEE POPULATIONS

Refugees are a global phenomenon. In the past few decades, they have included survivors of war, opponents of dictatorships, and victims of religious oppression. The most recent refugee populations in the United States are the Cubans and Haitians who arrived during the Mariel crisis, the refugees from Central and South American countries, and the Southeast Asian refugees who fled their homes in the aftermath of the Vietnam war.

The migration experience of refugees can be differentiated from that of immigrants on the basis of free choice. While immigrants have various reasons for migrating, refugees are usually "forced" to leave, with little or no hope of returning to their country of origin. In addition to the involuntary nature of their emigration, most refugees had encountered serious traumas and catastrophic life-threatening experiences—including war, torture, rape, hunger, persecution, imprisonment, confinement to concentration camps, deaths of family members and friends, and forced separation from their loved ones.

Sociocultural changes superimposed by the host country after resettlement add another dimension of stress. While still actively mourning their losses, refugees must also cope with the oppressive load imposed by the sheer need to survive in the process of reconstructing a new life during the postmigration period. They need to learn a new language, find jobs, adjust to different climates, locate housing, and deal with the "culture shock" in a foreign country.

Given these various stressors encountered by refugees, it would be reasonable to expect that they are a psychologically/psychiatrically at-risk population. In reviewing the literature on psychopathology and social disruption in refugees, Lin (1986) indicates that, over the past 40 years, researchers and clinicians alike have consistently noted that despite significant background differences, most refugees encounter similar kinds of adaptational difficulties and thus tend to develop similar problems.

The following mental health problems are more common in refugee populations as compared with the general population:

1. *Anxiety and depression.* The typical symptomatology includes a rich variety of complaints: headaches, dizziness, poor appetite, fatigue, aches and pains in the limbs, feeling of constant chills, poor concentration, sleep disorder, and suicidal thoughts (Kinzie & Manson, 1983; Nguyen, 1982; Lee & Chan, 1986).
2. *Posttraumatic stress disorder (PTSD).* Patients experience repetitive nightmares of catastrophic events, psychic numbing, intrusive thinking, restlessness, irritability, recurrent explosive anger, hyperalertness, poor concentration, and "survivor guilt."
3. *Somatization.* Patients present a description of "weak heart" (palpitations, fatigue), "weak kidney" (sexual dysfunctions, lower back pain, headache, decreased intellectual function), and "weak nervous systems" (inability to concentrate, irritability, poor memory) (Tung, 1985). Many patients hide their de-

pressive illness behind somatic complaints.
4. *Organic brain syndromes.* These are caused by beatings in prison, gunshot and explosion wounds, malnutrition, infectious disease, and so on.
5. *"Refugee neurosis."* Symptoms include an amalgam of insomnia, somatic complaints, mistrust and suspiciousness, nightmares, difficulty with interpersonal relationships, social isolation, and lack of enjoyment.
6. *Paranoid syndromes.* Common symptoms include delusions regarding the spouse's fidelity and government agencies. Somatic delusion is also common.
7. *Other psychiatric problems.* These include schizophrenia and schizophreniform psychosis, substance abuse, mania, bipolar disorder, panic disorder, and anorexia nervosa.

In addition to the individual and intraphsychic responses to stressors, attention should be paid to the impact of the refugee experiences on the family. There are some specific stressors encountered by refugee families:

1. *Intergenerational conflicts.* Brown (1982) and Stein (1986) observed that intergenerational conflicts attributable to different rates of acculturation resulted in strained relations with the entire family. Many refugee children and adolescents are under a strong double bind. On the one hand, their home culture expects them to be quiet, obedient, hardworking, humble, and respectful, whereas at school and with their peers, they learn American values, which have a strong emphasis on independence, self-reliance, and competition. Many English-speaking children become the "cultural broker" between their parents and U.S. society. Such role reversal weakens the authority of the parents and can evoke anger and resentment on both sides.
2. *Marital conflicts.* The traditional roles of husband and wife also undergo drastic changes after resettlement. The need to supplement family income has forced refugee women to seek employment. In fact, they often are more willing and able to accept low-status jobs, and frequently become the sole providers for their families. They often achieve a greater degree of initial adjustment than their husbands. Many are reluctant to regress

and assume their traditional submissive role. The upward social mobility of the wives and the downward mobility of the husbands become a source of family unrest. The unavailability of the extended family also deprives these couples of an important buffering and protective network.

3. *Conflicts with family members and relatives who are left behind.* Many refugees have an obsessive concern over separation from family members and a strong wish for reunification. However, the refugees' guilt and anxieties in not being able to bring their relatives to the United States are often mixed with anger and frustration. Very often, the relatives are unaware of the difficulties their American relatives encounter in the "promised land." They often make unrealistic demands for financial, material, and legal assistance. This inability of the American relatives to help their relatives abroad reinforces the sense of helplessness.

4. *Conflicts with the sponsor.* With no other alternatives, many refugees have to be quite dependent on their sponsor's financial, legal, and emotional support—especially when they first arrive. The role of the sponsor (usually assumed by the adult children or siblings who migrated here earlier than their parents) is at times in conflict with the traditional role in refugee families.

Most refugees tend to be very discreet about individual psychiatric problems and family conflicts. They enter counseling only on an involuntary basis or during crisis. In order to treat refugee families successfully, the therapist needs to understand their unique life experiences and world views, and to develop culturally attuned interventions at various phases in the helping process. The therapist should conduct a comprehensive assessment, taking into consideration the biological–psychological–sociological–cultural–political variables. The following areas of inquiry should be included beyond traditional intake data.

1. *Migration stress*
   Premigration experience (life in the homeland)
   This assessment should include:

- socioeconomic status of the family before the war
- type of community in which the family lived
- major caretaker(s) before the escape
- educational, medical, and recreational systems in the home country
- traumatic events in the family—death of family members, loss of significant relatives, loss of family properties, and so on
- significant physical injury and/or emotional difficulties
- traumatic events encountered—degree of exposure to death and dying, degree of torture, degree of assault, and so on

Migration experiences (the escape process and life in a refugee camp):

- decision to leave—why, when, and who?
- degree and type of trauma during escape, including attacks by pirates, rape, hunger, exposure to death
- refugee-camp experience—physical safety, psychological support
- separation and losses of significant others
- stress induced by legal immigration process—uncertainty of sponsorship, duration of waiting
- effect of specific traumas on individual and family
- effect of migration on individual and family life cycles
- acceptance of losses

2. *Acculturation stress*
   - problems caused by language difficulties
   - adjustment to new school, financial, and legal systems
   - culture shock and adjustment to new value system
   - changes in living environment and neighborhood
   - reception by the host country
   - adjustment to minority status

3. *Economic stress*
   - unemployment and underemployment
   - downward mobility and status inconsistencies

4. *Family stress*
   - intergenerational conflicts
   - role reversal of husband and wife
   - in-law conflicts

- conflicts with relatives who were left be-hind
- conflicts with sponsor
- degree of social isolation (for those refugees who left most of the family members in the homeland)

In addition to the assessment of the stressors, careful assessment needs to be made with respect to family strengths and support systems available in the refugee's cultural and religious community.

Generally speaking, most of the refugees are new arrivals who speak little or no English and are quite traditional in their beliefs. The therapist should be able to conduct skilled cross-cultural, cross-language therapy with the collaboration of a translator-interpreter, who can also serve as the "cultural broker." As indigenous healing practices are continuing to be used by many refugees, the therapist also needs to understand the refugee's cultural interpretation of mental health problems and traditional healing methods, and should work collaboratively with the folk healers in the refugee community.

One of the most difficult tasks for the therapist in the treatment of refugees is to discuss traumatic events with trauma survivors. Immature probing and too much disclosure may lead to serious and often unremitting emotional distress. On the other hand, avoidance of the topic may encourage pathological denial and repression. The therapist needs to assess the *readiness* of the client to explore such subjects. The gentle sharing of the trauma story after the establishment of trust, at the client's own pace and direction, can sometimes lead to healthy integration or resolution of the trauma experience and its positive effects on the self and relationships with significant others. During such discussions, the therapist needs to be aware of the issue of countertransference. Clinical contact with war survivors may stir up overwhelming feelings of horror, guilt, aggressiveness, or rage. A difficult but necessary task in the therapeutic process involves two delicate subtasks: to be able objectively to facilitate the client's search for understanding concerning the impact of the trauma, and, at the same time, to make the affective contact necessary to facilitate the treatment process.

TRAINING IN ETHNICITY

We believe that the best learning takes place in a context that allows for openness to new possibilities, not in a competitive, threatening context. We thus take the position that training should take a positive perspective to enrich the therapist's clinical repertoire. It does not help therapists to be told only what they are doing wrong, what does not work, and how inappropriate traditional therapies are for the clients they see. They need to be offered something new to try. We make it a point in all of our work to emphasize what can be done over what may go wrong.

We also believe that it is more useful to teach from the familiar, making it look unfamiliar as we apply a cultural lens, rather than to take unfamiliar cultural practices (e.g., voodoo, Irish superstitions) and make the clinician more familiar with them. If we start with familiar content, it is easier for trainees to realize that ethnicity applies to everyone, not just to ethnic groups that are very different from our so-called norms. In our view, one of the biggest disservices that is done in this area is to teach about ethnic beliefs as if we could learn about "strange and different" practices and not have to question our own values in the process.

Our training model requires that clinicians struggle consciously with their own subjectivity and recognize the limitations of their personal belief system. We believe training in culture should occur in the context of training about many differences: gender, class, religion, geography, and politics. Only when we come to realize the context-determined roots of all our values can we shift to a systemic view of ourselves as part of a helping context. Only then will we leave behind the dichotomized mythology of the doctor "diagnosing" and labeling the patient, as though by some objective measures of reality. We are always part of the systems we are trying to observe and our participation affects our observations. This perspective is a prerequisite for understanding and intervening in the complexities of human systems.

In our view, the most important part of ethnicity training involves the therapist's coming to understand his or her own ethnic identity in a differentiated way. This means that, ideally, therapists would no longer be "triggered" by ethnic characteristics they may have disliked in their own group or be caught in an ethnocentric view that their group's values are more "right" and "true" than others. Resolving the psychological issues of ethnic identity involves achieving a multiethnic perspective whereby we are open to understanding values that differ from our own and no longer need to convince others of our values or give in to theirs.

We try to teach a way of thinking more than providing specific information about different ethnic groups, but our experience has taught us repeatedly that theoretical discussions about the importance of ethnicity are practically useless in training clinicians. We come to appreciate the relativity of values best through specifics. Thus, in our training we work a great deal through detail. How do groups differ in their responses to pain and suffering, in their attitudes toward doctors? Do they prefer a formal or informal style in dealing with strangers? Do they tend to feel positive about their bodies? About work? About marital intimacy? About children expressing their feelings?

Our pilot study of mental health professionals' descriptions of their family experiences suggests that American ethnic groups do differ in their values, beliefs, and rules of family functioning along the lines of traditional stereotypes. Compared with other groups, for example, Jewish respondents more often reported that their families valued education, success, encouragement of children, verbal expression, shared suffering, guilt, and eating. WASP families emphasized personal control, stoicism, individuality, moderation, and keeping up appearances. The Irish reported more self-control, suffering, drinking, strength in women, and respect for the church's rules; Italians emphasized expressiveness, traditional sex roles, relatedness through eating, and getting things done through personal connections. With few exceptions, the differences were consistent with cultural stereotypes and with characterizations of ethnic American families in the family-therapy literature.

An important therapeutic implication of our data is that therapists and clients from different ethnic backgrounds can easily misunderstand each other. For example, Jewish and Irish respondents differed sharply on the item, "Chil-dren were encouraged to discuss and give their opinions on family problems." Jewish subjects rated this item higher than did the other groups, and the Irish rated it lower. On this basis, one could imagine a Jewish therapist encouraging children to give their opinions of family troubles and finding it problematic that Irish children were reluctant to respond. On the other hand, an Irish therapist might consider children in a Jewish family presumptuous or ill mannered because of their outspoken opinions on family problems. Another item, "You really got attention when you were sick," received a positive Jewish response, but a relatively negative WASP response. Imagine a WASP therapist's reaction to a Jewish patient's complaints about feeling sick, and that patient's reaction to the "withholding" therapist (McGoldrick & Rohrbaugh, 1987).

Obviously, the study of ethnocultural factors in therapy could hardly be based on encouraging therapists to learn the differences in values, family patterns, life-cycle rituals, religious practices, and attitudes toward seeking help of all groups. It would be a big mistake to suggest that therapists need to become cultural anthropologists in order to be effective clinicians. The best approach, we believe, is for clinicians to focus on the few groups to which they have considerable exposure (through their spouses, friends, travels, or clients) as a way of training themselves to be more aware of the cultural relativity of all norms and values.

Ethnicity, like family-systems training in general, may at times be a very loaded issue for trainees. Even an objective discussion of cultural differences may trigger disturbing feelings or memories of early ethnic experiences or exposure to prejudice. The psychological scars of negative stereotyping and discrimination are often still there—the cultural memory can readily come alive in response to a seemingly harmless joke or ethnic reference. For these reasons, we place great emphasis in our training on creating a context in which the leaders themselves expose their ethnic vulnerabilities as a model for others. We try to make the training situation a safe one for generalizing about cultural differences. Nothing would make training less likely to succeed than to begin with a description of the characteristics of different groups without making clear the need to use generalizations, which will reflect at best only partial truths. One of the best ways we know to do this is by describing our own reluctance to stereotype—our fears of being labeled as prejudiced or racist, and the alternative possibility of not talking about differences at all.

In our experience, presentations of one group alone are rarely successful because they lead trainees to think of the exceptions to the rule. Once a number of cultures are presented together, it is easier to recognize, for example, that while not all Irish are alike, they probably are a good deal more like each other than they are like Greeks or Russians or Chinese.

We have found that there are two major resistances to ethnicity training. The first is the attitude that ethnicity is a commonsense subject we all understand and that there is no particular need to develop a special program to study it when there are so many other critical priorities to be covered in training, although it would be all right to have a one-session training program for learning how to treat Hispanics, Blacks, and Asians successfully. While we consider it important to meet trainees where they are at, the risk of trying to focus all ethnicity training on minorities is that it allows clinicians from "non-minority" groups to maintain the idea that their own values are the norm and that these other groups have "deviant" or "different" values.

The second resistance, which is more difficult to address, is an active reluctance to define ethnic differences. At times, this may come from minority-group members who fear that in a discussion of ethnic differences in general, their own group will be lost. But more often, it comes from a deep-seated fear of generalizations. It is usually predictable that those who are most upset about discussions of ethnic differences have charged personal reasons for their reactions, such as an Irish woman who became incensed at the mention of drinking among the Irish, because, as she finally admitted, given her father's alcoholism, it made her feel that her family was "doomed."

In our training groups, we often ask participants to describe (1) themselves ethnically, (2) who in their family experience influenced their sense of ethnic identity, (3) which characteristics of their group they like most and which they like least, and (4) how they think their own family would react to having to go to family therapy and what approach it would probably prefer.

CONCLUSION

It is hard for us to remain open to cultural diversity. Ambiguity and difference are threatening, and we tend to close down emotionally when confronted with too much dissimilarity to our own experience. Understanding the relativity of our own ethnic biases is one of the best insurances against such rigidity. Yet this insight is hard to gain. There are particular difficulties for us as therapists in stepping outside our own belief systems. Not all cultures value the pursuit of insight, truth, "getting ahead," or sharing problems and feelings. By exploring our ethnic assumptions, we are led to question our primary therapeutic technique. It is no wonder we are threatened.

The extensive geographical and class mobility in American culture, while often cutting individuals off from their ethnic heritage, increases their contact with different ethnic groups. The high rate of interethnic marriage means that many Americans will learn about ethnic differences from marriage partners. But, at best, most Americans will probably come to understand well only three or four groups in the course of a lifetime. Obviously, no therapist can become an expert on all ethnic groups. What is essential for clinicians is to develop an attitude of openness to cultural variability and to the relativity of their own values.

Indeed, our ethnicity is rapidly evolving in new directions, where it becomes increasingly important to be able to define and differentiate the values and cultural patterns of those who live in the United States as we move toward the 21st century, compared with groups in Canada, Mexico, Japan, and elsewhere in the world.

Some potential negative consequences of emphasizing ethnicity must also be recognized. Overly strict adherence to a particular way of doing things, under the supposition that it is an "ethnic" value, can make an ethnic group resist change and thereby impede its development. Values that were functional in another place and time often become dysfunctional when translated into modern America. Ethnocentrism, clannishness, prejudice, fear, and distrust of outsiders can prevent cooperation, reinforce exclusivity, and deepen intergroup conflicts (Giordano & Giordano, 1977; Kolm, 1973; Mc-Goldrick, 1982a). The solution to these problems lies not in eradicating cultural differences, however, but in developing their potential to become a source of cultural enrichment.

REFERENCES

Abad, V., Ramos, J., & Boyce, E. (1974). A model for delivery of mental health services to Spanish speaking minorities. *American Journal of Orthopsychiatry, 44*, 584–595.

Ahren, F.M., Cole, R.E., Johnson, R.C., & Wong, B. (1981). Personality attributes of males and females marrying in the U.S. across racial/ethnic groups. *Behavioral Genetics, 11*, 181–194.

Aponte, H. (1974). Psychotherapy for the poor; an eco-structural approach to treatment. *Delaware Medical Journal, 46*, 432–446.

Barnett, L.D. (1963). Research on international and interracial marriages. *Marriage & Family Living, 25*, 105–107.

Bernal, G. (1982). Cuban families. In M. McGoldrick, J.K. Pearce, & J. Giordano (Eds.), *Ethnicity and family therapy*. New York: Guilford Press.

Bernard, M. (1980). *The family melting pot and the altar: Marital assimilation in early twentieth century Wisconsin*. Minneapolis, Minnesota: Univ. of Minnesota Press.

Billingsley, A. (1968). *Black families in White America*. Englewood Cliffs, NJ: Prentice-Hall.

Billingsley, A. (1976). The family and cultural pluralism. Address at Baltimore Conference on Ethnicity and Social Welfare. New York: Institute on Pluralism and Group Identity.

Boyd-Franklin, N. (1989). *Black families in therapy: A multi-system approach*. New York: Guilford Press.

Brown, G. (1982). Issues in the resettlement of Indochinese refugees. *Social Casework, 63*, 155–159.

Canino, I., & Canino, G. (1980). The impact of stress on the Puerto Rican migrant. Some treatment considerations. *American Journal of Orthopsychiatry, 50*, 164–186.

Carpenter, W., & Strauss, J. (1974). Cross-cultural evaluation of Schneider's first-rank symptoms of schizophrenia: A report from the international pilot study of schizophrenia. *American Journal of Psychiatry, 131*, 204–210.

Crester, C.A., & Leon, J.J. (Eds.). (1982). *Intermarriage in the United States*. New York: Haworth.

Crohn, J. (1986). Ethnic identity and marital conflict: Jews, Italians and WASPs. Institute for American Pluralism, American Jewish Committee.

Diner, H. (1983). *Erin's daughters in America*. Baltimore, MD: Johns Hopkins University Press.

Di Nicola, V.F. (1985). Family therapy and transcultural psychiatry: Parts 1 and 2, *Transcultural Psychiatric Research Review, 22/(2, 3)*, 81–113, 151–180.

Falicov, C.J. (1982). Mexican families. In M. McGoldrick, J.K. Pearce, & J. Giordano (Eds.), *Ethnicity and family therapy*. New York: Guilford Press.

Falicov, C.J. (Ed.) (1983). *Cultural perspectives in family therapy*. Rockville, MD: Aspen Systems.

Falicov, C.J. (1986). Cross-cultural marriages, In N. Jacobson & A. Gurman (Eds.), *Handbook of marital therapy*. New York: Guilford Press.

Fallows, M.A. (1979). *Irish-Americans: Identity and assimilation*. Englewood Cliffs, NJ: Prentice-Hall.

Fantl, B., & Shiro, J. (1959). Cultural variables in the behavior patterns of symptom formation of 15 Irish and 15 Italian schizophrenics. *International Journal of Social Psychiatry, 4*, 245–253.

Farber, B., Gordon, L., & Mayer, A.J. (1979). Intermarriage and Jewish identity: The implications for pluralism in American society. *Ethnic and Racial Studies, 2(2)*, 132–140.

Friedman, E.H. (1971). Ethnicity identity as extended family in Jewish–Christian marriage. In J.O. Bradt & C.J. Moynihan (Eds.), *Systems therapy*. Washington, DC: Georgetown Family Center.

Friedman, E.H. (1980). Systems and ceremonies. In E.A. Carter & M. McGoldrick (Eds.), *The family life cycle: A framework for family therapy*. New York: Gardner Press.

Friedman, E.H. (1982). The myth of the shiksa. In M. McGoldrick, J.K. Pearce, & J. Giordono (Eds.), *Ethnicity and family therapy*. New York: Guilford.

Gambino, R. (1974). *Blood of my blood: The dilemma of Italian-Americans*. Garden City, NY: Doubleday.

Garcia Preto, N. (1982). Puerto Rican families. In M. McGoldrick, J.K. Pearce, & J. Giordano (Eds.), *Ethnicity and family therapy*. New York: Guilford Press.

Gelfand, D.E., & Kutzik, A.J. (Eds.) (1979). *Ethnicity and aging*. New York: Springer.

Giordano, J. (1986). *The Italian-American catalog*. Garden City, NY: Doubleday.

Giordano, J., & Giordano, G.P. (1977). *The ethno-cultural factor in mental health: A literary review and bibliography*. New York. Institute on Pluralism and Group Identity.

Greeley, A.M. (1969). Why can't they be like us? New York: Institute of Human Relations Press.

Haskell, M. (1982). Her. *New York Times*, Feb. 25.

Heer, D.M. (1980). Intermarriage. In S. Thernstrom, A. Orlov, & O. Handlin (Eds.), *Harvard encyclopedia of American ethnic groups*. Cambridge, MA: Harvard University Press.

Heneggler, S.W., & Tavormina, J.B. (1980). Social class and race differences in family interaction: Pathological, normative, or confounding methodological factor? *Journal of Genetic Psychology, 137*, 211–222.

Herz, F.M., & Rosen, E.J. (1982). Jewish families. In M. McGoldrick, J.K. Pearce, & J. Giordano (Eds.), *Ethnicity and family therapy*. New York: Guilford Press.

Hines, P.M. (1989). The family life cycle of poor Black families. In E.A. Carter & M. McGoldrick (Eds.), *The changing family life cycle: A framework for family therapy*. Boston: Allyn & Bacon.

Hines, P.M., & Boyd-Franklin, N. (1982). Black families. In M. McGoldrick, J.K. Pearce, & J. Giordano (Eds.), *Ethnicity and family therapy*. New York: Guilford Press.

Hines, P., Richman, D., Maxim, K., & Hays, H. (1989). Multi-impact family therapy: An approach to working with multi-problem families. *Journal of Psychotherapy and the Family, 6*, 161–175.

Hsu, F.L.K. (1971). *Under the ancestor's shadow: Kinship, personality, and social mobility in China*. Stanford, CA: Stanford University Press.

Imber Coopersmith, E. (1983). The family and public sector systems: Interviewing and interventions. *Journal of Strategic and System Therapies, 2*, 38–47.

Jalali, B. (1982). Family therapy with Iranian American families. In M. McGoldrick, J. Giordano, & J.K. Pearce (Eds.), *Ethnicity and family therapy*. New York: Guilford Press.

Kiev, A. (1972). *Transcultural psychiatry*. New York: Free Press.

Kinzie, J.D., & Manson, S. (1983). Five year experience with Indochinese refugee psychiatric patients. *Journal of Operational Psychiatry, 14*, 105–111.

Kleinman, A.M. (1975). Explanatory models in health care relationships. In *Health of the family (National Council for International*

Health Symposium). Washington, DC: National Council for International Health.

Kolm, R. (1973). *Ethnicity and society: A theoretical analysis and its implications for the United States*. Rockville, MD: National Institute of Mental Health.

Lampiris, B.S. (1981). Cut-offs and Illnesses: A synopsis. In P.G. McCullough (Ed.), *Second Pittsburgh family systems symposium*. Pittsburgh: Western Psychiatric Institute and Clinic.

Lampiris, L. (1981). From a Greek tragedy to a Greek drama. In P.G. McCullough & J.C. Carolin (Eds.), *Pittsburgh family systems symposia collection of papers 1979–80*. Pittsburgh: Western Psychiatric Institute and Clinic.

Lee, E. (1982). A social systems approach to assessment and treatment for Chinese American families. In: M. McGoldrick, J. Pearce, & J. Giordano (Eds.), *Ethnicity and family therapy*. New York: Guilford Press.

Lee, E. (1988a). Family therapy with Southeast Asian refugees. In M. Mirkin (Ed.), *Social and political contexts of family therapy*. New York: Gardner Press.

Lee, E. (1988b). Assessment and treatment of Chinese American immigrant families. *Journal of Psychotherapy and the Family*.

Lee, E., & Chan, F. (1986). The use of diagnostic interview schedule with Vietnamese refugees. *Asian American Psychological Association Journal*, 36–39.

Lin, K.M. (1986). Psychopathology and social disruption in refugees. In C.L. Williams & J. Westermeyer (Eds.), *Refugee mental health in resettlement countries* (pp. 61–73). Washington, DC: Hemisphere.

Malzberg, B. (1963). Mental disease among the Irish-born and native whites of Irish parentage in New York State 1949–1951. *Mental Hygiene*, 48, 478–499.

Malzberg, B. (1973). Mental disease among Jews in New York State. *Acta Psychiatrica Scandinavica*, 49, 245–251.

Mays, V. (1989). AIDS prevention in Black populations: Methods of a safer kind. In V. Mays, G. Albee, & S. Schneider (Eds.), *Primary prevention of AIDS*. Newbury Park, CA: Sage Publications.

McAdoo, H. (1978). The impact of upward mobility of kin—help patterns and the reciprocal obligations in Black families. *Journal of Marriage and the Family*, 4(4), 761–776.

McGill, D., & Pearce, J.K. (1982). British families. In M. McGoldrick, J.K. Pearce, & J. Giordano (Eds.), *Ethnicity and family therapy*. New York: Guilford Press.

McGoldrick, M. (1982a). Ethnicity and family therapy: An overview. In McGoldrick, J.K. Pearce, & J. Giordano (Eds.), *Ethnicity and family therapy*. New York: Guilford Press.

McGoldrick, M. (1982b). Irish families. In M. McGoldrick, J.K. Pearce, & J. Giordano (Eds.), *Ethnicity and family therapy*. New York: Guilford Press.

McGoldrick, M. (1982c). Normal families. An ethnic perspective. In F. Walsh (Ed.), *Normal family processes*. New York: Guilford Press.

McGoldrick, M. (1989a). Ethnicity and the family life cycle. In E.A. Carter & M. McGoldrick (Eds.), *The changing family life cycle: A framework for family therapy*. Boston: Allyn & Bacon.

McGoldrick, M. (1989b). The joining of families through marriage: The new couple. In E.A. Carter & M. McGoldrick (Eds.), *The family life cycle: A framework for family therapy*. Boston: Allyn & Bacon.

McGoldrick, M., Almeida, R., Hines, P.M., Garcia Preto, N., Rosen, E., & Lee, E. (1991). Culture and mourning. In F. Walsh & M. McGoldrick (Eds.), *Living beyond loss*. New York: Norton.

McGoldrick, M., Braverman, L., Garcia Preto, N., Hines, P., Almeida, R., Schmidt, M., Taylor, J., Michaud, T., & Lee, E. (1990). Culture and mothers. *Journal of Feminist Family Therapy*,

McGoldrick, M., & Garcia Preto, N. (1984). Ethnic intermarriage: Implications for therapy. *Family Process*, 23, 347–362.

McGoldrick, M., Garcia Preto, N., Hines, P., & Lee, E. (1989).

Ethnicity and women. In M. McGoldrick, C. Anderson, & F. Walsh (Eds.), *Women in families*. New York: Norton.

McGoldrick, M., & Pearce, J.K. (1981). Family therapy with Irish Americans. *Family Process*, 20, 223–244.

McGoldrick, M., Pearce, J.K., & Giordano, J. (1982). *Ethnicity and family therapy*. New York: Guilford Press.

McGoldrick, M., & Rohrbaugh, M. (Eds.). (1987). Researching ethnic stereotypes. *Family Process*, 26, 89–99.

Midelfort, F.C., & Midelfort, C. (1982). Family therapy with Norwegian families. In M. McGoldrick, J. Giordano, & J.K. Pearce (Eds.), *Ethnicity and family therapy*. New York: Guilford Press.

Minuchin, S. (1974). *Families and family therapy*. Cambridge, MA: Harvard University Press.

Minuchin, S., Montalvo, B., Guerney, B., Rosman, B., & Schumer, F. (1967). *Families of the slums*. New York: Basic Books.

Mondykowski, S.M. (1982). Polish families. In M. McGoldrick, J.K. Pearce, & J. Giordano (Eds.), *Ethnicity and family therapy*. New York: Guilford Press.

Murase, K. (1982). Mental health treatment modalities of Pacific/Asian American practitioners. San Francisco: Pacific Asian Mental Health Research Project.

Murphy, H.B.M. (1975). Alcoholism and schizophrenia in the Irish: A review. *Transcultural Psychiatric Research*, 12, 116–139.

Myerhoff, B. (1978). *Number our days*. New York: Simon & Schuster.

Nguyen, S.D. (1982). The psychological adjustment and the mental health needs of Southeast Asian refugees. *Psychiatric Journal of the University of Ottawa*, 7, 26–33.

Nieves-Falcon, L. (1972). *Diagnostico de Puerto Rico*. Rio Piedras: Edil. (paperback).

Office of Refugee Resettlement. (1985). *Refugee resettlement programs: Report to the Congress*. Washington, DC: U.S. Government Printing Office.

Opler, M.K., & Singer, J.L. (1956). Ethnic differences in behavior and psychopathology: Italian and Irish. *International Journal of Social Psychiatry*, 1, 11–17.

Papajohn, J., & Spiegel, J. (1975). *Transactions in families*. San Francisco: Jossey-Bass.

Peterson, F.K. (1986). Race, adaptation, and family functioning: Testing the cultural variant hypothesis. Unpublished Psy.D. dissertation, College of William and Mary, Virginia.

Pinderhughes, E. (1982). Afro-American families and the victim system. In M. McGoldrick, J.K. Pearce, & J. Giordano (Eds.). *Ethnicity and family therapy*. New York: Guilford Press.

Pinderhughes, E. (1989). *Understanding race, ethnicity and power*. New York: Free Press.

Plath, D. (1985). Of time, love and heroes. In *Adult development through relationships*.

Preto, N.G. (1982). Family therapy with Puerto Rican families. In M. McGoldrick, J. Giordano, & J.K. Pearce (Eds.), *Ethnicity and family therapy*. New York: Guilford Press.

Rabkin, J., & Struening, E. (1976). *Ethnicity, social class and mental illness in New York City*. New York: Institute on Pluralism and Group Identity.

Ravich, R. (1969). The use of an interpersonal game-test in conjoint marital psychotherapy. *American Journal of Psychotherapy*, 23, 217–229.

Resnick, R.B. (1933). Some sociological aspects of intermarriage of Jew and non-Jew. *Social Forces*, 11, 94–102.

Rinder, I. (1963). Mental health of American Jewish urbanites: A review of the literature and predictions. *International Journal of Social Psychiatry*, 9, 214–220.

Roberts, B., & Myers, J.K. (1954). Religion, national origin, immigration and mental illness. *American Journal of Psychiatry*, 110, 759–764.

Rodman, H. (1967). Marital power in France, Greece, Yugoslavia, and the United States. A cross national discussion. *Journal of Marriage and the Family*, 29, 320–325.

Rotunno, M., & McGoldrick, M. (1982). In M. McGoldrick, J.K.

Pearce, & J. Giordano (Eds.), *Ethnicity and family therapy.* New York: Guilford Press.

Sanua, V. (1960). Sociocultural factors in responses to stressful life situations: The behavior of aged amputees as an example. *Journal of Health and Human Behavior, 1,* 17–24.

Sanua, V. (1978). The contemporary Jewish family: A review of the social science literature. In G. Bubis (Ed.), *Serving the Jewish family.* New York: Ktav Press.

Schwartzman, J., (1982). Creativity, pathology, and family structure: A cybernetic metaphor. *Family Process, 21,* 113–128.

Selvini Palazzoli, M., Boscolo, L., Cecchin, G., & Prata, G. (1978). *Paradox and counterparadox: A new model in the therapy of the family in schizophrenic transaction.* New York: J Aronson.

Shannon, W.V. (1963). *The American Irish.* New York: Macmillan.

Shibutani, T., & Kwan, K.M. (1965). *Ethnic stratification.* New York: Macmillan.

Shon, S., & Ja, D.Y. (1982). Asian families. In M. McGoldrick, J.K. Pearce, & J. Giordano (Eds.), *Ethnicity and family therapy.* New York: Guilford Press.

Singer, J., & Opler, M.K. (1956). Contrasting patterns of fantasy and motility in Irish and Italian schizophrenics. *Journal of Abnormal and Social Psychiatry, 53,* 42–47.

Spanier, G., Roos, P., & Shockey, J. (1985). Marital trajectories of American women: Variations in the life course. *Journal of Marriage and the Family, 47,* 993–1003.

Spiegel, J. (1971). In J. Papajohn (Ed.), *Transactions: The interplay between individual, family, and society.* New York: Science House.

Stack, C. (1974). *All our kin: Strategies for survival in a Black community.* New York: Harper & Row.

Staples, R. (1985). Changes in Black family structures: The conflict between family ideology and structural conditions. *Journal of Marriage and the Family, 47,* 1005–1013.

Stein, B.N. (1986). The experience of being a refugee: Insights from the research literature. In: C.L. Williams & J. Westermeyer (Eds.), *Refugee mental health in resettlement countries* (pp. 5–23). Washington, DC: Hemisphere.

Stoeckle, J., Zola, I.K., & Davidson, G. (1964). The quantity and significance of psychological distress in medical patients. *Journal of Chronic Disease, 17,* 959–970.

Tung, T.M. (1985). Psychiatric care for Southeast Asians: How different is different? In T.C. Owen (Ed.), *Southeast Asian mental health: Treatment, prevention, services, training and research* (pp. 5–40). DHHS Pub. No. HDM-1399. Washington, DC: U.S. Government Printing Office.

U.S. Bureau of the Census (1977). Persons of Spanish origin in the United States (Current Population Reports Series, No. 317:20). Washington, DC: U.S. Government Printing Office.

U.S. Bureau of the Census (1988) Current population reports, Series P-60, No. 161, Money income and poverty status in the United States; 1987 (advance data from the March 1988 Current Population Survey). Washington, DC: U.S. Government Printing Office.

U.S. Bureau of the Census (1989). *Statistical abstract of the United States: (109th ed.).* Washington, DC: U.S. Government Printing Office.

U.S. Department of Health and Human Services (1988). Annual summary of births, marriages, divorces, and deaths: U.S., 1987. *Monthly Vital Statistics Report, 36*(13).

Watzlawick, P. (1976). *How real is real?* New York: Random House.

Welts, E.P. (1982). Greek families. In M. McGoldrick, J.K. Pearce, & J. Giordano (Eds.). *Ethnicity and family therapy.* New York: Guilford Press.

Wills, G. (1971). *Bare ruined choirs.* Garden City, NY: Doubleday.

Winawer-Steiner, H., & Wetzel, N.A. (1982). German families. In M. McGoldrick, J.K. Pearce, & J. Giordano (Eds.), *Ethnicity and family therapy.* New York: Guilford Press.

Wylan, L., & Mintz, N. (1976). Ethnic differences in family attitudes toward psychotic manifestations with implications for treatment programmes. *International Journal of Social Psychiatry, 22,* 86–95.

Zborowski, M. (1969). *People in pain.* San Francisco: Jossey-Bass.

Zborowski, M., & Herzog, E. (1952). *Life is with people.* New York: Schocken Books.

Zola, I.K. (1966). Culture and symptoms: An analysis of patients' presenting complaints. *American Sociological Review, 5,* 141–155.

CHAPTER 19

A Family–Larger-System Perspective

Evan Imber-Black, Ph.D.

As family therapy has developed, increasing attention has been paid to the wider social context in which families live. A significant aspect of that wider context is the larger systems with which all families must interact. Such larger systems generally include work systems, schools, religious institutions, and health-care systems, and for some families may include public welfare, child welfare, foster care, courts, mental health clinics, and systems designed for special populations, such as agencies mandated to provide services to the mentally or physically handicapped or the aged.

For many families, such engagement with larger social systems is largely nonproblematic. A family may have an occasional difficulty with a particular larger system, or with a certain worker in such a system, but the problem does not absorb great amounts of energy, and the family feels able to solve it. Some families and larger systems, however, develop very difficult relationships that take a toll on normative development for family members and contribute to burnout and cynicism in the workers from the larger systems. Still other families must engage with larger systems more regularly and more intensely throughout their life cycle because of poverty, chronic illness, or other handicaps. This chapter will present a methodology for the family therapist who is working with families that are intensely involved with larger systems.

BACKGROUND

The family–larger-system literature has focused primarily on specific larger systems or particular presenting problems. The literature is mostly descriptive and case oriented, highlighting patterns that develop between families and larger systems.

An early reconceptualization of so-called "multiproblem" families as families with numerous agencies involved in their lives was made by Selig (1976). This perspective, expanded on by Imber Coppersmith (1985) is an examination of the interaction of families and multiple helpers, begins to shift the family therapist's attention from a sole focus regarding internal family process to a focus that includes family–larger-system interaction.

Family–health-care-system interactions have been discussed by Bell and Zucker (1968), who

583

highlighted how families and hospitals that share a common member, the patient, frequently develop patterns of mutual avoidance and distancing. Selvini Palazzoli, Boscolo, Cecchin, and Prata (1980) described problems that arise for the family therapist when a family is intensely involved with a physician who refers the family for family therapy. They referred to this as the "problem of the referring person," thus orienting the family therapist to see the issue as one of an "overinvolved professional" who had become a "family member." In their work, they describe interventions they had used to address this issue; however, they do not discuss ways to maintain viable relationships within the professional network. Harbin (1985) described problems arising between families and psychiatric hospitals, which he attributed to the meeting of an informal system (the family) and a formal, bureaucratic system (the hospital). Harbin's work is important in that it highlights the fact that neither system need be inherently dysfunctional for problems to arise in their interaction, thus orienting the family therapist to look for the strengths of each system. Imber-Black (in press) has discussed the importance of differentiating between those families that have temporary relationships with health-care systems and those that, by virtue of having a chronically ill member, must have permanent relationships with health-care systems, requiring altered boundaries between the family and the larger systems, and often placing particular stress on one member, who serves as a conduit between the family and the health-care system.

Problematic interaction between families and school systems have been discussed by Aponte (1976), Coleman (1983), Imber Coppersmith (1982a, 1982b), and Morawetz and Walker (1984). All of these works describe clinical cases that conceptualize a special triad of family–school–child, highlighting problems that arise, including mutual blame and mistrust and difficulties inherent in referrals for family therapy that ignore the macrosystemic level.

Several authors have examined the intricacies of particular presenting problems and the larger systems whose mandate it is to address those problems. Lack of a family–larger-system perspective in the work of such systems has been discussed as a crucial factor in the ways that larger systems can sometimes perpetuate the very problems they were intended to solve. The problems arising between families with handicapped members and the larger systems have been discussed by Berger (1984); Bloomfield, Neilson, and Kaplan (1984); Combrinck-Graham and Higley (1984); and Imber-Black (in press). Bokos and Schwartzman (1985), Harkaway (1983), Miller (1983), Schwartzman and Kneifel (1985), and Schwartzman and Restivo (1985) have examined the ways in which systems designed to address and alleviate the problems of drug abuse, obesity, alcoholism, residential care for children, and delinquency tend to perpetuate problems, often by replicating patterns of family interaction and contributing to a reified macrosystem that becomes less and less capable of change.

The often-used family-therapy concepts of triads and boundaries have been examined as useful concepts to apply at the family–larger-system level. Harrell (1980) studied families that were involved with larger systems over generations with no problem resolution and compared these with families that entered larger systems and exited with their presenting problem solved. He found enduring conflictual triadic patterns involving those families involved with larger systems for generations and the larger systems that precluded problem resolution. Imber Coppersmith (1983) utilized the concepts of triads and boundaries between families and larger systems as essential aspects of assessment of the family–larger-system relationship, moving these familiar family-therapy concepts to the more inclusive level of the macrosystem.

Finally, the family–larger-system–wider-social-context relationship has begun to be examined in a literature that describes the sociopolitical level at which larger systems operate and within which both families and larger systems are embedded. Here, institutionalized prejudice against particular populations—such as minorities and the poor (Imber-Black, 1987a), the mentally and physically handicapped (MacKinnon & Marlett, 1984), and women (Imber-Black, 1985)—has been examined as an underpinning to the very larger systems that were designed to work with these populations. These works are a call to examine the wider social context as an often invisible level in the work of family therapists who are seeking a macrosystemic perspective.

Rationale for the Family–Larger-System Perspective

A family–larger-system perspective enables the family therapist to conceptualize and intervene with those families whose past or current involvement with larger systems has resulted in a lack of problem resolution and in increased rigidity in patterns. Formerly, such families were designated as "multiproblem," "resistant," or "uncooperative" by therapists using a perspective that stops at the boundaries of the family, rather than a more complex perspective that includes the family's relationship to larger systems and multiple helpers.[1] Conducting a family–larger-system assessment enables a therapist to determine whether the *meaningful system* is the family alone or the family and its helpers.

A family–larger-system perspective also enables the family therapist to gather information regarding the place of larger systems in the family's life, determine viable points of entry that do not replicate prior treatment failures, cocreate family–helper relationships that are different and unanticipated, and conceptualize symptoms as these may function at the family–larger-system interface. Such a perspective also helps the therapist to account for macrosystemic constraints that are currently unchangeable, such as statutory issues or required family–larger-system relationships; design effective interventions at the macrosystemic level; and maintain viable relationships with other workers from larger systems.

A FAMILY–LARGER-SYSTEM ASSESSMENT MODEL

Assessing the family–larger-system relationship may occur at various points in family therapy. If a family is referred for therapy by another system, the family therapist should immediately begin to think in macrosystemic terms. A portion of a first interview with the family that is devoted to assessing the family's relationship with larger systems can frequently assist the therapeutic endeavor and avoid treatment failures that arise when one lacks such knowledge. If a family has a complicated and unsuccessful history with larger systems, then discussing its relationship with multiple helpers is generally an extremely engaging first step that can orient all subsequent work. Such an assessment may also inform the therapist that further macrosystemic approaches are unnecessary and a focus on the family will suffice. Family–larger-system assessment becomes part of any other individual and family assessment a therapist may do. Assessment information will also emerge over the course of therapy, both as the family and the larger systems involved begin to respond to the family therapy and if a family–multiple-helper interview is held.

Like all assessment in family therapy, family–larger-system assessment is interwoven into a process of initial engagement, interviewing, interventions, and responses to interventions. The elements of family–larger-system assessment are arbitrarily separated out here to enhance the clarity of presentation.[2]

What Larger Systems Are Involved?

The starting place for assessment begins with finding out which larger systems are currently

---

[1] *Editors' Note.* While we fully agree that the therapist's broadening of the clinical perspective beyond the nuclear and extended family is of extraordinary conceptual and practical significance, such a view does not, ipso facto, preclude the appropriateness of such designations; some families, their particular larger systems notwithstanding, *do* have multiple problems, *are* uncooperative, etc. It is not the use of such labels that is problematic, but the *misuse* that is, for example, when they are simply inaccurate, are used as rationalizations for the therapist's insufficient assumption of responsibility for the progress of treatment, reflect problems of countertransference, etc.

[2] *Editors' Note.* It is important to emphasize here that while this approach emphasizes a broadening of perspective for assessment purposes, it does *not* require that numerous members of the "larger systems" participate in ongoing therapy. Imber-Black's approach, in fact, seeks to find what Skynner (1981) calls the "minimum sufficient network" with the motivation to do try to solve the problem at hand, and the capacity to do so, and what Stanton (1981) calls the "systems of import," i.e., those persons involved in the maintenance of the problem.

involved with the family, as well as which larger systems the family has been involved with in the past. Here one begins to discover both the numerical and temporal dimensions of the family's involvement with larger systems. As a list of larger systems and workers is developed, one is able to discover key relational issues between the family and outside systems: *whether the family tends to engage and reengage with helpers with no change, whether involvement with larger systems is familiar across generations or a new experience, whether the family tends to involve outsiders at nodal developmental points, and whether one member is the conduit between the family and helpers.* That is, "family rules" regarding engagement with larger systems begin to emerge. As family members discuss their involvement with larger systems, the therapist will be able to discern a tone of optimism or pessimism, of hope or despair, of amiability or hostility regarding involvement with outside systems. Questions that shape this initial information gathering may include:

1. What larger systems are involved with the family?
2. How many agencies or subsystems of agencies regularly interact with which family members?
3. How has the family moved from one larger system to another?
4. Is there a history of significant involvement with larger systems? If so, regarding what issues?

Definitions of the Problem

When one has established that a family is or has been engaged with multiple larger systems, it is crucial to discover how these systems *and* the family are defining the problem and preferred solutions. This inquiry enables the family therapist to understand patterns both of conflict and of pseudomutuality between the family and helpers that may impede therapeutic progress. *Examining the macrosystem for definitions of the problem also enables the family therapist to see his or her own definition and preferred solution as one more point of view, rather than as the "truth."* Issues regarding the referral for family therapy often come alive during this inquiry,

since one may discover that representatives of the larger systems are far more upset and worried about a problem than the family is, or that the problem definition is statutory, or that the referral involves a hidden agenda for the family therapist to "uncover" that the referral source cannot. The locus of blame also becomes apparent during a discussion of problem definitions. Here one may find that different larger systems blame particular family members for the problems, while the family blames a particular worker. Or one may find total agreement, as when both the larger systems and the family blame all problems on the fact that the family is a single-parent family. When multiple larger systems are involved, each with its own mandate, language, and point of view, the family therapist will often find a variety of problem definitions and preferred approaches, so that the same child may be viewed variously as "mad," "bad," or "sad," and be engaged in different, and often conflicting, treatment approaches simultaneously.

Dyads

The family–larger-system relationship usefully can be conceptualized as an interacting dyad, using the familiar family-therapy constructs of complementarity and symmetry (Bateson, 1972, 1979; Lederer & Jackson, 1968; Watzlawick, Beavin, & Jackson, 1967). The culturally accepted definition of the client–helper relationship is a complementary one, in which the helper offers help, therapy, counseling, or advice, and the client receives such help. When one examines family–larger-systems relationships, however, one sees many variations on this pattern. Thus, one may see a pattern of escalating complementarity in which the more help that is offered, the more helpless the family appears, leading to the entry of more and more helpers. One also may see patterns that reverse the complementarity, so that the client helps the helper. Requests for more symmetrical relationships may be invoked, for instance, as clients refuse to do homework assignments or follow other suggestions, thus defining the relationship as one in which both client and helper may decide directions for the work. Such symmetry, unfortunately, may escalate into angry struggles between the family and the larger systems.

Patterns of complementarity or symmetry between the family and larger systems may replicate existing patterns in the family. Thus, a symmetrically struggling couple may develop a similar relationship with helpers. Patterns of complementarity and symmetry also exist among the workers in the various larger systems. Discipline lines (e.g., psychiatry–social work) may contribute to such patterns. It is important for the family therapist to remember that workers in various human-services systems tend to define their relationships with one another as symmetrical. Attempting to define a complementary relationship where the family therapist is "in charge" usually results in a deteriorating symmetrical struggle.

Examining the family–larger-system relationship for patterns of complementarity and symmetry enables the family therapist to remember that he or she, too, is part of the macrosystem, participating in such patterns with family and other helpers. Such information can assist the family therapist in deliberate choices of positioning and intervention design.

Triads

The use of aspects of triadic theory to understand family relationships has informed many models of family therapy. More recently, family–larger-system theorists have employed triadic theory to understand the complex configurations involving family members and multiple larger systems (Imber Coppersmith, 1983, 1985; Schwartzman & Restivo, 1985). Triads among family members and helpers may elaborate into complex patterns of interlocking triads. They may replicate intrafamily triadic patterns. It is not unusual to discover that a mother–father–child triad is mirrored by alliances between family members and helpers, such that any new helper who enters may be pressed to replicate preexisting triads. This isomorphism at multiple systemic levels contributes to an increasingly rigid macrosystem, as no new patterns become available.

The family therapist may also discover long-standing alliances and splits among various larger systems, so that shared cases immediately result in triads involving the family. When two larger systems that share a common case are at war with each other, the family begins to occupy a position similar to that of a child between two warring parents, unable to be loyal to both and unable to work well with either without alienating one or the other.

Family–larger-system functioning is usually deleteriously effected by ongoing triads, as problem-solving energy becomes absorbed in conflicts, the maintenance of alliances, mystification, and the increased disqualification of the self as the locus of responsible action. It is important for the family therapist to assess triadic patterns and to avoid joining preexisting triads.

Boundaries

The boundaries between a family and larger systems may be so diffuse that the larger systems intrude into aspects of the family's life that are well beyond their appropriate purview. Some larger systems are particularly intrusive, utilizing their mandate to enter more and more areas of the family's life. In turn, many families do not know how to protect their own boundaries from such intrusion. Often, the family's actions that are intended to keep larger systems at bay result in further intrusion.

Boundaries between a family and larger systems may also be too rigid, so that needed assistance is unavailable. Here, the family may not allow information from the larger systems to enter the family sphere, or the larger systems may distance from the family. Rigid boundaries may be the result of racial and ethnic prejudice that denies appropriate access to services.

With regard to the issue of boundaries, families that must have permanent relationships with larger systems because of handicaps or illness or poverty need to be distinguished from families that have temporary relationships with larger systems. Families with more permanent relationships with larger systems must negotiate boundaries in ways that allow access between the family and the larger systems. Initially, such families may distance from larger systems while they are adapting to an illness or handicap. If the larger system distances in turn, then a macrosystem with rigid boundaries between the subsystems will develop. The family therapist may need to help renegotiate such boundaries. While the role for the family therapist as negotiator of intersystem boundaries may be new, in actuality, it calls upon practiced skills utilized by family therapists in their usual intrasystem work. Additionally, the skills of "shuttle diplomacy" may be required, as one must enter both the family system and the larger system, assess the boundary issues, and be able to translate the needs of one system to another. The family therapist who begins to do such boundary negotiation work can expect to experience some initial anxiety; however, carefully acquired knowledge of the larger system's boundaries and their flexibility will facilitate the work.

Families engaged with multiple larger systems may "appoint" one member to span the boundary. It is important that the family therapist recognize who this person is, avoid designation of "overinvolvement," and help the family make optimal use of this conduit position, while making sure that the person is supported by family and helpers alike.

The family therapist also needs to assess whether a referral is an indirect attempt to renegotiate boundaries between a larger system and a given family. When a particular larger system whose mandate is social control cannot get information from a family, it may use a referral for family therapy as an attempt to gain greater access, expecting that the therapist will furnish reports on the family. It is crucial that such attempts to renegotiate boundaries indirectly be addressed as an issue in the macrosystem if the family therapist is to avoid joining an inadvertent alliance.

Assessing boundaries in the macrosystem will enable the therapist to discuss boundary issues with the family and to assist in the renegotiation of boundaries when necessary.

Myths and Beliefs

Families and larger systems encounter each other within a historical context of relationships that shape myths and beliefs. Thus, families that have had a significant amount of experience with helpers have formed myths and beliefs about larger systems, helpers in general, specific professions (e.g., psychiatry, education), and the helping relationship. Such myths may spring from an intergenerational legacy of beliefs or from cultural norms, including such beliefs as that outside helpers are to be avoided at all costs; that larger-system representatives are intrusive, or kind, or useless; or conversely, that engaging with larger systems is a mandatory part of family life. A family's myths may be specific about particular larger systems. For instance, a family may believe that school systems are "good" but medical systems are "bad." As with internal family myths, members will often focus on the information that supports the myths, ignoring that which challenges them.

In two-parent families, the intergenerational myths and beliefs about larger systems may differ, resulting in a mixed presentation to the larger systems, which, in turn, may join with that member whose belief about larger systems would lead to better cooperation. Such a move can easily alienate the member whose views may be more hostile toward larger systems, resulting in a self-fulfilling prophecy.

Family myths about larger systems also arise from critical incidents involving the family and larger systems. Such incidents often take place at key developmental points in the family's life, such as the birth of a child, the onset of a serious illness, or the leaving of a member. At these times, even brief negative interactions with larger systems can become fixed in family members' memories, affecting subsequent interactions with other helpers. Family members will recount such incidents vividly and with a high degree of emotion. It is important for the family therapist to hear these stories in order to differentiate himself or herself from these experiences and to establish a new relationship in the present.

Just as families have myths about larger systems, so larger systems have myths about families in general, specific families or members, and certain symptoms. Thus, in referrals, one may hear that a family is "uncooperative," "secretive," "hostile," or "hopeless." Larger-system myths may spring from theories that are accepted as "truth," from prejudices regarding racial or ethnic groups, from acceptance of stereotypical gender roles as the appropriate norm for families, from reports written about family members, from case conferences during which helpers exchange their myths and beliefs about a given case, and from particular experiences with a given family.

In assessing the myths and beliefs that families and larger systems have about each other, the family therapist should also be looking for myths that are similar and allow for no change, such as the myth shared by families and larger systems that "single-parent families need male role models," and for myths that are conflictual, such as a family myth that *no* therapy can be helpful encountering a larger-system myth that *only* therapy can solve certain problems.[3]

Family and Larger-Systems Solutions

Examining solution behavior has been highlighted by Watzlawick, Weakland, and Fisch (1974) as a pragmatic approach to understanding and intervening in ongoing interactional cycles that support symptoms. The family therapist assessing the family–larger-system relationship can profitably examine this relationship by looking for the "solutions" that families use in response to having larger systems in their midst and the "solutions" that larger systems use regarding families. Families that must have larger systems in their sphere often adopt solutions to this problem that paradoxically get them into more difficulty with the larger systems, which, in turn, adopt solutions that feed into escalating patterns of interaction.[4] Thus, a family wishing to avoid larger systems may adopt the solution of being secretive, withdrawn, or otherwise unavailable. The larger system, in turn, will often adopt the solution of pursuing the family further. A vicious circle of distance–pursuit–distance–pursuit easily develops as the family and larger system increasingly apply their solutions to each other.

A common larger-system solution to a family's problems is to engage more and more helpers, leading to a family–multiple-helper system. In response, some families' solution to having more and more helpers may be lovingly to absorb each one into the family, with no hint of change. Other families may respond with hostility that serves to distance the helpers, or may engage with larger systems only briefly during crises in order to reestablish a previous equilibrium.

A family therapist who can assess solution behavior between families and larger systems will be able to assist the family in developing more viable solutions to larger systems and to intervene effectively at the family–larger-system interface.

Family–Larger-System Transitions

As the family–larger-system relationship develops, the issue of transitions emerges in a number of dimensions. Many human-services systems have frequent changes of personnel. Such transitions are seldom marked. Families may even encounter a new worker without being told that the former worker is leaving. Such careless transitions can easily breed cynicism in family members. Other transitions occur because of policy changes in the larger systems. When such changes are not explained to families, a sense of mystification marks the macrosystem.

A family's transitional issues may be mirrored in the macrosystem. Thus, a family that has experienced a great many personal losses may be especially sensitive to unexplained losses of workers who leave. A family that was formed with larger systems in its midst, such as a family whose first child was born with handicaps, may have an especially difficult time with the transition of that child from the home to a group home, as this transition also involves a different, and usually less involved, relationship between the parents and helpers. Conceptualizing this as a family–larger-system transition issue, rather than as parental "overinvolvement," opens the therapist to creative interventions that mark and facilitate the transition. Finally, families and larger systems that have long-standing relationships with each other may need assistance with a family's transition to becoming more autonomous in its functioning.

---

[3] *Editors' Note.* To make a bad pun and borrow from a well-known maxim at the same time, we think this is a case of, "One person's myth is another person's persuasion." Thus, we see it as developmentally self-evident that single-female-parent families need a male role model, *and* that single-male-parent families need a female role model, not to perpetuate sex-role stereotypy, but to provide a model of intimate relating so essential to the development of later adolescent and adult competencies and comfort in close relationships.
[4] *Editors' Note.* For a more elaborated discussion of "solutions" in problem-maintaining cycles, see Segal (Chapter 6).

Predictions

All of the foregoing elements of assessment tend to focus on past and present family–larger system relationships. The final element of assessment deals with predictions regarding those relationships. As family members and larger-system representatives discuss their imagined futures, themes of hope versus despair, success versus failure, and long-standing future involvement versus eventual greater family autonomy all become clear. Fantasies of finding the "perfect" helper may emerge. Special alliances between family members and helpers, previously covert, may become overt as family and helper imagine disengaging from one another. Conflicting views of a family's future with larger systems may emerge, as the family predicts an attenuation of help, while the helpers predict further involvement. As the family therapist hears these future relationship predictions, he or she may be able to pose different, hypothetical future scenarios that serve as interventions in the macrosystem.

CASE EXAMPLE: A FAMILY HELPS THE HELPERS—ASSESSMENT

The utility of the above assessment format can be illustrated in its application to a complex family–larger-system relationship. The information was gathered first by interviewing the family about its relationship to larger systems, and subsequently in a family–larger-system interview. Information gathered in the family–larger-system interview will be discussed following the section on interviewing.

The family consisted of a young couple, Karen and Alex, and their two children, Jerod, 5, and Kim, 3. The family initially presented for family therapy because of the "aggressive behavior" of Jerod and the parents' request to learn "parenting." Karen and Alex did not tell the family therapist that they were involved with other systems. Over time, the family therapist discovered that the couple was experiencing many difficulties and had, in fact, engaged with multiple larger systems in an attempt to address these difficulties.

The difficulties included (1) Karen's past history as a child who had been sexually abused by her father; (2) severe fights between Karen and Alex, which often culminated in Alex's beating Karen; (3) fights with their respective families of origin, which always led to fights between the spouses; and (4) frequent threats of separation by each spouse that were never acted upon.

During an interview focused on the couple's relationships with larger systems, it was discovered that the spouses had the following larger systems currently in their lives: (1) a hospital-based group-therapy program for men who battered their wives; (2) a community-based group-therapy program for women who were beaten by their husbands or partners; and (3) a church whose minister counseled them frequently.

During the discussion of larger systems, the spouses said that they had previously seen only one counselor for all of their problems and had found that this did not work well, and that they preferred to see several different people. They said they believed that their problems were "too much" for any one helper to handle. They also believed that, as they met with the various helpers, they were discovering new problems that needed attention from new larger systems. For instance, their son's "aggression" had become more obvious to them following a discussion in Karen's women's group, where it was also suggested that he might benefit from a group for "aggressive" boys. Karen and Alex did not talk to the various helpers about the other helping endeavors. To the best of the couple's knowledge, the helpers did not know about each other until the family therapist began his inquiry.

Each larger system with which the couple was involved had offered a different kind of help as the solution to Karen and Alex's problems. Such help included group therapy with a behavioral and cognitive focus for Alex; group therapy with a personal-growth focus for Karen; individual therapy dealing primarily with incest, with a supportive and psychodynamic focus, for Karen; marital and family therapy with a Milan–systemic focus for the couple and the children; and individual and marital counseling with a Christian and spiritual focus.

Karen and Alex each came from a family that eschewed outside help for problems. Families-of-origin members knew about the couple's various involvements with outside helpers and disapproved. This led to further fights between the couple and their families of origin that usually culminated in the spouses' fighting with each other.

The couple had begun seeing outside helpers almost as soon as they married. Thus, larger systems were involved in their transition from their families of origin to early marriage and parenthood.

When the family therapist discovered the couple's relationship with other larger systems and multiple helpers, his own conceptualization of the issues began to shift from the family system alone to the macrosystem. Karen and Alex's strongly stated preference to work with multiple helpers regarding their problems rather than with one helper, coupled with the obvious lack of progress in an array of presenting problems, led the family therapist to seek consultation for a family–larger-system interview, to be described and discussed below.

FAMILY–LARGER-SYSTEM INTERVIEWING

Gathering information about and intervening in the family–larger-system relationship may be accomplished by interviewing the family regarding its past, current, and perceived future relationships with larger systems; interviewing family members and multiple helpers together; and interviewing larger-system representatives about their relationships with a particular family and each other. In all of these interviews, one is focused on the macrosystemic level and on patterns that may repeat at various levels. *Often, family–larger-system interviewing functions as an intervention into the macrosystem.*

Interviewing the Family About Its Relationship with Larger Systems

As one begins work with any new client system, it is advisable to devote time to discussing relationships with larger systems. It is important that this discussion be explained to the family as a way to facilitate the current therapy. The therapist's stance should be noncritical and exploratory and should not imply the termination of other relationships.

During this discussion, the therapist may discover a variety of possible relationships between the family and outside systems, including nonproblematic relationships with normative systems, such as health care and schools; a special and long-standing relationship between one family member and one helper; relationships with multiple helpers for a variety of problems with no hint of change; angry and hostile relationships between the family and statutory agencies, which the family experiences as intrusive; relationships with particular helping systems that involved critical incidents that may taint any new endeavor; or warm, seemingly benign relationships that function to maintain problems. One may also discover that the family is quite naïve regarding larger systems or has strong rules against engagement with outside helpers.

During a discussion of the family's relationship to larger systems, the therapist will begin to uncover myths and beliefs about helpers, alliances with and splits between the family and helpers, and multigenerational patterns involving the family and larger systems.

Families generally find such a discussion to be very engaging. Most often, they have not been asked about their relationships with larger systems in any detail, and many will have important stories to tell that metaphorically express key relationship issues in the macrosystem. Families that have had difficulties with larger systems are usually very eager to describe these, and in the telling, will usually guide the carefully listening therapist to alternative ways to relate more successfully.

While specific questions regarding the family–larger-system relationship must be tailored to each family, the following general questions can be used to orient the discussion to the macrosystemic level:

1. Who decided to go for outside help?
2. Who initiated the contact?
3. Who has been helped the most by the contact with outside help? Who has been helped the least?
4. What have various members of the extended family thought about your engaging with larger systems?
5. What do you think various helpers have thought of your family?

6. What might the other helpers tell me about working with you?
7. What are your ideas about why (a particular helper) referred you here at this time?
8. What do you understand other helpers' definition(s) of the problem to be?
9. What do you imagine your relationship with outside systems will be like in a year? In five years?
10. If the present problems are solved, what will happen to the relationship between (a particular family member or the whole family) and various helpers and larger systems?

These questions are usefully asked during a first or second session as part of any other assessment a therapist may be doing. Utilizing a temporal perspective, the therapist can examine past, present, and likely future relationships between the family and larger systems. Such early inquiry both implicitly announces to the family that the therapist's orientation to human problems and their solutions includes a macrosystemic view, and enables the therapist to begin to discover the meaningful system in which to do effective work. This initial inquiry may be very brief, as one discovers that involvement with larger systems is not salient, or such an inquiry may be more lengthy and may lead the therapist to a decision to hold a family–larger-system interview.

Interviewing Family Members and Multiple Helpers

Upon discovering that a family is involved with larger systems, the family therapist may want to telephone the other helpers in order to establish contact and further discern their roles in the case. Following such telephone contact, one may decide to hold an interview with the family and other helpers in order to clarify roles, expectations, and the nature of the referral in the presence of all concerned. Usually such an interview, held early in a therapy, can be conducted by the family therapist. The tone of the interview should be collaborative rather than interrogative. Any confusion the family may feel regarding the referral for family therapy should be addressed. This format, which clarifies what, if any, future contact will occur between the

therapist and other systems, can serve to demystify macrosystemic interaction for the family.

A second kind of family–larger-system interview may take place later in therapy and is useful if therapy is not progressing. Such an interview should be conceptualized as a consultation, in which the family therapist invites a consultant to conduct the interview, so that the therapist, who is part of the macrosystem, can also be interviewed. This format minimizes resentment on the part of the other helpers and maximizes cooperation.

As the family therapist invites various helpers to a family–larger-system interview, care should be taken to respect the scheduling requirements of various helpers and to avoid any criticism or blame. The family–larger-system interview should be presented as an opportunity for the family–larger-system network to learn about its relationships.

The act of family and helpers getting together for such an interview is generally an important intervention, as the occasion per se communicates unseen or unacknowledged connectedness, and usually brings together people who have never met, but who are all involved in the life of the family.

The consultant-led family–larger-system interview should focus on the macrosystemic level, rather than on the family level. Family issues are investigated only as these affect family–larger-system relationships. The consultant seeks to clarify repeating patterns, alliances, and splits; the roles of the various helpers and any role confusion; disparate definitions of the presenting problem and preferred solutions, myths, beliefs, and themes; and patterns of contact between family members and particular helpers that affect macrosystemic functioning, and, in turn, affect the family–family-therapist relationship and the family's own problem-solving capacity. While interviewing, the consultant watches for analogic messages, including seating arrangements and tone, that communicate the nature of relationships between the family and helpers.

At the beginning of the interview, the consultant should clarify his or her role as a person who has been invited by the family therapist to conduct the interview. The family therapist's reasons for requesting such a consultation should be described briefly. Care should be taken to communicate that the consultant has no intentions of telling anyone how to do his or her job. Respect for the assembled helpers is easily communicated by starting the interview with a portion devoted to each helper, describing his or her setting and job role. This discussion often leads to surprising comments by family members, who may have been confused regarding helpers' job roles. Helpers' embeddedness in their own systems comes alive, as participants describe being answerable to supervisors, regulations, and mandates. This part of the interview leads naturally into a discussion of various views of the family's problem, preferred solutions, and ideas regarding what has hampered such solutions. The consultant may explore participants' optimism or pessimism about change, the effects of change on various relationships between family members and helpers, and future hypothetical situations involving the family and helpers. Toward the end of the interview, it is useful to ask if any of the participants wish to raise any questions or issues.

CASE EXAMPLE: A FAMILY HELPS THE HELPERS—A FAMILY–LARGER-SYSTEM INTERVIEW

The family therapist working with Karen and Alex requested a family–larger-system interview. When he began to discuss this possibility with them, they were very enthusiastic about such a meeting, and it was at this point that they informed the therapist about their minister, who counseled them, and requested his presence at the interview. The discovery of more helpers is a common phenomenon when a family–larger-system interview is initiated, as is the family's enthusiasm for such a meeting.[5]

When the family therapist began to make calls to invite the participants, he discovered that the various helpers were not aware of each other.

Representatives of Karen's group-therapy program declined to attend, stating that Karen had finished her group and that they no longer considered her a client. In fact, she had finished just one week previously. If a helper declines an invitation to attend the interview, either because of anger, a wish to distance, refusal by a supervisor, a scheduling conflict, or a fear of vulnerability, it is important that the consultant remember the helper's presence in the macrosystem and ask questions that touch on this helper's relationship to the family and other helpers. In this case, all of the other helpers agreed to participate.

Several important aspects of the macrosystem emerged during the interview.

1. The family and the helpers, with the exception of the family therapist, believed the family needed many helpers. Each helper identified his or her own specialty (e.g., violence, incest, etc.) as an area in which the couple needed help, and each identified other areas (e.g., marital therapy) for which other experts were needed.[6] Most striking were the spouses' own beliefs about the need for multiple helpers. They stated that they felt that they had too many problems for one helper, and that they were concerned that if they only went to one, the helper would become "overloaded" and would not be able to cope. Karen said it was important "not to burden any one helper too much," and Alex remarked that in the past when they had gone to one helper, they had "confused him," and that they could tell that it was "hard on him." Thus, in a macrosystem whose verbalized *raison d'être* was for helpers to help the family, in fact, the couple saw its role as helping the helpers by giving only "manageable bits of information" in an effort not to "overload" any one helper. Here, the usual complementarity of helper and client surprisingly was being turned upside down. As the helpers listened to the couple's point of view that helpers should not be burdened or overloaded with the couple's problems, they appeared startled and expressed surprise.

---

[5] *Editors' Note.* While Imber-Black informs us (1990) that she has never had the experience of a family's refusing the family–larger-system interview, we have, and so we suspect there is some variability on this score, just as there seems to be in couples' responses to therapists' calling for family-of-origin sessions (Framo, 1981).

[6] *Editors' Note.* It has been our clinical impression on more than a few occasions that problems of the larger-system–family interface may be heightened by, or even generated by, the conflict that lurks between or among single-minded, overspecialized mental health workers (including, but not limited to, professionals) with one-factor axes to grind.

The tendency of the larger systems toward specialization and rigid boundaries between them had locked in with the couple's beliefs that "helpers needed to be helped" by giving each helping system only small amounts of information.

2. The various helping systems had conflicting beliefs about and approaches toward the couple's problems in two major areas, including the viability of the marriage and the locus of violence. The director of the program for men who batter their wives and the counselor from the sexual-abuse counseling center both had serious questions about whether Karen and Alex should stay together, while the minister and the family therapist were both working to keep them a couple. These same implicit alliances were seen during a discussion of the issue of violence, as the director of the men's group and the sexual-assault counselor believed that the violence was "in" Alex, while the family therapist and the minister believed that the violence was embedded in a pattern between the spouses. The spouses stated that they liked hearing these various points of view and that they did not find it confusing. Of central importance, however, was the fact that therapeutic progress was stalled in all of the treatment systems.

3. As the consultant inquired about patterns of contact between the partners after each had seen a helper, the couple described how in recent times each would come home from an appointment and describe what had occurred, and then a fight would ensue over the material raised. The various helpers had not known about this iatrogenic problem, and the couple had not recognized the pattern of the fighting after appointments with the various helpers until the discussion at the interview. This pattern had striking similarities to what would take place after the spouses had visited their families of origin. During the discussion, the couple and the helpers discovered that, in recent weeks, each helping system, unbeknownst to the others, had been working on increasingly difficult areas. Karen and Alex were, in fact, becoming overloaded with input, ideas, and directives, but felt that they should not complain to any of the helpers, since to do so might appear unappreciative of the help being offered.

4. Finally, the consultant addressed people's ideas regarding future family–helper relationships. Karen and Alex predicted that they would need less and less help, and that in about a year they would be able to go it on their own. Immediately following this prediction, two of the helpers began to offer other services that they felt they could provide once the current problems were in hand!

The consultant utilized the information from the interview to design an end-of-session intervention, to be discussed below.

Interviewing Larger-System Representatives Without Family Members Present

In family–larger-systems work, there are times when one may be asked to interview multiple helpers from one or more larger systems without family members present. As a consultant for a particular case or set of issues, one may also decide that it is effective to interview the helpers without the family members, in order to prepare for a subsequent family–larger-system interview.

When interviewing representatives from larger systems without family members present, one is particularly interested in how the participants view the agency's mandate; their relationships with clients in general as contrasted to the particular case under discussion; patterns of blame, overinvolvement, and overfunctioning; and themes of burnout, cynicism, or, conversely, of optimism.

When interviewing helpers about a family, it is useful to draw forth common elements of this particular case and other cases. Often, the helpers will begin to recognize repeating patterns of conflict or triads involving two agencies and several families. Such recognition begins to reconceptualize the problems at a family–larger-system level, rather than at the family level, and so provide for a wider range of solutions.

Working with multiple helpers from one or many agencies may also lead to the discovery that the family issues being identified are, in fact, metaphorical for serious organizational problems within the larger systems per se. Such recognition often leads to a larger-system consultation of a wider scope and longer duration.

FAMILY–LARGER-SYSTEM
INTERVENTIONS

Family–larger-system interventions are intended to address the macrosystemic level of organization and pattern. A specific intervention may be "given" to one person or a subsystem of the macrosystem, but the design of the intervention is such that other aspects of the macrosystem will be affected. Thus, one is seeking to discern and intervene in isomorphic patterns and themes that are replicated at various levels in the macrosystem, or one is seeking to discern and intervene in some significant feature of the relationship between family and larger systems that appears to be "stuck." Often, the family–larger-system interview serves as a powerful intervention in the macrosystem, as boundaries become less rigid, role confusion is clarified, and helpers and families hear ideas that each has about the other for the first time. If an end-of-session intervention is utilized that requires specific activities, it is often effective to give the intervention to family members, since they are the predefined client system, and because it is important to avoid interventions that tell other workers how to do their jobs. Such activities, however, should address macrosystemic relationships.

Several categories of interventions are useful for family–larger-system problems. These include (1) delineation and redistribution of tasks, which often occur spontaneously during a family–larger-system interview and simply need to be highlighted by the consultant at the end of the interview; (2) ritual interventions, including rituals to mark and facilitate transitions in the macrosystem, such as the entry and exit of members and the termination of long-standing relationships between family members and specific helpers, and belief-negotiation rituals that enable the family to deal effectively with competing beliefs in the macrosystem; and (3) postsession interventions that utilize the symbols of larger systems, such as memos and reports.

Task Delineation and Redistribution

It is common during family–larger-system interviews for both helpers and family members to discover that two or more people are doing the same jobs with the family, or that family members are confused about who to turn to in what circumstances, or that one helper has assumed all of the tasks, even though other helpers are involved in the macrosystem. For example, a family with a welfare worker and a therapist may call either or both in times of crisis, with each responding in areas that are not his or her actual mandate. Or a family may have a "favorite" helper, such as an adolescent's probation officer, and may attend other sessions only because the probation officer said to do so. Family-member confusion over "whose job is what" is usually clarified at family–larger-system sessions. Sometimes, a helper discovers that his or her presence in the macrosystem is redundant, and after a family–larger-system interview, will drop out of the treatment picture. Through careful questioning by the consultant, helpers may also discover that they have moved into areas of the family that go well beyond their mandate. Information generated in the interview often assists the helpers to make a decision to limit their involvement. The consultant does not tell the various helpers how to do their jobs, since this is an inappropriate role for the consultant, but the information discovered in the interview about role confusion, overinvolvement, continual crises that provoke responses, erosion of family responsibility for change, and so on, often lead to new decisions by the helpers, as, for example, when one probation officer remarked after an interview, "I learned that I'm working harder than the family is on this problem, and I'm not going to do that anymore!"

Opportunities for helpers to collaborate and obviate duplication of services also become apparent during interviews, and the consultant can facilitate limited-treatment partnerships as an intervention.

Rituals

Following family–larger-system interviews, rituals given to family members, but which address family–larger-system relationships, are useful interventions. Such rituals frequently utilize symbols and symbolic actions that characterize the family–larger-system configuration. Variations on the "odd days–even days" ritual

(Selvini Palazzoli et al., 1980) are particularly useful when a family is engaged with multiple helpers and is receiving simultaneous and contradictory messages, frequently resulting in increasing confusion and helplessness. Here, family members are asked to attend to ideas from a particular helper on certain days of the week, to attend to ideas from another helper on other days of the week, and then to make decisions based on what emerges. This ritual puts the family in charge of decisions again, while dramatically highlighting the divergent points of view in the macrosystem (Imber-Black, 1986). It effectively intervenes in patterns of triangulation, in which the family is being pressed to ally with mutually incompatible ideas and actions coming from two or more larger systems.

Rituals may be useful for key transition points in family–larger-system relationships, including at the point of referral, when a family may be leaving a favorite helper; at the point of entry into a new system; and at the point when a family terminates its relationships with larger systems, especially if these have been long-standing. The family therapist working with families that are involved with larger systems should be thinking about engagement rituals that function to engage the family in the new treatment. Often when a family is sent by another system to family therapy, there is a reluctance to engage or a misunderstanding about the nature and meaning of the referral. It is important that the family therapist not simply assume that treatment can commence immediately. After inquiring about other systems, the therapist may wish to give the family a time-bounded ritual to have a series of discussions on the pros and cons of entering family therapy, or of discussing sensitive issues openly, or of choosing a particular system with which to work. Here, the therapist should ask particular subsystems to get together for such discussions. This kind of ritual has the effect of involving the family in a discussion of its own needs *and* its engagement with other systems, including family therapy. Often, hidden agendas of the referral emerge at this point, as do issues of family anger or reluctance to engage in family treatment.

For families that have had long-standing relationships with larger systems and are able to function more autonomously, it is often effica-cious to design a ritual that will mark this major change in ways that the family can own and utilize to celebrate its own resources. Symbols of their own development can be given to the family members to take home and use in their own unique ways without helpers. For example, one single parent referred to helpers could guide the often chaotic conversations in her household. As she grew in confidence, she was able to guide such conversations herself, without them deteriorating into fights. However, she still believed that she needed to rely on multiple helpers. The family therapist presented her with a cookie jar at the close of therapy and suggested that when she wanted to lead family conversations, she could keep her hand on the cookie-jar lid and then pass the jar around accordingly. This became a termination ritual for a family that had had many years of involvement with therapeutic and welfare systems, as the mother took the symbol of her work with outside systems into her home to utilize autonomously with her children.

Another termination ritual that is especially useful when a family has had an effective relationship with outside systems, but either the family or helpers are having trouble saying goodbye and are finding new problems upon which to focus to sustain the relationships, involves the mutual exchange of small gifts between the family and helpers. This ritual defines the relationship as one of equals, as both are giving gifts, thus departing from the former complementarity of helper and client that marked the relationship. It is an effective way to express mutual appreciation.

Memos and Reports as Interventions

Memos and reports are useful interventions in the macrosystem, as they are a familiar way of communicating with helpers, but an unusual way of communicating with helpers *and* family members. Thus, memos and reports as interventions may combine the familiar and the unfamiliar, which is often an optimal combination to obtain systemic change.

At the end of a family–larger-system interview, the consultant may wish to transmit an opinion to all who came to the interview by sending a memo to the therapist who sought the consultation, with the suggestion that copies be sent to all the other participants. The memo may include a reframing, a positive connotation of the macrosystem, suggestions for the family therapist's role in the macrosystem, instructions to the family for a ritual that touches macrosystemic relationships, or some combination of these. Such a memo delineates the membership of the macrosystem and implicitly comments on the value of sharing information with both helpers and family members. This position runs counter to the usual definition of the relationship between helpers and clients in which the helpers are often privy to information that is kept from the clients. The memo symbolically offers a more symmetrical relationship between client and helpers. It generally functions to provoke new discussion in the macrosystem. Memos may also be used to send information to members of the macrosystem who did not or could not attend the family–larger-system consultation, thus preventing secrets.

Writing memos that will go to both helpers and family members is an artful task, since the consultant needs to use language that will be understood by both. The language of the memo should communicate respect for the members of the macrosystem.

Reports as interventions are best utilized in ongoing family therapy with clients who have a long history of relationships with larger systems, and who have frequently had reports written about them. Such reports, because they are written words on paper, often contribute to a reified view of a family. Subsequent reports are often written in the context of earlier ones. The family's one-down position is symbolized by its being the one about which reports are written. Here, the therapist may wish to ask the family to write its own report. This task often becomes a piece of the ongoing therapy, as the therapist and family work together on a new report or a "second opinion." Such reports may be sent to other systems, or they may be utilized as a termination ritual when a family has had and is completing long-standing relationships with larger systems. The family should receive its own copy of the report, with suggestions for updating it as relationships change.

CASE EXAMPLE: A FAMILY HELPS THE HELPERS—INTERVENTION

When the interview with Karen and Alex and the various helpers ended, the consultant requested that only Karen and Alex and the family therapist who requested the interview remain to hear the end-of-session intervention. The helpers were told that a memo would be sent detailing the consultant's impressions. This was done both because one of the helpers had to leave and because concluding the session in this way enabled the consultant implicitly to draw a boundary between the family and helpers. The family therapist was asked to remain because he had requested the consultation and would serve as a conduit between the consultant and the other helpers after the consultant left.

The intervention was based on many areas that arose during the session, including the competing definitions of the problem and the preferred solutions, the escalation of help, the triads formed by the couple and various helpers that resulted in more conflict between the spouses, the diffuse boundaries between the couple and helpers, and the unusual complementarity that resulted in the spouses' trying to take care of the helpers through their very careful parceling out of problems and concerns to various helpers. The intervention was intended to interdict the problematic patterns and to utilize the complementarity in the macrosystem by handing it back to the couple in a new way.

The consultant began by sharing with the spouses her impression that they had been able to gather a very fine group of helpers, and by stating her understanding that they preferred to have a number of people working with them on different areas. Thus, early in the intervention, Alex and Karen's preference for many helpers was positively framed. The consultant then highlighted the issue of Karen and Alex's fighting with each other regarding the input from the various helpers, and linked this to their wish not to upset any of the helpers by telling them that their ideas were contradictory or that too much help was being given at a particular time. They were then presented with a "tool" to assist them in their work with the various helpers. The word "tool" was specifically chosen, as this was the word the couple used to refer to what it was receiving from the various helpers. The consultant drew a large circle on the blackboard, and explained to the couple that this represented the various helpers with whom the couple was involved. The circle was drawn to cover an entire wall, thus metaphorically representing the size of the issues in the macrosystem. The couple's families of origin were also included as they were a major influence in provoking fighting between Karen and Alex, in a pattern similar to that involving the helpers. In addition to listing all of the helpers and the families of origin, one compartment was left blank to allow for the possibility of future helpers entering the sphere. (See Figure 19–1.)

The consultant told Karen and Alex that they would be given several copies of this large circle, and asked them to select a time once a week when they could sit down together and jointly discuss and evaluate where their work was with each helper in terms of intensity. Thus, a "1" or a "2" on the chart would represent the least intense work, and "9" or "10" would represent very "heavy," intense, and difficult work. As they filled in the chart, they were asked to observe how many areas were involving extremely intense work. The consultant suggested that very heavy work in more than one area at a time ran the risk of promoting conflict between the spouses, and that they should then decide which area they would like to concentrate on for the next period. They were then asked to communicate this to the helpers. Finally, Karen and Alex were told that the family therapist would send a copy of this chart to each of the helpers so they would know what Karen and Alex were doing. The consultant concluded by telling them that they would be "in charge of how much help you need, when you need it, and who you need it from." The intervention, then, was designed to put the couple in charge of the helping endeavor in a new way, replacing the earlier pattern of the couple "helping the helpers," with one of the couple deciding the direction and quantity of help. The intervention was designed to "go with," rather than directly challenge, the system of specialization and multiple helpers.

Karen and Alex returned to see the family therapist a month later. They reported that they had seen no helpers during that month. They had seen their families of origin, and had agreed prior to the visits to support each other. They also reported that their son was behaving better, and that they had dropped their plans to put him in a group for aggressive boys. They said they had gone out as a couple, which they had not done for a long time. They also reported making some friends at church, and Karen remarked, "Maybe if we had more friends, we would need fewer helpers!"

They told the therapist that they had used the tool given them by the consultant, but that they had implemented it separately and then sat together and shared their findings. It is important to note that this was the first time that they had not exactly followed instructions given to them by a helper.

Following the interview, the family therapist and the sexual-assault counselor agreed to be in touch with each other by telephone when the occasion warranted it. The psychologist from the men's group chose to distance from the macrosystem. The minister maintained his involvement solely with the couple.

The couple then gradually terminated its involvement with helpers. At a follow-up interview one year later, Karen and Alex reported that they were doing well and that the violence had not recurred. Their only involvements with larger systems were normative, including school and church. Karen remarked that she felt they had been "using helpers as parents" and that they had needed to "grow up." She also stated that she had confronted her father about the incest, and had done it on her own because she felt it was time to do so.

In this case, both the interview per se and the end-of-session intervention may be seen as provoking a reorganization of the macrosystem. The interview, like many family–larger-system interviews, was an intervention in boundaries between the helpers, who had never seen each other before this interview. Differences among the helpers, and the effect of these differences on the couple, were discussed openly for the first time in an atmosphere of respect. Information was generated that allowed a new way of seeing the couple's problems as being inadvertently supported by the macrosystem organization. The intervention implicitly and metaphorically commented on the complexity of the macrosystem, while providing a shift in boundaries and complementarity. Finally, the

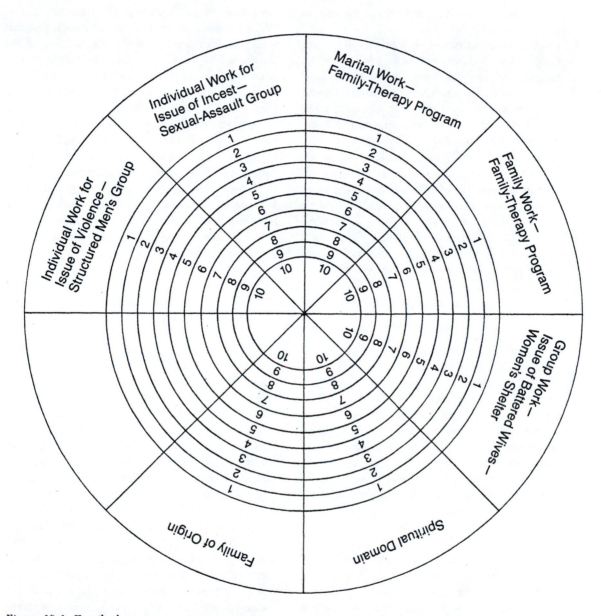

Figure 19-1. Family–larger-system intervention

couple was empowered to make future decisions regarding its relationships with helpers.

SPECIAL ISSUES IN LARGE-SYSTEM INTERACTIONS

The family therapist who works with families and larger systems will ultimately be working in a sociopolitical sphere, since most larger systems are organized according to assumptions that reflect more liberal social, political, and cultural norms. This issue becomes particularly salient for larger systems' interactions with women, families with chronically ill and handicapped members, and poor families. Here, the job of the family therapist is to be cognizant of the special issues relating to these populations and larger systems, and to be able to work in ways that empower the families in their often-required interactions with larger systems. Following a description of these issues, particular working methods for the family therapist will be delineated.

Larger systems that deliver health and human services, as well as public schools, tend to reflect norms that support traditional and nuclear family forms, even though the populations served by these systems often do not conform to such organization. Beginning with unexamined assumptions that "normal" families include two parents and are white and middle class, many larger systems postulate deficiency and pathology when families are of an ethnic minority, have a single parent, are poor, are headed by two women or two men, or vary in some other way. Thus, the initial encounter between a larger system and a family may be fraught with unacknowledged prejudice and stereotyping.

Women

Since larger systems tend to reflect social norms of the culture that creates and funds them, particular issues may arise in that many larger systems view problems in the family as the mother's responsibility. Appointments tend to be set with mothers, who are expected to take time off from jobs to keep them, whereas fathers are not. Responsibility for handling children's problems is assigned to mothers by the culture and by the larger systems representing the culture. Women may find that they are the recipients of binding messages from larger systems, as they are referred to multiple helpers and thus become the conduit between the family and the helpers, while simultaneously being criticized for "overinvolvement." Refusals to accept such referrals, however, may lead to families being labeled "resistant," "uncooperative," or "neglectful."

Stereotyping regarding the roles of women in family life become especially salient in larger systems' work with female-headed, single-parent households. Here, the wider culture's particularly mixed view of women—which holds them responsible for family functioning and, at the same time, considers them less capable than men—converges in a perspective that frames single-parent, female-headed families as inherently flawed. Strengths that may exist in this variant family form are not validated, and in-

quiries regarding the family's own natural network and ways to utilize it often are not made. Work to enhance existing competencies in the single mother is often eschewed in favor of referrals to "big brothers," and the single parent is encouraged to rely on helpers as "adult role models," rather than to view herself as such a model for her children. In addition, many larger systems ignore the reality that many "single parents," especially poor, minority women, in fact live with their own mothers, and the executive subsystem that requires validation consists of these two women who are raising the children. Schools or clinics often call the mother in for appointments and ignore or undermine the grandmother, whose place in the system may be crucial to its survival.

Families with Chronically Ill or Handicapped Members

Families with chronically ill or handicapped members generally find it necessary to maintain ongoing relationships with various larger systems, including health-care systems, special schools, and residential programs. Such ongoing relationships permanently alter the boundaries between the family and the outside world, as the family is required to have more permeable boundaries, particularly between itself and the larger systems. At the onset of the serious illness or handicap, the family may experience difficulty in altering its boundaries to accommodate the entry of larger systems. Distancing on the part of the family may be misunderstood as a lack of interest in the ill member, rather than as a difficulty with renegotiating boundaries with the outside world. The larger system may, in turn, distance, leading to a macrosystem marked by rigid boundaries and lack of information exchange. Many such families "appoint" one member, often the mother, to serve in a conduit or boundary-spanning role between the family and larger systems. Larger systems, which often do not conceptualize issues in terms of families or systems, are generally glad to have such a member with whom to interact, but may, at the same time, designate this person as "overinvolved" and ignore the stress of this position on the family member.

For the seriously ill or handicapped person,

the relationship between the family and the larger systems has special significance. Difficulties between the family and the larger systems may create triangles involving the ill or handicapped person that add to stress and contribute to dysfunctional behavior.

Families with ill or handicapped members often are stigmatized, an issue that is especially significant for families with "mentally handicapped" or "mentally ill" members, or with members with certain diseases, particularly the acquired immune deficiency syndrome (AIDS). This stigmatization comes not only from the general community, but also from workers in the larger systems, thus contributing to tense and angry relationships between families and these larger systems. It is crucial for family therapists who are working with such families to be cognizant of the process of stigmatization and to be able to discuss it with families, while seeking ways to influence and educate in the larger systems.

Families in Poverty

Families that are poor in our culture often have especially difficult relationships with larger systems. To be poor generally means to lack access to adequate health-care and competent educational systems, and to be required to interact with the welfare system. Interaction with these larger systems is often intimidating. Families whose children are removed by the state and put into foster care are more likely to be families that are poor. The stresses of poverty are compounded by the stresses of dealing with larger systems in a culture where families are expected to be autonomous and to function without outside help. The welfare system, which supposedly is organized to support families, in fact, frequently fragments them through practices and policies that ignore diverse family organizations, such as households headed by two women, or require men to leave in order for a family to receive aid. As the providers of financial aid, welfare systems often assume that this gives them carte blanche to penetrate the inner workings of families, taking a tremendous toll on privacy and family empowerment.

METHODS FOR THE FAMILY THERAPIST

When working with families that must interact with larger systems over many years because of illness or poverty, or when working with families in which family members, often women, have been ill served by larger systems, the family therapist requires methods to facilitate better relationships between the family and larger systems and to bring about family and specific-member empowerment. Following careful assessment of the family–larger-system relationship, during which a neutral position is useful in order to gather information in a nonblaming way, the family therapist may begin to function in a number of ways.

Family empowerment vis-à-vis larger systems may begin with the family therapist's designation of the family as the major expert on the family–larger-system relationship. Such a designation begins to shift the family from an enduring one-down relationship with helpers to a more collaborative relationship, at least with the family therapist.

The family therapist may serve as a negotiator between the family and the larger systems. Here, the therapist functions to reduce anger and misunderstanding, to mediate, to translate often obscure larger-system policies to the family in language that is understandable, and to resolve conflicts. Such work requires a position of credibility with both the family and the larger systems. The family therapist may be able to negotiate working partnerships between multiple helpers and family members that delineate particular areas of expertise and frame the involvement of all members of the macrosystem as required for successful problem resolution.

When attempts to facilitate a more effective family–larger-system relationship fail owing to the larger system's intractability, such as when a larger system continues to blame a family and/or to deny it adequate or legally required services, the family therapist will need to adopt the position of coach and advocate for the family. As coach, the therapist teaches the family about family–larger-system relationships and about the properties of interacting systems. He or she may rehearse family members for specific encounters with larger systems, such as school meetings, and plan strategies with them. The therapist also may assist the family in determining its rights under the law, advocate for these rights with the family, and coach the family in ways to advocate for itself. This coaching and advocacy should be undertaken with sensitivity to systemic processes in order to minimize blame and scapegoating in the macrosystem, and with the ultimate aim of empowering the family to advocate for itself.

BRIEF EXAMPLE—FACILITATING A FAMILY AND GROUP-HOME "LIMITED PARTNERSHIP"

An older couple, Mr. and Mrs. Cawley, were referred for therapy by a consulting psychologist who worked for a larger system that ran several group homes for "mentally handicapped" young adults. The referral letter stated that the couple was "having extreme difficulties adjusting to their son, William, 24, leaving home to live in a group home," thus locating the problem in the family. The group-home staff felt that these difficulties were adversely affecting William, who had moved into the home three months earlier. Several conflictual encounters had already occurred between the Cawleys and the group-home staff. William's behavior in the group home had started to deteriorate, and staff members said they noticed that it was especially bad after his visits home, and so blamed the parents. At the time of the referral, the group-home staff had just decided that William should not visit home for the next three months, and the Cawleys were considering removing William from the group home, which they were reluctant to do because he would also lose his vocational training slot.

The family therapist utilized most of the first session with Mr. and Mrs. Cawley to review their involvement with larger systems, which had begun at William's birth and had continued throughout his childhood and adolescence, culminating in the group-home placement. When William was born, and diagnosed shortly thereafter as "mentally retarded," the family was told

that not much help could be offered to him,[7] as little was available in the way of special education (and group homes had not yet been developed). Early interactions with professionals had left the Cawleys believing that William would be their sole responsibility. In their view, professionals had distanced from them. They recounted their own fears for William and for their family life. As a young child, William went to a special school for "mentally retarded" children, while living at home. The Cawleys were seldom consulted by the school personnel regarding their own impressions of William. No one advocated for the Cawleys, and there were no parents' groups in their community. During their son's growing-up years, however, services for the handicapped began to become available. With deinstitutionalization, a large group-home program developed in their city. When William was a teenager, the Cawleys were told by his school that William would be able to go to a group home eventually. Since William's leaving home had not been in the Cawleys' imagined future for him, it took a while to get used to the idea. They told the therapist that they felt that their attempts to find out more about what the group home could offer William were met with little response from the agency. They were given some pamphlets, and William was put on a waiting list. Each recollected interaction with larger systems had left the Cawleys feeling "pushed away."

When the time came for William to move into the group home, the family was given three weeks' notice. Thus, the ordinary preparation time that most families have when a young adult leaves home was lacking. The Cawleys went to an intake meeting for William, where they felt that their own views of William's needs and of their own were discounted. When they wanted

---

[7] *Editors' Note.* Imber-Black (1990) views "such diagnoses as our current best effort at describing cognitive differences in a society with little tolerance for such differences. Until better terminology comes along, I prefer the quotation marks." We earnestly agree that the use of such diagnostic labels can become a part of a problem-maintaining cycle, for example, by negatively affecting expectations for change. At the same time, the failure to use or consider such psychiatric diagnoses (i.e., without quotation marks) can result in suboptimal treatment, as has been shown clearly in the case of schizophrenia (McFarlane, Chapter 11; Grunebaum & Chasin, 1978).

to know when William would be visiting home and when they could visit him, a worker told them that they were being "too anxious" and that they needed to "let William grow up." When they told the worker that they were a religious family and that they wanted William to continue to go to church, they were told that William would decide that for himself. Thus, after many years of anticipating that William would never leave home, the parents were confronted with what felt like a precipitous leaving and a giving over of their son to strangers who did not want to know about their expertise as parents or their values.

The Cawleys also stated that they did not understand the referral for therapy, and that they felt blamed by it. They told the therapist that they wanted William to succeed in the group home, but that they did not want to be cut off from him.

The therapist conceptualized the issues here as appropriate for family–larger-system work. A triangle made up of Mr. and Mrs. Cawley, the group-home staff, and William had developed rapidly. Work with the parents alone would be intervention at the wrong level of the macrosystem. Following the meeting with Mr. and Mrs. Cawley, the therapist requested a meeting with the group-home staff. This meeting was held without the family in order for the therapist to join with the staff and not be seen initially as the family's advocate, but rather as a person who understood the difficult interactions that can occur between two systems that share a common member. It was clear from that meeting that the staff had very little understanding of how to work with parents or of the crucial developmental issues involved in a young handicapped person's leaving home. The therapist explained some of these issues in a manner that did not blame the staff members, but rather offered a framework in which they could begin to see the issues facing many of their clients. It was also clear that the staff wanted to work with William and to help him integrate successfully into the group home and the vocational program.

The therapist then requested a joint meeting of Mr. and Mrs. Cawley and the group-home staff. At this first meeting, the therapist took care to delineate particular areas of expertise regarding William, such that all who attended the meeting were seen as important contributors

to William's future. The group-home staff members began to learn about William through the parents' eyes. They were also able to hear about the experience of raising a handicapped son. The therapist also elicited important information regarding the parents' earlier expectations for William and how these had changed with the advent of the group-home program. The staff was given an opportunity to fully describe the program and what was planned for William. This first session began a longer process of lowering mutual suspicion between the family and the group home. William was present at subsequent meetings. As he began to see his parents and the staff cooperating, his own behavior began to improve. The family therapist continued to meet periodically with the family and the staff. This process terminated after a meeting of the family and the staff that the therapist could not attend, and that went well, prompting Mr. Cawley to tell the therapist in a telephone call that he now felt that the Cawleys and the staff were "partners" on William's behalf.

This case is an example of ongoing family–larger-system work, which differs from the one-session consultations described earlier. Here, the family therapist, after careful assessment, conceptualized the locus of continued work and intervention to be the family–larger-system relationship. Early efforts were directed toward gaining cooperation from all parties, as was possible in this case, and then creating a problem-solving system that could continue on its own after the therapist's exit. Very often, the sheer act of having a family and larger-system representatives sit down together in the presence of a family therapist, who will facilitate the non-blameful explaining of perspectives, begins a process of deescalation of conflict. In instances when such cooperation does not emerge, as when larger systems refuse to work with families and deny appropriate rights to clients, then an advocacy and coaching stance will be needed.

CONCLUSIONS

Over the past 35 years, family-therapy theory and practice have enabled effective intervention in a broad range of human problems. The logic of a systems perspective, however, implies that certain problems may not always lie neatly within the boundaries of a family, but that, instead, a family's complex involvement with other systems may provide the appropriate locus for assessment and intervention. While the ability to conceptualize problems and to intervene at the family–larger-system level is crucial for therapists committed to public-sector practice, family therapists need to develop the capacity to incorporate a family–larger-system perspective in order to determine when an intervention solely within the boundaries of the family is intervention at the wrong level of the system.

The family–larger-system viewpoint also highlights systemic connectedness at multiple levels, which go beyond families and larger systems to the wider social context. The family–larger-system perspective answers certain clinical questions, while posing new questions, including questions regarding access to service delivery, ways in which larger systems are carriers of particular cultural values, and ways in which larger systems may function to maintain an unexamined status quo for significant portions of the population. The next step in family–larger-system theory and practice must be the development of working methods that go beyond a case-by-case process, in order to facilitate effective collaboration among larger systems and to influence the development of larger systems whose *raison d'être* is empowerment for workers and clients alike.

REFERENCES

Aponte, H. (1976). The family-school interview: An eco-structural approach. *Family Process*, 15, 303–312.

Bateson, G. (1972). *Steps to an ecology of mind.* New York: Ballentine.

Bateson, G. (1979). *Mind and nature: A necessary unity.* New York: Dutton.

Bell, N., & Zucker, R. (1968–69). Family-hospital relationships in a state hospital setting: A structural-functional analysis of the hospitalization process. *International Journal of Social Psychiatry*, 15, 73–80.

Berger, M. (1984). Social network interventions for families that have a handicapped child. In E. Imber Coppersmith (Ed.), *Families with handicapped members.* Rockville, MD: Aspen Systems.

Bloomfield, S., Nielson, S., & Kaplan, L. (1984). Retarded adults, their families and larger systems: A new role for the family therapist. In E. Imber Coppersmith (Ed.), *Families with handicapped members.* Rockville, MD: Aspen Systems.

Bokos, P.J., & Schwartzman, J. (1985). Family therapy and methadone treatment of opiate addiction. In J. Schwartzman (Ed.), *Families and other systems: The macrosystemic context of family therapy.* New York: Guilford Press.

Coleman, S. (1983). A case of non-treatment of a non-problem problem. *Journal of Strategic and Systemic Therapies*, 2, 62–66.

Combrinck-Graham, L., & Higley, L.W. (1984). Working with families of school-aged handicapped children. In E. Imber Coppersmith (Ed.), *Families with handicapped members.* Rockville, MD: Aspen Systems.

Harbin, H.T. (1985). The family and the psychiatric hospital. In J. Schwartzman (Ed.), *Families and other systems: The macrosystemic context of family therapy.* New York: Guilford Press.

Harkaway, J. (1983). Obesity: Reducing the larger systems. *Journal of Strategic and Systemic Therapies*, 2, 2–14.

Harrell, F. (1980). *Family depency as a transgenerational process: An ecological analysis of families in crisis.* Unpublished doctoral dissertation, University of Massachusetts, Amherst.

Imber-Black, E. (1986). Women, families and larger systems. In M. Ault-Riche (Ed.), *Women and family therapy.* Rockville, MD: Aspen Systems.

Imber-Black, E. (1987a). Families, larger systems and the wider social context. *Journal of Strategic and Systemic Therapies*, 5, 29–35.

Imber-Black, E. (1987b). The family system and the health care system: Making the invisible visible. *Journal of Psychotherapy and the Family.*

Imber-Black, E. (1987c). The mentally handicapped in context. *Family Systems Medicine.*

Imber-Black, E. (1988). *Families and larger systems: A family therapist's guide through the labyrinth.* New York: Guilford Press.

Imber Coppersmith, E. (1982a). Family therapy in a public school system. In A. Gurman (Ed.), *Questions and answers in the practice of family therapy.* Vol. 2. New York: Brunner/Mazel.

Imber Coppersmith, E. (1982b). From hyperactive to normal but naughty: A multi-system partnership in delabeling. *International Journal of Family Psychiatry*, 3, 131–144.

Imber Coppersmith, E. (1983). The family and public service systems: An assessment method. In B. Keeney (Ed.), *Diagnosis and assessment in family therapy.* Rockville, MD: Aspen Systems.

Imber Coppersmith, E. (1985). Families and multiple helpers: A systemic perspective. In D. Campbell & R. Draper (Eds.), *Applications of systemic family therapy.* New York: Grune & Stratton.

Lederer, W.J., & Jackson, D.D. (1968). *The mirages of marriage.* New York: Norton.

MacKinnon, L., & Marlett, N. (1984). A social action perspective: The disabled and their families in context. In E. Imber Coppersmith (Ed.), *Families with handicapped members.* Rockwell, MD: Aspen Systems.

Miller, D. (1983). Outlaws and invaders: The adaptive function of alcohol abuse in the family-helper supra system. *Journal of Strategic and Systemic Therapies*, 2, 15–27.

Morawetz, A., & Walker, G. (1984). *Brief therapy with single parent families.* New York: Brunner/Mazel.

Schwartzman, H., & Kneifel, A.W. (1985). Familiar institutions: How the child care system replicates family patterns. In J. Schwartzman (Ed.), *Families and other systems: The macrosystemic context of family therapy.* New York: Guilford Press.

Schwartzman, J., & Restivo, R.J. (1985). Acting out and staying in: Juvenile probation and the family. In J. Schwartzman (Ed.), *Families and other systems: The macrosystemic context of family therapy.* New York: Guilford Press.

Selig, A. (1976). The myth of the multi-problem family. *American Journal of Orthopsychiatry*, 46, 526–531.

Selvini Palazzoli, M., Boscolo, L., Cecchin, G., & Prata, G. (1980). The problem of the referring person. *Journal of Marital and Family Therapy*, 6, 3–9.

Watzlawick, P., Beavin, J.H., & Jackson, D.D. (1967). *Pragmatics of human communications: A study of interactional patterns, pathologies and paradoxes.* New York: Norton.

Watzlawick, P., Weakland, J., & Fisch, R. (1974). *Change: Principles of problem formation and problem resolution.* New York: Norton.

EDITORS' REFERENCES

Framo, J.F. (1981). Marital therapy with sessions with family of origin. In A.S. Gurman & D.P. Kniskern (Eds.), *Handbook of family therapy.* New York: Brunner/Mazel.

Grunebaum, H., & Chasin, R. (1978). Relabeling and reframing reconsidered: The beneficial effects of a pathological label. *Family Process, 17,* 449–455.

Imber-Black, E. (1990). Personal communication.

Skynner, A.C.R. (1981). An open-systems, group analytic approach to family therapy. In A.S. Gurman & D.P. Kniskern (Eds.), *Handbook of family therapy.* New York: Brunner/Mazel.

Stanton, M.D. (1981). Strategic approaches to family therapy. In A.S. Gurman & D.P. Kniskern (Eds.), *Handbook of family therapy.* New York: Brunner/Mazel.

CHAPTER 20

Values and Ethics in Family Therapy

William J. Doherty, Ph.D., and Pauline G. Boss, Ph.D.

The inclusion of a chapter on values and ethics in this edition of the *Handbook of Family Therapy* reflects the considerable upsurge of interest in the topic since the first edition of the *Handbook* was planned in the late 1970s. At that time, there was a mere trickle of literature on ethics and values in family therapy. By the end of the 1980s, the trickle had become, if not yet a torrent, at least a steady stream of discussion in the family-therapy literature.

The goal of this chapter is to chronicle the development of concern with ethics and values in family therapy and to discuss the major areas of interest that emerged in the 1980s, including the role of therapist values, gender issues, confidentiality, informed consent, deception, and research. In addition, we discuss underlying ideological issues in the field and offer suggestions for further development in the area of values and ethics. The chapter will not discuss legal issues in family therapy, nor will it describe the activities of professional organizations that monitor ethical activities in the field.

HISTORICAL DEVELOPMENT

This section of the chapter gives a historical account of the development of thinking about values and ethics in family therapy, with particular focus on the crucial years 1978–1987, during which the field as a whole appeared to embrace the importance of these issues.

The founders of family therapy in the 1950s concentrated on creating a body of theory and technique for understanding and treating families. In this formative period, values and ethics were relegated to background considerations. This neglect no doubt reflected the prevailing scientific and philosophical emphasis on "value-free" research and professional activities (Krasner & Houts, 1984). As Drane (1982) has documented, most modern psychotherapies tend to follow the Western scientific/medical tradition of "bracketing" ethical concerns as separate from concerns of daily clinical practice. Like medicine, psychotherapy in the 1950s and 1960s was liberating itself from prescientific, often moralistic diagnoses and treatments. In this professional and cultural environment, there was little opening for intensive reflection on ethics and values in family therapy.

The first article on the topic of ethics in family therapy was published by Grosser and Paul in 1964 in the *American Journal of Orthopsychiatry*. They raised many issues that are still salient, including dealing with secrets and the potential for harm when highly negative affect is displayed in family-therapy sessions.[1] Their paper, however, did not stimulate further work in the area. By the late 1960s, Boszormenyi-Nagy, along with Spark, was developing a theory of intergenerational ethics in family therapy (Boszormenyi-Nagy & Spark, 1973). They viewed the therapist as an ethical broker with the family, striving to balance multiple claims and having special concern for the most vulnerable and dependent family members. Nagy's model, which is described in Chapter 7, has continued to develop through the 1980s as the only major family-therapy model with an explicit theory of the ethical dimensions of family life and therapy.

The next flowering of interest in ethics and values did not come until the late 1970s, with the works of Haley (1976) and Hare-Mustin (Hare-Mustin, 1978; Hines & Hare-Mustin, 1978). In a chapter in *Problem-Solving Therapy*, Haley offered a social-exchange framework for ethics in therapy: therapists are ethical to the extent that, in return for their monetary compensation, they deliver on the promise of expert help to solve the patient's problems. Haley also discussed the still-debated issues of manipulation, deception, and concealment in therapy. His specific arguments are described later in this chapter.

Rachel Hare-Mustin's work signaled the entry into the family-therapy literature of two important cultural issues in the 1960s and 1970s: feminism and concern that individual rights were being sacrificed to group needs. Family therapists for the first time were asked to question their assumptions about the value of unity for those couples and families considered toxic to individual members and to examine clinical attitudes and interventions that serve to perpetuate gender roles that limit women's rights and opportunities.

At the same time as the feminist critique of family therapy was launched, researchers were attending to the potential negative effects of family therapy. In 1978, Alan Gurman and David Kniskern published the first review of published evidence of deterioration effects in marital and family therapy (Gurman & Kniskern, 1978). Along with feminist critics, Gurman and Kniskern concluded that family therapy in some situations is hazardous to individuals and families. One senses in retrospect that 1978 marked an end to the age of innocence for the field of family therapy.

Along with these internal critiques, family therapists, like all mental health professionals, were forced to confront in the 1970s a changing legal environment for families and clinicians. States passed major legislation concerning divorce, custody, child abuse, and the regulation of therapists (Kaslow & Steinberg, 1982; Sporakowski, 1982). In addition, litigation and malpractice issues became more serious concerns for practicing therapists, who came to realize the power of the traditional axiom, "Ignorance of the law is no excuse" (Bernstein, 1982).

The year 1982 appears to have been a watershed for publications on ethics and values in family therapy. That year, Margolin published a comprehensive overview of family-therapy ethics in the *American Psychologist* (Margolin, 1982). She summarized the then-current state of the field in terms of several major questions that make family-therapy ethics more complex than those of individual psychotherapy: "Who is the client? How is confidential information handled? Does each family member have an equal right to refuse treatment? What is the role of the therapist's values vis-à-vis conflicting values of family members?" (p. 1. 788).

In 1982, the Aspen Family Therapy Collections series published a volume titled *Values, Ethics, Legalities and the Family Therapist*, under the editorship of Luciano L'Abate (1982). Several of the chapters in that book, such as those by Kaslow and Steinberg (1982) and Sporakowski (1982), provided the field's first intensive examination of the implications of the changing legal environment. The volume was also noteworthy for a chapter by Morris Taggart (1982)

---

[1] *Editors' Note.* This clinical theme was first explored in an empirical context by Gurman and Kniskern (1978a), in their examination of "deterioration effects" in marital and family therapy.

proposing the outlines of a systemic–ecological ethic for family therapy, one that transcends the individual–family dichotomy as well as the humanity–nature dichotomy. He argued for a uniquely systemic ethic for the field, as opposed to one borrowed from traditional, reductionist, and individually oriented professions.

Finally, 1982 was the year of publication of the first "Ethical Principles for Family Therapists" by the American Association for Marriage and Family Therapy (AAMFT) (1982, revised 1988). This document laid out binding norms for AAMFT members in the areas of responsibility to clients, competence, integrity, confidentiality, professional responsibility, professional development, research responsibility, and social responsibility. By 1982, then, ethics and values in family therapy had come of age.

In 1985, D. J. and R. J. Wendorf engaged in an exchange with Ivan Boszormenyi-Nagy about systemic ethics versus traditional relational ethics that emphasize individual rights (Boszormenyi-Nagy, 1985; Wendorf & Wendorf, 1985). The Wendorfs criticized earlier writings on family-therapy ethics for borrowing from a nonsystemic, linear, individualistic ethical tradition. They called for a radical rethinking of traditional ethics of human rights in view of systems theory. Although these authors did not lay out what such a new systems ethic would be, they did offer a systems-oriented discussion of secrecy, deception, and gender issues in family therapy. Boszormenyi-Nagy (1985), in a spirited rebuttal, argued that systems thinking does not eliminate the reality of interpersonal consequences of behavior and the need for an ethics of responsibility for these consequences. He affirmed the importance of holding individuals in the family systems accountable for their decisions and the consequences of those decisions.

The year 1985 was also marked by the publication of a special issue of the journal *Counseling and Values* on values and ethics in family therapy (Doherty, 1985). This special issue contained articles by Boss and Weiner (1985) on ethics and gender bias against women, by Ryder (1985) on professionals' values in family assessment, by Stein (1985) on the cultural assessment of therapist and family values, by N. Kaslow and Gurman (1985) on ethics and family therapy research, and by Christianson (1985) on ethical issues in family-centered medical care. In the editor's introduction, Doherty (1985) stated his belief that the area of ethics and values in family therapy had matured to the point in which in-depth analyses of specific topics were more useful than either overview articles summarizing many issues or edited books attempting comprehensive coverage of all relevant topics.

In 1986, Boszormenyi-Nagy and Krasner published a new formulation of a contextual ethic for family therapy. That book, *Between Give and Take*, clarified Nagy's theory and made it more accessible to clinicians. In the model of multilateral partiality, the therapist identifies with each person's vulnerability and resources, and then strives to balance them in the form of multilateral solutions. Therapist trustworthiness leads to greater trust among family members and improved balance of fairness. Boszormenyi-Nagy and Krasner (1986) stress that the therapist is accountable for the effects of therapy on family members and others who are not present, as well as those who are present in the therapist's office.

Unlike other work on family-therapy ethics, Nagy offers a theory of the ethical base of family relationships, rather than focusing only on therapist behavior. For Nagy, connectedness between the generations is a permanent, inescapable aspect of human life, as are the consequences of parents' ethical choices for their children. Bonds of ethical obligation, therefore, join individuals in a family, rendering issues of loyalty and indebtedness as core to family relationships. Parents are obligated to promote the welfare of their children, who, in turn, are obligated to be loyal to their parents. Spouses, through their act of commitment, likewise take on obligations and can expect loyalty (Boszormenyi-Nagy & Krasner, 1986). Judith Grunebaum (1987) used the example of incest treatment to demonstrate that Contextual Family Therapy, "with its dialectical approach to the 'interhuman' issues of fairness, family loyalty, and parental accountability . . . can transcend the limitations of both systems and feminist models while incorporating the important objectives and methods of those strategies" (p. 646).

After a period of relatively limited recognition in family-therapy training programs, contextual family therapy appears to be experiencing a renewal of interest as family therapists confront ethical challenges to systems theory. It will be interesting to see how this ethical framework struggles with the larger systems issues raised by feminists who assert that men and women have unequal power in society and, therefore, in families.

The year 1987 brought two important books on family-therapy ethics. Huber and Baruth's (1987) book was the first family-therapy-ethics text to be published in response to AAMFT's educational requirements for training family therapists. Their book, although lacking a philosophically oriented analysis, summarized the existing literature and offered a casebook format for discussing ethical dilemmas encountered by family therapists. The second book, edited by British therapists Waldron-Skinner and Watson (1987), was based on a series of workshops on family-therapy ethics. What is most distinctive about this volume is the presence of two chapters by moral philosophers. Lindley (1987) offered a sophisticated analysis of the issue of respect for people in family therapy and how deception can interfere with personal autonomy. Collier (1987) took up the ethics of language use in family therapy, arguing that "insofar as therapy works by means of language, the ethics of language use is also the ethics of therapy" (p. 124).

The year 1987 was also highlighted by Virginia Goldner's critique of the pragmatic approach to ethics in family therapy. She maintained that the emphasis on "what works is best" blinds therapists to the social and cultural factors that lie behind simplistic assumptions about the causes of human distress and the ease of potential solutions. In the prevailing culture, a moral relativism leads therapists to focus on the short view of helping people get over immediate problems while avoiding consideration of larger issues, such as gender bias, that permeate society and perpetuate human misery (Goldner, 1987).

To conclude this account of the first decade of literature on family-therapy ethics, we note the emergence of several interrelated emphases in the 1980s: the influence of personal and cultural values on family therapy, the existence of gender bias in the field, a focus on research ethics, and a controversy over deception. In addition, there was further delineation of thinking about the basic ethical issues of confidentiality, informed consent, and individual versus family needs. Because questions of values underlying family therapy are the foundation of the rest of the ethical issues, we will begin with that discussion, after dealing with definitional issues.

DEFINITIONS OF TERMS

Contemporary literature on professional ethics and values in family therapy, and in psychotherapy in general, tends to leave key terms undefined. Indeed, values and ethics are often used interchangeably in the literature. In defining our use of the term "value," we turn to guidance from Spiegel (1971), a family therapist with a lifelong interest in cultural values in therapy. He wrote that the central aspect of a value is "the ranking of an ordered set of choices from most to least preferable" (p. 53). Following anthropologist Kluckholn, Spiegel further proposes three tasks that values perform:

[Values] have an *evaluative* component—that is, they serve as principles for making selections between alternative courses of action; an *existential* component, which means that the value orientations help to define the nature of reality for those who hold the given values; and finally, they have an *affective* component, which means that people not only prefer and believe in their own values, but are also ready to bleed and die for them. For this reason, values, once formed, can be changed only with the greatest difficulty. (p. 190)

Values, then, refer to the cherished beliefs and preferences that guide human decisions. As Stein (1983) notes, however, this simple definition becomes more complex when one distinguishes between manifest and latent values, conscious and unconscious values, expressed and inferred values, and operant values and espoused values.

Furthermore, some values are held idiosyncratically, some are shared within the family system, and still others extend beyond the family to society. Finally, some values are uniformly adhered to and are thus (or appear to be) context-free, whereas others come into play only in certain contexts or situations. (Stein, 1985, pp. 209–210)

This chapter deals primarily with values shared by important segments of the American family-therapy community, values that reflect, in turn, mainstream cultural values in American society. Because there is still relatively little open presentation of the values underlying different approaches to family therapy—including their relevance to diverse populations and family types—we often will be inferring value positions rather than quoting them explicitly. Other observers no doubt may draw different conclusions from ours. As authors, we will make no attempt to disguise our own value positions. Writing this chapter has involved defining and debating our personal values about families and about therapy.

In this chapter, we use "ethics" in its traditional philosophical sense as referring to "reasoning about the right and wrong of actions" (Drane, 1982, p. 21). Ethics, then, is how we think about moral choice, i.e., good or bad, right or wrong. The term "ethical" will be applied to situations in which the family therapist makes a decision about a specific course of action in the moral domain, such as whether to break confidentiality when told a secret by a family member.

Values and ethics are closely related in the following way: values are the beliefs and preferences that undergird the ethical decisions made by individuals and groups. In other words, all ethical issues involve values as grounds for decision making, and all values that deal with social rights and obligations inevitably surface in ethical decisions.

PERSONAL AND CULTURAL VALUES IN FAMILY THERAPY

Shaped by the feminist critique and influenced by similar self-analyses in psychology, sociology, law, and other disciplines and professions, a strong consensus has emerged that family therapists inevitably engage in an active valuing process in treating families. Jacobson (1983) criticized his own model of behavioral marital therapy for ignoring the political (interpersonal power) dimension of the therapist's role. He challenged the notion of value neutrality in therapy: "By accepting whatever values the spouses

exhibit as legitimate, the therapist is in effect tacitly endorsing them" (p. 14). Ryder (1985, 1987) argued that family therapists frequently "encrypt" or bury their value positions behind supposedly descriptive statements about the family. In particular, terms such as "enmeshed," "dysfunctional," and "marital satisfaction" are often used to express culturally and personally derived value positions in the verbal form of descriptive facts. When such values are "encrypted" as facts, they tend to be invisible—and thus inaccessible to public scrutiny and debate. In Ryder's words:

If socially oriented therapy is not to pursue narrow ideological or other goals inadvertently, in the name of mental health, maturity, good coping, adequate functioning or adaptive behavior, the implicit evaluation in such terms might deserve more attention. (1987, p. 136)

In a similar vein, Aponte (1985) proposed that negotiation of values is a central, but often ignored, dimension of therapy. This negotiation requires that the therapist understand the inextricable link connecting the therapist's values with family assessment and intervention. Aponte (1985) argued that "values are integral to all social systemic operations and therefore to the heart of the therapeutic process. . . . Therapists do not have a choice about whether they need to deal with values in therapy, only about how well" (p. 337).

Other scholars have taken a more broadly cultural view of the intertwining of values and family therapy. Bernal and Ysern (1986), in a forceful analysis of the ideological content of family therapy, pointed out that even abstract forms of systems theory cannot extricate family therapy from its social and political milieu. The field's failure to engage in critical self-analysis, according to Bernal and Ysern, has contributed to its implicit acceptance of several ideological assumptions of contemporary American society, including: ignoring the structures of injustice and exploitation that affect families, the tendency to view family therapy as a commodity in a business relationship with clients, and the normative endorsement of the contemporary nuclear family and its traditional sex roles.

Cultural anthropologist Howard Stein has added his voice to this discussion as an observer of family therapy. He examined the "culture-bound metaphors of the machine and the computer" that shaped the field in its origins (Stein, 1983, pp. 282–283). According to Stein, unless family therapy engages in a careful examination of its own assumptions and metaphors about normal family functioning, it will inevitably engage primarily in a resocializing of families to the dominant culture of the time or to another ethnic culture favored by therapists. An example would be how White, middle-class therapists could view young adults living with their parents as indicating a lack of individuation when this living arrangement could be a product of the family's ethnic tradition or its employment or housing situation.

Although the debate has just begun on the clinical implications of the intertwining of therapists' values and therapy, there now is common agreement in the literature that family therapists take value positions continually in their thinking, their writing, and their clinical work. As of the early 1990s, the myth of value neutrality in therapy is dead—at least as an issue of professional debate. Whether it has died as an underlying and unspoken assumption is more doubtful, given the psychotherapy field's heritage in the medical model of diagnosing "objective" dysfunction and responding with value-free treatment. The challenge now appears to be to move from agreement at the theoretical level about the pervasiveness of value positions to the more difficult process of self-examination and the dialogue necessary to examine our values in the daylight instead of in the "crypt."

In the next section, we discuss two critiques of psychotherapy ethics that have emerged from social scientists and philosophers outside the therapy community, and we apply these critiques of value assumptions to family therapy.

IDEOLOGICAL ISSUES IN FAMILY THERAPY: A CHALLENGE FROM SOCIAL CRITICS

Two important books by social critics in the 1980s raised a serious challenge to the value assumptions of contemporary psychotherapies. First was *After Virtue* by the philosopher MacIntyre (1984), which contained a scholarly and scorching commentary on ethical relativism in contemporary moral philosophy and in society. Second was the award-winning book of social criticism *Habits of the Heart: Individualism and Commitment in American Life*, a cultural analysis written by the multidisciplinary team of Bellah, Madsen, Sullivan, Swidler, and Tipton (1985). These authors drew on MacIntyre's philosophical work in their analysis of the tension in American life between the individual and the community. We agree with the thrust of their general critique, which we will summarize first and then apply specifically to family therapy.

Both of these books offer a major critique of the role of therapy in contemporary America. Their analyses are echoed in the contemporary work of other critics from within the psychotherapy field, notably Sarason (1985) and Wallach and Wallach (1982). However, because of the germinal nature of *After Virtue* and *Habits of the Heart*, we will focus on these two books. Our discussion begins with these authors' central concern about American values, followed by their comments on the therapeutic community and then a discussion of the relevance of their points to family therapy.

Two Forms of Individualism in American Society

Both MacIntyre and Bellah and associates believe that contemporary America lacks a framework in which to understand the pursuit of personal gain in the context of social obligation. Having rejected the seemingly arbitrary imposition of moral rules from traditional religion and Victorian culture and having embraced the Enlightenment emphasis on individual rights, we have no common language for discussing the major moral issues in our communities and our professions. Bellah and colleagues (Bellah et al., 1985) propose that modern American values are dominated by two kinds of individualism: (1) utilitarian individualism, which emphasizes the pursuit of economic rewards; and (2) expressive individualism, which emphasizes the pursuit of psychological rewards. In both forms, social and community concerns are relegated to background considerations as they impinge on individual rights and preferences.

In both utilitarian and expressive individualism, according to Bellah and colleagues, interpersonal relationships are viewed in contractual terms rather than in terms of obligations and covenants. The utilitarian ideal aspires to a world where market rules permit the fair exchange of goods and services and where personal risk can lead to personal gain. The community is thought to prosper best when individuals are free to pursue private economic rewards. The expressive ideal, which developed in the 18th and 19th centuries in reaction to this utilitarian approach to life, aspires to a world in which individuals are free to develop their psychological well-being and to engage in relationships that promote this well-being. Social obligations are meaningful only to the extent that they are freely chosen by the individual; thus, they can be freely broken by the individual (Bellah et al., 1985, pp. 333–334). A basic assumption here is that of a "just world" in which individuals function in a fair and orderly social system where everyone has an equal opportunity for self-determination without being constrained by structures of inequality according to race, age, or gender (Boss, 1988, Chap. 8; Boss & Thorne, 1988).

Therapist and Manager as Modern Social Characters

MacIntyre proposed that each era in history has a "social character" type that crystallizes the dominant values of the time. For example, in the latter part of the 19th century, the principal social character was the Entrepreneur, who embodied cultural ideals and values about how the powerful individual could conquer the environment. In the 20th century, according to MacIntyre, we have two predominant social characters—the Manager and the Therapist—representing the values of utilitarian and expressive individualism, respectively. MacIntyre was not writing about family therapy specifically, but we believe that his ideas are relevant to our field. Although managers and therapists seek different kinds of rewards, MacIntyre (1984) believes that these two social characters are similar in the following important ways.

1. *Neither managers nor therapists, while in their culturally defined roles, have questioned the larger context of their professional interac-* *tions.* Bellah and associates (1985) agree with MacIntyre's point, which they restate as follows:

Like the manager, the therapist takes the functional organization of industrial society for granted, as the unproblematical context of life. The goal of living is to achieve some combination of occupation and "lifestyle" that is economically possible and psychically tolerable, that "works." The therapist, like the manager, takes the ends as they are given; the focus is upon the effectiveness of the means. (p. 47)

To MacIntyre and Bellah, such claims by managers and therapists to value-free effectiveness, and hence to the power to change human systems, constitute the most culturally powerful moral "fiction" of our age (MacIntyre, 1984, Chap. 6).

2. *Both managers and therapists have had difficulty with the language of morality.* This is not to suggest that managers and therapists are amoral, but that moral discourse about legitimate goals of production or therapy is outside of their traditions. Therapists, for example, have been trained to accept as unproblematic the goal of helping "maladjusted" people become better adjusted to their social and community situation. Furthermore, therapists tend to distrust in clients the language of moral "oughts" and "shoulds," often viewing these as forms of intellectualizing that are better stated as "wants" and "needs." Thus, the moral question, "Is this right or wrong?" becomes transformed into the tactical question, "Is this going to work for me now?" (Bellah et al., 1985, p. 129).

3. *Both managers and therapists have used contractual models of social relationships.* Therapeutic contractualism is the view that "interpersonal relationships are centered on contractual exchange, enacted in communication and negotiation, and grounded in each person's ultimate responsibility to himself or herself" (Bellah et al., 1985, p. 128–129). Each person in a relationship is expected to maximize personal rewards and minimize personal costs within a framework that allows the other party to do the same. (This is basic social-exchange theory, as in Thibaut and Kelley [1959].) Why should one choose to be committed to another? Because such commitment is important to one's own satisfaction in relationships. Such a purely contractual model, however, leaves every com-

mitment potentially unstable. This argument should not be reduced to the familiar saw that people are not committed enough these days. Rather, the point made by MacIntyre and Bellah et al. is that the predominant social ethic in psychotherapy lacks a language to explain and justify the permanent commitments we actually make. For example, an otherwise articulate therapist whom Bellah interviewed was unable to explain coherently her unbending sense of responsibility for the welfare of her children, since her language of psychological self-reliance and contractualism did not allow a coherent justification for permanent commitments that transcend personal payoff. As Bellah et al. write, "Perhaps a contract model, appropriate in the context of professional and managerial work, cannot carry the weight of sustained and enduring commitments" (1985, p. 130).

4. *Both managers and therapists have viewed societal obligations as outside their mission.* Business managers generally view social problems as the responsibility of government and charitable organizations. The manager's job is to mobilize human resources to produce goods and services and to earn profits that eventually feed back into the social system. In the same way, according to MacIntyre and Bellah et al., therapists have tended to view clinical work as isolated from political and community issues. Most therapists claim that their job is to help individuals and families, not to change society. What therapists do not realize is that they are opting for a culturally prescribed split between private and public, between personal friendship and "civic friendship." Thus, therapists embrace and unwittingly promote the privatization of family life at the expense of the seamless web that binds families and communities. We believe that what appears to be a truism of therapy—that it is concerned with personal and family pain and not with politics—becomes itself a profoundly political view that is beyond political debate.

Relevance of These Criticisms to Family Therapy

Family therapy, in our view, has escaped one of the most serious problems raised in the foregoing discussion, but it is susceptible to several others. On the positive side, family therapy has transcended the narrow focus on the individual that has characterized traditional psychotherapy since Freud. Family therapy arose out of the post–World War II culture that was discovering the interconnectedness of people in their close social ties. Some of Bellah et al.'s presentation of expressive individualism, with its emphasis on the authentic pursuit of one's own feelings and values, appears naïve from a family-therapy viewpoint. Family therapists would have no trouble embracing the following statement, in which the authors of *Habits of the Heart* (Bellah et al., 1985) suggest a postindividualist blending of individual and group identities.

This alternative sense of identity in which the person is never wholly separate from others is clearest in the family. It is a context in which identity is formed in part through identifying with and incorporating aspects of other members. When therapists see the family, and particularly the parent–child relationship, not only as the context in which external standards are imposed on the child but as one in which a person is formed and a character takes shape, then there are resources for a deeper understanding of what it means to be part of a group in general. (p. 135)

While family therapy appears to have transcended the cultural bias toward the atomic individual, we believe that family therapy, as part of the American culture and as an American clinical profession, has embraced a number of the value positions criticized by MacIntyre and Bellah and co-workers. Some of these criticisms have emerged from within the field, as cited before in the work of Hare-Mustin (1978), Jacobson (1983), and Bernal and Ysern (1986), and from friendly observers such as Stein (1983, 1985) and Whan (1985). First, family therapy has followed the other clinical professions in splitting therapy from larger social, cultural, and political issues (Sarason, 1985). *Family therapy thus has encouraged the privatization of both therapy and family life.* By and large, family therapy has adopted a modified version of the American medical model, in which clinical issues ideally are private matters between patients and clinicians. Matters of public welfare in medicine belong to specialists in public health, who generally do not see patients clinically. In the family field, therapists generally leave public issues to policy specialists and matters of prevention to churches, family-life educators, and marriage-enrichment professionals. We believe that family therapists have accepted this version of the American model—that families are the arena of private emotion and the community the arena of instrumental activity—with little thought as to alternatives.

Second, *important segments of family therapy have embraced a managerial, contractual approach to therapeutic relationships.* Haley (1976) is clearest about this, proposing a model for therapy ethics based on the fair exchange of expert intervention for client payment. Erickson (1984a, 1984b) has argued that a managerial model also underlies the thinking of ecosystemic therapists who emphasize organizational process in families to the neglect of individual actors and the wider social network. In Erickson's (1984b) words:

The whole of ecosystemic practice may be illuminated by a consideration of the epistemology as related to an industrial/business framework: the image seems apt of the ecosystemic therapist as a management consultant attempting to grasp the pattern of the *immediate* system of organization in which a process of concern is stuck and in which the producers and the product are of secondary importance (actually, not particularly visible) in order to offer an intervention to change the immediate set of relations. Both the base (person as subject) and the wider network may be chopped in the service of interventions to remove obstacles to "production." (p. 203)

A *third, related issue is the lack in the field, until recently, of moral debate about the ends or goals of therapy.* The debate in the 1980s concentrated on gender and culture: How much should these issues in the family and in the larger social sphere be included in setting goals for therapy? (See, for example, Goldner, 1988; Hare-Mustin, 1986; McGoldrick, Pearce, & Giordano, 1982.) Beyond these two issues, there has been relatively little discussion in the family-therapy literature about the legitimate ends of therapy and how these should be arrived at. Grunebaum (1987) offers a similar criticism of the field, noting that the prominent exception is contextual family therapy (Boszormenyi-Nagy & Krasner, 1986), which takes as its starting point the ethical connections among family members and between the family and the therapist.

In family-therapy models that have a developmental framework (such as psychodynamic and Bowen models), the goals of therapy are generally considered self-evident from the point of view of the model: to help clients get unstuck and further their development as individuals and as a family system. The values underlying these goals of therapy are not generally presented. In other, more problem-focused models such as strategic and behavioral therapies, the therapist is expected to accept the removal of the family's presenting problem—or some modification negotiated with the therapist—as the justifiable goal of therapy. Symptomatic individuals are to be helped become asymptomatic; distressed couples are to be helped to become more satisfied. Not all proponents of these models hold fully to all of these assumptions, but we believe that the above generalizations accurately describe the absence of explicit analysis of the values underlying the goals of family therapy.

How can these developmental and problem-solving family therapies become more sophisticated in the area of values? In light of MacIntyre's call for moral discourse about the ends or goals of therapy, we suggest that developmentally oriented family therapists need to engage in public dialogue about their value assumptions and ethical positions concerning their definitions of healthy, well-developed families and family members. For example, to what extent is "differentiation of self" a universally applicable goal for human life and thus for therapy? What other goals does it intersect with in a dialectical way, such as connectedness? Are there culturally different and acceptable ways to resolve the differentiation–connectedness tension, or is there one universal path of development? Is the path the same for men and women? When optimal differentiation of self is defined differently by the family and the therapist, how can such differences be handled ethically and respectfully unless the therapist has thought through these issues and is willing to conduct a dialogue about them with the family? We are not assuming that the treatment goal of self-differentiation could not withstand such an analysis, but only that this analysis would be most enlightening. Developmentally oriented family therapists tend to base the goals of therapy on clinical theories that "encrypt" major value assumptions about the goals of human life and family relationships. We still live with the legacy of Freud's belief that psychoanalytic diagnosis was scientifically objective and not value based.

In the same way, we suggest that problem-centered therapies should address their implicit assumptions about the legitimacy of goals brought by clients to therapy. Surely, some goals would be rejected by therapists, such as helping one to harm oneself or another. But suppose a family asked a therapist (of its own ethnic group) to help it prevent a young adult from disobeying by marrying outside the group. Would the therapist accept? In most segments of American culture, the therapist almost certainly would not agree to do so. But how does a problem-centered therapist decide on the worthiness or legitimacy of such goals? Problem-focused family therapists, in the end, need what all therapists need—an explicit position on normal or healthy family functioning and the morally acceptable activities of a therapist with a family. *Such theories are never perfect or complete, but without an attempt to create them, the field lacks the public moral discourse necessary for critical self-analysis. The result, we believe, is the moral fiction of clinical "effectiveness" backed by unexamined assumptions about human life and the relationships between therapists and clients.*

The fourth application of MacIntyre's and Bellah and colleagues' critique to family therapy refers to difficulties in seeing the individual family member as a separate moral agent. With the exception again of Nagy's work, family-therapy models either have no explicit theory of individual psychology (e.g., structural, strategic, Milan, behavioral) or lack an explicit moral dimension in their individual psychology (e.g., psychodynamic, Bowen). As Grunebaum (1986) has pointed out, systems theories generally have not made room for the ideas of justice and individual moral choice, which are fundamental to social groups. (We leave open the question as to whether such an integration of morality and systems theory is possible.) This issue goes to the heart of feminist critiques, which claim that family therapy has not attended to the unjust structures of equality and to the differential vulnerability of family members in contemporary society (Walters, Carter, Papp, & Silverstein, 1988).

If we therapists have had difficulty seeing ourselves as moral and valuing agents, not just as clinicians treating dysfunction, it is small wonder that we have had difficulty seeing family members that way. Thus, it is likely that most family therapists have been as uncomfortable as individual therapists have been with the language of moral "shoulds" in therapy, as in the following examples: after a divorce, both parents "should" remain committed to their children's welfare; children "should" remain committed to the welfare of their elderly, frail parents; even divorcing spouses "should" not deceive each other for the purposes of revenge or personal gain. The traditional languages of therapy make it difficult for family therapists to deal with these issues in moral terms—as ideals for family life and as shoulds for individual conduct. When pressed, most therapists would fall back on the language of expressive individualism, focusing on the personal losses to a client that might stem from cutting off a loved one. After a centuries-long legacy of moral injunctions handed down without debate by religious authorities, family therapists are understandably reluctant to serve as moral authorities in the lives of clients. What gets lost, however, is the ability to carry on a dialogue with clients about the moral choices they make in dealing with family members and other people in their lives.

In summary, the 1980s witnessed trenchant critiques of the psychotherapy enterprise in American culture. As a product of its context in American society, family therapy seems to have transcended some troublesome aspects of the larger culture, while, not surprisingly, adopting other aspects. The preceding discussion, of course, was influenced by the authors' own value concerns about the separation of the individual, the family, and the community in American society and in therapy and about the absence of moral debate in our field.

These ideological issues serve as a backdrop to the following discussion of common and practical ethical issues in contemporary family therapy.

DECEPTION IN FAMILY THERAPY

No area of family therapy has witnessed more disputatious ethical debate than that of deceptive practices by therapists. Deceptive practices have been identified most often with the strategic models of family therapy (Bodin, 1981; Stanton, 1981) and with paradoxical interventions. "Paradoxical" interventions generally involve a combination of explaining problems to the family in counterintuitive ways, deliberately escalating the symptoms, or redirecting the symptoms into new contexts (Fisher, Anderson, & Jones, 1981). Not invented by family therapists, paradoxical interventions have a long history in psychotherapy (Adler, 1928; Frankl, 1975). However, the use of paradox in systems-oriented therapy has been, for some, a hallmark in the development of family therapy.

A major ethical issue raised about paradoxical interventions concerns manipulation, usually defined by critics as tricking a family into taking a course of action desired by the therapist. Whan (1983), for example, maintains that the covert influence of paradoxical interventions undermines the value of the client's self-determination because the client is not informed about the mode of influence. When uncovered or sensed by the client, such manipulation damages the client's trust in the therapist, thus undermining a core healing ingredient in therapy.

In their defense of the ethics of paradoxical interventions, Brown and Slee (1986) contend that entering therapy necessarily involves the loss of some individual autonomy and freedom of choice. Furthermore, they maintain that responsible therapists explain paradoxical procedures in a way that contains part of the "truth" for the client, and that they ultimately form an explicit treatment contract that mitigates ethical concerns about indirect coercion. As to the issue of trust, Brown and Slee contend that trust is undermined only when the client perceives the therapist as dishonest. An alternative perception, according to Brown and Slee, is that the therapist is presenting a particular slant on reality that is not inherently dishonest (i.e., not believed by the therapist), but does capture one element of the therapeutic reality.

A further complication of this debate revolves around the therapist's intentions: two therapists may enact the same intervention but with different beliefs and intentions. Haley (1976) summarizes this situation nicely:

One therapist may encourage anxiety as a way of getting rid of it while another may do the same as a way of providing less pressure for the patient, or of allowing him to notice what he really feels, or for some other reason. In one case, an expert is deceiving a patient as a way of tricking him into being cured, while in the other case, the therapist is not deceiving a patient, at least not deliberately. Once again, we have the problem that "deceit" may be a matter of the therapist's awareness or ignorance of what he is doing. (p. 204)

Fraser (1984) dismissed the debate about the appropriateness of paradoxical interventions in family therapy by contending that "paradox is only paradox when viewed from an alternative orthodox" (p. 361). He pointed out that the notion of paradox presumes an established, "given" perspective in a particular cultural, personal, or therapeutic context. Thus, much second-order change may appear paradoxical from a client's perspective, even if the therapist's intention is more straightforward. In any event, according to Fraser, the culturally orthodox has no intrinsic ethical claim over the culturally paradoxical.

Extending Fraser's (1984) ideas, we propose that the ethics of paradoxical interventions should not be separated from therapy ethics in general. The former require the same justification as interventions that are culturally defined as "orthodox," such as insight-oriented or problem-solving techniques. The latter have no inherent claim to moral superiority over paradoxical interventions. For example, the act of prescribing a symptom for purposes of curing it is on the same ethical ground as advising a client how to avoid the symptom. Cautioning a recovering family to "slow down" requires no greater ethical justification than encouraging faster change. An intervention, of course, might be regarded as ethically unacceptable because it puts clients at risk of harm. However, both straightforward and paradoxical methods must pass the test of "do no harm."

In other words, we propose that, *in the absence of harmful clinical effects, paradoxical interventions require no more or no less ethical justification than conventional interventions.*

Critics of paradoxical interventions often assume that they are inherently deceptive. Note, however, the important distinction between paradox and deception described by philosopher Collier (1987):

The majority of 'paradoxical injunctions' . . . are injunctions, not statements. Telling someone to do something in the expectation that the outcome of the attempt will be to achieve some quite different result is not to tell a lie or to express feelings or opinions that one does not have. (p. 122)

We believe that the debate about the particular ethical justification of paradoxical interventions has distracted the family-therapy field from several larger ethical issues facing all therapeutic approaches. In the words of Brown and Slee (1986), "The dangers for the therapist who uses paradoxical techniques are the same as the dangers for any other therapist" (p. 490). *If paradoxical methods are used in a way that invades the autonomy of clients, deceives the client, or undermines the therapist's trustworthiness, then they are unethical. But these are also criteria for evaluating all therapeutic interventions.* The main issue, in our judgment, is not so much the *content* of the therapist's intervention—paradoxical or straightforward—but the moral aspects of the *therapist's intention* and *the interaction between the therapist and the client family.*

Having distinguished paradox from deception, we turn now to the literature on deception in family therapy, followed by our own analysis of the issues.

Deception in Family Therapy

We begin by summarizing the position of Haley (1976), who offered the first articulated theory of the ethics of deception in therapy. His starting point is that the therapist is entrusted by the client and by society with the authority and power to solve problems. Since "information and power are synonymous" (p. 218), the therapist's ability to reveal or conceal information is a cornerstone of therapeutic effectiveness. Haley contends that no therapist reveals all that he or she knows at a given time with the client. Even therapists who highly value openness with clients reserve the right to be selectively open at different times in therapy, in the interests of the client's welfare and the stability of the therapist–client relationship. All therapists, therefore, influence clients by sharing or withholding information about the therapist's thoughts and feelings concerning the client. The key question to Haley, then, becomes when it is ethical to reveal or conceal, not whether it is ever ethical to conceal. In Haley's words:

Whether a therapist is "honest" with his client or is "manipulating" him has been a source of controversy. It is now accepted that one cannot do therapy without manipulating people in the sense of influencing them to change since change is the purpose of therapy. The pretense that sitting with a deadpan expression and responding in monosyllables would not influence a patient's life decisions has been recognized as only a pretense. The question remains of how much of the therapist's maneuvering he should do outside the patient's awareness either by concealing information about his strategy or by using distraction techniques. (1976, pp. 199–200)

Haley has crystallized a key ethical issue in family therapy. Given the universality of therapist influence on clients, and given the therapist's continual decisions about what to disclose, what are the ethics of concealment? To return to our earlier argument, the issue is not whether the intervention is paradoxical or straightforward (neither being inherently deceptive), but whether any concealment involved is ethical and whether the therapist remains trustworthy.

Collier (1987), in a chapter on the language of objectivity and the ethics of reframing in family therapy, offers a distinction between deception and partial truths. Deception involves fact-language that implies to the client that the therapist is taking an objective position about the world, when the therapist is actually posing for the benefit of the client. Collier tweaks family therapists for using fact-language with clients but privately holding an epistemology that denies objectivity of description. It is not fair to have it both ways, says Collier: "To use language in this apparently objective way and then deny in one's second-order discourse that any account can be objectively true is to rob the original discourse of any content" (p. 123).

Arguments in the family-therapy field about deception frequently center around the twin issues of honesty and manipulation. Haley (1976) clearly views manipulation as synonymous with influence, and, therefore, as universal in therapy. The problem with Haley's definition is that the term "manipulation" is used so broadly as to make ethical distinctions nearly impossible to make; to do therapy is to "manipulate." We prefer Collier's understanding of manipulation, which he defines in terms of deception for the purpose of control: "Manipulation occurs when a person's actions are controlled by getting them to misunderstand the situation" (p. 124). It is the combination of deception and control that makes certain family-therapy practices ethically suspect. This use of therapist power is especially problematic when the clients are in socially disempowered situations, such as many women and minority families (Weiner & Boss, 1985). In our view, manipulation, defined as control through deception, requires extraordinary justification before its use by a therapist.

To return to the discussion of paradoxical methods, we believe that paradoxical interventions are not inherently manipulative to clients, although they can be used manipulatively by some therapists. One might even imagine a culture more mystically oriented than that of mainstream America in which prescribing symptoms, along with appropriate "go slow" incantations, would constitute the standard, orthodox treatment for emotional problems. In such a culture, offering direct psychological insight or teaching behavioral skills might appear disrespectful. The important ethical issue lies in the context of the intervention, namely, whether the therapist was assuming inappropriate power over the client through deceptive means that violate the autonomy of the client.

As to Haley's (1976) point that therapists inevitably engage in concealment because they cannot be expected to reveal every thought they have to the client, we offer Collier's (1987) distinction between deception and "tact," which involves sensitivity about the timing of disclosures to clients. Therapists, according to Collier, often "insert the wedge of truth thin edge first," with the hope that this tactful approach will facilitate their later efforts to inform the client of the whole truth. The therapist's intent is quite different here than in situations where keeping the client in the dark is essential to the treatment.

Lying in Therapy: An Analysis

Following are five examples of deceptive statements made by some family therapists in the interests of helping families. They are drawn from published case reports and from first-hand accounts by therapists to the first author.

1. "I once treated a family who. . . ." (The case example is fictitious or was treated by someone else.)
2. "I have two children the same ages as your children, so I know what it's like." (The therapist has no such children.)
3. "I have consulted with my colleagues behind the mirror about your situation, and they have advised me. . . ." (There is no one behind the mirror, but the therapist had consulted previously about the case.)
4. "I have consulted with several other therapists and they all agree with what I am about to say to you." (No such consultation occurred.)
5. "I want you and your mother to plan four eating binges this week. And I want you to keep careful written records about how your self-esteem is doing before and after each binge. The reason for this assignment is that I need more data about how your self-esteem is tied up with your binge eating, and the only way I can get this information is to read the records you keep for each binge. Then I can plan how to help you with your eating problem." (The therapist does not believe in the relevance of self-esteem to the client's problem and will not study the records for their diagnostic value. The therapist has chosen this approach to get the client, who believes that her problem stems from poor self-esteem, to comply with a paradoxical directive deliberately to enact her symptom.)

Each of these deceptive statements by therapists was presumably designed to help the clients. Such practices have been reported anecdotally by therapists to be highly "effective" when used at the "right time" with the "right family." For some therapists, some or all of these statements are ethically acceptable, while for other therapists, these statements represent an abuse of the therapeutic relationship. Frequently, professional dialogues degenerate into charges of "crass manipulation" versus "naïveté." We offer some perspectives borrowed from a moral philosopher to raise the level of discussion, if not to resolve the issues. We will present our own conclusions at the end of the discussion.

Following the analysis of Bok (1978) in *Lying: Moral Choice in Public and Private Life*, we define a lie as "an intentionally deceptive message in the form of a statement" (p. 16). "Deceptive," in turn, refers to "messages meant to mislead [others], meant to make them believe what we ourselves do not believe" (p. 14). Bok further limits her analysis to situations in which there is an intention to deceive, and in which there is no self-delusion about what the deceiver believes to be true. Thus, Bok's is a theory about "outright lies," which she believes are necessary to understand before the more borderline cases of half-truths and partial self-deception can be made clearer.

Note that Bok is referring to "truthfulness," which refers to a quality of the message sender, rather than to "truth," which refers to correspondence with "objective reality." *Truthfulness is an ethical issue referring to genuineness and trustworthiness, whereas truth is an epistemological issue about what is knowable. The issue of deception in family therapy becomes muddled when this basic philosophical distinction is not made, as when lack of truthfulness is justified on the grounds that the "truth" is inherently unknowable in an objective sense* (Weeks & L'Abate, 1982; Wendorf & Wendorf, 1985). Some authors make this distinction but proceed to dismiss the ethical debate about truthfulness by maintaining that the epistemological argument subsumes the ethical one. Bok, like all moral philosophers, keeps the distinction and regards the ethical sphere as crucial in its own right. To summarize, truthfulness concerns the correspondence between what I believe and what I tell you; thus, I may be wrong but truthful. We will not deal here with the intricacies of other forms of deception, as when I tell you what I believe, but with the purpose of misleading you about something else. The distinctions described by Bok and other philosophers have important relevance to the issue of deception in family therapy.

In her initial arguments, Bok (1978) points out that frequently the moral justification for lying concentrates on the intentions of the liar without considering the perspective of the one lied to, who is not given a choice. Lies, she maintains, give power to the deceiver, power the one lied to would usually not want to give up. In addition to taking the perspective of the one lied to, Bok asserts a community perspective: lies and patterns of deception must be evaluated not only for their harm to individuals, but also for their effect on the social fabric of trust in a community. She writes (Bok, 1978): "Trust in some degree of veracity functions as a *foundation* of relations among human beings; when this trust shatters or wears away, institutions collapse" (p. 33) (author's italics).

With these background assumptions, Bok lays out two principles for morally evaluating lies:

1. *The principle of veracity.* This principle asserts that truthful statements are preferable to lies in the absence of special circumstances. Stated differently, an initial negative weight accrues to the lie; liars hold the burden of proof. The reasons for this principle relate to the lack of consent by the one lied to, the unilateral assumption of power by the liar, and the overriding importance of veracity for the social fabric. Bok's conclusion is that lies should be considered only as a last resort, after truthful alternatives have been considered.

2. *Justification of lies and the test of publicity.* Bok proposes three levels of justification that are required for a responsible approach to deceptive practices. First is the *test of individual conscience*: one should stop to question oneself morally when considering a lie, rather than concentrate only on the pragmatic effectiveness of the lie. Second is the *test of group consideration*. Here a group of peers such as a professional community weighs the morality of the deception in light of moral principles and the ideals of the profession. Both of these levels of justification, however, are susceptible to self-serving biases. Hence, Bok proposes a third, crucial level of justification: the *test of publicity*, which refers to the public airing and consideration of a deceptive practice. This test rests

on the assumption that moral justification cannot be exclusive or hidden; it must be able to withstand a public debate. Bok (1978) explains the "public" in the following way:

The "public" required for the justification of deceptive practices should ideally be wider than our conscience and more critical than the imagined audience. . . . If the choice . . . forms part of a practice of deceit, then greater accountability should be required. Can the lie or the entire practice be defended in the press or on television? Can they be justified in advance in classrooms, workshops, or public meetings? (p. 105)

Bok does not assume that such public dialogue will inevitably lead to enlightened moral decisions, but rather that generally a more carefully defined and balanced moral choice is likely to eventuate. Deceptive practices that relate only to a minority of the population—for example, to schizophrenic patients or to minority populations—make the value of the publicity test problematic because most citizens cannot take the perspective of the minority group. However, Bok believes that the test of publicity is likely to be quite fruitful when the entire public—including men and women and racial and ethnic minorities—perceives itself as vulnerable to the deceptive practice, as in the case of medicine or therapy. She speculates that few deceptive practices by professionals would survive such a public debate. We agree. To exemplify Bok's point about the test of publicity, Doherty (1989) published a dramatization of a network television debate about deception in family therapy.

Through the use of a case example from Bok's book, we can summarize her thoughts about lying by professionals. The example concerns a physician who "cured" a young woman's anxiety attacks related to leaving home by prescribing a placebo. However, when her pills ran out and she was reexperiencing anxiety, she telephoned the doctor for a renewed prescription. Her doctor was out of town and she was referred to another physician. The upshot was her discovery of the placebo pills. She lost trust forever in her physician when she discovered that she had been deceived. The lie "worked," but the therapeutic relationship did not survive. Applying the principle of veracity, Bok contends that there was no effort by the physician to justify

resorting to a lie and that alternative treatments were available. In terms of the test of publicity, the deceptive use of placebos would be unlikely to survive public scrutiny, even if it could survive medical scrutiny. Public scrutiny sooner or later is likely to be an ultimate judge when professionals use deceptive practices. As mentioned earlier, however, public approval may not be reliable in the case of social groups that lack equal access to public attention and public power. The burden of justifying deceiving powerless people is extraordinarily high.

Bok (1978) concludes her argument against deception with the following statement:

It is not enough to look at each incident of manipulation in isolation, no matter how benevolent it may be. When the costs and benefits are weighed, not only the individual consequences must be considered, but also the cumulative ones. Reports of deceptive practices inevitably leak out and the resulting suspicion is heightened by the anxiety which threats to health always create. And so even the health professionals who do not mislead their patients are injured by those who do; the entire institution of medicine is threatened by practices lacking in candor, however harmless the results may appear in some individual cases. (p. 71)

Lindley (1987) agrees with Bok that deception is almost always harmful. "Full blown deception," he writes, "does harm to its victim, even if the victim is unaware of its having taken place" (p. 115). Autonomy is defined as the right to have one's own purposes and to have information upon which to base important decisions about one's welfare. Thus, he says, autonomy is essential to human dignity and must be treated with the greatest respect by therapists.

The following are our own conclusions about the ethics of deception in family therapy; they are offered in the form of ethical propositions for debate among our colleagues.

1. Truthfulness is a core dimension of therapy, exceptions to which must be carefully weighed and debated, both in the profession and with others outside the profession. Claims of "effectiveness" are not sufficient.
2. Therapists are not bound at all times to disclose all of their beliefs about the client family and its problems, but partial truthfulness should be used with the goal of eventual dis-

closure of all relevant information, especially when requested by the client family.

3. Lies can be justified only when no alternatives are available in the profession. This will be a difficult test for any deceptive practice to pass since family therapy has a plethora of techniques for any given problem. Note that it is not sufficient that the individual therapist have no personal alternatives, since failure to have learned alternative interventions is not an adequate justification for practicing ethically questionable ones. Alternatives in such cases include referral to another therapist, seeking consultation, or requesting a cotherapist who has different skills.

4. Lies in therapy are forms of coercion that require the same high degree of justification as the use of physical force. These might include certain emergencies where there is an imminent threat to life or health.

Example: A highly distressed client called her therapist after learning that she had been "dumped" by her lover. She said she had a handful of antidepressant pills and was about to take them. After several minutes of discussion, during which the client kept repeating her intention to kill herself, the therapist asked her whether anyone else was nearby. She said that she was calling from the lobby of a restaurant and that her sister was inside. The therapist told her to get her sister on the line. The client asked the therapist to promise not to tell her sister about her suicidal plan. The therapist promised not to tell, then proceeded to inform the sister about the client's plans, and asked her to stay with her sister to prevent her from taking the pills. The therapist also called the client's daughter and asked her to stay with her mother until the next morning's therapy session. The next day, the client, no longer acutely suicidal, was understandably furious at the therapist, but understood the therapist's reason for telling the lie. The therapeutic relationship—and the client—survived.

Returning to the five illustrations of deceptive practices given at the beginning of this section, we believe that none of the examples satisfies the criteria for justifying such deception. In all cases, there presumably were alternative, nondeceptive means to accomplish the therapist's goals of identifying with the family, adding credibility to the therapist's approach, or influencing a family to engage in a paradoxical task. Thus, these deceptive behaviors by the therapist constitute an ethically unacceptable infringement on clients' rights. In addition, there is reason to believe that the public's trust in the profession of family therapy would be seriously undermined if such practices became generally known. We believe that such public reproach would not stem simply from ignorance of systems thinking, but from a profound concern about the veracity of therapists in whom clients confide with so much trust.

Less clear-cut, in our opinion, are therapeutic "role playing" situations in which the therapist is speaking in an "as if" way at the metacommunication level, even though the messages literally are fact-statements. The key issue is the therapist's intention. When Carl Whitaker makes absurd-sounding statements of his beliefs (e.g., "You can never get divorced" or "Men are hopeless"), he presumably is not suggesting that the family accept his statements as literally true. He is not trying to deceive, but to speak at the unconscious level to reveal at the metaphorical level. In Lindley's (1987) words, "Works of fiction are literally false, but they are not deceptive, because authors do not intend their audiences to take them literally" (p. 114). As a mother in one family matter-of-factly told her son when he was puzzled by the therapist's contention that he was "conforming" by being rebellious, "That's family-systems talk." This family accepted the altered realities involved in family-systems therapy. The important ethical issue is that the therapist was not deceiving the family about the therapist's beliefs or intentions or concealing family realities that the family deserved to know about.

We believe that the issue of deception is, along with gender bias, the central ethical issue in contemporary family therapy. Our discussion is intended to introduce some new perspectives into the debate, and to offer some conclusions as departures for further dialogue. The stakes are high. We are not dealing with technical breaches of the virtue of truthfulness, or merely with "clumsy" interventions (Coyne, 1989), but with the foundations of trust that clients and society hold for family therapy.

INDIVIDUAL WELFARE AND
FAMILY WELFARE

All therapy is aimed at promoting the welfare of clients. Family therapy has the special burden of routinely treating multiple individual clients in a context in which a couple or family relationship is being treated. Family therapy, then, functions within the dialectic of individual welfare versus group welfare. In Green and Hansen's (1989) survey of AAMFT members, the ethical dilemma of "family versus individual needs" was rated the second most frequently encountered dilemma (out of 16), and the second most important one. Margolin (1982) has summarized the difficulty: "The therapist's primary responsibilities are to protect the rights and to promote the welfare of his or her clients. The dilemma with multiple clients is that in some situations an intervention that serves one's person's best interest may be countertherapeutic to another. Indeed, the very reason that families tend to seek therapy is because they have conflicting goals and interests" (p. 789). Margolin concludes her discussion by calling for family therapists to attempt to balance therapeutic responsibility toward individuals and the family as a unit.

The issue of individual welfare versus family welfare was first raised most explicitly by Hare-Mustin (1980) and Hines and Hare-Mustin (1978) in their feminist-inspired critiques of family therapy. Hare-Mustin posits that different family members are likely to benefit unequally from family therapy and that a pursuit of family-level goals (such as solidarity) can conflict with important individual rights and goals, particularly of women and most clearly in cases of abuse. She urges family therapists to be open with family members at the outset about possible conflict between individual and family goals.

Hare-Mustin's reasoning has been criticized by Taggart (1982) and Wendorf and Wendorf (1985) for reflecting the Western cultural bias toward considering rights only in terms of autonomous individuals. These authors call for a "systemic ethic." In Taggart's view of an evolutionary systemic ethic, "Values and ethics now refer to the dynamics of evolving systems and not to the vicissitudes of individual rights" (p.

32). On the other hand, critics of the systemic position, such as Boszormenyi-Nagy (1985) and Luepnitz (1988), maintain that patterns of victimization and asymmetrical vulnerability are realities in many families, and that individuals must be held accountable for their decisions and the consequences of their decisions. Hare-Mustin's later writings, furthermore, show that she does not hold a simplistic view of the importance of promoting individual autonomy as the goal of therapy, believing instead that autonomy and relatedness are impossible to conceptualize without each other, and that neither has been adequately addressed in the therapy literature (Hare-Mustin & Marecek, 1986).

At a more practical level, Sider and Clements (1982) offer a brief but well-nuanced discussion of the ethics of choice of an individual or a family approach to treatment. They maintain that most therapists avoid the dilemma by presuming harmony between individual needs and family needs, or by unilaterally assigning priorities to one level over the other—usually without a clear ethical justification. Sider and Clements conclude by proposing "an honest exploration of individual and social level good in all such cases, an explicit statement of the therapists' loyalty when there is conflict between levels, and a realization by both individual and social unit therapists that their choice of psychotherapeutic modality is not only a matter of personal preference or efficacy of technique. It is also a matter of ethics" (p. 1458).

This debate about individually oriented versus systemic ethics is a potentially enriching one for the field. At this point, we do not believe that the systemic ethic position has resolved the thorny issues of individual responsibility and of the therapist's duty to weigh individual needs as a separate category from family needs. Individual persons throw punches, and therapists must protect those who are vulnerable to being punched, no matter what the systemic factors are. On the other hand, Taggart (1982) and Wendorf and Wendorf (1985) have raised a crucial issue about how discussions of ethics in family therapy tend to reflect the prevailing American norms favoring individualism. In a classic book on the origins of the American health-care system, Freymann (1974) points out that the basic philosophy of Western medicine and the medical codes of ethics imply that a clinician's primary loyalty is to the patient as an individual. Broader issues of public welfare are relegated to the specialty of public health. In the Eastern European tradition, on the other hand, the clinician's first obligation was to the community, and secondly to the patient (Freymann, 1974, pp. 43–44).

This analysis suggests that the clear "givens" of an individual-rights orientation must be examined in a historical and cultural context and not taken as beyond debate and possible alteration. To conclude reflexively that the rights of autonomous individuals are always primary would undermine the special wisdom of family-systems theory. On the other hand, to collapse individual rights into the needs of the family group would turn our backs on an important tradition in the West that emphasizes the irreplaceable worth of individual persons. Somewhere in that dialectic lies the future development of family-therapy ethics. Examples of efforts at this integration are Boss' (1988) examination of the interplay between individual stress and family stress and Luepnitz's (1988) view that acts by individuals in families "are part of a long tradition of socially defining women and children as property of husbands and fathers" (p. 73). We add that this same social history has defined men as in charge, invulnerable, and in control. Given these traditions, it is not surprising that the issue of individual versus family welfare was raised first in our field by feminists, who have argued convincingly that balancing individual and family welfare requires therapists to see beyond the therapy room to the societal context.

INFORMED CONSENT IN FAMILY THERAPY

Like most treatment approaches in psychotherapy, family therapy was born in the era before concerns surfaced about clients' informed consent to enter therapy. The assumption was that troubled people asked for help and trusted the clinician to provide the best and most ethical care. The modern legal doctrine of informed consent was initiated by a 1960 court case that found a physician negligent in not informing a patient of the possible risks of treatment (Bray,

Shepherd, & Hays, 1985). The idea of informed consent is more than the commonsense notion that people should freely consent to treatment, but rather that consent involves "a knowledgeable decision based on adequate information about the therapy, the available alternatives, and the collateral risks" (Bray et al., 1985, p. 53).

The combination of state laws and professional associations' codes of ethical conduct have made informed-consent procedures standard in the practice of most therapists, often beginning with disclosure documents read by clients before seeing the therapist (Huber & Baruth, 1987, p. 27). Furthermore, there is little disagreement about the basic ingredients in informed consent. Hare-Mustin, Marecek, Kaplan, and Liss-Levenson (1979) propose three kinds of information that clients should have in making an informed choice regarding therapy: (1) the procedures, goals, and possible side effects of the therapy; (2) the qualifications, policies, and practices of the therapist; and (3) other available sources of help.

Complications for family therapists dealing with informed consent center around the issue of coercion of reluctant adults or children in the family. Experienced family therapists tend to have well-honed skills in helping the most eager family members to persuade the reluctant ones to enter therapy. The ethical gray area, in our view, is apparent when legitimate influence attempts become so coercive as to violate the autonomy of the skeptical family member. An example is when a therapist takes the position that no treatment will be given to anyone in the family unless all family members enter treatment. This stance may be coercive to willing family members by denying access to the therapist unless they make heroic and successful efforts to engage the other family members in therapy. We agree with Margolin (1982) that family therapists with this policy "should inform the family that other therapists do not necessarily share this preference and should have available a list of competent referral sources" (p. 795). We also add our view that refusing treatment without full family participation would be unethical in public mental health agencies, which are often the last resort for troubled families, or in communities with severe shortages of therapists.

The second troublesome issue in informed consent concerns the rights of children. Margolin (1982) points out that young children's limited ability to understand therapeutic procedures underlines their special vulnerability as a consumer group, since parents do not always know what is best for their children. We agree with her recommendation that therapists follow the example of researchers by informing children in simplified language what they can expect of family therapy, and ask for the "assent" to proceed with therapy. Assent is not legally binding in the way that "consent" is, but it nevertheless establishes the child as an active participant in agreeing to the treatment contract.

We believe that in the next decade family therapy's consideration of these difficult problems concerning informed-consent issues will be stimulated further by movements in the areas of patients' and consumers' rights, and of children's and adolescents' rights to make decisions concerning their health care—decisions that might not always be congruent with their parents' wishes (Gardner, Scherer, & Tester, 1989).

CONFIDENTIALITY IN
FAMILY THERAPY

Confidentiality between clinicians and patients had its origins in the 16th century, when physicians realized that persons with contagious diseases could face social ostracism if the community discovered their diagnosis (Huber & Baruth, 1987). The general point behind confidentiality in therapy is that the client has the right to be protected from the disclosure of information revealed in therapy, unless explicit authorization is given for this disclosure. As a general principle, there is no disagreement among therapists about the central value of confidentiality. However, for all therapists, judicial decisions have made the implementation of complete confidentiality impossible, as in the case of incest or child abuse or other clear dangers to a client or others. Third parties such as family courts and insurance companies have also established procedures that compromise the ideal of full confidentiality for clients.

Aside from these legal issues, the principal ethical challenges for family therapists concern the use of confidentiality in the multilateral relationship of family therapy. Margolin (1982) summarized three prevalent positions in the family-therapy field. The first position holds that the therapist should treat each family member's private revelations to the therapist in full confidence. This information is not to be divulged to other family members. The second position holds that the therapist should actively avoid learning secrets from one family member, and should not be bound to confidentiality if they are revealed. The rationale is that the secret information will create a special alliance that will be detrimental to therapy. The third position lies in between the other two. The therapist indicates to the clients that, in general, confidentiality does not apply, but that the client has the right to request that certain specific information be kept secret, and that the therapist will comply. No matter which approach is taken, we believe that it is essential for the therapist to communicate his or her policy on confidentiality; otherwise, family members may be operating on wrong assumptions. This disclosure of the therapist's policy on confidentiality should be part of informed consent for therapy. Thus, it is possible to distinguish between clinical judgment about which approach to confidentiality is most appropriate or effective and the ethical imperative to communicate the therapist's policy on confidentiality to the clients. The ethical and the clinical come together around the maintenance of trustworthiness in the therapeutic relationship, the quality that, as Karpel (1980) warns, is most apt to be compromised when secrets are mishandled by therapists.

ETHICAL ISSUES IN
FAMILY-THERAPY RESEARCH

From a historical perspective, the ethics of research procedures have been the subject of careful consideration only since the end of World War II, when the Nuremberg trials revealed the heinous pattern of human experimentation conducted by Nazi physicians. Strickler (1982) traces the path from the Nuremberg guidelines to the more elaborate Helsinki Code of Ethics on Human Experimentation, which was adopted by the World Medical Association in 1964. Psychotherapy research ethics were given their most elaborate initial statement in 1973 by the American Psychological Association (APA). Family-therapy researchers in the 1980s, following the lead of clinicians who were turning to ethical issues in family therapy, began more explicitly to concern themselves with the unique ethical challenges of conducting family-therapy research (Boss, 1987; Heatherington, Friedlander & Johnson, 1989; Jurich & Russell, 1985; Kaslow & Gurman, 1985; Ryder, 1987).

Most of this recent crop of writers about family-therapy ethics agree that there are many similarities between the ethics of therapy practice and the ethics of research. Responsibility for the well-being of family members and the family unit, confidentiality, and informed consent are core issues in both everyday clinical practice and family-therapy research. Interestingly, deception has not arisen as a major ethical concern in family-therapy research, probably because deception has not been a common feature there.

While the similarities with therapy ethics have been emphasized, a number of authors have highlighted several unique ethical challenges associated with family-therapy research. We will address these under the headings of informed consent, confidentiality, and potential risks and benefits. Following the discussion of these three commonly considered issues in family-therapy ethics, we will briefly describe some issues not so commonly considered.

Informed Consent in Family-Therapy Research

Heathingerton et al. (1989) summarize the limitations of ethical codes for traditional psychotherapy research in guiding family-therapy researchers in the area of informed consent. To begin with, when a researcher approaches a family to explain a study and to solicit participation, the family—especially a treatment family—is given an emotionally charged decision to make in a short time. Heatherington et al. give examples from their own research in which family members struggle over the question of whether anyone has something to "hide" by refusing to participate. Thus, even approaching a family to

explain a study is tantamount to an intervention in the family system. For this reason, Heatherington et al. recommend that families in treatment be approached first by their therapist, who can explain the study and learn whether the family members want to talk to the researcher. Of course, if the therapist has a major investment in the research, such an invitation can be potentially coercive. If the therapist is a participant in the study, the possible conflict of interest between the clinical role and the research role must be considered.

Once the researcher contacts the family, adequate informed consent procedures as established by the *Belmont Report* of the Department of Health and Human Services (DHHS, 1979) required three elements: information, comprehension, and voluntariness. Information appears more straightforward in principle than in practice. A central issue in research with families is that the researcher cannot fully explain what information might be revealed about family members. In research with individual subjects, the subject can be informed about the questions to be asked and, therefore, the aspects of self that will be revealed. In research conducted with interacting family members, the researcher cannot fully predict what family members may reveal about one another. For example, in a procedure calling for a discussion about mealtime activity, a family member might bring up a shameful episode of violence that occurred during a family meal. The group nature of family-interaction research makes full information about disclosures impossible to give in advance (Heatherington et al., 1989; Jurich & Russell, 1985; Kaslow & Gurman, 1985).

A practical ethical issue for many family-therapy researchers is how much to reveal as to why the family was recruited and why the therapist is doing the research procedure. Federal informed-consent guidelines require disclosure of both factors, but researchers may be afraid that subjects will not consent to be studied. For example, some researchers are tempted to state that their study is one of "parenting styles," with no reference to the fact that they are studying parenting styles in incest families and that the family has been recruited because of its history of incest. A professional and bureaucratic consensus has emerged that families have the right to know why they were selected and what the researcher is interested in finding out (DHHS, 1981). Although researchers fear that troubled families will not participate if fully informed, explaining the benefits of the research is often sufficient to encourage them to do so.

Comprehension is the second ingredient of informed consent. Here, family-therapy researchers have a unique challenge, since the family may consist of individuals of diverse ages with diverse life experiences, levels of intellectual ability, and mental conditions. Heatherington et al. (1989) embrace Margolin's (1982) recommendation for therapy, namely, that the research procedures be explained in different words to children and to adults, with follow-up questions to ensure that each family member understands. Except in advanced stages of illness, we believe that even mentally compromised family members, such as Alzheimer's patients, can be told what is happening and why. In addition, informed-consent documents must be written in everyday language without technical jargon.

Voluntariness is the third ingredient of informed consent. It means that there is no coercion, that subjects can withdraw without penalty, and that the subject's decision to participate will not affect access to services (DHHS, 1979). Kaslow and Gurman (1985) describe how researchers can present the option to participate in research in an intimidating way: "Families frequently report concern that if they refuse to participate, their treatment will be less adequate because of subtle changes in the behavior of the treatment team" (p. 52). This issue of subtle coercion is particularly difficult when the therapist is the researcher or has volunteered to be a therapist-subject in the research. The roles of therapist and researcher should be kept as separate as possible, with the therapist's first duty to be to the welfare of the client should a conflict between the roles arise.

In addition to dangers of coercion from the therapist, there is also the danger of coercion of individuals by other family members. We agree with the point made by Heatherington et al. (1989) that differential power and status among family members may compromise the voluntariness of certain members' choices to participate in research. The authors suggest that researchers make it a point to ask each family member for a decision. Although legally children do not have to give consent, Heatherington et al. (1989) strongly recommend that they be asked to "assent" to the procedures, and that researchers be reluctant to proceed without that assent. At the same time, these authors point out that indirect coercion is a dynamic in many families, and that it is not the responsibility of the researcher to protect family members from the subtle pressures that may characterize all family decisions. "The experimenters, however, should [assure] a reluctant family member that participation is voluntary and that it is fine to decline" (Heatherington et al., 1989, p. 380). In the second author's research experience with demented family members, consent is based on the same logic except when someone is in danger; then we view protection of a family member as the responsibility of the researcher and we refer the family members out to get help, even if that means losing them as subjects.

In general, the ethical mandate for free and well-informed consent for family-therapy research is even stronger than for therapy itself, since research is, by definition, designed more to meet the purposes of the researchers than those of the families. In our experience on human-subjects committees, investigators often must be pushed and prodded into giving subjects full disclosure of why they were chosen for the study, what the study is about, and what they can expect as research subjects.

Confidentiality in Family-Therapy Research

The issue of revealing family secrets surfaces in family research as well as in family therapy. In survey research, the problem is lessened by interviewing family members separately, with results not shared with other family members. The more serious problem with confidentiality arises when family members are studied in the same room at the same time and their answers are verbal rather than written. As mentioned before, this kind of research constitutes an intervention into a family system. Asking family members to discuss something they may never have discussed before opens the door to revelations that may surprise or shock other family members (Jurich & Russell, 1985; Kaslow & Gurman, 1985). Because the researcher has little control over spontaneous revelations by family members, it is necessary to include a warning about this possibility in the informed-consent procedures.

Another important confidentiality issue in family-therapy research concerns researchers' responsibility to report abuse that is revealed during the research process. Kaslow and Gurman (1985) affirm the requirement that the researcher inform the family in advance of potential legal limitations to confidentiality. They also refer to the more subtle confidentiality issues that surface when parents ask for access to research data on their children, when therapists request access to research data on clients, or when the researchers want to inform the therapist about the compromised well-being of a client. We strongly concur with Kaslow and Gurman's (1985) prescription for family-therapy researchers: "However the researcher chooses to handle the issue of confidentiality, it is incumbent on him or her to clearly convey that policy to the family. If there is to be an exception to the predetermined rules of confidentiality, everyone involved needs to be informed" (p. 51).

Risks and Benefits to Families

Because family-therapy research is designed more fundamentally to generate new knowledge rather than to help the families in the study, it carries a special burden of demonstrating that risks are minimized and that the potential benefits of the study are sufficient to justify what risks remain. A number of the risks of family-therapy research have been described in previous sections on informed consent and confidentiality, especially the ambiguity of what might be revealed and the unforeseeable emotional reactions family members might have to observational procedures.

The risks and benefits of family-therapy research no doubt differ across different types of study design. Simple questionnaire studies probably carry low risk if the data are kept confidential, but direct benefits to the research families are minimal. Observational research without an intervention component (e.g., where families are asked to discuss a topic or play a game) probably carry a somewhat greater risk of emotional discomfort and unintended disclosure, but some families may stand to benefit more from seeing themselves in action. Treatment research with experimental and control groups carries the greatest risks to and greatest benefits for the families involved. Risks of this kind of study include the possibility of deterioration while in a no-treatment group or a placebo control group.

As Jurich and Russell (1985) point out, families in treatment studies are assigned to treatments according to the needs of the study protocol rather than according to a therapist's judgment about which treatment or therapist might best fit the families' needs. Furthermore, they are likely to be involved in a more structured therapeutic experience (for the sake of the study protocol) than if they saw a therapist who was free to adapt his or her approach throughout the treatment. Finally, the research treatment might focus narrowly on a particular subsystem of the family (like the couple) and not attend to problems with other family members. Few research protocols give the therapist leeway to see different combinations of three-generational families at will. We agree with Jurich and Russell (1985) that the therapist's first mandate is to provide the best possible therapy for the client, while the researcher's first mandate is to demonstrate which treatment is most effective for a variety of clients. However, we believe that there are also similarities between the stances of therapists and those of researchers: both test hypotheses/clinical hunches and both must be accountable for the well-being of the families with whom they work even if this means losing them as clients or research subjects. The goal in family research is to, at least, do no harm.

Within this overall mandate to protect the well-being of the families in the study, the treatment researcher must develop specific plans and procedures rather than rely on good intentions. Gurman and Kniskern (1981) and Kaslow and Gurman (1985) discuss some of these procedures, such as: identifying the deterioration of families in any of the study groups and removing them from the study if they agree, and creating treatment-on-demand control groups in which families can request short-term help to get them over a rough spot while they are awaiting treatment. The second author used this approach in a study of families of Alzheimer's patients, and found that three of the 70 families did request treatment earlier than the study protocol called for. Kaslow and Gurman (1985) also point out that different kinds of study designs—say, with a placebo control group—are more ethically acceptable in formal research settings in which families volunteer in answer to newspaper advertisements than in community settings in which families contact their mental health center for treatment rather than to participate in a research study.

The three issues covered in this section on research—informed consent, confidentiality, and benefits versus risks—are the ones most generally discussed in the research ethics area. Three more subtle issues have been discussed by Boss (1987). First is the issue of interviewers' emotional reactions and attachments to subjects in qualitative family research, which can lead interviewers to experience anger, fear, or depression (LaRossa et al., 1981). Mishandled emotional reactions not only impede the research process, but may create risks for the family. Boss suggests that family-research interviewers work in teams of two in order to maintain a balance between caring too much and caring too little about the family. For example, an interviewer and a video-camera operator, both trained in clinical sensitivity as well as in research procedures, can provide important support to each other while doing sensitive in-home family research.

The second issue discussed by Boss (1987) is that of mutual benefit for the research interviewer and the subject interviewed. She challenges the traditional assumptions that interview research does not benefit both parties. Qualitative research with families that have suffered disasters has convinced many researchers that the interview process helps many family members to sort out their feelings, to feel more normal, and to have a sense of contributing to the welfare of others. Interviewers likewise often experience a sense of enrichment in being allowed to enter the lives of distressed families. Boss believes this mutuality is akin to how Whitaker and Keith (1981) describe how both therapist and family gain in family therapy.

The third neglected area of research ethics that Boss (1987) raises is that of the ethics of "discovery." She questions the assumption held by many researchers that only traditional empirical methods of research lead to new knowledge about families. She concludes:

> By so narrowing the definition of research discovery, we may be less than ethical in our responsibilities to the families with which we work. We are not listening to them or to our responses to them if we restrict ourselves to only one method of discovering *their* reality. If we are to work with them as researchers, we must not deceive ourselves that, by following the scientific method, we will know and represent their truth through the "hard data" we gathered from them. What we have measured may be only a partial truth. To be concerned with listening to, watching, and "feeling out" families may be just as important as operationalizing, quantifying, randomizing, and testing, especially in these early stages of discovery about stressed families. (p. 155)

Not all researchers will agree. For some, science and the discovery of new knowledge remains restricted to the scientific method with the belief that objectivity is attainable. Whatever the belief, research ethics and therapy ethics are intertwined and inseparable. Both involve a meeting between professionals and families, out of which, everyone hopes, greater knowledge and improved health will arise. The more researchers are involved in an in-depth way with research subjects—as in treatment research and qualitative interview research—the more the line between research and therapy becomes blurred and the more a finely tuned ethical sensibility is essential. This has important implications for the training of family researchers, who, we believe, must have enough sensitivity to clinical issues to be able to provide support to family members in immediate distress and to recognize which families require immediate referral to qualified professionals. The safety of family members must come before the perfection of a data set.

GENDER AND ETHICS IN FAMILY THERAPY

Earlier in this chapter, we described the origins of the feminist critique of family therapy. What has made this critique so powerful is that it is fundamentally an ethical critique as well as a theoretical and pragmatic one. More than other contemporary movements in family therapy, such as challenges to incorporate individual psychological issues and larger systems issues or more refined epistemological premises into the field, feminism in family therapy has raised questions about fairness and unfairness, justice and injustice, acceptance and prejudice. Feminists have criticized not only the stereotypical views of men and women held by family therapists, but also the moral underpinnings of the practice of family therapy itself.

In this section, we draw on the feminist literature in family therapy to describe a contemporary ethical position on gender ethics in family therapy. Prominent sources of our thinking have been Hare-Mustin (1986); Goldner (1987, 1988); Walters, Carter, Papp, and Silverstein (1989); Margolin (1982); Luepnitz (1988); Goodrich, Rampage, Ellman, and Halstead (1988); and Thorne (1982); Boss & Thorne, 1988).

In 1982, Margolin wrote that marriage and family therapists are most likely to perpetuate the following myths about gender roles and women's lives: a) maintenance of a marriage is usually best for a woman; b) a woman's career deserves less interest or sensitivity from the therapist than a man's career; c) child-rearing issues and children's problems are solely the mother's responsibility; d) the interpretation of extramarital affairs is subject to a double standard, based on gender; and e) a husband's needs are more significant than a wife's needs (Margolin, 1982).

Such myths about gender roles are easily maintained by therapists because they were embedded in our training. For example, traditional assumptions about women's development center on women as nurturers, thus excluding men from such experience. Boss and Weiner (1988) challenge the myths that only females can nurture and they must nurture to be normal, that women are less capable than men and thus men have to take care of them, that women should meet men's sexual needs but not reveal their own, that women are totally responsible for parenting and that women's roles are highly differentiated from men's roles—males must be instrumental, females must be expressive.

We continue the challenge to such outdated assumptions. Toward this end, we offer recommendations to stimulate thinking and discussion, following existing guidelines of the Ethi-

cal Principles for Family Therapist (American Association for Marital and Family Therapy (AAMFT) (1988), and the "guidelines for Therapy With Women" (American Psychological Association (APA) (1978). The AAMFT guidelines for ethics in therapy are stated first, followed by APA guidelines and finally our recommendations with the goal that they provide stimulation for debate.

I. Responsibility to Clients

A. "Marriage and family therapists are dedicated to advancing the welfare of families and individuals, including respecting the rights of those persons seeking their assistance, and making reasonable efforts to ensure that their services are used appropriately" (AAMFT, 1988, p. 1).

"The conduct of therapy should be free of constrictions based on gender-defined roles, and the options explored between client and practitioner should be free of sex-role stereotypes" (APA, 1978, p. 1122).

Our responsibility is to the client's welfare. Too often the welfare of the family is set above the welfare of the individuals within it, especially the woman's, since the family is more traditionally seen as her domain, with family welfare therefore identical with her own. "Exploration of roles should include an evaluation of marriage by the husband and wife as equal partners. Options for role flexibility (work, child care, sexuality, housekeeping) must be examined for biased assumptions that men are only instrumental and achieving and women are only expressive and dependent" (Weiner & Boss, 1985, p. 17).

On this basis, our ethical responsibility as family therapists is to:

1. Advance the welfare of individuals as well as the unit.
2. Make therapeutic decisions on the basis of what is life-enhancing rather than life-threatening for the individual within the family unit.
3. Support change rather than the status quo in abusive or life-threatening situations.
4. Be sensitive to individual as well as collective

perceptions, values, and belief systems within the parameters of what is life-enhancing rather than life-threatening to individuals within that system.

B. "Psychologists should recognize the reality, variety, and implications of sex-discriminatory practices in society and should facilitate client examination of options in dealing with such practices" (APA, 1978, p. 1122).

In a contextual perspective, politics sometimes cannot be separated from therapeutic issues. Discrimination against women is prevalent in housing, jobs, access to educational loans, pensions, and credit. Responsible therapists see couples and families in the context of their daily lives and are open to seeing contextual impediments (e.g., discrimination in employment) faced by women.

C. "The psychologist should demonstrate acceptance of women as equal to men by using language free of derogatory labels" (APA, 1978, p. 1122).

While psychologists, sociologists, and psychiatrists have in the past prescribed the role of family nurturer for a "normal" woman, at the same time, they labeled her pejoratively for this behavior. Clinical labels such as masochistic woman, schizophregenic mother, castrating female, engulfing mother, nagging wife, seductive woman, and penis envy are outdated and misogynist.

D. "The psychologist should avoid establishing the source of personal problems within the client when they are more properly attributable to situational or cultural factors" (APA, 1978, p. 1123).

Problems that therapists see in the interaction between family members may involve more than relational issues. Context matters. As Wiener and Boss (1985) have written: "The wife who is expected to run the home, rear the children, and provide consistent support for her husband as well as work for pay or as a volunteer outside the home may be mentally healthy but, because of her situation, is being asked to do the impossible. Depression in such a woman may be viewed as much as a response to unreasonable demands on her energy and resources as to a disorder of a psychogenic nature. Although both husband and wife may benefit from consciousness raising about situational or cultural demands on their time and energy, the wife is especially vulnerable since she is more likely to continue the 'supermom' role even when she is employed outside the home (p. 18)."

E. "The psychologist should recognize and encourage exploration of a woman client's sexuality and should recognize her right to define her own sexual preferences" (APA, 1978, p. 1123).

The residue of a double standard regarding sexual behavior for men versus women remains today. Family therapists of both genders must update themselves on the sexual needs of both genders and eliminate dichotomous thinking about women as either good women (asexual except for procreation) or bad (sexual beyond procreation). They must also eliminate the stereotype of the "healthy American male" as always sexual. For example, therapists often view extramarital affairs by the husband as more understandable than if the wife has an affair. Or, they are less likely to accept women who present bisexual or homosexual issues. Or, they take less seriously wives who complain of too little sex than husbands who complain of the same. Our ethical responsibility, regardless of our value stance, is to update ourselves about male and female sexuality and to be honest with our clients if our own personal values do not permit us to support their therapy. In this case, our ethical responsibility is to help them to find another therapist whose values more closely match their own. For a family therapist, this may mean calling in a consultant, referring a spouse out for individual therapy to supplement marital therapy, or seeking another family therapist who is more adept at addressing gender issues with both spouses present.

II. Competence

A. "Marriage and family therapists are dedicated to maintaining high standards of competence and services and using consultation from other professionals" (AAMFT, 1988, p. 3).

Competence means "having capacity equal to requirement," or, in other words, the legal capacity, qualifications, power, jurisdiction, or fitness to do therapy. We are not as concerned about the legal qualifications and jurisdictions as we are about the therapist's emotional power and fitness to do therapy. Indeed, issues of therapist emotional reactivity and projection are relevant for practicing ethically in the area of gender issues. The gender debate in family therapy has provoked so much emotional reactivity precisely because of its potential for projection and distortion. A therapist may be highly educated and trained and still be incompetent if moments of emotional overinvolvement or projection are not recognized when dealing with issues of fairness with all family members. Competent therapists should ask for help if they recognize slippage. Much therapist distortion has hidden comfortably behind gender stereotypes in the past, but a competent therapist must seek consultation when experiencing negative reactions to women (or men) in families.

B. "If authoritarian processes are employed as a technique, the therapy should not have the effect of maintaining or reinforcing stereotypic dependency of women" (APA, 1978, p. 1123).

According to Weiner and Boss (1985), "Any strategy that potentially disenfranchises a woman's status or power should be used with caution because of her prior socialization for dependency, inferiority, and subordination, and because of the broader social history that has made women particularly vulnerable to disempowerment" (p. 19). We believe the ethical goal of therapy is to empower rather than to make someone more dependent. While strategies of "one-upsmanship" may be useful with clients who are accustomed to being in charge, they are not useful with clients who are in subordinate positions in the outside world—most often, females. For example, therapists must examine their differential attitudes toward mothers who say they are too busy to keep a family therapy appointment versus fathers who say the same.

Often, the mother is labeled resistant and the father as simply, busy.

C. "The client's assertive behaviors should be respected" (APA, 1978, p. 1123).

As therapy progresses, a victimized woman's efforts to rebel should be viewed as healthy growth and should be nurtured. Her assertiveness in wanting to question the course of therapy or challenge the therapist's tardiness, for example, should be viewed as progress. It may be the first time she has asserted herself or set protective boundaries for herself.

III. Integrity

A. "Marriage and family therapists are dedicated to maintaining high standards of professional competence and integrity" (AAMFT, 1988, p. 3).

"The psychologist and a fully informed client should mutually agree upon aspects of the therapy relationship such as treatment modality, time factors, and fee arrangements" (APA, 1978, p. 1123).

What does integrity mean for the family therapist? It means being honest about therapy goals, therapist values, fees, appointment times, methods, and who is to be involved in the therapy. As discussed earlier in this chapter, truthfulness has a place of preeminence in therapy, exceptions to which must be carefully justified. This seems especially important in cases where women have been deceived and overpowered in the past. Manipulation does not promote empowerment.

In marital therapy, husband and wife should have equal input into any discussion about counseling goals, fees, appointment times, and who is to be involved. Too often, clinicians defer to the husband as the "head of the family" in such matters, even when the wife has instigated the therapeutic contact.

B. ". . . Sexual intimacy with clients is prohibited" (AAMFT, 1988, p. 5).

"The psychologist should not have sexual relations with a woman client or treat her as a sex object" (APA, 1978, p. 1123).

Above all, integrity means we are to be honest with ourselves about whom the therapy is benefitting; having sex with a client benefits only a needy therapist. Our existing codes of ethics make that answer clear. Because of the double power differential (between therapist and client and between a man and woman), therapist responsibility is magnified here, even if the client is seductive or consenting. This power differential varies with the gender and age of the therapist and client, but there is always a power differential between the two that puts full responsibility for prevention of sexual intimacy on the shoulders of the professional.

IV. Professional Development

A. "Marriage and family therapists remain abreast of new developments in family therapy knowledge through both educational activities and clinical experiences" (AAMFT, 1988, p. 4).

The therapist should be knowledgeable about current empirical findings on sex roles, sexism, and individual differences resulting from the client's gender-defined identity (APA, 1978, p. 1122).

All family therapists must take responsibility to update their knowledge base regarding gender (see Boss & Weiner, 1988). Proceeding without this new scientific knowledge is analogous to a surgeon's operating using outdated techniques. Professional competence must also include familiarity with published research and intervention strategies that address incest and other forms of victimization. Based on knowledge of this literature, therapists must routinely ask clients about incest, family sexual abuse, and rape experiences or other traumatizing experiences, such as in war. According to Weiner and Boss (1985), claims that such inquiries are too threatening to the client or the therapy process reflect the therapist's own resistance more than the client's. As part of professional development, family therapists must face their own abhorrence of family sexual pathology or war-time torture by increasing their knowledge and actively exploring their own fears and attitudes.

B. "The theoretical concepts employed by the therapist should be free of sex bias and sex-role stereotypes" (APA, 1978, p. 1122).

Theoretical assumptions underlying clinical practice and training should be regularly and rigorously discussed in public settings. Therapists working alone particularly need a peer consultation group where cases can be discussed and assumptions clarified and updated. Theories do not remain static; to avoid stereotyping and bias, therapists must participate in professional discussion about current changes in knowledge and beliefs about human diversity.

V. Social and Legal Responsibilities

A. "Marriage and family therapists recognize a responsibility to participate in activities that contribute to a better community and society, including devoting a portion of their professional activity to services for which there is little or no financial return" (AAMFT, 1988, p. 6).
"The psychologist whose female client is subjected to violence in the form of physical abuse or rape should recognize and acknowledge that the client is the victim of a *crime*" (APA, 1978, p. 1123).

A family therapist has a social responsibility to give something back to the community in which she or he works. Service might include sliding fee therapy or training, but involvement in political endeavors that would improve the community context may be even more important.
Legal responsibilities for family therapists to report abuse vary from state to state but, when abuse exists, it is both a moral and legal responsibility to protect the safety of family members at risk. Finding a safe haven for the abused and their children is a higher responsibility than beginning family therapy in the usual sense. The statistics regarding physical abuse of women and children in this country reflect a society that still has not given a clear message that it is unacceptable to hit women and children. Certainly, family therapists need to be explicitly clear to their clients and communities in this message.

A Note About Power, Gender, and Ethics

Underlying much of the prior discussion about gender and ethics in family therapy is the issue of power differential between men and women created by the larger social context. The therapist can examine this power differential in the family by asking the following questions: Who has the ability and resources to change if he or she wants to? Who has greater job skills and employment opportunities? Who has more access to financial resources—now, and if the couple divorces? Who carries greater care-giving responsibility for dependent children and elderly family members, and thus feels less able to leave the relationship? Who has the social license to exercise his or her wishes and to activate his or her resources? Generally, women in families fall on the less powerful side of each question.

An implication of this power differential can be shown in how the therapist perceives the appearance of passivity and overaccommodation in a woman. For a woman who experiences very limited access to economic self-survival, what appears to be an excessive degree of psychological passivity might represent a natural accommodation to a relatively dependent and powerless life situation. Since money and power are so equated in Western culture, the therapist might be best advised to assist this woman toward economic survivability, rather than focusing only on the interactional or intrapsychic dimensions of her situation. The power differential in society between men and women creates an ethical imperative for the family therapist to move beyond the traditional family-systems assumption of bilateral balance and equity between men and women in families.

A high percentage of people who come for therapy are women, but much of the theory in developmental psychology, counseling and family therapy has been biased against women. It is hoped therapists today will see it as an ethical responsibility to update their knowledge base and challenge their own biases. Without self-study and continuing education, therapists will repeat the prejudices of their trainers, thus perpetuating a context in which neither women or men will thrive (Boss & Weiner, 1988).

This discussion has used professional guidelines to focus specifically on ethical issues concerning women's issues in families. Perhaps it is not surprising that the APA's guidelines concerning women in therapy are better developed than those of the AAMFT. The analysis of gender, after all, is a more recent development in family therapy, as indicated by the fact that the APA guidelines were published the same year (1978) that the first feminist critiques began to be published in family therapy. The family field spent the 1980s catching up with the rest of psychology in the gender area. As the 1990s began, there was gratifying evidence that increasing numbers of men in family therapy were addressing men's issues in society, in the family, and in therapy (Meth & Pasick, 1990; Napier, 1991; Pittman, 1991).

FUTURE DIRECTIONS

We are encouraged about the new vigor of discussion and debate concerning values and ethics in family therapy. The literature is moving in a number of useful directions simultaneously. First is the more elaborate discussion of the ethics of specific dilemmas in family therapy, such as family violence (Willbach, 1989), and the use of the revised third edition of the DSM-III-R by systematically oriented therapists (Denton, 1989). Second is the application of ethical theories (Bailey, 1989) and ethical decision-making models (Zygmond & Borhem, 1989) to family-therapy ethics. Bailey's dissertation breaks new ground in examining the relevance for family-therapy ethics of two philosophical traditions: the relational ethics tradition of Martin Buber, and recently of feminist philosopher Noddings (1984), and the Aristotelian tradition recently explicated by MacIntyre (1984). Woody (1990) describes different implications of utilitarianism and contract theory for family therapy ethics, and distinguishes ethical theories from professional codes of ethics, professional theoretical premises, sociolegal context, and the therapist's personal and professional identity.

The third promising trend is the empirical study of family-therapy ethics in the form of surveys of therapists about the ethical dilemmas they face (Green & Hansen, 1986, 1989). Fourth is the development of curricula in family-therapy ethics (Piercy & Sprenkle, 1983). Fifth is the translation of the feminist critique into the form of case illustrations describing ethical decisions that therapists face in everyday practice (Goodrich, Rampage, C. Ellman, & Halstead, 1988), and into nuanced discussions of the clinical and ethical dimensions of gender and violence (Goldner, Penn, Sheinberg & Walker, 1990).

A major issue confronting the field of family-therapy ethics in the 1990s is the development of an ethical stance that is informed by systemic thinking yet does not vitiate centuries of tradition upholding individual rights and responsibilities, a tradition that only recently has begun extending rights to women. To accomplish this task, family-therapy ethicists might profitably place systems theory in dialogue with ethical traditions in philosophy that attempt to deal with individual and relationship dimensions of human life. To the extent that family therapy's philosophical paradigm has an ethical dimension, it has implications for everyone—for women, men, and children, for all races and ages and ethnic groups—not just for systemically sophisticated therapists in the privacy of our offices.

In the next decade, we should continue to hold our "in-house" debates about ethics, and certainly the issues discussed in this chapter should be part of student training and continuing education for professionals. But there should be new elements in the professional dialogue. One new element should involve a diversity of perspectives from both genders, from different racial groups, from ethnic minorities, from therapists of different ages, and especially from those groups whose voices have not been heard often enough in the ethics dialogue. The area of ethics and values is too important to leave to a handful of scholars who write articles and books on the subject. The discussion of critical issues must be joined by a pluralistic therapeutic community.

Another new focus to be explored is the growing literature on applied professional ethics, particularly work in the field of biomedical ethics. For example, the influential writings of Beauchamp and Childress (1979) have led to sophisticated analyses of ethical dilemmas in medicine according to the interplay of five principles: autonomy, beneficence, nonmaleficence, justice, and fidelity. Another example is the work of Pellegrino and Thomasma (1988), who have formulated a new theoretical basis for medical ethics, replacing the traditional emphasis on autonomy and paternalism with a model of beneficence-in-trust. Underlying some interesting new approaches to applied ethics are the writings of Alasdair MacIntrye (1984, 1986), a moral philosopher of considerable talent as a social critic, and Nel Noddings (1984), a feminist philosopher who has formulated an ethic of caring in contrast to an ethic based on abstract principles. These ethicists offer a rich grounding on which family therapists can develop more sophisticated approaches to ethics and values in the next decade.

Rather than confining discussions of ethics and values to the margins of family therapy, we would like to see them become assimilated into the central dialogue about our theories and practices as family therapists. The temptation has been to bring up ethics and values only in special cases when therapists are conscious of making specific ethical choices, or when they want to express personal disapproval of techniques with which they disagree. We have maintained in this chapter that values and ethics underlie everything we do in family therapy—theory, research, and practice. Now that these issues are more public in the field, their future development depends on our ability to maintain an open, thoughtful, and respectful dialogue, without resorting either to mindless relativism ("I do my thing, and you do your thing") or to mindless legalism ("Tell me how to avoid breaking the rules and getting sued").

This dialogue cannot be limited to professional concerns alone, because the issues we face as family therapists go to the heart of the human condition. For this reason, we must not only talk with one another, but also learn to engage with ethical traditions from philosophy and religion, to access the deep veins of human wisdom found in art and literature, and to participate actively in the broader social debate about human welfare and family life in our times.

ACKNOWLEDGMENTS

We thank John Bailey, Judith Grunebaum, Henry Grunebaum, Rachel Hare-Mustin, Marilyn Mason, Roger Knudson, and J. Pamela Weiner for reviewing preliminary drafts of this chapter.

REFERENCES

American Association for Marriage and Family Therapy. (1982, revised 1988). *AAMFT code of ethical principles for marriage and family therapists*. Washington, DC: AAMFT.

Adler, A. (1928). *Understanding human nature*. Atlantic Highlands, NJ: Humanities Press.

American Psychological Association. (1978). Guidelines for therapy with women. *American Psychologist, 30,* 1122–1123.

Aponte, H.J. (1985). The negotiation of values in therapy. *Family Process, 24,* 323–338.

Bailey, J.R. (1989). *Analysis of family therapy ethics*. Unpublished doctoral dissertation, University of Minnesota.

Beauchamp, T., & Childress, J. (1979). *Principles of biomedical ethics*. New York: Oxford University Press.

Bellah, R.N., Madsen, R., Sullivan, W.M., Swidler, A., & Tipton, M. (1985). *Habits of the heart: Individualism and commitment in American life*. New York: Harper & Row.

Bernal, G., & Ysern, E. (1986). Family therapy and ideology. *Journal of Marital and Family Therapy, 12,* 129–135.

Bernstein, B.E. (1982). Ignorance of the law is no excuse. In L. L'Abate (Ed.), *Values, ethics, legalities and the family therapist*. Rockville, MD: Aspen Systems.

Bodin, A.M. (1981). The interactional view: Family therapy approaches of the Mental Research Institute. In A.S. Gurman & D.P. Kniskern (Eds.), *Handbook of family therapy*. New York: Brunner/Mazel.

Bok, S. (1978). *Lying: Moral choice in public and private life*. New York: Vintage Books.

Boss, P.G. (1987, Spring/Summer). The role of intuition in family research: Three issues of ethics. In R. Garfield, A. Greenberg, & S. Sugarman (Eds.), Symbolic-experiential journeys: A tribute to Carl Whitaker (special issue). *Contemporary Family Therapy, 9,* 146–158.

Boss, P.G. (1988). *Family stress management*. Newbury Park, CA: Sage.

Boss, P.G., & Thorne, B. (1988). Family sociology and family therapy: A feminist linkage. In M. McGoldrick, F. Walsh, & C. Anderson (Eds.), *Women in families: A framework for family therapy*. New York: Norton.

Boss, P.G., & Weiner, J.P. (1988). Rethinking assumptions about women's development and family therapy. In C. Falicov (Ed.), *Family transitions*. New York: Guilford Press.

Boszormenyi-Nagy, I. (1985). Commentary: Transgenerational solidarity—therapy's mandate and ethics. *Family Process, 24,* 454–456.

Boszormenyi-Nagy, I., & Krasner, B.R. (1986). *Between give and take: A clinical guide to contextual therapy*. New York: Brunner/Mazel.

Boszormenyi-Nagy, I., & Spark, M. (1973). *Invisible loyalties: Reciprocity in intergenerational family therapy*. New York: Harper & Row.

Bray, J.H., Shepherd, J.N., & Hays, J.R. (1985). Legal and ethical issues in informed consent to psychotherapy. *American Journal of Family Therapy, 13,* 50–60.

Brown, J.E., & Slee, P.T. (1986). Paradoxical strategies: The ethics of intervention. *Professional Psychology: Research and Practice, 17,* 487–491.

Christianson, C.E. (1985). Ethical issues in family-centered primary care. *Counseling and Values, 30,* 62–73.

Collier, A. (1987). The language of objectivity and the ethics of reframing. In S. Walrond-Skinner & D. Watson (Eds.), *Ethical issues in family therapy*. New York: Routledge & Kegan Paul.

Coyne, J. (1989). Change the channel. *Family Therapy Networker, 13,* 40–41.

Denton, W.H. (1989). DSM-III-R and the family therapist: Ethical considerations. *Journal of Marital and Family Therapy, 15,* 367–377.

Department of Health and Human Services (1979). *The Belmont report: Ethical principles and guidelines for the protection of human subjects*. (DHEW Publication No. 1983, 381-132, 3205). Washington, DC: U.S. Government Printing Office.

Department of Health and Human Services. (1981). Final regulations amending basic HHS policy for the protection of human research subjects. *Federal Register, 46,* 8366–8392.

Doherty, W.J. (1985). Values and ethics in family therapy. *Counseling and Values* (Special Issue), *30,* 1.

Doherty, W.J. (1985). Values and ethics in family therapy: Overview. *Counseling and Values, 30,* 3–8.

Doherty, W.J. (1989). Unmasking family therapy. *Family Therapy Networker, 13,* 35–39.

Drane, J.F. (1982). Ethics and psychotherapy: A philosophical perspective. In M. Rosenbaum (Ed.), *Ethics and values in psychotherapy: A guidebook*. New York: Free Press.

Erickson, G.D. (1984a). A framework and themes for social network interventions. *Family Process, 23,* 187–197.

Erickson, G.D. (1984b). A menu note on the cybernetic network. *Family Process, 23,* 200–204.

Fisher, L., Anderson, A., & Jones, J.E. (1981). Types of paradoxical intervention and indications/contraindications for use in clinical practice. *Family Process, 20,* 25–35.

Frankl, V.E. (1975). Paradoxical intention and dereflection: Two logotherapeutic techniques. In S. Arietz & G. Chrzamowski (Eds.), *New dimensions in psychiatry: A world view*. New York: Wiley.

Fraser, J.S. (1984). Paradox and orthodox: Folie à deux? *Journal of Marital and Family Therapy, 10,* 361–372.

Freymann, J.G. (1974). *The American health care system: Its genesis and trajectory*. New York: Medcom.

Gardner, W., Scherer, D., & Tester, M. (1989). Asserting scientific authority: Cognitive development and adolescent legal rights. *American Psychologist, 44,* 895–902.

Goldner, V. (1987). Instrumentalism, feminism, and the limits of family therapy. *Journal of Family Psychology, 1,* 109–116.

Goldner, V. (1988). Generation and gender: Normative and covert hierarchies. *Family Process, 27,* 17–31.

Goldner, V., Penn, P., Sheinberg, M., & Walker, G. (1990). Love and violence: Gender paradoxes in volatile attachments. *Family Process, 29,* 343–364.

Goodrich, T.J., Rampage, C., Ellman, B., & Halstead, K. (1988). *Feminist family therapy: A casebook*. New York: Norton.

Green, S.L., & Hansen, J.C. (1986). Ethical dilemmas in family therapy. *Journal of Marital and Family Therapy, 12,* 225–230.

Green, S.L., & Hansen, J.C. (1989). Ethical dilemmas faced by family therapists. *Journal of Marital and Family Therapy, 15,* 149–158.

Grosser, G.H., and Paul, N.L. (1964). Ethical issues in family group therapy. *American Journal of Orthopsychiatry, 34,* 875–884.

Grunebaum, J. (1987). Multidirected partiality and the "parental imperative." *Psychotherapy, 24,* 646–656.

Gurman, A.S., & Kniskern, D.P. (1978). Deterioration in marital and family therapy: Empirical, clinical and conceptual issues. *Family Process, 17,* 3–20.

Gurman, A.S., & Kniskern, D.P. (1981). Family therapy outcome research: Knowns and unknowns. In A.S. Gurman & D.P. Kniskern (Eds.), *Handbook of family therapy*. New York: Brunner/Mazel.

Haley, J. (1976). *Problem-solving therapy*. New York: Harper & Row.

Hare-Mustin, R.T. (1978). A feminist approach to family therapy. *Family Process, 17,* 181–194.

Hare-Mustin, R.T. (1980). Family therapy may be dangerous for your health. *Professional Psychology, 11,* 935–938.

Hare-Mustin, R.T. (1986). The problem of gender in family therapy theory. *Family Process, 26,* 15–27.

Hare-Mustin, R.T., & Maracek, J. (1986). Autonomy and gender: Some questions for therapists. *Psychotherapy, 23,* 205–212.

Hare-Mustin, R.T., Marecek, J., Kaplan, A.G., & Liss-Levinson, N. (1979). Rights of clients, responsibilities of therapists. *American Psychologist, 34,* 3–16.

Heatherington, L., Friedlander, M.L., & Johnson, W.F. (1989). Informed consent in family therapy research: Ethical dilemmas and practical problem. *Journal of Family Psychology, 2,* 373–385.

Hines, P.M., & Hare-Mustin, R.T. (1978). Ethical concerns in family therapy. *Professional Psychology, 9,* 165–171.

Huber, C.H., & Baruth, L.G. (1987). *Ethical, legal, and professional issues in the practice of marriage and family therapy.* Columbus, OH: Merrill.

Jacobson, N.S. (1983). Beyond empiricism: The politics of marital therapy. *American Journal of Family Therapy, 11,* 11–24.

Jurich, A.P., & Russell, C.S. (1985). The conflict between the ethics of therapy and outcome research in family therapy. In L.L. Andreozzi (Ed.), *Integrating research and clinical practice.* Rockville, MD: Aspen Systems.

Karpel, M.A. (1980). Family secrets. *Family Process, 19,* 295–306.

Kaslow, F.W., & Steinberg, J.L. (1982). Ethical divorce therapy and divorce proceedings: A psycholegal perspective. In L. L'Abate (Ed.), *Values, ethics, legalities and the family therapist.* Rockville, MD: Aspen Systems.

Kaslow, N.J., & Gurman, A.S. (1985). Ethical considerations in family therapy research. *Counseling and Values, 30,* 47–61.

Krasner, L., & Houts, A.C. (1984). A study of the "value" systems of behavioral scientists. *American Psychologist, 39,* 840–850.

L'Abate, L. (Ed.) (1982). *Values, ethics, and legalities and the family therapist.* Rockville, MD: Aspen.

LaRossa, R., Bennett, L.A., & Gelles, R.J. (1981). Ethical dilemmas in qualitative family research. *Journal of Marriage and the Family, 43,* 303–313.

Lindley, R. (1987). Family therapy and respect for people. In S. Walron-Skinner & D. Watson (Eds.), *Ethical issues in family therapy.* New York: Routledge & Kegan Paul.

Luepnitz, D. (1988). *Family therapy revisited.* New York: Basic Books.

MacIntyre, A. (1984). *After virtue: A study in moral theory* (2nd ed.). South Bend, IN: University of Notre Dame Press.

MacIntrye, A. (1988). *Whose justice? Which rationality?* South Bend, IN: University of Notre Dame Press.

Margolin, G. (1982). Ethical and legal considerations in marriage and family therapy. *American Psychologist, 7,* 789–801.

McGoldrick, M., Pearce, J.L., & Giordano, J. (1982). *Ethnicity and family therapy.* New York: Guilford Press.

Meth, R.L., & Pasick, R.S. (1990). *Men in therapy: The challenge of change.* New York: Guilford Press.

Napier, A. (1991). Heroism, men and marriage. *Journal of Marital and Family Therapy, 17.*

Noddings, N. (1984). *Caring: A feminine approach to ethics and moral education.* Berkeley, CA: University of California Press.

Pelligrino, E.D., & Thomasma, D.C. (1988). *For the patient's good: The restoration of beneficence in health care.* New York: Oxford University Press.

Piercy, F.P., & Sprenkle, D.H. (1983). Ethical, legal, and professional issues in family therapy: A graduate level course. *Journal of Marital and Family Therapy, 9,* 393–401.

Pittman, F.S. (1991). The secret passions of men. *Journal of Marital and Family Therapy, 17.*

Rawls, J. (1971). *A theory of justice.* Cambridge, MA: Harvard University Press.

Ryder, R.G. (1985). Professionals' values in family assessment. *Counseling and Values, 30,* 24–34.

Ryder, R.G. (1987). *The realistic therapist: Modesty and relativism in therapy and research.* Newbury Park, CA: Sage.

Sarason, S. (1985). *Caring and compassion in the clinical professions.* San Francisco: Jossey-Bass.

Sider, R.C., & Clements, C. (1982). Family or individual therapy: The ethics of modality choice. *American Journal of Psychiatry, 139,* 1455–1459.

Spiegel, J. (1971). *Transactions: The interplay between individual, family, and society.* New York: Science House.

Sporakowski, M. (1982). The regulation of marital and family therapy. In L. L'Abate (Ed.), *Ethics, values, legalities and the family therapist.* Rockville, MD: Aspen Systems.

Stanton, M.D. (1981). Strategic approaches to family therapy. In A.S. Gurman & D.P. Kniskern (Eds.), *Handbook of family therapy.* New York: Brunner/Mazel.

Stein, H.F. (1983). An anthropological view of family therapy. In D. Bagarrozi, A. Jurich, & R. Jackson (Eds.), *Marital and family therapy: New perspectives in theory, research, and practice.* New York: Human Sciences Press.

Stein, H. F. (1985a) Therapist and family values in a cultural context. *Counseling and Values, 30,* 35–46.

Stein, H.F. (1985b). Values and family therapy. In J. Schwartzman (Ed.), *Families and other systems.* New York: Guilford Press.

Strickler, G. (1982). Ethical issues in psychotherapy research. In M. Rosenbaum (Ed.), *Ethics and values in psychotherapy.* New York: Free Press.

Taggart, M. (1982). Linear versus systemic values: Implications for family therapy. In L. L'Abate (Ed.), *Ethics, values, legalities and family therapy.* Rockville, MD: Aspen Systems.

Thibaut, J.W., & Kelley, H.H. (1959). *The social psychology of groups.* New York: Wiley.

Thorne, B. (1982). *Rethinking the family: Some feminist questions.* New York: Longman.

Walrond-Skinner, S., & Watson, D. (Eds.) (1987). *Ethical issues in family therapy.* New York: Routledge & Kegan Paul.

Wallach, M.A., & Wallach, L. (1983). *Psychology's sanction for selfishness.* San Francisco: Jossey-Bass.

Walters, M., Carter, B., Papp, P., & Silverstein, O. (1988). *The invisible web: Gender patterns in family relationships.* New York: Guilford Press.

Weeks, G.R., & L'Abate, L. (1982). *Paradoxical psychotherapy: Theory and practice with individuals, couples and families.* New York: Brunner/Mazel.

Weiner, J.P., & Boss, P.G. (1985). Exploring gender bias against women: Ethics for marriage and family therapy. *Counseling and Values, 30,* 9–23.

Wendorf, D.J., & Wendorf, R.J. (1985). A systemic view of family therapy ethics. *Family Process, 24,* 443–460.

Whan, M. (1983). Tricks of the trade: Questionable theory and practice in family therapy. *British Journal of Social Work, 13,* 321–337.

Whitaker, C.A., & Keith, D.V. (1981). Symbolic-experiential family therapy. In A.S. Gurman & K.P. Kniskern (Eds.), *Handbook of family therapy.* New York: Brunner/Mazel.

Willbach, D. (1989). Ethics and family therapy: The case management of family violence. *Journal of Marital and Family Therapy, 15,* 43–52.

Woody, J.D. (1990). Resolving ethical concerns in clinical practice: Toward a pragmatic model. *Journal of Marital and Familiy Therapy, 16,* 133–150.

Zygmond, M.J., & Boorhen, H. (1989). Ethical decision making in family therapy. *Family Process, 28,* 269–280.

EDITORS' REFERENCES

Gurman, A.S., & Klein, M.H. (1980). The treatment of women in marital and family conflict: Recommendations for outcome evaluation. In A. Brodsky & R. Hare-Mustin (Eds.), *Research on psychotherapy with women.* New York: Guilford Press.

Gurman, A.S., & Klein, M.H. (1984). Women and behavioral marital therapy: An unconscious male bias? In E. Blechman (Ed.), *Behavior modification with women*. New York: Guilford Press.

Gurman, A.S., & Kniskern, D.P. (1978a). Research on marital and family therapy: Progress, perspective and prospect. In S. Garfield & A. Bergin (Eds.), *Handbook of psychotherapy and behavior change* (2nd ed.). New York: Wiley.

Gurman, A.S., & Kniskern, D.P. (1978b). Deterioration in marital and family therapy: Empirical, clinical and conceptual issues. *Family Process, 17*, 3–20.

Jacobson, N.S. (1981). Behavioral marital therapy. In A. Gurman & D. Kniskern (Eds.), *Handbook of family therapy*. New York: Brunner/Mazel.

CHAPTER 21

Training and Supervision in Family Therapy: A Comprehensive and Critical Analysis*

Howard A. Liddle, Ed. D.

Few family therapists are aware of the emergence and scope of a specialty within their field. Supervisors themselves, when asked to name the source that has influenced them most, are more likely to cite a clinical paper or book than a reference from the training and supervision area. At workshops on supervision, a common participant lament can be heard: "I'm here to learn more about family-therapy supervision since there isn't much written on the topic."

There was a period when this conclusion was correct, but that time was long ago. Family-therapy training and supervision have been a viable

specialty area for over 15 years. Writings exist on a broad variety of topics. Beginning supervisors need not practice in the shadows of doubt and unclarity. Skills and methods of supervision, school-of-thought–specific models of training, and learning objectives have all been developed. The problems of training different populations, as well as the challenges of training in different contexts, have also been discussed. Not surprisingly, the latest developments in family therapy's clinical sphere have materialized in training and supervision. The epistemology debate, feminism, cross-cultures and ethnicity, and developmental thinking, for instance, are clearly represented in the training literature. Although still in its early stages, research has begun, with some of the most impressive work happening in the area of instrument develop-

* Acknowledgments are gratefully given to Gayle Dakof for her insightful comments on various versions of this chapter, and to Charlene Lapp for her tireless assistance in compiling references.

ment.[1] These psychometrically sound scales evaluate therapy and trainees as they progress toward proficiency in the complex craft of family therapy.

This chapter is a comprehensive critical analysis of the family-therapy training and supervision literature. Over a decade ago, a colleague and I reviewed over 100 articles on this topic (Liddle & Halpin, 1978). The first conclusion of the present effort concerned the growth of this content area. The current review covers three times as many contributions as the 1978 paper. There are many other ways in which the literature of training and supervision is different now from what it was at the time of the earlier review. This chapter considers these developments to arrive at a contemporary assessment of family-therapy training and supervision. It seeks to identify where we have been and where we are headed, and perhaps most important, where we need to go in this specialty that is vital to family therapy's future.

A SPECIALTY DEFINED: FAMILY-THERAPY TRAINING AND SUPERVISION

Historical Perspective

The first wave of papers in training and supervision reflected the early developmental stage of this family-therapy specialty area. While the early contributions may seem unsophisticated or obvious today, they must be comprehended in this developmental context. They were reflections of the broader field of family therapy as it existed at that time (which itself probably seems unsophisticated today). Let us trace the maturation of training and supervision into a bona fide area of specialization in family therapy.

Era I: Defining the Territory

The general literature on family-therapy training and supervision can be divided into two distinct eras or periods of development. There is a third era forming, which will be discussed at the end of the chapter. The first era would be characterized by the initial offerings to this literature (Ackerman, 1973; Ferber & Mendelsohn, 1969; Ferber, Mendelsohn, & Beels, 1972; Kempster & Savitsky, 1967; Mendelsohn & Ferber, 1972; Sander & Beels, 1970). These early writings seemed preoccupied with a narrow range of content. Further, some of these areas seem to be the ones that have lost their appeal today. Co-therapy as a training device represents one of these areas (Stier & Goldenberg, 1975; Tucker, Hart, & Liddle, 1976). Although it is still discussed today, it is only done so by minority schools of thought in the family-therapy field (e.g., Carl Whitaker's approach).

Another topic of early import that has received less discussion in recent years is the issue of personal therapy or family-of-origin work for trainees. Initially, there was a doctrinaire spirit to these writings that often recommended that trainees engage in marital or family therapy as a required part of training. Present-day training field consensus suggests a more measured tone to this recommendation. Therapy for trainees is now more likely to be framed in terms of the personal development issues of the therapist. There is more acceptance that there may be many paths to positive trainee growth and requiring therapy as part of training may be unnecessary, unproductive, or, as some have argued, unethical (Haley, 1976). The contemporary position still argues for the central importance of the person of the therapist in training, and the need for trainers to attend closely to this issue. The *requirement* of personal therapy or mandatory family-of-origin work for trainees is not seen as necessary, wise, or realistic in contemporary family-therapy supervision and training.

Bodin (1969) was among the first to outline many of the categories in this literature that would become standard, as well as more sophisticated, over the years. He briefly sketched trainee characteristics and context, the different professional settings and disciplines in which family-therapy training occurred, and different

---

training methods, many of which are still in use today (videotape, group supervision). The basic outline of what constitutes the training and supervision field is contained in this early publication. The difference between the Bodin article (and others of its era) and the field today, however, lies in the expanded degree of complexity, specificity, and sophistication in how training and supervision can be addressed. Modern-day training and supervision have become more specialized, complex, and sophisticated.

By the mid-1970s a significant literature was developing in the family-therapy training and supervision field (Kaslow, 1977; Liddle & Halpin, 1978). At this time, papers began to appear that covered a variety of content areas, including *techniques* (Bardill, 1976; Bodin, 1972; Hare-Mustin, 1976) and *models of supervision* (Ard, 1973; Birchler, 1975; Cohen, Gross, & Turner, 1976; Montalvo, 1973); *training-program descriptions* (Constantine, 1976; Hare & Frankena, 1972; Miyoshi & Liebman, 1969; Tucker et al., 1976), the *trainee's own family* as it relates to becoming a family therapist (Ferber, 1972; Framo, 1975; Guerin & Fogarty, 1972), *training as it exists in a variety of contexts* (Epstein & Levin, 1973; Malone, 1974; Talmadge, 1975); and the *problems and politics of training* (Ehrlich, 1973; Framo, 1976; Haley, 1976; Liddle, 1978; Shapiro, 1975a, 1975b; Stanton, 1975a, b). Although scattered in many places and lacking any coherent conceptual, technical or evaluative focus, sufficient literature accumulated to warrant major reviews of this specialized area. These will be discussed later.

Seminal Contributions

As we have said, more complexity gradually became evident in the training and supervision literature. Several seminal works of this era remain both historically and conceptually significant. The first of these offered a systematic way in which to think about training (Cleghorn & Levin, 1973). These authors identified and categorized three sets of skills for the family therapist—perceptual, conceptual, and executive. In their classification framework for the complex skills of family therapy offered trainers a conceptual scaffolding. The Cleghorn and Levin framework eventually allowed particular schools

of family therapy to classify the skills of their approach according to similar categories, making possible productive comparisons of models.

If the categorization and differentiation of family-therapy skills were major early advances in the training field, the specification of different schools of thought or approaches to training must be considered an equally significant development. A landmark work of its time and a contribution that endures as a helpful tool for the family-therapy trainer, is Haley's (1976) "Problems of Training Therapists." This work is an indispensable guide for the trainer wishing to clarify his or her orientation to training. The suggestions for selecting an orientation or choosing a place for training, for example, help in several ways. They enumerate some key domains that make up the training endeavor, clarify the trainer's personal supervision philosophy, and additionally, of course, specify Haley's recommendations for training family therapists.

Employing Haley's (1976) *schools of family therapy* training schema, Beal (1976) took the next logical step and, using the leading training centers of the time, provided specific examples of school-specific training approaches. Beal detailed how individual training sites represent a certain orientation, and classified each according to Haley's outline. Like the Cleghorn and Levin paper, the Haley and Beal contributions created organization and imposed conceptual logic on the burgeoning array of competing training philosophies and approaches. Haley's schema for drawing distinctions between training philosophies also prefigured the linking of training approaches to the theories of therapy that were being taught. This area of the field was to become known in family therapy as the isomorphic nature of training and therapy, and it will be covered later.

Two more papers are included in this section on seminal contributions to family-therapy training and supervision that would stand alongside the Haley, Beal, and Cleghorn and Levin articles as the most important early contributions in the family-therapy training field. One of these papers is a benchmark work by a man often referred to as a "behind the scenes" figure in the pioneer days of family therapy. Minuchin called him his most influential teacher.

In probably the most-cited paper in the training and supervision literature, "Aspects of Live Supervision," Braulio Montalvo (1973) articulated the supervisory method known as live supervision. Revolutionary in its day, and still considered so in many nonprogressive corners of the family-therapy field, live supervision allows the supervisor to guide the process of therapy as it occurs, giving help to the therapist when he or she needs it most—during the actual clinical interview. Montalvo's article presents the rationale for this method and the skills necessary to orient the supervisor.

Anchored with more or less equal values in economic and conceptual rationales, *group supervision* also has been a hallmark of family-therapy training, and its use was outlined in several early papers (Beatman, 1964; Kempster & Savitsky, 1967; Siegel & Dulfano, 1973). Stier and Goldenberg (1975) discussed several factors that make a group supervision seminar go smoothly. The use of a heterosexual cotherapy team, group versus individual supervision, the balance of technical or skill-focused versus personal feedback, and video playback were all recognized as critical elements that exist in the supervision context for better or worse. Although rudimentary by contemporary standards, the Stier and Goldenberg (1975) article was the first to offer empirical data on any aspect of supervision groups.

Era II: Critical Theory in Action

The family-therapy field in general has taken more of an appropriately critical approach toward itself in recent years. In parallel, the training and supervision field has begun to examine its assumptions, methods, and effectiveness in an equally evaluative way (e.g., Everett & Koerpel, 1986; Liddle, 1985). The second era of training and supervision development is related to this trend in the broader family-therapy context. The major reviews, in addition to taking turns at organizing the expanding supervision and training literature, increasingly assume more of a critical approach. That is, we are less likely to respond in awe or blindly accept any new method or idea that appears. Critique and analysis thus embody the spirit of this second era. While the force and degree of helpfulness of these various critiques vary considerably, they

share a concern about the current status of the quality of the training and supervision area (i.e., its published ideas, unpublished values, norms and beliefs, and its products—the waves of family-therapy trainees and supervisors that multiply the field's ranks). Let us examine these reviews, each of which has formulated several guidelines and recommendations.

Kaslow (1977)

The first paper that moved in this direction was the chapter by Kaslow (1977). She covered many of the key issues in the training field, such as the multifarious training contexts and their influence on training, supervisory techniques, some problems encountered by supervisors, and the trend to establish learning objectives. This review set the stage for the more comprehensive reviews that would follow. A strength of Kaslow's chapter is the articulation of her own position on and favorable reactions to such training issues as family-of-origin work for the trainee, the problems with overly regimented approaches to training, and the benefits of cotherapy as a training device.

Liddle and Halpin (1978)

A comparative review was offered by Liddle and Halpin (1978) in which the then-extant 100-plus–article literature was organized under six headings—goals of training and supervision, training supervision techniques, supervisor–supervisee relationship, personal therapy for trainees, politics of family-therapy training, and evaluation of training. Several problems with the literature were noted. These were discussed from the point of view of the fairly new area's stage of development. The most serious gaps in this literature included its fragmented and disorganized quality (i.e., the absence of organizing principles or purposes) and the lack of (1) specificity of methods and procedures, (2) building on the ideas and contributions of others, and (3) comprehensive overall theories of training and supervision that could guide trainers in their day-to-day work. Recommendations were made in several areas:

1. Evaluation of training and supervision should be considered one of the most important activities for the field.
2. Research should be carried out on the training and supervision processes in family therapy as they may be distinct from and similar to psychotherapy supervision.
3. Articulation of processes of supervisor development should receive priority, with particular attention given to the consequences of supervisor isolation and professional burnout.
4. Greater attention should be given to the quality of training and trainer qualifications.
5. More focus is needed on the area of political preparedness (i.e., incorporating our knowledge about the contextual reverberations of family therapy as a movement), as well as on the larger contexts in which family therapy is taught and practiced.

Everett (1980)

In the first of his two critical reviews of the marital and family-therapy (MFT) supervision literature, Everett (1980), as others had done before him (Kaslow, 1977; Nichols, 1979; Liddle & Halpin, 1978), examined the historical development of the marriage-counseling and family-therapy fields for clues to understanding the status of MFT supervision and training. Everett observed that concerns for clinical practice and theory development in family therapy preceded serious attention to training standards. In this sense, the *what* of training preceded the *how* to carry it out. Everett, with keen historical insight, wonders about the contemporary consequences of the fact that the first generation of family therapists was largely self-taught. Stimulated by this observation, a troubling issue emerges: Has this historical eventuality contributed to certain beliefs and values that many family-therapy supervisors have noticed and been worried about? Bluntly stated, this refers to the questions: "Who needs training to become a supervisor anyway?" "Isn't this something that one *just does*, learning how to do it along the way?" Unfortunately, questions of this nature rarely get posed as frankly as this for public discussion. They are more likely to remain unarticulated, emerging only among friends or in private conversations.

Liddle (1982)

As the training field became more complex and sophisticated, it was possible to articulate generic questions, those that apply to all trainers regardless of the approach being taught. Using an approach different from that in the 1978 review, Liddle (1982a) posed five generic questions. Each identifies basic issues for accompanying content domains and addresses the existing literature in each. They cover such areas as:

1. *Personnel.* Who should teach and be taught family therapy?
2. *Content and Skills.* What should the content of training be? How is this content translated into the corresponding skills that are needed to conduct therapy?
3. *Methodology.* What should our training methods be?
4. *Context.* How does the training influence the setting and the setting influence the training?
5. *Evaluation.* How should training be assessed?

Reviewing the literature under each of these questions yielded four basic issues: (1) individual learning styles (including cognitive styles); (2) the impact of various supervisory methods on the supervisee and the therapy, clarification of conceptual issues in training (e.g., the isomorphic nature of training and therapy; (3) a trend toward more sophisticated descriptions of the training process (e.g., multilevel and multisubsystem perspective and evaluation); and (4) a greater realization of the interconnection of the various domains of the family-therapy field (i.e., specifying mutually influencing processes among the conceptual, research, practice, and training subsystems).

Beavers (1985)

Haley's (1976) previously mentioned chapter contained a section on factors to consider in selecting a training context. On a broader scale, a family-therapy supervision "consumer's guide" was offered by Beavers (1985). He traced the distinctions between psychotherapy and family-therapy supervision, accurately characterizing family-therapy supervision as having three distinct features—including the heralding of a new era in openness to scrutiny and examination of the actual processes of supervision via videotapes and an emphasis on group supervision. Beavers also clearly articulates the importance of a contextual appreciation of supervision and the important role of organizations such as the American Association for Marriage and Family Therapy (AAMFT) in upgrading supervisory standards (others have emphasized this as well; see Hansen & Spacone, 1983; Kaslow, 1977; Everett, 1980; Nichols, 1979).

Everett and Koerpel (1986)

In a review and critique consistent with this second era in training and supervision, Everett and Koerpel (1986) offered a series of indictments against the status of the supervision literature from 1980 to 1985. They made the following key points:

1. Supervision is a critical aspect of the maturing MFT field. The education of MFT personnel provides "a milieu for the socialization of identity and the learning of skills" (p. 71). Supervision "provides the linkage between the various components of education. Thus, the supervisors become the gatekeepers of the profession" (p. 71).
2. As a result of family therapy's "continued preoccupation with competing loyalties to pioneers, or at least to differing conceptual or applied orientations" (p. 71), there has not yet emerged a careful and critical examination of the "internal processes of supervision" (p. 71).
3. The supervision literature does not appear to be integrated with the field within which it exists, and further, it "lacks a consistency of theoretical inquiry" (p. 71), as well as "a sophistication of research designs or methods" (p. 71).
4. Basic theoretical and research questions remain to be articulated.
5. Family-therapy supervision has remained isolated from related fields.
6. There is conceptual confusion, evidenced by a "serious blurring of broad training issues

and techniques with concerns of supervision and learning" (p. 71).
7. Theoretical issues need further exploration; for instance, "the reciprocal and circular interplay between roles and processes of supervisor, student and client family" (p. 71).

Piercy and Sprenkle (1986)

In their overview and organization of the training and supervision field, Piercy and Sprenkle (1986) offered a comprehensive treatment of the area (definitions of basic terms, history and overview, training programs, supervisors, methods and theoretical orientations of supervisors, research issues, and an identification of the major issues). Calling for an emphasis on research and evaluation, they found much of the training and supervision literature to be impressionistic, atheoretical, and inconsistent in quality.

Glick, Kessler, and Sugarman (1987)

Comparing the Sprenkle and Piercy overview of the family-therapy training and supervision literature with a review by Glick, Kessler, and Sugarman (1987) that appeared at about the same time reveals an interesting fact about this still-young field. Both of these reviews appeared in family-therapy textbooks. While both ostensibly cover the same portion of the field, very different interpretations can be obtained with even a cursory reading of these contributions. The reader of the Glick et al. rendition of family-therapy training would, on the basis of these authors' treatment of the topic, find this specialty area to be unsophisticated, certainly undeveloped, and perhaps even unexciting. Reading the chapter on the same topic in the Piercy and Sprenkle text would yield quite a different conclusion. This latter review characterizes training as a progressive specialty, active with development and challenging cutting-edge issues, many of which have begun to be explored in depth. Such discrepant coverage and interpretations of the same material are commonplace in our field today, and lead some to think of the area as unsophisticated, or at least encourage a conclusion that there is no consensus about crucial issues (Ganahl, Ferguson, & L'Abate, 1985; Haley, 1988).

Ganahl, Ferguson, and L'Abate (1985)

Ganahl et al. (1985) offer a pair of chapters that comprehensively cover family-therapy training and supervision issues and the "emerging (and emerged) field of family psychology" (Liddle, 1988a) and that provide a translation and integration of family systems ideas into mainstream psychology. A consistent theme running throughout the Ganahl et al. reviews is the plea for attention to quality in training. Like other reviewers who have stressed the field-shaping function of supervision (Everett, 1980; Liddle, 1988a), Ganahl et al. offer a high-level critical theory analysis of the training and supervision field. These authors are unequivocal about the importance of the interpenetration of theory and practice in training. They concur with others who condemn technique-focused training (Beavers, 1985; Everett & Koerpel, 1986; Kaslow, 1977; Nichols, 1979) and emphasize the necessity to ground therapy training more firmly in systematic training and supervision. They join authors such as Liddle (1982b), who calls for a personalized approach to training—one that factors in the personal style and abilities of trainees.

More than most other overviews and reviews, the chapters by Ganahl et al. offer numerous detailed recommendations as to how to upgrade the status of the training and supervision field. They urge attention to the following:

1. The family-therapy field has overemphasized practice and the development of therapy technologies to the exclusion of theory development, prevention, and empirical work.
2. There is a need to incorporate basic psychological knowledge into the family-therapy field. This, of course, has tremendous training implications. It relates to the questions of content or "what" needs to be taught during training (Liddle, 1982). Ganahl and colleagues are in accord with others who have argued that insufficient attention is being paid to the content of the training and supervision field, as well as with those who

advocate for the integrative movement in contemporary family therapy.

3. Values and belief systems are grist for the mill of training. Therapists need to be taught techniques or procedures for their work, but they also need to be able to think, to reflect, and to construct and evaluate their models in an intelligent and sensitive manner. Ganahl and associates cite the encroachment of third-party reimbursement systems and peer-review panels as warning signs. These developments may take final evaluation and determination of one's work out of the hands of individual providers.
4. Family-therapy curricula should be tied to the discipline in which the family-therapy training exists. That is, since these authors do not support the forming of a separate field called family therapy, they advocate family-therapy curricula emerging from the contexts, and indeed the contents, of the existing fields and specialties.
5. Family-therapy training should be both academic and experiential. This recommendation is consistent with the earliest formulations of family-therapy training, as well as with current practices.
6. In addition to the usual differentiation of training into experiential and academic components, Ganahl and associates also introduce other levels at which training should occur. These include:
   a. Technical training, which refers to the acquisition and practice of therapy skills in a protected environment.
   b. Clinical training, which puts students in an actual clinical context with clinical families that are seeking help. Trainees have experience with different supervisors and methods of supervision.
   c. Scientific training, which refers to the research orientation of the trainee and is linked to the trainee's discipline as well as to his or her personal interest in research experience.
   d. Professional training, which refers to the acquisition of professional skills (e.g., case management, fees, setting, ethical issues, case records, interprofessional relations, consulting, and supervising) and upgrading one's skills via continuing education.

Ganahl et al.'s (1985) final point concerns the issue of competence for the family therapist. In their view, completion of the above areas of training prepares the individual for becoming a competent family-therapy practitioner. This person is defined as one who not only is able to integrate current empirical and clinical practices, but also is able to change his or her understanding of the field as it changes. This concerns the evolving nature of a field and its practitioners. These authors strongly recommend adherence to these values of competence, attainment, and responsibility for self-improvement as a necessary and welcome fact of professional life.

CONCEPTUAL AND THEORETICAL ISSUES IN TRAINING AND SUPERVISION

As noted personality theorist Kurt Lewin once observed in his oft-cited quote: "There is nothing so practical as a good theory." Although family therapists are no strangers to theories and the conceptual implications of their work, the training and supervision area has been slow to accept the importance of theory and conceptual development. With Lewin's maxim in mind, we will examine conceptual foundations of training and supervision. We will describe some of the broad, guiding concepts that can help supervisors organize their work, and review some of the practically oriented conceptual developments in supervision.

Frameworks of Supervision and Training

Using the isomorphic nature of training and therapy as a base, Haley (1976, 1988) proposed a framework for considering training orientations. His schema is significant since it was the first of its kind. It also provides a useful contemporary guide to formulating one's orientation as a trainer. Haley compares and contrasts two positions about therapy, characterized in an intentionally extreme way.

"Orientation A" focuses on insight and growth (and represents the psychodynamic, experiential, and humanistic wings of family therapy), while "Orientation Z" emphasizes problem solving and behavior change (and represents the structural, behavioral, and strategic schools). These training and supervision orientations are characterized along four key dimensions.

Spontaneous Versus Planned Change

Within Orientation A, the responsibility for therapeutic change resides with the family and the job of the therapist is to help people change themselves. The supervisor helps the therapist to help clients help themselves. Supervisors from Orientation Z emphasize a planned versus spontaneous approach to training. Orientation Z supervisors assume primary responsibility for assessing the needs of the family and supervisee, and provide an intervention plan for both family and supervisee subsystems. In Orientation Z, failure is not seen as the fault of the trainee or the family, but as the inadequacy of the supervisor.

Growth Versus Problem Orientation

Training from Orientation Z teaches a specific set of interviewing and intervention skills that bring about change. Orientation A focuses on the personal development of the trainee, assuming, for instance, that the personal therapy of the trainee necessarily will have beneficial effects on the therapist's acquisition of skills and clinical ability.

Understanding Versus Action as a Cause of Change

Orientation A assumes that people in training and therapy should be made more self-aware, and that understanding is a primary mechanism of change. Orientation Z asserts that change results from altering behaviors in the present. It is assumed that neither understanding nor the expression of emotion causes therapists or clients to change. Supervisors plan a strategy and deliver directives requiring new behavior. Supervisors within this approach do not assume that a therapist's understanding or his or her own personal involvement with clients is related to becoming a competent therapist. Further, past history and insight play a limited role, or, in some cases, are counterproductive in producing therapist change. Orientation A tends to emphasize the importance of, if not necessity for, individual or family therapy for the therapist during the training process.

Self-Report Versus Observation

Orientation A tends to consider the ideas and fantasies of a person more relevant to therapy than the person's real-life situation. Self-report rather than observational or interactional data is primary. In Orientation Z, the main concern is the actual behavior of the parties involved rather than their descriptions of this behavior. Orientation A supervisors accept and rely on the self-report of the clinical situation from the therapist. The major methods of supervision are case notes and process recording. Orientation Z has supervisors observe therapists in action with the case, either in a live session through a one-way mirror or on audiotape or videotape. Orientation Z supervisors doubt a clinician's capacity adequately to report the clinical data of which he or she is a part, and prefer to have the action of therapy in front of them so that it can be specifically commented on and altered via live supervision. Therapist behavior is shaped by the supervisor's directive input.

Haley's (1988) extension of this training framework enumerated three dimensions of possible focus in training. These areas provide generic categories useful for helping supervisors to decide their philosophy and preferred methods of supervision. The *problem situation* refers, on the one hand, to a supervisory focus on the description of the client's situation and the specification of etiology. Alternatively, the supervisor may focus on formulating a treatment plan and strategies to implement this plan. The *therapist's personality* deals with the degree of supervisory focus on the personality of the therapist as a supervision goal versus an emphasis on family-of-origin work in training. In *skill supervision*, therapy is understood purely as an operational skill that requires practice under observation and direct guidance by the supervisor—the person charged with the responsibility for teaching the craft of therapy to the trainee.

While some training frameworks specify and teach therapist skills in a highly behavioral fashion, other frameworks emphasize the metaphoric and analogic side of human functioning. Whitaker has been a champion of the latter, with his best-known contribution in this regard provocatively titled, "On the Hinderance of Theory in Clinical Practice" (Whitaker, 1976). Perhaps the best-developed training framework representing this training orientation is that advanced by Duhl (1983) (also see Duhl & Duhl, 1979). Her book provides a trainer's epistemology from the experiential perspective, and includes a statement of the values and beliefs that are consistent with this model. Analogic and metaphoric exercises are included to help trainers access these less intellectual aspects of functioning. Duhl's work is a good example of how one's training values and beliefs can be clearly specified, as well as how these basic givens of a trainer are manifested in their selection of training methods.

Minuchin and Fishman (1981), having been influenced by both the experiential (especially Whitaker) and, to some extent, the behavioral traditions (cf. Minuchin, Rosman, & Baker, 1978), stake out an integrative position on this matter. Although they believe that training in specific skills is important, "training for spontaneity," as they call it, is vital. They describe this emphasis with a metaphoric tale of the training of the samurai warrior.

The training of the samurai, too, was a training for spontaneity. Only if the sword was a continuation of the arm could the samurai survive. The attention to detail that the samurai considered essential for achieving spontaneity was extraordinary. To become a master, he had to train as a warrior for three to five years. Then, having become a craftsman, he was required to abandon his craft and spend a number of years studying unrelated areas, like painting, poetry, or calligraphy. Only after achieving mastery in these different intellectual endeavors could the warrior go back and take up the sword, for only then had the sword become a continuation of the arm. He had become a samurai because he had forgotten technique. (p. 4)

There have been advances in trainers' capacity to specify their training assumptions, a task thought by many to be of critical importance in training and therapy. Piercy and Sprenkle (1984) and Nichols (1979), for instance, believe the apprenticeship model of training to be insufficient, and instead emphasize the importance of the education of family therapists. For these authors, classroom training, didactic instruction, and appropriate exercises are crucial if training is to be comprehensive. For Piercy and Sprenkle (1984), the process of family-therapy education includes several key elements: a synergistic interplay among theory, research, and practice; theory construction and criticism on the trainee's part; and a balance of professional input and student involvement. These authors also emphasize a frequently neglected proposition in training and therapy—the idea that excitement should be a by-product of family-therapy education (see also Whitaker, 1976; Duhl, 1983; Duhl & Duhl, 1979).

While the specific techniques of supervision have been described, they frequently have been fitted together in a piecemeal fashion, without an appreciation for their interdependence. One exception is a supervisory framework by Hodus (1985) that includes the complementarity of videotape and live supervision. This framework appreciates live supervision's proximity to the family phenomena and videotape review supervision's proximity to the therapist and to behaviors that need shaping.

Liddle's (1988) supervision approach stresses the importance of clarifying the supervisor's conceptualizations about and goals of supervision. This approach, relying on a developmental metaphor of the stages of training and trainee growth, details the different supervisor behaviors required at early and later stages of therapy and training.

Supervisor Thinking and Conceptual Development

This section considers the definition and treatment of the topic of supervisor thinking. How should the conceptual life of the supervisor be organized? What cognitive structures or thought rules guide the supervisory process? What frameworks or metaphors guide the supervisor in the process of monitoring and teaching family-therapy thinking and clinical practice?

Different orders or levels of learning are seen in supervision. It is important that the supervisor accurately discriminate the different but interdependent levels in the supervisory system. Berger and Dammann (1982) detailed the necessity for the supervisor's multidimensional vision of live supervision. Live supervision is simultaneously (1) the context in which different experiences of affect can exist on both sides of the one-way mirror, (2) a treatment setting, and (3) a training enterprise in which live supervision is used to change the thinking of trainees.

The conceptual framework of the live supervision context was offered in a skills-focused paper that included a flow chart for conducting live supervision. Liddle and Schwartz (1983) presented a step-by-step guide to the process of doing a live supervision session, suggesting factors that trigger supervisory intervention as well as guidelines for preparation and debriefing (post-) supervisory sessions. Heath (1983) proposed a writing schema that aids a supervisor's conceptualization of live supervision. Heath and Storm (1983) provide a general outline for preparing to become a supervisor, enumerating the things that one should do before and after one has started to supervise therapists. This topic of becoming a supervisor, unfortunately, has been underdeveloped. These authors have also been part of the movement to define how one's therapy theory can be used as a guide to one's supervisory and training models (Heath & Storm, 1983; Storm & Heath, 1985).

Anderson (1984) has creatively defined the supervisor's role, using the principle of isomorphism between therapy and supervision. Supervisory dimensions, such as hierarchical inevitability, the transmission of knowledge and skill from one person to another, and construction of certainty about a certain therapeutic path, are all called into question by Anderson and Rambo (1988). They demonstrate the redefinition of supervision assuming that the notion of the isomorphic nature of therapy and training is applied across all schools of thought. That is, when the systemic supervisory model matches the systemic therapy model, the rules of supervision change. Gelcer (1987) has also attempted to articulate a new framework for supervision within a systemic approach by adopting the invariant method of the Milan team. Although less successful than Anderson's efforts, the work of Gelcer and others (e.g., Gentry,

1986; Pearson, 1987) has clearly signaled an era in which the framework of isomorphism between therapy and supervision, at least in terms of the construction of a theory of supervision, is being advanced.[2]

Some authors have expressed concern about the lack of differentiation between administrative and clinical supervision (Goguen, 1986; Michalski, 1986). Others have noted other potentially confusing or ambiguous aspects of the supervisory situation, especially in terms of defining the common core of what a supervisor does (Aldefer & Lynch, 1986). Research by Saba and Liddle (1986) confirms this lack of clarity with a sample of AAMFT and American Family Therapy Association (AFTA) supervisors. In this study, supervisors stated the need for conceptual frameworks that would help define their training mission and guide them in day-to-day supervisory practice. The supervision model of Liddle (1988a), which offers conceptual guidelines for the supervisor on such matters as the stages of supervision and of supervisee development, and the ABCX model of Sharon (1986), which uses stress and coping theory to build a supervisory framework, are examples of attempts to help supervisors attain their desired conceptual guidelines. Patterson (1985) has attempted to offer a rationale for, as well as data on, the importance of adding an empirical perspective to supervision. His research has demonstrated, for instance, that supervision is a key variable in good outcome and low resistance in his social learning model of family therapy.

The Isomorphic Nature of Training and Therapy

There is probably no more misunderstood notion than the isomorphic nature of training and therapy. However, this arguably has been one of the most vital areas of thinking on how supervisors should conceive of their work. Historically and conceptually important, Doehrman (1976) conducted one of the earliest research studies on the connections between therapy and training.

Sluzki (1974a) offered one of the earliest state-ments about the usefulness of the isomorphism concept. His paper was one of the first to discuss the thinking process that leads to the shift to an interpersonal reality. In programs designed to alter the trainee's epistemology, such as a family-therapy training program, Sluzki stresses the importance of consistency in messages between content and structure by making sure that there is philosophical consistency at all levels of the program. In discussing another elemental aspect of the training experience, Haley (1980) echoes a general point made by Sluzki.

The professional setting of the therapist, particularly his supervisory relationship, is of basic importance. There is a reciprocal relation between the supervisory structure and the family structure. If the authority relationship between supervisor and therapist is clear, the hierarchy in the family will be more easily restructured. When the family hierarchy is in particular confusion . . . it is especially important that the hierarchical arrangement of supervisor and therapist be clear and firm. (p. 62)

Although it has been used in psychoanalytic writings on supervision for some time (i.e., the parallels of therapy and training; see Ekstein & Wallerstein, 1972), the family-therapy training and supervision literature has only gradually seemed to accept and utilize the isomorphism notion. It appeared in a number of early publications (Liddle & Halpin, 1978), and then slowly the value and use of the principle of isomorphism in the training and supervision of family therapists began to be defined (Andolfi & Menghi, 1980; Liddle & Saba, 1982, 1983, 1984; McGoldrick, 1982; Minuchin & Fishman, 1981; Storm & Heath, 1985). For some, the notion has been instrumental in their thinking about a broad framework for supervision and training. It has, for instance, been defined as an "overlay of overlays" (Liddle, 1985, 1988)—a framework in which other elements of the training process can be subsumed.

In an attempt to clear up some of the criticism and misconception of this concept (e.g., Everett & Koerpel, 1986) and to extend its definition and practical value, Liddle (1988a) has offered three points of clarification:

1. Parallel processes have referred mainly to a process-level *description* of interaction be-

tween subsystems. This usage minimizes the inherent intervention potentiality of the concept. No action or intentionality is attributed to the supervisor's *observation* of the parallel interactions. Here, parallel processes are phenomena that are meaningful only, or primarily, in a perceptual or assessment sense. Use of the term isomorphism, therefore, can include the notion that these interactions are also capable of being altered and shaped—they are subject to intentional supervisory intervention and change. Using isomorphism as a cognitive organizer, the supervisor transforms the assessment of parallel processes into an intervention, redirecting a therapist's behavior and thereby influencing interactions at various system levels.

2. The isomorphic nature of therapy and training is thus a principle that exists not only in the domains of observation and description, but also *in the domain of supervisory intervention*. Isomorphism does not simply refer to patterns that exist in an assessment-only sense: the replicating interactions are implicit as information that can be re-formed. They are realities that can be altered as assessment and intervention become blurred. With forethought and intentionality, the supervisor uses the interactional information (i.e., the way in which problem patterns are replicating in the training and therapy domains) to redirect the co-created course of the training-therapy system. Importantly, supervisors are not passive observers of pattern replication, but intervenors and intentional shapers of the misdirected sequences they perceive, participate in, and co-create.

3. Another useful aspect of the isomorphism concept refers to the interconnection and interdependence of the principles that organize therapy and training. One's principles about the goals, methods, and means of evaluation in therapy can be utilized as an aid to conceptualization and action in training.

McDaniel, Weber, and McKeever (1983) and Liddle (1980) have detailed the isomorphism idea from the point of view of different schools of family therapy and demonstrated the transtheoretical nature of the interconnectedness of training and therapy. Isomorphism (concordance between one's principles of therapy and

training) was found in an analysis of several school-specific training approaches (Liddle, Breunlin, & Schwartz, 1988). The explication of a number of training models demonstrated that despite an enormous range of training philosophies and methods, a clear correspondence between the trainer's theory of therapy and training philosophy could be found (e.g., Colapinto, 1988; Fisch, 1988; Haas, Alexander, & Mas, 1988; Nichols, 1988; Mazza, 1988; Papero, 1988; Pirrotta & Cecchin, 1988). We will examine the isomorphism notion again later, when comparing school-specific approaches to family-therapy training.

Training in Family Systems Thinking

Family therapy's foundation rests on the often-romanticized assumption that it represents a paradigm shift, a discontinuous way of conceiving human problems (Haley, 1963). Toward this end, it follows that the topic of teaching a therapist how to think along these radically different lines would hold a prominent place in the training and supervision literature. Here we examine the prevailing wisdom and predominant training techniques used in teaching a therapist how to think in family systems terms.

A preeminent characteristic of this literature is its heterogeneity. The contributions on the topic of teaching therapists how to think along family systems lines are varied and vibrant, and represent some of the most creative work in the entire area of training and supervision. Like much of the training and supervision literature, and like the early days of the family-therapy literature itself, the literature in this area is diverse and nonconformist. There is no consensus on how best to achieve the training goals regarding a therapist's conceptual shift.

In fact, there is no agreement on the overall importance of therapist thinking. Some have argued that overabundant therapist theorizing can lead to distance in the therapeutic relationship (a common problem of beginning family therapists, according to Napier and Whitaker, 1973), or worse, "downright therapist game-playing" (Whitaker, 1976). Along these same lines, Weakland (1976) worries about the dangers of exalting theory as something more than a point of view.

Under these circumstances, "theory tends to become an ultimate standard according to which all else must be decided, done and judged" (Weakland, p. 113).

Another common concern about another conceptual dimension of training is the so-called "cloning effect." While most concede that there is a phase in trainee learning that might be termed the puppet phase (Simon & Brewster, 1983), the trainee's conceptual development must not become retarded at this imitation stage of learning.

Grunebaum's (1988) paper, "The Relationship of Family Theory to Family Therapy," appearing 12 years after the Whitaker (1976) and Weakland (1976) papers, demonstrated how a simplistic either–or debate (i.e., clinical theory is good/clinical theory is not good) had been transformed. Grunebaum recasts the limited question of Whitaker's "hindrance of theory" into a new light. He asks what the knowledge base is that allows therapists to do therapy, and urges therapists to have many theories (i.e., concepts at different levels). Grunebaum's contribution moves the debate about the role of theory in clinical practice into a fresh, more productive and less extreme arena.

There is a growing consensus that a central training task is to produce therapists who can think for themselves. These clinicians can eventually construct their own "personal, evolving model of therapy" (Liddle, 1985). Contemporary therapists are taught to go beyond the existing schools and to incorporate extant frameworks into a personally compatible style and integrative theory of therapy. Having students articulate their personal assumptions about a theory of therapy has become standard, even preferred, training practice (Constantine, 1976; Liddle, 1982b). The process of blending personal values and style with standard schools of therapy remains an area in need of much greater specification.

Just as therapist conceptual development is important, the concept of unlearning has been proposed as equally essential to trainee development (Meyerstein, 1981). This position parallels that of Bateson (1979), who has always argued for the difficulty and, in his more pessimistic moments, the impossibility of ever truly changing one's personal epistemology. For Keeney (1979), the matter of a clinician's concep-

tualization is always a difficult and complex matter, since the therapist is "part in" as well as "part of" the system he or she is "treating," rather than an outsider or a spectator.

While the division of family therapy into competing approaches was a sign of progress, "schoolism," at least in its previous form, may have outlived its usefulness. Grunebaum and Chasin (1982) offered one of the first papers to deal with transtheoretical issues in the conceptual life of family therapists. They proposed a useful schema for comparing, contrasting, and integrating important elements of each school of thought. Developments such as the integrative movement in psychotherapy and family therapy and contributions such as that by Grunebaum and Chasin (1982), as well as those by others (Sluzki, 1983; Kantor & Neal, 1985; (1983), signal an end, it is hoped, to the negative aspects of the "schools of thought" regime in family therapy. This was an era in which turf wars and the personal charisma of our "Great Originals" (Hoffman, 1981) overshadowed careful model development and refinement.

This development within the training sphere has obvious implications for and connection with the integrationism movement in family therapy. Guidelines have developed for therapists to articulate their own therapy premises and personal therapy model (Liddle, 1982b; Lebow, 1987). A series of "family-therapy theory building questions" assist the developing clinician with the personal model articulation (Piercy & Sprenkle, 1985a, 1988). There is evidence that trainers in other fields also believe in the importance of activities that seek to help trainees develop independence and a personal way of constructing their own practice, regardless of their field (Argyris & Schon, 1974; Schon, 1984, 1987).

Clinical thinking and the development of the therapist's conceptual life have not always been dealt with in formal ways. A series of publications recently appeared that address therapist development, including, of course, aspects of therapist conceptual development. Senior clinicians, such as Anderson (1988), Carter (1982), and Minuchin (1984), have shared their developmental detours in personally open ways. In this new tradition, Patterson (1987) articulates six stances of the strategic family therapist—a proposed road map to the process of becoming a strategic therapist. Similarly, edited volumes by Coleman (1985), Efron (1988), and Kaslow (1990) offer a wealth of personal disclosures by family therapists of different theoretical persuasions and generations that deal with, among other things, the conceptual life and development of the therapist. These publications provide a refreshing contrast to the age in which a magical view of the family therapist prevailed. This period perhaps would be best exemplified by the edited, narrated video training tapes in which the therapist (apparently) negotiates every clinical curve with success.

Methods of Teaching Family-Therapy Thinking

Various training methods have been proposed to teach therapists how to think in family systems terms. These contributions are in contrast to those that address the therapist conceptualization process at more generic levels (e.g., Auerswald, 1985; Sluzki, 1974a). In general, these contributions would fall under the "learning by doing" tradition in family therapy, a philosophy embraced by representatives of diverse viewpoints and methods. (DeAth, 1979; Whitaker & Keith, 1981; Minuchin & Fishman, 1981).

Unfortunately, formalized family-assessment procedures generally remain in the realm of family research. A tool for teaching family assessment was offered by Meyerstein (1979) with her "family behavioral snapshot." Another outline for trainers, this one designed to help trainees plan clinical strategy and session goals, was proposed by Schwartz (1981). The practice effects of planning for each session in this kind of systematic way are discussed by Schwartz as a viable means of shaping a trainee's conceptual development. Therapist conceptual development—and, in particular, the integration of theory into practice—was the concern of Liddle (1980) in his "concept cards" supervisory method. Using index cards, therapists keep an ongoing file of the concepts/theoretical ideas that they identify as operational with any particular case. Drawing upon the tradition of training actors, Liddle (1981) also developed training methods that use mental imagery techniques to help therapists translate abstract concepts into practical terms.

Other broader, more comprehensive schemas

that aid therapist conceptualization have been offered by Sluzki (1983), with his demarcation of process, structure, and world-view conceptual lenses, and Kantor and Neal (1985), with their notion of therapist stances as an antidote to an overemphasis on technique. Sheflen's (1978) "Susan Smiled: On Explanation in Family Therapy" also has pragmatic relevance for training since it deals so exquisitely with therapist conceptualization and the still-underdeveloped link of thinking to clinical action. This classic paper addresses the relativistic nature of a clinician's perceptions and was one of the first to deal with the constructivist position in family therapy in a clinically useful way. A beginner's guide to the problem-oriented initial interview (Weber, McKeever, & McDaniel, 1985) exemplifies a model that can be captured with the phrase, "Teaching 'doing' also teaches 'thinking.'" Although these papers are examples of work not intended originally for an audience of trainers per se, they made significant contributions to the training literature.

There are other publications that also were not designed originally for an audience of supervisors, but should be considered contributions to the supervision literature. These deal with the frightening topic of failure in therapy, and offer well-organized principles for addressing this unpleasant but important subject. Bross (1980) gives some principles of failure from the point of view of a strategic therapist, while Coleman and Gurman (Coleman, 1985) present a comprehensive categorization of ideas about therapeutic failure generated by the contributors to Coleman's volume. Their questions on the factors in therapeutic failure constitute an important checklist that, if ignored or misplayed in therapy, could contribute to clinical disaster.

Focusing on the traditional importance of triadic theory in family therapy, Coppersmith (1985) devised a series of exercises to teach trainees to think in terms of triads. Street and Foot (1984) used videotape vignettes to help trainees practice formulation of a presenting problem in workable terms. Green and Sager (1988) created a series of writing assignments that orient the thinking of clinicians along family systems lines. Simulated family exercises, although severely criticized by some for their artificiality (Haley, 1976), also offer a way to teach clinicians about families and therapy (Weingarten, 1979). Working from a strategic therapy base, several authors have proposed specific methods to teach this clinical approach. For instance, the circular questioning method of strategic therapy has been refined in the form of a comprehensive teaching protocol by Fleuridas, Nelson, and Rosenthal (1986), and a step-by-step procedure for teaching positive connotation has been offered by Constantine, Stone-Fish, and Piercy (1984).

Also in the strategic tradition, Anderson and Rambo (1988) conducted an interesting experiment in applying strategic-therapy principles to the construction of a training model. Employing the dual-description focus of Bateson (1979), they provide parallel descriptions of the training process from trainer and trainee perspectives. Kantor, Bograd, and Markson (1987) also offer a creative example of how systems principles can be used to help therapists develop conceptual and clinical skills. Information about the therapeutic process, in the form of intersession feedback forms filled out by the supervisor and families, is shared with the therapist. By feeding back this frequently overlooked source of (potentially) corrective data to the clinician, therapists are helped with clearly targeted aspects of their development, as well as with their thinking about clinical situations.

Reamy-Stephenson (1983) provides an illuminating discussion of the importance of defining and teaching "the importance of a non-objective reality" (p. 56). She extends the definition of systemic thinking offered by Sluzki's (1974a) seminal paper, while giving concrete suggestions on how to facilitate the "epistemological transition" of therapists. Reamy-Stephenson assumes many pathways to teaching the systemic view, including using contemporary media or current events and developments in other fields and society in general as effective and ineffective models.

Therapist-conceptualization ability also assumes prominence in the Ericksonian-hypnosis tradition. Erickson valued the therapist's ability to exploit the nonlogical side of human thinking—the so-called "right brain" aspects of human functioning. This appreciation of the analogic and metaphoric in the training domain is well exemplified in the work of Duhl (1983). One way in which intermingling has begun in family therapy is in the intermingling of con-

tent areas such as hypnosis and therapy. Haley has long thought this confluence to be an enriching one for family therapy and for training family therapists. Hypnosis teaches a precision of language, a critical therapist skill (Haley, 1976).

Related Areas of Work in Therapist Thinking

It should be noted that significant work in therapist conceptualization is occurring in two other areas of the literature: the development of psychometrically sound instrumentation to assess therapist thinking (i.e., conceptual and perceptual skills), and learning objectives. The former topic is dealt with in detail in Avis and Sprenkle (1990), and learning objectives will be covered later in this chapter.

Therapy as Art or Science: In Search of a New Frame

"Is therapy an art or a science?" This question has long posed a puzzle for psychotherapy. Family therapy has had its own debate about this topic as well. Some emphasize the idiosyncratic creative aspects of being a therapist (Papp, 1984), while others focus on interview skills and techniques (Haley, 1976). Known as someone who liked to help people "think about their thinking," Bateson (1972) offered a metaphor that applies here. Bateson criticized the either–or debate on the problem and proposed a recasting of our thinking along less reductionistic lines. For Bateson, effective thinking processes, and by extension effective therapy, involve a dialectic between rigor and imagination. When both ways of thinking are available, they recursively affect and shape each other in positive ways. Rigor and imagination in one's thinking bring the best of both worlds, worlds that for Bateson were never apart.

Learning Objectives and Skill Articulation

The training and supervision literature has advanced considerably since early discussions about the skills of family therapy (cf., Ferber, Mendelsohn, & Napier, 1972). Although its degree of focus has varied since its introduction into family therapy, the specification of learning objectives and the articulation of family-therapy skills have made an impact on the literature. For example, we have already discussed the paper on learning objectives and skills paper by Cleghorn and Levin (1973). Using the Cleghorn and Levin perceptual, conceptual, and executive skills model as a guide, Tomm & Wright (1979) presented a comprehensive outline that offered examples of therapist functions, competencies, and skills in each category over the course of family therapy. Another important paper in this area was presented by Falicov, Constantine, and Breunlin (1981). While clearly in the tradition of the previous two contributions mentioned above, the Falicov et al. article was unique in several ways. It represented a first step in identifying family-therapy training objectives with the goal of *training evaluation* in mind. Next, it emphasized observational, conceptual, and therapeutic skills as existing within the context of a specific school of thought—which, in this case, was an integrative structural/strategic family-therapy model. Finally, it discussed the difficulties with learning objective approaches, such as the notion that different objectives and skills are often made to appear discrete. In practice, of course, they have considerable overlap.

Developments in approach-specific skills and learning objectives have continued although some schools emphasize this much more than others. As the field and its clinical models have become more complex, it is less likely that writing in this area could be done from a generic family-therapy perspective. While there is some impetus in the psychotherapy field, particularly within the integrative tradition, to develop a generic psychotherapy theory (Orlinsky & Howard, 1988), no parallel movement has yet begun in family therapy. However, school-specific approaches to learning objectives and skill articulation have begun in earnest in family therapy, with many of the major approaches represented (cf., Liddle et al., 1988a, pp. 11–148). Virtually all modern family-therapy approaches to training clearly reflect the theory of therapy being taught (e.g., strategic: Mazza, 1988; Milan: Pirrota & Cecchin; 1988; psychodynamic-systems:

Nichols, 1988; brief therapy: Fisch, 1988; Bowen-therapy: Papero, 1988)., with some emphasizing the delineation, definition, and transmission of particular skills or therapist behaviors (e.g., structural family therapy: Colapinto, 1988; functional family therapy: Haas et al., 1988).

In summary, recent work has evolved in articulating family-therapy skills and learning objectives and has become increasingly sophisticated. First, these efforts are now theory- and approach-driven, and thus contextualized within specific schools of thought. Next, there is an integration of different areas in discussing skills and learning objectives. Street and Treacher (1980) discuss the possible synthesis between the microcounseling or microtraining approaches and complex family-therapy skills. For instance, Street and Foot (1984) particularize the skill-training approach and identify methods for teaching observational skills; Jenkins (1984) discusses family-therapy skills within the more sophisticated context of value-laden decisions about choosing skills and methods of teaching them; and Kantor and Neal (1985) elaborate family-therapy skills and learning objectives within the complex context of therapist stances. This helps the field to move beyond unnecessarily rigid, pragmatically irrelevant or distracting distinctions among schools of thought. The Basic Family Therapy Skills Project (Figley & Nelson, 1989) is a research program designed to identify the most important characteristics of the beginning family therapist.

Lenses to Aid the Training and Supervision Process

Several content areas of family therapy are included here because they have been discussed as lenses that can inform, if not radically reform, the training process. These content areas are the developmental and family life-cycle perspective, cross-cultural and ethnicity training, and feminist theory's reformulation of the family systems paradigm. Each area can be incorporated into one's model and, more basically, into one's value system. Superimposing these overlays (Liddle, 1988a) onto the basic training task makes the work more complex, and allows it to keep pace with contemporary developments in different parts of the field and of society.

Developmental and Life-Cycle Thinking

Family therapy's tradition appreciates the conceptual importance of life-cycle thinking in clinical practice. The earliest work of Singer and Wynne in their theory of family dysfunction, for instance, included clear observations and conclusions about psychopathology in families within a developmental paradigm (Singer & Wynne, 1965). Work in this area has burgeoned over the years. Family therapy is increasingly advanced in its use of life-cycle theory and understanding of normal family functioning (Carter & McGoldrick, 1989; Falicov, 1988a; Karpel, 1986; Liddle, 1983; Walsh, 1987). Cautions have been raised, however, that balance the view of the strengths and limitations of life-cycle and developmental thinking (Gurman, 1983; Liddle & Saba, 1983). And, theory development in this area has been robust (cf., Breunlin, 1988; Combrinck-Graham, 1985; Falicov, 1988b; Kaye, 1985; Montalvo, 1986; Olson, 1988; Wood & Talmon, 1983; Wynne, 1984).

Although some in family therapy eschew normative conceptions of families and individuals and see no reason to include developmental thinking in therapy or supervision (e.g., Fisch, 1988), a growing body of work has examined the specific implications of informing the training process with lifespan content and thinking. Duhl (1983), Ferguson (1979), and Liddle (1988) described conceptual frameworks and rationales for including developmental content about normal families, and developmental thinking in general, into family-therapy training curricula and clinical supervision. Walsh (1987) emphasized the clinical usefulness of normal family research as well as the necessity of including such content in training. Liddle, Schmidt, and Ettinger (in press) discussed the general problems of research utilization in clinical practice and training, and provided a model of research translation for family therapists working with adolescents. Fulmer (1983) and Weingarten (1987a) developed teaching activities designed to sensitize participants to the family life-cycle concept and manner of thinking.

This trend in family-therapy training should not be surprising. The field has a legacy of using developmental concepts to organize its clinical practice, at least at a general level. *Uncommon Therapy* (Haley, 1973) was the first family-therapy text to structure a theoretical viewpoint (in this case, strategic therapy) along the lines of the life cycle. There remains a gap, however, between the concept or recommendation of integrating family life-cycle theory—or, as it has also been called, *developmental thinking*—into family-therapy practice. This gap also exists for the other overlays considered in this section: ethnicity/cross-cultural sensitivity and feminism. Although some have begun to specify the ways in which these content areas will be incorporated into the clinical models (Hughes, Berger, & Wright, 1978; Quinn, Newfield, & Protinsky, 1985; Stratton, 1988; Worthington, 1987), the work clearly has just begun. The reality or perception of an empirical base to such content may hinder the use of research findings in clinical practice. Clinicians, even those with doctoral training in a scientist-practitioner model, are notoriously difficult to interest in research findings. Most psychotherapists report that clinical research has little relevance to their practice (Morrow-Bradley & Elliot, 1986; Sechrest & Cohen, 1983). Thus, these content areas/lenses may not prove to be popular or easy to incorporate into practice. This may be due to a perception of an association with an empirical tradition (Liddle, 1991). The studies on the clinical-utilization problem by practicing psychotherapists may contain helpful hints in preventing what would be an unfortunate development.

This general content area has clear implications for activity in the theory and research arenas as well. How complex can our therapy approaches become? Is it possible to inform our models by the developmental, feminist, ethnic, and cross-cultural traditions without turning them into top-heavy monsters? Will this spirit of designing our theories with appropriate complexity and allowing them to be influenced by contemporary sensibilities create unwieldy and unrealistic "supertheories" (Liddle, 1983)?

Cross-Cultural and Ethnic Sensitivity

It is inconceivable to consider the family without using a developmental lens. Just so, it is now also increasingly difficult to condone what we might call the homogeneity myth regarding cross-cultural and ethnic issues. Simply put, clinicians are increasingly conscious of the need to have a cultural and ethnic template in their clinical work. A number of contributors have exhorted trainers and clinicians to expand their cultural and ethnic consciousness.

Despite the areas of activity, there is no consensus about how to train therapists for cross-cultural appreciation. Indeed, there is disagreement about what it means to be a clinician who is cross-culturally or ethnically aware. Some of the earliest contributions emphasized the characteristics of the different ethnic groups—differentiating one from another on the basis of history, traditions, and mores. These followed what might be termed a sociological tradition. The diverse, edited volume by McGoldrick, Pearce, and Giordano (1982) captured this spirit by bringing the similarities and differences of diverse cultures to the fore. *Ethnicity and Family Therapy* was a United Nations of content for the therapist to digest. Integration of this content into existing approaches to therapy was not emphasized, however, and it is on this score that controversy in this area exists.

Montalvo and Guitierrez (1983) suggest an alternative approach to teaching cultural sensitivity: "Since families can use their cultural repertoire and uniqueness to hide their basic patterns of functioning, a focus on interinstitutional dilemmas seems more useful for family therapists than a focus on cultural uniqueness" (p. 31).

Appreciation of this uniqueness does not require specialized training in the group's cultural and social traditions. Montalvo and Guitierrez believe that therapists will discover these traditions and customs during therapy by adopting the role of a learner.

To make the cultural dimension more central than the family's interactions with the surrounding institutions is to invite excesses, both emotional and technical. Emotionally, therapists will feel that unless they are within the skin of the culture, they understand little and can do less. Technically, therapists will require training in each particular ethnic and cultural background, confusing credentials on ethnicity with problem solving skills. The result would be a set of overspecialized baroque therapies in a field that still lacks basic research on methods as well as outcome. (p. 31)[3]

Montalvo and Guitierrez (1988) have been among the most critical about the misuse of the cultural identity emphasis. They note that while the cultivation of cultural and ethnic sensitivity as a core training concern is important, this noble goal can become misguided. Under such conditions, "problem solving becomes trivialized. The focus of accomplishment shifts to understanding the family from within the culture instead of helping them overcome the problem. Understanding based on the outside struggle between the two cultures—the family's and the host society's—is neglected" (p. 184).

Clinically speaking, these same authors argue, "The integration of openness to culture with clinical skills entails not allowing ethnicity to become an ascendant and overriding consideration. Underlying philosophy should be: People are more alike than they are different. Rapport does not depend on cultural attunement only" (p. 184).

Gradually, new emphases were given to the early focus on characteristic differentiation among cultural groups. Articles began to emphasize process dimensions between therapists and families, processes within families, and interactions between families and broader contexts (Falicov, 1983; Lappin, 1983). Warnings were given about the possible limitations of a cross-cultural "sensitivity" that preoccupies itself with content.

The danger of the interest in ethnicity is that it can distract us from the ways that poverty and social economic circumstances—and shortsighted policy makers—can smash and trample the family. *That* is not pretty, but ethnicity is pretty. I have nothing against the interest in ethnic patterns in families. I appreciate a good story on how one uses a family's ethnic background in treatment, but if you get too preoccupied with that sort of thing, you begin to miss the more

---

[3] *Editors' Note.* An even more extreme position against the need of therapists to receive specialized training in the area of ethnicity is taken by Friedman (Chapter 5) in his articulation of Bowen theory.

important social dynamics like making sure that the family gets decent health care or that it is not locked out of the job market. (Montalvo, 1986, p. 39)

In the spirit championed by Montalvo, Falicov (1988b) offered an intricate framework for teaching family-therapy trainees to think culturally. In merging the ecological developmentalism of Bronfrenbrenner with the macrosystemic influences of culture outlined by Sluzki (1979), Falicov presented a blueprint for training programs that want to take culture and ethnicity seriously enough to weave them into the fabric of the program. Also in this tradition, the work of Lappin (1983) deserves serious attention as well.

Feminist Thinking and Training and Supervision

The feminist political movement and intellectual tradition have changed American and worldwide cultures. In family therapy, these changes have been impossible to ignore, as the feminist debate has taken its turn on family therapy's center stage. Although it has shared the spotlight with other weighty topics such as constructivism and family therapy's relative influence on the traditional mental health and social service structures, feminism in family therapy has flourished. The literature on family therapy and feminism has exploded with books (McGoldrick, Anderson & Walsh, 1989; Carter, Walters, Papp, & Silverstein, 1988; Goodrich, Rampage, Ellman, & Halstead, 1988; Luepnitz, 1989), chapters, journal articles, and a new journal, *The Journal of Feminist Family Therapy*.

In family therapy, feminist thought has been evidenced by two kinds of contributions, one that deals with how feminist thinking can inform the field, and another that specifically attends to training and supervision issues. Family therapy has been challenged simply to keep up with the times and be true to its contextually sensitive heritage (Goldner, 1985). Feldman (1982) combined research findings with a discussion of the negative effects of traditional gender roles on family members. Another position asks that gender bias issues be more centrally placed in the field's thinking about training and supervision (Okun, 1983). In one of the earliest articles on this topic, Hare-Mustin (1978) made a series of recommendations as to the knowledge, skills, and attitudes necessary to confront sex-role stereotypes in one's clinical work (as well as in therapists' own lives). The caveat to be aware of one's own biases has been a consistent theme with family therapy's feminist authors. This is an area in which the trainer's level of functioning is important. Trainers are advised that in order to facilitate gender-bias freedom in their trainees, they first must be free of such biases themselves.

An important part of the feminist discourse has been the transformation of generic feminist principles into particular contexts of training and supervision. In a paper that makes clear progress along these lines, Caust, Libow, and Raskin (1981) define several major problem areas in training, including (1) the expression of authority and power, (2.) countertransference (trainees' feelings about power in families in the husband–wife relationship, etc.), (3.) sexual politics (power differentials when women are supervised by men), (4.) role-model issues (problems in using women supervisors as role models owing to sex-role biases), and (5.) boundary issues (related to the assertion that women have more difficulty in maintaining boundaries and the implications of this tendency in training and therapy).

Avis (1986) offers additional gender issues in training: (1) the failure to incorporate gender and power issues squarely enough into the training context; (2.) teaching theories that disadvantage women; (3) dealing with the fact that the goals of training may run counter to the socialization processes and outcomes with women; and (4) the realm of interactional processes in supervision between women and men.

Power and power differentials resulting from rigid gender-based roles are of major concern (Libow, 1985; Avis, 1986; Carter, Papp, Silverstein, & Walters, 1984). Interestingly, this problem has led to a resurgence of interest in and writing on this relatively neglected area of the field. The topic of power in relationships and families is often referred to as a great unresolved divide in family therapy (Dell, 1986; Rabkin, 1986).

Translating gender issues into the clinical sphere remains a challenge. One of these unresolved issues is how to handle gender content in family-therapy curricula. Should gender be included as one might include another course on the family life cycle or ethnicity, or should the integration be at a more basic, pervasive level? If the latter route is chosen, how will it be accomplished? While some have argued that it is acceptable to proceed on both fronts simultaneously (Avis, 1986), others contend that such changes are insufficient. They assert that only fundamental structural changes in programs and personal changes in individual trainers will do (Goodrich et al., 1988).[4]

Many of the feminist theory papers are in accord with this latter position. Several have pointed out the inadequacy of family systems theory (James & McIntryr, 1983), and family therapy in general (Goldner, 1985; Hare-Mustin, 1978), in dealing with contemporary changes in men's and women's roles.

The feminist movement not only has addressed macro issues in the family-therapy field, but it has also critiqued specific approaches and criticized them for sexist thinking and insensitivity to gender issues. Hare-Mustin (1978) was the first openly to criticize particular models on gender issues, citing the Bowen therapy and structural models as deficient in addressing sex-role issues. Gender biases in the behavioral marital and family-therapy approaches have also been discussed by several authors (Gurman & Klein, 1984; Jacobson, 1983; Margolin, Fernandez, Talovic, & Onorato, 1983). Along these same lines, Alexander's functional family therapy, a behavioral and social learning systems model, has been criticized by Avis (1986) as perpetuating traditional gender roles.

Perhaps the most extensive critique of family therapy approaches is contained in Luepnitz's (1988) outstanding volume. About a third of this book is devoted to a feminist critique of eight contemporary family-therapy approaches (i.e., those of Nathan Ackerman, Murray Bowen, Virginia Satir, Salvador Minuchin, Ivan Boszormenyi-Nagy, strategic family therapy,

Carl Whitaker, and Milan systemic therapy). Each model is evaluated in terms of, among other things, its ability to be transformed into a feminist-sensitive approach.

A noteworthy contribution to this literature is the paper by Wheeler, Avis, Miller, & Chaney (1985). Although it covers much of the same territory as others in its area (critique of systems theory, importance of understanding the sexism problem in families, and family therapy in its sociopolitical context), it is novel in its use of the perceptual, conceptual, and executive skills framework to discuss feminist family therapy. Further, these skills are grounded temporally— they are discussed in terms of three phases of therapy. The contribution by Wheeler and associates demonstrates how a feminist philosophy can be incorporated into training.

Some believe that it is the structure of training programs and the very content of training that must be transformed if a feminist viewpoint is substantively to change the field (Goodrich et al., 1988). These authors recommend that training programs use consultants periodically to check their progress in combating sexist philosophies and its change on feminist ideals.

Other aspects of training have been emphasized to demonstrate the manner in which feminist values can be used to change family therapy and family-therapy training. Reid, McDaniel, Donaldson, and Tollers (1987) considered skill development as it would relate to female trainees, and differential issues of career development for women and men trainees. Caust et al. (1981) stressed a multiple-context approach (individual supervision, group supervision, didactic presentations) to facilitate healthy sex-role attitudes.

Summing up this section, the contributions of the feminist family-therapy literature have been enormous. These books and papers have articulated the problem area from the macrosystemic levels of society and the field to the level of individual families, trainers, and trainees. They have reminded family therapy, and family-therapy training, of its political nature, urging family therapy to take its own clinical advice seriously—to pay attention to the sociopolitical and economic contexts in which it resides. The feminist dialogue in family therapy has contributed to the field's epistemological renewal. Its arrival was timely. The epistemology movement

---

[4] *Editors' Note.* While there is certainly value in the study of feminist theory per se, and the feminist mental health and psychotherapy literature, in general we lean toward preferring what Liddle calls "the more basic" approach. Thus, a separate chapter on feminism or gender does not appear in this *Handbook*, although pertinent matters are addressed in many of the chapters, as requested in our "Author's Guidelines," which appear at the front of this book.

seemed to be increasingly devoid of content, and intent on emphasizing theoretical elegance for its own sake. Feminist thinking in family therapy has operationalized the questioning of basic values and assumptions. Further, it promises to show how the inspection and alteration of these values can lead to needed change in a more contextually and gender-oriented direction. The sex-roles critique of specific models of family therapy is a welcome addition for trainers who worry about teaching outdated material to their students. It has also injected a much-needed critical theory perspective into family therapy, a field that, at its worst moments, too easily glides into a self-congratulatory posture.

METHODS OF TRAINING AND SUPERVISION

Live Supervision—Method and Symbol

Live supervision is generally considered simply as a *method* of training and supervision. This procedure, as we have seen, was first explicated by Montalvo (1973). It refers to the supervisor's observation of a session and the capacity to interrupt and guide the events and interactions of that same session, *as they happen*. Although live supervision as a method can be described in a straightforward way, it has come to represent much more than a single training technique in the world of family therapy. For Hoffman (1981), perhaps the field's most astute historian, "The advent of the one-way screen, which clinicians have used since the 1950s to observe live family interviews, was analogous to the discovery of the telescope. Seeing differently made it possible to think differently" (p. 3). Lewis and Rohrbaugh (1989) suggest that "the one-way mirror may be as basic to family therapy as the couch was to psychoanalysis" (p. 323). Live supervision has been characterized as a "hallmark of family therapy" (Nichols, 1984, p. 89). Simply put, the one-way mirror and its concomitant live supervision procedure have symbolic meaning in family therapy. They are synonymous with the advent and identity of the field.

Development

It was Charles Fulweiler, a psychologist, who first exposed Haley to the possibilities of a supervisor intervening during sessions (Simon, 1982). In 1953, Fulweiler was using the one-way mirror to teach psychological testing at the University of California, Berkeley. Seeing the families of the children that he tested, Fulweiler developed a style of observing the session, entering the room and offering some comments, and then leaving. Haley met Fulweiler in 1957 and became keenly interested in this procedure. Haley's observation that a supervisor's directives during a session were at once a supervisory and a therapeutic intervention led to one of the most important developments in family therapy. The procedure was refined and standardized for use with the telephone as part of the Institute for Family Therapy, a paraprofessional training program at the Philadelphia Child Guidance Clinic. Minuchin, Haley, and Montalvo were the key figures in the development of this program. At its cornerstone was the supervisory invention called live supervision.

Prevalence

Despite its apparent popularity, live supervision is not used as widely as some might think. Saba and Liddle (1986) and McKenzie et al. (198?) found that although live supervision (and videotape supervision) was believed by supervisors to be the most effective supervisory method, it is used less frequently than such methods as audiotape review and case notes. However, studies of supervision methods in training centers (Henry et al., 1986; Sprenkle, 1988) found a greater use of live supervision and videotape procedures. A study by Kaplan (1987) supports these findings. Within family-therapy training programs, especially those outside universities, live supervision plays a more central role.[5]

---

[5] *Editors' Note.* In nonuniversity training centers that specialize in family therapy, live supervision is more feasible and practical since such centers often carry a relatively small clinical caseload in comparison, say, with that found in a university medical center psychiatry department. In such settings, where large-scale service requirements exist alongside the training mission, live supervision as the *major* format is virtually impossible.

Although they used a sample that might not be representative nationally, Lewis and Rohrbaugh (1989) found only one third of a statewide group of Virginia AAMFT supervisors used live supervision. This intriguing finding, if supported by another study with a representative national sample, raises troubling issues for live-supervision proponents.

Criticisms

Live supervision has always had its critics, who have drawn up a list of complaints and cautions. These include: trainee dependence, intrusion into the privacy of the therapy, disruption of the natural rhythms and processes of sessions, family members' reactions to the call-ins, encouragement of trainee passivity, and a mechanical therapy approach, deskilling effects on trainees, boundary blurring between therapist and supervisor responsibility, and lack of opportunity for therapists to learn independent behavior (Beroza, 1983; Betcher & Zinberg, 1988; Hare-Mustin, 1976; Nichols, 1975, 1988; Russell, 1976; Simon & Brewster, 1983; Whitaker, 1976).

Others have responded to these criticisms. For instance, Westheafer (1984) defines a common process that occurs when live supervision becomes ineffective. In one situation, an incongruent hierarchy develops as a defense against issues of attachment in the supervisor–supervisee relationship. Schwartz, Liddle, and Breunlin (1988) take on two of the most common criticisms of live supervision—trainee robotization and problematic isomorphic sequences. They describe several common "muddles of live supervision," emphasizing the implementation dilemmas of this method and a supervisor's potential solutions. Additionally, careful research is emerging on the impact of live supervision on therapists and trainees (Cotton, 1987; Fennell, Hovestadt, & Harvey, 1986; Frankel, 1988; Gorman, 1989; Liddle, Davidson & Barrett, 1988; Piercy, Sprenkle, & Constantine, 1986; Wright, 1986). These empirical findings do not support the adverse opinions about and the emotional claims made for the harmful effects of live supervision.

Definitions and Uses

Those who have written about live supervision have used the field's key contributions (Haley, 1976; Montalvo, 1973) as benchmarks of creativity and clarity of expression. Over the years, the extensions of these earliest ideas have taken various forms. First, practical guidelines were formulated for the conduct of live supervision. The contributions in this category grow in their ability to define more precisely how live supervision is done (Birchler, 1975; Rickets & Turner, 1978). This is especially true in comparison with some of the earliest papers on the subject (Kempster & Stavitsky, 1967).

Taking a skills-definition approach and using therapy and training's interconnection as a guide to model construction, Liddle and Schwartz (1983) created a flow-chart framework for supervisory decision making in live supervision. Similarly, Kingston and Smith (1983) detail the factors that go into preparing for the live supervision session and give practical hints for supervisors.

Another extension of the live supervision method came in the conceptual realm. Berger and Dammann (1982) remind us always to conceive of live supervision in terms of its broader ecology. Live supervision is not only a training technique, but is also a context unto itself with certain characteristics (e.g., discrepancy in perception of affect between those in the therapy room and those behind the mirror), *as well as* a form of treatment (i.e., when live supervision is used, it cannot be separated from the therapy model but is one with the therapy).

For better or worse, live supervision becomes one with therapy. Piercy and Sprenkle (1986) offer some helpful conceptualizations concerning live supervision, and supervision methods in general. They define eight forms of live supervision. These vary according to dimensions called *temporal* (immediate or delayed), *spatial* (in or outside the room), and *personnel* (individual or team approach to supervision). Other conceptual developments in live supervision are discussed in the section on isomorphism between therapy and training.

The *earphone*, or the so-called "bug in the ear," is also considered a form of live supervision (Brown, 1985). It is thought to be most effective with beginning therapists. Byng-Hall (1982) details the earphone's advantages and disadvantages, as well as guidelines for its use. McGoldrick (1982) emphasized the effective aspects of the earphone method in situations that present particular difficulties for novice therapists (i.e., a case that might trigger personal issues). Because of the potential for many problems with this technique, however, earphone proponents recommend careful planning. This includes clarity with the trainees about the ground rules and procedures for earphone use, and consideration of the trainee's developmental level. Russell's (1976) critique of live supervision includes a strong dissent about the earphone method.

Peer Approaches/Group Supervision

From its earliest days, the literature has recognized the salience of peer influences in supervision. The practical realities of training settings dictated that training and supervision be done in groups (often in conjunction with individual supervision). To be sure, family therapy and family-therapy supervision appreciate how context considerations are all important. In this regard, the training literature demonstrates how not only to take into account, but also to *use, the presence of peers* in a training or supervision setting. This area's earliest papers focused on understanding and using the dynamic processes of the supervision group to facilitate training goals (Allen, 1976; Beatman, 1964; Cohen et al., 1976; Hare & Frankena, 1972; Siegel & Dulfano, 1973; Steir & Goldenberg, 1975; Tucker & Liddle, 1978).

Amplifying this tradition, Quinn, Atkinson, and Hood (1985) describe the organization and ground rules of operation for a stuck-case clinic that structures peer group influence into the training process. In this setting, therapists are responsible for bringing in difficult cases for consultation, and are also in charge of running the group discussion. The rules impose organization on the group members' roles (e.g., one member focuses on articulating the strengths of the case, another on sequences of interaction, and others with particular background or experience might tune in to their areas of expertise). The supervisor's role is to guide the group process and summarize the intervention that will be delivered. For Rabbi, Lehr, and Hayner (1984), the most important variable in the successfully functioning peer supervision group is the existence of a relatively equal competence level among the group members.

In summary, the presence of peers in the supervision group, and in the training context in general, has been discussed in the literature. While our previous review found this area to be underexplored (Liddle & Halpin, 1978), the same conclusion cannot be reached today because of the progress that has been made. Although no empirical conclusions have been reached, peers are believed to be a helpful— and for some, a necessary—component of therapist training (Brown, 1985; Liddle et al., 1984).

Team Approaches: Further Extensions of Live Supervision

Some of the most creative extrapolations of live supervision principles and methods have been in the area of peer and team approaches to family-therapy supervision. Our discussion of this topic, however, must be informed by the therapy model being taught. The structural model championed live supervision as we have described it thus far. But as Roberts (1981, 1983) has discussed, supervision can be either supervisor- or team-guided. The former approach tends more to resemble a structurally oriented approach, while the latter is more strategic. It has been within the strategic school of thought that these adaptations of live supervision have come. This generally has taken the form of having the team directly participate in the treatment. The observing team—or, as it is now known, the reflecting team—can send messages into the room, bypassing, supporting, or sometimes opposing the therapist's stance. This pushes team members (therapists who may serve as the therapist during the next interview) to be involved in the session in a more demanding and cognitive way. They will be called upon to offer ideas and to help formulate an intervention.

Another conceptual distinction needs to be made when discussing team supervisory approaches. This involves the boundary between supervision and therapy. Team approaches, by their nature, blur the division between therapy and training. In live supervision, the supervision method is not primarily a therapeutic intervention. However, live supervision is understood in a contextual manner, in which the very presence of the supervisor and the one-way mirror (along with the interventions to the therapist) creates an intervention. However, with team approaches, by design, there is more of an intentional and intervention component to the supervision method (team messages). In short, there is an intentional blending of the contexts of treatment and training in the team model. This innovation of accentuating the team's intervention potential is unique to family therapy.

The rise in the popularity of team approaches to training and supervision is related to the success of the team approaches to strategic therapy. The Brief Therapy Project of the Ackerman Institute in the mid-1970s pioneered team methods that not only were thought of as the core of treatment, but also were prized for their training advantages (Papp, 1977). These formulations were largely based on the therapeutic methods of the Selvini group in Milan. Later to be known as the "Milan model," this approach used the team as a *group mind* that would formulate hypotheses and construct interventions that were delivered by the therapist.

As we have seen, in the "classic" characterization of live supervision, messages are sent into the therapy room via telephone. These brief phone-ins are designed to provide the therapist and to alter his or her behavior. The phone-ins are not intended directly for the family, although the family certainly can be affected by the call's content. Team approaches to supervision, on the other hand, also are designed to send messages into the therapy room from behind the one-way mirror, but in this case, the messages are intended not only for the therapist, but also for the family.

While some emphasize a *therapy approach* that includes team interventions, minimizing or confusing the true supervisory or training aspects of the methods (Papp, 1980; Young et al., 1989), others are more interested in specifying guidelines for a distinct *training approach* (Pegg & Manocchio, 1982). For example, Olson and Pegg (1979) describe different supervisory interventions (authoritarian, supportive, explorative, and collaborative) made when the team and supervisor join the clients and therapist in the

therapy room. Carter (1982) illustrates this approach with guidelines for a supervisory discussion in the family's presence.

The simultaneity of training and treatment goals is a common theme with many authors. Coppersmith (1978) describes phone-ins to the therapist, phone-ins from the team to specific family members, and phone-ins between family members. Heath (1982) offers principles for organizing family-therapy teams in training, stressing the need to define clearly the training aspects of team use. (Recall the previously mentioned point about how some team approaches blur the distinctions and functions of the training and therapy functions of supervisory/treatment teams.) Suggestions are abundant on how teams ought to function (Cade, Speed, & Seligman, 1986; Heath, 1982; Landau-Stanton & Stanton, 1983, 1986; Roberts, 1981; Roberts et al., 1987; Young et al., 1989). Cornwell and Pearson (1981) offer novel hints on such matters as how to deal with common problems in using team approaches, including how to leave a session gracefully so that one can consult with the team ("withdrawal etiquette"), how to cope with the interruptions of the team, and how to use the data from a group of observers.

Another variation on the topic of teams concerns a procedure in which the *supervisor enters the room or is part of sessions* with the therapist and family. Smith and Kingston (1980) and Barnes and Campbell (1982) offer an approach in which the supervisor, in essence, assumes the place of a therapeutic team. Here, the supervisor sits in on the sessions, placing himself or herself off to the side of the therapist and family. There are variations on this method, related to the therapy approach being used. Writing from a structural-family-therapy perspective, Walters (1977) discusses the manner in which a supervisor joins a session to demonstrate use of parental authority. This supervisory method is not without its risks, and has received a good deal of criticism (cf., Beroza, 1983). "When a teacher doesn't know what to teach a student to do, he can have the student join him in a family session. Through osmosis the student is supposed to learn what to do. If the student is placed with an experienced person, he learns to sit back and not take the responsibility for what happens in the session" (Haley, 1974).

Haley has probably exaggerated the warning

necessary for using the sit-in method. There are occasions when it is warranted and useful. Just as live supervision does not seem to be an inherently helpful or harmful method, the supervisor sit-in procedure also is neither friend nor foe. The results of the sit-in method lie in its execution rather than in its nature. As the supervisory literature matures, we will witness how such methods can be discussed in greater depth. This will replace the either–or thinking of the past. Guidelines are needed that specify the conditions under which any given technique is and is not helpful. Ultimately, to add yet another perspective, these are empirical questions, and should be treated as such.

A final variation on the topic of teams concerns *cotherapy teams* as a training method. In family therapy, there has been no more vocal and visible proponent of cotherapy than Whitaker (Whitaker & Keith, 1981). Whitaker and Garfield (1987) offer cotherapy and consultation as a bona fide method of teaching psychotherapy. Although there are some exceptions, the supervision of cotherapy teams has received less attention than has the general topic of cotherapy (Berkman & Berkman, 1984; Latham, 1982; Tucker et al., 1976; Tucker & Liddle, 1978). How to facilitate the cotherapy relationship and to identify the problems that arise in cotherapy and supervision of cotherapy are issues that have been appreciated for some time (Jurasky, 1964; Sonne & Lincoln, 1964).

The literature on team approaches to training and supervision suffers from repetition. It seems to be an example of a more general trend in family therapy—the inability to integrate, comment on, and utilize the work of others. The redundancy on the topic of teams is puzzling since there are gaps in this part of the literature. Despite some noteworthy contributions, such as Roberts' pilot study and articulation of supervisor-guided and collaborative team groups, at least two areas need further specification.

For example, the developmental level of the therapist (advanced versus beginning) as a variable in considering a team's efficacy is insufficiently explored. An exception would be McGoldrick's (1982) discussion of this topic in relation to the earphone supervision method. Teams vary considerably and are run in very different ways. Some of them, for instance, are

structured with more experienced therapists in mind (Cade et al., 1986). These methods might be inappropriate or harmful with beginning trainees. Practical, empirically based guidelines for which kind of supervisory team is effective with which level of therapist/trainee need to be formulated.

Finally, the training group's developmental progress (and its management) is another area needing further inquiry. Despite early work on this important topic (Tucker et al., 1976; O'Hare, Heinrich, Kirschnor, Oberstine, & Ritz, 1975; Dell, Pulliam, Sheely, & Goolishian, 1977; Steir & Goldenberg, 1975), it now, unfortunately, commands only modest attention (Wendorf et al., 1985).

Videotapes in Family-Therapy Training

If live supervision is accepted as a hallmark of family-therapy supervision, the use of videotape in training must also be considered a defining feature of such training. Video training tapes have socialized an entire generation of clinicians wanting to work with families. Certain tapes became quite well known and were identified by their primary characteristics, which were often dramatic in-session therapist behaviors or events. Minuchin's "Taming Monsters," Montalvo's "Family with a Little Fire," and Haley's "Dog Phobia" became classics of the genre, invoked in the same way that one would recall a favorite film.

Although certain schools of thought—notably, the structural and strategic perspectives—pioneered video teaching material development, they were not alone in this contribution. The Georgetown Family Center developed a series of videotape lectures by Bowen, and Satir and Whitaker were often the subject of consultation session videotapes that were readily obtainable. In recent years, the AAMFT developed what it calls the "Masters Series." There are live demonstration interviews conducted at the annual national conference. Noted clinicians conduct a session in front of a large group of clinicians via closed-circuit television. These tapes are available for purchase through the association. What started with six published sources of videotapes (see Ferber et al.,'s *The Book of Family Therapy*) has now become a vibrant growth industry in the family-therapy field. As a review of today's family-therapy trade publications (*The Family Therapy Networker, Family Therapy News, Newsletter of the American Family Therapy Association*) indicates, dozens of video training tapes are available for purchase or rental.

Videotape Supervision

Despite the consistent presence of videotape as a characteristic feature of family-therapy supervision and training (Bodin, 1969, 1972; Hatcher, 1982; Perlmutter, Loeb, Gumpert, O'Hara, & Higbie, 1967), there have been remarkably few systematic descriptions or studies of videotape use in training and supervision. The earliest papers clearly had a psychodynamic slant (Berger, 1970), emphasizing how videotapes foster insight and understanding on the therapist's part (Alger & Hogan, 1970; Alger, 1973). This focus has continued in recent years. More recently, Kramer and Reitz (1980) have stressed the role of videotape playback in facilitating trainee self-awareness. Their method targets the therapist's subjective experience for supervisory intervention, and aims to increase the congruence between the inner experience and behavior of the therapist.

Gradually, the literature began to reflect recognition of videotape supervision's complexity and, in terms of its ineffectual application, limitations. Whiffen (1982) was among the first to offer a frank discussion of inept videotape supervision. One of the most common problems is the supervisor's lack of focus in using videotape. In this situation, the trainee becomes cognitively and emotionally overwhelmed. Hodas (1985) understands the interrelationship of videotape and live supervision complementary methods (not as isolated training techniques). Videotape supervision, as compared with live supervision, demands that the supervisor function as more of an analyst of the session's events. Videotape review permits the supervisor to challenge the supervisee to generate several therapeutic alternatives. Brainstorming possible strategies is more reasonable in this context than in the more pressured "do it now" arena of live supervision. In addition, videotape offers an important opportunity to address issues of therapist style (Hodas, 1985). In developments that will

parallel the integrative clinical models, the future will likely witness integrative, multicomponent models of supervision and training. These approaches will need to particularize the interrelationships among methods of video and live supervision, and group and individual supervision.

Other innovations might be in store as well. In what may be an idea whose time has come, but also something that will be difficult to implement, Fine and McIntosh (1986) describe the use of *interactive videos* to illustrate different approaches to family therapy. Along equally innovative, but more dramatic, lines, Haley claims to be the first to conduct *transcontinental live supervision*. The supervisors were in one part of the country watching a session via satellite and doing live supervision for an interview that was happening thousands of miles away.

Attempts to place the techniques of videotape supervision within a conceptual or theoretical framework have been rare. Breunlin, Karrer, McGuire, and Cimmarusti (1988), however, accomplish this and more in the most sophisticated treatment to date of videotape supervision. They offer second-order cybernetics as a theoretical framework for videotape supervision. In this way, the trainee's inner experience of the therapy and the interactional realities of the session can be addressed. These authors discuss the inadequacies of previous conceptions of videotape supervision (i.e., lack of conceptual framework, overemphasizing whether to focus on the interactions of therapy or on the inner experience or awareness of the supervisee). Breunlin and coworkers offer several guidelines for the effective use of videotape. These include: focused goal setting, attention to and a connecting of the inner experience of the trainee *over different contexts* (i.e., in-session experience of himself or herself versus experience of self as one watches the videotape), selection of tape segments that offer alterable therapist behaviors, and the supervisor's capacity to moderate the therapist's arousal in watching the tape and to moderate his or her self-evaluations.

Audiotapes in Supervision

Interestingly, although the use of audiotapes is common practice in psychotherapy supervision, it has never been popular in family-therapy training. Hatcher (1982) identifies audiotape supervision as a form of direct supervision in family therapy. Hart (1982) reviews the psychotherapy literature on the use of audiotapes in supervision and gives model-specific guidelines (e.g., audiotapes in task-focused and personal-growth approaches). This source gives family-therapy supervisors a reference to consult on the effective use of videotapes.

Simulation as a Method of Training

The running joke around some family-therapy training programs in the early days was that it was fine if families did not show up because simulations could always be used to demonstrate technique and provide practice opportunities. There are many, however, who have taken simulation seriously for some time (Bardill, 1976; Berg, 1978; Raasoch & Lacquer, 1979), despite active criticism (Haley, 1976). The earliest contributions used family sculpture as a primary way of teaching the complexity of family interactions (Duhl, Kantor, & Duhl, 1973). Specific simulation exercises have been proposed (Churven, 1977). These structured activities use the family life cycle as a way to organize simulations (Fulmer, 1983), for example. Other techniques allow trainees to experience four different family-therapy approaches (Israelstam, 1988). In addition to describing how simulation can be used in a live supervision preparation course, West et al. (1985) identify some of the skills that can and cannot be taught using simulation. This signifies the direction in which future writing on simulation must move. Evolution of this area demands a situation- and context-specific description of the advantages and disadvantages of the method, emphasizing the circumstances in which it works best. The live supervision literature, for example, is an area in which this kind of specification has already begun.[6]

---

[6] *Editors' Note.* This very well made point about specificity in training applies equally well, of course, to all training methods and techniques.

Other Methods Used in Training

The general area of methods illustrates how trainers have invented particular devices to remedy perceived gaps in training and supervision. Not surprisingly, they reflect the training orientations of the authors.

Piercy and Sprenkle (1985a) offer family-therapy theory-building exercises to introduce a personal, idiosyncratic approach to a student's development of a theoretical orientation. They also present a schema for classifying methods of training and supervision, using *spatial* (proximity), *temporal* (when the supervision occurs), and *personnel* (with whom) dimensions (Piercy & Sprenkle, 1986).

List (1986) addresses a neglected topic in this area—the usefulness of individual supervision. Providing an example of the kind of integrative emphasis mentioned previously, this paper discusses how individual supervision methods can be more fully developed and integrated with group supervision methods.

SCHOOL- OR APPROACH-SPECIFIC MODELS OF TRAINING AND SUPERVISION

Family therapy's differentiation into particular schools of thought represents a key developmental milestone. However, this progress has been accompanied by both positive and deleterious concomitants. On the advantageous side, it advanced the delineation of family-therapy training approaches, since it assumes that training in a generic, all-inclusive therapy model is unrealistic (or undesirable). To be specific about training necessitates that the trainer be clear about the content and methods of his or her particular therapy model. In this regard, particular training models, therefore, signify the existence of well-developed therapy approaches. The disadvantage is that such separation of therapy and training models into schools perpetuates rigid boundaries between approaches that, in practice, may not be so perfectly distinguished. In family therapy at least, the distinctions drawn among the many "schools" of family therapy remain a matter of opinion. Despite the popularity of the integration movement in psychotherapy and family therapy, it is likely that "schools of thought," in one form or another, will be with us for a while. This section highlights papers that describe training methods and procedures along the lines of particular models. A comprehensive comparative analysis of all the family-therapy training models has not yet been written. A beginning step has been to compare the major models on the dimension of live supervision and on the matter of hierarchy in the trainer–trainee relationship (Liddle et al., 1988b). This section highlights the key characteristics of primary family-therapy training perspectives.

The *Brief Therapy* training philosophy offers a no-nonsense, minimalistic approach to training. Training is done in a small group setting with an emphasis on supervision and providing techniques. Training in theory is not a major feature of the Brief Therapy training approach. Learning the Brief Therapy model is assumed to occur best by doing treatment under guidance with ongoing cases. Thus, Fisch (1988) notes, "While there is some initial didactic explanation of rationale and technique, the greatest bulk of the training involves direct supervision of treatment" (p. 81). The process of learning this approach relies on two key processes: unlearning one's previous model, and learning the new and, in most cases, radically different, principles. One of the more difficult premises for Brief Therapy trainees to accept is the model's "nonnormative aspect." According to Fisch (1988, p. 79), "We use no criteria to judge the health or normality of an individual or family."

This approach minimizes any claims of clinical wizardry, preferring to present its therapy and training in technical rather than artistic or personal (i.e., person of the therapist) terms. In the Brief Therapy approach: "The therapist's personality and psychological health play a relatively small role . . . except inasmuch as they may interfere with the disciplined focus required" (Bodin, 1981, p. 303). Training should dispel any belief that it takes a certain kind of character or artistry. A one-down stance is as applicable in training as it is in therapy. Selection of trainees is handled in a unique and characteristically lean—or what Hoffman (1981) termed parsimonious—manner: "We do not lay significant emphasis on selection interviewing of

trainees . . . Our criteria for selection are not complicated and we are principally interested in the above cited factors, the trainee's facility with English, their expectations regarding the training, and how they plan to use it" (Fisch, 1988, p. 86). Evaluation consists of the trainer's judgment about the trainee's use of key model elements in subsequent sessions, and in case discussions about cases seen outside of the training setting. This is intended to assess the generalizability of training to the trainee's work environment.

The *Milan systemic* (MS) training program, unlike the Brief Therapy approach, places a great deal of emphasis on trainees' theoretical development and epistemological shift. This conceptual shift is acquired via observation and participation on a therapy team. Trainees are taught to apply systemic thinking not only with their clinical families, but also in the agency structures in which the treatment exists.

Theory acquisition is facilitated by observation, by role playing, and eventually, in the later stages of training, by seeing families. It is the collective team that is emphasized rather than individuals (Pirrotta & Cecchin, 1988). Little regard is given to the acquisition of specific therapeutic skills, and the idiosyncrasies of therapist style are immaterial. Trainees see few families as part of their training, which is consistent with the point of view that it is the therapist's thinking and his or her membership as a team member that should be accentuated. The MS trainers attend to macro rather than micro levels of insession interaction. This level of attention also applies in the training approach, which is seen as isomorphic with therapy. For Cecchin (1987), one of the original four members of the Milan team: "We have become less interested in the small details. If we see that the therapist is missing some very important opening, something very obvious, we call the therapist out. But you can get obsessive, phoning in questions, 'Why don't you ask this . . . ? If I were there, I would have asked . . . ,' and so on. We don't do that so much anymore" (p. 119).

The trainee's task, according to this model, is to learn effectiveness in the admittedly difficult position between team and family. It is the therapist's responsibility to "learn how to be connected" (Boscolo, 1987, p. 120) with both of these subsystems. Todd (cited in Stanton, 1981) has expressed concern about the difficulty and complexity of training Milan therapists, especially therapists at beginning levels.

Trainers in this model are concerned about the generalizability of training. Although at least one group of MS trainees evaluated their program poorly in this regard (Pirrotta & Cecchin, 1988), trainers provide activities to facilitate application of the model across contexts. Trainees are given the opportunity early in training to present cases seen in their primary work setting rather than merely focus on training-setting cases. Role plays and videotapes also are part of the MS training program.

A trainer attitude of respect for the students is emphasized. The selection process is an important step in defining this attitude that is modeled as something the trainers want their trainees to convey to each other. Ideas and the intellect, rather than the personal characteristics of the trainees, are primary.

The trainers' nonjudgemental attitude toward their trainees, and their deemphasis of the individual in favor of the team process, allows the students more quickly to transcend the relational level of their participation in the training, and to focus on learning instead. There is no processing of the training group's interpersonal dynamics, as the group is seen as an epistemological tool rather than an end in itself. It is not considered important to examine how the individual fits into this particular group, or how the group process affects individuals. (Pirotta & Cecchin, 1988, p. 59)

The group becomes a thinking machine, a group mind, where matters of personality, personal style, and the modification of that style for therapeutic purposes become secondary or nonexistent.

Although "no formal follow-up study or survey has been conducted by the Milan group to quantify the effects of the training" (Pirrotta & Cecchin, 1988, p. 58), these authors offer impressionistic findings. They are remarkably candid in their revelations. Trainee response to the program is considered a function of the stage of involvement with the training. Initial reactions of delight and infatuation with the training process and the therapy are followed by several reactions. These include some disaffection with the therapy model itself, its apparent lack of

transferability to a wide range of clinical settings, the few actual number of families that get seen by the therapists, and the insufficient focus on skill development. In the words of Pirrotta and Cecchin (1988), "The emphasis on the collaborative group process left individuals to fend for themselves in their own learning process" (p. 59).

Probably the most comprehensive statement about the training of *strategic* therapists remains the contribution made by Haley (1976), in his classic chapter, "Problems of Training Therapists." In dealing with the issue of selection, Haley advises that strategic therapists in training should be mature and possess life experiences, and be intelligent with good interpersonal skills and a wide range of potential behaviors. These statements are made despite Haley's objection to a "personality supervision," a form of training in which the person of the therapist receives, in Haley's (1988) view, inordinate focus. Haley is concerned about competing contexts of influence in training. He advises that trainees be cut off from other supervisors and sources of therapeutic influence during training. Haley believes this prevents potential confusion of exposure and attempted adherence to contradictory approaches.

Haley's training philosophy contains several key ingredients. These include:

1. *Supervisor responsibility in skill development.* It is the supervisor's responsibility to protect clients from the inadequacies of beginning therapists, and to assist trainees to develop the skills that will solve clients' problems.
2. *Supervision methods.* Live supervision and direct observation of a therapist's work are essential and indispensable ingredients in training. Video supervision is also important. A supervisor must understand the trainee's ideological starting place. This is best accomplished by watching the trainee in action with a case. Supervisory discussions are diagnostic, but insufficient.
3. *Training philosophy.* Learning by doing is paramount. Minor emphasis is placed on didactics and theoretical acquisition. Theory grows out of action and experience. It is also important to teach a wide variety of therapy techniques, as well as ways of crafting them

to each case. One primary training goal is to expand the range of therapist skills and behavior available in clinical situations.

4. *Evaluation*. Therapy outcome is the *sine qua non* of effective training. If the clients do not improve, training and supervision are not successful. Obviously, from the standpoint of values, trainees in this approach are taught to take the outcome of their cases very seriously.

Mazza (1988), a former student of Haley and Madanes, provides a number of therapist typologies for the strategic supervisor (e.g., the overly eager, anxious, totally passive therapist). Mazza emphasizes the indirect techniques used in training strategic therapists, citing, as Haley has often done, the hypnosis tradition as a meta-framework of strategic therapy and strategic-therapy training. This training philosophy, another exemplification of the isomorphism principle in action, has also been advocated by Protinsky and Preli (1987) and Storm and Heath (1982). In discussing feedback received from strategic-therapy trainees, Storm and Heath make what will be seen as a controversial recommendation: They warn that supervisors should try to avoid getting caught using strategic techniques with their supervisees.

One dividing line between strategic-therapy trainers is the degree to which an epistemological shift is facilitated directly. That is, should the systems perspective be influenced through particular training exercises with videotapes, for example, or through the process of seeing cases under close supervision? The former philosophy is embodied in the work of such authors as Keeney and Ross (1983) and Reamy-Stephenson (1983). These authors are directly concerned with having access to and modifying the conceptual maps of their trainees. They advocate specific exercises, sometimes involving videotape viewing and discussion, to alter the conceptualization ability and targets of inquiry (e.g., question-asking strategies) of therapists in training. Strategic therapists such as Haley and Mazza, on the other hand, are less interested in the conceptual life of the therapist. They advise that interview skills are the essence of therapy and it is acquisition in this behavioral realm that changes a therapist's conceptualization ability.[7]

Structural family therapy has a tradition of ardent attention to training and supervision issues. It is a treatment model that has been taught extensively at preprofessional, allied, and continuing-education levels (Aponte & Van Deusen, 1981). It was one of the only family-therapy approaches to implement a program to teach minority, paraprofessional, indigenous community residents the skills of family therapy. The video teaching tapes of the Philadelphia Child Guidance Clinic (PCGC) should be considered, along with the seminal method of live supervision, to be foundational contributions.

In the early days of their training, the structural trainers had a strong emphasis on the technique of structural therapy. It was important, to invoke a Minuchin phrase of the era, to teach "the steps of the dance." A staff handout, "An Alphabet of Skills of Structural Family Therapy" ("a" stands for "accommodation," for instance) was used widely in Minuchin's years at PCGC. Despite this early emphasis on technique per se, there has been, more recently, a broadening of the training approach. Structural training has been increasingly attentive to the dangers of overfocusing on technique. Minuchin and Fishman (1981) assert that technique training must be balanced and sequenced with an equal emphasis on the self of the therapist. This focus expands the therapist's personal range of skill. Minuchin and Fishman discuss the inherently disruptive aspects of the inevitable transitional period of training in which new skills are practiced and the self of the therapist is emphasized. A good training relationship is vital throughout but particularly during these times. These authors discuss other hallmarks of the structural approach: direct observation and live supervision as fundamental to training, an ongoing theory/didactic seminar to integrate theoretical ideas with practice, and the need to take a long-term view of training and therapist development. In this regard, their thoughts on advanced therapists and the road to becoming a seasoned therapist are worthy of emphasis, in part be-

---

[7] *Editors' Note.* Perhaps the sequencing of interviewing versus conceptualization skills needs to vary with the model of treatment; for example, it would be inconceivable for a trainer to place interviewing skills before conceptual skills in psychodynamic methods, in Bowen therapy, etc.

cause this is an underdeveloped topic in the field:

On the way to becoming wise, the therapist finds himself moving from observations of particular trans-actions to generalizations about structure. He devel-ops ways of transforming his insights into operations that have the intensity necessary to reach the family members. In this process of achieving a wisdom be-yond knowledge, the therapist discovers that he has a repertory of spontaneous operations. Now he can begin to learn for himself. (Minuchin & Fishman, 1981, p. 10)

A second generation of structural therapists has written in excellent detail about the further applications of this training approach. This cir-cumstance yields an interesting development to monitor as the training field matures. We can trace a training model's evolution as a function of the therapy model's changes as well as the changes that accompany a new generation of trainers. Aponte and Van Deusen (1981), Hodas (1985), and Colapinto (1983, 1988) have added to this body of work. These contributions have developed vital topics in the training and su-pervision area, such as the interdependence of video and live supervision (Hodas, 1985). Co-lapinto (1988) gives a thorough treatment of the primary features of a structural training ap-proach. His discussion includes the process of learning, trainer–trainee relationships, the su-pervisor attitude, context factors in supervision and training, and the ingredients of trainee change.

Several common distinguishing characteris-tics can be said to identify the *transgenerational approaches* to therapy and training, which in-clude the contextual therapy of Boszormenyi-Nagy (1981), Bowen (1972) theory and therapy, and the couples group therapy and family-of-origin approach of Framo (1981). *Contextual therapy* trainees are required to have a basic knowledge of and commitment to the mandate of multidimensional partiality, a central precept of contextual work. An awareness of intraper-sonal events, in one's own life and with one's clients, is deemed important for the contextual therapy trainee. Personal therapy and the per-sonal growth of the trainee are central to this training philosophy. An integrative understand-ing of intrapersonal (psychodynamic), develop-

mental, and systemic transactional knowledge bases is also seen as vital. Combined didactic and clinical training is preferred. Cotherapy is endorsed as a viable learning context, in part, since it occurs in a variety of real-life applied settings. In short, contextual training clearly is consistent with its therapy. The principles used in the therapy context (e.g., fairness, account-ability) are also important to factor into training (Boszormenyi-Nagy & Ulrich, 1981).

The *Bowen approach* to training revolves around the central concept of differentiation of self (Kerr, 1981; Papero, 1988). This directly parallels the therapy model. As an approach to training, it has many unique features in com-parison with most other training models. First, therapy technique is deemphasized to the extent that some might characterize it as an *antitech-nique*. In a videotape review, for instance, su-pervisors are less concerned with a supervisee's ideas about the case than with his or her own reactivity or personal level of functioning. These reactions are seen as evidence of differentiation of self from one's family of origin (Papero, 1988). Clinical competence is directly related to com-petence with one's family of origin. Bowen the-*ory* is important to learn. As both Papero (1988) and Kerr (1981) explain, since it focuses so much on the therapist's personal growth, training is long term (e.g., three to four years) and, in most cases, open ended (Kerr, 1981). As Papero (1988) tells it, this process takes a very long time; indeed, it can be considered a lifelong quest. Differentiation of self is assessed in the trainee's clinical work and is monitored during supervi-sion meetings. Training in the Bowen approach seems indistinguishable from personal therapy for the therapist, since there is remarkably little emphasis on clinical skill and the methods com-monly used for teaching.

Papero (1988) cites an "observation" made by Bowen many years ago relating to the harm ther-apists can do with their "interventions." He adopts a naturalist's stance in defining the Bowen philosophy of therapy and training in which the emphasis is on the therapist's distant experimentation and curiosity, rather than on attempts to "change" or to "help" others. One could consider it an anti-intervention approach. Regarding the supervisor's role, hierarchy is scorned, and supervisors are required to mon-itor their own level of differentiation in the supervision relationship. In being vigilant about their personal differentiation of self, supervisors model appropriate behavior for their trainees.

Little role playing and no live supervision are used in this approach. As Papero notes, there are no observation rooms or observation mirrors in the Bowen family-therapy training center. They are seen as distractions from the real work of personal growth and differentiation of the supervisors' and therapists' selves. Evaluation is related almost entirely to the therapist's level of differentiation of self. Papero (1988) realistically cautions that perhaps the most reasonable outcome of training, as he and Kerr (1981) have described it, is the cognitive understanding of the concept of systems thinking. True differentiation of self, at least in the lofty but still underoperationalized ways they have discussed, is too ambitious a training goal. A clear understanding of theory is more important in this training approach than technique. Ultimately, trainees are led on a philosophical and intellectual quest that links the families they see, and families in general, to nature and the world of the natural sciences. Evolutionary biology, sociobiology, and genetics are examples of conferences held at the Georgetown center for family-therapy trainees. These therapists would seem to make up a select sample. This is a group whose mission is personal growth (differentiation of self), a quest that Bowen has declared to be the royal road to therapeutic effectiveness.

Framo's *intergenerationally oriented therapy,* one of the first integrative models, works at the interface of psychodynamic and interpersonal functioning. He sees both areas as keys to the content and personal-growth domains a therapist must master. Although a staunch proponent of such training activities as personal therapy (marital or family therapy rather than individual therapy) and the writing of a family autobiography, Framo believes that skills are also important, and it is here where he clearly diverges from another intergenerational model, Bowen theory. Framo believes that therapists are primarily "trained" by their families of origin. He believes more difficult family problems need treatment from a "natural," a person who has had good family-of-origin "training" as well as formal professional training in family therapy. Framo's model strikes a balance, at least at a philosophical level, between the importance of

the therapist's personal functioning and his or her skill level. His model has not, however, taken an aggressive approach to a precise articulation of therapist skills.

Another approach in the integrative tradition of training has been developed by Nichols (1988), who defines his model as an *integrative psychodynamic and systems approach.* Nichols believes it important to broaden training's definition. For example, training should include the education and career development of the therapist, a task that involves professional socialization and preparation in the most ecumenical sense. Nichols has described the principles of a flexible model that apply to the master's and doctoral level, as well as postdoctoral and free-standing institute settings. A family-therapy *educator* (a term he prefers to trainer) must flexibly craft the principles of teaching and therapy to the particular level of the trainee as well as to the training context.

In this approach, theoretical content is presented first, and is followed by the core of training—practical clinical experience with an experienced supervisor. Sequencing is important. Trainees are understood in terms of stages of personal development.

There should be a flexible use of learning objectives. The program's philosophy should embody a "hard but fair" attitude that is complemented by a spirit of "let's learn." Faculty should be reasonably diverse. Nichols advises against a guru or mentor system, worrying that this approach produces automated, nonindividualistic, technique-oriented clones. Content of training is important and trainers are advised to think seriously about their curricular content core. In this regard, an integrated developmental psychology component is seen as crucial.

Nichols does not avoid controversial positions. He believes that age and personal maturity are factors in trainee selection and training. He candidly questions whether anyone under 30 is mature enough to absorb all the knowledge that is relevant to family therapists, and perhaps to handle the personal issues of becoming a family therapist. This is a open question in the training field that has been the subject of debate for many years.

Another controversial position is Nichols' beliefs about a popular supervisory method. Nichols asserts that live supervision is done more for the benefit of the supervisor and family than the trainee. Regarding live observation and the supervisor's interventions, Nichols (1988) offers the following:

My experience was one could get quick change in the actions of trainee by modeling or intervening into the therapeutic work of the trainee. If, however, one looked carefully at the development of the student a year or so later, it generally turned out that the student had tended either to rebel against the stance taken by the supervisor or to slavishly follow the mentor's actions. In either instance, the student had not progressed in his or her own growth in the way that it is possible when the supervisor/teacher is absent. (p. 122)

Nichols pushes for variety in supervision in order to keep the trainee, and presumably the supervisor as well, at peak performance. Personal therapy or family-of-origin therapy during training is highly desirable but it can be over-recommended. For Nichols, the focus of training is not the personal growth of the trainees. In the available time, training should help the trainee become skilled in the technique, content, *and* professional demeanor that constitute family therapy. Over time, the hierarchical training relationship equalizes and a more collaborative, less directive set unfolds.

Finally, Nichols believes that training should influence clinicians to pursue a lifelong process of professional learning and improvement. This area, the supervisor's role in instilling values about such things as continuing professional education, is chronically underdeveloped in training. Perhaps the emerging literature on the mentoring process can provide clues as to how we can expand our definition of a trainer's mission.

A third example of integrative training blends psychodynamic concepts with family systems ideas (Stierlin, Wirsching, & Weber, 1982). Integration issues in training are also addressed by Todd and Greenberg (1987) in their cotrainer supervision that integrates structural-strategic and symbolic-experiential therapies.

While some family systems approaches emphasize articulation of content and skills, the *symbolic-experiential family therapy* (SEFT) approach, in a way that is similar to other major family-therapy models (e.g., Bowen's model), is a model that also deemphasizes behavioral skills and techniques of family therapy. Although the experiential therapy movement has been active since the 1950s (Whitaker & Malone, 1953), SEFT has had some degree of difficulty becoming systematized and developing in a coherent way (Connell, 1984). This has been due, in part, to such factors as the model's being so closely tied to the personhood of one individual, Carl Whitaker, as well as to the nature of this particular person. Certainly, when Hoffman (1981) coined the phrase the "Great Originals" to describe the senior generation of family-therapy innovators and clinical wizards, she must have had Whitaker, among a few others, firmly in mind. While useful for creating enthusiasm for a new field, one that had to compete for its place in the mental health marketplace, the emphasis on the Great Originals has proved deleterious (or at least is now anachronistic) to the evolution of the family-therapy field. This is particularly true in relation to schools that have had difficulties specifying what would constitute a true approach—replicable methods and not merely the idiosyncracies and personal style of a model's originator.

Gradually, however, Whitaker's students and followers have extended his ideas and approach, and their contributions of model refinement, extension, and articulation have been impressive (see, for example, Neill & Kniskern, 1982; Sugarman, 1987; Napier & Whitaker, 1978; Garfield, Greenberg, & Sugarman, 1989; Whitaker & Keith, 1981).

Learning to be a symbolic-experiential family therapist takes place in three stages. The first, *learning about family therapy*, is best accomplished in seminars and workshops. This is the time when the new language of the family systems orientation is learned. *Learning to do family therapy*, the second stage, requires direct clinical experience with cases. This is best accomplished in an outpatient setting. Several competencies are stressed. These include the ability to take a family history, understand basic systems thinking and its relationship to the mental health field in general, assess family structure and process, provide crisis intervention, do long-term couples therapy, organize a family conference around a crisis, and utilize consultation appropriately. The final stage, *being a family therapist*, involves "orienting one's clinical work around families", and consists of "a reorientation in which the therapist comes to believe in families rather than individuals" (Whitaker & Keith, 1981, p. 221).

Cotherapy is one of the most powerful and central methods and philosophical tenets of SEFT and has been discussed by many of Whitaker's proponents. More than any other contemporary family-therapy school, the Whitaker tradition has kept cotherapy alive for new generations of clinicians. Learning family therapy via cotherapy is seen as a valuable vehicle for the personal growth of the therapist, as well as a powerful force for change with the family. Since the creativity and freedom of the therapist (in terms of personal and professional role and interpersonal restraints) are primary in SEFT, cotherapy provides a way to release the therapist's full creative potentials. Additionally, since the growth of the therapist is critical in SEFT, cotherapy is believed to be a context that maximizes the potential learning in each therapeutic encounter.

Symbolic-experiential family therapy teaches that reliance on technique is harmful to one's health and growth as a therapist. In this school of thought, much emphasis is placed on the personal side and personal development of the therapist. Paraphrasing Whitaker to refer to training, Sugarman (1987) has referred to this with his notion that teaching SEFT resides in the personhood of the teacher. Whitaker has assumed an almost antitechnical stance since his earliest days in family therapy. In many ways, he seems actively to have resisted codifying his methodology, sometimes apparently out of the fear that therapists will use such specification as a way to hide behind method. For Whitaker, it is openness that is called for in the therapeutic encounter (Whitaker & Keith, 1981). "I have been hard put to explain what seems to work or how I end up operating in my role as a teacher. It seems more and more clear that I don't believe in supervision. Supervision is a process of looking over somebody's shoulder and telling what to do or how to maneuver. It's like teaching somebody to ride a bicycle. Advice may be useful, but also is constricting that its usefulness seems minimal" (Whitaker in Whitaker & Garfield, 1987, p. 106).

Symbolic experiential family therapy is quite concerned with what Whitaker believes to be

the cloning process that accounts for much of training. A mix of methods (live observation, cotherapy, group supervision, videotape, seminars, clinical experience with couples, couples groups, and families) makes sure that trainees do "not end up programmed to a set pattern" (Whitaker & Keith, 1981, p. 224). The role of the trainee's own experiences is key. Trainee involvement is vital and must be initiated from the trainees (as motivation must come from the family in Whitaker's first stage of therapy, "the battle for structure"). Teaching involves a continuous dialogue, as does SEFT, in which the teacher and trainee discuss assumptions, beliefs, values, fantasies, and notions about what might be best to do in therapy. The teacher "can only share his belief system, he cannot replicate it for someone else. Trainees have to build their belief systems through their own experience." (Whitaker in Whitaker & Garfield, 1987, p. 107).

Trainee anxiety should not be altered by the trainer, it is important to motivate the trainee to learn, grow, and risk. The personal-growth quest of the supervisor is connected to the goal of personal growth for the trainee. Cotherapy provides a context in which the supervisor models important traits such as imperfection, openness, caring, and self-disclosure. It is a context for learning about and experiencing the very qualities one is trying to infuse into therapy.

A therapist's conceptual confusion is not something to be avoided, but should be welcomed. It provides an opportunity for expansion, creativity, and growth. Trainees who are considered appropriate for this approach are mature and flexible, and have a tolerance for ambiguity and chaos (Whitaker & Keith, 1981). Responsibility is a prime notion: Each trainee is considered responsible for his or her own personal growth during—and, of course, beyond—training. This instills a valuable belief that is replicated in the therapy—patients are taught that *they* are responsible for themselves, and, therefore, *they* must act.

The SEFT approach represents another of the contemporary approaches that uses its therapeutic principles to guide its training principles. As has been observed, this isomorphism, however, can only be carried so far. Sugarman (1987) described his attempt to differentiate from the Whitaker charisma and still teach SEFT. Todd and Greenberg (1987) described their creative and personally growthful attempts at integration within the SEFT framework. Garfield et al. (1987), too, has described his struggle to break the personal replication of his mentor, Whitaker, and instead apply Whitaker's principles, such as personal growth and personal definition (also see Garfield, 1980, Garfield & Lord, 1982).

Connell (1984), writing from the SEFT tradition, defines a supervisory approach based on the ideas of Whitaker and his therapy. This paper represents the kind of next-generation thinking and model refinement that, although Whitaker may not approve because of its schematized nature, will be appreciated by many therapists who will never have the opportunity to be trained by Whitaker himself. Connell's contribution also answers those who have been skeptical about the repeatability of a Whitaker therapy approach. Taken together, this group of second-generation papers by SEFT proponents represents a major change in family therapy. We no longer simply copy styles or repeat the memorable lines of the Great Originals' videotapes. Thankfully, some of our therapy models have become more teachable and generalizable.

Let us close this section on SEFT, however, with a quote from Whitaker and Keith (1981), which is illustrative of so much about this approach.

Like becoming a parent in the nuclear family the qualitative effects of becoming a family therapist are often dramatic. Treating families is both painful and deeply moving. Doing psychotherapy is change-inducing in its symbolic effect on the therapist. The power of the family, like the power of the infant, is seductive and threatening. The therapist and the conceptual framework that emanates from his work live between the pressure for constructive narrowing toward more specific definition and allowing for more openness, vulnerability, which leads to growth and reparative experience. Next year we would not be able to write this chapter in quite the same way. (p. 224)

The unique contributions of SEFT to the training and therapy fields can be found in this passage. The therapist's personal level of functioning and growth, the powerful effects of being and becoming a family therapist, developmental (often parental) metaphors, symbolic representations in therapy, and the emphasis on the emotional side of a therapist's functioning are all covered and worthy of note.

Although not frequently referred to in the context of integrative approaches to family therapy, *Functional family therapy* (FFT) (Alexander et al., 1976) is a model that integrates principles of social learning, systems, and cognitive theories. It is also an approach that reveals many unique and exemplary characteristics of contemporary family-therapy approaches. Originally, FFT was tied closely to social learning theory and, of course, to family systems thinking. This model is a good example of how a model can change adaptively and creatively. In this case, the change has spanned the two decades of the model's existence. It has responded to feedback from the clinical and empirical arenas.

Functional family therapy is, among modern-day family-therapy approaches, an empirically formulated approach. Its principles and clinical and training methods have been developed and refined in clinical research settings. This has allowed for a systematic examination and reevaluation of the approach as the studies have accumulated. It has also been quite explicit, detailed, and systematic about the main training components.

In this approach, four elements of training are emphasized. The *conceptual element* is considered crucial since it provides the foundation of core concepts implemented in treatment. In true behavioral tradition, the techniques are explicitly defined, but equally important is the specification of the principles underlying the methods. Functional family therapy has a clear phase in which these concepts are taught. Didactic and modeling are primary training methods at the conceptual phase. Functional family therapy challenges a clinician's intellectual capacities as they stretch to incorporate principles of social learning theory and behavior analysis.

The *emotional element* of training refers to the trainee's ability to work with families in real-life conditions. This aspect of FFT training accepts the emotional stress brought on by doing family treatment. Functional family therapy appreciates how such therapist distress can lead not only to poor clinical performance, but also, potentially, to disastrous clinical outcome. Therapists need to develop sufficient emotional strength to cope with these clinical realities. The supervisor's job is to design an environment in which emotional resiliency can be acquired. This aspect of training should be highlighted and may help to address a common misunderstanding. Many people believe behavioral approaches do not attend to the therapist's (or the family's) internal or affective life. As the cognitive revolution in psychology continues to influence the field of psychotherapy (i.e., cognitive-behavioral treatments), previously underrepresented aspects of functioning such as attributional processes will increasingly appear in family therapy.

The *technical aspect* of FFT concerns the skills necessary to conduct a thorough assessment, and to engage in two other important aspects of the model,—therapy and education. This includes therapeutic skills in the relationship and structuring realm, skill clusters that have been linked empirically with positive outcome in the earliest work in FFT (Alexander & Parsons, 1973; Alexander, Barton, Schiavo, & Parsons, 1976).

The final core element of FFT training is known as the *relational realm*. This refers to the trainee's capacity to develop a relationship with the supervisor and to use this relationship to learn the skills of the approach. This approach appreciates the various *sets of skills* in the complex art of family therapy. Experience alone is not seen as sufficient for clinical success. Skill possession and articulation at various interconnected levels, including the affective and cognitive domains, are mandatory to effective work with real cases. At the important level of attitudes, FFT is interested in sweeping away family therapy's often unspecific, romantic notions about what produces good therapy. Its agenda is to make therapy skills transportable, as much as possible, and to leave the magical thinking accompanying guru worship to others (Warburton & Alexander, 1985).

Functional family therapy emphasizes the importance of the supervisor's role in helping therapists to motivate recalcitrant families to enter or remain in treatment. Motivation is a central concept in FFT, and it operates within the variety of interconnected systems of family, trainee, and trainer. Problems regarding motivation are defined as technical difficulties that require thought, analysis, and concrete solutions aimed at specific targets.

Trainers in this approach provide detailed feedback to their trainees so that trainee performance and skill level can be improved. Supervisors assess the clinician's ability to diagnose the interactional sequences and particular phases of therapy or intervention currently in operation. Conceptual ability on the therapist's part is crucial, as is the ability to operationalize these behaviorally oriented conceptualizations. Also important is the trainer's capacity to accurately assess this developing ability of the supervisee.

The FFT approach has detailed a theory of trainee learning and change, and further, related these processes to and distinguished them from a theory of change for families. Trainees change by *observational learning* (the staging or sequencing of training experiences is important), *cognitive restructuring* (supervisor feedback shapes trainees ideas), and *evaluative feedback*. In addition to its being an indispensable aspect of cognitive or conceptual change, constructive feedback is a powerful motivator for trainees to continue in their quest to improve.

The first phase of training does not include direct clinical experience with families. Trainees, in this didactic phase, learn the FFT theoretical content and skills of the approach. Clinical work begins in the second phase. A variety of supervisor formats are used, including live supervision, team supervision, videotape, and individual supervision (which is actually done with pairs of trainees). The trainer–trainee relationship is hierarchical, especially in the early phases of training. It is characterized by an expert–novice description. This relationship structure changes over time, becoming more egalitarian.

Trainers, from this perspective, need to have an understanding of the most common trainee problems. These are found in four areas.

1. *Demand characteristics of setting*: fear of evaluation, competition with peers, loss of status in attempting to learn a new approach, and unrealistic wishes about personal growth or problem solving as a result of participation in the training.
2. *Aspects of trainee style*: the emotional aspects of learning and conducting family therapy, and their effect on the developing clinician.
3. *Features of the FFT model*: difficulties with

learning the logic or mechanics of reframing, for example.

4. *Characteristics of trainer-trainee relationship*: excessive dependence on or an inability to understand the supervisor (i.e., poor communication in the supervisory relationship).

Just as the FFT clinician assesses problems of implementation in therapy (emerging from a conceptual model), the supervisor engages in the same behavior. Knowledge of common trainee difficulties sensitizes a supervisor to make early, preventive assessments of typical problem situations.

Firmly rooted in the scientist-practitioner tradition of the applied areas of psychology, the FFT training approach is a model with family systems concepts at its foundation. At the same time, it is a model that has expanded and refined this emphasis, unlike some other approaches to family therapy. Its empirical values and clinical research tradition, attention to feedback at model development and clinical levels, articulation of skills clusters, and recent attention to specifying the process of family treatment all stand as notable examples of why this model must be considered one of the premier approaches of contemporary family therapy.

In conclusion, the fortunes of the training models described in this section are inextricably tied to the school-specific movement in the clinical realm of family therapy. Contention exists about the future of school training and therapy. Clearly, one of the major issues and trends in family therapy, and psychotherapy at large, is the integrative movement. As new integrative models appear, concomitant integrative training and supervision approaches will also be developed. The particular problems of training integrative therapists has only begun to be addressed in the psychotherapy field (Halgin, 1988; Norcross, 1986, 1987; Robertson, 1986; Tennen, 1988) and has barely been raised in family therapy (Bagarozzi, 1980).

School-specific models are advantageous owing to their degree of specificity and the attempts to build inclusive models of training and supervision. That is, although we need contributions on the particular methods of supervision, at least one study showed the need for comprehensive and true models of supervision and training (Saba & Liddle, 1983). The school-specific

models have in general allowed for a close correlation between theories and methods of therapy and theories and methods of training. As the family systems approaches become more complex (e.g., production of treatment manuals to deal with specific clinical problems and populations), the corresponding methods used to training the clinicians in these more sophisticated models will need to follow suit.

DESCRIPTIONS OF TRAINING PROGRAMS

The history of training-program descriptions in family therapy is mixed in terms of quality of output, to say the least. Piercy and Sprenkle (1986) offer a forthright observation on this part of the field in their discussion of training programs that have not been accredited by the AAMFT: "Some, despite impressive brochures, are little more than a few course offerings offered by overextended, if well meaning, faculty members" (p. 290). This articulation of a frequently observed process, while quite a comment on the in-a-hurry attitude of many family therapists in the early stages of their and their field's development, also is a comment on the lack of training-program descriptions, or at least on the way in which training-program descriptions often appear.

In contemporary family therapy, training programs are hardly generic. The age of specialization dictates that a training program be tailored to the particular setting in which it exists. For example, training is given in academic contexts and in free-standing institutes, and the structure, mission, and methods of these various programs differ dramatically. The multiple contemporary contexts of training are described in detail in Liddle et al. (1988). This section covers some examples of training-program descriptions that illustrate how such descriptions have changed over the years.

In the early days of the family-therapy and training and supervision literature, as it pertained to training-program descriptions, many papers attempted to describe the training programs that it represented. These papers reflected the values and methods of the times in which they were written. For example, in one of the earliest descriptions of a training program, Mendelsohn and Ferber (1972) emphasize the personal-growth side of training, and indeed, of one's motivations to become a family therapist to begin with, suggesting that clinicians become family therapists to work on their personal issues from their families of origin. Constantine (1976) offers a more structured and sophisticated program description, yet, as the times dictated, it emphasizes the personal-growth side of training, minimizing such issues as learning objectives, or skills-based approaches, or the translation of training into the contexts in which the therapists will work.

As more training-program descriptions appeared, several changes can be noted in the ways in which they were presented. First, in general, such descriptions can be seen as becoming more sophisticated, as having more substance and breadth. As the field has matured and become more complex, so have the training programs, the vehicles to transmit the content and skills of the clinical side of the field (e.g., Falicov, 1988b; Kantor & Andreozzi, 1985).

Second, contemporary program descriptions have more of an appreciation of what has been called the politics of family-therapy training (Liddle, 1978). Trainers are more attuned to the realities of the clinical settings in which family therapy occurs and are more able to accommodate their training programs accordingly. Carpenter (1984) asserted that family-therapy training must become more relevant, advising that trainers need to pay closer attention in training programs to the contexts in which people work. Pilalis (1984), in a similar vein, argued for an antielitist stance to training, as well as for a need for those who design training programs to pay closer attention to the contexts of trainee practice.

Two fine examples of training program descriptions that demonstrate how to pay close attention to issues of trainee context are offered in a brief report by Menfi (1989) and in a more comprehensive presentation by Will and Wrate (1985). The Will and Wrate paper, in particular, provides perhaps the clearest example of a training program that is able to implement the value of preparing trainees to do family work in their natural contexts. Third, there would be the issue of appreciating the role of evaluation and research in training and supervision. Training-program descriptions now rarely do not include the importance of continuing evaluation and the important role that research in clinical and training matters plays in training programs. Will and Wrate (1985) describe the policy-level changes their program evolved after paying close attention to and conducting surveys of their former trainees.

Fourth, there is the matter of how specialized training programs have become. We no longer seem to be in the period in which a generic brand of family therapy could be taught. Training programs exist for specific purposes, in order to train a particular kind or discipline of trainees, and with a certain purpose or mission (Liddle, Breunlin & Schwartz, 1988a). Chable et al. (1988) present an example of a training-program description that does not lie in this new tradition. While asserting that the described training program is generalizable to other professional specialities, the authors present a family-therapy training model clearly and specifically designed for social workers. No mention is made of how this program would specifically fit into other training settings and with other disciplines of trainees. Many training-program descriptions can be found that appreciate the increasingly specialized enterprise that family-therapy training has become (e.g., Kaslow, 1985; Sprenkle, 1988; Herz & Carter, 1988; Combrinck-Graham, 1988; Wright & Leahey, 1988; Berger, 1988; Bardill & Saunders, 1988).

Fifth, the interconnection of clinical issues and training issues has transformed how training programs exist and develop. As integration becomes a more and more important topic for the clinical side of the field, it necessarily becomes important on the training side as well. Training-program descriptions will tend less to emphasize the so-called "pure" models of treatment with strong allegiances to the founders of those models, than to appreciate, if not emphasize, eclectic or integrative approaches in training (Lebow, 1984; 1987). Trainers clearly understand this seamless quality between the domains of clinical model development and training issues and methods.

Sixth, training programs tend to be more firmly grounded in a conceptual or theoretical base that matches the theory of therapy being taught. There is, in many training programs, then, a clear appreciation and implementation of the isomorphic nature of a theory of therapy and a theory of training (e.g., Colapinto, 1988; Fisch, 1988; Haas et al., 1988; Papero, 1988).

Seventh, a related point concerning theoretical and conceptual development in training programs would be how training programs are likely to adopt developmental models and metaphors in their design and implementation (Liddle, 1988a). Stages of training and trainee development are stressed, as is the distinct role and action and style of the adult learner-clinician. The role of cultural variables in training has also been emphasized as necessary to include in training contexts (Falicov, 1988). Clearly, there is also the welcome tendency to try to incorporate adult models of learning in the context of training (e.g., Duhl, 1983; Menfi, 1989; Will & Wrate, 1985).

Finally, training-program descriptions are now grounded more firmly in a temporal or evolutionary context. That is, they appreciate that a training program will change over time, accommodating to such major influences as the status of the family-therapy field, the local market, the realities of how professional life is organized, the level of development of the trainers and trainees, and the purposes and administrative support for training in this particular setting. The Will and Wrate (1985) paper provides one of the clearest and most useful examples of how a training program changes, partly in response to the ecological realities in which it exists and partly in relation to planning and design. Issues of trainer development also are a factor in why training programs evolve. In the context of a free-standing institute, Herz and Carter (1988) give a rare, candid glimpse of the economic and personnel factors that affect the changing shape and nature of institute-based training programs.

RESEARCH AND EVALUATION IN TRAINING AND SUPERVISION

Most Important Overviews

There is no other area in training and supervision that is as important and has been so underdeveloped as research and evaluation. Given the field's level of maturation, it is understandable

that this area has remained so ill formulated. However, there is an increasing appreciation of the importance—indeed, the necessity—of an attitude change toward research and evaluation. This section discusses the most important overviews to this content area (Avis & Sprenkle, 1990; Kniskern & Gurman, 1979, 1988; Street, 1988). Although we will cover specific examples of work in research and evaluation, these three contributions are significant in that they define what this content area needs to address. Together, they articulate the research agenda for training and supervision. Although training has been a subject of interest for family therapists for some time, there was a curious lack of reference to the need for training research and evaluation in the field's early days (cf., Ackerman, 1973; Beal, 1976; Ferber et al., 1972; Group for the Advancement of Psychiatry, 1970; Guerin, 1976; Zuk, 1975). Gradually, these attitudes and values were challenged (Everett, 1980; Liddle & Halpin, 1978). However, it was a seminal paper by Kniskern and Gurman (1979) that changed the nature of the discussion of what family-therapy training research needs to be. This contribution was the first to offer detailed guidelines, including many possible research questions and areas for training and supervision research. It was the most critical statement to date regarding the necessity of future attention on research in this area.

In characterizing "the field's empirical ignorance" (p. 83) on this topic, Kniskern and Gurman (1979) posed a series of research questions that could contribute to an empirical base for training decisions and actions. These covered several critical areas:

1. *Selection issues.* What roles should previous training, personality variables, and methods of selection such as personal interview or work sample play?
2. *Didactic methods.* What are the roles and impact of readings, sequencing of training methods, effects of observation of master therapists, and exposure to multiple methods?
3. *Supervision.* What consideration should be given to the impact, timing, and sequencing of audiotapes and videotapes; the comparative effects of supervisory styles (e.g., comparison of problem focused versus personal);

the number of cases that should be supervised; and the differential impact of various forms of supervision?

4. *Experiential methods*. It is not uncommon, despite protestations by some notable figures (e.g., Haley, 1976), to have psychotherapy be a required part of marital and family-therapy training (O'Sullivan & Gilbert, 1989). In this regard, Kniskern and Gurman (1979) pose the difficult but necessary questions: What are the changes of trainees relative to such personal therapy? Are there positive and/or negative effects of required personal therapy? At what stage might therapy be most helpful? And is it possible that activities such as work on the trainee's genogram affect the cognitive set of the trainees? (That is, is it this cognitive change that allows therapists to think more in terms of family systems rather than a family-of-origin intervention?)

Nearly a decade later, Kniskern and Gurman (1988) offered an update of their research recommendations. Their characterization of this area of the field became even more critical in their citation of a *"remarkable empirical ignorance* of what types of activity or styles of intervention should be fostered in trainees" (p. 372) (italics added). Kniskern and Gurman (1988) discuss the irony in the fact that although many of the field's pioneers worked in settings in which training was primary, the empirical evaluation of family-therapy training only recently has been appreciated as important enough to undertake. In this contribution, the authors' strategy, in family-therapy intervention terms, was to increase the intensity of their message.

Kniskern and Gurman (1988) recommend a five-step process of training program evaluation:

1. Identify and specify the training goals.
2. Develop the training model.
3. Develop measures that evaluate training-induced change.
4. Demonstrate the expected change in trainees.
5. Demonstrate that trainees who have shown the expected changes on the measures are better able to help families than are those who did not have the training.

The fact that the training and supervision area may now be sufficiently complex to warrant specific reviews of its specialty areas may not be news. The research and evaluation area is now adequately developed to merit such a review. This is a significant development in training and supervision. Avis and Sprenkle (1990) provided the field with its first review of training research. They reached conclusions and made recommendations in several realms:

1. *Design and methodology considerations*
   a. Several instruments with various degrees of reliability and validity appear able to distinguish between beginning and advanced therapists to measure the acquisition of conceptual or executive skills, and to offer therapists feedback on their in-session behavior.
   b. Despite this situation, there remains an urgent need for more psychometrically sound measures of trainee skill acquisition. Avis and Sprenkle have concluded that the instruments thus far are either problematic in terms of reliability and validity, or are too complex, cumbersome, and time consuming for the average trainer to use.
   c. In general, there is the strong need for controlled research. Only four studies used a comparison group, and only one had random assignment and adequate sample size. The empirically established connection between therapy outcome and training and supervision is a fledgling area of research.
   d. The following are examples of needed design improvements: specifying and controlling for trainer variables, including more follow-ups to determine the stability of training effects (cf., Schumm, Bugaighis, and Jurich [1985] for a discussion of repeated-measures designs in family therapy), using more adequate samples, and to avoid the bias present in many of the current studies, assuring trainer–investigator nonequivalence.
   e. Comparative studies will be increasingly necessary to answer the specificity question: What training is effective, and when, for whom, under what con-

ditions, and for what type of clinical situation?

f. There is a need for replications of existing studies; the findings of this research should be considered tentative given poor methodology and bias. These replications will require greater specification of teaching and supervisory methods, the contexts of training, and the conditions under which training occurs.

2. *Outcomes of training*

a. Various types of family-therapy training produce an increase in trainees' cognitive and intervention skills.

b. In-service training programs seem to be effective in having the agency staff see more families.

c. Traditional classroom methods are roughly equivalent to more extensive experiential methods in teaching beginning assessment skills.

d. The sequence of training activities may be an important variable in training.

e. Cognitive and intervention skills may develop independently of each other.

The final paper in this section also provides a critical analysis of the extant research literature on training and offers a conceptual model for organizing and running a training program. Adapting the work done in other contexts (Gottman, & Markman, 1978) to family-therapy training evaluation and design, Street (1988) proposes that family therapists use the systems approach first outlined by Zifferblatt (1972) in evaluating training. This procedure follows eight steps:

1. Selecting personnel in the training system.
2. Selecting the training context.
3. Outlining what is to be taught.
4. Selecting training methods.
5. Assessing training efficacy.
6. Assessing trainees' effectiveness.
7. Specifying program costs, benefits, and limitations.
8. Redesigning the program based on the feedback from the previous steps.

In addition, Street (1988) wisely reminds us of the context embeddedness of all training and the need for research to be sensitive in this regard. Research on training, therefore, will be quite complex, given the necessity of focusing on the interconnected subsystems of training, therapy, and surrounding setting, as well as their interactions.

The important contributions of Avis and Sprenkle (1990), Kniskern and Gurman (1979, 1988), and Street (1988) agree on several main points, and these are indicative of this content area's condition. First, research initiative in this area is desperately needed since the stakes are so high. Training, as well as therapy, should have an empirical foundation. Second, sufficient methodological advances have been made to permit the conducting of training research. Evaluation strategies and instruments are available, and enough knowledge and experience exist to pose important research questions. Third, the contributions thus far should be considered pilot work because of various problems. Fourth, the training research area will affect the clinical area, just as the clinical field affects the training field. Research on training has powerful implications not only for training sites, but also for mainstream family-therapy practice. Today's trainees are tomorrow's family-therapy constituency. Next, we will review the contributions in specific areas of research and evaluation.

Instruments to Measure Therapist Behavior

As Kniskern and Gurman (1979, 1988) and Avis and Sprenkle (1990) have observed, there is nothing more basic to achieving a more workable link between empirical work and training decisions than the development of therapist-behavior assessment. Consistent with the videotape utilization tradition of family therapy, many measures use videotape in their assessment design, although this was not always true of the earliest efforts in instrument development. Allred and Kesey (1977), for instance, developed a system for analyzing the verbal behavior of family therapists. Members of the Purdue University family-therapy group have been active in developing a similar coding format. Piercy, Laird, and Mohammed (1983) validated a scale that evaluates five categories of family-therapy skills spanning several theoretical orientations. This work would be considered in the tradition of psychotherapy research that uses paper-and-pencil instruments and observer-based coding schemas to rate therapist behavior.

There are two programs of research that deserve special mention with regard to instrument development. In their work, Pinsof (1979, 1980) and Breunlin and colleagues (Breunlin et al., 1983, 1989) are exemplary in their careful, patient, and thoughtful consideration of the great complexity that characterizes instrument development in training. Influenced by the Cleghorn and Levin (1973) approach to skill conceptualization and the McMaster model of family functioning and therapy, Pinsof (1979) first developed the Family Therapy Behavior Scale (FTBS). In an effort both to refine theoretically and make more manageable the FTBS, Pinsof (1980) then created the Family Therapy Coding System (FTCS). This instrument remains the most comprehensive and complex coding scale for family therapists' behavior (Street, 1988). This observer-based coding schema allows trained raters to assess the multidimensional nature of a therapist's interactions and interventions with a family.

Breunlin and colleagues (1983, 1989) have developed and continue to revise an instrument, the Family Therapy Assessment (FTAE), that assesses three levels of skill development in structural-strategic therapy. Like the FTBS, the FTAE has several psychometric strengths compared with other family-therapy training instruments. It consists of a videotape stimulus (an initial interview that uses actors following a script of an actual first session) and a corresponding multiple-choice-format paper-and-pencil instrument.

Generativity, the capacity of research to stimulate other work, is one indicator of productivity. Although people often think that research productivity depends on research grants, this is not necessarily the case. A number of doctoral dissertations have used the FTAE. These studies not only have produced some interesting findings, but they have helped to shape the instrument's development, which now is in its sixth version. In one of these dissertations, Hernandez (1985) conducted two validational studies on two instruments, the FTAE and the Piercy et al. (1983) measure of therapist level of sys-

temic thinking. The FTAE, except for one factor (observational dimension), successfully discriminated between novice and experienced therapists (conceptual and executive/therapeutic skills). Another dissertation, by Pulleyblank, while suffering from an inadequate sample size, used the FTAE to evaluate a structural-family-therapy training program (Pulleyblank & Shapiro, 1986). Although this dissertation found that the scores on the instrument differentiated between training program therapists and nontrainees, Kniskern and Gurman (1988) remind us to be cautious about the generalizability of this study.

In sum, while we have progressed in developing psychometrically sound measures to assess therapist behavior, the establishment of an empirical base for training remains a distant goal. Should family-therapy trainers choose to make a commitment in this direction, and it will take a multisystemic commitment with significant attitudinal and structural changes, then it would be well to study carefully the developments in the psychotherapy supervision literature. For some time now, this field has been producing fine quantitative and qualitative research on supervision and training.[8]

Program-Evaluation Studies

Training-program descriptions can be located with ease. Unfortunately, however, systematic evaluations of such programs are far more rare. The earliest efforts had characteristic flaws, including small sample sizes, a small or no comparison sample, relatively unsophisticated dependent variables (e.g., increase in number of families seen), and inadequate control for the variety of variables that could conceivably influence training outcome (Betof, 1977; Byles, Bishop, & Horn, 1983; Dowling, Cade, Breunlin, Frude, & Seligman, 1979; Flomenhaft & Carter, 1974).

Gradually, conceptualization about program evaluation became more sophisticated (e.g.,

---

[8] Robiner and Schofield (1990) offer a diverse bibliography of supervision in psychotherapy. Interestingly, most of the family-therapy supervision literature is neglected on this compilation—an unfortunate comment on the status of family therapy in certain quarters of psychotherapy.

Dowling & Seligman, 1980). In what Kniskern and Gurman (1988) recognize as the "first comprehensive empirical evaluation of any family-therapy training program," Tucker and Pinsof (1984) employed Pinsof's FTBS to assess the Family Institute of Chicago training program. The findings suggest that training can have a clinically meaningful effect on trainees. Training increased the systemic thinking, activity level, and the therapist's range of interactions with a simulated family. Training had limited effects as well, however, and did not always change trainees in desired directions. These findings are in accord with the later research of West, Hosie, and Zarski (1985), as well as that of Churven and McKinnon (1982), that suggested skill acquisition is to be an ordered, sequential process. The FTBS demonstrates differences between high- and low-experience trainees, both prior to and after training. The Tucker and Pinsof study and the Street (1988) paper were the first to discuss an important, sophisticated question about training outcomes, that is: *What is* the behavior that changes directly in relation to training per se, and what behaviors change in relation to therapist experience away from the training program? This issue also relates to a basic question about clinical change: *When* does change occur? (That is, to what degree does change occur within the context called psychotherapy and to what degree does it happen elsewhere?)

One other program-evaluation study deserves attention. In a study of 50 California-based master's-level MFT programs, O'Sullivan & Gilbert (1989) reached some distressing and politically sensitive conclusions. These authors concluded that the reality of many of these training programs often departs significantly from the ideals and suggested standards of the field.

Programs which carefully evaluate applicants before admission and state that they closely supervise and personally evaluate their students throughout their training are few and far between. . . . Academically, many of these programs hardly seem rigorous in terms of requirements for admission or graduation. Yet, they expect their graduates to eventually assume the role of independent mental health professional.

Of course, one wonders about this study's generalizability beyond the borders of California. Nonetheless, the implications of findings such as these are very disturbing for trainers, legislators who set policy and make licensing laws, the trainees in these programs, as well as for members of the public, who will presumably seek out therapists trained in these programs. While some family-therapy professional organizations have clearly decided to avoid dealing with the time-consuming, difficult, and economically and politically sensitive issue of training standards, one major organization—the AAMFT—has plunged headlong into accreditation, standard-setting, and credentialing activities. If the results of the O'Sullivan and Gilbert (1989) research have any validity, and it seems that they do, then it must be said that we all should be glad that someone has decided to be in the business of setting and enforcing standards for training and supervision.

Studies on Trainee Skill Development

Skill development, and, more basically, the skill-specification movement, has been a school-specific activity in family therapy. While certain models have been more adept at articulating skills than others, there is no agreement on this task's importance. Relatedly, the learning-objective movement in family therapy seems to reappear every so often in the context of pleas for a more consistent, integrated focus on teaching and learning objectives.

Using the innovative but controversial Delphi technique, Figley and Nelson's program of research (Figley & Nelson, 1989, 1990; Nelson & Figley, 1990) has begun to articulate the competencies of family therapists in an appropriately nongeneric, school-specific fashion. Although there is doubt about the usefulness of the school-specific framework in contemporary family therapy given the thrust toward constructing integrative models, this research is welcome since any effort systematically to particularize family-therapy skills is likely to yield fruitful results in the integrative-model-building realm.

Influenced by the microcounseling tradition of Ivey (Ivey & Authier, 1978), Street and Treacher (1980) reviewed the types of skill-training methodologies available to family therapy. These authors later specified ways of using a skill-identification, skill-training, practice, and close-feedback philosophy in family-therapy training. In a small study, they demonstrated the effectiveness of a microcounseling strategy to identify and use specific observational skills and family-therapy concepts (Street & Treacher, 1980).

Employing an interesting assessment device (Family Repertory Grid) that measures the trainee's capacity to articulate a series of constructs about the family, Zaken-Greenberg and Neimeyer (1986) demonstrated a positive impact of structural-family-therapy training. A strength of this study was the authors' emphasis on the importance of measuring training effects *specific to the program*. This is an elementary but often overlooked design issue.

Mohammed and Piercy (1983) compared the effectiveness of supervisor-led group discussions of a therapist's videotapes and a skill-based approach that used skills-training videotapes in group supervision. This study also addressed the important and underdeveloped issue of the order or sequence of training methods or activities. Although most of the study's findings were inconclusive, there does seem to be sufficient evidence to indicate that the order of training components (i.e., observation, use of videotape) may have an effect on skill acquisition. A study reported by West and colleagues (1985) also addressed the sequencing issue. These authors found that conceptual skills increased significantly from the beginning to midpoint of a training course, whereas observational skills increased from the midpoint to the end of the course. They conclude that conceptual frameworks are important in training. They believe these cognitive maps serve as a scaffolding that organizes observations of family process.

Of the hundreds of family-therapy workshops presented every year, very few are ever subject to anything other than a cursory, postsession consumer-satisfaction questionnaire. While the entertainment and self-promotion values of these events remain high (Madanes, 1988), the accountability and evaluation aspects are virtually nonexistent. In a study that runs counter to this troubling trend, Churven and McKinnon (1982) tested the effectiveness of a three-day workshop designed to teach basic family-therapy skills. Three measures (written case analyses, video interviews with simulated families, and self-ratings), which, unfortunately, were not subjected to validity and reliability checks, as-

sessed trainee change. Significant improvement was found on all three measures, with no differences among professional groups. A finding of note indicated that changes in cognitive and intervention skills were relatively independent. This conclusion was also reached by Pulleyblank and Shapiro (1986). Additionally, for Churven and McKinnon (1982), cognitive and intervention skill-assessment techniques evaluate different domains. These results reinforce the need to assess these dimensions with instruments that discriminate between skills. Additionally, there are implications here for the design of programs. Certain kinds of trainee learning can be targeted for change via specific training activities. Studies of this nature develop other versions of the specificity issue (i.e., *the* question for trainers in the years ahead): Which training techniques produce what kind of effects in which trainees?

Alexander, Barton, Schiavo, & Parsons (1976) and Barton and Alexander (1977) found structuring and relationship skills to be responsible for 60 percent of the variance in treatment outcome. The study identifies therapy skills that are related to therapy success in functional family therapy and provides a skill-evaluation framework.

Studies on Training Methods

Random assignment of subjects to different groups, as anyone who has taken Statistics 101 might recall, increases the chances of treatment- and control-group equivalence, thereby permitting the results of one's intervention to be fairly assessed. In a study that compared three methods of teaching, Tomm and Leahey (1980) provided the first training evaluation study that included random assignment of trainees to training groups—the random assignment of 72 medical students to three training methods. The students were assigned to one of the following situations: (1) traditional lecture with video examples, (2) small group of six students with two leaders and same video examples, or (3) small group with two leaders who interviewed and assessed families using the same videos. Results demonstrated that all groups improved over the period of the course, with no particular method evidencing superiority. While consistent with much of the comparative clinical trials literature that confirms the difficulty of obtaining robust differences among treatment groups, this study calls into question one of family therapy's earliest and most strongly held assumptions—that experiential learning is superior. This speculation, of course, must be qualified with a caveat regarding the generalizability of the Tomm and Leahey study (1980). The trainees were medical students and not family therapists. How equivalent this sample would be, for example, to a group of beginning clinicians is an open question.

Fennell, Hovestadt, and Harvey (1986) compared a group of trainees who received live supervision with one that got post hoc supervision. No significant differences were found between these two groups. Problems with the study make the results difficult to interpret (e.g., differential trainee experience levels, caseload differences).

Live Supervision

This method of supervision has been controversial for some time. Further, as in other areas of the literature, systematic studies have been rare. Wright (1986) published the first study analyzing phone-ins in a live supervision situation. Her findings were translated into recommendations for supervisors and were, unfortunately, less oriented toward charting the interconnections between the training and therapeutic systems. Some of her recommendations for supervisors using live supervision are: to be clear, to be positive, not to overload in content or frequency, to vary content, and to provide practice with phone-ins before a case starts.

In other research on live supervision, Liddle, Davidson, and Barrett (1988) interviewed 85 therapists who had just completed a live supervision clinic for a one-year or postdegree training program. This study indicates that trainees report taking less responsibility for the cases seen in live supervision than for those seen in private practice or at their agencies. Trainees voiced a concern about supervisor sensitivity to the students' wishes for autonomy. As training progressed, the more experienced students wanted more independence in case formulation and intervention generation. By the end of training, most students said they believed that live supervision could result in independent thinking

in trainees. However, dependency on the supervisor was found to be a potential problem. Experienced trainees moved from preferring tight control of their case at the outset of training to a position of increased dependence on the supervisor, in which they were more comfortable with supervisor input. Less experienced students began as much more dependent, and evolved toward increasing independence and shared control of the case.

Some of the best studies in family-therapy training and supervision are doctoral dissertations (Cotton, 1987; Frankel, 1989; Gorman, 1989; Hernandez, 1985; Moran, 1989; Ratlin, 1990; Sexton, 1989; Street, 1988). Dissertation research is sometimes unfairly perceived as a meaningless exercise in learning research skills (or, more cynically, as the final rite of graduate-school passage). This certainly has not been the case with this group of studies. Let us examine four of them.

In a benchmark study that might signal a new generation of research on family-therapy training, Frankel (Frankel, 1989; Frankel & Piercy, 1990)[9] explored one of the most commonly used (Saba & Liddle, 1986) but previously untested conceptual postulates in training—the isomorphic nature of training and therapy (Liddle, 1988). Kniskern and Gurman (1988) reminded us that there was, as yet, no empirical evidence that isomorphism between training and therapy would yield better outcome. Specifically, Frankel (1989) studied the extent to which supervisory phone-ins were related to change, both in immediate therapist behaviors and subsequently in resistant family behavior. She found the quality of supervisor behavior to be significantly related to the quality of therapists' behavior on the same dimensions. Further, she found that these behaviors, when positive, were related to positive influences on the clients. Frankel's study is the first research in family therapy to offer empirical support to isomorphism's relationship with outcome.

In a study of one type of one-time live supervision, Cotton (1987) found that calling a therapist out of a live session may be perceived

---

[9] This study was Frankel's doctoral dissertation, for which she received the AAMFT Graduate Student Research Award in 1989.

as abandonment and/or criticism by the patients. She found that this specific technique of live supervision did not result in short-term positive change and that the greatest impact seemed to be on the therapeutic process and therapist learning.

A strong tradition in psychotherapy supervision research has endorsed the importance of process dimensions such as the interactional process between therapist and supervisor (cf., Goodyear, Abadie, & Efros, 1984; Heppner & Handley, 1981; Holloway, 1982). Although this emphasis would be a welcome one in family-therapy supervision, there has been little work as yet in this area. Exceptions include the dissertation research of Gorman (1989) and Ratliff (1990). Gorman focused on what she termed the "moment-of-intervention" as a way of building a model for how supervisors make intervention decisions during live supervision. This qualitative study addresses one of Everett and Koerpel's (1986) important criticisms, namely, that research has been too focused on supervision as a technique rather than a process. In addition, it brings into family-therapy training and supervision research the relatively new process research tradition. Process research has great potential to transform the way therapists think about their work, as well as about research in general.

Gorman (1989) used videotape and transcription analysis, as well as interviews with the supervisors concerning their thinking process during the supervisory interventions. The clinical "training of origin" was found to have a powerful influence on the supervisory style and interventions of the supervisors. Additionally, issues of the treatment context were found pervasively to influence the supervisor's thinking and intervention rationale. Gorman (1989) concluded that her intensive process study of supervisors' *reflections on their actions*[10] yielded a view of supervision that is more complex than we may currently appreciate. Such analyses, for instance, show wide variability in supervisor behavior. This interesting finding needs expansion and further study.

Ratliff's dissertation research is also exploring an important dimension of the supervisory process, the management of consensus and disagreement[11] and this research may illuminate another overlooked aspect of family-therapy supervision—the supervisor–supervisee relationship. Although we are not guideless in this area (cf., Schwartz, 1987), a comprehensive understanding of the nature and variables of the supervisory relationship from a systemic perspective awaits further work.

Finally, in this section, we evaluate the current status of live supervision. Has live supervision fulfilled its promise to revolutionize training? Practically speaking, how much is live supervision used? Lewis and Rohrbaugh (1989) investigated these questions in a survey with a statewide group of Virginia AAMFT supervisors. Although it might not be representative of a national sample, this research revealed some disturbing findings about the current status of live supervision. Lewis and Rohrbaugh found that only one third of all supervisors used live supervision in any form. They speculate that if this low figure represents a trend, it might mean that live supervision is being practiced only by family-therapy purists. Since Rait's survey research (1988) has suggested that the predominant orientation in family therapy is "integrative" or "eclectic" Lewis and Rohrbaugh are concerned that this might signify that the family-therapy viewpoint has become diluted. The low frequency of use of live supervision is taken as further evidence of this change in the perception and status of family therapy.

Studies on the Use of Videotape

As practical guidelines for videotape supervision become more available (cf., Breunlin et al., 1988), evaluation models for this method must also be developed. In this regard, Street and Foot (1989) provide the kind of research that will advance us toward an empirical base for training. In studying the impact of watching a

---

[10] Schon's reflective practitioner paradigm fits nicely with this research. Supervisors would be wise to ask themselves: "Am I helping to produce 'reflective practitioners' or school-specific clones?"

[11] This dissertation proposal was the recipient of the 1990 AAMFT Graduate Student Research Grant Proposal.

live session versus watching a session on video-tape, they found some differences, depending on the nature of the interview and the family. For example, some families are inherently more difficult to assess than others, some concepts are more difficult to identify and discriminate than others, and some concepts are so linked with others that their independent assessment is impossible. Overall, however, they found a number of similarities in the judgments of the two groups. They conclude, therefore, that for training purposes, at least, clinically useful conclusions about family interaction can be made both from using videotape interviews and by live observation. This study's results, although they should be interpreted with caution, counter the oft-cited belief about the different ways in which live observation/supervision and video portray different realities (Berger & Dammann, 1982). The results caution trainers about the use of training materials we may take for granted (i.e., we assume certain training or experiential consequences that may or may not exist).

Studies of Personal Characteristics of Therapists/Trainees

While at least one prominent trainer has minimized the importance of personality factors in training family therapists (Haley, 1976), other authors, from a variety of orientations, have called for more attention to therapists' personal characteristics (Kniskern & Gurman, 1979, 1988; Lebow, 1987; Liddle, 1982a, 1982b; Liddle & Halpin, 1978; Minuchin & Fishman, 1981; Whitaker, 19??). Further, as family therapy rediscovers individuals, redressing the error of familial reductionism, the personality characteristics of family-therapy trainees have become a viable area of inquiry. For Heatherington (1987), clinical efficacy must be understood as an interactive consequence of a *particular approach* being carried out by a *particular person*. Kniskern and Gurman (1988) have recommended that we need to identify "the best matches between family therapist personality factors and particular methods and strategies of intervention" (p. 759). Although still in its early stages of formulation, this area has already evidenced itself as interesting, as well as one that is capable

of delivering some important findings for family-therapy trainers.

In an early study that included a control group, still more the exception than the rule in family-therapy training research, Walrond-Skinner (1979) reported on the personal changes in family-therapy trainees. Although Tucker and Pinsof (1984) sought to assess similar changes in their trainees, they did not achieve the gains reported in Walrond-Skinner. This was due, in part, to the high starting level (i.e., ceiling effects) of the therapists who entered the program (Tucker & Pinsof, 1984).

In a study of three groups of therapists who were trained in different schools of family therapy, Green and Kolevzon (1982) and Kolevzon and Green (1983) found greater divergence than convergence of therapist assumptions and styles. Street (1988) has cautioned, however, that this study ignored the context in which therapists practice their beliefs. Kolevzon and his colleagues have continued their focus on important topics, such as constructing an integrative model and professional development.

Kolevzon, Sowers-Hoag, and Hoffman (1989) explored the role played by a clinician's personality attributes in facilitating and/or inhibiting adherence to different therapy models. They found that personality attributes do play a role in predicting adherence to the belief and action systems unique to a particular approach to family therapy. Clinicians strongly allied to different models of family therapy will exhibit different—and, in some instances, oppositional—personality profiles. They conclude that (1) different models of family therapy may be learned best by different kinds of clinicians, and (2) personality variables should be considered important in model selection and in the course of subsequent training and supervision, as well as in the clinician's movement toward an integrative model. Although Kolevzon's work has been criticized for its underappreciation of the trainee's outside work context (Street, 1989), his research program merits serious consideration.

Studies of Trainee Perceptions of Training and Supervision

If there is one area of family-therapy training and supervision that has a history of consistent contribution, it would be this one. From family therapy's earliest days, trainers and trainees alike have hardly been shy in expressing their opinions about both sides of the training experience. Trainees have been surveyed about their impressions of a training program (Dowling et al., 1979), or specifically about live supervision (Liddle et al., 1988; Lowenstein, Reder, & Clark, 1982), and trainers and trainees have offered their views on the process of training (Dell, Sheely, Pulliam, & Goolishian, 1977; Henry, Sprenkle, & Sheehey, 1986; Wendorf, Wendorf, & Bond, 1985), and becoming a therapist from a variety of perspectives (Flores, 1979). Conceptualizations about trainee responses to the training process have ranged from the proposition of a parent–child metaphor for trainer–trainee (Kaslow & Gilman, 1983) to the stages of trainee response to training (Gershenson & Cohen, 1978).

This area of the literature suggests that trainees uniformly report the stress that accompanies training, especially when it includes live supervision and videotape. Further, trainees commonly have concerns about looking foolish in front of their peers and supervisors, and about sometimes being preoccupied with demonstrating their competence. Therapists in training recognize that dependence on the supervisor is a natural concomitant to being in training.

While helpful in a descriptive sense, the literature in this area is highly personal and impressionistic, often emotionally oriented, and not resting on a clear theoretical or conceptual base. In a paper that unfortunately provides an inaccurate representation of aspects of the training literature, Green and Kirby-Turner (1990) nonetheless offer a new contribution for conceptualizing the training experience.[12] Their paper begins with a theoretical framework that has only recently, with greater receptiveness to in-

dividuals, received attention in family therapy (Feixas, 1990), the personal construct theory of George Kelly. Their *repertory grid* (a self-characterization) and *trainee diary method* offer training research a much-needed new look[13] and give a needed substantive theoretical base to this topic. David Reiss' contention that, unlike psychoanalysis, family therapy does not have rich case studies—"a 'Little Hans' or a 'Dora' or a 'Rat Man' " (Reiss, 1988, p. 37)—to guide its theory development is equally applicable to family-therapy supervision. In applying what is, in family therapy at least, an underacknowledged theoretical system, personal construct theory, to the domain of training, the Green and Kirby-Turner paper gives us some fresh ideas about how to make sense of trainees' experience of their training.

CONCLUSIONS

This final section will briefly outline selected topics that on the basis of the foregoing review, should be considered areas that are important for every supervisor.

• *Research and evaluation.* Surely this represents what is perhaps the most important future area of development in training and supervision. Producing the next generations of family therapists, given the complexities of our world and field, will not be easy. We need to know what is effective and why. Questions about criteria and methods to determine effectiveness are now being asked and answered. A small revolution is happening in which practical instruments are being developed that can help us assess our work. This growing literature is becoming one of the most exciting areas of the field (cf., Kniskern & Gurman, 1979, 1980a, 1980b, 1988; Avis & Sprenkle, 1990; Breunlin et al., 1983, 1989; Zaken-Greenberg & Neimeyer, 1986; Churven & McKinnon, 1982; Crane, Griffin, & Hill, 1986; Dowling

---

[12] Green and Kirby-Turner (1990) report that trainees' views have been underrepresented in the literature, and how badly trainees and families react to live supervision. As the section on "Studies on Trainee Perceptions of Training and Supervision" indicates, there are numerous contributions of trainee perspectives. Additionally, although we certainly need more empirical work in this area, the available evidence suggests that the assertion by Green and Kirby-Turner of families' characteristic negative responses to live supervision is simply incorrect.

[13] See Kirchler (1989) for a discussion of the diary approach in marital research (an approach that has been used quite successfully in marital relationship research, for instance).

et al., 1979; Fennell, Hovestadt, & Samuel, 1986; Kolevson & Green, 1983; Tucker & Pinsof, 1984; Piercy et al., 1983; Pinsof, 1979; Pulleyblank & Shapiro, 1986; Street, 1988). Lastly, an exciting study by Strinhelber et al. (1984) investigates what might be considered the most vital question in all of this area: the relationship between supervision and clinical change.

• *Learning from psychotherapy.* Family therapy has maintained a separatist position for too long. It is time we began to understand and become more integrated with the psychotherapy field as a whole (Liddle, in press). Many developments in this field can help to shape and inform family therapy. The psychotherapy supervision literature is a case in point (Hogan, 1964; Hess, 1980). Long known for its empirical roots, studies on psychotherapy supervision can be found in virtually every issue of such publications as the *Journal of Counseling Psychology* and *Professional Psychology*. Specialized journals on supervision have existed for some time (e.g., *Counselor Education and Supervision, The Clinical Supervisor*). Additionally, the psychotherapy field is also sponsoring one of the most exciting areas of investigation and thinking to appear of late, namely, psychotherapy process research. This area of inquiry promises to make research clinically grounded and relevant (cf., Heatherington, 1989). The process-research writings of Greenberg (1986) and Pinsof (1981, 1988) deserve special attention. They cogently define the implications of process research for therapy-model construction and clinical practice.

• *Integrative models of supervision.* The issue of building integrative marital and family-therapy models has surely become one of the most important topics in the clinical realm of family therapy (Gurman, 1984; Lebow, 1984, 1987; Liddle, 1982b). In this chapter, we have touched on the difficulties of building integrative clinical models, as well as the issues involved in constructing integrative training models. This is another topic that has only recently begun to be defined in a helpful manner (cf., Duhl, 1985; Garfield, 1979). We are at an early stage here, still struggling to understand the nature of teaching integrative models. Again, developments in the psycho-

therapy field as a whole (cf., Wolfe & Goldfried, 1988) should be carefully followed and studied.

• *Treatment manuals.* Another exciting trend in the psychotherapy field was the introduction of treatment manuals into the therapy-outcome field, and more recently, into the training realm (Dobson & Shaw, 1988; Rounsaville, O'Malley, Foley, & Weissman, 1988). Family therapy has been slow to catch on to this important trend, and treatment manuals are not without their critics (cf., Stanton, 1988), but signs of family therapy's interest in this development can be found (Epstein, 1988; Jacobson, 1988; Wynne, 1988). Researchers conducting family-therapy treatment-outcome studies have begun to use treatment manuals in their work (Barton & Alexander, 1977; Henggeler et al., 1986; Joanning, Arrendondo, & Fischer, Quinn, 1984; Lewis, Piercy & Trepper Sprenkle, 1985; Liddle et al., 1991; Szapocznik et al., 1989). An understanding of the supervision implications of these developments awaits further inquiry.

• *Family life of the family therapist.* This area concentrates on the personal side of becoming and remaining a family therapist. Kaslow (1987) has contributed steadily to this topic. The area of family-of-origin work for trainees would also fit into this category (Forman, 1984).

• *Training trainers.* This chapter has focused on selected aspects of how to train family therapists, but what about training the trainers? What opportunities, body of knowledge, and frameworks exist for training those who do the teaching? Many aspects of these issues have been discussed in the literature (see Breunlin et al., 1988; Liddle, Breunlin, Schwartz, & Constantine, 1984; Constantine, Piercy, & Sprenkle, 1984; Draper, 1982; Fine & Fennell, 1985; Wright & Coppersmith, 1983).

• *Contexts of training.* Family-therapy practice and training and supervision takes place in a wide variety of settings, including free-standing institutes (Herz & Carter, 1988), hospitals, community mental health centers, universities (Berger, 1988; Sprenkle, 1988, Wright & Leahey, 1988), and in what is a virtually neglected area among authors, supervision in private practice (Kaslow, 1986). Training is a more diverse enterprise than ever

TRAINING AND SUPERVISION IN FAMILY THERAPY

before. Contributions such as these help us to understand this diversity and the ways in which context affects our work (cf., Shapiro, 1975a; Stanton, 1975b). This topic, of course, has long been a familiar one on the clinical side of the field.

• *Training within different disciplines.* Psychology (Berger, 1988; Green, Ferguson, Framo, Shapiro, & LaPerriere, 1979; Liddle, 1987; Liddle, Vance, & Pastushak, 1979; Stanton, 1975a, 1975b; *Journal of Family Psychology*, 1987), psychiatry (Combrinck-Graham, 1988), social work (Bardill & Saunders, 1988), nursing (Wright & Leahey, 1988), marriage and family therapy (Sprenkle, 1988), and family medicine (Ransom, 1988) are among the contemporary disciplines/professions involving training and supervision. How will the traditional disciplines relate to the inevitable growth of family therapy as a profession? Will family therapy continue to have difficulty making connections in the traditional mental health disciplines and delivery systems in which it must operate?

• *Special topics of supervision.* Critiques of the training area have been offered (Carpenter, 1984; Haley, 1974; Lask, 1989; Madanes, 1988; Werry, 1989). As training becomes more specialized, new problems become apparent (cf., Miller & Crago, 1989). The area of *ethics* in training and supervision has been drastically overlooked. A paper by Margolin (1982) still stands as the best articulation of the major dilemmas in this thorny area. Finally, the foundational topic of the trainer–trainee relationship has received remarkably little focus. One excellent exception is a paper by Schwartz (1987).

• *Supervisor development.* This is an area of the literature that deserves more attention. Since family therapy is finally able to discuss such constructs as personality again, what are the characteristics (Liddle, 1988a) and settings (see Stanton, et al. 1982) that produce good supervisors and supervision?

• *Accreditation and credentialing issues.* A movement is under way that has created a national written examination for the practice of marriage and family therapy. This is but one of the many issues for trainers to contemplate over the next few years (Keller, Huber, & Hardy, 1988; Smith & Nichols, 1979; Sporakowski & Staniszewski, 1980). The AAMFT

has been involved in the accreditation process for some time now, whereas the AFTA has declined, since its inception, to deal with credentialing issues. Controversies abound in this arena and will only become more pronounced, as the recent disturbing findings of a study on California-based MFT training programs can attest (O'Sullivan & Gilbert, 1989).

• *Mission of family-therapy training.* Challenges to the role, definition, and overall mission of family-therapy training have been made (Liddle, 1985). To what degree, for instance, are we preparing trainees for the realities of their everyday practice, in terms of the difficulty and variety of cases they will see? Further, are we readying these therapists for the political realities they will face as they attempt to practice family systems therapy? Moreover, do issues of discrimination (traditional practitioners making it difficult for family systems practitioners to do their work) still exist? Or are these romanticized fictions of a family-therapy era, a period in which family therapists felt persecuted, that no longer exists? What is the status of what has been called the politics of family-therapy training (Liddle, 1978), that area of the literature that has chronicled the early-stage difficulties of family therapy's establishment? (See Framo, 1976; Haley, 1975; Meyerstein, 1977; Shapiro, 1975b.)

• *The research-utilization problem in clinical practice.* Commonly referred to as the utilization problem in psychotherapy (Cohen, Sargent, & Sechrest, 1986), this issue refers to the continuing gulf between researchers and clinicians. Why do clinicians not know more about the relevant research findings of the day and incorporate them into their work? Similarly, do researchers have clinicians firmly enough in mind in the presentation of their findings, and is their research relevant to the average therapist? While this matter is considered by some to be an unsolvable problem, there are new ideas in this area. Although there are signs that the integration movement may be a way for this matter to receive some attention, family therapy has not yet caught on to this general topic. However, progress may be in the air: in 1990, the AFTA sponsored a conference that specifically addressed the clinician–researcher gap. Also, the Research Committee of the AAMFT has given this issue high priority in its upcoming work. This group routinely organizes a Research Institute at the AAMFT meeting. For the first time, a Research Track was introduced at the 1990 AAMFT annual meeting, and the AAMFT also sponsored Supervision Tracks at previous annual meetings.

In conclusion, the literature on family-therapy training and supervision is vast. Supervisors can no longer complain that their needs cannot be at least partially met by a careful study of this specialty area in family therapy. Of course, in this regard, the problem is more one of how to motivate experienced professionals to continue to learn (and to want to learn) about the new developments in their area. This is compounded by the necessity to remain current with the clinical developments in one's field in addition to those in the supervision and training area.

Gone are the days when supervision was seen as role that one simply graduated to, most frequently on a seniority basis. Supervision is not something that one learns on the job. Supervising family therapists requires great skill, both personal and conceptual. Supervisors must be formally trained, and by someone who can watch their work.

Being a skilled therapist is not enough. Clinical skill and knowledge are indispensable for, but no guarantee of, supervisory success. Without exaggeration, the success of the family-therapy field depends on the next generation(s) of supervisors. Our field can progress no further than do those who define it and teach it to others. These trainers represent what we have been and where we are going. It is they who carry the torch.

REFERENCES

Ackerman, N. (1973). Some considerations for training in family therapy. In *Career Directions* (vol. 2). East Hanover, NJ: Sandoz Pharmaceuticals.

Aldefer, C., & Lynch, B. (1986). Supervision in two dimensions. *Journal of Strategic and Systemic Therapies, 5,* A42–A45.

Alexander, J.F., Barton, C., Schiavo, R.S., & Parsons, B.V. (1976). Systems-behavioral intervention with families of delinquents: Therapist characteristics, family behavior, and outcome. *Journal of Consulting and Clinical Psychology, 44,* 656–664.

Alexander J.F., & Parsons, B.V. (1973). Short-term behavioral intervention with delinquent families: Impact on family process and recidivism. *Journal of Abnormal Psychology, 81,* 219–225.

Alger, I. (1973). Audio-visual techniques in family therapy. In D. Bloch (Ed.), *Techniques of family Psychotherapy.* New York: Grune & Stratton.

Alger, I., & Hogan, P. (1970). Use of videotape recordings in conjoint marital therapy. In M. Berger (Ed.), *Videotapetechniques in psychiatric training and treatment.* New York:.

Allen, J. (1976). Peer group supervision in family therapy. *Child Welfare, 55,* 183–189.

Allred, G., & Kersey, F. (1977). The AIAC, a design for systematical analyzing marriage and family counselors: A progress report. *Journal of Marriage and Family Counseling, 3(2),* 17–26.

Anderson, H. (1984). *The new epistemology in family therapy: Implications for training therapists.* Ann Arbor, MI: University Microfilms International.

Anderson, H., & Rambo, A. (1988). An experiment in systemic family therapy training: A trainer and trainees perspective. *Journal of Strategic and Systemic Therapies.*

Andolfi, M., & Menghi, P. (1980). A model for training in family therapy. In M. Andolfi & I. Zwerling (Eds.), *Dimensions of family therapy.* New York: Guilford Press.

Aponte, H.J., & Van Deusen, J.M. (1981). Structural family therapy. In A. Gurman & D. Kniskern (Eds.), *Handbook of family therapy.* New York: Brunner/Mazel.

Ard, D. (1973). Providing clinical supervision for marriage counselors: A model for supervisor and supervisee. *Family Coordinator, 22,* 91–98.

Argyris, C., & Schon, D.A. (1974). *Theory in practice: Increasing professional effectiveness.* San Francisco: Josey-Bass.

Auerswald, E. (1985). Thinking about thinking in family therapy. *Family Process, 24,* 1–12.

Avis, J. (1986). Feminist issues in family therapy. In F.P. Piercy, D.H. Sprenkle, et al. (Eds.), *Family therapy sourcebook.* New York: Guilford Press.

Avis, J.M., & Sprenkle, D. (1990). A review of outcome research on family therapy training. *Journal of Marital and Family Therapy.*

Bagarozzi, D. (1980). Holistic family therapy and clinical supervision: Systematic behavioral and psychoanalytic perspectives. *Family Therapy, 7,* 153–165.

Bardill, D. (1976). The simulated family as an aid to learning family group treatment. *Child Welfare, 55,* 703–709.

Bardill, D.R., & Saunders, B.E. (1988). Marriage and family therapy and graduate social work education. In H.A. Liddle, C. Barton, D.C. Breunlin, & R.C. Schwartz (Eds.). *Handbook of family therapy training and supervision.* New York: Guilford.

Barnes, G.G., & Campbell, D. (1982). The impact of structural and strategic approaches on the supervision process: A supervisor is supervised: Or how to progress from frog to prince: Two theories of change 1978–1980. In R. Whiffen & J. Byng-Hall (Eds.), *Family therapy supervision: Recent developments in practice.* New York: Grune & Stratton.

Barton, C., & Alexander, J. (1977). Therapist's skills as determinants of effective systems-behavioral family therapy. *International Journal of Family Counseling, 5,* 11–20.

Bateson, G. (1972). Experiments in thinking about observed ethnological materials. In *Steps toward an ecology of mind.* New York: Ballantine Books.

Bateson, G. (1979). *Mind in nature: Unnecessary unity.* New York: Dutton.

Beal, E. (1976). Current trends in the training of family therapists. *American Journal of Psychiatry, 133,* 137–141.

Beatman, F.L. (1964). The training and preparation of workers for family group treatment. *Social Casework, 45,* 202–208.

Beavers, W.R. (1985). Family therapy supervision: An introduction and consumer's guide. *Journal of Psychotherapy and the Family, 1(4),* 15–24.

Berg, B. (1978). Learning family therapy through simulation. *Psychotherapy: Theory, Research and Practice, 15(1),* 56–61.

Berger, M. (Ed.). (1970). *Videotape techniques in psychiatric training and treatment.* New York: Brunner/Mazel.

Berger, M. (1988). Psychology and family therapy training. In H.A. Liddle, D.C. Breunlin, & R.C. Schwartz (Eds.), *Handbook of family therapy training and supervision*. New York: Guilford Press.

Berger, M., & Dammann, C. (1982). Live supervision as context, treatment, and training. *Family Process, 21,* 337–344.

Berkman A., & Berkman, C. (1984). The supervision co-therapist teams in family therapy. *Psychotherapy, 21,* 197–205.

Beroza, R. (1983). The shoemaker's children. *Family Therapy Networker, 7,* 31–33.

Betcher, R., & Zinberg, N. (1988). Supervision and privacy in psychotherapy training. *American Journal of Psychiatry, 145,* 796–803.

Betof, N. (1977). The effects of a forty-week family training program on the organization and trainees. Unpublished manuscript, Temple University.

Birchler, G. (1975). Live supervision and instant feedback in marriage and family therapy. *Journal of Marriage and Family Counseling, 1,* 331–342.

Bodin, A.M. (1969). Family therapy training literature: A brief guide. *Family Process, 8,* 272–279.

Bodin, A. (1972). The use of video tapes. In A. Ferber, M. Mendelsohn, & A. Napier (Eds.), *The book of family therapy*. New York: Houghton-Mifflin.

Bodin, A.M. (1981). The interactional view: Family therapy approaches of the Mental Research Institute. In A. Gurman & D. Kniskern (Eds.), *Handbook of family therapy*. New York: Brunner/Mazel.

Boscolo, L. (1987). In Boscolo, L., Cecchin, G., Hoffman, L. & Penn, P. *Milan systemic family therapy: Conversations in theory and practice*. New York: Basic Books, Inc.

Boszormenyi-Nagy, I. & Ulrich, D.N. (1981). Contextual family therapy. In A. Gurman & D. Kniskern (Eds.), *Handbook of family therapy*. New York: Brunner/Mazel.

Bowen, M. (1972). On the differentiation of self in one's own family. In J. Framo (Ed.), *Family interaction: A dialogue between family researchers and family therapists*. New York: Springer. Also in M. Bowen (Ed.) (1978). *Family therapy in clinical practice*. New York: Jason Aronson.

Breunlin, D. (1988). Oscillation theory and family development. In C.J. Falicov (Ed.), *Family transitions: Continuity and change over the life cycle*. New York: Guilford Press.

Breunlin, D., Karrer, B., McGuire, D., & Cimmarusti, R. (1988). Cybernetics of videotape supervision. In H.A. Liddle, D.C. Breunlin, & R.C. Schwartz (Eds.), *Handbook of family therapy training and supervision*. New York: Guilford Press.

Breunlin, D., Liddle, H., & Schwartz, R. (1988). Concurrent training of supervisors and therapists: In H.A. Liddle, D.C. Breunlin, & R.C. Schwartz (Eds.), *Handbook of family therapy training and supervision*. New York: Guilford Press.

Breunlin, D., Schwartz, R., Krause, M., Kochalka, J., Puetz, R., & VanDyke, J. (1989). The prediction of learning in family therapy training programs. *Journal of Marital and Family Therapy, 15,* 387–396.

Breunlin, D.D., Schwartz, R.C., Selby, L., & Krause, M.S. (1983). Evaluating family therapy training: The development of an instrument. *Journal of Marital and Family Therapy, 9,* 37–84.

Bross, A. (1980). (Ed.). *Family therapy: Principles of strategic practice*. New York: Guilford Press.

Brown, M. (1985). I'll pitch, you catch: Substituting peer vision for live supervision of family therapy. *Family Therapy, 12,* 279–284.

Brown, M.S., Hirschmann, M.J., Lasley, J.H., & Steinweg, C.K. (1986). Annotated bibliography of key articles on the supervision and training of family therapy. In F.P. Piercy (Ed.), *Family therapy education and supervision* (pp. 139–145). New York: The Haworth Press.

Byles, J., Bishop, D., & Horn, D. (1983). Evaluation of a family therapy training program. *Journal of Marital and Family Therapy, 9,* 299–304.

Byng-Hall, J. (1982). The use of the earphone in supervision. In R. Whiffen & J. Byng-Hall (Eds.), *Family therapy supervision: Recent developments in practice*. New York: Grune & Stratton.

Cade, B., Speed, B., & Seligman, P. (1986). Working in teams: The pros and cons in F. Kaslow (Ed.) *Supervision and training: Models, dilemmas and challenges*. New York: Haworth.

Carpenter, J. (1984). Making training relevant—a critical review of family therapy training in the U.K. *Journal of Family Therapy, 6*(3), 235–246.

Carter, B., & McGoldrick, M. (Eds.) (1989). *The changing family life cycle.* (2nd ed.). Boston, MA: Allyn & Bacon.

Carter, B., Walters, M., Papp, P., & Silverstein, O. (1988). *The invisible web*. New York: Guilford Press.

Carter, E. (1982). Supervisory discussion in the presence of the family. In R. Whiffen & J. Byng-Hall (Eds.), *Family therapy supervision*. New York: Grune & Stratton.

Carter, E., Papp, P., Silverstein, O., & Walters, M. (1984). From ideology to practice: The women's project in family therapy. (An interview by R. Simon). *Family Therapy Networker, 8,* 28–40.

Caust, B., Libow, J., & Raskin, P. (1981). Challenges and promises of training women as family systems therapists. *Family Process, 20,* 439–448.

Cecchin, G. (1987). In Boscolo, L., Cecchin, G., Hoffman, L. & Penn, P. *Milan systemic family therapy: Conversations in theory and practice*. New York: Basic Books, Inc.

Chable, B. & students. (1988). The first phases of family therapy training. *The Australian and New Zealand Journal of Family Therapy, 9,* 209–215.

Churven, P. (1977). Role playing, deroling, and reality in family therapy training. *Australian Social Work, 30,* 23–27.

Churven, P., & McKinnon, T. (1982). Family therapy training: An evaluation of a workshop. *Family Process, 21,* 345–352.

Cleghorn, J., & Levin, S. (1973). Training family therapists by setting learning objectives. *American Journal of Orthopsychiatry, 43,* 439–446.

Cohen, H., Sargent, M., & Sechrest, L. (1986). Use of psychotherapy research by professional psychologists. *American Psychologist, 41,* 198–206.

Cohen, M., Gross, S., & Turner, M. (1976). A note on a developmental model for training family therapists through group supervision. *Journal of Marriage and Family Counseling, 2,* 48–76.

Colapinto, J. (1983). Beyond technique: Teaching how to think structurally. *Journal of Strategic and Systemic Therapies, 2,* 12–21.

Colapinto, J. (1988). Teaching the structural way. In H.A. Liddle, D.C. Breunlin, & R.C. Schwartz (Eds.), *Handbook of family therapy and supervision*. New York: Guilford Press.

Coleman, S. (Ed.). (1985). *Failures in family therapy*. New York: Guilford Press.

Combrinck-Graham, L. (1985). A model for family development. *Family Process, 24,* 139–150.

Combrinck-Graham, L. (1988). Psychiatry and family therapy training. In H.A. Liddle, D.C. Breunlin, & R.C. Schwartz (Eds.), *Handbook of family therapy training and supervision*. New York: Guilford Press.

Connell, G.M. (1984). An approach to supervision of symbolic-experimental psychotherapy. *Journal of Marriage and Family Therapy, 10,* 273–280.

Constantine, J., Piercy, F., & Sprenkle, D. (1984). Live supervision-of-supervision in family therapy. *Journal of Marital and Family Therapy, 10,* 95–98.

Constantine, J., Stone-Fish, L., & Piercy, F. (1984). A systemic procedure for teaching positive connotation. *Journal of Marital and Family Therapy, 10*(3), 313–316.

Constantine, L. (1976). Designed experience: A multiple, goal directed training program in family therapy. *Family Process,* 373–396.

Coopersmith, E. (1978). Expanding uses of the telephone in family therapy. *Family Process*, 17, 225–230.

Coopersmith, E.I. (1985). Teaching trainees to think in triads. *Journal of Marital and Family Therapy*, 11, 61–66.

Cornwell, M., & Pearson, R. (1981). Co-therapy teams and one-way screen in family therapy practice and training. *Family Process*, 20, 199–209.

Cotton, P. (1987). The impact of live supervision on family and couple therapy. Unpublished doctoral dissertation, Northwestern University.

Crane, R., Griffin, W., & Hill, R.D. (1986). Influence of therapist skills on client perceptions of marriage and family therapy outcome: Implications for supervision. *Journal of Marriage and Family Therapy*, 2, 91–96.

DeAth, E. (1979). Action models—Learning by doing. *Journal of Family Therapy*, 1(2), 231–239.

Dell, P.F. (1986). In defense of 'lineal causality'. *Family Process*, 25, 513–521.

Dell, P., Sheely, M., Pullian, G., & Goolishian, H. (1977). Family therapy process in a family therapy seminar. *Journal of Marriage and Family Counseling*, 3, 43–48.

Dobson, K., & Shaw, B. (1988). The use of treatment manuals in cognitive therapy: Experience and issues. *Journal of Consulting and Clinical Psychology*, 56, 673–680.

Doehrman, M. (1976). Parallel processes in supervision and psychotherapy. *Bulletin of the Menninger Clinic*, 40(1), 3–10.

Dowling, E., Cade, B., Breunlin, D.C., Frude, N., & Seligman, P. (1979). A retrospective survey of students' view on a family therapy training programme. In S. Walrond-Skinner (Ed.), *Family and marital psychotherapy*. London: Routledge & Kegan Paul.

Dowling, E., & Seligman, P. (1980). Description and evaluation of a family therapy training model. *Journal of Family Therapy*, 2(2), 123–130.

Draper, R. (1982). From trainee to trainer. In R. Whiffen & J. Byng-Hall (Eds.), *Family therapy supervision: Recent developments in practice*. New York: Grune & Stratton.

Duhl, B. (1983). *From the inside out and other metaphors: Creative and integrative approaches to training in systems thinking*. New York: Brunner/Mazel.

Duhl, B. (1985). Toward cognitive-behavioral integration in training systems therapists: An interactive approach to training in generic systems thinking. *Journal of Psychotherapy and the Family*, 1(4).

Duhl, F., & Duhl, B. (1979). Structured spontaneity: The thoughtful art of integrative family therapy at BFI. *Journal of Marital and Family Therapy*, 5, 59–76.

Duhl, F.J., Kantor, D., & Duhl, B.S. (1973). Learning, space, and action in family therapy: A primer of sculpture. In D. Block (Ed.), *Techniques of family psychotherapy*. New York: Grune & Stratton.

Efron, D. (1988). *Journeys*. New York: Brunner/Mazel.

Ehrlich, F. (1973). Family therapy training in child psychiatry. *Journal of American Academy of Child Psychiatrists*, 12, 461–472.

Ekstein, R., & Wallerstein, R. (1972). *The teaching and learning of psychotherapy* (2nd ed.). New York: International Universities Press.

Epstein, N. (1988). Dilemmas and choices in the design of family therapy research. In L.C. Wynne (Ed.), *The state of the art in family therapy research: Controversies and recommendations* (pp. 119–124). New York: Family Process Press.

Epstein, N., & Levin, S. (1973). Training for family therapy within a faculty of medicine. *Canadian Psychiatric Association Journal*, 18, 203–207.

Everett, C.A. (1980). Supervision of marriage and family therapy. In A. Hess (Ed.), *Psychotherapy and supervision* (pp. 367–380). New York: Wiley-Interscience.

Everett, C.A., & Koerpel, B.J. (1986) Family therapy supervision: A review and critique of the literature. *Contemporary Family Therapy*, 8, 62–74.

Falicov, C. (1988a). Family sociology and family therapy contributions to the family development framework: A comparative analysis and thoughts on future trends. In C.J. Falicov (Ed.), *Family transitions: Continuity and change over the life cycle*. New York: Guilford Press.

Falicov, C. (1988b). Learning to think culturally in family therapy training. In H.A. Liddle, D.C. Breunlin, & R.C. Schwartz (Eds.), *Handbook of family therapy training and supervision*. New York: Guilford Press.

Falicov, C., Constantine, J., & Breunlin, D. (1981). Teaching family therapy: A program based on training objectives. *Journal of Marital and Family Therapy*, 7, 497–505.

Falicov, C.J. (Ed.). (1983). *Cultural perspectives in family therapy*. Rockville, MD: Aspen Publications.

Feixas, G. (1990). Approaching the individual, approaching the system: A constructivist model for integrative psychotherapy. *Journal of Family Psychology*, 4, 4–35.

Feldman, L. (1982). Sex role and family dynamics. In F. Walsh (Ed.), *Normal family processes*. New York: Guilford Press.

Fenell, D., Hovestadt, A., & Harvey, J. (1986). A comparison of delayed feedback and live supervision models of marriage and family therapist clinical training. *Journal of Marriage and Family Therapy*, 2, 181–186.

Ferber, A. (1972). Follow the path with heart. *International Journal of Psychiatry*, 10, 6–22.

Ferber, A., & Mendelsohn, M. (1969). Training for family therapy. *Family Process*, 8, 25–32.

Ferber, A., Mendelsohn, M., & Napier, A. (Eds.). (1972). *The book of family therapy*. New York: Science House.

Ferguson, L.R. (1979). The family life cycle: Orientation for interdisciplinary training. *Professional Psychology*, 10, 863–867.

Figley, C., & Nelson, T. (1990). Basic family therapy skills, II: Structural family therapy. *Journal of Marital and Family Therapy*, 16, 225–240.

Figley, C.R., & Nelson, T.S. (1989). Basic family therapy skills, I: Conceptualization and initial findings. *Journal of Marital and Family Therapy*, 14(4), 349–366.

Fine, J., & Fenell, D. (1985). Supervising the supervisor-of-supervision: A supervision-of-supervision technique or an hierarchical blurring? *Journal of Strategic and Systemic Therapies*, 4(3), 55–59.

Fine, M., & McIntosh, D.N. (1986). The use of interactive videos to demonstrate differential approaches to marital and family therapy. *Journal of Marriage and Family Therapy*, 11, 85–90.

Fisch, R. (1988). Training in the brief therapy approach of the MRI. In H.A. Liddle, D.C. Breunlin, & R.C. Schwartz (Eds.), *Handbook of family therapy training and research*. New York: Guilford Press.

Fleuridas, C., Nelson, T., & Rosenthal, D.M. (1986). The evolution of circular questions: Training family therapists. *Journal of Marital and Family Therapy*, 12(2), 113–128.

Flomenhaft, K., & Carter, R. (1974). Family therapy training: A statewide program for mental health centers. *Hospital and Community Psychiatry*, 25(12), 789–791.

Flores, J.L. (1979). Becoming a marriage, family, and child counselor: Notes from a Chicano. *Journal of Marital and Family Therapy*, 5(4), 17–22.

Forman, B. (1984). Family of origin work in systemic/strategic therapy. *The Clinical Supervisor*, 2, 81–85.

Framo, J.L. (1975). Personal reflections of a family therapist. *Journal of Marriage and Family Counseling*, 1, 15–28.

Framo, J.L. (1976). Chronicle of a struggle to establish a family unit within a community mental health center. In P. Geurin (Ed.), *Family therapy: Theory and practice*. New York: Gardner Press.

Framo, J.L. (1981). The integration of marital therapy with sessions with family of origin. In A. Burman & D. Kniskern (Eds.), *Handbook of family therapy*. New York: Brunner/Mazel.

Frankel, B. (1989). Isomorphism in family therapy supervision: A study of the relationship among selected supervisor, therapist, and client behaviors". Unpublished doctoral dissertation, Purdue University.

Fulmer, R. (1983). Teaching the family life cycle: A guide for a workshop using simulated families. *American Journal of Family Therapy*, 11, 55–62.

Ganahl, G., Ferguson, L.R., & L'Abate, L. (1985). Training in family therapy. In L. L'Abate (Ed.), *The handbook of family psychology and therapy*. Homewood, IL: Dorsey Press.

Garfield, R. (1979). An integrative training model for family therapists: The Hahnemann master of family therapy program. *Journal of Marital and Family Therapy*, 5(3), 15–22.

Garfield, R. (1980). Family therapy training at Hahnemann Medical College and Hospital. In M. Andolfi & I. Zwerling (Eds.), *Dimensions of family therapy*. New York: Guilford Press.

Garfield, R., Greenberg, A., & Sugarman, S. (Eds.). (1987). Symbolic experiential journeys. A special issue of *Contemporary Family Therapy*, 9.

Garfield, R., & Lord, G. (1982). The Hahnemann masters of family therapy program: A design and its results. *American Journal of Family Therapy*, 10, 75–78.

Gelcer, E. (1987). Training in family therapy: Dealing with aspects of the invariant method. *Journal of Strategic and Systemic Therapies*, 6, 42–56.

Gentry, D. (1986). An introduction to brief strategic therapy supervision. *The Clinical Supervisor*, 4, 119–129.

Gershenson, J., & Cohen, M. (1978). Through the looking glass: The experiences of two family therapy trainees with live supervision. *Family Process*, 17, 225–230.

Glick, I., Kessler, D., & Sugarman, S. (1987). Family therapy training. In I. Glick, J. Clarkin & D. Kessler (Eds.), *Marital and family therapy*, 3rd edition. New York: Grune & Stratton.

Goguen, T. (1986). Psychotherapy supervision: Clarifying a complex task. *The Clinical Supervisor*, 4, 69–76.

Goldner, V. (1985). Feminism and family therapy. *Family Process*, 24, 31–47.

Goodrich, T., Rampage, C., Ellman, B., & Halstead, K. (1988). *Feminist family therapy*. New York: Norton.

Goodyear, R.K., Abadie, P.D., & Efros, F. (1984). Supervisory theory into practice: Differential perceptions of supervision by Ekstein, Ellis, Polster, and Rogers. *Journal of Counseling Psychology*, 31, 228–237.

Gorman, P. (1989). Family therapy supervision in an agency setting: An analysis of moments-of-intervention. Unpublished doctoral dissertation, University of Massachusetts.

Gottman, J., & Markman, H.J. (1978). Experimental designs in psychotherapy research. In S.L. Garfield & A.E. Bergin (Eds.), *Handbook of psychotherapy and behavior change: An empirical analysis*, 2nd edition. New York: Wiley.

Green, D., & Kirby-Turner, N. (1990). First steps in family therapy: A personal construct analysis. *Journal of Family Therapy*, 12, 139–154.

Green, R.J., Ferguson, L.R., Framo, J.L., Shapiro, R.J., & LaPerriere, K. (1979). A symposium on family therapy training for psychologists.

Green, R., & Kolevzon, M. (1982). Three approaches to family therapy: A study of convergence and divergence. *Journal of Marital and Family Therapy*, 8, 39–50.

Green, R., & Sager, K. (1982). Learning to think systems: Five writing assignments. *Journal of Marital and Family Therapy*, 8, 285–294.

Greenberg, L. (1986). Change process research. *Journal of Consulting and Clinical Psychology*, 54, 4–9.

Group for the Advancement of Psychiatry. (1970). The field of family therapy. GAP Report 78. New York.

Grunebaum, H. (1988). The relationship of family theory to family therapy. *Journal of Marital and Family Therapy*, 14, 1–18.

Grunebaum, H., & Chasin, R. (1982). Thinking like a family ther-

apist: A model for integrating the theories and methods of family therapy. *Journal of Marital and Family Therapy*, 8, 403–416.

Guerin, P. (1976). Family therapy: The first twenty-five years. In P. Guerin (Ed.), *Family therapy, theory and practice* (pp. 2–22). New York: Gardner Press.

Guerin, P., & Fogarty, T. (1972). The family therapist's own family. *International Journal of Psychiatry*, 10(1), 6–22.

Gurman, A. (1983). The virtues and dangers of a life cycle perspective in family therapy. *American Journal of Family Therapy*, 11, 67–72.

Gurman, A. (1984). Integrative marital therapy. In S. Budman (Ed.), *Forms of brief therapy*. New York: Guilford Press.

Gurman, A., & Klein, M. (1984). Marriage and the family: An unconscious male bias in behavioral treatment? In E.A. Blechman (Ed.), *Behavior modification with women*. New York: Guilford Press.

Haas, L., Alexander, J., & Mas, C. (1988). Functional family therapy: Basic concepts and training program. In H.A. Liddle, D.C. Breunlin, & R.C. Schwartz (Eds.), *Handbook of family therapy training and supervision*. New York: Guilford Press.

Haley, J. (1963). *Strategies of psychotherapy*. New York: Grune & Stratton.

Haley, J. (1973). *Uncommon therapy*. New York: Norton.

Haley, J. (1974). Fourteen ways to fail as a teacher of family therapy. *Family Therapy*, 1, 1–8.

Haley, J. (1975). Why a mental health clinic should avoid doing family therapy. *Journal of Marriage and Family Counseling*, 1, 3–12.

Haley, J. (1976). Problems of training therapists. In J. Haley (Ed.), *Problem-solving therapy*. San Francisco: Jossey-Bass.

Haley, J. (1980). *Leaving home: The therapy of disturbed young people*. New York: McGraw-Hill.

Haley, J. (1988). Reflections on therapy supervision. In H. Liddle, D. Breunlin, & R. Schwartz (Eds.), *Handbook of family and marital therapy*. New York: Guilford Press.

Halgin, R.P. (1988). Special section: Issues in the supervision of integrative psychotherapy: Introduction. *Journal of Integrative and Eclectic Psychotherapy*, 7, 152–156.

Hare, R., & Frankena, S. (1972). Peer group supervision. *American Journal of Orthopsychiatry*, 42, 527–529.

Hare-Mustin, R. (1976). Live supervision in psychotherapy. *Voices*, 12, 21–24.

Hare-Mustin, R. (1978). A feminist approach to family therapy. *Family Process*, 17, 181–194.

Hart, G. (1982). *The process of clinical supervision*. Baltimore: University Park Press.

Hatcher, C. (1982). Supervision of the double axis model of therapy. In R. Whiffen & J. Byng-Hall (Eds.), *Family therapy supervision: Recent developments in practice*. New York: Grune & Stratton.

Heath, A. (1982). Team family therapy training: Conceptual and pragmatic considerations. *Family Process*, 21, 187–194.

Heath, A., & Storm, C. (1983). Answering the call: A manual for beginning supervisors. *The Family Therapy Networker*, 7(2), 36–37, 66.

Heath, T. (1983). The live supervision form: Structure and theory for assessment in live supervision. In J.C. Hansen & B.P. Keeney (Eds.), *Diagnosis and assessment in family therapy*. Rockville, MD: Aspen.

Heatherington, L. (1987). Therapists' personalities and their evaluation of three family therapy styles: An empirical investigation. *Journal of Marital and Family Therapy*, 13, 167–178.

Heatherington, L. (1989). Toward more meaningful clinical research: Taking context into account in coding psychotherapy interaction. *Psychotherapy*, 26, 436–447.

Henggeler, S., Rodick, J., Borduin, C., Hanson, C., Watson, S., & Urey, J. (1986). Multisystemic treatment of juvenile offenders: Effects on adolescent behavior and family interaction. *Developmental Psychology*, 22, 132–141.

Henry, P.W., Sprenkle, D.H., & Sheehan, R. (1986). Family therapy training: Student and faculty perceptions. *Journal of Marital and Family Therapy*, 12(3), 249–258.

Heppner, P.P. & Handley, P. (1981). A study of the interpersonal influence process in supervision. *Journal of Counseling Psychology*, 28, 437–444.

Hernandez, K.K. (1985). *Validational studies on two instruments that measure therapists' level of systemic thinking*. Unpublished doctoral dissertation, Purdue University.

Herz, F., & Carter, B. (1988). Born free: The life cycle of a free-standing post-graduate training institute. In H.A. Liddle, D.C. Breunlin, & R.C. Schwartz (Eds.), *Handbook of family therapy training and supervision*. New York: Guilford Press.

Hess, A.K. (Ed.) (1980). *Psychotherapy supervision: Theory, research, and practice*. New York: Wiley.

Hodas, G. (1985). A systems perspective in family therapy supervision. In R.L. Ziffer (Ed.), *Adjunctive techniques in family therapy*. Orlando, FL: Grune & Stratton.

Hoffman, L. (1981). *Foundations of family therapy: A conceptual framework for systems change*. New York: Basic Books.

Hogan, R. (1964). Issues and approaches in supervision. *Psychotherapy: Theory, Research and Practice*, 1(3), 173–176.

Holloway, E.L. (1982). Interactional structure of the supervision interview. *Journal of Counseling Psychology*, 29, 309–317.

Hughes, S.F., Berger, M., & Wright, L. (1978). The family life cycle and clinical interventions. *Journal of Marriage and Family Counseling*, 4, 33–40.

Isaelstam, K. (1988). Contrasting four major family therapy paradigms: Implications for family therapy training. *Journal of Family Therapy*, 10, 179–196.

Ivey, A.E., & Authier, J. (1978). *Microcounseling: Innovations in interviewing, counseling psychotherapy and psychoeducation*. Illinois: Thomas Springfield.

Jacobson, N. (1983). Beyond empiricism: The politics of marital therapy. *American Journal of Family Therapy*, 11, 11–24.

Jacobson, N. (1988). Guidelines for the design of family therapy outcome research (pp. 139–158). In L.C. Wynne (Ed.), *The state of the art in family therapy research: Controversies and recommendations*. New York: Family Process Press.

James, K., & McIntyre, D. (1983). The reproduction of families: The social role of family therapy. *Journal of Marital and Family Therapy*, 9, 119–129.

Jenkins, H. (1984). Which skills how: Options for family therapy training. *Journal of Family Therapy*, 6(I), 17–34.

Joanning, H., Quinn, W., Arrendondo, R., & Fischer, J. (1984). Family therapy versus traditional therapy for drug abusers. National Institute on Drug Abuse Grant # R01 DA 03700.

Journal of Family Psychology (1987). Volume 1, number 2. Special section on training in family psychology and family therapy.

Jurasky, J. (1964). A sit-in method for training family group therapists. *Journal of Psychoanalysis in Groups*, 1, 109–114.

Kantor, D., & Andreozzi, L.L. (1985). The cybernetics of family therapy and family therapy research. In L.L. Andreozzi (Ed.), *Integrating research and clinical practice*. Rockville, MD: Aspen Publications.

Kantor, D., Bograd, M., & Markson, E. (1987). Somewhere over the rainbow: Beginning development of a cybernetic research team. *American Family Therapy Association Newsletter*, Spring, 8–9.

Kantor, D., & Neal, J. (1985). Integrative shifts for the theory and practice of family systems therapy. *Family Process*, 24, 13–30.

Kaplan, R. (1987). The current use of live supervision within marriage and family therapy training programs. *The Clinical Supervisor*, 5, 43–52.

Karpel, M. (1986). *Family resources*. New York: Guilford Press.

Kaslow, F. (1977). Training marriage and family therapists. In F. Kaslow (Ed.), *Supervision, consultation, and staff training in the helping professions* (pp. 199–234). San Francisco: Jossey-Bass.

Kaslow, F. (1985). An intensive training experience: A six day post-

graduate institute model. *Journal of Psychotherapy and the Family*, 1(4), 73–82.

Kaslow, F. (Ed.) (1986). *Supervision and training: Models, dilemmas and challenges*. New York: Haworth.

Kaslow, F. (Ed.). (1987). *The family life of psychotherapists: Clinical implications*. New York: Haworth.

Kaslow, F.W. (1990). *Voices in family psychology* (Vol. 1 & 2). Newbury Park, CA: SAGE.

Kaslow, N.J., & Gilman, S.R. (1983). Trainee perspectives on family therapy supervision. *American Journal of Family Therapy*, 11, 70–74.

Kaye, K. (1985). Toward a developmental psychology of the family. In L. L'Abate (Ed.), *The handbook of family psychology and therapy*, vol. 2. Homewood, IL: Dorsey.

Keeney, B. (1979). Ecosystemic epistemology: An alternative paradigm for diagnosis. *Family Process*, 17, 195–205.

Keeney, B., & Ross, I. (1983). Learning to learn systemic therapies. *Journal of Strategic and Systemic Therapies*, 2, 22–30.

Keller, J., Huber, J., & Hardy, K. (1988). Accreditation: What constitutes appropriate marriage and family therapy education? *Journal of Marital and Family Therapy*, 14, 297–305.

Kempster, S.W., & Savitsky, E. (1967). Training family therapists through live supervision. In N. Ackerman, F. Beatman, & S. Sherman (Eds.), *Expanding theory and practice in family therapy*. New York: Family Service Association of America.

Kerr, M.E. (1981). Family systems theory and therapy. In A. Gurman & D. Kniskern (Eds.), *Handbook of family therapy*. New York: Brunner/Mazel.

Kingston, P., & Smith, D. (1983). Preparation for live consultation and live supervision when working with a one-way screen. *Journal of Family Therapy*, 5(3), 219–234.

Kirchler, E. (1989). Everyday life experiences at home: An interaction diary approach to assess marital relationships. *Journal of Family Psychology*, 2, 311–336.

Kniskern, D., & Gurman, A. (1979). Research on training in marriage and family therapy: Status, issues and directions. *Journal of Marital and Family Therapy*, 5(3), 83–94.

Kniskern, D.P., & Gurman, A.S. (1980a). Advances and prospects for family therapy research. In J.P. Vincent (Ed.), *Advances in family intervention, assessment and theory* (Vol. 2). Greenwich, CT: J.A.I. Press.

Kniskern, D.P., & Gurman, A.S. (1980b). Future directions for family therapy research. In D.A. Bagarrozzi (Ed.), *New perspectives in family therapy*. New York: Human Sciences Press.

Kniskern, D., & Gurman, A. (1988). Research in family therapy training. In H.A. Liddle, D.C. Breunlin, & R.C. Schwartz (Eds.), *Handbook of family therapy training and supervision*. New York: Guilford Press.

Kolevzon, M.S., & Green, R.G. (1983). An experientially based inductive approach to learning about family therapy. *The American Journal of Family Therapy*, 11(3), 35–42.

Kolevzon, M., Sowers-Hoag, K., & Hoffman, C. (1989). Selecting a family therapy model: The role of personality attributes in eclectic practice. *Journal of Marital and Family Therapy*, 15(3), 249–25.

Kramer, T., & Reitz, M. (1980). Using video playback to train family therapists. *Family Process*, 19, 145–150.

Landau-Stanton, J., & Stanton, M.D. (1983). Aspects of supervision with the "Pick-a-Dial Circus" model. *Journal of Strategic and Systemic Therapies*, 2, 31–39.

Lappin, J. (1983). On becoming a culturally conscious family therapist. In C.J. Falicov (Ed.), *Cultural perspectives in family therapy*. Rockville, MD: Aspen.

Lask, B. (1989). Editorial-flying gurus and their recursive interactions. *Journal of Family Therapy*, 11, 315–318.

Latham, T. (1982). The use of co-working (cotherapy) as a training method. *Journal of Family Therapy*, 4, 257–269.

Lebow, J. (1984). On the value of integrating approaches to family therapy. *Journal of Marital and Family Therapy*, 10, 127–138.

Lebow, J. (1987). Training psychologists in family therapy in family institute settings. *Journal of Family Psychology, 1*, 219–231.

Lewis, R., Piercy, F., Sprenkel, D., & Trepper, T. (1990). Family based interventions for helping drug abusing adolescents. *Journal of Adolescent Research*, 5 82–95.

Lewis, W., & Rohrbaugh, M. (1989). Live supervision by family therapists: A Virginia survey. *Journal of Marital and Family Therapy, 15*, 323–326.

Libow, J.A. (1985). Training family therapists as feminists. In M. Ault-Riche (Ed.), *Women and family therapy.* Rockville, MD: Aspen Systems Press.

Liddle, H. (1978). The emotional and political hazards of teaching and learning family therapy. *Family Therapy, 5,* 1–12.

Liddle, H.A. (1980). Keeping abreast of developments in the family therapy field: The use of "concepts cards" in clinical practice. In A. Gurman (Ed.), *Questions and Answers in Family Therapy* (Vol. 1). New York: Brunner/Mazel. Also in *American Journal of Family Therapy,* 1980.

Liddle, H.A. (1981). In the mind's Eye: Use of visual and auditory imagery in creating therapeutic and supervisory realities. *American Journal of Family Therapy.*

Liddle, H.A. (1982a). Family therapy training and supervision: Current issues, future trends. *International Journal of Family Therapy, 4,* 81–97.

Liddle, H.A. (1982b). On the problems of eclectism: A call for epistemologic clarification and human scale theories. *Family Process, 4,* 81–97.

Liddle, H.A. (1982c). In the mind's eye: The use of imagery in training family therapists. In A. Gurman (Ed.), *Questions and answers in family therapy.* New York: Brunner/Mazel. Also in *American Journal of Family Therapy,* 1982.

Liddle, H.A. (Ed.). (1983). *Clinical implications of the family life cycle.* Rockville, MD: Aspen Publications.

Liddle, H.A. (1985). Redefining the mission of family therapy training. *Journal of Psychotherapy and the Family, 1*(4), 109–124.

Liddle, H.A. (1988). Family psychology: An emerging (and emerged) field [Review of L. L'Abate (Ed.), *The handbook of family psychology and therapy, Vols. 1 and 2*]. *Contemporary Psychology, 33,* 202–204.

Liddle, H. (1988a). Systemic supervision: Conceptual overlays and pragmatic guidelines. In H.A. Liddle, D.C. Breunlin, & R.C. Schwartz (Eds.), *Handbook of family therapy training and supervision.* New York: Guilford Press.

Liddle, H. (1988c). Use of the family life cycle paradigm in training. In C. Falicov (Ed.), *Family transitions.* New York: Guilford Press.

Liddle, H.A. (1991). Empirical values and the culture of family therapy. *Journal of Marital and Family Therapy.*

Liddle, H.A. (in press). What's wrong with family therapy. *Journal of Marital and Family Therapy.*

Liddle, H., Breunlin, D., & Schwartz, R. (Eds.). (1988a). *Handbook of family therapy training and supervision.* New York: Guilford Press.

Liddle, H.A., Breunlin, D.C., Schwartz, R.C., & Constantine, J. (1984). Training family therapy supervisors: Issues of content, form, and context. *Journal of Marital and Family Therapy, 10,* 139–150.

Liddle, H.A., Dakof, G.A., & Diamond, G. (1991). Adolescent substance abuse: Multidimensional family therapy in action. In E. Kaufman & P. Kaufmann (Eds.), *Family therapy with drug and alcohol abuse.* Boston: Allyn & Bacon.

Liddle, H., Davidson, G., & Barrett, M. (1988a). Outcomes of live supervision: Trainee perspectives.

Liddle, H., Davidson, G., & Barrett, M. (1988b). Pragmatic implications of live supervision: Outcome research. In H.A. Liddle, D.C. Breunlin, R.C. Schwartz, & J. Constantine (1984). Training family therapy supervisors: Issues of content, form, and context. *Journal of Marital and Family Therapy, 10,* 139–150.

Liddle, H.A., & Halpin, R. (1978). Family therapy training and supervision literature: A comparative review. *Journal of Marriage and Family Counseling, 4,* 77–98.

Liddle, H.A., & Saba, G. (1982). Teaching family therapy at the introductory level: A model emphasizing a pattern which connects training and therapy. *Journal of Marital and Family Therapy, 8,* 63–72.

Liddle, H.A., & Saba, G. (1983). On context replication: The isomorphic relationship of training and therapy. *Journal of Strategic and Systemic Therapies, 2,* 3–11.

Liddle, H.A., & Saba, G.W. (1984). The isomorphic nature of training and therapy: Epistemologic foundation for a structural-strategic training paradigm. In J. Schwartzman (Ed.), *Families and other systems.* New York: Guilford Press.

Liddle, H.A., Schmidt, S., & Ettinger, D. (in press). Adolescent development research: Guidelines for clinicians. *Journal of Marital and Family Therapy.*

Liddle, H.A., & Schwartz, R.C. (1983). Live supervision/consultation: Conceptual and pragmatic guidelines for family therapy training. *Family Process, 22,* 477–490.

Liddle, H., Vance, S., & Pastushak, R. (1979). Family therapy training opportunities in psychology and counselor education. *Professional Psychology, 6,* 45–49.

List, D. (1986). Bringing it all back home: Individual and group supervision in family therapy training. *Australian and New Zealand Journal of Family Therapy, 7,* 7–12.

Lowenstein, S., Reder, P., & Clark, A. (1982). The consumer's response: Trainee's discussion of the experience of live supervision. In R. Whiffen & J. Byng-Hall (Eds.), *Family therapy supervision: Recent developments in practice.* New York: Grune & Stratton.

Luepnitz, D. (1988). *The family interpreted: Feminist theory in clinical practice.* New York: Basic Books.

Luepnitz, D. (1989). *The family interpreted.* New York: Basic Books.

Madanes, C. (1988). Family therapy training: It's entertainment. In H.A. Liddle, D.C. Breunlin, & R.C. Schwartz (Eds.), *Handbook of family therapy training and supervision.* New York: Guilford Press.

Malone, C. (1974). Observations on the role of family therapy in child psychiatry training. *Journal of the American Academy of Child Psychiatry, 13,* 437–458.

Margolin, G., Fernandez, V., Taolovic, S., & Onorato, R. (1983). Sex role considerations and behavioral marital therapy: Equal does not mean identical. *Journal of Marital and Family Therapy, 9,* 131–145.

Mazza, J. (1988). Training strategic therapists: The use of indirect techniques. In H.A. Liddle, D.C. Breunlin, & R.C. Schwartz (Eds.), *Handbook of family therapy training and supervision.* New York: Guilford Press.

McDaniel, S., Weber, T., & McKeever, J. (1983). Multiple theoretical approaches to supervision: Choices in family therapy training. *Family Process, 22,* 491–500.

McGoldrick, M. (1982). Through the looking glass. In R. Whiffen & J. Byng-Hall (Eds.) *Family therapy supervision: Recent developments in practice.* New York: Grune & Stratton.

McGoldrick, M., Pearce, J., & Giordano, J. (Eds.). (1982). *Ethnicity and family therapy.* New York: Guilford.

McGoldrick, M., & Walsh, F. (1989). *Women in Families.* New York: Norton.

McKenzie, P.N., Atkinson, B.J., Quinn, W.H., & Heath, A.W. (1986). Training and supervision in marriage and family therapy: A national survey. *American Journal of Family Therapy, 14,* 293–303.

Mendelsohn, M., & Ferber, A. (1972). Is everybody watching? In A. Ferber, M. Mendelsohn & A. Napier (Eds.), *The book of family therapy.* New York: Science House.

Mendelsohn, M., & Ferber, A. (1972). Training program. In A. Ferber, M. Mendelsohn, & A. Napier (Eds.), *The book of family therapy.* New York: Science House.

Menfi, A. (1989). The family studies section: Bronx Psychiatric Center. In Continuing Education and Training, *American Journal of Family Therapy*, 17, 169–173.

Meyerstein, K. (1977). Family therapy training for paraprofessionals in a community mental health center. *Family Process*, 16, 477–494.

Meyerstein, I. (1979). The family behavioral snapshot: A tool for teaching family assessment. *American Journal of Family Therapy*, 7(1), 48–57.

Meyerstein, I. (1981). Unlearning myths about family therapy. *International Journal of Family Psychiatry*, 3/4, 203–219.

Michalski, A. (1986). Implications of collective agreements on supervision of structural family therapy. *Journal of Strategic and Systemic Therapies*, 5, A37–A41.

Miller, N., & Crago, M. (1989). The supervision of two isolated practitioners: It's supervision, Jim, but not as you know it. *Australian and New Zealand Journal of Family Therapy*, 10, 21–25.

Minuchin, S. (1984). Stranger in a strange land: An interview with Salvador Minuchin. (By R. Simon). *The Family Therapy Networker*, 8, 20–31.

Minuchin, S., & Fishman, H.C. (1981). Structured spontaneity, Chapter 1. In *Family therapy techniques*. Cambridge, MA: Harvard University Press.

Minuchin, S., Rosman, B., & Baker, L. (1978). *Psychosomatic families: Anorexia nervosa in context*. Cambridge, MA: Harvard University Press.

Miyoshi, N., & Liebman, R. (1969). Training psychiatric residents in family therapy. *Family Process*, 8, 97–105.

Mohammed, Z., & Piercy, F. (1983). The effects of two methods of training and sequencing on structuring and relationship skills of family therapists. *American Journal of Family Therapy*, 11, 64–71.

Montalvo, B. (1973). Aspects of live supervision. *Family Process*, 12, 343–359.

Montalvo, B. (1986, January-February). Lessons from the past: What have we learned about serving poor families. *The Family Therapy Networker*, 37–44.

Montalvo, B., & Gutierrez, M. (1988). The emphasis on cultural identity: A developmental-ecological constraint. In C.J. Falicov (Ed.), *Family transitions: Continuity and change over the life cycle*. New York: Guilford Press.

Moran, J. (1989). *Family therapy training and supervision*. Unpublished doctoral dissertation, Loyola University, Chicago.

Morrow-Bradley, C., & Elliot, R. (1986). Utilization of psychotherapy research by practicing psychotherapists. *American Psychologist*, 41, 188–197.

Napier, A.Y., & Whitaker, C. (1973). Problems of the beginning family therapist. In D. Bloch (Ed.), *Techniques of family psychotherapy: A primer* (pp. 109–122). New York: Grune & Stratton.

Napier, A.Y., & Whitaker, C. (1978). *The family crucible*. New York: Harper & Row.

Neill, J. & Kniskern, D. (1982). *From psyche to system*. New York: Brunner/Mazel.

Nelson, T.S., & Figley, C.R. (1990). Basic family therapy skills, III: Brief and strategic schools of family therapy. *Journal of Family Psychology*, 4(1), 49–62.

Nichols, M.P. (1984). *Family therapy: Concepts and methods*. New York: Gardner Press.

Nichols, W.C. (1979). Education of marriage and family therapists: Some trends and implications. *Journal of Marital and Family Therapy*, 5, 19–28.

Nichols, W. (1988). Family therapy education/training: An integrative psychodynamic and systems approach. In H.A. Liddle, D.C. Breunlin, & R.C. Schwartz (Eds.), *Handbook of family therapy training and supervision*. New York: Guilford Press.

Nichols, W.C. (1975). *Training and supervision*. Upland, CA.: American Association for Marriage and Family Therapy. (Audiotape #123).

Norcross, J.C. (Ed.). (1986). *Handbook of eclectic psychotherapy*. New York: Brunner/Mazel.

Norcross, J.C. (Ed.). (1987). *Casebook of eclectic psychotherapy*. New York: Brunner/Mazel.

O'Hare, C., Heinrich, A., Kirschnor, N., Oberstone, A., & Ritz, M. (1975). Group training in family therapy: The student's perspective. *Journal of Marriage and Family Counseling*, 1, 157–162.

Okun, B.F. (1983). Gender issues of family systems therapists. In B. Okun & S.T. Gladdings (Eds.), *Issues in training marriage and family therapists*. Ann Arbor, MI: ERIC/CAPS.

Olson, D. (1988). Family types, family stress, and family satisfaction: A family developmental perspective. In C.J. Falicov (Ed.), *Family transitions: Continuity and change over the life cycle*. New York: Guilford Press.

Olson, U., & Pegg, P. (1979). Direct open supervision: A team approach. *Family Process*, 18, 463–470.

Orlinsky, D., & Howard, K. (1987). A generic model of psychotherapy. *Journal of Integrative and Eclectic Psychotherapy*, 6(1), 6–27.

O'Sullivan, M.J., & Gilbert, R.K. (1989). Master's degree programs in marital and family therapy: An evaluation of admission and program requirements. *Journal of Marital and Family Therapy*, 15(4), 337–347.

Papero, D. (1988). Training in Bowen theory. In H.A. Liddle, D.C. Breunlin, & R.C. Schwartz (Eds.), *Handbook of family therapy training and supervision*. New York: Guilford Press.

Papp, P. (1977). The family who had all the answers. In P. Papp (Ed.), *Family therapy: Full length case studies*, (pp. 143–165). New York: Gardner Press.

Papp, P. (1980). The Greek chorus and other techniques of family therapy. *Family Process*, 19(1), 45–57.

Papp, P. (1984). Therapeutic creativity. *Family Therapy Networker*, 8.

Patterson, G. (1985). Beyond technology: The next stage in developing an empirical base for parent training. In L. L'Abate (Ed.), *Handbook of family psychology*, vol. 2. Homewood IL: Dorsey.

Patterson, R. (1987). Becoming a strategic therapist. *Journal of Family Psychology*, 1, 241–255.

Pearson, D. (1987). The strategic family therapy ritual as a framework for supervision. *Journal of Strategic and Systemic Therapies*, 6.

Pegg, P., & Manocchio, A. (1982). In the act. In R. Whiffen & J. Byng-Hall (Eds.), *Family therapy and supervision: Recent developments in practice*. New York: Grune & Stratton.

Perlmutter, M., Loeb, D., Gumpert, G., O'Hara, F., & Higbie, I. (1967). Family diagnosis and therapy using videotape playback. *American Journal of Orthopsychiatry*, 37, 900–905.

Piercy, F., Laird, R., & Mohammed, Z. (1983). A family therapist rating scale. *Journal of Marital and Family Therapy*, 18, 451–462.

Piercy, F., & Sprenkle, D. (1984). The process of family therapy education. *Journal of Marital and Family Therapy*, 10, 399–408.

Piercy, F., & Sprenkel, D. (1985a). Family therapy theory development: An integrated approach. In F.P. Piercy (Ed.), *Family therapy education and supervision*. New York: Haworth.

Piercy, F., & Sprenkle, D. (1986). Family therapy theory building: An integrative training approach. *Journal of Psychotherapy and the Family*, 1, 5–14.

Piercy, F., Sprenkle, D., & Constantine, J. (1986). Family members' perceptions of live observation/supervision: An exploratory study. *Contemporary Family Therapy*, 8, 171–187.

Piercy, F.P., & Frankel, B.R. (1989). The evolution of an integrative family therapy for substance-abusing adolescents. *Journal of Family Psychology*, 3, 5–25.

Pilalis, J. (1984). The formulation of family therapy training: Issues and implications. *Journal of Family Therapy*, 6, 35–46.

Pinsof, W. (1979). The family therapist behavior scale (FTBS): Developments and evaluation of a coding system. *Family Process, 18*, 451–462.

Pinsof, W.M. (1980). *The Family Therapy Coding System (FTCS)*. Chicago: The Family Institute of Chicago.

Pinsof, W. (1981). Family therapy process research. In A. Gurman & D. Kniskern (Eds.), *Handbook of family therapy*. New York: Brunner/Mazel.

Pinsof, W. (1988). Strategies for the study of family therapy research. In L.C. Wynne (Ed.), *The state of the art in family therapy research: Controversies and recommendations*. New York: Family Process Press.

Pirrotta, S., & Cecchin, G. (1988). The Milan training program. In H.A. Liddle, D.C. Breunlin, & R.C. Schwartz (Eds.), *Handbook of family therapy training and supervision*. New York: Guilford Press.

Protinsky, H., & Preli, R. (1987). Intervention in strategic supervision. *Journal of Strategic and Systemic Therapies, 6*, 18–23.

Pulleyblank, E., & Shapiro, R. (1986). Evaluation of family therapy trainees: Acquisition of cognitive and therapeutic behavior skills. *Family Process, 25*(4), 591–598.

Quinn, W.H., Atkinson, B.J., & Hood, J. (1985). The stuck-case clinic as a group supervision model. *Journal of Marital and Family Therapy, 11*, 67–74.

Quinn, W., Newfield, N., & Protinsky, H. (1985). Rites of passage in families with adolescents. *Family Process, 2*, 68–80.

Raasoch, J., & Lacquer, H. (1979). Learning multiple family therapy through simulated workshops. *Family Process, 18*(1), 95–98.

Rabkin, R. (1986). A tower of Babble: The sociology of body and mind. *Family Process, 25*, 153–163.

Rabi, J., Lehr, M., & Hayner, M. (1984). Study group II: The peer consultation team: An alternative. *Journal of Strategic and Systemic Therapies, 3*, 66–71.

Rait, D. (1988). A family therapy practice survey. *The Family Therapy Networker*.

Ransom, D. (1988). Family therapists teaching in family practice settings: Issues and experiences. In H.A. Liddle, D.C. Breunlin, & R.C. Schwartz (Eds.), *Handbook of family therapy training and supervision*. New York: Guilford Press.

Ratliff, D. (1990). *Managing consensus and dissensus in family therapy supervision*. Unpublished doctoral dissertation proposal, Texas Tech University, Lubbock, Texas.

Reamy-Stephenson, M. (1983). The assumption of non-objective reality: A missing link in the training of strategic family therapists. *Journal of Strategic and Systemic Therapies, 2*, 51–67.

Reid, E., McDaniel, S., Donaldson, C., & Tollers, M. (1987). Taking it personally: Issues of personal authority and competence for the female in family therapy training. *Journal of Marital and Family Therapy, 13*, 157–166.

Reiss D. (1988). Theoretical versus tactical inferences: Or, how to do family psychotherapy research without dying of boredom. In L.C. Wynne (Ed.), *The state of the art in family therapy research*. New York: Family Process Press.

Rickerts, V., & Turner, J. (1978). Through the looking glass: Supervision in family therapy. *Social Casework, 59*(3), 131–137.

Roberts, J. (1981). The development of a team approach in live supervision. *The Journal of Strategic and Systemic Therapies, 1*, 24–35.

Roberts, J., Matthews, W.J., Bodin, N., Cohen, D., Lewandowski, L., Novo, J., Pumilia, J., & Willis, C. (1987). Training with O (Observing) and T (Treatment) teams in live supervision: Reflections in the looking glass. Paper presented at the American Orthopsychiatric Association 64th Annual Meeting, March, 1987.

Robertson, M.H. (1986). Training eclectic psychotherapists. In J.C. Norcross (Ed.), *Handbook of eclectic psychotherapy*. New York: Brunner/Mazel.

Robiner, W.N. & Schofield, W. (1990). References on supervision in clinical and counseling psychology. *Professional Psychology: Research and Practice, 21*, 297–312.

Rounsaville, B., O'Malley, S., Foley, S., & Weissman, M. (1988). Role of manual-guided training in the conduct and efficacy of interpersonal psychotherapy for depression. *Journal of Consulting and Clinical Psychology, 56*, 681–688.

Russell, A. (1976). Contemporary concerns in family therapy. *Journal of Marriage and Family Counseling, 2*, 243–250.

Saba, G., & Liddle, H.A. (1983). On context replication: The isomorphic relationship of training and therapy. *Journal of Strategic and Systemic Therapies, 2*, 3–11.

Saba, G., and Liddle, H.A. (1986). Perceptions of professional needs, practice patterns and critical issues facing family therapy trainers and supervisors. *American Journal of Family Therapy, 14*, 109–122.

Sander, F., & Beels, C. (1970). A didactic course for family therapy trainees. *Family Process*, 411–424.

Scheflen, A.E. (1978). Susan smiled: On explanation in family therapy. *Family Process, 17*, 59–68.

Schon, D. (1984). *The reflective practitioner*. San Francisco: Jossey-Bass.

Schon, D. (1987). *Educating the reflective practitioner*. San Francisco: Jossey-Bass.

Schumm, W.R., Bugaighis, M.R., & Jurich, A.P. (1985). Using repeated measure designs in program evaluation of family therapy. *Journal of Marriage and Family Therapy, 11*, 87–95.

Schwartz, R. (1981). The pre-session worksheet as an adjunct to training. *American Journal of Family Therapy, 9*(3), 89–90.

Schwartz, R. (1987). The trainer-trainee relationship in family therapy training. In H.A. Liddle, D.C. Breunlin, & R.C. Schwartz (Eds.), *Handbook of family therapy training and supervision*. New York: Guilford Press.

Schwartz, R., Liddle, H., & Breunlin, D. (1988). Muddles of live supervision. In H.A. Liddle, D.C. Breunlin, & R.C. Schwartz (Eds.), *Handbook of family therapy training and supervision*. New York: Guilford Press.

Sechrest, M., & Cohen, L. (1983). Influence of psychotherapy research on clinical practice: An experimental survey. *Journal of Consulting and Clinical Psychology, 51*, 718–720.

Sexton, E. (1989). *A comparative examination of four models of family therapy supervision*. Unpublished doctoral dissertation, Temple University, Philadelphia.

Shapiro, R. (1975a). Problems in teaching family therapy. *Professional Psychology, 6*, 41–44.

Shapiro, R. (1975b). Some implications of training psychiatric nurses in family therapy. *Journal of Marriage and Family Counseling, 1*(4), 323–330.

Sharon, D. (1986). The ABCX model implications for supervision. *The Clinical Supervisor, 4*, 69–94.

Siegel, L., & Dulfano, C. (1973). Family therapy: An overview. In *Career Directions* (Vol. II). East Hanover, NJ: Sandoz Pharmaceuticals.

Simon, R. (1982, September-October). Behind the one-way mirror: An interview with Jay Haley, Part I. *The Family Therapy Networker, 6*(5), 19–25, 28–29, 58–59.

Simon, R., & Brewster, F. (1983, March-April). What is training? *The Family Therapy Networker, 7*(2), 24–29, 66.

Singer, M.T. & Wynne, L.C. (1965). Thought disorder and family relations of schizophrenics, IV: Results and implications. *Archives of General Psychiatry, 12*, 201–212.

Sluzki, C. (1974a). On training to think interactionally. *Social Science and Medicine, 8*, 483–485.

Sluzki, C. (1974b). Treatment, training, and research in family therapy. Paper presented at the Nathan W. Ackerman Memorial Conference, Carácas, Venezuela.

Sluzki, C. (1979). Migration and family conflict. *Family Process, 18*, 379–390.

Sluzki, C.E. (1983). Process structure and world views: Toward an integrated view of systemic models in family therapy. *Family Process, 22*, 469–476.

Smith, D., & Kingston, P. (1980). Live supervision without a one-way screen. *Journal of Family Therapy*, 12, 187–190.

Smith, V., & Nichols, W. (1979). Accreditation in marriage and family therapy. *Journal of Marital and Family Therapy*, 5, 95–100.

Sonne, J., & Lincoln, G. (1964). Heterosexual co-therapy team experiences during family therapy. *Family Process*, 4(2), 177–197.

Sporakowski, M., & Staniszewski, W. (1980). The regulation of marriage and family therapy: An update. *Journal of Marital and Family Therapy*, 6, 335–348.

Sprenkle, D. (1988). Training and supervision in degree granting programs in family therapy. In H.A. Liddle, D.C. Breunlin, & R.C. Schwartz (Eds.), *Handbook of family therapy training and supervision*. New York: Guilford Press.

Stanton, M. (1975a). Family therapy training: Academic and internship opportunities for psychologists. *Family Process*, 14, 433–439.

Stanton, M. (1975b). Psychology and family therapy. *Professional Psychology*, 6, 45–49.

Stanton, M.D. (1981). Strategic approaches to family therapy. In A. Gurman & D. Kniskern (Eds.), *Handbook of family therapy*. New York: Brunner/Mazel.

Stanton, M. (1988). The lobster quadrille: Issues and dilemmas for family therapy research. In L.C. Wynne (Ed.), *The state of the art in family therapy research: Controversies and recommendations* (pp. 5–32). New York: Family Process Press.

Stanton, M.D., Todd, T.C., & Associates. (1982). *The family therapy of drug abuse and addiction*. New York: Guilford Press.

Stier, S., & Goldenberg, I. (1975). Training issues in family therapy. *Journal of Marriage and Family Counseling*, 1, 63–68.

Steirlin, H., Wirsching, M., & Weber, G. (1982). How to translate dynamic perspectives into an illustrative and experimental learning process: Role play, genogram and live supervision. In R. Whitten & J. Byng-Hall (Eds.), *Family therapy supervision: Recent developments in practice*. New York: Grune & Stratton.

Storm, C., & Heath, A. (1982, July-August). Strategic supervision: The danger lies in the discovery. *The Family Therapy Networker*, 6(7).

Storm, C.L., & Heath, A.W. (1985). Models of supervision: Using therapy theory as a guide. *The Clinical Supervisor*, 3, 87–96.

Stratton, P. (1988). Spirals and circles: Potential contributions of developments in physiology to family therapy. *Journal of Family Therapy*, 10, 207–231.

Street, E. (1988). Family therapy training research: Systems model and review. *Journal of Family Therapy*, 10, 383–402.

Street, E., & Foot, H. (1984). Training family therapists in observational skills. *Journal of Family Therapy*, 6, 335–345.

Street, E., & Foot, H. (1989). The reliability of video viewing of family therapy interviews. *Journal of Family Therapy*, 11, 297–306.

Street, E., & Treacher, A. (1980). Microtraining and family therapy skills: Towards a possible synthesis. *Journal of Family Therapy*, 2, 243–257.

Strinhelber, J., et al. (1984). An investigation of some relationships between psychotherapy supervision and patient change. *Journal of Clinical Psychology*, 40, 1346–1353.

Sugarman, S. (1987a). Teaching symbolic-experiential family therapy: The personhood of the teacher. *Contemporary Family Therapy: An International Journal*, 9, 138–145.

Szapocznik, J., Rio, A., Murray, E., Cohen, R., Scopetta, M., Rivas-Vazquez, A., Hervis, O., & Kurtines, W. (1989). Structural family versus psychodynamic child therapy for problematic hispanic boys. *Journal of Consulting and Clinical Psychology*, 57, 571–578.

Talmadge, J. (1975). Psychiatric residents, medical students and families teaching family therapy to the uninitiated. *Family Therapy*, 2, 11–16.

Tennen, H. (1988). Supervision of integrative psychotherapy: A critique. *Journal of Intergrative and Eclectic Psychotherapy*, 7, 167–175.

Todd, T., & Greenberg, A. (1987). No question has a single answer: Integrating discrepant models in family therapy training. *Contemporary Family Therapy*, 9, 116–137.

Tomm, K., & Leahey, M. (1980). Training in family assessment: A comparison of three teaching methods. *Journal of Marital and Family Therapy*, 6(4), 453–458.18.

Tomm, K., & Wright, L. (1979). Training in family therapy: Perceptual, conceptual and executive skills. *Family Process*, 18, 227–250.

Tucker, B., Hart, G., & Liddle, H. (1976). Supervision in family therapy: A development perspective. *Journal of Marriage and Family Counseling*, 2, 269–276.

Tucker, B., & Liddle, H. (1978). Intra-and interpersonal process in the group supervision of beginning family therapists. *Family Therapy*, 5(1), 13–28.

Tucker, S., & Pinsof, W. (1984). The empirical evaluation of family therapy training. *Family Process*, 23, 437–456.

Walrond-Skinner, S. (Ed.) (1979). *Family and marital psychotherapy: A critical approach*. London: Routledge & Kegan Paul.

Walsh, F.W. (1982). *Normal family processes*. New York: Guilford.

Walsh, F.W. (1987). The clinical utility of normal family research. *Psychotherapy*, 24, 496–503.

Walters, M. (1977). On becoming a mystery. In P. Papp (Ed.), *Family therapy: Full length case studies*. New York: Gardner Press.

Warburton, J., & Alexander, J. (1985). The family therapists: What does one do. In L. L'Abate (Ed.), *The handbook of family psychology and therapy*. Homewood, IL: Dorsey.

Weakland, J. (1976). Communication theory and clinical change. In P.J. Guerin (Ed.), *Family therapy: Theory and practice*. New York: Gardner Press.

Weber, T., McKeever, J., & McDaniel, S. (1985). The beginning guide to the problem-oriented first family interview. *Family Process*, 24, 357–364.

Weingarten, K. (1979). Family awareness for nonclinicians: Participation in a simulated family as a teaching technique. *Family Process*, 18(2), 143–150.

Wendorf, D., Wendorf, R., & Bond, D. (1985). Growth behind the mirror: The family therapy consortium's group process. *Journal of Marriage and Family Therapy*, 11, 245–256.

Werry, J. (1989). Family therapy professional endeavour or successful religion? *Journal of Family Therapy*, 11, 377–382.

West, J., Hosie, T., & Zarki, J. (1985). Simulation in training family therapists: Process and outcome. *International Journal of Family Therapy*, 7(1), 50–58.

Westheafer, C. (1984). An aspect of live supervision: The pathological triangle. *Australian Journal of Family Therapy*, 5, 169–175.

Wheeler, D., Avis, J., Miller, L., & Chaney, S. (1985). Rethinking family therapy education and supervision: A feminist model. *Journal of Psychotherapy and the Family*, 1(4), 53–72.

Whiffen, R. (1982). The use of videotape in supervision. In R. Whiffen & J. Byng-Hall (Eds.), *Family therapy supervision: Recent developments in practice*. New York: Academic Press.

Whitaker, C. (1976). Comment: Live supervision in psychotherapy. *Voices*, 12, 24–25.

Whitaker, C., & Garfield, R. (1987). On teaching psychotherapy via consultation and co-therapy. *Contemporary Family Therapy*, 9, 106–115.

Whitaker, C., & Keith, D. (1981). Symbolic-experiential family therapy. In A. Gurman & D. Kniskern (Eds.), *Handbook of family therapy*. New York: Brunner/Mazel.

Whitaker, C.A., & Malone, T.P. (1953). *The roots of psychotherapy*. New York: Blakiston.

Will, D., & Wrate, R.M. (1989). Pragmatics and principles: The development of a family therapy training programme. *Journal of Family Therapy*, 11, 149–168.

Wolfe, B., & Goldfried, M. (1988). Research on psychotherapy integration: Recommendations and conclusions from an NIMH workshop. *Journal of Consulting and Clinical Psychology, 56,* 448–451.

Wood, B., & Talmon, M. (1983). Family boundaries in transition: A search for alternatives. *Family Process, 22,* 347–357.

Worthington, E. (1987). Changes in supervision as counselors and supervisors gain experience: A review. *Professional Psychology: Research and Practice, 18,* 189–208.

Wright, L. (1986). An analysis of live supervision "phone-ins" in family therapy. *Journal of Marriage and Family Therapy, 12,* 187–190.

Wright, L., & Coppersmith, E. (1983). Supervision of supervision: How to be "meta" to a metaposition. *Journal of Strategic and Systemic Therapies, 2,* 40–50.

Wright, L., & Leahey, M. (1988). Nursing and family therapy training. In H.A. Liddle, D.C. Breunlin, & R.C. Schwartz (Eds.), *Handbook of family therapy training and supervision.* New York: Guilford Press.

Wynne, L. (1984). The epigenesis of relational systems: A model for understanding family development. *Family Process, 23,* 297–318.

Wynne, L. (1988). An overview of the state of the art: What should be expected in current family therapy research. In L.C. Wynne (Ed.), *The state of the art in family therapy research: Controversies and recommendations.* New York: Family Process Press.

Young, J., Perlesz, A., Paterson, R., O'Hanlon, B., Newbold, A., Chaplin, R., & Bridge, S. (1989). The reflecting team process in training. *Australian and New Zealand Journal of Family Therapy, 10,* 69–74.

Zaken-Greenberg, F., & Neimeyer, G. (1986). The impact of structural family therapy training on conceptual and executive therapy skills. *Family Process, 25,* 599–608.

Zifferblat, S.M. (1972). Analysis and design of counselor-training systems: An operant and operation research project. *Counseling Psychologist, 3,* 12–31.

Zuk, G. (1975). *Process and practice in family therapy.* Haverford, PA: Psychiatry and Behavioral Science Books.

Name Index

Abad, V., 554
Abadie, P. D., 683
Abeles, G.,47
Abelsohn, D., 527
Ables, B. S., 116
Abrams, D. B., 88
Abramson, H. A., 389
Ackerman, N. W., 14, 20, 21, 22–23, 24, 25, 29, 30, 52, 284, 444, 639,657, 676
Adams, C., 9
Adams, H. E., 87
Adams, J., 458
Adler, A., 17, 21, 616
Ahren, F. M., 567, 568
Ahrons, C., 508, 522, 526, 527, 533
Aichorn, A., 445
Aldefer, C., 648
Alexander, F., 12
Alexander, J. F., 73, 85, 87, 88, 657, 672, 673, 681, 686
Alger, I., 663
Algie, J., 287
Allen, G., 276
Allen, J., 660
Allman, L. R., 58, 60
Allred, G., 678
Alouf, F., 438, 488
Ambert, A., 540
Andersen, T., 337
Anderson, 420
Anderson, A., 616
Anderson, C., 541
Anderson, C. M., 47, 363, 367, 368, 369, 371, 373, 375, 381, 385, 387
Anderson, E. A., 118
Anderson, H., 202, 209, 329, 335, 337–338, 339, 346, 647, 650, 652, 656
Anderson, J. Z., 538
Anderson, T., 202
Andolfi, M., 648
Andreas-Salome, L., 285
Andreozzi, L. L., 675
Annon, J., 499, 500, 504
Aponte, H. J., 419, 431, 562, 584, 610, 667, 668
Araoz, D., 240
Ard, D., 640

Argyris, C., 650
Arrendondo, R., 686
Arrington, A., 71, 74
Asarnow, R. F., 371
Ashby, W. B., 50
Ashikaga, T., 367
Atkeson, B. M., 73
Atkinson, B. J., 660
Atthowe, J., 276
Attneave, C., 31
Auerswald, E., 30, 32, 651
Authier, J., 680
Avis, J. M., 652, 656, 657, 676, 677, 678, 685
Azrin, N. H., 71

Bagarozzi, D., 674
Bailey, J. R., 633
Baker, B. L., 80, 83, 88
Baker, L., 31, 291, 420, 646
Baldwin, M., 52
Bales, R. F., 419
Balint, E., 20, 285
Balint, M., 20, 201, 285, 286
Bamrah, J., 88
Bandler, R., 239
Bandura, A., 68, 245
Bane, M. J., 508
Banerjee, S. P., 366
Baptiste, D., 539, 542
Barbach, L., 493, 502, 503, 504
Barcai, A., 421
Bardill, D., 640, 644
Bardill, D. R., 675, 687
Barker, R. L., 5
Barnes, G. G., 661
Barnett, I., 486
Barnett, L. D., 568
Barrett, M., 659, 682
Barrowclough, C., 88
Barrows, S., 330
Bart, P., 485
Barton, C., 73, 87, 673, 681, 686
Baruth, L. G., 609, 623, 624
Bateson, G., 27–29, 36, 41–43, 46, 47–48, 55–59, 172, 183, 192, 197, 198, 201, 228, 239, 241, 242, 326, 334, 338, 364, 444, 586, 650, 652
Bateson, W., 27
Baucom, D. H., 70, 98, 109, 126

Beal, E., 134, 640, 676
Beam, L., 15
Bean, W., 276
Beatman, F. L., 21, 641, 660
Beauchamp, T., 634
Beavers, W. R., 292, 642–643, 644
Beavin, J., 193, 586
Beavin, J. H., 17, 29, 32, 44, 326
Beck, S., 80
Beels, C. C., 365, 368, 639
Beer, S., 341
Bell, J., 14, 21–22, 28, 201
Bell, N., 5, 583
Bellah, R. N., 611, 612, 613, 615
Belle, D., 508
Bennett, H., 276
Bennum, I., 79
Bentovim, A., 284, 286–292, 299, 301, 304, 317
Berenson, G., 33
Berg, B., 664
Berger, 486
Berger, M., 584
Bergquist, B., 538, 647, 654, 659, 663, 675, 684, 686, 687
Berkman, A., 662
Berkman, C., 662
Berkowitz, R., 368
Berman, E., 500
Bernal, G., 215, 216, 219, 230, 553, 610, 613
Bernal, M. E., 87
Bernard, C., 43
Bernard, L. L., 8
Bernard, M., 568
Berne, E., 249
Bernstein, B. E., 607
Beroza, R., 659, 661
Bertalanffy, L. von, 42, 202
Betcher, R., 659
Betof, N., 679
Bettelheim, B., 180, 284
Beutler, L., 501
Billingsley, A., 548
Bion, W., 285
Birchler, G., 640, 659
Birchler, G. R., 86, 100, 102, 115, 116
Birley, J. L. T., 47, 367
Bishop, D., 679

Black, R., 353
Blanchard, P., 8
Blechman, E. A., 82
Bloch, D. A., 15, 30, 32
Bloomfield, S., 584
Blount, A., 335
Blumstein, 479
Boardman, W. K., 65
Bodin, A., 32, 173, 178, 616, 639, 640, 663, 665
Bogado, P., 457, 458
Bogle, 491
Bograd, M., 309, 652
Bohannon, P., 512
Bok, S., 619–620
Bokos, P. J., 584
Bond, D., 685
Booth, A., 538
Booth, P., 260
Borhem, H.,
Borstein, I., 33
Boscolo, L., 33, 54, 325, 326, 330, 331, 332, 333, 334, 336, 348, 355, 364, 459, 556, 584, 665
Boss, P., 543
Boss, P. G., 606, 608, 612, 618, 623, 625, 629, 630–633
Boszormenyi-Nagy, I., 29–30, 200, 201, 202, 203, 204–210, 213, 214, 216, 217, 222, 223, 225, 230, 231, 284, 286, 401, 444, 447, 448, 450, 468, 501, 607, 608, 614, 615, 622, 657, 668
Bowen, M., 18, 24, 25–26, 30, 60, 154, 159, 201, 202, 207, 214, 231, 286, 364, 444, 468, 500, 548, 657, 662
Bowlby, J., 20, 23, 284
Box, S., 286
Boyce, E., 554
Boyd, J. L., 72
Boyd-Franklin, N., 549, 557, 559, 562
Boyer, M. R. P., 485
Bradbury, T., 98
Brand, E., 540
Brandsma, J. M., 116
Bradt, J. O., 539
Bray, J. H., 623

Brecher, E. M., 16
Breier, A., 367
Breman, 491
Breunlin, D., 649, 653, 654, 659, 663, 675, 679, 683, 685, 686
Brewster, F., 650, 659
Broadhurst, B. P., 20
Broderick, C., 3, 240
Broderick, J. E., 71
Brodsky, M., 66
Brooks, G. W., 367
Bross, A., 651
Brown, E., 510
Brown, G., 366, 575
Brown, G. W., 47, 367, 371
Brown, J. E., 616, 617
Brown, M., 659, 660
Brown, R., 336
Browne, A., 371
Bruner, J. S., 418
Buber, M., 201, 231, 633
Buckley, W., 42
Budman, S., 181
Bugaighis, M. R., 677
Bullard, 491
Burck, C., 287, 306
Burden, S. L., 134
Burgess, A., 496
Burgess, J. M., 88
Butler, R., 486
Byles, J., 679
Byng-Hall, J., 301, 659, 660

Cade, B., 661, 662, 679
Cahill, M. F., 73
Calhoun, J. B., 136
Cambor, C. G., 20
Campbell, D., 325, 326, 328, 329, 331, 335, 336, 353, 364, 661
Campbell, R. V., 80
Capra, F., 196
Carkhuff, R. R., 85
Carnes, P., 495, 504
Carpenter, J., 675, 687
Carpenter, W., 548
Carroll, E. J., 20
Carstairs, G. M., 366
Carter, B., 505, 526, 528, 538, 539, 541–544, 615, 629, 650, 654, 661
Carter, E. A., 447, 468, 484
Carter, R., 679
Carver, G. W., 16
Castellucci, A., 335
Caust, B., 36, 656, 657
Cecchin, G., 33, 54, 56, 325, 326, 331–336, 348, 364, 459, 556, 584, 649, 653, 665, 666
Chable, B., 675
Chamberlain, P., 87
Chan, F., 575
Chaney, S., 657
Chaplain, 494
Chasin, R., 230, 309, 650
Chess, S., 71
Childress, J., 634
Chilgren, R., 491
Chilman, C., 538
Chock, P. N., 88
Christensen, A., 71, 73, 77, 103, 125
Christianson, C. E., 608
Churchill, W., 160
Churvin, P., 664, 680, 681, 685
Cimmarusti, R., 663

Cirillo, S., 330
Clark, A., 685
Clauson, J., 25
Cleghorn, J., 640, 653, 679
Clements, C., 622
Cleveland, M., 485
Clingempeel, W. G., 540
Cobb, J. A., 80
Cobb, J. P., 79
Coddou, F., 336–337
Cohen, C. I., 367
Cohen, H., 687
Cohen, J., 285, 286
Cohen, L., 654
Cohen, M., 640, 660, 685
Colapinto, J., 369, 417, 421, 432, 436, 440, 649, 653, 668, 676
Cole, J. O., 368
Cole, R. E., 567
Cole, T., 491, 492
Coleman, E., 488, 498
Coleman, M., 542, 543
Coleman, S., 584, 651
Comarr, 491
Collier, A., 609, 617, 618
Combrinck-Graham, L., 51, 584, 654, 675, 687
Condon, R., 389
Conger, R. E., 66
Connell, G. M., 670, 672
Conners, 389
Constantine, J., 652, 653, 659
Constantine, L., 640, 650, 675
Cooley, C. H., 18
Cooney, N., 88
Cooper, A. J., 502
Cooper, H., 542, 543
Cooper, L., 239
Copernicus, Nicolas, 196
Copley, B., 286
Coopersmith, E., 661, 686
Coopersmith, E. I., 651
Cornelison, A. R., 24, 48, 364
Cornwell, M., 661
Cotroneo, M., 29
Cotton, P., 659, 682
Cowgill, K. M., 526
Cox, M., 508, 529
Cox, R., 508, 529
Coyne, J., 621
Coyne, L., 366, 420
Crago, M., 687
Crane, R., 685
Crester, C. A., 568, 569, 570
Crohn, J., 567, 569
Cronen, V., 333, 334, 342, 354
Crosby, J., 511
Crow, T. J., 366
Crowe, M., 79, 88
Crutchley, E., 325, 364
Cuber, J., 11
Curran, J. P., 88
Czech, N., 240

D'Abro, A., 196
Dahl, A. S., 526, 539
d'Alembert, J. L., 196
Dammann, C., 240, 241, 647, 659, 684
Dangel, R. F., 80
Davidson, G., 549, 659, 682
Dawson, M. E., 367
Day, J., 25
Dearborn, L., 10, 15
DeAth, E., 651
DeKlyen, M., 127

DeLisi, L. E., 366
Dell, P., 194, 338, 424, 662, 685
Dell, P. F., 47, 48, 50, 656
Denton, W. H., 633
Descartes, 59, 60, 242
de Shazer, S., 57, 60
Detre, T., 365
Deutsch, M., 510
DiBlasio, P., 330
Dick, B., 457, 458
Dickenson, R. L., 10, 15–16
Dicks, 213
Dicks, H., 20, 284, 285
Dicks, H. V., 52
Diner, H., 550
Dinkmeyer, D., 21
Di Nicola, V., 330
Doane, J. A., 77, 87
Dobson, K., 127
Doehrman, M., 648
Doherty, W. J., 543, 606, 608, 620
Donaldson, C., 657
Dotti, D., 335
Dowling, E., 457, 679, 680, 685
Drane, J. F., 606, 610
Draper, R., 325, 326, 331, 336, 353, 364, 686
Dreikurs, R., 17, 21
Duberman, L., 539–540
Dubois, P., 4
Duhl, B., 29, 646, 647, 652, 654, 676, 686
Duhl, B.S., 664
Duhl, F., 31, 32, 430, 646, 647
Duhl, F. J., 664
Dulcan, M., 389
Dulfano, C., 641
Dumas, A., 195
D'Zurilla, T. J., 82

Eaustaugh, S. R., 389
Eddy, D., 407
Edgette, J. S., 275
Efros, F., 683
Ehrlich, F., 640
Einstein, A., 161, 169
Eisenstein, V., 20
Ekstein, R., 648
Elliot, R., 654
Ellis, A., 502, 503
Ellis, H., 6, 7, 15, 36, 480
Ellison, 494
Ellman, B., 629, 634, 656
Elwood, R. W., 69
Eno, M. M., 431
Ensminger, M. E., 69
Epimenides, 45
Epstein, N., 98, 640, 686
Erickson, E., 204, 240, 252
Erickson, G. D., 614
Erickson, M., 28, 54, 172–173, 184, 243, 244, 248, 257, 258, 259, 260, 274, 396, 403, 652
Erickson, M. H., 239, 240
Erikson, E. H., 284
Esterson, A., 364
Ettinger, D., 654
Euclid, 154
Evans, J. R., 368
Everett, C. A., 508, 512, 518, 519, 522, 641, 642, 643, 644, 648, 676, 683
Ezriel, H., 285

Fairbairn, R., 285

Fairbairn, W. R. D., 201, 213
Falicov, C. J., 553, 573, 574, 653, 654, 655, 656, 675, 676
Falloon, I. R. H., 65, 68, 71, 72, 74, 77, 78, 79, 80, 82, 83, 86, 87, 88, 371, 373, 384, 385
Fallows, M. A., 550, 567
Fantl, B., 548
Faraone, S. V., 88
Faustman, W., 82
Fay, L., 134
Feixas, G., 685
Felder, R., 445
Feldman, L., 656
Fellner, C., 464
Fennell, D., 659, 682, 686
Ferber, A., 30, 286, 639, 640, 653, 662, 675, 676
Ferenczi, S., 201
Ferguson, L. R., 644–645, 654, 687
Fernandez, V., 657
Ferrari, R., 335
Ferreira, A. J., 43, 44
Ferrier, M., 457
Fichter, M. M., 73, 88
Figley, C., 653, 680
Fincham, F., 98
Fine, J., 686
Fine, M., 686
Finkelhor, D., 484, 496
Fisch, R., 32, 50, 171, 173, 178, 184, 239, 240, 241, 242, 326, 396, 589, 649, 653, 654, 665, 676
Fischer, E., 367
Fischer, J., 330, 686
Fish, V., 338
Fisher, E., 510
Fisher, L., 291, 616
Fishman, H. C., 53, 420, 421, 422, 423, 424, 425, 429, 430, 432, 433, 434, 437, 439, 440, 441, 646, 648, 651, 667, 668, 684
Fithian, M. A., 480, 501, 503
Flanagan, S., 87
Fleck, S., 24, 48, 201, 364
Fleischman, M. J., 87
Fleuridas, C., 652
Flomenhaft, K., 368, 679
Flora, G. G., 389
Flores, J. L., 685
Floyd, J. F., 125
Flugel, J. C., 20
Foerster, H. von, 45, 56, 57, 172, 173, 194, 197, 336
Fogarty, T., 640
Foley, S., 686
Follette, W. C., 69, 88, 102, 121, 125
Foot, H., 651, 653, 683
Forehand, R., 73, 74, 75, 80, 82, 83, 87, 88
Forel, A., 6
Forgatch, M. S., 85, 88
Forman, B., 686
Fossum, M., 482, 501
Foster, S. L., 68, 70, 74, 76, 77, 82, 83, 85, 86, 87, 88
Foulkes, S. H., 285
Fowler, C. R., 10, 11
Framo, J., 29, 30, 33, 202, 231
Framo, J. L., 284, 286, 640, 668, 669, 687
Frank, K. A., 389

Frankel, B., 659, 682
Frankena, S., 640, 660
Frankl, V., 404
Frankl, V. E., 616
Franzen, G., 366
Fraser, J. S., 616
Fraunce, 32
Freeman, H. L., 88
Freymann, J. G., 622, 623
Friedlander, M. L., 625
Friedman, 31, 655
Friedman, E., 134, 143, 145, 146, 364, 466
Friedman, E. H., 134, 566, 569, 573, 574
Friedman, M., 201
Freud, S., 15, 17, 19, 169, 201, 242, 286, 422, 480, 500
Froiland, D., 512
Fromm, E., 18
Fromm-Reichmann, F., 18, 47, 201, 364
Frude, N., 679
Fruggeri, L., 335, 344
Fruzzetti, A. E., 127
Fry, W., 172, 242
Fuchs, 493
Fulmer, R., 654, 664
Fulweiler, C., 28, 658
Furniss, T., 301, 317
Furstenberg, F., 534, 538

Gadpaille, W., 484
Gage, B., 511
Gagnon, J., 500
Gaind, R., 367
Galileo, 196
Gallagher, M., 276
Gambino, R., 549
Ganahl, G., 644–645
Ganong, L., 542, 543
Garcia Preto, N., 546, 547, 552, 567, 571
Gardner, W., 624
Garfield, R., 662, 670, 671, 672, 686
Garrison, V., 367
Gebhard, P. H., 498
Gelcer, E., 647, 648
Gelder, M. G., 79
Gelfand, D. E., 573
Gentry, D., 648
Gershenson, J., 685
Gerson, R., 500, 529
Gilbert, R. K., 677, 680, 687
Gilligan, C., 207
Gilligan, S., 273
Gilman, S. R., 685
Gilmour, L. A., 287
Giordano, J., 35, 546, 548, 549, 614, 655
Glahn, T. J., 88
Glasgow, R. E., 73
Glen, 540
Glenwick, N., 537
Glick, I., 643–644
Glick, P. C., 388, 525, 532
Glover, E., 19
Glynn, T., 87
Godin, J., 276
Goguen, T., 648
Goldberg, 495
Goldberg, S. C., 365
Goldenberg, I., 639, 641, 660, 662
Goldfried, M., 686

Goldfried, M. R., 82
Goldner, V., 58, 217, 609, 614, 629, 634, 656, 657
Goldsmith, J., 527
Goldstein, 486
Goldstein, M. J., 87, 368, 371, 384, 385
Goldstein, S., 11
Goodman, E. S., 14
Goodrich, T., 656, 657
Goodrich, T. J., 629, 634
Goodwin, B. C., 146
Goodyear, R. K., 683
Goolishian, H., 202, 209, 335, 337–338, 339, 346, 662, 685
Gordon, D., 259, 567
Gordon, J. S., 70
Gorman, P., 659, 682, 683
Gossett, J. T., 292
Gottman, J., 99, 102, 103, 678
Gottman, J. M., 73, 99, 102, 103, 123, 125
Granvold, D., 515
Graves, D. J., 88
Greeley, A., 548
Green, B. L., 20
Green, D., 685
Green, R., 651, 684
Green, R. G., 686
Green, R. J., 687
Green, S., 37
Green, S. L., 8, 622, 633
Greenberg, D., 366
Greenberg, L., 670, 671, 686
Greenberg, L. S., 124, 126
Greene, B., 515
Greenley, J. R., 76
Grief, G., 535
Griest, D. L., 69, 71, 75, 76, 80, 82, 85, 87, 88
Griffin, W., 685
Grinder, J., 239
Gross, S., 640
Grosser, G. H., 607
Grossman, M., 485
Groves, Ernest, 7, 8, 9, 10, 11
Groves, Gladys, 7, 8, 10, 11
Grunebaum, H., 650
Grunebaum, J., 200, 203, 205, 206, 207, 209, 217, 230, 231, 232, 401, 608, 614, 615
Guerin, P., 640, 676
Guerin, P. J., 54, 134
Guerin, P. J., Jr., 6, 14, 21, 23, 25, 26, 27, 28, 30
Guerney, B., 31, 100, 116, 126, 503, 548
Guerney, B. G., 418
Guitierrez, M., 655
Guntrip, H., 201, 213
Gurman, A., 502, 503, 510, 651, 654, 657, 676, 677, 678, 679, 680, 682, 684, 685, 686
Gurman, A. S., 13, 14, 36, 44, 58, 118, 126, 181, 192, 607, 608, 625, 626, 627, 628
Guttman, H. A., 47, 48, 51, 58, 59, 60, 382
Gyarfasm, K., 201

Haas, G. L., 388
Haas, L., 649, 653, 676
Hadley, T., 491
Hafner, R., J., 79, 88
Hahlweg, K., 70, 78, 123, 126
Haley, J., 27–29, 30, 31, 32, 42,

43, 44, 46, 47, 50, 51, 54, 59, 60, 100, 172, 173, 182, 228, 239, 240, 241, 242, 246, 257, 258, 266, 286, 326, 364, 396, 397, 402, 403, 420, 449, 455, 548, 607, 614, 616, 617, 618, 639, 640, 642, 645, 646, 648, 649, 651, 652, 654, 658, 659, 661–662, 664, 666, 667, 684, 687
Halgin, R. P., 674
Halpern, R., 639, 640, 641–642, 648, 660, 676, 684
Halstead, K., 629, 634
Hammer, M., 367
Hand, I., 88
Handly, P., 683
Hanna, S., 539
Hannum, J. W., 457, 462
Hansen, J., 37
Hansen, J. C., 622, 637
Harbin, H. T., 584
Harding, C. M., 367, 390
Hardy, K., 687
Hare, R., 640, 660
Hare-Mustin, R., 505, 640, 656, 657, 659
Hare-Mustin, R. T., 35, 58, 59, 447, 622, 623, 629
Harkaway, J., 584
Harper, R., 503
Harrell, F., 584
Harris, S. L., 71, 79, 80, 82, 83, 88
Hart, G., 639, 664
Hartman, W. E., 480, 501, 503
Harvey, J. 659, 682
Haskell, M., 568
Hatcher, C., 663, 664
Hatcher, M. E., 389
Hawkins, N., 66
Hayner, M., 660
Hays, H., 562
Hays, J. R., 623
Heath, A., 647, 648, 661, 667
Heatherington, L., 663
Heer, D. M., 566, 572
Hegel, 59
Heiman, J., 486, 492, 493, 494, 500, 503
Heinrich, A., 662
Held, B., 56
Heller, S. S., 389
Henderson, C. R., 8
Henggeler, S., 686
Henry, P. W., 658, 685
Heppner, P. P., 683
Herbert, M., 82, 83
Hernandez, K. K., 679, 682
Herr, J., 396
Hershman, S., 239
Herz, F., 675, 676, 686
Herz, F. A., 533, 537
Herz, F. M., 549, 570, 572
Herzog, E., 549
Hess, A. K., 686
Hetherington, E., 508
Hetherington, E. M., 526, 529, 531, 532, 533, 534, 536, 537, 538, 540, 541, 625, 626
Hewlett, S., 530
Higbie, I., 663
Hightower, N. A., 458
Higley, L. W., 584
Hill, R., 484
Hill, R. D., 685

Hines, P. M., 546, 549, 552, 557, 559, 560, 562, 607, 622
Hippocrates, 489
Hirsch, S., 25
Hirsch, S. R., 367
Hirschfeld, M., 6–7, 9, 15, 36
Hite, S., 17
Hitler, 7, 18
Hochman, G., 134
Hoddas, G., 647, 663, 668
Hoenig, J., 7
Hof, L., 500
Hoffman, C., 684
Hoffman, H. J., 457
Hoffman, J. A., 126
Hoffman, L., 23, 48, 49, 50, 51, 194, 202, 326, 331–332, 337, 339, 350, 453, 650, 658, 665, 670
Hoffman, L. W., 457
Hogan, D. R., 502, 503
Hogan, P., 663
Hogan, R., 686
Hogarty, G. E., 363, 365, 367, 371, 384, 385
Hoier, T. S., 70
Holland, L., 276
Hollander, H., 276
Holloway, E. L., 683
Holmstrom, L., 496
Holtzworth-Munroe, A., 14, 96, 104, 111, 127, 332, 373, 504
Hood, J., 660
Hooley, J. M., 73, 371
Hoon, E. F., 501
Hoon, P. W., 501
Hops, H., 14, 66, 96, 99, 105
Horn, D., 679
Horney, K., 18
Hosie, T., 680
Houts, A. C., 606
Hovestadt, A., 659, 682, 686
Howard, K., 653
Howlin, P. A., 82, 83
Hozman, T., 512
Hsu, F. L. K., 564
Huber, C. H., 609, 623, 624
Huber, J., 687
Hudson, B. L., 82, 88
Huffington, C., 288, 326, 336
Hughes, J. B., 70
Hughes, S. F., 654
Hull, C., 240
Hume, 59
Humphrey, F., 498, 499
Humphrey, F. G., 10, 15, 16
Hurd, G. G., 367
Husted, 502, 503
Hyde, J. H., 490

Ievoli, R., 540
Ihinger-Tallman, M., 533, 538
Imber-Black, E., 48, 378, 533, 539, 583, 584, 593, 596
Imber Coppersmith, E., 336, 562, 583, 584, 587
Ingvar, D. H., 366
Irving, H., 518
Isaacs, M. D., 527, 531, 534, 535
Israelstam, K., 664
Ivey, A. E., 680
Iwaniec, D., 82, 83

Ja, D. Y., 570
Jackson, D. D., 14, 17, 18, 20, 23, 24, 25, 27–29, 32, 43, 44,

46, 47, 52, 67, 100, 172, 173,
    193, 201, 228, 242, 285, 286,
    326, 339, 364, 586, 613
Jacobs, B., 302
Jacobson, N. S., 14, 68, 69, 82,
    88, 96, 99, 100, 102, 103, 104,
    105, 109, 111, 114, 116, 118,
    119, 121, 125, 126, 127, 332,
    373, 504, 610, 657, 686
Jalali, B., 549
James, K., 657
Jenkins, H., 653
Jennings, G., 520
Jewson, R., 14
Joanning, H., 686
Johnson, C. L., 389
Johnson, D., 367
Johnson, R. C., 567
Johnson, S. M., 73, 124, 126
Johnson, Virginia, 4, 15, 16. See
    also Masters and Johnson
Johnson, W. F., 625
Johnston, D. W., 79
Johnston, J., 536
Jones, J. E., 616
Jones, R., 71
Jones, R. R., 66
Joy, V. D., 367
Jung, C., 17–18
Jurasky, J., 662
Jurich, A. P., 625, 626, 627, 677
Justice, R., 504

Kadden, R., 88
Kahn, L., 486
Kalter, N., 508
Kanfer, F. H., 68
Kant, I., 59, 242
Kantner, J. F., 485
Kantor, D., 31, 32, 650, 651,
    652, 653, 654, 675
Kaplan, A. G., 623
Kaplan, H., 480, 488, 492, 493,
    494, 500, 501, 503, 504
Kaplan, L., 584
Kaplan, R., 658
Karoly, P., 87
Karpel, M., 218, 654
Karpel, M. A., 624
Karrer, B., 663
Karrer, B. M., 435
Kasl, C., 495
Kaslow, F., 640, 641, 642, 643,
    644, 675, 685, 686
Kaslow, F. W., 6, 21, 23, 30, 31,
    508, 510, 607, 608
Kaslow, N. J., 625, 626, 627, 628
Katz, L., 543
Katz, S. E., 367
Kautsky, K., 7
Kaye, K., 654
Kautto, J. G., 134
Keeney, B., 242, 290, 331, 332,
    333, 334, 513, 650, 667
Keeney, B. P., 57, 58, 60
Keim, I., 407
Keim, J., 407
Keith, D., 446, 447, 448, 449,
    450–455, 458, 459, 461, 462,
    466, 467, 468, 470, 471, 651,
    662, 670, 671, 672
Keith, D. V., 26, 445, 628
Kellam, S. G., 69
Keller, J., 687
Kelley, H. H., 67, 99, 612
Kelly, J. B., 508, 509, 526

Kempster, S. W., 639, 641, 659
Kempton, W., 491
Kendler, K. S., 366
Kent, 484
Kent, R., 77
Kent, R. M., 76
Kent, R. N., 73
Kernberg, O., 285
Kerr, Michael, 134, 138–139,
    144, 150, 154, 165, 167
Kerr, M. E., 466, 668, 669
Kersey, F., 678
Kessler, D., 643–644
Kessler, S., 512
Kiev, A., 548
King, C., 30
King, H. E., 87, 88
Kingston, P., 659, 661
Kinsey, A. C., 7, 16, 496, 498
Kinston, W., 284–292, 297, 299,
    301, 304, 306, 315, 317
Kinzie, J. D., 575
Kirby-Turner, N., 685
Kirchler, E., 685
Kirsch, I., 276
Kirschnor, N., 662
Klein, M., 201, 284, 445, 657
Klein, N. C., 87, 88
Kleinman, A. M., 549
Klinnert, M. D., 87
Kluckholn, 609
Knaub, P., 539
Kneifel, 584
Knight, 491
Kniskern, D. P., 36, 126, 444,
    445, 447, 449, 451, 456, 465,
    468, 502, 503, 510, 607, 627,
    670, 676, 677, 678, 679, 682,
    684, 685
Knox, D., 14
Knudson, R. M., 118
Kockott, 502, 503
Koerpel, B. J., 641, 643, 644,
    648, 683
Koestler, A., 421, 423
Kohlenberg, 492
Kohut, H., 285
Kolevzon, M. S., 684, 686
Kolodny, R., 480, 486, 488, 489,
    493, 494, 495
Kopp, M. E., 7, 10
Kornfeld, D. S., 389
Koual, S. M., 389
Kraepelin, 367
Kraft, S. A., 104
Krafft-Ebing, 480
Kramer, C., 33
Kramer, D., 445, 451
Kramer, M., 363
Kramer, T., 663
Krasner, B., 29, 203, 206, 216
Krasner, B. R., 447, 448, 450
Krasner, L., 606, 608, 614
Kreisman, D. E., 367
Kressel, K., 510, 518
Krokoff, L., 103, 125
Krug, W. W., 82
Kubie, L. S., 19, 172
Kuipers, L., 368
Kuriansky, J. B., 389
Kvanli, J. H., 520

L'Abate, L., 68, 504, 607, 619
LaBurt, H. A., 365
Lacoursiere, R. B., 366
Lacquer, H., 664

Lader, M. H., 368
LaForge, R., 252
Laforgue, 19
Laidlaw, R., 10
Laidlaw, R. W., 20
Laing, R., 397
Laing, R. D., 243, 249, 364, 422
Laird, R., 678
Lama, R., 367
Lampiris, B. S., 573
Lampiris, L., 573, 574
Landau-Stanton, J., 661
Langdell, S., 276
Langsley, D., 368
Lankton, C., 261
Lankton, C. H., 239, 240, 241,
    243, 252, 258, 259, 261, 263,
    271, 483
Lankton, S. R., 239, 240, 241,
    243, 252, 258, 259, 261, 263,
    271, 483
LaPierre, K., 687
Laplace, 197
Lappin, J., 435, 655, 656
Laqueur, H. P., 365
LaRossa, R., 628
Lask, B., 687
Latham, T., 457, 662
Laver, M., 489
Lazarus, A. A., 480, 504
Leahey, M., 675, 681, 682, 686,
    687
Leary, T., 252
Lebow, J., 650, 675, 684, 686
Lederer, W. J., 100, 586
Lee, E., 546, 552, 565, 566, 575
Lee, R., 515
Lee, J., 47
Leff, J. P., 71, 73, 74, 76, 366,
    367, 368, 370, 384, 385
Lehr, M., 660
Lehr, W., 32
Leiblum, S., 486
Lentine, G., 407
Leon, J. J., 568, 569, 570
Leopold, J. V., 20
Lessler, K., 457, 458
Levenson, R. W., 103, 125
Leveton, 240
Levin, R., 489
Levin, S., 640, 653, 679
Leviticus, 489
Lewin, K., 27
Lewis, H., 365
Lewis, J. M., 292, 298
Lewis, M., 486
Lewis, R., 686
Lewis, W., 658, 659, 683
Liberman, R. P., 68, 70, 80, 82
Libow, J., 35, 656
Liddle, H. A., 638, 639, 640,
    641, 642, 644, 647, 648, 649,
    650, 651, 653, 654, 657, 658,
    659, 660, 662, 665, 674, 675,
    676, 682, 684, 685, 686
Lidz, R. W., 24
Lidz, T., 24, 25, 36, 48, 52, 201,
    284, 364
Liebman, R., 420, 640
Lillie, F. J., 80
Lin, K. M., 575
Lin, S. L., 525
Lincoln, 31
Lincoln, G., 662
Lincoln-Grossman, G., 29
Lindblad-Goldberg, M., 527, 533

Lindemann, Erich, 24, 31
Lindley, R., 609, 620, 621
Lipset, S., 27
Lipton, F. R., 367
Liss-Levenson, N., 623
List, D., 664
Loader, P., 287, 288, 289, 292
Locke, 59
Loeb, D., 663
LoPiccolo, J., 17, 480, 486, 492,
    493, 494, 500, 501, 502, 503,
    504
LoPiccolo, L., 17, 503
Lord, G., 672
Loreido, C., 240
Lovett, 490
Lovibond, S. H., 65
Lovitt, 491
Lowenstein, S., 685
Luepnitz, D. A., 419, 505, 533,
    622, 623, 629, 656, 657
Lustig, N., 20
Lutzker, J. R., J. R., 80
Lynch, B., 648

Mace, D. R., 11, 13, 14
Mace, Vera, 11, 13, 14
MacFarlane, W., 192
Machota, D., 368
MacIntyre, A., 611, 612, 613,
    615, 633, 634
Mackey, F., 489
MacKinnon, L., 54, 338, 353,
    584
MacKinnon, L. K., 58
Macy, J., 171
Madanes, C., 51, 54, 239, 286,
    364, 396, 399, 400, 402, 403,
    404, 405, 406, 407, 409, 411,
    415, 455, 667, 681, 687
Maddock, 484
Madsen, R., 611
Magagna, I., 286
Magner, 491
Mahlstedt, 485
Main, T., 285
Malan, 286
Malarewicz, J., 240
Malcolm, J., 418, 419
Malone, C., 640
Malone, C. A., 419
Malone, T., 444, 445
Malone, T. P., 670
Malzberg, B., 550
Manocchio, A., 661
Manson, S., 575
Marcus, R., 389
Marecek, J., 622, 623
Margolin, G., 14, 68, 82, 96, 99,
    100, 102, 103, 105, 114, 116,
    119, 125, 607, 622, 623, 624,
    626, 629, 657, 687
Markman, H., 70, 99
Markman, H. J., 99, 100, 104,
    125, 126, 678
Marks, I. M., 79
Markson, E., 652
Marlett, 584
Marmor, J., 58
Martin, B., 14, 102
Martin, C. E., 7, 496, 498
Marzari, M., 335
Marzill, R., 502
Mas, C., 649
Mason, M., 482, 483, 487, 501,
    502, 504

Mason, M. J., 479, 488
Masters, William, 4, 15, 16, 36
Masters and Johnson, 480, 485, 486, 487, 488, 489, 490, 492, 493, 494, 495, 496, 497, 500, 502, 503
Mathews, A., 503
Mathews, A. M., 79, 88
Matteini, M., 335
Matthews, W., 276
Matthews, 483
Matthews, W. J., 239
Maturana, H., 194, 242, 334, 336, 337, 341, 512
Maturana, H. R., 48, 51, 57, 59
May, P. R. A., 368
Mazza, J., 649, 653, 667
McAdoo, H., 549, 560
McAuley, R. R., 71
McCulloch, W., 172
McCurry, M. C., 80, 83, 88
McDaniel, S., 649, 651, 657
McDonald, D. W., 102
McDonald, R., 79
McEnroe, M. J., 82
McFarlane, W. R., 363, 364, 385
McGill, C. W., 72
McGill, D., 549, 571
McGimsey, J. F., 80
McGoldrick, M., 35, 134, 484, 500, 526, 528, 529, 532, 546, 547, 548, 549, 550, 552, 558, 566, 567, 570, 571, 572, 573, 578, 614, 648, 654, 655, 656, 659, 662
McGregor, R., 32
McGuire, D., 663
McGuire, L., 504
McIntosh, D. N., 663
McIntyre, D., 657
McKeever, J., 651
McKeever, Jr., 649
McKenzie, P. N., 658
McKinlay, 491
McKinnon, T., 680, 681, 685
McLean, P., 138
McLees, S., 88
McMahon, R. J., 74, 75, 80, 82, 83, 87
McNeal, S., 66
McRae, S., 80
Mead, G. H., 18
Mead, M., 27, 172, 332
Mehlman, S. K., 109
Meiselman, K., 488, 496
Meltzer, H. Y., 366
Mendelson, M., 30, 286, 639, 653, 675
Mendez, C., 336, 337, 341
Menfi, A., 675, 676
Menghi, P., 648
Menning, 485
Messerly, L., 101
Meth, R. L., 633
Meyerstein, I., 650, 651
Meyerstein, K., 687
Michaelson, R., 11
Michalski, A., 648
Midelfort, C. F., 23–24, 25, 549
Midelfort, F. C., 549
Miklowitz, D. J., 87, 371
Miller, D., 58, 338, 584
Miller, D. R., 18
Miller, L., 657
Miller, L. B., 287, 288, 292
Miller, M. D., 20

Miller, N., 687
Miller, S., 14, 503
Miller, V. H., 504
Milman, L., 420
Milne, A., 518
Mintz, J., 87
Mintz, N., 550
Minuchin, S., 23, 29, 30, 31, 34–35, 53, 70, 291, 403, 417, 418, 419, 420, 421, 422, 423, 425–430, 432, 433, 434, 437, 439, 440, 441, 450, 453, 548, 556, 562, 640, 646, 648, 650, 651, 657, 658, 662, 667, 668, 684
Mishler, E. G., 43
Mittlemann, B., 19, 20
Miyoshi, N., 640
Mohammed, Z., 678, 681
Monck, E. M., 366
Mondyknowski, S. M., 571
Montalvo, B., 31, 396, 417, 418, 420, 527, 548, 640, 641, 654, 655, 656, 658, 659, 662
Monti, P. M., 88
Mooney, T., 491
Moore, D., 99, 102
Moorman, J. E., 525
Moran, J., 682
Morawetz, A., 584
Moreland, J. R., 80
Moreno, J. L., 20
Morong, E., 365
Morris, S. B., 85, 86
Morrow-Bradley, C., 654
Mosher, D., 276
Moustaki, E., 286
Mowerey, J., 537
Moynihan, 539
Mudd, E. H., 8, 10, 11
Mueller, P., 457, 458, 464
Muney, 484, 491
Murase, K., 565
Murphy, H. B. M., 550
Murphy, M., 276
Myerhoff, B., 549
Myers, J. K., 550

Nadelson, C. C., 496
Napier, A., 286, 633
Napier, A. Y., 461, 462, 464, 468, 649, 670
Napoleon, 197
Naster, B. J., 71
Neal, J., 650, 651, 653
Neill, J., 670
Neill, J. R., 444, 445, 447, 449, 451, 456, 465, 468
Neilson, S., 584
Neimeyer, G., 681, 685
Neisser, V., 489
Nelson, J., 480, 481, 486
Nelson, T., 652, 653, 680
Neuchterlein, K. H., 367
Newfield, N., 654
Newman, 489
Newton, Isaac, 196, 198, 242
Nguyen, S. D. 575
Nichols, 436
Nichols, M., 23, 24, 25, 26, 31, 33, 43
Nichols, M. P., 658
Nichols, W., 11, 14, 649, 653, 669, 670, 687
Nichols, W. C., 642, 643, 644, 647, 659

Nieves-Falcon, L., 554
Nitzberg, L., 336
Noddings, N., 633, 634
Norcross, J. C., 674
Nord, C. W., 538
Norton, A., 365
Norton, A. J., 525, 532
Notarius, C., 99
Novaco, R. W., 123
Nugent, J., 101
Nugent, W., 276
Nunnally, E., 503
Nunnally, E. W., 14
Nusselt, 502, 503

Oberndorf, C. P., 19, 20
Oberstein, A., 662
Oblan, J. L., 31
O'Conner, D., 389
O'Dell, S., 82
O'Dell, S. L., 82, 87, 88
Offit, A., 500, 503
O'Hara, F., 663
O'Hare, C., 662
Okun, B. F., 656
O'Leary, K. D., 68, 71, 76, 77
Olson, D., 654
Olson, D. H., 46, 291
Olson, V., 661
Oltmanns, T. F., 71
O'Malley, S., 686
Omer, H., 276
Onorato, R., 657
Opler, M. K., 548
Oppenheimer, R. J., 196–197
Orfanidis, M. M., 457, 458, 464, 468
Orlinsky, D., 653
Ornstein, P. H., 285
O'Sullivan, M. J., 677, 680, 687
Otani, A., 276
Otto, H., 14

Pagel, M., 125
Paine, R. T., 4
Papajohn, J., 548, 554, 570
Papero, D., 134, 649, 653, 668, 669, 676
Papp, P., 55, 230, 396, 463, 467, 505, 615, 629, 652, 656
Parham, E. S., 389
Parker, V., 10
Parry, A., 353
Parsons, B. V., 87, 88
Parsons, T., 24, 25, 419
Pasick, R. S., 633
Pasley, 533, 538
Pastushak, R., 687
Patten, J., 336
Patterson, G., 648, 650
Patterson, G. R., 14, 66, 68, 70, 73, 74, 77, 79, 80, 85, 87, 88, 96, 99, 105
Patterson, J. N., 82, 83
Pattison, E. M., 367
Paul, B., 231
Paul, N., 231, 468
Paul, N. L., 52, 60, 607
Pearce, J., 35, 655
Pearce, J. K., 546, 548, 549, 550, 552, 571, 614
Pearce, W., 333, 334, 342, 354
Pearson, D., 648
Pearson, R., 661
Pegg, P., 661
Pellegrino, E. D., 634

Pendagast, E. G., 54
Penn, P., 55, 56, 331, 333, 634
Perlmutter, M., 663
Pert, C. B., 161
Pertras, 484
Peshkin, H. M., 389
Peter, 490
Petersen, 538
Peterson, J. A., 13
Phelps, R., 66
Phillips, C., 13
Phillips, S., 73
Phillips, V. A., 292
Piercy, F., 643, 647, 650, 652, 659, 664, 674, 678, 679, 681, 682, 686
Piercy, F. P., 504, 633
Pilalis, J., 675
Pincas, J., 492
Pinderhughes, E., 560
Pinhaus, V., 488
Pinsof, W., 679, 680, 684, 686
Pinsof, W. M., 36, 126
Pirrotta, S., 331, 332, 649, 653, 665, 666
Pittman, F., 499
Pittman, F. S., 633
Pitts, W., 172
Planck, M., 169
Plath, D., 547
Pollard, D., 326
Pols, B., 56
Polster, R. A., 80, 83
Pomeroy, W. E., 7, 496, 498
Popenoe, P., 8, 9, 10, 13, 15
Postpischil, F., 73, 88
Prata, G., 33, 54, 325, 326, 330, 332, 364, 459, 556, 584
Preli, R., 668
Preto, N. G., 549
Price, M. G., 102
Prigogine, I., 50, 56, 333, 335, 425
Prinz, R. J., 68, 73, 76, 77
Prochaska, J., 502
Protinsky, H., 654, 667
Pulleyblank, E., 679, 681, 686
Pulliam, G., 662, 685
Purcell, P., 411

Quinn, W., 654, 686
Quinn, W. H., 660

Raasoch, J., 664
Rabbi, J., 660
Rabin, C., 82, 491
Rabinowitz, C., 30
Rabkin, J., 550, 656
Rabkin, R., 396
Racker, 231
Rait, D., 683
Rambo, A., 647, 652
Ramos, J., 554
Rampage, C., 629, 634, 656
Rank, 18
Ransom, D., 687
Rank, Otto, 445
Raskin, P., 36, 656
Ratliff, D., 683
Ratlin, 682
Ravich, R., 571
Ray, R. S., 80
Raymond, M., 511
Reamy-Stephenson, M., 652, 667
Reder, P., 326, 685
Reid, E., 657

Reid, J. B., 66, 70, 87, 96, 99
Rein, L., 287
Reinman, 154
Reis, W. J., 20
Reiss, D., 43, 167, 291, 485, 685
Reiss, D. J., 363, 367, 371
Reitz, M., 663
Rembar, J., 508
Renshaw, D., 489
Resnik, R. B., 568
Restivo, R. J., 584, 587
Revenstorf, D., 123
Rhode, P. D., 367
Rice, D. G., 519
Rice, J., 519
Rich, M. E., 4
Richardson, H. B., 20
Richman, D., 562
Richmond, Mary, 4, 5
Rickets, V., 659
Ricoeur, P., 297
Rinder, I., 550
Riskin, J., 25, 32, 173
Risley, T. R., 65
Ritchie, A., 32
Ritterman, M., 239, 240
Ritz, M., 662
Roberto, L. Giat, 421, 434, 444,
    445, 446, 447, 450, 451, 453,
    454, 458, 466, 467
Roberts, B., 550
Roberts, J., 660, 661
Robertson, M. H., 674
Robin, A. L., 74, 77, 82, 83, 85,
    86, 87, 88
Robiner, W. N., 679
Robinson, B., 491
Robinson, E. A., 102
Robinson, Leon, 29
Rodgers, R., 508, 526, 527, 533
Rodgers, T. C., 20
Rodman, H., 571
Rodnick, E. H., 368
Rodriguez, S., 458
Rohrbaugh, M., 546, 567, 578,
    658, 659, 683
Roos, P., 558
Rosen, E. J., 549, 570, 572
Rosen, J., 27
Rosenbaum, L., 134
Rosenfeld, H., 285
Rosenthal, A., 22
Rosenthal, D. M., 652
Rosenthal, M., 87
Rosman, B., 3, 418, 420, 548,
    646
Rosman, B. L., 291
Ross, I., 667
Ross, J. M., 290
Rosser, R., 286, 299
Rossi, E., 239, 248, 257, 258,
    260, 274
Rossi, E. L., 239, 241, 245, 249,
    255, 258, 259, 260, 270, 272,
    273, 274, 275
Rossi, S. I., 239
Roth, R., 230
Roth, S., 309
Rotunno, M., 549
Rounsaville, B., 686
Rubinstein, D., 29
Ruddick, S., 208
Rue, J., 13
Ruesch, J., 27, 172
Runions, J. E., 59
Russell, A., 457, 659, 660

Russell, B., 27, 45
Russell, C. F. M., 79
Russell, C. S., 625, 626, 627
Russell, L., 457
Rutter, M., 75
Ryan, 239
Ryan, M. C., 444, 445, 454, 455
Ryckoff, 25
Ryder, R. G., 608, 610, 625

Saba, G., 648, 654, 658, 674, 682
Sachs, L., 160
Sager, C., 538, 544
Sager, C. J., 19, 20, 44, 52, 484,
    520
Sager, K., 651
Salasin, S., 508
Salerno, 489
Salter, A., 480
Salusky, S., 127
Samuel, 686
Sander, F., 639
Sanders, M. R., 87
Sanua, V., 550
Sarason, S., 611, 613
Sargent, M., 687
Sarrel, 499
Satir, V., 14, 27–29, 52, 60, 116,
    173, 184, 201, 239, 242, 657,
    662
Satir, V. M., 25
Saunders, B. E., 675, 687
Savitsky, E., 639, 641, 659
Sayer, J., 365
Sayre, P., 9
Schachter, F. F., 450
Scharff, D. E., 52
Scharff, J. S., 52
Scheflen, A., 27
Scheinkman, M., 526, 538
Scherer, D., 624
Schiavo, R. S., 87, 673, 681
Schiller, P., 16
Schindler, L., 123
Schmaling, K. B., 111, 127
Schmidt, 503
Schmidt, G., 240
Schmidt, S., 654
Schneidman, B., 504
Scofield, W., 679
Schon, D., 683
Schon, D. A., 650
Schooler, N. R., 363
Schover, L. R., 494
Schrader, S., 3, 240
Schultz, L. A., 87
Schumer, F., 31, 418, 548
Schumm, W. R., 677
Schwartz, 479
Schwartz, L., 508
Schwartz, L. H., 389
Schwartz, R., 649, 651, 659, 675,
    683
Schwartz, R. C., 647, 686
Schwartzman, J., 435, 572, 584,
    587
Schwebel, A. I., 80
Searles, H., 201, 231
Sechrest, M., 654, 687
Secter, I., 239
Segal, L., 32, 45, 57, 71, 173,
    195, 239, 364
Selig, A., 583
Seligman, P., 661, 679, 680
Selvini Palazzoli, M., 32–33, 54,

55, 325, 326, 327, 328, 329,
    331–332, 338, 344, 346, 347,
    349, 354, 364, 459, 467, 556,
    584, 596
Semans, J. H., 17, 493
Serber, M., 501
Sevitt, M. A., 288
Sexton, E., 682
Shakespeare, W., 184, 488
Shannon, W. V., 551
Shapiro, E., 207
Shapiro, R., 286, 640, 679, 681,
    686, 687
Sharon, D., 648
Sharp, 239
Sharpe, L., 389
Shaul, 491
Shaw, B., 686
Sheehey, R., 685
Sheely, M., 662, 685
Sheflen, 651
Sheinberg, M., 634
Sheldrake, R., 145, 147
Shepherd, J. N., 623
Sherman, R., 21
Sherman, S. N., 14, 21
Shiro, J., 548
Shockey, J., 558
Shon, S., 570
Siegal, L., 641, 660
Sigal, J., 50
Silber, T. J., 457, 458
Silverman, M., 21, 22
Silverstein, O., 505, 615, 629,
    656
Simon, F. B., 41, 48, 49, 56
Simon, R., 650, 658, 659
Singer, J. L., 548
Singer, M. T., 366, 371, 654
Singh, 491
Skeen, P., 491
Skinner, B. F., 98, 154
Skynner, A. C. R., 284, 285,
    585
Slee, P. T., 616, 617
Sluzki, C., 648, 652, 656
Sluzki, C. E., 15, 32, 34, 35,
    650, 651
Smith, D., 659, 661
Smith, V., 687
Smith, Z. D., 4
Snyder, D. K., 105, 126
Snyder, S. H., 366
Sobel, 23
Sobelman, G., 18
Sonne, J., 31, 662
Sorrentino, A. M., 330
Sowers-Hoag, K., 684
Spanier, G., 534, 558
Spanier, G. B., 105
Spark, G., 29, 30, 33, 202, 206,
    210
Spark, G. M., 286, 450, 501
Spark, M., 607
Speck, R. V., 31
Speed, B., 661
Speer, D. C., 49
Spiegel, D., 389
Spiegel, J., 548, 554, 570, 609
Spiegel, J. P., 5, 33
Spielman, M., 336
Spitzer, R., 505
Spohn, H. E., 366
Sporakowski, M., 607, 687
Sprenkle, D., 332, 504, 510, 518,
    643, 647, 650, 652, 658, 659,

664, 674, 675, 676, 677, 678,
    685, 686, 687
Sprenkle, D. H., 291, 633
Sprenkle, D. M., 57, 58
Stack, S., 508
Staniszewski, W., 687
Stanton, M., 640, 686, 687
Stanton, M. D., 441, 585, 616,
    666
Staples, R., 559
Steele, R. S., 297
Steenberg, M. R., 368
Steger, J. C., 501
Stein, B. N., 575
Stein, H., 610, 611, 613
Stein, H. F., 608, 609
Stein, S., 543
Steinberg, J., 517
Steinberg, J. L., 607
Stengers, I., 333, 335
Stern, B., 79
Stevens, B. C., 367
Stevens, J. R., 366
Stier, S., 639, 641, 660, 662
Stierlin, H., 41, 44, 205, 211,
    228, 284, 231, 406, 670
Stinnet, N., 539
Stoeckle, J., 549
Stolorow, R. D., 285
Stone, 486, 489
Stone, A., 10, 11, 15
Stone, I., 19
Stone, H., 10, 11
Stone-Fish, L., 652
Storm, C., 510, 518, 647, 648,
    667
Strachey, A., 19
Strachey, J., 19
Stratford, J., 287, 306
Stratton, P., 654
Strauss, J., 548
Strauss, J. S., 367
Street, E., 651, 653, 676, 678,
    679, 680, 681, 682, 683, 684,
    686
Strickler, G., 624
Streuning, E., 550
Strinhelber, J., 686
Stuart, R., 501
Stuart, R. B., 14, 67, 68, 70, 96,
    115
Stuckey, M., 389
Sturgeon, D., 368
Sugarman, S., 643–644, 670, 671
Sullaway, M., 71
Sullivan, H. S., 18, 27, 28, 201,
    419
Sullivan, W. M., 611
Sutherland, J., 21
Swidler, A., 611
Szapocznik, J., 686
Szasz, T., 243

Taggart, M., 58, 607–608, 622
Talmadge, J., 640
Talmadge, W., 504
Talmon, M., 424, 654
Talovic, S., 125, 657
Tannehill, R., 480
Tarasoff, 36
Tarrant, R., 515
Tarrier, N., 88, 368
Tecce, J. J., 368
Tennen, H., 674
Terry, Lidz, 24, 48
Tester, M., 624

Theodore, J., 156
Thilbaut, J. W., 67, 99, 612
Thomas, A., 71
Thomas, L., 156, 421
Thomasma, D. C., 634
Thompson, C., 17, 18
Thompson, K., 366
Thorne, B., 612, 629
Thorwarth, C., 71, 79
Tienari, P., 366
Tipton, M., 611
Titelman, P., 134
Todd, T., 420
Todd, T. C., 441
Tollers, M., 657
Tolsdorf, C. C., 367
Tomm, K., 55, 326, 328, 329, 330, 333–334, 336, 339, 342, 345, 347, 653, 681, 682
Toohey, M. C., 371
Toohey, M. L., 366
Treacher, A., 653, 680, 681
Trenkle, B., 240
Trepper, T., 686
Triescham, R., 491
Troll, 485
Truax, C. B., 85
Tucker, B., 639, 660, 662
Tucker, S., 680, 684, 686
Tung, T. M., 575
Turner, J., 659
Turner, M., 640
Turner, R. J., 69
Turpin, G., 368
Turquet, P., 285

Ulrich, D., 200, 401
Ulrich, D. N., 668
Ulrich, R. F., 367
Umbarger, C. C., 434

Vance, S., 687
Van Deusen, J. M., 667, 668
Van Trommel, M., 336
Varela, F., 242, 334, 336, 337, 512
Varela, F. J., 51
Vaughn, C., 47, 73, 368
Vaughn, C. E., 71, 73, 74, 76, 80, 88, 366, 370
Vemer, E., 542, 543
Viaro, M., 330
Vincent, J. P., 101, 102
Visher, E., 526, 528, 538

Visher, J., 526, 528, 538
Volgy, S. S., 508, 512, 519, 522
Von Glaserfeld, E., 195, 336, 341

Wackman, D., 14, 503
Wagener, D. K., 371
Wagner, 489
Wagner, R. L., 366
Wahler, R. G., 70
Waite, F. T., 5
Wald, E., 538, 539
Waldron, H., 85, 99
Waldron-Skinner, S., 609
Walker, G., 584, 634
Wallach, L., 611
Wallach, M. A., 611
Wallerstein, J. S., 508, 509, 526, 534
Wallerstein, R., 648
Walrond-Skinner, S. 684
Walsh, F., 208, 525, 526, 538, 539, 541, 656
Walsh, F. W., 654
Walters, L., 491
Walters, M., 505, 615, 629, 656, 661
Walters, R., 68
Wampold, B. E., 99, 102
Warburton, J., 673
Warkentin, J., 14, 26, 444, 445
Wasserman, I. M., 508
Watson, A. S., 20
Watson, D., 609
Watzlawick, P., 17, 29, 32, 44, 45, 50, 54, 57, 60, 171, 173, 178, 184, 193, 239, 241, 242, 274, 289, 326, 396, 502, 546, 586, 589, 649
Waxler, N. E., 43
Weakland, J., 27–29, 32, 171, 172, 173, 178, 184, 193, 228, 239, 241, 242, 364, 396, 446, 589, 649
Weakland, J. H., 47, 48, 326
Weakland, J. M., 50
Weber, G., 670
Weber, S., 649
Weber, T., 651
Webster, G., 146
Weeks, G., 494, 499
Weeks, G. R., 619
Weinberger, D. R., 366
Weiner, J. P., 608, 618, 629–633
Weiner, N., 172, 202

Weiner, O., 29, 31
Weingarten, K., 651, 654
Weinstein, C. D., 125
Weisman, R., 512
Weiss, R., 512
Weiss, R. L., 14, 99, 100, 102, 105, 114, 115, 116
Weiss, R. S., 534, 536
Weissman, M., 686
Weitzman, L., 533, 534
Wells, K. C., 69, 71, 75, 76, 80, 85, 87, 88
Wells, R., 80
Welts, E. P., 571
Wendorf, D., 37, 662, 685
Wendorf, D. J., 608, 619, 622
Wendorf, R., 37, 662, 685
Wendorf, R. J., 608, 619, 622
Werry, J., 687
Wertheim, E. S., 49
West, J., 664, 680, 681
Westheafer, C., 659
Wetzel, N. A., 572
Whan, M., 613, 616
Wheeler, D., 657
Whiffen, R., 663
Whisman, M., 127
Whitaker, C., 444–456, 458, 459, 460, 461, 462, 464–471, 621, 639, 646, 647, 649, 650, 651, 657, 659, 662, 670, 671, 672, 684
Whitaker, C. A., 26–27, 33, 58, 628
White, G. D., 538
White, L., 538
White, M., 450
Whitehead, A. N., 27, 45
Whiteside, J., 457, 458
Whiteside, M. F., 533, 539
Wiener, N., 41
Wig, N. N., 371
Wile, D. B., 124
Wilkinson, G., 88
Will, D., 675, 676
Willbach, 633
Williams, 505
Williams, C. D., 65
Wills, G., 551
Wills, T. A., 99, 102, 114
Wills, R. M., 126
Wilson, W., 530
Wilson, W., 530
Winawer-Steiner, H., 572

Wincze, J., 501
Windermand, L., 337–338
Wing, J. K., 366, 367
Winnicott, D. W., 201, 204, 216, 220, 284, 285, 286
Winter, W. D., 43
Wirsching, M., 670
Wolf, 486
Wolf, M. M., 65
Wolfe, B., 686
Wolpe, J., 17, 65, 480, 493
Wong, B., 567
Wood, B., 654
Woods, 486
Woody, J., 504
Woody, J. D., 633
Worthington, E., 654
Wrate, R. M., 675, 676
Wright, L., 653, 654, 659, 675, 682, 686, 687
Wyatt, R. J., 366
Wylan, L., 550
Wynne, L., 444
Wynne, L. C., 24–25, 36, 41, 48, 201, 284, 366, 371, 484, 654

Yalom, I., 44
Yalom, I. D., 389
Yamamura, H. I., 366
Yolles, S. F., 363
Young, J., 661
Ysern, E., 610, 613

Zaken-Greenberg, F., 681, 685
Zarit, J. M., 71, 73, 389
Zarit, S. H., 71, 73, 80, 82, 88, 389
Zarski, J., 680
Zborowski, M., 549, 590
Zeig, J., 241, 275
Zelnick, 485
Zilbergeld, B., 494
Zifferblatt, S. M., 678
Zill, 538
Zinberg, N., 659
Zinn, J., 286
Zola, I. K., 549, 550
Zucker, R., 583
Zuckerman, H., 139
Zuk, G., 29, 31, 676
Zwerling, I., 23, 30
Zygmond, M. J., 633

Subject Index

Abortion, 487
Acceptance-redefinition, 335
Ackerman Family Therapy Institute, New York City, 55
Ackerman group, 55–56
Ackerman Institute, 23, 54, 467
Acquired immune deficiency syndrome (AIDS), 479, 485, 489, 490–491, 498
Adaptation, 57
Adult Children of Divorce, 134
Adult development, autonomy and independence in, 70–71
Adult mental disorders, behavioral family therapy for, 88
Adult mentally ill, behavioral family therapy for, 68
African-American families, 556–562
  coping with poverty, 559–560
  death and mourning, 559
  economic factors, 558
  empowerment, 561–562
  engagement, 561
  expression of feelings, 559
  information gathering, 561
  kinship bonds, 557
  male-female relationships, 558–559
  role clarification/boundary setting, 562
  socialization to therapy, 561
  special issues of middle-income families, 560
  spirituality, 559
  treatment approaches, 562
  treatment implications, 560–561
After Virtue, 611
Agenda setting, 111
Aging
  men and, 486–487
  sex and, 486
  women and, 486
AIDS. *See* Acquired immune deficiency syndrome
Albert Einstein College of Medicine, 23, 30
Alcoholism, 488
"Alpha" prejudice, 447
Ambiguity, 398
Ambiguous function assignments, 271–272
American analysts, bias in, 18
American Association for Marital and Family Therapy Ethical Principles for Family Therapist, 629–633
American Association for Marriage and Family Therapy (AAMFT), 15, 510, 608

Code of Ethical Principles for Marriage and Family Therapists, 37
  standards for certification of training programs, 34
American Association of Marriage and Family Counselors (AAMFC), 15
American Association of Marriage Counselors (AAMC), 8, 9, 10, 11
  David and Vera Mace takeover of, 13
  establishment of, 10–11
  percent of members by primary professional identification, 13t
  purpose of, 10
  rejection of Masters and Johnson's membership, 15
  standards for marriage counselors, 12f
American Association of Sex Educators and Counselors (AASEC), 16
American Family Therapy Association (AFTA), 30, 33
American Fertility Society, 485
American Genetic Association, 9
American Institute of Family Relations (AIFR), 9, 13
American Journal of Clinical Hypnosis, 242
American Journal of Family Therapy, 607
American Journal of Orthopsychiatry, 607
American Orthopsychiatric Association, 5, 23
American Psychiatric Association, 19, 23, 25, 26, 495, 505
American Psychological Association (APA), 625
  "Guidelines for Therapy with Women," 629–633
American Social Hygiene Association, 9
American Society of Clinical Hypnosis, 242
Analogic communication, 44
Anger-management techniques, 123
Angst, 140
Anorexia nervosa, 31, 79, 325–326, 421, 471
Anorgasmia, 492–493
Anxiety, fear distinguished from, 140
Anxiety disorders, family behavioral intervention for, 88
Areas-of-Changes Questionnaire (A-C), 105
Assessment
  assessment procedure, 431–433
  family shape, 429–430
  focus of, 429–431
  points of entry, 430
  preplanning, 431

reframing problems, 432–433
staging enactments, 432
structural assessment and individual, 430–431
  in structural family therapy, 429–433
structural strengths and weaknesses, 430
tracking, 431, 432
unit of assessment, 431
Assessment of family functioning and dysfunction, 452–453
Assessment of system functioning, 250–254
  assessing family strengths and resources, 254
  assessment and treatment are inseparable, 253–254
  eliciting family reactions to illness and treatment system, 372
  evaluating present crisis, 372
  evaluation of family and social system, 372–373
  family psychoeducational treatment and, 371, 373
  psychological levels of assessment, 250–252
  role of verbal interview, 254
  testing tools and typical observations, 252–253
  unit levels of assessment, 250
Attention-arousal hypothesis, 367–368
Automatization, 243
Autopoeisis, 336

Battle for initiative, 462
Battle for structure, 462
Behavior
  as ideomotor communication, 260
  resistance behavior, 112
Behavioral, as term, 98
Behavioral assessment, characteristics of, 104–105
Behavioral assessment of marital discord, 104–108
  direct observation of problem solving and communication, 106–108
  interview, 105
  self report measures, 105
  spouse observation, 105
Behavioral change, 98
Behavioral communication training, 116–119
  feedback, 117
  instructions, 117

problem-solving training, 117–119
Behavioral exchange interventions, 110
Behavioral family therapy, 65–93
   behavioral analysis of family dysfunction, 72–74
   behavioral assessment of family functioning, 74–78
   boundaries in, 70
   case illustration, 89–93
   child-rearing issues and, 65–66
   coercion in, 66–67
   communication training, 81–82
   conducting sessions in home setting, 79
   contingency contracting, 84
   education of family, 81
   historical development, 65–69
   indications and contraindications for, 87–89
   modeling in, 68
   multifamily group sessions and, 80
   number of therapists in session, 80
   operant conditioning strategies, 83–84
   reciprocity in, 66
   role of therapist in, 84–86
   role rehearsal in, 68
   structure of, 78–80
   techniques of, 80–84
   as term, 65
   therapeutic factors in, 86–87
   therapist training in, 86
   therapy sessions, 80
   well-functioning family, 69–72
Behavioral family training, 82–83
Behavioral marital therapy (BMT), 96–131
   behavioral assessment of marital discord, 104–108
   behavior-exchange procedures, 113–116
   case illustration, 128–131
   cognition and, 98–99
   cognitive and affective exploration, 123–124
   combined treatment, success rate of, 126–127
   communication and problem solving training, 110
   criticism of, 97
   efficacy of, 126
   frequency of success of, 126
   generalization and maintenance, 110–111
   goal setting, 108–109
   identification of themes and modification of prototypical interaction patterns, 125
   politics of working with couples at thematic level, 125–126
   positive behavior change in, 110
   problem solving session, 119–123
   research on, 126
   role of therapist in, 111–113
   structure of, 109–110
   successful and unsuccessful marital relationships from behavioral perspective, 97–104
   and successful marriage, 99–102
   terminating, 123
Behavior exchange procedures, 113–116
   basic steps in, 113
   learning to ask for changes in behavior from partner, 115
   positive reinforcement, 113–114
   skill-training versus, 118
Behaviorism
   misconceptions about, 98
   objectivity and, 153–154
Beliefs and unconscious resources, 251

Belmont Report of Department of Health and Human Services (DHHS), 625
"Beta" prejudice, 447
Bethesda group, 25
Between Give and Take, 608
"Binuclear" family system, 522, 527
Biofeedback Frontiers, 134
Birth control, 484–485
Bisexuality, 497
"Blended family," 528
Blindness, sex and, 491
"Borderline personality," 537–538
Boston, in family-therapy movement, 31–32
Boston Family Institute, 31, 32
Boston State Hospital, 32
Boston Women's Health Collective, 496
Boundaries, in family, 423–424
Boundary making, 438–439
Bowen model, 53–54
Bowen theory and therapy, 134–170, 364
   asking questions and, 155
   basic premise of, 53
   books on, 134
   breadth of its perspective, 135–136
   continuity of emotional processes, 166
   dichotomies and, 168
   differentiation and, 137, 140–144
   eight basic concepts of, 139
   emotional as term in, 136
   emotional being of therapist in, 138–139
   emotional system in, 144–147
   emotional triangle in, 150–151
   family and culture in, 145
   family as unit of observation or treatment, 137
   family therapy and societal anxiety, 165–167
   four seminal constructs of, 139–151
   fundamental characteristics of, 135–139
   healing as self-regenerative phenomenon, 159–160
   "hostile environment," 143
   multigenerational transmission, 147–150
   natural systems view of healing, 161–164
   natural systems view of pathology, 160–161
   objectivity, 153–155
   perspective of universals, 136–138
   problems with, 169–170
   proximity and protoplasm, 155–159
   scale of differentiation, 142–143
   social science and, 168–170
   societal regression, 164–165
   three principles about conduct of, 152–153
Brain. See Human brain
Brainstorming, 121
Brief Therapy, 171–199, 287
   attempted solutions, 175–178, 181–182
   avoiding feared events, 188
   avoiding "the mine field," 183–184
   background of approach, 171–173
   Bateson, Gregory, 173
   Brief Therapy model, 175
   case example, 189–192
   case planning, 182–183
   client position, 178–179
   closure, 198
   confirming accuser's suspicions by defending oneself, 187–188
   constructivism, 194–196
   dangers of improvement, 188–189
   data collection, 180–181
   defining problem, 181
   demanding that self or others be spontaneous, 186

"do something different or more of the same," 185–186
   early goals of, 171
   epistemology, 192
   Erickson, Milton, 172–173
   family systems, 193–194
   family therapy as shift in epistemology, 192–193
   first telephone contact, 180
   formation of, 173
   general interventions, 188
   "go slowly" injunction to client, 189
   how problems arise and persist, 175
   integration of, 192
   interventions, 185–189
   interventions and patterns of attempted solutions, 186
   jamming, 187
   maneuverability, 179–180
   more on report and command, 183
   Newtonian revolution, 196–197
   nonrisk methods and inevitability of risk, 186
   other people's behavior as determinant of individual's behavior, 171
   paradox, 185
   problems of, 173–175
   reaching accord through opposition, 186–187
   reframing, 184–185
   setting goals, 182
   setting stage for treatment, 178
   techniques of, 178–185
   termination of, 189
   ultimate goal of, 185
   "U-turn," 189
Brief Therapy Center, 32
British Association for Family Therapy, 35
Bronx State Hospital, 30
Bulimia, 471

California Association of Marriage and Family Counselors, 13
California Family Studies Center, 13
Cancer, 487–488
   herpes and, 490
"Cartesian" stress model, 447–448
Case illustration of behavioral family therapy, 89–93
   assessment of family functioning, 90
   assessment of family members individually, 89–90
   presenting problem, 89
   treatment, 90–93
Causal doctrine, 196
Causality, 48
Center for Sexual Advice in Vienna, 7
Centrality, 439–440
Change, 272
   coercion in, 66–67, 70
   contingency contracting in, 67–68
   explaining, 50–51
   objectivity and, 153–154
   time necessary for, 163–164
   at unconscious level, 245
Change—Principles of Problem Formation, 32, 173
"Channels" in communication, 45–46
"Characterological growth," 52
Chicago, Illinois, in family-therapy movement, 33
Child/children
   child-rearing issues and behavioral family intervention, 65–66
   in contextual therapy, 227–229
   depression in mother and, 75

"difficult" to manage, 71
effects of custody arrangements on,
    535–536, 536–538
empathy between mother and, 18
exploitation of, 213
of intermarriage, 572
invisible loyalty, 211–212
mother in therapy of, 25
operant conditioning and, 96
parental conflict and personality of, 17–18
parentification of, 213–214, 451
parent-training approach to management
    of, 87, 88
schizophrenia in, 52
sexual abuse of, 484, 495–497, 504
split filial loyalty, 211
stepparent relationships and, 540–541
"symbiosis" between mother and, 25
trauma and, 285–286
Child counselors, licensing of, 13
Child-custody arrangements, 533–536
Child development, Sullivan's theories on,
    18
Child Guidance Clinic, 23
Child-guidance movement, 3
Chinese-American families, 562–566
    "Americanized" family, 563–564
    bicultural family, 563
    divorce in, 564
    family structure, 563–564
    life-cycle transitions, 564–565
    traditional family, 563
    transitional family, 563
    treatment implications, 565–566
Chinese Exclusion Act of 1882, 563
Chlamydia, 490
Chronically ill, larger systems and, 600–601
Chronic anxiety, 139
Chronic mental handicap, 71
Chronic physical handicap, 71
Circular causality, 193, 423
Circular feedback, 55
Circularity
    concept of, 58
    definition of, 328
Circular questioning, 346–347
Climacteric, 485
Cloning, 135
Closed system, 49
Closeness-distance conflicts, 125
Codependency behavior, 450
Coercion, in change, 66–67, 70
Coevolutionary model, 350–351
Cognition, BMT and, 98–99
Cognitive-affective change, 98
Cognitive therapy, 480
Colitis, family events and, 24
Collaborative set, 118–119
"Command" aspect of message, 45
Commands and reports, 183
Commission on Accreditation for Marriage
    and Family Education, 34
Communication: The Social Matrix of
    Psychiatry, 27, 172
Communication
    classifying, 45
    punctuation in, 46
    verbal versus nonverbal, 44–45
"Communication deviance," 371
Communication skills, in marriage, 100
Communication training, of family, 81–82
Community Child Guidance Center of
    Chicago, 21
Community Church of New York, 10
Comparison level, 99
Complementarity, 422–423

Complementary behavior, 42
"Concern of the Community with
    Marriage," 5
Conference on Conservation of Marriage
    and the Family, 10
Confidentiality, 36
    in family therapy, 624
    in family-therapy research, 626–627
Confirmation, 437
Conflict avoidance, 428, 451
    in men, 125
Conflict resolution, 100, 103
Conjoint Family Therapy, 29
Conjoint family therapy, 28–29
    background, 201
    individual therapy versus, 79
Conjoint marital therapy, 27
    extramarital sexual relationships and, 127
Conjoint therapy, 19
    as term, 20
Conjugal-therapy groups, 14
Connectedness, differentiation and, 434
Consensual domain, 336
Constructive anxiety, 454
Constructivism, 173, 194–196
Constructivists, 57
    on therapists, 75
Contextual therapy, 30, 200–237, 608
    applying partiality in, 224–225
    assessment of system functioning and
        dysfunction, 214–215
    asymmetry of parent-child relationship,
        206
    background to approach, 200–203
    basic relational context, 205–208
    bringing children into treatment, 227–228
    case illustration, 233–237
    conflicts of interest, 208
    curative factors and mechanisms of change
        in, 230–232
    current evolution of, 200–201
    detrimental relationship configurations,
        210–211
    development of approach, 201–203
    dysfunctional family, 209–214
    equitable symmetry, 227
    exoneration, 226–227
    family stagnation, 210
    feminist values and, 207–208
    goal of, 200, 202
    goals and goal setting, 215–217
    how to include children, 228–229
    intergenerational approaches, 231–232
    "interlocking-need templates," 213
    intimacy, 208
    invisible loyalty, 211–212
    ledger, 205–206
    legacy and ledger of merit and
        indebtedness, 205
    loyalty, 207
    loyalty context of therapy, 225–226
    marital relationships, 206
    multidirectional partiality, 222–224
    multigenerational perspective, 205
    multilateral concern of, 202
    parentification, 213–214
    relational definition of self, 207
    relational ethics, 204–205
    relationship with posterity, 209
    resistance, 229–230
    "revolving slate and destructive
        entitlement," 212
    role of therapist in, 219–221
    social context, 208–209
    special issues in marital treatment, 232
    split loyalty, 211

structure of therapy process, 217–219
    techniques of, 221–230
    termination of, 219
    treatment applicability, 232–233
    well-functioning marriage or family,
        203–209
Contingency contracting, 67–68, 84
Control, in family systems, 47–48
Conversations with Milton H. Erickson, 239
"Corrective loop," 333
"Correspondence theory" of knowledge, 194
Cotherapy, 457–459
    in BMT, 109
    in contextual therapy, 218–219
    mistakes in, 459–460
Cotherapy dyad, 457–460
Counseling and Values, 608
Countertransference, 19, 231, 259, 274
The Count of Monte Cristo, 195
Couple, as unit of diagnosis, 17
Couples Communication Program, 503
Couples communication workshops, 14
Couples Relationship Enhancement
    Program, 503
Crisis induction, 439
Critique of Pure Reason, 242
Cross-generational coalition, 426–427
Cutoffs, 53–54
Cybernetic epistemology, 331
Cybernetics, 27, 144, 171–172
    Gregory Bateson in early beginnings of,
        41–43
    as process, 41
"Cybernetics of cybernetics," 173, 332, 334,
    336
    basic premise of, 336
Cybernetic systems theory, 42

Deafness, sex and, 491
Defending oneself
    in Brief Therapy, 187
    in problem solving, 177–178
Demand-withdrawal pattern, 103
Denominationalism versus secularization,
    34–35
Depression, domestic conflicts following, 11
"Destructive entitlement," 206, 210, 212,
    226–227
Detouring-attacking triad, 429
Detouring-protecting triad, 429
Deviance, tolerance of, 71–72
Deviant behavior, recognition of, 73
Diabetes, 488–489
Diagnostic and Statistical Manual of Mental
    Disorders (revised third edition) (DSM-
    R-III), 174, 495, 505
Dialectical model, 201
Dichotomies, 167–168
Differentiation, 140–144, 203
    concept of, 137
    connectedness and, 434
    leadership and, 146–147
    as process, 141
    proximity and protoplasm, 156–157
    religious commitment in ministers and,
        148
    scale of, 142–143
    of self, 207
    as term, 140–141
    theoretical significance of, 141
    of therapist, 152, 157, 164
Digital communication, 44
Directive, as term, 98
Disabled, sex and, 491–492
Discontinuous change, 50
Disease, 209

Disengaged families, 426, 429, 434
Disengagement/enmeshment typology, 426
Disjunctive moves, 206
Distributive injustice, 225
Distributive justice, 210
Divorce, 508–523
    blended-family formation, 521
    in Chinese-American families, 564
    damaging effects of, 511
    decision to divorce, 516–517
    distancing, 514
    dual-family functioning, 522
    extramarital affairs and, 531
    heightened ambivalence, 514
    incidence of, 508, 525
    litigation, 518–519
    mediation, 518
    physical separation, 515
    postdivorce coparenting, 519–520
    potential disputes, 518–519
    predivorce fantasies, 516
    preparation fantasies and actions, 514–515
    pseudoreconciliation, 516
    recurring ambivalence, 517–518
    remarriage, 520–521
    repercussions of, 512
    second marriage, 521–522
    steps in process of, 513t
    suicide and, 508
Divorced and remarried families, 525–544
    child adjustment, 536–538
    child-custody arrangements, 533–536
    coevolutionary, developmental
        perspective, 528–529
    dysfunctional triangles, 542
    economic distress, 529–530
    emotional turmoil, 532
    facilitating divorce and remarriage
        processes, 543–544
    family belief system, 532–533
    family-life-cycle variables, 541–542
    family paradigms, myths, and realities,
        539
    intervention guidelines, 543
    kin and social support, 531–532
    language, beliefs, and practice, 527–528
    physical upheaval, 530–531
    postdivorce family organization, 529–538
    remarried-family adaptation, 538–544
    reworking previous divorce issues,
        539–540
    sibling relationships, 542
    stepparent relationships and child
        adjustment, 540–541
Divorce therapy, 510–511
Double bind, in schizophrenia, 28, 32
    defining conditions of, 46
    most quoted example of, 46
    proving existence of, 47
Double bind theory, 46–47, 364
"The Double Bind Theory of
    Schizophrenia," 172
Drug dependency, 488
Drugs, for schizophrenia medication, 377
Drug therapy, and biological research,
    365–366
"Dual therapy," 27
Dyadic Adjustment Scale (DAS), 105
"Dynamic equilibrium," 42
Dysfunction, defining, 72
Dysfunctional family
    behavioral analysis of, 72–74
    characteristics of interaction in, 299
    characteristics of, 449
    coalitions in, 450
    conflict avoidance in, 451

contextual therapy and, 209–214
description of dysfunctional structures,
    426–427
dysfunctional processes, 450
emotional communication among family
    members, 73
excessive expression of noncontingent
    positive feelings, 74
explanation of, 427–428
family context as "beneficiary" of
    symptom, 428–429
family context as ineffectual challenger,
    428
family context as "shaper" of individual,
    428
family psychoeducational treatment and,
    370–371
lack of clearly defined family rules, 73
Milan approach and, 340–342
nonfunctional subsystems in, 449–450
recognition of deviant behavior in, 73
relationship between structure and
    symptom, 428–429
role rigidity and sex stereotyping in, 450
specific correlations between structures
    and symptoms, 429
and structural family therapy, 425–429
structure of, 53
style of negative communication in, 73
symbolic-experiential family therapy and,
    449–452
symptom bearer, 429
Dyspareunia, 493

Eastern Pennsylvania Psychiatric Institute,
    Philadelphia, 29, 201
Ecosystemic epistemology, 57, 332
Education
    of family, 81
    on marriage, 8
    on parenting, 7–8
    in solving social problems, 7
Educational workshops for families,
    374–375, 380–381
Ejaculatory incompetence, 493–494
Emotional, as term in Bowen therapy, 136
Emotional system
    in Bowen theory, 144–147
    leadership and differentiation, 146–147
    similarity to field theory, 145–147
    as term, 144
Emotional triangle, 150–151
Empathic expression, 74
Empathy, 264, 415
Empirical measurement, 194
Empirical verification, 36
Enactive formulation, 418
Enactments, 420, 432, 438
Enmeshed families, 429, 434
Enmeshment, 156
Entitlement, as comotivator, 204
Environment, relationships and, 101
Epistemological truth, 57
Epistemology, of family theory and therapy,
    56–59
    definition, 56
"Epistemology of participation," 337
Equitable asymmetry, 206, 227
Equitable symmetry, 232
Ericksonian family therapy, 239–281
    acquiring experiential and interpersonal
        skills, 273–274
    ambiguous function assignments, 271–272
    assessment of system functioning,
        250–254
    case illustration, 276–281

common and serious technical errors,
    272–273
creating changes in family experience, 266
curative factors in marital-family therapy,
    273–275
dealing with times when change does not
    happen, 272
duration of therapy, 258
ethics of approach, 275–276
family problems, 245–250
goal setting, 254–257
homework and out-of-session tasks,
    270–272
hypnosis as modality for communication,
    266–270
importance of technique, 275
intake interview, 252
interpretations in, 273
question of standard structure, 257
rationale and philosophy, 240–241
role of psychotropic medications, 257–258
role of therapist in, 259–261
selection of particular techniques for
    specific goals, 264–266
skill-building assignments, 271
structure of therapy process, 257–259
techniques of Ericksonian marital and
    family therapy, 261–270
time between sessions and decisions about
    structure, 258–259
transference, 274
treatment applicability, 275–276
utilization in, 241, 261–264
variety in therapy session, 261
well-functioning marriage and family,
    243–245
Error-activated feedback, 43
"Error-activated" information, 50
Esalen Institute, Big Sur, Calif., 29
Ethical and legal issues, 36–37
"Ethical Principles for Family Therapists,"
    608
Ethics. See also Values and ethics
    in contextual therapy, 204–205
    definition, 610
Ethnic intermarriage, 566–574
    attitudes toward marriage, 570
    children of intermarriage, 572
    factors influencing, 567–568
    family context of marriage, 571–572
    life-cycle framework, 573–574
    male and female roles, 570–571
    patterns of, 568–570
Ethnicity, 546–580
    African-American families, 556–562
    assessment and treatment of recent
        refugees, 574–577
    Chinese-American families, 562–566
    defining, 547
    ethnic intermarriage, 566–574
    Irish families, 550–553
    mental health and, 547–550
    Puerto Rican families, 553–556
    training in ethnicity, 577–579
Ethnicity and Family Therapy, 550
Europe
    first organized family therapy training
        program in, 29–30
    sexual counseling in, 15
The Evaluation and Treatment of Marital
    Conflict, 134
Evolutionary feedback, 333
Exoneration, 226–227
Experiential alternatives, 458
Expert power, 36
Exploitation, 213

Expressed emotion (EE), 366–367
Extended-family reunions, 464
External-fixation methods, 270
Extramarital sex (EMS), 498–499
  conjoint marital therapy and, 127
  divorce and, 531

Families and Family Therapy,
  "Families of origin," 299
Families of the Slums, 30, 418, 419, 420, 426
Family. *See also* Dysfunctional family, *and*
    Well-functioning family
  age appropriate and age-inappropriate
      hierarchical arrangements in, 54
  behavioral analysis of family dysfunction,
      72–74
  behavioral assessment of family
      functioning, 74–78
  belief-action ecology of, 341
  boundaries of, 446
  chronological development of, 49
  clinical definition of, 27
  communication and metacommunication
      in, 44–46
  communication-interaction patterns, 78
  coping skills of, 77
  cutoffs in, 54
  as cybernetic system, 43
  definition, 69
  differentiation between members of, 53
  differentiation from, 18
  effect of schizophrenia on, 367–369
  ethnic and cultural expectations of, 69
  as "the family group," 52
  first-order change and, 51
  fragmentation of, 202
  function of, 422
  goals of, and therapist's goals, 433–434
  goals of individual members of, 77, 79
  homeostatic mechanisms of, 28
  as homeostatic system, 43
  interviews with, 11
  intimacy and members of, 70–71
  intrafamilial communication, 48
  life-cycle transitions in, 50
  limitations of morphogenesis, 51
  living in hospital with schizophrenic child,
      25–26
  maladaptive relationships in, 52
  mental disorders caused by interactions
      in, 28
  metaphor in, 399
  model of world of, 264
  morphogenesis in, 49
  morphostasis in, 49
  new information introduced into, 49–50
  normative data on, 69, 71
  organization of, 250–251, 252
  overinvolved interaction patterns in, 70
  pathology as byproduct of conflict in, 17
  permeable boundaries, 446–447
  points of entry into, 430
  power relations in, 55
  problem-solving skills of, 77, 78
  process of, 446
  psychoanalyzing members of same family,
      19
  reciprocal transactions in, 52
  recognition of deviant behavior in, 73
  reinforcing problem behavior in, 76
  as rule-governed system, 44
  schizophrenia and, 24, 25
  of schizophrenic, 43, 46, 47
  schizophrenic behavior in, 326
  second-order change in, 51
  self-governance in, 43

  shape of, 429–430
  social-skills training for, 82
  stagnation in, 210
  structural organization of, 446
  structure of, 53
  subsystems and boundaries, 423–424
Family functioning in focal family therapy,
    288–292
  concepts of interaction, 289–290
  episodes of interaction, 290
  holistic formulation, 291
  items of interaction, 290
  patterns of meaning, 290–291
  type formulation, 291
Family Games, 330
Family Group Therapy, 22
Family harmony, myth of, 44
Family Health Scales, 292–295
  affective life, 292–293
  alliances, 294
  boundaries, 293–294
  communication, 293
  family adaptability and stability, 294–295
  family competence, 295
Family-induced psychosomatic disorders, 31
The Family in Psychotherapy, 23
Family Institute, 23, 29
Family Institute of Chicago, 33
  as term used by Bowen, 144
  transactional patterns of, 422
  typing or categorization of, 291
  unconscious needs of members of, 52
  uncovering "truth" of, 56
  unemployment's effect on, 22–23
  as unit of treatment, 25
  unresolved issues with, 26
  will conflict in, 162
Family-counseling sessions, videotapes of,
    25, 28
Family counselors, licensing of, 13
Family Discussion Bureau, Tavistock Clinic,
    20
Family Evaluation, 134, 154
Family functioning, 74–78
  continual assessment, 78
  coping skills, 77
  functional analysis of family problems,
      75–78
  problem analysis, 74–75
  requisite formulation, 292
Family Institute of New York, 30
Family Institute of Philadelphia, 29, 31
Family interaction
  as homeostatic model, 52
  measuring, 32
  recording patterns of, 66
Family-larger-system assessment model,
    585–590
  boundaries, 587–588
  case example, 590–591
  definitions of problem, 586
  dyads, 586–587
  family and larger-systems solutions, 589
  family-larger-systems transitions, 589
  larger systems involved with family,
      585–586
  myths and beliefs, 588–589
  predictions, 590
  triads, 587
Family-larger-system interventions,
    595–597
  case example, 597–599
  methods for family therapist, 601–603
  rationale for, 585
  special issues in larger-system
      interactions, 599–601

Family legacy, 467
Family-life-education movement, 3, 6, 7, 9
Family-life educators, philosophy and goals
    of, 9
"Family management," as term, 79
Family Mental Health Clinic at Jewish
    Family Services, New York, 23
Family models, 51–56
  Bowen models, 53–54
  psychoanalytic model, 51–52
  strategic models, 54
  structural model, 53
  systemic model, 55–56
Family myths, 44
"Family of procreation," 299
Family problems, 245–250
  factors influencing type of symptom,
      249–250
  memos and reports as interventions,
      596–597
  rituals, 595–596
  task delineation and redistribution, 595
Family-larger-system interviewing, 591–593
  case example, 593–594
  interviewing family about larger systems,
      591–592
  interviewing family members and
      multiple helpers, 592–593
  interviewing larger system
      representatives without family
      members present, 594
Family-larger-system perspective, 583–604
  background, 583–585
  family-larger-system assessment model,
      585–590
  family-larger-system interventions,
      595–597
  family-larger-system interviewing,
      591–593
  how problems can develop, 247–248
  interactional nature of problems, 245–247
  symptom formation and identified
      patients, 249
Family Process, 20, 24, 25, 27, 30, 32, 33, 35
  first issue of, 29
  founding of, 21, 23
Family Psychiatric Unit, Tavistock Clinic, 20
Family psychoeducational treatment,
    363–393
  alterations of family interaction, 386
  assessment of system functioning,
      371–373
  attention-arousal hypothesis, 367–368
  background of approach, 363–368
  building social networks, 384, 386–387
  case illustration, 390–393
  community reentry, 381–382, 382–383
  controlling rate of change, 386
  core paradigm for treatment in single- and
      multifamily contexts, 37wf
  diagnosis, 388–389
  drug therapy and biological research,
      365–366
  dysfunctional family, 370–371
  early theories and practice, 364
  educational workshop, 374–375, 380–381
  education of family, 386
  effects of deinstitutionalization, 365
  effects of ongoing family intervention, 386
  ethical issues, 390
  family characteristics, 389
  format and social structure of sessions,
      374–376
  general definition of, 364
  goal setting, 373–374
  joining, 374, 379–380

levels of change, 384
mechanisms of change, 384–387
medication issues, 377
multiple-family therapy, 365
outcome evaluation, 390
psychosocial factors and course of illness, 366–367
reducing ambient stress and stimulation, 385–386
reentry and social-vocational rehabilitation phases, 375–376
role of therapist in, 377–379
social and vocational rehabilitation, 382, 383–384
special issues in marital therapy, 387–388
specific techniques in psycho-educational multiple-family groups, 382–384
structure of sessions, 376–377
structure of therapy process, 374–377
techniques in psychoeducation, 379–384
termination issues, 387
treatment applicability, 388–390
variables affecting change, 385
well-functioning family, 368–370
Family Service Associations of America, 5
Family system
in Brief Therapy, 193–194
change and status quo in, 49
Palo Alto's focus on whole family, 43
resistance to change, 55
as rule governed system, 193
Family theory, epistemology of, 56–59
Family therapists, 26
Family therapy
Adlerian thought in, 21
certification standards for training in, 34
clinical issues in, 492–499
confidentiality in, 624
deception in, 615–621
epistemology of, 56–59
evaluating lies in, 619–620
Gestalt therapy and, 52
importance of individual in, 43
indirect suggestions and binds in, 262–263
informational bind of, 144–145
informed consent in, 623–624
looking at whole family, 4
models of, 51–56
origin of, 4
as port of entry of cybernetic ideas, 43
psychoanalysis versus, 26
psychoanalytic origins of, 284–286
as shift in epistemology, 192–193
as subspecialty, 5
Family therapy as context for sex therapy, 479–505
alcoholism, 488
anorgasmia, 492–493
birth control, 484–485
cancer, 487–488
clinical decision making and sexual assessment, 499–502
couples issues, 483–484
desire-phase concerns, 494–495
developmental concerns, 484–492
diabetes, 488–489
drug dependency, 488
dyspareunia, 493
ejaculatory incompetence, 493–494
evolution of, 480–481
extramarital sex, 498–499
fertility issues, 485
gender issues, 505
heart disease, 489
homosexuality, 497–498

incest, 496–497
legal and ethical dimensions, 504–505
menopause, 485
parent education, 484
posttraumatic sexual-assault syndrome, 496
premature ejaculation, 493
presenting complaints, 481–482
prostatitis, 489
relationship issues, 482–483
sex and aging, 486
sex and disabled, 491–492
sex therapies, 502–504
sexual addiction, 495
sexually transmitted diseases, 489–491
sexual variations, 498
singles and, 487
vaginismus, 493
Family Therapy in Clinical Practice, 134
Family-therapy journals and newsletters, 35
Family-therapy movement, 20–33
Ackerman, Nathan W., 22–23
Bell, John, 21–22
Boston and, 31–32
Bowen, Murray, 25–26
Chicago, Illinois, in, 33
current scene: mid-1970s to present, 33–37
empirical verification, 36
ethical and legal issues, 36–37
feminist movement and, 35–36
first meeting of, 27
founding decade: 1952–1961, 21–30
Galveston, Texas, in, 32
gender issues, 35–36
homogenization versus specialization, 33–34
internationalization, 35
Lidz, Theodore, 24
Midelfort, Christian F., 23–24
Milan, Italy, in, 32–33
New York City in, 30–31
Palo Alto in, 32
Palo Alto Group in, 27–29
Philadelphia in, 31
Philadelphia Group in, 29–30
precursors, 20–21
"second wave," 1962–1977, 30–33
secularization versus denominationalism, 34–35
Whitaker, Carl A., 26–27
Wynne, Lyman C., 24–25
Family-therapy research, 624–628
confidentiality in, 626–627
informed consent and, 625–626
risks and benefits to families, 627–628
Family Therapy Techniques, 421
Fathers
in schizmogenesis process, 24
as sexual offender, 411
role of, in family, 425
Fear, anxiety distinguished from, 140
Federation of Parents and Friends of Lesbians and Gays, 491
Feedback, 42
Feminism
contextual therapy and, 207–208
family therapy and, 35–36, 607, 615, 623
sex and, 479
Feminists, on female sexuality, 17
Feminist therapists, 36
Fertility issues, 485
Field, definition of, 146
Field theory, 145–147
Filial loyalty, 205
First-order change, 49

First-order cybernetics, 339
Focal family therapy, 284–322
assessment for therapy, 305–309
case illustration: G. family, 317–322
derivation of meaning, 295–301
describing family, 288
detailed analysis of initial assessment, 310–311t
development of, 287–288
Family Diagnostic Interview, 306
Family Health Scales, 292–295
family pathology, classification of, 302
Focal (Family) Therapy Assessment Sheet, 307–309
focal formulation of G. family, 312–313f
Focal Therapy Record Sheet (FTRS), 315–317
historical perspective, 284–288
holistic formulation, 301–305
mechanism of change, 309–311
psychoanalysis and family therapy today, 286–287
role of therapist in, 315
seven-level description of family functioning, 288–292
social-systems model, 288, 289f
structuring therapy, 311–314
therapy process, 309–322
Framing statement, 28
Functional analysis
as behavioral marital therapy, 97–98
of family problems, 74–78
Functional family
adaptation and development, 424–425
hierarchy, 424
stages of, 424
Functional family and structural family therapy, 421–425
complementarity, 422–423
family function and individual, 422
generic and idiosyncratic constraints, 422
maintenance and change, 425
structure, 422–425
subsystems and boundaries, 423–424
Fundamentalism, 166
Fusion
Bowen's concept of, 156
with client, 157

Galveston, Texas, in family-therapy movement, 32
Gay couples, 469
parenting by, 536
Gender and ethics in family therapy, 628–633
competence, 630–631
integrity, 631–632
power and, 633
professional development, 632
responsibility to clients, 629–630
social and legal responsibilities, 632
Gender issues, 35–36, 103–104
Gender-role flexibility, 447
"Generalized other," 18
General systems theory. *See* Systems theory
Generation to Generation: Family Process in Church and Synagogue, 134
Genetic determinism, 146
Genograms, 54, 151
Genograms in Family Assessment, 134
Georgetown Family Center, 135
Georgetown University, 26
German Marriage Consultation Bureau, 7
Geschlechtskunde (Sex Education), 6–7
Goal setting, in Ericksonian family therapy, 254–257

cocreation in, 255–256
discussing treatment goals with family, 256–257
general treatment goals, 254–255
Gonorrhea, 489–490
Great Britain, marriage counselors in, 11
Growth, accomplishing, 247
Guidelines for Conducting Therapy, 346
Guilt feelings, 216–217
Gutmacher Institute, 485

Habits of the Heart: Individualism and Commitment in American Life, 611
Handicapped family members, larger systems and, 600–601
Healing
natural systems view of, 161–164
as self-regenerative phenomenon, 159–160
Heart disease, 489
Herpes, 490
Helsinki Code of Ethics on Human Experimentation, 624
Hispanic, as term, 553
Historical insight, 465–466
Holistic formulation, in focal family therapy, 301–305
current situation and link to past trauma, 303–304
disaster feared by family, 303
function of current interaction, 303
requisite changes, 304
summarizing focal hypothesis, 304
symptom as part of interaction, 301–303
Holon, 423
Homeostasis, 43, 67
as process in different contexts, 44
Homeostatic model, 52
"Home therapy sessions," 110
Homogenization, specialization versus, 33–34
Homosexuality, 497–498
AIDS and, 491
Havelock Ellis on, 6
Human brain
mechanical models of, 41
role of, 161
Human-growth movement, 29
Human Sexual Anatomy, 15
Human Sexual Inadequacy, 4, 16–17
Human Sexual Response, 16
Humor, in family therapy, 464
Hypersexuality. *See* Sexual addiction
Hypnosis, 265–266, 266–270, 274, 652
external-fixation methods, 270
induction-sequence outline, 268f
internal-fixation methods, 268–270
search phenomena in, 270
Hypnotherapy, 241

Identified patient, 75
Ideomotor response, 270
Illinois State Psychiatric Institute, 29
Illness, sex and, 492
Immune system, 209
self and, 156
Inanimate systems, as model, 50
Incest, 496–497
Index patient, 75
Individual
in family therapy, 43
as subsystem of family, 48
Individual therapy
conjoint family therapy versus, 79
limitations of, 201
Individuation and differentiation, 53–54

Induction, 439
Information
definition, 55
informational bind and family therapy, 145
origin of, 49–50
Information gathering, 334
Informed consent
in family therapy, 623–624
in family-therapy research, 625–626
principle of, 36
Inhibited sexual desire (ISD), 494–495
Inner life, 52
Inside the Family, 32
Insight, 87, 118, 230, 241, 349, 465–466
Institute for Family Studies in Milan, Italy, 33
Institute for Juvenile Research, Chicago, Illinois, 33
Institute for Social Psychiatry, London, England, 366
Institute of Sexual Science, 6
Instrumental behaviors, 100
Intake interview, in Ericksonian family therapy, 252
Interactional insight, 466
Intergenerational relatedness, 207
"Interlocking-need templates," 213
International Congress for Sexual Reform on a Scientific Basis, 6
International Congresses on Ericksonian Approaches to Therapy, 240
Internationalization, 35
Interpersonal checklist (ICL), 252–253
"Interventive interviewing," 334
Intimacy, 208, 448
conflict over, 125
expectations and definitions of, 70–71
marital distress over, 103
Intrafamilial communication, 48
Invariant prescription, 330
Invisible Loyalties, 30
Invisible loyalty, 211–212
Irish families, 550–553
family structure, 551
help seeking, 550
interactional style, 550–551
life-cycle transitions, 551–552
treatment implications, 552–553

Jamming, 187
Jewish Family Services, Family Mental Health Clinic at, 23
Jewish Institute on Marriage and the Family, New York, 11
Joining, 435, 437, 461
in family psychoeducational treatment, 379–380
as term, 181
Joining systems theory with psychodynamic understanding. *See* Focal family therapy
Josiah Macy conferences, 41
Journal of Divorce, 510
Journal of Heredity, 7, 10
Journal of Marital and Family Counseling, 14
Journal of Marriage and the Family, 510
Journal of Sex and Marital Therapy, 17, 501
Journal of Sex Education and Therapy, 17

Kegel exercises, 486

Ladies' Home Journal, "Can This Marriage Be Saved?," 10
Language
as consensual agreement, 336

symbolic function of, 466
"Law of nature," 198
Leadership, through self-differentiation, 146–147
Learning model, 100–101
Ledger concept, 205–206
"Left brain," 138
Legacy, as term, 205
Legacy-based treatment goals, 215–216
Lesbian couples, 469, 483–484
parenting by, 536
Libido, 140
Life-cycle transitions, in structural model, 53
Linear thinking, 48
Locke-Wallace Marriage Inventory, 501
Logical types, 27–28, 45
Longitudinal designs, in studies, 103
"Looking-glass self," 18
Loyalty, 207, 225–226
Loyalty conflict, 211
Lutheran Hospital, LaCrosse, Wisconsin, 23
Lying: Moral Choice in Public and Private Life, 619

Machismo, 554, 555
Maintenance, 437
Maladaptive relationships, 52
Male climacteric, 486
Male/female dichotomy, 168
Manipulation, in therapy, 617–618
Marital distress, 104–108
behavioral analysis of, 102–103
over amount of intimacy, 103
in women versus men, 104
Marital dyad, behavior exchanges in, 96–97
Marital enrichment movement, 14
Marital quid pro quo, 44
Marital relationships, 97–104
behavioral analysis of marital distress, 102
behavioral approach to marital therapy, 97–98
BMT and successful marriage, 99–102
cognition and BMT, 98–99
gender issues, 103–104
marital distress as outcome of conflict over intimacy, 103
symmetry of rights and responsibilities in, 206
Marital Satisfaction Inventory (MSI), 105
Marital therapy
applicability of, 127–128
behavioral approach to, 97–98
certification standards for training in, 34
for couples in acute crisis, 128
frequency of publications on, 13t
history of, 3–37
origin of, 4
politics and, 125–126
for schizophrenic patients, 387–388
separation or divorce versus, 127–128
Marriage
conflict resolution in, 103
education for, 8
Groves' "functional" approach to, 8
women's movement and, 102
Marriage and Family Counseling, 11
Marriage and Family Living, 9
Marriage Counseling, 11
Marriage counseling
licensing for, 13
professional articles on, 13–14
as subspecialty, 5
as term, 10
textbooks on, 11
Marriage-counseling movement, 4

Marriage Counseling Practice, 11
Marriage-counseling profession, 9–15
  Phase I: 1929–1932, 9–10
  Phase II: 1934–1945, 10–11
  Phase III: 1946–1965, 11–13
  Phase IV: Consolidation and maturation,
    13–15
Marriage counselors
  AAMC/National Council on Family
    Relations standards for, 12f
  standards for, 11
  training for, 13
Marriage Council of Philadelphia, 10, 11
Married couples, psychoanalysis of, 19
Married Guidance Council, 11
Massachusetts General Hospital, 31
Maturation, time necessary for, 162
Meanings and dimensions of family life,
    295–301
  common meanings, 297–298
  intersubjective meanings, 298
  proposed typology, 300–301
  stress and development of dysfunction,
    299–300
Mediating goals, 454–455, 469
Medication, prescribing, 344
Men
  aging and, 486–487
  conflict-avoidance in, 125
  marital power differential favoring, 125
  role of, 126
Menninger Clinic, Topeka, Kansas, 11, 23,
    25
Menopause, 485
Mental handicap, communication and, 82
Mental Research Institute (MRI), 29, 32, 54,
    71, 242. *See also* Brief therapy
  Brief Therapy Center at, 32
  founding of, 173
  goal of, 173
Mental retardation, sex and, 491–492
Merrill-Palmer School, Detroit, 11
Message, "command" aspect of, 45
Meta change, 329
"Meta" communication, 45–46
Metacomplementarity, 17
"Metamessage," 29
Metaphor, 466
Metaphor-construction protocols, 269f
"Metaphysics of pattern," 194
Metastatement, 28
Metasystem, 45
Milan approach to therapy, 325–360, 364,
    551
  aim of therapy, 349
  assessment of system functioning and
    dysfunction, 342
  background of, 325–338
  birth of, 325–327
  case illustration, 355–360
  circularity in, definition of, 328
  circular questioning, 346
  dysfunctional family and, 340–342
  ethical issues and, 354–355
  fifth stage (1979–present), 334–336
  five parts of family-therapy session, 326
  fourth stage (1979–present), 332–334
  "games" families play, 327
  goal setting, 343
  mechanisms of change, 348–351
  neutrality, 328–329
  rituals in families, 327
  role of therapist, 344–346
  second stage (1975–1979), 328–330
  sixth stage (1983–present), 336–338
  special issues in marital therapy, 351–353

structure of therapy process, 343–344
  techniques of marital family therapy,
    346–348
  terminating therapy, 348
  third stage (1979–1982), 330–332
  treatment applicability, 353–355
  well-functioning family and, 338–340
Milan, Italy, in family-therapy movement,
    32–33
Milan associates, 331
Milan Center for the Study of the Family,
    325
Milan group, 54, 55, 56, 467
Milieu interieur, 43
Milton H. Erickson Foundation, Phoenix,
    Arizona, 240
Minnesota Couples Communications
    Program, 14
Modeling, 68, 117
Morphogenesis, 49–51, 461
  limitations of, 51
Morphostasis, 49–51
Mother
  depression in, 75
  empathy between child and, 18
  parenting role of, 209
  primary object love for, 201
  schizophrenia and, 28
  "schizophrenogenic" mother, 47
  "symbiosis" between child and, 25
  in therapy of disturbed child, 25
MRI. *See* Mental Research Institute
Multidirectional partiality, 222–224
  application of, 233
  techniques of, 230
Multigenerational contractual ethics, 218
Multigenerational transmission, in Bowen
    theory, 147–150
  clinical example of, 148–149
  continuous natural process and, 148
  deemphasis on asymptomatology in, 149
  significance of, 148
  "working on one's family of origin," 148
Multilateral contract, 217
Multilateral contractual approach, 200
Multilateral therapeutic contract, 201, 202
Multiple therapeutic contract, 201, 202
Multiple family group sessions, 79–80
Multiple-family PE (MFPE), 373, 375, 378,
    384, 386
Multiple-family therapy (MFT), for
    schizophrenics and their families, 365
Multiple-impact family-therapy model
    (MIFT), 562
Multiple-impact therapy, 32
Multiple transference, 19
"Multiproblem" families, 583
"The Myth of the primary site," 149

Narcissism, 285
National Advisory Committee on Standards
    for Education and Training, 34
National Council on Family Relations, 9, 11
  Counseling Section of, 14
National family-therapy movements, 35
National Guidance Council of Great Britain,
    11
National Institute of Mental Health (NIMH),
    153
  Laboratory of Socioenvironmental Studies
    at, 25
Nature/nurture, 167
Naven ceremony, 42
Negative feedback, 42–43
Negentrop, 328
Negotiations and contracts, 403

Network coupling, 512
Network therapy, 31
Neuropsychiatric reductionism, 43
Neurotic Interaction in Marriage, 20
Neutrality concept, 328, 334, 355
New Jersey Neuropsychiatric Institute, 20
The New Sex Therapy, 493
Newtonian physics, 242
New York City, family-therapy movement
    and, 30–31
New York group, 15
New York Labor Temple, 10
New York Neurological Society, 19
New York Psychoanalytic Institute, 20
Ninth International Congress of
    Psychoanalysis, 19
Nodal events, 464
Nonnormative model, 174
Non-specific urethritis (NSU), 490
Nonverbal communication, 44–45
No-risk methods of problem solving, 176
Normative models, 174
Northwestern Medical School, Department
    of Psychiatry, 33
Nuremberg trials, 624

Oath of Hippocrates, 36
Objectivity. *See also* Differentiation
  asking questions and, 155
  change and, 153–154
  perception and, 195
"Objectivity in parentheses," 337
Object narcissism, 285–286
Object relations theory, 298
"Odd days and even days" prescription, 347
One-down position, 181
One-way mirror, 28
On Sex and Human Loving, 493
Open system, 50
Operant conditioning, 66, 67, 96
  strategies, 83–84
Opposition
  in reaching interpersonal accord, 177
  seeking accord through, 186–187
Optimal resource potential, 217
Oregon group, 14
Orgasmic dysfunction. *See* Anorgasmia
Orthopsychiatry movement, 5
Out from the Shadows, 495
Overfocusing on content, 440

Palo Alto, in family-therapy movement, 32
Palo Alto group, 14, 25, 27–29, 42
  causality issues, 48
  double bind theory, 46–47
  family as cybernetic system, 43
  family as homeostatic system, 43
  family as rule-governed system, 44
  family communication and
    metacommunication, 44–46
  issues of control and power, 47–48
  issues of levels and language, 48
  legacy of, 47–48
  role of, 43–47
  schizophrenia and, 28
Paradox, 153, 333
  in Brief Therapy, 185
  in systems theory, 55
Paradox and Counterparadox, 326, 327
Paradoxical injunction, 185, 326
Paradoxical interventions, 616
Paradoxical prescription, 267, 271, 326
"Parallel parenting," 527
Paraprofessionals, 11
"The Parental imperative," 205
Parental subsystem, 423

Parent-child relationship, asymmetry of, 206
Parent-education movement, 3
Parentification, 213–214
Parenting, education on, 7–8
Parents
    destructive relationship between, 24
    exploitation by, 213
    parent-training approach to child
        management, 87, 88
    sex education by, 484
Pathology, natural systems view of, 160–161
Patients Have Families, 20
Pennsylvania State University, 14
Persona (or mask), 18
Personality, as subsystem of family system,
    24
Philadelphia, family-therapy movement and,
    31
Philadelphia Child Guidance Clinic, 29, 31,
    419–420, 427
Philadelphia Group, 29–30
Philadelphia Psychiatric Center, 31
Pinpointing, 74, 120
P-LI-SS-IT model, 499–500
Postgraduate professional marriage
    counselors, 11
Position, as term, 178–179
Positive, deviation-amplifying feedback, 49,
    56
Positive behavior change, in BMT, 110
Positive communication, 73, 74
Positive connotation, 327
Positive feedback, 42, 49, 50, 51
    pragmatic importance of, 51
Positive framing, 261, 264, 267
Posttraumatic sexual-assault syndrome, 496
Posttraumatic stress disorder, 575
Poverty, families in, 601
Power
    in family systems, 47–48
    myth of, 338
    struggle for, 17
The Practice of Marriage Counseling, 11
Pragmatics of Human Communication, 32,
    326
Pregnancy, in teenagers, 485
Premature ejaculation, 17, 493
Pretreatment assessment, 108
    therapist contacts in, 107
    what to learn from, 106–107
Problem(s), 173–175
    attempted solutions, 175–178
    definition of, 174
    general definitions of, 174
    Haley's definition of, 397
    how problems arise and persist, 175
    therapeutic distinction and implications,
        174–175
Problem analysis, 74–75
Problem behavior, reinforcing, 76–77
Problem-determined systems, 338, 339
"The Problem of the Referring Person," 329
Problem-solution cycle, 182
Problem solving, 243–244
    fighting versus, 122
Problem-solving sessions, 119–123
    general guidelines, 119–120
    guidelines for defining problems, 120–121
    guidelines for reaching agreement, 121
    tendency of spouses to defend themselves,
        122
Problem-solving skills, 100
Problem-Solving Therapy, 607
Problem-solving training, 82–83
    in BMT, 110
    generalization, 123

pinpointing in, 120
    summary and conclusions regarding,
        121–123
    terminating, 123
Prostatectomy, 488
Prostatitis, 489
"Pseudomutuality" concept, 48
Psychiatric thinking, process and pattern in,
    43
Psychiatrists, power of, 48
Psychoanalysis
    and family therapy today, 286–287
    family therapy versus, 26
    on instinctual libidinal drive, 17
    objectivity and, 153–154
Psychoanalysts, fleeing Europe, 18
Psychoanalytic concepts, systems theory
    and, 52
The Psychoanalytic Study of the Family, 20
Psychoanalytic theory, 444
Psychodynamic (psychoanalytic) model, 193
The Psychodynamics of Family Life, 22, 23
Psychoeducational approach, 68
"A Psychogenetic Fantasy," 169
Psychosomatic Families, 420
Psychotherapy by Reciprocal Inhibition, 17
*Psychotherapy of Chronic Schizophrenic
    Patients*, 27
"Psychotherapy of the Absurd," 467
Psychotropic medications, 257–258
Puerto Rican families, 553–556
    divorce in, 555–556
    extended family, 555–556
    family loyalty, 554
    family structure, 554–555
    life-cycle transitions, 555
    machismo, 554, 555
    spirituality and individualism, 553–554
    treatment implications, 556
Punctuation, 46, 432

Rape, 496
Rational-emotive therapy, 480, 503
Reality
    consensual agreement and, 336–337
    constructivism and, 194, 195–196
    knowledge as, 194
    scientific method and, 196
    secular-scientific view of, 197
A Real Story of a Real Family, 4
Reciprocity, 66, 67, 70, 99
Referent power, 36
"Reflected appraisals," 18
Reflexive questions, 344, 347
Reframing, 435, 466–467
Refugees
    assessment, 576–577
    mental health problems in, 575
    stressors of, 575–576
Rejection-intrusion, 103
Rejunctive moves, 206
"Relational reality," 230–231
"Relational stagnation," 206
Relational therapy, interethnic issues in, 35
"The Relationship of Family Theory to
    Family Therapy," 650
Relationships
    distressed, 99
    environment and, 101
    lack of training in skills of maintaining, 100
    multilateral nature of, 204
    reward-cost ratio in, 99
    success of, 101
    trust in, 204
Remarriage, 469–470. *See also* Divorced and
    remarried families

"Remarried family," as term, 528
Remarried-family functioning model,
    544
"Report" aspect of message, 45
*Report of the FSAA Committee on Marriage
    Counseling*, 5
Reports and commands, 183
Rescuing maneuver, 440
Research and evaluation in training and
    supervision, 676–685
    accreditation and credentialing issues,
        687
    contexts of training, 686–687
    family life of therapist, 686
    five-step process of training program
        evaluation, 677
    instruments to measure therapist
        behavior, 678–679
    integrative models of supervision, 686
    live supervision, 682–683
    mission of family-therapy training, 687
    program-evaluation studies, 679–680
    research-utilization problem in clinical
        practice, 687–688
    reviews of specialty areas, 677–678
    special topics of supervision, 687
    studies of personal characteristics of
        therapists/trainees, 684
    studies on trainee skill development,
        680–681
    studies on training methods, 681–682
    supervisor development, 687
    trainee perceptions of training and
        supervision, 684–685
    training trainers, 686
    training within different disciplines, 687
    treatment manuals, 686
    videotape use, 683–684
Resistance, 272
    in contextual therapy, 229–230
    in symbolic-experiential model, 465
"Resistant family," 347
Reuniting family members, 405–406
Reversal, 153
Revolving slate, 226
Reward-cost ratio, in relationships, 99
"Right brain," 138
Risk, in problem solving, 176–177
Rituals, 403
Role rehearsal, 68
Roles, as defenses, 52
The Roots of Psychotherapy, 444
"Rotating scapegoat," 447
"Rubber fence" concept, 48
Rules
    governing marital relationships, 44
    in systems theory, 42

Saturday Evening Post, 25
"Schism" condition, 24
Schismogenesis
    definition of, 42
    fathers in, 24
Schizophrenia
    antipsychotics in, 365–366
    Bateson on, 172
    causality in, 370
    in children, 25–26, 52
    dopamine for, 366
    double bind in, 28
    double bind theory of, 172
    effect on family, 364, 367–369
    family and, 24, 25
    gliosis in, 366
    negative feedback and, 43
    Palo Alto group and, 28

prognosis for patients with, 363
psychotherapy for, 18
undifferentiated ego mass in, 53
ventricular enlargement in, 366
Schizophrenic, family of, 46, 47
"Schizophrenogenic" mother, 47, 209
Scientific method, 194
reality and, 196
Seal Island Conference, 1955, 446
Second-order change, 49
Second-order cybernetics. *See* "Cybernetics of cybernetics"
Second-order meaning system, 354
Secularization versus denominationalism, 34–35
Secular-scientific view of reality, 197
Self
concept of, 18
differentiation of, 207
evolutionary emergence of, 135
immune system and, 156
loss of, in relationships, 157
relational definition of, 207
Self-corrective feedback, 41
Self-delineation, 203–204
Self-fulfilling prophecy, 245
Self narcissism, 285
Self-object delineation, 207
Self Starvation, 325–326
Self-validation, 207
contextual therapy and, 216–217, 220
Sex
aging and, 486
disabled and, 491–492
as legitimate scientific research, 7
as metaphor, 479
singles and, 487
Sexological exams, 501–502
Sex therapy, 502–504
couples therapy, 503–504
goal meeting, 502
group therapy, 504
history, 15–17
individual therapy, 503
multiple-family groups, 504
standards of certification for, 16
structures of therapy, 502–504
Sex-therapy movement, 4
Sexual addiction, 495
Sexual Adjustment Inventory, 501
Sexual Arousal Inventory, 501
Sexual Behavior in the Human Female, 16
Sexual counseling in America compared with Europe, 15
Sexual dysfunction
as "anxiety," 480
chemical dependency and alcoholism and, 488
earliest understanding of, 480
as "moral degeneracy," 480
as "psychosexual immaturity," 480
Sexual genograms, 500–501
Sexual histories, 500
Sexuality
confusion regarding, 480
ethnicity and, 481
Sexual Interaction Inventory, 501
Sexually transmitted diseases, 487, 489–491
Sexual-marital-adjustment inventories, 501
Sexual problems
Freud on, 15
increase in, following World War I, 4
Sexual-reform movement, 6–7
Sexual revolution, 480, 481
Sexual variations, 498
Shaping procedures, 83

Sibling relationships, divorce and remarriage and, 542
Sibling subsystem, 423
Single-family PE (SFPE), 371, 373, 375
"Single-parent family," 527
Singles and sex, 487
"Skew" condition, 24
Skill, performance versus, 100–101
Skill-training, behavior-exchange procedures versus, 118
Smith-Hughes Act of 1917, 8
Smith-Lever Act of 1914, 8
Social context, families and, 419
Social Diagnosis, 4
Social-hygiene movement, 3, 9, 15
Socialization process, 100
Social-learning model, 104
Social organization, hierarchy in, 59
Social problems, intervention in, 3
Social psychiatry, 17–18
family therapy and, 4
marital therapy and, 4
Social psychology, 18
Social roles, in family, 251
Social work, as professional field, 4–5
Social workers, 4
relationship counseling and lack of involvement by, 5–6
training for counseling with couples, 5
Social-work movement, 4–6
Societal anxiety, 165–167
Societal regression, 164–165
Society of Medical Psychoanalysis, 20
Sociological literature, 8
Southard School, of Menninger Clinic, 23
Specialization versus homogenization, 33–34
Spinal-cord injuries (SCI), sex and, 491
Split filial loyalty, 211
Spontaneity
demanding, of self or others, 186
as solution to problems, 175–176
Spouse Observation Checklist (SOC), 105–106
Spouse subsystem, 423
Strategic approach, 364
Strategic family therapy, 396–416
case study, 411–416
changing benefits, 403
changing parent's involvement, 403–404
changing who is helpful to whom, 406
compassion and unity, 408–409
correcting family hierarchy, 402
creating positive frameworks, 408
domination and control, 402–403
empowering children to be helpful, 406–407
father as sexual offender, 411
finding protectors, 408
goals of therapy, 401–411, 415–416
helplessness versus power, 398–399
hierarchy versus equality, 400
hostility versus love, 400–401
involuntary versus voluntary behavior, 398
to love and protect, 405–407
to be loved, 403–405
metaphorical versus literal sequences, 399–400
orienting towards future and deeds of reparation, 407
personal gain versus altruism, 401
prescribing pretending of symptom, 405
prescribing symbolic acts, 404
prescribing symptom, 404
repentance and reparation, 409

to repent and forgive, 407–411
reuniting family members, 405–406
rituals and ordeals, 403
16 steps to reparation, 409–411
training and supervision in, 666–667
Strategic models, 54
Strategic therapy, 240
conceptualizing problems, 398–401
development of, 396
directives in, 397
goals of, 397
strategy chosen by therapist, 397
"Strategizing," 334
Stress
coping with, 72
and development of dysfunction, 299–300
emotional triangle and, 151
"String theory," 145, 148
Structural decoupling, 512
Structural family therapy, 417–442
assessment, 429–433
challenge to family's world view, 439
changing family structure, 438–439
clients, 434
common technical errors, 439–440
comprehensive model, 421
description of, 53
development of model, 417–421
dynamics of change, 440–441
dysfunctional family, 425–429
functional family, 421–425
goal of, 53
joining, 435, 436, 437
Philadelphia Child Guidance Clinic, 419, 420, 423
for Puerto Rican families, 556
role of therapist, 435–436
search for strength, 435
selective joining, 437
structure of treatment, 434–435
techniques of, 436–440
therapist, 434–435
time and space parameters, 435
treatment applicability, 441–442
treatment goals, 433–434
Wiltwyck School for Boys, 417–419, 420, 427, 429
working with couples, 441
Structural model, 53
Structural recoupling, 513
Structure-determined adaptation, 57
Structure-determined systems, 336
Structured fantasy technique, 230
Stuart Premarital Counseling Inventory, 501
Studies on Hysteria, 242
Subjective data, 50
Subsystems in family, 423–424
Successful marriage, defining, 99
Suicide, 406, 508
Summary Format of Family Functioning, 292
Surgery, sex and, 492
Symbolic-experiential family therapy, 444–475
assessment of family functioning and dysfunction, 452–453
background of approach, 444–446
case study, 472–475
cognitive mastery, 465–466
curative factors in marital and family therapy, 465–470
diagnosis in, 452
dysfunctional (marriage or) family, 449–452
early-phase, 461–462
effectiveness of approach, 471–472

expression of affect in, 468
gender-role flexibility, 447
irrationality or absurdity in, 467–468
late phase, 464
maturational growth as goal in, 467
middle phase, 462–464
resistance in, 465
role of therapist in, 459–461
setting and modifying goals, 453–456
special issues in marital therapy, 469–470
staged model of treatment in, 461
strengths of, 471
structure of therapy process, 456–459
techniques of therapy, 461–465
therapeutic suprasystem, 454–459
training and supervision for, 670–672
treatment applicability, 470–472
well-functioning marriage and family, 446–449
"Symbiosis" between mother and child, 25
Symmetrical behavior, 42
Symptom prescription, 185
Syphilis, 490
Systematic behavioral approach, 17
Systemic consultation, 335–336
Systemic family therapy, 154
Systemic messages, 467
Systemic models, 55–56
Systemic therapy, context and, 334
Systemic therapists, 344–346, 353
Systemic thinking, 335
Systems, hierarchical organization of, 45
Systems theory, 27
    circular feedback in, 55
    circularity in, 58
    family models and, 51–56
    levels and language in, 48
    paradox in, 55
    psychoanalytic concepts and, 52
    rules in, 42
    specific concepts of, 59

The Tactics of Change: Doing Therapy Briefly, 32
Tavistock Clinic, England, 20, 286
    Family Discussion Bureau, 20
Technical training, 644
Teen-age pregnancy, 485
Tetrads, 458, 459
Therapeutic alliance, 85
Therapeutic receptivity, 266
Therapeutic suprasystem, 454–459
Therapist
    compliance with directives of, 116
    dependence on, 66, 162–163
    differentiation of, 152, 157, 164
    family of origin and marriage of, 468, 686
    family therapy for, 468
    goals of, and family's goals, 433–434
    important qualities of, 274–275
    as modern social character, 612–613
    as narrator, 436
    personality of, 350, 646
    personal maturity of, 231
    personal participation of, 460
    personal values of, 256
    as producer, 435–436
    profile of, 436
    as protagonist, 436
    role of, 84–86

self-disclosure of, 460
skills of, 640
as stage director, 436
studies of personal characteristics of, 684
Therapist maneuverability, as term, 179
The Therapist's Own Family, 134
Therapy
    aim of, 349
    as art or science, 652
    frequency of, 162–163
    goals of, 83, 415–416, 614–615
    longevity of, 163
    resistance to, 86
    termination of, 86
Training and supervision in family therapy, 638–688
    audiotapes in, 663–664
    in Bowen therapy, 668–669
    in Brief Therapy, 665
    in contextual therapy, 668
    critical approach to, 641
    descriptions of training programs, 674–676
    developmental and life-cycle thinking, 654
    feminist thinking and, 656–658
    frameworks of, 645–647
    in functional family therapy, (FFT), 672–674
    historical perspective, 639–645
    in integrative psychodynamic and systems approach, 669–670
    in intergenerationally oriented therapy, 669
    isomorphic nature of training and therapy, 640, 648–649
    learning objectives and skill articulation, 652–653
    lenses to aid, 653–658
    literature on, 639–640, 643
    live supervision, 658–660
    methods of teaching family-therapy thinking, 651–652
    Milan systemic (MS) program, 665–666
    peer approaches/group supervision, 660
    related areas of work in therapist thinking, 652
    research and evaluation in, 676–685
    school-or approach-specific model of, 664–674
    seminal contributions to, 640–641
    simulation as method of training, 664
    in strategic therapy, 666–667
    in structural family therapy, 667–668
    supervisor thinking and conceptual development, 647–648
    team approaches, 660–662
    therapy as art or science, 652
    training in family systems thinking, 649–561
    videotapes in, 662–663
Transactional model, 194
Transcontinental live supervision, 663
Transference, 154, 222, 274
Transgenerational approaches, 668
Transgenerational family therapy, 466
Transgenerational patterns, 447
Transgenerational relationships, 202
Treatment manuals, 686
Troubleshooting, 124

Two-person system, 252–253

U.K. National Health Service, 288
Unbalancing, 439
Uncommon Therapy, 239
Undifferentiated ego mass, 53
"Unidisease," 167
Unified field theory, 136, 157
United Kingdom, analysis in, 284–285
"Unit of mind," 333
University of Wisconsin Medical School, Department of Psychiatry, 27
U.S. Bureau of the Census, 508, 555–556, 557, 558, 560
U.S. Department of Health, Education, and Welfare, 34
Utilization, as term, 241

Vaginismus, 493
Values, defining, 609
Values, Ethics, Legalities and the Family Therapist, 607
Values and ethics in family therapy, 606–634
    confidentiality in family therapy, 624
    deception in family therapy, 615–621
    definitions of terms, 609–610
    ethical issues in family-therapy research, 624–628
    future directions, 633–634
    gender and ethics, 628–633
    historical development, 606–609
    ideological issues in family therapy, 611–615
    individual welfare and family welfare, 622–623
    informed consent in family therapy, 623–624
    personal and cultural values, 610–611
Verbal versus nonverbal communication, 44–45

Watsonian behaviorism, 98
Wellesley, Human Relations Service at, 24
Welfare, beginnings of, 4
Well-functioning family, 69–72, 203–209, 243–245
    autonomy in, 448
    boundaries and alliances in, 245, 368–369
    communication, 369
    coping with stress, 72
    cultural adaptation, 449
    defining, 69
    differentiation and individuation in, 448
    expectations of, 69–70
    family psychoeducational treatment and, 368–370
    four dimensions of relationships, 203–205
    growth of, 244–245
    knowledge and coping skills, 370
    problem solving in, 448–449
    process characteristics of, 448
    sexual intimacy in, 448
    structure and style of, 70–71, 369–370
    tolerance of deviance in, 71–72
Wiltwyck School for Boys, 23, 30, 31, 417–419, 420, 427, 429
Women
    aging and, 486
    drug abuse by, 488
    larger systems and, 600
Women's Project in Family Therapy, 505